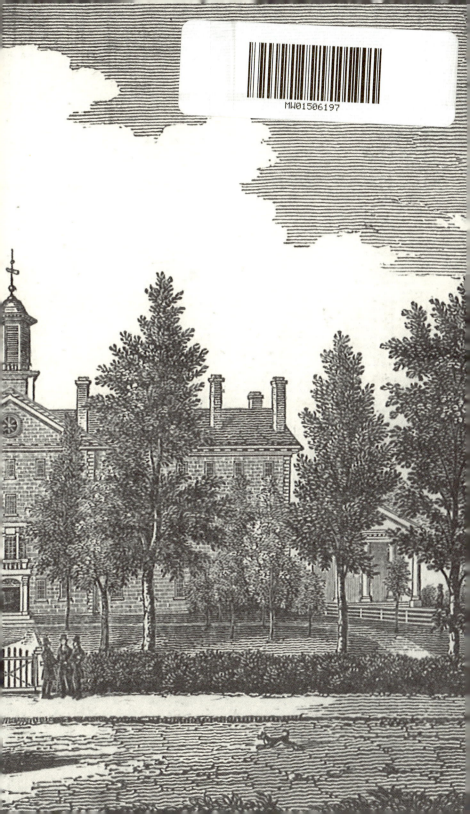

PRINCETON AND THE WORK OF THE CHRISTIAN MINISTRY

VOLUME I

PRINCETON
AND THE WORK OF THE
CHRISTIAN MINISTRY

*A Collection of Addresses and Articles
by Faculty and Friends of
Princeton Theological Seminary*

Volume 1

Selected & Introduced

by

James M. Garretson

THE BANNER OF TRUTH TRUST

THE BANNER OF TRUTH TRUST

Head Office	*North America Office*
3 Murrayfield Road	PO Box 621
Edinburgh, EH12 6EL	Carlisle, PA 17013
UK	USA

banneroftruth.org

© The Banner of Truth Trust 2012
Reprinted 2020

*

ISBN
This Volume: 978 1 84871 162 4
Two-Volume Ser: 978 1 84871 164 8

*

Typeset in 11/13 Adobe Garamond Pro
at The Banner of Truth Trust, Edinburgh

Printed in the USA by
Versa Press Inc.,
East Peoria, IL.

CONTENTS OF VOLUME I

Contents

FOREWORD

During its first century Princeton Theological Seminary was famous for biblical and theological orthodoxy and scholarship. Even today Christians remember with appreciation its 'majestic testimony' to the truth. Books by the Princetonians—Archibald Alexander, Charles Hodge, B. B. Warfield, J. Gresham Machen, and others—remain in print. The old Princeton theology, however, attracted little scholarly attention after the reorganization of the seminary in 1929 opened the door for a theologically diverse programme. Most books and articles that mentioned the Princeton theology disparaged it for its theological rigidity, biblical inerrancy, and Scottish Common Sense Philosophy. The first book-length introduction to Princeton theology did not appear until 1983—*The Princeton Theology 1812-1921: Scripture, Science and Theological Method from Archibald Alexander to Benjamin Warfield,* edited by Mark Noll. Thankfully, some recent books and articles have begun to present a more accurate and positive view of old Princeton's theology.

Princeton Seminary was more than a place for scholarly study of the Bible and theology, as essential as that was. It was also a place for training ministers in devotional living, missions, and pastoral work.

As Princeton approached its centennial in 1912, the seminary faculty put out a booklet called *A Modern School of the Prophets,* which stated: 'For almost one hundred years, this seminary has tried to be faithful to its trust and has furnished to the church that established it, men of missionary zeal, evangelistic fervour, pastoral loyalty and scholarly ability.' Scholarly ability, though very important, was not listed first in the faculty's description of the seminary's work. Missionary zeal, evangelistic fervour, and pastoral ministry were also major emphases of the seminary, as was the devotional life of its faculty and students. Until recently, the topics of piety, missions, and

Christian ministry have been neglected by those who studied and wrote about Princeton.

In 1981, a book by Andrew Hoffecker surprised many by its title and content—*Piety and the Princeton Theologians: Archibald Alexander, Charles Hodge, and Benjamin Warfield.*

My 1983 Princeton doctoral dissertation—'The Last Commmand: Princeton Theological Seminary and Missions'—explored the very impressive contribution of Princeton Seminary to the beginnings of the American missionary movement. (This story is summarized in my *Princeton Seminary,* volume 1, chapter 8.)

In 2005 James Garretson called attention to the seminary's training of preachers in his *Princeton and Preaching.* In *Princeton and the Work of the Christian Ministry,* Garretson has supplied us with more treasure from old Princeton. These two volumes contain over seventy sermons, addresses, and articles from Princeton faculty and friends, illustrating and defining the seminary's sustained commitment to the work of the Christian ministry. Garretson also provides a helpful introduction to this major aspect of the Princeton tradition.

Scholars of Princeton history will find these volumes instructive and insightful. Pastors, elders, and seminary students will be inspired and challenged. And anyone who loves the church and wants to see it at its best will be encouraged and blessed.

David B. Calhoun
Emeritus Professor of Church History
Covenant Theological Seminary
St Louis, Missouri
December, 2011

PREFACE

It is said that traditionalism is the dead faith of the living and that tradition is the living faith of the dead. The men of old Princeton Seminary, whose writings are found in this collection, knew this distinction and were well aware of the dangers of an orthodoxy not united to an orthopraxy rooted in a living piety.

As men of their times, they were shaped by the currents of theological thought which were forged in the fires of the Protestant Reformation and handed down as a living spiritual legacy by martyrs and godly churchmen who safeguarded the deposit of truth in their own generations.

As committed Christians and godly ministers faithful to the confessional standards of the Presbyterian Church, they viewed their calling and work as a sacred trust given to them by Christ and the church. All of their writings reflect this sense of sacred calling and partake of the spirit of those whose ministerial labours were carried out as acts of loving, loyal devotion to Christ and his Word.

The Princetonians high view of Scripture was accompanied by an equally high view of the calling and responsibilities associated with the ministerial office. Their collective writings on the pastoral office and their emphasis on the cultivation of 'eminent piety' in the life of the minister provide a rich theology of pastoral ministry—rich in wisdom as well as Christ-centred in focus. This pastoral theology is, for the most part, timeless in value and provides many useful insights for those whom the risen Lord has called into gospel work in the twenty-first century.

The friendship of the Rev. Mark Herzer has been a source of encouragement to the author and bears witness to the pastoral wisdom found in Princeton's past for ministry in today's world.

I would like to express my gratitude to Mr Ken Henke, Assistant Archivist in Special Collections at Princeton Theological Seminary,

Princeton, New Jersey, for his assistance in securing select manuscripts for this project. Thanks too to Dr David B. Calhoun for kindly providing the Foreword, and to the Banner of Truth Trust for undertaking publication of this collection.

A special word of thanks also goes to my daughters, Michaela and Rebekah Garretson, whose love and support for their father is a source of much joy and gratitude. It is my prayer that they would love and serve Christ all the days of their lives with the same passion and zeal that marked the lives of those whose writings are found within the pages of this book.

JAMES M. GARRETSON
Fort Lauderdale, Florida
December, 2011

INTRODUCTION

A MONG theological seminaries founded in the United States
in the past two hundred years, few have had world-wide influence as profound as Princeton Theological Seminary. Established in
1812 as The Theological Seminary of the Presbyterian Church in the
United States of America, few who witnessed the seminary's inauspi-
cious beginnings in the village of Princeton, New Jersey, could have
imagined the impact the seminary would have on American Christianity and culture and, through its graduates and publications, on the
church overseas.[1]

The decades leading up to the founding of the seminary were
marked by social change and political upheaval. The new nation,
born through the struggles of the American War of Independence,
now faced political and cultural challenges in both church and State.
Infidelity and scepticism were a serious threat to the moral foundations of society; Deism competed with Trinitarian Christianity

---

[1] For helpful overviews of the history of American Presbyterianism see D. G. Hart
and John H. Muether, *Seeking a Better Country* (Phillipsburg: P&R Publishing,
2007); Lefferts A. Loetscher, *A Brief History of the Presbyterians* (Philadelphia:
Westminster Press, 1983); James H. Smylie, *A Brief History of the Presbyterians*
(Louisville: Geneva Press, 1996). Hart and Muether are particularly good in
examining the theological currents that affected the development of Presbyterianism
in the United States. For a collection of primary source documents recording the
development of Presbyterianism in America see Maurice W. Armstrong, Lefferts
A. Loetscher, and Charles A. Anderson, *The Presbyterian Enterprise: Sources of
American Presbyterian History* (Philadelphia: Westminster Press, 1956). For a detailed
historical and theological analysis of the founding period in the history of American
Presbyterianism see Charles Hodge's important work, *The Constitutional History of
the Presbyterian Church in the United States of America,* 2 vols. (Philadelphia: William
S. Martien, 1839-40). For a study on the changing concepts of the Presbyterian
ministry between 1700 and 1900 see Elwyn A. Smith, *The Presbyterian Ministry in
American Culture* (Philadelphia: Westminster Press, 1962).

for religious allegiance in an era characterized by declining church attendance. Churchmen feared that the new nation was in imminent danger of abandoning the Christian heritage that had provided the foundation for its religious and political freedoms.[1] Yet in God's kind providence, the fortunes of the newly liberated colonies would not only be preserved but also strengthened by the Second Great Awakening. Radical political thought and deistical thinking soon encountered a revived Christian spirituality that would exert a widespread influence. Extending over a four-decade period (c. 1790-1830), churches, communities, individuals, and educational institutions all felt its power.[2] The debilitating effects of the revolutionary war had lowered moral standards, but declining church attendance was soon reversed as churches were significantly strengthened. Population growth, increased immigration, and, above all, personal experience of the new birth in Christ, all contributed to the growing influence of Christian belief and practice in the United States of America.

As the nineteenth century dawned, churches faced the new challenge of a rapidly expanding population that quickly outgrew the

[1] For a recent treatment of the Bible's role in shaping America's national history see Jerry Newcombe, *The Book that Made America* (Ventura: Nordskog Publishing, 2009). For background on this period in American history see Mark A. Noll, *America's God: From Jonathan Edwards to Abraham Lincoln* (Oxford: Oxford University Press, 2002); idem., *The Old Religion in a New World* (Grand Rapids: Eerdmans, 2002).

[2] For a helpful study on its strengths and weaknesses see Iain H. Murray, *Revival and Revivalism: The Making and Marring of American Evangelicalism, 1750-1858* (Edinburgh: Banner of Truth, 1994). For useful surveys see also John B. Boles, *The Great Revival: Beginnings of the Bible Belt* (Lexington: University Press of Kentucky, 1972, 1996); William G. McLoughlin, Jr., *Modern Revivalism: Charles Grandison Finney to Billy Graham* (New York: Ronald Press Company, 1959); Keith J. Hardman, *The Spiritual Awakeners: American Revivalists from Solomon Stoddard to D. L. Moody* (Chicago: Moody Press, 1983); idem, *Seasons of Refreshing: Evangelism and Revivals in America* (Grand Rapids: Baker, 1994); Paul K. Conkin, *Cane Ridge: America's Pentecost* (Madison: University of Wisconsin Press, 1990); Whitney R. Cross, *The Burned Over District: The Social and Intellectual History of Enthusiastic Religion in Western New York, 1800-1850* (New York: Harper & Row, 1965); Bernard A. Weisberger, *They Gathered at the River: The Story of the Great Revivalists and Their Impact upon Religion in America* (Boston: Little, Brown & Co. 1958); Benjamin Rice Lacy, Jr., *Revivals in the Midst of the Years* (Richmond: John Knox Press, 1943); J. F. Thornbury, *God Sent Revival: The Story of Asahel Nettleton and the Second Great Awakening* (Rushden: Evangelical Press, 1977).

existing provision of churches and pastors, especially along the ever-broadening western frontier. The old one-on-one mentoring models, which had worked so well in providing ministers for churches in the colonial period, simply could not supply sufficient numbers of pastors and preachers in such challenging circumstances.

Recognizing the need, a number of the new denominations acted to establish schools specifically dedicated to the training of men for the Christian ministry.[1] The seminaries were typically church-based institutions intended to contribute to the ongoing spiritual welfare of the respective denomination. Rooted in a shared Protestant heritage, they were established to preserve and perpetuate their own denominational distinctives in the new country.[2]

Each of the new denominational seminaries founded in this period shared a common commitment to the cultivation of Christian piety as well as an intelligent apprehension of the Christian faith. Truth was not only to be grasped by the mind, but embraced and believed by a receptive heart. Since the knowledge of the truth is, in the language of Scripture, 'unto godliness', a vigorous emphasis was placed on the cultivation of Christian piety in the life of the students, something that was seen to be essential for the true care of souls.

The core curriculum in the new schools reflected a historic four-fold division of study: Bible, Dogmatics, Church History, and

[1] For a comprehensive overview of the development of American seminaries see the multi-volume work by Glenn T. Miller, *Piety and Intellect: The Aims and Purposes of Ante-Bellum Theological Education* (Atlanta: Scholars Press, 1990); *idem., Piety and Profession: American Protestant Theological Education, 1870-1970* (Grand Rapids: Eerdmans, 2007). For a superb one-volume treatment on the history of clerical training and the role of the clergy in American society see E. Brooks Holifield, *God's Ambassadors: A History of the Christian Clergy in America* (Grand Rapids: Eerdmans, 2007). For an extremely useful overview of the history of the Christian ministry with chapters detailing its development in American church life see Richard H. Niebuhr and Daniel D. Williams, *The Ministry in Historical Perspective* (New York: Harper & Row, 1956, 1983).

[2] For important studies documenting the development of theology in America during this period see Paul C. Conkin, *The Uneasy Center: Reformed Christianity in Antebellum America* (Chapel Hill: University of North Carolina Press, 1995); E. Brooks Holifield, *Theology in America: Christian Thought from the Age of the Puritans to the Civil War* (New Haven: Yale University Press, 2003).

Practical Theology;[1] the cultivation and practise of Christian piety undergirded each department of study and served as the common bond in unifying the curriculum in its goal of preparing Christian men for the ministry of the Word.

Faculty selection also reflected the schools' purposes and goals. Most faculty were scholarly pastors, men who possessed pastoral experience and academic competency. Experience in church ministry brought a practical dimension to classroom instruction which enabled students to see the implications of formal theological study for ministry in local church settings.

Although there was a strong emphasis on the study of theological subjects, the seminary's goal was to produce gospel ministers rather than academic scholars. Academic study was never viewed as an end in itself; rather, rigorous and sustained academic study was seen as subservient to the goal of producing well-educated and pious students, approved unto God, workmen that need not to be ashamed, who rightly divide the word of truth. This was the focus maintained by such seminaries for most of the nineteenth century.[2]

* * * * *

With this historical context in mind, we can better understand the purposes behind the founding of Princeton Theological Seminary and the design of its curriculum. Alarmed by the inroads of infidelity and Deism in the academy and society, the founders of the seminary were also concerned that the Presbyterian-founded College of New Jersey had also made concessions to Enlightenment thinking; no longer did the college curriculum provide the biblical and theological teaching thought necessary for ministerial training.[3] In response, the

[1] For a suggestive and insightful study of the history of theological education see Edward Farley, *Theologia: The Fragmentation and Unity of Theological Education* (Philadelphia: Fortress Press, 1983).

[2] For helpful articles looking at the history of theological education in the evangelical tradition see D. G. Hart and Albert R. Mohler, *Theological Education in the Evangelical Tradition* (Grand Rapids: Baker Book House, 1996).

[3] For an account of the college's founding and development see Mark A. Noll, *Princeton and the Republic 1768-1822: The Search for a Christian Enlightenment in the Era of Samuel Stanhope Smith* (Princeton: Princeton University Press, 1989).

Presbyterian Church acted to preserve its past and protect its future by establishing a school that would reflect its confessional standards.[1] An 1811 committee report approved by the General Assembly of the Presbyterian Church details the process which led to the founding of the school and includes 'The Plan of the Theological Seminary of the Presbyterian Church in the United States of America' which established the goals and guidelines for the seminary's operation.[2]

Part apologetic in nature and part constructive in focus, the Plan details the founders' vision for the school. A careful reading of the document demonstrates the balance the founders sought to maintain between academic rigour and a life of 'vital piety'. The Plan emphasizes that which is to be believed and taught and the vital importance of Christian character for the work of ministry. The training envisioned would include: study of biblical languages and antiquities; exegetical studies; systematic and historical theology; church history and government; and pastoral theology, which would include homiletics and pastoral casuistry. Successful graduates were to be able divines, capable of explaining, proclaiming and defending the gospel as Christ's representatives; active churchmen committed to the Westminster Confession of Faith, the Larger and Shorter Catechisms, and the secondary standards of the Presbyterian Church; friends of revivals of religion, and enthusiastic supporters of missions.[3]

For a study examining the impact of Enlightenment thought on American college education see Douglas Sloan, *The Scottish Enlightenment and the American College Ideal* (Columbia University: Teachers College Press, 1971).

[1] For a brief account of the seminary's founding see Mark A. Noll, 'The Founding of Princeton Seminary', *Westminster Theological Journal*, 42 (Fall 1979): 72-110. For a history of the institutional development of the seminary through 1992 see William K. Selden, *Princeton Theological Seminary* (Princeton: Princeton University Press, 1992). For a comprehensive account of the spiritual life and culture that characterized the seminary from its founding in 1812 through its reorganization in 1929 see David B. Calhoun, *Princeton Seminary, vol. 1: Faith and Learning, 1812-1868; vol. 2: The Majestic Testimony, 1869-1929* (Edinburgh: Banner of Truth, 1994, 1996).

[2] See Samuel Miller, *A Brief History of the Theological Seminary of the Presbyterian Church, at Princeton, New Jersey; Together With Its Constitution, Bye-Laws, &c.* (Princeton: John Bogart, 1838); hereafter *A Brief History*. (See below, pp. 42-83).

[3] 'That, as filling the church with a learned and able ministry, without a corresponding portion of real piety, would be a curse to the world, and an offence to God and his people; so the General Assembly think it their duty to state, that in establishing

The Princetonians believed the study of theology was fundamental for understanding the nature of the Christian life.[1] The facts of God's self-revelation in history and Scripture were the foundation for theological reflection and formulation of doctrine. Thus a strong emphasis was placed on the mastery of Hebrew and Greek, the original languages of the Bible, in order to accurately exegete the text of Holy Scripture. Biblical antiquities were studied in order to understand the cultural context and social milieu of the ancient world. Systematic and historical theology organized the biblical data into its logical and linear development, while church history and government looked at the outworking of Christian doctrine throughout the centuries. Pastoral theology provided instruction in preaching and in ministerial etiquette,[2] while study of Puritan models of spiritual casu-

---

a seminary for training up ministers, it is their earnest desire to guard, as far as possible, against so great an evil. And they do hereby solemnly pledge themselves to the churches under their care, that in forming, and carrying into execution the plan of the proposed seminary, it will be their endeavour to make it, under the blessing of God, a nursery of vital piety, as well as of sound theological learning: and to train up persons for the ministry, who shall be lovers, as well as defenders of the truth as it is in Jesus; friends of revivals of religion; and a blessing to the church of God.' See Miller, *A Brief History*, p. 8 (see below, p. 47). The Plan lists the specific 'theological' categories as: Natural, Didactic, Polemic, and Casuistic Theology. It is an important historical point to note that the number of new seminaries established in the opening decades of the nineteenth century took place during, and one might argue, in consequence of the renewed spiritual vitality which accompanied the effects of the Second Great Awakening in church and society; the founders' appreciation for the beneficial effects of Holy Spirit-originated revival is evident in their desire that graduates would 'be friends of revivals of religion'. For a work representative of the Princetonians understanding of true and false revival see W. B. Sprague, *Lectures on Revivals of Religion* (Edinburgh: Banner of Truth, 2007).

[1] For a succinct summary of the 'scientific nature' of theological formulation see the inaugural address of B. B. Warfield, 'The Idea of Systematic Theology Considered as a Science', *Inauguration of the Rev. Benjamin B. Warfield, D.D., as Professor of Didactic and Polemic Theology* (New York: Anson D.F. Randolph & Company, 1888); reprinted in *Princeton and the Work of the Christian Ministry*, vol. 2 (Edinburgh: Banner of Truth, 2012), pp. 472-96, (herafter abbreviated as, PWCM)

[2] For a detailed treatment of the subject filled with much practical insight see Samuel Miller, *Letters on Clerical Manners and Habits Addressed to a Student in the Theological Seminary at Princeton, N.J.* (Princeton: Moore Baker, 1835).

istry gave insights into the application of Scripture to the spiritual needs of individuals and congregations.[1]

In addition to the academic emphasis, the Plan stressed the importance of the formation of Christian character and the cultivation of 'vital piety'. It was expected that the faculty would exemplify Christian piety both inside and outside the classroom.[2] The founders believed that godly mentors were among the primary means for the cultivation of Christian piety in the lives of the students. Thus, in the Plan we find a number of practical directives for cultivating, maintaining, and enlarging pious dispositions and actions of both faculty and students. Bible-reading, prayer, private and corporate worship, fasting, listening to sermons, and reading the best 'practical authors' were among the means recommended.[3]

[1] For authors and publications that shaped the Princeton approach to pastoral theology see the stimulating section 'Letters to Young Ministers', in James W. Alexander, *Thoughts on Preaching* (Edinburgh: Banner of Truth, 1975, 1988), pp. 101-69.

[2] For a study of the relationship between piety and doctrine in the lives of Archibald Alexander, Charles Hodge, and B. B. Warfield, see W. Andrew Hoffecker, *Piety and the Princeton Theologians* (Phillipsburg: P&R Publishing, 1981); *idem.*, 'The Devotional Life of Archibald Alexander, Charles Hodge, and Benjamin B. Warfield', *Westminster Theological Journal* 42 (Fall 1979): 111-29. For a treatment of Charles Hodge's approach to piety see Mark A. Noll, 'Charles Hodge as an Expositor of the Spiritual Life', *Charles Hodge Revisited: A Critical Appraisal of His Life and Work*, ed. John W. Stewart and James H. Moorhead (Grand Rapids: Eerdmans, 2002), pp. 181-216. Stewart and Moorhead's volume contains a number of valuable essays that examine Hodge's theology in relation to the intellectual and historical context of nineteenth-century culture.

[3] For a brief overview of the role of the seminary library in the cultivation of Christian piety among the students see the published paper by Michael J. Paulus, Jr., 'Spiritual Culture and the Theological Library: The Role of the Princeton Theological Seminary Library in the Religious Life of Theological Students in the Nineteenth Century', *(ATLA 2006 Proceedings)*. Paulus documents circulation records that indicate a sustained interest in the reading of devotional literature by the students. In the early 1820s, works by John Flavel, William Jay, John Bunyan, and Jonathan Edwards were in active circulation among students. Student interest in the reading of devotional literature prompted a complaint to the administration in 1830 that the library did not have adequate holdings in this field! For an overview of the role of devotional literature in American Presbyterianism see Mark A. Noll, 'A Precarious Balance: Two Hundred Years of Presbyterian Devotional Literature,'

The ministerial training model established at Princeton Theological Seminary sought to balance the objective and subjective aspects of Christian faith in a community-based learning environment that placed equal emphasis on piety and scholarship.[1] The training was intended to be practical and not merely theoretical. Directives in the Plan that obligated the faculty to inculcate 'practical religion in their lectures and recitations',[2] and expected the students to have the ability 'to support the doctrines of the Confession of Faith and Catechisms, by a ready, pertinent, and abundant quotation of Scripture texts for that purpose',[3] suggest a strong commitment to the application of the Bible to the student's preparation for ministerial service.

* * * * *

The delicate balance between piety and scholarship which the founders wished to retain was carefully safeguarded throughout the successive professorships of the men whose writings are included in this collection. Educational institutions inevitably change with the passing of time as they adapt to issues of institutional growth and cultural change. By the end of the nineteenth century, American

---

American Presbyterians, 68:3 (Fall 1990): 207-219; *idem.*, Mark A. Noll and Darryl G. Hart, 'The Language(s) of Zion: Presbyterian Devotional Literature in the Twentieth Century', *The Confessional Mosaic: Presbyterians and Twentieth-Century Theology*, ed. Milton J. Coalter, John M. Mulder, Louis B. Weeks (Louisville: Westminster John Knox Press, 1990), pp. 187-207.

[1] For a careful analysis of how Enlightenment and Pietistic thought had an impact on the model of ministerial training that Archibald Alexander developed at Princeton Seminary see Lefferts A. Loetscher, *Facing the Enlightenment and Pietism: Archibald Alexander and the Founding of Princeton Theological Seminary* (Westport: Greenwood Press, 1983). For an insightful article examining the relationship between piety and reason in the early Princetonians see Paul Kjoss Helseth, '"Right Reason" and the Princeton Mind: The Moral Context', *Journal of Presbyterian History*, 77 (1999): 13-28. For a recent and important collection of essays re-examining the inter-relationship between piety, Scottish Common Sense Realism, and the Reformed epistemological convictions that informed the Princetonians approach to the study and teaching of theology and apologetics see Paul Kjoss Helseth, *'Right Reason' and the Princeton Mind: An Unorthodox Proposal* (Phillipsburg: P&R Publishing, 2010).

[2] Miller, *A Brief History*, p. 21. (See below, p. 59.)

[3] Miller, *A Brief History*, p. 18. (See below, p. 56.)

seminaries were faced with significant academic challenges with the advent of the modern university educational model, the new field of the social sciences, and related developments in professional accreditation. Core values and curriculum were often modified in an attempt to accommodate these challenges as seminaries tried to keep pace with changing educational expectations.[1]

The Princetonians engaged with these challenges and yet sought to retain the core values upon which Princeton Theological Seminary had been founded. In 1896 at the fiftieth anniversary celebration of his appointment to the faculty of the seminary, Old Testament Professor, William Henry Green, made the following observation:

> Princeton Seminary stands, as it has always stood, for fidelity to the Word of God and the standards of the Presbyterian Church. At the same time it stands for the highest grade of biblical and theological learning. It welcomes all the light that can be thrown upon the Scriptures from every quarter, and does not shrink from the application of the most rigorous tests to the question of their origin or the nature of their contents. Convinced by the most abundant evidence that these Scriptures are the infallible Word of God, and that their teachings are the utterances of divinely sanctioned truth, this seminary has always maintained that sound learning will ever go hand in hand with implicit faith in this sacred volume.

Green continued his observations by noting that:

It was upon this basis that Princeton Seminary was originally

[1] For an analysis of these developments and their impact on theological education today see Daniel O. Aleshire, *Earthen Vessels: Hopeful Reflection on the Future and Work of Theological Schools* (Grand Rapids: Eerdmans, 2008). For a study examining the relationship between the modern research university and the divinity schools within the university system see Conrad Cherry, *Hurrying Toward Zion: Universities, Divinity Schools, and American Protestants* (Bloomington: Indiana University Press, 1995); for a related study examining developments in religious curriculum in American university education see D. G. Hart, *The University Gets Religion: Religious Studies in American Higher Education* (Baltimore: Johns Hopkins University Press, 1999). See also the observations by D. G. Hart, 'Overcoming the Schizophrenic Character of Theological Education in the Evangelical Tradition', *A Confessing Theology for Postmodern Times*, ed. Michael S. Horton (Wheaton: Crossway Books, 2000), pp. 111-30.

founded. It was with the unanimous purpose of establishing an institution where this cardinal position should be firmly held and faithfully inculcated that the Presbyterian Church resolved to plant here this its oldest seminary. This was the unwavering faith of those who were most directly instrumental in drafting its Plan, in laying its first foundations, in giving shape and direction to it in every respect at the outset of its career. This was the fixed and intelligent conviction of its first professors. That splendid quaternion of teachers, Drs Archibald Alexander, Samuel Miller, Charles Hodge, and Addison Alexander, were the glory and the crown of this seminary in former years, gave it its reputation before the church and the world, and in the protracted period during which they were spared to guide its affairs and to conduct its instruction, stamped their own character upon it, as I trust, indelibly. Under them Princeton Theology gained a definite and well understood meaning, which, it is to be hoped, it will never lose; from which may it never swerve. They whose privilege it was, as it was mine, to sit at the feet of those great and honoured preceptors, will bear their testimony that reverence for the revealed Word of God was a prominent feature of their instructions, and was constantly illustrated not only by the teachings of the classroom, but by their whole spirit and life. And all the wealth of their learning, all the fruit of their reflections, their studies and their researches were made to contribute to the exposition, the illumination, and the exaltation of the Bible.[1]

While academic specialization became more refined by the end of the nineteenth century, faculty such as William Henry Green and B. B. Warfield remained self-consciously committed to the integration of piety with learning.[2] Even with increasing curricular diversity

[1] See *Celebration of the Fiftieth Anniversary of the Appointment of Professor William Henry Green as an Instructor in Princeton Theological Seminary May 5, 1896* (New York: Charles Scribner's Sons, 1896), pp. 45-46.
[2] For a valuable introduction to Green's publications and his defence of the inspiration and authority of the Old Testament Scriptures see Marion Ann Taylor, 'William Henry Green', ed. Walter A. Elwell & J. D. Weaver, *Bible Interpreters of the 20th Century* (Grand Rapids: Baker Books, 1999), pp. 22-36. Green's supernaturalist approach to the use of modern scholarship as a 'believing critic' proved formative for successive generations of evangelical Old Testament scholarship in the twentieth century. Green's piety informed his scholarship and directed its approach to his study of the canon's formation, authority, and meaning. For a recent collection of essays

in elective courses that reflected a professor's specialization, issues of piety and spiritual growth remained at the heart of the instruction the students received in their classrooms.[1]

Perhaps what is most striking about the faculty is the way in which the needs of the church remained central to how they viewed their responsibilities as professors. Most had served as pastors before their appointment as professors in the seminary; as ordained ministers and professors, they viewed their work as a fiduciary trust given to them by Christ through the Presbyterian Church, for the faithful discharge of which they knew they must one day give an account to God. Their respective academic interests did not displace their focus on the application of scriptural teaching to the needs of the church and society. Their scholarship was carried out on behalf of the church and in the service of the church.[2]

on Warfield's background and theology see *B. B. Warfield: Essays on His Life and Thought*, ed. Gary L. Johnson (Phillipsburg: P&R Publishing, 2007). For a thorough and comprehensive overview of Warfield's theology see Fred G. Zaspel, *The Theology of B.B. Warfield: A Systematic Summary* (Wheaton: Crossway, 2010). For Warfield's careful analysis of the inter-relationship between piety and scholarship see especially 'The Religious Life of Theological Students' and 'Spiritual Culture in the Theological Seminary' in this collection. (See PWCM, vol 2, pp. 412-25 and 426-52.)

[1] The seminary faculty and core curriculum became objects of student criticism at the beginning of the twentieth century. While the emphasis on piety remained undiminished, the pastoral value of certain aspects of the instruction was a source of increasing concern on the part of students, faculty, and directors. Unlike sister institutions that dropped Hebrew language requirements and adopted a more comprehensive elective system of classes, Princeton maintained its rigorous academic standards even as it enlarged its offerings. Although a source of faculty tension, a department of English Bible was added to the programme to offset increasing student biblical illiteracy and to strengthen the practical aspects of the education students received. As the seminary responded to developments in educational technology and the professionalization of theological study, faculty interests often focused on issues of importance to the academy which, at points, overshadowed the learning acquirements necessary for effective pastoral ministry for which the school had been founded. Unfortunately, the benefits of academic specialization are often accompanied by an absence of pastoral experience and loss of pastoral focus in curriculum selection and classroom instruction—ministry skills which were effectively modelled and taught in Princeton's founding faculty. For perceptive observations on these changes and the challenges they created see Calhoun, *Princeton Seminary*, vol. 2, pp. 264-69.

[2] For observations on keeping the proper balance between piety and scholarship and

Princeton Theological Seminary is best remembered for the brilliant professors who graced its classrooms and whose prodigious and profound literary productions gave the school a reputation for conservative Reformed theology and academic excellence.[1] B. B. Warfield's exegetical studies on the inspiration and authority of the Bible[2] and Charles Hodge's three-volume *Systematic Theology*[3] are among the most notable and probably best remembered of these publications.

The Princetonians' voluminous literary output included grammars, commentaries, works on systematic and historical theology, church history, biblical theology, apologetics, biographies, sermons, and numerous journal articles, tracts, and occasional pieces. And yet for all their interest in the systematic formulation of scriptural teaching in creeds, confessions, and systematic theologies, the faculty never published a volume specifically devoted to a systematic exposition of a biblical, Reformed, and experimental pastoral theology. Archibald Alexander would have been the man most suited for this endeavour, but apparently felt that his literary efforts were best

---

maintaining the pastoral and ministerial priorities for which Princeton Theological Seminary was founded see the passionate remarks by William M. Paxton in 'The Ministry for this Age', 'The Charge', *Addresses at the Inauguration of Rev. Archibald Alexander Hodge, D.D., LL.D. as Associate Professor of Didactic and Polemic Theology, in the Theological Seminary at Princeton, N.J., November 8, 1877* (Philadelphia: Sherman & Co., 1877), pp. 5-16. (See PWCM, vol. 2, pp. 337-46.)

[1] For an introduction to the Princeton theology and collection of primary source documents on their view of Scripture, science, and theological method see Mark A. Noll, *The Princeton Theology 1812-1921* (Grand Rapids: Baker Book House, 1983, 2001). For select chapters dealing with the development of the Princeton theology in American Christianity see David F. Wells, ed., *Reformed Theology in America: A History of Its Modern Development* (Grand Rapids: Eerdmans, 1985). For a collection of primary source articles published in the 1830-40s from the *Biblical Repertory and Theological ['Princeton', from 1837] Review* confronting the theology of the 'New Divinity' see *Princeton vs. The New Divinity* (Edinburgh: Banner of Truth, 2001).

[2] See B. B. Warfield, *The Inspiration and Authority of the Bible* (Phillipsburg: P&R Publishing, 1948); see also *Revelation and Inspiration, vol. 1 of The Works of Benjamin Breckinridge Warfield* (New York: Oxford University Press, 1927; repr. Baker Book House, 1981).

[3] See Charles Hodge, *Systematic Theology* (Charles Scribner's Sons, 1872-73; repr. Eerdmans, 1979).

directed to a variety of publications rather than to a narrowly focused volume of this kind.[1]

The Princetonians did, however, think and write extensively on the subject of Christian piety and its bearing on the life of the Christian. Hodge's remarks about Princeton's approach to piety, made at the semi-centennial commemoration of his fifty years of service as a faculty member, April 24, 1872, provide helpful perspective on the spiritual legacy of the seminary's first professors:

> It is a proverb that the child is the father of the man. The same law controls the life of institutions. What they are during their forming period, they continue to be. This is the reason why this institution owes its character to Dr Alexander and Dr Miller. Their controlling influence is not to be referred so much to their learning, or to their superior abilities, as to their character and principles . . . It was of course not peculiar to them that they were sincere, spiritual, Christian men. This may be said of the founders of all our theological seminaries. But there are different types

---

[1] Commenting on Alexander's profound spiritual influence on the student body and his reticence to write on this subject, A. A. Hodge observed that: 'All the treasures of divine wisdom and grace, which the Holy Ghost communicates to life-long students of the Word, when to high intellect is added all the simplicity and docility of a little child, irradiated his soul and made it luminous to others. All the secrets of the human heart and its various experiences under the discipline of the natural conscience and of the Word and Spirit of God were known to him, and he possessed the finest skill in interpreting and in treating, with acute precision, the states and frames of all who sought his counsel or listened to his instructions . . . This utter simplicity, this all-penetrating insight, accompanied with a wonderful spontaneousness of thought, imagination and speech were personal attributes, inseparable from his presence and manner, and incapable of being transmitted to the printed page. During his later years, when urged to put the results of his studies and reflections in the permanent form of writing, he often said, "No, if I have any talent, it is to talk sitting in my chair." And however much he may have been mistaken in failing to recognize the value of his writings to the church, there is no doubt that his gifts as a talker on the themes of Christian experience were without parallel among his contemporaries. He, more than any man of his generation, appeared to those who heard him to be endued with the knowledge, and clothed with the authority of a prophet sent immediately from God. He was to us the highest peak of the mountains, on whose pure head the heavens, beyond the common horizon, pour the wealth of their iridescent radiance.' See Archibald Alexander Hodge, *The Life of Charles Hodge* (Edinburgh: Banner of Truth, 2010), pp. 487-88.

of religion even among true believers. The religion of St Bernard and John Wesley; of Jeremy Taylor and of Jonathan Edwards, although essentially the same, had in each case its peculiar character. Every great historical church has its own type of piety. As there are three persons in the Trinity, the Father, the Son, and the Holy Spirit, so there appear to be three general forms of religion among evangelical Christians. There are some whose religious experience is determined mainly by what is taught in the Scriptures concerning the Holy Spirit. They dwell upon his inward work on the heart, on his indwelling, his illumination, on his life-giving power; they yield themselves passively to his influence to exalt them into fellowship with God. Such men are disposed more or less to mysticism . . . There are others whose religious life is determined more by their relation to the Father, to God as God; who look upon him as a sovereign, or law-giver; who dwell upon the grounds of obligation, upon responsibility and ability, and upon the subjective change by which the sinner passes from a state of rebellion to that of obedience . . . Then there are those in whom the form of religion, as Dr Boardman has said, is distinctively Christological. I see around me Alumni whose heads are as grey as my own. They will unite with me in testifying that this is the form of religion in which we were trained. While our teachers did not dissuade us from looking within and searching for evidences of the Spirit's work in the heart, they constantly directed us to look only unto Jesus—Jehovah Jesus—him in whom are united all that is infinite and awful indicated by the name Jehovah; and all that is human, and tender, and sympathetic, forbearing and loving, implied in the name of Jesus. If any student went to Dr Alexander, in a state of despondence, the venerable man was sure to tell him, 'Look not so much within. Look to Christ. Dwell on his person, on his work, on his promises, and devote yourself to his service, and you will soon find peace.'[1]

Through sermons, lectures, essays, Sabbath Afternoon conferences, journal articles, and book-length contributions, successive

[1] See *Proceedings Connected With the Semi-Centennial Commemoration of the Professorship of Rev. Charles Hodge, D.D., LL.D in the Theological Seminary at Princeton, NJ, April 24, 1872* (New York: Anson D. F. Randolph & Company, 1872), pp. 50-51.

generations of Princeton professors examined piety's biblical, biographical, and experimental dimensions.[1] Particular emphasis was placed on 'eminent piety' as a foundational prerequisite for ministerial effectiveness.[2]

In their pulpit proclamation, classroom instruction, and literary publications, the Princetonians addressed individuals and children, husbands and wives, families, churches, ministers and church officers with the practical implications of the Bible's teaching for their lives. Rooted in a covenantal understanding of Christian discipleship, which recognized that all of life is lived in the presence of God and is therefore to be lived for the glory of God, the Princeton faculty sought to minister to people of every age and class. No one was outside their purview or interest.[3] The poor, the illiterate, and

---

[1] Representative publications include Archibald Alexander, *Thoughts on Religious Experience* (Philadelphia: Presbyterian Board of Publication, 1841; repr. Banner of Truth, 1978); *idem., Biographical Sketches of the Founder and Principal Alumni of the Log College* (Princeton: J. T. Robenson, 1845; repr. Banner of Truth, 1968); *idem., Practical Sermons: To Be Read in Families and Social Meetings* (Philadelphia: Presbyterian Board of Publication, 1850; repr. Solid Ground Christian Books, 2004); *idem., Practical Truths* (New York: American Tract Society, 1857; repr. Odom Publications, n.d.). For Samuel Miller see *Thoughts on Public Prayer* (Harrisonburg: Sprinkle Publications, 1985). For Charles Hodge see *The Way of Life* (Philadelphia: American Sunday School Union, 1841; repr. Banner of Truth, 1959); *idem., Conference Papers: Or Analyses of Discourses, Doctrinal and Practical, Delivered on Sabbath Afternoon to the Students of the Seminary* (New York: Charles Scribner's Sons, 1879); repr. *Princeton Sermons: Outlines of Discourses, Doctrinal and Practical, at Princeton Theological Seminary* (Banner of Truth, 1958, repr. 2011). For B. B. Warfield see *Faith and Life* (Edinburgh: Banner of Truth, 1974, 1990).

[2] See Archibald Alexander, 'An Address to Candidates for the Ministry, on the Importance of Aiming at Eminent Piety in Making Their Preparation for the Sacred Office', in *The Annual of the Board of Education of the General Assembly of the Presbyterian Church in the United States,* ed. John Breckinridge (Philadelphia: Russell and Martien, 1831), pp. 175-194. (See below, pp. 228-40.)

[3] Archibald Alexander's small systematic theology, *A Brief Compend of Bible Truth,* is an enlarged edition of an earlier work, published along with prayers and hymns, which was intended to aid the blind in their devotions. Alexander published a number of works intended for 'plain, common readers' without 'technical phrases and abstruse disquisitions' which could be read in short time periods. See Archibald Alexander, *A Brief Compend of Bible Truth* (Philadelphia: Presbyterian Board of Publication, 1846; repr. Reformation Heritage Books, 2005).

children were given special attention in their instruction and writings.[1]

In addition to their writings on piety, the Princetonians published a variety of occasional pieces on matters relevant to the pastoral office. Aspects of classroom instruction received by students at the seminary found opportunity for publication as chapter contributions and essays; some of the richest material is found among the published sermons delivered at the ordination or installation services of a minister. The published addresses especially capture something of the power of the preached Word and the impact the message would have had on the people who first heard them.

While a number of the more important books written by the major Princetonians have been reprinted, the majority of their printed sermon manuscripts, essays, and magazine articles addressing various aspects of the calling and work of the Christian ministry[2] and issues of Christian piety, have not seen the light of day since their original

[1] See Charles Hodge, 'Preaching the Gospel to the Poor', *Biblical Repertory and Princeton Review,* Vol. 43 No. 1 (1871): pp. 83-95. (See PWCM, vol. 2, pp. 242-53.) Beginning with Alexander through Warfield there was a recurrent interest in ministry to children. At the end of his life, Archibald Alexander remarked that if he could live his life over again he would devote it in ministry to children. In a letter of October 19, 1843, addressed to one of his sons pursuing ordination, Samuel Miller advised him to begin his ministry with a focus on the children in his congregation: 'Try and find them all out. Procure a little blank book, strongly bound in leather, which you may carry in your pocket for months and years together. Here insert the names of all the children of the congregation, with anything peculiar in the case of each which may be worthy of recollection. When you are about to visit a family, refer to this manual for the names of the children, inquire for them, speak kindly to them, calling them by name. Have a tract in your pocket for one, a little anecdote for another, *etc.* This will conciliate the parents, and bind them to your person; and it will still more conciliate the children and prepare them to attend on your ministry in a respectful and profitable manner. I am more and more persuaded, that that minister who neglects the children and young people of his flock, neglects one of the most—perhaps I may say the most important means of saving souls—of building up the church, and promoting at once the comfort and the success of his ministry.' See Samuel Miller, Jr., *The Life of Samuel Miller,* 2 vols. (Philadelphia: Claxton, Remsen & Haffelfinger, 1869; repr. Tentmaker Publications, 2002), Vol. II p. 458.

[2] For a study of Archibald Alexander's instruction on preaching and pastoral care see James M. Garretson, *Princeton and Preaching: Archibald Alexander and the Work of the Christian Ministry* (Edinburgh: Banner of Truth, 2005).

publication. Their value for understanding old Princeton's theology
of ministry, a theology that did so much to strengthen churches and
communities, calls for their reprinting.[1]

* * * * *

It is impossible, however, to understand the Princetonians' approach
to the work of the Christian ministry apart from their commitment
to Scripture. The Princetonians were Bible-based, theologically-
minded, and pastorally-focused educators.[2] Their commitment to
the Reformed faith and its expression in the formularies of the Westminster Confession of Faith and the Larger and Shorter Catechisms,
shaped their pastoral theology.[3] Business, corporate management,

[1] Over the years of their respective ministries, the Princetonians addressed a
variety of challenges to the Christian faith and confessional Presbyterianism:
infidelity and scepticism, Deism, anti-clericalism, anti-confessionalism, fanaticism
and enthusiasm, mysticism, rationalism, ritualism, the rise of religious cults and
new religions such as Mormonism and the Jehovah's Witnesses, Romanticism,
Unitarianism, Transcendentalism, the 'New Divinity' movement, revivalism, slavery,
secession, the reformulation of traditional theological categories and language in
the theology of theologians such as Schleiermacher and Horace Bushnell, the rise
of Higher Criticism, Darwinism, the emergence of the new social sciences, and
Protestant liberalism. Their literary productions address contemporary and historical
issues with intellectual acumen and spiritual sensitivity; in all their publications they
write as committed Christians seeking to advance Christ's kingdom in the hearts of
their readers as well as in the home, school, church, and society.
[2] The diversity and breadth of the Princetonians' interests can be examined in the
seminary journal founded by Charles Hodge in 1825. Published under a variety
of names, the *Biblical Repertory and Princeton Review* quickly became the most
distinguished Presbyterian and theological academic quarterly in the nineteenth
century. Edited by Hodge for over four decades, the journal chronicled the interests,
emphases, and challenges facing the Presbyterian Church and the work of theological
education in the United States. For a history of the *Princeton Review* through the
early 1870s see *Biblical Repertory and Princeton Review Index Volume from 1825-1868*
(Philadelphia: Peter Walker, 1871). For an introduction to the history of the journal
and its key articles and contributors see Mark A. Noll, 'The Princeton Review',
Westminster Theological Journal, 50 (1988): 283-304.
[3] The definition of 'subscription' to the Westminster Standards and the use of
creeds and confessions in general, was a topic of extended debate in nineteenth-
and early twentieth-century American Presbyterianism. It became a central issue
in the division of the American Presbyterian Church in 1837; was a debated issue

and therapeutic models of clerical instruction would have been alien to their approach. The minister as facilitator, comedian, or coach would have been anathema to them and so incompatible with their understanding of the high calling of the pastor and the dignity of the pastoral office. Scripture teaches that pastors and teachers are gifts from the ascended Christ to his church. They are given to shepherd, feed, protect, discipline, love, and even to die for the sheep for whom Christ himself laid down his life. As officers in his church, they have been entrusted with the keys of his kingdom to open the doors of salvation to the believing and to close them to the unbelieving. Their public ministry is a savour of life to some and a savour of death to others. At stake are the great issues of eternity; heaven or hell are the eternal destinies awaiting all to whom the minister preaches the gospel.[1]

---

in the reunion of the split church in 1869; and continued as a source of prolonged debate in discussions surrounding revision of the Westminster Standards at the beginning of the twentieth century. The Princeton faculty affirmed the validity of creeds and confessions; they viewed subscription to the Westminster Standards as an essential prerequisite for ordination as a Presbyterian minister and as a means of preserving the church's orthodoxy. For an argument defending their importance see Samuel Miller, *The Utility and Importance of Creeds and Confessions: Addressed Particularly to Candidates for the Ministry* (Philadelphia: William S. Martien, 1839). For an impassioned defence of the continued use of the Westminster Standards see B. B. Warfield, *The Significance of the Westminster Standards as a Creed* (New York: Charles Scribner's Sons, 1898). (See PWCM, vol. 2, pp. 453-71.) For a perceptive overview of Princeton's position on the debate see David B. Calhoun, 'Old Princeton Seminary and the Westminster Standards,' *The Westminster Confession into the 21st Century*, ed. J. Ligon Duncan (Fearn, Ross-shire: Christian Focus, 2005), pp. 33-61. For a summary of the debate's development and theological impact on American Presbyterianism from the 1850s through the end of the twentieth century see 'The Predicament of Pluralism: Theology and Confessions', *The Reforming Tradition: Presbyterians and Mainstream Protestantism*, ed. Milton J. Coalter, John M. Mulder, Louis B. Weeks (Louisville: Westminster John Knox Press, 1992), pp. 117-43.

[1] The Princetonians' passion for truth and the spiritual welfare of their hearers is captured in A. A. Hodge's remarks on his father's editorial leadership of the *Biblical Repertory and Princeton Review*: 'His religion was a personal experience. The most close and critical observer never in any moment of his living or dying hours saw in him the least symptom of doubt. That Christ is what he is set forth in the Scriptures to be, and that the Bible is the infallible Word of God, were facts inseparable from his personal consciousness. The logical force and habit of his mind made him see

The work of the preacher was to be undertaken as a physician of men's souls.[1] The pastor's visitation of his people in their homes was viewed as an essential accompaniment to his pulpit ministry. Students were taught to visit the people in order to discover their true spiritual condition and apply the Word of God to them accordingly. In home visits the Bible was to be opened, prayer offered, and the reading of the best devotional writers encouraged. By such means the pastor not only brought a blessing to his people but his love for them would be reciprocated in an affectionate and attentive hearing of the preached Word in church.

Most importantly, the students were impressed with the responsibility to cultivate a growing love for Christ. Love for Christ is at the heart of true discipleship; it is essential for growth in the Christian life and absolutely vital for the proper exercise of the pastoral office. Archibald Alexander's timeless counsel to students still speaks with fresh power to aspiring pastors today:

> The love of Christ ought so to predominate, so to possess his mind, and to bear him along, that every interfering, or opposing principle, should be neutralized or extinguished. This should suggest all his plans, guide all his operations, give energy to all his efforts, and afford him comfort under all his trials. Constrained by the love of Christ, he should cheerfully forgo all the comforts of ease, affluence, and worldly honour, to serve his Master in places far remote; or far removed from public observation. This holy affection should impel him to undertake the most arduous duties, and encounter the most formidable dangers; this should enkindle the ardour of his eloquence, and supply the pathos of his most tender addresses. This is the hallowed fire which should be kept bright and burning continually. All other warmth is no better than 'strange fire'. Nothing but the love of Christ, can

---

and grasp all things in their relations. All that he saw to be logically involved in a vital truth by which he lived, was to him part of that truth. Thus he experienced the whole Calvinistic system, and would defend it at all cost as the truth of God, from loyalty to Christ, and love for human souls. The whole was a matter of conscience and of life and death.' See A. A. Hodge, *Life of Charles Hodge*, p. 270.

[1] For an engaging overview of the minister's role in the exercise of pastoral care in American culture see E. Brooks Holifield, *A History of Pastoral Care in America* (Nashville: Abingdon Press, 1983).

make a truly faithful pastor, or evangelist, assiduous in all his services, and indefatigable in the most private and self-denying duties of his office.[1]

The principles of faith, hope, and love were woven deep into the tapestry of the instruction students received from men who possessed that rare combination of godliness and scholarship.[2] Their personal experience in ministry, knowledge of God's Word, and passion for the church inspired generations of students in the cause of Christ.[3]

Students graduated from Princeton Theological Seminary with an appreciation of the importance of sound theological foundations for faithful pastoral ministry. The study of theology was not seen as an impediment to effective ministry; rather, thinking theologically was the best foundation for practical, pastoral service.

* * * * *

[1] From Archibald Alexander, 'The Pastoral Office', quoted in Garretson, *Princeton and Preaching*, pp. 126-27. For the full text see, 'The Pastoral Office', in this collection, PWCM, vol. 1 pp. 253-74.

[2] The Sabbath Afternoon conference played a prominent role in cultivating the religious life of the seminary students. Commenting on its importance, A. A. Hodge remarked: 'The prominence and effectiveness of this weekly exercise was unquestionably for the last half-century a grand special characteristic of Princeton Seminary. During these past years it was in many respects the most remarkable and memorable exercise in the entire seminary course. They were held every Sabbath afternoon by the professors and students for the discussion and practical enforcement of questions relating to experimental religion and the duties of the Christian life. The members of all the successive classes will bear testimony to the unique character and singular preciousness of those Sabbath Afternoon Conferences in that sacred old Oratory, whose walls are still eloquent to them with imperishable associations. Here the venerable professors appeared rather as friends and pastors than as instructors. The dry and cold attributes of scientific theology moving in the sphere of the intellect, gave place to the warmth of personal religious experience, and to the spiritual light of divinely illuminated intuition. Here in the most effective manner they sought to build up Christian men rather than form accomplished scholars and to instruct them in the wisest methods of conducting their future work of saving souls and edifying the church of Christ.' See A. A. Hodge, *Life of Charles Hodge,* p. 485.

[3] For a collection of memorial addresses and funeral sermons eulogizing their influence see James M. Garretson, *Pastor-Teachers of Old Princeton: Memorial Addresses for the Faculty of Princeton Theological Seminary 1812-1921* (Edinburgh: Banner of Truth, 2012).

The selections that follow will give the reader opportunity to enter into the rich world of old Princeton Theological Seminary. Most of the material was written by the more prominent faculty who served from the school's founding in 1812 through the year of B. B. Warfield's death in 1921. Warfield is a key transitional figure whose life bridged the nineteenth and twentieth centuries and whose convictions were rooted in the theology and spirituality of the early faculty. Additional contributions come from men intimately associated with the seminary in its opening decades.

B. B. Warfield's death marked the end of an era in the history of the seminary. Commenting on Warfield's funeral in a letter to his mother, J. Gresham Machen, Professor of New Testament Literature and Exegesis at the seminary, felt that 'old Princeton . . . died when Dr Warfield was carried out'.[1] Although eight more years would pass before the institutional reorganization of the seminary in 1929, Machen believed the ideological convictions that had guided the seminary since its founding were being eroded with the passing of the older faculty and the new direction the seminary's administration and denomination's leadership were pursuing. While a number of the faculty remained sympathetic to the confessional convictions upon which the school had been established, the denomination and the seminary would soon formally reflect the convictions of theological modernism and would abandon the confessional orthodoxy that characterized Princeton's past. The doctrinal and ecclesiological issues which were at the heart of the division within the Presbyterian Church would prove determinative for the seminary's future. As the boundary lines of theological orthodoxy shifted, inevitable and accompanying changes also took place in the definitions, purpose, and practice of pastoral theology in the instruction students received.

The selections included in this collection provide a cross-section of articles, essays, chapters, and sermons which have a bearing on a theology of pastoral ministry as represented by the seminary's founders and faculty, whose theological convictions and approach

---

[1] Cited in Calhoun, *Princeton Seminary* vol. 2, p. 318.

to pastoral ministry predate the changes that took place within their denomination and at the seminary in the 1920s.[1] While for the most part timeless in value, each was written to address issues of pressing importance in the period in which the author lived. As with every piece of historical literature, it is important to keep this in mind as one reads through the collection. A number of the pieces are specifically directed to young men studying at the seminary in preparation of their future service as ministers and missionaries; some of the addresses were delivered to recent graduates at their ordination and installation services. Others address important issues facing the church and theological seminaries; several comment on trajectories in the field of theological studies and their accompanying impact on pulpit and pastoral ministry.

The first two chapters provide the historical background for the theology of pastoral ministry that emerged at Princeton. W. B. Sprague's commemorative address is a review of the first fifty years of the seminary's history. Delivered during the middle years of the Civil War (1861-65), the lecture is tinged with the emotions that a divided country brought to a church now divided too. Samuel Miller's history contains an account of the founding of the school but also provides a full transcript of the seminary's Plan—material which is essential reading to gain an understanding of the theological foundation upon which the Presbyterian Church established the seminary and how the founders intended it to function.

---

[1] For useful historical studies of the issues and events that precipitated the turbulence in the denomination and seminary see Lefferts A. Loetscher, *The Broadening Church* (Philadelphia: University of Pennsylvania Press, 1954); Bradley J. Longfield, *The Presbyterian Controversy: Fundamentalists, Modernists, and Moderates* (New York: Oxford University Press, 1991); Gary North, *Crossed Fingers: How the Liberals Captured the Presbyterian Church* (Tyler: Institute for Christian Economics, 1996); Edwin H. Rian, *The Presbyterian Conflict* (Grand Rapids: Eerdmans, 1940; repr. Committee for the Historian of the Orthodox Presbyterian Church, 1992). For a valuable biographical memoir that rehearses the story in the life of one of its leading figures see Ned B. Stonehouse, *J. Gresham Machen: A Biographical Memoir* (Grand Rapids: Eerdmans, 1954; repr. Banner of Truth, 1987). For a recent treatment of Machen and his time see D. G. Hart, *Defending the Faith: J. Gresham Machen and the Crisis of Conservative Protestantism in Modern America* (Baltimore: Johns Hopkins University Press, 1994; repr. Baker Books, 1995).

The next few selections bring us to the opening exercises of the new school. As part of the inaugural festivities that took place at the opening of the seminary in August 1812, a sermon, a lecture, and a charge to the new professor were delivered, and these set the tone and defined the direction of the school. The contributions from Samuel Miller and Philip Milledoler shed much light on the theology of ministry that would characterize the ministerial instruction students would receive. Archibald Alexander's message demonstrates the academic breadth and practical application that would characterize the seminary's biblical scholarship, rooted in a pious dependence on the ministry and work of the Holy Spirit.

The remaining selections demonstrate the integral relationship between theology and piety that characterized the publications of the seminary's founders, faculty, Board of Directors, and graduates. The majority of the selections address topics such as: a call to the ministry; the office and responsibilities of the ministry; sermon composition and delivery; the challenges and opportunities of the pastoral office; the means by which the minister can cultivate personal piety. Some of the essays address subjects which ought to be foremost in a minister's preaching. Additional essays examine how doctrine nourishes the Christian life, the important role confessions and catechisms serve in defining, defending, and explaining Christian belief and practice, and the purpose of church government and ecclesiastical polity in the life of spiritually healthy churches.

Viewed chronologically, the Princetonians' early writings address issues critical to the founding of the seminary. Writing as active churchmen and seasoned pastors, strong emphasis is placed on the value of theological study and the cultivation of ministerial piety for effective gospel service. Faced with an anti-clericalism that tended towards the democratization of the church and the downgrading of formal instruction for pastoral office, the Princetonians responded with articles and essays that expressed the biblical warrant for ministerial instruction and the divine calling of the pastoral office.[1]

---

[1] For a careful study of the cultural and theological shifts that took place at this time in American history see Nathan O. Hatch, *The Democratization of American Christianity* (New Haven: Yale University Press, 1989).

The first few decades of the nineteenth century were years of tremendous religious ferment. New religious sects such as the Mormons and Jehovah's Witnesses emerged challenging the basic tenets of Trinitarian orthodoxy and the redemptive accomplishments of Christ's substitutionary atonement. The period was also influenced by the Second Great Awakening, a movement of the Spirit of God, the effect and influence of which was examined in detail by the Princetonians. The early faculty at the seminary were men who had personal experience of revival. During these years they gave careful consideration to an examination of revival and expecially to the distinguishing of a genuine work of the Spirit from mere religious excitement. The new evangelistic methodology of Charles Finney, and the 'New Divinity' of Nathaniel Taylor were likewise subject to their critique.[1]

Samuel Miller's 'Ecclesiastical Polity: A Lecture', and Charles Hodge's 'What is Presbyterianism?' reflect debates taking place between the 1830s and 1860s regarding the biblical foundations and divine warrant for Presbyterian models of church government.[2] Notable emphases in this period can be found on the topics of public

---

[1] For Samuel Miller's analysis of the issues confronting the Presbyterian Church's identity and future see Samuel Miller, *Letters to Presbyterians on the Present Crisis in the Presbyterian Church in the United States* (Philadelphia: Anthony Finley, 1833). Some of Charles Hodge's best articles written for the *Biblical Repertory and Princeton Review* during this period were collected and published in a single volume in 1857. The volume provides an important overview of the key issues and individuals that the Princetonians addressed in the first half of the nineteenth century. See Charles Hodge, *Essays and Reviews: Selections from 'The Princeton Review'* (New York: Robert Carter & Brothers, 1857).

[2] For extended treatments of the topic see Samuel Miller, *Presbyterianism the Truly Primitive and Apostolical Constitution of the Church of Christ* (Philadelphia, 1835): idem., *The Primitive and Apostolic Order of the Church of Christ Vindicated* (Philadelphia: Presbyterian Board of Publication, 1840). Miller's most enduring work may well be his biblical and historical study on the office of ruling elder. See Samuel Miller, *An Essay, on the Warrant, Nature and Duties of the Office of the Ruling Elder, in the Presbyterian Church* (New York: Jonathan Leavitt, 1832; repr. *The Ruling Elder*, Presbyterian Heritage Publications, 1987). For a posthumous collection of Charles Hodge's writings on the doctrine of the church and its polity see *Discussions in Church Polity,* ed. William Durant (New York: Charles Scribner's Sons, 1878). The collection is intended as a supplemental volume to Hodge's three-volume *Systematic Theology* which as published did not include a section on the doctrine of the church.

worship, the missionary mandate, evangelistic outreach, the doctrine of the atonement, scriptural teaching on the doctrine of imputation, and catechetical instruction of the church. Charles Hodge's 1862 article, 'Are There Too Many Ministers?' illustrates the Princetonians' passion for missions and evangelistic outreach even as it indicts the Presbyterian Church for elitism in failing to provide sufficient ministerial support to sustain pastoral ministry among the poor. The Princetonians also entered into current debates regarding the propriety, benefits, and liabilities of the newly emerging Sunday School movement.[1]

A recurring emphasis throughout the decades is on the proper inter-relationship between theology and piety; A. A. Hodge's 1877 inaugural address, 'Dogmatic Christianity, the Essential Ground of Practical Christianity', is representative of the Princetonians' ongoing interest in maintaining the practical and pastoral implications of the formal study of theology in a period of increasing academic professionalization in seminary education. In two valuable addresses delivered to the student body in 1904 and 1911, Hodge's successor, B. B. Warfield, provides valuable insight on cultivating piety while pursuing theological studies in the academic atmosphere of campus life. 'Spiritual Culture in the Theological Seminary' and 'The Religious Life of Theological Students' represent the seminary's continuing commitment, in the opening years of the twentieth century, to the nurture of piety and sanctified learning as the fundamental educational ethos of the school.

The closing addresses by Maitland Alexander, grandson of Archibald Alexander, and Caspar Wistar Hodge Jr., grandson of Charles Hodge, reflect the challenges and changes facing the seminary in the early 1920s, precursors of events which would soon lead to the school's reorganization in 1929 and the subsequent exodus of several faculty to establish Westminster Theological Seminary in Philadelphia as a continuation of the principles and purpose for which Princeton Theological Seminary had originally been founded.[2]

[1] For a valuable history of the movement see Anne M. Boylan, *Sunday School: the Formation of an American Institution, 1790-1880* (New Haven: Yale University Press, 1988).
[2] The decade witnessed rapid changes. Hodge's 1921 inaugural address expressed confidence 'that here in America and in our church, the influence of Charles Hodge,

Although the selections were written over a period of a century by men who, in some cases, had never met, the spiritual continuity of their theological convictions is evident. Spiritual wisdom, fidelity to the biblical text, pastoral instinct, and confessional churchmanship anchor their scholarship and give direction to their ministerial instruction.

A noticeable feature of this collection is its pastoral warmth and depth of insight. The reader is made to feel the importance of the subject under consideration by the manner in which it is presented. Even the smaller contributions are packed with a pastoral wisdom that opens up whole horizons of understanding on the work of the Christian ministry.[1] Academic reviews become opportunities for

Robert Breckinridge, James Thornwell, Robert Dabney, W. G. T. Shedd, and B. B. Warfield, still lives on'. By 1929, Hodge's perspective had changed but his hope in God's promises had not diminished. In conclusion to an article similar to his inaugural address published in *The Evangelical Quarterly*, Hodge commented on the changes he witnessed: 'Doubtless this Reformed faith is suffering a decline in the theological world today. What has been termed a "Reformed spring time in Germany" we cannot regard as the legitimate daughter of the classic Reformed faith. In Scotland the names of William Cunningham and Thomas Crawford no longer exert the influence we wish they did. In America the influence of Charles Hodge, Robert Breckinridge, James Thornwell, Robert Dabney, William G. T. Shedd, and Benjamin Warfield, seems largely to have vanished. But though in theological circles and ecclesiastical courts the leaders of Reformed thought find scant recognition, wherever humble souls catch the vision of God in his glory and bow in humility and adoration before him, trusting for salvation only in his grace and power, there you have the essence of the Reformed faith, and God in his providence may yet raise up a leader of religious thought who shall once again make the Reformed faith a power in the theological world. If and when this happens we may confidently expect a true revival of religion in the Protestant world.' See Caspar Wistar Hodge Jr., 'The Reformed Faith', *The Evangelical Quarterly*, vol. 1 (1929): pp. 3-24.

[1] Archibald Alexander's wisdom is evident in his observations on the value of 'polished' manners for ministerial usefulness: 'In our opinion, true humility, meekness, and benevolence will produce the most genuine politeness, and if these dispositions are possessed in a high degree by the minister of the cross, the want of exterior accomplishments, though desirable, may easily be dispensed with. It is not intended to be intimated, that clerical manners are of trivial consequence; they are undoubtedly important, and when of the right kind, tend to promote the usefulness of ministers of the gospel. The idea which I intend to communicate is, that those manners which are in vogue among the higher classes of society are not exactly those which always become a preacher of the gospel. A young man who possesses

a fresh exposition of the topic under discussion; occasional pieces, addressing contemporary issues, provide helpful insights into the life and work of the church at that time. Throughout the collection, one senses being in the company of men who lived in the presence of God and who knew the sacred obligations entrusted to them as ministers of the gospel of Jesus Christ.[1]

---

genuine piety and good sense, will be likely, in the course of seven years' training, to acquire as much ease and polish of manners as are necessary, in a majority of clergymen; for, while a few have to mingle with the wealthy and fashionable classes of society, the greater number must labour among poor and plain people, with whom sincerity and friendliness are the qualities in a minister's conduct which serve best to recommend him to their esteem and confidence. And I venture to assert, that of the hundreds of students who have passed under my observation, those from rich families have possessed no superiority of manners over their poorer brethren.' See Archibald Alexander, *Thoughts on the Education of Pious and Indigent Candidates for the Ministry,* (Philadelphia: Board of Education of the Presbyterian Church, n.d.), p. 5. (See below, pp. 279-80.)

[1] One of the best summary statements of the Princetonians' convictions and sense of calling is found in Charles Hodge's reflections on the articles published in the *Biblical Repertory and Princeton Review.* As an academic extension of the seminary's goals, Hodge's remarks about the journal are equally representative of the Princetonians' understanding of the seminary's mission: 'The conductors of the *Princeton Review,* however, were Presbyterians. They firmly believed that the system of doctrine contained in the Westminster Confession of Faith, the system of the Reformed Church, and of Augustinians in all ages, is the truth of God revealed for his glory and the salvation of men. They believed that the upholding that system in its integrity, bearing witness to it as the truth of God, and its extension through the world, was the great duty of all those who had experienced its power. They believed, also, that the organization of the Presbyterian Church, its form of government and discipline, was more nearly conformed than any other to the scriptural model, and the best adapted for preserving the purity and developing the life of the church. It was, therefore, the vindication of that system of truth and of the principles of that ecclesiastical polity, the conductors of this journal, from first to last, had constantly in view. In this world life is a constant struggle against the causes of death. Liberty is maintained only by unsleeping vigilance against the aggressions of power; virtue is, of necessity, in constant antagonism to vice; and truth to error. That a journal consecrated to the support of truth should be controversial, is a matter of course; it is a law of its existence, the condition of its usefulness. The Bible is the most controversial of books. It is a protest against sin and error from beginning to end. To object to controversy, therefore, is to object to what is in this world the necessary condition of life. It is, consequently, no just ground of reproach to this journal that it has been engaged in controversy during the whole course of its existence. If it

* * * * *

The Princetonians were men who knew Christ's love and who loved him in return. They prayed, fasted, studied, and thought deeply on all aspects of the Christian life. Their theology of pastoral ministry was deeply rooted in the soil of their union with Christ, and from it grew a school of ministry which, through the power of Christ's Spirit, did much good for Christ's church. This is what God can do through the lives of men whose hearts are in heaven and whose hope is in Christ.

JAMES M. GARRETSON
Fort Lauderdale, Florida
December 2011

---

has always contended for the true and the right, and done this with due humility and charity, it has fulfilled its destiny. That it has often failed—at least in spirit and manner—may, and we fear must, be conceded. All such failures are to its surviving conductors matters of regret; but they can honestly say they have ever laboured to support the truth of God and to promote the interests of his kingdom to the best of their understanding and ability.' See Charles Hodge, 'Retrospect of the History of the Princeton Review', *Biblical Repertory and Princeton Review Index Volume from 1825-1868* (Philadelphia: Peter Walker, 1871), pp. 3-4.

REMEMBRANCE OF THINGS PAST

Alexander Hall, Princeton Theological Seminary, opened in 1817, from an old engraving. 'This building is of stone . . . It has been admired by all who have seen it, as a model of neat, and tasteful, and, at the same time, of plain, economical, and remarkably solid workmanship.' (Samuel Miller).

THE first signal manifestation of the divine favour to this institution was the selection of Dr Archibald Alexander and Dr Samuel Miller as it professors, and their being spared for nearly forty years to devote themselves to its service. It is admitted that the most important part of a man's life is the formative period of youth. The same is true of communities and institutions. If a college be dependent on the State, its character may vary with the change of parties in the State; but if it be independent, it bids fair to retain its original character from generation to generation. If a father commit his child to incompetent and wicked tutors and governors, the fate of the child is sealed; but if it be confided to faithful guardians, as a rule, it will grow up to be an ornament and a blessing. The favour of God to this infant seminary, was manifested in its being entrusted to the hands of men pre-eminently qualified for the sacred trust.

They were in the first place eminently holy men. They exerted that indescribable but powerful influence which always emanates from those who live near to God. Their piety was uniform and serene; without any taint of enthusiasm or fanaticism. It was also biblical. Christ was as prominent in their religious experience, in their preaching, and in their writings, as he is in the Bible. Christ's person, his glory, his righteousness, his love, his presence, his power, filled the whole sphere of their religious life. When men enter a Roman Catholic Church, they see before them a wooden image of Christ extended upon a cross. To this lifeless image they bow. When students entered this seminary, when its first professors were alive, they had held up before them the image of Christ, not graven by art or man's device, but as portrayed by the Spirit on the pages of God's Word; and it is by beholding that image that men are transformed into its likeness from glory to glory. It is, in large measure, to this constant holding up of Christ, in the glory of his person and the all-sufficiency of his work, that the hallowed influence of the fathers of this seminary is to be attributed.

CHARLES HODGE

WILLIAM BUELL SPRAGUE
1795-1876

PASTOR, author, and consummate theological biographer, William Buell Sprague was born in Andover, Connecticut in 1795. Sprague graduated from Yale College in 1815, and enrolled at Princeton Theological Seminary receiving his degree in 1819.

Sprague's first pastoral charge was with the Congregational Church in West Springfield, Massachusetts, where he served from 1820-29. In 1829 he accepted a call to Albany, NY, to serve as pastor at Second Presbyterian Church.

A beloved pastor and eloquent preacher, Sprague's forty years of ministry in Albany were also marked by tremendous literary productivity. His publications include sermons, biographies, historical pieces, lectures, and an important volume addressing a biblical and historical view of the origins, effects, and fruits of a Holy Spirit-originated revival, *Lectures on Revivals*.[1] The book also includes valuable essays

---

[1] W. B. Sprague, *Lectures on Revival* (Edinburgh: Banner of Truth, 2007).

on the subject from leading ministers who had personal experience of revival in their ministries.

A first-rate bibliophile, Sprague's personal library contained a massive collection of pamphlets, sermons, and other fugitive pieces of biographical and historical material often lost to future generations because of their ephemeral nature. His foresight for preservation of this material came to fruition in what is probably his greatest literary legacy to the Christian church—the massive nine-volume, *Annals of the American Pulpit,* published between 1857-69. The volumes record the history of the major denominations and religious groups in the United States through to the mid-nineteenth century. They are particularly valuable for the number of primary source documents included which give testimony to the vitality of Christian piety and its outworking in the lives of individuals, churches, denominations, and the nation. The volumes are a moving and spiritually enriching collection of biographical, historical, theological, and pastoral observations. They remain of enduring value for understanding the advance of Christ's church in America.

Sprague's moving retrospect on the first fifty years of Princeton Theological Seminary's history that follows provides helpful insights into Princeton's past and the reasons it had been so powerfully favoured by God in its mission to prepare future generations of pastors and preachers. Sprague cherished the teaching he had received at Princeton from the lips of men such as Archibald Alexander and Samuel Miller, and sought to preserve and perpetuate its ministerial heritage in his own life, ministry, and writings.

A GOLDEN JUBILEE[1]

F ELLOW Alumni and Dear Brethren: It would be an offence against the proprieties of the hour, against the instincts of nature, and even the dictates of religion, to suppose that our hearts were not now moved by a common impulse, and our thoughts flowing in the same channel. In coming back to this endeared spot, to keep this commemorative day, we have, I suppose, by common consent, left all matters of private and individual interest behind us. We have come to unite in an offering of reverence, and gratitude, and filial devotion to the mother who has cherished and trained us, and then dismissed us with her blessing, and sent us forth to our work. We have come to offer to God thanksgiving, not only for his manifold tokens of kindness to ourselves, in the various fields we have occupied, but for that unbroken stream of bounty and grace, which, during all these years, he has been pouring upon our beloved seminary. We have come to look on each other's faces again in the land of the living; to refresh our spirits by the interchange of kind thoughts and grateful remembrances; and though we shall meet the graves of many of our brethren on the field we are to traverse, and cannot but pause in tenderness and sadness by the side of them, yet the transition to the glorious world beyond is too easy to allow them to cast upon us more than a momentary shadow. It is chiefly a work of the heart then, in the form of communion with each other, and, may I not add, with a portion of the general assembly and church of the firstborn, that we are assembled here to perform.

The occasion, you perceive, gives me no choice of a subject. There are numerous topics, bearing more or less directly on the general

---

[1] William B. Sprague, *A Discourse Addressed to the Alumni of the Princeton Theological Seminary, April 30, 1862, on Occasion of the Completion of its First Half Century* (Albany: Steam Press of Van Benthuysen, 1862).

subject of theological education, from which I might perhaps select, without doing any great violence to the occasion; but I am sure you would regard any abstract discussion as but a poor response to the distinctive claims of the day. In your heart, if not with your lips, you would be quoting Solomon against me, where he says, 'To every thing there is a season.' You would say, Other themes for other places and other times; but here, today, the only befitting theme is the *Princeton Theological Seminary*. I do not complain of the restraint which the occasion imposes upon me—I am rather glad to be shut up in so green a pasture.

The thought which I propose now to illustrate, is at once the most general and the most obvious that suggests itself in connection with the occasion—namely, that *this institution is a might power*—mighty in its *elements* and *operations*.

The first element of this power is to be found in *the spirit in which the institution originated*. The spirit of any age, or of the church, or any portion of the church, at any given period, is never a matter of accident, or the product of causes that have had only a brief existence—on the contrary, it has had a long train of antecedents, and is the result of the combined influences of many minds, and perhaps of several generations. The Presbyterian Church in this country, from her beginning, was marked by true Christian nobility: on the very first page of her records are names which will always remain proof against the oblivious influence of time. While she was yet in her minority, unhappily she stood forth before the world as a house divided against itself; but, even then, she had her noble spirits on each side; and, though they were not working *harmoniously,* the Head of the church was overruling their independent and even conflicting movements for the correction of her errors, and the ultimate increase of her energies. As the re-union marked a bright period in her history, so it proved a starting point for yet more signal triumphs; and though, in common with every other Christian denomination, she had a thorny path to traverse during the War of the Revolution, yet, besides showing herself baptized with the fire of Christian patriotism, she was prosecuting her appropriate mission up to the full measure of her ability. And in the generation that came out of that conflict, as well as in the one that immediately succeeded, our church had many choice

spirits, to whose influence in guiding, controlling, elevating, it were
not easy to fix a limit. Here we reach the point where the great idea
of establishing a theological seminary, to meet the increasing wants
of the church, was first developed. Three generations at least had
performed their work and passed away, leaving the results in a widely
extended ecclesiastical body, in an elevated tone of public spirit, and
in a just appreciation of an enlightened as well as earnest ministry.
And now that the fulness of the time for this great work had come,
not only was the general state of the public mind, in a good degree,
prepared for it, but there were men found suitable to conduct the
enterprise;—men who united to a sober, comprehensive, far reaching intellect a heart in which the love of Christ and of his church was
the ruling passion. The Presbytery of Philadelphia, of which Doctors
Green and Janeway were prominent members, had the honour of
originating the overture to the General Assembly, in which this noble
conception was embodied; and it was certainly highly creditable to
the catholic spirit of the Assembly of 1809, that the chairman of the
committee, to whom this important subject was referred, was Dr
Dwight, President of Yale College, who was a delegate that year from
the General Association of Connecticut. The report of the committee
was marked by great wisdom, and suggested three different ways in
which the exigency might be met—namely, the establishment of one
seminary that should be central in the church; or the establishment
of two,—one in the north and one in the south; or the establishment
of one within the bounds of each synod. Agreeably to the suggestion
of the committee, these several plans were referred to the consideration of all the presbyteries, with a request that they would respectively signify their preference at the next meeting of the Assembly;
and, when the returns came to be made in 1810, the question was
decided in favour of the one central institution. The next step was
the drafting of a Plan of the proposed seminary; and to this service
Doctors Green, Woodhull, Romeyn, Miller, Alexander, Richards,
and Armstrong—all men of note in the church, and some of them
men of extraordinary power—were designated. Of the instrument
which they produced (said to have been from the pen of Dr Green),
I will only say that it was worthy of the honoured names affixed
to it. Thus it appears that, while this institution had its origin in a

watchful regard to the interests of the church, its foundations were laid by some of the master-builders in Zion; and I am sure you will agree with me in recognizing in this fact one of the leading elements of its power.

I find another in *the felicitous selection of the place where the institution should be located*. It might seem, at first, that the prevalent idea of the presbyteries, which was also sanctioned by the General Assembly, that there should be one great central institution for the accommodation of the whole church, was not very rigidly adhered to, inasmuch as the position actually selected had a large majority of presbyteries, as well as a much more extended territory, south of it. This arrangement doubtless had its origin in the spirit of fraternal conciliation, and in the general desire to accomplish the greatest amount of good. It was perceived at once that this place offered facilities for the establishment and growth of such a seminary, that were to be found nowhere else; and to this weighty consideration our fathers were willing to sacrifice all personal preferences. Besides, they were well aware that they were making provision for the church as she then was, and not as she would be at some distant day; and doubtless they foresaw what has actually come to pass,—that, as she extended the bounds of her habitation, she would plant other similar institutions to meet her increasing necessities. Nor is it to be supposed that they wholly ignored the fact that this place is easily accessible from the New England States; for there was a relationship existing then between our denomination and the Congregationalists of New England, that has since ceased; and, though the Andover Seminary was at that time in successful operation, it was doubtless anticipated—and the event justified the anticipation—that many young men from among our Northern neighbours would prefer an education here to one in their own well-endowed and honoured institution. These, it may be presumed, were some of the considerations that led the Assembly to that more liberal construction of the expressed will of the church, that fixed the seminary so far north of the actual centre of the domain of Presbyterianism.

But what were the particular circumstances which combined to give this place an advantage over any other that could be selected? First of all, it is a *lovely* spot; where nature has been even prodigal of both her bounties and her beauties; where there is a healthful atmosphere to breathe, and rich prospects to gaze upon and admire. So, too, it is a *retired* spot, and therefore favourable to study, to devotion, to the general culture of both the intellect and the heart. It cannot be denied that a theological seminary, in the midst of a crowded population, has some advantages peculiar to itself; particularly in the opportunities it affords for active usefulness in ministering to the spiritual wants of the ignorant and depraved; but is it not at least questionable whether these advantages are not more than counter-balanced by the distraction and turmoil, and especially the manifold temptations to a spirit of worldliness, incident to a great city? But this institution, though exposed to few disturbing influences, is far from occupying a too-secluded position—here and hereabouts are all the advantages for social enjoyment and culture that any student can reasonably desire. And then it is to be borne in mind that this quiet place is about equi-distant from the two largest cities on the continent; that as either can now be reached in a couple of hours, so the advantages of both are easily accessible; and that our students can procure books, or anything else, from either of these cities just about as readily as if they lived on Broadway or Chestnut Street. But probably the controlling circumstance that led to the selection of this spot, was that here was *already established a great literary institution,* which had, from its beginning, been identified with the Presbyterian Church; an institution whose history was, to a great extent, the history of illustrious names; and whose fame and influence had already penetrated to the extremities of the land. When the seminary was born, the college threw a protecting arm around her, as if she had been an adopted child. The college library was our library. Our recitation room was in one of the college buildings. Our place of worship was the college hall. One-third of the preaching we listened to on Sabbath morning was from the venerable president of the college. Our evening discussions were often enlivened by the wit and genius of one of the college professors,—I mean the lamented Lindsly. In short, it is not too much to say that the benign influence of the college was all-pervading. As the seminary grew in years, she grew also in strength, and, after a while, she went up and took possession of her own noble home; and, in process of time, she became independent in respect to all her accommodations. But she has never cut loose from the college in any such sense as to forget her early debt of gratitude, or to decline or undervalue the benefits of an enduring intimacy. The professors in the seminary and the officers of the college have always been fellow-helpers in every good work; and I venture to say that there are few who cherish a more grateful remembrance of Carnahan, and Dod, and Hope, than our surviving professors who were associated with them. The truth is that the two institutions have, in various ways, ministered to the advantage of each other; and each of them holds a higher place today,—the one in the world of letters, the other in the domain of theology,—than if they had not been walking together for half a century in one another's light.

There is yet another circumstance, worthy of being noticed, that designates this place as peculiarly fitted to be the seat of a theological seminary—I refer to the fact that it is *the depository of so much venerable dust.* Our fathers, in fixing upon this spot, did not forget that the graves of Burr, and Edwards, and Davies, and Witherspoon were here; and that the illustrious Samuel Stanhope Smith was lingering in the twilight of life, just ready to be gathered; and, if they could have thrown themselves forward, fifty years, they would have found that family of honoured graves more than doubled. Those graves are the silent representatives of some of the brightest spirits which have emigrated from earth to heaven; and, to every minister of the gospel, and every candidate for the ministry, they speak most impressively of being faithful unto the death, and of the crown and the throne, with which fidelity shall be rewarded. Is it not a privilege to be living within a few moments' walk of a group of monuments, that have names inscribed upon them, which are as household words all over Evangelical Christendom? Is it not reasonable to believe that many a young man who comes hither to be trained for his sacred work, while he sits with docility and delight at the feet of the living teacher, sometimes gets a fresh baptism of spiritual influence by waiting at the graves of the glorified dead? Is it too much to suppose that the very atmosphere of this institution has been rendered more pure from its connection with the memories of these departed sages and saints?

Enough, I trust, has been said to show that the power of this seminary is derived partly from its favourable position. A yet more important element of this power is the character of the minds that have controlled it.

The conception, the beginning, even the establishment, of a great institution is nothing more than the opening of a field for gifted and well-trained minds to labour in; and unless the services of such minds can be put in requisition, the design of the institution can never be accomplished. Great moral enterprises do not work out their legitimate results by mere mechanical force: even the Almighty Architect of the Universe, though he has been pleased to subject the kingdoms of both nature and providence to fixed laws, yet never, for a moment, withdraws his eye from the minutest of his works, or leaves a single event to occur without his guiding and controlling agency—surely then it were preposterous to imagine that human wisdom should breathe into any of its plans or its works a principle of life, which, if not absolutely self-sustaining, would require but little care or effort for its preservation. After this seminary had been created, by an Act of the General Assembly, and the whole church had pronounced the work very good, the enterprise might have been rendered utterly abortive by being confided to an inadequate supervision and direction. But, instead of that, the same noble spirits that had projected and founded it, became its guardians and professors; and, as they passed away, others, upon whom their mantles fell, entered into their labours; and thus the seminary has passed the perils of youth, and reached a vigorous and prosperous manhood. Never could this point have been attained but for the large measure of intellectual foresight, and comprehensiveness, and accomplishment, of love to the church, of reliance on the wisdom, and power, and grace from above, and of harmony of counsel and effort, which have characterized those to whom the destinies of the institution have thus far been committed.

If we glance at the list of the *directors* of the seminary, the first name on which our eye rests, is that of the venerable Ashbel Green,—whose majestic bearing seemed to say that he was born to rule; and who, during many of his later years, stood as an almost solitary representative of the ministry of a preceding generation. His commanding presence fitly represented his force of intellect and force of will. He was sternly unyielding in his regard to what he believed right, and in his opposition to what he considered wrong; and some of his demonstrations might have indicated, especially to those who saw him only at a distance, that there was an excess of iron in his moral constitution; but those who were privileged to get nearer to his heart, and to witness the air of graceful kindness which he diffused around his own fireside; who knew the comforting words that he uttered to the sorrowful, and the encouraging words that he addressed to the desponding, and the large charities that he dispensed to the poor, needed no other evidence that there was strung in his bosom a chord, not only of high generosity but of tender sympathy. Besides serving the college in this place, in the relations of both professor and president,—the latter for a long course of years, he exercised his ministry, for a quarter of a century, in connection with one of the most influential churches on the continent, and at a period which identified him with some of the leading events of both our civil and ecclesiastical history. He shone, perhaps, nowhere more brightly than in the pulpit. His discourses were simple and natural in their construction; of a deeply evangelical and practical tone; full of appropriate and luminous thought; and delivered with an air of dignity and impressiveness that scarcely left it at anyone's option whether or not to be an attentive hearer. The clouds of old age had settled around him some time before his departure; but I believe they were at no time so dark and heavy but the beams of the Sun of righteousness passed through them into his soul. It was an auspicious omen to the seminary that such a veteran in wisdom and piety should have had such a place assigned to him, and especially that he should have occupied the chair of the President of the Board of Directors for so long a period.

The name of Dr Green, at the head of the list of directors, is followed by more than a hundred other names, some of which are associated with princely liberality and public spirit, others with the highest order of pulpit eloquence, or executive power, or both combined, while most of them have commanded, in a high degree, the respect and confidence of the church. In looking over this honoured list, I find not a few, who, for their exalted character as well as faithful services, are well worthy of grateful commemoration; and, but for the invidiousness of making a selection, and the fear of exhausting your patience, I would gladly pay a passing tribute to a goodly number of them. Indeed, there are two bright names on this catalogue, which have so lately become associated with the grave, and which, withal, suggest such precious memories, that I am sure you would not be willing that I should pass them without at least a kindly commemorative word. Need I say that I refer to Van Rensselaer and Murray.

Cortlandt Van Rensselaer had his birth and education amidst decidedly Christian influences, and yet amidst those temptations to a life of indolent ease, which are always incident, especially in this country, to a condition of great opulence and worldly consideration. Happily, in his case, Christianity early assumed the dominion in his heart, so that he passed safely the ordeal to which providence subjected him, and came out of the walks of the most elegant refinement into one of the humblest of all the fields of ministerial labour. And that mission of good-will to the poor slaves he would gladly have continued, but for the appearance of certain clouds in the distant horizon, that have since covered the whole heavens, and are now discharging their contents in a tempest of fire. We find him next engaged in planting a Presbyterian Church in a beautiful village in this neighbourhood, where none had before existed, and, after a few years of self-denying and eminently useful labour there, he took the responsible position of Secretary of the General Assembly's Board of Education, which he held until the disease of which he died had well-nigh run its course. As he was not only a director, but an Alumnus, of the seminary, so he was always devoted to its interests; and the office which he held during the greater part of his professional life,—discharging its duties not only most faithfully but gratuitously, placed him at the head of one of the great fountains of influence by which the seminary is sustained. Who that knew him will ever forget the fertility of his mind in projects of Christian usefulness, and the exuberance of his charity in carrying them into effect? Who can forget the kindliness of his smile; the meekness and modesty of his spirit; the firmness with which he adhered to his own mature convictions, and the graceful facility and generous indulgence with which he met the adverse opinions of others; his practical obliviousness of worldly rank; his wit, sometimes taking the form of a delicate innuendo, and sometimes doing the work of a two-edged sword; his zeal and energy, shrinking from no sacrifices, halting at no obstacles, and revealing a heart deeply in communion with him, who, though he was rich, for our sakes became poor? His death was the signal for mourning much beyond the limits of his own communion. The marble that marks the place of his grave, might well bear the inscription, 'An exalted specimen of sanctified humanity.'

But scarcely had the mind of the church been withdrawn from the heavy calamity sustained in his death, before the tidings were flying over the land that Nicholas Murray, a kindred spirit, had, by a single step, passed from the fulness of health and usefulness to his reward. Murray was born with extraordinary qualities of both mind and heart; but he was born, and had his early training, amidst the cold shadows of Romanism. By a train of circumstances which were little of his own devising, he was separated from his earliest religious associations, and was brought across the ocean, first to cast away his inherited errors, and then to be baptized with the Holy Ghost. In due time, he went forth from this school of the prophets, and, like the great apostle, whose spirit he so largely shared, became an earnest and powerful defender of the faith which he had seemed born to oppose. For upwards of thirty years, and until his Master called him home, he was always in the high places of Zion, and always had his armour on, ready to obey any summons. He had strongly marked national characteristics, but they were so many irresistible attractions. His face reflected not only his clear and comprehensive intellect, but his genial, loving and sympathetic spirit. No child of sorrow, no victim of temptation, no subject of poverty, could ever be brought to his notice, but his heart, his lips, his hand, involuntarily opened to administer the needed consolation, counsel, or relief. In the pulpit he spake words of wisdom and of weight, and with an air of authority that continually pointed upward to his divine commission. In the deliberative assembly his presence was always recognized as a power. Through the press his intellect delivered itself of much profound practical wisdom, and the elements of conviction were lodged even in the corruscations of his wit. When his work was done, his hands were still nerved to do more. The church gazed wishfully after him, and felt that one of her strong rods was broken.

In connection with the Board of Directors, I may mention the Board of Trustees also,—on whom devolves the chief management of the financial interests of the seminary. And here we find another noble body of men,—some of whom have been conspicuous in the different professions, some in the field of judicial honour, some in the circles of commercial enterprise, some in the walks of general philanthropy, while all have been skilfully, watchfully, earnestly engaged in placing the institution on higher and firmer ground, by the successful disposition and gradual enlargement of its pecuniary resources. At the head of this list, and as a fitting representation of it, stand the justly cherished names of Andrew Kirkpatrick and Samuel Bayard,—both synonyms for wisdom and purity, benevolence and honour.

Such, then, are the minds by which this institution, in respect to its outward and more general concerns, has been controlled; and, surely, under a conduct so wise and energetic, it were reasonable to suppose that, by this time, it should have reached a vigorous maturity. But it is the character, not of its directors and trustees merely; but especially of its *professors,* to which we are to look for the secret of its rapid and healthful development. I cannot speak of them all in detail, as my feelings would incline me, because—thanks to a gracious providence—a portion of them are yet alive to hear the testimony I should render; but I may say of them, in general, that, though they have exhibited a diversity of gifts, yet all have had the same spirit;—a spirit of singular devotedness to the interests of the institution—all have been men who have well established their claim upon the gratitude of the church, and whose memory the church will treasure, as a sacred deposit, in her own bosom. The day will come—though I would fain hope it may be distant—when the characters of those who now occupy these chairs of honourable usefulness, will become legitimate subjects for delineation; and I have no fear that those on whom the office shall devolve, will find it other than a grateful and easy one; but, meanwhile, we may be allowed to linger for a little among the graves of the departed, and refresh both our memories and our hearts by calling up some of their admirable characteristics.

First on the starred list appears the venerable name of Archibald Alexander;—a circumstance that reflects double honour upon the church at that period; for it was alike creditable to her that she had such a man within her limits, and that she had the wisdom to place him where his influence would operate with the greatest power. He came hither with the benefit of a large experience, both academic and pastoral; and the event more than justified the high expectations which had been founded upon his reputation, both in Virginia and in Philadelphia. The feature of his character, which was perhaps more obvious and all-pervading than any other, was a well-nigh matchless simplicity. You saw this, first, in all that pertained to his exterior—the movements of his body, the utterances of his lips, the very expression of his countenance, you felt were in perfect harmony with the laws of his own individual constitution. And the same characteristic impressed itself upon the workings of his mind. Though the best productions of many of the best writers, in every part and every period of the church, lay in his memory as so much well-arranged material, and though he knew how to appropriate it to the best advantage, and it had even become essentially incorporated with his own thoughts, yet it never interfered in the least with the perfect individuality of his intellectual operations. Whatever he produced, whether orally or with his pen, had his own image and superscription so deeply wrought into it that its genuineness could hardly become a matter of question. And his simplicity was perfected in the movements of his moral nature—and here it discovered itself in a frankness that never dissembled; in an independence that never faltered; in an integrity that would have maintained itself even in the face of martyr fires. In all the appropriate duties of his professorship, he was alike able and faithful. Not only his lectures, but his less formal communications to the students—his criticisms upon their performances, his solution of their difficulties, and, above all, those never to be forgotten Sunday afternoon talks on practical and experimental religion, all showed a richness and promptness of thought, and a depth of piety, which, I am sure, none of us can recall without admiration. 'What he was as a preacher you who have heard him can never forget; and you who have not heard him can never know. I will only say that here, as everywhere else, he was the very personification of naturalness; and when his inventive and richly stored mind was set vigorously to work in the pulpit, under the combined action of physical health and strong moral forces, he sometimes held his audience by a power absolutely irresistible. The great and good Dr John H. Rice told me that he once heard him preach to a few people assembled in a private dwelling in Virginia, when he became perfectly transfigured, and his

audience as perfectly electrified; and he did not hesitate to pronounce
it the highest effort of pulpit eloquence to which he had ever listened.
In his descent to the grave, there was a beautiful demonstration of his
humility, his faith, his love to God and man,—of all those qualities
which had constituted the strength of his character and the glory of
his life.

Dr Alexander was sole professor but a single year. In 1813, the
revered and beloved name of Samuel Miller became associated with
his; and the relation, thus established, continued a source of mutual
blessing, and a field for cordial co-operation, for nearly forty years.
I will venture to speak of some of the different phases of Dr Miller's
character somewhat in the order in which they presented themselves
to me. In the summer of 1813, and a few weeks only before he entered
on his professorship, I passed a Sabbath in New York, and the excellent report of him which I had often heard in New England, took
me to the then new church in Wall Street, one part of the day. I
saw before me in the pulpit a man of a perfectly symmetrical form,
of a countenance expressive at once of mildness, dignity and intelligence, and altogether, as it seemed to me, of rare personal attractions.
Though his voice was not powerful, or susceptible of any great variety
of inflection, his utterance was perfectly distinct, and his whole manner evinced thoughtfulness and culture. His discourse (I speak of it
with the more confidence, for I heard it again after I became a student
here) was distinguished for lucid arrangement, for impressive scriptural thought, for great propriety and elegance of diction, for being
thoroughly exhaustive of its subject, and in some parts for the very
sublimity of pathos. It is due to candour to say that I always regarded
this as one of his most felicitous efforts; and yet, in its general character, it was but a fair specimen of his preaching. The next time I
saw him was three years later, in his own study, when I presented to
him a letter designed to procure my introduction to the seminary.
His kindly and almost paternal spirit, breathing through his polished
and dignified manner, awakened in me a feeling at once of reverence
and affection; and this mingled feeling never forsook me in all my
subsequent intercourse with him; and it is the offering which I love
to make to his memory to this day. Those fine qualities of mind and
heart which were so beautifully reflected in his manners, constituting

him the highest type of a Christian gentleman, rendered his presence anywhere a benediction. There was a singular grace and fitness in all his words and actions. He had much of the spirit of generous conciliation and forbearance, but it was qualified by an unwavering fidelity to his own well-considered and conscientious judgments. His character, as it came out in his daily life, was, to his students, one unbroken lesson of love and wisdom. And his meetings with us in the recitation room were as creditable to his intellect as I to his heart: for, while the influence of his bland and considerate manner, there as everywhere, operated as a charm, we always had presented to us a luminous, well-digested and highly satisfactory view of the subject which engaged our attention. Dr Miller lived to feel the infirmities of age, but not to be the subject of a paralysed intellect, or to witness any waning of the interest of the church in respect to him. I was one of those who were privileged to see him, when he was standing almost in the presence of death. I never heard such sublime words, expressive at once of trust and victory, as then fell from his lips. The chariot was already there; and it was but a few days after that I heard he had ascended.

There is yet another professor, who has died while in connection with the seminary, and so recently that the numerous tributes which his death called forth are still fresh in the memories of all of us—I refer, as you know, to the gifted and accomplished Addison Alexander. I suppose I may say, without the fear of contradiction, that a nobler specimen of the divine workmanship has rarely appeared, in the form of a human mind, than he exhibited. To have possessed any one faculty in the measure in which he possessed all, would have been enough to constitute a man of mark. His facility at acquiring knowledge of every kind, and especially language, was perhaps without a known parallel; and this, in connection with an untiring industry, gives us the clue to his vast acquisitions. His genius was alike brilliant and powerful—it was equally at home in the heights and in the depths—it could breathe in the zephyr; it could flash in the lightning; it could ride in the storm. The effect of his preaching is thought to have been lessened by the rapidity of his utterance; but his published discourses are a model in respect to both beauty and strength. As a teacher, he not only communicated from stores that seemed inexhaustible, and with a fluency that never hesitated, and a perspicuity that forbade misapprehension, but, by an almost magical influence, he quickened the minds of his pupils into a fervid enthusiasm, which was at once a stimulus to their faculties, and a pledge of their success. He was shy and distant in common intercourse; but those who knew him well, testify that he had not only a large and generous heart, but a strong susceptibility to social enjoyment. For more than twenty years, he shone here, a star of the first magnitude; and the day that saw that star sink beneath the horizon, was a day of deep and widespread mourning.

There have been two other professors in the seminary, who have finished their earthly course, though neither of them died until some time after his connection with the seminary ceased—I refer to John Breckinridge and James W. Alexander. Both of them performed good service here; but as each resigned his professorship after two years, we must doubtless look elsewhere for the monuments of their highest usefulness. Dr Breckinridge was a man of brilliant and attractive qualities, of commanding presence, of an earnest, heroic and generous spirit, and of great control of the popular mind. For several years he held the pastoral office in a large city, discharging its duties with great acceptance and success; but perhaps the years in which he accomplished most for the church, were those in which he was employed in aid of two of our most prominent objects of Christian benevolence. Some of his discourses and especially of his anniversary speeches, in behalf of these objects, have rarely been exceeded as specimens of manly and effective eloquence.

Dr Alexander inherited many of the fine qualities, not only of his father, but, it is believed, of his maternal grandfather also,—the far-famed Dr James Waddell. Like his father, he was a model of simplicity in everything; while he had probably more of graceful culture than his father could claim. He had a mind of great richness, great delicacy, and exquisite susceptibility to every form of beauty. His thoughts always seemed fresh and glowing. His pen rarely moved but it flew; and yet in the record which it made, we sometimes recognize the ingenious speculations of the philosopher, and sometimes the gorgeous creations of the poet. He was distinguished for habits of sanctity and devotion; but there was born with him, and there always remained with him, a vein of playful humour, that he knew better how to control than others knew how to resist. His preaching was at once attractive and instructive. Multitudes thronged to hear him, and not a few met in his ministrations the converting and sanctifying power of God. Both these eminent ministers, though the period of their actual connection with the seminary was brief, were yet always on the alert to promote its interests, and carried a strong affection for it to their graves.

Estimate now the evidence which has been presented that the character of the professors of this seminary forms a mighty element of power. Can anyone believe that men of so much intellectual and moral force can have been here,—some of them for so long a period,—in the vigorous and diligent use of their faculties, without making this institution one of the strongholds of Zion? Especially can anyone believe this, when the influence of the directors and trustees is taken in connection with that of the professors, thus securing the wisest management, as well as the most faithful guidance and the ablest instruction?

Yet another element of strength in this institution is *the bounty by which it has been sustained.* We all know that such an institution as this could never be established and maintained but at a vast expense. Here is a capacious and commodious building devoted to the use of the students. Here are dwellings for the occupancy of the professors. Here is a fine, tasteful edifice for the accommodation of the library; to say nothing of the choice and extensive library which it accommodates. Then again, here are five well-endowed professorships; and probably about thirty scholarships (though the number is nominally considerably greater), which meet, in a great measure, the exigencies of an equal number of indigent students. Surely, all this could never have been done, if the bounty of the church had not flowed hither as a river. The seminary has had, still has, individual benefactors, whose donations are not only honourable but princely; and though delicacy forbids me here to pronounce their names, gratitude has already inscribed them on an imperishable record. And I cannot forbear to refer to the fact, the announcement of which, a few moments since, has filled us with admiration and gratitude, that two of these benefactors have impressed their own bright mark upon this day, by making it the occasion of an offering that is itself grand enough to form an epoch in the history of the institution.[1] And the church, as a body, or at least no inconsiderable portion of it, has, with a willing mind, sent hither large offerings, sanctified by faith and prayer.

Is it too much, then, to say that the mighty power in whose presence we stand, has its being, at least in a subordinate sense, in the spirit of Christian charity?

The last element of this power which I will ask you to consider, is *the influence of the great numbers who have been educated here, reacting upon the institution itself.* I do not say that every individual who has had his training on this ground, has gone away satisfied; for I well know that there are some, who, if there was nothing on earth to find fault with, would vent their spleen against the sun, moon and stars: but I do say with confidence that our students have, with very few exceptions, carried away with them a grateful sense of the benefits received here, which has manifested itself, as opportunity has presented, in substantial acts of good-will. You do not expect a child, of even ordinary sensibility, to forget his early home,—no matter how great may be the distance that separates him from it. You do not expect even the alien, if he has the heart of a man, to ignore the hand that has been stretched out for his guidance, or opened for his relief, as soon as he has passed the range of its movements—and not more reasonable were it to expect that those who have been theologically nurtured here, should forget the helping, forming influence, as soon as they have passed from under it. I tell you, again, they do not forget it—and, more than that, it weighs upon them as an ever present, cherished obligation, keeping their hearts strong, and their hands nerved, for any good service it may be in their power to render. Indeed, they are always serving the seminary just in proportion to the measure of their fidelity and usefulness in the church; for they are its

[1] It may not be improper here to state that the donation referred to was $50,000, from Messrs Robert L. and Alexander Stuart, to be applied, in several different ways, for the benefit of the seminary. Another donation, of $35,000, has been recently made by Mr John C. Green, for the endowment of a new professorship. Each of these gentlemen had so signalized himself by his previous benefactions to the seminary, that these generous and graceful gifts were less a matter of surprise than of thankfulness and rejoicing. It is well known that the beautiful building, containing the library, is but a magnificent item in the sum of the contributions of Mr James Lenox.

epistle, known and read of all men. Wherever you meet one of its Alumni, you have a right to assume, until it is proved to the contrary, that you have found one who always bears it on his heart, and is ready, according to his ability, to lend a helping hand for the promotion of its interests. Well may an institution, with such an army of auxiliaries scattered all over the land, repose securely in a sense of its own stability.

I have endeavoured to show that this seminary is a power mighty in its elements—let us see now whether it is not equally mighty in its *operations*.

I say, then, the influence which this institution has exerted, still exerts, is *diversified,* and yet *harmonious*. Its records show that there is scarcely a department of ministerial or Christian usefulness in which it has not been largely and most creditably represented. Of course its grand object is to make able and faithful ministers of the gospel; and the great business of the ministry is to fulfil the divine ordinance in the preaching of the gospel. Nevertheless, the sacred office, in respect to its particular duties, is somewhat modified by a variety of circumstances; and, in some instances, it becomes incorporated with other kindred vocations. While the individuals concerned appear occasionally, perhaps frequently, in the pulpit, they are entrusted with the supervision and direction of the different branches of the machinery by which the church is doing her great work; and it may be that, while the literal preacher may seem to be almost lost,—perhaps in the quiet round of a teacher's duties, perhaps in the conduct of some grand evangelical enterprise, he may really be accomplishing more for the church than if he could multiply himself into half a dozen stated preachers. I know not whether the office of a Christian minister ever combines more of privation and self-sacrifice with more of efficiency and glory, than when held by the faithful foreign missionary;—the man who goes forth, in the strength of God's grace, to battle with the prince of darkness in the very heart of his earthly dominion. It devolves upon him to strike the first blow for the deliverance perhaps of a vast empire from the deepest intellectual and moral degradation; to supply the first material for the mind to act upon, as it is waking out of the slumber of ages; to commence the re-construction of the whole fabric of society, by substituting a Christian for

a heathen basis—but no less than 127 of our students have become
foreign missionaries; besides seven more who have already been designated to the same office—that is, they have gone, or are going,
to carry the gospel either to the savages on our borders, or the far-
off pagans,—both sitting alike within the shadow of death. No man
occupies a place of higher responsibility than he who superintends
the education of young men for the sacred office; for the influence
of his instructions, and counsels, and spirit, instead of terminating
upon them, diffuses itself all over the church—but this seminary has
supplied twenty-eight professors to different theological institutions,
some of whom, I need not say, have attained to great eminence in
their respective departments. What vast importance attaches to our
colleges,—those nurseries of the very flower of the country's intellect;
and how directly is the hand of those who conduct them upon the
springs of our national prosperity—but of those who have had their
training here, thirty-six have occupied the presidential chair, and
ninety-four have held professorships, in these higher seminaries,—
most of them, at the same time, being, either statedly or occasionally, engaged in preaching the gospel. Who can measure the amount
of service which they perform for the church, who have a primary
agency in directing our great benevolent institutions—but twenty-
nine of our Alumni have held the secretaryship of some or other of
these societies, thus directly identifying themselves with the progress
of the gospel at home or abroad. The influence of an editor of a
widely circulated religious newspaper or other periodical is exerted
so quietly that perhaps the multitude take little note of it; and yet
that same editor may have a sort of ubiquity in the church,—even
in the nation—he may be in contact with men's minds as a guiding,
irresistible power, where his name has never been heard—he may sit
by his desk, and change the current of public opinion, or forestall the
decisions of ecclesiastical judicatories, without opening his lips; and,
when the Sabbath comes, he may be in his own or some other pulpit,
proclaiming the glad tidings, like any other minister of Christ—but
here again, no less than twenty-nine whose names are enrolled on our
catalogue, have held this responsible position; and among them are
several of our most highly endowed and cultivated minds,—some of
whom weekly, and others quarterly, strike chords that vibrate, not

now indeed to the extremities of the land, but up to a certain dark, revolting, bloody boundary. And I must not forget to add that the seminary, especially through its professors, has contributed largely, in other ways, to our theological and historical literature. If all the books, which have been written on this ground, were gathered, they would not only go far towards forming a library, but among them would be found some of the best productions, in their respective departments, that any language can furnish.

But in all this variety there is perfect *harmony;*—not only no interference, but cordial co-operation. The end aimed at in each of these several departments of active usefulness is the same—all have in view the intellectual and moral renovation of the race, in connection with the progress of a pure Christianity. It is like some great piece of machinery, each part of which not only performs its own appropriate work, but helps to maintain the harmonious and efficient action of the whole. The stated pastor, the foreign missionary, the theological professor, the president of a college, the secretary and leading spirit of a great benevolent institution, the editor of a religious newspaper or other periodical,—each has his distinct office, while each becomes, in some sense, an auxiliary to the rest;—sometimes directly,—by supplying the requisite material for others to work upon, or becoming identified with some important effort out of his own immediate range; and sometimes indirectly,—by an example of vigorous application, or perhaps brilliant success.

The influence of this seminary, I remark again, has been a conservative, and yet not an unduly restrictive, influence—it has been adverse to a reckless spirit of innovation, but favourable to healthful progress. The tendency to extremes is one of the qualities that mark the imperfection, not to say perverseness, of our common humanity; but never, perhaps, has this tendency manifested itself so palpably, or in so great a variety of forms, as since this seminary has been in existence; and hence, to meet the exigency hereby created, we have the new and expressive word, *ultraism*. It is worthy of remark that this spirit always contemplates, originally, a good object—it always has its basis in truth and right; but, from being exclusively or disproportionately contemplated by an ill-balanced mind, the object either acquires an undue relative importance, or else it suggests the use of unjustifiable means for its accomplishment. I will instance only a single case—that of revivals of religion. A genuine revival we all recognize as the richest blessing that God bestows upon his church; and, in the multiplication of these scenes, we get a foretaste of millennial, even of heavenly, glory. But who needs be told that, in what has been called a revival, fanaticism has sometimes performed some of her wildest and most revolting feats; and all the solemnities, even the decencies, of religious worship have been sacrificed; and Satan has counted almost as many self-deceivers as the conductor of the work has counted converts. With this spirit, in none of its various manifestations, has this seminary ever had any sympathy—its sound, scriptural teachings have been a perpetual rebuke to it; and the impress of sobriety, which its students have received here, has, with comparatively few exceptions, been decisive of their future course. But then, on the other hand, the seminary has never been alarmed because the world does not stand still—it has never suggested the expediency of stopping short of the point of duty, lest there should be found some temptation there to pass on into the region of extravagance—it has never been slow to admit new thoughts, or to encourage new projects, where they have seemed to originate in wisdom or tend to usefulness. In short, it has sought not to stay the advancing spirit of the age, but to direct it; and sure I am that the verdict of the whole church is that it has been eminently successful.

It is only an extension, or rather a specific application, of this thought, to say that this seminary, *while it has been true to the interests of the Presbyterian Church, which it represents, has yet been catholic in its bearing towards other denominations.* That it has always been the faithful supporter and defender of the Presbyterian faith and order, everyone, who has been a student here, knows from the character of its teachings; and the whole church has evidence of it in the general character of those of her ministers who have been educated here; in the manner in which the seminary has been represented, in her highest judicatory, on questions touching vitally her prosperity; in the fact that the first Professor of Church History and Church Government, while he was yet a pastor, as well as during the period of his professorship, published several elaborate and highly popular works, vindicating the claims of Presbyterianism; and, finally, in the many luminous and forcible articles, bearing more or less directly on this subject, which have appeared, from time to time, in the *Biblical Repertory*. But, while the seminary has shown itself thoroughly Presbyterian, in character as well as in name, it has never assumed that Presbyterianism is the only divinely accredited form of Christianity—while it has maintained that it is the most perfect embodiment of Scripture truth, in respect to both doctrine and order, it has never set up any exclusive banner; never made its own shibboleth a term, either of fraternal communion, or of admission to its privileges. Even in the fierce controversy, connected with the second great disruption of the Presbyterian Church, it never placed itself in any needlessly offensive attitude, or counselled to any rash or uncharitable measures; and I venture to say that those of its Alumni, who, by that act, were thrown into another body, never lost their filial regard for this their *Alma Mater;* and that those of them who are with us here today, are just as earnest in their devotion, and just as cordial in their congratulations, as if the Assembly of 1837 had confined itself to its ordinary routine of business. But the most decisive testimony on this subject is to be gathered from our general *Catalogue;* and, if you will glance over it, you will find a large number of names, whose only connection with Presbyterianism is in having a place there. For instance, in the very first class, there was a man who came hither an Episcopalian, and subsequently became a Baptist—the same man has been, and, for aught I know, still is, one of the lights of the Baptist denomination in the South. No less than forty-two, who have been educated here, have found their home, and their field of labour, in the Episcopal Church—and, of these, three have become bishops;—men, known and honoured by the wise and good of every name; and I doubt not that their large hearts would respond gratefully to our kind remembrances of them. Ninety-two have become ministers in the Congregational Church; fifty-six in the Reformed Dutch Church; thirty-two in the Baptist Church; eleven in the Associate Reformed and United Presbyterian Church; seven in the German Reformed Church; and five in the Lutheran, and an equal number in the Methodist Church. A portion of these, indeed, changed their ecclesiastical relations after leaving the seminary; but many of them did not; and the fact that they could, without embarrassment, pursue their studies here preparatory to the ministry, proves, beyond all question, that they found here an atmosphere, tempered, in a high degree, by the spirit of Christian catholicism. Their distinctive peculiarities they did not indeed hear vindicated—they may have even heard laboured arguments to disprove them; but there has always been a measure of decorum, and dignity, and generous indulgence, pertaining to the spirit of the place, that has made it a happy home even for those whose denominational views are at the greatest remove from those which are here inculcated.

I cannot forbear to say that this seminary is exerting a *loyal and patriotic, but not an intemperate or indiscriminately condemnatory, influence*. It seems to be the order of providence that everything on earth that hath life, whether physical, intellectual, or moral, should have its times for going to sleep. Thus it has been with American patriotism—the spirit, which worked as fire in the bosoms of our revolutionary fathers, had not only lost much of the glow in which it then manifested itself, but had so long been exposed to the wild storms of party, that it seemed threatened with absolute extinction. Wise and thoughtful men were not without fears that patriotism, in respect to a large part of our population at least, was sinking into her last iron slumber, if she had not actually been arrayed in her death-robes. But the memorable 13th of April, 1861, put to flight that delusion. The balls that struck upon Sumter did a much more potent work than they had bargained for; for, besides achieving an inglorious triumph over a handful of brave but defenceless men, who were on the eve of starvation, they turned the heart of the whole loyal part of the nation into steel. Patriotism had now no longer a dubious existence. Quick as the lightning, she multiplied herself into a host of bright angels, who were going to and fro, delivering lessons upon our perils and duties, and inspiring courage and hope. I do not mean to intimate that this seminary had ever been indifferent to the interests of the country—she stands too near the spot where Washington commanded, and Mercer fell,[1] to be readily suspected of that—but until now there has never been any great occasion to put her to the test: and, since the occasion has come,—thanks to a

---

[1] The memorable battle of Princeton was fought within a few hundred yards of the site of the seminary.

gracious providence,—she does her work nobly; not by stepping out of her sphere, but by being a unit for the country's unity; especially by sending forth mature thoughts, well considered and weighty arguments, bearing upon the crisis, for the nation to digest and apply. Patriotism, bold, earnest, effective, but yet thoughtful and forbearing, has inscribed her name on the walls, even the very door-posts, of this seminary; and, in her light, well may the whole country see light and rejoice.

But a painful question here forces itself upon me—How is it that so large a number who have been educated here, with whom many of us have taken sweet counsel, and some of whom we have all delighted to honour,—have identified themselves with an enterprise, designed to lay waste this goodly inheritance which our fathers bequeathed to us? I know many of them so well, and they have had a place in my heart so long, that I could not, if I would, answer this question in any other spirit than that of the most-enlarged charity. The thought, which I am sure it is most grateful for us to indulge, is, that many of them have just silently bowed to influences which they could not control; and that, when the external pressure comes to be withdrawn, we shall find that, though they have been in the rebellion, they have not been of it. And then again, in respect to the large numbers, who, we know, have assumed an attitude of declared hostility to the government, who needs be told of the blinding influence of circumstances; of the mighty power of hereditary prejudices, of social and domestic relationships, of long-established associations, of the eloquence of statesmen, of the general current of example, of the pleas of imagined self-interest, to render both the intellectual and moral vision so confused that good and evil shall seem to have changed places? Who of us can be certain that an influence, which has been so universal, would not have included himself among its victims, if he had come within its range? I am not attempting to make out a justification of our brethren for having fallen into this mad and desolating current;—for that my conscience would not allow me to do—but I submit it to you whether there is not that in their circumstances, which should at least qualify our censure. As for those who have not only been educated here, but have been born and had their home in the North, and are perfectly conversant with Northern manners, and institutions, and influences, and yet have pronounced anathemas upon us in their pulpits,—strengthening the popular delusion that the heart of the whole North never rests from breathing out threatenings and slaughter against the South,—it would be too much to ask for *them* any large measure of indulgence; and yet is it not better to study them as an anomalous specimen of the workings of human nature, than to reciprocate their abuse and crimination? I confess there is not a fact in the whole history of the church, that confounds me more, than that our Southern brethren should, with such apparent cordiality and unanimity, have lent themselves to this unnatural rebellion; and yet, I say again, if we obey the dictates of wisdom, we shall forbear all bitter and hostile demonstrations, and shall hold ourselves ready to resume fraternal relations with them, whenever providence shall open the way for it. Or if that day should never come, we shall go down to our graves in a brighter light, and leave a better example to those who come after us, if, while we have been true to our country, we have never cast needless reproaches upon our mistaken brethren.

I only add that this seminary exerts *a widely extended and constantly extending influence*. It has drawn its students, not only from nearly every State in the Union, but from several European countries; and from almost every college, from venerable old Harvard down to those comparatively new lights, which the spirit of Christian enterprise has kindled up in the far West. Here, too, there has been a gathering from all the different classes of society—the sons of the rich and the great have been here—those who have had their birth and training in the middle walks of life, where there is least of temptation and most of comfort, have been here in crowds—those whose education has been little else than a constant battle with adverse circumstances, have been here; and, last of all, the descendants of Ham have not been without an honourable representation here,—a fact to which we appeal with confidence as proof that this seminary has never endorsed the doctrine that, because, unhappily, a dark skin has become with us an emblem of servitude, it therefore necessarily involves the curse of ignorance and degradation. Now, between each district, each college, each class in society, that is thus represented in the seminary, and the seminary itself, there is opened, in proportion to the extent of the representation, a channel of reciprocal influence. And then trace the influence which this great body of students, gathered from the four winds, and from such a variety of social positions, exerts, as they go forth to their several fields of labour. There is not a city of any extent in the land, where the gospel has not been sounded forth by some voice or voices that hail from this seminary. Travel in whatever direction you will, you cannot go far, but that its influence will meet you, either in the form of the living preacher, or in the auspicious results of some ministry upon which the grave has closed. If it were not for the iron gate which the spirit of rebellion has set up, you might go to the extreme southern or south-western boundary of the country, and find churches not a few, which were supplied, the very last Sabbath, by men whose names appear on our catalogue. If you make your way into the wilderness, the native home of savages, where, half a century ago, the first sign of civilization had not appeared, but where now Christianity holds her well-established dominion, there, again, you will find that this seminary has had her full share in accomplishing these blessed results. And, finally; if you cross the ocean, and explore the dark domain of foreign paganism or spurious Christianity, you can scarcely pause in any country, and look around you, without finding yourselves in contact with an evangelizing influence that has emanated from Princeton: and if, before you return, you visit the land of our fathers, and put yourselves into communion with the great and good spirits there, you will quickly discover that they are scarcely less familiar with the masterly biblical, theological, historical, and practical works, that our professors have sent forth, than we are with the choicest of *their* productions. Verily the influence of this seminary has diffused itself everywhere, and mingles with everything! If there is no part of our own country too distant or inaccessible to be reached by it; if it moves upon the great deep of ignorance and superstition in China and India, in France and Italy; if it penetrates into the very darkest part of the heart of Africa; and, finally, if it brings us into close fellowship of thought and feeling with the wise and good all over the world, who will venture, even now, to fix its boundary?

And yet this has been, still is, a *constantly increasing* influence. Some of us remember the time when this great tree, some of whose branches now overshadow other countries, was a mere sapling. We knew then, however, that its seed was good, having been deposited here by the faith and prayers of the church—we knew that the most skilful hands were employed for its culture, and that the enriching dews of heavenly grace were not withheld from it; and we had a right to anticipate for it a vigorous and substantial growth; but I doubt not that its history has far more than realized the most-sanguine expectations of the most hopeful of its friends. At the time of my own admission to the seminary, in the fall of 1816, the number of students, if my memory serves me, was about twenty-five; whereas the present number is 168; and I hazard nothing in saying that this numerical increase is a fair index to its general progressive prosperity. I do not say that each successive year has been, in all respects, more prosperous than the one immediately preceding; but I do say that, on the whole, it has been constantly growing, not only in numbers, but in resources, in usefulness, in favour with God and man.

And now, in view of the ground we have so rapidly passed over, are we not brought irresistibly to the conclusion that the Princeton Theological Seminary is a mighty power,—well worthy to have attracted us hither on this grateful, commemorative errand? Is there not essentially inherent in it an energy that must necessarily work out grand results? And have not those results already become matter of history, to a sufficient extent to fill us with gratitude for the past, with hope for the future?

My Friends, could we have a more impressive lesson of the vanity of this life of ours, than is found in the fact that, in speaking of this seminary at the close of the first half century of its existence, we have seemed to be holding converse much more with the dead than with the living? Does not the vast accumulation of stars on our catalogue, diffusing over it an air of funereal gloom, invite us to pause, not more in tender remembrance than solemn reflection? If we glance at the list of our directors, we find that sixty-three out of 113 have finished their course; and of the twenty, who constituted the original Board in 1812, one venerated name[1] only remains, unassociated with the grave.

[1] Rev. John McDowell, D.D., whose untiring devotion to the interests of the seminary, as well as of the Presbyterian Church at large, is already a matter of history. It was a subject of general regret that he was prevented, by the infirmities of age,

On the list of the Board of Trustees, twenty-seven out of fifty-two are starred; and, of the sixteen who composed it in 1825, the name of only one stands without the significant prefix, and he the solitary survivor of the other Board. Of the ten, who have held professorships here, only half survive. Of the 2,422, who have received their theological education here, either partly or wholly, no less than 485 have gone to give an account of their stewardship. And we, my Brethren, are all in the current, which is thus sweeping onward to eternity. When the Centennial Celebration comes round, who of us all, think you, will be here to welcome it? There will be a joyful meeting of kindred spirits then, but they will belong to another generation. May our gracious Master pour upon us the spirit of wisdom, and strength, and earnest devotion to our high calling, so that, before our places on earth are vacated, we may build some new monuments of fidelity in his service, which will at once reflect fresh honour upon the institution at which we have been trained, and encourage and animate those who shall come after us.

I am quite aware that I have passed the legitimate limit of this exercise, and yet I find other topics crowding upon my mind, upon which, under other circumstances, I would gladly speak, and to which I have no doubt you would heartily and warmly respond. For instance, I should love to present to you the seminary in her relation to other similar institutions, showing you how nearly she stands at the head of the list in the order of time, and tracing her influence in the healthful growth of some of her younger sisters. I should love to call your attention to the signs of promise in respect to the future; to show you that it is scarcely more certain that the order of providence will proceed, than that this seminary will develop new powers, and gather increasing glory, in her onward course. I should love, especially, to try to reproduce, to those of my own classmates and contemporaries in the seminary who are present, some of the cherished scenes of those early days; to remind them of the splendour of Larned's eloquence; of the charm of Nevin's wit; of the apostolic simplicity of Newbold; of the thoughtful, earnest and intensely devout spirit of Armstrong. But into neither of these fields, attractive as they are, do I feel at liberty to

---

from being present to share in the services and enjoyments of the Semi-centennial Jubilee.

enter. Nothing remains, then, but that we leave our united benediction upon the seminary, and bid her *adieu*. We thank the directors and trustees for the wisdom, vigilance, energy, with which they have ordered her movements, husbanded her resources, and ministered, in various ways, to her efficiency and strength. We thank the professors for the ability, fidelity, constancy, which have ever characterized their labours, as well as for the cordial welcome with which they have now greeted us. We congratulate the present generation of students on their advantages, their attainments, their prospects, and we counsel them to gird themselves with strength from on high, that they may be prepared to meet the high demands of the age. We give and record our pledge to the seminary that her interests shall be our interests, and that, when we forget our obligation to her, our right hand may forget her cunning. We tender our acknowledgments to the inhabitants of this ancient and honoured town for the cordial and graceful hospitality which we have found in their dwellings, and in which some of us recognize only a reproduction of what we used to witness in their fathers and mothers, who have fallen asleep. We ratify afresh our vows of fraternal fellowship with each other, thanking God for this happy meeting, and sending our thoughts and hopes forward to a glorious renewal of our intercourse, where the meeting shall be, not for a day, but for eternity. The hallowed scenes through which we are now passing shall never fade from our memories,—no, never. We will dwell upon them—we will cherish them—we will embalm them—they shall make all our thoughts of this beloved spot more precious; and we will gather from them a fresh stimulus to the prosecution of our onward, upward journey.

APPENDIX[1]

The celebration of the fiftieth anniversary of the establishment of the Theological Seminary of the Presbyterian Church in Princeton, took place on April 30, 1862, agreeably to a plan, of which notice had been extensively given. The day was one of the most beautiful and

[1] This account of the proceedings of the day is taken, substantially, from the *New York Observer*.

balmy of the whole year. Many hundreds of the Alumni of the seminary were present, and with them many brethren of other denominations, who joined heartily in all the exercises of the occasion. There were many clergymen from the Congregational, the Episcopal, the Reformed Dutch, the Baptist churches, and the several families of Presbyterians, who seemed as much at home on that delightful spot and in that goodly company, as if they had not only been born and nurtured, but always dwelt, in the same ecclesiastical household.

The Alumni met at eleven o'clock in the First Presbyterian Church. The Rev. Dr Magie, of Elizabeth, New Jersey, was chosen to preside, and the Rev. Dr Paxton, of the Allegheny Theological Seminary, was appointed secretary. Dr Magie, on taking the chair, made a few pertinent remarks, expressive of the great pleasure it afforded him to mingle in the exercises of the day, and of his deep sense of obligation to the seminary, which he should carry with him to his grave.

The Rev. Dr Yeomans, being called upon, led in prayer.

The committee, who had arranged the meeting, stated that no order of exercises had been agreed upon, but that they had prepared a report, leaving it to those who should speak on the resolutions to select their own topics. The following is the report submitted, and subsequently adopted:—

1. The Alumni of the Princeton Theological Seminary, assembled to celebrate its fiftieth anniversary, record with devout gratitude their sense of the great goodness of God to this institution. We especially recognize his beneficent providence in raising up those two venerated men, Archibald Alexander and Samuel Miller, to become its first professors, and in sparing them to conduct its affairs with pre-eminent wisdom and fidelity for forty years.

2. In the general *Catalogue* of the seminary just issued, we find the following summary of its history:—

> Whole number of students—2,422
> Dead—485
> Connected with the seminary the present year—168
> Foreign missionaries 127
> Appointed foreign missionaries—7
> Professors in theological seminaries—28

Presidents of colleges—36
Professors in colleges—94
Directors of this seminary—17
Moderators of the General Assembly—8

We refrain from any attempt to gather up the weighty results which a half century must have accumulated in the train of an army of faithful labourers like this. A glance at the table will show that the healthful influences, emanating from this source, have radiated far and wide in every direction; that, apart from the spiritual benefits conferred on some thousands of churches, this seminary has had an important agency in moulding our systems of popular education, and in training the public men of the country, and that many a pagan land has reason to bless God that it has been established. We rejoice in all the good which has been effected through these various channels; and we reassure our brethren, especially those in heathen countries, that they are not forgotten as we gather around our *Alma Mater* today.

3. It is a matter of sincere gratitude with us, that our seminary has never faltered in its maintenance of the ancient faith of the apostolic church, and that, through the writings of its professors and Alumni, it has made large and valuable contributions to biblical criticism and theological science; achieving for itself a reputation in these departments which has commanded the respect of the best scholars of Europe and of our own country.

4. In view of the distrust so often expressed respecting theological seminaries, we deem it proper to reaffirm our hearty approval of the principles embodied in the Plan of this institution and illustrated in its history: the system adopted here commends itself to us, at the close of a half century, as eminently wise, scriptural and efficient: and the seminary was never more worthy of the confidence of the church than it is at this moment. In accounting for this result, we may refer not only, under providence, to the eminent learning and ability of the professors who have filled its various chairs, but to the spirit of genuine piety which has uniformly pervaded and controlled its entire administration. While keeping well abreast with the age in the general progress of biblical science and polite literature, it has

been the paramount law of this school of the prophets to subordinate the intellectual to the spiritual, and never to exalt speculative theology at the expense of personal religious experience. This is the true glory of our seminary, and herein, under God, lies the secret of its power and success.

5. In the pervading spirit of our venerable seminary we recognize that true catholicity of feeling, combined with an inflexible adherence to sound doctrine, by which our church has always been distinguished. And in this characteristic we find an explanation of the grateful fact, that our sister churches are so often represented on its catalogues; as they have also sent some of their most honoured sons to take part in this commemoration.

6. We record with reverence and submission the ravages which death has made among the directors, the faculty, and the Alumni of our seminary. May we pay the best of all tributes to their memory, by following them in so far as they followed Christ.

7. We offer our united and hearty thanks to the numerous benefactors of our beloved seminary. We respectfully remind the church it has so long adorned and blessed, that its funds are still very inadequate to its needs. And we propose to our fellow Alumni, whenever the dark cloud which now overshadows the land shall have passed away, that a united effort be made to complete its endowment, and establish its financial interests upon a broad and generous foundation.

All the exercises of the morning, with the exception of the above resolutions, though highly felicitous, were evidently unpremeditated; and, as no provision was made to secure the speeches at the time of their delivery, all that can be done is to barely hint at them. Dr Hodge was called upon to speak, as having been the associate of Dr Miller and Dr Alexander; and, though he responded reluctantly, from being impressed with the idea that it was unsuitable that his voice should be heard on the occasion, his remarks were characterized by great appropriateness, and by a pathos that was quite irresistible. He remarked that when the two venerable men, who had been named, were made professors, he was but a mere youth, and that when he was elected to be associated with them, he felt like sitting on a stool at their feet. Dr Alexander took him by the hand as if he were a child, and in that relation he had always loved to regard himself; and for him to speak on this occasion was like making remarks at the funeral of one's own father. He paid a touching tribute to the memory of both these admirable men. He had seen them under various forms of trial, but had never heard a word from either which the purest angel would have stopped on their lips, nor any manifestation of feeling toward each other, which God himself would not approve. It was a pleasure to him to bear such a testimony concerning these holy men in the presence of such an audience, before he died. The seminary had now a history, world-wide, that could not be altered—and who had given it such a history? Dr Alexander and Dr Miller, whose shoes' latchet he was not worthy to unloose.

The Rev. Dr Charles Beatty, of Steubenville, Ohio, said he was one of the earliest of the Alumni, and reared almost in sight of the seminary; and, when he was licensed to preach, Dr Alexander came to him, and, taking him by the hand, said 'God bless you, my son'; 'and I feel that grasp', said he, 'as though it had been but yesterday'.

The Rev. Dr. Howard Malcolm, of the Baptist Church, said there were two features in the character of the seminary and its professors, to which he wished to bear testimony; and his testimony was as follows:—

It is an eminently catholic institution. I am a Baptist. I came hither a Baptist, and went away a Baptist. I never heard anything here that injured my feelings. The subject of infant baptism was discussed, but never in an unkind spirit. I have two sons who are Baptists, and both of them were educated here. 2nd. I have never known an institution where personal piety was more studiously cultivated. The whole surrounding atmosphere seemed impregnated with the spirit of devotion.

The Rev. Dr Chickering, of Portland, Maine, being called upon as a minister of another denomination, (Congregational), said that some who had preceded him apologized for not having expected to speak, 'but if any have come thus', said he, 'I more'—and besides he had come almost out of breath, for he had travelled three hundred and fifty miles in twenty-four hours, stopping four hours in Boston, and one in Jersey City. He counted it a joy to be there. He had not come as a denominational representative. New England had heard of

Dr Miller and Dr Alexander, and he had found himself so much at home that he had quite forgotten that he was not an Alumnus, and had detected himself in voting on the resolutions. 'And', said he, 'I like the name of your great annual assemblage, the General Assembly—it is both scriptural and impressive.'

The Rev. Dr Plumer repeated the names of many of the early Alumni, who, with the venerated Professors, had gone to the heavenly mansions; among whom were the beloved Nevins, and Douglass, and Graham—but it was not of those of whom he wished then to speak—it was of his *Elder Brother,* the Lord Jesus Christ—to him belonged the glory of all the influence and success of the institution. It was on his head that he wished to place the crown.

Interesting and impressive remarks were made by Professor Fisher, of Yale College, who paid a beautiful tribute to the memory of Dr James W. Alexander; by the Rev. Dr Baird, who related a conversation that he had with Dr Chalmers, in which the great Scotch divine spoke in most glowing terms of both Dr Alexander and Dr Miller; and by some others.

The following interesting letter was received from the Rev. Dr Swift, of Allegheny City:—

Allegheny, April 18, 1862.
The contemplated meeting of the Alumni of the Theological Seminary at Princeton:

Honoured and Dear Brethren: I feel it a privation to be unable to mingle my fraternal congratulations with yours, and share with you in the sacred and congenial pleasures of this fiftieth anniversary of our venerated seminary. Surely you will find it intellectually and spiritually 'good to be there', and may our blessed Lord be with you and refresh your hearts. When I recur to the fact that I became a member of the seminary in 1814, about eighteen months after its opening, and when Dr Miller had just arrived to assume the duties of his office, and our entire roll of students numbered but little over twenty, I am reminded solemnly that, if I were present with you today, I should find few of my contemporaries to greet. If I asked for Blain, and Blatchford, and Huntington, and McDowell, and Stanton, and Wood, and Cruikshanks, and Edgar, and Green, and Searle, and Smith, and Talmage, and Wilbur, and Chamberlain, and Crow, and Gilbert, and Henry, and Mills, and Judd, and Larned, and others, this side the grave and of heaven, I should ask in vain. The dwelling I might perhaps find, where our class, for a time, met for recitation in Dr Miller's parlour, and the other humble dwelling where Dr Alexander lived, and where one of our number instructed his sons, James and Addison, then but sprightly lads. Without an edifice and without a library, we borrowed our common recitation room and our books from the College of New Jersey: and the life of our infant seminary was a life of faith and of hope, having indeed a pledge of a continued and growing life in the possession of two of the ablest and best instructors which Protestant Christendom then contained.

It was on a spring morning, during the period of our residence in the seminary, that the village population beheld the novel yet noble spectacle of our little band, without pomp or music, emerging from the college campus, and marching out, headed by Drs Green, Alexander, and Miller, and a few directors, to an adjacent field, where, with devout supplication, the first named was to lay the cornerstone of the seminary edifice.

In the comparative destitution of funds to erect this single building; in the fewness of the spectators and the simplicity of our little, feeble host of students, there was, in that scene, to the eye of mere worldly aspiration, perhaps an almost ridiculous absurdity in the act of beginning to build with such a prospect. But when these venerable men uncovered their heads, and the words of faith, and prayer, and consecration of all to Christ, broke upon the air of that calm and tranquil morning; when it was asked, in tones of mellowed and holy earnestness, that this intended edifice (itself as yet but the object of faith) might be reared up as a lasting monument of God's goodness to the Presbyterian Church, and that, for Christ's glory, it might be the educational home of many generations of his ministers who should carry the everlasting gospel to all nations, there was in those utterances of humble confidence in Christ, and lofty expansive expectation, a sublimity and power which every heart must have felt. That morning the Mediator of the new covenant was there, and ever since he has been fulfilling the petitions of that hour. The years which we have since seen, have, many of them, been years of disaster and trial to our Zion; and large portions of it, then represented there, have been sundered from its pale; and these noble devoted fathers, and almost all the brethren then present, have passed away; but the venerable seminary has moved on with unfaltering prosperity, and expanding usefulness: and it is a source of gratitude to God that, for these fifty years, no one of her professors has, either by defection in doctrine or inconsistency of practice, brought the slightest stain upon her honoured name. Her pupils also have, to a remarkable extent, been free from cases of apostasy; and have faithfully served the church at home and in distant lands.

Some fifteen or twenty years ago, in a casual conversation, the present senior professor, with his characteristic humility and self-distrust, said to me, 'When these well-known and eminent fathers shall be gone, Princeton, away from the geographical centre of the church, will no longer have the attractions and the central influence which she once had.' I did not tell him what I thought of this. I did not tell him that I had been present on that morning when its corner-stone was laid, and felt assured that, as to Princeton, her onward career was then written in heaven.

In the progress of events, I have been called to co-operate in founding and sustaining another seminary of our church; and have, with my brethren, rejoiced and given thanks to Christ for its success hitherto; but I have, in doing this, lost nothing of my earliest love to Princeton. My faith would not permit me to think, nor my heart permit me to desire, that anything should impair the influence, or impede the growth, of this our first and model institution. Much we may, my beloved Brethren, yet do for it, in our various spheres of duty, and we who are old, by our fervent prayers.

The close of another fifty years none of us will be here to witness; but if we are faithful, what a glorious epoch may it be amidst the long hallowed scenes of Princeton! How many distant lands will have pronounced its name! How many additional venerated dead will have bound the sacred memories of the church to the cemetery which slumbers at its side!

Beloved Brethren, may our gracious Lord bless your happy and sacred convocation with his especial presence, and make your communion sweet. May your rejoicings for what he has already done for Princeton be as the gladness of a morning, whose light shall shine more and more unto the perfect day.

With Christian love and fraternal salutations,

Yours, truly,

E. P. Swift.

At the close of the meeting, the Alumni of the seminary, together with all the strangers present, were invited to the seminary grounds, where a bountiful and even splendid dinner had been provided, of which several hundred partook, the occasion being one of rare social enjoyment. An hour or more was here spent in reviving old associations, the ladies, in the meantime, having been invited to the houses of the professors and other citizens, which had been thrown open to all who were disposed to share their hospitalities.

The interesting scene at the seminary grounds was very agreeably varied by an announcement, coming from the Board of Trustees, that Messrs Robert L. and Alexander Stuart, of New York, had just contributed $50,000 to the funds of the seminary, in honour of its fiftieth anniversary. It was received with shouts of applause, and added not a little to the enjoyment of the occasion.

At three o'clock in the afternoon, the Alumni, according to previous arrangement, reassembled in the church, and with them a large number of the inhabitants of the town, and of strangers from various parts of the country,—filling the edifice to its utmost capacity. The commemorative discourse was preceded by a prayer from the Rev. Dr Jacobus, Professor in the Allegheny Theological Seminary, and followed by another, from the Rev. Dr Potts, of New York; after which, the Rev. Dr Backus, of Baltimore, offered a resolution for the printing of the discourse which had been delivered, which was unanimously adopted. The exercises were concluded by the singing of the doxology, by the immense congregation, and the pronouncing of the benediction, by Dr Potts. The multitude of brethren then dispersed, with their hearts filled with gratitude and gladness by the hallowed exercises of the day.

A BRIEF HISTORY OF PRINCETON THEOLOGICAL SEMINARY[1]

THE importance of the union of piety and learning in the holy ministry, is one of those radical principles of ecclesiastical wisdom, which the experience of ages has served more and more to confirm. If the priests' lips were, of old, to keep knowledge; if the ministers of the gospel are bound to feed the people with knowledge and with understanding; then nothing can be plainer than that ignorance, or small and indigested knowledge, is, next to the want of piety, one of the most serious defects in a candidate for the sacred office. It is equally plain, that if this great concern be properly directed, especially if it be directed with order and uniformity, it must be attended to by the church herself. That which is left to individual enterprise and caprice, may sometimes be well managed, but will seldom be managed in any two cases alike. Besides, unless the church take this matter into her own hands, she cannot inspect and control the education which her candidates for the holy ministry receive. Her most precious fountains may be poisoned without her being able to apply an effectual remedy. No church, therefore, which neglects the proper education of her ministers, can be considered as faithful, either to her own most vital interests, or to the honour of her divine Head and Lord.

Impressed with these solemn convictions, a number of the ministers and other members of the Presbyterian Church, long before the establishment of their seminary, deeply lamented the want of such an institution, and saw with much pain the extreme disadvantages under

[1] Samuel Miller, *A Brief History of the Theological Seminary of the Presbyterian Church, at Princeton, New Jersey; Together With Its Constitution, Bye-Laws, &c.* (Princeton: John Bogart, 1838). For a biographical sketch of Samuel Miller see below, p. 383.

which their candidates for the ministry laboured, in pursuing their theological studies. They saw young men, with very small previous acquirements in literature and science, after devoting only twelve or eighteen months, and in some instances much less, to the study of theology; and even for that short time, almost wholly without suitable helps, taking on themselves the most weighty and responsible of all offices.

They saw, at the same time, the 'Reformed Dutch Church', the 'Associate Reformed Church', and the descendants of the venerable Puritans in New England, all going before them in an honourable and successful career of exertion, to remove these disadvantages, and to establish seminaries for the instruction of their candidates for the ministry: and they perceived, that, unless the Presbyterian Church should imitate their example, while other denominations rose and flourished, and became the means of extensive blessings to their country, she must inevitably decline, and fall into a state of discouraging weakness, inferiority, and comparative uselessness.

Accordingly, after long waiting, and after much counsel and prayer, the proposal to establish a theological seminary for the Presbyterian Church, was first introduced into the General Assembly, during the sessions of that body in May, A.D. 1809. It was introduced in the form of an overture or proposal from the Presbytery of Philadelphia. This overture was so far countenanced by the Assembly as to be referred to a select committee, who, after due deliberation on the subject, brought in the following report, which, being read, was adopted, and became the act of the Assembly, in the following words, *viz.*—

The committee appointed on the subject of a theological school, overtured from the Presbytery of Philadelphia, report,

That three modes of compassing this important object have presented themselves to their consideration.

The *first* is, to establish one great school, in some convenient place near the centre of the bounds of our church.

The *second* is, to establish two such schools, in such places as may best accommodate the northern and southern division of the church.

The *third* is, to establish such a school within the bounds of each of the synods. In this case, your committee suggest the propriety of leaving it to each synod to direct the mode of forming the school, and the place where it shall be established.

The advantages attending the first of the proposed modes, are, that it would be furnished with larger funds, and therefore with a more extensive library and a greater number of professors. The system of education pursued in it would therefore be more extensive, and more perfect: the youth educated in it would also become more united in the same views, and contract an early and lasting friendship for each other; circumstances which would not fail of promoting harmony and prosperity in the church. The disadvantages attending this mode would be, principally, those derived from the distance of its position from the extremities of the Presbyterian bounds.

The advantages attending the second of the proposed modes and the disadvantages, will readily suggest themselves, from a comparison of this with the other two.

The advantages which would attend the third, to wit, the establishment of theological schools by the respective synods, would be the following. The local situation of the respective schools would be peculiarly convenient for the several parts of a country so extensive, as that for the benefit of which they were designed. The inhabitants having the seminaries brought near to them would feel a peculiar interest in their prosperity, and may be rationally expected to contribute much more liberally than to any single school, or even to two. The synods, also, having the immediate care of them, and directing, either in person or by delegation, all their concerns, would feel a similar interest, and would probably be better pleased with a system formed by themselves, and therefore peculiarly suited to the wishes and interests of the several parts of the church immediately under their direction. Greater efforts, therefore, may be expected from ministers and people, to promote the prosperity of these schools, than of any other. The disadvantages of this mode would be, the inferiority of the funds, a smaller number of professors; a smaller library, and a more limited system of education in each. The students, also, as now, would be strangers to each other.

Should the last of these modes be adopted, your committee are of the opinion, that everything pertaining to the erection and conduct of each school, should be left to the direction of the respective synods.

If either of the first, the whole should be subject to the control of the General Assembly.

Your committee also suggest, that, in the former of these cases, the funds for each school should be raised within the bounds of the synod within which it was stationed. In the latter, they should be collected from the whole body of the church.

Your committee, therefore, submit the following resolution, to wit:

Resolved, that the above plans be submitted to all the presbyteries within the bounds of the General Assembly, for their consideration; and that they be careful to send up to the next Assembly, at their sessions in May, 1810, their opinions on the subject.

Agreeably to this resolution, the three alternate plans which it contemplates, were sent down to all the presbyteries, to be considered and decided upon by them.

At the meeting of the next General Assembly, in May, 1810, the presbyteries were called upon to state what they had respectively done with respect to the recommendation of the last Assembly, relative to the establishment of a theological school. The reports from the several presbyteries on this subject, having been read, were referred to a select committee to consider and report on the same. This committee made a report, which, being read and amended, was adopted, as follows, *viz.*—

The committee, after maturely deliberating on the subject committed to them, submit to the Assembly the following results.

I. It is evident, that not only a majority of the presbyteries which have reported on this subject, but also a majority of all the presbyteries under the care of this Assembly, have expressed a decided opinion in favour of the establishment of a theological school or schools in our church.

II. It appears to the committee, that although according to the statement already reported to the Assembly, there is an equal number of presbyteries in favour of the first plan, which contemplates a single school for the whole church; and in favour of the third plan, which contemplates the erection of a school in each synod; yet, as several of the objections made to the first plan, are founded entirely on misconception,[1] and will be completely obviated by developing the details of that plan; it seems fairly to follow that there is a greater amount of presbyterial suffrage in favour of a single school, than of any other plan.

III. Under these circumstances, the committee are of opinion, that, as much light has been obtained from the reports of presbyteries on this subject, as would be likely to result from a renewal of the reference: that no advantage will probably arise from further delay in this important concern; but, on the contrary, much serious inconvenience and evil; that the present General Assembly is bound to attempt to carry into execution some one of the plans proposed; and that the first plan, appearing to have, on the whole, the greatest share of public sentiment in its favour, ought, of course, to be adopted.

IV. Your committee, therefore, recommend, that the present General Assembly declare its approbation and adoption of this plan, and immediately commence a course of measures for carrying it into execution, as promptly and extensively as possible; and, for this purpose, they recommend to the Assembly the adoption of the following resolutions, *viz.*—

Resolved, 1. That the state of our churches, the loud and affecting calls of destitute frontier settlements, and the laudable exertions of various Christian denominations around us, all demand, that the collected wisdom, piety, and zeal of the Presbyterian Church, be, without delay, called into action, for furnishing the church with a larger supply of able and faithful ministers.

2. That the General Assembly will, in the name of the great Head of the church, immediately attempt to establish a seminary for securing to candidates for the ministry more extensive and efficient theological

[1] Some of the presbyteries objected to a single theological seminary, for the whole church, because they apprehended that, if this plan were adopted, every presbytery would become thereby bound to send all their candidates to study in it, however inconvenient or expensive it might be. Others were fearful, that the professors, in such a seminary, if they were not formally empowered to license candidates to preach the gospel, might be clothed with powers out of which such an abuse would naturally grow, thereby endangering both the purity and peace of the church, and giving to a few men very dangerous influence. It was for the purpose of obviating those, and other objections to a single seminary, that the sixth, seventh and eighth resolutions, in a subsequent page, were adopted by the General Assembly.

instruction, than they have heretofore enjoyed. The local situation of this seminary is hereafter to be determined.

3. That in this seminary, when completely organized, there shall be, at least, three professors; who shall be elected by and hold their offices during the pleasure of the General Assembly; and who shall give a regular course of instruction in divinity, in oriental and biblical literature, and in ecclesiastical history and church government, and on such other subjects as may be deemed necessary. It being, however, understood, that, until sufficient funds can be obtained for the complete organization and support of the proposed seminary, a smaller number of professors than three may be appointed to commence the business of instruction.

4. That exertions be made to provide such an amount of funds for this seminary, as will enable its conductors to afford gratuitous instruction, and, where it is necessary, gratuitous support, to all such students as may not themselves possess adequate pecuniary means.

5. That the Rev. Doctors Green, Woodhull, Romeyn and Miller, the Rev. Messrs Archibald Alexander, James Richards, and Amzi Armstrong, be a committee to digest and prepare a plan of a theological seminary; embracing in detail the fundamental principles of the institution, together with regulations for guiding the conduct of the instructors and the students; and prescribing the best mode of visiting, controlling, and supporting the whole system. This plan to be reported to the next General Assembly.

6. That, as filling the church with a learned and able ministry, without a corresponding portion of real piety, would be a curse to the world, and an offence to God and his people; so the General Assembly think it their duty to state, that, in establishing a seminary for training up ministers, it is their earnest desire to guard, as far as possible, against so great an evil. And they do hereby solemnly pledge themselves to the churches under their care, that in forming, and carrying into execution the Plan of the proposed seminary, it will be their endeavour to make it, under the blessing of God, a nursery of vital piety, as well as of sound theological learning: and to train up persons for the ministry, who shall be lovers, as well as defenders of the truth as it is in Jesus; friends of revivals of religion; and a blessing to the church of God;

7. That as the constitution of our church guarantees to every presbytery the right of judging of its own candidate, for licensure and ordination; so the Assembly think it proper to state most explicitly, that every presbytery and synod will, of course, be at full liberty, to countenance the proposed Plan or not, at pleasure; and to send their students to the projected seminary, or keep them, as heretofore, within their own bounds, as they may think most conducive to the prosperity of the church.

8. That the professors in the seminary shall not, in any case, be considered as having a right to license candidates to preach the gospel; but that all such candidates shall be remitted to their respective presbyteries to be licensed, as heretofore.

The committee appointed to prepare a constitution in detail for the contemplated seminary, made report to the General Assembly which convened in 1811; which report, after being duly considered, was amended and adopted, as follows.

PLAN OF THE
THEOLOGICAL SEMINARY
OF THE PRESBYTERIAN CHURCH
IN THE UNITED STATES OF AMERICA

INTRODUCTION[1]

Inasmuch as the obtaining of salvation through Jesus Christ our Lord, to the glory of the eternal God, is the chief object which claims the attention of man; and considering, that in the attainment of this object the dispensation of the gospel is principally instrumental, it is manifestly of the highest importance, that the best means be used to insure the faithful preaching of the gospel, and the pure administration of all its ordinances. With this view, therefore, institutions for the education of youth intended for the holy ministry, have been established in all Christian countries, and have been found, by long experience, most eminently conducive to the prosperity of the church.

[1] The Plan, as here given, includes all the amendments which have been made in it, by successive Assemblies, from 1811 to the date of the present publication [1838].

48

Hence the founders of the Presbyterian Church in the United States of America, did, from its very origin, exert themselves with peculiar zeal to establish and endow colleges, academies, and schools, for the education of youth for the gospel ministry. So rapid, however, has been the extension of this church, and so disproportionate, of late, has been the number of ministers educated, to the call which has been made for ministerial service, that some additional and vigorous efforts to increase the supply are loudly and affectingly demanded. Circumstances also do imperiously dictate, not only that the labourers in the vineyard of the Lord should be multiplied, but that they should be more thoroughly furnished than they have ordinarily been for the arduous work to which they must be called. Influenced by the views and considerations now recited, the General Assembly, after mature deliberation, have resolved, in reliance on the patronage and blessing of the great Head of the church, to establish a new institution, consecrated solely to the education of men for the gospel ministry, and to be denominated, *The Theological Seminary of the Presbyterian Church in the United States of America.* And to the intent that the true design of the founders of this institution may be known to the public, both now and in time to come, and especially that this design may, at all times, be distinctly viewed, and sacredly regarded, both by the teachers and the pupils of the seminary, it is judged proper to make a summary and explicit statement of it.

It is to form men for the gospel ministry, who shall truly believe, and cordially love, and therefore endeavour to propagate and defend, in its genuineness, simplicity, and fulness, that system of religious belief and practice which is set forth in the Confession of Faith, Catechisms, and Plan of Government and Discipline of the Presbyterian Church; and thus to perpetuate and extend the influence of true evangelical piety and gospel order.

It is to provide for the church an adequate supply and succession of able and faithful ministers of the New Testament; workmen that need not to be ashamed, being qualified rightly to divide the word of truth.

It is to unite, in those who shall sustain the ministerial office, religion and literature; that piety of the heart, which is the fruit only of the renewing and sanctifying grace of God, with solid learning:

believing that religion without learning, or learning without religion, in the ministers of the gospel, must ultimately prove injurious to the church.

It is to afford more advantages than have hitherto been usually possessed by the ministers of religion in our country, to cultivate both piety and literature in their preparatory course; piety, by placing it in circumstances favourable to its growth, and by cherishing and regulating its ardour; literature, by affording favourable opportunities for its attainment, and by making its possession indispensable.

It is to provide for the church, men who shall be able to defend her faith against infidels, and her doctrines against heretics.

It is to furnish our congregations with enlightened, humble, zealous, laborious pastors, who shall truly watch for the good of souls, and consider it as their highest honour and happiness to win them to the Saviour, and to build up their several charges in holiness and peace.

It is to promote harmony and unity of sentiment among the ministers of our church, by educating a large body of them under the same teachers, and in the same course of study.

It is to lay the foundation of early and lasting friendships, productive of confidence and mutual assistance in after-life among the ministers of religion; which experience shows to be conducive not only to personal happiness, but to the perfecting of inquiries, researches, and publications advantageous to religion.

It is to preserve the unity of our church, by educating her ministers in an enlightened attachment, not only to the same doctrines, but to the same plan of government.

It is to bring to the service of the church genius and talent, when united with piety, however poor or obscure may be their possessor, by furnishing, as far as possible, the means of education and support, without expense to the student.

It is to found a nursery for missionaries to the heathen, and to such as are destitute of the stated preaching of the gospel; in which youth may receive that appropriate training which may lay a foundation for their ultimately becoming eminently qualified for missionary work.

It is, finally, to endeavour to raise up a succession of men, at once qualified for and thoroughly devoted to the work of the gospel ministry; who, with various endowments, suiting them to different stations in the church of Christ, may all possess a portion of the spirit of the primitive propagators of the gospel; prepared to make every sacrifice, to endure every hardship, and to render every service which the promotion of pure and undefiled religion may require.

ARTICLE I
Of the General Assembly

Sect. 1. As this institution derives its origin from the General Assembly, so that body is to be considered at all times as its patron, and the fountain of its powers. The Assembly shall, accordingly, ultimately sanction all its laws, direct its instructions, and appoint its principal officers.

Sect. 2. The General Assembly shall choose a Board of Directors, consisting of twenty-one ministers, and nine ruling elders, by whom the seminary shall be inspected and conducted. Of this number, one-third, or seven ministers and three elders, shall be chosen annually; to continue in office three years. And if any vacancy shall occur in the Board, by death, resignation, or incapacity to serve, the Assembly may annually fill up such vacancies.

Sect. 3. All professors of the seminary shall be appointed by the Assembly. But in cases of necessity, the Board of Directors may employ a suitable person to perform the duties of a professor, till a meeting of the Assembly shall take place.

Sect. 4. The General Assembly shall, at all times, have the power of adding to the Constitutional Articles of the seminary, and of abrogating, altering, or amending them; but, in the exercise of this power, the contemplated additions, abrogations, alterations, or amendments, shall, in every case, be proposed at one Assembly, and not adopted till the Assembly of the subsequent year, except by a unanimous vote.

ARTICLE II
Of the Board of Directors

Sect. 1. The Board of Directors shall meet statedly, twice in each year; once in the spring and once in the fall, and oftener on their own adjournments, if they shall judge it expedient. Nine members of the

Board shall be a quorum; provided always, that of this number, five, at least, be ministers of the gospel, and the president, or, in case of his absence, one of the vice presidents, be one.

Sect. 2. The Board shall choose out of their own number, a president, two vice presidents, and a secretary. In the absence of the president and vice presidents, the senior member present shall preside.

Sect. 3. The president of the Board, or in the event of his death, absence, or inability to act, the first vice president shall, at the request of any three members, expressed to him in writing, call a special meeting of the Board of Directors, by a circular letter addressed to each; in which letter notice shall be given, not only of the place and time of meeting, but of the business intended to be transacted at the meeting notified; and this letter shall be sent at least twenty days before the time of said meeting.

Sect. 4. The secretary of the Board shall keep accurate records of all the proceedings of the directors; and it shall be his duty to lay these records, or a faithful transcript of the same, before the General Assembly, annually, for the unrestrained inspection of all the members.

Sect. 5. Every meeting of the Board of Directors shall be opened and closed with prayer.

Sect. 6. The Board of Directors may make rules and regulations for the performance of the duties assigned them, or for the preservation of order, not inconsistent with the prescriptions of this plan, or the orders of the General Assembly.

Sect. 7. At the commencement of each stated spring meeting, the whole Plan of the Seminary shall be distinctly read before the Board of Directors.

Sect. 8. The Board shall direct the professors of the seminary, in regard to the subjects and topics on which they are severally to give instructions to the pupils, so far as the same shall not be prescribed by this Plan, or by the orders of the General Assembly.

Sect. 9. It shall be the duty of the Board of Directors to inaugurate the professors of the seminary, and to direct what forms shall be used, and what services performed, on such occasions.

Sect. 10. Every director, previously to his taking his seat as a member of the Board, shall solemnly subscribe the following formula, *viz.*— 'Approving the Plan of the Theological Seminary of the Presbyterian

Church in the United States of America, I solemnly declare and promise, in the presence of God and of this Board , that I will faithfully endeavour to carry into effect all the articles and provisions of said plan, and to promote the great design of the seminary.'

Sect. 11. The Board of Directors shall inspect the fidelity of the professors, especially in regard to the doctrines actually taught; and if, after due inquiry and examination, they shall judge that any professor is either unsound in the faith, opposed to the fundamental principles of Presbyterian church government, immoral in his conduct, unfaithful to his trust, or incompetent to the discharge of his duties, they shall faithfully report him as such to the General Assembly. Or if the longer continuance of a professor be judged highly dangerous, the directors may immediately suspend him, and appoint another in his place, till the whole business can be reported, and submitted to the Assembly.

Sect. 12. It shall be the duty of the Board of Directors to watch over the conduct of the students; to redress grievances; to examine into the whole course of instruction and study in the seminary; and generally to superintend and endeavour to promote all its interests.

Sect. 13. The Board of Directors shall make, in writing, a detailed and faithful report of the state of the seminary, to every General Assembly; and they may, at the same time, recommend such measures for the advantage of the seminary, as to them may appear proper.

Sect. 14. At every stated meeting of the Board of Directors, unless particular circumstances render it inexpedient, there shall be at least one sermon delivered in presence of the Board, the professors, and students, by a director or directors, previously appointed for the purpose.

ARTICLE III
Of the Professors

Sect. 1. The number of the professors in the seminary shall be increased or diminished, as the Assembly may, from time to time, direct. But when the seminary shall be completely organized, there shall not be less than three professors: one of Didactic and Polemic Divinity; one of Oriental and Biblical Literature; and one of Ecclesiastical History and Church Government.

Sect. 2. No person shall be inducted into the office of Professor of Divinity, but an ordained minister of the gospel.

Sect. 3. Every person elected to a professorship in this seminary, shall, on being inaugurated, solemnly subscribe the Confession of Faith, Catechisms, and Form of Government of the Presbyterian Church, agreeably to the following formula, *viz.*—'In the presence of God and the Directors of this Seminary, I do solemnly, and *ex animo* adopt, receive, and subscribe the Confession of Faith, and Catechisms of the Presbyterian Church in the United States of America, as the confession of my faith; or, as a summary and just exhibition of that system of doctrine and religious belief which is contained in holy Scripture, and therein revealed by God to man for his salvation; and I do solemnly, *ex animo* profess to receive the Form of Government of said church, as agreeable to the inspired oracles. And I do solemnly promise and engage, not to inculcate, teach, or insinuate anything which shall appear to me to contradict or contravene, either directly or impliedly, anything taught in the said Confession of Faith or Catechisms; nor to oppose any of the fundamental principles of Presbyterian church government, while I shall continue a professor in this seminary.'

Sect. 4. The salaries of the professors shall be recommended by the directors; but they shall be fixed only by a vote of the General Assembly.

Sect. 5. The professors may accompany their lectures and recitations with prayer, as frequently as they may judge proper, in addition to those daily seasons of prayer in which all the students will unite.

Sect. 6. Each professor shall lay before the Board of Directors, as soon as practicable after his appointment, a detailed exhibition of the system and method which he proposes to pursue, and the subjects which he proposes to discuss, in conducting the studies of the youth that shall come under his care: and in this system he shall make such alterations or additions as the Board shall direct; so that, eventually, the whole course through which the pupils shall be carried, shall be no other than that which the Board of Directors shall have approved and sanctioned, conformably to Section 8. Article II. And as often as any professor shall think that variations and additions of importance may be advantageously introduced into his course of teaching, he shall submit the same to the Board of Directors, for their approbation or rejection.

Sect. 7. Every professor shall, if practicable, have at least one lecture or recitation every day, on which the pupils, in his branch of instruction, shall be bound to attend; and on which the other pupils of the seminary shall attend as often, and in such manner, as may be directed by the majority of the Board of Directors.

Sect. 8. Any professor intending to resign his office, shall give six months notice of such intention to the Board of Directors.

Sect. 9. The professors of the institution shall be considered as a faculty. They shall meet at such seasons as they may judge proper. In every meeting the professor of didactic and polemic divinity shall preside, if he be present. If he be absent, a president shall be chosen *pro tempore*. The faculty shall choose a clerk, and keep accurate records of all their proceedings; which records shall be laid before the directors at every meeting of the Board. The president of the faculty shall call a meeting whenever he shall judge it expedient, and whenever he shall be requested to do so by any other member. By the faculty, regularly convened, shall be determined the hours and seasons at which the classes shall attend the professors severally, so as to prevent interference and confusion, and to afford to the pupils the best opportunities of improvement. The faculty shall attend to, and decide on all cases of discipline, and all questions of order, as they shall arise. They shall agree on the rules of order, decorum, and duty, (not inconsistent with any provision in the Plan of the Seminary, nor with any order of the Board of Directors), to which the students shall be subjected, and these they shall reduce to writing, and cause to be publicly and frequently read. They shall determine the hours at which the whole of the pupils shall, morning and evening, attend for social worship, and the manner in which, and the person or persons, of their own number, by whom, the exercises of devotion shall be conducted.

Sect. 10. The faculty shall be empowered to dismiss from the seminary any student who shall prove unsound in his religious sentiments; immoral or disorderly in his conduct; or who may be, in their opinion, on any account whatsoever, a dangerous or unprofitable member of the institution.

Sect. 11. Each member of the faculty shall have an equal vote.

Sect. 12. It shall be the duty of the professors, under the direction of the Board of Directors, to supply the pupils of the institution with the preaching of the gospel, and the administration of the sacraments of the Christian church; if this supply shall not, in the judgment of the directors, be satisfactorily furnished by a church or churches in the place where the institution shall be established.

ARTICLE IV

Of Study and Attainments

As the particular course of study pursued in any institution will, and perhaps ought to be modified in a considerable degree by the views and habits of the teachers; and ought, moreover, to be varied, altered, or extended, as experience may suggest improvements; it is judged proper to specify, not so precisely the course of study, as the attainments which must be made. Therefore,

Sect. 1. Every student, at the close of his course, must have made the following attainments, *viz.*—He must be well skilled in the original languages of the Holy Scriptures. He must be able to explain the principal difficulties which arise in the perusal of the Scriptures, either from erroneous translations, apparent inconsistencies, real obscurities, or objections arising from history, reason, or argument. He must be versed in Jewish and Christian antiquities, which serve to explain and illustrate Scripture. He must have an acquaintance with ancient geography, and with oriental customs, which throw light on the sacred records.—Thus he will have laid the foundation for becoming a sound biblical critic.

He must have read and digested the principal arguments and writings relative to what has been called the Deistical controversy.—Thus will he be qualified to become a defender of the Christian faith.

He must be able to support the doctrines of the Confession of Faith and Catechisms, by a ready, pertinent, and abundant quotation of Scripture texts for that purpose. He must have studied, carefully and correctly, natural, didactic, polemic, and casuistic theology. He must have a considerable acquaintance with general history and chronology, and a particular acquaintance with the history of the Christian church.—Thus he will be preparing to become an able and sound divine and casuist.

He must have read a considerable number of the best practical writers on the subject of religion. He must have learned to compose with correctness and readiness in his own language, and to deliver what he has composed to others in a natural and acceptable manner. He must be well acquainted with the several parts, and the proper structure of popular lectures and sermons. He must have composed at least two lectures and four popular sermons, that shall have been approved by the professors. He must have carefully studied the duties of the pastoral care.—Thus he will be prepared to become a useful preacher, and a faithful pastor.

He must have studied attentively the form of church government authorized by the Scriptures, and the administration of it as it has taken place in Protestant churches.—Thus he will be qualified to exercise discipline, and to take part in the government of the church in all its judicatories.

Sect. 2. The period of continuance in the theological seminary shall, in no case, be less than three years, previously to an examination for a certificate of approbation. But students may enter the seminary, and enjoy the course of instruction for a shorter time than three years, provided they in all other respects submit to the laws of the seminary, of which facts they may receive a written declaration from the professors.

Sect. 3. There shall be an examination of all the pupils in the seminary, at every stated meeting of the Board of Directors. Those pupils who shall have regularly and diligently studied for three years, shall be admitted to an examination on the subjects specified in this article. All examinations shall be conducted by the professors, in the presence of the directors, or a committee of them. Every director present shall be at liberty, during the progress of any examination, or after the same shall have been closed by the professors, to put to any pupil such questions as he shall deem proper. Every pupil that shall have passed his final examination to the satisfaction of the directors present, shall receive a certificate of the same, signed by the professors, with which he shall be remitted to the presbytery under whose care he is placed, to be disposed of as such presbytery shall direct. Those who do not pass a satisfactory examination, shall remain a longer space in the seminary.

Sect. 4. It shall be the object of the professors to make such arrangements in the instruction of their pupils, as shall be best adapted to enable them, in the space of three years, to be examined with advantage on the subjects specified in this article.

ARTICLE V

Of Devotion, and Improvement in Practical Piety

It ought to be considered as an object of primary importance by every student in the seminary, to be careful and vigilant not to lose that inward sense of the power of godliness which he may have attained; but, on the contrary, to grow continually in a spirit of enlightened devotion and fervent piety; deeply impressed with the recollection that without this, all his other acquisitions will be comparatively of little worth, either to himself, or to the church of which he is to be a minister.

He must remember, too, that this is a species of improvement which must of necessity be left, in a great measure, with himself, as a concern between God and his own soul.

It is proper, however, to delineate the path of duty, to express the wishes and expectations of the founders of the seminary, and to make such requirements as the nature of the subject will permit.

Sect. 1. It is expected that every student in the theological seminary will spend a portion of time every morning and evening in devout meditation, and self-recollection and examination; in reading the holy Scriptures, solely with a view to a personal and practical application of the passage read, to his own heart, character, and circumstances; and in humble, fervent prayer and praise to God in secret.

The whole of every Lord's day is to be devoted to devotional exercises, either of a social or secret kind. Intellectual pursuits, not immediately connected with devotion, or the religion of the heart, are on that day to be forborne. The books to be read are to be of a practical nature. The conversations had with each other are to be chiefly on religious subjects. Associations for prayer and praise, and for religious conference, calculated to promote a growth in grace, are also proper for this day; subject to such regulations as the professors and directors may see proper to prescribe. It is wished and recommended, that each student should ordinarily set apart one day in a month for special prayer and self-examination in secret, and also that he should, on suitable occasions, attend to the duty of fasting.

Sect. 2. If any student shall exhibit, in his general deportment, a levity or indifference in regard to practical religion, though it do not amount to any overt act of irreligion or immorality, it shall be the duty of the professor who may observe it, to admonish him tenderly and faithfully in private, and endeavour to engage him to a more holy temper, and a more exemplary deportment.

Sect. 3. If a student, after due admonition, persist in a system of conduct not exemplary in regard to religion, he shall be dismissed from the seminary.

Sect. 4. The professors are particularly charged, by all the proper means in their power, to encourage, cherish and promote devotion and personal piety among their pupils, by warning and guarding them, on the one hand, against formality and indifference, and on the other, against ostentation and enthusiasm; by inculcating practical religion in their lectures and recitations; by taking suitable occasions to converse with their pupils privately on this interesting subject; and by all other means, incapable of being minutely specified, by which they may foster true experimental religion, and unreserved devotedness to God.

ARTICLE VI
Of the Students

Sect, 1. Every student applying for admission to the theological seminary, shall produce satisfactory testimonials that he possesses good natural talents, and is of a prudent and discreet deportment; that he is in full communion with some regular church; that he has passed through a regular course of academical study; or, wanting this, he shall submit himself to an examination in regard to the branches of literature taught in such a course.

Sect. 2. The first six months of every student in the seminary shall be considered as probationary; and if, at the end of this period, any student shall appear to the professors not qualified to proceed in his studies, they shall so report him to the Board of Directors, who, if they are of the same opinion with the professors, shall dismiss him from the seminary.

Sect. 3. The hours of study and of recreation for the students shall be fixed by the professors, with the concurrence of the directors; and every student shall pay a strict regard to the rules established relative to this subject.

Sect. 4. Every student shall be obliged to write on such theological and other subjects, as may be prescribed to him by the professors. In the first year, every student shall be obliged to produce a written composition on such subjects, at least once in every month; in the second year, once in three weeks; in the third year, once in two weeks. Each student shall also commit to memory a piece of his own composition, and pronounce it in public, before the professors and students, as frequently as, in the judgment of the professors, this exercise can properly be performed, when a due regard is had to the numbers who must engage in it, and to the other duties of the seminary.

Sect. 5. Every student shall not only preserve an exemplary moral character, but shall be expected to treat his teachers with the greatest deference and respect, and all other persons with civility.

Sect. 6. Every student shall yield a prompt and ready obedience to all the lawful requisitions of the professors and directors.

Sect. 7. Diligence and industry in study shall be considered as indispensable in every student, unless the want of health shall prevent, of which the professors shall take cognizance, and make the suitable allowance.

Sect. 8. Strict temperance in meat and drink is expected of every student, with cleanliness and neatness in his dress and habits; while all excessive expense in clothing is strictly prohibited.

Sect. 9. Every student, before he takes his standing in the seminary, shall subscribe the following declaration, *viz.*—'Deeply impressed with a sense of the importance of improving in knowledge, prudence, and piety, in my preparation for the gospel ministry, I solemnly promise, in a reliance on divine grace, that I will faithfully and diligently attend on all the instructions of this seminary, and that I will conscientiously and vigilantly observe all the rules and regulations specified in the Plan for its instruction and government, so far as the same relate to the students; and that I will obey all the lawful requisitions, and readily yield to all the wholesome admonitions of the professors and directors of the seminary, while I shall continue a member of it.'

Sect. 10. There shall be three vacations in the seminary every year. The spring vacation to continue six weeks; the fall vacation six weeks; and the winter vacation two weeks. The vacations to commence at such times as the Board of Directors shall deem most expedient.

ARTICLE VII[1]
Of the Library

Sect. 1. To obtain, ultimately, a complete theological library, shall be considered as a leading object of the institution.

Sect. 2. It shall be the duty of the directors to present to the General Assembly, a catalogue of the most necessary books for the commencement of a library, and recommend the purchase of such a number as the state of the funds will permit.

Sect. 3. It shall be the duty of the professors to procure and keep a large folio, to be denominated, *The Prospectus of a Catalogue of a Theological Library.* In this folio, divided into proper heads, each professor shall, at his pleasure, enter, in its proper place, the title of such books as he shall deliberately judge to be proper for the library. The Board of Directors, or the members of it individually, may do the same. From this folio it shall be the duty of the directors to select such books as they think most necessary, and as the sum appropriated for the current year will purchase, and recommend their purchase to the Assembly. The Assembly shall, annually, decide by vote, what sum of money, for the current year, shall be laid out in the purchase of books.

Sect. 4. A suitable room or apartment shall be assigned for the library. The shelves for the books shall be divided into compartments or alcoves; and if anyone of them be filled, or nearly so, by a donor, his name shall be conspicuously placed over it.

Sect. 5. A librarian shall be appointed by the Assembly.

Sect. 6. No book shall be permitted, on any occasion, to be carried from the seminary.

Sect. 7. A book of donations shall be carefully kept by the librarian, in which shall be entered, by him, the books given to the library, the time when, and the name of the donor.

[1] This article is laid over for the consideration of a future Assembly.

Sect. 8. Regulations for the use of the library, not inconsistent with the provisions of this article, shall be detailed in a system of by-laws, for that purpose; to be drafted by the first librarian, and occasionally modified and added to, as circumstances shall require, by his successors; which regulations, after being ratified by the Board of Directors, shall be authoritative.

ARTICLE VIII
Of the Funds

Sect. I. The funds of the institution shall be kept, at all times, entirely distinct and separate from all other monies or funds whatsoever; and they shall be deposited in the hands of such corporation, or disposed of for safe keeping and improvement, in such other manner as the General Assembly shall direct.

Sect. 2. The Board of Directors shall, from time to time, as they may see proper, lay before the Assembly plans for the improvement of the funds, and propositions for the appropriation of such sums as they may think necessary for particular purposes.

Sect. 3. No money shall, at any time, be drawn from the funds, but by an appropriation and order of the Assembly for the purpose.

Sect. 4. A fair statement shall annually be laid before the Assembly, by the proper officer, of the amount of the funds belonging to the seminary, of the items which constitute that amount, and of the expenditures in detail for the preceding year.

Sect. 5. The intentions and directions of testators or donors, in regard to monies, or other property, left, or given to the seminary, shall, at all times, be sacredly regarded. And if any individual, or any number of individuals, not greater than three, shall, by will, or during his or their lives, found or endow a professorship or professorships, a scholarship or scholarships, or a fund or funds, destined for special purposes, said professorships, scholarships, or funds, shall forever afterwards be called and known by the name or names of those who founded or endowed them. And if any congregation, presbytery, synod, or association, shall found a professorship or professorships, scholarship or scholarships, fund or funds, said professorship or professorships, scholarship or scholarships, fund or funds, shall forever afterwards be called or known by such name as the body founding them shall give.

Sect. 6. After supporting the professors, and defraying the other necessary charges of the seminary, the funds shall be applied, as far as circumstances will admit, to defray or diminish the expenses of those students who may need pecuniary aid, as well as to lessen, generally, the expense of a residence at the seminary.

* * * * *

After adopting the foregoing Plan, the General Assembly which met in 1811, did little more than take measures for collecting funds for the proposed institution, by appointing a number of agents in all the synods for that purpose; who were instructed to proceed with as little delay, and as much energy, as possible, and to report to the Assembly of the next year. They also appointed a committee to confer with the trustees of the College of New Jersey, at Princeton, respecting any facilities and privileges which the said trustees might be disposed to give to a theological seminary, if located in Princeton.

At the meeting of the next Assembly, in May, 1812, the location of the seminary was fixed at Princeton, in New Jersey; a Board of Directors was elected; and the Rev. Archibald Alexander, D.D., a native of Virginia, for some time President of Hampden Sidney College, and at that time pastor of the Third Presbyterian Church in Philadelphia, was appointed Professor of Didactic and Polemic Theology. On the last Tuesday of June following, the Board of Directors held their first meeting, at Princeton. On the 12th day of August, of the same year, the Board of Directors met again, and Dr Alexander, the Professor Elect, was solemnly inaugurated, and entered on the duties of his office. The number of students at the opening of the institution, on the day last mentioned, was *three*.

At the meeting of the Assembly, in May, 1813, the number of students had increased to *eight*. By this Assembly, the Rev. Samuel Miller, D.D., a native of the State of Delaware, and, at the time of his election, pastor of the First Presbyterian Church in the City of New York, was elected Professor of Ecclesiastical History and Church Government, and was inaugurated by the Board of Directors on the 29th of September following. By this Assembly also, the location of the seminary in Princeton, which had been before temporary, was now made permanent.

The General Assembly which met in May 1815, taking into consideration the great inconveniences resulting to the institution from the want of suitable apartments for the recitations, and other exercises of the seminary; and more especially the numerous privations, and even danger to their health, to which the students were subjected by the want of convenient places of lodging; determined to erect a public edifice in Princeton, which should contain all the public apartments indispensably necessary for the present, and also lodging rooms for the comfortable accommodation of the pupils. Accordingly, this edifice was commenced in the autumn of that year; was first occupied by the professors and students in the autumn of 1817, when about one-half of the apartments were prepared for their reception; and was soon afterwards completed. This building is of stone; one hundred and fifty feet in length, fifty in breadth, and four stories high, including the basement story. It has been admired by all who have seen it, as a model of neat, and tasteful, and, at the same time, of plain, economical, and remarkably solid workmanship. Besides the apartments necessary for the library, the recitations, the refectory establishment, and the accommodation of the steward and his family, this edifice will furnish lodgings for about eighty pupils.

During the first year after the establishment of the seminary, the Professor of Didactic and Polemic Theology, besides his own appropriate duties, discharged, as far as practicable, those also, pertaining to the Professorship of Oriental and Biblical Literature. And on the appointment of a second Professor, in 1813, they divided the whole course of instruction, prescribed by the Plan of the Seminary between them. But the Assembly which met in May 1820, finding that the health of the Professor of Didactic and Polemic Theology, as well as his other duties, did not admit of his longer continuing to conduct the instruction in the original languages of Scripture, resolved to authorize the professors to appoint an assistant teacher of those languages. And to this office, Mr Charles Hodge, a native of Pennsylvania, then a licentiate, under the care of the Presbytery of Philadelphia, but since ordained to the work of the gospel ministry, and a member of the Presbytery of New Brunswick, was soon afterwards accordingly appointed. By the Assembly which met in 1822, he was elected Professor of Oriental and Biblical Literature, and was solemnly inaugurated in the following September.

Professor Hodge, soon after his appointment to the office of Professor of Oriental and Biblical Literature, with the consent of the Board of Directors, visited Europe; and, after spending some time in Great Britain and France, devoted himself more particularly to biblical studies in the Universities of Berlin and Halle. He was absent about two years.

The General Assembly which met at Pittsburgh, in the year 1835, appointed two new professors, *viz.*—the Rev. John Breckinridge, D.D., a native of Kentucky, and for several preceding years Corresponding Secretary of the General Assembly's Board of Education, to be Professor of Pastoral Theology; and Mr Joseph Addison Alexander, A.M., of Princeton, to be Associate Professor of Oriental and Biblical Literature. Dr Breckinridge accepted his appointment, and was inaugurated on the 26th of September following. Mr Alexander declined accepting his appointment to a professorship, for the present, and preferred occupying the place of instructor in that department, at least for a time. It is expected that he will, ultimately consent, formally and officially, to occupy, as he does now virtually, the place to which he was chosen. Mr Alexander enjoyed, prior to his entering on the duties of instructor in the institution, very gratifying opportunities of extensive travel in Great Britain, and on the continent of Europe; and of study in the Universities of Halle and Berlin.

The following rules for regulating elections of directors and professors of the seminary, were adopted by the General Assembly in 1812.

1. When the Assembly shall proceed to the election of directors of the theological seminary, the clerk shall call on the members severally, to nominate any number of persons, not exceeding the number to he elected, if he shall think it expedient to make any nomination.

2. When the members have been severally called upon in the order of the roll, to make a nomination agreeably to the above rule, the names of the persons nominated shall be immediately read by the clerk for the information of the members, and on the day following the Assembly shall proceed to elect, by ballot, the whole number of directors to be chosen.

3. Two members shall be appointed to take an account of the votes given for the candidates nominated for directors, and to report to the Assembly the number of votes for each of the said candidates, who have a plurality of votes, who shall be declared duly elected:—but if the whole number to be elected, should not be elected, and two or more of the candidates should have an equal number of votes, then, in that case, the house shall proceed to elect from the nomination a sufficient number to complete the Board; and shall continue to vote in this manner, until the full number specified by the constitution of the seminary be completed.

4. When the votes shall have been counted, and the requisite number of directors shall have been elected, in the manner above specified, the moderator shall announce to the Assembly the names of those persons who shall appear to have the highest number of votes, and are thus elected.

5. Whenever a professor or professors, are to be elected, the Assembly, by a vote, shall determine the day when said election shall be held; which day shall be at least two days after the above determination has been made. Immediately after the vote fixing the day has passed, the Assembly shall have a season for special prayer, for direction in the choice. The election, in all cases, shall be made by ballot. The ballots having been counted by two members previously appointed, they shall report a statement of said votes to the moderator; and in case there shall appear to be an equal number of votes for any two or more candidates, the Assembly shall proceed, either immediately, or at some subsequent period of their sessions, to a new election. The choice being made, it shall be announced to the Assembly by the moderator.

The theological seminary, though located in Princeton, is altogether independent of the college located in the same town, and separate from it. No officer of the one is, as such, an officer of the other. There is, in fact, no connection whatever between the two institutions, excepting what arises out of certain articles of agreement between the trustees of the college and the General Assembly, formed in 1812; in virtue of which the theological students, for a short time, boarded at the refectory, and lodged in some of the spare rooms of the college: and in consequence of which also, for about four years, the lectures and recitations of the seminary were conducted in the public rooms of the college. Everything of this kind, of course, terminated, when the public edifice of the seminary was opened for the reception of its students. And of these articles, the only one of which the theological seminary has availed itself, for several years past, or is likely ever again to avail itself, is that which gives to the students of the seminary the use of the college library, which consists of about seven thousand volumes. This article is in the following words:—

> The trustees grant to the professors and pupils of the theological seminary, the free use of the college library; subject to such rules as may be adopted for the preservation of the books, and the good order of the same.

There has been a slow but steady increase of the number of students in the seminary, from the opening of the first session until the present time. It began, as we have seen, with three. It has since risen gradually to one hundred and thirty, which may be regarded as the present average number, The whole number of students who have belonged to the institution, from its commencement is more than one thousand. Of these, forty have engaged in the work of foreign missions. A number more have in view, and are preparing for the same field of labour. Considerably above one hundred and fifty have been engaged in domestic missions. The remainder are, or have been, pastors of churches; and a large portion of those who employed the first years of their ministry in missionary labour, have since been settled in pastoral charges.

Library

The library of the seminary was commenced soon after the commencement of the institution. One of the earliest and most liberal contributors to its formation, was the Rev. Dr Ashbel Green, the first President of the Board of Directors, and one of the most prominent and active of the original founders of the seminary. As a memorial of his zealous and eminent services, it was called the Green Library. This collection of books may now be estimated at about six thousand volumes, and is annually increasing. When the Synod of the Associate Reformed Church, a few years ago, voted to become united with the Presbyterian Church, it also voted to deposit its library in the theological seminary at Princeton, for the use of that institution forever. That library having been chiefly collected in Great Britain, by the Rev. Dr John M. Mason, one of the most distinguished ornaments of the Associate Reformed Church, and, for many years, the principal professor in her theological seminary;—it was thought proper to give this collection of books his name. Accordingly, soon after it was deposited in Princeton, it received, and has since been known by the name of the Mason Library. The number of volumes in this library may be estimated at near four thousand.

These two libraries have ever been kept perfectly distinct. This is proper in itself; and is the rather necessary, because that portion of the Associate Reformed Church which refused to acquiesce in the union with the Presbyterian Church, several years since, commenced a suit at law for the recovery of the Mason Library, which has been lately decided in favour of that Synod; so that it is expected that that collection of books will be, in a few months, removed from Princeton.

Funds

The funds of this institution have never been adequate to its support. It has been necessary to have recourse, from time to time, to annual collections; and this necessity still exists. Measures have been taken for the endowment of three professorships, and considerable progress made in the enterprise. But no one of them has been completely filled. There is a prospect that, before long, these endowments will be completed. The number of scholarships endowed by different liberal individuals, for the support of as many students in the institution, is twenty-six.

The following is a catalogue of both these classes of funds.

Professorships

In 1821, it was announced to the General Assembly that foundations for three professorships had been commenced by the following bodies.

The two Synods of North Carolina, and of South Carolina and Georgia, resolved to raise $15,000 each; so as to constitute a fund for a joint professorship of $30,000.

The Synod of Philadelphia resolved to endow a professorship with a capital sum of $25,000.

The Synod of New York and New Jersey resolved to endow a professorship with a capital sum of $25,000.

No one of these professorships has been fully completed: though much the greater part toward the completion of each has been actually paid. It is due, however, to the Synod of New York, which since the date of the resolution above alluded to, has been erected into a separate synod, to state, that her portion of the promised endowment has been fully paid.

Scholarships

The scholarships which have been founded are the following.

1. The Le Roy scholarship, founded in 1816, by Mrs Martha Le Roy, of the City of New York.

2. The Banyar scholarship, founded in 1816, by the same.

3. The Lenox scholarship, founded in 1816, by Robert Lenox, Esquire, of the City of New York.

4. The Whitehead scholarship, founded in 1817, by John Whitehead, Esquire, of Burke County, Georgia.

5. The Charleston Female scholarship, founded in 1817, by the Congregational and Presbyterian Female Association of Charleston, SC, for assisting in the education of pious youth for the gospel ministry.

6. The Class scholarship, founded in 1819, by the first class in the seminary of that year.

7. The Nephew scholarship, founded in 1821, by James Nephew, Esquire, of M'Intosh County, Georgia.

8. The Woodhull scholarship, founded in 1823, by Mrs Hannah Woodhull, of Brookhaven, Long Island, New York.

9. The Scott scholarship, founded in 1823, by Mr William Scott, of Elizabethtown, New Jersey.

10. The Van Brugh Livingston scholarship, founded in 1823, by Mrs Susan U. Neimcewiecz, of Elizabethtown, New Jersey.

11. The Augusta Female scholarship, founded in 1823, by ladies of Augusta, Georgia.

12. The Jane Keith scholarship, founded in 1823, by Mrs Jane Keith, widow of the late Rev. Isaac S. Keith, D.D., of Charleston, South Carolina.

13. The Gosman scholarship, founded in 1825, by Robert Gosman, Esquire, of Upper-Red-Hook, Dutchess County, New York.

14. The Wickes scholarship, founded in 1825, by Eliphalet Wickes, Esquire, of Jamaica, Long Island, New York.

15. The Othniel Smith scholarship, founded in 1825, by Mr Othniel Smith, of Jamaica, Long Island, New York.

16. The John Keith scholarship, founded in 1825, by Mr John Keith, of Bucks County, Pennsylvania.

17. The Hester Smith scholarship, founded in 1826, by Miss Hester Smith, of Carmel, Mississippi.

18. The Anderson scholarship, founded in 1827, by James Anderson, Esquire, of the City of New York.

19. The Kennedy scholarship, founded in 1827, by Mr Anthony Kennedy, of Frankford, Pennsylvania.

20. The Colt scholarship, founded in 1829, by Roswell L. Colt, Esquire, of Baltimore, Maryland.

21. The Boudinot scholarship, founded in 1830, by the Hon. Elias Boudinot, LL.D. of Burlington, New Jersey.

22. The Ed scholarship,[1] founded in 1830, by Mr Robert Hall, and his sister, Mrs Marion Hall, of Newburgh, New York.

23. The Kirkpatrick scholarship, founded in 1830, by William Kirkpatrick, Esquire, of Lancaster, Pennsylvania.

24. The Stille scholarship, founded in 1834, by John Stille, Esquire, of Philadelphia.

25. The King scholarship, founded in 1835, by Mr Gilbert King, of Newburgh, Orange County, New York.

26. The Benjamin Smith scholarship, founded some years since, by the will of Mr Benjamin Smith, of Elizabethtown, New Jersey, deceased, and the sum bequeathed expected soon to be actually paid in.

---

[1] For an explanation of this name, which was selected by the founders, see *Josh.* 22:34.

Rules of Decorum, Order and Duty for the Students

1. It shall be the duty of every student to attend punctually at the hour appointed for each recitation or lecture to begin.

2. Every student who shall be absent, without leave, from the recitation or lecture of any professor, shall assign to such professor, the reason of his absence.

3. It shall be the duty of every student, when, in the course of recitation, he shall be addressed by the professor, to rise, and remain standing, while he is answering the questions, or performing the part assigned him; unless the professor shall particularly request him to remain seated.

4. If any student desire to obtain leave of absence, if he contemplate absence from only one recitation or lecture, it shall be his duty to apply only to the professor who is to conduct the recitation or lecture in question. But if it be his wish to be absent from two or more recitations, it shall then be his duty to apply to all the professors from whose exercises he wishes to be absent.

5. No conversation shall be allowed during any recitation or lecture, nor any reading, excepting that which relates immediately to the subject of the lecture. This rule, however, shall not be considered as prohibiting any pertinent questions which any student may be disposed to ask respecting the subject at any time under consideration.

Rules for the Regulation of the Students in the Public Edifice.

1. Morning and evening prayers shall be attended by the students of the seminary, at the hours appointed by the professors.

2. In conducting the devotions of the morning, the students of the first class shall preside in rotation, except when one of the professors is present.

3. Evening prayers shall be regularly attended by one of the professors.

4. It shall be left to the professors to accompany prayer with such other exercises as to them may seem proper.

5. From morning prayers until breakfast; from nine o'clock until twelve; and from two o'clock p.m. until five, shall be hours of study.

6. In the hours of study, the students shall not be unnecessarily

absent from their respective rooms; nor shall there be any passing from room to room, unless on special business.

7. It shall be the duty of the students to preserve their rooms neat and clean, and carefully to avoid defacing or injuring any part of the edifice.

8. All unnecessary noise within the edifice, is prohibited at all times, but especially in the hours of study.

9. It shall be the duty of each student to spend some portion of each day in wholesome exercise.

10. The professors shall have a general power to preserve order and decorum in the house; to inspect the rooms of the students; to appoint monitors or censors; to direct and govern any person or persons, who may be employed as servants in the house, and to dismiss the same whenever they shall judge it proper.

11. It shall also belong to the professors to prescribe rules for the preservation of order and decorum in the attendance of the students at their meals.

12. The students shall, at all times, treat the steward of the seminary with respect; and they shall not, on any occasion, infringe on the regulations which, with the approbation of the professors, he may make for the government of the servants, or the refectory, or kitchen.

13. It shall be the duty of the professors of the seminary to enforce these rules; and to exercise such discipline, in case of an infringement of any of them, as to them may seem proper; not inconsistent with the Constitution of the seminary.

Rules for the Regulation of the Students in the Dining Room

1. The students shall, at the proper signal, assemble in the dining room, in as quiet and orderly a manner as possible.

2. A member of the first class, in alphabetical order, shall preside at each meal. The presiding student shall ask a blessing, and shall call upon any other whom he may think proper, to return thanks.

3. The members of each class, as far as circumstances will admit, shall sit together at table.

Rules for the Preservation and Security of the Public Edifice, etc.

1. Every student, at the commencement of every session, shall contribute to the 'General Expense Fund', the object of which is to clean, light and warm the public rooms, and to keep in repair the public edifice. Those who occupy rooms in the public edifice shall pay ten dollars per annum, and those who room elsewhere, nine dollars, to this fund. Of this sum six dollars shall be paid by all the students, in advance, at the commencement of the winter session, and the balance, also in advance, at the commencement of the summer session. This payment to be made to the treasurer of the trustees of the seminary, and the receipt for the same produced to the professor who officiates, as clerk of the faculty of the seminary.

2. If any student shall, accidentally, or from any cause whatever, injure any part of the public edifice, or its furniture, he shall immediately report the same to the Steward of the seminary, who shall cause the injury to be repaired, at the expense of him who caused it.

3. If any student shall desire to alter the fire place, or any other fixture in his room, or to fix a grate, or introduce a stove, he shall inform the steward of his purpose, and obtain his permission to execute it: and no stove shall be set in any room without placing it on some metallic, or other incombustible substance.

Admission into the Seminary

The Plan of the institution requires that 'every student applying for admission, shall produce satisfactory testimonials that he possesses good natural talents, and is of a prudent and discreet deportment; that he is in full communion with some regular church; that he has passed through a regular course of academical study; or, wanting this, he shall submit himself to an examination in regard to the branches of literature taught in such a course.'

'Every student, before he takes his standing in the seminary, shall subscribe the following declaration, *viz.*—"Deeply impressed with a sense of the importance of improving in knowledge, prudence, and piety, in my preparation for the gospel ministry, I solemnly promise, in a reliance on divine grace, that I will faithfully and diligently attend on all the instructions of this seminary, and that I will conscientiously and vigilantly observe all the rules and regulations specified in the Plan for its instruction and government, so far as the same relate to the students; and that I will obey all the lawful requisitions, and readily yield to all the wholesome admonitions of the professors and directors of the seminary, while I shall remain a member of it.'"

When a student has been received under the care of a presbytery, and has passed his examination on the studies usually pursued in colleges with approbation, a certificate from the presbytery declaring this fact, is received as sufficient to answer every requisition in regard to testimonials.

When a student, who has been connected with any other theological seminary, seeks admission into this, he must produce testimonials of his good standing, and regular dismission, before he can be received.

The proper time for entering the seminary is at the commencement of the winter session, which begins early in November. It is important that students should be present at the opening of the session.

Vacations

There are three vacations in the seminary every year. The spring vacation of six weeks; the autumnal vacation of six weeks; and the winter vacation of two weeks;—to commence at such times as the Board of Directors shall deem expedient.

The Board have accordingly ordered the following arrangement:—the spring vacation to commence the first week in May; the fall vacation the Monday evening preceding the last Wednesday in September; and the winter vacation on the first day of February.

Course of Study in the Seminary

First year—Hebrew Language; Exegetical Study of the Scriptures; Sacred Rhetoric; Biblical Criticism; Biblical Antiquities; Introduction to the Study of the Scriptures; Mental and Moral Science; The Evidences of Natural and Revealed Religion; Sacred Chronology; Biblical History.

Second year—Exegetical Study of the Hebrew and Greek Scriptures continued; Didactic Theology; Ecclesiastical History; Missionary Instruction.

Third year—Exegetical Study of the Scriptures continued; Didactic Theology continued; Polemic Theology; Church Government; Pastoral Theology; Composition and Delivery of Sermons.

Members of the first class are required to exhibit original compositions once in two weeks; those of the second class once in three weeks; and those of the third class once in four weeks.

Necessary Expenses of the Seminary

There is no charge made either for tuition or room-rent; but each student pays $10 per annum to the 'General Expense Fund', the object of which is to defray the contingent expenses of the institution. Students who may prefer rooming out of seminary building can be accommodated in the village and vicinity.

Indigent students are aided either by the General Assembly's 'Board of Education', the 'American Education Society', or the funds of the seminary.

The expense of board in the Commons varies from $1.25 to $1.75 per week. Board may be obtained in private families at from $1.50 to $2.50 per week. Expense of fuel from $6 to $10 per year. Washing $8.

The students, in addition to the libraries attached to the seminary, have access to that of the college; and, on application to the several professors of that institution, can have the privilege of attending lectures on natural philosophy, chemistry, and natural history.

Gentlemen well qualified to teach the German and French languages are resident here, and will give instruction in those branches to such students as desire it, at their own expense.

Wants of the Seminary

Although this institution has been in operation for more than twenty-five years, yet a variety of circumstances have served to show that the public are very imperfectly informed of its situation. That its friends may be the better able to judge of its wants, and of the various ways in which the wealthy and the pious may contribute to its benefit, it may not be improper to exhibit, in detail, the following items, with a distinct explanation connected with each.

I. *The Support of the Professors*

This is mentioned first, because it is the most vital and indispensable part of the whole. A theological seminary without adequate instructors, would, of course, be a name without a reality. It would be possible to get along—inconveniently and imperfectly, indeed; but still to get along, without public buildings, without a public library, and without funds for the support of the students. But without instructors, nothing, it is evident, in the form of a seminary of learning, can be carried on at all. And it is equally evident, that capable instructors cannot be expected to quit other important stations, and devote themselves, for life, to this object, without some good prospect of a comfortable and permanent support. Yet it has been, for some time, a matter of wonder and regret to the friends of the seminary, that it has been, for so many years, a candidate for the favour of the religious public, without obtaining a single permanent and adequate endowment, for the support of even one professor. Almost all other institutions of a similar kind have been built up by the large donations of liberal benefactors. Toward some of them there has been a liberality of this kind displayed, which reflects the highest honour on a number of distinguished individuals. The names of Hollis and Boylston, of Hancock, Hersey, and Erving, designating so many different professorships in the University of Cambridge, in Massachusetts, have long been monuments of splendid munificence, and will be transmitted with honour to the end of time. And in the Theological Seminary at Andover, the professorships of Christian Theology, of Sacred Rhetoric, and of Sacred Literature, confer on the names of Bartlett and Abbott, of Brown and Norris, an illustrious immortality. But, while so much has been done, by Christian liberality, for other institutions, it is a humiliating fact, that no individual has been hitherto found, in all our large and wealthy bounds, who has manifested a disposition to endow a single professorship. Can the thought be admitted that there is less-enlightened attachment to the church of Christ, or less disposition to exercise munificence in the best of all causes, in the bosom of the Presbyterian Church, than among our Congregational brethren of New England? May we not rather hope, that the deficiency hitherto acknowledged and lamented, has been owing to a want of acquaintance with the necessities of the institution, rather than to the want of a disposition to patronize it? May we not cherish the hope, that when the object is fairly presented, and the urgent necessities of the seminary fully made known, there will also be found among Presbyterians an amount of Christian liberality and public spirit, commensurate with the demand for its exercise?

It will be observed, that the Plan of the Seminary provides, that 'if any person or persons, not exceeding three, shall, by will, or during his or their lives, found or endow a professorship or professorships, said professorship or professorships shall forever afterwards be called and known by the name or names of those who founded or endowed them; and also that presbyteries, synods, or associations of any kind, may enjoy the same privilege.' And in connection with this, the General Assembly of 1815, resolved, 'that a sum not less than $25,000 should be considered as requisite to endow a professorship.'

Wealthy individuals, by coming forward and endowing one or more professorships themselves, may not only endear their names to Christians of the most distant posterity; but may also render it unnecessary for the synods, who have resolved to endow professorships, to collect monies for the accomplishment of their purpose from the poor as well as the rich, within their respective bounds. Or those whose pecuniary means do not allow of so large an enterprise, may, by throwing in a few hundreds, or a few thousands, into the synodical appropriations for this purpose, happily assist in expediting the attainment of their object.

II. *The Support of Students*

A number of the students belonging to the seminary are unable to provide the means of their own support; and unless these means were furnished from other sources, would be obliged to withdraw from the institution, and from all the advantages which it affords. This generally has been, and is now, the case with a majority of the whole number. But, after all that has been done in this way, many pious and promising young men, in different parts of our church, who desired to come to the seminary, have been prevented from enjoying the privilege, because no encouragement to hope for adequate support could be held out to them; and, in some cases, it is feared, the church has been altogether deprived of the services of precious youth, who might have adorned her ministry, but who saw no door open for pursuing the studies necessary to qualify them for the sacred office.

It is of the utmost importance, then, that funds be furnished for the support of indigent students; for the entire support of those who need it, and for the partial aid of those whose circumstances are straitened. Indeed, the seminary cannot be considered as accomplishing all that it is intended to accomplish, until it shall be able freely to open its doors to all the youth of piety and talent, who may desire the holy ministry; affording gratuitous instruction to all without exception, and gratuitous boarding to all who may need such assistance.

For this purpose, it will be observed, that the Plan of the Seminary provides for the endowment of scholarships, that is, devoting a principal sum, the interest of which shall be sacredly applied, forever, to the support of an indigent student. These scholarships, it is further provided, shall forever bear the name of their founders respectively. A number of scholarships have been already founded, by distinguished friends of the seminary, as has been seen in the preceding history; and it is earnestly hoped that their number will be increased. Can a Christian of wealth and public spirit devote a portion of his property to a more interesting purpose? While so much pains and expense are bestowed on sending the Bible, in all languages, to every part of the world; can it be forgotten that the *living teacher* is an appointment of God, for converting the nations, no less important than the written word? And can anyone, who has eyes to see, and ears to hear, fail of knowing, that while Bibles are multiplying rapidly, there is not a corresponding multiplication of ministers of the cross? Is it not an object, then, worthy of the best efforts of every believer in Christ, to do all in his power to add to their number? And how can he do it better than by founding scholarships in theological seminaries? To establish a fund for the education of one minister of the gospel after another, in an unbroken succession, to the end of time, is surely one of the most desirable achievements of Christian charity which a pious mind can easily contemplate. Perhaps there is no other object to which such a sum can be appropriated; that will be likely so extensively to promote the glory of God, the good of souls, and the eternal reward of the pious donor.

The General Assembly have determined, that a sum not less than $2,500 shall be considered as requisite to endow a scholarship. It is evident, however, that the annual interest of $2,500, especially at the present low rate of interest, is not sufficient for the entire support of any young man in a theological seminary, even in the most economical manner. It is desirable, therefore, that a few scholarships of higher amount, say of $3,000 and $3,500, be established. For while some students are able to furnish a part of what is necessary for their own support, others are totally destitute, and, of course, must be furnished with a full support, if any.

For a number of years after the establishment of the seminary, a large part of the support furnished to indigent students was derived from Female Cent Societies, and other Female Associations, in different parts of our church. For seven or eight years past, these societies have, in a great measure, ceased to furnish their wonted supply. Either from a decline of their zeal, or from an impression that their efforts were no longer needed, but few of them are any longer in the habit of transmitting the fruits of their annual liberality. Only two or three of all the former number continue to transmit their contributions. This decline is deeply to be lamented. These contributions are greatly needed. It would gladden many a student's heart, and prevent many a painful privation, if they could be resumed and continued. And if one or two ladies, in each church, who take an interest in the welfare of Zion, and who desire to see the number of pious and well furnished ministers greatly increased, would undertake to manage the affairs of these associations, to recollect the return of their anniversaries, and to collect their dues, they might, with very little effort, be kept in regular and most useful operation.

III. *The Purchase of an Adequate Library*

A good library is a matter of vital importance in a theological seminary. Without it, both professors and students are subjected to privations and embarrassments of the most serious kind, at every step of their course. There ought to be in every such institution, a library of sufficient extent to furnish every standard work which may be quoted or recommended on every subject which may become matter of discussion in the institution. Compared with what it ought to be, the library at present possessed by the seminary is very small and imperfect. Many of the most important works recommended to the pupils are not to be found in it, and are, of course, beyond their reach. Instead of 100,000 volumes, which the institution ought to possess, it has less than a twelfth part of that number. And now that the library of the Associate Reformed Synod is no longer ours, the scantiness of our supply in this respect must strike unfavourably every beholder, and give pain to every friend of the seminary.

There certainly ought to be placed, in some such central situation as that of Princeton, a great library, to which students and writers on all subjects might resort; and where might be found every important work needed, either for perusal or reference, in all departments of literature and science. And of some works recommended to the perusal of whole classes of students, instead of one, there ought to be, on the shelves of such an institution, several dozens of copies. This object ought to engage the immediate attention, and the efficient liberality of every friend of the seminary, and, indeed, of every friend of literature. A few thousand dollars devoted to the enlargement of the library, would be most usefully bestowed. Donations in books, or in money to be appropriated to the purchase of books, would be gratefully acknowledged by the directors and officers of the seminary.

The apartment in the public edifice, destined for the library, is entirely too small for the reception of such a collection as every theological seminary ought to possess. Nor is this all: an extensive and valuable library ought never to be deposited in any other than a fireproof building. It is exceedingly desirable, therefore, that some individual or individuals, friendly to the seminary, should erect a suitable building, for the reception of a large library, in the vicinity of the main edifice, and constructed, as nearly as possible, upon the principle of being proof against fire, while it should admit of being comfortably warmed. The destruction of the greater part of the library of Princeton College, by the memorable fire which consumed the public edifice of that institution in 1802, furnished a very instructive admonition on this subject.

The Officers of the Seminary in January 1838

Directors
MINISTERS

Gardiner Spring, D.D.
William A. M'Dowell, D.D.
William Neill, D.D.
William Latta.
William D. Snodgrass, D.D.
Joseph M'Elroy, D.D.
George Musgrave.
Benjamin H. Rice, D.D.
John M'Dowell, D.D.
William H. Sprague, D.D.
Cornelius C. Cuyler, D.D.
George Potts.
Elias W. Crane.
John N. Campbell, D.D.
Ashbel Green, D.D.
William W. Phillips, D.D.
John Johnston.
Asa Hillyer, D.D.
Robert M'Cartee, D.D.
Henry A. Boardman.
Nicholas Murray.

RULING ELDERS

John T. Woodhull, M.D.
Hugh Auchincloss.
Alexander W. Mitchell, M.D.
Benjamin Strong.
Samuel Bayard.
Ambrose White.
Alexander Henry.
Moses Allen.
James Lenox.

Trustees

Samuel Bayard, Esq., *President.*
Hon. Samuel L. Southard, *Vice-President.*
Rev. John M'Dowell, D.D., *Secretary.*

Alexander Henry, Esq.	John J. Bryant, Esq.
Benjamin Strong, Esq.	Rev. Ashbel Green, D.D.
John T. Woodhull, M.D.	Rev. William W. Phillips, D.D.
Solomon Allen, Esq.	Rev. David Comfort.
Lewis W. R. Phillips, Esq.	Rev. Nicholas Murray.
Jabez G. Goble, M.D.	Rev. Isaac V. Brown.
James Lenox, Esq.	Rev. James Carnahan, D.D.
Job Squier, Esq.	Rev. Joseph M'Elroy, D.D.
Henry W. Green, Esq.	Rev. Eli F. Cooley.

James S. Green, Esq., *Treasurer of the Board of Trustees.*
Josiah Cary, Esq., *Steward.*

Professors

Rev. Archibald Alexander, D.D.,
Professor of Didactic and Polemic Theology.
Rev. Samuel Miller, D.D.,
Professor of Ecclesiastical History and Church Government.
Rev. Charles Hodge, D.D.,
Professor of Oriental and Biblical Literature.
Rev. John Breckinridge, D.D.,
Professor of Pastoral Theology and Missionary Instruction.
J. Addison Alexander, A.M.,
Associate Professor (elect) of Oriental and Biblical Literature.

Form of a Devise or Bequest for the Seminary

'To the Trustees of the General Assembly of the Presbyterian Church
in the United States of America, I give and bequeath the sum of (here
designate the property, personal or real), to be added to the Permanent
Fund of the Theological Seminary, at Princeton, New Jersey, under
the care of the said Assembly; *Or* to the Contingent Fund of the said
Seminary; *Or* toward the establishment of a Professorship, or Scholarship, in said Seminary; *Or* toward the increase of its Library, *Or* the
support of its indigent students, &c.' according to the wish of the
donor;—and the corporation are bound by charter to apply the donation accordingly.

The above form may be used by a Testator residing in the State of
Pennsylvania, where the Trustees of the General Assembly have been
incorporated; but, in the other States of the Union, the following
form is recommended, *viz.*—

In Cases of Real Estate.

'I give and devise unto A. B. and C. D. the survivors and survivor
of them, and the heirs of such survivor (describe the real estate), for
the use of, and in trust for, the Trustees of the General Assembly of
the Presbyterian Church, to be applied to the use of the Theological
Seminary of the said church, now located at Princeton, New Jersey',
&c. &c.

In Cases of Personal Estate

'I give and bequeath unto (as above, excepting instead of the heirs
of such survivor say,) executors, administrators, and assigns, of such
survivor.'

INAUGURAL ADDRESSES
AT THE OPENING OF PRINCETON
THEOLOGICAL SEMINARY
1812

The oldest Presbyterian graduate school of theology
in the United States, the Princeton Theological Seminary
was founded by the General Assembly of
the Presbyterian Church.

Three students were present when the school opened
on August 12, 1812.

Until the first building was completed in 1817,
classes met in faculty homes and in facilities of the
College of New Jersey, now Princeton University.

*Wording on a commemorative plaque at
Princeton Theological Seminary.*

THE DUTY OF THE CHURCH[1]

And the things which thou hast heard of me among many witnesses, the
same commit thou to faithful men, who shall be able to teach others also.

2 Timothy 2:2

THE Apostle Paul received, both his knowledge of the gospel, and his commission to preach it, immediately from the great Head of the church. Yet, notwithstanding the extraordinary circumstances which attended his theological instruction, and his official investiture, that all things might be done decently and in order, he submitted to the laying on of the hands of the presbytery, before he went forth on his great mission to the Gentiles. In like manner, Timothy, his own son in the faith, to whom the exhortation before us is addressed, was set apart to the work of the holy ministry, by the presbytery, in which body, on that occasion, the apostle himself seems to have presided.[2] Timothy was now at Ephesus; and being the most active and influential member of the presbytery which was constituted in that part of the church, his spiritual father directed to him, as such, and in him to the church in all succeeding times, the rules and instructions contained in the epistles which bear his name. Among these we find the passage which has just been read: 'And the things which thou hast heard of me in the presence of many witnesses, the same commit thou to faithful men, who shall be able to teach others also.'

---

[1] Samuel Miller, 'The Duty of the Church to take Measures for Providing An Able and Faithful Ministry: A Sermon', *The Sermon, Delivered at the Inauguration of the Rev. Archibald Alexander, D.D. as Professor of Didactic and Polemic Theology, in the Theological Seminary of the Presbyterian Church, in the United States of America. To Which are Added, the Professor's Inaugural Address, and The Charge to the Professor and Students* (New York: Whiting and Watson, 1812), pp. 5-54.

[2] Compare *1 Tim.* 4:14 with *2 Tim.* 1:6.

It is impossible, within the limits of a single discourse, to do justice to a portion of Scripture replete with such various and important matter, as the slightest attention will discover in this text. Of course, much of what properly belongs to its illustration, must be either wholly omitted, or very briefly noticed, on the present occasion. That the Christian ministry is an institution of Jesus Christ; that this institution is essential, not only to the well-being, but also to the very existence of the church, as an organized body; that Christ has promised that there shall always be a succession of ministers in his church, to the end of the world; and that none have a right to enter on the appropriate functions of this sacred office, without having that right formally and officially 'committed' to them, by men who are themselves already in the same office; are great, elementary principles of ecclesiastical order, which are all fairly implied in the passage before us; but which, I trust, it is not necessary for me to attempt either to establish or to illustrate before this audience. They are so plainly laid down in Scripture, and so evidently reasonable in themselves, that I shall, at present, take them for granted.

Neither will it be deemed necessary, at present, to dwell on the numerous and important benefits of an able and faithful ministry. It may be said, without exaggeration, that every interest of man is involved in this blessing. The order, comfort, and edification of the church; the progress in knowledge, the growth in grace, and the consolation of individual believers; the regularity, peace, polish, and strength of civil society; the extension of intellectual and moral cultivation; the glory of God; and the eternal welfare of men; are among the great benefits which an able and faithful ministry is, ordinarily, the means of promoting; and which, without such a ministry, we cannot hope to attain, at least in any considerable degree. If it be acknowledged that the sanctions of religion exert a mighty, and most benign influence on the order and happiness of society; if the observance of the Christian Sabbath be as really a blessing to the world as it is to the church, if the solemnities of public worship, be a source of moral and temporal benefit to millions, who give no evidence of a saving acquaintance with the power of the gospel; if the weekly instructions of the sanctuary have a native tendency to enlighten, refine, and restrain, those whom they are not the means of converting; and if it please God 'by the foolishness of preaching to save them that believe'; then, it is evident, that an able and faithful ministry, next to the sanctifying operations of the Holy Spirit, is the greatest benefit that can be conferred upon a people. And, if these great institutions of heaven are likely, other things being equal, to be beneficial, in proportion to the clearness, the force, the wisdom, and the fidelity with which they are exhibited, as both common sense and the Word of God evidently dictate; then it is plain, that the *more* able and the *more* faithful that ministry, with which any people is blessed, the more extensive and important are likely to be the benefits resulting from it, both to the church, and the world. The father of a family, as well as the professor of religion, has reason to desire the attainment of such a ministry. The patriot, as well as the Christian, ought earnestly to wish, and be ready to contribute his aid, that the church may obey the precept of her Head and Lord: 'the same commit thou to faithful men, who shall be able to teach others also'.

I say, that the church may obey this divine precept; for it is, undoubtedly, a mistake, and a very grievous mistake, to imagine, as many seem to imagine, that precepts of the kind before us, are addressed to ministers alone. It is freely granted, that ministers are the appointed agents for training up those who are to succeed them in this holy vocation; and for imparting to them the official pow-ers, which they have themselves received. Yet it is, unquestionably, in the *name,* and as the constituted executive and organ of that part of the church which they represent, that they perform this service. If, therefore, as I take for granted all will allow, the design of the pre-cept before us did not cease with Timothy: if both its reason and its obligation be permanent; then the church of Christ, at this hour, is to consider it as directed to her. It is the church that is bound to take order, that what she has received be committed to faithful men, who shall be able to teach others also.

The doctrine of our text, then, is, *that it is the indispensable duty of the church of Christ, in all ages, to take measures for providing an able and faithful ministry.*

The great fact, that this is the duty of the church, I shall consider as sufficiently established by the plain and unequivocal precept before us; and shall employ the time that remains for the present discourse, in inquiring,

What we are to understand by an able and faithful ministry? And, *What are the means which the church is bound to employ for providing such a ministry?*

I. *What are we to understand by an able and faithful ministry?*

It is a ministry, at once qualified and disposed to perform, with enlightened and unwearied assiduity, all the duties, whether of instruction, of defence, or of discipline, which belong to ambassadors of Christ, to pastors, and rulers in his church.

This general character implies *piety, talents, learning,* and *diligence.*

1. The first requisite to form a faithful and able minister, is *piety.* By this I mean, that he be a regenerated man; that he have a living faith in that Saviour whom he preaches to others; that the love of Christ habitually constrain him; that he have himself walked in those paths of humility, self-denial, and holy communion with God, through our Lord Jesus Christ, in which it is the business of his life to endeavour to lead his fellow men.

I shall not now speak of the necessity of piety, to a minister's personal salvation; nor of its inestimable importance to his personal comfort. I shall not dwell on the irksomeness, nay, the intolerable drudgery, of labouring in a vocation in which the heart does not go along; nor on the painful misgiving which must ever attend preaching an unknown Saviour, and recommending untasted hopes and joys. Neither shall I attempt to describe, tremendous and overwhelming as it is, the aggravated doom of that man, who, from the heights of this sacred office, shall sink into the abyss of the damned; who, after having preached to others, shall himself become a castaway (*1 Cor.* 9:27). But my object is, to show the importance, and the necessity, of this best of all attainments, in order to qualify any man for discharging the duties of the ministerial office. It is to show, that, without piety, he cannot be an able minister. He cannot be a workman, that needeth not to be ashamed, rightly dividing the word of truth, and giving to each his portion in due season (*2 Tim.* 2:15).

How can a man who knows only the theory of religion, undertake to be a practical guide in spiritual things? How can he adapt his instructions to all the varieties of Christian experience? How can he direct the awakened, the inquiring, the tempted, and the doubting?

How can he feed the sheep and the lambs of Christ? How can he sympathize with mourners in Zion? How can he comfort others with those consolations wherewith he himself has never been comforted of God? He cannot possibly perform, as he ought, any of these duties, and yet they are the most precious and interesting parts of the ministerial work. However gigantic his intellectual powers; however deep, and various, and accurate his learning, he is not able, in relation to any of these points, to teach others, seeing he is not taught himself. If he make the attempt, it will be the blind leading the blind; and of this, unerring wisdom has told us the consequence (*Matt.* 11:15). It were rash, indeed, and unwarranted, to say, that a man who knows nothing of the power of godliness, may not be employed, by a sovereign God, as the means of saving benefit to others. God undoubtedly may, and probably sometimes does, 'by way of miracle, raise a man to life by the bones of a dead prophet' (*2 Kings* 13:21). He may, and, there is reason to believe sometimes does, 'honour his own Word so far as to make it effectual to salvation, even when it falls from unhallowed lips'. The ministry even of Judas Iscariot was, probably, not without its benefit to the church of Christ. But such a result is not, in ordinary cases, and certainly not in any considerable degree, to be expected. When unsanctified ministers are introduced into the church, we may generally expect them to prove, not only an offence to God, but also a curse to his people. Piety, orthodoxy, practical holiness, and all the spiritual glories of the household of faith will commonly be found to decline in proportion to the number and influence of these enemies in disguise.

And here I cannot help bearing testimony against what appears to me a dangerous mistake; which, though it may not be common, yet sometimes occurs among parents and guardians of the more serious class. I mean the mistake of destining young persons to the gospel ministry, from a very early period of life, before they can be supposed, from any enlightened view of the subject, to concur in the choice themselves; and before they give any satisfactory evidence of vital piety. Brethren, I venerate the parent who desires, and daily prays, that it may please God to prepare and dispose his child, to serve him in the ministry of reconciliation. Nay, I think that parent worthy of the thanks of every friend to religion, who solemnly devotes his child, even from the earliest period of life, to the service of the church, and avowedly conducts every part of his education with a view to this great object; provided the original consecration, and every subsequent arrangement, be made on the condition, carefully and frequently expressed, as well as implied, that God shall be pleased to sanction and accept the offering, by imparting his grace, and giving a heart to love, and desire the sacred work. But there is a wide difference between this, and resolving a particular son shall be a minister, in the same manner, and on the same principles, as another is devoted to the medical profession, or to the bar, as a respectable employment in life; without recognizing vital piety, and the deliberate choice of the ministry, from religious motives, as indispensable qualifications. This kind of destination to the sacred office, is as dangerous as it is unwarranted. Let the Christian parent, however solemnly he may have devoted his child to the work of the ministry, and however fondly he may have anticipated his entrance on that blessed work; if he find, at the proper age for deciding the question, no comfortable evidence of a heart regenerated, and governed by the spirit of grace; let him deliberately advise—though his heart be wrung with anguish by the sacrifice—let him deliberately advise the choice of another profession. When young men begin to enter the gospel ministry, because they were early destined to the office; because it is a respectable profession; or because they wish to gratify parents and friends; rather than because they love the office, and its work, and have reason to hope that God has been pleased to call them by his grace, and reveal his Son in them (*Gal.* 1:15, 16); we may consider the ministry as in a fair way to be made, in fact, a secular employment, and the church a prostituted theatre for the schemes and ambitions of worldly men.

So deeply and vitally important is piety in forming a faithful and able ministry; and so often has it appeared to be forgotten, or, at least, undervalued, amidst the brilliancy of more splendid accomplishments; that there cannot be too strict a guard placed on this point, both by public sentiment, and by ministerial fidelity. Many very excellent men, indeed, have felt a jealousy of theological seminaries, as such, as if they were calculated for training up learned and eloquent, rather than pious ministers. Though I believe that this jealousy has been sometimes indulged unjustly, and often carried to an unwise and mischievous extreme; and though there appears to me no other ground for it, than the melancholy fact, that the best human institutions are liable to perversion and degeneracy; yet I cannot find in my heart to condemn it altogether. Nay, I trust that a portion of it will always be kept alive, as a guard, under God, against the evil which it deprecates. For I persuade myself that every minister of the Presbyterian Church, in the United States, is ready to adopt the language, with a little variation, of that great and excellent man, who, for near thirty years, adorned the American church, and the presidential chair of this college.

> Accursed be all that learning which sets itself in opposition to vital piety! Accursed be all that learning which disguises, or is ashamed of vital piety! Accursed be all that learning, which attempts to fill the place, or to supersede the honours, of vital piety! Nay, accursed be all that learning, which is not made, subservient to the promotion and the glory of vital piety![1]

But piety, though it hold the first place among essential qualifications here, is not all that is necessary. It is not every pious man, nay, not every fervently pious man, that is qualified to be a minister, and far less an able minister. Another essential requisite to form the character of such a minister, is,

2. *Talents.* By which I mean, not that every able minister must, of necessity, be a man of genius; but that he must be a man of good sense; of native discernment and discretion; in other, words, of a sound respectable natural understanding.

When our blessed Lord was about to send forth his first ministers, he said unto them: 'Be ye wise as serpents, as well as harmless as doves' (*Matt.* 10:16). And, truly, there is no employment under heaven, in which wisdom, practical wisdom, is so important, or rather, so imperiously and indispensably demanded, as in the ministry of reconciliation. A man of a weak and childish mind, though he were pious as Gabriel, can never make an able minister, and he ought never to be invested with the office at all: for with respect to a large portion of its duties, he is utterly unqualified to perform them; and he is in constant danger of rendering both himself and his office contemptible.

[1] See Witherspoon's sermon on 'Glorying in the Cross of Christ'.

No reasonable man would require proof to convince him, that good sense is essential to form an able physician, an able advocate at the bar, or an able ambassador at a foreign court. Nor would any prudent man entrust his property, his life, or the interests of his country, to one who did not bear this character. And can it be necessary to employ argument, to show that interests, in comparison with which, worldly property, the health of the body, and even the temporal prosperity of nations, are all little things, ought not to be committed to any other than a man of sound and respectable understanding? Alas! if ecclesiastical judicatories had not frequently acted, as if this were far from being a settled point, it were almost an insult to my audience to speak of it as a subject admitting of a question.

Though a minister concentrated in himself all the piety, and all the learning, of the Christian church; yet if he had not at least a decent stock of good sense, for directing and applying his other qualifications, he would be worse than useless. Upon good sense depends all that is dignified, prudent, conciliatory; and respectable in private deportment; and all that is judicious, seasonable, and calculated to edify, in public ministration. The methods to be employed for winning souls are so many and various, according to the taste, prejudices, habits, and stations of men: a constant regard to time, place, circumstances, and character is so essential, if we desire to profit those whom we address: and some tolerable medium of deportment, between moroseness and levity, reserve and tattling, bigotry and latitudinarianism, lukewarmness and enthusiasm, is so indispensable to public usefulness, that the man who lacks a respectable share of discernment and prudence had better, far better, be in any other profession than that of a minister.[1] An able minister he cannot possibly be. Neither will anything short of a sound judgment, a native perception of what is fit and proper, or otherwise, preserve any man who is set to teach and to rule in the church, without a miracle, from those perversions of Scripture, those ludicrous absurdities; and those effusions of drivelling childishness, which are calculated to bring the ministry and the Bible into contempt.

---

[1] Though a Christian would have expressed himself in different language, there is much weight in the maxim, of the heathen satirist, *Nullum numen abest si sit prudentia.* ['No protecting power is wanting, if prudence be but employed.'] Juvenile, *Sat.* x:365.

3. A third requisite to an able and faithful ministry is *competent knowledge*. Without this, both piety and talents united are inadequate to the official work. Nay, without cultivation and discipline; without a competent store of facts and principles, to regulate the mind, the stronger the talents, the more likely are they to lead their possessor astray, and to become the instruments of mischief, both to himself and the church.

The first ministers of the gospel were divinely inspired; and, of course, had no need of acquiring knowledge by the ordinary methods. They were put in possession by miracle, and perhaps in a single hour, of that information, which, now can only be gained by years of laborious study.[1] It were well if this fact were remembered and weighed by those who plead, that, as the gospel was first preached by fishermen and tax-gatherers, so it may be as well preached, at the present day, by persons of fervent piety, and plain sense, who have never enjoyed any greater advantages of scholastic learning, than the apostles did. The supposed fact, which these vain and ignorant pleaders assume, is utterly unfounded. The apostles were not an illiterate ministry. They were the soundest, and best-informed divines that ever adorned the Christian church. So indispensable did it appear to infinite wisdom, that they should be such, that they were thus accomplished by the immediate inspiration of the Holy Ghost. And we have reason to believe, that men, before unlearned, were chosen to be the subjects of this inspiration, in preference to others, that the miracle might be the more apparent; that it might be the more clearly seen that the excellency of the power was of God, and not of man (2 *Cor.* 4:7). Let this inspiration, confirmed as it then was by miracle, be now produced, and we will acknowledge it as more than an adequate substitute for the ordinary method of acquiring knowledge, by books and study.

But if, as we all allow, the age of inspiration and of miracle be long since past; and if it be still necessary, notwithstanding, that the preachers of the gospel possess, substantially, the same knowledge

---

[1] There is no intention here to exclude daily, or frequent conversations with our Lord, as one important means of instruction which the apostles enjoyed. This, however, though not, strictly speaking, a miraculous mode of acquiring knowledge, was yet wholly extraordinary.

that the apostles had; then, undoubtedly, it is to be acquired in a different way from theirs, that by the diligent use of ordinary means. If ministers must be 'apt to teach', as the Spirit of God has declared,[1] they ought to be capable of teaching. If the priest's lips ought to keep knowledge (*Mal.* 2:7), he certainly ought to possess knowledge. And if Timothy, though he lived in the days of inspiration, and was the immediate and favourite disciple of an inspired man, was yet enjoined, by that very inspired man, to give himself to reading, as well as to exhortation; to meditate upon these things and to give himself wholly to them, that his profiting might appear to all (*1 Tim.* 4:13, 15); how much more necessary are similar means of acquiring knowledge, to those who are called to labours of the same nature, and quite as arduous, without possessing the same advantages.

But what kind, and what degree of intellectual cultivation, and of acquired knowledge, may be considered as necessary to form an able minister of Jesus Christ? That we may give a more enlightened answer to this question, let us inquire, what such a minister is called, and must be qualified to perform? He is, then, to be ready, on all occasions, to explain the Scriptures. This is his first and chief work. That is, not merely to state and support the mere simple and elementary doctrine of the gospel; but also to elucidate with clearness the various parts of the sacred volume, whether doctrinal, historical, typical, prophetic, or practical. He is to be ready to rectify erroneous translations of sacred Scripture; to reconcile seeming contradictions; to clear up real obscurities; to illustrate the force and beauty of allusions to ancient customs and manners; and, in general, to explain the Word of God, as one who has made it the object of his deep and successful study. He is set for the defence of the gospel (*Phil.* 1:17); and, therefore, must be qualified to answer the objections of infidels; to repel the insinuations and cavils of sceptics; to detect, expose, and refute the ever varying forms of heresy; and to give notice, and stand in the breach, when men, ever so covertly or artfully, depart from the faith as delivered to the saints (*Jude* 3). He is to be ready to solve the doubts, and satisfy the scruples of conscientious believers; to give instruction to the numerous classes of respectful and serious

[1] *1 Tim.* 3:2; *2 Tim.* 2:24.

inquirers; to 'reprove, rebuke, and exhort, with all long suffering and doctrine' (*2 Tim.* 4:2). He is to preach the gospel with, plainness, dignity, clearness, force, and solemnity. And, finally, he is to perform his part in the judicatories of the church, where candidates for the holy ministry are examined and their qualifications ascertained; where a constant inspection is maintained over the faith and order of the church; where the general interests of Zion are discussed and decided; and in conducting the affairs of which, legislative, judicial, and executive proceedings are all combined.

This is but a very brief and imperfect sketch of what a minister is called to perform. Now, it is evident that, in order to accomplish all this, with even tolerable ability, a man must be furnished with a large amount of knowledge. 'He must' (and on this subject I am happy in being able to fortify myself with the judgment, and to employ, for the most part, the language of the General Assembly of our church),

he must be well skilled in the original languages of the holy Scriptures. He must be versed in Jewish and Christian antiquities. He must have, a competent acquaintance with ancient geography, and oriental customs. He must have read and digested the principal arguments and writings, relative to what has been called the Deistical controversy. He must have studied, carefully and correctly, natural theology, together with didactic, polemic, and casuistic divinity; and be able to support the doctrines of the gospel, by a ready, pertinent, and abundant quotation of Scripture texts for that purpose. He must have a considerable acquaintance with general history and chronology; and a particular acquaintance with the history of the Christian church. He must have studied attentively the duties of the pastoral office; the form of church government authorized by the Scriptures; and the administration of it as practised in the Protestant churches'.[1]

He must have become well versed in moral philosophy, as an important auxiliary in studying man, his constitution, the powers and exercises of his depraved and sanctified nature, and his duties thence arising. To all these, he must add, a respectable share of the knowledge, in general grammar, in logic, metaphysics, natural philosophy, mathematical science, geography, natural history, and polite literature.

[1] *Constitution of the Theological Seminary of the Presbyterian Church,* Article 4th.

Several of these branches of learning are, indeed, only auxiliary to the main body, if I may so express it, of ministerial erudition. But they are important auxiliaries. No man, it is true, can be a complete master of them all; and it were criminal in a minister to attempt so much. The time requisite for this, must be taken from more important employments. Of some of these departments of knowledge, general views are sufficient; and of others, perhaps, an acquaintance with nomenclature and first principles ought to satisfy the theological pupil. But so much of them ought to be acquired as may enable their possessor the better to understand the Scriptures, and the better to defend the gospel. I repeat it, every branch of knowledge is helpful and desirable to the Christian minister. Not to enable him to shine, as a man of learning: this were infinitely beneath the aim of an ambassador of Christ: but to make him a more accomplished and useful teacher of others. For it is certain that the more he attains of real, solid science, provided it be sanctified science, the more clearly will he be able to explain the sacred volume, and the more wisely and forcibly to preach that 'gospel which is the power of God unto salvation to every one that believeth' (*Rom.* 1:16).

4. Once more, it enters into the character of a faithful minister, that he is *active, diligent* and *persevering* in the discharge of his multiplied and arduous duties. However fervent his piety; however vigorous his native talents; and however ample his acquired knowledge; yet, if he be timid, indolent, wavering, easily driven from the path of duty, or speedily discouraged in his evangelical labours, he does not answer the apostle's description of a faithful man. The minister who is, in any good measure, entitled to this character, is one who carefully studies to know, and to the best of his knowledge, declares the whole counsel of God, without fearing the frowns, or courting the smiles, of men; who shrinks not from any self-denial, labour, or danger to which the will of his Master, and the interests of religion, evidently call him; who abhors the thought of sitting down in inglorious ease, while thousands are perishing around him; who does not allow himself to be diverted by secular or minor objects from his grand work; who is instant in season and out of season, in all the diversified and momentous labours of his holy vocation; and the object of whose steady exertion, as well as supreme desire, it is, that the church may

be built up; that souls may be saved; and that Christ in all things may be glorified (*1 Pet.* 4:11).

Such is a faithful and able minister. A minister fervently pious; eminently wise, discerning, and prudent; extensively learned, especially mighty in the Scriptures; abounding and prevalent in prayer; a bold, energetic, instructive, experimental preacher; a zealous, affectionate, condescending, laborious pastor; a friend to revivals of religion; a firm and persevering contender for the truth; one, in short, who devotes all his talents, all his learning, all his influence, and all his exertions, to the one grand object, fulfilling the ministry which he has received of the Lord Jesus.

Such a minister, to select an example, was the Apostle Paul. With a heart warmed with the love of Christ; with an understanding vigorous, sound, and comprehensive; and with a store of various and profound knowledge, he went forth to meet and to conciliate the enemies of his divine Master: and in the course of his ministry, he manifested the importance of every qualification with which that Master had furnished him. Let us follow and observe him a little in the discharge of his ministerial labours. 'Now we see him reasoning with Pagans, and then remonstrating with Jews: now arguing from the law of nature, and then from the Old Testament Scriptures: now appealing to the writings of heathen poets and philosophers, and then referring to the traditions of the fathers, of which he had been exceedingly zealous: now stating the arguments with all logical exactness, and then exposing the sophistry and false learning of his adversaries:[1] now pleading with all the majesty and pathos of unrivalled eloquence, upon Mars Hill, and before Felix and Agrippa, and then instructing, from house to house, the young and the aged, with all the tenderness of a father, and all the simplicity and condescension of a babe. And what was the consequence? With these qualifications, he laboured not only more abundantly, but more successfully, than all the apostles; and has probably been the means of richer blessing to the church and the world, than any other mere man that ever lived.

But you will, perhaps, ask, 'Ought all these qualifications to be considered as indispensable for every minister? For example, ought

---

[1] Stennett's Sermon before the Education Society, p. 12.

no one to have the ministry "committed" to him, unless he have acquired, or be in a fair way to attain, the whole of those literary and scientific accomplishments which have been recounted as desirable?' It is not necessary, perhaps it is not proper, at present, to give a particular answer to this question. My object has been to describe an able and faithful ministry. To my description I am not conscious of having added anything superfluous or unimportant. Such a ministry it ought to be the aim and the endeavour of the church to train up. Yet, it is certain that under the best administration of ecclesiastical affairs that ever existed, since the days of the apostles, or that is ever likely to exist, all ministers have not been alike able and faithful: and it is equally certain that cases have occurred in which individuals with furniture for the sacred office inferior to that which is desirable, have been in a considerable degree, both respectable and useful. But still a character something resembling that which has been drawn, ought to be considered as the proper standard, and exertions made to attain as near an approximation to it, in all cases, as possible. And after all that can be done, exceptions to a rigid conformity with this standard, will be found in sufficient number, without undertaking to lower the standard itself, in such a manner as to provide for their multiplication. But,

II. *What are the means which the church is bound to employ, for providing such a ministry?* This question was assigned as the second subject of inquiry.

And here, it is perfectly manifest, that the church can neither impart grace, nor create talents. She can neither make men pious, nor give them intellectual powers. But is there, therefore, nothing that can be done, or that ought to be done by her? Yes, Brethren, there is much to be done. Though Jehovah the Saviour has the government upon his shoulder, his kingdom is a kingdom of means; and he is not to be expected to work miracles to supply our lack of exertion. If, therefore, the church omit to employ the means which her King and Head has put within her power, for the attainment of a given object, both the sin and the disgrace of failing to attain that object will lie at her own door.

What, then, are the means which the church is bound to employ for providing an able and faithful ministry? They are such as these:

looking for, and carefully *selecting* young men of piety and talents for the work of the ministry; providing *funds,* for the temporary support of those who may stand in need of such aid; furnishing a *seminary,* in which the most ample means of instruction may be found; and, having done all this, to guard, by her *judicatories,* the entrance into the sacred office, with incessant vigilance.

1. The church is bound, with a vigilant eye, *to search for, and carefully to select, from among the young men within her bosom, those who are endowed with piety and talents, whenever she can find these qualifications united.* Piety is humble and retiring; and talents, especially of the kind best adapted to the great work of the ministry, are modest and unobtrusive. They require, at least in many instances, to be sought out, encouraged, and brought forward. And how, and by whom, is this to be done? The children of the church are, if I may so express it, the church's property. She has a right to the services of the best of them. And as it is the part, both of wisdom and affection, in parents according to the flesh, to attend with vigilance to the different capacities and acquirements of their children, and to select for them, as far as possible, corresponding employments; so it is obviously incumbent on the church, the moral parent of all the youth within her jurisdiction, to direct especial attention to such of them as may be fitted to serve her in the holy ministry. And it may be asserted, without fear of contradiction, that whenever young men are found, who unite fervent piety, with talents adapted to the office, it is the duty of such to seek the gospel ministry; and it is the duty of the church to single them out, to bring them forward, and to endeavour to give them all that preparation, which depends on human means, for the service of the sanctuary.

2. The church is bound to *provide funds for the partial or entire support of those who need this kind of aid, while they are preparing for the work of the ministry.* Some of the most promising candidates for this holy work have not the means of supporting themselves, while they withdraw from the world, and give up its emoluments, for the purpose of becoming qualified to serve God in the gospel of his Son. These persons must either abandon their sacred enterprise altogether, or receive, from some other source, adequate aid. And from what source can they so properly receive it, as from their moral parent, the

church? Nature, reason, equity, parental affection,—all conspire in pointing to this parent, as the most suitable provider. The aid which flows only from the hand of individual and occasional bounty, may be withdrawn, or grudgingly continued: but the church can never be weary, as long as ability is given her, of providing for her beloved children. The aid which individuals, as such, furnish, may excite, in delicate minds, a painful sense of dependence: but children ought to feel, can feel, no pain in receiving from the hand of parental affection.

Nor is it any valid objection to the furnishing of this aid, that the objects of it may not always be found, when their character shall be completely developed, either ornaments to the church, or worthy of so much exertion and expenditure. As well might parents according to the flesh decline to provide for the support and education of their children in early life, lest peradventure they might afterwards prove neither a comfort nor an honour them. In this respect every faithful parent considers himself as bound, in duty and affection, to take all possible pains for promoting the welfare of his offspring, and having done so, to leave the event with God.

Neither ought the church to consider this provision as a burden, or imagine that, in making it, she confers a favour. It is as clearly her duty—a duty which she as really owes both to her Master and herself, as the ordinary provision which she makes for the support of the word and ordinances. Or rather, it is to be lamented that she has not been accustomed always to consider it, as an essential part of her ordinary provision for the maintenance of the means of grace.

3. A further means which the church is bound to employ for providing an able and faithful ministry, is, *furnishing a seminary in which the candidates for this office may receive the most appropriate and complete instruction, which she has it in her power to give*. In vain are young men of fervent piety, and the best talents, sought after and discovered; and in vain are funds provided for their support, while preparing for the ministry, unless pure and ample fountains of knowledge are opened to them, and unless competent guides are assigned, to direct them in drinking at those fountains. This, however, is so plain, so self-evident, that I need not enlarge upon its proof.

But perhaps it may be supposed by some, that there is no good reason why these means of education should be provided by the church, as such. It may be imagined, that they will be as likely to be provided, and as, well provided, by private instructors, as by public seminaries. But all reason, and all experience, pronounce a different judgment, and assign as the ground of their decision, such considerations as these.

First, when the church herself provides a seminary for the instruction of her own candidates for the ministry, she can at all times inspect and regulate the course of their education; can see that it be sound, thorough, and faithful; can direct and control the instructors; can correct such errors and make such improvements in her plans of instruction, as the counsels of the whole body may discover. Whereas, if all be left to individual discretion, the preparation for the service of the church may be in the highest degree defective, or ill-judged; not to say unsound, without the church being able effectually to interpose her correcting hand.

Again, when the church herself takes the instruction of her candidates into her own hands, she can furnish a more extensive, accurate, and complete course of instruction than can be supposed to be, ordinarily, within the reach of detached individuals. In erecting and endowing a seminary, she can select the best instructors out of her whole body. She can give her pupils, the benefit of the whole time, and the undivided exertions, of these instructors. Instead of having all the branches of knowledge, to which the theological student applies himself, taught by a single master, she can divide the task of instruction, among several competent teachers, in such a manner as to admit of each doing full justice both to his pupils and himself. She can, form one ample library, by which a given number of students may be much better accommodated, when collected together, and having access to it in common, than if the same amount of books were divided into a corresponding number of smaller libraries. And she can digest, and gradually improve a system of instruction, which shall be the result of combined wisdom, learning, and experience. Whereas those candidates for the sacred office, who commit themselves to the care of individual ministers, selected according to the convenience or the caprice of each pupil, must, in many cases, at least, be under the guidance of instructors who have neither the talents, the learning, nor the leisure to do them justice; and who have not, even a tolerable collection of books, to supply the lack of their own furniture as teachers.

Further, when the church herself provides the means of instruction for her own ministry, at a public seminary, she will, of course, be furnished with ministers who have enjoyed, in some measure, a uniform course of education; who have derived their knowledge from the same masters, and the same approved fountains, and who may, therefore, be expected to agree in their views of evangelical truth and order. There will thus be the most effectual provision made, speaking after the manner of men, for promoting the unity and peace of the church. Whereas, if every candidate for the holy ministry, be instructed by a different master, each of whom may be supposed to have his peculiarities of expression and opinion, especially about minor points of doctrine and discipline, the harmony of our ecclesiastical judicatories will gradually be impaired; and strife, and perhaps eventually, schism, may be expected to arise in our growing and happy church.

It is important to add, that when the church provides for educating a number of candidates for the ministry at the same seminary, these candidates themselves may be expected to be of essential service to each other. Numbers being engaged together in the same studies, will naturally excite the principle of emulation. As 'iron sharpeneth iron', so the amicable competition, and daily intercourse of pious students, can scarcely fail of leading to closer and more persevering application; to deeper research; to richer acquirements; and to a more indelible impression of that which is learned, upon their minds, than can be expected to take place in solitary study.

Nor is it by any means unworthy of notice, that, when the ministers of a church are generally trained up at the same seminary, they are naturally led to form early friendships, which bind them together to the end of life, and which are productive of that mutual confidence and assistance, which can scarcely fail of shedding a benign influence on their personal enjoyment, and their official comfort and usefulness. These early friendships may also be expected to add another impulse to a sense of duty, in annually drawing ministers from a distance to meet each other in the higher judicatories of the church;

and, which is scarcely less important, to facilitate and promote that mutual consultation, respecting plans of research, and new and interesting publications, which is, at once, among the safeguards, as well as pleasures, of theological authorship.

These, Brethren, are some of the considerations which call upon every church, to erect, and to support with vigour and efficiency, a theological seminary for the training of her ministry. If she desires to augment the number of her ministers; if she wishes their preparation for the sacred office to be the best in her power to give, and at the least possible expense; if she desires that they may be a holy phalanx, united in the same great views of doctrine and discipline, and adhering with uniformity and with cordial affection to her public standards; if she deprecates the melancholy spectacle of a heterogeneous, divided, and distracted ministry; and finally, if she wishes her ministers to be educated under circumstances most favourable to their acting in after life, as a band of brethren, united in friendship as well as in sentiment; then let her take measures for training them up under her own eye, and control; under the same teachers; in the same course of study; and under all those advantages of early intercourse, and affectionate competition, which attend a public seminary.

In favour of all this reasoning, the best experience, and the general practice of the church in different ages, may be confidently urged. 'It has been the way of God', says the pious and learned Dr Lightfoot, 'to instruct his people by a studious and learned ministry, ever since he gave a written word to instruct them in.' 'Who', he asks,

> were the standing ministry of Israel, all the time from the giving of the law, till the captivity in Babylon? Not prophets, or inspired men; for they were but occasional teachers; but the priests and Levites, who became learned in the law by study. Deuteronomy 33:10. Hosea 4:6. Malachi 2:7. And for this end, they were disposed into forty-eight cities, as so many universities, where they studied the law together; and from thence were sent out into the several synagogues, to teach the people.

They had also, the same writer informs us, 'contributions made for the support of these students, while they studied in the universities, as well as afterwards when they preached in the synagogues.' He tells us further, in another place, 'that there were among the Jews, authorized individual teachers, of great eminence, who had their *Midrashoth,* or divinity schools, in which they expounded the law to their scholars or disciples.' 'Of these divinity schools', he adds, 'there is very frequent mention made among the Jewish writers, more especially of the schools of Hillel and Shammai. Such a divinity professor was Gamaliel, at whose feet, the great Apostle of the Gentiles received his education.'[1]

Under the Christian dispensation, the same system, in substance, was adopted and continued. At a very early period, there was a seminary of high reputation established in the city of Alexandria, in which candidates for the holy ministry were trained up together, and under the ablest instructors, both in divine and human learning; a seminary in which Pantaenus, Clemens, Alexandrinus, Origen, and others, taught with high reputation. Eusebius and Jerome both declare, that this seminary had existed, as a nursery of the church, and had enjoyed a succession of able teachers, from the time of Mark the Evangelist.[2] Writers on Christian antiquities also assure us that there were seminaries of a similar kind very early established at Rome, Caesarea, Antioch, and other places;[3] and that they were considered as essential to the honour and prosperity of the church.

At the period of the Reformation, religion and learning revived together. The Reformers were not less eminent for their erudition, than for their piety and zeal. They contended earnestly for an enlightened, as well as a faithful ministry; and, accordingly, almost all the Protestant churches, when they found themselves in a situation to admit of the exertion, founded theological seminaries, as nurseries for their ministry. This was the case in Geneva, in Scotland, in Holland, in Germany, and, with very little exception, throughout Reformed Christendom. And the history of those seminaries, while it certainly demonstrates, that such establishments are capable of being perverted, demonstrates, with equal evidence, that they have been made, and might always, with the divine blessing on a faithful administration, be rendered extensively useful.

[1] Lightfoot's *Works,* vol. 1., 357, 574.
[2] *Euseb:* Lib. v. c. 10. *Hieron.* Oper. i. 105.
[3] Bingham, *Origines Ecclesiastica.* Book III. Chap. 10.

And what have the most eminently pious and learned ministers, that ever adorned the American church, thought on this subject? Let, yonder venerable walls tell! Yes, Brethren, it was because Tennent and Dickinson, and Burr, and Edwards, and Davies, and Finley, and Blair, and other champions of the cross, were deeply impressed with the truth, that learning and talents, united with piety, are of the highest importance to, the Christian ministry, that they laboured and prayed so much for the establishment and support of Nassau Hall.

May their spirit and their opinions revive; and more and more pervade our church, until the dawning of the millennial Sabbath!

In establishments of this kind, in more recent times, our congregational brethren, in New England, and our brethren of the Dutch and Associate Reformed churches, have gone before us, and set us noble examples. We have, at length, awoke from our sleep; and with tardy, but, as we hope, with firm, with well-advised, and with heaven-directed steps, have begun to follow them. In the name of Jehovah Jesus, the King of Zion, we lift up our banner! May his blessing descend, and rest upon the transaction of this day, as a pledge that he is about to visit our church in his abundant mercy!

4. The last means of providing an able and faithful ministry, on which I shall insist, is *fidelity on the part of the judicatories of the church in guarding the entrance into the sacred office.* It is our happiness, that, according to the truly apostolic and primitive constitution of our church, the power of licensing candidates, and of setting apart to the work of the holy ministry, is not given to any individual, by whatever name he may be called. Nay, while the church provides a seminary for the instruction of her candidates for the sacred office, she does not give even to the conductors of that seminary, however pious, learned, or venerable, the right ultimately to judge of the qualifications of those candidates, and to admit or reject them, at their pleasure. This is the prerogative of her appropriate judicatories; and the manner in which it is exercised, is all-important. However vigilantly and perseveringly other means for attaining the object proposed, may be employed, if there be a failure here, the most calamitous consequences may be expected. If presbyteries be superficial in their examinations of candidates; if they be too ready to lay hands on the weak, the ignorant, the erroneous, or those of doubtful piety; or if, for the

sake of attaining an occasional purpose, or meeting a temporary diffi-culty, they at any time suffer the barriers which have been erected for excluding the incompetent or the unworthy, to be removed or tram-pled down, they are taking the direct course to bringing the ministry and religion into contempt.

I know that, on this subject, pleas are often urged which it is extremely difficult to resist. Some good qualities in the candidates; private friendships; an unwillingness to give pain; the scarcity of ministers; and the necessities of the church, are all alternately employed as arguments for the admission of unsuitable characters into the ministry. But it is a most important part of fidelity in the work of the Lord, to oppose and reject every plea of this kind. Pri-vate friendship ought not to interfere with a supreme regard to the Redeemer's kingdom. It is better, much better, to inflict pain for a time, on an individual, than to wound the church of Christ. And by introducing into the ministry those who are neither faithful, nor able to teach, judicatories are so far from supplying the wants of the church, that they rather add to her difficulties, and call her to struggle with new evils. To be in haste to multiply and send out unqualified labourers, is to take the most direct method to send a destructive blast on the garden of God, instead of gathering a rich and smiling harvest.

On the other hand, when judicatories, with enlightened vigilance, and fidelity, guard the entrance into the sacred office; when they exert the authority committed to them, keep out of the ministry, incompetence, heresy, levity, and worldly mindedness; they obey a divine precept; they support the real honour of the gospel ministry; they constrain those who are looking toward that blessed work, to take a higher aim, and to seek for higher attainments; they give the churches 'bread instead of a stone, and fish instead of a serpent'; and though they may appear, to those who make haste, to be tardy in supplying the public demand for ministers, they are taking one of the most effectual methods, under God, for raising up a numerous, as well as an able an faithful ministry.

Let as now turn our attention to some practical inferences from the foregoing discussion. And,

1. If the representation which has been given be just, *then our church has been, for a long time, almost entirely, and very criminally, negligent of a great and important duty.* While she has directed much laudable attention to other objects, she has, in a great measure, suffered the most promising means of providing an able and faithful ministry, to take care of themselves. Other churches have also been guilty, in a considerable degree, of similar negligence; a negligence for which, alas! our country mourns; and would mourn much more, if the importance of the subject were understood, and appreciated as it ought to be; but our church has been pre-eminently guilty! Though among the largest Christian denominations in the United States; though possessing, in its individual members, perhaps more wealth than any other; though favoured, in many respects, with ample means for every kind of generous ecclesiastical enterprise; and though often and solemnly warned on the subject; she has yet been among the very last of all the evangelical denominations among us, to commence a course of efficient exertion for raising up a qualified ministry. We have slumbered, and slumbered, until the scarcity of labourers in our harvest has become truly alarming! God grant that we may testify by our future conduct, that we remember, with unfeigned humiliation, our former negligence; and that we are resolved, as his grace shall enable us, to make amends for it, by redoubled zeal and diligence in time to come!

2. From what has been said, it appears, that *the solemnity to attend on which we are this day assembled is a matter of cordial and animating congratulation to each other, and to the church of Christ in the United States.* We are convened, under the authority of the General Assembly of our church, to organize a theological seminary, and to inaugurate the first professor in that seminary. Though later, much later, in commencing this establishment than we ought to have been; we trust it is about to commence under the smiles of the great Head of the church; and that we confidently regard it as a token for good to the Redeemer's kingdom. Yes, Brethren, we have more reason to rejoice, and to felicitate one another, on the establishment of this seminary, than on the achievement of a great national victory, or on making a splendid addition to our national territory. It is the beginning, as we trust, of an extensive and permanent system, from which blessings

may flow to millions while we are sleeping in the dust. Let us, then, rejoice and be exceeding glad; and in the midst of our joy, let us look up to the Source of blessing, who can cause the walls of our Zion to rise even in troublous times.[1] While we gratulate each other, let our petitions ascend, with our praises, to the throne of grace, that the seminary this day established, and, as we verily believe, founded in faith and prayer, may be a fountain, the streams of which shall make glad the city of our God; flowing in every direction, and abundantly watering the abodes of Zion's King, until all flesh shall taste his love, and see his glory!

3. If what has been, said be correct, *then those who are more immed-iately charged with conducting this seminary, whether as directors or pro-fessors, ought to consider themselves as honoured with a very solemn and weighty trust.* The design of the supreme judicatory of our church, in founding this seminary, is nothing less than to train up an able and faithful ministry; a ministry on whose piety, talents, and learning, the temporal and eternal welfare of thousands, now living, may, speaking after the manner of men, depend; a ministry, whose character may have a commanding influence, in forming the character of others, and they again of those who may successively fill the same office, until the end of time! The design is interesting beyond expression; and the task of those who are appointed to carry it into execution, is serious and important to a degree which mortals cannot estimate. When I cast an eye down the ages of eternity, and think how important is the salva-tion of a single soul; when I recollect how important, of course, the office of a minister of the gospel, who may be the happy instrument of saving many hundreds, or thousands of souls; and when I remember how many and how momentous are the relations, which a seminary intended solely for training up ministers, bears to all the interests of men, in the life that now is, and especially in that which is to come; I feel as if the task of conducting such a seminary had an awfulness of responsibility connected with it, which is enough to make us trem-ble! O my Fathers and Brethren! let it never be said of us, on whom this task has fallen, that we take more pains to make polite scholars, eloquent orators, or men of mere learning, than to form able and

---

[1] War had been declared, by the United States, against Great Britain, a few weeks before this discourse was delivered.

faithful ministers of the New Testament. Let it never be said, that we are more anxious to maintain the literary and scientific honours of the ministry, than we are to promote that honour which consists in being full of faith and of the Holy Ghost, and the instruments of adding much people to the Lord. The eyes of the church are upon us. The eyes of angels, and, above all the eyes of the King of Zion, are upon us. May we have grace given us to be faithful!

4. This subject *suggests matter for very serious reflection to the youth, who are about to enter as students in this seminary, with a view to the gospel ministry.* Behold, my young Friend, the high character at which you are called to aim! You have come hither, not that you may prepare to shine; not that you may prepare to amuse men by philosophic discussion, or to astonish them by flights of artificial eloquence: but that, by the blessing of God, upon the use of means, you may become faithful men, who shall be able to teach others also; that you may become wise in winning souls to Christ; that, you may prepare to go forth, defending and proclaiming the messages of grace to guilty men, and persuading them to be reconciled to God. Seek to excel. It is noble to excel. But let it be always for the edifying of the church. This, my young Friends, this it the object which is recommended to your sacred emulation. We charge you, in the presence of God, to let all your studies and aims be directed to this grand object. Seek with humble, persevering, prayerful diligence, to be such ministers as you have heard described; and you will neither disappoint yourselves, nor the church of Christ. Seek to be anything else, and you will be a grief and a curse to both. May God the Saviour bless you, and prepare you to be workmen that need not be ashamed!

5. From this subject we may derive *powerful excitements to young men of piety and talents, to come forward and devote themselves to the gospel ministry.* We trust no young man will ever think of that holy vocation, until he has first given himself up a living sacrifice, holy and acceptable to God, by Jesus Christ. We would not, for any consideration, be accessory to the sin of alluring into the sacred office, those who know nothing of the power of godliness, and who, on the most favourable supposition, can be nothing better than miserable retailers of cold and unproductive speculations. But while we say this, and repeat it, with all the emphasis of which we are capable, we assert,

with equal confidence, on the other hand, that wherever fervent piety appears, in any young man, united with those talents which are adapted to the office of an ambassador of Christ, it is incumbent on their possessor, without delay, to devote himself to the work of the ministry. There are only two questions which need be asked concerning any youth on this subject. Has he a heart for the work? And has he those native faculties, which are susceptible of the requisite cultivation? If these questions can be answered in the affirmative, I hesitate not to say, that in the present state of the church, it is his duty to seek the ministry. Young men of this college! have none of you any desire to serve your fellow men, and to serve Christ, in this exalted office? You have but one short life to live in this world; and you must, in a very little time, decide how you will spend that life.

> We confidently pronounce, that it can be spent in no manner so desirable, so noble, so godlike, as in the gospel ministry. If then, you love the Lord Jesus Christ, come—we affectionately invite you to come, and take part with us in the ministry of the grace of God. The example of Christ invites you to come; the tears of bereaved churches, who can find none to break unto them the bread of life, entreat you to come; the miseries of wandering souls, who find none to lead them to heaven, plead with you to come. Come, then, and take part with us in the labours and rewards of the ministry of reconciliation.[1]

6. Finally, if the representation which has been given be correct, *then the church at large ought to consider it as equally their privilege and their duty to support this seminary.* If one may judge by the language and the conduct of the generality of our church-members, they seem to consider all regard to institutions of this kind, as the province of ministers only. They readily grant, that ministers ought to be prompt and willing, to give their time, their labours, and, where they have any, their substance, for this end; but for themselves, they pray to be excused. They either contribute nothing toward the object; or contribute in the most reluctant and sparing manner, as if they were bestowing a favour, which they have a perfect right to withhold. My dear Brethren, it is difficult to express in adequate terms either the

[1] See 'Address of the Presbytery of New York, on educating poor and pious youth for the gospel ministry', p. 14.

sin or the folly of such conduct. Seminaries of this kind are to be founded and supported by the church, as such. It is the church that is bound to take order on the subject. It is the church that is responsible for their establishment and maintenance. And if any of her members, or adherents, when called upon, will not contribute their just portion of aid for this purpose, the Head of the church will require it at their hands. Professing Christians! look upon the alarming necessities of the church; upon destitute frontier settlements; upon several hundred vacant congregations, earnestly desiring spiritual teachers, but unable to obtain them. Look upon the growing difficulty, with which the most eligible and attractive situations in the church are supplied; and then say whether those who still remain idle can be innocent? Innocent! Their guilt will be greater and more dreadful than can be described. Come, then, Brethren, humbled by the past, and animated by the future, rouse from your lethargy, and begin to act in earnest! Your Master requires it of you! The aspect of the times requires it of you! The cries of the neglected and the perishing require it of you! Your own privileges and blessings require it of you! Yes, ye who call yourselves Christians! If you love the church to which you profess to belong: if you possess a single spark of the spirit of allegiance to her divine Head and Lord: nay, if you desire not a famine of the word of life; if you desire not the heaviest spiritual judgments to rest upon you, then come forward, and act, as well as speak, like friends of the Redeemer's kingdom. Come forward, and give your influence, your substance, and your prayers, for the help of the Lord, against the mighty (*Judg.* 5:23). Amen!

AN INAUGURAL DISCOURSE[1]

Search the Scriptures.
John 5:39

HIGHLY Respected and Venerable Directors of the Theological School, and other Learned and Respectable Auditors, convened on the present solemn occasion!

The institution and commencement of a theological seminary, under the patronage and direction of the General Assembly of our church, ought to be a subject of mutual congratulation to all its members. But it cannot be concealed, that the same causes which have operated to render such an institution urgently necessary, have also opposed serious obstacles in the way of carrying it into effect. The deficiency, among us, of that kind and extent of learning requisite to confer dignity and respect, as well as usefulness, on the professor's chair, is too obvious to require remark. But every important institution must have its infancy and growth, before it can arrive at maturity; and however long we might have deferred this undertaking, the same difficulties would probably have met us at its commencement, which we are now obliged to encounter. The sentiments and emotions by which my own mind is agitated, in consequence of the new and important station in which I find myself placed by the choice of my brethren, and especially, the deep sense which I entertain of

[1] Archibald Alexander, 'An Inaugural Discourse, Delivered in the Church at Princeton, New Jersey, in the Presence of the Directors of the Theological Seminary, on the 12th of August, 1812.' *The Sermon, Delivered at the Inauguration of the Rev. Archibald Alexander, D.D. as Professor of Didactic and Polemic Theology, in the Theological Seminary of the Presbyterian Church, in the United States of America. To which Are Added, the Professor's Inaugural Address, and the Charge to the Professors and Students* (New York: Whiting and Watson): pp. 55-104. For a biographical sketch of Archibald Alexander see below, p. 155.

my insufficiency for the work, I shall not attempt to express. If the design be of God, he will prosper the undertaking, notwithstanding the weakness of the instruments employed in carrying it on; and will crown our feeble efforts with success. On him therefore may our hope and confidence be firmly fixed; and may his 'will be done on earth as in heaven'!

I have selected, as the subject of the discourse now required of me, the words of our *Lord,* recorded in the 6th chapter and 39th verse of the Gospel according to John:

Ἐπαυνᾶτε τὰς γραφάς. *Search the Scriptures.*

The verb here used, signifies, to search with diligence and attention. Its literal meaning appears to be, to pursue anyone, by tracing his footsteps. Thus it is employed by Homer to express the lion's[1] pursuit of the man who had robbed him of his whelps, by his footsteps; and the dog's[2] pursuit of his game, by his track. The precise meaning of the word, therefore, both in its literal and figurative application, is expressed by the English word, investigate. It may be read, either in the indicative, or in the imperative mood. Dr Campbell, in his new translation of the Gospels, prefers the former, and renders the passage, 'Ye do search the Scriptures'; but Wetstein and Parkhurst consider it to be in the imperative, agreeably to our version: and certainly this rendering gives more point and force to the sentence, 'Search the scriptures, for in them ye think ye have life, but they are they which testify of me.'

Although the word, γραφάς, scriptures, is of such general import, as to include writings of any kind; yet there can be no doubt but what the Scriptures of the Old Testament were here intended. This phrase is used in the New Testament, as we use the word Bible, which, though literally signifying any book, yet is now appropriated to designate the volume of inspiration.

The history of the origin of alphabetical writing is involved in considerable obscurity. The first notice which we find of the existence of such an art, is contained in the command given to Moses, in the 17th chapter of Exodus; to write a certain transaction in a book:[3]

[1] *Il.* xviii. line 321.
[2] *Odys.* xix. 1. 436.
[3] *Exod.* 14:14: כְּתֹב זֹאת זִכָּרוֹן בַּסֵּפֶר

and soon afterwards, we read that the law was written by the finger of Jehovah, on the two tables of testimony.[1] To me, it appears very probable, therefore, that it was about this time a subject of revelation to Moses. As a precise pattern of the tabernacle was shown to him in the mount, and as certain persons were inspired with wisdom to fit them for the execution of that work, why may we not suppose that this wonderful art, so necessary for recording the revelations received from God, for the use of posterity, was also made known to Moses? One thing is certain; that all the alphabets of the western portion of the globe, and probably those of the eastern also, have had a common origin: and we have no authentic account of the invention of an alphabet by any people; so that whenever this art of writing may have had its origin, I am persuaded it was no invention of man, but a revelation from God.

With respect to the antiquity of these writings, I know of none which can bear any competition with the Pentateuch. Some, indeed, have supposed, that some part of the Vedas of the Brahmins, was written before the books of Moses; but there is no historical evidence on which we can depend in support of this opinion. And we are too well acquainted with the fraudulent pretensions of the Hindus to antiquity, to place any confidence in their assertions. The ultimate opinion of that incomparable scholar, Sir William Jones, on this subject, was, that the writings of Moses were the oldest of any in the world:[2] and a more competent and impartial judge could not easily be found.

As the words of the text are indefinite, they should be considered as imposing an obligation on all sorts of persons, according to their ability and opportunity, to search the Scriptures. We cannot help therefore being struck with the impiety, as well as absurdity, of the practice of the Papists, in withholding the Scriptures from the people.

Will it be said, that when they misinterpret and pervert them, they should be taken away? But such was the conduct of the persons here addressed by Christ. They were so blinded by prejudice, that they could not perceive in the Scriptures, that person, who was the

[1] *Exod.* 34.
[2] See *Asiatic Researches,* vol. 1 and 2.

principal subject of them. But does the divine Saviour forbid them the use of the Scriptures, on this account? No; he enjoins it on them, *to search them*. To study them with more care, and with minds more free from prejudice.

Though the duty of searching the Scriptures is common to all Christians, yet there are some on whom it is more peculiarly incumbent. Teachers of religion, and candidates for the sacred office, are bound by an obligation of uncommon force to attend to this duty. In particular relation to such, I propose to consider the subject, in the sequel of this discourse. But before I proceed further, I would observe, that although the words of our Lord, in the text, refer to the Old Testament (for at the time of their being spoken there were no other scriptures extant), yet the reason of the command will apply with full force, to other inspired writings, as soon as they are promulgated. We shall therefore consider the Scriptures of the New Testament, as well as the Old, embraced within the scope of our Saviour's command.

It will be important to bear in mind, that there are two distinct things comprehended in the object of this investigation. First, to ascertain that the Scriptures contain the truths of *God:* and, secondly, to ascertain what these truths are.

Let us now suppose the two volumes containing the Old and New Testaments, the one in the original Hebrew, the other in the Greek, to be put into the hands of the theological student, accompanied with the command of Christ, search the scriptures. Investigate these volumes with diligence. What should be the first step in this investigation? Ought he not to be well satisfied of the identity of these books, with those which formerly existed? Here is a Hebrew volume; but does it contain the same writings to which our Saviour referred? And does this Greek volume comprehend the very books which were received as inspired in the apostolic age? In this inquiry, the biblical student may obtain complete satisfaction. With respect to the canon of the Old Testament, one fact will be sufficient to remove all doubt. These books have been in the possession of both Jews and Christians ever since the commencement of the gospel dispensation; and they now agree in acknowledging the same books to be canonical; which, considering the inveterate opposition subsisting between them, is a convincing evidence, that the canon of the Old Testament has undergone no change, since the introduction of Christianity. And that it had undergone none before that period may be proved from this circumstance, that although our Lord often upbraids the Jews with having *perverted* the Scriptures, he never insinuates that they had *altered* or *corrupted* them.

In confirmation of what has been said respecting the canon of the Old Testament, we might adduce the testimony of Josephus, and of the Christian Fathers; who not only agree with one another in their catalogue of the books of the Old Testament but with the canonical list which we now hold. The books called *Apocrypha* were never received into the canon by the Jews, nor by the earlier Christian Fathers and councils, and have therefore no just claim to be considered as belonging to the Old Testament.

With regard to the New Testament, the evidence is equally convincing. The Christian church was, in a short time, so widely extended, and embraced so many different languages and nations, that a universal agreement, in this whole body, through all the successive periods of the church, in acknowledging the same books to be canonical, must satisfy every impartial mind that our New Testament is the very same which was received and held sacred by the primitive church. To strengthen this conclusion, it may be added, that at a very early period, these books were translated into many different languages; several of which early translations, either in whole or in part, have come down to our times; and some of them have been preserved among Christians unknown to their brethren of other countries, for many centuries.

In addition to this, it may be observed, that accurate lists of the books of the New Testament were made by early ecclesiastical writers, and also by general councils, which are still extant, and agree with our catalogue of canonical books. It deserves to be mentioned also, that the churches in every part of the world held copies of these Scriptures, which they preserved with the utmost vigilance; and quotations were made from them by all the fathers; so that a large portion of the New Testament might be collected from the works of the early ecclesiastical writers. Besides there are still extant manuscript copies of the whole, or a part of the New Testament, from 1,200-1,500 years old, which contain the same books that are comprehended in our printed volumes.

What has now been asserted, respecting the universal consent with which the books of the New Testament were received by the ancient church, in its all its parts, must be admitted, with the exception of those few books, which have been termed *Antilegomena,* because their divine authority was denied or disputed by some. Impartiality requires us also to state, that these books are not found in some of the oldest versions, as the Syriac, for instance; and therefore it must be admitted that the evidence for their canonical authority is not so complete, as of the rest, which were ever undisputed. At the same time, it ought to be observed, that the chief reason of doubting was, because these books, for a while, were not so generally known to the churches: but as soon as they were accurately examined, and their evidence weighed, opposition to them ceased; and at no late period, they obtained an undisturbed place in the sacred canon.

The theological student, having obtained satisfaction respecting the perfection of the canon of Scripture, the next step in his investigation should relate to the *integrity* of the sacred text. For it is possible that the canon might be complete, and yet the text might be so corrupted and mutilated as to leave it uncertain what the original of these books might have been. It is of importance, therefore, to be able to prove, that the Scriptures have suffered no material injury, from the fraud of designing men, or from the carelessness of transcribers. In the former part of the last century, this was a subject of warm altercation in the church. For whilst some maintained that the sacred text had not received the slightest injury from the ravages of time, others boldly asserted that it was greatly corrupted. The agitation of this question led to a more extensive and accurate examination and collation of manuscript codices than had been before made, and gave rise to that species of biblical criticism, which has, within the last half century, assumed so conspicuous a place in theological science. Distant countries were visited, the dark cells of cloisters and monasteries explored, and all important libraries ransacked, in search of copies of the Scriptures. Learned men, with unparalleled diligence, employed their whole lives in the collation of manuscripts, and in noting every, even the smallest variation, in their readings. Their indefatigable labour and, invincible perseverance in prosecuting this work, are truly astonishing. It has indeed, much the appearance of laborious trifling; but upon the whole, though not always so designed, has proved serviceable to the cause of truth. For though the serious mind is at first astonished and confounded, upon being informed of the multitude of various readings, noted by Mills, Wetstein, and Griesbach, in the codices of the New Testament; and by Kennicot and De Rossi, in those of the Old; yet it is relieved, when on careful examination it appears that not more than one of a hundred of these, makes the slightest variation in the sense, and that the whole of them do not materially affect one important fact or doctrine. It is true, a few important texts, in our received copies, have by this critical process, been rendered suspicious; but this has been more than compensated by the certainty which has been stamped on the great body of Scripture, by having been subjected to this severe scrutiny. For the text of our Bibles having passed this ordeal, may henceforth bid defiance to suspicion of its integrity. And with respect to the disputed texts referred to above, one thing should ever be kept in mind; that, granting that the evidence from the present view of ancient manuscripts, is against their genuineness, yet this may not be decisive. The learned Cave lays it down as a rule to direct us, in judging of the comparative excellence of the editions of the fathers, 'That the older the editions are, by so much the more faithful are they.'[1] And he assigns this reason for the rule, that the first editions were made from the best manuscripts, which were commonly lost or destroyed, when the edition was completed. And I see not why the same reason will not equally apply to the early editions of the Scriptures. In fact, there is historical evidence, that the manuscripts used, by Cardinal Ximenes, in his *Polyglot,* have been destroyed, and they appear, from several circumstances, to have been both numerous and ancient: and I am persuaded also, notwithstanding what Wetstein and Michaelis have said to the contrary, that some of those used by Stephanas, in his editions of the New Testament, have also been lost.

---

[1] *Historia Literaria Proleg.* See v T. 1.

We cannot tell, therefore, what the evidence for these texts might have been to these learned editors. Certainly very strong, or they would not have inserted them.

The next step in this investigation, would be, to ascertain, that these books are genuine; or were written by the persons whose names they bear; but as this appears to me to be substantially answered, by what has been already said, and by what will be added under the next article, I will not now make it a subject of particular discussion; but will proceed to inquire into the *authenticity* and *inspiration* of the Scriptures. I join these two things together, because, although a book may be authentic without being inspired; yet if the Bible be authentic, it must have been given by inspiration, for the writers profess that they were inspired.

The truth of this point may be established by several species of evidence, quite distinct from each other.

It may, in the first place, be demonstrated by proving the *truth of the facts recorded* in the Scriptures. These facts, many of them, being obviously of a miraculous nature, if admitted to have existed, will indubitably prove, that those persons by whom they were performed, must have been sent and assisted of God: for, as the Jewish ruler rightly reasoned, 'no man could do these things unless God were with him'. Now the truth of these miracles may be established by testimony, like other ancient facts; and also by the history of them being so interwoven with other authentic history, that we cannot separate them: and especially, by that chain of events, depending on them, and reaching down to our own time, which has no other assignable origin but the existence of these miracles. For, to believe in the events which the history of the church presents to us, and yet deny the miracles of the gospel, would be as absurd, as believing that a chain which hung suspended before our eyes, had nothing to support it, because that support was out of sight. As to the witnesses of these facts, they are such, and deliver their testimony under such circumstances, and in such a manner, as to *demand* our assent. The impossibility of successfully impugning this testimony, obliged the most insidious enemy of Christianity to resort to the principle, that no testimony is sufficient to confirm a miracle: but the absurdity of this position, has been fully demonstrated by Campbell, Vince, and others, and it has also been shown by an ingenious writer,[1] that the gospel was true, even upon this author's own principles, because its falsehood would involve a greater miracle than any recorded in it.

The next species of evidence in support of the proposition under consideration is derived from *prophecy*. If the Scriptures contain predictions of events which no human sagacity could have foreseen; if they have foretold events the most improbable, which have occurred in exact conformity with the prediction; and if they have described a person combining in his character and life, traits and events apparently incompatible and inconsistent; and yet a person has appeared answering literally to this description, then certainly the writers of these predictions were inspired. But such is the fact. 'This sure word of prophecy' is, indeed, like 'a light that shineth in a dark place'; but it is also like the light of the dawn which 'shineth more and more unto the perfect day'. Other evidence may lose something of its force by the lapse of time, but this grows brighter and stronger with every revolving year; for the scope of prophecy comprehends all ages; and new events are continually occurring which had been long foretold by the oracles of God.

The third species of evidence for the authenticity and inspiration of the Scriptures arises out of their *contents*. The extraordinary, and superlatively excellent nature of the Christian religion, proves that it could not have been the production of impostors, nor of unassisted fishermen; nor indeed, of any description of uninspired men. Its doctrines exhibit that very information, which is necessary to satisfy the anxious inquiries of man, conscious of his guilt and desirous of salvation. Its precepts are so sublimely excellent, so marked with sanctity and benevolence; and at the same time so perfectly adapted to human nature and human circumstances, that the brightest wit can detect no flaw, nor suggest any improvement. 'The heavens declare the glory of God'; and so does the holy page of Scripture. It bears the stamp of divinity in its face; and breathes a spirit which could originate no where else but in heaven.

Another evidence, but connected with the last, is the *blessed tendency and holy efficacy* of the gospel to reform the hearts and lives

[1] *Vide Brit. Encyclop.* vol. 14.

of men, and to produce peace and joy in the mind and conscience; which effects never could result from any false religion.

The success of the gospel, in its commencement, is also an important consideration. When we contemplate the resistance which was to be overcome, both external, from religious and civil establishments, and internal, from the inveterate prejudice and vices of men; and then take into view the means by which all these obstacles were surmounted, we cannot refuse to admit that the power of the Almighty accompanied them.

The beneficial effects of Christianity on those nations which have received it, is a striking fact, and furnishes a strong argument in favour of the authenticity and inspiration of the Scriptures. Under their benign influence, war has become less sanguinary and ferocious; justice has been more equally distributed; the poor have been more generally instructed, and their wants supplied; asylums have been provided for the unfortunate and distressed; the female character has been appreciated and exalted to its proper standard in society; the matrimonial bond has been held more sacred; and polygamy, the bane of domestic happiness, discountenanced. In short, the whole fabric of society has been meliorated; and real civilization promoted by Christianity, wherever it has been received: and the above mentioned effects have borne an exact proportion to the purity in which this holy religion was preserved, and the degree of conformity to its precepts which has existed among any people,

The next question which should engage the attention of the theological student, is, *for what purpose were the Scriptures given?* In answer to this, all are ready to agree, that they were intended to be a guide to man in matters of religion; *a rule of faith and practice*. But here several important questions occur. Are the Scriptures the *only* rule? Are they a *sufficient* rule? Are they an *authoritative* rule? and were they only designed to guide us in matters of religion?

Our first controversy is with the Romanists, who maintain that tradition is also a rule of faith; and the Scriptures without tradition are neither a sufficient nor intelligible rule. But this opinion takes away all that fixedness and certainty, which a written revelation was intended and calculated to give to religion. Wherein consists the advantage of having a part of the will of God committed to writing, if the interpretation of this depends on the uncertain and varying light of oral tradition? We might as well have nothing but tradition, as be under the necessity of resorting to this uncertain guide to lead us to the true meaning of the written Word. But had it been intended to make this the channel of communicating the divine will to posterity, some method would have been devised to preserve the stream of tradition pure. No such method has been made known. On the contrary, the Scriptures predict a general and awful apostasy in the church. It could not be otherwise, but that during this period, tradition would become a corrupt channel of information. This apostasy has taken place; and the stream of tradition has, in fact, become so muddy, and so swelled with foreign accessions, from every quarter, that Christianity, viewed through this medium, exhibits the appearance of a deformed and monstrous mass of superstition. But, if we should admit the principle, that the constant tradition of the church should be our guide, where shall we go to look for it? To the Greek, to the Latin, or to the Syriac Church? To the fourth, ninth, or fourteenth, century? For there is no uniformity; not even in the infallible Catholic Church. Everyone in the least acquainted with ecclesiastical history, must know, that not only has the practice varied, at different times, in very important matters; but also the bulls of popes, and decrees and canons of councils, have often been in perfect collision with one another: and, what is worst of all, have often been in direct hostility with the Word of God. For the same thing has happened to tradition in the Christian, as formerly in the Jewish church. 'It hath made the word of God of none effect', 'teaching for doctrines the commandments of men'.

But whilst we reject tradition as a rule of truth, we do not deny the utility of having recourse to the early practice of the church, for the illustration of Scripture, where there is any doubt respecting apostolic practice or institution.

There are two other opinions, by which the sufficiency and authority of the Scriptures, as a rule of faith and practice, are invalidated. These, though held by persons erring on opposite extremes, agree in derogating from the respect due to the Scriptures.

The first is, the opinion of those who will not believe anything, though contained in Scripture, which *does not correspond with their own reason*. If, for instance, a thousand passages of Scripture could be adduced, explicitly teaching the doctrine of the Trinity, of original sin, of efficacious grace, of vicarious sufferings, or eternal punishments, they would not admit them, because they have determined all these to be contrary to reason; and therefore the Scriptures must be so interpreted, as to exclude all such doctrines; and the texts which support them, must be tortured by the critical art, or perverted by the wiles of sophistry, until they are silent, or speak a different language. Now, the only mystery in the religion of these sons of reason, is that they should want a revelation at all. Certainly it would be more consistent to reject Christianity wholly, than whilst professing to receive it in the general, to deny almost all the particular doctrines of which the general system is composed. For my own part, I cannot consider Socinianism in any other light than Deism masked. At any rate, they are nearly related. If that has a little stronger faith, this has the advantage on the score of consistency.

The other opinion referred to, is that of fanatics in general, who, whilst they confess that the Scriptures are divinely inspired, *imagine that they are possessed of the same inspiration.* And some, in our own times, have proceeded so far, as to boast of revelations, by which the Scriptures are entirely superseded as a role of faith and practice.[1] Now, the difference between these persons, and the holy men of God who wrote the Scriptures, consists in two things. First, the inspired writers could give some external evidence, by miracle or prophecy, to prove their pretensions; but enthusiasts can furnish no such evidence: and secondly, the productions of the prophets and apostles were worthy of God, and bore his impress; but the discourses of these men, except what they repeat from Scripture, are wholly unworthy of their boasted origin, and more resemble the dreams of the sick, or the ravings of the insane, than the 'words of truth and soberness'.

But, on the other hand, there have been some who believed, that the Scriptures not only furnish a rule to guide us in our religion, but a complete system of philosophy; that the true theory of the universe

---

[1] Vide *The Testimony of Christ's Second Appearing,* by the people called 'Shakers'.

is revealed in the first chapters of Genesis; and that there is an intimate connection betwixt the natural and spiritual world. The one containing a sort of emblematical representation of the other; so that even the high mystery of the Trinity is supposed to be exhibited by the material fluid, which pervades the universe, in its different conditions, of fire, light, and air. John Hutchinson, Esq. of England, took the lead in propagating this system, and has been followed by some men of great name and great worth. Jones, Horne, Parkhurst, Spearman, and Bates, would be no discredit to any cause. But, although, we acknowledge, that there is something in this theory which is calculated to prepossess the pious mind in its favour; yet it is too deeply enveloped in clouds and darkness to admit of it becoming generally prevalent. And if what these learned men suppose, had been the object of revelation, no doubt, some more certain clue would have been given to assist us to ascertain the mind of the Spirit, than the obscure, though learned, criticisms of Hutchinson.

The next question which occurs, in the course of this investigation, is very important. How should the Scriptures be interpreted, in order that we may arrive at their *true* and *full* meaning? The obvious answer would be, by attending to the grammatical and literal sense of the words employed, to the force and significance of the figures and allusions used, and to the idiom of the languages in which they are written. But here we are met by a very important and embarrassing question. Is the literal meaning of Scripture, always, or generally, the principal and ultimate sense; or, are we to suppose that under this, there is a recondite, spiritual meaning contained? Most of the Fathers considered the Scriptures to contain a double sense; the one literal, the other mystical or allegorical; and they regarded the first very little except in relation to the second. The Romanists maintain an opinion very similar; but the mystical sense they divide into several parts. And among, Protestants, there are many who discover a strong predilection for this mode of interpretation.

But this principle, admitted without limitation or qualification, has a direct tendency to overthrow all certainty in divine revelation. For, as there is no certain key to this mystical or spiritual meaning, every man makes it out according to the liveliness of his own imagination:

and weak men by their fanciful expositions greatly degrade the dignity and mar the beauty of revealed truth.

The followers of Baron Swedenborg, not contented with two, maintain that the Scriptures contain three senses, the celestial, spiritual, and natural, which are connected by correspondences. This doctrine of correspondences is, according to them, the only key to open the true meaning of Scripture; which was, for many ages, lost, but recently was made known to this extraordinary nobleman. Notwithstanding the extravagance of this system, it has charms for some persons, and these not of the illiterate vulgar. It is a sort of refined mysticism, which corresponds with the peculiar turn of some minds, that are fond of novelty, and disdain to walk in the old beaten track. Reasoning or argument, with those who profess to hold familiar intercourse with angels, would, I presume, be superfluous. We shall leave them therefore to enjoy their visions of a terrestrial heaven, without interruption, whilst we proceed to observe,—

That among the orthodox themselves, there is no small difference of opinion respecting the extent which may be given to the meaning of Scripture. The celebrated Cocceius laid it down as a rule, that Scripture should be considered as signifying all that it could be made to signify. The whole of the Old Testament, in his opinion, was either typical or prophetical of Messiah and his kingdom. Here, as in a glass, he supposed the future destinies of the church might be viewed. The learned Grotius verged to the very opposite extreme, in his ideas of the interpretation of Scripture. This gave rise to a saying which became proverbial, respecting these two great men; and which is highly creditable to the piety of the former; *'Grotius nusquam in sacris literis invenire Christum Cocceium ubique'.* 'That Grotius could find Christ no where in the Bible, Cocceius everywhere.'

This rule of Cocceius, however, is liable to great abuse; and as Limborch justly observes, 'is calculated to make of the Scriptures a mere Lesbian rule,[1] or nose of wax, which may be bent into any shape; and seems to be no other than the old allegorical method of interpretation, introduced under a new name'.

---

[1] An adaptable standard, from the pliable leaden rule of masons of the ancient Greek island of Lesbos. *Ed.*

But, on the other hand, it is certain, that many of the persons, occurrences, and ceremonies of the Old Testament are typical; and some things are thus interpreted in the New Testament, which we never should have conjectured to possess any meaning beyond the literal, unless we had been otherwise taught by inspiration. Besides, all judicious commentators are forced to admit, that many of the prophecies have a primary and secondary reference; even the most important of those which relate to Messiah are of this description. Those who insist that one meaning and no more belongs to every text are greatly at a loss how to reconcile with their opinion the quotations made from the Old Testament in the New where they are expressly said to be fulfilled, though certainly, many of them, not in their primary and literal sense. Under the guidance of sound sense and just criticism, we should pursue a middle course between these two extremes. But although we cannot admit the rule of Cocceius in all its latitude, nor go the whole way with his followers; yet it is but justice to acknowledge, that some of them deserve to be ranked with the first expositors and theologians who have appeared in the church. As long as truth, piety, and solid learning shall be held in esteem, the names of Witsius, Vitringa, Burman, Van Til, and Braunius will be dear to the theological student.

Upon the whole, our conclusion respecting this matter is, that every particular passage of Scripture should be interpreted according to the peculiar circumstances of the case: the literal should be considered as the true and only meaning, unless some remoter sense be indicated by some peculiar aptitude, correspondence, or fitness, in the words and ideas of the text; or unless it be referred to something else in the Scriptures themselves. Good sense and the analogy of faith are the guides which we should follow in interpreting the Bible.

We come now to consider the *helps* which the biblical student needs, to enable him to search the Scriptures with success. The volumes which we have already supposed to be put into his hands, are not written in our vernacular tongue. We have, it is true, an excellent translation of the Scriptures; but this was not made by inspiration, and cannot therefore possess the same authority and infallibility, with the originals. We admit the lawfulness and utility of translations for the use of the people; but nothing can be more evident, than that the expounder of Scripture should be well acquainted with the very words by which the Holy Ghost teacheth us the will of God. The knowledge of the Hebrew and Greek languages, therefore, is a necessary prerequisite to the successful study of the Scriptures. I think I may venture to assert, that this single acquisition will be of more importance to the theological student, than all the commentaries which have ever been written. By this means, he will be able to see with his own eyes; and will be qualified to judge for himself.

Every person who has had experience will acknowledge, that even in reading the plainest texts, there is a satisfaction and advantage to be derived from the original, which cannot easily be explained. It becomes therefore a duty incumbent on all who are candidates for the sacred office, or invested with it, to endeavour to become acquainted with the original Scriptures.

But in all writings, and especially such as contain historical facts, there are frequent allusions to the existing customs of the country, and to the prevailing opinions of the people, where the book was written. The same is found to be the case with the Scriptures. Many passages would be quite unintelligible, without some acquaintance with Jewish antiquities. The customs and manners of that people should, therefore, be studied with particular attention.

And as scriptural history frequently refers to the condition, character, and transaction of cotemporaneous nations, it is of importance to be well acquainted with their history, as delivered to us by profane authors. There is, however, a more important reason why the biblical student should be well versed in history, ancient and modern; and that is, because there he must look for the accomplishment of many important prophecies. Even the fulfilment of the remarkable prediction of Christ, respecting the destruction of Jerusalem, is not recorded in Scripture, but must be sought in the Jewish and Roman historians.

Chronology and geography are also requisite helps, to enable us to understand many parts of Scripture. These have been called the eyes of history; and they are not more so of civil, than sacred history.

Even modern travels have been turned, by some learned men, to a very important account, in explaining the Scriptures. For oriental customs and modes of living have not been subject to the same capricious changes, which have prevailed in the western nations. And therefore, by observing carefully what oriental customs are, at this day, a very probable opinion may be formed, of what they were two thousand years ago. This observation holds good, particularly, in relation to such Eastern nations as have never been conquered, nor incorporated with any other people; as the Arabs, for instance.

Indeed, to speak the truth, there is scarcely any science or branch of knowledge, which may not be made subservient to theology. Natural history, chemistry, and geology have sometimes been of important service, in assisting the biblical student to solve difficulties contained in Scripture; or in enabling him to repel the assaults of adversaries, which were made under cover of these sciences. A general acquaintance with the whole circle of science is of more consequence to the theologian, than at first sight appears. Not to mention the intimate connection which subsists between all the parts of truth, in consequence of which important light may often be collected from the remotest quarters; it may be observed, that the state of learning in the world requires the advocate of the Bible, to attend to many things which may not in themselves be absolutely necessary. He must maintain his standing as a man of learning. He must be able to converse on the various topics or learning with other literary men; otherwise the due respect will not be paid to him; and his sacred office may suffer contempt, in consequence of his appearing to be ignorant of what it is expected all learned men should be acquainted with.

But next to the knowledge of the original languages, an acquaintance with early translations is most important. The Septuagint, the Chaldaic paraphrase, the Syriac, and the Vulgate, deserve to be particularly mentioned.

The Septuagint is an invaluable treasure to the student of sacred literature. Most of the Fathers, and several learned moderns, believed it to have been made by inspiration; and others, as well as these, have preferred it to the Hebrew original. But this is certainly attributing too much to it. The fabulous account of the miraculous manner in which it was executed, given by Aristeas, which misled the Fathers, is now generally exploded; and this was the principal ground on which the opinion of its inspiration rested. It has been pleaded also, that this version was constantly quoted by Christ and his apostles; but our Lord himself could not have used it, as he spoke and conversed not in the Greek but the Syriac language. And although it is true, that the apostles and Evangelists commonly quote from it, yet not uniformly. Sometimes they differ from it, and give a better translation of the original. It has also been plausibly stated, that the manuscripts from which this version was made, must have been much more perfect than any now extant, after the lapse of two thousand years. But it ought to be remembered, that the copies of the translation have been as liable to the injuries of time, as those of the original: and indeed much more so; for providence raised up a set of men, who watched over the Hebrew text with unceasing and incomparable vigilance. The Masorites devoted their lives to this object; and to prevent all possibility of corruption or alteration, they numbered not only the words, but the letters, of every book in the Bible. No such means were employed for the preservation of the text of the LXX; and accordingly the various readings in the copies of this version, are far more numerous and important than those of the Hebrew original. But whilst we reject the high claims for this version, which go to place it on a level with, or give it the preference to, the original; we willingly acknowledge its importance; and what is remarkable, is, its utility is greater in relation to the New Testament, than the Old; for it is written in that very dialect of the Greek language, in which the books of the New Testament are written; that is, the words are Greek, but the idiom Hebrew. It is therefore of more importance in assisting us to understand the language of the New Testament, than all other Greek authors beside.

This version has, by the consent of all, been considered the oldest extant; but a recent writer in *The Christian Observer*[1] asserts that the Syriac translation of the Old Testament, contains internal marks of an antiquity superior to that of the Septuagint. The evidence of the fact, if it be so, must be internal; for I believe it is certain, that there is no external testimony which will, support this assertion.

The Chaldaic paraphrase has commonly been referred to the time of Christ's advent, or to a period a little earlier; but the above-mentioned writer asserts that it is nearly as old as the time of Ezra.

[1] No. for July 1811.

131

Without stopping to inquire into the validity of this opinion, I would observe, that these paraphrases are of no small importance to the interpreter of Scripture, as they serve to show how the Jewish doctors understood certain passages prior to the birth of Christ; and clearly prove, that they referred to the expected Messiah, all or most of those prophecies, which we apply to Christ.

The Syriac version of the New Testament is very valuable, on account of its antiquity; and has some shadow of claim to the authority of an original; for it is written in the same, or very nearly the same language, which our Lord used when he delivered his sermons and instructions to the people; and may therefore be supposed to contain, in many instances, the identical words which he uttered. In the opinion of some, it was made at the close of the apostolic age, or at furthest some time in the second century: but others refer it to the third, fourth, or even the fifth, century. However these things may be, it cannot be doubted, but that much advantage may be derived from this version in searching the Scriptures; and accordingly much use has been made of it by the learned, of late, in solving difficulties and elucidating obscure passages, which occur in the New Testament: and being written in a language possessing a near affinity with the Hebrew, it is easily accessible to the Hebrew scholar.

The Vulgate, is commonly supposed to have been made by Jerome, and to have succeeded to older Latin versions. It was, for many ages, the only medium through which the revelation contained in holy Scripture, was viewed in the western part of the church. The Romanists, considering that this version could be made to favour their pretensions and corruptions, more than the original, bent all their force to the support of its authority; whilst at the same time, they let slip no opportunity of disparaging the Hebrew text. At length they proceeded so far as to decree, in the Council of Trent, 'that it should be reckoned *as the authentic standard by which, all disputations, preachings, and expositions, should be judged; and that no person should dare to reject its authority on any pretext whatever.'* The more liberal Catholics themselves, are ashamed of the unblushing effrontery of this decree; and what slender foundation there was for so high a claim, may be conjectured from this circumstance, that a learned man[1] of their own

---

[1] Isidore Clarius.

communion declares, that he had himself noted 80,000 errors in this version. But, nevertheless, it may be useful in many ways to the biblical student, and being written in Latin, is accessible to every scholar. And here I will take occasion to remark, the great importance of a familiar acquaintance with the Latin language, to the theologian. Although no part of Scripture is written in that language, yet it is almost essentially necessary to pass through this vestibule, in order to arrive at the knowledge of any other ancient language; most valuable grammars and dictionaries being written in Latin: and almost all theological works, not designed for the immediate use of the people, were composed in this language, prior to the middle of the last century, a very small portion of which have been translated into English. The course of theological study would indeed be very much circumscribed, if we were destitute of this key to unlock its rich treasures. It would lead me into a discussion too long, to consider, what assistance may be derived from the writings of the Fathers; what from the Schoolmen; what from the Reformers; and what from more modern commentators and critics, in the interpretation of the Scriptures. The time allotted for this discourse would be entirely insufficient to do justice to this subject. I shall therefore leave it untouched, and proceed to mention,—

A help, which, though put in the last place, in this discourse, is of more real importance than all the rest; and that is, *the illumination and assistance of the Holy Spirit*. Illumination differs from inspiration in this respect; that whereas by the latter we are made acquainted with truths before unrevealed, or unknown, by the former we are enabled to discern the beauty and real nature of the truths contained in a revelation already made. It is obvious, that in the study of divine truth, much depends on the temper and condition of the student's mind. A proud and self-sufficient person, however endowed with acuteness of intellect, and furnished with stores of literature, is continually prone to fall into pernicious error; whilst the humble man occupies a station from which truth may be viewed to advantage. Prejudice, proceeding from education or passion, blinds the mind, and warps the judgment; but the sincere and ardent love of truth disposes us to view the whole evidence, and impartially to weigh the arguments on both sides of any question. As much therefore depends upon preserving our own minds in a proper state, as upon the diligent use of external means of information. The conclusion from these premises is, that the student of sacred literature should be possessed of sincere and ardent piety. He should be a man 'taught of God', conscious of his own insufficiency, but confident of the help of the Almighty. Indeed, when we consider the weakness of the human intellect, and the various prejudices and false impressions to which it is constantly liable, we must be convinced, that without divine assistance, there is little hope of arriving at the knowledge of truth, or preserving it when acquired. He, who would understand the Scriptures, therefore, ought not to 'lean to his own understanding', but by continual and earnest prayer, should look unto the 'Father of lights', from whom proceedeth every good and every perfect gift; and who hath promised to give wisdom to those who lack it, and ask for it.

There is no person who needs more to be in the constant exercise of prayer, than the theological student: not only at stated periods, but continually, in the midst of his studies, his heart should be raised to heaven for help and direction. A defect here, it is to be feared, is one principal reason why so much time and labour are often employed in theological studies with so little profit to the church. That knowledge which puffeth up is acquired; but charity, which edifieth, is neglected.

When the serious mind falls into doubt respecting divine truths, the remedy is not always reasoning and argument, but divine illumination. The mind may be in such a state, that it is rather perplexed, than relieved, by mere human reasoning; but at such times a lively impression made by the Spirit of truth banishes all doubt and hesitation; and then, the same texts or arguments which were before unavailing to our conviction and satisfaction, exhibit the truth in a light as clear as demonstration. This may appear to some to savour of enthusiasm. Be it so. It is, however, an enthusiasm essential to the very nature of our holy religion, without which it would be a mere dry system of speculation, of ethics and ceremonies. But this divine illumination is its life, its soul, its essence. It is true, this influence is not peculiar to the theologian. Every sincere Christian, in his measure, partakes of this 'anointing', by which he is taught to know all things; but the teacher of religion needs a double portion of this spirit. How often does the minister of the gospel labour and toil with all his might, without producing anything of importance, for edification! But if he receive the aid of the Spirit, his text is opened and illustrated, without any painful exertion of his own. He is conscious, indeed, that he is a mere recipient. The train of thought which occupies his mind, appears to originate in some occult cause, which he cannot trace. And happy would it be for preachers, happy for their hearers, if there were more dependence on divine assistance, not only in the composition, but in the delivery of sermons! When God shall appear in his glory, to build up Jerusalem, he will raise up, I have no doubt, a race of preachers, who shall partake of this heavenly gift, in a much higher degree than has heretofore been common. He will bring forward to the sacred office, men possessing *boldness,* founded on their reliance upon divine assistance; *clearness,* proceeding from divine illumination; and that *unction* which flows from the sweet and lively experience of the truth delivered, in the heart of the preacher. The solicitous, and often unsuccessful, effort to rise to some artificial standard of oratory, shall then yield to nobler motives; and the preacher, like Paul, shall be willing to make a sacrifice of his own reputation for learning, and refinement, at the foot of the cross: and to count all things but loss for the excellency of the knowledge of Jesus Christ his Lord. Gospel simplicity and sincerity, shall then be preferred by the Man of God, to all the soaring flights of eloquence, and to all the splendid trappings and tinsel of human science. May it please the Lord of the vineyard speedily to send forth many such labours into his harvest; for the harvest is great, and the labourers are few!

I will now bring this discourse to a conclusion, by offering some motives to excite the theological student to diligence in the perusal of the sacred Scriptures.

A book has a claim upon our time and study, on account of the authority by which it comes recommended, the excellency of the matter comprehended in it, and the interest which we have involved in the knowledge of its contents. On all these accounts the Bible has the highest possible claim on our attention. It comes to us, as we have proved, authenticated as the Word of God; stamped as it were with the signature of heaven; and recommended to our diligent perusal by the Lord Jesus Christ. The matter which it contains, is, like its origin, divine: *truth,* pure, glorious and all important truth, constitutes the subject of this book. The saying ascribed to Mr Locke, when he took leave of a beloved relation, shortly before his end, was worthy of that profound genius; 'Study', said he, 'the sacred Scriptures; they have God for their author, truth without mixture of error for their matter, and eternal life for their end.' If we should take the lowest view of the subject, and form our opinion of the Scriptures by the same rules by which we judge of human compositions, they will be found to transcend the highest efforts of human genius, as far as the heavens are above the earth. Hear on this subject, the decision of a scholar; in whom learning and taste in their highest perfection were combined; 'I have regularly and attentively read these holy Scriptures, and am of opinion that this volume, independently of its divine origin, contains more sublimity and beauty, purer morality, and finer strains of poetry and eloquence, than can be collected from all other books, in whatever age or language they may have been composed.'[1]

But the excellency of the Scriptures cannot be appreciated by the rules of human criticism. As well might we think of judging of the proportions of the celestial arch, or the location of the stars in the vast expanse, by the roles of architecture. The Word of God, like his works, is on a plan too vast, too sublime, too profound, to be measured by the feeble intellect of man.

Fully to explain how worthy the Scriptures are of our attention, on account of the matter comprehended in them, would require us to exhibit all the truths which they contain; but as this cannot be done in one, or a few discourses, I will now content myself with mentioning a few leading points, on which the Scriptures furnish us with information of the most important kind.

In the first place, then, it is here, and here alone, that we can learn the true character of God. The indistinct outline, which may be traced in the works of creation, is here filled up. The knowledge of God, which could be derived from a view of his works, would not be sufficient for man, even in a state of innocence; and much less

---

[1] Found written in his own hand, on a blank leaf of Sir William Jones's Bible, after his death.

so when he is fallen into sin. None have ever been able to form just conceptions of the Deity from the light of nature alone. A revelation was absolutely necessary to teach man what God is; and the Bible contains all the information which we need on this subject. Here the divine glory is revealed. The moral attributes of Deity, especially, are represented in the clearest, strongest light. Truths respecting the divine nature are here revealed, concerning which, reason and philosophy could never have formed a conjecture. The glorious and mysterious doctrine of a Trinity in unity, is taught from the beginning to the end of the Bible; a doctrine offensive to the pride of man, but one which will afford subject for profound contemplation through eternity. From the Scriptures we learn, not only that God is holy, just, merciful, and faithful; but we behold these attributes harmonizing in a work which, according to all the views that finite wisdom could have taken of it, must have placed them in a state of complete variance; that is, in the justification and salvation of a sinner. In the redemption of Christ these divine perfections not only appear harmonious;—'mercy and truth having met together, and righteousness and peace having kissed each other'; but in the cross are exhibited with a lustre and glory, which, according to our conceptions, could not have been given to them, in any other circumstances. If we would know *the only true God,* then, we must 'search the Scriptures'.

In the next place, we obtain from the Bible a satisfactory account of the origin of evil, natural and moral. Not, indeed, an explanation of the reason why it was permitted; but such an account of its introduction, as is perfectly consistent with the honour and purity of the divine government. We here learn that God created man 'in a state of innocency, with freedom and power to will and do that which was well pleasing to himself, but yet mutable, so that he might fall from it.' This liberty was abused by man: sin therefore owes its origin to the creature, who is wholly chargeable with its blame; although it did not take place without the knowledge, nor contrary to the purpose, of the infinite God. The first man being the root of all his posterity, and being appointed to act for them as well as for himself, they are involved with him in all the consequences of his fall; for 'they sinned in him and fell with him in his first transgression'. All the streams of sin and misery in the world, flow, from this original fountain. And so deep and dreadful is this fall of man, that he is utterly unable to recover himself from the guilt and depravity into which he is by nature sunk.

The last mentioned article of information would be only calculated to plunge us into the depths of misery and despair were it not that the Scriptures teach us the consoling doctrine of redemption. Indeed, the whole Bible may be considered as a history of *redemption*. Here we can trace the wondrous plan up to its origin, in the eternal counsels of peace. Here we read of the early development of this plan, after the fall, in paradise. The incarnation and victory of the glorious Redeemer was clearly intimated in the promise, 'that the seed of the woman should bruise the serpent's head'. To this object, the faith of the pious was directed, by every new revelation and institution. Prophets, in long succession, with lips touched with hallowed fire, described and predicted Immanuel. Although their prophecies are often expressed in dark symbolical language, yet sometimes, from, the midst of this darkness, there are vivid coruscations of light, which exhibit the promised Messiah as visibly, as if he had already come. At length the fulness of time arrived, and 'God sent forth his Son made of a woman, made under the law, to redeem them that were under the law.' 'God was now manifest in the flesh.' And, he 'who being in the form of God, thought it not robbery to be equal with God, made himself of no reputation, and took upon him the form of a servant and was made in the likeness of men; and being found in fashion as a man, he humbled himself and became obedient unto death, even the death of the cross; wherefore God also hath highly exalted him, and given him a name which is above every name.' The redemption of the church by the blood of the Son of God is a subject on which angels look with wonder; and it is a subject, which, through eternity, will furnish a theme for the songs of the redeemed of the Lord.

But the Scriptures give us information, not only of the work of the Redeemer in procuring for us an 'everlasting righteousness'; but also of the work of the Spirit, in uniting the redeemed soul to Jesus Christ; in regenerating, sanctifying, supporting, guiding, and comforting it; until it is 'made meet for the inheritance of the saints in light'.

Another important article of information which we find in the Scriptures of truth is a clear expression of the will of God, in relation to the duty of man. There are, it is true, traces of the law of God still remaining on the heart of every man; but these are far from being sufficient to show him the full extent, and the spiritual nature, of the duties required of him. And what might be known from honestly inquiring of our own consciences, respecting our duty, is often missed through the influence of false principles, instilled into the mind by a defective education, and by customs become universally prevalent, through the corruption of human nature. But we need be no longer at a loss about the law of God. He condescended to publish it, with his own voice, in the hearing of all Israel; and to write it with his own finger, on tables of stone. To explain this law, we have many comments from inspired men; but especially we have the lucid exposition of the Law-giver himself; and, what is more important, we behold it fully illustrated and exemplified, in the obedience which he, in our nature, and for our sakes, rendered to it; so that, if we now wish to know our duty, we have only to contemplate the character of Jesus Christ. If we wish to do it, we have only to walk in his footsteps.

Finally, the Scriptures contain a distinct and full revelation of futurity, as far as it is necessary for us to know what is to be, hereafter. In them, 'life and immortality are brought to light'. Full assurance is given, by the testimony of one who, cannot lie, that 'an exceeding great and eternal weight of glory' is reserved for the people of God in another world. In the New Testament, we are made familiar with heaven, by the frequency with which it is mentioned and described. The existence of a future world is no longer left to be collected by uncertain reasoning, and probable conjecture. It is now a matter of testimony. Faith has a firm ground on which to rest; for this truth is linked with every fact and doctrine of the gospel; is seen in every promise and threatening under the new dispensation. But the Scriptures reveal not only a heaven of glory, but a hell of horror; a dark and 'bottomless pit', where 'the worm dieth not, and where the fire is not quenched', and where 'there is weeping and wailing and gnashing of teeth'. They give us the certain assurance, also, of a day being appointed in which God will judge the world in righteousness by that man whom he hath ordained; and in which they that are in their graves shall rise, some to everlasting life and glory, and others to everlasting, shame and contempt.

From this brief survey of what the Scriptures teach us, we must be convinced of the great importance of being well acquainted with them. Our own salvation is involved in the right knowledge of this book; and if we are teachers of others, how important is it, that we 'as good stewards of the mysteries of God', be 'able rightly to divide the word of truth, giving to every one his portion in due season'. We should, therefore, 'meditate on these things, and give ourselves wholly to them, that our profiting may appear unto all'. We must 'take heed unto ourselves, and to our doctrine, and continue in them; for by so doing we shall both save ourselves and them that hear us.'

But we shall not only find the Scriptures to be a source of profitable instruction; a rich mine of truth which has never yet been fully explored; but also a source of pure and permanent delight.

As the natural light is pleasant to the eyes, so is truth to the understanding, unless some moral disease render its approach unacceptable. 'They whose deeds are evil, love darkness rather than light'; but the regenerate soul 'rejoices in the truth'. Food to the hungry is not more pleasant, nor cold water more refreshing to the thirsty, than evangelical truth to the pious mind. It is, indeed, the bread of life which cometh down from heaven; the 'hidden manna' with which the spiritual Israel are fed, whilst they sojourn in this wilderness. The person who has been taught of God, prefers the truths of his Word to all earthly treasures, and to all the sweets of nature. 'More are they to be desired, than gold, yea, than much fine gold: sweeter also than honey and the honey comb.' 'The law of thy mouth is better unto me than thousands of gold and silver.' 'Thy statutes have been my song in the house of my pilgrimage.' How delightful must it be to sit as a disciple at the feet of Jesus, and with a childlike docility, imbibe precious instruction, from his Word and Spirit! When we fall under the power of some overwhelming temptation, or when dark clouds of adversity thicken around us, in the truths and promises of our God, we find our only refuge. In the sanctuary, when the oracles of God are delivered, doubt and unbelief, sorrow and despair, are driven away. Here divine beauty beams with mild effulgence on the soul, and the troubled spirit is charmed to rest. 'One day in thy courts is better than a thousand.' 'One thing have I desired of the Lord, that will I seek after, that I may dwell in the house of the Lord, all the days of my life, to behold the beauty of the Lord.'

When Jesus joins himself to his disconsolate disciples, how soon is their sorrow turned into joy! And whilst he opens their understandings to understand the Scriptures, how do their hearts burn within them! That which above all things makes the Scriptures precious, and the study of them delightful, is, that there we can find Jesus Christ. We have no need to say, 'who shall ascend into heaven, that is, to bring Christ down from above; or who shall descend into the deep, that is, to bring up Christ, again from the dead?' For, 'the word is nigh us, even in our mouth, and in our heart; that is, the word of faith which we preach': 'Christ and him crucified' is the centre of the Christian's religion, the foundation of his faith and hope, and the perennial spring of all his pleasures and his joys. When, at any time, it pleases God to shine upon his Word, whilst the believer reads its sacred contents, what a divine glory illuminates the holy page! What attractive beauty draws forth the best affections of his heart! What wonders do his opened eyes behold in the cross! He seems to be translated into a new world, and is ready to exclaim, 'I have heard of thee by the hearing of the ear; but now mine eye seeth thee.' 'Old things are passed away, and behold, all things are become new.' O! could the pious reader of the Scriptures constantly retain these spiritual views, and these holy impressions, heaven would be begun. This wilderness would 'bud and blossom as the rose', and paradise be renewed on earth. But 'this is not our rest, it is polluted'; that remaineth for the people of God; even 'an inheritance incorruptible, undefiled, and that fadeth not away, reserved in the heavens for us, who are kept by the power of God through faith unto salvation, ready to be revealed in the last time.'

But whilst we are on our pilgrimage to this promised land, the Scriptures will be 'a light to our feet and a lamp to our path'. They will, answer the same purpose to us, which the pillar of cloud and of fire, did to the Israelites. They will guide us in the right way, through all our journey. Let us, then, be persuaded diligently 'to search the Scriptures'.

I beg leave to conclude this discourse in the words of the pious Weller, the friend and disciple of Luther:

I admonish you again and again, that you read the sacred Scriptures in a far different manner from that in which you read any other book: that you approach them with the highest reverence, and most intense application of your mind; not as the words of a man, nor an angel, but as the words of the divine Majesty, the least of which should have more weight with us, than the writings of the wisest and most learned men, in the world.[1]

[1] *Consilium De Studio Theologia.*

PHILIP MILLEDOLER
1775-1852

DUTCH Reformed minister, educator, and college president, Philip Milledoler was born in Rhinebeck, New York. His parents were of Swiss descent, having fled to the Rhinebeck area when British soldiers occupied New York City in 1775. Affiliation with the German Reformed Church provided him with the opportunity for a good theological grounding at an early age. Converted at fourteen years of age, he graduated from Columbia College in 1793. Eager to pursue a ministerial calling, Milledoler joined the Nassau Street German Reformed Church of New York City in 1793 or 1794, and read theology under its pastor, the Rev. John D. Gros. Licensed in 1794, he began work with the Nassau congregation; in 1795, aged just twenty, he became sole pastor of the congregation. In 1800 he transferred his ministerial credentials to the Dutch Reformed Church, while taking new employment as pastor of the Pine Street Presbyterian Church, Philadelphia; by 1805 he had returned to New York City to serve as pastor of the Rutgers Street Presbyterian Church. From 1813-25 he served the

Collegiate Dutch Reformed Church of New York City, after which he became President of Queen's College (later renamed Rutgers College), serving simultaneously as Professor of Didactic and Polemic Theology at the Theological Seminary of the Reformed Church in America, New Brunswick, New Jersey. Milledoler retired from both positions in 1840 and returned to New York City, where he lived the remainder of his life, maintaining an active preaching ministry among the city's congregations.

His preaching was marked by evangelical fervour and deep piety. A man of prayer, his congregations were noted for their evangelical emphases, strength of membership, and numerous conversions. Throughout his ministry Milledoler's preaching was blessed to the reviving of a number of his hearers and stirred interest in the religious reform activities of the early nineteenth century. He served as Moderator of the General Assembly of the Presbyterian Church in 1808. He founded the American Bible Society in 1816, founded and was President of the American Society for the Evangelization of the Jews, and also served as Secretary for the United Foreign Missionary Society. His publications include a variety of sermons and addresses.

Milledoler also played an important role in American Presbyterian history, helping to plan and establish Princeton Theological Seminary. His other accomplishments notwithstanding, he is best remembered for the stirring charge he delivered to the new professor and students of divinity at the inaugural service and installation of Archibald Alexander as the seminary's first Professor of Theology in August 1812.

A CHARGE TO THE PROFESSOR
AND STUDENTS OF DIVINITY[1]

REVEREND and Dear Brother, the engagements you have formed this day, are peculiarly solemn and affecting. The charge devolving on the pastor of a congregation, in entering upon the duties of his office, is deeply interesting, but not so interesting as yours. You are not called by a particular branch of our church to minister in holy things, but by her highest ecclesiastical judicatory, to superintend the education of her sons. Under the direction, we trust, of the great Head of the church, you have been invited to train up for her service, bands of intelligent, intrepid, and faithful champions of the cross. The characters you are to form for active service, are the flower of our youth; young men from whose lips, at some future, and not far distant period, multitudes of souls may receive instruction; who may be destined to fill the chairs of teachers and professors in our schools, and on whose fidelity, under God, may depend the future peace and prosperity of the church, and the salvation of thousands, perhaps millions, yet unborn.

Suffer me, under these circumstances, to give a brief exhibition of the views of the General Assembly in founding this institution, and to point out some duties incumbent on you, in the accomplishment of those views. The Assembly, in founding this school, are desirous of securing and perpetuating to the church, a learned, orthodox, pious, and evangelical ministry.

We want a learned ministry.

---

[1] Philip Milledoler, 'The Charge to the Professor and Students', *The Sermon, Delivered at the Inauguration of the Rev. Archibald Alexander, D.D. as Professor of Didactic and Polemic Theology, in the Theological Seminary of the Presbyterian Church, in the United States of America. To which Are Added, the Professor's Inaugural Address, and the Charge to the Professors and Students* (New York: Whiting and Watson): pp. 107-22.

Whatever mischief has been done to the world by philosophy, falsely so called, we are persuaded that true learning has never injured the church, and never will. Such is the harmony existing between the works and Word of God, that, discoveries in the former will never cease to promote our regard for the latter. It has been said, that ignorance is the mother of devotion; that aphorism we utterly and indignantly reject. To instruct others, and especially in divine things, men must first be instructed themselves. On this principle God himself has acted from the beginning of the world to the present day. In former ages, he himself spake directly to the prophets. The messages they delivered were formed under the immediate influence of his grace, and the inspiration of his Spirit. 'For the prophecy came not in old time by, the will of man; but holy men of God spake as they were moved by the Holy Ghost' (*2 Pet.* 1:21).

At the entrance of our Saviour upon his ministry, he chose twelve disciples. These were prepared by himself for their work, and that too especially in the first instance by a regular course of instruction. It was after that course of instruction, and not before, that they were sent out to evangelize the world. Of completing the designs of God toward our race, in their day, these servants of Christ had no expectation. Their number was small, their lives precarious, the opposition they met with, powerful and constant; and their influence confined to regions which, however extensive in themselves, were yet small when compared to the whole world. They were, therefore solicitous to provide for the future, wants of the church, and took immediate steps for transmitting their power and authority to others. Hence, that charge of Paul to Timothy: 'And the things that thou hast heard of me among many witnesses, the same commit thou to faithful men, who shall be able to teach others also' (*2 Tim.* 2:2). Thus early provision was made for the supply of the church with an able and faithful ministry. Beside the instruction they had received from their Lord, the apostles and their immediate successors were qualified in a miraculous manner for their work. They were endowed with the gift of tongues. Devils fled at their rebuke; diseases, the most inveterate, were healed by a word or by a touch. They had also the power of discerning spirits (*1 Cor.* 12:10); a power which gave them no small advantage over ordinary teachers. All these gifts, from their extraordinary nature, and the well-known disposition of mankind, were calculated to excite curiosity, to attract attention, to draw men within the sphere of the gospel, and to carry home, by divine grace, irresistible conviction to their understandings and hearts. They enjoyed another advantage; they were under the influence of the Spirit of God, to a degree, of which now, alas! owing to our most awful supineness, we can hardly form a conception. This inference of the Spirit gave dignity to their manners, intrepidity to their zeal, and a general character to their ministry, which commanded the admiration of both friends and foes. With such advantages, it is not to be wondered at, that they towered with eagles' flight above the philosophers of their day, and outstripped in their progress all the wisdom of the sages, and all the eloquence of the schools. But the gift of tongues, with other miraculous endowments of the Holy Spirit, began gradually to disappear, with the extension of the gospel. This circumstance had a considerable influence in changing the face of the church, and especially in regard to the education of her ministers. That the Scriptures might be read in the languages in which they were originally penned, or translated into the tongues of foreign nations; that young Gentile converts might become mighty in the Scriptures; and that the sons of the church might be qualified to contend for the faith once delivered to the saints, against learned and subtle adversaries without, as well as against sectaries in her own bosom, it was soon perceived that a learned, as well as pious, ministry, was indispensably necessary. The most distinguished of the primitive fathers were advocates for a learned ministry. They well knew that learning without piety might be abased to the worst of purposes; but they were willing to allow that the abuse of what is good in itself, can never detract from its intrinsic value. In this view of the object, they were followed by the Reformers; and it is a principle which has been acted upon, and contended for, from that day to the present, by the best and purest churches in Christendom. In the careful instruction, then, of our youth, dear Sir, for the work of the gospel ministry, you will neither stand upon new or untenable ground. And, assured as you may be, that you are doing the will of Christ, you may safely employ in it all the stores of your learning; all the resources of your genius, and all the powers of your soul. But whilst there can be no doubt, either of the lawfulness or expediency of such a work, it is not to be concealed, that it is a task of great labour and difficulty. To say nothing of that diversity of disposition, taste, and intellect, in students themselves, which renders the art of teaching, as well as government, so exceedingly intricate; waving also at present all observations on *methods* of instruction, I will venture to say, that the work itself is one of the most arduous in the world. The Scriptures are a mine of inexhaustible wealth, but to be enriched with their treasures will require close and constant application. To exhibit divine truth in a lucid and systematic manner; to show the unity of Scripture in the connection and dependence of its parts; to make of our young men sound biblical critics, and able casuists; to furnish them with gospel armour of proof, offensive and defensive; to give them an extensive acquaintance with church history and government; but especially so to indoctrinate, and, if I may use the expression, leaven them with heavenly truth, that they may ever after hold, and defend it for themselves, as well as communicate it to others; is a work indeed of no small magnitude. In this work you will soon, we hope, be aided by faithful colleagues; but a large and important part of it will still rest, under God, upon yourself. To cultivate such a field as this; dear Sir, will be sufficient to call forth the exertions of the most active and enterprising mind; it will therefore behoove you, notwithstand-ing *all* your present acquirements, not only to cherish the attainments you have already made, but, also further to enrich your mind with the spoils of science, and to extend your inquiries into almost every department of literature, sacred and profane.

Another charge devolving upon you with peculiar weight, dear Brother, is the faithful maintenance, of that system of doctrines handed down to us by our fathers, and for which in numerous instances they have sacrificed 'their fortunes, their liberties, and their lives'. Strongly attached to the doctrines of the Reformation con-tained in her standards, jealous of innovation, and anxious to trans-mit the truth as it is in Jesus inviolate to posterity, the Presbyterian Church will expect, and permit me to add, Sir, after the signal mark of her confidence reposited in you, will have a right to expect that her doctrines, and especially her distinguishing doctrines, will be taught in this school without adding to, or taking aught from them in any wise, or under any pretext whatsoever. It is also expected that these doctrines will be explained in terms used by her best writers from almost time immemorial, and which from long use have become familiar, to, and are best understood by, her members. By observing this plan, there will be an agreement of theological terms used in the instruction of our youth, with those used in our standard books, as well as an agreement of terms used by our future licentiates and ministers, with those to which our congregations are accustomed. An object this, of no small importance to the future harmony of our churches. The Confession of Faith of the Presbyterian Church, and form of government connected with it, will be an important book in this seminary. Containing a form of sound words drawn from the lively oracles of God, and tested by experience, it has long served, and will hereafter, serve, as a bond of union to the churches. As every minister in our connection is required, to subscribe this Confession, they should be well acquainted with its contents. When adopted, it cannot be renounced without renouncing our communion; nor invaded, without a species of sacrilege. If important doctrinal errors are ever introduced into our churches, they will be introduced by a gradual departure from our standards. These should be guarded, therefore, with inviolable care. Is any man dissatisfied with them, he is not bound to receive them; and if he does receive them, he is by that very act sacredly bound to cherish and maintain them. To surrender truths deemed of *minor importance* is only to prepare the way for other demands, and greater sacrifices; and if first attempts are not repelled, they will soon be followed by others, till all is gone that is worth contending for. To give our young men an early acquaintance with these standards is therefore an object of primary importance; and should they be required during their theological course, to commit to memory the greater part, if not the whole, of our confession and book of discipline, it would be attended with incalculable advantage. It would not only give them a decided superiority over others in ecclesiastical councils, but would also tend to guard them against error, as well as to secure their attachment to the truth. Peculiarly set for the defence of the gospel, it will be expected of you, dear Brother, that you will stand as a bulwark for truth against the encroachments of error. In this respect also, the Assembly have deposited in your hands a most sacred trust; and one we are persuaded, that will never be abused. With pleasure we anticipate the period when the youth of our seminary will not only exhibit sound principles themselves, but will also be disposed, and prepared to hand them down inviolate to others.

And as it is desirable that we should have a learned and orthodox, so we also need a pious and evangelical, ministry. Whatever may be the talents of ministers, they are like, without personal piety, to be of no lasting advantage to the church; nay, such characters have often inflicted upon it deep, and almost incurable wounds. That they are utterly unfit for the sacred office is manifest. How shall they feed the flock of Christ purchased with his blood, who have no interest in that purchase? How shall they sympathize in the sufferings of God's people, who have no spiritual feeling? Or how shall they speak a word in season to weary and tempted souls, who themselves never felt, and therefore never mourned, under the awful pressure of their sins? Their godly hearers can be satisfied with them no longer than they shall have address enough to conceal their real characters, and they not infrequently become the scorn even of the careless and impenitent. We hope the time is far distant, when our churches will be satisfied with mere exhibitions of learning, or eloquence, or with the substitution of dry moral lectures for the preaching of the cross. The Apostle Paul was determined to know nothing among his hearers but Jesus Christ, and him crucified. He was convinced that nothing under heaven could exhibit the divine character in a clearer light, and that nothing had equal influence on the human mind, to control, reform, and change it into the image of God. He had fairly made the experiment, and hath taught us, both by precept and example, that the true ministry of reconciliation must be pious and evangelical. In preparing such a ministry for the church, it is desirable that such, and such only, should be sent forward to the school as are hopefully pious. What remains to the professors of the institutions is continually to insist upon the necessity of it, to cultivate it where it exists, by precept and example; to honour it with marked respect, and in every instance in which they shall be satisfied of the want of it in any pupil, to take effectual steps to prevent his entrance upon an office, for which in such case he is so evidently disqualified.

Thus, reverend and dear Brother, I have endeavoured to mark out your glorious work, and have ventured a few thoughts on the best means of its accomplishment. We want a learned, orthodox, pious, and evangelical ministry. To such, and such only, can we confidently and comfortably commit the affairs of the church; and to leave another ministry in it, if we ourselves are faithful, would plant thorns in our dying pillows. As no greater curse can fall upon a people than to commit its spiritual interests into the hands of weak and unskilful, but especially of unprincipled, men; so, on the other hand we are persuaded that an able and faithful ministry, is one of the most distinguished blessings to the world. Its influence in the church must be obvious to all; and its benign influence on our schools, as well as on the general good order and happiness of society, will be denied only by the thoughtless or the profligate. This seminary then, even in its infant state, is an object of public interest; an object not only: calculated to call forth the good wishes of our own church, but of the church at large, and even of the nation. Though its origin be small, the voice of its sons, we trust, will one day be heard to advantage from one extreme of these United States to the other; nay, the time may not be far distant, when they will vie with their transatlantic brethren, in carrying the lamp of eternal truth, and planting the standard of the cross, on the remotest shores of heathen lands. The blessings that flow from such a ministry, are not blessings of a day, of a year, or even of an age. These men will in due time transmit their knowledge and authority to others, and these again to their successors, to the final conflagration of the globe. In this view of the subject, Reverend Sir, you will feel a weight of responsibility upon you sufficient to bow the shoulders of an angel. The infant state of the institution will add to that weight. The General Assembly have stamped it with grand and impressive features, but they have only drawn the great outlines of its character. Much yet remains to be done. The perfection of their plan will be result of time and experience, and will greatly depend on the wisdom and diligence of their profession. In all this work, dear Brother, you will have the eyes of God, of angels, and of men, upon you; but you enter upon it with great encouragement. You may promise yourself the good wishes and prayers of the whole church of God. You may also promise yourself the cordial co-operation of your brethren in the Lord. In their personal friendship, as well as interest in the work, you will find pledges of future consolation and support.

But above all, you may promise yourself, if faithful, the constant blessing of the great Head of the church: there lies your strength, your wisdom, your every qualification for the work. The promise, 'I am with you always', has never been forgotten by him, and never will. I have only to add a wish that when the book shall be opened that records the transactions of this day, that you may have cause to rejoice in them for ever.

Permit me, also, young gentlemen, on this solemn occasion, to address myself to you. You will have the honour of being the first whose names are enrolled in the register of this seminary. They will stand, we hope, at the head of a host of worthies, whose future labours shall bless the church of God, and do honour to their country. As you are first in order of time, so we pray, that you may be numbered with the first, in devotion to God, and usefulness to mankind. The studies in which you will be engaged, are not only delightful, to the pious mind, but are also calculated to enlarge your souls; to ennoble and transform them into the very image of God. The privilege you will enjoy, of consecrating your time to the study of the Scriptures, and your persons to the service of Christ, is too great for expression. You are now, young gentlemen, to lay the foundation of your future character and usefulness in life; and, in some measure, at least, as connected with it, of your future and eternal felicity. Permit me then to urge, with all possible earnestness, a diligent improvement of time and opportunities afforded you in the good providence of God. Your stay in this seminary may seem long in prospect, but it is really short; short in itself, and especially so, when compared with the work you have to do. Observe the plan of education marked out by the Assembly, and you will see at once, that the most diligent application will barely suffice, to give you, not to say a perfect, but even a competent knowledge of the subjects it embraces.

If any suppose that occasional application, or superficial reading, will constitute an eminent divine, they are exceedingly mistaken. In searching after, illustrating, or defending truth, the whole circle of the sciences may be pressed into the service of Christ. The study of the Scriptures, especially in their original languages, is a work of time, as well as of deep research. To obtain an accurate knowledge of Scripture types, prophecies, and doctrines; to be acquainted with the sophistry of enemies, and qualified to expose it; to be well informed in church history and government; and to acquire facility in collecting, judgment in arranging, and gracefulness in the delivery of your thoughts, will all require time and labour.

But whilst I thus urge preparation for the altar in the acquirement of useful knowledge, let me also insist, particularly insist, on the cultivation of personal piety. As you are now to lay the foundation of solid learning, and literary eminence, so also of good character. Many eyes will be upon you, and more expected than from other young men of the same age, engaged in other pursuits. To the youth of this venerable seat of learning and the arts, you are especially called, to set examples of piety worthy of imitation. Not to speak of actions grossly derogatory to your Christian character, and the stain of which might follow you to your graves; remember, that you have in great measure passed that period of life, in which folly is extenuated by juvenile indiscretion. A short time will place you, God willing, upon the theatre of the world, under the august character of ambassadors of Christ. Bear this in constant remembrance; and if you ever hope to fill that station with dignity to yourselves, usefulness to others, and glory to God, learn now to live by faith in the Son of God; govern your passions; deny yourselves, and consecrate your whole souls to the service of the Redeemer. Whatsoever things are true, just, lovely, and of good report, if there be any virtue, and if there be any praise, think on these things. Let the world take knowledge of you, that you have been with Jesus; let it appear evident to all that you have entered upon your work with due reflection, and from proper motives, and you will in no wise lose your reward.

With piety toward God, my young Friends, be careful to cultivate respect for your instructors. It is the sign of an ingenuous mind, and a debt of gratitude you owe them. They will deserve well at your hands. The hero of Macedon revered his father much, but he revered his instructor more. He viewed him as a second father; as one who had formed his mind; and acknowledged a debt of gratitude he never could repay. Christian youth, in regard to their Christian teachers, must not be outdone by the gratitude of a heathen.

Beloved pupils, who have commenced with me your theological course—I now resign you with pleasure into other hands. Divided between parochial duties, and the care I owed you, I have found the task of instruction difficult, and sometimes oppressive; your future teacher, unencumbered by other cares, can, and will cheerfully, devote his whole time to your improvement. I am happy to bear this public testimony to your former diligence and good conduct, and trust you will secure, by your future deportment, the approbation of your teachers, of the public, of your conscience and your God.

ARCHIBALD ALEXANDER
1771-1851

Virginian by birth, Archibald Alexander was raised in a godly Presbyterian home. A gifted student, he received a classical education at Liberty Hall Academy, a regional preparatory school, under the mentorship of the Rev. William Graham. Deepening familiarity with Reformed 'experimental piety', the witness of evangelical friends and mentors, and developing awareness of his inherent sinfulness accompanied by a season of religious awakening in and around the area in which he lived, culminated in his conversion in 1789. Subsequent theological instruction with Graham led to licensure and ordination as a minister in the Presbyterian Church. Alexander soon found service as an itinerant missionary along the Virginia/North Carolina border. After serving as President of Hampden Sydney College and as minister of a combined pastoral charge in his native State, he accepted a call, in 1807, to the Third Presbyterian Church, Philadelphia. In 1812 Alexander was elected by his General Assembly to serve as the first professor of theology at the newly founded Princeton Theological Seminary. Alexander remained at Princeton until his death in 1851. While at Princeton, he earned a reputation as an outstanding educator, writing a number of books and articles on theology, apologetics, church history, and what today would be classified as 'Christian spirituality'.

During the course of his lifetime, Alexander became renowned for his understanding of the nature and effects of biblical piety. As a teenager, he had opportunity to witness first-hand the outbreak of local revivals. These outpourings of the Spirit were part of a larger movement of the Spirit of God breathing new life into individuals and communities and producing large numbers of new converts, a movement that historians now characterize as the 'Second Great Awakening' (c. 1790-1830). Alexander's itinerant missionary labours, subsequent pastorates, and opportunity to preach and counsel during a season of revival occurring in the winter of 1814-15 at Princeton College (the converts including the young Charles Hodge), provided him with a wealth of personal experience and ripened his wisdom on the differences between true and false conversion and the biblical characteristics of genuine and spurious religious awakenings. His works, *The Log College* and *Thoughts on Religious Experience,* provide valuable insights into the nature of experimental piety in relation to the Spirit's work in the conversion of individuals and its related impact on church and society during times of 'spiritual refreshing'.

As the first faculty member at Princeton, Alexander was responsible for organizing the curriculum and teaching all the classes. Alexander's commitment to the integration of faith with learning in the shaping of an intelligent and informed piety came to expression in important theological volumes such as *Evidences of the Authenticity, Inspiration and Canonical Authority of the Holy Scriptures* and a popular treatment of systematic theology, *A Brief Compend of Bible Truth.* Alexander's interest in foreign missions is evident in his *A History of Colonization on the Western Coast of Africa.* In addition to important articles and book reviews in the *Biblical Repertory and Princeton Review,* Alexander published works of biography and a variety of essays on preaching and pastoral care. Toward the end of his life a number of his sermon manuscripts were printed in *Practical Sermons: To Be Read in Families and Social Meetings;* his lectures on moral science were published posthumously in 1852 as

Outlines of Moral Science, as was a volume of collected articles, tracts, and essays on Christian piety a few years later, *Practical Truths.*

Archibald Alexander's personality, piety, and pastoral perspective left an indelible imprint on the model of ministerial training that Princeton Theological Seminary developed. A gifted teacher and outstanding extemporaneous preacher, Alexander's presence at Princeton played a prominent role in shaping American Presbyterian pulpit and pastoral practice.

PREFACE TO THE MEMOIRS OF THOMAS HALYBURTON[1]

A LL the truths necessary to the illumination, sanctification, and consolation of Christians, are contained in the sacred Scriptures, and are exhibited in divers ways, and under many different aspects. Divine truth is to the mind, what light is to the eye: it reveals to us all those objects with which it is important that we should be acquainted. It is impossible that error, however sincerely believed, should answer the end of truth. Right affections are so intimately associated with the belief of the truth, that there is an absurdity in supposing them to exist without this foundation. Every divine truth revealed in Scripture is calculated, either singly, or in connection with others, to make a salutary impression; but when any part of the system of divine truth is obscured by ignorance, or distorted by error, there will be a corresponding defect in the moral exercises of the individual. The relation of sound doctrine to pious feeling and moral character, may be compared to that between the types used in printing, and the impression on the paper. If there be any defect or disorder in the types, it will appear on the corresponding page. It may not be such as to destroy, or entirely obscure, the meaning of the whole passage; but still it is the cause of a defect, which mars the beauty of the impression; and often renders the sense uncertain. I am of opinion, that no Christian can be in ignorance or error respecting any portion of revealed truth, without injury. The precise evil we may be unable to define; it may be imperceptible, yet it has its effect on the system. Obliquities in moral conduct, if we were capable of ascertaining their cause, might often be traced to errors in opinion.

---

[1] Archibald Alexander, 'Preface', *Memoirs of the Rev. Thomas Halyburton* (Princeton: Baker & Connolly, 1833), pp. v-xiii.

It is evident, therefore, that he who trifles with the truth, trifles with his own life. To be indifferent about truth, is a folly of the first magnitude. To be governed by mere inclination, taste or fashion, in the adoption of our religious opinions, is indicative of a diseased and dangerous state of mind. Truth is so vital and so necessary to the existence and perfection of a pious character, that we cannot be too solicitous to acquire correct knowledge. Pride, prejudice, and partiality, should be laid aside, and the love of truth should be kept alive in our souls. Mere intellectual vigour, and extensive erudition, are no effectual security against error. Honesty and deep humility are essential prerequisites to the successful pursuit of truth.

As the truth makes an impression on the mind in accordance with its own nature, and modified by the various circumstances of individuals; and as these salutary effects taken together, constitute the Christian character, and furnish the only certain evidences of a work of grace on the heart, it is of immense importance to be able to delineate, and ascertain, with as much precision as possible, these characteristics; that we may know, in our own case, and that of others also, whether spiritual life has commenced, and is progressive in our souls. Now, as in water face answereth to face, so the heart of man to man. The impressions of truth on different minds will be substantially alike. There will indeed be varieties arising from the degree of knowledge, and the peculiar temperaments and habits of individuals; but these minor differences will not affect the general similarity. Though in one case the impression made by the seal is deeper and more distinct than in another; yet by comparing them, we may be able readily to conclude, that they have been produced by the same seal. Thus, when the truth of God is made effectual by the Holy Spirit, to regenerate and sanctify the hearts of men, there may be, and are, endless varieties in the minor traits, but the leading features are the same in all. It will be seen, as far as these effects can be made evident, that they are all the children of the same father, and all bear the family likeness. The great difficulty in this business, is to ascertain the precise nature of the effects produced. In regard to our own minds, this investigation is attended with no small perplexity; but in relation to others, the subject does not admit of absolute certainty. One man, however perspicacious and discriminating his intellect, and however well acquainted with the Word of God, and with the genuine impression which it makes when it takes effect, cannot directly examine the sentiments and feelings of another. He can only form an opinion of what is in the hearts of others, by their words and actions: but the same words may be used, and the same external appearances exhibited, when the internal exercises of the soul are specifically different. For example, a man may declare that his heart overflows with love and gratitude to God, or that he is full of the joy of the Holy Ghost, and godly sorrow for sin, and yet all this may be said in hypocrisy; or what is more common, the person may be conscious of feelings, which, through ignorance, he calls by these names; and yet the emotions which he experiences may be mere counterfeits of those graces, the names of which he appropriates to them.

The Scriptures furnish us with many clear delineations of the exercises of the true believer. These are our safest guide, and only unerring standard of experimental religion. By meditating by day and night on the contents of the sacred pages, we may become so familiar with the characteristics of genuine piety, that we may find it easy to determine, that the same lineaments have, in some faint degree, been drawn on our own souls. But in examining into our true character, we may be much assisted by reading the memoirs of men of distinguished judgment and eminent piety. Many such works are now in circulation, and are adapted to promote, in high degree, the edification of the reader; but I am acquainted with no production of this kind in which the exercises of the human heart, both before and after regeneration, are so distinctly described, as in the following biography of the Rev. Thomas Halyburton, written by himself. We have here the faithful narrative of the views, feelings, conflicts, temptations, victories, and consolations of a man of eminent piety, and uncommon soundness of judgment, made at a period when he was most capable of forming an impartial opinion. He has portrayed the unregenerate heart in its deceitfulness and corruption, without disguise. From his own experience, he clearly testifies the inefficacy of a religious education, while unaccompanied by the grace of God. He, in the next place, teaches us, how powerfully the truth of God operates on the natural conscience, and how strongly it restrains even the unregenerate heart, from rushing into all the excesses of wickedness. Under the light of truth, and the lashes of a guilty conscience, the soul naturally seeks some refuge, some place where it may be sheltered from the thunderings of Mount Sinai.

The distinct and satisfactory narrative which the author gives of the changed views and exercises of his mind, at the time of his conversion, and afterwards, ought to be deeply pondered by every professor; but especially, by all candidates for the sacred office. While, in our day, conversions are multiplied beyond all former precedent, there is much reason to fear, that many of them will not bear to be brought to the touchstone of God's Word. With many, conversion has become a slight and easy thing, the mere hasty purpose of an hour; and unaccompanied by those deep views of depravity, and those soul-comforting views of Jesus Christ, which are here described.

The consequence is, that multitudes who profess conversion, do not exhibit, in any satisfactory degree, the spirit of Jesus Christ, in the meekness, humility, benevolence, and self-denial of their character. There is much reason to suspect that in the religion of many who now enter the church under a momentary excitement, Christ has no place. They speak nothing of the spiritual glory of the Mediator, in the account which they give of their experience. Their exercises would seem to have as little relation to the distinguishing doctrines of Christianity, as to those of the Qur'an. Of what account is it that multitudes cry, 'Lord, Lord', and yet do not evince, that they are truly born of God? Their zeal, their bustling activity and their flaming profession of attachment to the cause of Christ, will answer no purpose, while they indulge a self-sufficient, self-righteous, censorious, and turbulent spirit. Between the fervour of fanaticism, and the glow of holy benevolence, the difference is immense. The one is the wild-fire which consumes and desolates the church of God; the other is like the hallowed flame on the altar of God, which causes a sweet odour to ascend to heaven, with all the sacrifices which are offered.

In these memoirs, we have, also, a fuller and more particular description of the conflict between light and darkness, faith and unbelief, sin and holiness, than can readily be met with elsewhere. Many sincere believers have sad experience of the power of atheism, and the buffetings of Satan, and they often meet with but little sympathy or relief, from books or preachers. In consequence they are tempted to think that their case is altogether peculiar, and are ready to sink into hopeless discouragement; believing, that their 'spot is not the spot of God's children'; but fearing, lest these temptations and conflicts are the mark of his reprobation. Let such take comfort when they here read, what dreadful conflicts with unbelief, pride, and atheism, were endured by this distinguished servant of Jesus Christ.

There are two kinds of knowledge displayed, in a remarkable degree, in this book: the one is the knowledge of the Holy Scriptures, in their application to the various conditions and exigencies of believers; the other, an extraordinary insight into the deceitful windings, doublings, and complicated foldings, of the human heart. I see not how anyone who is sincerely desirous of knowing what he is, and what the Word of God requires him to be, can rise from the perusal of this little volume, without real and sensible benefit. There is a penetrating power in the words of a man who believes, in good earnest, all that the Word of God relates, and speaks the sentiments of his inmost soul.

The circumstances attending the death of this distinguished man, are such as to attract the attention of every reader. His dying words were faithfully recorded at the time, and they serve to show, in the clearest manner, the power of the gospel, to inspire with confidence, the soul of the believer, in the last conflict. The triumphs of faith, in this case, were signal and glorious. Through all his sickness, his reason remained undisturbed. In the whole scene there seemed to be less than usual of an excited imagination; but the realities of the eternal world, were contemplated soberly, by a steady faith. When first seized, his evidences were clouded, and his conflict with his spiritual enemies, tremendous; but in a short time, the storm passed over, the clouds were dissipated, and the clear sunshine of divine favour dawned upon his soul. From that time, he enjoyed uninterrupted peace, and unwavering assurance, until he fell asleep in Jesus. I do not know that I have ever read a narrative of the last moments of any saint, which were to my mind more satisfactory; or of any death which was more in accordance with the exceeding great and precious promises of God. I have read of exercises of a more ecstatic and rapturous kind, but never of any, where the comfort and confidence of the person, seemed to depend more entirely on the simple, sober exercise of faith. Who will not exclaim upon perusing this narrative, 'Let me die the death of the righteous, and let my last end be like his!'

As in the original *Memoirs of Mr Halyburton,* there are many Scoticisms; many obsolete expressions; and frequently, such a confused collocation of words, as to render the sense obscure, it has been judged expedient, to make such alterations in the style, as would remove these blemishes, without the least addition to the sentiment, or the least diminution from the ideas of the author. Indeed, the author's own words have been invariably retained, even when quaint and antiquated, if the sense was perspicuous. We like to see an old author in the dress and fashion of his own times, rather than decked in the finery of the moderns. It was also found that the reader was rather obstructed than aided by the numerical subdivisions, which so much abound in the work; these therefore have been mostly omitted as also the references to chapter and verse of Scripture; especially, where the passage is not cited. These alterations have been made with care and diligence, by a young gentleman, a student in the theological seminary, who has been at the pains of re-writing the whole book; and has thus prepared the work to be read with ease and pleasure, buy those to whom the Scottish idiom and dialect are obscure and harsh. If this effort should prove successful, he will probably undertake to perform a similar service for 'Halyburton's Great Concern'. Having derived benefit myself from the work now presented to the public, I feel it to be a duty to recommend it to others; and especially, to all young ministers of the gospel, and to all candidates for the holy ministry. Let our young theologians be such as Halyburton was, and error will hide its head as ashamed; and genuine piety will be inculcated and exemplified. That the blessing of God may accompany the reading of this little volume, to all into whose hands it may come, is the sincere prayer of

A. ALEXANDER
Princeton, NJ,
May 1833.

ON THE NATURE OF VITAL PIETY[1]

On the nature of vital piety; —its sameness in all ages and countries— and its various aspects in different circumstances.

TRUE religion not only enlightens the understanding, but rectifies the affections of the heart. All genuine feelings of piety are the effects of divine truth. The variety and intensity of these feelings depend on the different kinds of truth, and the various aspects in which the same truth is viewed; and also, on the distinctness and clearness with which it is presented to the mind. In a state of moral perfection, truth would uniformly produce all those emotions and affections which correspond with its nature, without the aid of any superadded influence. That these effects are not experienced by all who have the opportunity of knowing the truth, is a strong evidence of human depravity. In a state of moral depravity, the mind is incapable alike, of perceiving and feeling the beauty and excellence of divine truth. The dead neither see nor feel, and man is by nature 'dead in trespasses and sins'. Hence the necessity of the agency of the Holy Spirit to illuminate and regenerate the mind. The nature of divine agency, in every case, is inscrutable by mortals. 'The wind bloweth where it listeth, and thou hearest the sound thereof, but canst not tell whence it cometh, or whither it goeth: so is every one that is born of the Spirit.' We know, however, that the work of the Spirit, in the regeneration of the heart, is adapted to the rational nature of man. The thing to be accomplished is not the creation of some new faculty; it is a moral renovation; and all moral changes must be effected by understanding and choice. To put the soul, therefore, in that state

[1] Archibald Alexander, 'An Introductory Essay', *Advice to a Young Christian, on the Importance of Aiming at an Elevated Standard of Piety.* By a Village Pastor (New York: G. & C. & H. Carvill, 1831), pp. 5-32.

in which it will rightly understand the truth, and cordially choose the highest good, is the end of regeneration. Truth, therefore, must be the means by which actual conversion to God takes place. 'Being born again, not of corruptible seed, but of incorruptible, by the word of God, which liveth and abideth for ever.' 'Of his own will begat he us with the word of truth.' 'Sanctify them through thy truth: thy word is truth.' Although piety in the heart is the effect of a divine operation, yet all its exercises take place agreeably to the common laws of our rational nature. The understanding is enlightened, the judgment is convinced, motives operate on the will, and conscience approves or disapproves. That the soul, in the exercises of piety, is under the renovating influences of the Holy Spirit, is not known by any consciousness which it has of these divine operations, but by the effects produced in a change of views and feelings; and this change is ascribed to God, because no other is able to produce it; and his Word assures us that he is its author.

Now, as all men are endowed with the same natural susceptibilities, and as all Christians contemplate the same fundamental truths, the work of grace in the hearts of all, must be substantially the same. All have, by the knowledge of the law, been convinced of sin; have been made to feel sorrow, shame, and compunction, upon the recollection of their transgressions; and to submit to the justice of the sentence of condemnation, which the law denounces against them. All have been made sensible of their own inability to save themselves, and under the influence of these humbling and penitent feelings, have been led to seek refuge in Jesus Christ, as the only hope of their souls. This plan of salvation appears glorious and suitable to all believers; so that they not only acquiesce in it, as the only method of salvation, but they are so well pleased with it, that they would not have another if they could. And, in the acceptance of Christ as a complete Saviour, there is, in every case, some experience of joy and peace. Connected with the views which the true believer has of Christ as a Saviour, there is also a discovery, more or less clear, of the glory of the divine attributes, especially of those which are most conspicuously manifested in the cross of Christ. Holiness, justice, mercy, and truth, shine, in the view of the sincere convert, with a lustre surpassing all other excellence; and God is venerated and loved for his own intrinsic excellence, as well all for the rich benefits bestowed upon us. But, although these views may be distinguished, yet in experience, they are not separated. The brightest discovery of divine excellence ever made, is God's love to our miserable race. The law of God is also viewed to be holy, just, and good, by every regenerated soul. The unrenewed heart never is, nor ever can be, reconciled to the law; 'it is not subject to it, nor indeed can be', but the 'new man' delights in the law of God, and would not have one precept of it altered; and while it condemns all his feelings and works as imperfect, he approves of it still, and blames himself for his want of conformity to a rule so perfect.

Another thing in which the experience of all Christians is uniform, is that they all are brought to a deliberate purpose to be on the Lord's side. On this point there is no hesitancy. Many are affected, and much agitated with religious impressions, and yet never come to a full decision to choose God and his service. They halt between two opinions, and have a divided mind. Such persons, however lively their feelings, are not yet truly converted: all true converts, after counting the cost, have settled this point for ever. And they can say with the psalmist, 'My heart is fixed, O God, my heart is fixed.' They are, therefore, prepared now to comply with the terms of discipleship laid down by Christ himself. They are willing to 'deny themselves, to take up their cross, and follow him; to forsake father and mother, wife and children, houses and lands, yea also their own lives, for the sake of him, who gave himself for them.'

Out of such views and feelings as have been described, arises, an ardent hungering and thirsting after righteousness, an intense desire to know more of God, and to be admitted into closer union and more intimate communion with him. These habitual desires of the renewed soul, find their proper expression in prayer, and lead to a patient and earnest waiting upon God in all the ordinances and means of his appointment. True piety, however, does not stop in mere desires, or in attendance on religions duties; it seeks to glorify God by action. The earnest inquiry of every soul, inspired with the love of God, is, 'Lord, what wouldst thou have me to do?' And wherever there is piety towards God, there will exist benevolence towards men. One of the most sensible emotions of the young convert is, 'goodwill to men'; a sincere desire of the welfare and eternal salvation of all, not even excepting its most inveterate enemies. And towards the children of God, there springs up a strong and tender affection. Such seem to be brethren indeed, because they are the brethren of Christ, and bear something of his image, in the humility, meekness, and benevolence of their character. In short, genuine piety disposes and determines all who are its subjects, to obey and respect all the commandments of God, and to hate and avoid all sin, according to that declaration of David, 'I esteem all thy precepts concerning all things to be right, and hate every false way.'

In all the above-mentioned essential characteristics of piety, there is a perfect sameness in the exercises of all true Christians. The same impression has been made on every renewed heart, and the only difference is, that it is imprinted more deeply on some, than others; but, still, the characters are identical; and, therefore, the evidences of a work of grace, contained in the Holy Scriptures, are equally applicable to all persons who have been brought from darkness to light. There often is, moreover, a striking resemblance in those accompanying exercises and circumstances, which are not essential. Awakened sinners are liable to the same erroneous conceptions, and usually fall into the same mistakes. They are all prone to think, that by reforming their lives they can restore themselves to the favour of God. They commonly apply to the works of the law for relief, in the first instance; and when driven from this false refuge, by a clearer view of the spirituality and extent of the law, and the depth of their own depravity, they are apt to give up all for lost, and seriously to conclude that there is no hope in their case. They are all prone to misapprehend the nature of the gospel: of its freeness they can at first form no conception; and, therefore, they think it necessary to come with some price in their hands—to obtain some kind of preparation or fitness, before they venture to come to Christ. And when it is clear that no moral fitness can be obtained, until they apply to him, this legal spirit will lead the soul under conviction to think, that very deep and pungent distress will recommend it to Christ; and thus many are found seeking, and praying for a more deep and alarming impression of their sin and danger. It is, also very common to place undue dependence on particular means; especially on such as have been much blessed to others. Anxious souls are prone to think, that in reading some particular book, or in hearing some successful preacher, they will receive the grace of God which bringeth salvation; in which expectation they are always disappointed, and are brought at last to feel that they are entirely dependent on sovereign grace; and that they can do nothing to obtain that grace. Before, they were like a drowning man catching at every thing that seemed to promise support; but now, they are like a man who feels that he has no support, but is actually sinking. Their cry, therefore, is, now truly a cry for *mercy*. 'God be merciful to me a sinner!' 'Lord save, I perish!' And, it has often been proverbially said, 'man's extremity is God's opportunity', which is commonly realized by the soul cut off from all dependence on itself—the arm of the Lord is stretched forth to preserve it from sinking; the Saviour's voice of love and mercy is heard; light breaks in upon the soul, and it finds itself embraced in the arms of the Saviour; and so wonderful is the transition, that it can scarcely trust to its own experience.

This similarity of feelings in the experience of the pious has often been remarked; and has been justly considered a strong evidence of the divine origin of experimental religion: for how, otherwise, can this uniformity of the views and feelings of the pious, in all ages and countries, be accounted for? Enthusiasm assumes a thousand different shapes and hues, and is marked by no uniform characteristics; but scriptural piety is the same now, as in the days of David and Asaph; the same, as when Paul lived; the same, as experienced by the pious Fathers of the Christian church; the same, as described by the Reformers, by the Puritans, and by the evangelical preachers and writers of the present day. When the gospel takes effect on any of the heathen, although it is certain that they never had the opportunity of learning anything of this kind from others, yet we find them expressing the same feelings which are common to other Christians. Persons from different quarters of the globe, whose vernacular tongue is entirely different, yet speak the same language in religion. Members of churches, which hold no communion; and which, perhaps, view each other, when at a distance, as heretics, often, when brought together, recognize in one another dear brethren, who are of one mind in their religious experience.

The late eminently pious and learned theologian, the Rev. Dr Livingston, related to me, not many years before his decease, a pleasant anecdote, which will serve to illustrate the point under consideration; and which I communicate to the public the more willingly, because I do not know that he has left any record of it behind him. While a student at the University of Utrecht, a number of pious persons, from the town and from among the students, were accustomed to meet for free conversation on experimental religion, and for prayer and praise, in a social capacity. On one of these occasions, when the similarity of the exercises of the pious, in all countries and ages, was the subject of conversation, it was remarked by one of the company, that there was then present, a representative from each of the four quarters of the world. These were Dr Livingston from America, a young man from the Cape of Good Hope in Africa, another student from one of the Dutch possessions in the East Indies, and many natives of Europe of course. It was therefore proposed, that at the next meeting, the three young gentlemen first referred to, together with an eminently pious young nobleman of Holland, should each give a particular narrative of the rise and progress of the work of grace in his own soul. The proposal was universally acceptable; and accordingly, a narrative was heard from a native of each of the four quarters of the globe—of their views and feelings, of their trials and temptations, *etc*. The result was highly gratifying to all present; and I think Dr Livingston said, that it was generally admitted by those present, that they had never before witnessed so interesting a scene. And since I have taken the liberty of mentioning the name of that venerable and distinguished theologian, I beg leave to add, that I have never seen a man who appeared to love vital piety more, or to understand its nature better.

But the identity of religious feeling which has been described above, is consistent with a great variety in many of the accompanying circumstances. Indeed, it seems probable, that each individual Christian has something distinctly characteristic in his own case; so that there exists, at least, as much difference in the peculiar features of the inner as of the outward man. The cause of this diversity are manifold; as first, the different degrees of grace received, in the commencement of the divine life; secondly, the extent to which they have respectively run in sin, and the suddenness, or gradual nature of their change;

thirdly, the degree of religious knowledge which is possessed; and finally, no small diversity arises from the various constitutional temperaments of different persons, which must have a powerful effect in giving complexion to the exercises of religion. To all which may be added, the manner in which persons under religious impressions are treated by their spiritual guides; and especially the manner in which the gospel is preached to them.

It has been remarked by men of exact observation, that particular revivals of religion are often marked by something peculiar in the exercises, and in the spirit of those who are the subjects of them. In some revivals, convictions are more pungent and awful, or continued for a longer time, than in others; and the converted, in some revivals, appear to acquire a much deeper and more abiding impression of the reality and glory of divine things, and are evidently more under the constraining influence of the love of Christ, than is observable in other cases. These are subjects which deserve a careful investigation; and as revivals are increasing in frequency and extent in our churches; and as different modes of conducting them are in use, it is highly important, that some man of deep experience, and sober, impartial judgment, should make observations extensively, and communicate them to the religious public; which is, in many places, perplexed and distracted, with the different methods of treatment recommended by different persons, and different parties. It may, however, be laid down as a sound maxim, that in proportion as the truth of God is clearly brought to view, and faithfully applied to the heart and conscience the good effects will be manifest. Erroneous opinions, although mingled with the essential truths of the gospel, will ever tend to mar the work or God. The good produced on any individual, or on a society, must not be judged of by the violence of the feelings excited, but by their character. Men may be consumed by a fiery zeal, and yet exhibit little of the meekness, humility, and sweet benevolence of Jesus. Great pretenders and high professors may be proud, arrogant, and censorious. When these are the effects, we may, without fear, declare, 'that they know not what manner of spirit they are of'. Any religion, however corrupt, may have its zealots; but true Christianity consists in the fruits of the Spirit, which are 'love, joy, peace, long suffering, gentleness, goodness, faith, meekness, temperance'.

Piety seems also to assume an aspect somewhat different, in different ages and periods of the church. There is in human nature a strong tendency to run to extremes; and from one extreme, immediately to the opposite. And as the imperfections of our nature mingle with everything which we touch, so piety itself is not exempt from the influence of the tendency above mentioned. In one age, or in one religious community, the leaning is to enthusiasm; in another, to superstition. At one time, religion is made to assume a severe and gloomy aspect; the conscience is morbidly scrupulous; things indifferent are viewed as sins; and human infirmities are magnified into crimes. At such times, all cheerfulness is proscribed; and the Christian whom nature prompts to smile, feels a check from the monitor within. This alloy of genuine piety is also often connected with bigotry and censoriousness. Now, when true religion is disfigured by such defects, it appears before the world to great disadvantage. Men of the world form their opinions of the nature of piety, from what they observe in its professors; and from such an exhibition of it as we have described, they often take up prejudices, which are never removed. There is, however, an opposite extreme, not less dangerous and injurious than this—when professors of religion conform to the world, so far that no clear distinction can be observed between the Christian and the worldling. If the former error drives men away from religion, as a sour and miserable thing, this leads them to the opinion, that Christians are, actuated by the same principles as they are; and therefore they conclude that no great change of their character is necessary. It is sometimes alleged by professors who thus accommodate themselves to the fashions and amusements of the world, that they hope by this means to render religion attractive, and thus gain over to piety those who neglect it; but this is a weak pretext, for such conformity always tends to confirm people in their carelessness. When they see professors at the theatre, or figuring in the ballroom, their conclusion either is, that there is no reality in vital piety, or that these professors act inconsistently.

The religious habits of some serious professors of religion, are adapted to make a very unfavourable impression on the minds of sensible men. They assume a demure and sanctimonious air, and speak in an affected and drawling tone; often sighing, and lifting up their eyes, and giving audible utterance to their ejaculations. Now these persons may be, and, I doubt not, often are, truly pious; but the impression made on most minds, by this affectation of religious solemnity, is, that they are hypocrites, who aim at being thought uncommonly devout. It appears to me, that religion never appears so lovely, as when she wears the dress of perfect simplicity. We ought not, indeed, to be ashamed of our religion, before the world; but it behooves us to be very careful, not to give to others an unfavourable opinion of serious piety. The rule is, 'Let your light *so* shine that others seeing your good works may glorify your Father, who is in heaven.' 'Let not your good be evil spoken of.'

But the aspect and character of the piety of one age; may differ from that of another, more from the peculiar circumstances in which Christians are placed, than from the prevalence of erroneous views or incorrect habits. In one age, vital piety seeks retirement, and runs in hidden channels. At such a time, the attention of Christians is turned chiefly on themselves. Much time is devoted to devotional exercises; often whole days. The secret recesses of the heart are explored with diligence and rigour; indwelling sin is detected in its multiform appearances, and is mortified with invincible resolution; the various means of personal growth in grace are studied, and used with persevering assiduity; and much useful knowledge of the nature of the spiritual life in the soul is acquired. But while vital piety is thus carefully cultivated, and the attention is earnestly turned to the exercises of the heart, there may be very little display of active, enlarged benevolence; there may be few vigorous efforts made to meliorate the condition of the multitudes perishing in sin. Under the influence of these defective views of the nature of religion, many pious persons, in the early ages of Christianity, withdrew entirely from the world, and lived in the wilderness; which mistake occasioned innumerable evils to the church, the effects of which are not yet obliterated.

The spirit of piety among the Reformers, seems to have been pure and vigorous, but not as expansive as it might have been. They seem scarcely to have thought of the hundreds of millions of heathen in the world; and of course, made no efforts to extend the knowledge of salvation to them. Indeed, they were so much occupied at home, in contending for the faith against the Romanists, that they had little time left for benevolent enterprises at a distance; but if that zeal which was worse than wasted in controversy with one another, had been directed to the conversion of the heathen, their usefulness would have been far greater than it was.

The Puritans also, although profoundly acquainted with experimental religion, seemed to have confined their attention too exclusively to themselves. Their ministers were, it is true, silenced, and driven into corners and into exile, by an ungrateful and tyrannical government; but it seems wonderful to us, that when prevented from preaching the gospel to their own countrymen, they did not turn to the Gentiles. But the era of mission had not yet arrived, and probably they had but small opportunity, in their persecuted state, of uniting their counsels or combining their energies in schemes of distant benevolence. One thing, however, is now manifest, that the providence of God overruled the retirement and leisure of those godly ministers, who were ejected from their charges, so as to render their labours more useful to the church, than if they had been permitted to spend their lives in preaching the gospel; for, when deprived of the liberty of employing their tongues, they betook themselves to their pens, and they have left to the church such a body of practical and casuistical theology, as all ages before or since, cannot equal. I have no doubt, that such men as Owen, Baxter, Flavel, Bunyan, Goodwin, Manton, Howe, and Bates, have effected much more good by their practical writings, than they could possibly have done by their preaching, supposing them to have been ever so successful.

But our lot is cast in a different age, and in a different state of the church. After a long slumber, the attention of Christians has been aroused to consider the perishing condition of the heathen. We live in a period when great designs are entertained, and plans formed for the conversion of the whole world,—when one benevolent enterprise or institution follows another in rapid succession, until the Christian community begins to exhibit an entirely new aspect, from what it did within our own remembrance. Christians have begun to feel, that by a combination of effort, they have power to accomplish much. The public attention is kept awake by the frequent recurrence of public meetings of an interesting kind, and by that more potent engine, the wide circulation of religious periodicals, by which interesting intelligence is conveyed to almost every corner of our extensive country. The duty of Christians to be active is now inculcated, in almost every form; tracts are multiplied; the Scriptures are circulated; the young and ignorant are instructed, by new methods; and many are found running to and fro to promote the propagation of evangelical truth. Revivals of religion also are exerting a mighty influence on the church. The number of serious Christians is vastly increased; and many youth are brought forward to a course of preparation for the gospel ministry. A spirit of liberality also is witnessed, unknown to our fathers; and the duty of consecrating to the Lord a reasonable proportion of all their increase, is beginning to be extensively felt among serious Christians. And such is the spirit of enterprise, that no undertaking appears too arduous, which has for its object the advancement of the Redeemer's kingdom: and such is the favour of heaven towards benevolent enterprises in our day, that scarcely one has failed of accomplishing some good; and although the schemes of benevolence are so various and so multiplied, yet there has occurred no sensible interference of one with another. As they all aim at the same object, so they are all viewed as parts of the same great system of operations. Now, in all these favourable appearances and benevolent exertions, every pious heart must and will rejoice.

But is there no danger, that many who feel interested in the operations of the day, and contribute to their advancement, should be mistaken as to their true spiritual condition? When a powerful current takes a set, many will be carried along with it, whichever way it may run. And is there no danger that Christians themselves, while they seem to flourish in external profession, zeal and activity, may be decaying at the root, for want of sufficient attention to their own hearts, and to the duties or the closet? There is indeed much reason to fear that many professors now exist, who confine their religion too much to those external acts, which may be performed from motives no higher than those which operate on unrenewed men. The danger now is, that the religion of the heart will be neglected, and that many will feel well satisfied with themselves, on account of their activity and zeal, who are yet strangers to a work of grace. This being the point on which Christians of the present day are liable to err, it is a matter of congratulation, that some writers seem disposed to turn the attention of the Christian public, to the importance of diligence and punctuality in performing the duties of the closet. The following letters are well calculated to produce this effect. They were forwarded to me by an esteemed young clergyman, who is settled as a pastor in a distant and retired village. They were addressed, as the author has stated in his preface, to a young lady of highly respectable connections, upon the occasion of her making a public profession of religion. The father of this young lady, who is distinguished for his benevolence and evangelical piety, was unwilling that the pious and judicious counsels and affectionate exhortations which they contain should be limited to an individual, since they are so well adapted to be useful to Christians generally; and especially to the young, placed in circumstances similar to those of the person to whom they were originally addressed. A request was, therefore, made for their publication. The author through modesty has withheld his name, but has requested me to introduce them to the public with some preliminary essay of my own; with which request I have here complied, believing that the letters of my young friend are seasonable, judicious, and pious, and that as they are written in an ornate and animated style, they will be extensively perused by the young.

EVIDENCES OF A NEW HEART[1]

MAN was, in the beginning, created in the image of God, which consisted in 'knowledge, righteousness, and true holiness'. By the fall, the human race have lost that crown of glory with which the first man was adorned, and have become corrupt and blind.

The chief end of the gospel is to restore man to holiness, and thus to make him happy. To bring about this, much was requisite. Sin must be atoned for, and a new creation must take place. The first of these ends was effected by the one offering of Jesus Christ, as a lamb to take away the sins of the world. The great work is finished, and there remaineth no place for any other sacrifices; the way into the most holy is now laid open; that is, a door is opened by which believers, who are sprinkled with the blood of Christ, can enter into the highest heavens. But the restoration of the image of God by the new creation, is a work which is carried on from age to age, upon all who become heirs of salvation; and is now carried on by the conversion of sinners through the preaching of the Word of Life.

If man were made perfectly holy by his regeneration, there would be no difficulty in knowing certainly, when this good work had been wrought; or if there were no counterfeits of piety, or if the heart of the renewed was not still in a measure deceitful, it would be easy for the children of God to arrive at a satisfactory assurance, that they had passed from death unto life; and there would remain no ground on which the unconverted could persuade themselves that they had been the subjects of this change. But still, although difficulties stand in the way of complete assurance, and many deceive themselves with the name, the form, and the counterfeits

[1] Archibald Alexander, 'Evidences of a New Heart', *Biblical Repertory and Theological Review*, Vol. 6 No. 3 (July 1834), pp. 353-65.

of piety; yet there are marks of regeneration so plainly laid down in Scripture, and presented in so many aspects, that the honest and diligent inquirer will not be disappointed in obtaining such a degree of comfortable evidence of the favour of God towards him, as will be of more value than all the treasures of this world. And the hypocrite, or formalist, may, by the application of Scripture marks, determine, that he is still 'in the gall of bitterness and in the bonds of iniquity'. It may be stated as a truth, that if the truly pious remain in distressing doubt respecting their spiritual state, it is owing to some want of diligence in searching their own hearts, and comparing them with the Word of God; to some erroneous opinions which they have imbibed; to some melancholy humour in their constitution; or, they are fallen into some woeful declension, or they have been overcome by some powerful temptation which has produced a sense of guilt in the conscience, and spread darkness through the whole soul. And on the other hand, there is no unregenerate man, however amiable, moral, and benevolent he may be, who does not constantly carry about with him clear, legible marks of his being in an unconverted state. All that is wanting to bring conviction to his mind, is a conscientious application of the Word of God to his heart. Every deceived soul is, therefore, its own deceiver. No man with the Scriptures in his hands, is under any necessity of remaining in error, on this all-important subject.

From what has been said, it is obvious, that it is a very useful and necessary thing to understand what the Scriptures teach on this point. And as some aid may be afforded to the ignorant, to the doubting, and to all who are not familiar with their Bibles, by drawing out, and clearly setting forth the testimonies of the Word of God, in regard to this matter, we have attempted to render some assistance in this way, in the essay which is here presented to our readers, and to which their candid and earnest attention is requested.

On this subject, so vital to our best interests, we shall not indulge in speculation, nor even lay any stress on human reasoning, but endeavour clearly to exhibit what the Scriptures teach, with all simplicity; and as a systematic method can be of no service in this case, we shall not resort to it in communicating the truths which we wish to address to the reader.

We have already observed, that the new creation is intended to restore to the human soul, the lost image of God. We now remark, that the holy law of God furnishes the most correct standard, by which to judge of the reality of this renewal of the mind. The law is the perfect measure of the creature's duty. Conformity to the law is the exact image of God; for the law is a transcript of his moral attributes. Now conformity to the law consists, in 'loving God with all the soul, and heart, and mind, and strength, and our neighbour as ourselves'. If then, our hearts have been brought to love God and our neighbour, we have been renewed in the spirit of our minds; for, in our carnal, which is our natural state,—'the heart is enmity against God and not subject to his law'. But, lest any, who are not renewed should persuade themselves that they possess this characteristic, let us mention some of the prophecies and evidences of the love of God.

1. *It must be sincere and genuine love,* felt in the heart, and not a mere animal commotion, or a mere profession of the lips. Sincere love stands opposed, both to that which is pretended, and to that which is spurious. It is easy to say with the mouth, 'I love God', but our love must not be *in word,* but *in deed,* and *in truth.* Our love must be a real emotion of the heart, and not a dissembled affection.

But it must also be genuine. A man may call any feeling by the name of love. He may experience a feeling of exhilaration diffused through his frame, he knows not how; and knowing that he did not produce it by any voluntary effort of his own; and, observing, that it came on him suddenly after much distress; and that it causes him to feel happy, he may call it, *the love of God,* when it may be nothing more than a flash of joy, produced by some physical change in the animal frame, especially in the nerves. We know that there are natural causes which will produce such effects. Or it may be nothing more than an exercise of self-love, arising from some persuasion that the danger which he supposed to be hanging over him, has passed away. As if a man under conviction of sin should imagine, that he heard a voice saying, 'thy sins are forgiven thee', or should have a text of Scripture of similar import, to occur to his mind, he may be led, without examination, to think that he is a converted man; and may feel a joy proportioned to his former sense of danger, or desire of happiness. Now, we do not deny that something like this may accompany a sound conversion, yet it is manifest that all that has been mentioned may be experienced without any change of heart—it may be nothing but nervous exhilaration, or the gratification of self-love, neither of which surely are evidences of piety. And, O, that they who are the guides of immortal souls would duly consider this, and not become accessory to the delusion of multitudes!

2. *Love to God must be founded on a just view of his character, as revealed in the Scriptures.* It must be love to God, not only as good to all, but as just and holy; we must love God as sin-avenging, as well as sin-pardoning. What we mean is, that the object of our esteem and love must be the whole character of God, as he has revealed himself to us in his Word. If we have true love to God, we shall rejoice that such a being exists, and that he is what he is; we shall delight to meditate on all his perfections; the awful as well as the amiable. Now, this is only saying, that our love must be fixed on the true and living God, and not on an idol; for is it not most manifest, that if we love him not in his true character, however strong our affection, it is directed to another being—to an idol of our own imagination; and it matters not whether our idols be material or spiritual.

3. *Our love to God must be the predominant affection of our hearts.* Whether it is possible to exercise love to God in any degree, while other affections have the ascendency, it is not necessary to inquire; for the Scriptures are most express in declaring, that no other love but that which is supreme, and prevails over every conflicting passion, will be of any avail. 'He that loveth father or mother more than me', says Jesus, 'and he that loveth son or daughter more than me, is not worthy of me.' And the same thing is expressed in the strongest possible manner, in another place. 'If any man come unto me and hate not his father and mother, and wife, and children, and brethren, and sisters, yea, and his own life also, he cannot be my disciple.' The young man who came to Christ was put to this test, which, with all his amiable qualities and high professions, he was unable to endure. And Christ recognizes the same principle in his solemn interrogation addressed to Peter: 'Simon, son of Jonas, lovest thou me more than these?' Indeed, if this were not the fact, the love of God would not form and mould the character and govern the life of Christ's disciples; for every one knows that the strongest affection does always govern.

This is a test to which all must come; and if we are found wanting, when tried by this touchstone, our hearts are still unrenewed—the heart of stone remains, with all its hardness.

4. Again, *true love is constant.* The soul may be agitated by feelings which are attended with much greater commotion, and which may be accompanied with more ecstatic joy, but these are transient; like the morning cloud and early dew, they pass away. But the love of God in a renewed heart, takes root and abides. Temporary faith is not distinguished from that which is saving, by the liveliness of the feelings or the fair external appearance, for the seed which fell on the stony ground grew up as quickly and flourished, for a while, as luxuriantly as that on good ground. Its defect was want of root, and therefore it soon withered away. In revivals of religion it has often occurred, that some of those who seemed to feel the most, and who attracted most attention, after a while, decline and turn back. It is he that persevereth to the end, that shall be saved. We lay it down, therefore, as one property of true religion, that it is permanent. But this constancy of love is not at all inconsistent with great vicissitudes of feeling, and frequent fluctuation of frames. When the soul mourns an absent God, love is not extinct; nor its evidence obscure; true love discovers itself as manifestly, by uneasiness, on account of the absence of a beloved object, as by joy at his presence. When many seem to begin well, and to run well in the way which leads to Zion, be not too sanguine of the event. Many blossoms drop and produce no fruit, but where the heart is really renewed, there it will appear by a steady continuance, and gradual progress in piety. They, therefore, who have been long travelling on the pilgrimage to the new Jerusalem, have much better evidence of piety, other things being equal, than they who are just setting out.

5. *Genuine love to God inspires the soul with a desire to please God.* This is the nature of love, that it desires a return of affection from the person beloved. This leads to the use of every means to please that person. On this principle is founded the injunction of Christ, 'If ye love me keep my commandments'; and the declaration, 'He that hath my commandments and keepeth them, he it is that loveth me.' Now what would seem to be easier than to know, whether, indeed, we were habitually desirous of pleasing God, by keeping his commandments?

If we truly love God, this desire will have more influence over our conduct than any other.

6. *But love to God also produces a fear of offending him.* The pious man is characterized by being in the fear of the Lord, all the day long. He feareth always, not with a slavish dread, but with a holy reverence. He fears to give offence. And when he is convinced that he has in any way done what he habitually wishes to avoid, it is to him a subject of unfeigned grief. He mourns in secret places, and obtains the blessing which Christ has promised to Zion's mourners. He sorrows after a godly sort, and finds in his own experience that godly sorrow is efficacious to work repentance unto life, or a change of mind which is connected with eternal life.

7. *The desire of communion with God, and joy in his presence,* are strong evidences of love to God. The ardour of this desire for the sensible and comfortable presence of God is various. Sometimes it is exceedingly great, so that it is expressed, by the panting of the heart after water-brooks—by longing, thirsting, and even fainting. But when there is *a new heart,* it will give indication of its heavenly origin by pointing its desires towards God. How can that soul be renewed, which is unconscious of all such desires? Yea, that does not feel them daily? We might discourage and distress the timid Christian, by laying down the sensible enjoyment of communion with God as an inseparable attendant on piety (and we must not break the bruised reed, nor quench the smoking flax), but certainly, we must insist on *the desire, the habitual desire* of such communion, as an evidence of piety, which all must be conscious of, except those who are fallen asleep, or gone far back in the way of declension. And whatever may be the real condition of these backsliders in the sight of God, there are no evidences of piety applicable to them while they remain in that state.

We need say nothing about the joy experienced from the sensible manifestation of God's presence, and from the light of his countenance lifted up on the soul; for there our aid is not needed, for the soul enjoys already a blessed assurance of the divine favour, and is not only conscious of loving God, but feels the love of God shed abroad in the heart, and can say in the language of the spouse, 'My beloved is mine and I am his.'

8. The last particular which we shall mention is, *the fixed purpose and ardent desire to glorify God.* Love identifies the honour and interest of the person beloved with our own. It is even possible that we should love another with an affection so strong, that in our zeal for his honour we almost forget ourselves. Such a strength and fidelity of attachment has been observed in inferiors towards their superiors. But if even there is room for such a sacrifice, and a reasonableness in it; it is when God, our Creator, Benefactor, and Redeemer is the object of our love. This love to Christ has, indeed, a constraining power. It makes us willing to be anything, or suffer anything, that God may be glorified in us, and by us, living and dying.

The desire to glorify God then, with our bodies and spirits, which are his, which he hath bought with a price, is the best evidence of love to God; and consequently the best evidence of a new heart. If there be a new heart without this aim at God's glory, it is not from the regeneration of the spirit. It may, like Saul's be another heart, but the love of God is not in it; and wherever the renewing spirit comes, there is love, for the fruit of the spirit is love, joy, peace, *etc.* This same heart causes us to rejoice when God is glorified, whoever may be the instrument; and to mourn when his name is dishonoured. 'Rivers of waters', says David, 'run down mine eyes because they keep not thy law.' The Lord directed the man clothed with linen, and having a writer's inkhorn, to 'set a mark on the foreheads of the men that sigh and that cry for all the abominations that be done' (*Ezek.* 9:4). That heart which thinks nothing, and cares nothing for God's glory is a base, worldly, selfish heart, and has no resemblance to the new heart of the gospel.

Christ's kingdom on earth is that in which the glory of God is more involved, than in anything within our reach. Every renewed heart loves the church, and desires, and rejoices in its advancement. Every article of intelligence which relates to the conquests of the Redeemer, the triumphs of the cross and the conversion of men is cheering to his spirits, and grateful to his heart. For this cause he is willing to labour, to suffer, and to die. Whatever of talents, of learning, of influence, of wealth, God has given him, he considers all as consecrated to the service of God. And his language is, 'Lord what wilt thou have me to do?'

There are, indeed, many nominal Christians, and many strict professors, who feel differently; who will scarcely stir a finger, or give a dollar, to promote the kingdom of Christ. But we read in the Scriptures, that while many are called, few are chosen; that but few of those who seek to enter in at the strait gate are able to find it; that many draw nigh to God with their lips while their heart is far from him. We judge no man in particular, but, lay it down as a decisive mark of a renewed heart, that the man will make God's glory the chief end of all his actions and plans; and that the advancement and prosperity of this object will be very dear to him and will greatly rejoice his heart.

Here we might finish our labour, for he who truly loves God has every other mark of piety, and undoubtedly is possessed of a new heart; but as the Scriptures present this subject under many different aspects, it will be proper to give some other views of it, that everyone may have the best opportunity of determining what his own spiritual condition is.

A sincere love of the truth, and inflexible attachment to it under all temptations to deny to abandon it, is one evidence of a new heart. The new man is born of the incorruptible seed of the Word of God, is begotten by the word of truth, and sanctified, and guided, and comforted by the truth; it is natural for him therefore to love the truth. It is the food by which he lives. It is sweet to his taste, sweeter than the honeycomb, and more desirable than fine gold. There is a sweet accordance between the truth of God, and the feelings of the new heart. His language is, O, how I love thy law! it is my meditation day and night. He that abideth in the doctrine of Christ he hath both the Father and the Son. I rejoiced greatly that I found of thy children walking in the truth. The real Christian will part with life sooner than relinquish the truth of God. If all should forsake it, yet by the help of God, will not he. This then is his characteristic.

The Apostle Paul declares, that, 'If any man be in Christ he is a new creature, old things are passed away, behold all things are become new.'

Here we may observe that this change cannot take place in a person arrived at the years of discretion, without his observation. In the *new creation* old things are passed away, and all things are become new.

Now as this complete revolution takes place in a man's own mind, of all the exercises of which he must be conscious, it is clear that he cannot have been the subject of such a new creation, without some knowledge of the fact. The renewed man may, indeed, sometimes doubt whether what he has experienced is a genuine conversion, but he cannot doubt that he has undergone a change. He cannot but remember the various impressions, convictions, conflicts, discouragements, heart-troubles; and also the light, the truth, the hopes, the sweet meltings of soul, the feelings of gratitude, love, and confidence, which have at one time or another occupied his mind. Those, therefore, who cannot look back to a great change in their views and feelings, either gradual or sudden, ought not to entertain, for a moment, the hope that they have received a new heart.

To this there is one exception. There may be some now, as in former times, who have been sanctified from their birth, or from the womb. But such cases, when they occur, will carry with them their own evidence. From childhood, from the earliest dawn of reason, such persons will manifest such a love of divine truth, such a tenderness of conscience, such a readiness to perform all known duties, such a fondness for the people and ordinances of God, such a delight in hearing of Christ and heaven, and such an exemption from the common predominant vices of children, such as lying, vanity, envy, ill will, attachment to their own interest, that the new creation, although we cannot observe its commencement, will show itself by the light, beauty, and order which surround it, and are impressed upon it. When any person, then, has now, and always has had, a heart to love God, and delight in his service, he may without scruple believe, that this good work was wrought upon him prior to his recollection. But let no one deceive himself with a vain delusive hope, who has only been preserved from gross immoralities, and has often been the subject of religious impressions from his youth up; for it may be presumed, that this is the case with the majority of those who have had the advantages of a religious education. Let everyone, then, look back with serious impartiality, and inquire what change of views and feelings he has experienced, which corresponds with the new creation, in which old things have passed away, and all things have become new.

The same apostle, in his Epistles to the Ephesians and Colossians, uses language of this sort, in relation to this change; 'And that ye put off, concerning the former conversation, the old man, which is corrupt according to the deceitful lusts; and be renewed in the spirit of your mind: And that ye put on the new man, which after God, is created in righteousness and true holiness.' 'Seeing that ye have put off the old man with his deeds, and have put on the new man, which is renewed in knowledge, after the image of him that created him.' And again, he describes those who are 'made alive' and 'saved by grace', as persons 'created in Christ Jesus unto good works'. Among the deeds of the old man, specified as those which must be put away are, lying, cherished anger, stealing, corrupt communications, bitterness, wrath, clamour, evil speaking, and all malice. Now, from these passages we learn, that the Christian has become a new man, in principle and practice; and that a reformation of life, by which he turns away from all his former vices, of whatever kind and decree they might be, is an essential thing in his character, according to the Scriptures. Those professors, therefore, who retain any of their sins, and habitually practise them, secretly or openly, have not 'put on the new man', and are not renewed 'in the spirit of their minds'. As the 'putting off the old man' is nothing else than forsaking all our former sins, of every sort, so 'putting on the new man' is acquiring the habits and exercising the graces of a holy life. These are too numerous to be here specified, the principal are faith, love, humility, charity, meekness, temperance, thankfulness, prayer, *etc.* Now let everyone who wishes to decide whether he has a new heart, turn to those passages where the fruits of the Spirit, and Christian graces are enumerated, and ask himself, as he reads each particular, does my heart produce this fruit? Let us be assured, that religion is the same now that it was in the days of the apostles. And if our religion will not bear the scrutiny of Scripture marks, it is false; and our hearts are not renewed.

Another evidence of a renewed heart, which is much insisted on by the Apostle John, and is indeed laid down by Christ himself, as a distinguishing mark of a true disciple, is love to the brethren. 'He that saith he is in the light, and hateth his brother, is in darkness even until now. He that loveth his brother abideth in the light.' 'We know that we have passed from death unto life, because we love the brethren: he that loveth not his brother abideth in death.' And Christ says, 'These things I command you, that ye love one another. Hereby shall all men know that ye are my disciples, if ye have love one to another.' Without this brotherly affection, all gifts, and all knowledge, and all sacrifices, even of all our goods, and life itself, will profit nothing.

Some think that this is so low a mark of piety, that there is danger of announcing it, lest unconverted men should be led to think well of their condition. But our wisdom is, implicitly to follow the Scriptures. If Christ and his apostles have insisted especially on this evidence of piety, we need not be afraid to depend on it as certain. But although unrenewed men may and will deceive themselves, by supposing that they possess this and other marks of piety, the children must not be deprived of their allotted food, because dogs snatch at it. The truth, however, is that there is no characteristic of piety of which carnal men are more utterly destitute than of love to the brethren. They may love them with a natural affection because they are relatives, or be pleased with them because they are amiable, or be attached to them because they do not stand in the way of their ambition; or because they receive benefits from them; they may, moreover, feel respect for the consistency of their religious character, but they have no complacency in their holy character—they feel no fervent affection for them because they are Christ's. On these accounts they are hated of the world. But the new heart cleaves to the people of God, like Ruth to Naomi, who said, 'thy people shall be my people and thy God my God'. There is among sincere Christians, a peculiarly strong, tender, and pure affection. No bond on earth is so close and sacred. They are 'taught of God to love one another' 'with a pure heart fervently'. Such is the strength of this love that he who feels it is ready to lay down his life for the brethren. This renders the communion of Christians delightful. They have the same Saviour, and being animated by the same spirit, their mutual intercourse is sweet, and they continually endeavour not to please themselves, but their brethren for their good. They 'weep with them that weep, and rejoice with them that rejoice'; and are 'kindly affectioned one to another, in honour preferring one another'. If it be said, that few possess this temper, then we must conclude, that there are few real Christians.

If brotherly love waxes cold in any church or society, most certainly true religion is at a low ebb in that society. Love of a party is a quite different thing. Brotherly love embraces with kind affection Christians of other denominations, and is exercised towards the poor and afflicted, as well as the rich and prosperous. It is attended also with good works. It does not say, 'Go, be fed and clothed', but is ready to administer to the wants of Christ's needy followers. The strongest recommendation of this grace is found in the words which Christ will address to his disciples at the last day. 'Then shall the king say to them on his right hand, Come ye blessed of my Father, inherit the kingdom prepared for you from the foundation of the world, for I was an hungered and ye gave me meat, I was thirsty and ye gave me drink; I was a stranger and ye took me in; naked and ye clothed me; I was sick, and ye visited me; I was in prison, and ye came unto me. Verily I say unto you, inasmuch as ye have done it unto one of the least of these my brethren, ye have done it unto me.'

Another characteristic of a new heart is, *trust in God and submission to his will*. 'Thy will be done' is the sincere language of the pious heart, at all times, and when heavy afflictions press on the soul, it may cry out in agony, 'If it be possible let this cup pass from me': but soon it rejoins, 'Not my will, but thine be done.' And when sore bereavements deeply wound the tenderest feelings of nature, the language of the renewed heart is, 'It is the Lord, let him do what seemeth him good.' The strokes of God's chastising rod irritate the proud, and sink others into hopeless sorrow, but they drive the pious closer to his God; for as he knows by experience that there is shelter under the wings of his mercy, he flies thither as to a safe refuge.

But that mark on which the Scriptures lay the greatest stress, is one of a general nature, which includes all others, it is *a good life*. The tree is known by its fruits. A good man, out of the good treasure of his heart, bringeth forth that which is good. In this sense a man is justified by works, for he must prove the reality of his faith by his works; for faith without works is dead. God's redeemed sons are 'zealous of good works'. 'Beloved', says the Apostle John, 'follow not that which is evil, but that which is good. He that doeth good is of God; but he that doeth evil hath not seen God. Whoso keepeth his word, in him verily is the love of God perfected.' All they that are in Christ, 'walk not after the flesh but after the spirit'. Christ says, 'If ye love me keep my commandments.' 'If ye keep my commandments ye shall abide in my love.' 'He that abideth in me and I in him, the same bringeth forth much fruit.' 'Herein is my Father glorified that ye bear much fruit, so shall ye be my disciples.'

Saul, of Tarsus, was a persecutor, and a blasphemer, and a murderer, hurried on by false zeal, but when he was on his way to Damascus, he received a new heart. And from that day and hour he was an humble, zealous, laborious, patient, and devout man. He spent his life in travelling and preaching in the midst of cruel enemies, who often scourged, beat, and imprisoned him. But his purpose never wavered, his zeal never abated, his patience and fortitude never gave way, but he went on praying for blessings on all, and sacrificing everything that men count dear, for the promotion of the gospel. Through a long life, he exhibited, in spirit, and conduct, a bright example of piety. His zeal for God's glory, his love to the Saviour, his affection for all true Christians, his benevolence to all men and tender concern for their salvation. His spirit of devotion, his indefatigable labours, his patience, his self-denial, his trust in God, and contempt of worldly honours and possessions, do all most clearly manifest a heart renewed by the grace of God. All Christians, it is true, do not come up to the standard of Paul's experience and excellence; but all truly converted persons have something of the same spirit which was in this apostle; for true religion, though it differs in degree, is every where the same in kind.

Many persons, also, in modern times, give indubitable evidence of a new heart. Their whole views and tempers are changed. The tiger becomes a lamb. The proud, vindictive, covetous, and unclean, become humble, meek, contented, pure, benevolent, and devout. The change is often so remarkable, that all around observe it, and cannot but wonder at the alteration. Such monuments of the reality and power of the grace of God are, happily, to be met with in almost every place where the gospel is faithfully preached.

It may be proper now to adduce some examples to show, how a renewed heart shows itself in the life.

A woman who had been a sinner, that is, a great sinner, having become penitent (and repentance is nothing else than receiving a new heart), felt such love to Christ that it constrained her to follow him into a house, where she knew that her presence would be detestable to the master of the house; but being filled with penitential grief for her past sins, she poured out a flood of tears on the Saviour's feet as they lay extended on the couch, and then kissed his feet and wiped them with her hair. Here was a new heart, for there was much love, and much humility and godly sorrow; and accordingly, her forgiveness was prompt and full. (See *Luke* 7.)

The publican who prayed at the same time as the Pharisee in the temple, smote upon his breast and cried, 'God be merciful to me a sinner', had a new heart, for it was an humble, penitent, and believing heart; and accordingly he went down to his house justified.

The Syro-phoenician who would take no denial of her suit, but made a new plea of every objection, discovered evidence of a new heart, for no other heart professes such faith as this, or perseveres so importunately in prayer. And the nobleman who sent for Christ, but thought himself unworthy that he should come under his roof, had a new heart, for no one unrenewed is so bowed in humility.

On the other hand, Peter, although under the power of sudden temptation, wickedly denied his Lord with curses and oaths; yet showed that he had received a new heart, for when his Master looked upon him, and he was led to think of his conduct, his heart was melted into contrition, and he went out and wept bitterly.

Mary, the sister of Lazarus, was so filled with desire of learning from Jesus, when he lodged at her house, that she omitted all attention to common business, that she might fully improve the precious privilege of hearing the instructions of her Lord: for while her more careful worldly sister was cumbered with much serving, she sat at Jesus' feet and heard his words. Mary had received a new heart, for she chose the better part which shall never be taken away from her.

Judas discovered that his heart was unrenewed because he was deliberately and habitually a thief, and for the love of money betrayed his Lord. And when convinced of his great sin, he did not repent with a godly sorrow, but with guilty despair, and went away and hanged himself. But Peter gave evidence that the root of the matter was in him, for even when he fell foully under the power of temptation, he almost instantly repented, and wept bitterly on account of his transgression.

Two thieves were crucified with Christ; one of them reviled him, but the other reproved his companion, and prayed to Jesus to remember him when he came into his kingdom. This was a prayer of faith. It proceeded from a renewed heart, and was graciously heard and fully answered. 'This day', said the dying Jesus, 'shalt thou be with me in paradise.' Was ever scene like this? One dying man prays to another, who was also in the agonies of death, for a blessing, when he should receive his kingdom, and immediately, has a promise of an immediate entrance into paradise!

THE CURE OF SOULS[1]

THERE is a striking analogy between the office of a pastor and that of a physician. They both have respect to the welfare of men; and while the one seeks to heal the diseases of the body, the other aims at restoring to health the disordered souls of men. It belongs to each, not only to cure, but to prevent diseases; and to soothe and comfort such patients as it may be found impossible to cure. As the physician cannot safely follow his profession without an accurate knowledge of the human frame, so the pastor ought to be well acquainted with the constitution of the mind, and with all its faculties, susceptibilities and passions. And as the body and mind are intimately but mysteriously united, it appertains to both these professions to be acquainted with the effects of this union in their reciprocal influence on the constituent parts of our nature; therefore the knowledge of physiology is important to both. I have often been struck with admiration at the ardour and self-denial manifested by the students of medicine, in acquiring the requisite knowledge of the anatomy of the human body, and in making themselves acquainted with the pathology of the most loathsome diseases. They learn to enter cheerfully into the wards of hospitals, alms houses, and asylums for the insane, that they may become acquainted with the symptoms of all classes of disease to which the human frame is liable; and they spare no pains in making experiments, and ascertaining the efficacy of particular remedies and modes of treatment. And I have desired to witness something of the same diligence and self-denial in candidates for the holy ministry, that they might become better qualified to deal with the moral diseases of those souls which are committed to their care. Every pastor should study to become a skilful casuist; for if he

---

[1] Archibald Alexander, 'Introduction', *Pastoral Reminiscences,* Shepard K. Kollock (New York: M. W. Dodd, 1849), pp. v-ix.

is a faithful shepherd, he will meet with a great number and variety of cases of conscience, which will call for both his tenderest compassion and spiritual skill, in the treatment. Well authenticated cases of particular diseases, and an account of the method of treatment which has proved successful, are justly held to be highly valuable, especially to the young physician; because, as yet, his own experience is too small to guide him to a judicious practice; and it is always found unsafe to trust to mere theory. And I am certain that young clergymen stand in as much need of such helps as the young physician. I have often pitied the condition of a young pastor, when he first takes upon him the care of souls, and has devolved upon him the duty of a spiritual physician to a large number of immortals; whose everlasting welfare may depend very much on the treatment which they receive from their spiritual physician. It is therefore, exceedingly important that pastors should avail themselves of every opportunity to make themselves acquainted with casuistical theology; and after conversation with experienced Christians and exercised souls, on experimental religion, there is no better means than a faithful report of cases which have actually occurred in the experience of pious and faithful pastors. On this account, I greatly approve the design of the Rev. S. K. Kollock, to publish a volume of *Pastoral Reminiscences* or a detailed account of certain interesting cases of experience which occurred, and of which he was a witness, while a pastor of a Christian church. Several of these I have had the opportunity of seeing in manuscript; and cannot but think that their publication will be attended with beneficial effects to many. With the case of the poor widow, who died so triumphant a death, I was particularly interested.

Her religion, in my judgment, was of the right kind; its chief characteristics were, strong faith, pure love, deep humility, and entire resignation to the will of God. Her pastor, at her bedside, was rather a learner than a teacher; and there is no place on earth where instruction can be more effectually obtained, than at the dying bed of such a saint. I was particularly struck with the account which she gave to her pastor, in answer to his inquiry, of the way by which she obtained and preserved that strong assurance of the favour of God, which she habitually enjoyed. It was not by poring over her past experience, but by *direct acts of faith* on the Son of God, and steady reliance on his all-sufficient righteousness.

I have also perused with much satisfaction, the narrative of the conviction and conversion of the sea captain; and with the scriptural and judicious method of the pastor in answering his objections, and opening up to him the plan of God's mercy, and exhibiting clearly before him the riches of divine grace, and the absolute freeness of the blessings of the everlasting gospel. This narrative, I am of opinion, will be very serviceable to young ministers, when called to direct anxious, inquiring souls, in the way of salvation. And as the exercises of this seaman were very similar to those of other convinced sinners, the method pursued so successfully in dealing with him, will be found well adapted to other cases.

As two of the narratives of this volume relate to seamen, it is to be hoped that it will circulate among this class of people, and be useful to many, both as containing an awful warning from the example of the 'Naval Apostate'; and great encouragement from that case of conversion which was proved to be genuine by the fruits of holiness which ensued. The theological sentiments of the author appear to me to be uniformly sound and evangelical; and I am persuaded that there is nothing in the volume which will be found offensive to any real Christian of any denomination; and I shall be disappointed if the book does not meet with a ready sale and general approbation.

Mr Kollock never manifests any ambition to say *fine things;* but his style is always plain and perspicuous, and at the same time, neat and correct.

Upon the whole, I consider this volume a real accession to our stock of religious reading; and I do cordially recommend it to the attention and careful perusal of all into whose hands it may come; and especially, to young pastors, and candidates for the ministry.

PASTORAL FIDELITY AND DILIGENCE[1]

IF any minister of modern times had a right to admonish pastors, and to prescribe to them rules to be followed in the management of their flocks, that man was Richard Baxter. For he exemplified in his own conduct everything to which he exhorted others; and his success was equal to his fidelity and diligence. The fruits of his labours at Kidderminster were very remarkable, and they were permanent; for the change produced by his ministry in the religious and moral condition of that town are not entirely worn out to this day. And we are happy in having his own account of the means used, which were attended with such signal success.

> Every Thursday evening, such of his neighbours as were desirous of it, met at his house for conversation and religious exercises; each one having liberty to propose his doubts, or to ask any questions. To those he gave suitable answers; and before they separated, it was his custom to call first upon one and then another, to lead in prayer, besides praying with them himself. This, with the singing of a psalm, was all that was done. On another evening, some younger persons met and spent two or three hours in prayer. On every Saturday evening, it was customary to meet at each other's houses, to repeat the sermon of the preceding Sabbath and to prepare for the duties of the next day. Once in a few weeks they had, on one occasion or another, a day of humiliation and prayer. Every religious woman who escaped the dangers of childbirth, kept, with a select company of her neighbours, a day of thanksgiving for God's mercy in her safe deliverance. Every week, he and his assistant took fourteen families each, for catechising and conference; the assistant going into the country, and Mr Baxter attending

---

[1] Archibald Alexander, 'Review of *Gildas Salvianus;* or, *The Reformed Pastor. By Richard Baxter.*' *Biblical Repertory and Princeton Review,* Vol. 13, No. 1 (January 1841), 11-29.

to such as were in the town. He first heard them recite the words of the Catechism, and then examined them about the sense; and lastly, urged upon them the state of mind and practice which corresponded with the truths recited. He was careful not to press them hard, when through ignorance they were unable to answer, but passed them by, and said something by way of exhortation. He spent about an hour with each family, and permitted no other persons to be present, lest through bashfulness any should be embarrassed and prevented from answering freely; or lest one should be led to speak of the ignorance and mistakes of his neighbours. Every Monday and Tuesday afternoon was spent in these family visitations; and the mornings of the same days were spent by his assistant in the same exercises.

Every first Wednesday in the month, a meeting was held for parish discipline; and every first Thursday of the month was the ministers' meeting for discipline and disputation. His public preaching met with an attentive, diligent auditory. Before he entered the ministry, God blessed his private conversation to the conversion of some who continued to be exemplary Christians. These, in the beginning of his ministry, he was wont to number as his jewels; yet, after a while, they so increased that he could not keep count. His church was commonly very full, and the hearers so increased, that it was found necessary to erect several additional galleries, for the accommodation of the people. On the Lord's day, there was no disturbance to be seen in the streets; and, as one passed along, he might hear a hundred families singing psalms, or engaged in repeating sermons. When he first came to Kidderminster, there might perhaps be found one family in a whole street who worshipped God. When he left the place, there were some whole streets in which there could not be found a single house in which the worship of God was not maintained. Even in those houses which were the worst, such as taverns and ale-houses, there were commonly found one or more who feared God and called upon his name. Such as conducted themselves scandalously were excommunicated; and of six hundred communicants, there were not twelve of whose piety he did not entertain a good hope.

Some of the poor men of the congregation competently understood the body of divinity, and were able to judge in difficult controversies; and some of them were so able in prayer, that very few ministers were equal to them in order and fulness. Abundance of them were able to pray in a very proper manner with their families or others, possessing a remarkable gift and lively utterance, which rendered it edifying to hear them, and the innocency of their lives, and the temper of their minds, were such as to call forth the praises of all who regarded the truth. The professors of religion were generally of humble mind and carriage, of meek and quiet behaviour to others, and of blameless conversation.

The account which he gives of the means made use of to produce such a blessed state of things, is also worthy the attention of every pastor. The people among whom he was settled had not been previously hardened under the preaching of the gospel. They had never before enjoyed an awakening ministry; but only a few formal, cold sermons. Baxter himself was in his vigour, and full of ardour and animation. His voice too was naturally penetrating and moving, which with common hearers is a great matter. He preached also with the feelings of a dying man; for, on account of his bodily infirmities, he had the prospect of death continually before him; for his impression at this time was, that a year or two would terminate his earthly labours.

But the circumstance which seemed to gain him the most ready access to the hearts and consciences of his people was, the impression made on their minds that he sincerely sought their good. If the people had entertained the least suspicion of the purity and benevolence of his motives; if they had supposed that he was erroneous, scandalous, or covetous, the effect of his ministry would have been small. 'A bishop must have a good report from those that are without.' He was also greatly aided by the prayers and efforts of the godly in the place. They thirsted after the salvation of their neighbours, and being dispersed all over the town, they were everywhere ready to discountenance vice and error, to justify piety, and to convince, reprove, and exhort men, as occasion offered, and as there was need. They also inculcated the duty of prayer, and the sanctification of the Lord's day. And it was a custom for those who were intelligent and serious, when they had a meeting at their houses, to repeat sermons, *etc.* They invited their ignorant neighbours to attend, so that often the houses of the better sort of people, on such occasions, would be crowded with poor people. Their holy, humble, and exemplary lives were of the greatest advantage to the success of his ministry. Nothing so convinces men of the truth and reality of vital religion as the living example and meek and humble spirit of its professors; while, on the other hand, there is no greater obstruction to the gospel than the inconsistent lives and unsavoury spirit of many who are in the communion of the church. The unity and concord which were preserved among the pious were also of great benefit. The place was also, in a good degree, exempt from those sects and heresies which abounded at this time in most places of the land.

> Private meetings were found to be an effectual help to piety in the place, for by this means the truths that had slipped away were recalled, and serious impressions which were in danger of being worn away were renewed, and good desires cherished. These meetings were found also greatly to increase the knowledge of the people; and by the continual exercise of the gift of prayer, many improved in their gifts, and the younger learned to pray, by hearing those that were older. They furnished the preacher also with an opportunity of knowing the persons who were beginning to be serious; for, if anyone was wounded by the arrows of truth, in the public dispensation of the Word, he would be sure to drop into these meetings. By the means of these also, idle meetings, and the loss of time, were prevented; and so far were these religious meetings from producing schism, that they were the chief means of preventing anything of the kind; for the pastor was commonly there in the midst of them; solving their doubts, silencing their objections, and moderating them in all things.
>
> It gave him also no small advantage, that being a single man, and spending little on himself, he was able to distribute the larger part of his income among the poor. And when he found any of their children possessing promising talents, he would, by means of his own funds and the aid of his friends, send them to be educated at the university. Several of these became useful preachers, and with their brethren were ejected by the Act of Uniformity; while others conformed and remained in the ministry. In giving charitable relief to the indigent, he never made it a question whether they were good or bad; for he

thought the bad had souls and bodies which needed charity most. And he left this encouraging and important fact on record, '*That what little funds he ever acquired were obtained when he gave most away', and that when he has been able to give little his increase has also been diminished.*

He also promoted the good work, by giving away good books. Most of these he wrote himself; and of some small books which he published, he gave every family one, which amounted to near eight hundred.

It was a saying of Baxter, verified in the experience of many pastors, 'That freeholders and tradesmen are the strength of religion, and of the community, while gentlemen, and beggars, and servile tenants, are the strength of iniquity.'

Another great help to his success was the practice already mentioned, of dealing with every family apart, catechising and instructing them. That which was spoken to them personally, seemed to awaken their attention much more than the same truths heard from the pulpit.

The faithful exercise of church discipline also, was no small furtherance of the people's good; for Baxter found, that without discipline he never could have kept the religious part of the church from divisions and separations. Pious people have, from their very character, an inclination to separate from the irreligious and profane; and if they had not seen a disposition to separate such from the communion, they would have been disposed to withdraw from the society. Many abstained from coming to the Lord's table for fear of discipline, for out of 1,600 of proper age to come to the Lord's table, there were no more than six hundred communicants. It was the custom, however, for all to come that would, so that their exclusion was their own act; and as to the posture in partaking of the ordinance, everyone acted according to his own judgment. He baptized the children of all sorts, but he required the parents to give him, privately or publicly, an account of their faith, and if any father was a scandalous sinner, he made him confess his sin openly, before he would baptize his child. If the father refused, the administration of the ordinance was postponed until the mother brought the child; for he says, he rarely found both father and mother so destitute of knowledge and faith, as in a *church-sense* to be incapable of receiving this ordinance for their children.

Another thing which facilitated his success as a pastor, was the manner in which he brought forth the truth in his preaching. He adapted his sermons to the peculiar circumstances of the flock. The subject of his preaching was the fundamental doctrines of the gospel, which were so frequently exhibited that they became familiar to the thoughts of the people. But to keep his hearers humble, and to prevent vain self-sufficiency, he was accustomed to put something in every sermon, which they did not know before. By this means they were kept in a learning state, and their thirst for knowledge was both excited and gratified. For he thought, if preachers tell their people but what they know already, they will be tempted to turn preachers themselves, and suppose that they have learned all the minister can teach them, and have become as wise as he is. Ministers will be despised if they do not possess knowledge superior to that of their people, but if he communicates to them things which they did not know before, by a daily addition to their former knowledge they will be led on with desire and delight. He never thought it expedient to take up their time with unprofitable controversies, which could not produce edification; nor did he affect novelties in doctrine, contrary to the received opinions of the universal church; but such things as tended to illustrate the great doctrines of the gospel.

One important circumstance connected with the success of this eminent pastor was, *that he kept himself free from all worldly entanglements,* so that his whole time was devoted to his ministry, except what was taken up by sickness. Personally he had nothing to do with the tithes of the parish; everything of this kind he committed into the hands of others; and he directed that where his parishioners were poor, the debt should not be exacted, but entirely remitted.[1]

The preceding account of Baxter's labours is taken from the history of his own life and times, written by himself; and it contains the best practical commentary which can be given of his *Reformed Pastor*. And a better model can scarcely be found for the imitation of the clergy of all denominations in our day. It is true, that Baxter was a man of great abilities and extensive learning; but these qualifications do not appear to have been those which contributed most to his success.

---

[1] See Baxter's *Life* abridged for the Board of Publication.

His fervent zeal, his tender compassion for souls, his manifest sincerity, his wise selection of appropriate means, and his indefatigable diligence, were the true reasons of his success. And can it be shown, that any minister ever possessed these qualifications of an evangelical pastor, and yet laboured without effect? Why may not that which was done by Baxter be done by every pastor? Perhaps few can preach so well as he did; but if the hearts of ministers were now as much in their work as was his, their preaching would be with power, and a blessing would attend it. And if they would 'watch for souls as they that must give account', they would find work enough to occupy their hearts and their hands.

Entire devotedness to the duties of their office seems essential to an efficient ministry. Their worldly pursuits and avocations may be in themselves very innocent; but it is enough to condemn them that they are *avocations* which call them away from their proper work. When it was recently announced by a clergyman from the other side of the world, that the missionaries of a certain society had been deeply engaged in land speculations, how did it shock all our best moral feelings? And if it should be told that any of our American missionaries had so managed their small salaries that by judicious speculation they had become rich, and were living in splendour, what should we think? How should we feel? But who will undertake to prove, that pastors at home are not bound to be as dead to the world, and as much devoted to their work, as any missionary? Is not the ministerial character as sacred here as in foreign countries? and is not the salvation of the souls committed to them as important as the salvation of an equal number of the heathen?

There is little doubt, but that the true reason why missionaries do commonly excel in piety, is because they are entirely cut loose from the possessions of the world. They give up all prospect of owning property. They have made up their minds to sacrifice entirely what the world calls *independence,* and to expect to have nothing but food, raiment, and shelter from the weather; and for these necessaries they are content to rely upon the free will offerings of the church. If they can turn any talent to profit, it is not for themselves, but for the common cause. What a noble example, to see the venerable Carey labouring assiduously in teaching, not to enrich himself, but to bring every dollar of a large salary and cast it into the common treasury; and contented to receive from them no more than the common share of the poorest missionary. O, could we see such examples at home, of self-denial and disinterestedness, we might begin to hope that Zion was about to arise from the dust, and that God had put a new spirit into her watchmen.

There is no vice, perhaps, which the clergy in our country are so liable to be infected with as covetousness; and yet this is no less a crime, according to the Word of God, than idolatry. Ministers, it is true, are generally poor, but they may be greedy of gain notwithstanding this, and may neglect the responsible duties of their awful calling, for the sake of filthy lucre. The necessity which is often laid upon them by the unjust parsimony of their people, to provide by their own exertions for their own households, often becomes a snare to them. They get accustomed to worldly business, and perhaps expert in managing pecuniary matters, and when any man once gets his hand in, in the way of making money, by lawful means, it will be difficult for him to relinquish the pursuit. And as to stopping when he has a *sufficiency,* this he is no more likely to do than other men who make riches the object of their pursuit. That point of sufficiency is a vanishing point; when the man approaches it, it recedes from him, and still keeps as far ahead as at the beginning; so that the pursuit which at first promised to be short and soon ended, proves to be interminable. 'Ye cannot serve God and mammon', says our Saviour. This is eminently true as applied to the ardent pursuit of wealth, and the duties of the holy ministry. No man can be much occupied with worldly cares and business, and at the same time have his heart duly engaged in the duties of his pastoral office. These last will either be neglected, slightly performed, or the genuine spirit which should pervade and animate the whole service, will be wanting. And then it will be like a body without a spirit.

Another danger is, that the leading and wealthy part of his parishioners, wanting an apology for their own love of the world, will be secretly delighted to find their minister, who should be their reprover, animated by the same spirit, and as thoroughly engaged in the pursuit of wealth as themselves. And how can he be faithful in declaring the whole counsel of God concerning the love of riches? Will not his mouth be stopped? Or, if inconsistently he performs his duty in the pulpit, will not everyone be ready to apply to him that proverb, 'Physician, heal thyself'? 'Thou that teachest another, teachest not thou thyself?' The worldly minister, when he meets his parishioners from time to time, has so much to say about the common objects of their attention, that he cannot edge in a word of admonition or divine instruction. Indeed, such ministers have commonly little talent for religious conversation; and people do not expect it of them; or if, against the current of their thoughts and affections, they force themselves to give utterance to some common-place remarks on this subject, they come out so dryly and formally that, instead of warming, they freeze the feelings of their people. Such ministers would relinquish the sacred office, if they could do it honourably; and surely it would be more consistent for some to give up the office than nominally to continue to wear the clerical character, while they perform scarcely any of its duties. Here is the secret of the frequent dissatisfaction between pastors and their flocks, and the cause of such frequent disruption of the sacred bond cast around them at their installation. When has it been known, that a people have been solicitous to be freed from the oversight and preaching of a truly devoted, faithful, and laborious minister? Though he may not be a first-rate man as to talents, yet if he is humble, affectionate, sincere, and laborious, in the study, in the pulpit, and in the family, such a man will find himself seated in the affections of his flock; and if a few fastidious and conceited hearers wish for more learning, more eloquence, and a more fascinating style of preaching, the great body of the people will cleave to him, and with docility receive the word from his mouth; and will always rejoice to see their pastor entering their dwellings. The poor, among whose humble cottages he often directs his steps, will hail him as a friend and benefactor, and will bless God for giving them so faithful a guide and instructor.

While some pastors are rendered almost useless by worldly entanglements, others sink into a state of discouragement. When preparing for the sacred office, they pleased themselves with the hope of doing much good. In prospect, everything looked fair and pleasing; and they anticipated that their labours would produce a great visible effect. But when they go forth, and are fixed in a charge where the people are careless and ignorant, and pay little attention to their instructions, and afford no visible fruits of their labours, they become disheartened; and perform their parochial duties with languor, because without hope of success. Fault is found with the situation of the parish, or the character of the flock; and some other place must be sought. But they cannot find a congregation of angels, or even one made up of saints; and they are never likely to be suited. We entertain the opinion, that more than half the cases of the removal of ministers will not be sanctioned by the great Head of the church, who sees and observes all the affairs of his kingdom on earth. Good men often make sad blunders in this matter. They literally *go from home,* because annoyed by some perverse neighbours, or unreasonable parishioners, who, finding how easily their sensibility is wounded, take pains to vex them. They cannot bear this thorn in the flesh, the piercings of which are not deep and dangerous, but constant, and they cannot get clear of it. O, if they would look to that God whose grace is sufficient to enable them to bear all trials, they would not leave their place to escape an evil which very probably, in the end, would do them good. We are much inclined to the opinion, that when a minister has been called, in providence, to take charge of a people, if he would resolve to lay himself out to promote their best interests of every kind—if he would begin to instruct the ignorant, to train the youth, to warn the unruly, to feed the flock with the pure milk of the Word, to make every sacrifice for their benefit, and to bear with unmurmuring patience all their ill treatment—still praying for them, and tenderly watching every opportunity to do them good, his difficulties in time would be removed or lessened; his enemies would become reconciled; the careless would take on them the serious profession of religion, and what was like a wilderness would become like the garden of the Lord. Who had a harder lot than Oberlin and Neff, among the wild rocks of the Alps, and a people as wild as the land which they inhabited? and yet, by patient endurance—by unceasing effort—by wise measures of improvement—and by the spirit of ardent, inextinguishable piety, they were enabled, by the blessing of heaven, which is sure to attend such labours, to see the work of God prospering in their hands. They had the pleasure of beholding such a transformation in the aspect of society as filled their hearts with joy and gratitude, and their mouths with praise. And what was there in Kidderminster, when Mr Baxter began his labours there, which promised much comfort or success? But by faithful, persevering labours—such labours as are within the reach and ability of any pastor, if only his heart be right,—he accomplished a glorious work of reformation, and was the honoured instrument of saving a multitude of souls, who are now as stars in his crown, while he rejoices with them before the throne of God.

To some, this kind of life, replete with labours, and cutting off the preacher from all the advantages of earthly gain, honour, and comfort, seems to be unreasonable. They are ready, not merely to apologize for the course pursued by ministers who engage in worldly pursuits, but to put in a plea of justification. Ministers are but men, and too much ought not to be expected of them. They commonly have families for which they are bound to provide, or be worse than infidels. They are educated men, and possess feelings as refined as others of this class; and why should this profession be doomed to a life of self-denial and hardship? If their people are unable or unwilling to make provision for them, they have a right, and are bound to attend to worldly affairs, in that degree which is necessary to furnish them with a sufficiency of this world's goods, if not an independence. And by mingling with the people in the commerce and common intercourse of life, they conciliate the men of the world, and remove the prejudice so extensively imbibed, that religion renders men austere and unsociable, and is inimical to the innocent pleasures of life. And if, under the favour of providence, they acquire property by lawful exertions, they should not be censured for that which all other men are indulged to pursue and possess. Now, in this defence, there is so much truth and error mingled, that we will not undertake to discriminate between them. But, let us suppose that a fragment of authentic ecclesiastical history had come down to our times, containing the following statement of facts.

> The Apostle Paul, though much devoted to his Master's service, yet was not inattentive to his own worldly interest. Travelling much, he had the opportunity of seeing the improvements of one country, and introducing them into another. By watching his opportunities of

increasing his fortune, he was able to lay up money enough to purchase a handsome house at Corinth, which he furnished in a plain, but rich and elegant manner; and, while at Ephesus, he found an opportunity of making a very favourable speculation in some lots and houses, which were brought to the hammer, through the failure in business of their former owners. Some of his brethren, who were less skilful in trade, or less favoured with opportunities of making valuable acquisitions of this kind, seemed disposed to censure him as acting inconsistently with his high vocation; but he despised such censures, as knowing that they proceeded from envy of his success in business. And as long as he lived, though he met with some losses, he continued to increase in wealth; so that when he suffered martyrdom at Rome, he was worth an estate valued at ——.

But we must stop. No Christian feelings can endure such a representation, either in the case of Paul, or Peter, or John, or Apollos, or Timothy, or any other primitive preacher. Such a narrative as the above, if it had been contained in the Acts of the Apostles, would have ruined the Christian religion. And our feelings are so correct on this subject, that any representation of a similar kind of traffic in the world, and acquisition of wealth by any of our missionaries abroad, would raise such a hue and cry against them, that the missionary cause could not sustain itself, in these circumstances, for a single year. But on what principles do we make so wide a difference between what was unbecoming and inconsistent with the sacred office, in the apostles' days, and in our times? Is it not the same Lord that we serve? Is it not the same gospel which is entrusted to us? Is not eternity as near to us and as important as to them? And is not the day of judgment many hundred years nearer? Is not the salvation of immortal souls as deeply interesting now as it ever was? And do not ministers now take upon them as solemn ordination vows as were ever assumed by men? Where, then, is the ground of our different feelings, in regard to certain courses of conduct? It has no just foundation. It may be traced to our own selfishness, which blinds us in regard to all that relates to our own interest or ease. But if it might be supposed that the circumstances of the apostles and primitive teachers, exposed as they were to persecution, and having the whole world opposed to them, might make them indifferent to worldly things, which, if they possessed, they could not retain; yet how shall we account for the high requisition which the Christian world makes on the missionary, compared with the pastor at home? Do ye not condemn our own worldliness, self-indulgence, and indolence, while we would censure in a missionary what we, as a matter of course, allow ourselves to pursue or to enjoy? Certainly, ministers at home are as much bound to be self-denying, faithful and laborious, as those who go to foreign countries. The missionary may be exposed to more hardships necessarily; but we defy any man to show, that the minister at home is not under obligations to labour as faithfully, and to make for the cause of Christ as great sacrifices, as those beloved men, who have forsaken their native land, and all their dear relatives, without the expectation of ever seeing them again. Indeed, as these painful sacrifices are such as ministers are not required to make, they seem to be bound, in other ways, to show an equal attachment to Christ's kingdom; and to labour more indefatigably for the conversion of souls, perishing all around them. There is no escape from self-condemnation in this case; and the only way by which we can evade the condemnation of our Judge is, to condemn ourselves, and humble ourselves in penitence before him, lest he deal with us according to our sins, and reward us according to our iniquities. Let us remember, that the time is short; and that what we do must be done quickly. We must work while the day lasts, for soon the night cometh when no man can work. Is it not a sign of God's displeasure that he is calling off from the harvest field, some of the most faithful and efficient labourers? But there is slight lamentation in the churches, for these great losses. 'The righteous perisheth and no man layeth it to heart; and merciful men are taken away, none considering that the righteous is taken away from the evil to come.' And let the ministers of God begin to lay to heart their true condition, and the evils which threaten the church. The enemy is coming like a flood, and yet the watchmen hold their peace—they are asleep—they sound no alarm—they appear to be at ease in Zion. 'Let the priests, the ministers of the Lord, weep between the porch and the altar, and let them say, spare thy people, O Lord, and give not thine heritage to reproach, that the heathen should rule over them. Wherefore should they say, among the people, where is their God?'

Let us indulge our imagination for a moment, in conceiving of two ministers of equal talents and opportunities, but one of whom only has been faithful, self-denying, and laborious, entering together into the presence of their common Lord, and appearing before his judgement seat. The first is accosted in a language which surprises him, 'Well done, good and faithful servant, enter into the joy of thy Lord'; the other is confounded and abashed before he hears his sentence—his own conscience has already anticipated his doom. We need not be surprised that he trembles, and would gladly hide himself in some secret cavern. But stern necessity is laid upon him, and he is arraigned, and the charge against him is not for any enormous crime. No, his conduct was always moral and decent, but it is for sloth and unfaithfulness. He had a talent, and did not improve it. He was a steward, and yet he was unfaithful in dispensing his Lord's goods; and the dreadful sentence is, 'take the wicked and slothful servant who neglected to do his Lord's work, and cast him into outer darkness, there shall be weeping and gnashing of teeth.' O, wretched man! where now are your treasures, your houses and lands, and all your earthly possessions, for the sake of which you betrayed your Master, and ruined your soul?

There is a class of ministers whose situation is truly deplorable. We know of no set of men who claim our compassion more. They are such as having been invested with the sacred office, by ordination, are unable to find any people willing to accept of them as their pastor; or, if they should happen to obtain a settlement, for want of acceptableness, are speedily pushed off, and sent afloat upon the wide world without the means of comfortable subsistence for their families. They wander about in search of a place of rest, and after spending much time, and being at inconvenient expense, in visiting vacant churches, are after all disappointed, and are often reduced to great straits to obtain the bare necessaries of life. No doubt there are good men, who have gone through the usual course of preliminary studies, and have had the hands of the presbytery laid upon them, who, nevertheless, are entirely unfit for the work, and however they may be regularly called by men, have never received the call of God to be ministers of his church; for, when God calls a man to any work, he always furnishes him with the necessary qualifications. If any person is found destitute of these, and cannot acquire them, though he may be, in the sight of the church, a regular minister, and his ministrations valid, yet he has mistaken his road; and sometimes such persons are convinced of this, when it is too late. For, according to the doctrine commonly received among us, the ministry can be laid down only by a regular deposition from office, by the competent authority.

Whether this be a correct doctrine, has been with us a matter of serious and increasing doubt. If deposition were not attended with lasting disgrace, we should not be disposed to dissent from the received opinion. But take this case: A young man is put to learning by his parents, that he may become a minister, and when he arrives at the proper age, he makes a serious profession of religion. His intellect may be sound, and his literary acquisitions may be good, but he speaks in a way so stammering and so cold and uninteresting, that it is painful to everyone to hear; and to be obliged to do this once a week would not only be unedifying, but would be a penance, which few persons would be contented to endure long. Now, this young man ought to have had his attention directed by his friends and advisers, to some pursuit not requiring public speaking. And the presbyteries and classes, when candidates appear before them, on trial, should make particular experiment of their gifts in this respect; which, however, is much neglected, and young men, who are scarcely ever proper judges of their own defects, are introduced to an office for the duties of which they possess no competency. Formerly, it was a part of every candidate's trials for the ministry, to preach in public, and the sermon was, on this account, called 'a popular discourse'; but this salutary custom begins, at least in the presbyteries in this section of country, to be laid aside; and the candidate is only required to read his popular sermon before the presbytery, as he does any other written discourse required of him. In consequence of this, no proper trial is made of the candidate's capacity to speak audibly and fluently in public. But the point to which we wish to direct our remarks is, that a conscientious person, who has been induced to enter the ministry without the necessary qualifications, when he is convinced of his incompetency, should be permitted, with the consent of the presbytery, to resign his office. If he may not, then a man who has become a preacher without the call of God—and all will acknowledge that such a case may occur—must be forced to remain in an office, the duties of which he is unable to fulfil, and which he ought never to have entered. And hence it comes to pass, that there are among us many presbyters who preach not at all, and hang heavily on the skirts of the church, and are an encumbrance to our ecclesiastical bodies. We see not why, even in cases of confirmed ill health, which disqualifies a man from preaching, as when the voice is lost, a minister should not be permitted to resign his office. But what if he should so recover it again as to be able to preach? We answer, that all that would be necessary would be to recognize him again as a minister. He would need no new ordination; as, indeed, the custom is not to re-ordain a minister who has been deposed and excommunicated, when he is restored to his office and standing in the church.

We are aware that our Book of Discipline makes no provision for a minister's resigning his office after ordination; but the question is, would it not be well to have such a provision? and do not the circumstances of our church call for something of the kind? What we have said on this point, we wish to be considered as not the expression of a decided opinion on the subject, respecting which probably the conductors of this *Review* would not entirely agree; but as intended to turn the attention of the church to the point, and to elicit discussion, which may lead to the adoption of a new section in our Book of Discipline; or may confirm us more fully in the doctrine which has been commonly received, and in favour of which we are aware that there are some able advocates.

We would take this occasion to declare, that we hardly know a more responsible and awful duty, which men are ever called to perform, than the conferring the sacred office on a fellow creature. The regulations of our church on this subject are truly excellent; and if they were always carried into effect with that strict fidelity which the importance of the transaction demands, all would be well—at least, as well as human wisdom and care could make it. But we seriously apprehend that these trials are too often but superficially entered into; especially as it regards personal piety. If a young man is a member of the church—if he has been through college, and the theological seminary and seeks to be a minister, it is thought to be hard to throw any obstacle in his way after his having spent so much time and expense in preparation. We think that the laxity of presbyteries does not relate so much to the literary qualifications and orthodoxy required, as to the examination on experimental religion, and making a thorough trial of the ability of the candidate to preach to the acceptance and edification of the people. In regard to the first, we remember a case in which a young man of education presented himself before a large and respectable presbytery, and when called upon to give some account of his experimental acquaintance with religion, had literally nothing to say, and could only answer to some leading questions—which is a very unsatisfactory method of examination. The presbytery hesitated, and called him in again, but still there was nothing like a narration of a work of grace: they voted to receive him on trial, and in due time he was licensed. He had been but a short time a probationer, before he declared himself an infidel. Afterwards, indeed, it was reported that he had repented, and renounced his errors; but surely he ought never to have been licensed.

In regard to the ability of the candidate to preach to the acceptance of the people, this it may be said is sufficiently provided for by his licensure, when he enters on this part of his probation. But we are of opinion, that it is attended with great evil, even to license a man as a probationer, who is not fit for the ministry; for if we bring a man thus far, unless he commit some scandalous offence, he will contrive to get into the ministry. And people generally are accustomed to make very little distinction between a licentiate and an ordained minister. Let the man be fairly, but strictly tried before he is sent out. Presbyteries are not restricted to the particular trials specified in the Book of Discipline; they are at full liberty to institute other trials, if they think it necessary. And why, we ask, would it not be expedient, to have some trial of the ability of the candidate in extempore speaking; and in giving the sense of passages of Scripture, without the opportunity of recourse to commentaries? for who is so dull, that he cannot write down what he finds in books of exposition? We are of opinion, that no man is truly qualified for the ministry, who is not able to express himself promptly and clearly on any plain subject, without having recourse to books, or to his pen. Not that we would discourage the use of the pen; but we would have the tongue trained to ready utterance, as well as the hand to compose.

But to return to the subject of pastoral duty. We entertain the opinion, notwithstanding the fierce opposition to the clergy which is rising and organizing itself in the east, that the pastoral office is the most honourable, the most useful, and, when rightly filled and executed, the most happy office in the world. But, at the same time, we are ready to admit, that to a man destitute of genuine piety, it must be a heavy yoke, and intolerable drudgery; and that to the man who serves God in it, with a mind divided between its duties and the pursuit of the world, and distracted with secular avocations, it must be a painful service; that the conscience of such a man must be ill at ease, and his comfort in the exercise of the office very small. To enjoy this holy service, the heart must be unreservedly devoted, and everything made subordinate to its claims upon our time and our energies.

Let us then again bring into view, what is required by the great Head of the church, of those who undertake to be ministers of the gospel. We shall say nothing at present of the missionary service; our concern is with the ministry at home, and especially with the pastors of the churches. And to such, we would affectionately, but solemnly, say, divest yourselves at once of all worldly engagements and entanglements, that interfere with your making full proof of your ministry. Though avarice may plead—though the love of ease and pleasure may solicit—be resolved and cut off the right hand, and pluck out the right eye, which offend, and begin your work anew; not under the influence, of a momentary impulse, but from a conviction that God calls you to engage in this work with renewed zeal and effort. An account of your stewardship must be tendered, and that soon; and surely you ought to desire to be in a situation to give this account with joy and not with grief. Set apart a day for humiliation and prayer, and for the solemn consideration of your past ministerial life. Be determined to look honestly into the case; and if you have been remiss—if you have been unfaithful in 'warning every man, and teaching every man'—determine now that you will hereafter keep your great business so habitually on your mind, that you will not suffer any opportunity of doing good to escape you. Never be in any company without recollecting that you are there as the ambassador of Jesus Christ, and that you have a commission to seek the eternal salvation of every man, woman, and child, with whom you may meet at any time. Be 'fishers of men'. Throw out your bait, and draw into the gospel net as many as you can. Omit nothing which promises to be a means of winning men to Christ. Personally address such as in your conscience you think will be benefited by such application. Let not the fear of giving offence, or of hurting the feelings of your friends, prevent you from kindly admonishing them, and patiently instructing them. Go around among your people—begin with the poor—pass not by the wretched dwelling of the profligate. Who knows but you may save a soul from death, and cover a multitude of sins? Sometimes, the blaspheming drunkard has a wife, whose heart, broken with afflictions of the heaviest kind, is prepared to receive the consolations which the gospel brings. Learn to bear with patience the abuse and even the curses of the wicked. Make no other return, but to bless, and pray for those who despitefully use you. Remember, that great will be your reward in heaven.

Try to engage others to co-operate with you. Go to your elders, and exhort them to untiring diligence and conscientious fidelity in performing the duties of their office. Make it a point to convene them once a week for prayer and conference, in relation to the affairs of the church, of which you and they are appointed rulers. Instruct them in their duty, and urge them to go among the poor and ignorant, and to visit the sick and afflicted. But your best hopes must rest upon the training of the young. Catechise them in the family—catechise them in meetings appointed for the purpose, and also in the church. Enlist others in the work. Give a class to pious young women to instruct. And whatever you do, do not neglect to form your young people into classes for Bible instruction. Try every lawful method to make your instructions interesting to the young. Enter into the service with all your heart. Prepare yourself for the meeting. Communicate as much solid instruction as you can, and the good seed lodged in the tender minds of youth will not be wholly lost. And when their minds are open to receive instruction, will be the best opportunity to make effectual addresses to the heart and conscience. One such opportunity affords fully as hopeful a prospect of saving benefit, as a public discourse to a promiscuous multitude. If your people are distinguished into ranks, who do not mingle together in social intercourse, have different classes in different places, and become all things to all men. Some ministers who profess to be great friends to revivals, seem to think that nothing can be done until the revival comes; and therefore when they have preached on the Sabbath, they sit down and fold their arms and complain. People should be prepared for a revival by sound instruction, or they will get little good from having their feelings powerfully excited, or even their consciences awfully awakened. The main thing that men do is to sow the seed and water it, and to look to God, by incessant prayer, that he may give the increase.

When ministers live near each other it answers an excellent purpose to aid one another in preaching and visiting. Two ministers are enough, or three, at most. The same truths inculcated every Sabbath by the pastor will sometimes come with a new power when uttered by the voice of another. And a stranger can often take greater liberty in reproving some sins, and treating some subjects, than the pastor; and while the preaching of one is suited best to one class of hearers, the preaching of another, though inferior, will make a deeper impression on another class. Let ministers join, on these occasions, in visiting each others' congregations.

And when ministers meet in presbytery, let it be a main object to stir up and edify one another, and to promote religion in the parish where they are convened. How delightful and how profitable these ecclesiastical meetings of ministers might be, if, exempt from all jealousy, envy and ill will, they should come together in the true spirit of their Lord and Master.

THE CHARACTER OF THE
GENUINE THEOLOGIAN[1]

This article which follows is a translation from the Latin of Witsius. The elevated thought and ardent piety of the whole together with the manifest importance of the subject and the known wisdom of the author, will suggest themselves to the reader as sufficient reasons for its insertion. As the original discourse is an inaugural oration, pronounced when Witsius assumed the theological chair at Franeker, there are local allusions which are entirely omitted. A few paragraphs have been passed over for the sake of brevity. The date of the discourse is April 16, 1675.

THE theologian, as I use the term, is one imbued with the knowledge of God and divine things, under the teaching of God himself; who celebrates his adorable perfections, not by words alone, but by the ordering of his life, and is thus entirely devoted to his Lord. Such, of old, were the holy patriarchs, the inspired prophets, the apostles by whom the world was enlightened, with some of those luminaries of the primitive church, whom we denominate the fathers. Their knowledge consisted, not in the acute subtleties of curious questions, but in the devout contemplation of God and of his Christ. Their chaste and simple method of illustration did not gratify the itching ear, but by scaling the impression of sacred things on the heart, enkindled the soul with love of the truth. Their blameless life was apprehended even by their enemies, and being in correspondence with their profession, fortified their teaching with irrefragable evidence, and was a manifest token of intimate communion with the Most Holy God.

[1] Herman Witsius 'The Character of the Genuine Theologian', tr. Archibald Alexander, *Biblical Repertory and Theological Review*, Vol. 4, No. 2 (April 1832), 158-70.

In contemplating the character of such a theologian, let us inquire first in what schools, under what teachers, by what methods he attains to a wisdom so sublime; secondly, in what manner he may best communicate to others what he has thus acquired; and finally, with what habits of mind and excellence of life he may adorn his doctrine. Or, more concisely, let us view the genuine theologian, with reference to his *learning,* his *teaching,* and his *life.* For no one teaches well, who has not first learned aright. No one has learned aright, who has not learned for the purpose of teaching others. And both are useless, unless reduced to practice.

To begin then, at that which is fundamental; the man who merits the honourable title of a genuine theologian must have the basis of his learning in the lower school of nature, and must gather from the structure of the universe, and the wonders of divine providence, from the monuments of ancient and modern history, the recesses of the several arts, and the beauties of various tongues, those things which, deposited in the sacred treasury of memory, may become the foundation of a nobler edifice, when he advances to a higher school. It is not without design that God has impressed upon his works the visible tokens of his attributes; that he has introduced man endowed with sagacity of mind into the august theatre of the universe. It is not without design that all things in the government of the world, and the changes of human affairs are conducted with so harmonious a variety, and so wise a choice. It is not without design that he hath so ordered the works of nature, as to afford some type of the works of grace and glory, and as it were, the rudiments of a better world. It is his will, that we should learn, from an attentive observation of these things, what and how great he is; eternal, infinite, most almighty, most wise, at once the greatest and the best, most fully sufficient for his own plenary happiness, since he gives to all life and breath and all things; most worthy, in short, to be served and imitated, and to be supreme in our love and our fruition. It is his will, that we should contemplate his majesty diffusing the beams of its effulgence in our inmost hearts, there giving laws, awarding swift vengeance to sin, and to good works the mildest approbation, and the sweetest tranquillity of soul. He has chosen, that in view of the transitory, evanescent and glass-like frailty of things which have been falsely deemed eternal, we should aspire to that which is heavenly, and thus to himself the Lord of heaven, who remaining unmoved is the cause of all motion.

Nor should the theologian limit himself to the works of God, but labour to discover all that the industry of men has effected for leading the soul in pursuit of truth, and for so perfecting language as to render it the suitable interpreter of the mind. He should most assiduously consult the masters in logic, grammar, and rhetoric; using these as Israel used the Gibeonites, who were hewers of wood and drawers of water for the sanctuary. The first of these will deliver to him precepts for definition, division, and arrangement; the other will instruct him in the art of uttering his sentiments, purely, tersely, elegantly, and persuasively—both herein ministering to the ministers of the sanctuary. He should glean precepts of virtue from the sayings of philosophers, and examples from the records of history; these will condemn the baseness of languor and inaction, though they may not avail to incite him towards more sublime objects. He should sedulously acquire various languages, especially those in which God has chosen to convey his sacred oracles, so as to understand them in their own proper idiom, and that God may not need an interpreter with him whose office it is to interpret the divine will to others. All that is sound and reasonable in human arts, all that is elegant and graceful in the array of refined literature, emanates from the Father of lights, the unwasted fountain of all reason and truth and beauty; this should therefore be collected from every source, and instantly be consecrated to God. Are these things minute and earthly? Minute and earthly as they are, they are the glasses by which the most refined images of supernatural things may be more clearly discovered by our renovated eyes.[1] These are the rudiments of the future theologian; if they are superciliously contemned, he will hardly find the desired fruit when called to higher walks, or answer to his title and his office. Yet these are merely the rudiments.

The theologian is not to spend his life in these things. Let him ascend from these lower instructions of nature to the higher school

[1] There is a figure in the original which can scarcely be admitted into grave discourse in our language: *Attamen minuta ista acus sunt, quibus aurea veritatum coelestium fila introducamus, et animis nostris firmiter insuamus.*

of revelation; and sitting at the feet of God his Master, learn from his mouth those hidden mysteries of salvation, which eye hath not seen nor ear heard; which none of the princes of this world have known; which no reason, however disciplined, can reach; which angelic choirs, even in contemplation of the face of God, desire to look into. In the secret books of the Scriptures, and nowhere else, at the present time, the mysteries of the more sacred wisdom are unfolded. Whatever is not derived from these, whatever is not founded on them, whatever does not exactly agree with them, is vain and futile; even though presenting a show of more sublime knowledge, or corroborated by antiquity of tradition, consent of doctors, and cogency of argument. 'To the law and to the testimony.' Whoso speaks not in accordance with this judgment shall never greet the brilliant dawn. These celestial oracles, the theologian would embrace; these he should ply with daily, and with nightly toil. In these he should be conversant, from these he should learn; with these he should compare every sentiment, nor embrace aught in religion which is not to be there found.

Let his belief be dependent on no man, no prophet no apostle, nor even on angelic teaching, as though the dictates of man or angel were to be his standard. In God, and God alone, must his faith be reposed. For the faith in which we are instructed, and which we inculcate, is not human but divine; and is so jealous of mistake, as to account no basis sufficiently firm, except that only foundation—the authority of the infallible and ever true God. There is, moreover, in the insidious study of the Scriptures a certain indescribable fascination.[1] It fills the intellect with the brightest ideas of heavenly truth, which it teaches purely, soundly, with certainty and without mixture of error. Soothing the mind with ineffable sweetness, it allays the craving of the soul as with streams of honey and of oil; penetrates the intimate seclusions of the heart with insuperable efficacy, and so firmly engraves its instructions on the mind, that the believer as confidently acquiesces in them, as if he had heard them uttered in the third heaven by the voice of God himself. It influences the affections, and everywhere exhaling the fragrance of holiness, breathes it forth upon the pious student, even in cases where he does not realize all that he learns.

[1] ἑλχυστιχον.

No one can tell how much we impede our own progress by a preposterous method of study, which is too prevalent, and according to which we first form our conceptions of divine things from human writings, and then, in confirmation of them, seek for passages of Scripture, or, without further examination seize upon those suggested by others, as referring the question in hand: whereas we should deduce our ideas of divine truth immediately from the Bible itself, using the compositions of men simply as *indices,* allotting these passages to the several topics of theology, from which we may learn the doctrine of the Lord.

And here, I cannot forbear adducing the opinion of the subtle Twiss, with reference to John Piscator, and his method of study. After having stated what was remarkable in his doctrine and religious science, he proceeds thus:

> I shall only add, that I look with high regard upon the theologian, who, professing sacred letters alone, and using the ordinary discipline of grammar, rhetoric, and logic (in which he is a proficient) as merely subsidiary, has attained to such a method of treating theology, not in a popular but scholastic way, as leaves him without a superior, and almost without an equal among the Schoolmen. As if, in this speculative age, so ambitious to blend secular with sacred erudition, it had pleased the Father of mercies to afford us an example of what we might attain of accurate and scholastic learning, in things pertaining to life, by the simple study of the Scriptures, assiduous meditation, and exposition—with the total neglect of all the Schoolmen, summists, and masters of sentences.[1]

So thought, and so spake this undaunted champion, concerning the method of study which we commend. His words are not cited with the view of banishing the commentaries of the learned from the hands of the theologian, and thus leaving him to learn from the worst of all teachers—*himself,* that is, from mere presumption, with the Scriptures misunderstood as a cloak for his errors. Great men of the church, raised above the cares of life and devoted wholly to God, loving him, and beloved by him, have discerned many things in Scripture, which they have extracted, and presented in the clearest light.

[1] *Vind. Grat.* 254. col. i. c.

Amidst the darkness of life, these things might have remained forever hidden from us; and we might never have discovered them, by our unassisted powers, in the depths of their concealment. And although, we may discover, much by our own study of the Scriptures, it is, nevertheless, delightful, and corroborative of our faith, to see, that the manifestation of the same truth, from the same source, has been previously granted to others by the same Lord, who has vouchsafed to shed light on our difficulties. We admire the modesty of Jerome, who professes that, with regard to the sacred volume, he never confided in his own single abilities, nor formed an opinion from his own simple endeavours; but, that he was accustomed to take counsel, even on those passages which he supposed himself to understand, but especially on those of which he was dubious. And Athanasius, in the beginning of his *Oration against the Gentiles,* applauds a Christian friend to whom he was writing, because, though himself competent to discover in the Scriptures those doctrines about which he consults Athanasius, he still listened with modesty to the opinions of others. This one idea I would reiterate, that the asseveration of no mortal, as to the sense of Scripture, is to be believed, unless he fixes conviction on the mind from the Scripture itself, so that while man is the *index,* we may become wise unto salvation, from the teaching of God himself. This is loudly proclaimed by the most eminent expositors. 'I would not', says Cyril of Jerusalem, 'that you should give credence to my simple declarations of these things, unless you obtain from the Scriptures a demonstration of what I preach': adding a sentiment which deserves to be perpetuated: 'For, the saving efficacy of our faith arises not from any eloquence of ours, but from the demonstration of the Holy Scriptures.'[1] With this the remark of Justin Martyr is coincident, 'I assent not to men, even though multitudes concur in their declarations: since we are taught by Christ himself, to yield our faith, not to the doctrines of men, but to those which were preached by the prophets, and revealed by himself.'[2] It is wisely observed by Athanasius, who has been already quoted, that even the Apostle Paul did not make use merely of his own authority, but confirmed his doctrine by the Scripture. And if this was done by one who was permitted to

[1] *Catech*. iv. Cap. de Sp. Sancto.
[2] *Dial. cum Tryph*. p. 63. edit. Steph.

hear ineffable words, who was the interpreter of mysteries, and who had Christ speaking in him, how perilous, in this day, to rely on any authority but that of the Holy Scriptures! The sum of what has been said is this, that the genuine theologian is an humble student of the Word of God.

The Scriptures, then, are the sole standard of what is to believed; but in order to a spiritual and saving understanding of their contents, the theologian must commit himself to the inward teaching of the Holy Ghost. The student of the Bible must be at the same time the disciple of the Spirit. No who regards heavenly things with the perverted eye of nature can perceive their native splendour and beauty; he contemplates only a mistaken image; for they differ greatly in themselves from the impression made on the minds of such as view them so obliquely. In order to apprehend spiritual things, there must be a spiritual mind. The mysteries of Scripture elude the perspicacity of the most penetrating human intellect; and the natural mind perceives them no more than one sense can receive the objects of a different sense. The Holy Spirit, the great Instructor of the soul, coming in aid of this infirmity, communicates to his disciples a new and heavenly mind, on which he pours a most clear illumination, so that celestial mysteries may be seen in their true light. Together with divine things, he bestows a mind to appreciate and comprehend them. He grants the things of Christ together with the mind of Christ. Taught in this spiritual and heavenly school, the theologian not only learns to form correct ideas of divine objects, but is made to participate in these very objects, a treasure truly above all price. The teaching Spirit does not present mere words, and naked dogmas, nor vain dreams and empty phantasms: but, if I may use the expression, the solid and permanent substances of things; introducing them to the soul which truly comprehends them, and embraces them with every affection and in every power of the heart. The pupil of this school does not merely know, nor merely believe, but sometimes realizes what is meant by remission of sin, adoption, communion with God, the gracious indwelling of the Spirit, the love of God shed abroad in the heart, the hidden manna, the sweet tokens of Christ's love, and the pledge and earnest of perfect bliss. There are in this mysterious wisdom many things which you can never learn but by having, feeling, tasting them. The new name is known only by him who possesses it. And the spiritual Teacher causes his disciples to taste and see the preciousness of the Lord. He leads them into his banqueting house, his banner over them is love; he saith, Eat my friends, yea drink my beloved; and then crowned, not with heathen garlands, but with those of the Redeemer, they acquire a clear vision of celestial things.

The truths which are thus learned by experience, are so deeply fixed in the soul, that no subtlety of argumentation, no assault of the tempter, shall avail to remove the impression of the seal. To all objections there is a triumphant reply at hand; for it is vain to dispute against experience. For we have not followed cunningly devised fables, will such be able to say, when we have believed the power and coming of our Lord Jesus Christ, but have been eye-witnesses of his majesty; and we cannot but believe those things which we have heard, which we have seen with our eyes, and our hands have handled of the Word of life. Since, then, it is only in the school of the Spirit that these things are learned, so clearly, so purely, so happily, is it not evidently necessary above all thing, that the theologian should consign himself to the guidance of this Instructor? To be here received, he must renounce his own wisdom and in his own estimation, become a fool that he may be wise. The world of theology is created, like the natural world, out of nothing. By actual love draw near to God, and love will be followed by the communication of his counsel: 'If a man love me, my Father will love him, and we will make our abode with him'—is the promise made by the faithful Jesus to his disciples. Lay up the instructions of the Spirit in a retentive mind, and recall them again and again to view by frequent meditation. Pursue this study, not by reading only, but by prayer; by communion not merely with men in ordinary discourse, but with God in supplication, and with the soul in devout thought. The soul of the saint is like a little sanctuary, in which God dwells by his Spirit and where the Spirit, when sought unto by ardent prayer, often reveals those things which the princes of this world, with all their efforts, are unable to attain. In a word, give all diligence to keep the mirrors of the soul untarnished, and spiritually pure, that it may be fitted to receive that pure Spirit, and his spiritual communication. 'Blessed are the pure in heart, for they all see God.' By these several steps, under the guidance of the Holy Ghost, the theologian will at length reach such knowledge, that, in the light of God, he shall contemplate God, the fountain of light, and in God and the knowledge of him, shall rejoice with joy unspeakable and full of glory.

From this celestial teaching of the Spirit, the theologian will acquire the happy *art of instruction,* which we have already noted as the second requisite. There is a marked difference between the veteran commander, who has led armies, possessed cities, disclosed the stratagems of the foe and made himself an adept in all the tactics of war—who has often forced his way through opposing hosts, and by long use learned *Res gerere et captos ostendere civibus hostes,*[1] and the loud and swaggering Thraso, who, with an unstained shield, wages a war of words, but has beheld battles only in description. Such is the difference between the disciplined theologian, who, like Paul, has traversed the course of Christianity, and by honour and dishonour, by evil report and good report, is as dying, yet alive, as unknown, and yet well known, as sorrowful yet always rejoicing, as poor, yet making many rich, as having nothing, and yet possessing all things—and the scholastic pedant, and index-learned rhapsodist, who, feeble in mind and heart, but mighty in memory and words, deems himself the very alpha of theologians.

It is not enough for the Christian teacher to proclaim truths with which he is familiar, unless he does this with pure love. If he regards with affection the divine Giver of all wisdom, and those committed to his charge, as sons or brethren, and also the truth consigned to him, he cannot but strive with all his powers to gain many for God; that there may be many who with him shall adore that sole wisdom, which he can never alone glorify to his own satisfaction.

The same love will prevent him from declaring anything except what may be sure, sound, solid, promotive of faith and hope, tending to piety, unity, and peace; avoiding all prejudice, abstaining from unfairness and perversion, most sedulously omitting novelties of expression, and unmeaning verbiage; and holding himself aloof from the odious strife of words, and from curious, idle, or irregular

---

[1] To perform deeds and show the citizens their enemies captured.

controversies, which disturb the minds of the simple, rend the church, fill it with suspicions and surmisings, *within,* and present a delightful spectacle to enemies, and to Satan himself *without.* O man of God, flee these things, nor ever catch at the disgraceful reputation which springs from novelty of inventions! Through divine grace, we possess, in our churches and seminaries, a precious deposit of heavenly truth, so clearly demonstrated by Scripture, so ably defended against every adversary, approving itself to the conscience by so rich in exuberance of consolation, and so great power of promoting holiness, and confirmed by the blood of so many martyrs, beloved of God that it cannot be doubted, that we have all which is necessary to conduct believers to salvation, and to perfect the man of God for all good works. The mind is ungrateful, and unobservant of its own good, which complains of darkness in the very midst of such evangelical light; and which, in our Reformed churches, trembles, as if the path lay through mansions unvisited by the sun, *Et loca senta situ, noctem que profundam.*[1]

What, then, shall we say of that unseasonable prurience of innovation, by which truths long since delivered to us safely, plainly, and cautiously, are sometimes destroyed, sometimes deadened, and sometimes implicated in strange and unprecedented forms of expression? We might exclaim to the actors in this work, as did Chrysostom to the innovators of his time: 'Let them hear what Paul saith, that they who innovate in the smallest degree, pervert the gospel.'[2] Let it not however be supposed that we desire to stand in the way of improvement. Nothing can be more delightful to the believing soul, nothing more advantageous to the church, than to make daily increase of scriptural knowledge, to form more clear ideas of spiritual things, to descry more distinctly the concatenation of salutary doctrines in one chain of admirable wisdom, and with evident and ingenious arguments to corroborate the ancient truth; to shed light upon obscurities, to search with fear and trembling into prophetic mysteries, to apply to the conscience the powerful demonstrations of Christ and the apostles, to compare the symbols of ancient ceremonies with Christ the anti-type, and in this cause to act as a scribe well instructed

[1] And places rough with neglect, and deep night.
[2] Chrys. *ad Galat.* i. v. 9.

in the kingdom of heaven, bringing forth from his treasury things new and old. On this point let us concentrate all that we possess, of erudition and diligence. Let this be done, and no good man will object, the church will rejoice, Satan will be disappointed, the efforts of the saints will be prospered by God, who has predicted that in the latter time many shall investigate and knowledge shall be increased. Yet away with these idle, curious, rash, and perverse speculations, flattering some with the mere charm of novelty, and attempted by others from party zeal, which result in no profit, but rather engender strifes, than 'godly edifying which is in faith'.

In seeking this edification, the theologian should hold truth in its purity, without the interposition of trifles from human philosophy, which disfigure the oracles of God. The great things of God need not swelling words, but rest on their own strength, and transcend all understanding: these should not be reduced to the categorical arrangements of the logicians, nor should the attempt be made to invest the Master with the livery of the servant. The things of God are best explained in the words of God. And he errs, who supposes that he can expound the secrets of theology more accurately, clearly, and efficaciously or intelligibly, than in those terms and phrases, which the apostles (after the prophets) made use of; terms dictated by him who gave the faculty of language, who formed the hearts of all, and who therefore best knows, in what manner the heart should be instructed and moved. He that speaketh, let him speak as the oracles of God, not as the idle and repulsive barbarity of the Schoolmen, but as the Holy Ghost giveth utterance. Let the man of God believe me, that it is neither for his own honour, nor that of the wisdom which he professes, to vex these august mysteries with the obscure forms of dialectic skirmishing, to bring in the tedious comments, the grandiloquence, the ludicrous expressions, and the sonorous emptiness of the schools, as the very vitals of theology, and to bind the queen of sciences with pedantic fetters of clanking technicalities.

Speak simply, if you would duly maintain the honour which has been mentioned; not with enticing words of man's wisdom, but in demonstration of the Spirit and of power. Aim, in all your instructions, not to fill the minds of your hearers with vain fancies, but to edify them in faith, to excite them in love, that they may shine in holiness, and rise to the likeness of God. O that henceforth that holy method of theologizing, longed for by so many saints, might prevail in the Reformed seminaries, which should not sink into servile musing, nor evaporate in litigious strife, but shine with vivid lustre in the mind, light up living fire in the heart, and transfuse our Nazarites into the mould of heavenly truth! But with what feelings, and with what success, will that man labour, who has not first framed his own life in a manner conformable to God? And this brings us to the last thing mentioned as requisite to complete the theologian,—*an unblemished purity of morals answerable to his profession.* It is the Lord's will to be sanctified in all that draw nigh unto him, and that his priests should be clothed with righteousness. Unless they are examples to believers in every Christian virtue, and can say with Paul, 'Those things which ye have learned, and received, and heard, and *seen in me,* do': and 'Be ye followers of me, even as I also follow Christ',—they destroy more by a bad life, than they build up by sound doctrine; they disgrace religion, insinuate a scepticism as to what they preach, and open a wide door to libertinism and atheism. And indeed I might ask, how is it possible for one who knows the truth as it is in Jesus, not to be inflamed with the love of Christ—not be made holy in the truth? Surely he in whose tabernacle God vouchsafes communion must needs walk with him, as did Enoch and Noah. He whose soul has experienced and tasted heavenly things must have his conversation in heaven. He who daily contemplates the attributes of God, shining in the face of Jesus Christ, and is surrounded on every side by the light of grace, cannot but be transformed into the same image from glory to glory, even as by the Spirit of the Lord. So that I hesitate not to asseverate, that he is no genuine theologian, and has seen no ray of the divine mysteries in any suitable manner, whose knowledge of truth has not led him to escape the pollutions of the world and the dominion of sin. For thus saith the Lord: Ye shall know the truth and the truth shall make you free. *Intellectum intelligendo omnia fieri,*[1] is an ancient axiom of the philosophers. It was this which the Platonists chiefly sought in the contemplation of the divine ideas, by the sublime knowledge of which man becomes a god, so far as man can

---

[1] Understanding comes about by understanding everything.

be made participant of the divine condition, as Hierocles elegantly remarks. But that which philosophy could not accomplish for her followers, exhibiting the divine perfections only by the unfavourable light of nature, theology richly furnishes to hers, displaying to their contemplation the glories of God and of his Christ in the refulgence of grace, and thus making them partakers of a divine nature; as the inspired Apostle Peter speaks. For God is holiness. By holiness, I intend the sum of all virtues, which it would be here inappropriate to discuss particularly. Desire of heaven; contempt of the world; unfeigned sobriety; modesty, diligent in its own affairs, and not prying into those others; a temper as studious of peace as of truth; fervent zeal, attempered with bland lenity; long suffering under rebuke and injury; prudent caution, as well with regard to times as actions; rigid self-inspection, with forbearing mildness towards brethren; and whatever else pertains to this sacred constellation—these, these not only *adorn,* but *constitute* the theologian. I figure to myself a man, who while intent on heavenly meditations, simulates no gravity of visage or garb, but panting for high and eternal things, holds in contempt the splendour of the rich, and the earth with all its gold and silver. Contented with the grace of Christ the Saviour, and the fellowship of the indwelling Spirit, he looks from an eminence down on all the blandishments of earthly vanity, and craves no wealth, nor pleasure, nor fame. Fully intent upon the care of souls, and the guarding, protecting and extending of Christ's spiritual kingdom, and on beautifying what is already possessed, he owes nothing to the forum, the camp, or the court. He looks for no office, preoccupies no rostrum, courts no patronage, seeks favour of no authority, plays no oratorical part, but justly discriminating between the church, the college, and the court, limits himself to the pulpit or the chair. The higher his flight in the contemplation of heavenly things and the practice of piety, the less does he seek to obscure a brother's honour; measuring himself not with himself, but with those who are above him, and especially with the perfect law of God. In all that concerns the cause of God, the salvation of souls, the defence of the church, and the protection of divine truth, he is all on fire with zeal for God and would rather endure a hundred deaths, than concede one iota to an adversary in that which is not his own but the Lord's. Yet for

himself he avenges no wrongs, meekly bears the maledictions which
are hurled at his head, and in the warmest contest, lays no stress
on his own imaginations, but yields everything for peace and concord. Such an one, to use the expression of the ancients respecting
Athanasius, is to those who strike, an adamant; to those who differ,
a magnet. With prudence in counsel, he attempts nothing rashly,
accomplishes nothing turbulently; and with a humility not feigned
nor outward, but with all the simplicity of candour, casts himself at
the feet of all, exalts himself above none, and prefers each to himself.
Show me such an one and I will salute him as the genuine theologian.
With veneration, with embraces, acknowledging that he is the glory
of Christ, and that the glory of Christ is in him.

ON THE IMPORTANCE OF
AIMING AT EMINENT PIETY[1]

WHETHER an unconverted minister may be the instrument of the conversion of others, is a question which has sometimes been agitated; but although the answer should be in the affirmative, yet it can afford very slender ground of consolation to one who has assumed the office of the gospel ministry, without possessing genuine piety. To be the instrument of bringing others to heaven, and yet to be cast down to hell ourselves, is, surely, one of the most appalling considerations which can possibly be presented to the human mind. A sovereign God may, indeed, employ any instrument he pleases for the conversion of sinners; but it would be unreasonable to expect, that, commonly, he would make use of unsanctified men in this holy work. A greater calamity to the church could not easily be conceived, than the introduction of a multitude of unregenerate men into the sacred ministry; for, such as is the ministry, such will be the people. Such men will ever be disposed to corrupt the simplicity and purity of the gospel, which the carnal mind cannot love; and even if they should preach the true doctrines of the Bible, their own hearts can never be in accordance with them; and although their words may be the truth of God, yet its good tendency will be counteracted by their proud and earthly spirit. Besides, it cannot be expected that the Holy Spirit will usually accompany with his sanctifying influences the labours of men, who, even when they preach the Word of God, are not actuated by a desire to promote the

[1] Archibald Alexander, 'An Address to Candidates for the Ministry, on the Importance of Aiming at Eminent Piety in Making Their Preparation for the Sacred Office', *The Annual of the Board of Education of the General Assembly of the Presbyterian Church in the United States,* ed. John Breckinridge (Philadelphia: Russell and Martien, 1831), pp. 175-94.

glory of God, or to rescue men from the ruins of sin, but are all the time seeking their own glory, or aiming at their own emolument.

That genuine piety is an essential characteristic of a preacher of the gospel, all men seem now to admit; for all are shocked when they observe a wicked life in one who ministers in holy things. Piety is expected as a matter of course in all those who have it as their official duty to inculcate piety; and even the profane despise the wretch who dishonours his sacred calling by a course of conduct at variance with the holy precepts of the gospel. However men of the world may be gratified to find ministers coming down to their own level, and however they may enjoy the company and lively wit of an ambassador of Christ; yet, in their sober judgment they cannot but perceive the glaring incongruity between his character and profession; and none, except the most hardened in iniquity, would be contented to have such a man for their spiritual guide. In extreme distress and mortal sickness, none would send for such a one to comfort them; but then they wish—if they desire any religious conversation—that the most godly minister be brought them. In our church, the possession of true religion has been considered a matter of so much importance in the ministry, that she permits no candidate to be taken on trial by any presbytery, until, by a free and full conversation on experimental religion, he satisfies them that he has more than the name or form of godliness; and that he has, as far as human judgment can determine, experienced in his own soul, that blessed change, which is called the new birth. And it is a matter of vital interest to the prosperity of the church, that this salutary provision of our fathers be not suffered to degenerate into a mere formality. If the time should come—which may God avert!—when vital piety shall not be deemed an essential prerequisite to an entrance on the sacred office, *Ichabod* may be written on our church, for the glory will have departed from her.

Whether, now, this duty is performed by presbyteries, with as much fidelity as its importance demands, I shall not take it upon me to determine; but it cannot be amiss to submit it to their consideration, in the form of an inquiry. In some presbyteries, the salutary practice of conversing freely and frequently with candidates during the period of their continuance on trial, has been introduced, and is calculated to produce the happiest effects. It cannot for a moment be supposed, that such a continued scrutiny would be ungrateful to the feelings of pious young men. They are often involved in perplexing difficulties in relation to their call to the ministry; and most commonly their difficulties arise from doubts respecting the genuineness of their religious experience. To such it would often be of incalculable importance to be permitted freely to expose their exercises to the view of experienced ministers of the gospel, that they might enjoy the benefit of their counsels.

But my object in addressing you at present, my young Friends, is not to insist on the necessity and importance of genuine piety in the sacred office, but to offer some considerations to show the advantages of eminent piety to the right and successful discharge of the duties of the ministry.

I. The first remark which I would make on this subject is, *that without some degree of eminence in our piety, it is scarcely possible, that we should possess satisfactory evidence of its reality.* And this results from the very nature of the evidence which we must possess, in order to be satisfied, on solid grounds, respecting the goodness of our spiritual state. A man can in no other way know that he is renewed, and in the favour of God, but by the exercise of faith, repentance, love to God and his people, humility, meekness, submission, *etc.,* but the certainty, that we do repent, believe, and love God and the children of God, must depend on the strength and constancy of these exercises; therefore, they alone who have attained to some eminence in piety will possess that assurance, which is so desirable to every Christian, but especially important to the minister of the gospel. When the principle of piety is feeble, the remaining corruption of nature will be proportionally strong, and, consequently, it will be exceedingly difficult to ascertain whether this weak faith, encompassed by so many infirmities, is indeed a saving faith. This difficulty is increased by the consideration, that there are counterfeits of piety so imposing, that, if it were possible, they would deceive the very elect. Some, indeed, will be disposed to allege, that the witness of the Spirit is sufficient to furnish undoubted evidence of our being the children of God, even if our exercises of faith and love be very feeble. I have no doubt that the Spirit does often give his decisive testimony to the fact that a person is passed from death unto life; but it may well be doubted whether the witness of the Spirit is ever given independently of the actual exercises of piety. It seems to me much safer, and more reasonable, to believe, that this testimony is afforded by calling into lively exercise the graces of the Holy Spirit; and, although it is true, that the Holy Spirit does shine upon his own work in the heart, and enable the pious soul to see clearly that its past views and exercises were of a truly spiritual and evangelical kind; yet, it is reasonable to think, that when these satisfactory views of past experience are enjoyed, the present state and exercises of the mind are more than usually elevated. When we are in darkness, and our faith is feeble, we are unable to recognize the character even of those holy affections, which, at the time, appeared most clearly to be the fruit of the Spirit; but it is a matter of common experience with the exercised Christian, that when he has a renewal of these pious emotions, he can look back and clearly discern the nature of similar exercises which were formerly enjoyed. But conceding that the Holy Spirit may produce in us immediately, a joyful persuasion that we are the children of God—and I do not deny that this may be the fact—to whom is it most probable that this favour will be granted? To him whose pious affections are lively and vigorous, or to him who is weak in the faith, and dull and irregular in all the exercises of religion? Undoubtedly to the former. It is not God's method of dealing with his children, to encourage sloth and unfaithfulness, by connecting assurance with a low state of piety; but this is the gracious reward of the watchful, diligent, persevering believer. When the exercise of piety is low, anxious fear is made to operate on the sluggish mind. And if there are cases which seem to be repugnant to the statement here given, they may, nevertheless, be reconciled with it; especially, when it is considered how incapable we are of ascertaining the real spiritual state of others. In order to this, it would be necessary that we should see the person in his private devotions; yea, that we should be able to examine the daily feelings of his heart. Some persons who are truly and ardently pious, and who hold much communion with God and their own hearts in private, do not exhibit to others as much appearance of lively piety as many others, who, in fact, are greatly inferior to them. This is sometimes owing to a constitutional reserve and diffidence, or to a natural buoyancy of spirit, which, when the person is in company, has the appearance of levity. And again, it ought to be considered, that as none are more confident of their good estate than deluded souls, many of those who seem to maintain assurance without much appearance of elevated piety, may belong to this class. In general it will be found, that a rational scriptural assurance is the result of much self-examination, reading the Scriptures, and prayer, and that those who enjoy this delightful persuasion habitually, are persons in whom genuine piety has been assiduously cultivated, and has acquired deep root, and is in a healthy, vigorous state. If, then, you would gain a comfortable assurance of being the children of God, you must aim at a high standard of piety.

II. Eminent piety is not only necessary to the peace and personal comfort of the minister of the gospel, but *it is requisite to prepare him for the faithful, diligent, and successful discharge of the duties of his office.* Pastoral duties are often exceedingly difficult to be performed. They require so much self-denial, so much benevolence and compassion, and so much spiritual wisdom, that it may be calculated on as a matter of certainty, that they will be neglected, or carelessly performed, unless the minister be actuated by deep and strong feelings of piety. It requires an habitual impression of divine things, and a continual sense of the responsibility of our office, to keep up our minds to that lively tone of feeling which is necessary to lead us forward in our work with alacrity, energy, and perseverance. The temptations to indolence and self-indulgence, are so powerful from without and from within, that you will undoubtedly grow remiss, unless you are sustained by more than common piety. Some will, for want of this, be led away by the spirit of the world around them, and will be satisfied with such attainments as the low state of piety in their people demands. They sink down to the level of the church, which they serve, instead of endeavouring to raise the standard of piety among those committed to their charge. Others become discouraged at the apparent want of success from their labours, and nothing more effectually cuts the nerves of effort than despondency. Such ministers may be thought very pious, because they are low-spirited, and indulge gloomy anticipations; but there are few things more inimical to lively piety and to ministerial fidelity, than this moping, desponding temper. Few things have a greater tendency to harden the heart, and to render the man reckless of consequences, than this discouraged state of mind. The talents of such ministers are permitted to rust for want of exercise, and all their efforts are slow and feeble. Others again will engage with ardour in literary pursuits, and while they are gratifying a mere natural thirst for knowledge, or a vicious ambition of pre-eminence, persuade themselves that they are occupied with the labours of their high vocation. Many pastors neglect the spiritual welfare of their people upon pretence of study, when, if their literary pursuits were impartially examined, they would be found to have little or no connection with their great work; yet these are more respectable and more useful, than the class of indolent loungers, who are seldom in their studies, and who have the temerity to serve God in his sanctuary with crude, undigested discourses, which cost them no labour in the preparation. Now, the remedy for all these evils, and scores of others, is the possession of higher degrees of religion. This will make the indolent man, industrious; the careless man, serious; the ambitious, humble. This will induce the servant of the Lord to watch for souls as one that must give an account. Who, except the man who has his heart touched with a tender compassion for perishing souls, will sufficiently exert himself to rescue them from ruin? The minister of Christ should be ever on the watch for favourable opportunities of winning souls. He is a fisher of men, and must study the arts of drawing them into the gospel net; accommodating himself to the tempers, conditions, and circumstances of all, that he may win some. Many of the duties of the pastor are of such a nature, that nothing but the warm feelings of piety will lead him to the regular performance of them; and, indeed, if they should be performed from other motives, it would be in such a manner as would be productive of no good. Love to God and to the souls of men, is the very principle which gives activity to the faithful minister. This leads him to patient perseverance in sowing the seed of the Word; this makes him apt to teach, and willing to condescend to men of low estate, to give them the needed instruction. Under this fluence the spiritual physician will be found in the hovels of the poor, at the beds of the sick, and in the house of mourning; but there is no other principle strong enough or pure enough, to lead to the faithful discharge of such duties; and that it be efficient, it must be kept in a lively, growing state.

But eminent piety is not only important for the discharge of the more private duties of the pastoral office, but also for the composition and delivery of sermons. Preaching is the noblest and most useful institution among men. It is God's great means of saving sinners, and edifying his own people: but in order to answer the end for which it was designed, the preaching of the gospel must be rightly performed. Many things, it is true, are requisite to make a truly good preacher; but after all other qualifications have been mentioned, and duly appreciated, it will be found, that, unless eminent piety is superadded to them all, there will be a great, and indeed, an essential defect. The true spirit of preaching cannot be described in words, but it can be perceived and felt; and this spirit is nothing else but the manifestation of those emotions and desires of the heart in which genuine piety consists. The pious man speaks from the heart; and there is a mysterious sympathy between the soul of the speaker and those of his hearers. Men need no instruction to enable them to understand the language of genuine feeling, and where that feeling is the exercise of the pure love of God, and humble penitence, it reaches the heart of the attentive hearer, and communicates by sympathy something of its nature, so far as there exists any susceptibility of a kindred emotion. If sermons were always composed under the influence of pious sentiments, they would never be those cold, formal, lifeless things which we often find them to be. And it is one of the strongest arguments in favour of extempore preaching, that the speaker is more likely to feel the truth which he utters, than when he sits down to write in his study. But this is not always the fact, for the extempore preacher may fall, and often does fall, into a round of commonplace ideas, or mere generalities, by which he is in no degree affected himself; and which, however he may exert his voice, and assume the appearance of earnestness, never can affect the intelligent hearer. The true remedy, and the only remedy, against cold, formal, and uninteresting written sermons, and against unmeaning and unimpressive extempore harangues, is the possession of lively feelings of piety when the minister sits down to compose, or when he stands up to speak. O how precious would the Word of God be to the pious hearer, if it was always delivered with the proper spirit! How much more would preaching attract the attention of the careless, and how much deeper would be the impression on their minds, if the dispenser of the Word not only delivered the truth, but poured forth with it a flood of pious affection. The low state of piety in ministers is the chief reason of the want of success in preaching. It is true, God must give the increase; but when he gives it, he prepares suitable means beforehand. It is not analogous to his method of dispensing divine influences, that the cold and formal preacher should be made the instrument of much good. It is found, in experience, that God blesses most the labours of those whose hearts are most sincerely and deeply engaged in their work. Men of eminent abilities without lively piety, make poor and dry preachers. They may compose rhetorical discourses, and deliver them eloquently, but the spirit is wanting; and while the taste of the refined may be gratified, and many may admire the ingenuity of the preacher, the pious are not fed, and the blessing of God does not commonly accompany such preaching. That man who does not seriously aim at the conversion of sinners, is not likely to be the instrument of this great change. This leads me to observe,

III. In the third place, that *eminent piety will make you mighty in prayer, and this will give success to all your other labours.* The most accomplished minister is entirely dependent on God for every degree of success in his ministry. Even the apostles could not convert a single soul by all their miraculous gifts, and by all their inspiration; by all their fervent zeal and indefatigable labours. This heavenly birth is not of the will of the flesh, nor of the will of man, but of God. 'Paul may plant, and Apollos water, but God giveth the increase; so then neither is he that planteth any thing, neither he that watereth; but God that giveth the increase.' Since, then, you are entirely dependent on the grace of God for your success in your work, is it not exceedingly important, that you should have skill and energy in using the instrument by which divine influences maybe brought down upon your ministrations? And you need not be informed, that the prayer of faith is the instrument by which the kingdom of heaven may be, as it were, invaded, and taken by violence. God cannot resist (I speak it with reverence), the force of a holy, believing, untiring importunity, which resolves to give him no rest, until he grants the blessing. Why are the labours of ministers so frequently barren of fruit? Why are they still destined to cry, 'Who hath believed our report?' The fault is not principally in the preaching: this is sound, and evangelical; but probably the great deficiency lies in the feebleness of our prayers. God is waiting to be gracious; but he will be inquired of by the house of Israel for these things, that he may do it for them. If the good seed of the Word were soaked in prayer before it is dispensed, and then watered with prayer after it is sown, it would oftener be seen to spring up and bring forth abundant fruit. The man of God must be a man of prayer—he must be instant, unceasing, and fervent in prayer; and then he will be able to open heaven, and call down showers of divine influences upon his other labours. But how otherwise can this grace and gift of prayer be obtained but by attaining to eminence in piety? On this subject Christ himself, who is the fountain of life, and himself the giver of all spiritual blessings, has set us a perfect example that we should follow his steps. At this day, especially, we need men, not only mighty in the Scriptures, but mighty in prayer. In conducting the public prayers of the congregation, how much the comfort and edification of the pious depends on the spirit of him who is their mouth to speak unto God, must be obvious to all. Our mode of offering up our prayers without a preconceived form, can commend itself to enlightened and spiritual men, only when our ministers shall possess the true spirit of prayer, and shall pray with the spirit and with the understanding. Cultivate piety, then, in all its parts, for prayer is nothing else but the natural language of the pious heart; it is the breathing of the new man; or rather the inexpressible groaning and sighing of a soul sick of sin, and panting for deliverance. O that young men who seek to be useful in the ministry would spend more time in communion with God in prayer, than they commonly do! To be eminent in piety and mighty in prayer are identical.

IV. *The example and daily walk of a pastor is of the utmost importance to his usefulness among his people.* The sentiments of a large majority of the people, respecting the nature of piety and the correct standard of life, will be taken rather from the example than the discourses of their pastor. A holy life preaches to the consciences of men as nothing else does; and it gives weight and influence to every word which he speaks; whereas, if a minister's conduct be not exemplary, he may speak with the eloquence of men and angels, and it will be disregarded. The wickedest men in society feel the force of a consistent and holy life. They may hate the man because he reproves their sins; but in their inmost souls they fear and respect him; and are more persuaded of the reality of true religion by one such example, than by a thousand arguments. The pious are continually edified and comforted by seeing the godly walk of their spiritual guide. As he appears to follow Christ, so they will endeavour to follow him. They see by his conduct what manner of persons Christians ought to be; for duty is much more evident when it is distinctly drawn out and exhibited in the life, than when inculcated in words. Now it may be laid down as a maxim, that a man's life will be as is his inward piety. No man ever did lead a holy life who had no experience of the power of true godliness. And that pastor who possesses eminent piety, is the only one whose example will produce much effect on the minds of men. Others may make an external show of zeal, and may abound in religious duties, but the sweet savour of piety will be wanting, and the uniform consistency of the mature Christian will not be found, when their whole conduct is scrutinized.

It ought also to be kept in mind, that no man can leave any security that he will not fall into disgraceful sins, but by aiming at a high standard of piety. The power of temptation is too great to be resisted by a weak and irregular faith; and no men are exposed to more dangerous temptations than are some ministers of the gospel. And, alas! many stand as beacons to warn those who come after them of the dangerous rocks and quicksands which beset the course of the minister of the gospel. Some who went out of port with swelling sails and fearless confidence, are seen, after being tossed and driven with a succession of fierce tempests, reduced almost to the condition of a wreck. 'Let him that standeth take heed lest he fall.' But when gross misconduct is avoided, there may be so much appearance of vanity, of levity, of indolence, of peevishness, of worldly mindedness, or of unsteadiness in principle and practice, that no one is edified by the example and conversation of their pastor. While the devoutly pious weep in secret over his foibles and deficiencies, the wicked secretly triumph and take confidence, because they see so little in the man of God which distinguishes him from themselves. The example of the pastor, instead of elevating the standard of piety among the people, is continually pleaded by professors and others as sanctioning their self-indulgent and careless manner of living. Be persuaded, my young Friends, to 'let your light so shine before men, that they seeing your good works may glorify your Father who is in heaven'. 'Be an example of believers, in word, in conversation, in charity, in spirit, in faith, in purity.' 'Follow after righteousness, godliness, faith, love, patience, meekness.' Nothing upon earth is so lovely as the mild but steady light of a holy life. And to exhibit such a life, you must become eminent in piety.

V. Another consideration which will confirm what has been said respecting the importance of eminent piety to ministers is, that *without this no man can be qualified to solve cases of conscience, and to direct the perplexed and troubled spirit in the way of peace.* One great end of the ministry is to bind up the broken-hearted, and to comfort mourners in Zion; but how can that shepherd heal the diseased of the flock, and guide the weak and ignorant, who is but little experienced in the divine life? 'The secret of the Lord is with them that fear him.' The man who knows not the conflicts of the Christian life, the buffetings of temptation, and the succours of grace, cannot be a skilful spiritual guide. Many young preachers who may attract much admiration by their pulpit performances are, nevertheless, poorly qualified to deal with diseased consciences, or to guide those Christians who have made great advances in the divine life. And no human learning can fit a preacher for this part of his work; he must be taught of God; and should seek to know the hidden life of communion with God, by a rich and growing experience.

VI. Finally, *uniform and exalted piety is the only thing which can render your work delightful.* To such as do not live habitually under a sense of divine truth, the duties of the ministry must be exceedingly irksome, and almost intolerable. To a heart unreconciled to God, and destitute of all relish for divine things, what enjoyment can there be in prayer, in preaching, and catechising, and attending on the beds of the sick and the houses of poverty and mourning. It is, indeed, strange, that such men should ever think of the ministry of the gospel, as a profession for life. But ambition and vain glory may find gratification in the opportunity which the pulpit affords for the display of learning, ingenuity, and eloquence, and in the respect and sanctity which, in the view of many, is attached to the sacred office;

but without lively piety, there can be no delight in the more private and self-denying duties of the pastoral care. It is love which makes every burden light, and every yoke easy. To one who loves the Lord Jesus Christ supremely, no work can be more pleasant than the feeding of his sheep and lambs. The good pastor loves the sheep for the sake of their owner, the great and good Shepherd, who laid down his life for them. For his sake, labour, and toil, and sorrow, and persecution are not only borne with patience, but welcomed and rejoiced in.

Animated by this living principle of love to the Lord Jesus Christ, the pious missionary shuts his eyes on all that the world esteems good and great, and embraces a life of poverty, toil, and suffering, in far distant lands. The endearments of home, and relatives, and country, he relinquishes, and becomes, for life, a voluntary exile. To the men of the world, his conduct appears wrapt in mystery. They cannot understand the nature of his feelings, and call them by the opprobrious name of enthusiasm. To them it seems to be an unnatural sacrifice of happiness; for they cannot imagine, that he has any compensation for his losses. But the truth is, no men on earth enjoy more pure happiness than devoted missionaries. They do actually receive a hundredfold for all the sacrifices which they have made. I speak of such as are actuated by deep and ardent feelings of piety; for, strange as it may seem, it is possible for men to become not only missionaries, but martyrs, and yet be utterly destitute of true religion. But such instances, it may be presumed, are rare. That which moves, supports, animates, and consoles the laborious preacher among the heathen, is the warm and steady glow of love to the Redeemer, and to the souls of men. The more a Christian is cast upon religion alone for his happiness, the more does he enjoy its pleasures. For this reason, the pious missionary, although surrounded with dangers and difficulties, and often almost overwhelmed with sorrow and discouragement, upon the whole, is among the happiest of mortals; and he would be unwilling to exchange his condition for one of the greatest affluence and ease.

It was nothing but the constant exercise of eminent piety which animated the apostles and primitive Christians with such an inextinguishable ardour; and which caused them to rejoice even in reproaches and persecutions. There was no miracle necessary to enable the martyrs to rejoice at the stake, and even in the flames; the shedding abroad of the love of God in their hearts was sufficient to produce all the effects which were witnessed; and the same would now result from the same cause.

Be assured, my dear young Friends, that without genuine piety, the office of the holy ministry will not be tolerable, unless the conscience be seared as with a hot iron; and without eminent piety, your work will not be pleasant; but if your hearts are deeply affected with the truths which you profess to love, and which you expect to preach, nothing will be able to prevent or materially to disturb your peace of mind. This is a joy which is full, and which no man taketh away from you. If, therefore, you wish for a happy life and a peaceful end, cultivate piety and daily study to become eminent in every branch of the Christian character. Remember, too, that you must soon appear before the judgment seat of Christ to render an account of your stewardship. When that solemn hour shall have come, the advantages of eminent piety will be most conspicuous. The difference between the faithful and diligent, and the wicked and slothful servant will be manifest to all; the one will be for ever comforted, and the other tormented. To the one, the Lord will say, 'Well done, good and faithful servant, enter into the joy of thy Lord'; to the other, 'Depart from me, I never knew you.' Through eternity shall the pious and devoted minister rejoice in the presence of God, with those redeemed spirits, whom he has been the instrument of rescuing from hell and conducting to heaven. But who can describe the anguish and the wailings of unfaithful ministers, when, with Judas, they lift up their eyes in the deepest regions of despair. 'Hell', said one of the Fathers, 'is paved with the skulls of ungodly ministers.' O, then, be in earnest about your work. Let divine love glow in your own bosom. Regard not the world nor the things in the world. Be instant in season and out of season. Live near to God, and keep up a lively sense of divine things on your minds. Exert every faculty and employ every talent and opportunity in promoting the glory of God and the salvation of men. Be faithful unto death, and ye shall receive the crown of life.

RIGHTLY DIVIDING
THE WORD OF TRUTH[1]

Study to show thyself approved unto God, a workman that needeth not
to be ashamed, rightly dividing the word of truth.
2 Timothy 2:15.

SOME parts of Holy Scripture seem not at any time to have received as much attention as their importance merits, nor as much as is given to other passages, of no greater moment. As an example of what is here asserted, may be adduced the solemn admonition of Paul, in the verse immediately preceding the text, in which he directs Timothy to charge the preachers over whom he had superintendence (and of course all), 'before the Lord, that they strive not about words to no profit, but to the subverting of the hearers'. Mere logomachies, or contentions about words have been productive of incalculable mischief in the church of God. These unprofitable disputes among the professed followers of Christ, have not only unsettled and subverted the minds of many within the pale of the church, but have been the occasion of deep-rooted prejudice in those who were without; by which their conversion has in many cases been prevented or hindered. It has long been remarked, that no spirit is more pungent and bitter than that of theologians in their contentions with one another; and it has often happened, that the less the difference, the more virulent the acrimony. When the controversy relates merely, or principally, to words, the strife is more obstinate than when it relates to things, for in that case both parties may be in the right.

[1] Archibald Alexander, 'Rightly Dividing the Word of Truth', *The Princeton Pulpit,* ed. John T. Duffield (New York: Charles Scribner, 1853), pp. 29-47.

But it may be asked, must the servant of God yield the truth to anyone who chooses to impugn it, or is he at liberty to make a compromise with error for the sake of peace? I answer, by no means. He is bound to contend for the faith once delivered to the saints, and to hold fast the form of sound words which he has received. Controversy will be necessary so long as error exists, but two things are strictly forbidden: first, unprofitable contention, the tendency of which is 'to subvert the hearers'; and, secondly, angry contention, for 'the servant of the Lord must not strive, but be gentle to all men'. No man has a right to compromise a single truth, for this is the sacred deposit which he, in common with other ministers, holds for the edification of the church; and which they are bound to commit to other faithful men, to be transmitted to those who may come after them.

It is not our duty to enter into controversy with all those who may differ from us in matters not fundamental. 'Him that is weak in the faith receive ye, but not to doubtful disputations.' 'For one believeth that he may eat all things; another, who is weak, eateth herbs. Let not him that eateth despise him that eateth not; and let not him that eateth not judge him that eateth, for God hath received him. Let every man be fully persuaded in his own mind.' In all such cases, if God's glory be the end, the person will be accepted, although he may be in trivial error. To seek the honour and glory of God, is the grand characteristic of all true Christians. 'For none of us liveth to himself, and no man dieth to himself. For whether we live, we live unto the Lord; and whether we die, we die unto the Lord; whether we live, therefore, or die, we are the Lord's.'

In our text, Timothy is exhorted 'to approve himself to God as a workman'; this term carries with it the idea of skill in his calling. He cannot with propriety be called a workman who undertakes a business which he knows not how to execute. At any rate, the 'workman who needeth not to be ashamed', must be skilled in what relates to his profession. Two sorts of men should, therefore, be excluded from the gospel ministry: first, those who will not work; secondly, those who know not how to perform their work aright. Any man who fails in either of these particulars, will bring shame upon himself. It appears to be implied that peculiar wisdom is requisite in discharging the duties of this office, for it is added, 'rightly dividing the word of truth'. Accurate discrimination is here evidently required. Not every ignorant declaimer is capable of doing this. He who would 'rightly divide the word of truth' must, unless he be inspired, diligently and for a long time study the Bible. He should study it with all the aids which can be obtained, human and divine. The body cannot be dissected by one who has never studied anatomy, and it would be reckoned great presumption in an ignorant person to undertake to perform the most difficult surgical operation. His motives might be good, and he might be persuaded that he was doing a good thing, but that would not alter the nature of the case, nor render quackery the less dangerous. Such a man could not rightly divide, or dissect the parts, so as to do no injury to the vital organs. But does it not argue greater presumption, for ignorant men to thrust themselves into the office of the holy ministry? Is it true that this is a work which can be performed without learning? Or that little danger is to be apprehended from the mistakes into which unskilful workmen may fall? We shall be better able to answer these questions, when we have considered what is requisite in 'rightly dividing the word of truth', which is the single object which it is proposed to keep in view in the remainder of this discourse.

Truth is of various kinds—physical, mathematical, moral, *etc.;* but here one particular kind of truth is referred to, called the *word of truth*—that is, the truth of the Word of God—the truth of divine revelation—*theological truth*. The Bible was not given to teach men philosophy, or the arts which have respect to this life; its object is to teach the true knowledge of God, and the true and only method of salvation. I might here spend time in showing how much preparatory learning and study are requisite to such a knowledge of the Bible as he ought to possess, who undertakes to be an expositor of its truth. But I will pass all this over, as sufficiently evident, and proceed to make some observations on the important duty of 'rightly dividing the word of truth'.

1. The truths of God's Word must be carefully distinguished from error. Light and darkness are not more opposite than truth and error. In some cases, error comes forth into the open light of day, in its native deformity, avowing its hostility to the Word of God, and professing it as its object to subvert the Holy Scriptures, under the pretext of

delivering the world from bondage, and obtaining liberty for men to live as they list. With regard to this species of error, there is no need of much skill to run the line of division between it and truth. Every honest mind can at once perceive the wide difference; and, as for those who have pleasure in unrighteousness, it is often the judgment which they incur from a just God. It has often been observed, that infidels are as incapable of *perceiving* as of *loving* the truth. But sometimes error assumes the garb, and uses the language of truth. Satan himself is transformed into an angel of light; no marvel, therefore, that error and falsehood should wear a disguise fitted to deceive the unwary, and, if it were possible, the very elect. In all ages of the world, false teachers have existed, and often abounded. False apostles, false prophets, deceitful workers have ever been the pests of the church of God, under every dispensation. And the earth is still inundated with floods of error. Through pride and licentiousness, men of corrupt minds still endeavour insidiously to sap the foundation of gospel truth; the time is come when many will not endure sound doctrine. Here the skilful workman must be on the alert. Here all his wisdom must be put in requisition, to detect, expose, and refute every form of error and heresy which may arise. By his skill, fidelity, and vigilance, the tender flock of Christ must be preserved from 'wolves in sheep's clothing'. By a clear exhibition of gospel truth, on all the important points of religion, the people should be so instructed, and so imbued with the truth, that error shall make no impression on them. Error is a creeping pestilence; no error can promote holiness. The connection between truth and holiness is most intimate and indissoluble.

2. But it is necessary to divide the truth not only from error, but from philosophy, and mere human opinions and speculations. Many who do not reject the truth, yet so cover her with robes of their own weaving, that she cannot be seen in her lovely simplicity. They are forever connecting with the doctrines of God's Word, their own wire-drawn and uncertain speculations. We have too much metaphysical reasoning in our theology. The truth of God is not illustrated by such methods; it is rather obscured and adulterated. Thus, it often happens, that a sermon contains very little Scripture truth. After the text is uttered, the preacher has done with the Bible, and the hearers are fed, or rather starved, by some abstruse discussion of a subject, not

treated of in the Word of God; or which is there taken for granted as a thing which requires no discussion, or which is above the human intellect. Now, whether these speculations are true or false, is of little consequence; for they serve neither to confirm our faith, nor to strengthen our love to God and man. This is not the pure wheat of the divine Word; it is chaff, and 'what is the chaff to the wheat?' This is not rightly to divide the word of truth. The spiritual workman must take pains to separate the Word of God from all admixture of mere human philosophy, and metaphysical speculation. It is the 'sincere milk of the word' after which the new-born child of grace thirsts, and by which he grows.

3. The skilful workman must be able to distinguish between fundamental truths and such as are not fundamental. All Bible truth is important and no part is to be rejected or neglected. But some truths must be known and believed, or the person cannot be saved; while there are other truths which true Christians may be ignorant of, and while ignorant may deny. There are two grand marks of fundamental doctrine. (i) That the denial of them destroys the system. (ii) That the knowledge of them is essential to piety. All truth is essential to the perfection of the system; fundamental truths, to its existence.

4. Rightly to divide the word of truth, we must arrange it in such order, as that it may be most easily and effectually understood. In every system some things stand in the place of *principles,* on which the rest are built. He who would be a skilful workman in God's building must take much pains with the foundation; but he must not dwell forever on the first principles of the doctrine of Christ, but should endeavour to lead his people on to perfection in the knowledge of the truth.

5. A good workman will so divide the word of truth, as clearly to distinguish between *the law and the gospel;* between *the covenant of works and the covenant of grace.* No mistakes in religion have been more frequent or more fatal, than those which relate to the terms of a sinner's acceptance with God, or the true method of justification. These mistakes are the more to be dreaded, because they seem to have the sanction of reason which dictates that a just God will treat men according to their works. Upon a superficial view, it would seem as if the doctrine of grace, or justification by faith alone, was unfriendly

to holiness. More than one-half of the Christian world, therefore, are misled by error, more or less dangerous, on this point of vital importance. Some are so blinded to the deficiencies of their own righteousness, that they place their whole dependence on their own good deeds: while others are willing to compromise the matter, and if their own merit may be permitted to come in for a principal share in the honour of their salvation, they are willing that Christ should obtain the second place, and that by his merits their own small deficiencies should be covered. By a correction of error on this point of doctrine Luther began the Reformation, and called it *the article of the standing or falling of the church.* And this was correct, for an error here vitiates the whole theology of the man who holds it; and the minister who does not clearly preach the doctrine of justification by faith in the righteousness of Christ, though he be as learned as Paul, or as eloquent as Apollos, is not such a workman as needeth not to be ashamed. Such a one can never rightly divide the word of truth. If he miss the mark on this cardinal point, you will find him bewildered and bewildering his hearers everywhere else. The gospel in his mouth will give no distinct and intelligible sound, but will be a vague and confused report; and if he *essentially* err, in regard to the method of a sinner's justification, he brings himself under the anathema of Paul for preaching another gospel—which, however, is not another, for it brings no good news to lost sinners; but sets men at work to get into paradise at the old gate, which was long ago shut up, and has for thousands of years been guarded by the fiery-flaming sword of divine justice. Here, again, men are prone, when driven from one error, to fly to the opposite; or rather in shunning one extreme to run upon the other. For while some seek salvation by the works of the law, others deny that we have anything to do with the law, and actually 'by faith make void the law', pretending and teaching that the obligation of the moral law has ceased, since Christ has obeyed it in our stead. Now, this antinomian leaven is a sweet morsel to the appetite of the carnal professor; for he loves safety and ease, but hates self-denial and holy living. Others again talk of a *new law* for Christians, which they call the law of liberty or sincerity, because it does not condemn for every transgression, as does the moral law, and does not require absolute perfection in our obedience, but is satisfied with sincerity; just as if God could change the requisitions of his law without changing his own nature, or as if it were not most absurd to suppose that any law could require less than perfect obedience to its own precepts. But we hear from another quarter that the minister of Jesus should preach *free grace,* and finished salvation, but not utter the thunders of the law, and thus produce a spirit of bondage by bringing back the terrors of Sinai. Such persons may suppose that they are the only friends of free grace; but that minister who ceases to exhibit the holy law of God in its spirituality, extent, and binding obligation, may cease to preach the gospel also; for where there are none sick, there will be no need of a physician; and where no law is preached, there will be no conviction of sin, and none crying out 'what must we do to be saved?'—so that it is most evident the law must precede the gospel in the sinner's experience, and also in rightly dividing the word of truth. I do not mean to sanction the absurd practical error, that for a time, and it may be a considerable time, the gospel should be withheld from the people. For what is this but to usurp the prerogative of God? In any audience, who can tell but there may be at least one convinced sinner, who needs instantly the consolations of the gospel? And they who have already believed, need continually the sprinkling on their heart and conscience of the same blood which at first gave them peace. Let no minister of Christ, therefore, presume to keep back, during a single sermon, the precious gospel of Jesus Christ, which, probably, some poor sinner is hearing for the last time. Who that has read the Acts of the Apostles, does not know that days and weeks are not necessary for the conversion of a soul by Almighty grace? Conviction by the law, and reconciliation by the gospel, may sometimes take place in a few minutes. The spiritual workman, therefore, who wields the two-edged sword of the Spirit, must so direct and manage this weapon of proof, as to render it most efficient in penetrating between the joints and marrow; yea, between the soul and the spirit, so that the very thoughts of the heart may be made manifest.

Let the law be faithfully proclaimed, as binding on every creature, and as cursing every impenitent sinner; and let the utter inability of man to satisfy its demands be clearly set forth, not as an excuse, but as a fault; and then let the riches of grace in Christ Jesus be fully exhibited and freely offered, and let all—however great their guilt—be urged to accept of unmerited pardon, and complete salvation.

6. Another thing very necessary to a correct division of the word of truth, is that the promises and threatenings contained in the Scriptures be applied to the characters to which they properly belong. How often do we hear a preacher expatiating on the rich consolations of the exceeding great and precious promises of God, when no mortal can tell, from anything which he says, to whom they are applicable. In much of preaching, there is a vague and indiscriminate application of the special promises of the covenant of grace, as though all who heard them were true Christians, and had a claim to the comfort which they offer. This is not a skilful division of the word of truth. In such a division, the saint and the sinner are clearly distinguished by decisive Scripture marks; so that every one may have a fair opportunity of ascertaining to which class he belongs, and what prospects lie before him. Rightly dividing the word of truth includes, therefore, what may be termed *characteristical preaching*—that is, a clear and just delineation of character, by using the pencil of inspiration. For if, in this business, men follow their own fancies, and lay down marks of piety not authorized by the Word of God, they will often cry peace to those to whom God has not spoken peace, and will give unnecessary pain to the children of God by obscuring their evidences, and perplexing their minds with fears and scruples by a false representation of the true characteristics of genuine piety. It is much to be regretted that this accurate discrimination in preaching has gone so much out of use in our times. It is but seldom that we hear a discourse from the pulpit which is calculated to afford much aid to Christians in ascertaining their own true character; or which will serve to detect the hypocrite and formalist, and drive them from all their false refuges. In the best days of the Reformed churches, such discriminating delineation of character, by the light of Scripture, formed an important part of almost every sermon. But we are now more attentive to the rules of rhetoric than to the marks of true religion. How do Owen, Flavel, Boston, and Erskine abound in marks of distinction between the true and false professor? And the most distinguished preachers of our own country—the Mathers, Shepards, Stoddards, Edwardses, as also the Blairs, Tennents, Davies, and Dickinsons,—were wise in so

dividing the word of truth, that all might receive their portion in due season. But certainly the word of truth should be so handled, that every person who does not turn away his eyes may see the lineaments of his true character, reflected from the Word, as the image from the glass. This, indeed, requires something more than a fertile imagination and a ready utterance—more than the learning of the schools, or profound critical acumen. It requires that the preacher study much upon his knees, that he examine his own heart with unceasing care, that 'the word of God dwell in him richly, in all wisdom and spiritual understanding'; and also that he converse frequently and freely with experienced Christians. In these matters there are many private persons who are wiser than their teachers; and a preacher, of true humility, will be often glad to learn from those who have had longer or deeper experience than himself. When others are seeking his counsel in regard to their spiritual condition, he is learning from them, for these are lessons which we can best learn from the living subject.

7. But finally, the Word of God should be so handled, that it may be adapted to Christians in different states and stages of the divine life; for while some Christians are like 'strong men', others are but 'babes in Christ, who must be fed with milk, and not with strong meat'. Christ taught his disciples as they were able to bear it, and reserved many things which he wished to say, to the time when they were capable of understanding his meaning. The same course was pursued by Paul. We are bound, indeed, 'to declare the whole counsel of God', but in due order, at proper times, and with a wise reference to the strength and spiritual attainments of our hearers. We must 'keep nothing back which is profitable', but he who is wise to win souls, will judge correctly when, and in what way, particular parts of the system of truth should be inculcated. Christ will not have the bruised reed broken, nor the smoking flax quenched.

Again, respect must be had to the condition of Christians, as they are found advancing in the divine life, or falling into a state of backsliding and declension. The former should be stimulated to persevere; the latter should be plucked as brands from the burning. The word of truth ought also to be so divided as to be adapted to the external circumstances of Christians. When in prosperity and honour, they should be admonished not to be high-minded, but fear; not to trust in uncertain riches, but in the living God, who giveth us all things richly to enjoy. They should be exhorted to rejoice with trembling, and to use the world as not abusing it, and should be reminded that by worldly prosperity, many professors have sunk low in piety, have become infatuated with the gaiety and pageantry of a vain world. Their affections fixed too intensely upon the creature, piety often withers under the sunshine of prosperity, and they become conformed to the world, participate in its pleasure, and court its honours. Even the real Christian, in this condition, has a morbid sensibility, which exposes him to take offence at the wounds inflicted by brotherly reproof, and friendly warning. Here the knife of the spiritual surgeon is wanted. A dangerous gangrene has arisen on the inner man, which must not be suffered to grow. Let the faithful warnings of the pulpit ring in the conscience of the professor who exhibits a character so doubtful, and stands in a position so dangerous. By fidelity ministers may give offence to their best supporters, and cause them to forsake their ministry; it may be so; it has been so, but he must approve himself to God. Whenever a minister of the gospel makes it his chief aim to please men, he ceases to be the servant of God. He must therefore reprove, rebuke, exhort, with all long suffering and doctrine. Whether men will hear or forbear he must be faithful to his Master and to their souls; and must, at every risk, clear his skirts of their blood, 'warning every man, and teaching every man, with all meekness'.

But God's people are often in affliction, and are led through deep waters. One billow succeeds another in quick succession, until they are almost overwhelmed, and, ready to sink, they cry out of the depths. Or, long-continued judgments press them down, until their spirits are broken with sorrow. 'Many are the afflictions of the righteous.' 'Whom the Lord loveth, he chasteneth, and scourgeth every son whom he receiveth.'

But under all these sorrows he has provided for them refreshing cordials in his Word, that their fainting spirits may be relieved, and their broken hearts healed. These must be administered by the spiritual physician. These disconsolate and afflicted members of the flock are those who most need the pastor's care. Over these he must exercise a watchful and tender supervision; and however humble their habitation, and obscure their condition, they must be sought out and visited. Here you may see the difference between the man-pleasing, time-serving preacher, and the humble, faithful man of God; for while the former is continually courting and flattering the great, and feasting with the rich, the latter is searching for the sheep and lambs of his Master's flock, that he may feed and comfort them, in imitation of the Great Shepherd. He must condescend to men of low estate—remember the poor—visit the sick—and have a word in season for every weary soul; yea, he must pilot the departing pilgrim over Jordan to the land of promise,

There is a portion for the dying which must not be withheld. When heart and flesh fail, and the spirit is on the wing, and just ready to take her flight into unknown worlds, then must the guide of souls hold up the torch of truth to enlighten her as she passes through the 'valley and shadow of death'. Then let the voice of the Great Shepherd be heard in his word of promise, saying, 'I will never leave thee nor forsake thee.' 'In my Father's house are many mansions'; 'Father, it is my will that where I am, there my disciples may be also, that they may behold my glory.'

The exhortation of Paul to Timothy is to study to show himself approved unto God, a workman that needeth not to be ashamed: and he points out the method by which he might thus meet with the divine approbation, *viz.*, by rightly dividing the word of truth. What is included in this duty, we have now considered, and will leave the application to those who are interested in the subject. Ministers, who are accustomed to teach others, ought to be willing to teach themselves also. They who have the skill and fidelity to apply the truth to the consciences of their hearers, should also be faithful to their own souls in detecting and censuring their own failures in time past, and should to the last day of their ministry endeavour to improve in every pastoral qualification, and in fidelity and skill in dividing the word of truth. Many useful inferences might be deduced from this subject, but I forbear to bring them forward, first because I have already consumed as much of your time as is proper; and, again, because I would not trench upon the ground which will more properly be occupied by those brethren who have been designated to take part in this solemn service.

I would conclude by remarking that my own ministry in the Word is coming fast to a close; and one of my greatest consolations is to see younger ministers raised up by the great Head of the church, to fill the places of us who must soon leave the stage. I consider the preaching of the gospel to be the most honourable and important work in the world. The exigencies of the church now demand ministers of the highest qualifications; and of all qualifications none is so indispensable as deep, unfeigned, spiritual piety—a heart imbued habitually with the Spirit of Christ, and disposed to count all things but loss for his sake; and willing to count not their own lives dear to them, so that they may finish their course with joy, and the ministry received of the Lord Jesus, to testify the gospel of the grace of God.

The wise, faithful, and laborious workman may be enabled to say with Paul, shortly before the close of his ministry,

> I am now ready to be offered, and the time of my departure is at hand. I have fought a good fight, I have finished my course, I have kept the faith. Henceforth there is laid up for me a crown of righteousness, which the Lord, the righteous Judge, will give me at that day; and not to me only, but unto all them also that love his appearing.

Then, indeed, will the Supreme Judge manifest his approbation of all his faithful servants who have rightly divided the word of truth.

THE PASTORAL OFFICE[1]

Feed my sheep.
John 21:16

ALTHOUGH the Lord Jesus Christ treated all his disciples with condescending and affectionate familiarity, yet some of them he distinguished with more marked attention, and with more intimate access to himself than the rest. On what ground this preference was manifested, it is not for us to inquire; it is sufficient that we are sure that all his actions were guided by perfect wisdom, and sprung from the purest motives. Of the whole number, John only had the appellation of 'the disciple whom Jesus loved'; and to him it was granted, not only to be present at those interesting scenes in our Lord's life and sufferings which were exhibited to few witnesses, but also to lean on his breast at the sacred supper, and to receive, as a legacy, the charge of the blessed virgin from Jesus while dying upon the cross.

But Peter also received many marks of special attention from his Master. He was applauded and honoured for his noble confession, that Jesus was the Messiah, the Son of the living God; was severely rebuked for his cowardly and carnal policy in endeavouring to dissuade his Master from meeting the sufferings which he had foretold; was forewarned of his shameful and ungrateful denial of his Lord; and was the object of the special prayers of the great Intercessor, that his faith might not entirely fail in this hour of temptation and discomfiture. And when he had verified the prediction of Jesus, by thrice denying him, he was brought to a penitent sense of his sin by a reproving but gracious look from his suffering Lord.

[1] Archibald Alexander, '*The Pastoral Office*'. *A Sermon, Preached at Philadelphia, before the Association of the Alumni of the Theological Seminary at Princeton on Wednesday Morning, May 21, 1834* (Philadelphia: Henry Perkins, 1834).

After the resurrection, also, Peter, notwithstanding his fall, was not overlooked. The angels who appeared at the sepulchre to the women, charged them to inform his disciples of the event, and *Peter;* not naming any other. And it seems that Christ appeared to Peter before he had been seen by any other of the apostles. And here, at the sea of Tiberias, a place consecrated by the residence, the miracles, and sermons of Jesus, he directed his conversation, in a very special manner, to Peter; asking him three times, whether he loved him, and at each answer giving him a charge to 'feed his lambs', or to 'feed his sheep'.

The first thing which claims our attention in these words is, the tender solicitude which the great Shepherd feels for his flock; a solicitude, which has no measure, abatement, or termination. 'A woman may forget her sucking child, but I will not forget thee', is the language which he uses to them. In life, in death, and after his resurrection, he still bears them on his heart; just as the high priest of the Jews bore the names of the twelve tribes on his breast-plate, when he appeared before God.

But who are they whom Christ denominates 'my sheep', 'my lambs'? They are undoubtedly 'a peculiar people', 'a chosen generation'. Christ always makes a wide distinction between his sheep and the rest of the world. They are the elect people, 'whom God foreknew, and whom he predestinated to be conformed to the image of his Son: who were chosen in Christ before the foundation of the world, that they should be holy and without blame before him in love'—'being predestinated to the adoption of children by Jesus Christ to himself, according to the good pleasure of his will'—'to the praise of the glory of his grace'. They are the persons given by the Father to Christ, not one of whom can be lost; for Christ giveth eternal life to all that were given to him (*John* 10:28). 'And I give unto them eternal life, and they shall never perish; neither shall any man pluck them out of my hand.' They are such as from eternity were beloved of the Father and the Son: for whom the good Shepherd layeth down his life. 'I am', says he, 'the good shepherd; the good shepherd giveth his life for the sheep'. And again, 'I lay down my life for the sheep.' The Apostle Paul seems to have had the words of our text in his mind, or rather the sentiment which they express, when he addressed the elders of Ephesus in this solemn exhortation: 'Take heed, therefore, unto yourselves, and unto the flock, over the which the Holy Ghost hath made you overseers, to feed the church of God which he hath purchased with his own blood.' This is that 'little flock', to which it is the 'Father's good pleasure to give the kingdom'.

The sheep of Christ do all, sooner or later, 'hear his voice and follow him'. Before he goes after them, to call them by his Word and Spirit, they know him not, although they are known to him. During this time of ignorance, they wander far from the fold, and the pastures of the good Shepherd; have no delight in his Word and service; but when he draws them to himself, and reveals to them his love and his glory, they leave all for his sake, and are ready to follow him wherever he goeth; 'through evil report and good report'.

While on earth, they are the objects of his special care. For their sake the church was established; and all its ordinances and institutions are intended for their nourishment, growth, and consolation. In their seasons of darkness and tribulation, he never forsakes them; but his arm is continually stretched out for their protection, against the ravenous beasts of the wilderness, which are ever 'going about, seeking whom they may devour'. After conducting them safely through the perils of the wilderness, they pass 'the valley and shadow of death', under his guidance; but even there, 'they fear no evil', for he is with them, and with his rod and staff he comforts them.

From what has been said, it appears, that the sheep of Christ are now in three states, widely different from each other. One part are not yet in the fold, and know nothing of the good Shepherd, that bought them with his blood. Another part are in the church, or at least in a state of grace, and hear the voice of the Shepherd, and follow him; but are still liable to many diseases and disasters, and exposed to many fierce and powerful enemies. The third class are safely gathered into the general fold above, and feast in celestial pastures, where no ravening beast enters, and where they are exempt from all disease, and from all danger.

Another prominent truth, in these words, is, that *love to Christ —supreme love to Christ*—is the most important qualification of a pastor of Christ's flock. The question is thrice put, 'Simon, son of Jonas, lovest thou me?' And in each case, after receiving an affirmative answer, the Lord Jesus commands him to feed his sheep, or to feed his lambs. Is not this as much as to say, none are qualified to feed my sheep, who have no love to me? And the thing is sufficiently evident to reason; for he who has no love to the owner, will have no real regard for the safety and health of the flock. Among men of the world, it sometimes happens, that one passion becomes so strong, that it nearly swallows up all others. Thus, avarice in the miser, is found potent enough to counteract the strongest propensities of nature. Ambition, also, in others, carries all before it. Everything subserves the one pursuit, or yields to it. Now, such should be the case with the minister of the gospel. The love of Christ ought so to predominate, so to possess his mind, and to bear him along, that every interfering, or opposing principle, should be neutralized or extinguished. This should suggest all his plans, guide all his operations, give energy to all his efforts, and afford him comfort under all his trials. Constrained by the love of Christ, he should cheerfully forego all the comforts of ease, affluence, and worldly honour to serve his Master in places far remote; or far removed from public observation. This holy affection should impel him to undertake the most arduous duties, and encounter the most formidable dangers; this should enkindle the ardour of his eloquence, and supply the pathos of his most tender addresses. This is the hallowed fire which should be kept bright and burning continually. All other warmth is no better than 'strange fire'. Nothing but the love of Christ, can make a truly faithful pastor, or evangelist, assiduous in all his services, and indefatigable in the most private and self-denying duties of his office. Other motives may lead a man to great diligence in preparing for his labours in the pulpit, where splendid eloquence wins as much applause as anywhere else. Other motives also may stimulate a minister to great public exertion, and give him all the appearance of fervent zeal and devotedness to God, in the eyes of men; but if supreme love to Christ be wanting, he is, after all, nothing; or, at best, a mere 'sounding brass or tinkling cymbal'. Genius, learning, eloquence, zeal, public exertion, and, great sacrifices, even if it should be of all our goods, and of our lives themselves, will be accounted of no value, in the eyes of the Lord, if love to Christ be wanting.

The church is now using laudable exertions to increase the number of ministers; but, we may multiply preachers; we may educate them well, and they may be acceptable to the people; but, alas! if they love not the Lord Jesus Christ, Zion will not be built up. The great harvest will not be gathered.

But I proceed now to what is my principal object, to inquire how the sheep of Christ's flock should be fed. Or, in other words, to give an outline of the duty of a pastor to his flock.

Our blessed Lord, here employs two words to signify his flock, 'lambs' and 'sheep', that it might appear, that he would have Peter, and other pastors, to overlook none, however weak they may be. He also uses two words to express the duty of pastors, in taking care of the flock. First, he says, Βόσκε τὰ ἀρνία μου, *feed my lambs;* next, he says, ποίμαινε τὰ πρόβατά μου, *perform the office of a shepherd* to my sheep. The only reason for bringing the original into view here is, that the difference between the extent of the meaning of these two words is not preserved in the English version. The second word, here employed, has a much more extensive sense than the other. It is often used to express the idea of government and guidance, as well as feeding. No word is more common with classic writers, to express the whole duty of a king in governing and providing for his people. This word, therefore, properly includes the whole duty of a pastor to his flock.

It will be no how necessary to take notice here of the extravagant claims which the Romanists found on this text, in favour of the regal power of their pontiff, over the whole church. It is sufficient to observe, in regard to such claims, that no one would ever have thought of looking to this text for support to them, unless there was a great deficiency of other evidence.

It would be presumptuous to undertake to give a full view of pastoral duties, in the time allotted for this discourse. Volumes have been written on the subject, and it would not be difficult to fill many discourses, with the detail of the various and important duties of the pastoral office; but my object is only to bring forward a few things—a mere outline, which each of you is capable of filling up; and which, I trust, you do fill up, not merely in theoretical knowledge, but in the daily practice of the duties of your office.

1. This duty of feeding the sheep of Christ, implies, that we should endeavour to gather them into the fold, and introduce them to the

pastures which he has provided. Christ said to the Jewish people, 'other sheep I have which are not of this fold. Them also I must bring.' He meant the people whom he had chosen, who were then scattered among the heathen, in different countries. These were not of the Jewish fold, but they were his sheep. They were not yet brought home, and had not yet heard his voice, but he claims them as his own. To gather in these, was the first object of the ministry of the apostles. 'Go', says Christ, in giving the commission, 'Go into all the world, and preach the gospel to every creature.' 'Go teach, or make proselytes, of all nations'; and, accordingly, 'they went everywhere, preaching the word', and the Lord was with them, and great was the company of disciples. The sheep were now gathered into the fold of Christ by thousands. The gospel net was seldom cast in vain, but under the direction of the Master, it enclosed a multitude of men. And why may we not hope to see similar effects from the preaching of the gospel, accompanied by the outpouring of the Holy Spirit, in these latter days. Most assuredly, if the world is to be filled with the knowledge of God as the waters cover the sea; if all nations are to be given to Christ as his inheritance; if all shall know the Lord, from the least to the greatest, then the ingathering of souls in all former seasons, is nothing more than the first fruits of the glorious harvest which is yet future. God's arm is not shortened that it cannot save; the Word has lost nothing of its energy; and the residue of the Spirit is with him. Why then are we so unbelieving, and so easily discouraged, as though Zion would never arise; as though the fulness of the Gentiles would never come in; as though the promise would never be fulfilled, that all Israel shall be saved?

If this good work had been prosecuted as it was begun, by this time, there would have been none left in the wilderness; the whole world would before now have been included in the visible church. But alas! although the church has changed its situation, yet it is doubtful whether it is much more extensive than at the close of the apostolic age. Much the greater part of the world is still unoccupied ground; and the commission to go into all the world to call in the lost sheep, has devolved upon the present ministry, in all its force. This long-neglected duty, has of late engaged the attention of the church, and some have felt the constraining obligation of the divine command, and have gone forth, to preach the gospel among the heathen. (May the King of Zion prosper them in their work!) But still little, comparatively, has been done. Professing Christians, in general, are not as deeply interested in promoting this object as they should be. Ministers are not sufficiently impressed with the duty which is incumbent on them. The lost sheep ought to be gathered from the east and the west, and the north and the south; but when the inquiry is made, 'Who will go for us?', we do not hear a sufficient number promptly saying, 'Here are we, send us.'

This is undoubtedly the most important and glorious work, about which the minds of men can be occupied. All other enterprises, whether scientific, political, or economic, terminate on some benefit or convenience which relates only to temporal things; but the conversion of the world to Christianity is connected with the eternal welfare of mankind, and at the same time, would promote their happiness in this life, more than all other causes which can be put into operation; for 'godliness hath the promise of the life that now is, as well as of that which is to come'; and is in all respects the greatest gain. And this great and glorious work is predestinated. The Scriptures must be fulfilled, and God is able to accomplish all his richest promises to the church. This dark world shall be enlightened. This corrupt world shall be regenerated. This confused and deformed world shall be restored to order and clothed with beauty, and this miserable world be filled with joy and rejoicing. Glorious things, indeed, are spoken, in the volume of God's prophecies, respecting Zion: she shall become the joy of the whole earth, and all nations shall unite in calling her blessed. And these extraordinary benefits shall be conferred by the preaching of the everlasting gospel; and this inestimable treasure is not committed to angels, but to men. You are the ambassadors of Christ, by whom a rebellious world is to be reconciled. You are of the number of the workmen by whom this spiritual temple is to be built; and as your season of labour is circumscribed within narrow limits, it behooves you to work the work of God while the day lasts, for the night cometh on apace, when no man can work. You will never have another opportunity to glorify your Lord upon earth. Whatever you may do, others will arise who will be honoured with glorious success in the advancement of the

Redeemer's kingdom. The sheep must be gathered into the fold, and the good Shepherd will cause them, even from the ends of the earth, to hear his voice and follow him. Happy, indeed, will those pastors be, who, when he appeareth, shall be able to exhibit a multitude converted by their ministry.

And when missionaries offer themselves, there is not that promptness in the churches, to contribute liberally to their support which is desirable. And perhaps there is not always that self-denial and readiness to endure hardship, in the missionary, which the nature of the service requires. There ought to be more expedients to lessen the expenses of our missionary stations; for upon the scale of expense on which they have been conducted, it is certain, that operations of this kind must be circumscribed within very narrow bounds.

If the Christian church felt her obligations to her Lord and Redeemer as she ought, the whole body would be like a great missionary society, whose chief object was to spread the gospel over the whole world.

It was the last public act of a greatly respected and highly gifted servant of Jesus Christ, personally known to many of you, and by character to you all, when on his deathbed, and when heart and flesh were failing, to dictate a set of resolutions[1] to be laid before the General Assembly of our church, the object of which was, to make a public and solemn declaration, that the church consider herself as a great missionary society, instituted for the conversion of the world; and that henceforth she would make that her great object. The Moravians have effected more than all other Protestants, although few in number, because they have made the extension of the Redeemer's kingdom, the primary object of their association.

But how many of Christ's sheep may be still uncalled in our own land? Is there zeal enough, and exertion enough, in supplying the destitute around us, and in our frontier settlements, with the means of grace? Are not large districts of country lying desolate, as it relates to the institutions and instructions of religion? Consider, dear Brethren, what should be done, and what duty devolves upon each of you in this respect. Foreign missions, and home missions,

---

[1] The reference is to the Resolutions dictated by the late lamented Rev. Dr John H. Rice, during his last painful illness.

ought never to be viewed as rival or interfering objects. They are only different departments in the same great field of labour; and success in the one has a direct tendency to promote the prosperity of the other.

2. Next, let us consider the manner in which the sheep, when gathered into the fold, should be fed. The Word of God is, in general, the food with which his people must be fed. The knowledge of the truth, is the proper nutriment of the spiritual life.

Now, to feed the flock of God, the pastor must understand the Scriptures. And he must feel in his own soul the experience of the efficacy of the truth. 'For if the blind lead the blind, will not both fall into the ditch?' A guide of the children of God, ought to have a deep and rich experience of the manifold grace of God; and should be well acquainted with the various cases of conscience, which are common among the sheep of his pasture. His very soul should be imbued with the spirit of the gospel. And he should be of a very tender and compassionate disposition, towards all persons labouring under trouble of mind.

To feed the church of God, it is necessary, that the *truth of the gospel* be preached. Error can never nourish the soul. Error, even when mingled with truth, is like poison in our food. It is a thing much to be dreaded and avoided, to preach what is not true; or, what God has never commanded us to teach. The pastors of Christ's flock, have the strongest motives to induce them to 'take heed to themselves and to their doctrine'. They should be exceedingly solicitous to know what the truth is, not only for their own sakes, but for the sake of the people; and when they do know the revealed will of God, woe be unto them, if they do not preach it faithfully.

The whole counsel of God should be declared. Nothing that can be profitable should be kept back. The scribe well instructed in the kingdom of God, brings out of his treasure things new and old. The Old Testament and the New; the law and the gospel; the promises and the precepts; the predictions and the histories; the justice and the grace of God;—in short, everything which the Scriptures have it as their object to reveal, we must preach. Yet as in every system, while all parts are necessary in their place, some are more absolutely essential, and occupy a more central, and more prominent place;

so, in the system of scriptural doctrines, some truths must be made more conspicuous than others; and must be more frequently and earnestly inculcated, because on the knowledge of these, salvation is suspended. But every part of divine revelation should receive proper attention. The people need to be instructed in all that God has revealed for the edification of his church.

The Word of God must be exhibited in its genuine simplicity. The babes of Christ grow and thrive only by the 'sincere' (*i.e.,* untainted, unmixed) 'milk of the word'. This celestial nutriment will not bear to be mixed with human inventions and philosophy, without great injury. There should be no adulteration of the truth. No diluting of it. No combination of it with things foreign to its nature. Clear, sound, simple expositions of divine truth, should form the basis of the pastor's instructions from the pulpit.

The truth should be preached in a discriminating manner, with adaptation to the state and capacities of the particular flock to which it is addressed, and with seasonable and powerful application.

A mere general exhibition of the truth, without skilfully dividing it, so as to give every one his proper portion, is such a method of feeding the sheep of Christ, as will bring shame on him who thus dispenses the Word. What should we think of the skill and fidelity of a physician, who should mix up good medicines and dispense them indiscriminately to all the patients in a hospital? Very much like this is the conduct of the preacher who deals out the Word of God, without regard to the different characters of his hearers. Careless sinners must be awakened and persuaded by having the terrors of the Lord set before them. The watchman must not fail to sound the alarm, and testify against the sins of the people. 'He should cry aloud and spare not.' For if he fail of being faithful, their blood will be required at his hands (*Ezek.* 3:17-21).

Gainsayers must be convinced, and their mouths stopped with solid argument. And yet we must instruct those, who oppose themselves, with meekness. 'The weapons of our warfare are not carnal.' 'The servant of the Lord must not strive', but yet he must 'earnestly contend for the faith once delivered to the saints.' The ignorant must be instructed. The babes in Christ must be fed with milk; the mature believer with strong meat.

The mourner must be comforted, and the weak and faint supported and refreshed, with an application of the free and gracious promises of God.

But in order to adapt his instructions to the various classes of persons in his charge, and to meet the various exigencies of the people, the pastor must descend from the pulpit; he must follow his flock to their homes. He must teach not only 'publicly', but also 'from house to house'. He must find out, by personal acquaintance, the wants and diseases of mind under which they suffer. He must patiently, assiduously and perseveringly set himself to feed the sheep of Christ; and not to overlook the 'lambs', who are first mentioned in our Lord's charge to Peter. It matters not whether by these we understand the weak in faith, or those of tender age; both must be carefully nourished. The youth form the most interesting part of the flock of every pastor. On them rest the hopes of the church. They must soon stand in the places of their fathers. They will very shortly have the whole concerns of the church of Christ in their hands. How important is it then, that they be trained up in the way they should go; 'brought up in the nurture and admonition of the Lord'.

Among all the 'signs of the times' which are encouraging, there is no one more calculated to inspire hope, than the attention paid to youth in Sabbath Schools and in catechetical and Bible classes.

This is, indeed, to begin to build on a good foundation. If we would have the tree to grow strait, we must attend to it when young and tender. Let these efforts then be continued and multiplied. This is so far a compliance with the command of Christ, 'feed my lambs'.

By means of Sunday Schools, now so widely extended over the church, the faithful pastor is furnished with a troop of auxiliaries, in the faithful discharge of his duty, unknown to our fathers, and which should be appreciated as one of the distinguishing blessings which God has granted to his church in our days. That pastor who does not cherish and patronize this catholic institution manifests an ignorance or indifference in regard to the welfare of the lambs of his flock, little consistent with sincere love and fidelity to the great Shepherd. The superintendence of these schools, within the bounds of his charge, properly belongs to the pastor, and his assisting elders; and when the actual duties are transferred to other competent hands, the direction and government should remain with him. But I must not omit, what has long been with me a favourite opinion, that these Sunday Schools should include persons of all ages: all your people, even though grey-headed, should be in a course of regular instruction. The truth is, that most adults need to have the same lessons inculcated, which are given to the children. This, moreover, is no impracticable theory. The experiment has been tried, in a number of congregations in Massachusetts, and the result, as far as is known, is delightful. It is not necessary for adult men and women to be catechised as children are, but they might be formed into classes; might appoint a leader, or take this office in turn, and might prepare a certain number of chapters, on the contents of which they might freely converse, for an hour or two; and such as desired it, might be permitted to propose questions, to be answered on the spot, or to be reserved until the next meeting. We are, in fact, all children, while in this world, and need to learn something from God's Word every day; and such an employment would fill up the vacant hours, and enliven the spirits of the aged, when they are so apt to become torpid, for want of interesting objects of attention. And I verily believe, that it would be the means of preserving their powers from sinking into dotage.

And if parents could be induced to co-operate more zealously in this work; if mothers, especially, would be persuaded to be more earnest and assiduous in instilling divine truth into the infant mind, who can tell what a reformation might be wrought in one age? And I cannot but hope, that maternal affection, which is one of the strongest as well as tenderest feelings implanted in the human constitution, begins already to be directed into its appropriate channel. The existence and success of 'Maternal Associations', intended for the mutual assistance of pious mothers, encourages me to believe, that this powerful and inextinguishable yearning of the maternal heart, the nature and force of which mothers only can appreciate, is about to be sanctified to the great object of promoting early piety, and sowing the seed which may ripen into religion in mature age, when this effect fails in earlier life. If I were called on to declare what means of conversion, beside public preaching, had been most blessed of God, I should unhesitatingly answer, *maternal instruction*.

The pastor of a flock may well be compared to the physician of a hospital. It is important for him, as far as possible, to know the case of each individual under his charge; and especially to search out such as are labouring under peculiar maladies. He must not only be ready to visit his people, but prompt to enter into religious conversation with them. Not merely of a general and uninteresting kind, but relative to their own state,—their various spiritual troubles, conflicts and temptations; and having learned the cases of spiritual disease, he should study them with care, and bring them specially and individually before the throne of grace; and should not cease to visit such persons, however weak and erroneous their views may be. And even if they seem to derive no benefit from his conversation, he must not forsake or neglect them. Like a kind physician, he must show his sympathy, when he can apply no effectual remedy.

The sick, also, he must visit, and deal with them faithfully, skilfully and tenderly, according to their respective characters and states of mind.

The poor of the flock must never be forgotten by the faithful pastor. Many of the most precious of Christ's sheep and lambs, are found in this class. 'God hath chosen the poor of this world, rich in faith, and heirs of the kingdom.' It was a distinguishing proof that Jesus was the true Messiah, 'that the poor had the gospel preached unto them'. And when the other apostles had no other instruction to give Paul, they earnestly requested, that he would 'remember the poor'. 'The same', says he, 'which I also was forward to do.' Religious influence is said rather to ascend than descend. It is, I believe, a fact, that a pastor's influence over the higher classes of society, will be greater, if he pays chief attention to the poor, than if he assiduously courted the rich. The poor are much more accessible than the rich, who are fenced round by so many forms of etiquette, that to address them personally and pointedly is considered as a want of good manners; but, generally, the poor can be approached without danger of giving offence; and they consider the attentions of a minister as a condescension and favour. They also need religious instruction more than others, because their time is commonly completely occupied and their education defective. It is of high importance to guard the poor against habits of idleness and intemperance. These vices are the source of most others. To which may be added, the spending of the Lord's day in an improper manner. No evil is more threatening in free countries than the increase of pauperism: unless a check can be given to it in England, the country must be ruined; and its progress here is alarming. Pastors have more in their power, in regard to this branch of political economy, than any other class of men. Experience has fully shown the inefficacy of legal provision for the poor. The true remedy can only be found in raising their character, by instilling into their minds sound religious instruction. There is a culpable negligence, in most of our churches, in making suitable provision for the accommodation of the poor. In most Protestant churches in our large cities, you see very few of the poorest of the people. They have no place, and they are ashamed to appear in such well-dressed assemblies, with their tattered garments. It is said that in no country in the world, is there such an exhibition of fine clothing in the house of God, as in these United States. Does not this, in connection with what has been said, deserve the attention of the pastor? I consider unbounded luxury, in dress, furniture, and equipage, as one of our crying sins.

Here, it would be in place, to speak of the exercise of Christian discipline, if time would admit of our taking up this interesting subject. But we must pass it over with one or two remarks.

All discipline is intended for edification, and not for destruction. Even when one who had been in the church, was delivered to Satan for the destruction of the flesh, the end aimed at was, that 'the spirit might be saved in the day of the Lord Jesus'.

Discipline, seasonably and faithfully administered, would produce a most salutary effect. It would, indeed, sometimes offend the pride, and rouse the wrath of false professors; but by this means they are led to manifest their true character, and show what manner of spirit they are of. But on the minds of sincere believers, though erring, discipline will generally, sooner or later, produce the happiest effects. They may wince under the rod; and, for a time, a rebellious spirit be manifested, as when a child is corrected; but if the rod of discipline be applied in a firm and judicious manner, the proud spirit bends, and humble penitence ensues. But, when I speak of discipline, I take the word in its full latitude. I do not mean, principally, the arraigning of church members before the church, or church courts. This is the last resort, and should never be used till other methods have proved ineffectual. That discipline which is most likely to be salutary is that of personal admonition and reproof. If when a brother commits a fault, he should be admonished for it by anyone who is the witness of it; or if the pastor, or some of his assistants in government, would go to an offending brother, and affectionately warn, exhort, or rebuke him, as the case might require; how much evil might be prevented! 'Let the righteous smite me, it shall be as an excellent ointment, which shall not break my head.' The pastor, by a vigilant inspection of his flock, might observe the incipient tendency to go astray, and by using what may be with propriety called, preventive discipline, they might be entirely restrained from wandering, or reclaimed as soon as they had begun to deviate from the right path. The true way to prevent the disagreeable necessity of formal trials before church courts, is to be faithful and vigilant in administering that discipline which consists in a personal application of the truth of God, to such as are beginning to slide. And this, though peculiarly incumbent on pastors, and other officers of the church, is not confined to them. To neglect it towards any brother, even under the Mosaic economy, was reckoned equivalent to hating him. And there is nothing in the way of exercising this discipline, but culpable pride, and a weak tenderness, or aversion to give present pain, though the effect should be ever so salutary. 'Reprove, rebuke, and exhort, with all long suffering and doctrine.'

1. If the Great Shepherd of the sheep took so lively an interest in the welfare of the flock when he was upon earth—if they were peculiarly his object when he endured the pains of death on the cross,—if he directed his chief attention to the same subject after his resurrection, while he conversed with his disciples on earth—then, we may infer, that he still bears his people on his heart. But we are not left to inference; we have positive proof, that the salvation of his purchased flock is the object which he is continually promoting before his Father's throne. The case of every one of them he presents in his prevalent intercessions. And in the exercise of his mediatorial government, he protects, guides, and comforts every one of his sheep and lambs. The character given of him by Isaiah, he still verifies. 'He shall

feed his flock like a shepherd, he shall carry the lambs in his bosom, and gently lead those that are with young.' The situation which he occupies is the best possible for exercising a general superintendence over all his people, and providing for all their wants.

The opinion of Christ's reigning personally and visibly upon earth before the day of judgment, which at an early period of the church prevailed, and which has been zealously revived in our day by the *prophetic* men of Great Britain, is destitute of all solid foundation. In that case, he must, as when formerly upon earth, take up his residence in some particular country, where, to the churches on the opposite side of the globe, he would be as invisible and inaccessible as he is while seated at the right hand of God. The same reasons which rendered it expedient for him to leave this world, and ascend to heaven, still exist in all their force, for his continuing there. Faith does not require that its object be visible to sense: it is the property of faith to see those things which are invisible, and the greatest blessing is not to those who have seen and believed, but to those who have not seen, and yet have believed.

Thence he sends down the *Comforter,* who never leaves them, but abides with them forever. And for their edification he hath established numerous helps and means to aid them in making good their way to heaven. In particular, he has instituted the ministry of reconciliation. When he ascended up on high, he gave gifts unto men:

> Some apostles, and some prophets, and some evangelists, and some pastors and teachers, for the perfecting of the saints, for the work of the ministry, for the edifying of the body of Christ, till we all come in the unity of the faith and of the knowledge of the Son of God, unto a perfect man, unto the measure of the stature of the fulness of Christ.

To each of these under-shepherds he gives commandment, *'Feed my lambs, feed my sheep';* and his eyes, which are like a flame of fire, are ever on these watchmen. He sees how every one fulfils his duty as a pastor or evangelist. He takes notice of all their exertions, and scrutinizes all their motives. If they are found faithful, he will not fail to encourage and prosper them. 'Lo', says he, 'I am with you always, to the end of the world'; and when our work is done, he will express his approbation of every faithful servant, in a manner which will astonish them. He will say, 'Well done, good and, faithful servant, enter into the joy of your Lord', and will exalt them to such glory and felicity, as it is not now in their power to form an idea of. But he also follows with a keen eye of displeasure, all slothful, unfaithful, and self-seeking pastors. And O! how he will resent their neglect of his beloved sheep and lambs, at a future day. Dreadful will be the retribution, when unfaithful ministers shall be called to give an account of their stewardship. Much is committed to their care and fidelity. They are the 'light of the world', and the 'salt of the earth'; but if their own light be darkness, and the salt become insipid, how miserable is the situation of those for whom they are appointed to watch!

Dear Brethren, let us remember that our time of exertion will soon be over; the day of reckoning must soon come to us as well as others. Let us deal honestly with our own souls, and detect and condemn our own negligence and unfaithfulness, and be more engaged in our appropriate work, than we have ever yet been. Many of Christ's sheep are yet in the wilderness. They have never yet heard one call from the Shepherd's voice. Many for whom we ought to entertain lively hopes that they are of the destined number of the Redeemer's flock are still among us, wandering in devious and dangerous ways. Can nothing more than has been attempted be done to reclaim them? Many of them are the children of the church, who have the badge of discipleship upon them. Do pastors deal with such, with sufficient earnestness and tenderness? Do they bear them on their hearts before the mercy-seat, as the great High Priest bears all his sheep? Is there among us no remissness, no forgetfulness, no turning aside to vain jangling, no undue attachment to the world? While we preach to others, and are ready enough, perhaps, to denounce upon them the terrors of the Lord, are we not cold and formal and insensible, too often living far from God, without free access to his presence, or enjoyment of fellowship with him.

2. When I see before me so many of the Alumni of our beloved seminary, I am conscious of various and strong emotions. In the number, I observe some who were among our earliest pupils, who can no longer be addressed as young men. Middle age has been reached, and grey hairs already begin to appear, and furnish the solemn admonition, that life is on the wing; and that ere we are aware, old age is

coming on apace. When I look over the list of students, who were once connected with the seminary, I cannot avoid an impression of deep sorrow, upon observing how the ranks have been thinned by the relentless hand of death. For several years after the seminary was in operation, it was often a subject of remark, that not an individual of our number, had been taken away by death; but now, after the lapse of twenty-two years, I find, upon examination, that the number of students, who have deceased, amounts to more than sixty. Yes, it is a solemn fact, that more than sixty of the Alumni of the institution, have been snatched away from their earthly labours! Some, indeed, were cut down before they had entered on their public work; while others were permitted to preach the gospel successfully for a number of years.

The fact which has now been stated, cannot fail to be received by you who survive, as a solemn admonition to be ready also; as 'you know not the day nor the hour' when your Master will call for you, to render up an 'account of your stewardship'. Another grave lesson which it teaches is, that you should work while the day lasts, as the night rapidly approaches, when no work can be done. 'Whatever your hand findeth to do, do it with your might.' When this short span is gone over, there will be no possibility of returning to correct the errors, or compensate for the defects of your ministry. If we could only appreciate the value of our time and opportunities of usefulness, what energy would it not communicate to our efforts! Permit me then, in the view of the shortness and uncertainty of life, to exhort you most earnestly to exert all your faculties, and improve all your opportunities, to promote the kingdom of your Lord and Saviour. 'Be fervent in spirit', constant in affection, wise in your plans, and indefatigable in your labours. Some of you may have what the world would call a hard lot. You may be subjected to many privations, and to heavy toils, in obscure stations; where, separated from polished and enlightened society, and even from much intercourse with your brethren, your hearts may become discouraged, and you may feel as if you were forgotten by all; but remember, that however you may live unnoticed by men, there is *One* whose watchful eye never loses sight of you, and whose sympathizing heart bears a part in all your sorrows. There is *One,* who has promised, that he 'will never leave you nor forsake you', and that he will 'be with you always, even to the end of the world'. This friend, 'who sticketh closer than a brother', has power as well as compassion; and has pledged his word, that all things shall work together for good, to them who love him. And in due season, he will reward you openly, for all the sufferings and labours endured for his sake.

3. As you are now met to renew your feelings of mutual friendship, and to revive your affection towards our beloved seminary, I would call to your remembrance some of the objects contemplated by the founders of this institution, as expressed in the Plan which you often heard read when students. These objects are,

> To furnish our congregations with enlightened, humble, zealous, laborious pastors, who shall truly watch for the good of souls, and consider it as their highest honour and happiness, to win them to the Saviour, and to build up their several charges in holiness and peace.

> To promote harmony and unity of sentiment among the ministers of our church, by educating a large body of them under the same teachers, and under the same course of study.

> To preserve the unity of our church, by educating her ministers in an enlightened attachment, not only to the same doctrines, but to the same plan of government.

These important and desirable ends, it is your solemn duty to promote; and, perhaps, the responsibility was never greater on any ministers of the Presbyterian Church, than on those of you who are now members of her supreme judicatory. The crisis is most interesting. Much, very much, depends upon the decisions of this body, at the present sessions. It does not behoove me to dictate, or even suggest to you, what in particular should be done; but it is right that I should exhort you to lay aside all prejudice, passion, and party spirit, and with sincere and honest hearts, in the fear of God, to consult and act for the real welfare and best interests of our beloved Zion, as you will answer for it at the tribunal of Jesus Christ, before which we must all soon appear. If now, while the ark of God is in your keeping, you should give it a wrong touch: if your measures should tend to destroy the purity, disturb the peace, or break the unity of this extended section of the Christian church, how awful your accountability. If through any want of wisdom or fidelity on your part, this well-organized society should fall into dissension or disunion, what a triumph will you afford to the enemies of our common Christianity, and to those religious sects, which cherish feelings of envy and jealousy towards the Presbyterian Church. The enlightened friends of religious liberty in Great Britain, have their attention intensely fixed on the important experiment which we are engaged in making in this country, whether the church can exist and flourish, without a connection with the State; and as our denomination is among the largest and most influential, they are observing our progress with deep interest, and shall we, by our ill-timed disssensions and innovations, dash all their fond hopes, and cause them with sadness to admit the necessity of a religious establishment? Even the Protestants of Germany, are at this time observing, with excited interest, the acts and proceedings of the Presbyterian Church in America, not only as furnishing a solution of the grand problem, that religion can exist and flourish without the aid of the support and coercion of civil enactments, but also because in settling their own church polity, many of the most evangelical of their ministers are disposed to look to us as a model of the wisest ecclesiastical organization. Shall we disappoint the raised expectations of them also?

The interest which our dissenting brethren of the Congregational Union in England takes in the progress and condition of the American churches is manifested, not merely by the report of others, but by a delegation which have reached our shores, and have already expressed in strong and affectionate terms, the sentiments and sympathies of this large and respectable body of orthodox, evangelical Christians. This fraternal communion of churches, separated by the wide ocean, is truly delightful and affords a happy anticipation of that blessed time when all the real members of Christ's household, too long sundered from each other by misapprehension and prejudice, shall be united in one holy family; one pure church, which shall acknowledge 'one Lord, one faith, one baptism', and shall ever 'keep the unity of the Spirit in the bond of peace'. May these beloved brethren who are now among us, be privileged to carry back to their native country, such a report of our ecclesiastical state, as will cause the hearts of God's people, in the land of our forefathers, to rejoice.

4. Dear Friends, and once beloved pupils, advancing age and debilitated health admonish me that my continuance here will probably not be long. My race is nearly run, and if it would tend to edification, I could fill your ears with lamentations, that I have felt so little and laboured so imperfectly for the honour of the Redeemer. But I forbear to dwell on this sorrowful theme. In regard to myself, I have only to ask an interest in your daily prayers. Most of you will probably see my face no more after our parting on this occasion. As my closing exhortation, therefore, I would say, 'Trust in the Lord and do good.' Be faithful, be diligent, be humble, be zealous for the truth and honour of God. Seek the wisdom which cometh from above, and which God has promised to give to the prayer of faith. Love one another and pray for one another. Remember also continually in your supplications those who are preparing to follow you into the ministry; especially bear on your hearts before the throne of grace, the seminary which you love, and the dear youth who are there collected in successive companies. And surely I need not exhort you to remember Zion. Her very dust and stones, I trust, are precious in your eyes, and her prosperity you esteem above your chief joy. But the times in which your lot is cast are characterized by peculiar and striking signs, which it behooves you carefully to observe. The cry for help from afar is borne to you almost on every breeze. The demand for the messengers of truth begins to be made by the heathen themselves. The door for preaching the gospel is, in the providence of God, opened in almost every pagan land. The islands of the sea have already, many of them, been converted unto God, and have received in their own tongues, the law of the Lord. Many are running to and fro and knowledge is increased among the people. The church begins to feel her responsibility, and to be conscious of her power. At the same time the enemy comes in like a flood; let it be your care that the standard of the Spirit of the Lord be lifted up against him. Satan rages with more than wonted fury, because he perceives, that his time is short. Christ, the King, has need of every talent which any of you possesses. He that has ten talents, and he that has one, are equally required to occupy and improve them to the utmost; and every poor service performed

in, faith and sincerity, shall meet a divine reward. Let no discouragement, nor distrust, in relation to the church, find a place in any of your minds. The cause is God's and he is able to maintain it, and has sworn that it shall never fail. The gates of hell shall not prevail against the church, for it is founded on a rock. Be strong in the Lord, and in the power of his might. Fight the good fight of faith. Watch for souls as they that must give an account. Care only for the things of Christ, and nothing for your own things. If you make it your first and great business to seek the kingdom of God, all other things shall be added unto you. What may not you, who are now before me, and others of like character, effect for the building up of the waste places of Zion, and for the conversion of the world! Permit me then to conclude in the valedictory address of Paul to the Corinthians. 'Finally, brethren, farewell. Be perfect, be of good comfort, be of one mind, live in peace, and the God of peace shall be with you.'

THOUGHTS ON THE EDUCATION OF PIOUS AND INDIGENT CANDIDATES FOR THE MINISTRY[1]

THERE is in the minds of many a strong prejudice against the whole plan of educating young men for the ministry, on the funds of the church. Of this prejudice, the writer confesses that he once was a partaker, owing to his education among the descendants of the Scotch, who generally entertain a strong aversion to every idea of depending on others for their subsistence. There can be no doubt that this feeling of independence has been of great service to the Scottish nation, in leading the poor everywhere to struggle hard to maintain themselves. This is, therefore, a feeling which should be respected and cherished; and all persons should have it instilled into their minds in their early education. I have known many young men, who were so much under the influence of this sentiment that they have rejected all offers of gratuitous aid, and have laboured for years to acquire the means of finishing their education. And although I cannot but respect the character of such, I am now of opinion that an enlightened and enlarged view of all the circumstances which should regulate the conduct of candidates for the ministry would lead to a different conclusion.[2]

The true state of the case is this. The church wants ministers, and must languish and decline, if she does not obtain a sufficient supply. Every pious young man who has talents to be useful in the ministry,

---

[1] Archibald Alexander, *Thoughts on the Education of Pious and Indigent Candidates for the Ministry*, (Philadelphia: Board of Education of the Presbyterian Church, n.d.).

[2] The Free Church of Scotland has adopted the system of aiding her indigent candidates for the ministry.

has the ability to make for himself a comfortable living, in some secular business; and in a worldly point of view, every young man of vigorous mind and enterprising disposition makes a sacrifice of his temporal interest by becoming, in this country, a candidate for the ministry. If then, a sufficient number of candidates, from the class able to support themselves, do not offer, is it not the duty of the church to assist in the education of indigent and pious youth, possessed of good natural abilities? The question to be decided is extremely plain and simple—shall the church do without a sufficient supply of ministers, or endeavour to obtain such a supply by educating pious young men who are unable to gain an education by their own means? Suppose the church to proceed on the principle involved in the objection to this mode of procuring a supply of ministers, what will be the consequence? The appeal must here be made to facts. What has been for twenty years past, the proportion of candidates who have had it in their power to support themselves? Upon looking over the catalogue of our students, from the commencement of this seminary, I find that at least one half the whole number have required to be aided by the funds of the church or by benevolent individuals. Some of these, by spending years in teaching, might have found their way into the ministry, but the greater number would have been discouraged, and would have turned their attention to some other pursuit; or, they would have sought an entrance into the sacred office, without any suitable and thorough preparation. Certainly, we have not had a superabundance of good ministers: and surely, no one would wish to see our church filled with men imperfectly prepared. With all our exertions by means of the Board of Education, the number of our ministers falls far short of the demand.

Perhaps, there is a lurking idea, in the minds of many, that some disgrace attaches to this plan of education. As it would be a disgrace to an able-bodied man to live upon the charities of his neighbours, so it is thought that something of the same disgrace must attach to the young man, who is able to provide for himself by honest industry in some lawful occupation, to live on the funds of the church. Now this would be a fair statement of the case if nothing else was to be taken into consideration but the interest of the person himself. But if the church needs his services, and if in order effectually to serve her, he must be educated, the case is entirely changed. While she is educating these youth, she is preparing ministers for her own use, and whose services are necessary to her prosperity. If the State needs skilful officers and expert engineers for her defence, she finds it expedient to institute military schools for the education of such as are willing to turn their attention to the military profession: and no question is asked about their wealth or indigence, because the good of the country is the object in having them thus educated. This is right; and no one ever thinks that any disgrace attaches to those young men who are thus educated at the public expense. And if the church were able, it would be justice for her to educate all, of whatever external circumstances, who were qualified to do her service. But this is not demanded; all that she is requested to do is to support or aid such young men as are unable to furnish the means of their own education.

What has now been said will answer an objection often made by plain, well-meaning people, when applied to, to contribute to this object. They say, 'Our sons have to labour for their living, and what obligation is on us to give money to educate other men's sons.' To such, we would respectfully say, Have you a minister who preaches the gospel to you on the Sabbath, and do you value this privilege? Or, if you are destitute of the stated dispensation of the world, do you not desire it, as the richest privilege you can possess in this world? Well, if you need ministers, where do you think they are to come from? If all are of your mind, and refuse to aid in preparing young men for the ministry, the consequence will be that there must be a great deficiency of educated ministers; and your children may be brought up without the regular administration of the Word and ordinances of God, which you must esteem a great calamity, if you have any just estimation of the worth of their souls. But if you are so situated as to be sure of enjoying the means of grace, do you feel as a Christian, no compassion for the extensive regions in our own country, which are destitute of the regular preaching of the gospel? Do you never consider the case of the millions, and hundreds of millions, of benighted heathen, who are now on their way to the great tribunal? If in the sovereign dispensations of divine mercy, we have received and enjoyed the preaching of the Word, shall we be so selfish, as not to be willing to send it to those who are perishing for lack of knowledge; who are suffering a dreadful famine, not for the want of bread, but for the want of the Word of the Lord?

Perhaps, you say, that you are the friend of missions and willing to contribute to this object, but not to the Board of Education. But permit me to ask how the missionary enterprise can proceed without devoted ministers? The cry every year of the Missionary Boards is, 'Who will go for us?' But how can they go unless they be sent? And how can they be sent, unless they are prepared and educated for the work? The truth is, that without the Education Board, your other Boards would be, in a great measure, useless. Look over the wide missionary field at home and abroad, and ask yourselves where these men, who are bearing the heat and burden of the day, were obtained? The answer will be, from our colleges and seminaries, and a large portion of them were beneficiaries of Education Boards. They exercised the pious self-denial, to become beneficiaries of the church, that they might have the opportunity of preparing themselves for the arduous work in which they are now wearing out their lives. I have called them *beneficiaries,* but I doubt the propriety of the term; *they* are not the obliged persons; but the church is their debtor. And their sacrifice is far greater than that of the most liberal contributor to their support. And let our farmers and mechanics, when called on to contribute to this object, not consider it as a gratuity to the individuals aided, about as a necessary means of keeping up a supply of faithful pastors for our increasing churches, and as the only effectual method of obtaining missionaries to carry the gospel to the destitute, both on our continent and in foreign lands. Let it be considered, also, that if God should favour their sons by calling them to prepare for the work of the ministry, other people will be solicited to assist them in obtaining the requisite education.

And here it may be proper to remark, that many pious parents ought to seek this honour for their sons; and every congregation should have pious young men in a course of education for the ministry. The neglect of some large congregations in this respect is great and surprising. They may have experienced frequent revivals of religion and yet have never sent forth a single minister from their bounds; whilst other churches have, within the last half century, sent out dozens. In reading the *Life of the Late Dr Proudfit,* nothing struck me more forcibly, than the fact that from the single church of which he was pastor, thirty or forty young men had entered the ministry; probably a larger number than from any single congregation on the continent; or perhaps in the world. Every parent or pastor, who furnishes a good minister to the church, becomes thereby a rich benefactor to the whole body. And if they have not the ability to give a good education to the promising youth who may rise up among them, the church is bound to aid them; and in order to this, application must be made to all our congregations for their contributions.

Another objection to this mode of obtaining candidates for the ministry is, that poor young men taken up to be educated, are commonly rude and unpolished in their manners, having grown up among rough, unmannered people. And it is remarked that such seldom acquire the refinement and polish of manners, which are expected and should be found in ministers of the gospel. If this objection had weight, it would operate powerfully against the selection of the apostles, by our blessed Lord; for they were all taken from the humbler walks of life; and although their Master miraculously supplied their want of learning, by endowing them with supernatural knowledge and the gift of tongues, yet we do not read that he wrought any miracle to give them the manners of polished gentlemen. Perhaps the objector lays too much stress on the mere polish of manners. In our opinion true humility, meekness, and benevolence will produce the most genuine politeness, and if these dispositions are possessed in a high degree by the minister of the cross, the want of exterior accomplishments, though desirable, may easily be dispensed with.

It is not intended to be intimated, that clerical manners are of trivial consequence; they are undoubtedly important, and when of the right kind, tend to promote the usefulness of ministers of the gospel. The idea which I intend to communicate is that those manners which are in vogue among the higher classes of society are not exactly those which always become a preacher of the gospel. A young man who possesses genuine piety and good sense will be likely, in the course of seven years' training, to acquire as much ease and polish of manners as are necessary in a majority of clergymen; for, while a few have to mingle with the wealthy and fashionable classes of society, the greater number must labour among poor and plain people, with whom sincerity and friendliness are the qualities in a minister's conduct which serve best to recommend him to their esteem and confidence. And I venture to assert, that of the hundreds of students who have passed under my observation, those from rich families have possessed no superiority of manners over their poorer brethren.

And this leads me to notice another objection of a still more serious nature. It is, that a dependence of this kind for the means of education must have a debasing effect on the minds of youth, and detract from that manly independence which is an estimable trait in the character of any man, and especially of a minister. Now, in my judgement, this objection is utterly without confirmation from the facts which have fallen under my observation. The circumstance of indigence may, indeed, have the effect of keeping down that spirit of pride and arrogance. Which is so apt to arise in the minds of youth born to affluence; but this is a real benefit. But as to any spirit of meanness generated by this mode of education, it has no existence, except in the imagination of those who make the objection. If the candidate is actuated by the elevated aims and pious motives which should govern all who aspire to this office, he will not be liable to any influence of the kind supposed. Indeed, commonly, the funds of the church are so dispensed, that the beneficiary seldom knows the individual to whom he owes his support: he receives the aid needed as coming from the church, through the agency of the Board of Education.

From the origin of this seminary as was before stated, at least one half the students have been more or less dependent on charitable funds for their support; and yet it has never been observed by the professors that these were, as a body, inferior to the others in any respect whatever. Certainly their being beneficiaries has not lowered them in the opinion of their fellow students, as far as the fact was known; for in a majority of cases, the wants of the needy are supplied without giving such publicity to the transaction that it becomes known even to their fellow students.

If we should now take a survey of all the pastors and evangelists in connection with the Presbyterian Church, whether labouring at home or in the foreign field, there would be found no marked inferiority in those educated on the funds of the church in manners, piety, talents, or usefulness. If all who were thus educated should at once be withdrawn from the field of labour, it would leave such a chasm, or rather such a desolation, as would fill every pious mind with grief and discouragement. If then, this plan of providing a supply of ministers for the church has been found necessary in times past, why should it not be equally, yea more necessary hereafter, as the field is every day widening both at home and abroad, and the demand for labourers more urgent, every succeeding year?

Contributing to aid pious students in their preparation for the gospel ministry has ever been considered a laudable species of benevolence; and the establishment of scholarships and bursaries in colleges and universities has been with a direct view to this object. From the biography of the Reformers, and other eminent men since their time, it appears that they felt a deep interest in the subject, and often used their influence to obtain aid to enable candidates for the ministry to pursue their theological studies to their completion, without interruption.

There is scarcely any plan to which objections may not be made: but if this plan be essential to the prosperity of the church—I had almost said, to its existence—why make objections? They may injure a good cause, but cannot possibly do any good. In these cases, it has been truly remarked, that those who contributed most largely to education funds were not the persons who usually find fault, but such as desired an excuse for not giving. Now, as charity ought to be free and unconstrained, let such keep their money, but let them not influence others, by their objections, to hold back their contributions. If there be anything wrong in the management of this business, let it be pointed out, that it may be corrected. If any improvement in collecting and disbursing these charitable funds can be devised, let it be suggested, that it may be adopted and carried into effect. But we earnestly beseech all the friends of our church not to raise nor listen to a clamour against this necessary scheme of benevolence, at a time when the demand for labourers is greater than it ever has been. To hinder or discourage the education of poor and pious youth of good talents for the holy ministry is actually to oppose the vital interests of Christ's church; and when this is done by Presbyterian ministers, it is a species of ecclesiastical suicide. It is virtually to cut the nerves by which our efforts in advancing the kingdom of the Redeemer must be made.

Here we might leave the subject, but it is our wish to meet every objection which has been made, or can be made to the principles and plan of our Board of Education; for we are both sorry and surprised to learn, that in some quarters, and with some persons, this Board has become unpopular. It is alleged, that there cannot be a very urgent need of our multiplying ministers, while there are so many unemployed, hanging about our large cities; and whenever a church becomes vacant, immediately a swarm of candidates are found seeking a place and a living. For such ministers we have no apology to offer, except that many will get into the ministry, who have not popular talents, and therefore do not readily find a field where they can do good and support their families. Such are sometimes truly pious men, and if they had a charge would be faithful and edifying pastors. And they are not to be blamed for seeking a place in which they may be useful, and at the same time gain a living for their dependent families. Again, settled pastors are often, through the caprice of their people, obliged to resign their charge and being cast out, without means of subsistence; it is natural and reasonable for them to seek another situation. Often they are not censurable for being without charges, but the people to whom they ministered, and who had engaged to afford them a support. Cases are known, in which a single person has had influence to occasion a severance of the sacred bond which subsists between a pastor and his flock. But after all, this thing is greatly exaggerated. Look into our cities and large towns, and how many unemployed Presbyterian ministers do you find? Some, indeed, are engaged in teaching; and in whose hands can youth be more safely and advantageously placed than in those of ministers? It is devoutly to be wished that pious ministers were so abundant that every school in the land might have one at its head. But what connection has this with educating poor and pious youth? These, when received into the ministry, are not usually the persons who spend their time in idleness. Let facts be ascertained and you will find that poor ministers are the most laborious and the most ready to go on foreign missions. Christ himself was, as to worldly goods, the poorest of the poor; and by choosing that condition he has sanctified a state of poverty and rendered it honourable in ministers of the gospel to be poor. He, therefore, commonly calls his most faithful servants from this class; but as he himself subsisted on the charities of his devoted friends, he would have his church to be liberal in the support of poor ministers, and in aiding pious students to prepare for their sacred work.

Another objection is that many of those youth selected to be educated for the ministry, do not possess sufficient strength of mind to avail themselves of the advantages to be derived from a liberal course of learning; so that, when they have passed through all the schools, they are found poorly qualified to be useful ministers of the gospel. It must be confessed that there has not always been sufficient caution in receiving young men on the funds of the church. There has not been, in many cases, a sufficiently rigid scrutiny into the natural capacity of the candidate. Some pious persons are so destitute of the powers of mind requisite to profit by a liberal education, that after passing through all the usual stages of a literary course, they are almost as little qualified for the work of the ministry, as if they had remained at the plough or in the counting-house. Though there has been a fault in regard to this matter, yet the blame does not lie at the door of the Board of Education, but with the too partial friends of the youth who recommended him. And, perhaps, there has been some want of vigilance and care in the committees of presbyteries, who have had committed to them the responsible duty of examining and recommending beneficiaries to the Board. For some years, the Board have, very properly, devolved the whole responsibility of receiving beneficiaries on the presbyteries, and have resolved to take all who are thus recommended, and they will receive none but such as are under the care of the presbytery. Here it may be remarked, that when a youth is once put on a course of learning, with a view to the ministry, it is extremely hard to drop him, unless he should be found guilty of immoral or very imprudent conduct. When he has been induced to relinquish the business for which he was preparing, and has been encouraged, and perhaps, persuaded, to turn his attention to the ministry, to drop him is not only cruel, but a severe injury, which none are willing to inflict unless the unfitness of the person is most manifest. And, indeed, with every degree of caution, it is impossible to judge certainly of the capacity of candidates, in the commencement of their course; for while some are so dull, that they never can be made anything of, there are others whose minds are developed very slowly, and who improve under culture, to a degree far above what was anticipated. The fact is, that in all cases, the education of youth is an experiment. What any individual will be, cannot commonly be known prior to the trial. In all institutions of learning it will often happen that many who enjoy the advantages of instruction do not profit much, either for want of capacity, or habits of study. We must educate a multitude in our schools and colleges, in order to bring out the talents of a few.

In regard to moral delinquency, the cases have been so few, that it is a matter of sincere thankfulness, that out of the hundreds of youth educated for the holy ministry, so few have acted in such a manner as to render it necessary to cast them off. In general, the beneficiaries of the Board have exhibited an exemplary behaviour during the whole course of their education.

Some time ago it was a matter of serious consideration, whether young men educated on the funds of the church should not be brought under obligations to repay all that they receive. Our church determined that this was not expedient. To send out our young ministers under a heavy load of debt, is surely to place them in a very undesirable situation; and although they have personally received a rich benefit in their education, yet it should be remembered that they were aided in acquiring learning, not for their own benefit, but for the service of the church. Every man of right moral feelings, will be sensible, however, of an obligation which he will be disposed to discharge in some way whenever providence shall put it in his power; and we do find that, frequently, pecuniary returns are made by some who have been the beneficiaries of the Board. Most of our young ministers receive so meagre a support that it should not be desired, if they were willing, that they should think of repaying what they have received. And there are some who, though they have not repaid the church in kind, have more than done it by services rendered to this cause, and especially, by aiding other young men in obtaining an education.

It is true, however, that there are persons in affluent circumstances, who were aided through their whole course by the funds of the church, who have never made any return, or even acknowledgment, of their obligations. Concerning such, we would only say that their moral sensibilities are not as strong and delicate as they might be. But what would be thought of the man who after having been essentially aided by the Board of Education, should refuse his aid and co-operation in its benevolent exertions?

There is also another case, in which real injustice is done to this Board. It is when a young man, after receiving aid from its funds, through his whole course, as soon as he enters the ministry, leaves our connection and joins some sister denomination. Now we do not censure the young minister for entering a field more important and more inviting than he can find in our church; but it is our deliberate and we think impartial judgment, that in such a case, he is bound in conscience to repay all that he has received.

In conclusion, we would address ourselves to the ministers and members of the Presbyterian Church. We entreat you, dear Brethren, to look at this subject seriously, and you will find that there is no institution more vital and more necessary to our prosperity, as a church, than the Education Board. It has been said, that compared with our other Boards, this is unpopular with many of our churches and with many individuals, who are able to aid it. But why so? Whence this prejudice? So you wish our churches to be furnished with able, well educated pastors, and how are they to be obtained? Perhaps, your opposition is to a public education in theological seminaries. Well, propose some better plan, and we shall rejoice to adopt it; but the church has been fully persuaded that such institutions were necessary to the best preparation of the greatest number of candidates for the ministry. But there is no compulsion in regard to this matter. Any who choose to pursue their studies in private, or with private pastors, are at liberty to do so: only we ask you to give your aid to enable poor and promising youth to acquire the requisite training to become useful ministers of the gospel. The place of study is a secondary thing. The work of missions, foreign and domestic, is becoming every year, more important, and pious, faithful men are demanded for this service; and where will you find them, unless you assist young men who are willing to devote themselves to this important work? Nearly all the missionaries in the foreign and domestic field, have come out of your theological seminaries; and the fact is, that most of them imbibed the missionary spirit while in these institutions, and a large proportion of them were educated, too, on the funds of the church. If this department is neglected, or should become unpopular, one of two things will be the consequence; either, there will be a deplorable deficiency of labourers in the vineyard of the Lord; or, the church will be filled with imperfectly educated men. In either of these cases, the cause of our Zion must decline. Other denominations will reap the harvest; for they are becoming more and more attentive to the education of their ministers. Yea, several large denominations, which some years since seemed to entertain a very low estimate of the necessity of learning in the ministry, are now straining every nerve to promote a liberal education among their ministers. If we do not come forward liberally and vigorously in support of this scheme of benevolence, we shall undoubtedly fall into the background, in comparison with our sister denominations. While we sincerely rejoice in the more correct views which some of them entertain on the subject of ministerial qualifications, we do not wish to see our own beloved church retrograding in this matter. If the Presbyterian Church has been more distinguished for any one thing than another, it is the uniform zeal which she has cherished for the education of her ministers, and her unceasing exertions to bring promising and pious men into the ministry, who were destitute of the means of obtaining a thorough education.

It will not be a matter of surprise, that if our church neglects her duty in relation to this matter, God, in righteous judgment, may so order things that we shall have few pious young men to educate. Already, the number of candidates is said to be diminishing. Let us beware of incurring the displeasure of the Lord of the harvest.

It may be proper to say a word respecting the way in which this business has been managed by the Board of Education. The writer, while he seldom ever meets with the Board, has been in a situation to observe its proceedings, and he is free to declare, that in his opinion, much zeal, wisdom, and diligence have uniformly characterized the management of the Board and their Executive Committee. And our secretaries and agents have been indefatigable in their exertions. The Presbyterian Church is under unspeakable obligations to a few working men, in Philadelphia, who have for years served on her Boards and her committees. The sacrifice of other benefactors of the church is small when compared with the weekly labours of some of these devoted men. I know that some jealousy exists in other parts of the church on account of so many of our Boards having their seats in Philadelphia, as though the power of the church was too much concentrated in a few persons. And if it were not that the true interests of the church would suffer by their removal, it would be desirable to have them distributed among the principal cities, included in our bounds. This is desirable not for the reason hinted at, but because a disproportioned requisition is made on a few benevolent men, for their time and labour. These men can have no other than benevolent motives for their long-continued and faithful services. They attend to the business of the church weekly without any compensation, except the satisfaction of doing good. And as to honour or applause, they neither seek it nor receive it; their names are scarcely known to the church, for which they so assiduously labour. Though equally faithful men might be found in other cities, yet I am persuaded that there is a great advantage in having the business of the church, concentrated in the place where the General Assembly generally meets.

If it were in my power to suggest any improvements in the system pursued by the Board of Education, I would willingly do it; but on an impartial survey of the rules of the Board, I am of opinion, that they approximate as near perfection as can be expected in any affairs conducted by fallible men. If every church in our connection would do its duty in regards to this matter, we should not only have funds enough, but candidates enough; for then every church would feel the obligation not only of contributing money to support indigent students, but of endeavouring to supply the church with a succession of pious youth, to be educated for the sacred work of the gospel ministry.

A MISSIONARY SERMON[1]

Go ye into all the world and preach the gospel to every creature.
Mark 16:15

T HE promulgation of this command marks a new and important era in the history of the church and of the world. These
words may be considered as the public and formal abrogation
of the Mosaic economy; and the authoritative annunciation of the
new order of things under the gospel.

The first communications of divine truth, through Adam and
Noah, were made indiscriminately to the human family; but, in both
instances, the precious deposit was generally adulterated, and nearly
lost. The wisdom of God, therefore, saw it to be necessary to select
and separate from the idolatrous world, a particular family which
might serve as a repository of the divine oracles and institutions; until
that 'seed of the woman' should come, of whom it was predicted, that
he should 'bruise the serpent's head': and that 'seed of Abraham', in
whom all the families of the earth should be blessed.

During this period the church of God was, for the most part, circumscribed within the limits of the elect nation. Its institutions were
not designed nor calculated for general use; but were local, temporary,
and burdensome in their nature, yet well adapted to the purposes for
which they were appointed. It is true, a permission was given to the
Israelites, to receive proselytes from other nations, of such as resided
among them, or should choose, for the sake of the worship of the
true God, to come to them; but they never received a command to
propagate their religion among the surrounding nations. They were
not authorized to send out missionaries to convert the world. These

[1] Archibald Alexander, *A Missionary Sermon, Preached in the First Presbyterian Church in Philadelphia, on the Twenty-third of May, 1814* (Philadelphia: William Fry, 1814).

were the 'times of ignorance' which God 'winked at'. He would leave the world to make a fair experiment of its own wisdom, and to exhaust all its own resources; that it might ever afterwards appear evident, that the world by wisdom did not know God; and that a divine revelation was absolutely necessary for its instruction.

But *now* the middle wall of partition was broken down; the law of commandments contained in ordinances, being abolished in the flesh of Christ; that is, this law received its accomplishment, when the body of Christ was lifted up on the cross, as a propitiatory sacrifice for sin. By this means, those who were far off are made nigh, by the blood of Christ. That the kingdom of God, or gospel dispensation, was not fully introduced until after the death of Christ is evident, because the Mosaic institutions until that time continued in full force, and Christ himself rendered obedience to the ceremonial law until the very day of his passion. The kingdom of heaven, indeed, was preached; that is, it was announced to be at hand, by John the Baptist, and by our Lord and his disciples. The nature of this kingdom was unfolded, and its future condition in the world predicted; but no new laws were promulgated, nor any new institutions set up, which in the least interfered with, or superseded the ceremonial liturgy of the Jews.

But when Jesus Christ, our great high priest of good things to come, had, through the eternal Spirit, offered himself without spot to God to bear the sins of many; and had by this one offering of his own body, perfected forever them that are sanctified, the service of the first tabernacle was set aside, and as to any utility, or divine authority, ceased forever; as an emblem of which, the veil of the temple was rent in twain from the top to the bottom, at the very moment of expiation; when Christ our high priest, by shedding his vital blood and pouring out his soul unto death, offered his one great sacrifice for sins.

At the rising of the sun, the feeble light of the stars is lost in the superior splendour of his beams. When a living person is before us, we no longer want an obscure delineation of his features. The shadow may serve to give us a faint idea of the substance; but when the substance is come, we may be content that the shadow should flee away. The restrictions, tutors, and governors, requisite in a state of minority, are not needed by the man of mature age. So, when Christ was manifested as our priest and sacrifice, the twinkling of the types, and the obscure sketch of the ceremonies of the law, were wanted no more.

The King Messiah, had already, by a series of stupendous miracles, and by completely fulfilling the prophecies which related to him, established his claim to the high character and office which he assumed; and having laid an ample foundation for the kingdom which he was about to establish, he now issues his commission to those, whom he had chosen to administer and act in his name, and by his authority, upon earth, and says, 'Go ye into all the world, and preach the gospel to every creature.'

As his kingdom was not of this world, he would not avail himself of the powers of the earth in its establishment: as it was his purpose that his religion should not stand in the wisdom of man, but in the power of God, he rejected the aids of human learning and eloquence; and selected, as his ministers, rude and illiterate men, taken from an unimproved part of the country, and from the lowest occupations in society;—men totally unversed in the policy of the world, and incapable of speaking even their own vernacular tongue with propriety. To such ministers did Christ commit the management of his kingdom, and sent them forth into all the world, to preach, without any earthly protection or patronage. This little band of heroes went forth to achieve the conquest of the world, with no other aid than the help of God, with no other armour than the panoply of the gospel. Their weapons were not carnal but spiritual, yet mighty through God to the pulling down of strong holds.

But we are not to suppose that our Lord Jesus Christ sent out these men to instruct and convert the world, without qualifying them for their work. Whom he sends, he calls; and whom he calls, he qualifies. The apostles were therefore directed to tarry at Jerusalem, until they should be endued with power from on high. Accordingly, on the day of Pentecost, they were thoroughly baptized with the Holy Ghost and with fire. The effects of this baptism were, that they were enlightened to understand the sacred Scriptures of the Old Testament. They were enabled to recollect distinctly and comprehend generally the meaning of all the discourses, which they had heard from the lips of Christ. Their faith, love, fortitude, patience, and assurance of the favour of God were wonderfully strengthened and increased. They were endowed with the extraordinary faculty of speaking with perspicuity and propriety, languages, which they had never learned, nor heard; and with the power of healing the sick, dispossessing the demoniac, and raising the dead. There was moreover given to them a mouth and wisdom which none of their enemies could withstand; and a presence of mind and promptitude of utterance, which enabled them to defend themselves with composure and dignity, and plead the cause of their Lord with convincing force, however suddenly called upon, or however august and imposing their audience.

So great, however, was the power of early and national prejudice, that the apostles did not, for some time, understand the extent of their commission. They had, before, been sent on a short mission, on which occasion it was ordered, that they should not go into the way of the Gentiles, nor even enter into any city of the Samaritans; and they seem to have thought, that by going into all the world, and preaching to every creature, no more was intended, than that they should go to the seed of Abraham now widely dispersed among the nations. But this veil was soon removed, by a particular revelation made to Peter in a vision; and by the calling of Paul to the apostleship, who, from the beginning, received commission to go to the Gentiles, and was, in a peculiar manner, designated and directed, to preach among the Gentiles the unsearchable riches of Christ.

We read in history of many persons travelling into foreign countries to acquire curious and useful knowledge, and of their imparting their dearly purchased treasure to a few chosen disciples on their return; but I believe this is the first instance on record of any persons leaving their own country, and visiting foreign parts, with no other than the benevolent purpose of communicating important information to their fellow creatures. The very novelty and sublimity of the project of reforming a world lying in wickedness, bespeaks a divine impulse; but the success of these first missionaries stamps the gospel with such a seal of authenticity, as neither the lapse of ages, nor the sophistry of its enemies can ever obliterate.

The apostles divided the world amongst them, and whilst some went to the East, others directed their course to the North, the West, the South. They turned their back upon all their earthly friends and prospects, and went forth to meet sufferings and death in their most frightful forms; but they were supported by the conviction that they forsook nothing, but what was perishable; and in the confidence that heaven was before them, whichever way they turned their faces; and near, wherever they might breathe out their souls.

Discouraged by no difficulties, and appalled by no dangers, they penetrated into countries not described by the geographer, and whose story has not been told by the historian: and even the record of their own labours is only in heaven. Suffice it to say, that they proved faithful unto death, and have gone to receive a crown of life. Most of them it is believed, received also the crown of martyrdom: but where, or how, or when, we cannot with any certainty say.

In further considering this subject, it shall be my object—

I. To show that this commandment imposes an obligation on the ministry and on the church, now existing, to propagate the gospel among the nations, who are not yet blessed with its light.

II. Endeavour to answer the question, What is the present duty of the American churches, and particularly of our own, in relation to this command?

III. Conclude with some considerations and motives to stimulate and encourage us to exert ourselves in carrying our Lord's will into effect.

I. In the first place then I am to show, that this command imposes an obligation on the ministry and on the church to propagate the gospel among the heathen. The proof of this proposition is so plain, that few remarks will be necessary to establish the point.

It is evident from the tenor of this commission, that it did not respect the apostles only, but their successors in the ministry; for the work here prescribed was too great to be completed by so small a number of labourers. What could be done by zeal, diligence, and perseverance, they effected: but the world was too wide, and the life of man too short, to admit of a few persons preaching the gospel to all the tribes and nations, scattered over the surface of this globe. As our Lord intended that this work should be accomplished, we may conclude, that the commission to execute it, extended to the successors of the apostles, as well as to themselves.

Again, every authorized minister of the gospel, derives his author-ity to preach and baptize, from this commission which Christ gave to his apostles. He has received his office, it is true, immediately from the hands of others, already in the ministry; but all the authority which they possessed to confer such an office is derived from the original commission. Otherwise the office of the gospel ministry would be merely of human and not divine appointment. But Christ is king in his church, and is the fountain of power as well as honour.

Now, that instrument which gives authority must be allowed to regulate its exercise. If we receive the office, we of course take upon us the obligation to fulfil its duties. But the commission says, 'Go ye into all the world, and preach the gospel to every creature.' The con-clusion therefore is inevitable, that every minister is bound, by the very nature of his office, to use his best efforts to propagate the gospel through the whole world.

To this it may be objected, that that part of the commission, which directs the conversion of the nations, was peculiar to the apostles and other extraordinary ministers of that age; but of this there is no proof: and if it were true, the consequence would be, not only that other ministers were not bound to execute this work, but it would be unlawful for them to attempt it. And, conversely, if it be lawful to preach the gospel to the heathen, it must be because it is included in our commission; and if comprehended in our commission, then we are bound to its performance.

But a more plausible objection is, that, according to this view of the subject, it would follow, that every preacher of the gospel must become a missionary, and go to preach to the heathen. But this dif-ficulty will vanish, if we consider the commission as given to a body of men, that is, to the ministry of reconciliation, who are to act in concert in carrying it into effect: and also if we interpret it agreeably to the great end which was designed to be accomplished.

Suppose a literary society were directed by authority, to commun-icate the knowledge of some art or science to the whole world, and also to preserve a lively recollection of the truths communicated on the minds of their disciples; it is plain, that, whilst it would be expedient for some to go into foreign parts, others should commence their work at home; and whilst some were engaged in teaching those

PRINCETON AND THE CHRISTIAN MINISTRY

who had never learned, others would be as properly employed in keeping up, and increasing, the knowledge of those already initiated.

Such is the state of the case with the ministry, who are commissioned to preach the gospel to all nations.

The ground which has been gained must not be abandoned for the hope of gaining more. The knowledge of evangelical truth must be preserved; and those who have heard and believed must be further instructed, and their children, as they become capable, must also be taught. This requires a stationary ministry. And so we read that, when Christ ascended up on high, he gave not only some apostles, prophets, and evangelists, but also pastors and teachers, for the perfecting of the saints for the work of the ministry, and for the edifying of the body of Christ. Accordingly, the apostles ordained elders in every city, where they collected churches. But all are comprehended under the general commission; and however it may fall to the lot of some to be stationary, they are, nevertheless, as a part of the body, bound to promote the diffusion of the light of the gospel, by every lawful and practicable means.

But to establish the point under discussion beyond all possibility of doubt, I will adduce the promise of our Lord, which he annexed to the commission, for the support and encouragement of those appointed to execute it. The command of Christ, on this occasion, is not expressed in the very same words by the Evangelists, Matthew and Mark; or rather, they have recorded different parts of the discourse, which the risen Saviour delivered on this occasion. In Matthew, Christ says, 'Go teach all nations, baptizing them in the name of the Father, and of the Son, and of the Holy Ghost, teaching them to observe all things whatsoever I have commanded you: and lo! I am with you alway, even to the end of the world.' Now these last words clearly ascertain the extent of the commission. Christ well knew that none of those persons then in his presence would live to the end of the world; but he addressed the apostles as standing at the head of a long succession of preachers, which should not cease, until he should come again, when the world would be at an end.

Now it is plain, that the promise and command are of equal extent: for they are addressed to the same persons, at the same time, and the one was intended to encourage those, who should obey the other; but the promise reaches through every age to the end of the world; therefore so also does the command. We think ourselves authorized to plead this promise; but as surely as we do so, we recognize the obligation of the command: for, those with whom Christ hath promised to be alway, are such as are engaged in propagating his religion over the world.

If more were needful to be said on a subject already sufficiently plain, I would argue from the circumstances of the case. The work commanded to be executed is not yet completed. It is agreeable to the will of God that it should be done. It is predicted that it shall be accomplished. Those therefore who manage the affairs of Christ's kingdom, are bound, by every lawful means, to comply with the revealed will of God, and to fulfil his unchangeable purpose, of giving the heathen to his Son for an inheritance, and the uttermost parts of the earth for his possession.

The only thing which remains under this head is to show that the obligation of this command extends to the private members of the church as well as to the ministry. Not that they are bound to preach the gospel; for no man taketh this honour unto himself but he that is called of God, as was Aaron. The nature of the duty incumbent on the church, in relation to this object, can easily be made apparent. If a king should send forth heralds through the whole extent of his dominions, to announce some important intelligence to his subjects, it would be the duty of all not only to avoid throwing any obstacle in the way of the royal messengers, but to facilitate their progress by every means in their power, and to give them every encouragement and support whilst engaged in the king's business. Well, Zion's king, who is the King of kings, and Lord of lords, hath sent forth his heralds, and commissioned them to go to the ends of the earth, announcing everywhere the glad news of salvation: are not all the subjects of this King, then, under obligations to promote this object? And how will they answer for it, to the great King, who throw obstacles in the way of the preachers of the gospel, or who are negligent about affording them assistance? This is a great work which is undertaken, deeply involving the honour of God, the interest of the Redeemer's kingdom, and the salvation of souls. The call is loud for everyone to come to the help of the Lord against the mighty. Everything which can contribute to the accomplishment of the important end in view, is put in requisition. Power, influence, talent, learning, wealth, navigation, commerce, medicine, ought all to lend their aid in propagating the gospel.

How much might a Christian government effect by friendly negotiation with heathen powers for the introduction of the gospel, and for the liberty and security of missionaries! What a blessing to the world, if commerce, so often stained with injustice and cruelty, should be sanctified to this glorious end! What a noble return for the precious commodities of the East, to send them the Word of God and preachers of salvation! What a change in the affairs of men, if our merchants esteemed the diffusion of truth, and the salvation of the heathen, a merchandise better than the merchandise of silver, and the gain thereof preferable to the gain of fine gold! Thanks be to God! some such merchants there are on both sides of the Atlantic! But oh! may he increase their numbers an hundredfold!

But not only those possessed of power and wealth may promote this great work, but every humble, pious Christian, is permitted and enjoined to bring his offering. If they cannot make large contributions in silver and gold; or if they do not possess talents, learning, and power, yet they have access to a throne of grace, and may employ humble, fervent prayer, the most effectual of all means, in promoting the cause of God.

II. I come now, in the second place, to inquire, What is the duty of the American churches, and particularly of our own, in relation to this command?

1. I have had occasion, already to observe, that this command does not oblige us to abandon the vineyard which has been planted in this western world, and that it is as much the duty of one portion of the ministry to feed the flock of Christ, already gathered unto the fold, as it is of another to go in pursuit of the lost sheep, which are still wandering in the wilderness. Nay more; this is our first duty. To leave the churches without any regular supply of the means of grace, for the sake of planting new churches among the heathen, would be no less absurd, than for the husbandman to relinquish a field already enclosed and cultivated, to clear and plant new ground

in the wilderness. Besides, it ought to be taken into serious consideration, that in the increasing and widely expanded population of this extensive country, there are multitudes destitute of the regular administration of the Word and ordinances: and this is true, not only in regard to our frontier settlements, but to the very suburbs of our largest cities. How many thousands, in this land, scarcely hear the sound of the gospel once in a year! Without the most energetic exertions, there is much reason to fear that some large districts of our country will sink into a state of ignorance and indifference on the subject of religion, equally as fatal as paganism itself. The souls of our neighbours and countrymen are as precious as those of the heathen; and they are more within our reach; to these, therefore, we should first devote our attention and exertions.

The blacks and people of colour also, in a peculiar manner, demand our attention. They have been a highly injured people, and justice, as well as humanity, demands that we should in some way afford them redress; and what better can we do for them, than to convey to them the knowledge of a crucified Saviour, in whose precious blood they may find a balm for all their bleeding wounds, and in whose gracious promises, a cordial to revive their fainting hearts, under the various afflictions which they are destined to endure. These people are amongst us, understand our language, are easily accessible, and willing and desirous to hear the gospel. Let us not, therefore, overlook them because they are a degraded people, but let us rather pity their miserable condition, and provide for them the rich consolations of the grace of God.

2. Again, it must appear obvious to all, that the heathen of our own continent, and on our own borders, have a peculiar claim on our benevolence. Without a divine warrant we have driven them from this land. The fine country which we now occupy was theirs, as much as any country can be ours. But what have we given them in return? The gospel, the richest treasure which we could communicate, and the communication of which would not have rendered us the poorer, we have in a great measure kept back.

How little have we, as a nation, been concerned for their conversion to Christianity, although the propagation of this religion was made the ostensible reason, by the governments of Europe, for taking possession of all these countries. This is a national sin, the guilt of which is probably, at this moment, imputed to us by him who weighs the actions of men, and renders righteous retribution unto nations as well as individuals.

Let it not be said, that the savage habits and roaming life of the western Indians render their conversion impracticable. The gospel, accompanied by the power and blessing of God, has a thousand times triumphed over obstacles equally as insurmountable. Obstacles as formidable existed in the case of our own heathen ancestors, before the gospel was propagated among them. Had those men of apostolic spirit, who preached the salvation of Christ among them, been as easily discouraged as we are, how miserable might our situation have been at this moment!

Let it not be said, that they must first become civilized before they can receive the gospel. This is a mere refinement of modern times, totally unsupported by historical testimony. What, in fact, has been the great means of civilizing Europe, but Christianity? What, in the nature of things, has such a tendency to subdue the ferocious passions of savages, as the doctrines and institutions of our holy and benevolent religion? Have not the Caffres and Hottentots, the Greenlanders and Eskimo, the most degraded of all savage tribes, embraced the gospel in our own times? Let us then hear no more of waiting for the civilization of the Indians, before we attempt their conversion. Let us rather believe that the truest and most effectual instrument of civilization is the Word of God; and that the renovation of the heart, which it produces, will do more to mitigate savage ferocity, than all the arts in the world.

If, therefore, we possess any zeal for the salvation of the heathen, let us endeavour to propagate the gospel among the aborigines of this continent.

3. But, is it the duty of the American churches to send missionaries to the East? This question has of late engaged the attention of the Christian public; and is of great importance. Previously to expressing an opinion, I would premise, that, if there existed any proportion between the labourers and the harvest, according to every principle of judicious distribution, the heathen on this continent, would, undoubtedly, fall to the lot of the American churches; and would

furnish a field sufficiently large, for all their zeal and exertions. But at present, the harvest truly is great, and the labourers are few. As in a great field, which cannot all be reaped, it matters little where you thrust in the sickle. The only question of any importance is, in what part will our labour be likely to produce most fruit? Or, what part of the harvest is most ripe for the sickle? Such is the present state of the great harvest of souls, which lies before us. The little band of missionaries, who have gone forth, or who are likely to go forth from Christendom shortly, to labour in this field, are not adequate to the thousandth part of the work to be performed. They should, therefore, commence and prosecute their labours, wherever the harvest is richest and ripest. When I turn my eyes to the East, two considerations strike my mind with great force. The one is, the multitude of people who inhabit those regions, most of whom are still sitting in darkness, and in the region and shadow of death. Hundreds of millions of immortal souls, hastening to eternity, without any knowledge of the only name given under heaven, among men, whereby we must be saved. How overwhelming the thought! If our object be, according to the tenor of our commission, to preach the gospel to every creature; here, here is the place to publish the glad tidings, where millions, in a short time, might be made to hear the joyful sound.

The other consideration is, that there appears to be a great and effectual door opened in the East, at this time, for the propagation of the gospel.

For many years past, providence seems to have been preparing the way of the Lord. The Bible has been recently translated into many eastern languages, and the Word of life begins to be extensively circulated among the heathen. The attention of the Christian world has, after a long sleep, been awakened, and directed to this portion of the globe; and by the gracious interposition of providence, favouring the exertions of the pious and benevolent, those odious and disgraceful restrictions, which prevented the introduction of missionaries in the East, are now, in a great measure, removed.

The loud call, which the present dispensations of providence seem to send forth to all Christian nations in behalf of the millions of Asia, is, Go over and help them. Some of our sister churches have not been disobedient to the heavenly call. Our brethren in the eastern States have made a magnanimous beginning, and have set us a noble example worthy of imitation. Another large Christian society seems to have felt the divine impulse, and is at this moment in motion. Many sober Christians are of opinion that the awful darkness of a long night begins to break. Undoubtedly, a new era has commenced in regard to the propagation of the gospel. And shall our church, as numerous as any in the Union, remain idle spectators of the exertions of others? Shall we only, pay no regard to the signs of the times? Can we be contented, to prosecute the great business of missions, in the same cold and circumscribed manner as we have hitherto done? I trust not. I sincerely hope, that the General Assembly, which constitutes the missionary society of our church, will, at their present sessions, take the subject of foreign missions into serious consideration; and that they will resolve to co-operate cordially and energetically, in carrying on this glorious work.

To this, I am aware, there are some plausible objections, the principal of which I will now endeavour to obviate.

The first is, the want of funds. If our efforts hitherto have been barely adequate to collect sufficient funds to defray the expense of missions to our frontier settlements, how can we expect to carry on, successfully, an expensive foreign mission?

To which I answer, that our churches have proportioned their contributions to the object which we have held up to their view. But, if we should determine on a foreign mission, it will excite the attention of many who have never yet been pervaded by a missionary spirit; and will bring into operation a liberality which only waits for an opportunity to discover itself. But, whether sufficient funds can be obtained for this purpose, is a problem which experience alone can certainly solve. But, if I am not deceived, there is at present a disposition in the people of this country to promote this object. It has been evinced in every instance in which any call has been made on their liberality for the dissemination of evangelical truth in those populous regions. The success of our brethren in the eastern states in collecting funds is calculated to afford ample encouragement. Only let the people know that you mean to send missionaries to the East, and many will be forward to contribute.

If this respectable audience were assured, that the collection of this evening would be appropriated to a foreign mission, I have little doubt that their contributions would be doubled. Nay, I believe I should not misrepresent the sentiments and feelings of some of my hearers if I should assert, that with this object in view, they would increase their contributions tenfold. Many have begun to taste the refined luxury of beneficence. Experience has taught them the truth of that saying of our Lord, 'It is more blessed to give than to receive'; and of the aphorism of Solomon, 'There is that scattereth and yet increaseth, and there is that withholdeth more than is meet, but it tendeth to poverty.' For the liberal soul has been made fat, and those who have lent unto the Lord have been repaid with large interest. It seems to be a principle in the conduct of providence, that they who give most liberally, shall have the more to give.

Wealth has acquired a new value with those, who have learned this exquisite mode of enjoying it; for no treasures ever afforded such delicious gratification as those which are dedicated to the Lord. That surplusage of wealth, which has commonly been employed in feeding vanity and gratifying ambition, would be abundantly sufficient to promote all the important objects of real benevolence. Indeed, if only the one hundredth part of the money expended in dissipations and luxuries hurtful to health and morals, were reclaimed for missionary purposes, it would be more than adequate to all our wants.

One resource may, I think, be depended on, if others fail. When the expensive work of the Levitical tabernacle was on hand, the fair daughters of Israel, not only performed much by the labour of their hands, but with a willing heart brought their most valuable jewels of gold, and precious stones, and dedicated them to the service of the Lord; and we read that, the laver, a very costly and important part of the sacred furniture of the court of the tabernacle, was made out of the looking glasses, or brazen mirrors, of the women who were accustomed to assemble at the door of the tabernacle. The dignity, happiness, and usefulness of the female sex, are intimately connected with religion. It has often been mentioned to the praise of Christianity, that wherever it has been received, woman has arisen from her degradation and assumed her proper rank in society. To which we may add, that in proportion as the genuine spirit of this religion is prevalent, the importance of the exertions of the female sex become evident. Not to detain you with accounts of their frequent instrumentality in the introduction and propagation of the Christian religion, which are recorded to their honour in the early history of the church, I will only advert to their recent exertions in this city, which furnish a noble pledge of what may be expected from them in this glorious cause.

But another objection is, that we cannot obtain missionaries willing to go among the heathen, in lands so distant. A few years since, this would have appeared an insurmountable obstacle; but a great change has taken place. We have not only heard of some of the inhabitants of Europe leaving their native shores, but we have seen the youth of America willingly offering themselves to go and preach the gospel to the heathen, on the other side of the globe. And even delicate females, influenced by the love of Christ and the ardent desire of promoting the salvation of the heathen, have broken asunder the tenderest bonds of human nature, and have deliberately forsaken affectionate parents and beloved brothers and sisters, to go into the remotest lands, never, never to return.

The same hallowed flame by which they were inspired, glows at this moment in many a youthful bosom. The language of their hearts is, Here am I, send me. Open the way, provide the means, and missionaries will not be wanting.

But the most formidable objection is that by sending missionaries abroad, we will rob our own vacancies, and retard the propagation of the gospel, among the aboriginal inhabitants of this country. If I believed that this consequence would follow, I should feel myself bound to protest against foreign missions. But, before this objection be admitted, let it be considered that the number of preachers, who might be expected to go on a foreign mission, would be too inconsiderable to produce any sensible effect on the churches here; but whilst the labours of less than half a dozen persons would scarcely be missed at home, they might perform the most important services as missionaries in the East. But this measure would not diminish the number of faithful labourers in our churches. There is the strongest reason to believe that the effect would be exceedingly beneficial in many ways to professing Christians. It would excite a missionary spirit, which is the true spirit of Christianity. It would raise the tone of religious feeling many degrees. It would tend to the destruction of bigotry and of a narrow sectarian spirit. It would promote peace and harmony in the churches. If Christians had their minds properly occupied, and their hearts suitably expanded, with this noble object of propagating the gospel among the heathen, they would not, they could not, spend their lives in petty contentions.

The adoption of this measure would excite a spirit of prayer for the heathen among God's people. If they had missionaries labouring in the East, they would frequently and earnestly be endeavouring to hold up their hands by prayer. And so far will our sending missionaries to the East be from diminishing the number of preachers, for the supply of our vacancies and churches, that I sincerely believe, it would be the best measure which we could adopt for the increase of candidates for the sacred ministry. One successful missionary sent to the East, would also enable us to do something more effectually for the conversion of the heathen on our own borders, than has hitherto been done. It would produce that very ardour, which is necessary for the commencement and vigorous prosecution of such a work. It would not be long before enterprising missionaries would explore our western wilds, and visit the many tribes of Indians who are scattered over this vast continent: and the labourers in the West would soon begin to emulate those in the eastern parts of the vineyard.

III. But in whatever way, or among whatever people, we may think it most expedient to propagate the gospel, let us without delay be active in the fulfilment of this most important duty. The motives, which should urge us to activity and combined exertion, are of the most forcible kind. The honour of our God and Redeemer are deeply concerned in this matter. The consideration of so many millions, giving that worship to dumb idols which is due to God only, ought deeply to affect our hearts, and will if we really love his name. Our bosoms should glow with inextinguishable zeal to overturn, by the artillery of the gospel, those monstrous temples, and hideous idols, on whose altars such multitudes of our degraded fellow-creatures are daily offering their polluted worship, and their sacrifices of cruelty.

And is it no dishonour, think ye, to Christ, that, although he offered himself a propitiation, for men of every nation, that so many have never yet heard his name. When oppressed with a sense of sin's desert, when wounded and stung with remorse, they pine away and die in their sins, and no messenger of mercy comes near, to speak to them in words of consolation. Did not Christ come to destroy the works of the devil, and yet are not four-fifths of the population of the world under the baleful influence of this prince of darkness? Consider, I beseech you, the value of one immortal soul; which nothing could redeem from death, but the precious blood of the Lamb of God; and which is destined to an immortal existence, in glory and happiness or in darkness, disgrace, and everlasting misery! Calculate how many souls are, every year, perishing for lack of that knowledge, which, by sending the gospel, we might convey to them. I have no wish to enter into the discussion of the question whether the salvation of some of the heathen be possible without the knowledge of a Saviour, in some extraordinary way unknown to us. In whatever way this question may be decided, it will have little or no influence in altering the motives which should impel us to seek the conversion of the heathen; for it will be admitted by all, that they who are abandoned to gross and abominable idolatry, or to enormous vices against the law of nature, cannot be saved in that state. If they could, it would be a great blessing for multitudes in Christendom to be converted back again to paganism, because under the gospel, it is plain, that he who believeth not shall be damned. What then, I would ask, is the condition of the heathen in regard to religion and morality? Are they not almost universally either idolaters, or enslaved to the most degrading vices? No words are sufficient to describe the abyss of depravity into which most heathen nations are sunk. Their moral condition is wretched and disgusting beyond anything that the imagination can easily conceive. All those encomiums which philosophers of a certain school, and for a certain purpose, have lavished on distant savage tribes, are proved to be false—utterly false.

Now, prejudice and system aside, I appeal to your good sense—I appeal to the benevolent feelings of your hearts—I appeal to your conscience to decide, whether it be more charitable to neglect the conversion of the heathen, on the supposition that they may possibly be saved without the gospel; or to carry to them the Word of God, which we know is able to make them wise unto salvation? The apostles certainly acted under the belief that the knowledge of Christ by the gospel, was ordinarily necessary to the salvation of sinners; otherwise they would never have sacrificed their lives in endeavouring to bring the heathen to the knowledge of the truth. They believed that there was but one name given under heaven, by which men could obtain salvation; and therefore they exerted themselves to the utmost, to spread abroad, in all lands, the savour of this precious name, knowing that men could not believe on him, of whom they had not heard; and that they could not hear without a preacher.

O ye ministers of the gospel! the successors of the apostles! imitate their praiseworthy example. To you now, are the treasures, and the keys, of the kingdom of heaven, committed. Have compassion, I beseech you, on your fellow creatures and brethren, in whose veins the same common blood circulates, and who are destined to the same immortal existence. O pity their wretched condition, and endeavour to rescue them from impending ruin.

And ye people of God! who have tasted the sweetness, and experienced the power of the gospel, you know how dreadful a thing it is to stand exposed to the sentence of a broken law; and how inexpressibly delightful, by faith, to view 'the lamb of God who taketh away the sin of the world'. Your feelings have been made alive to what concerns the glory of God, and the honour of your Redeemer, and the welfare of immortal souls. Can you therefore remain at ease? Can you cease from exertion? Can you restrain your prayers? Will you suffer your silver and gold to canker in your coffers? Or will you any longer lavish your treasures on inferior and unnecessary objects, when you enjoy such an opportunity of applying a portion of your wealth to the most excellent of all objects? God in his providence is in our times wonderfully opening a door for the propagation of the gospel among the heathen. The long, dark night of superstition and error, we trust, is drawing to a close. The morning star already appears in the Eastern horizon; and ere long, we hope, that the Sun of righteousness will arise on the millions of Asia, with healing under his wings; and will extend his benign influences over the whole habitable world. The sound of the trump of jubilee, proclaiming the day of salvation and acceptable year of the Lord, is now heard on the plains of Hindustan, in the deserts of Africa, and in the remote and far-separated isles of the Southern Ocean. The Indian, the Negro, the Hottentot, and Otaheitean, begin to emerge from the dismal darkness of barbarism, and to assume the dignity of man, and enjoy the privileges of the Christian. They begin to taste the sweetness of redeeming love, and sing the praises of the Prince of life in their own native tongues.

The Bible, which contains the words of eternal life, has been circulated of late to an extent, and with a success, which fills the world with astonishment. A few years ago, we would have deemed incredible, that which we have lived to witness;—and if an angel from heaven should declare the events, which will occur during the next half century, perhaps our faith would stagger at the wonderful report. But however great and glorious the events, which may be evolved by the revolutions of the great wheel of providence, they will probably be effected by the means, which God has already appointed, and which have been commonly employed. The churches will be roused to exertion. A spirit of prayer and supplication will be granted. A liberality, unknown to former ages, will be called into exercise. Many will be stirred up to offer themselves as missionaries. Christians, agreeing in the great fundamental doctrines of the gospel, will become more united in spirit and more harmonious in operation. The aspect of the nations will be changed. Wars will cease and the sword be turned into the plough-share, and the spear into the pruning hook. National animosities and antipathies will be extinguished or mitigated. Kings will then esteem it their highest honour to become nursing fathers, and queens nursing mothers to the church. There will then be no occasion for pathetic addresses to the passions to extort a scanty pittance from the pockets of the avaricious. The people will offer to the service of the Lord, as of old, when they were obliged to tell them to stay their hand—that it was enough.

Whether any anticipation of the spirit of these future times is possessed by my present audience will now be put to the test. The object is now before you. Funds are needed for missionary purposes—perhaps, to send missionaries to the East. I will not urge you to give, nor attempt any appeal to your passions: 'the Lord loveth a cheerful giver'. Let every one then, according as the Lord hath prospered him, and according as he hath purposed in his heart, bring his oblation to the treasury of the Lord. The ponderous gift of the man of wealth and the widow's mite will both be acceptable. Of one thing however you may rest assured, that no one will become ultimately the poorer, for giving liberally to such an object. And this I believe would be the result, if your contributions should be increased tenfold. Finally, remember that the principal fruit of your liberality will be enjoyed in heavenly blessings. 'He who soweth sparingly shall reap also sparingly; and he who soweth bountifully, shall reap also bountifully.'

And now may God make all grace abound toward you, that ye always having all sufficiency in all things, may abound to every good work; being enriched in every thing to all bountifulness, which causeth through us thanksgiving to God.

CHRIST IN THE MIDST[1]

C HRISTIAN Friends—you are convened on a very interesting occasion. You are met here, not to transact any secular
business, but to lay the foundation of a house to be dedicated
to the worship of the living God—your almighty Creator, kind Preserver, and Benefactor, and most gracious Redeemer. The eye of the
omniscient Jehovah looks with favour on such an enterprise, because
it is intended to promote his own glory and the salvation of men, in
which he delighteth. If public worship be a duty, which all Christians
admit, then there must be a place in which the people may assemble;
and a house consecrated to the worship of God should be decent
and commodious, and we ought not to desire to serve God with that
which costs us nothing. We may be parsimonious in what relates to
personal accommodation and self-indulgence; but in what regards
the service of God, we should be liberal. David said, 'Neither will I
offer burnt offerings unto the Lord my God of that which doth cost
me nothing.' And all the immense wealth which this devout king
acquired in a long reign, and in many successful wars, he dedicated
to the service of God, for the erection of the temple. And when the
people as well as himself, had a heart to give willingly for this object,
he considered it a matter of special thanksgiving; although it was
but returning to the Lord what properly belonged to him. 'Now,
therefore, our God, we thank thee and praise thy glorious name. But
who am I, and what is my people, that we should be able to offer
so willingly after this sort? For all things come of thee, and of thine
own have we given thee.' After the return of Israel from their Baby-
lonish captivity, they were severely reproved for their negligence in

[1] Archibald Alexander, 'Address', in *A Lecture by the Late Hon. James M'Dowell, of
Lexington, VA, and An Address by the Late Rev. A. Alexander, D.D.* (Philadelphia:
Joseph M. Wilson, 1851), pp. 43-48.

rebuilding the temple of the Lord. Some said, 'The time is not come, the time that the Lord's house should be built.' And what answer did the Lord return to this, by his prophet Haggai? 'Is it a time for you, O ye, to dwell in ceiled houses, and this house lie waste?' And for this neglect, the bounties of God's providence were, in a great measure, withholden from them. Their agricultural labour was unproductive, 'They sowed much and brought in little.' And so it will ever be. If we neglect our duty in regard to his worship, or are niggardly in making suitable provision for it, he will manifest his displeasure by withholding his favours, or by sending upon us his righteous judgments. The exhortation of God to the people, then, we may apply to ourselves, 'Consider your ways.' 'Go up to the mountains and bring wood, and build the house, and I will take pleasure in it, and I will be glorified, saith the Lord.'

I said that the founding of a church, or a house for the worship of God, was an interesting transaction; and I now will show why.

In the first place, it is, as it were, bringing God to dwell among you and to bless you. We all know, that Jehovah dwelleth not in temples made with hands. And as Solomon said in his prayer at the dedication of the temple, 'But will God, indeed, dwell on the earth. Behold the heaven and heaven of heavens cannot contain thee, how much less this house that I have builded.' God is not confined to any place; no, not even to the highest heavens; yet he does condescend to take up his abode in particular places. For, after Solomon had ended his prayer, the glory of the Lord filled the house, and resided there in the inmost, or *Most Holy Place:* which glorious presence, or indwelling, the Jews called *Shekinah.* This was a miraculous manifestation; and we look for nothing of the kind now; but there is a presence, or ind-welling, a *spiritual* Shekinah, which is still more glorious and more beneficial; and this is in his church, in all ages. 'Wherever two or three are gathered together in my name', says Christ, 'I am in the midst of them.' Certainly, then, where a church of true believers meet for his worship, there is he, their Head. The most important society in the world is the church, and it is a high privilege to have a branch of it established in our midst, to which we and our children can have free access. For wherever there is a church of Christ, there Christ will be present; and he never comes to any place without bringing a blessing with him. 'In all places where I record my name, I will come unto them, and I will bless them.' This is a promise of a general nature, not confined to any one time or dispensation. Wherever, then, a church is organized, and a house of prayer erected, there the name of God is recorded, and his promise sure. He will come and bless the people who assemble there for his worship, and to hear his holy Word. No greater blessing has God given to men than the *glorious gospel* of his grace. Wherever it comes, it sheds light on all around. It holds forth *Christ,* who is the Sun of righteousness, the light of the world. The beams of divine truth, when they shine into any place, disperse the mists of ignorance, error, and prejudice; and if the natural light is sweet, and pleasant to our eyes, how much more the light of divine truth? How happy are they who know the Lord, and are illumined with the rays of spiritual light?

The gospel is, moreover, a healing medicine for the diseased souls of men. It is an effectual remedy for maladies incurable by any other means. It is the balm of Gilead, and Christ is the great Physician, who has procured the remedy, and knows how to apply it. Suppose your families were down with some fatal disease which baffled all the skill of physicians, and one should come among you who possessed a sovereign remedy, which no other knew or could administer, how would the dwelling of such a physician be surrounded! and from morning to evening applicants would throng around him. Well, spiritual health is more important than bodily; and men are all deeply diseased with the mortal leprosy of sin, though many are insensible of their miserable condition. How desirable to have a dispensary in your midst, where all may come and be gratuitously supplied with medicine, which will heal their souls! Such a dispensary will be a gospel church in the midst of you.

But more, the gospel is *the word of life.* It is the voice of God for raising the dead. Men, by nature, are not merely sick, but dead—'dead in trespasses and sins'; but the Word attended by the power of the Spirit, which always accompanies it, communicates spiritual life to the dead. It inspires men with new principles of action—not selfish, and sordid, and carnal; but holy, benevolent, and useful. They actually become, under the influence of the gospel, 'new creatures'; 'old things are passed away, behold all things are become new'. No other means has ever produced a thorough reformation of heart and life. The gospel is also the harbinger of peace. It is the 'word of reconciliation'. By it the breach between God and the sinner is made up; 'Being justified by faith, we have peace with God, through our Lord Jesus Christ'. It brings peace to the troubled conscience, and harmonizes the discordant passions of the soul. And it produces peace among men, just so far as it is embraced and obeyed. It removes those malignant passions, which are the sources of strife of every kind. 'Whence come wars and fightings, but from your lusts?' Eradicate or subdue these evil passions, and the peace of society is secured. What is the proper remedy for those evils which have so frequently disturbed the peace of society in this great city, the very name of which should put men in mind of the duty of loving one another? The conservative politician says, 'We want a faithful, vigilant, and strong police.' Very good; but this can only *restrain* the evil—we want a remedy that will *eradicate* it—which will correct the evils of the *heart*—which will inspire men with goodwill to one another, and cause them to live in the fear of God. If you want good order, peace, the pleasures of friendship, and good society, introduce the gospel; and let its sacred truths be impressed on the minds of the rising generation. Let children early receive lessons from the sacred Scriptures. Let them hear these truths from their parents and from their Sunday School teachers. Our safety as a nation depends upon the right education of our children; and I know of no good system of education, which is not based on the truths of the gospel. You have already the blessed institution of the Sabbath School among you; gather into it all the youth who are running wild on the Sabbath, and, if needful, setup 'ragged schools', where the very offscouring of our race may be collected and instructed.

My Christian Friends, you are mostly strangers to me; but once I was well acquainted with Southwark, and all its streets and lanes. I considered it as part of my charge; for many of my parishioners inhabited this district. The church which I served, had more members here than all others put together. Forty years ago, much prayer was offered up for Southwark. During the whole period of my ministry, we kept up a prayer meeting, in this district, at the house of two pious widows. That prayer meeting was attended by many, and there was more appearance of the presence of God in it, than in any of our other meetings. The pious of other denominations frequently met with us there, and united their prayers with ours. Excuse me, if I mention the names of some who delighted to attend in that retired spot. Joseph Eastburn, though residing far away, was often in our midst, with his warm heart, affectionate voice, and tearful eye. There he poured out his feeling heart in many a fervent prayer and earnest exhortation. The case of the neglected seamen had not then engaged his attention. And I must mention two of the elders of the Pine Street Church, of which I was pastor, John McMullin and James Stuart. If they were ever absent, it was from sickness or some providential hindrance. Stuart, I understand, has recently been called home. He was, indeed, a man of fervent spirit—more earnest and affecting prayers than his, I never heard. And John McMullin, of Front Street, was certainly, in temper, in conversation, in his whole behaviour toward God and man, one of the most consistent, perfect Christians with whom I have ever been acquainted. Weekly, these men, with others, offered up their earnest prayers in this district, and for its inhabitants, which, I trust, are now about to be answered more fully than before.

We had connected with our church a company of poor widows, who were supported by the alms of the church. These pious women were mostly inhabitants of Southwark. I used to think, that those poor women, instead of being a burden, were a treasure to the church; for they prayed day and night for her prosperity. Guided by the faithful elders above-mentioned, I sometimes visited them in their garrets or cellars; and these visits were always edifying to me. One afflicted Scotch widow, who lived in a poor garret, I particularly remember. Her soul appeared to be alive to God. The prayers of the Lord's poor are powerful; and no doubt some of them remain to be answered, in behalf of the inhabitants of this place.

Finally, I would say, Arise and build. Let every man, woman, and child do something to help forward the house of the Lord. And to whomsoever the missionary applies for aid, for Christ's sake, let him not be sent empty away. It is for the Lord's house that he solicits. And when such an enterprise is on foot, so necessary to supply the spiritual wants of a destitute district, let all Presbyterians in the city of Philadelphia feel it to be not only a duty, but a privilege, to lend their aid. Let them desire to have at least a nail in the house of God about to be erected. Let them rest assured, that, in the end, they will be no losers by contributing to such an object.

Dear Friends, when the missionary of Southwark applies to you for aid in erecting this church, send him not empty away. According to your ability, and according as God has blessed you, give—give liberally—give cheerfully, and the Lord will reward you with blessings a hundredfold more valuable.

LECTURES ON THE SHORTER CATECHISM: A REVIEW[1]

WITH pleasure we hail the appearance of these *Lectures on the Shorter Catechism,* and we are gratified to see them comprised in so handsome a volume; for we are more and more persuaded, that nothing is gained to any body by coarse paper and a bad type. A perspicuous and orthodox commentary on this concise but rich system of gospel truth, cannot but be a valuable present to the Christian public, and especially to the members of the Presbyterian Church. Such a work we have now before us, which, in our opinion, supplies an important desideratum in our theological literature. For although we have several expositions of the Westminster Shorter Catechism which are sound and pious, yet, having been written a long time since, their language is now uncouth, and the whole style of composition antiquated; so that they are little read, and indeed are for the most part out of print. The whole body of Presbyterians, therefore, of every sect, who use this Catechism, will feel themselves under special obligations to the venerable author for producing what, we hope, will become a sort of standard work for the instruction and edification of their youth; and certainly it is matter of congratulation with the friends of orthodoxy, that the execution of such a work has fallen into hands so competent to do it justice. The reader, it is true, will not, in those lectures, find much discussion of abstruse and difficult points in theology, nor any great parade of critical learning: both of which would have been entirely out of place in a work addressed to youth, and intended for the edification of persons of all classes in society. But we are far from intimating that

[1] Archibald Alexander, 'Review: *Lectures on the Shorter Catechism,* by Ashbel Green', *Biblical Repertory and Theological Review,* Vol. 2 No. 2 (1830), pp. 297-309.

the young theologian may not study these lectures with profit. We do believe, that often the student of theology spends his time and wastes his strength in reading authors which have no other recommendation but that they are abstruse, obscure and learned; while he neglects and perhaps despises works which are rich in truth and strong in argument, merely because they are plain and unpretending. We do not hesitate, therefore, to recommend this volume to the careful and repeated perusal of our candidates for the holy ministry. In fact, it comprehends all the truths which they will ever have occasion to teach.

It is no part of our object, in this review, to enter into a critical examination of the style and composition of these lectures. This is altogether unnecessary at this time; for although they now appear for the first time collected into a volume, the whole of them have been twice before the public; first, when they were orally delivered by the author to his own catechumens, and secondly, when published in numbers in *The Christian Advocate,* of which valuable miscellany the author of this volume is the well known editor. It will be sufficient to remark, in general, that the style of these lectures is remarkable for correctness, perspicuity and force; the language is well adapted to the subjects treated, and while it furnishes a good example of purity and neatness, it is every where intelligible to the humblest capacity.

But if we do not entirely misinterpret the temper and taste of the times in which we live, doctrinal catechisms, and lectures explanatory of such catechisms, are not the books which will be sought after and read with avidity. The religious taste of most readers is, we fear, greatly vitiated by works of fiction and other kinds of light reading. Nothing will now please, unless it be characterized by novelty and variety; and while many new means of instruction have been afforded to our youth, in which we sincerely rejoice, we are so old fashioned in our notions, as to feel regret that in our own church those excellent little summaries of Christian doctrine, the Westminster Catechisms, are falling with many into disuse. Our numerous periodicals, coming out weekly, monthly, and quarterly, and often presenting much that is interesting, so occupy our leisure, that works of solid instruction are now read by few. Even the theologian, who is devoted to sacred pursuits, unless he is very economical in the distribution of his time, will find, that after perusing all the pamphlets which fall from the press in such abundance, he will have a small portion left for the more deep and solid works of theology; it is well indeed if by this means the Bible itself is not neglected. There is, doubtless, a great increase of reading among the population of this country within a few years; yet we cannot but fear that didactic and practical works of sound theology have, in too many instances, been excluded by the religious novel and the religious newspaper. And here, again, we must enter a caution against being misunderstood; as though we wished to proscribe all attempts at promoting a taste for reading by well composed fictitious narratives; or, that we would, if we could, diminish the facilities which now exist, of conveying religious intelligence to every corner of our country. We assuredly entertain no such feelings: but what we regret is, that while on the one hand we are gaining many advantages which our fathers did not enjoy, on the other we are losing benefits which they did possess, and which they highly prized. For we see no good reason why the acquisition of new privileges should lead us to relinquish the old. There is certainly no necessary repugnance between different approved methods of religious instruction. In the circumstances in which the rising generation are placed, there may be abundance of shallow, showy, bustling, active piety; but the ripe fruits of profound spiritual knowledge, and of deep practical experience, will be rare. In process of time, we apprehend, the strong lines of demarcation between truth and error, on many important points, will become more and more indistinct: and not only so, but many precious evangelical doctrines will be held in low estimation; because, perchance, they are not embraced by every denomination of Christians. Creeds and catechisms, so highly appreciated by our ancestors, are in danger of being cast aside like old-fashioned furniture, which is too cumbersome for modern use. Many are not at all aware that there is an increasing tendency to these consequences; while others foresee them, and rejoice in what they consider the extinction of a sectarian spirit; and fancy they see, in the course of things, an approximation to that happy state of the church, predicted in Scripture, when all sects shall be melted down into one harmonious, united society. Now, although we respect the motives by which such persons are actuated, and would as truly rejoice in the universal peace and unity of Christ's body on earth as any others, yet, we are persuaded, that union which has not gospel truth as its foundation, is worthless, and in the nature of things cannot be lasting. When that happy period of the church shall arrive, which has been alluded to, Christians will be better acquainted with all the doctrines of the Bible than at any former time, and will be more attached to them. As long as error exists in the world there must be a collision between it and truth: for light and darkness cannot dwell together; and no church will really be promoting unity and peace by relinquishing or neglecting what she believes to be truth, because some sections of the church do not view these points in the same light. If these doctrines are true, all will eventually embrace them; and the sooner, if they are clearly and faithfully exhibited. We think, then, that the true policy for every Christian denomination to pursue, is to maintain firmly and faithfully the doctrines which are believed to be scriptural; and at the same time, to treat other denominations who do not differ from it in fundamental points, with a kind, paternal, and liberal spirit; but while real differences exist, not to attempt an amalgamation, or even too close an union; for bodies which continue very peaceable towards each other when at a proper distance, may, when placed in too close contact, be thrown into a state of violent collision.

Catechetical instruction must have been coeval with the human family. At first all knowledge was communicated orally, and handed down by tradition. The first man delivered a stock of important ideas to his children; and they again to theirs, with different degrees of ability and fidelity. The most usual place of instruction was, doubtless, for a long time, the domestic circle. Here the pious patriarch would spend much time in dealing out to his listening children the lessons which he had learned in his youth from his predecessors, and those which he had been taught by his own experience. These instructions were properly of the nature of *catechising*, which may be defined to be 'the familiar communication of knowledge, orally'. As long as this duty was faithfully performed by parents, the darkness of ignorance and idolatry was prevented, but as soon as it fell into neglect, error and vice must have been the consequence. Of Abraham, God certifies, 'I know that he will command his children, and his household after him, and they shall keep the way of the Lord, to do justice and judgment' (*Gen.* 18:19). And God, by Moses, insisted more upon no duty than this, of domestic instruction in the truths of religion. 'And the words which I command thee shall be in thy heart, and thou shalt teach them diligently to thy children, and shalt talk of them when thou sittest in thy house, and when thou walkest by the way, and when thou liest down, and when thou risest up.' Again, 'Only take heed to thyself, and keep thy soul diligently, lest thou forget the things which thine eyes have seen, and lest they depart from thy heart all the days of thy life; but teach them, thy sons, and thy son's sons' (*Deut.* 4:9, 10; 6:7). To these precepts the psalmist refers, when he says, 'He established a testimony in Jacob, and appointed a law in Israel, which he commanded our fathers, that they should make them known to their children: that the generation to come might know them, even the children which should be born, who should arise and declare them to their children' (*Psa.* 78:5-6). The word *catechise,* is properly Greek, derived from the verb κατεχιω, 'to instruct with the voice', which is found, in some of its parts, six or seven times in the New Testament, but is commonly translated 'to instruct': because in English, the word *catechise* has somehow acquired a narrower signification than the original term, and conveys the idea of *instruction by question and answer;* whereas, the word in Greek includes all manner of elementary, oral instruction: and it would be desirable to bring back the word to its original meaning. This, however, is of small moment. The passages in which the original word is found, are the following: *Luke* 1:4; *Acts* 18:25; 21:21, 24; *Rom.* 2:18; *1 Cor.* 14:19; *Gal.* 6:6.

It appears, therefore, that this mode of instruction is fully recognized in the sacred Scriptures. Indeed, if no other methods of inculcating divine truth were resorted to, than delivering elaborate and continued discourses from the pulpit, very little information would be gained by the young and the ignorant. Preaching supposes and requires some preparatory knowledge in the hearers, to render it useful in communicating religious knowledge. Elementary principles must be acquired in some other way; and this was more especially the case before the invention of printing, when books were very scarce, and few persons were able to read. It seems that the apostles and first teachers of the Christian religion were much occupied in giving religious instruction, from house to house; and we know, from undoubted authorities, that in the earliest times of the primitive church, all who applied for admission into the church, from among the heathen, and all the children of Christians, were carefully instructed by catechising; that is, by a course of familiar teaching, *viva voce.*[1] To every church a class of catechumens was attached, and formed a kind of school, in which the first principles of religion were inculcated, and certain formulas of Christian doctrine, such as the early creeds, carefully committed to memory, together with portions of the sacred Scriptures. In some places these schools for catechumens became very famous, and were supplied with teachers of the highest character for learning and piety; so that they were frequented by the lovers of sacred literature from other countries. A celebrated institution of this sort flourished for several ages at Alexandria, in Egypt, in which Origen was educated, and of which he became the most distinguished teacher. A large number of the treatises written by the Fathers in different countries, and in different centuries, were composed expressly for the instruction of the catechumens. And until darkness overspread the church, and her unnatural pastors deprived the people of the Scriptures, the church was, as it ever should be, like a great school, where holy men of God devoted their time to the instruction of the rising generation, and of converts from paganism.

In catechetical, or elementary instruction, the grand secret is, 'little at a time, and often repeated'. Whoever would successfully instruct children and very ignorant adults, should avoid the error of crowding too many things into their minds at once. It is as preposterous a practice as it would be to attempt to increase the activity, vigour, and size of the body, by cramming the stomach with as much food as it could hold. Moreover, the truths first communicated should be as simple as possible. Tender minds must not be fed with strong meat, but with pure milk. To accommodate instruction to the state of advancement in knowledge, and to the degree of development of the mental faculties, is certainly that part of education which is most difficult, and at the same time most important. That historical facts should form the commencement of a course of religious instruction,

[1] That is, 'with living voice' or 'by word of mouth'.

is indicated, first, by the method pursued in the Bible; and secondly, by the predilection of all children for this species of knowledge. But, at a very early period, moral and doctrinal instruction of the most important kind may be connected with the scriptural facts inculcated, and may always be most advantageously engrafted on them. Doctrinal catechisms are, it is admitted, not commonly understood well by children; but it can do them no harm to exercise themselves in committing the words to memory; for it is universally admitted, that to strengthen the memory, it must be frequently and vigorously exercised: and will it not be much better to have it stored with words, which contain the most salutary truths, rather than those which may, by some association, prove injurious on the recollection? Sometimes the having committed to memory such a system as the Shorter Catechism, is of the utmost importance to an individual when his lot is cast where he has no means of correct information; or in case the person should lose his sight or hearing. We once noticed an exemplification of this in the case of a man of strong mind, who had led a busy life, without much concern with books, and who in his latter years was entirely blind. In conversation on the most important topics of religion, in which he took a deep interest, he would continually recur to the answers in the Shorter Catechism, which he had learned when young; and which now seemed to serve as a guide to his thoughts in all his meditations. But the true reason why so many children learn the Catechism without understanding its meaning, is, that no pains are taken to explain its doctrines, and to illustrate them, in a way adapted to their capacity. Parents are, for the most part, either incapable of giving such instruction, or negligent in the performance of this important duty. Most parents then need just such a help, for the discharge of this duty as is here provided for them. Why then should not every Presbyterian family possess itself at least of one copy of these *Lectures,* which are handsomely printed, and sold at a very reasonable rate? And why may not this become an important aid to the teachers in Sunday Schools, where these schools consist of the children of Presbyterian parents? We do earnestly hope that attention to doctrinal instruction will not be relinquished, nor diminished, in our church. Hitherto Presbyterians have been distinguished above all people in the world, for a correct and thorough knowledge of the

tenets of their own church. No people on earth are so well indoctrinated in the principles of religion, and in the proof of the doctrines
believed, as the Scotch, and their descendants in Ireland and America.
Other people far exceed them in metaphysical speculations, and in
the knowledge of other matters: but for sound religious knowledge,
commend us to Scotch Presbyterians of every sect.

The benefits of thorough instruction in the doctrines of religion
cannot be calculated. The truths thus received into the mind may
prove ineffectual, in some cases, to restrain from open sin; but even
in these, the force of the truth is often felt, and the person thus situated, is much more likely to be convinced of the error of his ways
than those transgressors whose minds are almost totally destitute of
the knowledge of the doctrines of religion. There is, moreover, an
unspeakable benefit from the possession of correct doctrinal information, when the mind falls under serious impressions of religion; for,
then, truths which had been early inculcated, and long forgotten,
will revive in the memory, and serve to guard the anxious mind from
those enthusiastic errors into which ignorant persons are so prone to
fall when they are deeply exercised on the subject of their salvation.
Let not the members of the Presbyterian Church, therefore, become
remiss in that which has ever been her most honourable distinction;
the careful initiation of children into the doctrines of religion, contained in her catechisms; than which, we believe, a sounder system of
theoretical and practical theology, cannot be found in any language.
It may appear rather extraordinary, that the assembly of divines at
Westminster, should have prepared two catechisms, as this seems
rather calculated to distract than edify the church. But the history
of this matter is simply this. The Larger Catechism was first composed by a committee of three members; Dr Tuckney, Dr Arrowsmith, and the Rev. Mr Newcomen; though there is good reason to
believe that the first named had the chief hand in the composition.
The work was highly approved, but was thought to be too long to
be generally committed to memory by children; the committee was
therefore directed to prepare a catechism containing the same truths,
in a more condensed form. The Shorter Catechism is therefore an
abridgment of the Larger, and by comparison it will be found to
contain the substance of the Larger, expressed with more brevity, but

containing, for the most part, the very language of the original. It was formerly a frequent thing for young persons of both sexes, in our church, to commit to memory, accurately, the whole of the Larger Catechism. Whether this practice is continued in many of the Presbyterian congregations, under the care of the General Assembly, our information is not sufficient to enable us to declare; but we cannot but believe that young persons who have accomplished this object, have acquired a treasure which may be to them of more value than thousands of silver and gold. One thus armed with the panoply of divine truth, will not be liable to be 'carried about with every wind of doctrine', and every wild spirit of enthusiasm which may be abroad in the world; and when he reads religious books, or hears discourses from the pulpit, he will be not only capable of understanding them better than others, but will carry about with him a test, by which he can make trial of the correctness of what he hears or reads, and thus be in a situation to obey the apostle's exhortation, 'Prove all things, hold fast that which is good.' We cannot be contented to let the opportunity pass of bestowing merited commendation on those denominations of Scotch Presbyterians who are not in communion with the General Assembly, for their indefatigable industry and care in giving doctrinal instruction to their children. In this respect, it must be acknowledged, they greatly excel all other denominations of Christians in our country. Among them, we have reason to believe, there has been no falling off in attention to the catechisms; and few instances ever occur of the members of these churches being seduced by the insidious arts of the propagators of error and infidelity.

The question may occur to some, To whom does it belong to give catechetical instruction? We answer, to all who are capable of teaching anything of divine truth correctly. But, especially, it is the duty of parents, guardians, masters, schoolmasters, elders, and ministers. All who can be enlisted in the service should be engaged to teach those more ignorant than themselves. And we feel constrained to give our testimony strongly in favour of Sunday Schools, in which so many persons are employed, so beneficially to themselves and others, in giving instruction out of the Bible. When this is called a new institution, it surely is not meant that any new instruction is given; or that there is anything new in the manner of communicating religious knowledge. The whole novelty of the thing consists in the success of the attempt to engage such a multitude of teachers in giving lessons, and such a multitude of scholars in learning them. But we would respectfully ask, whether parents, and ministers, and elders, have not become more remiss in catechising since the introduction of Sunday Schools?

In order to render the public catechising of children profitable, the pastor of the flock must manifest a deep and lively interest in the exercise. If he should appear indifferent, and attend on catechetical exercises in a formal, or careless manner, no great good can be expected to arise from such meetings: but if he will take pains to arrange all the circumstances of such exercises, so as to render them interesting to old and young;—if he will propose special subjects of inquiry, refer to proper books, and converse freely with his people on this topic, a spirit of investigation will be excited, religious knowledge will be pursued with diligence and alacrity, and catechising will be found to be the most effectual means of diffusing correct information on the doctrines of religion.

If common schools were what they ought to be, seminaries in which Christian doctrine was carefully taught, then our schoolmasters would all be catechists, and the children would be trained in the knowledge of God, and their duty. The business of catechising youth seems also to be one of the appropriate duties of the eldership: for surely these officers ought not to be restricted to mere matters of order and government. As leaders of the people, they should go before them in religious instruction; and it would be an expedient, as it is a common arrangement, to have each parish so divided into districts, that every elder would have a little charge of his own to look after, the families within which he might frequently visit, and where he might frequently collect and catechise the youth. If ruling elders are commonly incompetent to perform such a work as this, they are unfit for the office which they hold, and can be of little service in the church in other respects. It is now becoming matter of common complaint, that our ruling elders are not generally sensible of the important duties which belong to their office, and are not well qualified to perform them. But how can this evil be remedied? We answer, that the effectual remedy will be found in an increased attention to instruction in the doctrines of the church, by which means many will acquire a taste and thirst for religious knowledge; and whenever this occurs, there will be rapid progress in the acquisition of such a fund of sound theology, as will qualify them to communicate instruction to the young and ignorant. In the meantime, let every pastor meet with the elders of his church, once in the week, for the express purpose of discussing questions which relate to the duties belonging to their office; and thus those who are really desirous of executing their office in a faithful and intelligent manner, will become better and better prepared for their important work every year.

The question has often been agitated, whether it would not be expedient to have an order of catechists, whose duty it should be to attend to this whole concern; and the idea has been favourably entertained by some in the Presbyterian Church. But to us it appears, that such an office would be worse than useless: for, if the catechist be taken from among the members of the church, where he is expected to officiate, and this must be the case if every church is supplied with one or more, then why not constitute him at once a ruling elder? Surely the mere name of *catechist* would not qualify him to give instruction; and if he is qualified, would he not be as able to teach, if called by the name elder as catechist? And if the office is judged to be expedient, because we cannot obtain well qualified elders, how can it be supposed that competent catechists could be found? The idea of some, however, is, that to perform the duties of catechising well, requires much more time than men can commonly afford from their own business; and, therefore, proper persons should be employed, at a reasonable salary, to devote their whole time to this important branch of instruction. Now all this is very reasonable, and brings us to the very point mentioned before, *viz.,* that schools, among Christians, should have it as their chief object, to bring up children in the knowledge of divine things; and the proper catechists of the church would be the teachers of these schools. If it be said, that school masters are often incompetent to perform this part of their duty; we reply, that the same thing would be true, if they were called catechists; or if other persons were sought for, in the present state of the church, there would exist the same difficulty in obtaining them as there is now in finding well qualified school masters. The truth is, the church should take pains to train men for this very office; and parents should set a much higher value on it, than they have been accustomed to do; and the office ought to be rendered more respectable, and more desirable than it is at present.

It may, perhaps, be thought by some, that the prevalence of Sunday Schools renders it unnecessary for church officers to concern themselves with the instruction of the youth under their charge. If, indeed, the schools of this description within the parish are under the special superintendence and tuition of the pastor and elders, there is no good reason why catechetical instruction should not be given in a Sunday School as well as anywhere else. Catechizing is an exercise peculiarly suited to the Sabbath, and if the officers of any church should agree to conduct this part of instruction in their valuable institutions, it would certainly be an improvement on the plan on which they are commonly conducted. But when, as is commonly the case, these schools are made up of children of different denominations, and are under the direction of persons not connected with any one church, their existence and prosperity, while it will greatly facilitate pastoral labours, ought not to be considered as a substitute for catechising. We are afraid, however, that some pastors, as well as many parents, have become remiss in this part of their duty, from the mistaken idea, that their labours in this field are now superseded. This mistake should be carefully counteracted; and while the benefits of Sunday Schools are gratefully acknowledged, the instruction of our youth in the catechisms of our own church should be pursued with increasing diligence.

The old Presbyterian plan of conducting catechising did not confine this method of instruction to children and youth, but extended it to all persons except the officers of the church. And certainly one of the chief hindrances to the success of catechetical instruction has been that it commonly terminates too soon. When children have arrived at the age of twelve or fourteen years, they take up the opinion that they are too big and too old to repeat the Catechism; in consequence of which, until the institution of Bible classes, our youth received no appropriate instruction, in many congregations, in that period of their lives which of all others is most important for improvement in knowledge. While we are strong advocates for catechetical instruction, we are at the same time warm friends to the method of instruction pursued in Bible classes; and we should be pleased to see both these methods of instruction extended to all ages and conditions of men; for who is there that has not something yet to learn? And what upon earth is so worthy of time and pains as the knowledge of God's Word, and the doctrines of his wonderful love and grace? Every man who contributes to the increase of this kind of learning by his writings, should be deemed more a public benefactor than he who invents the most useful machine. Let all, then, whom God has entrusted with so excellent a talent as that of writing well on theology, take heed that they do not hide it in a napkin or bury it in the earth; for never was there a time when there was greater need of good books and tracts to counteract the floods of error which are issuing from a thousand sources; and never was there a period when the effect of good writing was so extensive. By means of the improvements in printing, and the facilities of conveyance in our day, opportunity is afforded of circulating opinions throughout the land; and if religious men sleep, there is no doubt that the enemy will sow his tares plentifully. Let the friends of truth, therefore, be watchful and wise, and ever on the alert, in seizing opportunities of enlightening the world with the pure doctrines of the Word of God.

THE DUTY OF
CATECHETICAL INSTRUCTION[1]

THE Word of God describes various evidences of a renewed heart. That we may know our true spiritual state, it is important to try ourselves by them all. Each evidence is also to be examined in its particular exercises. As regards love, for example, the professor of religion is to inquire, not only have I, in general, a benevolent spirit; but do I love God, his people, law, service, kingdom, and the doctrines of his holy Word? Love, as a 'fruit of the spirit', exercises itself toward all its appropriate objects. The Christian under its influence will not love one proper object, and be averse to another; love God, but withhold his affections from some child of God; or love one precept and not another; one doctrine of the Bible and not another. If you are a true Christian, you will give evidence of it in this, that you love all that God requires you to love; himself, each child of his family, each precept and each doctrine of his holy Word.

The object of the present tract is to consider 'the love of the truth',—attachment to the doctrines of the Bible—as an evidence of grace in the soul. God has set forth in his Word a system of holy and glorious truths, toward which no Christian can feel indifference or aversion; some of these are, the doctrines of the Trinity, the deity of Christ and of the Holy Spirit; the sovereignty of God, as displayed both in his moral government, and in the accomplishment of his own most holy will and pleasure; as comprised in this last, the doctrines of decrees and election; the free moral and accountable agency of man; the universal, native and total depravity of mankind; regeneration, by the special and supernatural agency of the Holy Ghost; the atonement of Christ for man's sins by his sufferings and death; justification

---

[1] Archibald Alexander, *The Duty of Catechetical Instruction*, (Philadelphia: Wm. S. Martien, 1836).

by faith in Jesus Christ alone; the final perseverance of the saints; the judgment of the world by Jesus Christ at the last day; and the future and eternal punishment of the wicked and blessedness of the righteous. The subject named as the title of this tract, is discussed with particular reference to these doctrines; for reasons which will be obvious. They, with others, compose the system sometimes called 'evangelical', or 'orthodox'; sometimes 'the doctrines of the Reformation'; but a better, and an apostolical appellation, is that given by Paul, *viz.,* 'Christ crucified'. Even some sceptical men, denying the inspiration of the Scriptures by the Holy Ghost, but interpreting Scripture language as they do that of other books, have candidly acknowledged that they teach this system of doctrines. If so even they judge, the man who professes himself a pious believer in the Bible as God's Word, can withhold neither his faith in these doctrines, nor his love to them, and at the same time make good his claim to being considered a Christian.

Here we should distinguish between love to the doctrines of the Bible, and some things men are in danger of mistaking for it, to their ruin. An assent of the understanding, simply, to a truth of the Bible, it scarce needs be said, is not love to it. Men's understandings are often convinced of things as true, which they oppose, and from which they are utterly averse. This is true in relation to doctrines of the Bible, in many men. They regret that they are true, and their feelings are against them; while knowing in their own consciences that they are immutable truths. Love to the doctrines of the Scriptures should also be carefully distinguished from that preference which arises from some selfish or sinister reason. In the controversies respecting religious doctrines, it is not infrequent that feelings of partisanship enlist unconverted men on the side of the truth. Do not boast that you are ready to contend for the truth. Do you love it? An orthodox head, as well as an Arminian or Pelagian one, may be associated with an unrenewed heart. A devout Christian can find no more complacency in orthodoxy itself, united with heartlessness and inactivity in the service of Christ, than in a blustering and denunciatory Pelagianism or Arminianism. Love to the truth is also to be distinguished from that kind of intellectual interest which arises from seeing its positions ingeniously proved or ably defended in argument. It is also to be distinguished from simple hereditary preferences. Men are sometimes found preferring the faith of their fathers or ancestors; without any satisfactory evidence that they love the truths of the Bible therein set forth, for their own sakes. Some probably die in the speculative faith of their fathers in the very truths of God, and 'die in their sins', and are forever lost.

Love to divine truth is an affair of the heart, as renewed by the Holy Spirit. It fixes the mind, the whole soul on the instructions of God's Word. The sincere lover of the divine doctrines says of God, 'I have esteemed the words of his mouth as more than my necessary food.' 'I rejoice at thy word, as those that find great spoil.' 'Thy words were found and I did eat them; and thy word was unto me the joy and rejoicing of my heart.' His preference of divine truth is decided; 'I have chosen the way of truth.' He earnestly desires and prays for increased knowledge of it and guidance into it; 'O send out thy light and thy truth, let them lead me, and let them bring me unto thy holy hill, and to thy habitation.' He finds sacred satisfaction in seeing others receiving, honouring, and obeying it; says, with that apostle whose character seemed all love, 'I rejoiced greatly, that I found of thy children walking in the truth'; 'I have no greater joy than to hear that my children walk in the truth.'

This Scripture account of love to divine truth, is attested by the experience of all who have been renewed by the Holy Ghost. It is deeply interesting to trace in the religious exercises and character of devoted Christians, their love to the doctrines of God's Word. They describe their feelings not only respecting divine truth in general, but particular doctrines in which they have found peculiar satisfaction and to which they had great aversion, before they became Christians. They are not only convinced of them in their understandings and consciences, but rejoice in them, with an affectionate joy. Doctrines which they once regarded with indifference; or at which they were uneasy and jealous, and against which, perhaps, they often contended with all their powers; the Spirit of God has taught them to see in an entirely different light, and to esteem them as cause of gratitude and love to God. We might give, did our limits permit, multitudes of most instructive examples from the Scriptures, and from Christian biography, showing affectionate delight in divine truth generally, and in many particular doctrines, as an evidence of grace, prominent, bright and beautiful.

The reasons of this holy affection to the doctrines of the Bible are various. It is God's truth. In every Scripture account of it, he hears the voice of his Father and his God. He also perceives the character of God, which he supremely loves, as reflected by each truth of his Word. There is also an excellence in the nature of divine truth itself, to his spiritual taste. 'How sweet are thy words unto my taste; yea, sweeter than honey to my mouth.' Its effects also render it inestimable in its value. Its adaptedness to humble, quicken, sanctify him, and render him conformed to the character of his Lord and Saviour, renders it precious to his soul. He loves it also for its effects on others, as the instrument of their conversion and sanctification to eternal life. He looks upon a world in sin and rebellion against God; sees everywhere the 'stout-hearted and far from righteousness'. What, he asks, shall break the power of this rebellion, bring down these stout hearts, stay the enmity of these spirits, bring back these wanderers to God? He remembers 'the sword of the Spirit, which is the word of God', and joins in the prayer of David, 'Gird thy sword upon thy thigh, O most mighty, in thy glory and in thy majesty'; 'thy right hand shall teach thee terrible things'; 'let thine arrows be sharp in the hearts of the king's enemies, whereby they fall under him'; fall to be subdued, brought to obey and love him. His heart delights in such truths; gives glory to God for them, and for all they accomplish by the power of the Spirit of grace, to the salvation of man and the glory of God. In short, the Christian feels that his heart is attached to the doctrines of God's Word, by cords which nothing can sunder. As he loves the divine character, so he loves divine truth. As he finds satisfaction in contemplating it here, he lives in happy anticipations of spending eternity in the contemplation of it, amidst the glories of heaven. And it is an animating reflection, that if here, where he 'sees through a glass darkly', the doctrines of God's Word appear so lovely, sublime, glorious; what will they be, when contemplated in the light which, to eternity, shall beam from the throne of his Redeemer and his God.

We consider, more particularly, the influence of love to the doctrines of the Bible on the Christian's character, habits of thought, feeling, and action. We shall find this part of the subject to have close application for the consciences of professors of religion in this day of fondness for modifications of doctrine, and of professions of new discoveries respecting religious truth.

Love to the doctrines of God's Word will lead to prayerful and diligent searching of the Scriptures, to know more of them. The true Christian will desire to be an intelligent one, respecting divine truth. He will be content with no past attainments in the knowledge of it. 'I follow after'; —'I count not myself to have apprehended.' With the fervent desire to know the truth better, which he so much loves, he will look up to his Father and his God, saying, 'lead me in thy truth, and teach me, for thou art my God; thy Spirit is good, lead me into the land of uprightness'. In forming our opinion of Christian character, we are warranted in building our judgment respecting individuals, as regards this evidence,—love to the truth,—very much on the devotedness and diligence with which we find them inquiring for it in 'the lively oracles of God'. The professed Christian who lives upon opinions he has gathered, and from lack of interest, or from disinclination, spends little time in his closet with his Bible and his God, is one whose love to the truth is very questionable. For where there is grace in the heart, there is implanted a spiritual taste; and that taste will seek its gratification in an increasing knowledge of these beloved truths.

It will also lead the Christian to seek satisfaction in the various means of advancing in knowledge of it. Conversation with intelligent Christians, the writings of devout and able men, plain, faithful preaching of the truth, will all be highly prized. He finds, with other Christians, satisfaction, like that of the disciples on the way to Emmaus, in 'talking together of all these things'; and his heart will burn within him, through this means, as owned of the Spirit for his quickening. Such a Christian will naturally and easily fall into conversation upon divine truth. He prizes next to the Bible, the books which are enriched by large drafts from the pure Word. A text of Scripture is a bright spot to his eye, shedding light all around it. The preaching and writings of good men are valued by him, according as they help his conceptions of divine truth. He will sit in the sanctuary with devout satisfaction while he hears 'the voice of the Lord', in his proclaimed truths. It will be to him like the 'voice from the excellent glory', which the disciples heard in the mount of the transfiguration. Spoken by a frail and imperfect man like himself, it may be; yet he will listen to it, 'not as the word of man', but as the voice of God speaking through the lips of an 'ambassador for Christ'. The messenger will be forgotten in the message. He will be conscious, that on the one hand, his devout affections for the truth and the feasting of his soul upon it, will be observed by him to whose eyes, 'all things are naked and open'; and that, on the other, if there lurk in the most secret recess of his soul a feeling which is reluctant at the reception and approval of 'jot or tittle' of the doctrines of God's Word; that too will be known to him 'whose eyes are as a flame of fire'.

Another influence of love to the truth will be its inducing a jealous care that the head and the heart shall go together. The real lover of the truth will never be satisfied with mere intellectual progress and attainment in it. 'Though I understand all mysteries and all knowledge, and have not love, I am nothing.'

Another influence of love to the doctrines of the Bible will be to inspire perfect confidence in their adaptedness to do good to the souls of men. Many calling themselves Christians, and among them some ministers, question or deny the profitableness of doctrinal instruction; and assert the hurtfulness of it; especially of certain doctrines. Those of the original and total depravity of man, divine sovereignty, decrees, election, the work of the Holy Spirit in renewing the soul, and the perseverance of the saints, are more frequently distrusted, as to their effects, than others. Respecting these, or any other doctrines set forth in the Bible, it will be the last question a lover of divine truth will ask, 'Will they do any good? Will they not do hurt?' His confidence in the eternal and 'only wise God' will be too childlike, implicit, and firm, to permit him to believe that in putting his holy Word into the hands of men, he has given them instruction which will 'do no good', and may or will 'do hurt', as is a frequent allegation in these days. He will remember that which is written, 'if our gospel be hid, it is hid to them that are lost; in whom the God of this world hath blinded the eyes of them that believe not, lest the light of the glorious gospel should shine unto them'; and that also which is written respecting the very ministry of the truth, as being to some, 'a savour of death unto death'. He will remember that it is not through the unhappy tendencies of these doctrines that any are driven away from Christ and lost; but because they turn them into the means of injury to themselves, by 'wresting the Scriptures to their own condemnation'. If men will not submit to be slain by the 'sword of the Spirit', as wielded by 'the power of the Spirit', that they may live unto God; but will violently use it by perversion, to slay their own souls; the Christian proves that 'their blood will be upon their own heads'. His confidence in it, as of salutary efficacy, is implicit and happy, while he considers the good which it has done to his own soul; and to the thousands on earth, and the 'ten thousand times ten thousand, and thousands of thousands' now in glory. In view of the strange opinions of some, that there are doctrines in the Bible which do hurt; he may ask himself, 'Is it possible that I have entered the kingdom of heaven, not only under hazards from my own wicked heart, the world, and Satan; but in hazard too from some of the very doctrines of the Bible?' And his whole soul will recoil at the thought, as if Satan had whispered blasphemy in his ears. No. The Christian, loving the doctrines of God's Word, will be willing to leave the effect of every one of them to him, in the sure confidence that God can and will take care of his own truth.

Love to divine truth is a steadfast principle. We see changes in the midst of professors of religion, at the present day; from professed belief of the doctrines of the gospel, to an unsettled state of mind, and scepticism respecting them; and then to positive aversion. This is a dark sign, as respects the true spiritual state of anyone. That doctrine of the gospel which a Christian has once loved, he will no more cease from loving, than he will 'fall from grace'. What is an apparent change, from loving any given doctrine, to distrust of it, and aversion, is only the manifestation of the solemn fact that it never has been loved. Love to the truth is not a thing which will, 'like a vapour continue for a little time and then vanish away', leaving the Christian to be 'tossed to and fro, and carried about by every wind of doctrine, by the sleight of men and cunning craftiness whereby they lie in wait to deceive'; and at the sport of the feelings of uneasiness, prejudice, and aversion. The truths which the Christian begins to love, he will love to all eternity. The very thought of a change of the state of his affections towards any truth of God, would distress him like the undermining of the foundation of his hope.

The true Christian, as loving the doctrines of the Bible, will be willing to have them embraced in his confession of faith; and when he joins himself to the visible church, will be willing to declare to men, before God and all heaven, that he believes them. There is in our churches at the present time a singular sensitiveness respecting creeds and confessions. Now if a Christian has 'received the love of the truth'; if the doctrines of the gospel have done his soul good; if he expects to be sanctified and saved through their means; what motive can he possibly have for keeping his belief of them secret. If he believes they have been to him 'a savour of life unto life', why should he not tell the world so, with the explicitness of language, and the frankness of feeling, which become one who supposes himself to have 'passed from death unto life'! Does the man who has been rescued from the borders of the grave, feel ashamed to tell his fellow men what was the medicine which has ministered to his restoration? And shall the converted man, in whom, through the instrumentality of the holy truths of God, has been laid the foundation of eternal health,—immortal vigour—be ashamed to tell the world from which he separates himself, in a Christian profession, the doctrines of God which have been blessed to his regeneration? And shall a church of the Lord Jesus Christ, bought with his blood and renewed and sanctified by his Holy Spirit, be unwilling to record in their creed, and show to the world, the doctrines by which they live and grow and thrive; and in which they hope to rejoice eternally in the presence of 'the Lord God and the Lamb'. No. That Christian who loves the holy truths of God, will take sacred and sweet delight in giving honour to them and their author, by a full and ingenuous showing of it in his confession of faith. And a church which has not travelled down into the darkness and delusion, for which that of Laodicea was so solemnly rebuked, would shrink from the crime of revising any truth of God out of their symbols of faith. Secrets to keep, in matters of faith! Ashamed to tell the world what they believe! If the love of God and of the truth be in them, and in exercise, they would as soon think of making a secret of their hope of eternal life; as soon think of being 'ashamed of Jesus'. To those whose breasts have been the seats of such unhappy workings, and whose declarations to the world respecting their faith have become equivocal, we commend the solemn consideration of that word of Christ, 'Whosoever therefore shall be *ashamed of me and of my words,* in this adulterous and sinful generation, of him also shall the Son of Man be ashamed when he cometh in the glory of his Father with the holy angels.'

Love to the doctrines of the Bible will forbid the substitution of anything else which professes to be a part of Christian character, instead of a cordial belief of those doctrines. Here is a point of imminent danger with multitudes who are considered converts, and who enter the church at the present day. Much is said, and with propriety, of 'coming out on the Lord's side', of 'being for God', 'working for God', and 'coming up to the help of the Lord against the mighty'. Along with this however we also have—what surely does not well comport with these things,—much said in depreciation of the importance of doctrines and doctrinal instructions,— and of those doctrines especially which prostrate the pride of the human heart, and show the sinner to himself as in the hands of a holy and sovereign God. The popular voice calls loudly for what is termed practical preaching, as invidiously contrasted with doctrinal. The professed fears of many attribute to some of those holy truths of God, at which the human heart most reluctates, tendencies which hinder or check revivals of religion, perplex young Christians and introduce disputes. *Do duty, and let alone the truth,* is the substance of too much of the pulpit preaching and private advice which is given to dying men; on whose knowledge and obedience of the truth is solemnly depending the eternal life of the soul. Thus, as it has been well remarked by a sound and discerning minister, 'religion is made to condemn the truth'. These questions are serious in their bearing on this great practical error. Is it the love of God which thus in effect attempts to set *doing* at variance with *believing,* which puts zeal instead of knowledge and 'sanctification through the truth', which professes to bring out the *commands* of God to bear on the consciences of men, while it shuts up the *doctrines* of God, by silence concerning them, or by cautious and timid presentations of them, in which their meaning is misunderstood; or caricatures of them, which hold them up to derision and contempt? Love to the truth will be found allied with a belief in such a thing as integrity of Christian character,—of the importance of both doing the commands and believing the doctrines of the sacred Word. The true Christian will feel and act on the feeling, that love to all divine truths is one of the chief corner-stones which constitute the basis of Christian character. The conviction will be settled and immutable in his mind and heart, that he can no more preserve the integrity and consistency of his character as a Christian without being a cordial lover and believer of the whole truth, than he can be a Christian without repentance or 'faith toward the Lord Jesus Christ'.

Love to divine truth will be an effectual preventive against all uneasiness and dissatisfaction with its doctrines. It is an absurdity in terms,—the idea of a Christian being uneasy and dissatisfied with what he professes to love,—and love to which is an essential element of Christian character. What does one who professes himself a follower of Christ declare to a sinful world, which is worthy of a declaration, if not that he is attached to the truths of God's Word? There are doctrines in relation to which the feelings of the professor of religion will assist him easily to perceive the relevancy and importance of this point. Take, for example, the doctrine of the deity of Christ. If you are a true Christian, this is the truth which you love, and in relation to which you feel no uneasiness or dissatisfaction. So of the atonement of Christ; if there be a doctrine of the Bible which you love, surely it is this. So of the free moral agency and accountableness of man; your mind is in no balancing of uneasiness, has no dissatisfaction with this. Here, now is the doctrine of God's sovereignty, including among other things, 'his having mercy on whom he will have mercy'; the doctrine of the original and total depravity of mankind; the doctrine of regeneration, as declaring man's dependence on the renewing power of the Holy Spirit. These are as clearly doctrines of the Bible, as the first named. They have God for their author; are as holy in their character; as essential in the great system of divine truth, are as important to the production of given effects on the heart and conscience of the sinner. They are also to be loved by the Christian. They are so loved. There is scarce a doctrine in the Bible with which Christians have testified stronger satisfaction, than with the doctrine of divine sovereignty, for example: if you are a Christian, you include these last named among the truths which you approve and love. If you call yourself a Christian, and still are averse to these truths, explain this to yourself, if you can, and still keep hold of your hope. If you do love these truths, how is it possible that uneasiness or dissatisfaction with them can have place in your breast? What kind of a Christian must he be, who unites in his experience these strange contrarieties, love to divine truth, and also uneasiness and dissatisfaction with some of its grand articles. We press this, as a point for consideration, because we see multitudes who are professedly the friends of God and his truth, who sit with a most mysterious uneasiness under the preaching of certain doctrines, and have a very singular sensitiveness respecting their holding a place in their articles of faith.

In this connection we remark, that love to divine truth will utterly forbid all disposition to be excused from receiving any given doctrine of the Bible, because that difficult questions can be raised respecting it by sceptical men; or because God has not stripped it of mystery, and laid it open to human conceptions. It will also most authoritatively repress all inclination to assent to the cavils of unbelieving men, respecting the doctrines of the Bible. A *Christian* is the last man on earth from whom to expect such things.

Love to the doctrines of the Bible will constrain the Christian to a faithful and fearless defence of them, whenever he hears them reproached or denied. The true Christian is of a tender spirit, respecting everything which touches the honour of God. Of the doctrines of his Father's Word, which he has received in love, and in which his soul rejoices, he says, 'He that toucheth you, toucheth the apple of mine eye.' His soul is hurt, 'cast down within him', when he sees them dishonoured by unbelief, held up to ridicule, and contemned; and, above all, when he sees these things in men professing the religion of Christ; perhaps even in the sacred office of the ministry. Living in a world where God speaks by his Word, and writes out upon its pages as with a sun-beam, his glorious 'mind and will', he cannot withhold himself from 'contending earnestly for the faith once delivered to the saints'. He hears a voice saying to him, 'Speak, and hold not thy peace, for I am with thee.' He feels that silence would be to betray the truth. For is not the truth worthy of defence? Is not the God of truth to be feared? Must great doctrines of the gospel, 'pertaining to life and godliness', be cast down, and trampled upon, and that too, in the church, and in the pulpit; and not a son of God lift his voice in their defence? Shall the church yield by one inch after another, 'the ground of the truth'; or let presumptuous and unholy hands take away the pillars of its temple, and prostrate it in the dust? Have Christians nothing to do, but to believe the truth for their own good; and may they quietly suffer dying men, with whom they are soon to stand before God in judgment, to trifle with it, to treat it with indignity, and to cast out its name as evil? No; the love of Christ in his true friends will constrain them to do their duty. Girding themselves 'with all prayer and supplication in the Spirit', and watching for the divine honour, 'with all diligence', they will ever be ready. In every conflict respecting the doctrines of the sacred Word, they will be seen wielding 'the sword of the Spirit, which is the word of God'; moving on, firm, faithful, 'valiant for the truth'. The Captain of their salvation will go before them; lead them, encourage their spirits; and make 'the weapons of their warfare mighty, through God, to the pulling down of the strongholds'.

But the Christian is not one who delights in controversy, except called to it for the honour of his Lord. He will, therefore, covet more the delightful employment of propagating the knowledge of the truth among men. If his faith in the doctrines of the gospel is not to be hidden in a corner; neither will he shut up the knowledge of them from others. 'To do good, and to communicate, forget not', applies to importing the knowledge of truth, as well as to alms giving. In this he will have regard not only to the propagation of the gospel in heathen lands, but the promotion of the pure faith among all around him. The very church sometimes becomes in a measure corrupt in the faith; and there arises occasion for saying to many professing Christians, 'For whereas, for the time, ye ought to be teachers, ye have need that one teach you again, which be the first principles of the oracles of God.' But not more imperious is the necessity for communicating the truth to the nations which 'sit in darkness', than it sometimes is to *re*-communicate it to those who have once seemed to know it. There is an indistinctness of view in individual Christians, and pervading many of the churches of our land, respecting divine truth, which is both surprising and alarming; and in many professors of religion, an ignorance of truth, and an aversion to it, which is almost heathenish. The Christian enters into the desire of his Lord, to have 'all men come to the knowledge of the truth'. Therefore, he will seek in various ways to aid men's acquaintance with it; will promote their study of the Scriptures as the great depository of divine doctrines; will 'reason with men out of the Scriptures'; will promote publications which set forth plain, scriptural, instructive delineations of divine truth; will uphold the preaching of the truth, and endeavour to bring all he can to attend upon its ministrations. In whatever the good knowledge of God's holy truth can be advanced among men, in that he will labour, cheerfully, diligently, humbly; and God will make it to be successfully. For 'the truth is great, and must prevail'. God may, for a time, permit men to rage against it, and their opposition to check its progress; and the subtlety and ingenuity of false philosophy to perplex and try men's minds, and to lead away into the dark mazes of error, those who have 'not received the love of the truth'. And those who thus sin may, for a time, feel encouraged to think, that they shall 'cast down the truth to the ground', and yet prosper. But God is all this time saying, 'in his secret place of thunder', 'I know thy going out and thy coming in, and thy rage against me.' And the time is coming, when he will make them tremble and submit; or, as 'despisers, wonder and perish'. 'He hath given a banner to them that fear him, that it may be displayed, because of the truth.' And 'yet a little while, and he [the King of truth] that shall come, will come, and will not tarry'; and will gather around their banner, multitudes that know and rejoice in the truth; and the enemies of it he will clothe with shame. While these things are certain, the lovers of his truth have nothing to do, but to move steadily onward, labouring to scatter the 'light of the knowledge of the glory of God'. Their hearts desire and prayer to God shall be answered; and his knowledge will yet fill this fallen world.

There are modes of thinking, and attitudes of mind, in many churches in our country at the present time, respecting several of the doctrines of the sacred Word we have named, which make necessary a close application of the subject of this tract.

Respecting those who 'receive not the love of the truth', it is a solemn, fearful declaration, 'For this cause, God shall send them strong delusion, that they should believe a lie; that they all might be damned who believed not the truth, but had pleasure in unrighteousness.' If men sin against God, persisting in their feelings of aversion to the doctrines he has taught, let them be well aware of the fearful danger to which they expose themselves. If they continue averse to them, their doom is thus foretold. God will not permit men to trifle with his truth. Mark the expression, 'strong delusion'. Error, inasmuch as it is opposed to the powerful truth of God, is brought forth with the best strength of the human mind, and rendered plausible and almost irresistible, by sophistry and ingenuity. See how one whose mind is not the residence of 'the love of truth', is enticed, led, overcome, ensnared, as he looks upon the plausible delusion of error, in which while the *name* of a holy truth is perhaps retained, its *character* has undergone a complete transformation, so that it is no more the truth. He says in himself, 'How reasonable this looks; how consistent with the feelings of my heart; how clear; here is no mystery; here are no "hard sayings"; all meets my mind.' And with some wrested Scriptures, to sustain the ingenious sophistries of unbelief, he draws the conclusion: 'This must be the truth.' He sits down satisfied, because he has succeeded in getting away from doctrines which were unwelcome to his feelings. 'Strong delusion'! binding the soul with its cords of iniquity, perhaps never to be sundered, till death separates his body to the grave, and his soul to the scenes of eternity. Take heed how by 'receiving not the love of the truth', you provoke God to send upon you 'strong delusion'.

The professor of religion has occasion to fear respecting his own spiritual state, who finds himself uneasy, dissatisfied, disposed to dispute against any of the doctrines of the Bible we have named. Ask yourself, 'Is my heart right with God?' What must be the state of your affections toward him whom you call your Father in heaven, if you find yourself excepting against any portion of his revealed will!

That professor of religion has occasion to be anxious respecting himself, who wishes to set aside any doctrine of God's Word, on the plea that it is unessential to be believed, in order to salvation; or, that it is a point of difference between man and man, on which true wisdom is silence. There is in use much language of this description, respecting some doctrines we have particularly stated. The remark is

a common one, as a short-hand way of putting down a doctrine,—
'This is one of those points which are of no great importance.' Points!
The whole truth of God is made up of 'points'; and every one of them
is designed by the Spirit of God, to be 'sharper than any two-edged
sword'. God has filled his Word with these, that they may take effect
on the soul of the sinner, and test the state of the professed Christian.
And the moment a man winces under their effect, and endeavours
to get away from it, he is trying to get away from the sword of the
Spirit. And if he succeed, he will at last find that he succeeded, most
fearfully, in getting away from being converted to God. It is an opinion gaining considerable credence, and that, too, among those who
would feel themselves injured by any question about their orthodoxy,
that they have been converted, and that others can be, without concerning themselves with the doctrines we have mentioned. Such will
find in the end, that they are to prove converted through the means of
these as well as other doctrines, and brought into harmony of feeling
with them, or that they have not been converted at all. The only wise
God knows what effects need to be accomplished upon your heart;
and what truths are adapted and necessary to the accomplishment of
these effects. If you are to be born again, it will be through the means,
and into the belief of these much despised truths. God will not commit himself to the dictation of any sinner, as to the means by which
he will be converted. You must submit to the means he has appointed
in his *whole* and holy truth.

The opinion has place in the minds of some men in the sacred
office, that it is practicable to modify or lay aside these 'offensive
doctrines', or interweave them with others, so that they shall not be
distinctly perceived; that there is what a sensible writer calls 'a certain
wise way', in which their offence shall be made to cease. Others there
are, who go farther, and pronounce them the needless peculiarities
of a system; and hold them up to ridicule, under some opprobrious
epithet or appellation; and pronounce preachers of them enemies
of the conversion of sinners, and of revivals of religion; and pride
themselves on converting sinners by an easier way, and in the taking
up of the stumbling-blocks out of their path to the cross, by keeping
or putting these hated doctrines out of sight. And multiplied conversions are counted, as produced by this more excellent way. It is proper

to remind such, that the day is approaching, when God has declared, that 'the fire shall try every man's work, of what sort it is'; when it will be seen whether such ministrations have been, truly, building on the foundation God has laid, that which shall abide; or that which God will 'consume with the breath of his mouth, and destroy with the brightness of his coming'. Take heed of the impiety of the attempt to be wiser than God, in fixing upon the means by which men shall be brought to his footstool.

The assumption is made by those who talk of doctrines which are not essential, or 'minor points', that though God has revealed by the inspiration of the Holy Ghost, and preserved almost miraculously in the world, for 6,000 years, his announcements of these truths; yet that it is man's right to sit in judgment on their real value; and if he pleases, to pronounce them unessential. It is a strange fact, that men confessedly unconverted and out of the church, oppose these doctrines as of some importance; while men professing themselves Christians and in the church seek to degrade them from their dignity and hide their glory, by pronouncing them unimportant,— 'non-essentials'. We are constrained to ask whether of these twain is the greatest offender against God; he who opposes a truth in the acknowledgment of its magnitude, or he who despises it under the pretext of its insignificance?

Now we ask for that Scripture which warrants this so common and popular notion, that there are doctrines in the Bible unessential to be believed. Which is the doctrine of God's Word, on which a minister can be silent and yet blameless? Which is the truth so unessential, that, respecting it a man may live in unhappy, spirit-chafing prejudice, and yet not have to 'give account thereof in the day of judgment'? Tell us what is that doctrine of God with which a man may contend, secretly or openly; which he may shut up in studied silence, or openly malign; and yet lie down on his death bed in peace, feeling that he owes to God no repentance, and to man no acknowledgment of dishonour done to the Bible? Can a man pass from fighting against a truth of God, to the bliss of saints and angels bowing before the throne in adoration of his truth?

The plea of the unessentialness of given truths goes upon a principle which would excuse almost any errorist who ever rejected a truth of the Bible. If I may with impunity pronounce one truth unessential; another may declare another so. If I may set aside one truth, which I call unessential and not endanger my soul; why may not another do the same by two, three, five, which he pleases to consider so, and be as safe as myself? Where is the line which separates between me and the Universalist, the Deist, yea, even the Atheist in this matter?

No: let no man who calls himself a Christian, and a lover of divine truth, talk of unessential truths of the eternal God: of the majesty of heaven sending down from amidst the brightness of his glory, a book in which he trifles with men, by giving them their choice what portion of its announcements they will believe, and what they will set aside as being of sufficient importance to be believed. If you are a sincere lover of divine truth, you will spend no time, and commit no sin, in making exceptions to doctrines of the Bible; nor in searching for excuses to quiet conscience in withholding your assent from any given truth. On the contrary, you will embrace in the range of your holy affections, the whole. You will fear breaking in upon the perfections and harmony of the great system of divine truth, by thus taking away *one*. And if you expect to meet God in heaven as your reconciled Father, and to be owned and blessed, through eternity, as a child of his love—believe him in all the declarations of his truth; and love them, as you are bound to love himself, with all your soul, mind and strength. And be yours the blessedness of the blissful contemplation of all God's glorious truths, in the light which shall beam from his eternal throne.

SUGGESTIONS IN VINDICATION
OF SUNDAY SCHOOLS[1]

THE importance of the general diffusion of religious knowledge seems now to be universally admitted. No longer is
it pretended that ignorance is the mother of devotion, or
that real knowledge can be injurious to any portion of the community. Experience teaches that the more ignorant men are the more
liable are they to be hurried into acts of violence and excess, or to
be seduced into vice by the persuasions and example of the wicked.
Most malefactors, who are condemned by the laws of the country,
are exceedingly ignorant of religious truth: the mob, often influenced
and led on to acts of shocking outrage, is everywhere composed of
the least informed of the people. An ignorant multitude is always
liable to be misled by designing demagogues, or seduced by artful
impostors. A regard to character, and a respect for the opinions of
others, is greatly strengthened by an increase of knowledge, and this
is one of the strongest barriers against infamous vice. Conscience,
the most powerful of restraints, possesses force in proportion to the
light of truth in the mind. Superstition may, indeed, be promoted
by ignorance, but true religion never. Fanaticism also is closely allied
to ignorance, but the most effectual remedy against enthusiasm is
genuine piety. Scepticism, it is true, is often associated with a considerable extent of knowledge, but the cure of infidelity must be found
in a correct acquaintance with the truth; and the best preventive of
this evil is early religious instruction. It cannot be doubted, that the
manners of men are polished by education. Where do you find manners the most sordid and brutal, but among those who have never

[1] Archibald Alexander, *Suggestions in Vindication of Sunday Schools, but More Especially
for the Improvement of Sunday School Books, and the Enlargement of the Plan of
Instruction,* Miscellaneous Pamphlet Collection (Library of Congress) DLC (1829).

been instructed? Ferocious passions naturally spring up in minds entirely uncultivated. And it need not be feared that instruction will render the poor more miserable by making them more sensible of their humble condition. Sound religious knowledge will teach them that happiness may be enjoyed as fully in a cottage as in a palace; that contentment with our condition is the duty of all; and that want and affliction furnish a very salutary discipline, by which faith is tried, virtue improved, and the soul prepared for a better world. The discontented, envious poor, are not commonly those who have been religiously educated, but the ignorant and profligate. It can admit of no doubt, therefore, that the diffusion of knowledge, and especially of religious knowledge, among all classes of people, is a thing to be desired; and that no pains and labour can be considered too great, which are the means of accomplishing this end.

But how this can be most successfully effected, is a question which demands the serious consideration of every friend of man. God has, indeed, appointed the preaching of the gospel as the great instrument of the instruction and moral reformation of men, and nothing should be allowed to supersede this; for God is wiser than man, and will, moreover, honour and bless his own institutions. Let it be admitted, then, that the faithful preaching of the gospel is the *great means* to which all others should be subordinate. But God has also directed Christians to give mutual instruction to one another, and 'to hold forth the word of life' to those who are in darkness. Private instruction is as much authorized as public preaching, and, in its place, is as necessary. Indeed, without private instruction public preaching will be in a great measure useless. One who is totally uneducated, cannot understand the purport and connection of a sermon. The people must, by some means, be prepared by elementary education to profit by the public teaching of the church; and the want of this elementary knowledge, is one great reason why so many hear to so little profit. They hear, but they understand not; and thus the good seed is lost. This preparatory instruction ought to be given in every family; but alas! I need not say how commonly this is neglected, or so imperfectly attended to, that our youth are, in many places, growing up in shameful and dangerous ignorance. But if parents and masters will not perform their duty in this respect, can no remedy be devised?

Can no substitute be proposed? Yes; God, in his kind providence, has directed the attention of his church to a remedy which may be considered effectual, if it be diligently and universally used. This is the Sunday School system of instruction. Although this method of teaching the young and ignorant is so simple, yet it deserves to be ranked second to no discovery of our age. I do not know that the beneficence of providence has been more manifest in anything which has occurred in our day than in the general institution of Sunday Schools. Other benevolent institutions provide the means of religious instruction; but the Sunday School makes the application of them. Indeed all others require this for their successful operation. Bibles and tracts cannot be useful to those who cannot read; but in these humble seminaries the ignorant are taught to read. Pious youth are wanted to be educated for pastors and missionaries; and where will you go to find them, but to the Sunday Schools? Here will often be seen the first buddings of that piety, which expands in the performance of faithful missionary labour in some heathen land. A large majority of the missionaries now in the field were nurtured in Sunday Schools. Here will be sown, in many a heart, the precious seed which will germinate in a thousand benevolent efforts, and bring forth fruit unto eternal life. While the civilian is earnestly employed in devising plans for prisons, and dungeons for solitary confinement, let it be the noble object of the patrons of Sunday Schools, to render all such institutions, if possible, unnecessary. And this is not a vain hope, if all the children in the country could be brought under the regular influence of this mode of instruction. Scarce any of those taught in these schools have ever been disgraced by a condemnation for crime.

We are, as the voice of experience teaches, never less liable to lose the fruit of our labour, than when we instil religious instruction into the susceptible minds of children. This precious seed is seldom entirely lost; for although it may lie long buried, as it were, under the dust, it may spring up at a late day and flourish long after the hand that sowed it is laid in the grave. Besides, we are not aware how much positive evil is prevented by the impressions of religious truth on the minds of youth. In the Sabbath School the little boy is taught the Ten Commandments; it is moreover inculcated on him, that God is angry with the wicked, and that his curse will follow the evildoer. Also, he learns there, that the evil of sin is so great, that God's own Son came into our world, and died on the cross, to make an atonement for it. In his Bible, which he here learns to read, he finds it written, that 'the wicked shall be turned into hell'; and that the ungodly shall not inherit eternal life. Now, when this boy goes into the world, and meets with dissolute companions, who tempt him to steal, or murder, or bear false witness, will not these solemn truths which he has learned at school, rush upon his mind, and operate as strong restraints to preserve him from the commission of crimes, under the power of which he would easily fall, were it not for these salutary impressions?

Sunday Schools were originally instituted with a special view to those unhappy children, who through the ignorance, or profligacy, or carelessness of their parents have no religious instruction, but on the contrary, are brought up under the influence of evil counsels and worse examples. And such children ought still to be considered the direct object of these institutions; but it has been found, that they may be rendered highly useful to children of every description. Often it happens, that well disposed and pious parents are poorly qualified to communicate religious instruction to their own children; and not infrequently, children are more attentive to lessons of morality and religion coming from others, than to those which they learn from their own parents. From these they are so accustomed to hear advice and reproof, that they are very apt to contract a habit of heedlessness when admonished by them; but when another, who claims no authority but that which is founded on kindness, speaks affectionately to these children, they are mute with attention, and seem to be tenderly affected with what they hear from their beloved Sunday School teachers. The good order and solemnity maintained in these schools has a great effect in predisposing the youthful mind to be attentive and serious; and also the gentle emulation which is properly excited gives a spring and alacrity to the spirits which is favourable to improvement. There are few parents, I believe, who can instruct their own children as well as they may be taught in many of our Sabbath Schools.

But the good effect of this institution is nearly as conspicuous, in regard to the teachers, as the pupils. It has been long a maxim, that to know a thing accurately, the best method is to teach it. And with respect to religious knowledge it has ever been found very difficult to induce people generally, whether old or young, to give such patient attention to divine truth, as to become well acquainted with the doctrines and precepts of the Bible. Now this difficulty is happily obviated in regard to the teachers in our Sunday Schools. The necessity which they are under of teaching the lesson, furnishes a motive sufficiently strong, to induce them to study it with diligence, and by the aid of all the helps to which they can have access. Thus many of our intelligent young people are actually becoming accurate Bible theologians. They are acquiring divine knowledge, in that way, which leads them thoroughly to understand what they learn, and to fix it indelibly in the memory. I do not know any better school in which these persons could be placed for their own improvement, than to enjoy the privilege of teaching the children in Sunday Schools. The advantages of this situation, I am persuaded, have not been overrated. The good resulting from this benevolent employment has not been confined to mere improvement in sacred knowledge, but in many instances, has issued in the conversion of the heart to God. There can, I believe, be no doubt but that a larger proportion of Sunday School teachers have become truly pious, within a few years, than of persons of any other class or description. God fulfils his own gracious promise, that they that water shall themselves be watered. The benefits derived from these blessed institutions to teachers, are, themselves, a rich compensation for all their labour, and for all the expenses incurred, in keeping them up.

But Sunday Schools have not only been beneficial, in a high degree, to the pupils, and the teachers, but also to the parents and other relatives of the children. Many parents are so hostile to religion and to religious men that they can scarcely be approached in any other way than through their children. All such persons view religion, distorted and deformed, through a medium of dense prejudice; but when their children repeat their lessons in their hearing, and read to them from the sacred Scriptures, new light often darts into their minds, and speedily a great change takes place in their sentiments. Sometimes, also, ignorant or profligate parents will accompany their children to a Sabbath School, who can by no other means be induced to enter the walls of a church. When there, their attention is riveted, while they listen to the answers of their own children; and thus the truth finds access to minds long estranged from God, and deeply buried in ignorance.

But it is not the ignorant and vicious parent only, that derives benefit through the attendance of his children at Sunday Schools; many well-informed and respectable people are led by the inquiries of their children, to search after many things which they never knew before, or had forgotten. In families where much attention is paid to the lesson for the week, all hands are set to work to find out appropriate answers to the questions. Commentaries are consulted, and I have no doubt, that, in many cases, the exercises of the Sunday Schools have been the means of bringing these valuable books into families where they would not otherwise have been found. And it is much to be desired, that we had a commentary, sound and concise, evangelical and practical, adapted to Sunday Schools. If such a book were placed in every family from which children come, how extensively would Bible knowledge be diffused in a short time?

It may, moreover, be mentioned as one of the minor advantages of Sunday Schools, that they promote neatness and decency of dress and personal appearance among the poor. The moral, pious, and industrious poor are generally remarkable for cleanliness and for being tidy in their dress when they go out from home: but the idle, intemperate, and profligate, are usually disgustingly filthy, and their children are squalid in their whole appearance. Now, how close the connection is between neatness and purity of mind I shall not attempt to determine; but that every step in civilization is favourable to virtue and religion, there is no doubt: and whatever will have the effect of inducing parents to exercise some care and industry in attending to the personal appearance of their children, so as to put them into decent trim, has, in the my opinion, a very salutary result.

But my object in this essay is not merely to decant on the utility of Sunday Schools: I wish to enter somewhat particularly into the principles on which these institutions should be conducted; and the improvements, which may, without difficulty, be engrafted on the existing system. Not that I mean to give any precepts relative to the minute regulations of these institutions. My experience does not enable me to judge or direct anything on this subject: and it is one on which teachers and superintendents are better capable of directing than other persons. But although I have no experience in the management of Sunday Schools, I have not been an uninterested spectator of their origin and rapid progress; and the more I reflect upon the subject, the more important does the institution appear. I confess, therefore, that I feel no small solicitude that nothing should occur which would have a tendency to retard its advancement or prevent it from attaining to that perfection, and accomplishing that measure of good, of which the system is capable. My zeal in the cause of Sunday Schools, therefore, together with the request of some respected persons who are devoted to this object, must be my apology for offering my opinions freely to the public on this interesting subject.

1. I have observed, with pleasure, that the system of Sunday School benevolence, in its most prominent features, is catholic. It willingly embraces all who receive the Bible and are willing to use it. It has, therefore, been considered a desirable object to combine as many religious denominations in this enterprise as possible; and it is not perceived that with prudent management there can exist any ground of unpleasant collision. The American Sunday School Union, as a society, professes no creed but the Bible; although the individuals who are concerned in its management, belong to several distinct denominations, to the forms and peculiar opinions of which respectively, they adhere. But, in conducting Sunday Schools they know no sect but Christianity, no creed but the Bible.

The object of Sunday Schools, is, to communicate that knowledge which is common to all who hold the fundamentals of Christianity. There is, undoubtedly, in our time, some approach to the spirit of unity and catholicism; and, certainly, this spirit, when genuine, should be cherished as pertaining to the gospel of Christ. In whatever institutions, therefore, Christians of different denominations can combine their benevolent and pious efforts with an increase of strength and without compromising their peculiar tenets, they ought to unite; and it partakes of the nature of schism to break this union on account of narrow sectarian feelings and interests. While schemes of close connection between those who differ in matters viewed to be of some importance to the purity of faith and worship are only adapted to produce collision, and greater alienation than before existed, it is delightful to see those, who have long been too far apart, drawn near together by the power of their mutual love to Christ and by the sweet bands of brotherly love. Why should those who are so soon to inhabit one house in heaven treat each other as aliens and enemies or spend their time in building up high walls of separation? Let each section of the church catholic maintain, with becoming firmness and zeal, what they honestly believe to be the truth of God, and no imputation of bigotry can justly be charged upon them while they pursue this course: but, as the points of difference between evangelical Christians are trivial, compared with the important and fundamental truths in which they agree, brotherly kindness ought not to be interrupted on account of their differences; and whenever any occasion offers, on which they can cordially unite their efforts, it is manifestly their duty to receive one another as Christ has received them, and to show to a world which is ever cavilling on account of the dissensions of Christians, that real Christians can love one another still, although partially separated by names and forms.

It is manifest, from an examination of the constitution of the Sunday School Union, that all its articles are catholic: no preference is there shown to any one denomination. And it is equally evident, from a consideration of the character of the gentlemen who compose the Board of Managers, that no partiality has been exhibited. It would scarcely be possible to form a board with a more equal respect to the several denominations concerned in this enterprise; and, as far as is known to me, the same impartiality is manifest in the proceedings of the Board, both in the selection of their officers and committees, and in the books selected for publication.

I have been led to make these remarks, because it has been objected, by some, to this society, that while it professes catholic principles, it is in fact merely an instrument for building up one denomination. But how is this possible when no one denomination has a majority in the Board? Will all parties, retaining their peculiar sentiments and attachments, concur, in promoting the separate interests of a society different from their own? And I would ask of those who make this objection, what single act of the American Sunday School Union has even the semblance of partiality for a particular sect? I am verily persuaded that no such act can be pointed out. It may be true, indeed, that some denominations enter more zealously and generally into the enterprise than others, but this argues no fault in the constitution, or partiality in the Board; or in their agents. The remedy is—and it would be a most desirable one—that all denominations emulate each other in zeal and energy in promoting Sunday Schools in their respective churches. Here is a wide field for a noble, a holy competition. But surely, there exists no ground of complaint, and no reason for objection to the constitution or administration of the society.

2. But while the American Sunday School Union have been scrupulously careful to maintain impartiality, as it relates to the several religious denominations united in this scheme of benevolence, it is probable that they have not been sufficiently aware of another objection, which has recently been made by some warm friends of the institution. It is alleged that there is danger lest the American Union should establish a system of religious instruction everywhere, independent of the regular and authorized pastors of the church. It is said that their agents penetrate into the parishes of every denomination, and there establish their schools without the consent, or concurrence of ministers, or other church-officers; and that by this means, the religious instruction of the youth is likely to be taken out of the hands of those to whom, according to the economy of Christ's house, it has been regularly committed. And, moreover, that we have no security for the soundness of the doctrines inculcated by the teachers of a society, which may propagate just what opinions it pleases; and so it may happen, that the children of a parish may, in the Sunday Schools, be taught doctrines directly repugnant to those held by the minister and by the church to which he belongs. I bring forward this objection with all its force, that its weight may be duly appreciated by the managers of the Union.

Now, in answer to this, it can be truly stated, that the managers of the American Sunday School Union have ever been solicitous to obtain the co-operation of the clergy in their respective spheres of action and influence; and they have not only invited their aid, but have even, in some instances, given offence to some clergymen by one of their standing questions, which they regularly call upon the schools under their care to answer; which is, 'How far are the ministers engaged in promoting the schools? Have you taken any steps to

interest ministers in your vicinity to promote Sunday Schools?'[1] But
if ministers, generally, have paid little or no attention to the subject,
and the schools have gone forward without their aid or inspection,
surely the blame does not lie at the door of the American Sunday
School Union. If the clergy of the different denominations will not
take hold of this thing, and give it a direction within their own parishes or preaching districts, it is impossible for the American Sunday School Union to compel them to perform their duty. And if
the minister of a parish will not come forward and lend his aid and
counsel, must the work stop? Must the Sunday School agent make
no effort to provide for the instruction of those who are willing to
be taught within those bounds? Surely, no sincere friend to the rising
generation would affirm this. And candour compels me to declare,
that when at the late meeting of the delegates of auxiliaries with the
Board in Philadelphia, this subject was brought up and discussed,
the managers discovered every disposition to adopt any resolution, or
take any measures, which would have the effect of enlisting the clergy
of the several denominations, cordially in this work: and when a resolution was proposed and voted by the delegates of the auxiliaries, to
urge this matter again and more earnestly on the pastors and other
church-officers, it received the decided approbation of the Board of
Managers of the American Sunday School Union. But the aspect of
the question which is most important is, not who have been remiss in
the discharge of duty in time past, but what can be now done to avert
the danger and prevent the evil which it has been seen is imminent.
In observing on this subject, I beg leave respectfully to say to the
ministers of the gospel of every denomination:—

Dear Brethren, I scarcely know a pastoral duty of higher responsibility,
than to lend your utmost aid and influence to give efficiency and a
right direction to Sunday Schools within the limits of your parishes
and your vicinity. You have known and felt how difficult or rather
impossible it is, for one man to instruct effectually all the youth of

---

[1] The following is one of the duties enjoined in the commission which the managers
give to their agents:—'It will be your special duty to wait on all ministers of the
gospel, and make known particularly to them, the nature and objects of your
mission, and use your influence to interest them in promoting Sabbath Schools in
their respective congregations, towns, and counties.'

a large parish. If you should do nothing else, it would still be imperfectly done. Under these discouraging prospects, some of you have probably been driven almost to despair of effecting anything; while others have endeavoured, by occasional catechising, and by paying an annual pastoral visit to the families under your care, to accomplish what seemed practicable: but you know, that unless parents, guardians, and masters will do their duty faithfully, in the domestic instruction of their families, these occasional exercises never can be effectual to feed the lambs of Christ's flock. O! how much would many of our fathers in the ministry have given for a half-a-dozen faithful coadjutors in communicating elementary knowledge to the young? But in their time, such aid could not have been obtained. No young person, nor scarcely any elderly one, could have been persuaded to become teachers. Such a thing was unknown and uncustomary, and no one thought of it. But, now, providence has provided you with a piece of moral machinery, which, if rightly directed, will be of as much avail to you, as the labour-saving machines to the mechanic in our extensive manufactories. It will not answer for you to leave it in the hands of others. They may direct it well, or they may not; but as it is to operate on the youth of your charge, for whom you have an account to give, you ought yourself to attend to its operation. You ought to be solicitously attentive to, and be found in the midst of, all Sabbath Schools within your own charge—watching, from week to week, with that deep interest and anxiety which you cannot but feel, the course of instruction—the conduct and character of teachers and scholars—and the progress and prospects of the school; admonishing in love and pastoral faithfulness the labourers who may seem to be remiss—giving encouragement to the faithful and a word of exhortation to all. Thus you will make one of their number,—you will be intimately acquainted and connected with all their plans and proceedings, and may exercise over them all the kind care and salutary influence which belong to your place and duty, and for which they will return kindness, confidence, and gratitude. It is this faithful, constant, official inspection, which the officers and managers of the American Sunday School Union greatly desire to see exercised over their schools by every minister of the *Lord Jesus Christ;*—they feel as if this was the right and province and duty of ministers, and they have often mourned over the distance which has seemed to separate the chief labourers in the vineyard from those whose design, responsibility, and success are so nearly allied to their own. Others may perform the laborious parts of the service, but it belongs to you, and it behooves you, to inspect these schools, and see that nothing is inculcated which is contrary to sound doctrine, and that no spirit of wild fanaticism is introduced by ignorant zealots. As a watchman on the walls of Zion, you cannot, you must not remain an indifferent spectator of this powerful system. It will go forward whether you lend your assistance or not; but it is your incumbent duty to give it direction, so far as its operation affects those under your care.

Why is it that some of you, my Brethren, have so little discerned the signs of the times, as not to perceive, that a mightier moral engine has not been set in operation for ages? That it affords to the faithful pastor greater facilities for the instruction of his people than anything before discovered? And is it possible that any of you have paid no serious attention to the progress of Sunday Schools, and have given no effectual aid to their establishment in your parishes? or that, having them there, you are contented that they may take their course (and whoever will, may have the superintendence of their instruction?). I respectfully ask you, who have hitherto neglected this subject, what you could desire in the way of aid to your arduous pastoral duties, more convenient and effectual than Sabbath Schools in every district of your congregation? By their means you enjoy the assistance of ten, twenty, thirty, or forty persons, every Sabbath, earnestly and diligently engaged in giving religious instruction to the children of your charge; and giving it to multitudes whom your instructions would never have reached. And your young men and women, instead of spending the Sabbath idly or unprofitably, are now, many of them—if Sunday Schools abound with you—in a train of useful learning and improvement, which will every year be rendering them more capable of being useful and respectable members of the church, and will qualify them for becoming heads of families with a good prospect of being able to teach them the way of life, and to bring up their children in the nurture and admonition of the Lord.

I am acquainted with one large congregation, where the pastor, until lately, neglected Sabbath Schools, and they languished until they were near extinction; but now he feels their importance, and devotes himself to promote their prosperity, visiting one of them and lecturing to children and parents every Sabbath, and the whole aspect of this congregation is changed. The desire of learning has extended itself to all ages; and there is, throughout the congregation, a lively attention and alacrity in relation to sacred things, which is very different from the apathy and lukewarmness of their former condition.

I confess, I do not see how any man having the care of souls, can reconcile it to his conscience, or how he will answer it to his Master, if he continues to be indifferent to this important concern. But it is not sufficient that you approve the institution, and speak well of it, and give free consent to its introduction into your parish: much more than this is incumbent on you and expected from you. It is a duty, the obligation of which you cannot evade, to give your personal aid and counsel to carry on this important work. Many ministers begin to have their eyes opened to see this business in a far different light from what they formerly did, and begin to look upon Sunday Schools as the most important auxiliaries to their great work of rescuing immortal souls from everlasting destruction: and I hope the time is at hand, when every clergyman and every church-officer will be found taking an active and a leading part in the affairs of this institution, so far as it is connected with their respective churches.

And, here, I beg leave to state, that the American Sunday School Union prescribe no standard of doctrine to the schools in their connection. Their object is to bring their scholars to a knowledge of the *Bible,* the great repository of all religious truth. The Sunday School teacher who seeks wisdom from on high, and draws his instructions from this pure fountain, will not be likely to be misled, or to mislead others, in any matter of importance. But it behooves the pastors of the churches to see to it, that nothing is inculcated on the youth under their charge, which is inconsistent with that form of doctrine which he himself esteems and teaches to be truth. And it is a fact too well known to be here repeated, that the catechisms of different evangelical churches have been frequently and willingly used as books of instruction, whenever this has been requested by parents or others having the right to direct the religious instruction of children. And if this long approved method of instruction has been less attended to than its importance demands, the reason may be found in the diversity of religious denominations, which are frequently mingled in the same school; or, where this does not exist, in the inattention of the clergy to the schools established within the precincts of their pastoral charges. For, I may venture to affirm, that no evangelical pastor will ever meet with any difficulty in having the catechism or form of doctrine adopted by his own church, inculcated on the youth of his own parish. I am, at this time, acquainted with a large and flourishing Sunday School, containing above a hundred scholars, in which the catechism of the church to which they belong is made an object of attention and instruction on one Sabbath in each month. But in schools unconnected with the pastoral charge of any minister—of which there are many—the superintendents and teachers must of course pursue that mode of religious instruction which to them appears best: and as long as all the books of instruction used in Sunday Schools are published, and may be examined by all who feel an interest in this subject, there can be no danger that error will be circulated by means of this institution.

3. Another important subject connected with this institution, is the publication and circulation of books. As much has been said of late respecting the character of the books issued from the Depository of the American Sunday School Union, I will take the liberty of expressing my opinion of the manner in which this department of the business should be conducted.

Although the preparation of books was not originally contemplated as a part of the Sunday School system; yet, in the progress of the enterprise it has grown up to an importance which is fully equal to that of any other department. Indeed, when we reflect upon the recent origin of this institution, and upon the smallness and obscurity of its commencement, we cannot but be astonished at the extent of its operations in the circulation of books. If we except the book establishment of the Methodist Episcopal Church, I believe, there is no other society in this country which supplies so large a portion of the population with its reading. And, certainly, they who select and distribute the books which are perused and studied by the people, and especially by the young, will have a greater influence in forming the character of the nation than any other persons, let them use what other means they may.

The plan of connecting libraries with each school and establishing depositories in convenient situations is characterized by wisdom. It has long been a desideratum to have congregational libraries for the use of the people; and, frequently, attempts have been made to establish them, but with very little success. The people have not taken a lively interest in these institutions, and where they exist, do not generally make much use of the books. The reason of this seems to be that the authors selected for such libraries, though valuable, are not suited to the taste, nor level to the capacity of common people. Few have leisure or inclination to go through ponderous volumes, or to peruse books of deep reasoning and replete with learning. The experiment made by the American Sunday School Union, evinces, that small books, written in a lively style, and rendered interesting by pleasant narratives, are the kind of reading which is adapted to the taste of a large part of our adult as well as youthful population. For, although the libraries are intended particularly for the use of the children, yet it is found, that when the books are brought into the families to which the scholars belong, they are read with avidity by persons of all ages. By this means, the books published and distributed into every nook and corner of the United States, by the American Sunday School Union, are producing a great effect on a vast multitude of people. The management of this business has been committed, by the Board of Managers, into the hands of a publishing committee, who have, without the least prospect of personal emolument, devoted to it their time and attention, with an untiring assiduity which demands the gratitude of all who are friendly to the universal diffusion of knowledge. The caution exercised by this committee will be manifest when it is understood that no work is sent to the press to which any of the committee objects. The demand for books, however, has increased so rapidly, and the call for variety, as well as numbers, has been so urgent and incessant, that it may not have been practicable for the publishing committee, in every instance, to furnish the most suitable works. They have done, perhaps, the best that could be done in their circumstances; and while they have merited our warmest commendation for their disinterested labours, there seems to be no just ground for censure, because they have not done what it was impossible to do. I think it necessary to enter thus far into a vindication of the publishing committee, since much has been said respecting the character of the books published under their inspection; and complaints are still abroad on this subject. But while I would cheerfully award unqualified commendation to this respectable committee, I do not mean to say, that they have fallen into no mistakes in managing this momentous concern. But it should be kept in mind, by those inclined to find fault, that this responsible business has devolved upon them unsought and unexpected. Indeed, there is something wonderful in the rapid increase of everything connected with this institution. The persons who now have the management of this great concern began their labours in obscurity, neither desiring nor seeking the notice of the world; but God has abundantly prospered their humble and disinterested efforts, so that now they find themselves, without having aspired to it, placed at the head of one of the most useful institutions in the world. They feel their responsibility to be great beyond expression, and are deeply sensible, I trust, of their need of wisdom from on high; and, at the same time, will be thankful for any suggestions which the friends of the cause are disposed to make to aid them in their arduous work. I am not apprehensive, therefore, of giving any offence to the Board, or their committee by the freedom of my remarks.

The principal objection in regard to the books issued from the Depository is, that, too generally, they were of a light and fictitious character. Now, I am not sufficiently conversant with all the publications of the Union to judge correctly on this subject, but I am inclined to believe, that there has existed a mistake on this point. Too many fictitious stories, and some of them containing few lessons of moral or religious instruction, have been put into circulation. The tendency of this is to vitiate the taste of the rising generation, so that while they are greedy after fiction, they will have no appetite for solid, instructive reading. And, I believe, the committee themselves have for some time been turning their attention to works of more substantial value.

But, it is evident that no course which can be pursued in this business, will unite the suffrages of all good people; for some object to all fictitious writings as having in the main a bad tendency, and as incompatible with the simplicity and sincerity of the Christian religion. It seems necessary, therefore, to say a few words on this subject;—but it would require a volume to discuss it fully.

I would, then, observe, that we cannot proscribe all writings in which fictitious personages are introduced, without passing a sentence of condemnation on various parts of sacred Scripture, and particularly on the parables of our Lord Jesus Christ. These must fall under the denomination of fictitious discourses; or discourses in which unreal personages are introduced, and represented as speaking and acting, that by this means important truth might be conveyed to the minds of men, in such a manner as to be understood, to obviate prejudice and to create interest. The Song of Solomon, also, a canonical book of Scripture, is from the beginning to the end a spiritual allegory. This method of instruction seems also to be dictated by nature; for fables or apologues and allegories are in use among all nations; and the severest moralists have never supposed that there was anything inconsistent with the strictest regard to truth in the introduction of fictitious personages: for where there is no purpose to deceive, and where no one is deceived, there can be no violation of truth and sincerity. Words are but the signs of our ideas, and it matters not what language we use, if it fairly conveys our true meaning to others. When a man employs words ironically, the literal sense is absolutely false if the irony be just; and yet the meaning of the person is as clear, and more forcible, than if the truth were simply uttered.

Again,—a fictitious narrative, used as a vehicle for important moral instruction, bears a strong analogy to the use of general terms in common speech. We know that all things in existence are particular or individual things; but finding a great many individuals which bear a striking resemblance to each other, we give a common name to the whole. In like manner, there are many individual persons of similar character; there are many courses of conduct, which, with their causes and attendant circumstances, are of usual occurrence; and it is important to collect these features of human life, and so embody them, that they may be useful to those who are yet without experience. Now, this may be done in several ways, as by general maxims or aphorisms; by narratives of real facts; or connecting those common matters of observation and experience with fictitious personages, which, as it leaves the moral instructor at liberty in the selection of circumstances, possesses some advantages over the simple narrative of facts in the order, and with the circumstances, in which they occur. When, however, the picture of human manners or character is fairly taken from nature, it is, what may with propriety be called, *general history;* it is a representation of what often actually happens, without the peculiar circumstances of any single case; and the difference between a judiciously constructed fictitious narrative, intended to convey moral instruction, and real history, is no greater than between the use of a proper name and a common appellative, when we speak of any individual. In this way much might be taught, which, in common, is learned by painful experience. And this mode of instruction being capable of being rendered highly interesting to the young especially, ought not to be relinquished, or given up to those who will employ it for the mere indulgence of fancy and feeling, and frequently to the real injury of the reader. It is impossible to suppress all fictitious writings, or to restrain young people from reading them; is it not then the dictate of wisdom to provide them with such as are not only innocent but instructive? Is not this the most probable method of weaning our young people from the fondness for novel-reading, the effects of which are sometimes so fatal, and most commonly injurious? But, I am aware, that the land of fiction is a dangerous ground to travel over. There is no species of writing so liable to abuse; and none so difficult to execute with judgment. The imagination, when indulged, is prone to extravagance; and is as liable to become wild on religious subjects, as any others. A vivid fancy is often without the guidance of sound judgment and correct taste; and when a writer begins to feel a deep interest in the personages of his own imagination, the great end of writing is apt to be forgotten, and the narrative be so woven as to create interest and afford pleasure, rather than to convey moral instruction. It should also be remembered that fictitious writings should never be permitted to form the principal reading of the young; and they should be prepared with much judgment and care, and used with great caution. A judicious parent will not refuse to indulge his child, occasionally and moderately, with wholesome sweetmeats, creams, and comfits; but who would think it wise to feed him with nothing else? Just so, writings of this description may be useful to interest young people, and to form a taste for books in those in whom it does not naturally exist, and to convey moral instruction in a grateful vehicle; but the books commonly used should be of a more solid and didactic kind.

Upon the whole, then, I would give it as my opinion, that while fictitious works should not be altogether proscribed, they should not form a large proportion of the books issued from the Depository; and that in the selection of those to be put into the hands of children, the utmost caution should be used. It would be a real loss to the rising generation, to call in all the delightful and instructive little stories of Mrs Sherwood and Miss Edgeworth. Who would object to the *Shepherd of Salisbury Plain,* or other stories of Miss Hannah More, in the 'Cheap Repository', because they are not real histories? For a long time it was commonly supposed, that that tract of unrivalled excellence, *The Dairyman's Daughter,* was a fictitious story; and now, when it is known, from the best authority, that it contains a history of real facts, its effect is probably no greater than before; although it affords us much pleasure to be assured, that the persons in whom we have taken so lively an interest did actually exist. One thing, in my opinion, ought faithfully to be done by authors: they should inform their readers whether the personages and occurrences of their narratives are real or fictitious; for whatever be said of the lawfulness of fictitious writing, it never can be consistent with truth to palm on the public a tale of the imagination for historic truth.

It may occur to some, that there does not exist sufficient security, that the books selected for publication will uniformly be of the proper character. It may be alleged, that the committee of publication, consisting of gentlemen engaged in secular business, who can only devote their leisure hours to the examination of books, there is reason to apprehend that an injudicious selection will often be made. And, moreover, it may be thought, that as clergymen as a class are better acquainted with religious books and better judges of their adaptation to be useful to the rising generation than any other description of men, that it would be wise to submit all contemplated works to them for their opinion and advice before publication. To which I would reply, that several of this committee are men of liberal education, and are so situated as to have it in their power to devote much of their time to this interesting work. Moreover, they have constantly the aid and advice of the Corresponding Secretary of the Society and of the Editor of the Magazine, who are not only pious but literary men whose whole time is devoted to the interests of the Union. But still, I am pleased to find that the public mind is awake to the importance of this subject, because it is evident, that the same power of multiplying and distributing books which is calculated, under a wise direction, to be the means of so much good, is equally capable, under a different guidance, to become an engine of incalculable evil. It gives me pleasure, therefore, to have it in my power to state, that the committee are so deeply sensible of the high responsibility of their office, and of their own liableness to error, that they have been in the habit of subjecting those works, concerning which there could be any doubt, to the judgment of men in whose opinion the religious public repose the greatest confidence. And it is still their wish and purpose, as far as possible, to avail themselves of the suggestions and counsels of such men, both of the clergy and laity, so as to secure, as far as human frailty will permit, the selection of those books for publication which will be best adapted to promote the edification of all who read them.

4. I will now proceed freely to inquire, whether the system of instruction in Sunday Schools admits of any improvement or enlargement. And here, before I go farther, I would remark, that my observations on this subject must be considered theoretical, rather than practical: but the benefit of theory is, that it often suggests what, in practice, is found to be easiest and best.

Again, I would observe, that it is not contemplated as practicable that the whole system which I am about to delineate should be everywhere introduced, or that it should be carried into complete effect anywhere, immediately. Improvements in such institutions require time and experience; and I doubt not, that, in some respects, better plans and arrangements than those here specified will be discovered. My object will be accomplished if improvements be commenced; and in some measure answered, if I can succeed in turning the public attention to the subject.

It appears to me, then, that the system of Sunday School instruction might be greatly enlarged, both as it relates to the pupils received under their tuition, and as it relates to the subjects of instruction. In regard to the former, my plan would be so large as to include all persons who need instruction, from the infant of two years up to the man of a hundred years of age. Infant schools are now in a rapid progress of being established, and they are filling the minds of the Christian and philanthropist with pleasure and surprise. And there is no reason why there should not be Sabbath Schools for infants as well as for children of greater age. In giving instruction, age should make no distinction. Infant schools should therefore be a regular part of the Sunday School system. It is true, they are kept through the week; and so are other schools; but their teachers, during the week, may give them no religious instruction. If the American Union does not gather these tender little ones under her fostering wing, they may fall into the clutches of those who will seek to devour them; their infant minds may be made to imbibe the poison of error instead of the sincere milk of the Word.

Again,—the Sunday School system ought to embrace all those youth who are included in Bible classes. There never can be any definite line of distinction drawn between the appropriate studies of Sunday Schools and Bible classes. In practice, all distinction is already confounded; and why should the instructions of Sunday Schools stop at a particular point? Why not instruct the pupils as long as they are willing to remain? The objections that might be conceived to this amalgamation will, I trust, be obviated by the plan which will be submitted immediately for consideration.

But I would not confine the instruction of Sunday Schools to youth; I would have it extended to all who are willing to be taught. The fact is that multitudes of adults need instruction as much as the youth, and many would be delighted to have the opportunity of learning. Pride and false modesty would prevent some from coming forward, lest their ignorance should become manifest; but I would spread a mantle over their weakness, and devise a method of instruction which would require from adults nothing else but to hear, with the privilege of asking questions as often as they might be disposed to do so.

Having developed my plan for the enlargement of the system, as respects the pupils, I will add, that the execution would require a correspondent enlargement in regard to teachers. It would require that the pastor and his coadjutors, by whatever name called, should all become active teachers in these institutions. My idea is that the whole church should form one great Sabbath School, and that all the people should be disciples or teachers; or sometimes the one and sometimes the other, according to circumstances. Knowledge, like wealth, is not acquired merely for ourselves; it should be like the light of a candle, for the benefit of all in the house. Every man and woman is under sacred obligations to teach those more ignorant than themselves. There is no good reason why the instruction of Sunday Schools should be confined to a few young people, as is commonly the case. Let the aged fathers and mothers, who have been learning for more than half a century, impart of the rich stores of their experience to the young. Let the learned, if there be such in the parish, not disdain to instruct in the higher branches of liberal knowledge; and, especially, let the pastor consider the Sabbath School as one principal field of his labours. Here the whole work of catechising and of instructing Bible classes may be advantageously performed. Here he may preach to the young far more effectually than from the pulpit.

5. But it is time that I should develop the proposed plan as it respects the enlargement of the studies pursued in these schools.

This has already been hinted at in speaking of Bible classes, but I will now enter more into detail. After mature deliberation, I am of opinion that all the pupils who can ever be taught in Sunday Schools might be conveniently arranged into six different classes; and supposing a child to enter the first or lowest class, and to go through the whole system, he would rise, by regular gradations, through the whole of the six classes in succession.

The first class would include infants and others, who were learning to spell and read.

The second class, such children as were able to read, but not sufficiently advanced in age and intellect, to study the lessons contained in the prepared books of questions. These children should be furnished with a simple, historical catechism, containing questions and answers; and also plain moral precepts, with a reference to the retributions of eternity.

The third class should embrace all children and others who are capable of learning the select lessons: in short, most of those who now attend Sabbath Schools.

The fourth class should comprehend all those who have gone over the selected lessons which relate principally to historical passages; and they should be furnished with a similar book of selected lessons relating to the doctrines and moral precepts of the Bible. Their answers to these doctrinal questions ought to be in the words of Scripture. After which, they should learn the catechism of the church to which they belong, with such explanatory lectures, or exposition, as might be provided.

The fifth class would consist of such young persons as are commonly included in Bible classes, who would be instructed in the emblems, figures, parables, types, and most remarkable prophecies of Scripture. This would include biblical antiquities, and many other interesting matters which do not fall under that denomination; especially a short system of sacred geography, and a concise and perspicuous view of the collateral history of the Bible: by which I mean, such historical facts as are referred to in the Scriptures, or may serve to elucidate the sacred history.

The sixth class should be instructed carefully in the evidences of divine revelation, external and internal; in the nature and proof of divine inspiration; and in the history and canonical authority of all the books contained in the Old and New Testaments; together with the reasons for rejecting apocryphal books of every description.

The obvious objection to this system is that it is too much extended: but is there any one thing included in it which every intelligent Christian ought not to know? Is there any part of this system, which, in a regular course of Christian instruction, can be dispensed with? And if we cannot communicate as much religious instruction as is desirable, that need not hinder us from forming a complete system, and from carrying it into effect as far as we can. It cannot, indeed, be expected that all, or even a majority of scholars, will go through the whole course; but some will be found willing to do so; and as the value of biblical knowledge comes to be more highly appreciated, the number of thorough, persevering scholars will increase every year.

Another objection to a plan of instruction so extended is that competent teachers cannot be obtained to communicate instruction on all the points mentioned. The answer to this objection has already been given in part, when we spoke of the part which it was expected the pastor and other well-informed persons in the parish would take in the instruction of Sunday Schools. To which I will now add, that with a proper apparatus of suitable books on the subjects mentioned, some of which are now in readiness, and others are in a course of being prepared by the American Sunday School Union, there will be found no great difficulty in carrying the plan into full accomplishment.

Moreover, if we create a demand for teachers of higher attainments than are now needed, many of those already in office will take much pains to prepare themselves for this work; and thus the extension of the plan of instruction will have a most favourable effect on the improvement of many young persons of both sexes, who are now devoted to this employment.

Besides, it would be one advantage of this plan, that those teachers who should instruct the three lower classes, might be scholars in the three higher, if such an arrangement should be made as would allow of the lower classes reciting in the morning, and the higher in the afternoon or evening.

If, for example, in villages and the country, the Sabbath Schools should meet at nine o'clock in the morning, at which time the three younger classes would be instructed, and at which the attendance of the pastor ought not to be expected. Supposing, then, the public service to commence, as is usual, at eleven o'clock, the children might all attend in the church, under the inspection of their teachers; but let the afternoon be devoted entirely to the instruction of the higher classes and of adults, at which time let the pastor and his assistants attend, and aid in the instruction of the school. And it may here be remarked, that however numerous the schools may be for younger children in the morning, it would generally be expedient that all the teachers and advanced scholars should meet together in the church, or some other central place, in the afternoon; because this description of learners will be less numerous than the younger, and the minister cannot instruct in more places than one. This arrangement would, it is true, exclude the afternoon sermon where such a service is usual; but it would furnish a substitute far more effectual for the instruction of the people. In cities and large towns this plan may not be considered expedient, or where the people have always been accustomed to a regular afternoon service in the church; but if once the instruction of adults as well as children was made a part of the exercise of Sunday Schools, it would be found, on trial, to be far more beneficial to all concerned to attend these, than to hear an additional sermon; and especially as the usual service of prayer and praise might be as solemnly performed in the Sabbath School as in the church. And on all these occasions there ought to be some kind of lecture delivered by the pastor. But in regard to the particular arrangement, every congregation could determine it best for themselves. All that I mean by the above observations is to show that the plan proposed may, without any great inconvenience, be reduced to practice, as in cities and large towns the evening might be occupied with the exercises of the Sabbath Schools, if that was preferred to the afternoon.

In regard to the instruction of adults, several methods might be proposed which would render the service both pleasant and profitable. They might meet, on some convenient time in the week, in little knots, or on Sabbath morning, and converse freely on the subject of the lesson prescribed, whatever it might be; and in the time of the regular meeting of the Sabbath School, such as were willing might be questioned by some elderly person, or by the pastor, and the others might be permitted to hear and to learn. Having studied the lesson, they would be nearly as much instructed by the examination of others as by their own; a plan of this sort is now in operation in a very large and respectable congregation in New Jersey. But should none of adult age consent to be publicly catechised, it need create no discouragement; for the pastor, or other teacher, might propound the questions and answer them himself, allowing all persons freely to make any inquiry, or ask for any explanation. It is scarcely conceivable what a spring this practice would impart to the minds of the people, which are commonly left to stagnate; and as it would undoubtedly increase their knowledge, so it would add much to their happiness, by leading them to shake off that inertness which is so unfavourable to real enjoyment. It is not necessary, however, to establish any uniform method for the instruction of adults; what would be well suited to one people, would not be adapted to another: a judicious pastor would be able to regulate this matter in his own flock. Let the experiment be fairly made, and if it do not result in much good, I shall confess myself disappointed.

6. The only other subject on which I wish to make any remarks, is that of agents and auxiliaries. To carry into full effect the plans of the American Sunday School Union, many prudent, industrious, and persevering agents will be requisite. It has hitherto been common to look to the profession of the ministry alone for agents; but experience teaches that they cannot be supplied in sufficient numbers from that quarter; and considering the want and importunate demand for preachers in the destitute regions of our country, they ought not, except in extraordinary cases, to relinquish the appropriate duties of their office to become agents for this or any other society. Here the question meets us, whether pious, active, and judicious laymen would not answer for Sunday School agents as well, and in some respects better, than clergymen? Of this, I have myself no doubt. But can they be obtained? Why not? There are scores of young men in our principal cities who have been long experienced in conducting Sunday Schools, and who take a deep interest in their furtherance and prosperity. Undoubtedly some of these zealous men will cheerfully offer their services as soon as the door shall be opened for their employment. I know, indeed, that on their part it would require a sacrifice of worldly prospects for the sake of Christ and his cause: but, I ask, are they unwilling to make this sacrifice? I should be grieved to think that that was the fact. Why should it be required of ministers alone to exercise self-denial and make sacrifices for the promotion of the Redeemer's kingdom? Did Christ give one set of terms to ministers and another to private Christians? Or rather did he not require of every disciple the same disposition to deny himself and to renounce the world, by taking up his cross and following him? It cannot reasonably be supposed, that the employment of pious laymen on agencies will in any way infringe on the sacred office of the ministry. He will have nothing to do with the peculiar duties of a preacher. He must

often, indeed, give public statements to the people, and it may often be convenient to use the pulpit for this purpose; but an exhibition of the views and plans of the American Union will no more interfere with the duties of those ordained to the sacred office than speaking at the bar, or in the senate. And as there does exist a jealousy among the several denominations, or at least among some who belong to them, respectively, it might have some tendency to obviate the difficulty which has been felt on this point if well qualified laymen should be commissioned as agents.

In regard to auxiliaries, it seems to me, that at present the organization of the Union is very incomplete. Their connection with the parent, or central society is by far too loose and undefined to enable the whole body to exert that energy which she would be capable with a more perfect organization. One thing is clear, that all the agents of the auxiliaries ought to be appointed by the Board of the American Union, and should be amenable to this body. Unless it is intended to carry on the operations of Sunday Schools by societies perfectly independent of each other, something ought to be done speedily to draw the bands of connection closer, to enable the General Union to aid more effectively the exertions of the auxiliaries; and to render the auxiliaries in fact, what they are in name, aids to the parent society in her arduous and extended operations. But while local societies appoint agents to traverse large portions of country, and carry on their measures without consulting or even informing the American Union of their plans and operations, it is just the same as if there existed no connection whatever. As far as I can learn, there is not even any systematized plan of increasing the funds of the general society by the numerous auxiliaries. It would require more wisdom and more time than the writer can command, to devise an effective plan of union and co-operation between the general society and its auxiliaries. All I intended was to bring the subject before the public; and I do solemnly hope, that it will engage the earnest attention of the General Union, and of all the local Unions in the land.

And now I would appeal to the pious and benevolent of all denominations, to say whether this institution, so extensive in its operations, so multiplied in its ramifications, and so beneficial to all classes of society in its results, shall be cramped or retarded in its career of usefulness for want of adequate pecuniary aid? Seldom, since its earliest existence, has the American Sunday School Union made any appeal to the public for this species of aid: the operations of this society have been, not to draw anything from the people, but to confer benefits upon them; and still it contemplates no other system; for while tens of thousands are every week deriving rich blessings from the institution, those persons engaged in managing it give the strongest possible evidence of disinterestedness;—personal emolument, or advantage they neither expect nor are willing to receive. Now, it is evident that the principal burden of sustaining an institution in which the whole community have so deep an interest, ought not to devolve upon a few persons: but, hitherto, this has been very much the case. When it is considered how small a sum from every Sunday School, or even from every auxiliary, regularly forwarded, annually, to the parent society, would enable them not only to carry on, but greatly to enlarge their operations, especially in the publishing department, I cannot persuade myself that there will be found any reluctance in the public to contribute the funds requisite for the energetic and extensive operation of this powerful engine for doing good. There can be no doubt, that the American Sunday School Union is highly in favour with all the friends of religion and sound morality in our country. Perhaps no other institution has so universally conciliated the affections of the people. It is with confidence, therefore, that I make this appeal to the public, to render promptly and liberally all the pecuniary aid which is needed. No permanent funds are contemplated by the society. Whatever sums may be received will be immediately applied to the important purposes of sustaining and enlarging the system of Sunday Schools. That I am not mistaken in supposing that the society needs pecuniary aid is evident from the fact revealed at the last anniversary by the worthy president of the American Sunday School Union, that the treasurer of the institution was $17,000 in advance for the Union. It is true, indeed, that the sums due to the institution are considerably more than what they owe, but these are widely scattered, and the collection of them very slow. For their valuable building, the Union is indebted almost entirely to the liberality of a few devoted friends in the city of Philadelphia: but a large part of the purchase money of this property is still due. From this brief statement of facts, it will be evident to all the friends of Sunday Schools in our country, that the time has arrived when it has become an imperious duty for the Christian public to step forward and relieve the Board from their pressing embarrassments, and to take effectual measures to prevent the recurrence of the same in future.

In conclusion, I have only to say, that the more I reflect on the power and salutary influence of the Sunday School system, the more am I convinced, that it has been raised up by a benignant providence to be one of the most effective engines in overthrowing the kingdom of Satan, and promoting a general reformation in society, especially in that class of people who have evaded the influence of other means of improvement. If what I have written may contribute in some small degree to the furtherance of this good cause, I shall think that my time was well employed, and that I have received a rich remuneration for my labour.

THE USE AND ABUSE OF BOOKS[1]

A S books are the scholar's armour with which he fights, and as they furnish the implements with which he performs his work, I have selected for the subject of this introductory lecture, 'The Use and Abuse of Books'.

Books are the scholar's armour. They are the implements with which he performs his work. In the early ages of the world, when the life of man was protracted through many centuries and human knowledge was confined within narrow limits, books were not necessary. The memory of the aged served as a sufficient repository of facts and oral traditions as an adequate means of their communication.

But at an early period in the history of the world it appeared good to infinite wisdom to direct that the revelations which were made to man should be committed to writing. As there is no evidence of any more ancient writings than those of Moses, it is reasonable to conclude that the making of books originated in divine appointment and was performed by divine assistance. There can therefore exist no doubt as to the importance and utility of this means of instruction. The Bible, the first and best of books and heaven's richest gift to man, contains treasures of wisdom and knowledge.

But a doubt might possibly arise whether any other books were useful or necessary, especially as it is maintained that the written revelation of God's will is perspicuous and complete. But such a doubt would readily be dissipated by considering that the evidence of the Bible's authenticity depends on the knowledge of facts which must be learned from other books—that reference is often made

[1] *The Princeton Seminary Bulletin,* Vol. 26, No. 3 (2005), carried a previously unpublished lecture by Archibald Alexander on 'The Use and Abuse of Books'. The article was based on a transcription by Michael J. Paulus, Jr., Technical Services Librarian, Special Collections, Luce Library, Princeton Theological Seminary, and contained an Introduction by him. Reproduced here with permission.

in scriptural history to transactions as if they were known but with which we can be acquainted only by other books. The same may be said of ancient customs and opinions. The prophecies contained in the Bible foretell the destinies of many nations and cities, and of the church even to the end of the world; in most cases the fulfilment of these predictions must be watched for in other writings than the sacred Scriptures.

Besides, the Bible was not given to teach us everything, but only to point out our duty and show us the method of salvation; our other knowledge is useful and even necessary to the enjoyment of those comforts which a beneficent God allows his creatures in this world, and also to the propagation of the gospel through the world. The knowledge of agriculture, of architecture, of the arts by which clothing is prepared, of geometry, geography, navigation, *etc.,* is highly useful. But this knowledge is not contained in the Bible; for it, therefore, we must have recourse to other books.

The reasoning of Omar the successor of Mohammed respecting the celebrated library at Alexandria was not sound, who, being consulted respecting the disposal of the books, directed them to be burned, saying, If they contain anything different from the Qur'an they are false and pernicious—if the same, they are useless.

The state of literature, in regard to books, is greatly changed from what it formerly was. When it was necessary to make books by the slow process of writing every letter with the hand, and when the materials with which they were made were with difficulty acquired, books must have been rare and costly. None but the man of wealth could acquire any considerable number. But since the invention of printing, which must be considered the most important after the discovery of the alphabet, books have been multiplied to such a degree that a sufficient number are within the reach of every scholar. Indeed, as benefits seldom fail to be accompanied with some inconvenience, this multiplicity of books is calculated greatly to perplex and sometimes to discourage and mislead the studious scholar. He finds himself overwhelmed by a sight of this vast mass of literature which he beholds in public libraries and in bookstores. He is at a loss where to begin, or what to select, and sometimes thinks it is vain to begin at all, as he is sure he can never get through so many volumes.

It is a matter of importance, therefore, that the young student should be furnished with a guide in his literary pursuits. He should also obtain the knowledge of such general rules as may be useful to direct his course when he may not enjoy the privilege of living instructors. To afford some little assistance on this subject is the design of this introductory lecture.

I will begin, then, by distinctly stating some of the principal ends which can be answered by books; for unless we keep these in view, we shall often wander at random and spend our time and labour without profit.

1. Books serve in the first place as a repository of facts which occurred before we existed or beyond the sphere of our observation. It is worthy of observation that the Book of God consists chiefly of facts. These are made the foundation of that system of instruction with which we are presented in the Bible. From this we may take a hint that the knowledge of facts is the most important branch of human knowledge. History, therefore, holds a high place among the objects of human knowledge.

2. Books are necessary to furnish us with the knowledge of languages without which ancient books, divine or human, cannot be read. We should go to the sources.

3. They furnish us with new, perspicuous, and enlarged views of truth by admitting us to an acquaintance with the opinions and reasonings of men of the most profound and extensive research. By [these] we are often enabled speedily to arrive at conclusions which otherwise we could not have reached at all, or only after a tedious and perplexing pursuit. In knowledge one man has the advantage of standing, as it were, upon the shoulders of his predecessors: and though not possessing greater nor equal capacity, yet he may go much further. By this means sciences have been perfected by the labours of successive generations which otherwise must have remained in their infancy. And this applies in some degree also to subjects of revelation. For the sacred Scriptures give us general principles from which we are bound to derive legitimate inferences and which we must apply, according to our thrift, to the various relations and circumstances of human life.

4. Books also answer the purpose of resolving our doubts, which are often attended with painful perplexity.

5. Books also serve to confirm us in the truth of our own reasonings by exhibiting to us the progress of other minds in the same pursuits.

6. They assist, moreover, to detect our errors into which through ignorance or inadvertence we may have fallen.

7. They also save us much time and trouble by presenting truth in a methodical and apprehensible form.

8. Books are also useful in forming the taste by presenting to us models of good writing.

9. They also enrich the mind by furnishing it with a variety of figures and illustrations, which might not have occurred to it without such aid.

10. By reading we obtain, too, a preciseness of language.

11. Books furnish an innocent pleasure which can be enjoyed in solitude. They serve to amuse and relax the mind when fatigued with intense studies and arduous pursuits.

12. They improve the heart by presenting forcibly and impressively the motives which are adopted to excite pious affections and lead to good resolutions.

These are the principal ends which can be answered by authors, of which we should never lose sight.

In the next place I proceed to lay down *some maxims which should govern us in the use of books.*

1. Reading must not be substituted for thinking. Books are not properly used but abused when they are allowed to supersede the exercise of our own faculties. We must cultivate independence of mind.

2. We must not read too much. To read a great deal without exercising our own thoughts on subjects is like eating a great deal which the stomach cannot digest. The food in neither case turns to nutriment, and instead of strengthening weakens the system. Some men are constantly devouring books; without discrimination they swallow everything which comes in their way. An unnatural appetite is created, but no advantage is acquired. The man becomes little the wiser for all his reading. To burden the memory with a multitude of undigested and unanalysed things is of no use. It would be better to leave them in books.

3. We should select with judgment and care the books which we read. Many books are worse than useless—they are pernicious. Others would be good if there were none better on the same subject; but it is a waste of time to read an inferior author when you might have access to one much more excellent. We should endeavour, therefore, to find out the merits of books on subjects in which we are interested.

4. An important species of knowledge to the student is, therefore, the character of books and what they contain. This may be obtained by conversations with the learned by reading judicious reviews—not only such as are recent, but the old; and by examining the contents and indexes of books; and, frequently, by reading a few chapters in a book we may ascertain its character.

5. All well-written books we are not bound to read—if we are already acquainted with the subject, or if we are capable of thinking for ourselves on the same, we may dispense with reading a book. Often, however, it is necessary to read so much of it as to form a judgment of its merits so that we may recommend it or affix on it our censure.

6. Many books of the most valuable kind are needed only for occasional reference.

7. Many books can only be read with profit by those whose minds are prepared for the subject. It is, therefore, a disadvantage to read some books too soon, especially if they are never read again. In every science it is hurtful to dash into the more difficult before we have well learned the elementary parts.

8. Some books should be read not only with care but perused over and over again.

9. When a book is our own property, it is useful to mark in the margins with a pencil those passages which we wish to remember or review so that we can go over the book a second time with a glance.

10. The making of long extracts from books is of little use. If our extracts become very voluminous, it is as easy to turn to what we want in the book as in our commonplace book. It is often sufficient to know where certain things are to be found. Facts and dates should be marked with precision, and of them it is always of advantage to make a record. But elegant expressions and fine reasonings it would be better to read again in their proper place in the authors. It will,

however, often be useful to make an abstract of what we read, so far as to serve as a table of contents of the volume.

11. In regard to the form of a commonplace book, it is not of much importance. Every man can invent one to suit his own taste, or he may consult such authors as have prescribed a form.

12. By encyclopedias and dictionaries and periodical works, general knowledge is rendered more accessible than it formerly was; but on subjects in which we wish to be truly learned we must take a different course. These works have undoubtedly extended knowledge, but they have also made scholars superficial. Compends are useful to those who have learned a science, but the more a thing is learned in detail at first, the better.

13. In selecting books, we should not blindly attach ourselves to the ancients or moderns, to writers of this or that nation or sect, to the exclusion of all others.

14. In our reading, we should be careful not to scatter our labours over too wide a field. We must not attempt more than we can accomplish. To become profoundly and accurately learned in every department of science is, in the present extended state of literature, too much for any man. To excel in any branch requires that many others be comparatively neglected. By aiming at too much, we become superficial in everything. There must be a division of labour, even to understand what those have done who have gone before us. Nevertheless, general knowledge is very necessary to an accomplished minister of the gospel. He should not remain wholly ignorant of any important and useful branch of human knowledge. But whilst he cultivates the field of universal science superficially, he ought to be accurately acquainted with all the learning which belongs to his own profession. Much useful knowledge may be acquired in the hours of relaxation. Follow your own authors.

15. We should be constantly on our guard lest other books lead us away from the study of the Bible or interfere in any degree with our habitual perusal of that sacred record, which contains the substance of all our theology and foundation of all our hopes. All our studies should be subordinate to that of the sacred Scriptures. Better read nothing else than neglect this; other books are useful just in proportion as they aid us in understanding the Bible. No man can use too

much diligence in digging in this field. It contains a treasure which never can be exhausted. Even those parts which we have studied most frequently will continue to afford us new light, if we come to them with due reverence and docility.

16. As the world is so full of books and as the number is increasing every day, it seems needful to be given in advice to young men engaged in literary pursuits not unnecessarily to increase the number of books. It is not a sufficient reason for a man to become an author that he can write well; unless he can really cast new light on some subject, it will be better for him to retain his compositions for his own use and that of his people. With many, however, there is an itch of writing and a desire to be known to the public, which induces them to commence [as] authors when they are no how qualified for the task. In most cases it is imprudent for young men to commit themselves by publishing their sentiments, for in a series of years their minds undergo a considerable change and the old man would willingly recall what the young man has said. [*E.g.,*] *Augustine. Baxter.*

A man may be placed, however, in such circumstances as will justify his publishing his compositions although he may know that they possess no superior excellence. As, for example, when his people or his acquaintances are furnished with few books and would be more disposed to read his, from personal attachment to the author, than others as good or better. Or when truth is in danger of suffering by the introduction of erroneous opinions which are disseminated by means of popular books or pamphlets, it may become the duty of a man to repel these attempts by publishing a refutation. Or again, if a man has made himself master of some particular branch of knowledge on which there is not in print any convenient treatise, he may become very useful by imparting his acquisitions through the medium of the press. Or finally, if a man can write sermons or tracts adapted to the capacities of common people and is able to impress into them much of the savour of true piety, he ought to write, for such books are greatly needed. But what is more useless and what more absurd than to publish discourses which contain nothing new—nothing but what may be read in hundreds of books already in the hands of the public, and especially if all their excellence consists in their being coldly orthodox or in possessing the shadow of eloquence.

17. In purchasing books, select rather such as you have not read than those with which you may be well acquainted, although you may know them to be valuable. And endeavour to buy such as are scarce if valuable in preference to others equally valuable, which are common. Sometimes it is easier to borrow a book than to buy it, not for sake of economy (for this would be meanness) but because you will use more diligence in reading it than if it were your own. Be not anxious to procure an extensive library at once, unless you are going to a place where books cannot easily be obtained. You will probably read with more care when you have a few well-chosen books than when you have before you a great number which will tend to discourage you. Your desire to read a volume will be greatly diminished if it lies on the shelf before your eyes for years before you find opportunity of perusing it. Get the best editions of every valuable work.

18. In making up a library lose no opportunity of securing such books as may be often needed for reference, such as valuable dictionaries, lexicons, *etc.*

19. As I have mentioned the borrowing of books, I would take occasion to censure the too common practice of neglecting to return borrowed books. It should be one of our fixed rules when we borrow a book to read it speedily, use it carefully, and return it certainly.

20. Accustom yourselves to attend with care to the preservation of all useful books which you use, whether they are your own or the property of others. In order to do this, habituate yourselves to keep all the books which you have about you in good order. Let each one have its proper station, and when you have finished reading at any time, let the author be respectfully returned to his appropriate place. I have seldom known a person who profited much by books who treated them rudely. A real scholar contracts a friendship for the very volume which has contributed to his information and edification. It is indeed provoking to see how some persons deface and injure valuable books, especially when they belong to others. Benevolence should lead them to hand down unimpaired to posterity every means of useful instruction enjoyed by themselves.

21. Converse together on the subjects of your reading. Much benefit may be derived from this practice. It is like holding up several lights around an obscure object; the part which is not illuminated by

the rays of one may catch those of another. The collision of minds is often like that of flint and steel, productive of a spark of light which otherwise would have continued latent. By means of the ideas of others we are often led to views which they do not possess and are wiser. But to render such discussions useful or even safe, they must be conducted with candour and good humour. If ambition to conquer takes the place of the love of truth, instead of friendly discussion there will be disgraceful contention.

22. But finally, in all your reading and studies, bear it in mind that all true wisdom cometh down from above. Ask of God, therefore, to bestow upon you the knowledge of the truth. Habituate yourselves to ejaculatory prayer in the midst of your studies. When you take a book in your hand, lift up your heart to God for a blessing; and often as you read let your desires ascend to the source of light, that your minds may be irradiated with beams from the Sun of righteousness.

SAMUEL MILLER
1769-1850

PRESBYTERIAN minister, author, historian, and educator, Samuel Miller was the fourth son born to the Rev. John and Margaret Miller. His father served many years as the pastor of the Presbyterian Church near Dover, Delaware. Miller's early education in the parsonage prepared him for graduation with honours from the University of Pennsylvania in 1789. Returning to Dover, he studied theology under his father until 1791, whereupon, following his father's untimely death, he continued this theological studies under the Rev. Charles Nisbet, the first President of Dickinson College in Carlisle, Pennsylvania.

Ordained in 1793, Miller served a collegiate pastorate of three congregations (Wall Street, Brick, and Rutgers Street) in New York City with the Rev. John McKnight and the Rev. John Rodgers. He continued to pastor the Wall Street congregation (later renamed First Presbyterian Church) following the separation of the three churches in 1809.

Miller gained reputation as a competent cultural historian with the 1803 publication of his *Brief Retrospect of the Eighteenth Century*. In 1813 Miller was elected by the Presbyterian Church to serve alongside Archibald Alexander as Professor of Ecclesiastical History and Church Government at Princeton Theological Seminary. He remained in this position until his death in 1850.

Miller was a respected preacher and beloved pastor. Miller's written sermons were thoroughly biblical and yet stately and elegant in expression. His dignified view of the ministerial office was reflected in the literary composition of his sermons. As a pastor, Miller ministered in New York City during periods of illness and yellow-fever epidemics that decimated large numbers of the city's population, including his own congregation. His pastoral background, high view of the ministerial office, and experience of the brevity of life are evident in the passionate appeals and sense of urgency that mark his sermonic exhortations and more popular writings.

A prolific author, Miller's literary output included works on church history, Presbyterian church government, biography, and a variety of occasional sermons and lectures. Miller's *The Ruling Elder*, is a detailed biblical and historical defence of the doctrine of the eldership; his volume on *The Utility and Importance of Creeds and Confessions* is a well-argued explanation of their value and validity. Several books were written to explain, defend, and vindicate Presbyterian church government and polity—a subject of significant disagreement among Presbyterians in the early nineteenth century that would ultimately lead to the division of his denomination in 1837. His volume on ministerial etiquette, *Clerical Manners and Habits,* was a standard treatment in its field.

Miller also wrote major spiritual-biographical treatments of Charles Nisbet, John Rodgers, and Jonathan Edwards. Miller's personal commitment to the importance of private and public prayer is found in the final publication from his pen, *Thoughts on Prayer,* published not long before his death.

An active churchman who loved and sought to preserve the Reformed and Presbyterian confessional heritage, Miller was a humble and pious man whose sermons and publications did much to influence the direction of his denomination and influence ministerial training, not only at Princeton but also at countless other institutions. Students who sat under his instruction graduated as those who knew the importance of the ministerial office and the requirements of an able and faithful ministry.

THE FORCE OF TRUTH[1]

To the Chairman of the Executive Committee of the Board of Publication of the General Assembly of the Presbyterian Church, in the United States:

REVEREND and Dear Brother,
It is extensively known that the pious and eminently useful Dr Thomas Scott, the commentator, who for a number of years, occupied so high a place in the confidence and affections of the friends of evangelical truth and of vital piety, entered the sacred office, without any practical acquaintance with the religion of which he undertook to be a teacher. For several years after his ordination, and after he had made the solemn subscription to the Thirty-nine Articles, *etc.*, required of those who are received into the ministry of the Church of England, he was, in spirit and in creed, a *Unitarian and Pelagian,* and deliberately acting upon the most selfish and worldly principles in all his studies and pursuits. From this dream of proud self-confidence it pleased God to awaken him, by a series of events apparently accidental, to lead him to renounce his errors one after another, and eventually to enable him to repose and rejoice in that precious system of free and sovereign grace, which once he despised.

With the account which he has himself given of this change in his views under the title of *The Force of Truth,* you have been long acquainted; and, if I mistake not, more than one edition of this account has, within the last twenty years, been given to the American public. Still the work has not that general circulation which its deeply

[1] Samuel Miller, 'Recommendatory Letter', *The Force of Truth: An Authentic Narrative. With a Recommendatory Letter, by Rev. Samuel Miller, D.D. to which Are Added Eight Letters Addressed to Dr. Scott, by Rev. John Newton,* Thomas Scott (Philadelphia: Presbyterian Board of Publication, 1841), pp. 9-20.

interesting character renders desirable. I could earnestly wish to see it take a place among the volumes issued by our Board of Publication, and finding its way to every Presbyterian family in the land. I am persuaded it is in your power greatly to extend its circulation; and, in my opinion, it is hardly possible unduly to multiply the copies of a work so eminently adapted to illustrate and magnify the grace of God.

What though the venerable author of this narrative belonged to a different ecclesiastical pale from that in which it is our happiness to find ourselves, and to labour? This circumstance does not, with me, form the least deduction from its value. Perhaps it may be said to be one of the chief glories of that system which we adopt, as Presbyterians, that it turns away the minds of men from an undue regard to the external forms of the gospel, to that simple purity of evangelical truth, which is 'the power of God unto salvation to every one that believeth'; that it guards us against the miserable worship of heartless rites and genealogies, as a ground of hope towards God, and teaches us to place all our confidence on the atoning sacrifice and perfect righteousness of 'him who, through the eternal Spirit, offered himself without spot, the just for the unjust, that he might bring us to God'. May it ever be so! I regard every man as my brother in Christ, however he may differ from me in other respects, who teaches me to 'glory in nothing save in the cross of the Lord Jesus Christ'; and who represents salvation, in its beginning, its sum, and in completion, as wholly of free, rich and sovereign grace 'abounding, through righteousness unto eternal life by Jesus Christ our Lord'; and who, while he unceasingly proclaims, that my *title* to heaven rests solely on the ground of the atonement and righteousness of the Redeemer as my surety, ceases not to insist that my *preparation* for heaven can be effected only by the renewal and sanctification of my heart by the power of the Holy Spirit, and inclining me to 'deny ungodliness and worldly lusts, and to live soberly, righteously and godly, in this present evil world', and to walk before God in all the ways of holy obedience.

When, therefore, I open the volumes of such men as Scott, and Newton, and Cecil, I entirely forget, the system of prelacy with which they happened to be connected, and drink in the precious streams of evangelical and experimental truth which they pour forth, without thinking that they belonged to a different fold from myself; or rather feeling that they and I belong, in reality, to *the same church,* the same precious body which the Redeemer has purchased with his blood, and sanctified by his blessed Spirit. Let my soul be with the souls of such men, in whatever ecclesiastical connection they may be found, and by whatever name they may be called! If the inspired Apostle Paul preached the true gospel, *these men preach it,* for their language and spirit are all as exactly his, as if he spoke by them. The remark made, many years since, in regard to their great predecessor, the celebrated George Whitefield, of the same ecclesiastical connection with them, applies here with equal force. More than seventy years ago, while that 'prince of preachers' was daily addressing admiring crowds in the city of Philadelphia, a group of his opposers was seated in the coffee house in that city, listening to an animated harangue of Mr P. who sustained an important office, and a high secular character. He was loading the person and the ministry of Mr Whitefield with abuse, and warning his hearers against his alleged errors and fanaticism. In the midst of this harangue, Dr Chovet, an eminent physician, but a bold and profane infidel, entered the coffee-house, and, after listening for a few minutes to the violent language of the speaker, broke out upon him in the following homely but pointed style:

P. I am surprised at you! *You* profess to believe the New Testament. Now I do not; but *you* do. I am amazed that you can speak as you are doing against a man who preaches as *Whitefield* does. I do not undertake to decide who is right and who is wrong, for I consider it all as a fable; but if the Apostle *Paul* was right, *Whitefield* is right, for he preaches as much like him as if Paul had spit him out of his mouth.

The verdict of the coarse and blunt infidel was undoubtedly correct. I can never open the pages of Scott, or those of the affectionate friends, contemporary with him, already named, without feeling confident that, if the holy Apostle of the Gentiles were now to rise from the dead, and revisit our earth, he would, without hesitation, recognize them as sincere and enlightened fellow disciples, and fellow workers in the cause of their common Master.

It is no doubt true, that the doctrines usually denominated *Calvinistic,* which Dr Scott slowly, but firmly embraced, are everywhere unpopular, and ever will be so as long as human nature remains what it is. All men are by nature proud and self-righteous, and whenever their minds are turned towards the great question concerning the way of salvation, they are prone to imagine, that they can, in part, at least, if not in whole, save themselves. When, therefore, they hear doctrines proclaimed which lay the sinner in the dust before God, and ascribe all the glory of his salvation, from first to last, to the merit and power of Christ; when they hear it maintained, that 'by the works of the law shall no flesh living be justified', but that we are 'justified freely by the grace of God, through the redemption that is in Christ Jesus', they are offended. They cannot consent utterly to renounce their own merit and strength, and to accept of salvation as a mere gift of free and sovereign grace. 'The carnal mind is enmity against God; for it is not subject to the law of God, neither indeed can be.' Almost everywhere, then, the popular voice is against the genuine doctrines of the gospel; and if the question, whether they are true or not, were put to vote before the mass of society, the decision would probably be two to one, if not three or four to one against them. If the Bible be true, the human heart is on the side of error. We are all, by nature, *Pelagians,* or *Semi-Pelagians,* until the grace of God teaches us better. This fact, however, instead of being a solid objection to the doctrines in question, obviously furnishes one out of many proofs that they are of God. For the Word of God everywhere declares that 'the truth as it is in Jesus', is distasteful to the carnal heart; that to the children of this world it is everywhere a 'stumbling-block and foolishness'. Of course, if the doctrines for which we plead were generally acceptable and popular among the unrenewed and worldly, it would show conclusively that they were not such as the apostles preached.

Dr Scott found this attestation given to his new creed, as soon as his having embraced it was made known. The great majority of his early friends and acquaintances, especially the wealthy, the refined, the honourable, almost with one voice condemned it, and considered him as a sort of degraded man. Only a small number, and those by no means among the world's favourites, felt prepared to approve the change, and to bid him 'God speed'. So it was in the beginning; so it is now; and so it ever will be, as long as man is by nature an 'alien from the commonwealth of Israel, and a stranger to the covenant of promise'.

It is generally known that the brother in the ministry with whom Mr Scott corresponded, while his mind was undergoing that conflict which issued in his conversion, was the venerable John Newton, whose works have been so eminently popular and useful among the friends of vital piety. This correspondence undoubtedly had no small influence among the means which were blessed to the benefit of Mr Scott. In most of the editions of *The Force of Truth* which I have seen, the name of Mr Newton is not given. I hope, if your committee should concur with me in judging that this work ought to be made one of the standing publications of our Board, that they will introduce that venerated name at full length in its proper place. I can think of no good reason why it should any longer be withheld.

It is an interesting fact in the history of the following 'Narrative', that, in drawing it up, the author consulted William Cowper, the celebrated English poet, his friend, and, at that time, his neighbour. The eminent talents, the ardent piety, and the deplorable mental sufferings of that great and good man, from a morbid physical constitution, are well known to every admirer of genius where the English language is spoken. That he gave to this work his friendly supervision; that he advised in regard to its style and arrangement; and that he gave to the whole his cordial imprimatur, will be regarded with interest by every intelligent reader.

One suggestion more. Allow me to recommend that the eight letters of Mr Newton, addressed to Mr Scott, while he was anxious and inquiring, be added at the end of the volume. They are so excellent, both in matter and manner, that they are well worthy of accompanying the narrative with which they were, historically, so closely connected. They may be, in a few cases, in a small degree abridged, if there be a fear of swelling the volume too much. I am persuaded that all its readers will thank you for the addition. Scarcely any religious letter-writer ever exceeded Mr Newton. Those in question, in particular, have one excellence which renders them a model in this class of writings. Forty-nine fiftieths of all the controversial writings on the subject of religion, that I have ever met with, in the course of a long life, have been by far too polemical in their language and spirit. That is, they too often reminded the reader, however decent, and even polite the style, of 'the tug of war'. Newton had the rare talent of arguing with an errorist with so much paternal benignity, as well as force, and of conducting all his controversial arguments with such constant practical appeals to the heart, as entirely to disarm the polemical spirit. This is a happy art; or rather, I should say, a precious gift of grace, which nothing but a large measure of the Spirit of Christ can enable any man with entire success to exhibit. We are never so likely to convince and win an adversary, as when we can so address him as to make him forget that we are arguing against him, and open his whole heart to our affectionate appeals. Newton had this talent in as great a degree as almost any man ever had.

Dr Scott has given a very satisfactory note in regard to the popular use of the name *Methodist,* as a term of reproach in England. If our reading population were as familiar with the state of things there as here, nothing more would be necessary; but as they cannot be supposed to be, I will take the liberty of adding one word of caution. In this country the name *Methodist* is never applied to any other religious denomination than that which was originally founded by the Rev. John Wesley. Whereas, in England, this name is applied, not merely to the Wesleyan body, but also to all ministers and members ever so closely connected with the Established Church, who hold evangelical sentiments, and contend for the reality and necessity of heart religion. Dr Scott had no connection with the Wesleyan Methodists. He was as much opposed to their Arminianism as any Calvinist in the land. Still, in that country, where the name in its popular application, is *generic,* rather than *specific,* he was constantly reproached as being a Methodist.

Persuaded that you will concur with me in my general estimate of this work, and hoping that you will be disposed to adopt it as one in your catalogue of publications, I am, reverend and dear sir,

Your brother in Christ,

SAMUEL MILLER
Princeton,
January 12, 1841

THE LIFE OF M'CHEYNE[1]

EVEREND and Dear Brother,

I have received, within a few days, from a valued correspondent in Scotland, a biographical work which I have read with peculiar pleasure, and which I could earnestly wish might be circulated throughout the bounds of our beloved church. The work to which I refer is entitled, *Memoir and Remains of the Reverend Robert Murray M'Cheyne, Minister of St Peter's Church, Dundee,* by the Rev. Andrew A. Bonar, Minister of the Free Church of Scotland, Collace.

Although Mr M'Cheyne was a young man, not extensively known to fame, who died last year at the early age of twenty-nine, yet he was so highly esteemed and confided in by his brethren of the Church of Scotland, that in 1838, when in the twenty-fourth year of his age, he was chosen, in connection with three older ministers, on a delegation to the Jews of Europe and Asia; to inquire into their condition, and to report on the prospects and best means of calling their attention to the character and claims of the religion of Christ. This commission he fulfilled with an ability and faithfulness which, together with the preceding and subsequent character of his ministry, caused his death, which took place in 1843, to be regarded as a great calamity to the cause of truth and of vital piety in North Britain.

The impression left by Mr M'Cheyne on the minds of those who were most intimately acquainted with his person and ministry, is strongly portrayed in the following representation, found in a review of this memoir, contained in a periodical published in Edinburgh, and evidently written by one who had the best opportunity of knowing the whole character of the deceased, in all its aspects. The extract will speak for itself. Such language could not have been prompted by an ordinary man.

[1] Samuel Miller, 'Introductory Letter', *Memoir and Remains of the Rev. Robert Murray M'Cheyne,* Andrew A. Bonar (Philadelphia: Paul T. Jones, 1844), pp. vii-xviii.

ROBERT MURRAY M'CHEYNE! To dwell on his saintly character would be a pleasant theme. At this realizing moment to produce his effigy seems a possible task. That countenance so benevolently earnest, with its gleams of brightness flitting over its settled pensiveness;—that eye so mild and penetrating, as of one who had seen through the world's vanity before he had discerned the Saviour's beauty;—that forehead familiar with high and holy thoughts;—that disentangled pilgrim-look which showed plainly that he 'sought a city';—the serene self-possession of one who walked by faith;—and the sequestered musing gait such as we might suppose the meditative Isaac had;—that aspect of compassion, in such unison with the remonstrating and entreating tones of his melodious and tender voice;—that entire appearance as of one who had been with Jesus, and who would never be right at home till, where Jesus is, there he should also be:—these things we think we could delineate; for associated as they are with some of the most solemn and delightful hours of personal history, they come back on memory with a vividness which annihilates the interval since last we saw them, and with that air of immortality about them, which says, joyfully, 'He is not dead, but sleepeth.' To know him was the best interpretation of many texts. At least, we have a clearer conception of what is meant by a 'hidden life', and a 'living sacrifice', and can better understand the sort of life which Enoch led, since we made the acquaintance of Robert M'Cheyne.

Happy would it have been for Scotland had all its churches and manses witnessed the scenes with which St Peter's, Dundee, and the abode of its minister had become familiar. So heart-deep and humbling were the confessions of sin in Mr M'Cheyne's family prayers and in public worship; so far did he descend into the inward abysses of atheism, and carnality, and hypocrisy; and so faithfully and mournfully did he lay before the Lord these hidden plagues, the perversities of motive, and the intricacies of self-righteousness, that nothing was so fitted to convince of sin and destroy confidence in the flesh. Then in his prayers he held such reverential and endearing communion with a reconciled God;—he pressed so near the throne; there was something so filial in his 'Abba, Father'; it was so obvious even to lookers-on, that he was putting his petitions and praises into the golden censer;—so express, and urgent, and hopeful were his supplications, that it was awakening to hear him pray. It was enough to make some Christians feel, 'Hitherto we have asked nothing in Jesus' name'; and enough to prick the heart of prayerless worldlings. His preaching was a continuation of his prayers. In both he spoke from within the veil, his hand on the mercy-seat, and his eye fixed on the things invisible. His usual address was calm and evenly, but arresting and enchanting. His hold of the truth gave him a hold of his hearers. He was at home in the pulpit. He did not need to bestow that care on composition which is incumbent on less gifted men. His poetic fancy and instinctive taste, with a steady flow of thoughts and words, saved him much trouble in this respect. But that was all. He did not avail himself of his fine genius and happy power of language, to procure a name for eloquence. He was content that the subordinate end was answered, and that even in extempore addresses he could proceed without embarrassment or hesitation. His eye was single; his aim was souls—souls for Jesus' sake. He had some other use for his bow than to entertain his hearers with the twang of the sonorous string. The salvation of souls was his object; and in his study preparing for the pulpit, and in the pulpit looking down upon his people, all his anxiety was to find truth that would penetrate the conscience—the unawakened consciences of all kinds of people, and truth which would lead anxious souls to the desired landing-place of peace with God. This unity of purpose gave a continuous earnestness and solemnity to his ministry. His feeblest appeal was more personal and importunate than the most pointed exhortations of vaguer ministers in their most faithful moods. His solicitude for the salvation of his hearers made him affectionate even beyond his natural tenderness. Sometimes a smile of momentary bitterness would be provoked when depicting the absurdity of sin and the infatuation of sinners; but it instantly subsided into the habitual compassion with which he yearned over souls. So well understood was his errand;—so accustomed were they to the entreating voice and expostulating attitude of this ambassador of Christ;—so thoroughly aware that he was seeking their immediate conversion were the most careless in his congregation, that any disquisition which had not a present and practical bearing, a sermon without Christ or without earnestness, would have astonished the most indifferent among them, and made them fear that their minister was no longer himself.

Commending the truth to every man's conscience in the sight of God, a demonstration of the Spirit seldom failed to accompany his preaching. His ministry at Dundee was a constant awakening, and he seldom addressed an auditory elsewhere without its proving to some a time much to be remembered. Nay, a demonstration of the Spirit accompanied his presence. His visits to pious families were hallowing, and his casual contact with secular men was solemnizing; and even those who only 'wondered and perished' knew that a prophet had been among them indeed.

But his character has been so often delineated already, and the materials for knowing him better which these volumes supply, are so abundant, that we shall not pursue this personal portraiture any further. Nor shall we fill our pages with extracts from a book which we hope every reader of this *Review* has, by this time, either read or begun to read. His school-companion, his fellow-pilgrim to Palestine, his near neighbour in the ministry, and most frequent coadjutor in each labour of love, is his biographer. No one who knew how undivided in his life Mr M'Cheyne and Mr A. Bonar were, thought that any other should attempt the record of that life; no one who reads it could wish that any other had. By natural talent fitted to notice the finer features of character, and to fathom some of its abstruser depths, and by a better taste accustomed to observe the rise and progress of religion in the souls of men, and peculiarly happy in describing things as he sees them, Mr Bonar is a fit biographer in any case where eminent piety reigned in a delicate and accomplished mind. In the present case, so intimate and like-minded were they, that the narrative derives much of its beauty from the congeniality between the subject and its narrator. The only fault is one, into which a stranger could not have fallen. Some of the more obvious features of Mr M'Cheyne's character are hardly noticed. To Mr Bonar they were so habitual that they had ceased to be observable. They would have impressed a stranger. The ordinary aspect of the man, his in-door life and daily walk, his manner of conversation in the world and among his Christian friends, such scenes as have seldom transpired, except in the prayer meetings and at the communions of St Peter's;—more of his sayings and deep remarks on Scripture, and, if possible, more of the special instances of his success in winning souls, we should have gladly obtained, and some of these a distant on-looker would have been apt to give. The work does not absolutely lack these things, and it possesses the surpassing value of revealing the interior growth of that eminent piety which produced his eminent usefulness. And altogether, the memoir is a faithful and effecting record of as beauteous a character, and as effective a ministry as he who holds the seven stars has exhibited to the church in these last days.

To give this article a practical tendency, we may be allowed to mention what we believe to have been the secret of Mr M'Cheyne's uncommon usefulness. The subject is seasonable, at this time when so many ministers, and elders, and private Christians are inquiring by what means they may extend their personal efficiency, and become, in the hands of the Spirit, the agents in adding to the church of such as shall be saved. From what we know of Mr M'Cheyne, and have read in these memoirs, we are persuaded that next to his habitual dependence on the Spirit of God, the occasion of his uncommon success was *the consistency and conspicuousness of his Christian character*. He lived in the eye of his people. Though his house had been a glass-fronted cabinet, they could scarcely have been more minutely cognizant of his movements and whole manner of life. They knew that his week days were but a sequel to his Sabbaths, and what they saw him in the pulpit, they found him in his study and among his friends, by the way-side, and in their own houses. He was everywhere 'the man of God'. His preaching was impressive, for his life applied it. His everyday demeanour exemplified 'and adorned his doctrine'.[1]

Such is the attestation of the contemporaries and intimate friends of this extraordinary man, who had marked his spirit, and listened to his instructions, in public and in private for years together; in all the various circumstances which 'try men's souls'. Can any one who appreciates the value of Christian character, doubt that such an example ought to be portrayed for the benefit of the church and of the world; and that such a spirit ought to be studied as deeply, and recommended as widely as possible?

One of the most promising and gratifying features in the present aspect of the Free Church of Scotland, and one of the most precious

[1] *The Presbyterian Review and Religious Journal.* No. LXV, July 1844. Edinburgh.

pledges of the blessing of God on her noble enterprise, is the evident revival of a spirit of vital piety among her members, and especially among her ministers and elders. This revival has gone hand in hand with her faithful struggle for maintaining the truth and order of Christ's house. Nor is the connection between these two objects of attention either remote or unimportant. For as, on the one hand, the prevalence of vital piety cannot be expected to be found in any church in which the pure doctrines of the gospel are not held fast and faithfully preached; so, on the other, where a sound faith at present exists, it will assuredly, not long continue to be maintained, after vital piety declines. As men are 'sanctified by the truth', so none but sanctified men will be disposed for any length of time together, to 'contend for the truth' and to preach it with simplicity and clearness. In the early history of the Reformed churches of France, we find orthodoxy and vital piety maintaining a joint reign to an extent as benign and happy as in any other portion of Protestant Christendom. One of the first symptoms of a departure from their original purity, was a disposition manifested by some of their ministers of questionable piety, to explain some of the articles of the Confession of Faith which they had solemnly subscribed, in a latitudinarian manner. Deviation followed deviation; synodical bodies began to tolerate serious error; an evangelical spirit declined with evangelical truth; until, at length, they ceased to occupy the place and to maintain the character of 'witnesses' for 'the faith once delivered to the saints'. The history of the Church of Scotland is in melancholy accordance with the same great principle. With the growth of 'Moderatism', orthodoxy and piety sunk together; until 'the things which remained were ready to die'. At this juncture God was pleased to interpose for her help. Faithful men were raised up; men 'full of faith and of the Holy Ghost'; men who remembered the orthodoxy and piety of their fathers; men trained in the school of experience and of sound doctrine, and willing to give up all for Christ. The sublime spectacle which these devoted men have since exhibited,—in abandoning all the endowments and comforts of the established church, for the sake of fidelity to their Master in heaven—has been, since the era of its occurrence, the admiration and joy of a large part of the Protestant world. Of this blessed revival and triumph of Christian principle, M'Cheyne and his memoir may be considered at once as a fruit and a specimen.

I write these lines, and recommend this work, my dear Brother, under the deep impression that we cannot pray for greater blessing to our beloved church than that the mantle of this holy man may rest upon all our pastors and elders, exciting them to the zeal, the unceasing diligence, and the entire consecration to their Master in heaven which were so conspicuous in his short course. We need—greatly need—large additions to the number of our ministers; but we still more urgently need a higher standard of piety among those that we have. Often, in reading this delightful memoir, have I said to myself, 'O, if all the pastors of our church, or a large portion of them, were such as M'Cheyne, as dead to the world as he was; as full of sanctified unceasing ardour to do good to the souls of men; as watchful to instruct and edify the young and the old; as much like Christ in all their habits and efforts—what a different aspect would our portion of the religious community wear? How much more elevated would be the eloquence of our pulpits! An eloquence not growing out of the principles and rules of art, but governed and animated by that heart-felt sense of the infinite importance and preciousness of evangelical truth which never fails to reach the heart. How much more frequent would be revivals of religion! or rather, how much would most of our congregations resemble that of the subject of this memoir, in which those who knew it best have told us there was a gentle, noiseless, but almost constant awakening! If such men presided over all our churches, what a hallowed impulse would be given to the missionary cause, and to all the scriptural plans for diffusing the knowledge of salvation throughout the world! How easy would it be to do without public agents for stirring up the people to sustain the cause of Christian benevolence! The pastor and the eldership of every church would be a source of hallowed influence in regard to that great cause, adapted under God, to keep every church awake and alive to its claims. M'Cheyne, while he lived, needed nobody to come in and remind the people of his charge, that the church was bound to send the gospel to every creature; and that every individual member of the church was under obligation to take an active part in this work. The habitual preaching, the public and private prayers, and the daily example of this heavenly-minded pastor were at once a constant memento of their duty, and a powerful stimulus to its performance.

While I lament that there is not more of this spirit reigning among the ministers and elders, and members of our beloved church, I consider the appearance and the popularity of such works as this memoir, as a pledge that the gracious King of Zion will revive us. Some of us who are old and grey-headed, and have been permitted to preach the gospel for more than half a century, so far as the eye of man can discern, have been instrumental in winning much fewer souls, and have done far, far less for the honour of our blessed Master, than this youthful servant of Christ in a ministry of less than a fifth part of the same length. Surely the contemplation of such a portrait as that presented in this memoir, ought to fill us with humiliation and shame.

My hope is, that the great Head of the church will speedily raise up a race of ministers more holy, more zealous, more wise, more diligent, and more entirely devoted to their work than their fathers have ever been.

Blessed day! when the watchmen on the walls of Zion 'shall never hold their peace day nor night; when they that make mention of the Lord shall not keep silence, nor give him any rest, until he establish and make Jerusalem a praise in the earth; until the righteousness thereof go forth as brightness, and the salvation thereof as a lamp that burneth.' Come, Lord Jesus, come quickly thus to bless thy church and people; 'even so, come, Lord Jesus!'

With fervent prayers that we may all lay to heart our duty and our responsibility more deeply than we have ever yet done,

I am, Reverend and Dear Brother, your fellow servant in the gospel of Christ,

SAMUEL MILLER
Princeton,
September 19, 1844

THE DIFFICULTIES AND TEMPTATIONS WHICH ATTEND THE PREACHING OF THE GOSPEL IN GREAT CITIES[1]

So, as much as in me is, I am ready to preach the gospel to you that are
at Rome also: for I am not ashamed of the gospel of Christ.
Romans 1:15, 16

IT is not known when, or by whom, the gospel was first preached in the city of Rome. Indeed the whole of the early history of the Church of Rome is involved in great obscurity; as if it had been expressly designed by infinite Wisdom, to discredit the claims of those who pretend to trace a regular descent, and to derive supreme ecclesiastical power, through the first bishop of that church. It was probably, however, one of the first planted of the Gentile churches; perhaps by some of those who were scattered abroad by the persecution which followed the death of Stephen; or possibly earlier than even this: for among those who heard the Apostle Peter preach on the day of Pentecost, and who were converted on that memorable occasion, are mentioned strangers of Rome. These Roman Jews, on their return home, would not fail to proclaim to others the same precious gospel which they had heard in Jerusalem; and, we may suppose, were instrumental in making a number of converts to the Christian faith. It is highly probable that the Church of Rome was founded thus early; for the historian Tacitus tells us, that in the time of Nero,

---

[1] Samuel Miller, *The Difficulties and Temptations which Attend the Preaching of the Gospel in Great Cities: A Sermon, Preached in the First Presbyterian Church, in the City of Baltimore, October 9, 1820; at the Ordination and Installation of the Reverend William Nevins, as Pastor of Said Church* (Baltimore: J. Robinson, 1820).

the Christians in that city were a 'very great multitude':[1]—And when the apostle wrote his epistle to them (which is generally supposed to have been about the year 57, or 58), their faith, we are informed, was spoken of throughout the world.

The city of Rome was now at the height of its glory. It was the metropolis of the world:—the great centre of all that was refined, scientific, splendid, luxurious, and fashionable in the whole Empire. There the wisdom of the wise, the power of the mighty, the magnificence of the rich and noble, and the licentious refinements of the sensual, held a sovereign and most imposing reign.

The Apostle Paul, at the date of this epistle, had never been in Rome. He had, indeed, as he tells the Romans in this chapter, long earnestly desired, and often intended, to pay them a visit, but had been hitherto prevented. But he was still, as he intimates, ardently desirous of going, and intent upon it. As much as in me is, I am ready to preach the gospel to you that are at Rome also; for I am not ashamed of the gospel of Christ. As if he had said—'Notwithstanding all the splendour and luxury, and fashionable philosophy, and hostility to the religion of Jesus Christ, which I know reigns at Rome, I am ready to go thither, and bear my simple, humbling message. I am ready to go even to imperial Rome, though I am aware that the rich, the great, and the learned of that splendid metropolis will all be likely to be arrayed against me;—still I am ready and desirous to go thither and preach the gospel: for I am not ashamed of the gospel of Christ; for it is the power of God unto salvation to every one that believeth, to the Jew first, and also to the Greek.'

By the 'gospel' we are to understand the glad tidings of salvation by a crucified Redeemer. That wonderful message, which informs man that he is a guilty, depraved, and miserable sinner; but which, at the same time, announces to him, that there is 'redemption through the blood of Christ, even the forgiveness of sins, according to the riches of his grace':—which proclaims, that in consequence of the fall of the first man, his posterity are, by nature, condemned, polluted, and utterly unable to deliver themselves; but that 'God so loved the world that he gave his only begotten Son, that whosoever believeth

---

[1] *Annal.* xv. 44.

in him might not perish, but have everlasting life'. That this eternal Son of God, equal with the Father in all divine perfections, in the fulness of time, appeared in our world, in the nature and likeness of man; that in this mysterious union of very God and very man in the same glorious person, he obeyed and suffered as the substitute of his people; that, as their covenant-head, he made a complete atonement for all their sins, and brought in everlasting righteousness for their justification; and that all who, from the heart, believe in him, whosoever will accept of mercy, whether Greek or Jew, Barbarian, Scythian, bond or free, are washed and justified, and sanctified, in the name of the Lord Jesus, and by the Spirit of our God; and shall be made perfectly blessed in the full enjoyment of God to all eternity.

This is that gospel which shines in every page of Paul's epistles; which he solemnly resolved to preach, and to preach nothing else; and which he was earnestly desirous of proclaiming in Rome.

I propose to embrace and illustrate the leading thoughts implied in our text, in the following propositions.

I. There are *peculiar difficulties and temptations* which attend the preaching of the gospel in *great cities;*—and

II. It is of *peculiar importance* that the gospel *be plainly and faithfully preached* in such places.

I. There are peculiar difficulties and temptations which attend the preaching of the gospel in great cities.

It is not my purpose, at present, to speak of the difficulties and temptations which attend the gospel ministry in general, and everywhere; but of those alone which may be considered as, in some degree, peculiar to great cities.

And, in entering on this branch of the subject, I need not say, that human nature is the same, both in city and country; and that the same general virtues and vices are to be found in both. But it can scarcely, I think, be doubted, that particular circumstances in both, are productive of appropriate effects, and confer upon the state of society in each an appropriate aspect. There is, if I mistake not, a sort of *intensity of character* imparted to the inhabitants of great cities; an intensity generated and nourished, by the almost constant intercourse of persons of like taste and employment, and by the unceasing stimulants which such intercourse is calculated to apply. In no places on earth, assuredly, do we find such extremes of character; such exalted virtue, and diabolical vice; such fervent piety, and daring profaneness; such noble generosity, and sordid selfishness, as in great cities. We are told, that, in the land of our fathers, the phrase, 'London piety', is often employed to express the highest degree of heavenly-mindedness; and 'London vice', the most degrading and shocking depravity. We may apply the same remark, with some degree of propriety, to every great city. Cities are commonly the grand theatres on which both the good and the bad display their greatest energies. Now, as in all society, the bad form by far the larger part; and as their follies and vices are heightened by the circumstances in which they are placed in a great city; there, of course, we must expect to find, in its most concentrated virulence, whatever is hostile to the purity and simplicity of the gospel, and whatever is opposed to the success and the enjoyment of a gospel minister.—But to be more particular.

1. The accumulated *wealth,* and the consequent *luxury* and *dissipation* of a great city, form a serious obstacle to the plain and faithful preaching of the gospel.

If wealth were *generally* employed, as *some* pious individuals have employed it, to promote the spread of the gospel, and the happiness of mankind; it would indeed be a real blessing, and its increase highly to be desired. But, alas! in this depraved world, how seldom is wealth thus employed! It is too commonly made to minister to the vanity and the lusts of its possessors; and thus becomes a curse both to them, and to all around them. But in great cities, where many wealthy individuals are brought together, and where the principle of competition and display maintains such a peculiarly powerful influence; there the 'pomps and vanities of the world' hold an almost undisputed reign. There magnificent houses, grand equipages, splendid dress, and expensive entertainments, form, with multitudes, the ambition, and the business of life. There the unceasing effort of many, to rival those above them, to outstrip equals, and to dazzle inferiors, is the grand object, which keeps up the constant fever of anxious pursuit.

While splendid living is the idol of one class, various kinds of amusement, commonly called pleasure, employ and corrupt a much larger class. The theatre, the card table, the dance, the midnight revel, and every form of dissipation are summoned to their aid to kill time, or to season the insipidity of sober life. Amusements are multiplied, and combined, and varied, and reiterated, until they become the chief, and, with many, the sole employment. And even some of those who are not engaged in these pursuits themselves, are so connected by various ties with those who are that they cannot escape the contagious influence. Cast an eye, my Friends, over any populous city, and say whether the picture is not below rather than above the reality.

Now, need I say, that all this is directly contrary to the spirituality and self-denial of the gospel? Need I say, that a person who walks in such a course, even though he be a stranger to gross vices, cannot be a disciple of Jesus Christ? No, Brethren, as long as the Bible is our guide, it is impossible to decide otherwise. And I have sometimes thought that there is no class of persons more difficult to be approached and impressed by a minister of Christ, than your genteel, decent worshippers of luxury and fashion. We cannot denounce them as immoral, in the popular sense of the term; and they are apt to imagine that they are *saints* because they are not *profligates*. As long as this impression remains, there is no hope of their being profited by anything we can say. With what an anxious and trembling heart, then, must a minister of the gospel go to proclaim his message in a place where such society abounds! He needs not only all his fortitude as a man, but also all his confidence as a believer, and all the gracious aid promised by the Master whom he serves, to support and animate him in the undertaking. He, of course, takes no pleasure in delivering an unwelcome or offensive message, as such; but would much rather, if it were possible, please all his hearers. How painful the task, then, to go to the tribes of vanity and frivolity, however elevated in their own estimation, and address them plainly and faithfully, as Paul would have done, on the sinfulness and danger of their course! How hard to natural feeling, to go to those who, it may be, a few days or hours before, caressed him, and perhaps loaded him with civilities at the hospitable table, and tell them, that except a man be born again, he cannot see the kingdom of God; that he that believeth not on the Son of God, shall not see life, but that the wrath of God abideth on him; that we must not be conformed to this world; but must deny ungodliness and worldly lusts, and live soberly, righteously, and godly in this present evil world!—O, what a temptation is here to soften or keep back the truth! What a temptation to avoid dwelling on those great practical, gospel doctrines, which he knows are so grating and offensive to many of his hearers!

But, alas! even this temptation, fearful as it is, is not the whole of his danger. It will be well if, besides softening or keeping back the truth, he be not gradually and insensibly drawn to adopt in his own person and family, those very worldly habits, against which he was bound to have lifted up both his voice and his example. It will be well, if, instead of being a faithful reprover of prevailing vanities and follies, he be not, in effect, their daily patron. There is, I am persuaded, no harder trial of a minister's graces, than to mingle continually with the members of a wealthy, polished, and fashionable congregation, and at the same time to keep himself unspotted from the world. Truly it requires the firmness, as well as the prudence of an apostle, to be surrounded with the spirit of conformity to the world, and yet, without giving just offence, to have no fellowship with it: to be continually solicited by worldly blandishments; and yet to maintain that holy elevation of sentiment and conduct which becomes an 'overseer of the flock', a 'steward of the mysteries of God'.

2. The *refinements of philosophy*, falsely so called, which are apt to reign, in a peculiar degree, in great and polished cities, are unfriendly to the preaching, and the success of the gospel.

A variety of circumstances concur in drawing to large cities, a greater number, not only of the truly learned, but also of vain pretenders to knowledge, than are commonly found in other situations. In great cities, men of both these descriptions, are most apt to find appropriate society, and appropriate employment. There they find excitement, and gratification, and scenes in which to display their talents, or their vanity. Of course, places of this kind are generally found to be the favourite theatres of their association and enterprise.

But need I remark, that persons of this character are peculiarly apt to be found arrayed against the simplicity and purity of the gospel? Not that I suppose genuine philosophy to be unfriendly to the religion of Jesus Christ. The real and profound science of such men as Bacon, and Boyle, and Newton, and Locke, and many more, demonstrated that knowledge, in itself, is a handmaid to religion; a friend to faith. But the pride of knowledge, and the speculation of false science, are diametrically opposed to the humility and simplicity of the gospel. They are perpetually disposed to wage, a concealed, perhaps, but real, and malignant warfare, against the Spirit, and all the distinguishing and most precious doctrines of Christianity. For example, the doctrine of the divine existence in a Trinity of persons, that fundamental doctrine in the system of redemption:—The doctrine of the fall and ruin of our race in Adam, our federal head and representative; without which I will venture to say, both the language and the offer of the plan of mercy are unintelligible:—The doctrine of atonement by the vicarious sufferings, and of justification by the imputed righteousness of the Surety, which may be said to be the life and glory of the gospel:—And, finally, the doctrine of regeneration and of progressive sanctification by the power of the Holy Spirit, 'without which no man shall see the Lord'—are all doctrines which the spirit of false and vain philosophy regards with aversion, if not with contempt. When, therefore, a minister of the gospel goes to a place where large numbers of those who possess this spirit are collected and embodied must he not, of necessity, meet with peculiar obstacles, with peculiar temptations? If, indeed, he will consent to betray his Master with a kiss, and to preach another gospel, all will be quiet; this kind of opposition will totally cease. But he dare not do it. If he would save himself and them that hear him, he must not think, for one moment, of such complicated treachery.

This consideration appears to have deeply impressed the mind of Paul, in the prospect of going to Rome. He was perfectly aware that the proud philosophers of that great capital would regard with disdain a man, who came to them preaching salvation in the name of a despised Jew, who had been crucified at Jerusalem as a malefactor; and preaching a salvation, too, which in all its features was adapted to abase human pride. He was sensible that he must go, calculating and contented, to be reckoned a fool and a madman, for coming with such a message to men who accounted themselves more wise than the rest of mankind. So he had found it in the polished and learned Athens; so he had found it in the proud, luxurious Corinth; and so he expected to find it, wherever he went among the great ones of the world. And, let me add, Brethren, so must every ambassador of Christ expect to find it in every age and clime, if he resolve to preach the gospel of the grace of God, in all its plainness and primitive simplicity. He must calculate on being regarded by the vain, the conceited, the proud, the self-righteous, wherever he finds them, as a weak, prejudiced, sour, puritanical enthusiast: and it will be well if he be not loaded with still more opprobrious names. But he must be willing to encounter all this, and more, for the sake of his Master. He must be ready to say, with the same apostle, who penned the words of our text—'We are counted fools for Christ's sake: we are made as the filth of the world, and as the offscouring of all things. But none of these things move me, neither count I my life dear unto myself so that I might finish my course with joy, and the ministry which I have received of the Lord Jesus.'

3. Another difficulty and temptation in the way of a city pastor, closely allied to the last which was mentioned, is—That, in polished and fashionable society, there is always a peculiar demand for *smooth and superficial preaching*.

It is not only the spirit of proud philosophy that is hostile to the gospel. The spirit of luxury, and worldly refinement is equally so; and is often a more dangerous foe for being more plausible and insidious. The votaries of pleasure and ambition delight in that kind of preaching which will not disturb them in their unhallowed course. They say, 'Prophesy to us smooth things.' The more a sermon is decorated with the charms of a splendid rhetoric, the more it contains of the 'enticing words of man's wisdom', and the less of plain, and pungent gospel truth, the better adapted it is to their taste. In short, they will not fail to be pleased with a preacher, who gratifies their fancy with brilliant imagery and language, and their ears with fascinating tones, and says little or nothing to make them displeased with themselves.

Search Christendom over, my Friends, and you will find this to be one of the grand temptations in preaching the gospel to the luxurious and fashionable, especially in large cities. And, alas! how many ministers who set out with the purpose and promise of being faithful, have fallen into the snare! They have begun, perhaps, with that most vain and delusive of all calculations (for such I verily believe it to be), that the doctrines of the gospel are never so likely to find their way to the hearts of the gay and the worldly, as when they are covered and disguised with artificial ornament. Hence they have insensibly contracted the habit of preaching,—the truth, perhaps,—but truth so gilded over,—so loaded with ornament,—so studiously divested of everything adapted to give it edge and effect, as to be little if any better than keeping it back. This kind of preaching is greatly admired by the people of the world; but it leaves the pious to starve and mourn. It excites no alarm. It produces no complaint on the part of the unbelieving and impenitent. It allows every hearer, who is so disposed, to slumber in security; and is adapted, ultimately, to make those who statedly attend upon it, Christian in name but heathen in reality.

Such have been the guilty course, and the fatal influence, of many a polished, courtly preacher, from the age of Paul of Samosata[1] to the present hour. If you doubt the fact, search with impartiality the records of Jerusalem and Antioch, of Carthage and Alexandria, of Constantinople and of Rome; and you will doubt no longer.

But, from a courtly, flattering mode of preaching the transition is easy and natural to erroneous opinions. And, accordingly, great cities have commonly been, in all ages, the hot-beds of error. Because there have been displayed most frequently the pride of intellect, and those splendid temptations which are apt to beguile from the simplicity that is in Christ. In the great cities of the Roman Empire began that clerical ambition, which invaded the primitive parity of gospel ministers, and which finally issued in the Papal usurpation. In great cities, likewise, or, at least, in states of society similar to what is commonly found in such places, has generally commenced that fatal decline from orthodoxy, which began, perhaps, with calling in question some of what are styled the more

---

[1] Paul of Samosata was so called from the place of his birth. He was the Bishop of Antioch, about A.D. 260. Queen Zenobia, who then reigned in Syria, had a great esteem for him, on account of his eloquence, though she preferred the Jewish religion to all others. Paul, being a great courtier, in order to gain the favour of the queen, and to win her over to the Christian faith, endeavoured to accommodate his system of doctrine, and his mode of preaching to her taste. He denied the doctrine of the Trinity, as held by the orthodox, and also the proper divinity of Christ; and took great pains to add new splendour to the public worship of his church. He at first attempted to conceal, or explain away his opinions, and gave much trouble to the clergy of his time and neighbourhood; but was, at length, detected, and deposed from the ministry. See the accounts given of this man and his errors, by Eusebius, Athanasius, Nicephorus, Theodoret, Chrysostom, *etc.*

rigid peculiarities of received creeds, and ended in embracing the dreadful, soul-destroying errors of Arius or Socinus.[1] We might easily illustrate and confirm this position, by examples drawn from our own country, had we time to trace the history of several sects among us, and especially of American Unitarianism. But I forbear to pursue the illustration farther: and shall only take the liberty to ask, as I pass along—How it is to be accounted for, that the preaching of those who deny the divinity and atonement of the Saviour, and who reject the doctrines of human depravity, of regeneration, and of justification by the righteousness of Christ—How, I ask, is it to be accounted for, that such preachers, all over the world, are most acceptable to the gay, the fashionable, the worldly minded, and even the licentious? That so many embrace and eulogize their system, without being, in the smallest perceptible degree, sanctified by it? That thousands are in love with it, and praise it; but that we look in vain for the monuments of its reforming and purifying power? I will not pretend to answer these questions; but leave them to the consciences of those who believe, that the genuine doctrines of the gospel always have had, and always will have, a tendency to promote holiness of heart and of life; and that we must all speedily appear before the judgment seat of Christ.

---

[1] The above language, concerning the destructive nature of the Arian and Socinian heresies, has not been adopted lightly; but is the result of serious deliberation, and deep conviction. And in conformity with this view of the subject, the author cannot forbear to notice and record a declaration made to himself, by the late Dr Priestley, two or three years before the decease of that distinguished Unitarian. The conversation was a free and amicable one, on some of the fundamental doctrines of religion. In reply to a direct avowal on the part of the author that he was a Trinitarian and a Calvinist, Dr Priestley said—'I do not wonder that you Calvinists entertain and express a strongly unfavourable opinion of us Unitarians. The truth is, there neither can, nor ought to be, any compromise between us. If you are right, we are not Christians at all; and if we are right, you are gross idolaters.' These were, as nearly as can be recollected, the words, and, most accurately, the substance of his remark. And nothing, certainly, can be more just. Between those who believe in the divinity and atonement of the Son of God, and those who entirely reject both, 'there is a great gulf fixed' which precludes all ecclesiastical intercourse. The former may greatly respect and love the latter, on account of other qualities and attainments; but certainly cannot regard them as Christians, in any correct sense of the word; or as any more in the way of salvation, than Mohammedans or Jews.

The preacher then, who goes to a polite and luxurious capital, ought to be most vigilantly on his guard against the tendency and the influence of which I have spoken. He ought to be constantly aware of the difficulty and of the temptation before him: and while he endeavours to gratify, as far as is lawful, the taste for elegance and refinement in his public services; he ought, at the same time, so to preach as to be able, with truth, to say—'I preach Christ crucified, not with the enticing words of man's wisdom, but in demonstration of the Spirit, and of power.'

4. A fourth obstacle to the success of gospel ministers in populous cities is the tendency of particular circumstances, in such places, to *harden the heart.*

Of these circumstances I have only time, at present, to mention two—*viz., familiarity with death,* and the *frequency and publicity of gross vices.*

Few things have a greater tendency to impress and soften the heart, than death, and the various attendants on the close of our earthly pilgrimage. The coffin, the shroud, the funeral procession, and the open grave, all tend to inspire deep reflection and serious-ness, in every man who has not become obdurate as a brute. Nay, the most abandoned profligate, and even the atheist, are compelled to be thoughtful while they stand over the house appointed for all living. Such, in fact, is the impression made on the minds of most persons, by a death and a funeral, in those places in which occurrences of this kind are comparatively rare. But probably everyone who has had an opportunity of making the observation, has remarked, that in large cities, where deaths and funerals, and sometimes large numbers of them, occur every day, they, in a great measure, cease to make the impression which is proper and desirable. The scene is familiar. The mind becomes, in this respect, hardened. And that whole train of motives which the gospel preacher is wont to draw from the consid-eration of death and eternity, and which ought to be among the most awfully powerful, make, for the most part, but little impression.

The same general remarks may be applied to gross vices. In the retirement of the country, when such vices seldom occur, and when they do occur, are in a great measure concealed from public view, they are regarded with a kind of instinctive horror. But, in great cities, where they occur every day, and sometimes every hour, and frequently court the public eye, they are, insensibly, regarded with less and less horror. And it will be well if the minds of many, who once thought themselves beyond the reach of such an effect, are not gradually poisoned by the contagious example. It will be well if practices once considered as unquestionably and highly criminal, be not, by and by, so familiar to the mind, as to appear scarcely criminal at all, and as hardly a proper object of ecclesiastical discipline.

Now, it cannot be questioned, that whatever hardens the heart—whatever renders death and eternity less impressive, and sinful practice, of whatever kind, less abhorrent to the soul, forms a real obstacle to the success of the ambassador of Christ. It can scarcely, I think, be doubted, that this was one of the difficulties which the apostle contemplated in the prospect of preaching the gospel at Rome. There, he knew, that many of those practices which he must denounce as unchristian, were not only loved, but sanctioned by public opinion, and by general habit. But in spite of this, and of every other obstacle, he declared himself ready to go forward; ready to put his reputation, and even his life in jeopardy, to plead the cause of his Master against all opposition.

5. The only other peculiar difficulty which I shall mention, as attendant on the labours of a minister of the gospel in a great city, is that *love of variety,* and that *fondness for religious dissipation,* if I may so speak, which are apt to prevail in populous places.

When a minister is settled in a retired situation, or in a town where there is but a single church, and but seldom an opportunity of comparing the ministrations of others with his, he has, comparatively, an easy task. He is, in a great measure, free from that peculiar pressure, which a very different state of things imposes on the city pastor. In great cities there is created a sort of morbid appetite for variety, and for an excessive quantity, as well as delicacy, of public preaching. There is such an easy access to every sort of talent and manner, that it cannot fail of being extremely difficult for any one man to keep together, and to satisfy, a large congregation. If he hope to do it, he must not only preach the pure gospel, with diligence and with power; but he must also labour, as far as is lawful, to give his people that variety and richness of matter, which may be adapted to the various tastes of those who attend on his ministry. He must labour, as our Lord expresses it, like a good householder, 'to bring forth out of his treasure things new and old'. He must, as the apostle, in writing to Timothy, exhorts, give attention to reading, as well as to exhortation: he must meditate upon these things, and give himself wholly to them, that his profiting may appear unto all.

But that love of variety, which is peculiarly strong in the inhabitants of great cities, and which a city pastor must make peculiar exertions to consult, and, as far as is proper, to satisfy, is not the whole of his difficulty. There is also a tendency in large towns, where public exercises of religion abound, and where some churches, of one denomination or another, are almost always open; there is a tendency among many professors of religion, otherwise exemplary, by far too much to neglect the duties of the closet, and of the family, and to be almost perpetually engaged in attending on public services. I am a warm friend, not only to a punctual attendance on the stated service of the house of God on the Sabbath; but also to an attendance on prayer meetings, and other similar exercises, as providence may afford an opportunity, in the course of the week. The person who has it in his power to attend such meetings, but has no taste for it, and seldom or never appears at them, gives too much reason to fear that if he have real religion at all, it is at a very low ebb in his soul. Nay, I have no doubt that, where the principle of piety is in a lively and growing state, such meetings will be regarded as a feast, and there will be a desire to enjoy them as often as is consistent with the other duties of the Christian life. But this desire may be, and often has been, indulged to excess; especially by parents and heads of families. Many hasten from church to church, and from one social meeting to another, until every hour on the Sabbath, and every evening in the week, are employed in public services. In fact, they seem to think that they serve God acceptably just in proportion to the number of public exercises on which they can attend. This religious dissipation—for it really appears to me to deserve no better name—is productive of multiplied evils. It interferes, almost entirely, with that calm self-examination, and self-converse, which are so essential to a life of growing piety. It abridges, or prevents, in a most fatal degree, that faithful instruction of children and servants, which is indispensable to training up a family in the nurture and admonition of the Lord. And it tends to surcharge the mind with an amount of spiritual provision which is never properly digested, or likely to be advantageously applied. The consequence is, that the young and rising generation, in such families, are never prepared by adequate training at home to hear the gospel with profit. While those who are more advanced in life, taking little or no time for meditation and reading in private, do not grow as they ought in scriptural knowledge, and remain but babes while they ought to be strong men in Christ.

Hence arises what is alleged by many to be a fact, and what, I suspect, is really so; that among the mass of the professors of religion in great cities, there is, commonly, less accurate and digested knowledge of Christian doctrine, than among an equal number of professors in the country. Not that there is less general intelligence, or less access to books, in the former than in the latter: but, on the contrary, more, usually, of both. But because there is more mixed society; more of those distracting interruptions which multifarious society cannot fail to produce; and, of course, less retirement, less religious reading, and less leisurely digestion of what is read and heard.

Now, it is perfectly obvious that all this is unfriendly both to the comfort and the success of a Christian pastor. Whatever has a tendency to interrupt or to abridge the exercises of retirement and devotion; whatever has a tendency to prevent professors of religion from enjoying much deep, undisturbed converse with themselves, their Bible, and their God; and whatever tends to interfere with the patient, laborious pursuit of family instruction, and family discipline, will always be found to have an equal tendency to increase the toil, and at the same time to diminish the fruit of a minister's work: will render the closet a less edifying preparative for the sanctuary, and the parental mansion a less wholesome nursery for the church of God.

Such are some of the peculiar difficulties and temptations, which beset the ambassador of Christ in a great city; and which either hinder his success, or increase his labour, or tempt him to employ unhallowed means for avoiding the trouble which they induce.

It cannot be necessary to add, that, these things being so, the situation of a city minister is, by no means to be coveted or envied. If he have a more comfortable temporal support than usually falls to the lot of his country brethren (though this is by no means always the case, and perhaps more seldom than is imagined, when everything is taken into the account); and if he enjoy the advantage of more intelligent society, and of greater literary privileges; he has at the same time, if he be faithful, more severe labour; more perplexing care; more distracting interruptions from unprofitable company; less command of his time, for either study or devotion; and less ministerial comfort. He is like a soldier, who is not only always on duty, but always in the front of the battle; often on the forlorn hope; and if he be sometimes cheered with the voice of approbation, and the shout of victory, he is, perhaps, still more frequently assailed by the murmurs of complaint, and discouraged by the fruitlessness of his toils.

I have dwelt so long on this branch of the subject, that less time than I could wish is left for considering the second proposition, which is

II. That, as peculiar difficulties and temptations attend the preaching of the gospel in great cities; so *it is of peculiar importance that the gospel be plainly and faithfully preached in such places.*

It is of unspeakable importance that the gospel be plainly and faithfully preached everywhere. 'For it is the power of God unto salvation, to every one that believeth.' If the salvation of the soul be of infinite moment; if the gospel of the grace of God be the only message of life and peace to fallen man; and if he that believeth this gospel hath life, but he that believeth it not, shall not see life, but hath the wrath of God abiding on him;—then no tongue of men or of angels can tell the importance of preaching the gospel, in its simplicity and purity, to every creature.

But the thought which I wish to illustrate and enforce is, that there are some considerations which render it *peculiarly important* that the gospel be plainly and faithfully preached in *great cities*. Among many which might be suggested, I will only request your attention to the following.

If there be any justness in the remark offered in a former part of the discourse, that there is a certain *intensity of character* usually observable among the inhabitants of great cities; that, especially, their luxury and dissipation, their follies and vices are, in common, more strongly marked, than in the more spare population of the country; then it follows that there is, humanly speaking, more *need* of the gospel in the former than in the latter: a more imperious call for exhibiting, in all its solemnity and power, that most potent of all means for opposing and subduing the depravity of man. It is a maxim among physicians, that the most strongly marked diseases, call for the most bold and vigorous treatment. To counteract a poison of peculiar virulence, remedies of the most active character must be employed. So it is in the moral and spiritual world. Where difficulties more than commonly powerful and obstinate exist, remedies of corresponding potency ought to be sought and diligently applied. Since, then, the gospel of Christ exhibits the only adequate remedy for human depravity and misery, it ought to be preached with peculiar plainness, fidelity and perseverance, wherever the diseases which it is intended to heal reign with more than ordinary malignity.

Again, it is of peculiar importance that the gospel be faithfully and powerfully preached in great cities, because *there it is commonly addressed to greater numbers at once than in more retired places.* There the preacher has a more favourable opportunity of doing good upon a large scale: and, of course, the result of a given amount of labour, other things being equal, will be likely to be more extensively useful. When Peter preached at Jerusalem, and Paul at Antioch and Corinth, they seem to have accomplished more by single sermons, than by many, in the smaller settlements which they visited.

A large city, likewise, forms, as it were, the heart, the most vital portion of the state or country to which it belongs. It gives fashion, and almost law, to the surrounding districts. A favourable impression made here, will be extended in every direction. A happy impulse given here, will vibrate, and be beneficially felt to the remotest bounds of the social body. How important, then, that in the metropolis of a state or nation, the truth be known and honoured, and orthodox churches established and edified! How peculiarly desirable, that in such a great centre of action and of influence, there be able, faithful men, well qualified to be guides of the faith and practice of those around them!

Further, in a great city, there is special need of instructive, faithful preaching, because, as you have heard, *there is apt to be less reading, less retired devotion, less patient use of the private means of growing in scriptural knowledge,* than are commonly found in other places, where the means of grace are statedly enjoyed. It often happens, in large cities, that the instructions given from the pulpit, form the greater part of what many professors of religion and others, ever receive. Of what unspeakable importance is it, then, that the preaching, in such circumstances, be plain, clear, sound, able, faithful, and edifying! How important that preachers be scribes, well instructed in the kingdom of God; qualified rightly to divide the word of truth, and give to every one his portion in due season!

In a large city, moreover, the faithful, popular preacher will, almost every Sabbath, address *a number of strangers,* who flock to the metropolis, on business or pleasure, from every part of the surrounding country; and who, if they be benefited themselves by his labours, will earn with them a portion of the sacred treasure, wherever they sojourn, or wherever they abide. When Peter preached in Jerusalem, on the day of Pentecost, he was an instrument of saving benefit to many who resided in almost every part of the Roman Empire. Some of the inhabitants of Egypt and of the Lesser Asia, of Crete and Arabia, of Rome and of Parthia, were found together, drinking in the word of life from his lips; and each, afterwards, going to his own home, we may suppose, became a means of saving knowledge to many around him. O how animating and, at the same time, how solemn, is this thought to one who, from Sabbath to Sabbath, proclaims the message of salvation in a populous city! Every time he enters the pulpit, he will, perhaps, preach to some who never heard him before, and will never hear him again; and who may carry away an impression eternally beneficial or injurious, according to its character, not only to themselves, but also to many others over whom they may exert an influence!

Finally, in a large city, as we have seen, there is generally collected *a much greater amount of intellectual power, of literary acquirement, and of pecuniary means, than are to be found in other places.* Of course, if a right direction be given to public sentiment by the faithful preaching of the gospel (and we cannot hope that it shall be given by any other means), we may expect to see a much greater amount of talent, of learning, of wealth, and of exertion devoted to the cause of the Redeemer, to the promotion of human happiness, than could otherwise be reasonably expected. The servant of Jesus Christ, then, who takes the oversight in the Lord of a large and wealthy city congregation, may consider himself as called to preside over the movements of an engine of mighty power, which, under wise guidance, may accomplish more than can easily be estimated;—not for his own personal aggrandisement;—not to gratify the littleness of sectarian bigotry;—but to support and extend those great plans for building up the church of God, at home and abroad, which now do honour to those who engage in them, and which will promote the happiness of unnumbered millions in time and eternity.

It is plain, then, that the labours of a gospel minister, in a great capital, are more important than those of most others in the sacred office:—That greater benefits, or greater mischiefs are likely to flow from them, according to their character!—And that, as he is called to struggle with many peculiar and most painful difficulties; so he has, also, peculiar inducements to be faithful, and may expect peculiar rewards for his fidelity.

This subject appears to me to be replete with instruction both to our young Brother, who is this day to be invested with the sacred office; and also to that portion of the inhabitants of this great city, who are statedly to attend on his ministrations.

First, let me apply the remarks which have been made to the youthful candidate, whose investment with the office of an ambassador of Christ, and whose pastoral charge over this people, are this day to begin. My beloved Brother! the great Head of the church has cast your lot in a most important and interesting station. He has been pleased to place you on one of the most conspicuous hills of Zion. You have heard of the difficulties and temptations which will attend you. Contemplate them without self-flattery, but, at the same time, without dismay. They are real. They are formidable. Nay, the half has not been told you. Allow one who himself resided more than twenty years in a large city, to speak with some degree of confidence on this subject. Rely upon it, the splendour of wealth, the fascinations of refined and elegant society, the charms of luxury, the caresses of respect and kindness, and the insinuating voice of popular applause are more truly dangerous to a minister of Christ, than the terrors of persecution. More dangerous to his ministerial fidelity,—more dangerous to his ultimate peace. Turn not away, I beseech you, from a distinct view of this danger; but, in the name and in the strength of your Master, regard it with a steady eye, and as a good soldier of Jesus Christ, gird on your armour.

Preach the simple and pure gospel. Be not ashamed of it; though the children of gaiety and dissipation call you rigid, and even fanatical; and though the self-righteous and philosophical consider the cross as folly;—be not ashamed of it. Let your resolution be that of Paul—'For I determined to know nothing among you, save Jesus Christ and him crucified.' Whether men will hear, or whether they will forbear, hold forth the word of life. Hold it forth, without disguise or concealment; in all its majesty and purity; in all its humbling and elevating character. And be careful not only to *preach the gospel,* but also to *live the gospel.* Let all your deportment be a living, striking comment on the holy, humbling, and self-denying doctrine which you will preach. Remember, that, not only every sermon you deliver, but every word you utter, and every part of your example, on this hill of Zion, will be of peculiar importance; nay, perhaps, will be for the rise or fall of many in Israel. Let them all, then (more I cannot say, and more I need not say), let them all be such as becometh the gospel of Jesus Christ.

In pursuing this course, you will gain with all, and lose with none. It is a common opinion, that when a minister of Christ is in the company of the gay and the worldly, he conciliates their respect by as much conformity to their practices as decorum will permit. There never was a greater mistake. I grant, that, by pursuing this course, he may conciliate their prevailing *taste,* and their present *wishes, but not their judgment,* or their *respect.* They never fail to *think* the less of him, at the time, for all his concessions to their habits of life; seldom fail to *speak* of it to his disadvantage when he has withdrawn. No; the judgment and the conscience of every worldly man, nay, of the most profligate man in this city, are strongly in favour of a pure, holy, retiring, self-denied character on the part of ministers of the gospel. When such a character is exhibited, it invariably extorts even from the licentious, the homage of respect and admiration: and they are among the first to remark with severity on every departure from it. Be assured, then, that a minister of the gospel, by every act of conformity to the maxims and manners of the world, loses in the estimation of the worst of men, and grieves to the heart the generation of the righteous.

When I think of your ministry in this place, my dear young Brother, I am ready fondly to hope that we may apply to you the same exhortation, and the same encouragement, which were given by the Saviour himself to the Apostle Paul, when he was about to preach in the city of Corinth. 'Be not afraid', said the ascended Redeemer; 'Be not afraid, but speak, and hold not thy peace; for I am with thee, and no man shall set on thee to hurt thee; for I have much people in this city' (*Acts* 18:9, 10). So, in my Master's name, I would say to you: *Be not afraid; but speak, and hold not thy peace; for the Lord is with thee. Be faithful; for the Lord, I trust, has much people in this city. Be faithful unto death, and thou shalt receive a crown of life.* Remember that the true honour of a gospel minister consists, not in receiving greetings in the markets, or in being invited to the uppermost rooms at feasts, or in being called of men, 'Rabbi, Rabbi.' No, his honour consists in doing good; his laurels are *conversions;* the highest eulogium that can be bestowed upon him is that which is recorded of a minister of old—'He was a good man, and full of the Holy Ghost and of faith, and much people was added to the Lord.'

Remember, also, the shortness and uncertainty of life; and endeavour every Sabbath to preach, and every day to live, as if it might be your last. O what an affecting comment on this counsel is the early removal of that precious young minister of Christ, who, not long since, proclaimed his Master's message within these walls, but has recently been translated to another, and, we trust, a better world! Yes, the pious, the eloquent, the noble-minded, the beloved Larned,[1] your brother, and companion in study, is no more! 'Even so, Father, for so

---

[1] The Rev. Sylvester Larned, late pastor of the Presbyterian Church in the city of New Orleans, who a few weeks before the delivery of this discourse, in the 24th year of his age, and in the midst of high promises of usefulness, fell a victim to a malignant fever, which was epidemic in the place of his residence. He and Mr Nevins were fellow-students at the theological seminary, of which the author is one of the professors, and were much attached to each other. Mr Larned, not long before his death, had been invited to the First Presbyterian Church in Baltimore to be their pastor; but with a disinterestedness, as striking as it is rare, he resolved not to forsake a congregation which he been instrumental in forming, and which he considered as still urgently needing his labours. Few young ministers of the present day have accepted a higher place in the public regard, or died more unfeignedly and generally lamented.

it seemed good in thy sight'!—Make it your daily and hourly care, my Brother, to be ready to follow him; ready to obey the summons to yourself, whenever it may arrive. 'And when the chief Shepherd shall appear, may you receive a crown of glory that shall not fade away'!

In the second place, let me apply the subject before us to *the members of this congregation.*

You are not to imagine, my Friends, that the discussion in which we have been engaged, is applicable only to him who is about to become your pastor. It has a direct, and very solemn application also, to the flock of Christ, of which he is to be an overseer. You reside in a great, rich, polished, and luxurious city; a city which appears destined to become one of the greatest in this western world. While this circumstance will be, as you have heard, a source of difficulty and of temptation to your pastor, it will be a source of no less temptation to yourselves. O my Friends! such a situation is a trying, a peculiarly trying one to professing Christians. They walk every hour in the midst of contagion and of danger. 'Watch and pray without ceasing', I beseech you, against the unhallowed influence of the worldly splendours and attractions which surround you. Cherish in your persons, and in your families, those Christian virtues of moderation, simplicity, self-denial, and purity, which are so essential to social and ecclesiastical happiness. Guard against a criminal *conformity to the world,* that reproach and bane of the church of Christ. Above all, invite the holy, sanctifying Spirit of God into your city, and into your church; and then from this great centre of life and activity, healthful influence will be pouring forth in every direction, and diffusing blessings far and wide.

You have invited this young brother, greatly beloved and respected by his teachers, to be your pastor. Despise not his youth. Receive him as *an ambassador of Jesus Christ;* for he comes in his name, and bears his message. Remember the difficulties and temptations which will await him in this wealthy capital, and add not to their number by your manner of treating him. Instead of weakening his hands, or tempting him, by any conduct on your part, to be ashamed of the gospel, or to keep back, or disguise it, let your treatment of him and his ministrations be always such as to excite and animate him to greater fidelity and holy seal. Make a point of encouraging and supporting him in the exercise of enlightened *Christian discipline*. Without some good measure of discipline, there may be a *congregation*, but I venture to say, there cannot be a *church*. Never account him your enemy because he tells you the truth. When he sets before you your guilt and depravity by nature; when he reminds you of your sins and your danger; when he describes to you the terrors of the judgment day, and the miseries of the damned in hell,—be not offended. He will take no pleasure in dwelling on these things for their own sake: but only that by exhibiting your danger, he may constrain you to flee from the wrath to come, and to lay hold on the hope set before you in the gospel. And surely, my Friends, if the danger of impenitent sinners be as great, as tremendously great, as the Word of God declares it to be, that minister who should fail to warn them, and to set before them their real situation, would deserve to be accounted their worst enemy, and to be abhorred for his want of fidelity.

When I look round on this great city, I think of Rome, as it was when Paul went thither to preach the gospel. I think of its prosperity and grandeur in that day; and I ask myself—Where is it now? Alas! its glory is departed! Had Rome been faithful to its privileges, it had retained its glory to this day. But it became corrupt and corrupting; and the righteous Governor of the world brought upon it his destroying judgments. My dearly beloved Brethren, read in the history of that city, at once what will be your happiness and safety, and where your danger lies. Your happiness and safety will consist in cherishing the gospel; in opening your houses and your hearts, as well as your church, to its blessed influence. Your danger will lie, in rejecting that gospel, or in turning away from its spirit and power, while you bear its name. 'Behold, I set before you, this day, life and death, blessing and cursing: Therefore choose life, that your souls may live.' 'The Lord bless you and keep you. The Lord make his face to shine upon you, and be gracious unto you. The Lord lift up the light of his countenance, and give you peace.' Amen.

THE WORK OF EVANGELISTS
AND MISSIONARIES[1]

And they shall build the old wastes; they shall raise up the former
desolations; and they shall repair the waste cities,
the desolations of many generations.
Isaiah 61:4

O UR blessed Saviour, in the synagogue at Nazareth, expressly
decided that these words refer to gospel times, and to the
benign influence of his ministry and his truth. It is probable, indeed, that the primary reference of the verse immediately
under consideration is to the return of the Jews from captivity in
Babylon, and the restoration of their lands and cities, which had been
long lying desolate, to a state of prosperity. But no one, I think, can
doubt, that it has a far wider scope, and is intended to convey an
infinitely more precious meaning. The Saviour himself is here introduced as the speaker. He refers to his own coming in the flesh, and
to the calling of the Gentiles. He exhibits himself as 'anointed', or
'set apart', to be the Friend and Restorer of ruined man; to preach
good tidings to the meek; to bind up the broken-hearted; to proclaim
liberty to the captives, and the opening of the prison to them that are
bound; to be the Comforter of mourners; to give unto them beauty
for ashes, the oil of joy for mourning, the garment of praise for the
spirit of heaviness.

---

[1] Samuel Miller, *A Sermon, Delivered in the Middle Church, New Haven, Connecticut,*
Sept. 12, 1822, at the Ordination of the Rev. Messrs. William Goodell, William Richards,
and Artemas Bishop, as Evangelists and Missionaries to the Heathen, (Boston: Crocker
and Brewster, 1822).

But the effects of the Redeemer's ministry were not to terminate with his personal presence on earth. He not only declares that he is to enlighten, to restore, to sanctify, to elevate the subjects of his immediate gracious ministrations; but that those who are thus brought into the church, and saved by his mighty power, are to be made, in their turn, instruments for converting and saving others. These converts, he informs us, shall not only be called themselves, trees of righteousness, the planting of the Lord, that he may be glorified; but they shall build the old wastes; they shall raise up the former desolations, and they shall repair the waste cities, the desolations of many generations.

We have, in these words, two subjects, which demand our attention; both of which appear to me to form topics of address appropriate to the solemn occasion on which we are convened.

First—*the condition of those who are destitute of the blessings which the Saviour has to bestow.* And,

Secondly—*the promise that they shall be delivered from this condition; and the means by which their deliverance shall be effected.*

I. Let us contemplate the *condition of those who are destitute of the light and sanctifying energy of the gospel.* They are represented, in our text, as in a state of 'waste', and 'desolation'. 'They shall build up the old wastes, they shall repair the desolations of many generations.'

This representation applies, not only to the ancient covenant people of God; but also to all the heathen nations, and, in general, to all who are strangers to the light and the practical influence of our holy religion.

When we speak of the 'old wastes', and of the 'desolations of many generations', we, of course, mean to convey the idea, that the places, or the people of which we speak, were once in more favourable circumstances; that they once enjoyed advantages which they no longer possess; and, in consequence, have sunk into darkness and ruin. Now this representation precisely corresponds with plain, undoubted fact. When we take the slightest survey of the history of our fallen race, we shall see that very precious privileges and blessings have been, at different times, either actually enjoyed by all the families of the earth, or placed fairly within their reach: and that these blessings have been either ungratefully rejected, or stupidly squandered away and lost. In reply, therefore, to the old and impious cavil,—'Why has not God given the gospel to all mankind?'—we may confidently assert, and appeal to history for an ample confirmation of the fact, that he has, from time to time, imparted the knowledge of the true religion to the *whole human family;* so that they are altogether without excuse.

That the knowledge of the true method of salvation was imparted to our first parents, no Christian will deny. They were originally formed in a state not only of immaculate, but of high perfection. Brought into existence in the perfect maturity of all their powers; in the image of God; with a happy balance between their sensitive, intellectual and moral faculties; surrounded with ample light, and with all those expressions of divine love, which are adapted to make creatures blessed; their happiness was without interruption or alloy. Reposing under the 'blissful bowers of paradise', all was innocence, all was enjoyment, and every creature was a minister to their comfort. Nor was this all. No sooner had their Creator made them, than he began to speak to them, and, of course, immediately instruct them in language (the real origin, I have no doubt, of articulate speech), in all the duties to himself and to one another; and in everything necessary to their temporal and eternal happiness. I am aware that some theoretical philosophers have given a very different representation of this matter. They contend that the original state of man was exceedingly degraded: that he occupied a rank, at first, little if any above that of the beasts of the field: that all intelligence, the power of communicating his thoughts by speech, and even his erect posture, are the result of his own long continued efforts; and that having, by his own exertions, gradually escaped from the state of brutality, silence and solitude in which he was originally found; he is in a constant course of improvement, by the same exertions, which will ultimately issue in a state of perfection in this world. I will only stop to say, that all this is as contrary to sober, uninspired history, as it is to the Word of God. The latter distinctly informs us, that the primitive state of man, with respect to his intellectual, moral, and social character, was the highest that he has ever enjoyed, or ever will enjoy on this side of heaven; and that, since the fall, his natural course, when left to himself, is not to rise in knowledge, virtue and enjoyment; but, on the contrary, to sink deeper and deeper into darkness, corruption and misery. And this testimony, I fearlessly assert, is amply confirmed by all other authentic records, so far as they speak at all on the subject.

When our guilty progenitors had broken the law of their God; had ungratefully trampled on their most precious privileges; and had lost their innocence, and with it every blessing; the God of all grace did not, as he might justly have done, inexorably cast them off. The fall had scarcely occurred, before a method of deliverance was announced, as wonderful as it was gracious. In the first promise, we see the first dawn of gospel light, the first pledge of gospel blessings. Adam was placed under a dispensation of mercy. A visible church was founded in his family, of which he and his partner in sin, together with their children, were members. Sacrifices were offered, in obedience to God, and in token of their humble acquiescence in the terms of the new covenant under which they were placed; and the Lord smelled a sweet savour in the contrition and offerings of his penitent children.

But again was the divine goodness abused, and his authority trampled under feet. The light of the primitive revelation, though at first respectfully received, became less and less regarded. The true religion gradually lost its hold on the hearts and lives of men; and unbridled sin, and its necessary offspring, misery, soon began to gain a melancholy prevalence. Even during the lives of our first parents, who, no doubt, faithfully instructed and exhorted their posterity, impiety, crime and suffering awfully reigned. Men set at nought counsel and rebuke. All flesh corrupted their way. The earth was filled with violence. Among the immense and highly cultivated population of the antediluvian world (for such there can be little doubt it was), Jehovah was generally forgotten, or remembered only to be insulted. Here and there a pious man, like a few feeble and glimmering stars in a dark night, only served to render the surrounding darkness more intense and melancholy. Enoch, and afterwards Noah, and probably others, taught and warned in vain. Until, at length, the wickedness of men rose to such an enormous height, that a Being of infinite wisdom and benevolence determined to destroy the world of the ungodly by a flood. Only a single family of all the corrupt millions on our globe escaped; and even of that family, a part only appear to have been truly pious.

After the deluge, the moral and religious interests of men were placed upon a new footing, and commenced a new career, with more favourable prospects. The visible church was continued in the family of Noah with additional light and privilege, with additional covenant engagements, and with additional experience of the evil of sin, and the necessity of unreserved obedience. That this religious knowledge was imparted, in all its fulness, to the posterity of Noah, for several generations, there can be no reasonable doubt; and, of course, all the inhabitants of the earth were, once more, instructed in the true religion, the religion of Jesus Christ, for such it really then was, the same in substance as at the present day. And who would not have expected this precious deposit to be gratefully retained, and sacredly transmitted to the remotest posterity? But, alas! the inhabitants of the earth almost immediately commenced again the downhill course. Instruction and warning were vain. Even the terrors of the deluge were soon forgotten. The religion which came out of the ark, before the last of the occupants of that ark was dead, seems to have nearly vanished from the earth. Forgetfulness of God; gross idolatry; moral corruption; and all their attendant evils of discord, strife and war, overspread the nations; and rendered necessary another interposition on the part of the Most High to save the church from utterly perishing.

When Jehovah chose for himself a peculiar people;—when he committed to them his truth and his ordinances;—when he recorded his name, and, from time to time, displayed his glory among them, they became, at once, a light and a warning to all the surrounding nations. But did the world profit, as might have been expected, by all these means of instruction; by all these proclamations of the way of mercy by a Saviour to come? No; far from it! the corrupt Canaanites; the refined and scientific Egyptians; the idolatrous nations round about Palestine; the polished and splendid Babylonians, Persians, Greeks and Romans—all—all, in succession, turned their backs on the offers of mercy; hardened themselves against God; and chose darkness rather than light. The multiplied and most impressive miracles which Jehovah wrought for the support of his truth, in the sight of the nations, in Egypt, at the Red Sea, in the wilderness, and in Canaan, were regarded only with stupefying terror, or hardening rage. And even when, at length, the Old Testament Scriptures were translated into the most rich, polished, and extensively diffused language then on earth, and thus the knowledge of the sacred oracles conveyed to many thousands, perhaps millions, of the most enlightened and reflecting part of the heathen world;—still the church of God seems to have received no cordial accessions from that quarter. The word of life seems to have been studied only by their *Literati;* and by them as, at best, only a curious history, or a singular, superstitious fable. With one accord they closed their eyes against its precious light, and sunk down into the most deplorable moral corruption and desolation. So that, when the Saviour came in the flesh, whatever lustre the refinements of luxury, the ingenuity and elegance of art, or the splendours of literature and science, may have shed on a few countries—on Egypt, Babylon, and Syria; on Asia Minor, Greece, and Italy, the whole world was, without exception, a spiritual 'waste'. Even the chosen people of God had sunk into the most humiliating corruption and degradation. In whatever direction the eye of piety was turned, men were seen to have fallen ignobly from their high privileges, and to have become, even where society appeared in its best form, a mass of splendid putrefaction and ruin. The Jews, with the Word of God in their hands, had become, in some respects, worse than the surrounding heathen; and the latter, with all their boasted wisdom, had never been able to reach that great, fundamental fact, on which all revealed religion rests, that there is but one God, the maker of heaven and earth; or rather, it had been imparted to them, but they lost it again and again. Not liking to retain God—mark that expression—*Not liking to retain* God in their knowledge, he gave them up to a reprobate mind, leaving them to a wretched system of polytheism, on which the merest babe in Christ looks back with wonder and horror, and which produced effects worthy of its character. Their very religion directly inculcated and nurtured, pride, ambition, malevolence, cruelty, deceit, and sensuality; and thus, instead of promoting their happiness, was constantly dragging them still lower in crime and wretchedness.

But, in these deplorable circumstances, in a manner still more marvellous than ever, did a gracious God again interpose, for the benefit of the human family. A messenger more dignified, and a light more abundant, than before, were presented to the inhabitants of the earth.

In the fulness of time, the Desire of all nations came, and completed that great sacrifice for sin, which had been so long the object of prayer and expectation. Now the meridian light of gospel day shone on the church. That which had been before taught under types and shadows, was now manifested with unveiled glory. And that which had been hitherto, chiefly confined to a single nation, was now directed to be proclaimed to all people. Accordingly, the command of the Saviour to his apostles, when he left the world, was, 'Go ye into all the world, and preach the gospel to every creature.' This command was, in some good measure, obeyed. Within two centuries, the gospel was preached, and large and respectable Christian churches formed, in almost all parts of the then known world. And who that witnessed the triumphs of the cross, in the days of the apostles, and of their immediate successors, could have doubted for a moment, that, long before this time, the church, glorious in strength and beauty, would have been the joy of the whole earth? In fact if Christian parents, and Christian ministers, in early and subsequent times, had not been awfully unfaithful to themselves and their solemn trust, the religion of Jesus Christ had, long since, covered our globe. And that it is not so, is the sin as well as the misery of man himself, and not the fault of God. As long as the gospel was preached with zeal, in its simplicity and purity, it had free course and was glorified. But when Christians began to grow cold and selfish; when they divided into sects and parties; when the ministers of Christ began to waste their strength in doting about questions and strifes of words, or in contests about titles and places; when they began to adulterate the doctrines of the gospel with the refinements of philosophy falsely so called; when emperors and kings perverted the religion of Christ into an engine of State; and when those who ought to have been propagating the gospel abroad, found abundant employment at home, in contriving uncommanded rites and forms, in struggling for power and wealth, and in toiling through the childish fooleries of superstition; then, indeed, as might have been expected, the ardour of missionary zeal rapidly declined; the progress of truth was arrested; the daughter of Zion was covered with a cloud; and the nations called Christian, instead of prizing the liberty wherewith Christ had made them free, willingly subjected themselves to the yoke of bondage, and gave their strength and power to the beast.

And here it may be worthy of notice, as we pass along, that there has always been a tendency in man to add to the appointments of heaven, under the notion of rendering them more popular and acceptable. It seems to have been an opinion entertained by many, in all ages, that a dress of superstitious trappings is necessary as a kind of vehicle for the truth; 'that a simple and rational religion cannot attract and fix the mass of mankind; that either pageantry, or mysticism, or both, must be employed, if we would impress the minds of the generality of men; in short, that the common people must be, in some degree, deceived for their good'. But never was there a more wretched mistake. As long as the religion of Jesus Christ retained its primitive simplicity, both in doctrine and ritual, it made, as has been said, rapid progress; and wherever it found its way, demonstrated, that it was the power of God unto salvation. Amidst the sneers of the wise, the frowns of the mighty, and the terrors of martyrdom, it went on conquering and to conquer. But when the simplicity of the gospel gave place to the inventions of men, Christianity immediately declined. It lost its power over the hearts and lives of men. It fell, if I may so speak, by its own weight. Just in proportion as it was divested of its genuine character, its progress was retarded: until, at length, the missionary spirit, and missionary triumphs of primitive times, were no longer known in the church—proclaiming to us the decisive and wholesome lesson, that we are never so likely to succeed in the propagation of the gospel, as when we hold it forth in all its native simplicity, without attempting to make it better, or other, than our Master left it in his Word.

Alas! what a scene of spiritual desolation at this hour broods over the greater part of Christendom, in consequence of acting on a different principle! The wisdom of this world, which is ever foolishness with God, with the view of adorning the religion of Jesus Christ, and recommending it to the world, has gone on, step by step, to load and deform it by additions, and to pollute it by unhallowed admixtures, until it is no longer the gospel of the grace of God; until it has lost all that attraction and power which once caused it to triumph among the heathen; and until, indeed, it is no longer, as some calling themselves Christians present it, worth the acceptance of the heathen. To this it is, no doubt, owing, that, since the rise of the Papal Beast, the gospel, in the hands of its votaries, has made absolutely no conquests which deserve to be set down to the score of Christianity. To this, in a great measure, is it owing, that, to the present hour, but *little more than a fifth part of mankind so much as bear the Christian name;* and that, of this small portion, probably *two thirds, at least, need instruction in the gospel almost as much as the benighted pagans themselves.*

The 'wastes' and the 'desolations' spoken of in our text, are called 'old wastes', the 'desolations of *many generations*'. And truly, if this language were proper in the days of the prophet, it is still more emphatically proper at the present day. Age after age have this darkness, depravity and misery been brooding over the nations. One blind and corrupt generation after another has existed its little day, and then passed off the stage, to make way for the following, as dark, as corrupt, and as miserable as themselves. Who that remembers how early, and how long, the children of Abraham enjoyed the light of life—the adoption, and the glory, and the giving of the law, and the promises,—can avoid weeping over that righteous dispensation of God, by which, for so many centuries, they have been scattered abroad, a hissing and a by-word, among all nations; without a temple, without a priest, without a sacrifice, and without a ruler? Who that recollects what Jerusalem was, when Solomon wielded the sceptre of his father David, can avoid the most melancholy reflections, when he beholds it, according to the divine prediction, so completely trodden down of the Gentiles? Who that has read of the large and flourishing churches, which were once the glory of Antioch and Ephesus, of Smyrna and Sardis, of Corinth and Philippi, can forbear to mourn with bitterness over them now, when their glory is departed, and when their very light is as darkness? How many ages, too, have elapsed, since the millions who follow the false prophet of Mecca, have been slumbering, the miserable victims of imposture, sunk under the blinding and degrading influence of error, and of those wretched vices, which error naturally generates! Above all, how long and how sad is the story of pagan 'desolation'! Truly it is an 'old waste', the 'desolation of many generations'. Century after century—in a world on which the light of the gospel has beamed—have the poor pagans been going on in the same melancholy round, living and dying without God, and without hope; covered with ignorance; besotted with sensuality; reeking with crime; bowing down to stocks and stones; worshipping them with rites cruel, bloody, impure, or, at best, senseless; strangers to rational enjoyment in this world, and passing every day, by thousands, with prospects still more gloomy, into the world to come. O that my head were waters, and mine eyes a fountain of tears, that I might weep day and night over this awful waste, this mighty desolation!

Can we contemplate, my Friends, the picture which has been drawn—and I am not conscious of having added a single shade which does not properly belongs to it—or rather I am conscious of having fallen utterly short of adequately representing its dark colours—Can we contemplate, I say, such a picture, without perceiving, and being ready to acknowledge, in all its humiliating extent, the deep depravity of our nature, and the innate tendency of man, in all ages, to depart from God, and from true dignity and happiness? Can we hesitate a moment to confess, that the children of men are, themselves, wholly to blame, for the darkness and desolation of our world; that we can charge no part of it on the Most High; that they have corrupted *themselves*, degraded *themselves*, destroyed *themselves?* And can we forbear, while we cast an eye over the appalling and heart-sickening scene, to ask, with the deepest interest, Is there no hope? Can these dry bones live? Can these regions of widespread waste and death, ever be restored to life and health, and beauty and happiness? Yes! all glory to the riches of divine love and mercy! our text gives us an answer at once decisive and animating. For it declares,

II. That the 'waste places' which have been described shall be 'built up', and these 'old desolations' happily 'repaired'. And it also informs us by *what means* restoration shall be effected.—To a brief consideration of this part of our subject let us now proceed.

That there is a time coming, when this world, so long the theatre of rebellion against God, and of all that complicated suffering which is the natural offspring of such rebellion,—shall be restored to the reign of truth, and purity, and peace and blessedness, is, if I am not deceived, the almost unanimous expectation of all who bear the Christian name. And that this blessed renovation of our world will appear, in all its glory, in less than two centuries from the present time, is also, if I mistake not, generally agreed, even among those who place it at the greatest distance: and some pious and learned interpreters of prophecy believe that it is nigh, even at the door. Let no despondency, or timidity, or secret scepticism lead any one to doubt whether this blessed prospect will be realized. The mouth of the Lord hath spoken it. The Father hath given to the Son, from eternity, the heathen for his inheritance, and the uttermost parts of the earth for a possession. The whole earth is plainly included in the covenant grant; and the whole earth shall, assuredly, be included in the promised blessing. Hath he said it, and shall he not do it? Hath he spoken, and shall he not make it good? Heaven and earth may pass away; but one jot or tittle shall in no wise pass from his promise, till all be fulfilled.

Hear what the Lord hath spoken! 'The Lord of hosts will destroy the face of the covering cast over all people, and the veil that is spread over all nations' (*Isa.* 35:6, 7). 'The earth shall be filled with the knowledge of the glory of the Lord, as the waters cover the sea' (*Hab.* 2:14). 'For from the rising of the sun even unto the going down of the same, my name shall be great among the Gentiles; and in every place shall incense be offered unto my name, and a pure offering: for my name shall be great among the heathen saith the Lord of hosts' (*Mal.* 1:11). 'The kingdoms of this world shall become the kingdom of our Lord and of his Christ' (*Rev.* 11:15). 'For he must reign until he hath put all enemies under his feet' (*1 Cor.* 15:25). 'The wilderness and the solitary place shall be glad, and the desert shall rejoice and blossom as the rose' (*Isa.* 35:1). 'The Lord will make bare his arm in the sight of all the nations. Nation shall not lift up the sword against nation; neither shall they learn war any more' (*Isa.* 2:4). 'For the glory of the Lord shall be revealed, and all flesh shall see it together, for the mouth of the Lord hath spoken it' (*Isa.* 11:5).

These precious and animating Scriptures have never yet been fulfilled. They plainly imply, that the period is approaching, when there shall be a general prevalence of the profession and the power of religion over the whole earth. Not that every Christian will then be perfect, or even every professor of piety, truly pious: but that the visible church shall fill the world; that all infidelity, heresy, superstition, profaneness, and open vice, shall be banished from the earth; and that religion shall be everywhere honoured, and every where prosperous. Before the accomplishment of these predictions, we are assured that the Man of Sin, the Son of Perdition, shall be brought down; that the kingdom of Antichrist shall be utterly overthrown; and that the kings of the earth, who had given their power and strength to the mother of harlots and abominations, shall then hate her, and make her desolate, and burn her with fire (*Rev.* 17:16). Another preliminary to the introduction of this glorious day—to be accomplished about the same time with the destruction of the Papal power—is bringing to an end the Mohammedan imposture; when all the unclean spirits which have been cast out of the mouth of the false Prophet, as well as out of the mouth of the Beast, and which have gone forth deceiving the nations, shall be finally destroyed. These events will prepare the way for the general conversion of the ancient covenant people of God; for grafting them in again into their own olive tree, from which they have been broken off by unbelief; *and restoring them, as a body, to the possession of their own land.* 'For, thus saith the Lord, the children of Israel shall abide many days without a king, and without a prince, and without a sacrifice, and without an image, and without an ephod, and without a teraphim. But afterward they shall return, and seek the Lord their God, and David their king, and shall fear the Lord and his goodness in the latter days' (*Hos.* 3:4-5). And again; 'Behold, I will take the children of Israel from among the heathen, whither they be gone, and I will gather them on every side, and will bring them into their own land. Moreover, I will make a covenant of peace with them, even an everlasting covenant; and the heathen shall know that I, the Lord, do sanctify Israel, when my sanctuary shall be in the midst of them forever more' (*Ezek.* 37:22-28). Again, thus saith the Lord to Israel—'Whereas thou hast been forsaken and hated, so that no man went through thee, I will make thee an eternal excellency, a joy of many generations. The sons also of them that abided thee, shall come bending unto thee, and all they that despised thee, shall bow themselves down at the soles of thy feet; and they shall call thee. The city of the Lord, the Zion of the Holy One of Israel' (*Isa.* 40:14ff.).

And allow me to observe here, my Friends, if these things be so, what a deep and affectionate interest ought Christians of the present day to take in the children of Abraham, still beloved for the Father's sake; and in that land in which they are again to be gathered! Surely on *them,* and on *that country,* which we may still call *their land,* the eyes of every disciple of Christ ought now to be intently fixed; for them his prayers ought daily to ascend; and for their conversion every friend to the church of God, and to the ultimate happiness of man, ought to be willing to contribute and to labour to the utmost. For *until the Jews are brought in, to say the least, the full splendour of millennial glory cannot arise upon our world.*

The conversion of the Jews, and their restoration to their own land, we learn from the sure word of prophecy, shall be the signal for the universal preaching of the gospel, and the bringing in of all the Gentile nations. For, says the apostle, if the fall of Israel be the riches of the world, and the diminishing of them the riches of the Gentiles, how much more their fulness! If the casting away of them be the reconciling of the world, what shall the receiving of them be but life from the dead? (*Rom.* 11:12, 15). For the kingdom, and the greatness of the kingdom, under the whole heaven, shall be given to the people of the saints of the Most High, and all dominions shall serve and obey him (*Dan.* 7:27).

Blessed renovation! Happy world! when these prospects, in which the Lord causes his people to hope, shall be gloriously realized! I will not attempt to describe the scenes which the generations of the Millennium are destined to witness. I dare not venture on the task. Take away from the world all the malignant and violent passions, which now disquiet and degrade the children of men;—take away the intemperance, the impurity, and the injustice, which are daily destroying individuals and families; take away the bigotry, party spirit, discord, and strife, which unceasingly agitate society, ecclesiastical as well as civil;—take away the war, famine, pestilence, oppression, and slavery, which have been, for so many generations, the scourges of our race;—take away earthquakes, tempests, drought, blasting and mildew, which so often destroy 'the hopes of man':—take away all these things—and suppose the general reign of truth, righteousness, order and peace:—suppose the people of God everywhere to see eye to eye, and the visible church to be harmoniously united all over the world:—suppose the earth everywhere cultivated and fruitful—the air salubrious—the seasons always favourable—tranquillity, plenty, temperance, health and longevity, universally to prevail—and all accompanied with constant and abundant influences of the Holy Spirit, *constituting one continual and universal revival.*—Imagine a scene like this; and then say, whether our world, during such a period, would not deserve to be called, as it is called in the sacred volume, the new heavens, and the new earth, wherein dwelleth righteousness? Whether it would not deserve to be considered what it is, doubtless, intended to be, the vestibule of that mansion of rest, which is not made with hands, eternal in the heavens?

But by *what means* shall these promises be fulfilled—these blessed prospects realized?

Not by the mere prevalence and power of human reason. Many, who profess to have no belief in the Christian's Millennium, yet dream of something equivalent to a pagan Elysium on earth. They talk of the perfectibility of man; of reaching a period in which all diseases, and all misery shall be unknown; and when death shall be no more triumphant over our race. And they suppose that all this will be accomplished by the progress and influence of Reason, gradually regenerating and restoring the world. But all experience, to say nothing of the Bible, pronounces this a vain hope. The experiment has been making on the power of Reason to restrain, purify, and elevate man, for nearly 6,000 years; and the result is as mortifying as it is decisive. All that it could ever accomplish, by its best influence, was to soften and polish, but not to remove, the moral desolation: to paint and whiten the sepulchre, while its interior remained filled with dead men's bones, and all uncleanness. It has ever been a fact, and will ever remain a fact, to the end of time, that the world by wisdom knows not God. Never did this boasted Reason teach a single nation, or a single individual, of all the children of men, to deny ungodliness and worldly lusts, and to live soberly, righteously, and godly, in this present evil world.

Nor yet again, will the blessings which we anticipate be attained by the progress of *literature and science.* Although when sanctified, that is consecrated by real religion, literature and science are a blessing—an inestimable blessing—yet alone they never led an individual to true holiness, or a nation to virtue and happiness:—A fact which is as notorious, as, upon the principle of the sufficiency of natural religion, it is incapable of a satisfactory solution. If it had been otherwise, we might have expected always to find the purest religion among those pagan nations, who carried the refinements of literature and science to the highest pitch of perfection. But was this, in fact, the case? Directly the reverse! The worship of the Great Spirit, by the American or African savage, is unspeakably less removed from the simplicity of the true religion, than the 30,000 deities of the Greek or Roman philosopher.

Quite as little reason, as from either of the foregoing, have we to expect the attainment of our hopes by the restraining and regulating efficacy of *human laws*. Human legislation may prohibit, may threaten, may, to a certain extent, coerce; but its utter—utter insufficiency to reach the seat and throne of human depravity,—to purify the heart,—to curb the restless appetites,—to restrain the rage of clamorous passions,—and to arrest the artful plans, and busy prowlings of secret villainy—has been painfully felt and confessed in every age. So that he who can hope for any effectual relief from this quarter, must have a hardihood, not to say, an absurdity of credulity, nearly allied to the hallucination of the bedlamite, who, on his pallet of straw, insists that he is hastening to the occupancy of a throne.

None of these things, then, can bring on the latter-day glory, or, by themselves essentially meliorate the condition of man in this world. As auxiliaries they are valuable—highly valuable—and, as such, will certainly be prized by every enlightened friend of human happiness. But they cannot be the chief confidence of any rational man. Nothing can be considered in this light but the religion of Jesus Christ;—the glorious gospel of the blessed God, which is the power of God unto salvation to every one that believeth;—which alone can reach the heart—act upon its inmost recesses—purify its blackest pollutions—and control its fiercest passions. Men may dream of other remedies; but there is no other really effectual remedy for the disease of man; no other helper, amidst its dismal ravages, than this. His disease has ever absolutely laughed to scorn all other remedies; and it ever will laugh them to scorn. But here is effectual help. Here and here alone we find light for human darkness, pardon for human guilt, cleansing for human depravity, consolation for human sorrow, strength for human weakness, and a complete repairer of human ruin. Only suppose the principles and the power of the religion of Christ to be universal, and this world would exhibit, everywhere, a foretaste of heaven. They *shall* be universal. The mouth of the Lord, I again assert, hath spoken it. Nor shall this blessing be attained without means—without human means. It is by the preaching of the gospel, by men, like ourselves, that the prophetic Scriptures every where represent it as to be expected. It is when the rod of Jehovah's strength shall be sent out of Zion, that the nations are to be made willing in the day of his power.

That eminent and elegant critic, Bishop Lowth, translates the former part of our text thus—And they that spring from thee—that is, from the children of Abraham, when converted (for to them the prophecy was directed) shall build up the ruins of old times, shall restore the ancient desolations. From this and a few other passages, in the Old Testament, some pious and learned men have supposed, that the great body of the missionaries who shall be made most successful in converting the Gentile nations to Abraham's God and Saviour, shall be converted Jews. On this point I shall, at present, express no decisive opinion. It is true, that some of the Scriptures usually quoted to establish it, may be considered as sufficiently explained by the fact, that all the first missionaries employed in propagating the gospel, both before, and immediately after our Lord's ascension, were, native Jews. But other passages have been thought not very naturally to admit of this explanation; and, of course, to suggest the opinion just mentioned. I cannot help regarding the opinion as having some degree of probability in its favour. And, certainly, if it be taught in Scripture, it is well calculated, on various accounts, deeply to interest the pious mind.

But perhaps it will be asked, what reason have we to expect such blessed effects from the preaching of the gospel in time to come? We have seen that the same gospel has been, long since, preached to all nations; and yet it has been generally rejected; and oh! how much 'waste' and 'desolation' still remain! What reason have we, then, to expect a more favourable result in future? I freely acknowledge, Brethren, that, on the principle of mere human calculation, we have no such reason. If we had no other ground of confidence, our hopes would certainly be altogether extravagant. But our expectations are founded entirely on the promise of God. The promise has passed his lips, that the time shall soon come, when the gospel shall be crowned with universal success; when the complaint shall no longer be made. Who hath believed our report? and to whom is the arm of the Lord revealed? Nay, when it shall be so universally received that it shall be no longer necessary for men to teach every one his neighbour, and every one his brother, saying, know ye the Lord; but when all shall know him, from the least of them even unto the greatest of them (*Jer.* 31:34). Not that we are to suppose, that when the Millennium opens, ministers will no longer be necessary. This would be to suppose, that the preaching of the gospel, and the administration of the sacraments will then cease. Whereas the whole tenor of Scripture leads to the conclusion, that, during the period in question, all the ordinances of religion will be more universally enjoyed, and more highly prized, than ever; and, consequently, that the ministers of religion will be more numerous, more sought after, and more beloved, than in any former period. The children of men will then come into the world depraved as well as now. The same means of grace which are now made effectual to the conversion of sinners, and to the edification and comfort of believers, will then, no doubt, be employed, and made effectual for the same purposes. The chief point of difference will be, that they will then, very seldom, fail of success. And, surely, this circumstance will not be likely to make them less esteemed. But when it is said, that, at that time, men shall not any longer need to teach every man his neighbour, and every man his brother, saying, know the Lord, we are to understand the prediction as meaning, that Christian light shall then be so universally diffused, that no part of the population of the globe, shall need that instruction in the knowledge of the true God, as distinguished from idols, which we now impart to the pagan nations.

Perhaps my hearers will expect me to say something more particular than I have yet said, as to the time in which the glorious day of which I have been speaking, shall be ushered in. On this subject, I profess to know so little, and feel myself so little entitled to speak with confidence, that I shall, of course, forbear to pronounce positively. That it will arrive, and before a long lapse of time, I have no more doubt than I have that the judgment of the great day will arrive. But perhaps we may say of the former, as we certainly must of the latter—Of that day, and of that hour knoweth no man. Possibly some of your children's children may see it, if not in its meridian glory, yet in its early dawn. But he that believeth shall not make haste. Let us patiently wait the Lord's time. Of one thing we may be certain, that it will be brought on as fast and as soon as infinite Wisdom sees best; and faster or sooner no enlightened believer would allow himself, for a moment, to desire. The vision is for an appointed time; but, at the end it will speak and not lie. Though it tarry, wait for it, for it will surely come, it will not tarry (*Hab.* 2:3).

But I ought in candour to say, that, before the Millennium can arrive, there are, I fear, yet to be exhibited in our world, and especially on the old Latin earth, scenes from which, if we could fully anticipate them, the stoutest heart would turn away appalled and shuddering. Yes; scenes of which to hear, in the most distant manner, will make the ears of the men of that generation tingle! The great day of the battle of God Almighty is yet to come: a battle which must rage with peculiar violence on the site of that empire of persecution and blood, over which Satan, for so many ages, reigned. God grant that our beloved country, which has so little of the blood of the saints in its skirts, may be in a great measure exempted from the horrors of that awful scene! But, however this may be, let no man's heart fail him on that account; nay, let no effort be paralysed by the anticipation of the dreadful conflict. For the elects' sake, it shall be shortened. And I had almost said, Let Christians of the present day be united and diligent in doing their duty,—in spreading the gospel,—and in besieging the throne of grace—*and the conflict shall be made shorter still!* And even amidst the utmost fury of its rage, let it never be forgotten, that it is the indispensable harbinger of blessings unparalleled and glorious! Again, then, I say, Let no man's heart fail him at the prospect. 'The Lord of hosts is with us; the God of Jacob is our refuge. *Selah' (Psa.* 46:11).

From what has been said, we may learn,

1. *How great a blessing it is to be favoured with the gospel of Christ!* It is almost as incredible as it is humiliating, how prone we are, when a blessing is familiarly enjoyed, to forget its value, and to forget our obligations for it. So it is with the light of day. So it is with the vital air which we breathe, and with our daily food. And so it is, pre-

eminently with the light and the privileges, of the gospel. We have enjoyed them so long and so constantly, that we are ready to consider them, not only as matters of course, but almost, in a sort, as our right. We forget that to them we are indebted for our personal safety, for our domestic purity and peace, and for our social order, and happiness, as well as for all our spiritual knowledge and hopes. But, to correct this error, let us often think of the darkness and desolation of the poor pagans. And let us again recollect that our ancestors were once in the same situation. Yes, Brethren; within the reach of authentic history, the inhabitants of the British Isles were miserable savages and idolaters, offering human and other sacrifices to dumb idols, and sunk in all the sottish corruption and misery of paganism. Such were our fathers! But God had mercy on them, and sent missionaries to them, to teach them the way of life. And from them the blessing has been transmitted to us. Through the tender mercy of our God, the dayspring from on high has visited us, to guide our feet in the way of peace. The lines have fallen unto us in pleasant places, yea we have a goodly heritage. Blessed are our eyes, for they see, and our ears, for they hear; for many prophets and righteous men desired to see the things which we see, but never saw them, and to hear the things which we hear, but never heard them. Bless the Lord, our souls, and all that is within us, bless his holy name; bless the Lord, O our souls, and forget not all his benefits (*Luke* 1:78; *Psa.* 16:6; *Matt.* 13:16; *Psa.* 103:1-3).

2. We learn, from the foregoing remarks, that *the cause of missions is decisively the most important and interesting cause in the world; and that the duty of prosecuting it as extensively as possible, is, at once manifest, and most imperative.*

To show the unspeakable greatness and importance of the cause of missions, nothing more, I am persuaded, is necessary before a Christian audience, than to remind them what that cause is; to remind them that it is the same cause in which the eternal counsels of peace were engaged; the same cause for which the divine Redeemer descended from heaven, and underwent all the humiliation and sufferings of his incarnate state. It is the cause which has for its object the extension of the Saviour's reign, and raising millions of our fellow men from deplorable darkness and desolation, to temporal and eternal blessedness. Yes, it is the *great cause,* in comparison with which *all others sink unto nothing.* Let the worldly philosopher and statesman, dazzled with the artificial splendour of their respective little worlds, imagine that the subject of missions is a minor matter, which nothing but fanaticism magnifies into much importance. Alas! they know no better. They are blind to the real character of this great object. The cause which they undervalue, will, in a little while, be seen and acknowledged to be the cause of God, of glory, and of eternity, when all the petty plans and efforts which now fill their vision and their hearts, shall be lost in oblivion.

No Christian is at liberty to consider himself as discharged from the duty of aiding in this great cause. Every disciple of Christ under heaven is bound to do *all in his power* to impart the glad tidings of salvation to all others who have it not. And never will this obligation cease, until the gospel has been actually preached to every nation, and kindred, and tongue and people. As long as there is a single nation remaining pagan, our efforts to send them the gospel, ought not to be abandoned, or even relaxed. Nay, as long as a single individual of our species is known to be ignorant of Christ, it would be worth while to go to all the expense and trouble of circumnavigating the globe, to carry to that individual the knowledge of salvation.

I am aware that some who profess to love the cause of missions, have seriously questioned the wisdom and the duty of sending missionaries to Asia and to the islands of the Pacific Ocean, while there remain so many literal heathen, as well as so many destitute frontier settlements, in our own land, to whom the heralds of salvation are yet to be sent.

Into the general discussion of this subject, it is impossible, at present, to enter. A word or two only can be indulged. It is manifest that if the apostles and primitive Christians had acted upon the principle of these objectors, the progress of the gospel would have been much more slow, and confined within much narrower limits, than it was. But, blessed be God! they did not act upon it. They sent forth missionaries to distant regions, passing by, for a time, many waste and desolate places in their more immediate neighbourhood; and establishing a number of great centres of evangelical light and action in the midst of Satan's empire. This was a wise plan at that time, or else inspired men would never have adopted it, and it is a wise plan still. And, for myself, I have no fear, that following their example, will prevent, or, for an hour, retard the progress of the gospel among the frontier settlements, or the heathen on our borders. On the contrary, I am persuaded, that from every foreign missionary station on which God is pleased to pour out his Spirit, a blessed influence never fails to react, not only all around it, but also, and in no small degree, upon the Christian population of our own land; exciting on the subject of missions a deeper interest, and more fervent prayers; and eventually calling forth larger contributions, and more missionaries, for domestic as well as for foreign purposes. All experience demonstrates that we are never so likely to receive an ample blessing at home, as when we open our hearts, and send help to our brethren abroad.

My *Honoured and Reverend Associates of the Board of Missions!* The trust reposed in us is solemn and interesting in the highest degree! To be called especially and jointly to engage in this noblest of all causes, is a privilege and an honour which we can never adequately prize. If we made the estimate of it which we ought, we should come, every successive year, to the discharge of our duty, with augmented pleasure and zeal, and never think that we had done, or could do a thousandth part enough in such a cause. Oh! if the glorified spirits of our departed fellow-members could speak to us from their mansions of rest: if the beloved and venerated Dwight and Worcester could re-visit our Board, and tell us what their estimate now is of that cause in which they were once engaged with us here;—would it be, think you, to intimate that they had loved it too much, or had been more devoted to it than it deserved? Oh, no: on the contrary, it would be to say, that they now see in it an importance and a glory unspeakably greater than they ever saw in this world; and to conjure us to pursue it with growing ardour and affection.

3. We may learn from this subject, not only the importance of the missionary cause; but also *the great encouragement which we have to persevere in the pursuit of it.*—We have the best encouragement in the world; the encouragement derived from the assurance that we shall not labour in vain. We know that it is a cause which must and will succeed. The promise of him who cannot lie has gone forth: and will

anyone dare to say either that he cannot or will not accomplish what he has promised? Let us, then, hold on our way, with all the alacrity and confidence of those who anticipate a speedy and a glorious conquest. Let us be steadfast, unmovable, always abounding in the work of the Lord, forasmuch as we know that our labour shall not be in vain in the Lord (*1 Cor.* 15:58). What though apparently adverse dispensations of providence now and then occur? What though some of those missionaries, from whose labours much was expected, are taken away, prematurely as it appears to us, by death? What though that ample success, for which we have been waiting and praying, be delayed longer than we had confidently anticipated? Still let none be discouraged. The Lord is not slack concerning his promise, as some men count slackness. Let us, therefore, be patient. Behold the husbandman waiteth for the precious fruit of the earth, and hath long patience for it, until he receive the early and the latter rain. Let us also be patient, and stablish our hearts, for the coming of the Lord draweth nigh.

And, while we are thus waiting, let us remember where our only hope and encouragement be. Only in the power and faithfulness of our covenant God. Without Jehovah, the king of Zion, we can do nothing. Except the Lord build the house, they labour in vain that build it. Unless the Spirit of God preside in our counsels, and go forth with those whom we send, as a Spirit of counsel and of might, of understanding, and of the fear of the Lord, all that we attempt will be in vain. Yes; all the wisdom which this age of literature and of science can produce; all the funds which the east and the west, the north and the south can furnish, will prove altogether ineffectual, unless the Almighty King of Zion add his blessing. While we plan and labour, then, let us pray without ceasing for that blessing. Let us constantly look, and long, and entreat for the display of that mighty power of God, which is, after all, our only hope. Awake, awake, put on strength, O arm of the Lord! Awake, as in the ancient days, in the generations of old. Art thou not it that hath cut Rahab, and wounded the Dragon? Art thou not it which hath dried up the sea, the waters of the great deep; that hath made the depths of the sea a way for the ransomed to pass over? (*Isa.* 51:9, 10).

4. We learn, again, from what has been said, *how great is the privilege and the honour of being a missionary*. When I speak of the honour of being a missionary, I have no reference to the applause of men; no reference to that sort of reputation which he may derive from having his name emblazoned in every gazette and magazine and his labours and success lauded by the reports and orators of respectable societies. This is a kind of honour, which principles greatly inferior to those of Christianity ought to teach every man to value at a very low rate. But I speak of honours infinitely more valuable; honours which, though they have nothing attractive or desirable in the eyes of an unbelieving world, will be estimated above all price by men of true wisdom;—the honour of receiving the approbation of God—the honour of being employed as instruments to build up his kingdom, and promote his glory. These are the honours, my respected and beloved young Friends, who are this day to be set apart for missionary work,—these are the honours which, I trust, will be yours. You are going forth to attempt, as God shall enable you, to repair the 'waste places', to build up the 'desolations of many generations'. You are going forth to be, as your Master was, the restorers of paths to dwell in. The predecessors of all those to whom you are about to be sent once enjoyed the true religion, or had it placed within their reach. But they rejected the precious offering, and sunk down into darkness, corruption and misery. You go, if, happily, you may be made, by the blessing of God, instrumental in raising them from their degradation, pouring light on their darkness, comforting them in their sorrows, delivering them from their old desolations; in a word, teaching them how to be happy in this world, and eternally blessed in the world to come. What a noble, what a delightful, what a godlike employment is here! and yet how arduous! Who is sufficient for these things? If you desire, in any measure to attain the object for which you are sent, be careful to carry, wherever you go, the pure gospel. Know nothing but Jesus Christ and him crucified. Hold forth, with simplicity and fidelity, the Word of life. And, having done this, place all your reliance on the power of God to crown your work with success. Paul may plant, and Apollos may water, but God giveth the increase. Neither is he that planteth anything, nor he that watereth anything, but God that giveth the increase (*1 Cor.* 3:5-7). Difficulties and trials will certainly await you.

Nothing great or precious, in this lost world, was ever accomplished without them. But if they are made the means of keeping you more humble, and nearer to God, they will become, however painful, the means of promoting the grand object which you seek—the furtherance of the gospel. Go in peace; and may the God of love and of peace go with you!

5. Finally, *while we are taking measures for sending the gospel to others, have we all embraced it practically and savingly for ourselves?*

We have heard of great things, my Friends, which God will certainly accomplish for his church. But there is every reason to believe, that before they can be completely accomplished, all of us, who are now seated before the Lord, shall have gone to judgment, and have entered on our eternal state. Are we prepared for that judgment? We speak much, and we, perhaps, give something, for sending the gospel to the heathen; but are there no heathen in this audience? O, my fellow Mortals! that very Saviour whom we wish to proclaim to the benighted nations, must be cordially embraced by us, or we shall never see life. That same pardoning mercy and sanctifying grace, which we are desirous of having preached in the dark places of the earth, must be experimentally known by us, or we shall die in our sins. All our privileges, however rich and various, will fall utterly short of saving us. Saving us, did I say? If not practically improved, they will but sink us into a deeper perdition than we should have incurred if we had never enjoyed them. We must be washed, and justified, and sanctified, in the name of the Lord Jesus, and by the spirit of our God. Then, if we die before the Millennium arrives, it will be to go to a brighter and better world, than even millennial glory can render this theatre of rebellion and suffering. Then, from the heights of the upper sanctuary, we shall look down on the Saviour's triumphs here below, with joy unspeakable and full of glory. In the meantime, let us aspire to the honour of being workers together with God, in hastening on those triumphs. Let the language of our hearts, and of our conduct, as well as of our lips, unceasingly be—Come, Lord Jesus! come quickly; even so come, Lord Jesus! Amen.

THE PUBLIC WORSHIP OF GOD[1]

Now, therefore, arise, O Lord God, into thy resting place,
thou, and the ark of thy strength.
2 Chronicles 6:41

T HE history of buildings and places devoted to the worship
of God, especially in the earlier periods of the church, is very
obscure. In the patriarchal age, we have no distinct record of
anything of this kind. That the pious, from Adam to Moses, were no
strangers to the social exercises of religion, can hardly be doubted:
and if they had stated social worship, we must suppose they had particular places to which they resorted for that purpose. Accordingly,
when Cain, by murdering his brother, had forfeited his former standing as a professor of religion, we are told that 'he went out from
the presence of the Lord'; by which commentators have generally
understood to be meant, that he no longer associated with the people
of God; that he no more frequented the place where sacrifices were
wont to be offered; but became, literally, excommunicated from the
visible church. In subsequent times we find the pious, wherever they
sojourned, or fixed their residence, erecting altars, at which they, and
probably their households, worshipped God. Thus did Noah, and
thus, after him, did Abraham and Jacob, on a variety of occasions.
The tabernacle, reared by divine direction in the wilderness of Arabia,
on the journey of the chosen people of God from Egypt to Canaan,
more than twenty-five centuries after the visible church was established, seems to have been the first movable structure, and the temple

[1] Samuel Miller, *A Sermon, Delivered June Seventh, 1823, at the Opening of the New
Presbyterian Church, in Arch Street, in the City of Philadelphia, for the Public Worship
of God* (Philadelphia: T. T. Ash, 1823).

446

of Solomon, at Jerusalem, the first fixed edifice that was ever erected for a religious purpose.

The temple of Solomon has been justly styled the wonder and glory of the East. It was certainly, on many accounts, the most remarkable edifice that was ever erected. Imagine, for a moment, a building of which 'Jehovah himself condescended to be the architect.' A building, in the construction of which, scarcely anything appeared of less value than silver and gold. A building on which was bestowed the labour of 180,000 workmen for more than seven years. And a building in which there was, no doubt, a greater display of grandeur, taste, and beauty than in any other structure that was ever raised by the hand of man.

But all this external splendour and glory did not satisfy the pious mind of Solomon. After bestowing upon the outward adorning of this temple, all that his exalted genius and his royal treasures, under the special direction of God, enabled him to afford, he still acknowledges, in his prayer at its dedication—of which our text is a part— that the ornament, the glory which he values most, is the presence of Jehovah in the house which he had erected to his name. 'Now, therefore, arise, O Lord God, into thy resting place, thou and the ark of thy strength!' As if he had said—The art of man has done all that it can accomplish. But vain will be everything, unless the Lord himself come and take up his abode in the temple which we have raised to his glory. Come then, thou God of the house, and crown our labours with thy presence! Come, thou, and enter in, and dwell here: and this will be the consummation of our desires.

The ark of God, to which the royal suppliant here refers, was the ark of the covenant, originally formed by divine direction in the wilderness, and deposited in the Most Holy Place, first in the tabernacle, and afterwards in the temple. On the interesting occasion on which the words of our text were delivered, this ark was with much solemnity brought, and, for the first time, placed in the house of God, as the most precious part of its furniture. It was called the ark of Jehovah's strength, because it was a pledge of his presence; and because it was attended, whithersoever it went, with most remarkable manifestations of divine power. And the temple, in which it was now deposited, is represented as the resting place of God and his ark, because, after many removals, for the space of several hundred years, this symbol of the divine presence and glory, was, at length, fixed in the Most Holy Place in the temple, as its permanent and final abode.

Although, in this prayer of Solomon, there was, no doubt, something asked which was peculiar to the temple, and to the dispensation under which it was erected; and for which we, of course, cannot ask in behalf of any place of worship under the Christian dispensation; yet there is also something in its import common to all ages, and which applies to every place in which God is worshipped. It, therefore, forms a proper subject of discourse at this time.

The blessing here implored is the presence and power of God; and that to be displayed in a house devoted to his worship. Let us inquire into the *nature* and the *value* of this blessing. And while we speak of it, may the great Master of assemblies cause us to experience its blessed reality, to the glory of his holy name!

I. The first question which arises is, *what is the nature of the blessing here implored?* What are we to understand by that *presence* and *power* of God, in a house devoted to his worship, which, under the gospel dispensation, we may properly ask and hope to receive?

God is everywhere present. There is a sense in which, according to the language of the Apostle Paul, in his sermon at Athens, 'He dwelleth not in temples made with hands';—that is, he is not, as the pagans imagined, concerning their deities, confined to particular buildings or places. All space is his temple. Every part of the universe is his abode. This most impressive, and incomprehensibly glorious doctrine is suggested by Solomon in the very prayer of which our text is a part. 'Will God, in very deed', he asks, 'dwell with man on the earth? Behold, the heaven, and the heaven of heavens cannot, contain thee; how much less this house which I have builded!' This is the *essential presence* of God. It is the same at all times, and in all places. It is the same in heaven, earth, and hell, it pervades the universe; supporting, actuating, and controlling all creatures, and all their actions. The Most High can no more cease, for a moment, to be present everywhere, than he can cease to be God.

There is another sense in which God was present in certain buildings and places, under the Old Testament dispensation; and which, so far as we know, was confined to that dispensation, I mean the manner in which he was present, and manifested his power at Luz, in the wilderness, when the patriarch Jacob cried out under a sense of it—'How dreadful is this place! Surely the Lord is in this place! Verily, this is none other than the house of God, and this is the gate of heaven!' (*Gen.* 28:16, 17). Jehovah was also present, in a similar manner, at the burning bush in Midian, when he appeared and spoke to Moses, and said,—'Put off thy shoes from off thy feet, for the place whereon thou standeth is holy ground' (*Exod.* 3:5). Another example of this solemn presence and manifestation of the divine glory, was exhibited at Mount Sinai, when the people were forbidden to approach the mountain on account of it; when thunderings, and lightnings, and earthquake, struck terror into the whole congregation of Israel, and constrained even Moses, with all his piety and heroism, and all his holy familiarity with God, to say—'I exceedingly fear and quake' (*Heb.* 12:21). And, finally, of this presence and manifestation of the divine glory, we have a signal example in the Shekinah, or visible token of the majesty of God, which, for ages, appeared over the mercy-seat, in the Most Holy Place in the tabernacle, and afterwards in the temple. For, although there was considerable diversity of mode in which the divine presence was manifested in each of these several cases; yet they may all be regarded as coming under one general law, as referable to one general class. This may be called the *miraculous,* or *extraordinary presence* of God. It was a presence which addressed itself to the external senses. It was visible and audible; and it imparted a relative holiness to the places in which it was manifested. This relative holiness, in some cases at least, depended not upon the presence of worshippers. It was adherent, if I may so express it, to the buildings and places themselves. They were, properly speaking—especially those which were last mentioned—*consecrated* buildings and places. Whether there was a worshipper or not in the tabernacle, or in the temple, still the Shekinah, or visible glory of God, overspread the mercy-seat; and anyone who profanely entered the sacred apartment, or even glanced an eye, contrary to the divine injunction, on the august symbol, was considered as a capital offender against the majesty of heaven, and inevitably perished.

In this sense, we are not to expect, or to ask, the Most High to dwell in any building, or in any place, under the gospel dispensation. That particular mode of manifesting the divine glory to the church, was chiefly, if not entirely, confined to the ceremonial economy, and, of course, terminated when that economy was abolished.

But there is a *third sense,* in which God may be said to be present, in those places or buildings which are devoted to his worship. I refer to his spiritual and *gracious* presence. Jehovah dwells, by the power of the Holy Spirit, in every sanctified heart. 'Thus saith the high and lofty One that inhabiteth eternity, I dwell in the high and holy place, and with him also that is contrite, and of an humble spirit, and that trembleth at my word' (*Isa.* 57:15; 64:2). And in conformity with this representation, the Apostle Paul says to believers, 'What, know ye not that ye are the temple of God, and that the Spirit of God dwelleth in you?' 'As God hath said, I will dwell in them, and walk in them, and I will be their God, and they shall be my people' (*1 Cor.* 3:16; *2 Cor.* 6:16). Wherever, then, there is an humble, contrite, believing heart, there Jehovah is spiritually and graciously present; present to enlighten, to sanctify, to comfort, and to bless. Wherever a sincere and devout worshipper lifts up his soul in faith and love to heaven, whether in the closet or in the field; on the trackless ocean or in the lonely desert, he may find and enjoy a present God. In this respect, as was said with regard to his essential presence, God is confined to no times, to no places, to no forms. Wherever there is a holy heart, of whatever kindred or people, or nation, or tongue, he comes in to him, and makes his abode with him.

But, as Jehovah always has had, and always will have, a respect to his covenant, and will put honour upon the ordinances of his own appointment; so wherever his people are assembled for acts of social worship, he has promised to favour them, in a special manner, with his gracious presence:—and, in attending on the ordinances of his house, they are encouraged to expect the divine presence, in a manner which they may not ordinarily hope for in the neglect of these ordinances. 'Where two or three are gathered together', said the Saviour, 'in my name there am I in the midst of them' (*Matt.* 18:20). 'The Lord', says the psalmist, 'loveth the gates of Zion more than all the dwellings of Jacob. The Lord hath chosen Zion: he hath desired it for an habitation: this is my rest forever; here will I dwell, for I have desired it' (*Psa.* 87:2; 132:13, 14). Yes, my Christian Friends—in the sanctuary, that is, in the place where the people of God habitually convene, wherever that may be, to hear his holy Word, to sing his praise, to pour out the prayer of faith, and to receive the sacramental seal—there, in a special manner, Jehovah, the King of Zion is present with them: there he accepts both their persons and their offerings: there he manifests himself to them, as he does not to the world: there he draws near to them in mercy, and enables them to draw near to him in the lively exercise of grace: there he lifts upon them the light of his countenance, and gives them joy and peace in believing: there he brings them into his banqueting house, and his banner over them is love.

The foregoing principles and remarks will, I conceive, enable us to determine in what sense we are to invoke, and to expect, the presence and the power of God, in places devoted to his worship, under the gospel dispensation, and in what sense we are not. We are not, by any means, as I just intimated, to invoke, or to expect this blessing in the same mode in which it was manifested in a number of cases, under the Mosaic economy, and especially in the tabernacle and temple of old. We are not to invoke or to expect it in any sense which implies either intrinsic or relative holiness in such buildings or places. *Intrinsic* holiness can be ascribed to nothing but the real, spiritual church,—the body of believers, whom the Redeemer hath purchased with his blood, and sanctified by his Spirit: and *relative* holiness can be ascribed to nothing but that which is devoted exclusively to holy purposes. The Most Holy Place, under the ceremonial economy, could be entered by only one individual of all the nation of Israel, and by him only once a year. And even into the Holy Place none might enter or so much as look, but those who bore the sacerdotal character. But a little reflection will convince us that our places of public worship cannot be holy, even in this latter sense, so long as they are open to the worldly as well as the pious; so long as we permit the profane and unbelieving to come and mingle in our assemblies, with the most spiritual and exemplary worshippers. When, therefore, we adopt the prayer of our text in reference to this house, it is not, that its seats and aisles, its columns and arches may have some mysterious sanctity impressed upon them, but that God may be pleased to manifest his spiritual presence—his gracious power to his people, when they shall assemble here from time to time: that here sinners may be convinced and converted, and saints edified and comforted; that here he may bless the provisions of his house, and satisfy his poor with bread: that here he may clothe his ministers with salvation, and cause his saints to shout aloud for joy. And the more frequently and powerfully these manifestations of his gracious, life-giving, and sanctifying influence are enjoyed, the more largely is the blessing implored in our text conferred.

It was said by the inspired prophet Haggai, concerning the second temple, erected by a set of impoverished returning captives—'The glory of this latter house shall be greater than the glory of the former' (*Hag*. 2:9). What was the prophet's meaning? The temple of which this was spoken, was greatly, I had almost said infinitely, inferior to that which Solomon dedicated, when he uttered the words of our text. Inferior in cost, in splendour, in furniture, and in all its outward glories. It even lacked that ark of Jehovah's strength, which adorned the first edifice, and that symbol of the divine presence which over-spread the mercy-seat above. Yet still it was really more glorious than the former temple. Why so? Because it was favoured with the pres-ence of Christ himself, in a sense more truly valuable and glorious than anything vouchsafed under the ceremonial dispensation. The Redeemer was present *personally*, and by his *blessed Spirit* in this sec-ond temple:—present in a manner far more adapted to enlighten, to purify, to elevate, and to bless, than that presence which had been the honour of the original structure. And, let me add, that the humblest and meanest edifice which is favoured with the spiritual presence of the King of Zion is, in all cases whatsoever, beyond comparison, more glorious than the most magnificent temple, the glories of which are all of the outward and secular kind.

The primitive Christians, my Friends, had no such temples for the worship of God, as that in which we are now assembled. They held their solemn assemblies in private houses,—in retired upper cham-bers,—in cellars,—in caves,—and even in vaults, in which the dead were deposited. It was not, as is generally believed, until some time in the latter half of the third century, that they began to erect houses for the express purpose of public worship. And even these, at first, were of the most plain and simple kind. It was *then*—mark it well—when the disciples of Christ were persecuted on every side, and when they had neither the means nor the privilege of raising those expensive and splendid structures for the worship of God, which afterwards became so common—it was *then* that they enjoyed, in a pre-eminent degree, the presence and the gracious power of their ascended Master. It was then that the blessing implored in our text, in its proper gospel sense, was, perhaps, more happily and gloriously realized than ever before or since. Yes, Brethren, it was in those early times, when the church had none of that external splendour thrown around her, which dazzles the eyes, and attracts the admiration of the worldly minded; when magnificent temples and rich ecclesiastical endowments were unknown; when all was simple and unostentatious, and humble:— it was *then,* pre-eminently, that the King of Zion dwelt among his people. Then the word of the Lord had free course, and was glorified. Then the churches were built up in the most holy faith—and converts, walking in the fear of the Lord, and in the comfort of the Holy Ghost, were multiplied. Then, in a word, the Spirit and presence of Christ, dwelling and reigning among his people, and manifested in all the ordinances of his appointment, and in holy tempers and practice formed the brightest era in the history of the church.

But when, in the fourth century, the fires of persecution were quenched; when the wealth and grandeur of the world began to take the side of Christianity; when Constantine the Great loaded ecclesiastics with multiplied honours, and lavished his imperial treasures on the erection and endowment of splendid cathedrals; when the ministers of the sanctuary, instead of directing all their attention to the true spiritual interests of the Redeemer's kingdom, began to expend their energies in the pomp and toil of a gaudy ritual, and to exceed paganism itself, in outward glory;—then the spirit and power of Christ, in the same proportion, departed from the church. As the ceremonial of piety increased, the reality of it gradually declined. The more splendid professions and mock consecrations were multiplied, the less power did real holiness maintain over the hearts and lives of men. In short, the more laboriously men strove to impart holiness to those things to which it never was, or could be imparted, the more miserably did they fail of manifesting it in those things to which it did properly belong, and in which it ought to have been manifested. Hence arose, in this century, for the first time, so far as history informs us, the pompous consecration of churches, with many superstitious notions relative to their holiness; and several centuries afterwards, the consecration of church-yards, church bells, and church vessels;—notions and practices which have generally had most stress laid upon them in those churches and times in which the genuine spirit of the gospel had least practical influence.

I mention these things, my Friends, not by any means for the purpose of imputing blame to those who may differ from us in opinion on this subject; but merely to show how prone professing Christians have been, in all ages, to mistake the real nature of that blessing of which we are speaking, and which it is a part of the appropriate service of this day to implore. To show that, in fact, where there has been most external magnificence and splendour, most laboured ceremonial, and outward glory, there has commonly been least of that spiritual presence and power of the King of Zion, which is the true happiness and glory of the church. And, on the contrary, that some of those periods which have been most remarkable for affliction and depression, with respect to the external church, have been distinguished by the most signal displays of her Master's power and love;—the Word and ordinances have been accompanied with a peculiar divine energy;—vital piety has been more deep and prevalent; the flame of faith, and love, and universal holiness, have risen far higher, and shone with a far brighter lustre than in more externally prosperous seasons. And happy is that church, the members of which, understanding the real nature of the blessing in question, and holding everything else subordinate to it, cease not to pray for its attainment, and to pursue that humble, spiritual course, which is adapted, under the government of a faithful and prayer-hearing God, to draw it down in its most plenteous effusions!

Having thus briefly considered the nature of this blessing, let us,

II. Attend to its *value*. The wise man prays for it as for a most important object; as something which he deemed far more desirable and precious than all the outward splendour that the wealth and the art of man could confer.

Need I stop, my Friends, to show, by formal reasoning, that the wise man's estimate of this matter was correct;—that the presence and the gracious power of the great Head of the church, is the richest, the most precious blessing that any church can receive;—that, however poor and depressed in her external condition, if she be favoured with a large measure of this blessing, she is rich indeed; but that, if she have it not, though loaded with all the wealth, and honours, and outward prosperity that a flattering world can bestow—she is poor and miserable, and would appear so in her own view, if she could see herself in a just light?

What, let me ask, is the great design of the church? If it be, indeed, as many seem to imagine, an institution the chief object of which is to polish and adorn the surface of society:—if its grand purpose be merely to furnish objects which shall dazzle the senses, gratify the imagination, cultivate the taste, and soften the manners of men:—if it be intended, in short, to furnish a place for an elegant and entertaining lounge on the Lord's day; to supply on special occasions the pageant of an imposing ceremonial; to seal us with the Christian name, when we enter the world, and to solemnize with appropriate exercises our sepulture, when we leave it:—if such be the chief design of the church—then, indeed, we might suppose, that the greater its external glory, the more perfectly it would answer the great purpose which it was intended to subserve; and that nothing else was really essential to the attainment of its highest benefits.

But if the church has been established by its all-wise and all-gracious Master, that it may be a nursery for heaven;—if, to this end, everything respecting it has been so prescribed by infinite Wisdom and Love, as to render it admirably adapted to become the birth-place of souls;—the means of convincing and converting sinners, and of enlightening and comforting believers;—if, in a word, the great design of the church is to be the depository of Jehovah's truth and ordinances;—to bear witness to his gospel and his glory, before an unbelieving world;—and to become the means of sanctifying the hearts and lives of men, and thus preparing them to be happy members of the society of their fellow men, in this world, and above all to be partakers of the holy joys of his presence in the world to come:—if such be the great design of the church; the great purpose for which it was originally founded, and for which it is still preserved and sup-ported;—then, surely, the gracious presence, the sanctifying power of Christ, is the most invaluable blessing that can be conferred on the church at large, or on any particular branch of it. It is the grand bless-ing which the friends of Zion ought to desire above all others, and for which they are bound to labour and pray without ceasing.

It is only so far as the gracious presence and blessing of Christ are vouchsafed to his church;—it is only so far as the King of Zion con-descends to come and dwell in it, with the 'ark of his strength', that any real spiritual benefits are enjoyed by his people. Without his gra-cious presence, there is no true spiritual worship, no profitable hear-ing of the Word, no real benefit in ordinances. We may write upon them all—*Ichabod*—'for the glory is departed!' But when the King comes, in the power of his grace and love, into those places in which his name is recorded,—then his Word is quick and powerful,—reli-gion is revived,—times of refreshing come;—many hear the voice of the Son of God, and they that hear are made to live; multitudes are seen asking the way to Zion, with their faces thitherward, and say-ing—'Come let us join ourselves to the Lord in a perpetual covenant never to be forgotten.'

Further, it is the gracious presence and blessing of Christ which renders the service of the sanctuary *delightful,* as well as beneficial to his people. Without this blessing, all is dull and comfortless; but with it, all is light, and peace and joy. When this is enjoyed, and then only, the pious can say, with experimental pleasure, How amiable are thy tabernacles, Lord of hosts! A day in thy courts is better than a thou-sand. My soul thirsteth, yea even longeth, for the courts of the Lord. My soul is satisfied as with marrow and fatness. I sat down under his shadow with delight, and his fruit was sweet to my taste.

In short, what the light and genial warmth of the sun are to the natural world, that, and unspeakably more, is the presence of Christ with his church and people. It brings life, and growth, and fruitful-ness, wherever, and in proportion to the degree in which it is con-ferred. It quickens the spiritually dead;—warms and excites to activ-ity the cold and ice-bound believer; and causes fruit to abound where all had been barrenness and sterility before. What is *hell,* but being banished forever from the presence of the Lord, and from the glory of his power? And what is *heaven,* and the *heaven of heavens,* but the uninterrupted and everlasting enjoyment of him whose favour is life, and whose loving kindness is better than life? What is the essence of the celestial blessedness, but enjoying without a cloud, and without measure, that gracious presence of God which is vouchsafed in a degree whenever a soul dead in trespasses and sins, is raised to newness of life, or a child of God filled with joy and peace in believing? 'I shall be satisfied', says one, 'when I awake with thy likeness.' 'In thy presence is fulness of joy, and at thy right hand are pleasures forever more' (*Psa.* 17:15; 16:11).

Permit me, now, Brethren, to employ the foregoing illustration of the text for the purpose of enforcing several practical considerations, which appear to be suggested by what has been said, and by the solemnities of this day.

1. And the first practical lesson which our subject suggests is, that *professing Christians are everywhere bound, as far as possible, to provide themselves with commodious and comfortable houses for the purpose of worshipping God.* We are not, indeed, bound, nay, I think, we are not at liberty, under the simple spiritual dispensation in which our lot is cast, to emulate, even if it were in our power, the splendour or expense of the Old Testament temple. The unrivalled richness and glory of that wonderful edifice, were intended to answer great typical and ceremonial purposes, which called for everything that was bestowed upon it. But the same thing, I apprehend, would not be lawful, without a special divine warrant, under the present dispensation. To expend millions upon a single place of worship now, while thousands of poor around us are suffering for bread, and while a great majority of our race are still covered with pagan darkness, and perishing for lack of knowledge,—appears so unreasonable and criminal, that I hope we are in no danger of going to that extreme. But another, and perhaps, a much more common extreme, especially in our church, taken at large, is, contenting ourselves with mean and uncomfortable houses in which to worship God. Nay, it is not very uncommon, in some districts, for a number of the opulent members of our truly primitive and apostolical church, to dwell themselves in ceiled houses, while the house of God lies, comparatively, waste. This, I will venture to say, is both disreputable and criminal. We ought always

to be ready to serve God with *the best that we possess*. No worshipper ought ever to be willing to live in a better house than that which he, with others, has devoted to his Maker and Redeemer.—And while, on the one hand, that splendour and magnificence of architecture, which is adapted to arrest and occupy the mind, and to draw it away from spiritual objects, ought carefully to be avoided; and avoided, not merely on the score of expense, but of Christian edification; so, on the other hand, that simple tasteful elegance, on which the eye is apt to rest with composed satisfaction; that studious provision for perfect convenience and comfort, which is calculated to place every worshipper in circumstances favourable to tranquil, undivided and devout attention, ought to be always and carefully consulted by every congregation, that is able to accomplish what is desirable in these respects.[1] And perhaps it may not be improper to add, that all this

[1] May it not be questioned, whether the principles which ought to regulate our conduct in relation to this subject, have been at all times duly regarded? It is a law of our mental, as well as of our physical nature, that two classes of emotions cannot be in a high, certainly not in a governing, degree of exercise at the same time. Whenever, therefore, we assemble for the worship of God in situations in which we are constantly surrounded and addressed by the most exquisite productions of art, which arrest and engross the mind, we are, plainly, not in circumstances favourable to true spiritual worship. Would any rational man expect to find himself really devout in St Peter's, at Rome, even if the most scriptural service were performed within its walls, until he should have become so familiar with the unrivalled specimens of taste and grandeur around him, as to forget or cease to feel them? Or, would anyone be likely to 'make melody in his heart to the Lord', while the most skilful and touching refinements of music saluted and ravished his ears? Thrilled and transported he might be; but it would rather be the transport of natural taste, than the heavenliness of spiritual devotion. There never was a sounder maxim than that delivered in the plain and homely, but forcible, language of the celebrated Mr Poole, the learned compiler of the *Synopsis Criticorum,* so well known throughout the Christian world, in the preface to a sermon, entitled 'Evangelical Obedience', and preached before the Lord Mayor of London, in 1660. Amidst much other excellent matter, the author observes—'the more inveiglements there are to sense, the more disadvantage to the spirit'. No one, of course, will consider this maxim as intended to teach, that, in order to promote the spirit of true devotion, it is necessary or desirable to be surrounded with that which is mean, irregular, or disgusting to the mind of taste. On the contrary, the fact is, that such mean and disgusting objects tend to arrest and draw away the mind in an opposite and painful manner; and are thus, perhaps, with respect to many persons, quite as unfriendly to the exercises of calm piety, as

is, in my judgment, peculiarly important in *great cities,* where the point of taste is more generally consulted, and where the style and magnitude of surrounding objects seem to demand more attention to appearances, than may be absolutely necessary, or even truly useful, in a different situation.

You have, therefore, in my opinion, acted wisely, my Friends, in the erection of this edifice. It was a measure which you owed to yourselves, to your children, and to the church of God. Some of you have already vested, and others will vest, no small amount of property here. I pray you grudge not the investment. Perhaps it will prove to be the best part of your estate. It certainly *will* prove to be so, if you honestly desire and implore that blessing from the King of Zion of which we have been speaking. And, at any rate, if, by aiding to erect such a temple to the living God, as will be likely to attract and fix within the sound of the gospel, many a wavering family or individual, you are made instrumental in conferring benefits, inconceivably precious in their nature, and endless in their duration, on many immortal souls, think you that you will ever regret the expenditure? No, my Friends, rather will you have reason to rejoice in it more and more forever!

2. The spirit of our text seems evidently to intimate, that *the practice of opening houses of public worship with appropriate religious exercises, is a rational and laudable custom.*

I am no friend, my respected hearers, to many of those ideas, in relation to this subject, which have had much currency among serious people, in different ages, and which are now received by no small portion of the community; as if, by the solemnities which attend the first opening of a church for public worship, it became, properly, a consecrated building; in other words, as if there were a kind of inherent sanctity imparted to the edifice itself; a sanctity which communicated some mysterious efficacy to the religious services

---

the utmost fascinations of art can be. The obvious inference from the whole, then, is, that, for the house of God no style of architecture or of music is so favourable to the most elevated exercises of pious affection, as that simple, correct, tasteful style, on which the mind rests with tranquil, composed gratification, without being either painfully occupied with emotions of disgust, or captivated and borne away by those of sensitive pleasure. The happy medium, in this, as in most things, is conducive to the highest degree of edification: while all short of it, and all beyond it, will seldom fail of proving injurious.

performed within its walls. I know of nothing, either in Scripture, or in the records of the primitive church, which gives the smallest countenance to ideas of this kind. I know of no warrant, as I before intimated, for believing that holiness can be imparted to the walls, or arches, or seats, within which we assemble to worship God. And when we recollect the mischievous superstitions, and delusive hopes which have been so extensively generated, in all ages, by the doctrine in question, it surely cannot be considered as a very profitable, or even innocent doctrine.

But, in receding from an error on this side, let us not fall into one on the other. Because the idea of 'consecrating a church', as that phrase is commonly understood, is really objectionable; because we cannot conceive of holiness, strictly speaking, being imparted to a material building,—let us not imagine that there is anything, either unscriptural or unreasonable, in entering on the occupancy of a house intended for public worship, with appropriate exercises of religion, and, by these exercises, solemnly devoting or dedicating it to God. Is it unreasonable or unscriptural, when we commence the public occupation of such a house, to thank God for the power and the privilege of erecting it? Is it unreasonable or unscriptural to pray, that his blessing may rest upon the erection of it;—that he may meet his people there, from time to time, with the manifestations of his grace and his love;—and that his Word preached, and his ordinances administered there, may be attended with power from on high? Is it unreasonable or unscriptural to begin by imploring from him who has all hearts in his hands, that a building erected for his service, may, as long as it shall stand, be devoted to his glory;—that no false doctrine may ever be proclaimed, or criminal practice ever recommended within its walls;—and that it may always be the resort of spiritual worshippers, and the scene of glorious triumphs over sin and Satan? No, my Friends, I must believe that this is all rational and scriptural. Nay, allow me to ask—Does any Christian dare to enter on the occupancy of a house of any kind, as the residence of *himself* or his *family*, without beginning that occupancy with fervent prayer for a blessing upon it; without asking the God of all grace to smile upon his residence in it, and to make it, in the best sense, a place of comfort and prosperity to him and his, without in fact, in a sense, dedicating it to God? I say,

does any Christian dare to enter on the occupancy of any *house* without this? I hope not. And if not, can he give vent to the best feelings
of his heart, if he open the doors, and enter the seats of the house of
God, without exercises of a similar kind, but, of course, more public,
more formal, and, therefore, more solemn?

Accordingly, it has been customary, I believe, in all ages, in which
the people of God were allowed and were able to erect houses for his
stated worship, to open them with appropriate exercises of religion. It
would seem, indeed, to be a dictate of nature, and to be no less countenanced by the Word of God. That it is a practice liable to abuse,
is no valid objection to its proper and enlightened use. Intelligent
Christians can easily distinguish between entering on the occupancy
of a place of worship in the fear of God, and with a suitable acknowledgment of God; and cherishing those superstitious sentiments, and
adopting those superstitious forms, in relation to this subject, which
may be attached to anything, and which few of the institutions of
religion, however precious, have entirely escaped in certain periods
and portions of the church.

3. Again, it appears to me to follow, from what has been said, that
after a house erected for the worship of God has been solemnly set
apart for that purpose, *it is not desirable or proper, in ordinary cases, to
employ it for any other purpose.*

Although neither intrinsic holiness, nor relative holiness can, properly speaking, be ascribed to the buildings or places in which God
is worshipped, but only to the worshippers themselves:—although
there are no buildings or places known to me, under the present dispensation, into which, like the Holy Place, or the Most Holy Place,
in ancient times, it is lawful for none but consecrated persons ever
to enter:—yet we are by no means, to think, to infer from this, that
there are no sentiments of *reverence* and *solemnity* which ought *always*
to be connected with those places in which holy services are statedly
performed. There is, my Friends, a principle deeply implanted in our
nature, which we commonly denominate the principle of association. This principle will always lead serious, devout minds to connect
feelings of reverence with an edifice in which the people of God statedly meet for public worship. They will always enter with mingled
emotions of solemnity and pleasure, within those walls which have

long and often resounded with the glad tidings of salvation:—they will contemplate with delight those seats in which the pious have often found communion with their God and Saviour; and they will look with sentiments of sacred veneration toward that pulpit from which they have statedly heard the instructions and consolations of divine mercy. Are these feelings superstitious? Are they to be proscribed? Far, very far from it! They are natural; they are commendable; they are scriptural feelings. They ought unquestionably to be cherished. Nay, I will venture to say, that the person who can enter a church without experiencing any of the devout and reverential emotions to which I have referred has not in exercise the proper feelings of a man, certainly not those which become a Christian man.

Now, when houses devoted to the worship of God are frequently, or even occasionally, employed for other and secular purposes, and especially for purposes connected with noise, disorder, and unhallowed mirth, the effect cannot fail of being unhappy. It breaks that devout, reverential association of which I have just spoken. It connects ludicrous images and recollections with the house of God. It takes away from the affectionate respect and awe with which it is always desirable to enter the sanctuary. And it will be well if, the next time it is entered, after such an incongruous scene, there be not a struggle before the mind can resume its wonted tranquil devotion. Would any good man, who was at the same time a wise and prudent one, be willing that the closet, to which he was accustomed daily to retire for secret devotion, should be frequently employed for purposes which, so far as he thought of them, were calculated to disturb or banish every devout feeling? Surely I need not wait for an answer.

Guard, then, against everything of this kind as far as possible. There are obstacles enough to a spirit of elevated devotion in the house of God, without unnecessarily adding to their number. Let nothing ever enter these walls, if you can possibly exclude it, that tends to inspire levity, to pollute the imagination, or to give you pain in recollecting it, when you afterwards come to worship God. Let nothing be exhibited here, which will render it difficult for you or your children, when you tread these courts, to feel as if you were withdrawn from the world. Let nothing, in a word, be transacted here, but what has a tendency to compose and spiritualise the mind, and to raise it from earth to heaven.

4. Finally, my Friends, from what has been said, it appears, that the object of your most earnest and tender entreaty, this day, and at all times, ought to be, *that God may here be pleased graciously and liberally to dispense his spiritual blessings.*

Methinks the great Head of the church, today, addresses every devout worshipper who has an interest in this edifice, in the language which an eastern monarch addressed to his beloved companion, as recorded in the sacred history,—'What is thy petition, and what is thy request?'—Happy will it be for this church of Christ, if the hearts of all are united as one man in replying—'Now, therefore, arise, Lord God, into thy resting place, thou and the ark of thy strength!' While you are thankful that the Lord has prospered you thus far, imagine not that your work is done, when the house which you have raised for God, is opened and dedicated to him. Your work, in fact, in reference to this sanctuary, is only now begun. Let it be your care, not only once, but constantly and perseveringly, to implore that spiritual presence of the King of Zion, which is the richest of all blessings that can be conferred on a church, and which alone can render this edifice, and the occupancy of it by you and your children the means of real and lasting benefit.

Do you ask, *how* you are so to conduct yourselves as to invite, from time to time, this invaluable blessing? I answer—Besides continually asking for it, in humble, unceasing, persevering prayer;—let a diligent discharge of duty constantly testify that you really desire to obtain it. See that everything be done for the welfare of the church which fidelity to our common Master requires. Study, at all times, to co-operate with your beloved pastor in promoting your own best interests. While he preaches the gospel with faithfulness and zeal, and dispenses the sacramental seals committed to him, with an enlightened fidelity; be it your care, my Friends, to attend upon all his ministrations with punctuality, with meekness, and with love; to support him continually by your prayers; to encourage the hearts, and strengthen the hands of him and your other ecclesiastical rulers, in the maintenance of discipline; to stimulate one another to every good word and work; and, in one word, to endeavour, by all the means which the Head of the church has appointed, to draw down the blessing of God upon your solemn assemblies, and upon all the individuals who compose them.

If ever the time should come in which the simple and pure doctrines of the gospel shall be either corrupted or kept back, by those who minister here in holy things:—if the divine glories, the vicarious atonement, or the justifying merits of the Lord that bought us, shall ever be denied by those who occupy this pulpit:—if the sacraments of Christ's house shall ever be habitually neglected or profaned within these walls:—or if the body of worshippers shall ever become cold, prayerless, and secular in their character:—whatever outward glory may continue to surround this house, I proclaim to you this day, that the Lord will depart from it, and that the, ark of his strength will no more display its power here.

God grant, my Friends, that the blessed reverse of all this may be your happy lot, to the latest generations! Peace be within these walls, and prosperity within these palaces! May you, and your children, and your children's children, long come to this house of God, and never come to it without a blessing! As the external glory of this latter house is greater than the glory of the former occupied by you, may the latter, in *spiritual glory* still more eminently excel the former! May the eye of Jehovah be ever open upon it, and his ear be ever attent unto the prayer that may here be offered up! May the Word and ordinances here dispensed, from Sabbath to Sabbath, be attended with power from on high! May this devoted edifice, as long as it shall stand, be a means of Christian sanctification, a seat of Christian enjoyment, and a centre of Christian action! May revival after revival fill it with devout and holy worshippers! And when they shall successively take leave of it, may it be to enter a house of infinitely greater glory; a house not made with hands, eternal in the heavens! Amen, and Amen!

CHRISTIAN WEAPONS NOT CARNAL BUT SPIRITUAL[1]

For the weapons of our warfare are not carnal,
but mighty through God to the pulling down of strong holds.
2 Corinthians 10:4

AS long as man retained his primitive innocence, he loved truth, and was ever ready to give it a cordial welcome. But the moment he fell from God and from holiness, truth became painful, and, of course, odious to him. He felt that he could no longer listen to it as a friend, speaking peace; but must henceforth regard it as an enemy, which could deliver no other than a hostile message. Accordingly, when we read that the holy and happy tenants of Eden had become rebels by eating the interdicted fruit, the next thing we read of is, that, on hearing the voice of the Lord God walking in the garden, they hid themselves from the presence of the Lord among the trees of the garden. And the Lord called unto Adam, and said unto him, Where art thou? And he said, I heard thy voice in the garden, and I was afraid, and I hid myself.

From that fatal hour, all efforts to impress moral and religious truth on the minds of men, have been, properly speaking, a warfare; that is, in whatever direction they have been applied, they have never failed to meet with resistance. As all men, by nature, hate the truth as it is in Jesus; and as all men, quite as universally, are opposed to the spirit and the demands of gospel obedience; it follows that all

---

[1] Samuel Miller, *Christian Weapons Not Carnal, But Spiritual: A Sermon, Delivered in the Second Presbyterian Church, in the City of Baltimore, October 13, 1826; at the Installation of the Reverend John Breckinridge, as Colleague with the Reverend John Glendy, D.D. in the Pastoral Charge of the Said Church* (Princeton Press: D. A. Borrenstein, 1826).

attempts to procure the reception of the one, or to enforce the practice of the other, must be made in the face of hostility: a hostility not, indeed, always equally bitter in its hatred, or gross in its violence; but still real hostility, which nothing can appease but a surrender of Jehovah's claims to the inclination of the rebellious creature. Hence, whenever the banner of truth and righteousness is raised in any place, opposition never fails immediately to arise: and however unreasonable its character, or revolting its aspect, in the view of the truly spiritual mind, it usually bears away the multitude, and would always do so, did not divine power interpose to prevent it. The human heart, left to itself, is ever ready to bid welcome any plausible flatterer, who will prophesy deceits, and say, in the language of the first deceiver, Ye shall not surely die.

Of the truth of these remarks, we have a striking example in the history of the church of Corinth. The apostle Paul had laboured in the ministry of the gospel in that city for a considerable time; and his labours had been crowned with success. Numbers were added to the professing people of God. Soon after he left them, however, a false teacher came among them, who appears, from various hints dropped by the apostle, to have been a man of honourable birth; of fine talents; of polished education; and of great skill in all the arts and refinements of Grecian eloquence. He was evidently, also, as such impostors commonly are, a man of lax principles; ever ready to accommodate his doctrines to the pride, the prejudices, and the corrupt passions of those whom he addressed. This artful deceiver, on the one hand, set himself with peculiar bitterness against the apostle; found fault with his birth and education; alleged that his bodily presence was mean, and his speech contemptible; and insinuated that he was really no apostle. On the other hand, he boasted much of his own origin, learning, eloquence, and other accomplishments, and endeavoured to persuade the people of Corinth that he was, in every respect, Paul's superior.

Unhappily, the situation of the Corinthian church at this time was peculiarly favourable to the views of such an impostor. In consequence of the surrounding wealth and luxury, and the remarkable exemption from persecution which it had for some time enjoyed; a large number of its members were deeply tinctured with a worldly spirit. In fact, the church there seems to have been full of professors who were far from having either the knowledge, the steadiness, or the spirituality which became them. No wonder, therefore, that this false teacher found admirers and followers. He raised a considerable party, which gave much trouble to the friends of truth, and which, for a time, threatened the peace, if not the existence of the church in that city.

The inspired apostle, in the passage of which our text makes a part, seems to be directly addressing this false teacher and his adherents, and repelling some of the insinuations which he had made against himself. In reply to the charges,—that he was destitute of the credentials of an apostle,—and that he had none of those decisive and energetic means of resisting opposers, and supporting his authority, which they supposed a teacher sent from God ought to exhibit; the apostle declares,—Though we walk in the flesh, that is, though we inhabit mortal bodies, and are compassed about with fleshly infirmities;—yet we do not war after the flesh,—or according to the flesh. For the weapons of our warfare are not carnal, but mighty through God to the pulling down of strongholds.

In the passage of holy scripture before us, there are two points which demand our particular notice, *viz.*:

I. The *weapons* which the apostle employed, and to which alone he gave his sanction; and,

II. The *great efficacy* of those weapons: they were *mighty through God*.

I. Let us first contemplate the weapons which the apostle speaks of himself as employing. The weapons of our warfare are not carnal.

The word carnal means fleshly. It is opposed in Scripture to spiritual or holy; and is generally employed by the inspired writers to designate the principles of our depraved nature. Thus, when it is said, that the carnal mind is enmity against God (*Rom.* 8:7); and that to be carnally minded is death (*Rom.* 8:6);—the language is evidently meant to express the dominion of that corrupt disposition which men bring with them into the world, and on which the sanctifying grace of God has not yet taken effect. Of course, by the phrase, carnal weapons, is meant, such weapons as our corrupt nature forms and furnishes. In other words, it is intended to designate all those means of recommending and propagating religion which the great Author of that religion has not prescribed, but which the wisdom of this world has invented. Such weapons have been employed in all ages. They are the favourite weapons of carnal men: or rather, they are the only weapons which such men are either qualified or disposed to employ. But they are not confined to carnal men. Even some of those who sincerely love the Saviour, may be, and have been, betrayed into the use of means for promoting his honour, which may well deserve to be styled carnal, and which, in themselves, are not the less carnal, or the less criminal, because they are employed by good men. In short, every method, of propagating truth, or of recommending duty, either real or supposed,—which unhallowed principles suggest, or unhallowed motives prompt, or which, in one word, is not in conformity with the Word and Spirit of God, may be pronounced a carnal weapon, the use of which our text indirectly, but most solemnly, forbids.

But it may not be unprofitable to specify, a little more in detail, some of those means which are frequently resorted to, for the professed purpose of propagating religion, and which evidently belong to the class proscribed by the apostle in the passage before us.

And at the head of the list, may be placed persecution, whether in its more gross and violent, or in its more mitigated forms. By the former, you will readily understand to be meant all those cases in which the 'secular arm' has interfered to enforce the claims of a particular religious denomination, or of a particular set of opinions, by fire and sword,—by fines and forfeitures,—by racks and chains, and banishment, and all the various penalties which oppressive governments, civil and ecclesiastical, have so often, and so grievously inflicted. By the latter are intended all that molestation, abuse, or temporal inconvenience, of whatever kind, which have been heaped upon men on account of their religious opinions. The narrative of these inflictions, and of the diabolical fury with which they have, in countless instances, been executed, forms one of the most melancholy chapters in the history of that which calls itself the church of God. A narrative the more unspeakably revolting, from the fact, that the most shocking atrocities which it displays were perpetrated in the name, and by the alleged authority, of a God of mercy, and from a professed regard to his glory! Before this enlightened audience I

468

need not say, that persecution for conscience sake, in all its forms, is one of the greatest absurdities and abominations that ever disgraced the Christian world;—that it is contrary to reason, to justice, and to humanity, and certainly not less contrary to the Word of God, and to all the radical principles of our holy religion.

To the same interdicted class of weapons, we may refer all civil establishments of religion. Whatever may be their form, or the degree of their rigour: whether they are intended to operate by force, by fear, or by allurement: whether we consider them as a tax on error, or as a bounty on faith; as a legal provision for instructing the people in what the civil magistrate (who may be an infidel or a heretic) chooses to say is truth; or as a convenient engine in the hands of government, for reaching and controlling the popular mind: in all cases, they are unhallowed in their principles, and pernicious in their tendency: calculated to generate and encourage hypocrisy; to corrupt the Christian ministry; to make the care of souls an affair of secular merchandise; and to prostrate the church of God, with all its officers and ordinances, at the feet of worldly politicians.

Again, all human inventions in the worship of God are liable to the same general charge. The object of these, in every age, has been to consult carnal prejudices, and to accommodate carnal feelings: of course, they are carnal weapons. When, therefore, professing Christians began, soon after the apostolic age, to introduce into the church rites which the Saviour never instituted, for the purpose of assuaging the enmity, or conciliating the affections of Jews and pagans: when they borrowed, from either or from both, without scruple, and without the smallest warrant, as they fancied an inducement—the smoking incense; the worshipping toward the East; the bowings; the adoration of images; the purgatorial fire; the merit of bodily maceration; the celibacy of the clergy; the splendid garments; the holy days; the exorcisms; the processions and all the endless array of superstition; insomuch that, as early as the close of the fourth century, the venerable Augustine complained that, for one institution of God's they had ten of man's, and that the presumptuous devices of men were more rigorously pressed than the divine prescriptions;—who can doubt that they were chargeable with employing carnal weapons? And when Christian churches or individuals, at the present day, aim to allure the gay and the worldly, by pomp and splendour of ceremonial, by that studied address to the senses in the public service of the sanctuary, which the primitive and purest periods of Christianity never knew; who can doubt that they also lay themselves open to the same charge? They undertake to be wiser than God; they employ means, which, however well intended, can result in nothing but mischief. The church has no power to 'decree rites and ceremonies'. If she had, there would be no other bounds to the multiplication of them, than the ever varying, and ever teeming figments of human vanity or caprice. To claim such a right is rebellion against her Master. To exercise it, is systematically to introduce superstition and complicated corruption into his sacred family.

Further, even ecclesiastical confessions and formularies may be so perverted as to become carnal weapons. No one is a warmer friend to these summaries of gospel truth, properly understood, and in their proper place, than he who now addresses you. When they are faithfully drawn from the Word of God; when they claim no authority but that which is founded on their conformity to that Word; when they are imposed upon no man's conscience; but are honestly and simply employed for the purpose of excluding from the visible church those who are really enemies to her radical truth and order; then reason, Scripture, and experience all bear witness in their favour. But when they are erected into an ultimate rule of faith; when they claim an inherent authority; when they are set above the Bible, or on a par with the Bible; when they are imposed on the consciences of men, as indispensable passports to the honours and emoluments of an established church; and even employed to ensnare the minds of unread and inexperienced youth, as a term of admission to literary privileges; then, instead of promoting truth, and cherishing piety, they are hostile to both. Instead of maintaining the unity of the spirit in the bonds of peace and love, they fetter the mind; they ensnare the conscience; they engender division and strife; they become instrumental in corrupting, rather than preserving the simplicity that is in Christ.

The next weapon, of this unhallowed class, which demands our notice, and which the faithful minister ought to reject, is the introduction of the subtleties of philosophy into the simple doctrine of Christ. The religion of the Bible is one thing: the philosophy of it, is quite another. And although it is not always easy, and perhaps not necessary, or even proper, for a student of the Bible, in his closet, to banish from his mind every inquiry which encroaches on the latter; yet, in my opinion, it is the former, and the former only, which ought to be presented in preaching the gospel. And whenever the ambassador of Christ, instead of proclaiming the simple gospel, entertains his hearers, either in whole, or in part, with the refinements of philosophical speculation, with the presumptuous efforts of carnal reasoning, he is guilty of substituting something in place of the gospel, he cheats them with chaff, instead of feeding them with Zion's provision.

Again, in close connection with this, we may remark, that the pride and ostentation of unsanctified learning, are carnal weapons, which have produced countless evils in the church of God. Genuine learning, and even profound learning, when united with vital piety, is an instrument in the propagation of religion, of inestimable value. To despise it, is at once, to insult our reason, and the almighty Author of reason. To decry it, is one of those devices of Satan, by which he ensnares even good men into the service of his kingdom. But while all this may be confidently maintained, still nothing is more certain than that perverted learning, unsanctified learning, has been the means of turning millions away from the kingdom of Christ, rather than bringing them into it. It has been the means of inflating with pride; of corrupting truth; of leading ministers and others to rely upon intellectual attainments and efforts, rather than upon the Word and Spirit of the living God, to bring men to the knowledge and enjoyment of his glory.

No less liable to the same charge, is the general idolatry of talent in the church, and especially all reliance on mere human eloquence as a means of converting men to the belief and love of the gospel. That God daily honours talents, and sometimes those of the most transcendent order, by using them for the extension of his kingdom, it is impossible to doubt. And when they are devoutly regarded as his instruments, and employed in humble reliance on his grace, as that which alone can render them truly useful, they are genuine Christian weapons. But when they become objects of idolatrous worship and dependence, they lose their Christian character, and degenerate into carnal weapons. And, in this case, they are probably none on which the great Head of the church is seen more frequently and more severely to frown. For his glory he will not give to another. Among these talents, perhaps eloquence is the most ensnaring, because most rare, and most fascinating. No man who had either an intellect to perceive, or a heart capable of emotion, ever undervalued genuine eloquence. It is that unaffected, powerful utterance of thought and of feeling, which meets a response in every mind in which thought and feeling find a place. And yet, eloquence itself, however genuine and perfect, can never change a single heart; and to rely upon its efficacy in persuading any man to be reconciled to God, is to rely upon a carnal weapon. Above all, does this appellation belong to the employment, in the kingdom of Christ, of those artificial refinements and pomp of rhetoric; those profane and vain babblings, and oppositions of science falsely so called; that affectation and parade of oratory; which so often usurp the name of eloquence. My preaching, says the inspired author of our text, in another place—was not with enticing words of man's wisdom, but in demonstration of the Spirit and of power. And again—Christ sent me to preach the gospel, not with the wisdom of words, less the cross of Christ should be made of none effect (*1 Cor.* 2:4; 1:17).

Nor can we, for a moment, hesitate to give the name of carnal weapons, to the 'pious frauds', the refined cunning, dissimulation, and stratagem, the carnal policy, and all the crafty management, practised on men, for the alleged purpose of promoting their benefit. All these, even when viewed under the most favourable aspect, are liable to the general charge of doing evil that good may come; an abomination in the church of Christ, which has corrupted and disgraced it from the beginning; which is not the less abominable, however, because it is old; and of which the inspired apostle, in writing to the Romans, speaks in terms of the severest reprobation (*Rom.* 3:8). How often a disingenuous, crooked policy, calling itself wisdom; and a timid, temporizing, unfaithful course, disguised under the name of prudence, have been adopted, with temporary success, by ecclesiastical men, every student of history, and every observer of daily occurrences, has noticed and deplored. Yet they are really, as remote from true wisdom, as different from genuine Christian prudence, as the basest counterfeit is from authorized coin.

All such weapons, the Christian, and more particularly the Christian minister, if he would partake of the spirit of Paul; if he would not disgrace that worthy name by which he is called, must abhor and avoid.

Thus far, my Friends, according to the plan of the apostle, I have treated the subject negatively. I have told you what his weapons were not, and have given you a specimen of those which the spirit of our text forbids. The weapons of our warfare, says this enlightened and faithful minister of Jesus, speaking of himself and his brethren—the weapons of our warfare are not carnal. What kind of weapons, then, did they employ? For the answer to this question, we are not left to conjecture. We find ample instruction respecting it in our context, and in the other apostolic records.

Some, indeed, suppose that the apostle refers primarily and chiefly, in this passage, to the exercise of those miraculous powers, with which he and his brother apostles were endowed; by means of which they were enabled, when they thought proper, to silence opposition, and effectually to display that authority which their divine Master had given them for edification and not for destruction. Those who adopt this opinion consider the apostle in our text as declaring, that the weapons which he wielded were not those of feeble flesh; but such miraculous, supernatural weapons, as his enemies could neither sustain nor resist, when he chose to put them forth. That there may be some reference here to miraculous gifts is, perhaps not improbable; but that they are principally intended, we can by no means admit. This appears to be conclusively decided by the strain of the verse immediately following our text. The weapons employed were such as were adapted, to cast down imaginations, and every high thing that exalteth itself against the knowledge of God, and to bring into captivity every thought to the obedience of Christ. Now, obviously, the only weapons adapted to produce these spiritual effects, are spiritual weapons. Miraculous powers, we know, were not always connected with cordial subjection to Christ, even in those who possessed and exercised them; nor are they ever represented in Scripture as the means of effecting true sanctification in others. Spiritual weapons alone are God's ordinary means of producing this blessed effect. These, then, are here chiefly intended by the apostle. Weapons addressed to the intellectual and moral part of our nature. Weapons which make their appeal to the reason and the heart of man. Weapons which depend for all their efficacy on the Spirit and grace of God; and which are daily made the power of God unto salvation to every one that believeth.

The same apostle who penned our text, in the sixth chapter of his Epistle to the Ephesians, speaks at large of the Christian armour; describing its several parts, and showing the use of each. In that place it served his purpose to speak chiefly, though not exclusively, of the Christian's defensive armour; such as the girdle of truth, the breastplate of righteousness, the shield of faith, and the helmet of salvation; which belong to all believers. But, in the passage before us, he had occasion to refer particularly to the weapons of Christian ministers, and more especially to those of the offensive kind; or those which are important, not merely for the protection and defence of their own persons; but also for attacking and vanquishing the enemies of their Master. Even these weapons, however, are not carnal, but spiritual: not intended to injure, but to save; not to inflict violence on the persons of those to whom they are directed; but to enlighten, to convince, to sanctify, to comfort, and lead to perfect and eternal blessedness. Let us take a cursory survey of some of these weapons, as we find them enumerated in the inspired volume.

And the first of these spiritual and potent weapons which I shall mention, is *the Word of God;* the Word of truth and grace contained in the Holy Scriptures. This holy Word, when applied by the Spirit of God, is indeed a powerful weapon. Hence, in the strong language of inspiration it is called the rod of Jehovah's strength; and in another place, it is represented as the sword of the Spirit (*Eph.* 6:17); and again, it is said to be quick and powerful, and sharper than any two-edged sword, piercing even to the dividing asunder of soul and spirit, and of the joints and marrow, and to be a discerner of the thoughts and intents of the heart (*Heb.* 4:12). Again, the entrance of this Word, we are told, giveth light; it converteth the soul; it maketh wise the simple; it rejoiceth the heart; it enlighteneth the eyes; it is able to make us wise unto salvation (*Psa.* 119:130; 19; *2 Tim.* 3:15). Accordingly, this is the grand weapon on which the primitive ministers of Christ were directed to rely, under God, for extending his kingdom. Go ye, said the Master himself, into all the world, and preach the gospel to every creature. And to this day, he who preaches the genuine Word of God; that is, who preaches the gospel—the simple, pure gospel; without the admixture of carnal reasonings or vain philosophy; he who does this faithfully, fervently, and affectionately; does that which is much more likely to be effectual in extending the religion of Jesus Christ, in its power, than if he were to erect a thousand splendid temples for the solemnities of public worship, or to found a thousand sumptuous benefices, for the temporal support of ecclesiastics.

Another weapon, by means of which the ambassadors of Christ are bound to plead the cause and extend the reign of their Master, is *the right administration of the sacraments which he has appointed.* As the church is a body of professing people, called out from the world, and united under Christ, their only King and Head, there seems to be, upon every principle, a call for those badges and seals of the covenant under which they are constituted, by which we find that it has pleased their infinitely wise Sovereign actually to distinguish them. By means of these, among other things, a visible line of separation is drawn between the church and the world. The visibly 'precious', are separated from the 'vile'. The 'sacramental host' of God's people are embodied and arrayed, in the sight of the enemy's camp; and an epitome of their religion, as it were, addressed to the senses of every beholder. These seals, therefore, the servants of Christ are commanded to administer to the end of the world. And by the enlightened and discriminating application of them, they employ, as long experience has proved, a gentle, but most potent weapon, not only for exciting, sustaining, and comforting the friends of their cause; but also for drawing multitudes from the hostile ranks, and enlisting them under the banner of the Prince of Peace.

A further weapon, which Christ has been pleased to appoint by his authority, and to crown with his blessing, is *the holy discipline of the church.* By this is meant that system of regulation and correction, which infinite wisdom has established in his professing family as one of the great means of promoting its purity and edification. A system which makes no pecuniary exactions; which resorts to no secular penalties; which neither sells nor gives 'indulgences' to the systematic sinner; which invades no man's civil or religious rights; but which, by moral power alone, that is by instruction, by entreaty, by admonition, by rebuke, by warning, by suspension, and, in extreme cases, by exclusion from the visible church,—removes offences, vindicates the honour of Christ,—causes the wicked to fear,—and promotes the benefit of the offenders themselves. There can be no question, then, that the discipline of the church, when properly understood, and wisely conducted, may be made as really the means of convincing and converting sinners, and building up believers, as the faithful preaching of the gospel. I know, indeed, that worldly men both dread and hate discipline. They are in the constant habit of considering and representing it, as mere 'punishment'; as a 'hard and tyrannical exercise of ecclesiastical authority'. But I know, too, that the enlightened Christian loves it. He regards it as one of the means of grace, and as a precious privilege. He knows, that if the church be a 'garden', as the Scriptures represent it,—'the garden of the Lord'—it must be defended by an enclosure; or else—to keep up the figure—every beast of the field would waste it. But a spiritual enclosure without discipline, would be an absurdity in terms, as well as contradictory to the Bible. The Christian, then, who has learned to contemplate the professing family of Christ with the spirit of a disciple, regards the discipline of that family with peculiar interest. He is ready to say, even when the case becomes his own,—Let the righteous smite me; it shall be a kindness: and let him reprove me, it shall be an excellent oil (*Psa.* 141:5). Accordingly, in the very epistle from which our text is taken, we have an account of a case of discipline, which the officers of the church of Corinth were commanded to exercise; which they did exercise; which was blessed to the benefit of him who was the subject of it; and after the beneficial operation of which, he was restored to the fellowship and privileges of the church.

Another of those weapons with which the ambassadors of Christ are to go forth to their warfare, is *fervent, importunate prayer.* Prayer for the pardon and salvation of the enemies of the church. Prayer for the success of all the means of grace. Prayer for the universal spread of the gospel. Thus the same inspired apostle who penned our text, after elsewhere describing and recommending the whole Christian armour, closes all by the exhortation—'Praying always, with all prayer and supplication, in the Spirit, and watching thereunto with all perseverance and supplication for all saints.' And, surely, if divine aid be constantly necessary, and ought to be unceasingly implored, in the ordinary warfare, of which the apostle is here speaking; it cannot be less needful in the still more arduous warfare, in which those whose office it is, to win souls to Christ, are daily engaged. While, therefore, every other prescribed weapon ought to be used with as much diligence, and indefatigable perseverance, as if all depended on the human agent; the divine blessing should be continually invoked, with as much earnest importunity, as if means were excluded. Every plan should be formed with prayer; every effort nerved by prayer; every address, if I may so express it, enclosed in prayer; and every service followed by prayer.

I shall only mention one more of those spiritual weapons, by which the enemies of Christ are overcome, and his religion effectually propagated. I mean *holy example*. It was long ago enjoined by the Saviour himself—'Let your light shine before men, that others, seeing your good works, may glorify your Father in heaven.' And often, since that injunction was given, has the bright example of Christian meekness, purity, humility, and benevolence, been the means of silencing the gainsayer; of extorting a reluctant homage from the infidel; and even of melting into cordial penitence and love the hardest heart. Many a man, who had resisted with apparent ease every other weapon, has been overcome by the power of embodied, living religion, and been constrained to confess with trembling—Truly, this is the finger of God! A distinguished unbeliever, of the last century, after spending a few days at the residence of an eminently pious minister, was so deeply impressed with his pure, benevolent and heavenly conversation, that he said—I must leave this house. If I remain here a day longer, I shall become a Christian in spite of myself.

Such are the principal weapons which it becomes Christian ministers to employ, and which we may confidently hope the great Head of the church will bless. For, says the apostle,

II. They are *mighty through God* to the pulling down of strongholds. This is the second point demanding attention.

This form of expression plainly implies, that carnal weapons are not mighty; that they are not powerful to promote the great ends of overcoming the enemies of the cross, and extending the reign of pure and undefiled religion. And, accordingly, all testimony serves to show that this is really the case: that for effecting these objects they are the most powerless imaginable. Racks, gibbets, the magistrate's sword, and 'Acts of Uniformity' have made hypocrites by thousands; but they have never yet made a Christian; and they never will or can make one, as long as the nature of man, and the kingdom of God retain their essential characters.

Let those who doubt this, recollect for a moment, the nature of the strong holds which Christian ministers are commissioned to pull down. They are not those of physical, but of moral power. They are those of pride, unbelief, self-righteousness, love of the world, super-stition, sensuality, and all that enmity to God, his truth, and his commandments, which every where characterize unsanctified men; together with all those vain pleas by which they are wont to excuse, if not justify themselves in their rebellious course. In these strong-holds, the children of this world are, as it were, entrenched. And the success of the 'good soldier of Jesus Christ', consists in pulling down their unhallowed fortifications, and constraining them to surrender themselves willing captives to the blessed Redeemer: or, as our con-text expresses it, in casting down imaginations, and every high thing that exalteth itself against the knowledge of God, and bringing into captivity every thought to the obedience of Christ.

Such being the nature of the conquest to be effected, it is perfectly manifest that carnal weapons are by no means adapted to accomplish the end. A free, unconstrained choice is essential to moral agency. Our Creator has made it the duty of every man to engage in his serv-ice, as matter of enlightened conviction and deliberate, voluntary, cordial preference. If we were required to give a definition of true religion, we should answer—'It is receiving and obeying the gospel in the love of it.' Or, we should say, 'It is voluntarily choosing, and heartily following Christ, as our Teacher, Redeemer, and Sovereign.' But how can this be wrought in the mind, or enforced, by carnal weapons? Such weapons cannot, in the nature of things, reach the object. Men may, indeed, be constrained to perform certain external acts, by the dread of secular penalties, or by the hope of temporal rewards. But is this true religion? It may be policy, or hypocrisy, or priestcraft, or statecraft; but true religion it cannot be. The idea of compelling men to believe, or of bribing or forcing them to love is, surely, in the very first rank of absurdities.

But further, the use of carnal weapons, for promoting religion, is not only, in its own nature, absurd and preposterous; but it is also an unhallowed attempt to usurp the authority of God. He alone is Lord of the conscience. To attempt, therefore, to tamper with it by secular weapons, or to apply means of external coercion, where the devotion of the heart is the service required,—is a presumptuous interference with the divine prerogative. It is like endeavouring, by pillars of brass or marble, to prop up the heavens.

Nor is this all; the use of carnal weapons, in moral and spiritual concerns, is not only absurd and impious; but experience has shown that they can never answer the end which those who employ them profess to seek. They have invariably proved themselves to be worse than useless in promoting the cause of genuine Christianity. The moment they began to be used for promoting the spread of the gospel, its lustre began to be dimmed, and its power to decline. Men found that when they employed unhallowed means to fill the house of God, they seldom failed, by those very means, to empty it. I grant, indeed, that power, and wealth, and splendid civil establishments, may appear to be effectual, for a time, in building up what many suppose to be, and call, religion. They may multiply and adorn gorgeous edifices for worship; they may found rich endowments for enabling ecclesiastics to live in luxury; they may impart to all the outward accommodations and ceremonial of religion, an imposing magnificence; and they may allure multitudes of the affluent and the learned into the church, and many a graceless votary of ambition into the sacred ministry. But this is not promoting real religion. It is, in truth, pursuing a course directly calculated to destroy it. When Christianity, in primitive times, had nothing to depend upon, under God, but her moral power, that is, the simplest moral means; then, in the midst of persecution, she made a progress, and displayed a power more astonishing to the contemplative heathen, than the most signal miracles of her inspired ministers. They saw the servants of Christ, going forth, without the least aid from the great ones of the earth; nay, in direct opposition to all the wealth, the power, and the superstition of the world. They saw them bearing no fleshly weapons;

nothing but the simple gospel of the grace of God, to the Jews a stumbling-block, and to the Greeks foolishness. Yet they saw this simple weapon triumphant over all that flesh and blood could oppose to it. They saw the religion of Christ making its way in spite of the allurements of sense, the frowns of power, and the fires of martyrdom. They saw it converting the bloodthirsty savage, into a model of clemency and benevolence; transforming the hardened blasphemer into a devout worshipper, and the bitter persecutor into a zealous apostle of that faith which once he destroyed; making the abandoned voluptuary temperate and pure; the fraudulent, just; the avaricious, charitable; the passionate, meek and placable; and the proud infidel, an humble suppliant for pardon through that blood which cleanseth from all sin. Then the word of the Lord had free course and was glorified. Then multitudes were added to the church of such as were saved. Then the churches, blessed with an humble, spiritual, and devoted ministry, and walking together in the fear of the Lord, and in the consolations of the Holy Ghost, were edified and comforted. In short, then the church probably held a more exalted station with regard to vital piety; the holy flame of faith, and love, and spiritual obedience, rose higher and shone brighter, than at any period since that time. But whenever carnal weapons began to interpose:—when imperial power and splendour began to take the side of the church; when emperors began to invite ecclesiastics to their courts, and to load them with emoluments and honours; when the doctrines and claims of the church began to be enforced by civil penalties; when a pampered priesthood began to exhaust their ingenuity in rendering the public service a gaudy and dazzling ritual:—from that hour, real religion declined. The fire of love and zeal was extinguished. Ministers, in a great degree, lost their spirituality. The mass of the people soon became like their teachers. And the church, instead of continuing to be that holy, spiritual body which she once was, became a splendid, rich, corrupt, worldly church, over which, while the gay and ambitious rejoiced, the truly pious were constrained to mourn.

And in all cases in which the same simple spiritual weapons, which wrought such moral miracles in the primitive church, have been faithfully employed, the same blessed results have been invariably, in a greater or less degree, manifested. Yes, Brethren, wherever and whenever the same weapons, which in the hands of the primitive ministers of Christ, were so powerful, are honestly and diligently wielded, in the same spirit as by those devoted men; they will assuredly be found, as then, mighty through God to the pulling down of strong holds. The proudest columns of the enemy, however apparently formidable, will melt away before them. I will not, indeed, undertake to define the measure of success, which will attend the ministry of him who faithfully, consistently and constantly plies the genuine weapons of the gospel. I cannot assert that success is the natural effect of fidelity; for I know that without the blessed power of God, it will not follow the very best endeavours. Nor can I venture to pronounce that success will be, in all cases, in exact proportion to fidelity; for I recollect that God is a sovereign. But I have no doubt, at the same time, that all Scripture, and all experience warrant us in laying it down, with confidence, as a general principle, that eminent personal holiness and official fidelity in ministers of the gospel, will usually be found connected with eminent success in winning souls to Christ. It can by no means, indeed, be maintained, that, whenever a revival of religion occurs, and the strong holds of sin and Satan are pulled down, it follows, of course, that the minister who is instrumental in this work, is himself, certainly, a pious man, and his weapons all purely spiritual. A man who is utterly graceless, may be made, in the dispensations of a sovereign God instrumental in imparting grace to others. But my position is, that where his spirit, his life and his weapons are all, in a good measure, such as they ought to be, he will not fail of being successful. I repeat it, Brethren, if a minister of the gospel will, simply, humbly, wisely, steadily, affectionately, and perseveringly, employ those weapons of which the apostle speaks, and, at the same time, honour God by unfeignedly looking to him alone to make them effectual; I could as soon doubt that Jehovah has made promises to his church, and that he will be faithful to what he has said, as doubt that a revival of his work, and a display of his glory, will be in a greater or less degree, the blessed result.

It appears to me that the whole history of the church confirms this position. In what part of Christendom was there ever an enlightened, spiritual, exemplary, faithful ministry at work without many visible and precious seals to its fidelity? Even when apparent exceptions have occurred, have they not proved, on examination, to be rather apparent than real? A preacher, indeed, may declare the truth in its purity every time he opens his mouth; and yet he may do it in so cold, pointless, and uninteresting a manner, that no rational man could expect him to make an impression. Or, he may preach the truth, and do it with inimitable force, fervour and skill; and, at the same time, out of the pulpit, manifest so little of the Christian spirit, and, perhaps even so much of the opposite spirit, as to counteract all his public labours. Or, he may be faithful as a preacher, and exemplary as a man; and yet be so habitually indolent as entirely to neglect the children of his charge, and by no means to follow up, by his efforts from house to house, what he may have begun in the sanctuary. Can it be wonderful, or is it in the least degree adverse to what seems to be the spirit of our text, that such men have little or no success? It is only where the weapons in question are, all of them, honestly, consistently, and with some tolerable degree of diligence, employed, that we have a right to anticipate the plenary blessing. If, in such case, there has ever been a failure of the blessing, it is more than has ever come to my knowledge, or, as I verily believe, to the knowledge of any other man.

But we are reminded by our text, that this happy result, whenever it occurs, is not of man, or by man; but all of God. Mighty through God, says the apostle, to the pulling down of strongholds. That is, the weapons of our warfare do not produce their effect in virtue of their own natural energy, or in virtue of the wisdom or power of us who wield them; but they are mighty through that God whose power works by them. Not by might, nor by power—that is, by human might or power, but by my Spirit, saith Jehovah (*Zech.* 4:6). We have this treasure—the treasure of the gospel—says the apostle—in earthen vessels, that the excellency of the power may be seen to be of God, and not of us (*2 Cor.* 4:7). Even when the inspired Paul planted, and the eloquent Apollos watered, God gave the increase. So then, neither is he that planteth anything, neither he that watereth, but God that giveth the increase (*1 Cor.* 3:7).

The foregoing illustration of the spirit of our text, suggests to us a variety of practical inferences, to some of which, allow me, before I close, to solicit your serious attention.

1. The principles laid down seem to me instructive as to the question, What, and how far Christians, as Christians, have to do with civil government.

The kingdom of Christ is not of this world. And if all carnal weapons are prohibited in promoting the extension, and in conducting the affairs of this kingdom, then it is evident that the civil magistrate, as such, has no right to interpose in the affairs of the church, either with his sword or his regulations; that he has no right either to reward or to punish men for their religious opinions, in any case or way whatever. Man is accountable to God alone for his religious creed, and his religious practices. As long as he disturbs not the peace of society, no one has a right to call him to an account for either. But, on the other hand, to say, as some have done, that Christians have nothing to do with civil government, is to say, that, in becoming Christians, they cease to be men; and that the Bible contains no instructions or precepts applicable to Christians as members of civil society. The church, and the states or kingdoms of this world, are entirely separate governments. Neither can ever be subjected to the other, as such, without mischief. But the members of both being, in many cases, the same; and the laws of Christ extending to all the relations and duties of men; it can, in no case, be strictly said, either that Christians have nothing to do with politics, or that the magistrate has nothing to do with religion. Every Christian, indeed, ought to recoil with instinctive dread and horror from every attempt on the part of civil government to interpose in the affairs of the church, even to help her. As members of the church of Christ, we need no other help, we wish no other, than to enjoy an equal protection with others in all our civil rights. Nay, we deprecate the thought of more than this. When more is attempted, there is death in the unhallowed touch;—not merely to one of the parties, as in the case of Uzzah of old; but, I had almost said, to both: and to both it certainly would be, if it were possible even for the gates of hell to prevail against the church. Truly, we ought to be jealous of everything which brings civil government into contact with the church. Rather, much rather, let the church have the frowns than the caresses of the world. There is far less evil to be apprehended from the former than from the latter. Yet, while we say this, it is nevertheless true, on the one hand that every civil magistrate ought to be a Christian, to love the church, and to seek to promote her interests: and, on the other, that every Christian ought to be a vigilant and active patriot, loving his country, and endeavouring to secure her welfare continually, by faithfully discharging all the duties of a good citizen. That man ill, indeed, estimates or discharges the duty which he owes to him who is Head over all things for the church, who acts upon the principle, that he has no concern with the civil government under which he lives; and who deliberately abandons the elective franchise, the hall of legislation, and the court of justice, to the enemies of his Saviour. Instead of this, let him faithfully attend, according to the call of providence, on every civil, as well as ecclesiastical duty; being careful, to whichever of them he addresses himself, to employ no other weapons,—to take no other course, than those which become him as a Christian.

2. We may learn from this subject the true ideas that ought to be annexed to what are called the rights of conscience;—the rights of private judgment.

There cannot be a plainer principle than that the rights of conscience are inalienable. No man has a right, if he could, to force my conscience; nor have I a right to force that of any other man. Nay, strictly speaking, the thing is impossible. I may coerce his body; I may tamper with his conscience; I may tempt it, and even corrupt it; but coerce it, I cannot. The very term conscience, implies that internal conviction, which it is physically impossible for one man either to form, or to control, for another. But while we admit, nay strenuously maintain, the sacredness of the rights of conscience; is it any violation of those rights, for the church to exclude any man from her communion for heresy or immorality? Certainly not. There is a striking analogy, in this respect, between religious and civil concerns, which may serve to illustrate the subject. Every man, for example, has an undoubted right to dispose of his own property as he pleases. That is, no human power has a right to control him in this matter, as long as he does not invade the peace of society. Yet if he spend his property in degrading licentiousness, and prodigality, every sober-minded person will consider him as sinning both against God, and against society. And if he go on to a certain length in this course, though the law of the land may not take hold of him, he must not be surprised or complain, if all decent people drop his acquaintance, and decline receiving him into their families. In vain will he appeal to the public, and say that this treatment is persecution; for that he has a perfect right to regulate his own expenditures as he thinks proper. True; and his neighbours have the same unquestionable right to bestow their respect and countenance on whom they please, and to withdraw them from whom and when they please. So it is in spiritual concerns. All men, undoubtedly, have a right to believe what doctrines they choose, and to embrace what form of religion they choose. God forbid that this right should ever be called in question; or ever for one moment assailed with carnal weapons. But the church, which is an assemblage of individuals, must have the same right to judge whether she can agree with another individual in opinion, and walk with him in fellowship, or not. Of course, if any man connected with the church become corrupt, either in principle or practice, he surely has no reason to complain if the church admonish and entreat him as a brother; and, if he persist in his unhallowed course, if she withdraw from him, and disown him. For if it be a violation of the rights of conscience for the church, in such case, to withdraw from him; then it is an equal violation of the rights of conscience for an individual to withdraw from a corrupt and apostate church, with which he has on the best grounds, become disgusted, and with which he can no longer worship in comfort. And thus, acting on the principle which some contend for, instead of the rights of conscience being maintained, all real enjoyment of those rights would be banished from the world. No individual, or body of men whatever would have a right to choose their religious principles or connections for themselves!

3. The principles involved in our text plainly teach us, that it is wrong to vindicate any doctrine, or any practice, merely on the ground of human authority. If good men have used carnal weapons, we may allow them to have been good men; but we must not imitate them, or be governed by their authority, in that which was manifestly contrary to the spirit of the gospel. This is one of the principal ways in which error has obtained currency, and even the most zealous support, and sometimes from those who verily thought they were thereby doing God service. The inspired Paul, in writing to the very church to which our text is directed, warns it against referring to human

names, when the great principles of duty are in question. To some
who had said, I am of Paul, and I of Apollos, and I of Cephas, and I
of Christ, he makes the solemn appeal—Was Paul crucified for you?
or were ye baptized in the name of Paul? – Call no man master, my
Friends, one is your master, even Christ. What though Origen was a
pious man, and the most eminently learned and ingenious divine of
his age; and what though Augustine was, perhaps, the most illustrious name for sound theology, erudition, zeal, spirituality, and usefulness, in the annals of the church, from the second to the sixteenth
century? Yet, when the former gave himself up so unworthily to alle-
gorising dreams, and philosophical speculations; and when the latter,
amidst all his pre-eminent worth, yielded to so many of the popular
superstitions of the day; we must by no means attempt to justify all
that they taught. What though Luther, Calvin and Cranmer were
inestimably precious men, and worthy of being held in everlasting
remembrance; the first, for a piety, holy courage, and decision of
character, for which the whole Christian world ought ever be thankful; the second, for a depth of penetration, a soundness of judgment,
an extent of learning, and an ardour of zeal for Christ, which the
friends of the Redeemer's kingdom are bound to remember, to the
end of time, with the deepest veneration; and the third, for a pious
devotedness and fidelity which should never be alluded to by a duti-
ful son of the Reformed church without some epithet of honour? Yet
when Luther indulged in irascible passion, and permitted almost all
his polemical writings to be tarnished with opprobrious language:
when Calvin's name and influence were implicated in the burning of
a heretic; and when Cranmer took a still more immediate and active
part in burning at least four persons for their religious belief; let us
not attempt their justification. Their error, indeed,—I speak more
particularly of the error of the two latter,—was rather that of the age,
than peculiarly of the men; for the rights of conscience were then
understood by none. Still they erred—greatly erred. They used carnal
weapons; and, for this are, of course, to be censured, not imitated.
Again I say, my Friends, we are not to be governed by human authority. As Protestants, as disciples of Christ, the Bible is, to us, the only
infallible rule of faith and practice. The first, and grand question for
us to ask, therefore, is, not—whether any of the rulers have believed

a certain doctrine, or adopted a certain course? Not, whether this or that distinguished man has embraced a particular opinion? Not even, how the church has decided respecting it; but—What saith the Scripture? Let the Word of God be our rule; let it furnish all the weapons we employ; and we may confidently look for a blessing.

4. We may learn from this subject, in what consists that success in his official work, which a minister of the gospel ought to desire and seek. Not in merely collecting and attaching to his person a large and admiring congregation. Not in making his own learning, talents, and accomplishments, the objects of popular applause and idolatry. Not even in filling the church with multitudes of decent professors. A minister may attain all these, in as high a degree as man ever did; and yet, in the most important sense, be wholly without success in his ministerial work. The most precious kind of success; that which he ought to desire, and to pray for without ceasing, consists in his ministry being blessed to the conversion of sinners; in pulling down the strong holds of enmity and disobedience in which they are entrenched; in drawing them away from their infatuated connection with sin and Satan, and all that is corrupting and degrading in their subjection to both; in leading them to a vital union and obedience to the Saviour: in short in bringing the impenitent to the true knowledge and love of the gospel, and in building up believers in faith and holiness unto salvation. This is the success for which a gospel minister should look, and labour, and pray, and nothing short of which ought ever to satisfy him.

I grant, indeed, that an enlightened and faithful gospel ministry may be, and constantly is, productive of many subordinate effects, which are of great value in society. It tends to advance the interests of general knowledge in the world. It promotes order, polish, and decorum in social intercourse. It makes better members of the society of men on earth, thousands and millions who will never be prepared for the inheritance of the saints in light. But still, the higher effects which I have mentioned, are the great and most blessed constituents of success. Where they are never attained, the most important ends of the ministry of reconciliation are never attained. And where this is the case, even the subordinate benefits of which I have spoken, generally fail in a corresponding degree.

5. We learn, from the spirit of our text, what minister is most likely to be successful in his ministerial work. Not, by any means, as a matter of course, he who is the most learned divine. Not he who dwells most, in his public or private instruction, on the philosophy of religion. Not, in all cases, the most eloquent preacher. Not he who is most confident of success. Not he who feels most self-complacency in the contemplation and prospect of success. But he is most likely to be successful in his ministerial work, who himself most cordially loves the gospel; who enters most deeply into its power and sweetness, as a matter of practical experience; who preaches it most simply, intelligently, earnestly and affectionately; who prays most fervently for the manifestation of its saving power; and who exemplifies its benign effects most uniformly in his own temper and life. That man may hope for a blessing on his ministry. Such a man, I will venture to say, never failed of being favoured with times of refreshment and revival from the presence of the Lord. In short, if the faithful minister can have, and ought to have no other influence than that which is of a moral kind; if moral weapons are the only weapons which he ought to attempt to wield; then it is plain that he who displays, both in speech and action, the largest portion of moral truth, moral beauty, and moral glory, will be most likely to exert that happy moral influence, which of all others, is most desirable and precious. This is a kind of exertion, which, when genuine, was never lost. And, as long as God is faithful, he who is steadfast, unmovable, always abounding in the work of the Lord, will find that his labour is not in vain in the Lord. On the other hand, that minister who expects to have a particle of salutary influence in the world, beyond his own solid moral worth, and moral influence; in other words, beyond the degree in which he preaches the Saviour's truth, and manifests the Saviour's loveliness, in his own spirit and practice, will be likely to be most egregiously disappointed. There is a power in consistent holiness, which belongs to nothing else beneath the throne of God.

6. Our text affords many important suggestions to the young servant of Christ, who is about, today, to be constituted a pastor of this church.

My dear Son, both the language and the spirit of the text admonish you, that your ministerial work, if you be faithful in it, will be found a continual warfare; a warfare against all that is hostile in the heart of man to the pure gospel of Christ; a warfare against pride, and unbelief, and appetite, and passion, and avarice, and selfishness, and all that exalteth itself against God and holiness. Whether you have respect to your own heart, or the hearts of others, every inch of ground that is gained, from conversion to glorification, is to be gained by fighting. Go forth, then, to your work with the spirit of a 'soldier'—expecting to fight; willing to fight; and confidently anticipating the victory. Not, indeed, anticipating it, as a celebrated young Reformer, in the beginning of his course did; who felt as if the force of his preaching must bear down all opposition; but who was afterwards constrained to confess, that old Adam was too strong for young Melancthon. Let your anticipations be rather founded on the mighty power of God, and on the promise of his grace to those who employ with fidelity the armour which himself has furnished.

But our text further admonishes you, in this warfare, to beware of the weapons you employ. As to the weapons of persecution, of secular penalty in any form, I bless God that they are equally precluded, by your own disposition, and by the political charters under which it has pleased him mercifully to cast our lot. But think not that these are the only weapons interdicted by your Master. Beware of carnal wisdom, carnal passion, carnal reasoning, carnal prudence, carnal management, carnal substitutes of any kind, for those simple, spiritual weapons which Jehovah hath authorized. Never attempt to promote religion by any other methods than those which the Word of God warrants. Go not forth with Saul's armour; but with the simple sling and stone with which it becomes the good soldier of Jesus Christ to meet those who defy the armies of the living God. The great Head of the church has not authorized you, or any other minister, to lord it over the consciences of men, or to hurt a hair of any man's head on account of his religious belief. The only means entrusted to you are moral means. You are called to beseech men, by the meekness and gentleness of Christ, to be reconciled to God; to instruct them, to persuade them, to entreat them, to pray for them, and to win them by the lustre of your example. These alone are your weapons. Whatever form of opposition you may be called to encounter, never think of employing any other. Employ these, however, with indefatigable diligence. Whether men will hear, or whether they will forbear, follow them, with your instructions, your entreaties, and your prayers, meekly and patiently, to your latest breath. And even if some, in the bitterness of their hostility, should be prompted to oppose you with personal violence (in supposing this possible, I, of course, refer to none in this congregation), say, with the illustrious heathen chief, Strike, but hear me! or rather, with One greater than any mortal champion—Father, forgive them, for they know not what they do!

While on the subject of the weapons you employ, allow me again to put you on your guard, in preaching the gospel, against substituting the refinements of philosophical speculation, for the plainness and simplicity of Bible truth. The latter is adapted to every capacity; is suited to every age, clime, and state of society; and is never truly presented without beneficial effects. The former is often little better than a caricature of the gospel; and, in many cases, is much more fitted to make sceptics and infidels than to bring men to sit, as little children, at the feet of Jesus. The history of religion in our own country presents many an instructive lesson on this subject. Learn wisdom from those lessons. If you wish your preaching to be most useful, let it be as much as possible conformed to the apostolic model. If you are bound as to the matter, why not equally as to the manner, to preach the preaching which your Master bids you?

And while our text warns you against the use of unhallowed weapons, it reminds you where your reliance ought constantly to be placed for success in your work. When David went forth to meet the proud Philistine, he said, in reply to his insolent defiance, I come to thee in the name of the Lord of hosts, the God of the armies of Israel. Such ought to be the language and the dependence of every minister of religion, in going forth to his warfare. There can scarcely be a more unpromising appearance than to see him who undertakes to fight the battles of the Lord, confident in an arm of flesh, and relying on the potency of his own efforts. Very different was the spirit of the apostle Paul. When I am weak, said he, then am I strong. Plainly implying, that when he was most sensible of his own weakness, and most completely divested of all reliance on himself, he enjoyed the firmest confidence in divine aid, and the most comfortable anticipations of ultimate victory.

Thou, therefore, my Son, be strong in the Lord, and in the power of his might. Be of good courage; for the battle is his; and he will never send you awarfaring on your own charges. We shall all look with the deepest interest to the result of your labours in this place. You are about to be connected with one of the most important congregations on this hill of Zion; and to be united with a venerable colleague, whose age and experience will enable him to give you many a valuable lesson, and with whom it will be your privilege to labour as a son with a father. Our prayer is that the Captain of salvation may gird you with strength, and inspire you with wisdom; and that the ecclesiastical relation which is this day formed may be productive of lasting comfort, and an abundant blessing.

7. Finally, our text furnishes matter of serious address to the members of this congregation, who are this day to receive a collegiate pastor.

You have heard that it becomes ministers to employ no other than spiritual weapons in their warfare with human corruption. If so, it becomes those to whom they minister, to be workers together with them, and, as far as possible, to alleviate all the burdens and dangers of their warfare. If your pastors will be bound to labour and pray without ceasing, for the spiritual welfare of yourselves and your children; can it be necessary to employ arguments to show that you ought to encourage and aid them in the most interesting of all work on this side of heaven? In addressing you, my respected Friends, I am persuaded that argument is not necessary. As the only weapons they will ever think of employing will be of a spiritual kind; so these are precisely those in reference to which it will be most in your power to help them. You can help them much by yielding yourselves to God, as those who are alive from the dead; much by your prayers; much in early and faithfully training up your children in the nurture and admonition of the Lord; much by diligently and consistently maintaining family religion; much by exhibiting a bright example of Christian holiness in all your temper and practice. In all these ways, you may hold up their hands, and impart a joy to their spirits, which none but faithful ministers can adequately feel.

Remember, too, my dearly beloved Brethren, that you also, as well as your ministers, if you are Christians, are engaged in a warfare, each one for himself, against sin and Satan, and all the powers of error and wickedness. In this warfare, never forget that spiritual weapons alone can avail you anything. If you desire to mortify corruption, to resist temptation, to overcome the world, and to grow in grace, rely not upon human inventions or strength to accomplish the work. Imagine not that spiritual maladies can ever be reached by carnal weapons; or that real sanctification is ever likely to be promoted by observances which God never appointed. But be unceasingly diligent in the use of all those spiritual means, which the great Author of salvation has instituted, and which alone we have reason to expect he will bless. Look to him. Let his word dwell in you richly, in all wisdom and spiritual understanding. Abound in prayer. Make new and daily application, by faith, to that blood which cleanseth from all sin. Let the love of Christ constrain you to affectionate and holy obedience. Let all his ordinances be precious. Put on the whole armour of God. Fight the good fight of faith. Quit you like men; be strong.

Soon will the solemnities of this day, with all their momentous results, pass in review before a higher tribunal than that which is now assembled in the house of God. Then the Chief Shepherd shall appear, to take an account of his servants, and of those to whom they have ministered. There you and your children must meet these under shepherds, and answer for the use which you shall have made of their labours for your benefit. O, may it be to every one present a meeting replete with joy and with glory! Amen!

THE IMPORTANCE OF
THE GOSPEL MINISTRY[1]

BELOVED Candidates for the holy ministry, it is evident that ministers of religion must have been coeval with the first acts of social worship. Long before the institution of the Levitical priesthood, there were, undoubtedly, persons who 'ministered in holy things', that is, who presided in offering sacrifices, and in conducting the exercises of public instruction and devotion. Even among the antediluvians, we read of those who 'preached' and 'prophesied' in the name of the Lord; and after the flood, before the commencement of the Mosaic dispensation, we find mention made of Melchizedek, a priest of the Most High God; and also of Jethro, a priest of Midian, who was, evidently, a worshipper of Jehovah.

After the establishment of the Aaronic priesthood, the line was more distinctly drawn than ever between the ministers at the altar, and those in whose behalf they ministered. New barriers were raised against all unauthorized intrusion on the appropriate duties of the priestly office; and weighty and most momentous was the trust committed to those who bore that office. When the New Testament church was organized, the same general feature was impressed on the more spiritual dispensation. Still a class of men was set apart for the service of the sanctuary; and their essential functions, as before, appropriated to them alone. In several respects, indeed, did the ceremonial priesthood differ from the New Testament ministry. The latter were no longer confined to a single family. They were no longer called 'priests' but 'ministers', 'servants', 'stewards of the mysteries of God', 'ambassadors of Christ', *etc*. They were no longer distributed

[1] Samuel Miller, *The Importance of the Gospel Ministry: An Introductory Lecture, Delivered at the Opening of the Winter Session of the Theological Seminary at Princeton, New Jersey, Nov. 9, 1827* (Princeton: D. A. Borrenstein, 1827).

into several orders. And a variety of ceremonial observances relating to their qualifications, investiture, and succession, ceased to be obligatory.

Mr Gibbon, indeed, asserts, that the distinction between 'clergy' and 'laity' was unknown in the primitive church, and was not introduced until the second century. If by this assertion he meant, that we do not find these precise terms, to distinguish between ecclesiastical men and others, in familiar use, in any Christian writings earlier than those of Tertullian, Origen, and Cyprian; and, especially, that the proud and arrogant claims with which one of these terms was afterwards connected, were, before their time, in a great measure, unknown;—he is probably correct. But if his meaning be, that the Christian ministry is not an institution of Jesus Christ; that he did not, from the beginning, annex to it a specific spiritual authority; that ministers were not, from the very origin of the church, designated by appropriate titles; that there were not appropriate functions assigned to them; and that these functions were not, in the primitive church, confined to them, but were common to all Christians;—if this be his meaning, there could hardly be a statement more palpably erroneous; —a statement more unequivocally contradicted by the New Testament itself, and all the most authentic records of early antiquity.

And, as the office of which we speak has, either substantially or formally, existed in all ages, so its object has been ever the same. Not to establish a set of lords over God's heritage; not to form a 'privileged order' in the community; not to exercise a spiritual despotism over the understandings and consciences of men; not even to supersede the attention of men to their own spiritual interests; but to stimulate, to guide, and, in various ways, to assist them in this attention. Every private individual, indeed, is, of course, responsible for his own moral character. Every one who comes within the reach of the gospel, is to inquire, to believe, and to obey for himself, and for himself to receive the reward of his deeds; and if he neglect his duty, no diligence on the part of others can avail him. Yet, at the same time, every minister of religion is no less responsible for all the instructions which he gives, and for all his fidelity, or the want of it, in leading those around him into the way of truth and salvation. And if any perish through his unfaithfulness, their blood will be required at his hands.

My object, my beloved young Friends, in the present address, is to call your attention to the unspeakable importance of the sacred office to which you aspire; to show that the character of those who bear it, is vitally interesting to the church of God; that whenever the church is extended and built up, ministers are instrumental in conferring the blessing; that whenever she is corrupted and degraded, ministers are the guilty agents in accomplishing the mischief: and, in short, that what ministers are, the church will always be.

This, I have no doubt, will appear if we consider,—

I. *The great design of the office itself.* The importance of any institution is plainly to be measured by the objects which it is intended to promote; by the purposes which it is appointed and adapted to accomplish. Estimated by this standard, the importance of the gospel ministry is literally infinite. What is its great design? It is nothing less than to publish, explain, and recommend the religion of Jesus Christ; to proclaim its glad tidings, and to extend its holy reign. But, is this religion of any real value to mankind? Is it of any importance that the children of men be instructed in the way of salvation; that they be brought under the genuine power of the gospel; that their sins be pardoned; that their hearts be sanctified; that their evil habits be subdued; that their unhallowed affections and lusts be crucified; and that they be prepared for every holy duty and enjoyment here, and for eternal blessedness hereafter? Nothing can be plainer than that these are matters in comparison with which all the temporal interests of men are as the small dust of the balance, weighed against the everlasting mountains. Yet these are the great matters about which ministers of the gospel are primarily and constantly conversant. The grand object of their commission is to turn men from darkness to light; from Satan to God; from pollution, condemnation and misery, to purity, pardon and happiness; and finally to the enjoyment of an incorruptible crown, an undefiled inheritance, an exceeding and eternal weight of glory in the heavens.

It might be supposed, indeed, that a system so pure, reasonable and glorious as the gospel of Jesus Christ, when once made known, would always be found to work its own way in the world, without the efforts of the living teacher to urge it on the attention and the consciences of men. But the Word of God gives us no warrant to expect such a result, and all experience is equally against it. The carnal mind is enmity against God. The natural man receiveth not the things of the Spirit of God; they are foolishness unto him. So that, left to himself, no one would embrace or obey the gospel. To say nothing, therefore, of the unnumbered millions of our world's population, who have never heard the gospel, and who can never be expected to hear it 'without preachers', ministers may be said to be indispensable for maintaining the power of the gospel, even where it is already established. To keep alive religion in the world; to prevent Christian knowledge, public worship, the Sabbath, and the various ordinances of social piety from utterly perishing among men; in short, to preserve those who have enjoyed Christianity from relapsing into real heathenism, it is necessary that ministers of religion be constantly employed to rouse men to a sense of their condition. It is necessary not only that the people be furnished with the written Word, but also with the living teacher, who shall, from Sabbath to Sabbath, and from house to house, bring their minds, if I may so express it, into contact with that Word, and constrain them to give it their serious and practical attention. It is necessary that they be called together, instructed, warned, entreated, conjured, again and again, day by day, to attend to the things which belong to their peace. For nearly eighteen centuries, the standing means both of maintaining and extending the knowledge of Christ and his salvation in the world, has been the preaching of the gospel. And without the use of this divine ordinance still, we have no reason to expect either that sinners will be converted, or saints edified and comforted. It is not, of course, meant to be intimated, either that no conversion is ever effected but by means of the authorized ministry; or that this ministry is ever made effectual by any virtue or power of its own. But the position meant to be maintained is, that God, in his sovereign wisdom, hath appointed and promised by the foolishness of preaching to save them that believe; that consequently, on the one hand, where the gospel is not preached, we have no reason to expect that the work of conversion and salvation will, to any extent, go forward; and that, on the other, where it is faithfully and ably dispensed, it will generally be accompanied in a greater or less degree with a sanctifying and saving power.

Now, if these things be so, then it follows that the best interests of the community, and especially the vital interests of the church of God,—her orthodoxy, purity, life, peace, and enlargement, may be said to be suspended on the character of her ministry. Where there are no ministers, it is obvious that there can be no church, no organized, visible Christianity. And where there is an existing ministry, it is equally evident that the church must, from the nature of things, bear the same character with those who are the appointed medium for conveying to her the aliment on which she lives, and the principles by which she is guided. If men be either not instructed at all, or taught erroneously, the consequences may be equally fatal. If the blind lead the blind, we know what infinite wisdom has told us will ensue. None under the name of ministers can hope to be instrumental in promoting the true welfare of men, but those who have both the ability and the disposition to lead them in the right way. If they be, generally, enlightened, fervently pious, and really faithful, not only in preaching the pure gospel, but also in the discharge of all their public and private duties; true religion both in principle and practice, will be extensively understood, valued, and prevalent. But if, on the contrary, they be, as a body, ignorant, unfaithful, erroneous in doctrine, or corrupt in practice; if they be proud, ambitious, worldly minded, contentious, and negligent of the best interests of men; real religion will as certainly be despised and decline, as any necessary effect will result from the presence of its cause. Nay, only let ministers be indolent, and forgetful of the great end and duties of their office, and spiritual desolation and death will as assuredly reign around them, as darkness will ensue in the absence of the solar rays. In short, if human nature be such as the Bible represents it,— earthly, sensual, proud, selfish, and backward to all that is spiritually good; if no other remedy than that which the gospel furnishes, be either adapted or effectual to the healing of our moral disease; and if all Scripture and all experience teach us that this remedy cannot be expected to display its healing power, any further than it is unremittingly exhibited and applied, by those who are appointed to execute this holy and benevolent office; then nothing can be plainer than that, if they be essentially deficient, either in orthodoxy, skill or fidelity, the moral pestilence which they are commissioned to cure, must rage with uncontrolled fury. It would require a constant course of miracles to prevent consequences the most disastrous from covering the face of society.

When we consider, moreover, that the public preaching of the gospel is almost the only means of instruction in morals and religion which a large portion of mankind enjoy; when we reflect that the minds of men, if not occupied with truth and holiness, will be unavoidably occupied with falsehood, with superstition, and with numberless forms of corruption; and when we remember, too, that the eyes of all, enemies as well as friends, are habitually turned toward ministers of religion, either for the purpose of imitating their example, or of deriving from their delinquencies encouragement in infidelity and sin;—when these things are considered, surely it is not easy to overrate the importance of the sacred office to all the best interests of the church, and of mankind. Surely, it is of unspeakable, nay of infinite moment, that the man who undertakes to instruct his fellow men in the things of God, and salvation; who is, as it were, their mouth in speaking to God, and the mouth of God in speaking to them; who dispenses the sacraments to them and their children; who administers instruction and consolation to the sick and the dying; who undertakes, in a word, to be the teacher, the counsellor and the guide of his fellow sinners, in seeking temporal and eternal happiness;—surely it is of infinite importance that he who is charged with these high duties, should be wise, holy, faithful, diligent, self-denied, and exemplary. On his character and conduct, the interests of eternity as well as of time, are every hour suspended. A minister of religion cannot be a neutral or indifferent member of society. He will be a blessing or a curse wherever he is. And a blessing or a curse, in most cases, proportioned to the degree in which he is pious and faithful, or the reverse.

II. Let us next attend to *some of the statements of Scripture on this subject.* These correspond, most perfectly, with the foregoing representations:—importing, that when the spiritual guides of the people are wise and faithful, the church is always blessed; and that when they are ignorant, selfish, and corrupt, she never fails to suffer, and generally in direct proportion to the degree of their delinquency.

On the one hand, faithful ministers are promised in Scripture as a great blessing, and their labours represented as a pledge of rich benefits, both temporal and spiritual. I will give you pastors, saith Jehovah, by the prophet, after mine own heart who shall feed you with knowledge and with understanding. And again, by the same prophet, 'I will set shepherds over them, which shall feed them. And what is represented as the consequence to those who are thus fed? They shall fear no more, nor be dismayed, neither shall they be lacking, saith the Lord. And again, the great Head of the church, in describing that period when Zion shall eminently flourish, says, I have set watchmen upon thy walls, O Jerusalem, which shall never hold their peace, day nor night:—and concerning that period, he adds, Behold, the Lord hath proclaimed unto the end of the world, Say ye to the daughter of Zion, Behold, thy salvation cometh; behold, his reward is with him, and his work before him. Thou shalt no more be termed Forsaken; neither shall thy land any more be termed Desolate: but thou shalt be called Hephzibah, [that is—My delight is in her], and thy land Beulah, [that is—Married]; for the Lord delighteth in thee, and thy land shall be married (*Jer.* 3:15; 23:4; *Isa.* 62:4, 6, 11).

On the other hand, the unfaithfulness of ministers is, everywhere, represented in Scripture, not only as an aggravated sin; but also as a source of incalculable injury to the church, and to all the interests of social order. The following specimen of inspired language on this subject, is of the most decisive character.

Thus saith the Lord, the pastors are become brutish, and have not sought the Lord; therefore they shall not prosper, and all their flocks shall be scattered. Mine heart within me is broken because of the prophets; for both prophet and priest are profane: they walk in lies; they strengthen the hands of evil doers, so that none doth return from his wickedness. Thus saith the Lord, from the prophets is profaneness gone forth into all the land. If they had stood in my counsel, and had caused my people to hear my words, then they would have turned them from the evil of their doings. But they have caused my people to forget my name. Therefore, I am against the prophets, saith the Lord. Pastors have destroyed my vineyard; they have trodden my portion under foot; they have made my pleasant portion a desolate wilderness.

Son of man, prophesy against the shepherds of Israel; prophesy and say unto them, Thus saith the Lord God unto the shepherds—Woe be to the shepherds of Israel, that do feed themselves. Should not the shepherds feed their flocks? Ye eat the fat, and ye clothe you with the wool; ye kill them that are fat; but ye feed not the flock. The diseased have ye not strengthened, neither have ye healed that which was sick, neither have ye bound up that which was broken, neither have ye brought again that which was driven away, neither have ye sought that which was lost; but with force and with cruelty have ye ruled them. And they were scattered, and they became meat to all the beasts of the field, when they were scattered. Hear this, O ye priests, and hearken; for judgment is toward you, because ye have been a snare on Mizpah, and a net spread upon Tabor. My people are destroyed for lack of knowledge; because thou hast rejected knowledge, I will also reject thee, that thou shalt be no priest unto me: seeing thou hast forgotten the law of thy God, I will also forget thy children. There shall be, like people, like priest; and I will punish them for their ways, and reward them for their doings. Thus saith the Lord God, Woe unto the foolish prophets, that follow their own spirits, and have seen nothing. O Israel, thy prophets are like the foxes in the deserts. Therefore, thus saith the Lord, because they have spoken vanity, and seen lies, therefore, behold, I am against them, saith the Lord God. Because they have seduced my people, saying, Peace, peace, when there was no peace; and one built up a wall, and lo, others daubed it with untempered mortar. Therefore, I will break down the wall, and it shall fall, and ye shall be consumed in the midst thereof; and ye shall know that I am the Lord. O ye priests, ye have departed out of the way; ye have caused many to stumble at the law. Therefore have I made you contemptible before all the people, according as ye have not kept my ways (*Jer.* 10:18, 21; 12:10; 22:9, 14, 15, 23, 27, 30; *Ezek.* 34:2-5; *Hos.* 4:6, 9, 10; 5:1; *Ezek.* 13:4, 8-10; *Mal.* 2:8).

It were easy to fill many pages with quotations from the Old Testament, which speak in a similar strain. And the same language is continued in the New Testament. There we read of false teachers; of teachers reprobate concerning the truth; of men who, by their false doctrines, and unhallowed practices, overthrew the faith of those around them; of men who sought their own, not the things which are Jesus Christ's. And we are assured, that such, not only brought upon themselves swift destruction; but that many followed their pernicious ways, and that, on their account, the way of truth was evil spoken of. In short, in every part of Scripture, we find error in doctrine, and corruption in practice, in the church, uniformly traced to the ignorance, unfaithfulness, or profligacy of those, whose office and whose duty it was to have been teachers and guides of the people. The language before quoted of the inspired prophet—like people, like priests, may be considered as an epitome of all the scriptural statements on this subject.

III. The great principle which it is my present object to establish, is further confirmed *by all the analogies and facts which pervade every species of society.* In the family circle—if the parents, the natural instructors and guides of youth, be ignorant, unprincipled, profane, or profligate; who does not expect as a matter of course, to find the children walking in the same steps of ignorance, pollution and shame? And if they be found to possess the opposite character, who does not regard it as a kind of moral miracle? Nay, in the estimation of the wise, it is not necessary that a parent be profligate, in order to be a curse to his children. Such is the tendency of human nature to sink down into darkness and ruin, that indolence alone, on his part, may effectually destroy them. Only let him entirely neglect their intellectual and moral culture, and he will probably train them up to be miserable vagabonds, a disgrace to himself, and the pests of society.

In like manner, in a seminary of learning; do we not always find the attainments and character of the taught, to bear a distinct proportion to those of the teachers? If those who occupy the place of instructors be grossly defective either in scholarship or diligence, who can reasonably suppose that they will succeed in the propagation of sound knowledge? If preceptors be ignorant, it were strange, indeed, to find their pupils well instructed. If those who are employed to cultivate the minds, and form the habits of the young, be incompetent to the discharge of their duties, and set an unworthy example, how can learning, and virtue, and order, be expected to reign among those committed to their care? As well might we expect darkness to beget light, or vice to propagate virtue. And if the degeneracy should become so widespread, as that the whole body of literary teachers in a country, at the same time, should be unqualified and unfaithful, would not the general interests of literature necessarily, and as a matter of course, be everywhere utterly degraded? If the fountains be corrupt, the streams, surely, cannot be pure and salutary. It is impossible. What the former are, the latter will ever be.

The same principle applies to the civil community. Legislators and magistrates give law to those around them, not only by official enactments, but also by their example, and by the incalculable power of their influence. When, therefore, they throw the whole weight of their example and influence, whatever may be their amount, into the scale of order, virtue, and true religion, the consequence is always happy. There never was an instance of this being thoroughly done, by leading men, as a body, without giving a tone to public sentiment and practice of the most benign character. And, on the contrary, there never was an instance of their generally taking an opposite course, without producing effects of the most injurious kind on public morals and happiness. If it be true, in every walk and connection of life, that one sinner destroyeth much good; it is equally true, that one truly pious and exemplary man produceth much good. But when that sinner, or that pious man, holds a conspicuous and influential place in society, who can set bounds to the good or the evil which he may, and probably will, occasion? Every additional degree of elevation which he holds, or of influence which he possesses, will render him a greater blessing, or a heavier curse, each day that he lives. In a word, as the general character of the rulers of a nation is, so will the nation itself certainly prove.

But if this principle apply to every other class of rulers and leaders among men, much more essentially and solemnly does it apply to ministers of the gospel. Because the great interest, entrusted to their official administration, are infinitely more momentous than the highest of those which secular men, as such, can ever pursue; because, in spiritual things, we stand in more pressing need of stimulants, and guidance, and aid, than in temporal pursuits; and because the consequences of the influence which ministers exert, and of the impressions which they make, not only affect this mortal life, but stretch into eternity. The highest object which kings, emperors, and legislators ever propose to themselves, in their fondest plans, is the advancement of population, wealth, external tranquillity, and temporal happiness. None of them ever sought the sanctification of the human heart, and the everlasting welfare of men, as the ultimate end of their plans. But the great end of that kingdom which faithful ministers recommend and promote, while it includes many subordinate benefits, is moral and eternal blessedness. Of this kingdom alone it may be said, that it is not meat and drink, but righteousness and peace and joy in the Holy Ghost. And to him alone who is immediately instrumental in saving or destroying a soul, do the highest responsibilities attach of which man is capable. When other leading men in the community act their part, they will, no doubt, exert some degree of influence on the moral as well as the secular interests of men; but the activity of ministers of the gospel is primarily destined to affect, and, to the whole extent of its influence, does affect the spiritual and eternal interest of all within the sphere of their ministrations. I have only to add,—

IV. That all these reasonings are abundantly *confirmed by the voice of history*. The direct declarations of Scripture on the general truth before us, have been already considered. Its historical information is equally striking and decisive. Search the inspired history, from beginning to end, and you shall find, that just in proportion as ministers of religion were enlightened and holy, faithful and diligent, the purity and prosperity of the church were established. Whether during the patriarchal or Mosaic dispensations; whether under judges or kings, it was ever the same. Wherever the spiritual instructors and guides were sound and devoted men, religion, in a considerable degree, flourished; truth was maintained; idolatry was frowned upon; and order and happiness abounded. And whenever God, after long spiritual declension among his people, intended mercy for them, and a happy revival in their bondage, we never find him accomplishing his purpose by miracle, but always by the use of human instruments, and generally by his commissioned servants. He seldom failed to raise up able and devoted men to enlighten, reform and sanctify the people. But whenever the prevailing character of those who bore the sacred office became corrupt, a scene the sad reverse of all this was disclosed on every side. Truth and justice were trodden down in the streets, divine institutions were dishonoured. Idolatry lifted its head, and public profligacy and misery followed in its train. This was so steadily the course of things throughout the whole of the Old Testament economy, that to quote all the examples of it on record, would be to repeat the greater part of the Jewish Scriptures. On the one hand, the revivals of religion which occurred repeatedly, under the auspices of faithful men, raised up by God for the purpose, in the time of the Judges, and afterwards in the time of Ezra, of Nehemiah, and of the Asmonean witnesses of the truth; and, on the other hand, the pernicious influence of unsanctified teachers, from time to time; the conduct of Hophni and Phinehas, who, by their unworthy conduct, caused the people to despise the offerings of the Lord; the conduct of the sons of Samuel, who became sources of deep corruption and disaffection among the people; and the deplorable spirit, habits and influence of the priests and scribes, before the captivity, after the captivity, and during our Lord's ministry on earth,—all bear witness to the correctness of the principle which I am endeavouring to establish.

When the New Testament church was set up under a more spiritual form, the ministers commissioned to go forth, and preach the gospel, with Paul at their head, were men, we know, of a peculiarly devoted spirit. They were endowed not only with extraordinary gifts, but also with large measures of grace. They meddled not with the kingdoms of this world. They aspired to no earthly distinctions. They employed no 'carnal weapons'. They undertook not to be 'judges or dividers' among the people. But setting one object alone before them—the advancement of the kingdom of Christ, in all its simplicity and purity, they pursued that object with zeal, with indefatigable labour, and with unceasing prayer, day and night; giving themselves wholly to their work; shrinking from no privation; intimidated by no danger; counting all things but loss for the excellency of Christ; and not regarding even their lives as dear to them, so that they might finish their course with joy, and the ministry which they had received of the Lord Jesus. How striking the delineation of the character, and the narrative of the ministry of these holy men! What sacred elevation of sentiment and affection! What zeal! What humility! What disinterestedness! What abstraction from the pleasures and honours of the world! What devotedness to their Master's glory, and to the salvation of souls! What unwearied labour in preaching and instructing from house to house! What holiness of example in all manner of conversation!

And what were the effects of the ministrations of such men? The most decisive and happy. The Lord followed their labours with an abundant blessing. More was done in the propagation of the genuine gospel, during the first century, than in any other, from that period to the present hour. None of those devoted missionaries laboured in vain. The Word of the Lord had free course, and was glorified. Much people were added to the Lord. As long as the ministers of Christ maintained this character, not all the wisdom of philosophy falsely so called; not all the frowns of an antichristian government; nay, not all the terrors of martyrdom, could obstruct the course of the new and heaven-born system which they taught. Though they were persecuted from city to city; persecuted to prison and to death; hated of all men, and their names cast forth as vile, for the sake of the holy and gracious message which they proclaimed; still that message went on conquering and to conquer. Great multitudes believed and were added to the Lord, both men and women: And the Word of God increased, and the number of the disciples multiplied greatly; and great companies became obedient to the faith. And the churches had rest and were edified, and walking in the fear of the Lord, and in the comfort of the Holy Ghost, were multiplied. Nor was this the case merely in Judea, in Samaria, and in Galilee, but also in Syria, in Asia Minor, in Rome, in Greece, and, indeed, throughout the greater part of the known world.

It is not denied, indeed, that in several of the churches of which we have accounts, during the lives of these devoted ministers of Christ, we read of dissensions arising, of false doctrines being introduced, and of corrupt practices gaining ground. But, while we admit that the apostles were not perfect, more than other men; and that, as long as human beings preach, and administer the affairs of the church, some degree of imperfection may be expected to mark every work and society with which they are connected; still it may be confidently asserted, that the difficulties and corruptions which arose in the apostolic churches, were in no wise inconsistent with the doctrine which I maintain. For, in every instance in which heresy, division, or immoral practices marked the character of any church in the apostle's days, it was, evidently, the work of weak or wicked ministers; of false apostles, judaizing teachers, or men otherwise unsound and unfaithful; who, coming in, brought with them error, strife, and every evil work. I cannot recollect a single exception to this statement. Corrupt occupants of the sacred office, or miserable pretenders to that office, were always the authors of the mischief.

In the second and third centuries, we mark a gradual, but very distinct and melancholy decline, both in faith and practice, throughout the whole church. And when we carefully scrutinize the causes, as well as the circumstances of this decline, it is impossible not to consider it as connected with a corresponding decline in the character of the clergy. When Justin Martyr, Clement of Alexandria, and Origen, together with other ministers, whose taste and character they became instrumental in perverting, had tarnished the simplicity and purity of the gospel; they opened the way for more mischief in the church of God, than, with all their learning they were able to estimate, or, with all their good intentions, to counteract. The following strong picture from the pen of Cyprian, will show that there was at that time clerical degeneracy enough to account for all the corruption, in doctrine and practice, which then existed, or which soon followed.

A long continuance of peace and security had relaxed the rigour of that holy discipline which was delivered to us from above. The religion of the clergy slackened and decayed; the faith of priests and deacons grew languid and inactive; works of charity were discontinued; and an universal license and corruption prevailed. Divers bishops, who should have taught both by their example and persuasion, neglecting their high trust, and their commission from above, entered upon the management of secular affairs, and leaving their seat, and their charge with it, wandered about, from place to place on mercantile business, and in pursuit of disreputable gain. Thus the poor of the church were miserably neglected, while the bishops, who should have taken care of them, were intent upon nothing but their own private profit, which they were forward to advance at any rate, and by any, even the foulest methods.[1]

[1] *Dr Lapsis,* Sect. 4.

Origen speaks of the clergy of his day in language no less pointed and revolting. 'If Christ', says he,

> justly wept over Jerusalem, he may now, on much better grounds, weep over the church, which was erected to the end that it might be an house of prayer; and yet, through the filthy usury of some (and I wish that these were not even the pastors of the people) it is made a den of thieves.[1]

Eusebius, who lived in the next century, writes in the same strain concerning the age of Cyprian.

> When, through too much liberty, we fell into sloth and negligence; when everyone began to envy and backbite another; when we waged, as it were, an intestine war amongst ourselves, with words as with swords; pastors rushed against pastors, and people against people, and strife and tumult, deceit and guile advanced to the highest pitch of wickedness.—Our pastors, despising the rule of religion, strove mutually with one another, studying nothing more than how to outdo each other in strife, emulations, hatred, and mutual enmity; proudly usurping principalities, as so many places of tyrannical domination. Then the Lord covered the daughter of Zion with a cloud in his anger.[2]

If such were the character of the clergy in the days of Origen and Cyprian, we have, surely, no reason to wonder at the deep degeneracy, both in doctrine and morals, which all the records of that time show to have begun in every part of the church, and which prepared the way for the still deeper degeneracy which marked the succeeding age. The teachers and leaders of the church, as a body, were no longer faithful; and it would have been miraculous, indeed, if the church herself had remained pure and harmonious.

In the fourth century, when Christianity became, for the first time, the established religion of the Roman Empire, both the causes and the symptoms of spiritual corruption, became, everywhere, more prevalent, and more strongly marked. And the first and most prominent fact which strikes us, in the gloomy scene which followed, is the degeneracy of the clergy. Christ's kingdom is not of this world. Of

[1] In *Mett.*, p. 441.
[2] *Hist. Eccles.* Lib. viii. cap. 1.

course, the moment the church becomes united with the civil government, under whatever form, she suffers a kind of spiritual prostitution, which is invariably productive of both pollution and degradation. When Constantine professed to be a convert to the religion of Christ (and he was, probably, never more than a mere worshipper in the 'outer court' of the Christian temple) he immediately began to bestow upon its institutions and ministers all the splendour of imperial munificence. The emperor, and his subordinate officers, courted and flattered the clergy; and the clergy, in their turn, courted and flattered the great men of the empire;—sought their smiles;—accepted secular endowments with greediness;—were found in places at court;—and became the sycophants and tools of men in power. Their suppleness, luxury, unhallowed emulations, and consequent unfaithfulness led, as might have been expected, to a corresponding character among the body of visible Christians. Again the Old Testament adage, 'like people, like priest', became unhappily and signally realized. The church exchanged the simplicity of truth, and the beauty of holiness, for the habiliments of secular splendour. And then set in that full tide of corruption in doctrine, order and morals, which, after receiving one serious check in the time of Augustine, soon issued in the Papal apostasy; and transformed the chaste virgin, as left by our Lord and his apostles, into the mother of harlots and abominations.

During the Dark Ages, the general character of the clergy was such as we might suppose likely to produce, and be produced by, the character of the church. Ignorant, voluptuous, ambitious, contentious, and profligate, as the great body of them were, to an almost incredible degree, they continually shed a baleful influence all around them; and instead of being teachers of truth and purity, and guides to heaven; they became, everywhere, instructors in the most childish superstitions, panders to lust, and ringleaders in all wickedness. If truth, and decency, and, especially, anything like Christian character existed anywhere, they were sure to be found in the respective neighbourhoods of some pious ministers of Christ, scattered here and there, who, like glimmering stars in a dark night, were lighting a few humble souls to glory.

Time would fail me in entering into those minute details of historical induction which serve to illustrate and confirm our general position. But, if I mistake not, the further we penetrate into the recesses of ecclesiastical history, the more numerous and glaring will be found to be the facts, which establish, not only the reality, but also the importance of the doctrine which it is my aim to impress upon your minds.

Who were the authors of ninety-nine parts out of an hundred, of that enormous mass of superstition, which now forms, and has for ages formed, the contents of that Augean stable, which the inspired apostle styles the man of sin, the son of perdition? Beyond all controversy, ecclesiastics—ignorant, deluded, vain, or profligate ecclesiastics.

With whom have originated all the heresies, which, from the birth of Christ to this hour, have corrupted and divided the church, and given rise to some of her most fearful calamities? In almost every instance, their authors have been ecclesiastics—philosophical or ambitious ecclesiastics.

Who have created the most mischievous parties and schisms, which have distracted and torn the body of Christ; alienated his ministers from each other; and filled Christendom with the most bitter and unrelenting warfare? A regard to truth still constrains me to say, that selfish, proud, turbulent ecclesiastics have been the ringleaders in all the mischief.

Who have been, in almost all cases, the haughty and cruel persecutors of the meek, pious, and faithful witnesses of the truth? Who have been most active in conducting those of whom the world was not worthy, to prison and to death, for their fidelity to God and his people? It is painful to repeat the sentence;—but it is impossible to avoid still saying—ecclesiastics.

Who can take the most cursory glance at the ecclesiastical history of Great Britain, in the seventeenth century, without perceiving how possible, nay, how easy it is for a bigoted, proud, and worldly clergy to destroy, in a few years, the spirituality of a church, to banish her most faithful ministers, and to cover her with darkness and desolation? And who can study, ever so slightly, the rise, progress, and disasters of the French Huguenots, so conspicuous, at one period, among the pious followers of the Lamb, without being convinced that the gradual departure of their ministry from the doctrines and spirit of the Reformation, was the principal means of drawing down upon them those awful judgments, by which a righteous God was pleased to reduce and scatter them, and from which they have never recovered to the present day?

On the contrary, who have been chiefly instrumental, under the divine blessing, in accomplishing all the happy reformations which have, at any time, blessed the church? Who have been instrumental in forming new and thriving congregations; in restoring weak and declining ones; in healing ecclesiastical divisions; in promoting happy revivals of religion; in transforming an ignorant, unpolished, and heathen population, into an enlightened, orderly, and pious community; in raising the standard of intellect; in promoting the growth of knowledge; in encouraging and regulating the education of youth; in diffusing a spirit of sound morality; in teaching men the rights of conscience, and extending a love of civil and religious liberty;—in a word, in promoting the reign of truth, order, and happiness, in church and State? To these questions, if I mistake not, the voice of history returns a very unequivocal response. In particular, the more closely you scrutinize the history of the Waldenses and Albigenses in remoter periods; and of the Protestant churches of England, France, Geneva, Germany, Holland, Scotland, and New England, in more modern times, the more clearly you will find them to speak a language in perfect harmony with the great principle which I maintain: viz., that no church was ever ruined, or essentially injured, but by her own ministers: or signally blessed, but through a revival of their zeal and fidelity.

If the foregoing representation be correct, then we may infer,

1. *That the ministerial office is the most interesting, the most responsible, the most awful under heaven.* Every minister of the gospel bears a resemblance to his Master in this respect, that he is set for the rise and fall of many in Israel. What he is, the portion of the church with which he is connected, will probably be. Most other men may go through life without exerting such a vital influence, both for time and eternity. But on his character, example, spirit, and preaching are continually suspended the everlasting realities of salvation or perdition, and that to an extent which no human arithmetic can calculate. He does not deliver a sermon, or take a step, or live an hour,

which may not take hold of heaven or hell. To him the ark of God is committed, and an unhallowed touch may draw down destruction, not only on himself, but on thousands. Can a candidate for the ministry think of this, and not tremble? Is not this a charge weighty enough, and momentous enough in its consequences, to make even an angel tremble? No wonder that some great and good men have shrunk from the thought of accepting this office out of pure conscientiousness. And, let me add, that that youth who, in contemplating this office, does not look forward to it with a sacred awe; who does not sit down, and solemnly count the cost of his undertaking; and, while he reposes, with confidence in the power and faithfulness of his God, does not often ask himself, with the most tender and prayerful solicitude—Who is sufficient for these things?—discovers but little acquaintance either with his own heart, or with the magnitude and awfulness of the trust which he seeks. But, while I say this, in fidelity to you, my young Friends, I must also, in fidelity to my Master, say—Let no young man who sincerely loves Christ and the souls of men; who earnestly desires the gospel ministry; and to whom the great Head of the church opens the regular door of entrance into the office;—let no such young man say,—The work is so awful, that I dare not venture upon it. Of every such youth it may be said, The Lord hath need of him: and for discharging the duties of this high trust, he may safely cast himself on the power and grace of him who said concerning his ministers—Lo, I am with you always, even unto the end of the world.

2. From the view which has been taken of this subject we may infer, *how various, extensive, and difficult of attainment, are the qualifications which fit any man to be useful, and, especially, in any eminent degree, useful, in the ministerial office!*—The man who undertakes to instruct hundreds, and, perhaps, thousands, of the learned as well as the ignorant, in the most important of all knowledge:—the man who offers himself as an expounder of the Bible, the most difficult book, in some respects, in the world, to be understood and explained:—the man who proposes to act as a spiritual guide to immortal souls; to enlighten the perplexed; to counsel the tempted; to satisfy the doubting; to silence the bold and literary infidel; to refute the learned and ingenious heretic; and to stop the mouth of the artful caviller:—

the man who undertakes to be a watchman on the walls of Zion, to discern when danger is approaching; to estimate its nature and magnitude, and to give warning accordingly:—the man, in a word, who is preparing to go forth into the church, and the world, as an adviser, a guide, and a helper, in all that is good; as a centre of light, and counsel, and instruction, and consolation, and holy activity to thousands:—surely such a man ought to have many qualifications which do not belong, and are not necessary, to common Christians. What various, and extensive knowledge; especially, what familiar acquaintance with Scripture; what deep and ardent piety; what prudence; what knowledge of the world and of the human heart; what command of his own spirit; what zeal; what patience; what capacity for labour; what diligence; what perseverance, are indispensable here? That no man without unfeigned and even ardent piety ought to engage in the duties of this office, is conceded, even by those who have no piety themselves. But there may be truly pious men, who are, nevertheless, totally unqualified for the ministerial work. No ignorant man; no strikingly weak man; no imprudent man; no habitually indolent man; no rash, headstrong, turbulent, contentious man, is fit to be a minister, even if we could suppose him to have the piety of an angel.

3. From the representation which has been given, we may infer, *that candidates for the holy ministry ought to be in no haste to terminate their preparatory studies, and to enter on the active duties of the sacred office.* When we reflect on the various attainments and qualifications which are indispensable to the able and faithful discharge of ministerial duties; how much digested knowledge, sacred and profane; how much Christian experience; how much familiarity with Christian casuistry; how much self-command; and what long and unwearied labour is to be gone through, not only in storing the mind and the heart with all requisite ministerial furniture; but also in forming such habits and manners as shall be adapted to promote official usefulness.—When we reflect on this, it appears equally wonderful and humiliating, that any candidate for the sacred office should imagine that he can be prepared for the pulpit, and the pastoral charge, in a few brief months after commencing his professional studies! It is difficult to conceive of more deep delusion. Does not the apostle expressly prohibit laying

hands on a 'novice?' And what is a 'novice', but one who labours under that deficiency in knowledge and practical experience which usually characterizes a recent convert?—It is impossible for any man, whatever may be his talents, to acquire, in so short a time, the requisite amount of various knowledge. But even if he could do this, still he ought to be deterred from contenting himself with so hasty and compendious a course. For he has much to gain besides mere knowledge, and much that requires time, toil, and conflict. He is called to study his own heart; to ascertain his own defects and foibles; to discipline his own feelings and habits; to study clerical character, under its various aspects, as it is, and as it ought to be; to become acquainted with the state, and the wants of the church; and, in a word, to lay a deep and broad foundation for every superstructure of intellectual, moral, and spiritual attainment, which it is his duty to raise.

You, no doubt, remember, that the priests, under the Old Testament dispensation, were not permitted to enter on the public duties of their office, until they had reached the age of thirty years. I will not say, that, under the New Testament economy, we ought to be rigidly governed by the same rule. But I can by no means regard with approbation the conduct of some modern candidates for the sacred office, who have prematurely pressed into the pulpit, at the age of twenty, or twenty-one, after an extremely hurried and imperfect course of study. I will only say, that, in ordinary cases, nothing can justify such presumptuous haste. No young man, unless his circumstances be very peculiar, ought ever to be licensed to preach the gospel under twenty-four, or twenty-five years of age; or to be ordained to the work of the ministry under twenty-six, or twenty-eight. Men seldom have, at an earlier age, that deep, steady, enlightened piety; that amount of Christian experience; that maturity of judgment; that established gravity and prudence; that acquaintance with men and manners, and those stores of practical wisdom, which are so desirable, even in the first acts of evangelical and pastoral duty. Many a juvenile candidate for the sacred office has entered on his public duties so strikingly deficient in knowledge, in maturity of judgment, and in practical experience, as to draw a heavy cloud, not only over the outset but also over the whole course of his professional life. To this source, I have no doubt, we may trace many of those personal indiscretions and theological and ecclesiastical vagaries, which have destroyed the usefulness of many a young minister. To this source, also, we may trace the early decline of popularity, and the disreputable dismission of many a promising young pastor who, with all his sprightliness and confidence, never had a stock of knowledge adequate to the demands of the stated ministry. To this we must ascribe the poor, jejune, and unprofitable preaching of hundreds, who maintain their places, and wear the clerical garb. And to this, among other things, we may refer the rashness, and the melancholy triumph of zeal, over knowledge and wisdom, in undertaking to guide the interests of religion, in times of extraordinary awakening and revival. The narratives of the unscriptural devices, and unskilful management of ministers, pious, indeed, but totally lacking in information, experience, and mature wisdom, form some of the most melancholy pages in the history of the church.

4. If the doctrine on which I have been insisting be correct, then, *how great is the guilt of unfaithful ministers!* He who has taken on himself the vows, and all the tremendous responsibilities of this office; and yet, from indolence, or from spiritual indifference, neglects the souls committed to his charge:—or, from a desire to please, flatters and deceives them in the great concerns of salvation,—daubing with untempered mortar, and crying, peace, peace, when there is no peace;—incurs a degree of guilt which it is impossible to express or measure. We speak of the thief, the murderer, and the perjured person, in civil life, with abhorrence; but what is their guilt, when compared, in the light of God's Word, with that of the unfaithful minister? The one robs his fellow men of a portion of perishing wealth;—the other robs them of all that is precious in the hopes of the soul. The one kills the body, and after that, has no more that he can do;—but under the murderous hand of the other, the immortal spirit dies, and is plunged into the abyss of the damned. The one tramples on a solemn appeal to God about some temporal trifle;—the other daily violates oaths and vows which have for their object the church of the living God, the pillar and ground of the truth, and all the mighty interests of thousands throughout an unwasting eternity. A wicked minister is the most wicked of all men. His sins are more extensively and permanently mischievous than those of other men. He sins against greater

light, and stronger obligations, and more solemn engagements than
other men. And, therefore, it appears to me highly probable, that
the lowest depths in the prison of eternal despair, are occupied by
unprincipled, unfaithful ministers. And, let me ask—Is not this
peculiar guilt likely to rest with especial weight on such unprincipled
and unfaithful ministers as hold an orthodox creed, and go down to
perdition from orthodox churches? Surely those whose theory is most
spiritual; whose profession is most strict; and whose excitements to
fidelity are most solemn, incur a proportional degree of guilt in setting them all at naught. If this suggestion be well founded, there are,
probably, no men on earth, at this hour, whose situation is more
responsible, and who are called upon more deeply to ponder it in
their hearts, than the ministers, and candidates for the ministry, of
the Presbyterian Church in the United States.

5. In the light of this subject *we may see why it is, that the clergy
have been so much despised, and made the objects of so much contemptu-
ous sneer, in all ages, by infidels and worldly men.* That assailing, and
endeavouring to depreciate the character of ministers, has long been
a favourite method of attacking Christianity itself, both on the part
of some who professed to believe it, as well as of open infidels, is well
known. The unfairness of this method of attack is, indeed, manifest.
The Bible is our rule of faith and practice; not the character of those
who undertake to expound and publish it. Still, however plain, and
however reasonable this distinction, it is often entirely overlooked.
Religion always has been, and ever will be, to a great extent, judged
of by her ministers. And, alas! that they have, in so many instances,
given occasion to the enemy to 'speak reproachfully'! Among the
many millions of ministers who have officiated in the sanctuary since
the establishment of a visible church on earth, how large a number,
with the language of holy exhortation on their lips, have been grossly
immoral! How many more, while directing the attention of others
to a better world, have manifested that they were selfish, worldly
minded, and supremely devoted to the ambitious pursuits of the
present life! O how small has been the proportion in any age or
country, who have preached and lived as if they really believed the
great things which they professed to be desirous of inculcating on
those around them! The truth is, the great body of the clergy have

never acted in character; and, therefore, no wonder they have been treated with contempt and ridicule. It is not in the nature of things that men so inconsistent, should be really respected in their official character. Worldly men sometimes, indeed, honour ministers, who have little apparent piety, for their talents, their learning, or their attractive social qualities: but they seldom fail to discern their official defects, and, no doubt, are often hardened by them in unbelief and impiety. I freely grant, indeed, that if ministers were heavenly purity itself embodied, infidels and worldly men would dislike and malign them. When infinite Purity was manifest in the flesh, they did cry out, Crucify him, crucify him. Still, however, there is such a thing as the apostle speaks of, when he exhorts Timothy, by well doing to put to silence the ignorance of foolish men. Blessed be God! it has been often done; and we may hope, that, through his grace, it will be still more frequently done hereafter. If the ministerial character were presented under its genuine, scriptural, and primitive aspect, it would extort a reluctant homage, even from the most abandoned votaries of sin. Only let ministers lay aside all worldly policy and habits; let them demonstrate by their conduct that their treasures are in heaven; let them show, by their simple scriptural piety, their zeal, humility, purity, meekness, self-denial, and deadness to the world that the imitation of Christ is their habitual study, and doing good their 'ruling passion'; and we shall soon cease to hear of the charge of 'priestcraft', and the sneer, that the clergy of all religions are alike. Too much 'alike', a great majority of them have, indeed, been, in selfishness, indolence, and unfaithfulness to their trust! But the purity of the divine Word, and the glorious beauty of the Spirit of Christ, by which they professed to be guided, have been ever the same. A sufficient number, too, have been really guided by them, to show that, amidst a multitude of counterfeits, there has been much true coin. And the time is coming when the clerical character shall be, everywhere, so much in harmony with the spirit of the Bible, as to redeem itself from every reproach, and to be universally acknowledged as a blessing to the world.

6. We may see, from this subject, *why there is so little truly good and profitable preaching*. An anonymous writer, in a late number of a distinguished foreign journal, remarks, that the eloquence of the

pulpit, generally speaking, turns very peculiar advantages to a very moderate account. Although I have no doubt that my estimate of true excellence in gospel preaching, would be found to differ greatly from that of the writer in question; yet the remark just quoted, however humiliating, is, doubtless, founded in fact. Considering the amount of preaching; and considering, too, the scope, the subjects, the opportunities of leisurely preparation, the excitements, and the almost unlimited field of usefulness, furnished to the Christian preacher, I do think the examples of high excellence, and of extensive benefit, in this department of exertion, are wonderfully few and small, compared with what might be reasonably expected. It is by no means a sufficient answer to this complaint, to say, that great talents are extremely rare; and that a very high grade of eloquence, in any profession, is still more rare. This is, no doubt, true. And if distinguished genius, and first-rate eloquence, measured by the precepts of Cicero, Longinus, or Quintilian, were necessary to form a good preacher; the great majority of clerical men might hold themselves guiltless in being very inferior preachers. But these, however, desirable and useful in their place, are far from being necessary, to great excellence, and eminent usefulness in gospel preaching. A man of enlightened, fervent piety, medium talents, and mature biblical and theological furniture, may preach well;—sufficiently well to be a rich blessing to any community. There is not one of you, my young Friends, who, if his heart were warmed and elevated as it ought to be, with living, active piety, and if he took suitable pains to store his mind with appropriate knowledge, might not be a preacher of great excellence, and of extensive usefulness. The fire of zeal would supply the lack of artificial refinements, and pour forth a constant stream of eloquence, irregular, perhaps, and plain, but truly sanctified, feeling, and, therefore impressive in its character. The true reason, then, why we have so little good and profitable preaching, is, that, among those who attempt to perform this service, there is so little deep, warm, heart-felt piety; and so little of that patient, indefatigable labour, to store the mind with knowledge, and to attain an easy, natural, forcible method of communicating it, which are within the reach of most ordinary minds, supremely intent on doing good. Some of the most useful preachers that ever entered the pulpit, have been men not at all distinguished either for great genius, profound learning, or striking elocution. But they never failed to be distinguished for good sense, Christian prudence, fervent love for their Master's cause, and for immortal souls, and untiring perseverance in holy labour. And, rely upon it, whoever will steadfastly exhibit these, in any church or country, will attain high excellence, and great acceptance and usefulness as a gospel preacher.

7. From what has been said, it is evident, that, *while we greatly need a much larger number of ministers; we still more urgently need an increase in ministerial piety, zeal, and fidelity.* That there is a real, nay, a most distressing deficiency in the number of labourers employed in the 'great harvest', in almost every part of our country, every well-informed person knows to be a fact. Taking into view the missionary, as well as the pastoral service, it is probably safe to affirm, that if we had a thousand able and faithful men added, at once, to our present number of ministers, they might all be usefully employed. This, I am aware, is doubted by some, because they, now and then, find a candidate for pastoral settlement, or for some other branch of evangelical service, unemployed. But the inference drawn from this fact is, undoubtedly, delusive. May it not be said of a portion of those unoccupied candidates, that they are not worth employing? That they are so strikingly deficient in the most important qualifications as to be little if any better than none? And of the rest, that they are not willing to go where they are pressingly invited and greatly needed? But if some, evidently wanting in the furniture requisite for instructing and edifying the people; and others, not willing to labour where they are called, are standing idle; does either case afford evidence that able, willing, and faithful labourers, and even large additional numbers of them, are not greatly needed? Certainly not. Every enlightened friend of religion, then, will pray without ceasing that more labourers may be raised up, qualified, and thrust forth into the harvest. But the friends of piety ought to pray still more earnestly, that all who are sent forth may be of the right stamp. It is unspeakably more important that ministers be men of the proper spirit, than that they be very numerous. Many people appear to speak and act as if it were desirable to obtain a large number of ministers of almost any sort. But, truly, this is a great mistake. Of what advantage is it to any church to

add to her ministry a drone, an ignoramus, or a learned formalist? A thousand such additions to her clerical ranks would do her no good. Good did I say? The more such ministers are multiplied, the worse it is for the church. They draw down upon her blasting and desolation, rather than a blessing. What the church needs is a greater number of pious, humble, enlightened ministers, who know how to labour, and who love to labour, for Christ, and for immortal souls. One such man, a Brainerd, or Whitefield, or Tennent, or Martyn, is worth fifty, or a hundred of your cold, timid, indolent men, although they go through a formal round of duties, without any disreputable deficiency, and preach the truth, and nothing but the truth, every time they enter the sacred desk. One such man as the Apostle Paul, has been, and may be again, the means of regenerating a nation: while scores or hundreds of men calling themselves ministers, but either bloated by sacerdotal pride, or paralysed by frigid indifference, may slumber through their miserable routine for years, without witnessing the regeneration of a single soul.

8. We may learn, from what has been said, *what that kind of honour is to which ministers of the gospel ought to aspire*. Clergymen, in all ages and countries, have unhappily degraded their office, while they intended to 'magnify' it. They have sought wealth, or secular station, or affected splendour in living, or courted the patronage of great men, or aspired to high rank in the walks of literature, or, if no more elevated honours were within their reach, to occupy the uppermost rooms at feasts, to receive greetings in the markets, and to be called of men, Rabbi, Rabbi. Need I say, that all these will be regarded by an 'ambassador of Christ', who has the genuine spirit of his office, and who wishes, with Paul, to 'magnify it', in reality, as infinitely beneath his 'sanctified ambition'? That illustrious gospel hero, Martin Luther, was accustomed to say—God will sometimes endure a love of worldly honour in lawyers and physicians: but in ministers of the gospel he will in no case endure it. Let this sentiment sink down into your hearts, with the weight of an incontrovertible maxim. History has, undoubtedly, set upon it the stamp of truth. Every effort that ministers make in secular aspirings, and every step they gain in secular greatness, though it may not bring upon them the visible judgments of the Almighty, will assuredly diminish their zeal, reputation, and

usefulness, in the sacred office: and, if indulged to a considerable extent, will effectually destroy them all. The true honour of a minister of reconciliation lies in possessing all the qualifications proper for his official work, and in devoting them supremely and unceasingly to the advancement of the Redeemer's kingdom. The servant of Christ never miscalculates more egregiously than when he undertakes to be a competitor for worldly titles, places, or distinctions of any kind. The more entirely he is withdrawn from the world, the more perfectly he lives above it, and the more completely he is absorbed in the great work of seeking the salvation of men, the more wisely he consults his reputation, as well as his duty and his happiness. Let Lord Bolingbroke, and the thousands of nominal Christians, who, though they reject the name of infidel, have the same spirit; let them sneer at what he somewhere calls the sublime passion for saving souls. It is a sublime passion;—the most sublime that can actuate the bosom of a mortal. It was this that brought the Saviour from heaven. The highest honour of a minister consists in doing good. His noblest laurels are conversions. The best eulogium that can be pronounced upon him, is that which was passed on a minister in primitive times—He was a good man, and full of the Holy Ghost and of faith; and much people was added to the Lord.

9. If the leading doctrine of this lecture be correct, then *there is nothing (humanly speaking) more urgently needed for promoting the best interests of the Redeemer's kingdom in the United States, than that the clergy, as a body, should possess a proper spirit, and be fully roused to the faithful discharge of their momentous duties.* When we deliberate about plans for promoting the great cause of truth and piety, we are apt to talk of almost all other means, excepting precisely those which are most radical and essential. We speak much of helping the cause forward by funds, and societies, and annual sermons, and multiplying auxiliary associations, and making eloquent addresses at annual meetings, and a variety of such popular means. Of all these I most cordially approve, as highly useful in their respective places. But I will venture to say, we need nothing so much, so far as instrumental agency is concerned, as that the body of Christ's ministers among us be fully awakened to a sense of their obligations and their duties, and embark, with humble dependence on their Master, and with

their whole hearts, in their appropriate work. Until this shall, in some degree, take place, even supposing all the wealth of the world to be put at the disposal of the church, the work of bringing men under the genuine influence of the gospel will go tardily on. But until this take place, adequate funds for carrying on this great work cannot be furnished; for until ministers be previously imbued with the proper spirit, we must not expect our churches to be roused to that state of spiritual sensibility and exertion, which is indispensable, and which will, one day, be realized. It would be a strange phenomenon, indeed, to see the churches going beyond their leaders in knowledge, feeling, zeal, and effort. As reasonably might we expect to see armies pressing forward to conquest and triumph, when their officers timidly refused to lead them, or were ignobly slumbering in the rear.

How large a number of the ministers of the Presbyterian Church in the United States (for I will not speak of any other church) are fully awake, and on the field of battle, properly armed and accoutred, and with the spirit of good soldiers of Jesus Christ burning in their bosoms, I dare not venture to estimate. That all are not so; that all are not engaged, to the extent of their strength, in instructing, rousing, and leading on 'the sacramental host' of God from grace to grace, and from victory to victory, is a melancholy fact too evident to be denied by the most careless observer. When this desirable state of mind and of habit shall be realized with respect to the great body of them, then the time, even the set time to favour Zion, will have come. Then shall the signal be given for the whole body of our population to come up, willingly and efficiently, to the help of the Lord against the mighty. For, that the mass of our professing people have not made higher attainments in Christian feeling, and Christian effort; that they have not more knowledge of truth; more piety; more zeal; more comprehensive views of the deplorable state of the world; more deep sympathy for the destitute and the perishing; and a more active spirit of benevolent exertion for enlightening the world—I hold to be more owing to a defect of zeal on the part of the clergy themselves, than to any other single cause, next to the native depravity of the human heart. If the great body of our ministers were thoroughly imbued with the apostolic spirit, and animated to a corresponding tone of habitual exertion, we should soon witness glorious days in our beloved country.

10. Finally, in the views which have been taken of this subject, *you, my young Friends, may find much matter for serious personal application.* The great office, the awful office which we have been contemplating;—the office on which so much depends in reference to unnumbered millions,—for soul and body, for time and eternity;—this is the office which you seek;—for which you have come hither to prepare;—to which all your studies and intercourse here will be, or ought to be, directed. Solemn undertaking! Momentous enterprise! Oh, if you could foresee the unutterable consequences which will result from this enterprise, to yourselves, and to all the multitudes whom you may, in the course of your lives, approach and influence, the present would be an hour of deep solemnity with everyone whom I address. May the Lord give you grace to ponder well in your hearts what you are about, and what is before you! May the Lord give you grace to consider seriously the furniture which you need for this mighty work; especially that deep, ardent, active piety, which lies at the foundation of all other useful furniture. You need, it is true, other attainments, and much of other attainments; but without this, you will be of little use as ministers of Christ. Without this, directing, warning, animating, and sanctifying all your other accomplishments, they will be as a sounding brass and a tinkling cymbal.

Think, I pray you, what a day it is, in which the Head of the church has cast your lot! No preceding generation of ministers ever saw such a day as this! Such openings for usefulness; such calls to exertion; such multiplied and extensive fields whitening to the harvest; such abundant and potent means for doing good to mankind. To live now, is a talent put into your hands, for which you must give an account. Have you an ardour of piety, a tone of moral sentiment, a spirit of enterprise corresponding with this day? If not, give yourselves no rest till you in some good measure attain them all. If an ancient heathen rhetorician, in giving directions for the attainment of the 'sublime', in writing, could say—Spare no labour to educate your soul to grandeur, and to impregnate it with great and generous ideas; much more may the same language be addressed to a candidate for the gospel ministry, in the present stage of the church's progress. Take unceasing pains to get large views of ministerial furniture, ministerial duty, and ministerial success. Strive to educate your souls to grandeur of conception, and grandeur of wishes, and hopes, and enterprise for the moral benefit of your fellow men. Aim high. Let no petty plans satisfy you, either as to acquirement or exertion. Every one of you, however humble his talents, if really disposed to make the most of what God has given him, might cause his influence to be felt to the ends of the earth.

Think, further, what a weight of responsibility, if you live to sustain it, will soon devolve upon you. When I see more than a hundred theological students before me, amounting to nearly a thirteenth part of the whole number of our ministry; and recollect that, in a little time, the reins of ecclesiastical administration will drop from the hands of those who now bear them,—and who, alas! have so much reason to mourn over the defective manner in which they have borne them;—and that a large part of the weighty trust will devolve on you, I can scarcely express my emotions. Is it so, my young Friends, that this beloved church; this truly primitive and apostolic church; this church for which our fathers have prayed and laboured so much; this church, which, though repeatedly involved in the flame of controversy and trial, yet, like the 'burning bush' at Horeb, has not been 'consumed', but has been mercifully brought forth more thrifty and flourishing; this church, in the future destiny of which the peace, edification, and eternal welfare of so many myriads are involved;—is soon to be committed, under God, to your management, associated with those who, in other places, are, like yourselves, training up for the work? And is it true that so much, under God, depends upon your spirit, attainments, and character? that what you shall be, fifteen or twenty years hence, the Presbyterian Church will be? O, then, gird up the loins of your minds; be sober and watch unto prayer. Let a sense of your incalculable responsibility daily rest upon you. Let it impel you in your studies, give new fervour to your devotions, and impart a deeper tone of solemnity to all your intercourse, both with one another, and with all around you. Remember, in going out, and in coming in, in sitting down and in rising up, that you are consecrated men, bound to live and to die for the church of God. Cultivate a deep and habitual spirit of prayer. Covet earnestly the best gifts; and shrink from no labour, either in study or in self-denial, that will prepare you to perform with more efficiency your Master's work. Consider no sacrifice as too great for the promotion of the Redeemer's kingdom. Set up no banner, in any case, but that of Christ. Let all carnal ambition, pride, envy, contention, and unhallowed emulation be put away from among you. Be always ready to surrender every personal feeling for the sake of brotherly love and edification. Cherish more and more the feelings of a holy brotherhood, pledged to Christ, and to one another by indissoluble ties. Remember that, united, you will stand, and by the spirit and strength of Christ, can do all things; but that, divided, you must fall; and that in every fall of the Christian ministry, the cause of the Redeemer bleeds and mourns. Resolve, that, if the church be corrupted with error, agitated by controversy, or torn by schism, the sin shall not lie at your door. If her walls be broken down, by folly or wickedness, see that you be found in the breach, fighting and praying for her restoration. And if ever a time should come in which you can do nothing more, at least be found weeping between the porch and the altar, saying, Spare thy people, O Lord, bless thy heritage, save them, and lift them up for ever! But, if you are faithful, my young Friends, such a time will never come. Yes, if only the little band, now seated within the sound of my voice, should all happily prove to be animated with the spirit of the primitive heralds of the cross, there is no presumption in saying, that, you alone, under God, would form a pledge to our beloved church of her spiritual prosperity.

The God of all grace grant that you may act a part more worthy of the sacred office than we, who have preceded you, have ever done! May he preside over your studies; endow you with all those gifts and graces which will fit you for the faithful performance of his great work; and form you to be 'chosen vessels' for building up his church, and bearing the treasures of his love to a dark and miserable world: and to his name be the glory! Amen!

NOTE

A few remarks on the distinction between the clergy and the laity, which it was not convenient to introduce into the body of the lecture, it is deemed proper to present in this place.

It is impossible to read the Acts of the Apostles, and the several epistles, especially those to Timothy and Titus; and to examine, in connection with these, the writings of the 'Apostolic Fathers', without perceiving that the distinction between ministers of religion and private Christians, was clearly made, from the very origin of the Christian church, and uniformly maintained. That the terms, *clergy* and *laity* were not used at first, is of no importance in any view; since the distinction intended to be expressed by them, has undoubtedly and uniformly existed from the commencement of the New Testament dispensation to the present day. The titles of 'rulers' in the house of God;—'ambassadors of Christ';—'stewards of the mysteries of God'; 'bishops, elders, shepherds, ministers', *etc.*, as distinguished from those to whom they ministered, are so familiar to all readers of the New Testament, that further elucidation of that point is altogether unnecessary.

The word κλῆρος properly signifies a lot. And as the land of Canaan was divided among the Israelites by lot, the word, in process of time, came to signify an inheritance. In this figurative, or secondary sense, the term is evidently employed in 1 Peter 5:3. Under the Old Testament dispensation, the peculiar people of God were called, (Septuagint translation) his κλῆρος, or inheritance. Of this we have examples in Deuteronomy 4:20, and 9:29. The term, in both these passages, is manifestly applied to the whole body of the nation of Israel, as God's inheritance, or peculiar people. Clemens Romanus, one of the 'Apostolic Fathers', speaking of the Jewish economy, and having occasion to distinguish between the priests and the common people, calls the latter λαϊκοί. Clemens Alexandrinus, toward the close of the second century, speaks of the Apostle John, as having set apart such persons for clergymen (κλῆροι) as were signified to him by the Holy Ghost. And in the writings of Tertullian, Origen, and Cyprian, the terms clergy and laity occur with a frequency which shows that they were then in familiar use. Jerome observes, that ministers are called *clerici*, either because they are peculiarly the lot and portion of the Lord; or because the Lord is their lot, that is, their inheritance. Hence the learned and pious father takes occasion to infer, 'That he who is God's portion, ought so to exhibit himself, that he may be truly said to possess God, and to be possessed by him' (*Epist.* 2. *ad Nepotian.* 5). Others have thought, that, in giving this title, some regard was had to the ancient custom of electing persons into sacred offices by lot.

And as we have abundant evidence that ecclesiastical men were familiarly called *clerici,* or clergymen, from the second century; so we have the same evidence that this term was employed to designate all ecclesiastical men. That is, all persons who had any public employment in the church, were called by the common name of *clerici* or clergymen. It was applied, continually, to elders and deacons, as well as to bishops or pastors. Nay, in the third century, when not only prelacy had crept in, and obtained a general prevalence; but when the same spirit of innovation had also brought in a number of inferior orders, such as sub-deacons, readers, acolyths, *etc.,* these inferior orders were all styled *clerici.* Cyprian, speaking of a sub-deacon, and also of a reader, calls them both *clerici.* The ordination of such persons (for it seems they were formally ordained) he calls *ordinationes clericae;* and the letters which he transmitted by them he styles *literae clericae.* The same fact may be clearly established from the writings of Ambrose, Hilary, and Epiphanius, and from the canons of the Council of Nice. Indeed there seems reason to believe, that, in the fourth and fifth centuries, and subsequently, the title of *clerici* was not only given to all the inferior orders of ecclesiastical men, but was more frequently applied to them than to their superiors: who were generally addressed by their more distinctive titles. Those who recollect that learning, during the Dark Ages, was chiefly confined to the clergy; that few, excepting persons of that profession, were able to read and write; and that the whimsical privilege, commonly called 'benefit of clergy', grew out of the rare accomplishment of being able to read;—will be at no loss to trace the etymology of the word *clerk* (*clericus*) or secretary, to designate one who officiates as the reader and writer of a public body.

To distinguish the mass of private Christians from the clergy, they were designated by several names. They were sometimes called laymen, from *populus;* sometimes private men, from, *privatus* (see *Acts* 4:13); sometimes *seculars,* from which signifies a secular life. Soon after the apostolic age, common Christians were frequently called— *men of the church*—that is, persons not belonging either to Jewish synagogues, or heathen temples, or heretical bodies, but members of the church of Christ. Afterwards, however, the title, *ecclesiastics* became gradually appropriated to persons in office in the church. See *Stephani Thesaurus.* Bingham's *Origines Ecclesiasticae,* 13.1.

THE IMPORTANCE OF MATURE PREPARATORY STUDY FOR THE MINISTRY[1]

BELOVED Pupils, the subject to which I have resolved to direct your attention on the present occasion, is the great importance of candidates for the holy ministry going through a mature and adequate course of professional study before entering on their public work. The friends of this institution have often remarked, with surprise and regret, how very small a portion of those who study here can be prevailed upon to remain for three years, and to complete the regular course. Seldom, if ever, I think, have we been able to persuade as many as one half of any class to continue their studies to the close of the prescribed period. Many stay but half the usual time; others not more than a third part; and some, after spending with us a single short summer session, have gone forth, and announced themselves to the churches as pupils of our seminary. Against this great and, I fear, undiminishing evil, the professors have, from time to time, raised the voice of solemn remonstrance: the Board of Directors have, once and again, recorded their pointed testimony: and the General Assembly have expressed their utter disapprobation, in terms which might have been expected to be decisive in their influence on all considerate minds. Still the deplorable evil in question continues to prevail. Presbyteries either give their direct countenance, or cannot be prevailed upon to set their faces, with sufficient firmness, against it; and short-sighted or infatuated young men, setting at naught the counsels of experience, and urged on, either by inconsiderate friends,

---

[1] Samuel Miller, *The Importance of Mature Preparatory Study for the Ministry: An Introductory Lecture, Delivered at the Opening of the Summer Session of the Theological Seminary at Princeton, New Jersey, July 3, 1829* (Princeton: Princeton Press, 1829).

or their own impatience, ascend the pulpit, and undertake to teach others, while they need to be taught themselves the first principles of the oracles of God.

I shall not at present, detain you with any comments on the tendency of this practice to injure the seminary itself; to render it both less useful, and less respectable, in the eyes of an enlightened religious public. I forbear to urge this consideration, not because it is a matter of small moment; for the character of an institution like this, is always of real importance, not only to the particular branch of the Christian family with which is it more immediately connected, but also to the whole church of God:—but because this is a topic, concerning which we might be suspected of partiality; and, more especially, because there are other considerations, still more momentous, on which I consider it as my duty now to enlarge.

I shall employ the present lecture, then, in endeavouring to impress upon the minds of those whom I address, that the preliminary studies of a candidate for the holy ministry ought to be as mature and complete as he can make them; and, of consequence, that nothing less than what is commonly styled a 'regular course', either here or elsewhere, under the direction of some approved teacher or teachers, ought to be considered as sufficient, by any theological student, who wishes to be, permanently, either acceptable or useful in the sacred office. And in support of this position,—

I. My first argument shall be drawn from a consideration which I take for granted none will controvert, viz., *That we are bound to serve Christ with the very best faculties and attainments that we possess, or can possibly acquire.*

That we are really bound to serve God with the best that we have or can gain, I hold to be, upon Christian principles, a self-evident proposition. If so, then the young man who does not honestly endeavour to make the most of those faculties which God has given him; who does not cultivate, and enlarge, and enrich them to the highest degree which his circumstances render practicable; and who, having done this, does not devote them all in the best manner that he is able, to the service of his Master, undoubtedly commits sin; and a sin proportioned to the degree in which he fails of doing in this respect, what he might and ought to have done. Has God given us talents, accompanied with the command, 'Occupy till I come'? Are we commanded to make the most that we can of these talents by 'trading', that is, by laborious culture and exertion? And are we informed that our reward will be in proportion to our fidelity in trading, and our guilt in proportion to our negligence and unfaithfulness? Then there can be no hesitation in pronouncing, that he to whom God has given good talents, who sits down contented with a small amount of mental culture; who, when he might gain one hundred degrees of knowledge, with which to serve the church, contents himself with fifty, or twenty, or, alas! as many do, with ten, or, peradventure, even with five, commits a grievous sin against God, against the church, and against his own soul.

That intellect is power, and that knowledge is power, will not be denied by any of those whom I now address. Power to enlighten; power to exert influence; and, consequently, power to do good. Of course, the more a minister of the gospel has of both, provided they be under the sanctified guidance of genuine piety, the better is he qualified to serve the church of God; and the more likely will he be, other things being equal, to promote its best interests. There is no doubt, indeed, that the real success of all Christian ministrations depends on the mighty power of the Spirit of God, accompanying them, and making them effectual. But still, as long as God's kingdom is a kingdom of means, and as long as the good done, is ordinarily proportioned to the character of the agency employed in accomplishing it, we must suppose that of two ministers equally pious, he who is best instructed in the things of the kingdom of God, most at home in the great system of his truth, and most 'mighty in the Scriptures', will be most likely to be a successful servant of the church.

I would, then, appeal to the conscience of every candidate for the holy ministry, whether he can voluntarily and deliberately permit himself to form a plan for his theological education, which will, if I may be allowed the expression, stint and abridge all his preparation for public work, and deprive him, it may be, of three-fourths of that amount of qualification with which he might and ought to come forth to the service of the church? Can he, as a conscientious man, allow himself, when it is possible to order it otherwise, to enter the sacred office with slender acquirements, when, by doing so, he will, in all probability, render himself less acceptable to the church; less useful in his day; less capable of defending the gospel against gainsayers; less able to instruct, and mould, and influence the rising generation; less able to take the lead in diffusing sanctified science around him; less able to benefit, in any respect, the kingdom of his divine Master, and the world in which he lives? It is no valid plea to say, in answer to this reasoning, that an individual, in a given case, cannot pursue a more adequate course of study, without much difficulty, and at the expense of many sacrifices. Be it so. The service of God daily calls for labour and sacrifice. And he who refuses to sustain them, when it is in his power, and when there is an evident call of duty, is unfaithful to the highest obligations.

II. The next argument which I would urge in favour of a mature and thorough course of preliminary study, shall be drawn from *the consideration of the extent, difficulty, and importance of the various departments of knowledge which are necessarily included in such a course.*

Multitudes of secular men, and too many who are turning their eyes to the sacred office, seem indeed, to think that the preparatory studies of a minister may be brought within a very narrow compass. In fact, they seem to imagine that a careful perusal of the Bible; of some one systematic work on theology, such as that of Turretin or Ridgely; and of Mosheim and Milner on ecclesiastical history, together with a few more single volumes on detached theological subjects, is quite enough to prepare any man for the pulpit. All that can be said of such persons is, that they betray an ignorance as wonderful as it is disreputable. As well might a man dream that he was qualified to be a physician, by the perusal of Cullen's *First Lines,* or of Thomas's *Practice of Physic;* or a lawyer, reading Blackstone's *Commentaries.* Surely such calculators never penetrated beyond the surface of any single question in biblical or theological inquiry. Let me request you to glance over the catalogue of studies prescribed in this seminary, as detailed in the chapter entitled, 'Of Study and Attainments', and then to say, whether any one of them can be wisely or safely left out of the list; and further, how much time is necessary to go over them, I will not say deeply, but even in the most cursory manner that admits of real intelligence. When we recollect that every candidate for the ministry is called upon by our Plan to make himself familiar with the original languages of Scripture; with biblical history; with biblical antiquities; with the principles and details of biblical criticism and interpretation; with didactic and polemic theology, in all their diversified and interesting branches, including the Deistical controversy, the Unitarian controversy, the Pelagian and Semi-Pelagian controversies, to say nothing of many other departments of this boundless subject. When we recollect that to these must be added ecclesiastical history, church government, the composition and delivery of sermons, the pastoral care, and a variety of other subjects which cannot be minutely specified;—I say, when we recollect that all these branches of study are indispensable; that they ought all to be made objects of attention by every candidate for the holy ministry; that he is really not prepared even to begin his work as an interpreter of Scripture, and a professional counsellor and guide of immortal souls, without some good acquaintance with every one of them;—is it possible for anyone, who knows what study and knowledge mean, to think of gaining any valuable acquaintance with these various and extensive departments of knowledge, in less than three or four years of diligent application? It is impossible. They are subjects in respect to which no talents can supersede the necessity of patient and protracted labour. Nay, it is evident that a tolerably comprehensive acquaintance with any one of them, cannot be acquired by the finest mind without months of devoted study. He, then, who thinks so far to master them all, as to be prepared to be a teacher in the house of God, at little expense of time and toil, labours under a delusion which would be a proper subject of ridicule only, were it not so destructive in its consequences to the most precious interests of men.

If there be, then, in the bosom of the church a melancholy spectacle, it is that of a rash, self-confident young man, who presses forward to the awful station of a spiritual teacher, when he has not been taught himself; who is not qualified, perhaps, to illustrate and guard a single point in theology; who, of course, must be a superficial preacher; and who cannot fail of being liable to all the crude thinking, and the doctrinal inconsistencies and aberrations, which so frequently mark the character of those who thus prematurely intrude into the sacred office. How it is that young men apparently conscientious, can deliberately consent to go forth as public instructors in the church of Christ; to open and apply the Scriptures; to meet and confute the learned sceptic; to silence the ingenious caviller; to solve delicate and momentous questions of casuistry; to counsel the anxious, the perplexed, the tempted, and the doubting; and adapt themselves to all the variety of characters and duties which a large congregation presents, while they are, comparatively children, both as to knowledge and experience,—is indeed wonderful, and as humiliating as it is wonderful!

What an impressive comment on the presumptuous readiness with which too many young men, in modern times, venture on the arduous and awful labours of the gospel ministry, with the slenderest furniture, were the fears and the hesitations of the illustrious Calvin, as recorded by his biographers! After that celebrated Reformer had published the first edition of his *Institutions of the Christian Religion,* when Joseph Scaliger supposes him to have been the most learned man in Europe, and when he was importuned, and finally constrained to settle, as a pastor in Geneva, he was actually on his way to Strasburg, for the purpose of further pursuing his theological studies, under the impression that he had not yet obtained mature scriptural knowledge enough to warrant his undertaking the stated exercise of the pastoral office!

III. A third consideration which shows the importance of having the preparatory studies in theology as thorough and complete as possible is, *that he who does not lay a good foundation in the beginning, will never be likely to supply the deficiency afterwards.*

Many candidates for the ministry, no doubt, content themselves with what they acknowledge to be a short and very superficial course of study at the outset, because they imagine they will have an ample opportunity of supplying all deficiencies after entering on their official work. They flatter themselves that, after they have actually entered the field of public labour, they will have at once better facilities, and stronger excitements to study, than they now enjoy; and that, then, they will make up, and more than make up, whatever may now be wanting. But it is easy to show that this expectation generally proves, in fact, and in most cases must prove, altogether delusive. Rely on it, my young Friends, if you leave this seminary with a mere smattering of theological knowledge; with what you know to be a scanty and inadequate foundation, there is every probability that you will go through life, and to your graves, with very little more. The superstructure concerning which you anticipate so much, will, pretty certainly, be of the same miserable, scanty, and insufficient character.

For, in the first place, when a young preacher, at the present day, goes out to serve the church,—if he have talents, and be popular,—and especially if he have ardent piety, and a heart to perform his work with zeal, he will have so much to do; will be so incessantly called upon in every direction; will be constrained to preach so much in season, and out of season, that he will hardly find time enough to prepare, even in the most hasty and superficial manner, for the pulpit; much less to engage in other studies in which he might have found himself deficient when he began to preach. And, what is worthy of particular notice here, the more ardent his piety, and the more animated, interesting, and popular his preaching, the worse, as to the point in question, it will be for him:—that is, the more incessant will be his interruptions, and the more difficult he will find it to redeem any time for real study. I say for real study; for those little snatches of reading and writing, all of which, and more, are indispensably necessary for preparation for the pulpit, and which are seldom enjoyed with a perfectly composed mind, are really not worthy of the name of study. The consequence is, that nine out of ten, perhaps nineteen out of twenty, of those who engage in preaching with very slender furniture, go through the whole of their ministerial life with lean, unfurnished minds. Their profiting does not appear to all. Not having the habit of close study, it is not easy to begin. They, perhaps, hope for much, and promise much in the way of future improvement, but never find time for it. The result is, they are not instructive or interesting preachers. The small stock with which they begin is soon exhausted. Their popular acceptance soon declines or ceases. They are seldom long settled in one congregation, the people everywhere discovering, in a short time, that they know but little, and cannot feed them with knowledge and with understanding. They remove, ignominiously, from place to place. Instead of being attracted and edified, the people to whom they minister are scattered, and perhaps perish under their feeble ministrations. Premature dotage creeps on:

and they die, in many cases, rather a burden than a blessing to the church. It is truly melancholy to think how often this has been the real history of ministers who entered the sacred office without proper furniture, and who, for want of time or inclination afterwards, never made up their early deficiency.

We know that if a common mechanic learn his trade well in the beginning, and go forth from his apprenticeship a good workman, he is not only able to do his work better, but also to do more work in a given time, and to do it with far more ease and comfort to himself, than if he had gone out a bungler, and but half-taught. The same principle, in all its extent, applies to the intellectual and moral workman. When the candidate for the sacred office allows himself to engage in the duties of that office but half-prepared, all his subsequent work will be performed with more difficulty, more tardily, and probably with less usefulness. His preparations for the pulpit will cost him more time and toil, and will be less satisfactory to himself, as well as to others. Whereas, if he delay going forth to his work until he be really ready, his comfort, his reputation, and his benefit to the church and the world, will be likely to be proportionably increased.

But, even supposing that he who enters on the duties of the holy ministry with slender furniture should afterwards be determined, whatever it may cost him, to make up his deficiency by unwearied and extra efforts. Still his task will be difficult, and his prospect gloomy. He can only take one of two courses, either of which will probably be fatal. He may attempt, amidst all his multiplied active labours, and distracting cares, by night studies, and by urging nature in every way, and beyond her strength, to gain that which he ought to have acquired before he entered the pulpit. In this case he will, pretty certainly, destroy his health, and either sink into a premature grave, or reduce himself, for the remainder of his days, to a state of languor and protracted disease, which will render existence a burden, and all comfortable and efficient discharge of duty impossible. O how many miserable and hopeless invalids for life might have avoided the calamity of which they are victims, by gaining, in the preliminary part of their course, that which they unwisely left to be accomplished by subsequent efforts! Or, the delinquent in question may choose another alternative. He may, after entering the ministry, confine himself to his study, neglecting family visitation, neglecting family instruction, neglecting the anxious inquirer, neglecting the sick and the dying; in short, neglecting all pastoral duties, excepting those of the pulpit. The consequences of adopting this alternative, may be even still more deplorable than in the former case. While the other course would, probably, be fatal to his health, this would be fatal to his usefulness, fatal to his character, and fatal to the best interests of the souls committed to his charge.

But it will be asked,—Have not individuals been frequently known, who entered the office of the holy ministry with very small theological furniture; but who afterwards, by extraordinary efforts, became not only respectably, but some of them even richly furnished for their work? I answer, such instances have now and then occurred. But they have been generally men of peculiar intellectual vigour and perseverance; of great decision of character; and placed in circumstances which, in a great measure exempted them from the daily and hourly calls of pastoral duty. Of such a man in the American church, within the last twenty years, since the additional claims on the time and efforts of ministers have become so numerous and importunate, I know of no example. And I have no doubt that, if the whole history of those men, who, in other times and countries, have presented such examples, were impartially examined, they would be found powerful witnesses not against, but for, the doctrine which I am labouring to establish.

IV. Further, a mature and leisurely training for the gospel ministry is highly important, not merely for the purpose of storing the mind with knowledge, but also *for the purpose of that intellectual and moral discipline,* which is of no less value, to a minister of Christ than theological learning.

Many seem to imagine that the only use of a regular and complete course of preparatory study is the mere attainment of knowledge. And, therefore, when a candidate for the ministry, after completing his collegiate course, is exhorted to spend at least three years in a theological seminary, or in some similar situation, it is thought, by many serious people, to be almost a criminal sacrifice to mere learning. But such persons forget that the discipline of the mind, and especially of the heart, the temper, and the general character, is among the most important parts of professional preparation. They forget that even if the requisite amount of fact and principles could be crowded into the mind of a young man in six months, or even in six weeks, still one essential object of theological education would be unattained; which is casting the whole man, if I may be allowed the expression, into the proper mould for a minister of religion. This includes the correction of bad habits; the formation of new and better ones; the gradual discipline and ripening of the intellectual powers; mellowing, softening, and at the same time invigorating, the graces of the heart; bringing down high thoughts of himself; ascertaining his own defects and foibles; learning the value of gravity, self-command, prudence, and Christian dignity; studying human nature and the world; studying clerical character as it too commonly has been, and as it ought to be; in short, unlearning many things which have been learned amiss, and correcting many erroneous views, and juvenile propensities, which nothing but time, and suitable associations, accompanied with much observation, watchfulness, prayer and conflict can possibly, under God, enable him to accomplish. Suppose a young man to enter a seminary like this, to be trained up for the gospel ministry. Suppose him to have lively, vigorous talents, and unfeigned piety; but at the same time to be rash, impetuous, indiscreet, ignorant of the world, elated with ideas of his own powers and importance, and ready on all occasions, to dash forward for the attainment of his object. Now, if such a young man had read all the books in the world, and heard and treasured up all the learned lectures that ever were delivered, within these or any other walls, he would still be unfit to go forth as a minister of the gospel;—to be a teacher, an example, and a guide in the church of God. Such an one needs the friendly hints, the fraternal counsel, the gentle Christian attention of a band of fellow-students. He needs to be taught by experience, and sometimes by very painful experience, to be admonished, and mortified, and humbled again and again, before he can be brought to 'think soberly', to feel what his own defects and foibles are, and to acknowledge that others are greater and better than himself; before he can learn habitually to respect the feelings of others, to treat all around him with delicacy, to be swift to hear, slow to speak, slow to wrath. And all this is not, ordinarily, to be acquired in a year, or in two years. It is, usually, a slow process; and the longer it can be continued, within reasonable limits, the better. It will indeed be well if the close of the most protracted course in the seminary, should find those who pass through it in any good measure, mature, or even advanced, in these attainments. For it is certain that all who enjoy the opportunity are by no means so happy. In fact, with many, this intellectual and moral discipline is far more needed, and far more important, than mere knowledge. The want of it is their most prominent and radical defect; and will be likely, perhaps, more than any other (next to a defect in piety) to interfere with their acceptance, their comfort, and their usefulness to the end of life.

The truth is, many of the ministers of our church, enter on their public work by a good deal too early in life. Not only before they have taken time to become sufficiently furnished with biblical and theological knowledge, but before their character is properly formed and matured. Like the unfledged young of the feathered tribes, they have ventured forth, and attempted to fly, before their wings were ready to sustain them. The consequence is, that like them also, many an ignoble fall, and many a sad bruise and wound, are found to be the result. It is really very seldom that any man has such maturity and solidity of judgment, such habitual gravity and prudence, such a knowledge of himself and of the world, and such a store of the various and important information which he needs, as to qualify him for entering the pulpit before twenty-five or twenty-six years of age, and especially for undertaking a pastoral charge before twenty-seven or twenty-eight. Nor even then is he ready for such delicate, difficult and momentous work, unless he have spent years in steadily contemplating its nature, and in preparing and disciplining his whole mind and habits for its performance.

V. A further argument in favour of a regular and complete course of theological study, may be drawn from *the opinion and practice of our fathers in all past ages.*

In the ancient Jewish church, no priest could enter on the full and active duties of his office, until he was thirty years old; and of the preceding years, the last fifteen, and especially the last ten, were devoted to diligent study and preparation for his official work. Of course, I hardly need add, that the course of study in the divinity schools under the Old Testament dispensation was long, leisurely, and mature.

In like manner, after the advent of the Saviour, when the church became organized and settled, careful study as a preparation for the sacred office was continued, and that by divine direction. For although the first preachers were illiterate fishermen, yet they were supernaturally instructed by their Master, and endowed with the power of working miracles, and speaking with tongues, in aid of their ministry, and long before this period of miracle and inspiration was ended, we find careful study and mature knowledge enjoined by an apostle, who knew their value by experience, and inculcated them upon principles which apply to all ages. He had himself been brought up at the feet of Gamaliel; and seems to have been well skilled in every branch of literature and science then taught. And, what is particularly worthy of our notice, this only man, among all the apostles, who was favoured with ample and ripe learning, was by far the most eminently useful of the whole number. Accordingly he gives directions which plainly establish, not only the truth but also the importance of the doctrine for which I am contending. The candidate for the ministry, according to the direction of this apostle—is not to be a novice,—but to be apt to teach—and able to teach;—he is to give himself to reading, and to let his profiting appear to all.

In the second, third and fourth centuries, study for the holy ministry seems to have been considered as a serious thing, by no means to be hurried over, or regarded as a small affair. Several years of laborious study were not thought too much to be submitted to for this important object. By some of the early councils it was solemnly decided that no man ought to be ordained to the work of the ministry under thirty years of age; because they thought that none could be qualified for the office at an earlier period; because the Lord Jesus Christ himself began his ministry at that age; and because they considered it as the most perfect age of man.

When the modern theological seminaries, or rather theological courses of instruction, in the universities of Europe were established, the same general plan was adopted. In none of them, I believe, is a less time than three years considered as sufficient for a regular course— and in some much more is required. And, what is remarkable, even

in those universities in which the professors in the theological department, complete their whole course of lectures in a single year, as I
believe, is the case in Holland, and some other countries, still at least
three years are considered as requisite for a complete professional
course. It being supposed of essential importance that every student
should travel repeatedly over the same ground, that his knowledge
might be more thoroughly digested, and more deeply impressed on
his mind.

When the Seminary of the Associate Reformed Church in the United
States was first established, a period of three years was assigned for the
regular course. Yet, in a little time afterwards, the venerable synod of
that church, extended the course to four years, finding, by experience,
that three were altogether inadequate to the purpose intended.

Now, the use which I wish to make of these facts, and others of
a similar kind, which might be detailed, is the following:—If our
fathers in all ages, if the wisest and best of men, both under the Old
and New Testament dispensations, have judged that a number of
years of close application to study were necessary to a suitable course
of preparation for the ministry, shall we be arrogant enough to suppose that they were all wrong, and that we understand the subject
better than they did? Is the field of knowledge now less extended than
it was then? Or shall we be vain enough to imagine that we have better talents, and better capacities for acquiring knowledge than they
had; and that we can accomplish as much as they did in less time? It
is probable that we shall none of us think of adopting either of these
suppositions. No; they had as vigorous and active minds as we possess; they were at least as diligent in study as we are; they were quite
as much averse, as we are, to the waste of time; they felt as much as
we probably feel, for the salvation of souls perishing around them:—
and yet, after much experience, they found the time which has been
mentioned necessary to them. Rely on it, my beloved pupils, if you
had the same experience, you would be of the same mind with them:
and if you have not the same convictions now, you will, I doubt not,
adopt them by and by; perhaps some of you when it shall be too late
to profit by the conviction.

VI. Another consideration in support of the doctrine for which I
contend is, that *the present state of the world, and especially of our own*

country, calls for more various and profound knowledge in ministers of
the gospel, than was demanded in former times.

It is not, I think, speaking extravagantly to say, that where one
person in the United States half a century ago, received a liberal education, at least ten, perhaps fifteen, in one form or another, receive
it now. In every part of our country, even in the newest and most
remote settlements, there are numbers of professional and other individuals of shrewd and active minds, well informed, and qualified to
judge with intelligence and correctness of the talents and learning
of those who appear before them as ministers of the gospel. Some
of these men are friendly to the religion of Christ and its preachers;
but a much larger number are, at heart, hostile to both. A minister,
then, can hardly go into the most remote and unenlightened districts
without meeting with some, and often with many, who are able and
very much disposed to scrutinize all that he delivers, and to detect all
his ignorance and mistakes. A smattering, and more than a smattering in the languages, in the sciences, and in all those departments of
knowledge, from which infidels are wont to draw some of their most
perplexing objections, is almost everywhere diffused from Canada to
Mexico, and from the ocean to our remotest Western settlements.
Now, ought ministers of religion to consider themselves as qualified
to engage in the public discharge of the duties of their office, until
they have gone through such a course of mature study as will qualify
them to appear with tolerable advantage before such men; to instruct
them in divine things; to refute them; and to defend the cause of
Christ against their attacks? Are they really prepared to be heralds
of the cross; to be watchmen on the walls of Zion; to be shepherds
of the flock; to be leaders and guides of the people without such
furniture as I have described? They certainly are not.

I am aware that some candidates for the holy ministry, who deliberately content themselves with small preparation for their work, are
frequently heard to say, that they do not aspire to any conspicuous
station; that their utmost hope is, that they may, perhaps, be qualified to serve the church in an humble way, among some poor and
plain people, where preachers are few and greatly needed. But how
can such a candidate know where the Lord of the harvest may assign
to him his field of labour? He is not his own master, nor will he

mete out the bounds of his own habitation. His duty, therefore, is not to say,—I will go to some obscure place, and will only aim to be qualified for such a place; but, rather,—I will go wherever the great Head of the church, in his infinite wisdom may send me, and will labour, to the extent of my opportunity and ability, to be prepared for any place. Besides, this whole plea is delusive in another view. It is an utter mistake to suppose that persons of small talents, and slender furniture, are adapted to new settlements, and destitute regions. There the best talents, the best acquirements, and the most prudent, judicious men are most indispensably required. Men of feeble minds and small attainments may, perhaps, do good by sitting down in old settlements, where there is much knowledge, prudence, and piety, and where other ministers are at hand to counsel and aid them. In circumstances of this kind, I have known such men truly useful in the ministry. But they are by no means adapted to be sent as pioneers into new and destitute regions where everything is to be commenced and organized; and where all the skill, address, learning, prudence, piety and knowledge of the human heart, and of the wiles of Satan, that a minister can possible bring to his aid are greatly, nay, indispensably needed.

To this fact, the attention of the professors of this seminary has been drawn with a frequency and a force, which could not fail of making a deep impression on their minds. In the course of eight or ten years past, we have received many, very many applications to recommend candidates for settlement in feeble congregations and remote places, both in the new and the old States, accompanied, at the same time, with a detail of circumstances, concerning the situation and character of the people, which convinced us that no candidates would answer the purpose excepting those who had much knowledge, prudence and piety; nay, which convinced us, that sending candidates of any other character would rather hinder than promote the progress of the Redeemer's kingdom. Candidates we had, and, in some instances, in considerable numbers; but few or none fit to be sent to such scenes of labour; and so we were obliged to inform our importunate applicants. The truth is, many of the people in these remote districts desire—and it is a reasonable wish—that the ministers sent them should be qualified to take the lead in all the ecclesiastical organizations and proceedings, not merely of a single church, but of several neighbouring churches, starting into life and activity; to be the counsellors and guides of townships, and sometimes, perhaps, of counties; to mould a heterogeneous population into a harmonious and comfortable mass; to give advice, go forward, and command respect in difficult and delicate cases; and to take an active part in promoting sound literature as well as religion, in the respective neighbourhoods in which they may be placed. Indeed to much of this work every itinerant missionary is called; and it is of the utmost importance that he be able to perform it with acceptance and usefulness. And that candidate for the ministry who is either too lazy, or too narrow-minded to take the requisite pains to qualify himself for these various and momentous duties, may think himself very conscientious, and may give himself great credit for being moderate and humble in his views; but he is an infatuated man. He is not merely under a mistake; he is unfaithful to himself, to the church, and to the Master whom he professes to love.

VII. The position which I wish to establish, is still further confirmed, and its great importance illustrated by *the humiliating fact, that learning is, at present, at a low ebb among the clergy of the Presbyterian Church.*

This assertion will, probably, be considered as a paradox by some who now hear me, especially when taken in connection with what was before advanced respecting the growing literature and intelligence of our country. Have not lawyers and physicians become more learned and able, as well as more numerous, than they were forty or fifty years ago? In general I believe they have. And have not our clergy you will ask, made a corresponding improvement? In general, I am persuaded they have not. Whatever may be the reasons of it, the humiliating fact, I apprehend, is really so. They have not made a corresponding improvement. Other causes may be assigned for this fact—if it be a fact—but I really believe one great cause is the prevailing excessive and criminal haste to be licensed, and to get into the field of active labour. The means of more mature study, and the excitements to more mature study, have been constantly increasing; but both the means and excitements have been lost upon a large number of our candidates. And when a rapid improvement might have been expected, a real decline, if I mistake not, has been silently and insensibly going on.

A little more than three quarters of a century ago, there was a considerable number of ministers in the Presbyterian Church in this country, who deserved to be called illustrious. As to the reality of this fact, you will not hesitate, when I mention, as a specimen, the names of President Dickinson, the elder President Edwards, President Burr, the Tennents, Mr Blair, President Davies, President Finley, and a number more scarcely inferior; men, most of them, at once eminent for the fervour of their piety, the activity of their zeal, the vigour of their talents, the extent of their erudition, and their commanding influence. The distinguished usefulness of these holy, apostolical men, in giving a tone to the preaching, the discipline, and the character of the church to which they belonged, it would not be easy to estimate. They were felt to be workmen that needed not to be ashamed, qualified rightly to divide the word of truth; and the churches, and their younger brethren confided in them, and looked up to them, and, under the divine blessing, were guided aright. They were men fitted to have influence, and they had it, and employed it for the glory of God, and the best interests of mankind.

The generation of ministers next to them were, as a body, little, if any less distinguished. Then we had Strain, and Duffield, and Witherspoon, and McWhorter, and Waddell, and Wilson, and Rodgers, and Hoge, not to mention others of equal claims; men of wisdom, piety, prudence, dignity, and peace;—men who commanded the veneration and confidence of the churches; men, who, whenever they appeared in ecclesiastical judicatories, especially in the higher ones, seemed as if they were sent to enlighten, and guide, and bless the family of Christ.

Of the present state of our church in reference to this point, it is both difficult and delicate to speak. But I ask—Have we an equally illustrious list to show at this hour, in proportion to our greatly augmented numbers and advantages? The ministers of our church are nearly ten times as numerous as they were sixty years ago; and the facilities for obtaining books, and pursuing study, are also greatly multiplied. Upon every principle of proportion, we ought to be able now to bring forward a catalogue of Presbyterian apostles at least ten times as large as could have been produced in the days of Edwards, Davies, and Finley. But can we produce such a catalogue? It would rejoice my heart if I could think it possible. We cannot, however, I think, so far impose upon ourselves as to deem it possible. The most mortifying facts of a contradictory character stare us in the face. How difficult is it, even in this day of theological seminaries, some of which have been nearly twenty years in operation, to supply an important vacant congregation with a pastor in whom the union of eminent learning, talents and piety is considered as indispensable? How much more difficult still to find a proper head for a college, to take a goodly portion of the rising generation under his care, and train them up to sound learning, and enlightened virtue and piety? And if a professor in a theological seminary be needed, it seems he can only be had by robbing some other institution, or some important post in the church; and thus, perhaps, inflicting a certain and immediate injury more than sufficient to countervail even the anticipated advantage; I should really tremble for the interests of Christian literature, and of sound theological knowledge in our church, and in our country, if I did not cherish the hope that he who sits as king upon the holy hill of Zion will give an effectual impulse to the hearts of at least a few of the present generation of candidates for the sacred office, and by their means to the hearts of many others, and thus effect a happy revolution in the current of our affairs.

VIII. Let me, once, more, entreat you to consider, as a further argument on this subject, *that our country, and especially some part of it, stand in need of nothing at this moment (next to the sanctifying grace of God) so much as a larger supply of truly able, pious, and well-trained ministers of the gospel.*

There is, in my opinion, a great and grievous mistake prevailing in regard to this matter. Many youthful and unfurnished candidates for the ministry profess to be anxious to get into the field of labour, because, say they, the harvest is so great and the labourers so few. They feel for the spiritual desolation which they witness, and of which they hear. They figure to themselves thousands perishing for lack of vision; and they sometimes imagine that, in circumstances so urgent, it would be almost criminal in them to remain poring over their books, while so many souls are passing daily into eternity, without any to tell them of him whose blood cleanseth from all sin. But this reasoning is founded on a total misapprehension. The harvest is indeed great, and it is distressing to think that the labourers are so few. The harvest, however, is not greater than it was in the days of our Lord's personal ministry. The whole world was then in a state of even more complete moral desolation than at present. And yet he did not think proper to enter upon his public ministry until he was full thirty years of age. The harvest is not greater, or more distressingly in need of labourers, than it was in the days of Paul; and yet that holy man, immediately taught of God, would receive no novice to the work of the ministry, would lay hands suddenly on no man, even for the purpose of sending forth a messenger of life to the perishing. The number of ministers, my beloved pupils, is unspeakably less important than their character. There is indeed the most pressing want of more labourers to go forth and feed the destitute and perishing millions in every part of our revolted world. But I will venture to say there is a still greater want of well-qualified labourers in whom piety, wisdom, prudence, zeal and learning are conspicuously united. One such man will really be likely to do more good—far more good—than fifty unqualified men, or men not furnished, in some measure, as public teachers and guides ought to be. One such man as Brainerd, or Edwards, or Buchanan, or Martyn, would be really more useful to the church, and to their generation, than many scores of weak and ignorant men, and especially men of dubious piety, under the name of ministers. So the Word of God teaches; and so we judge concerning other professions. Suppose a population of 10,000 families to be labouring under a contagious and mortal disease. Would it be better to send among them half a dozen wise and skilful physicians, or fifty or even a hundred miserable quacks, who would be likely to kill more than they would cure? Surely no thinking man can hesitate a moment about the proper answer. The truth is, there are unqualified men enough in the ministry. Other denominations are furnishing them in abundantly sufficient numbers. The task seems to be incumbent on us, under God, to train up for the service of the church, ministers of a more mature, scriptural and elevated character; and if the proper qualifications are not insisted on, and provided for by our church; if the great mass of those sent out by us are not able as well as pious and faithful ministers of the New Testament, I know of no denomination of Christians likely to supply the deficiency.

Look abroad, my young Friends, upon this nation, in all its settlements, in the length and breadth of them. Contemplate the number, the character, and the wants of our population. Behold the melancholy reign of ignorance and vice. Contemplate the learning, the boldness, and the industry of heresy on every side. Mark well the prevalence, the unwearied diligence, and the eloquence of infidelity. Think how much able writing, as well as skilful and powerful preaching, is called for by the shrewd and hostile millions within our widely extended territory. Advert for a moment, to the mighty influence which the press is destined to exert over this people, and how deadly that influence must be, if it be not guided and sanctified by the religion of Jesus Christ. Think of the interests of literature as well as of piety. Count the number of the youth who are to be trained up either for usefulness and heaven, or profligacy and perdition. Ponder well the necessities of our seminaries of learning, if they are to be made a blessing and not a curse. Look at these things, beloved candidates for the holy ministry, and consider seriously what must be the consequence, without a series of miracles, unless the young soldiers now coming forward to the service of the church take care to be adequately girded for the mighty warfare before them;—and if your spirits are not stirred within you by the sight, to take high aims in preparing for your work; to aspire to elevated attainments in knowledge, and in piety, you are but ill fitted for this age, or for the office which you seek.

With these impressions, when I see young men, under the notion of serving the church and of supplying the urgent demand for ministers, prematurely, and without proper furniture, pressing into the pulpit, instead of rejoicing, I mourn. They may have pious intentions, and may sincerely think they are promoting the welfare of the church; but they are preparing, in all probability, to inflict upon it a real injury. They may think the Lord hath need of them. But they are deceived. The Lord is a God of order, and not of confusion, in all his churches. He has never made mental imbecility, ignorance, rashness, and incompetence, proper qualifications for doing his work. If the Lord had need of them, he would not only open the door for their entrance, but would also qualify them for their work. In short, it cannot be too strongly impressed on the mind of the youthful candidate for the sacred office, that it is not mere additions to our numbers—a larger list of ministers of any sort that we need; but more ministers of the right stamp; men really fitted by the union of holy zeal, sound wisdom, and solid knowledge, to enlighten, counsel, guide, and bless the church; and that if they be essentially wanting in the qualifications necessary for this purpose, they had better be in any other profession than that of the holy ministry. The truth is, if we had but half our present number of ministers, yet, if that half were all men of the primitive, apostolic spirit, our beloved church and country would be far more richly blessed than they are at this hour. We should soon witness scenes which have seldom greeted the eyes of Christ's ambassadors, since the days of apostolic zeal and triumph.

The inference from all this is, that every candidate for the holy ministry who desires to serve the church of Christ in the most acceptable and useful manner; who wishes to be a rich and extensive blessing in his generation; who would be suitably prepared to meet the character and the demands of the age in which he lives—ought by all means, if it be possible, to go through a regular and mature course of preparatory study; that he is bound to exert himself to the utmost to attain this object; that his duty to God, to the church, to his country, and to himself—all conspire to show the criminality, as well as the folly of resting contented with anything short of it, if it be within his reach.

And by going through a regular and full course of study, I do not mean a mere nominal course; but a real, and faithful devotion to the prescribed studies, during the whole time assigned for them. Students may be three full years in a seminary, and yet, by that unsteadiness of application, which is either the original weakness, or the unhappily contracted habit of so many serious young men;—by yielding to every solicitation, which wears the remotest aspect of a call of providence, to break in upon their daily task; by accepting agencies, which commence a little before, and extend a little beyond the limits of their vacations; by allowing almost any plausible object, either of curiosity or of business to prevent their punctual return at the opening of each session; by forming engagements of different kinds, in the neighbourhood of the seminary, which frequently, and perhaps statedly, interfere with some of its appointed duties; by attending anniversaries, and other religious meetings; and in ways almost too numerous to be specified, scarcely suffering a month or even a week to pass, without permitting some unnecessary inroads to be made on the time professedly devoted to study;—I say, in these ways, they may reduce the real value of their nominal three years, to what a student of diligent habits would easily have found in two-thirds, or even in one-half of that time. Remember that a prescribed time and course of study are merely deceptive, if they be not as diligently and constantly occupied as health will permit. God forbid, my young Friends, that I should discourage your attention, even now, to any proper object connected with the eternal well-being of your fellow men. But recollect that for everything there is a season, and a time for every purpose under heaven. Remember that you have come hither to prepare for the ministry, not to commence its duties. Remember that engagements out of the seminary, even of a religious nature, may be improper for you at present; and that they certainly are so if they are either unseasonable or excessive in their encroachments on your time; or if they are calculated, in any way, materially to interfere with the regular course of study, which you have voluntarily brought yourselves under solemn obligations to pursue.

Prize every moment, then, of your three years' course as a precious treasure. Avoid wasting one of those moments with as much care as a miser would avoid throwing away a piece of gold. Rely upon it, you have not a moment to lose. Your whole time will be found too little for the great objects which you profess to have in view. Constantly bear in mind the purpose for which our venerable church has incurred the expense of founding and supporting this institution, and also the professed purpose for which you have entered it; and recollect that every engagement, either in or out of this house, which is not really subservient to the great object for which you have come hither, is something like a fraud upon your own consciences, and upon the church who claims your time, your talents, and your best services, as all her own.

Whatever may be the grade of your talents, my young Friends, or the peculiar character of your minds, respectively, the course which

I recommend may be said to be equally necessary to you all. On the one hand, those whose powers are of the moderate and solid kind, rather than the brilliant,—and this has been the character of some of the most eminently useful men that ever lived—ought to be aware that they need all the excitement, the invigoration, and the culture which the most mature and diligent study can give them. And, on the other hand, those who are endowed with remarkably lively, vigorous, and even brilliant talents, should recollect that they need all that I have been recommending, on some accounts, even more than others. For I hold that no class of men are more likely to do harm in the sacred office, than your striking, splendid, popular preachers, who have power to excite strong feelings, but not wisdom, prudence, and knowledge enough to regulate and direct them. A ship that carries much sail, and but little lading, is always in more danger in traversing the ocean, than the vessel which spreads less canvass to the winds, and at the same time bears an equal, or even a less cargo. An ample lading is, of course, more necessary to the safety of the former than of the latter. Let no candidate for the ministry, then, imagine that the sprightliness and force of his talents can supersede the necessity of mature study. Nay, so far from this, careful study and training are, to him, on that very account, the more indispensable. The more vigorous, powerful and active his mind, the more he needs the directing, restraining, and sanctifying influence of much study, prayer, retired communion with God, and counsel with age and experience. Without these, he is in far more danger than the man of dull and feeble powers, of falling into the varied evils which are apt to flow from eccentricity, impetuosity, or, the pride of talent.

I hope no one will so far misunderstand my main purpose in this lecture, as to suppose that I would bind every theological student to pursue the course which has been recommended; or that I would refuse admission to the sacred office to all, without exception, who have not enjoyed this privilege. The contrary may be inferred from several things which I have said, but I choose to be explicit on this point. The old law maxim, *Summum jus, summa injuria,*[1] may be applied here. To press a general principle too far, is to pervert and

---

[1] Literally, 'Extreme right, extreme injury.'

abuse it. Some have not health enough to sustain them in such a course as has been urged. Others are unavoidably shut out, by the providence of God, from that measure of temporal support which is indispensable to their prosecuting such a plan of preliminary study as they themselves earnestly desire. In such cases, if there be uncommon ardour of piety, joined with uncommon judiciousness, prudence and zeal, they ought to be admitted, after a shorter and more imperfect course of study than is commonly and properly deemed regular. Still, in every such case, the privation of the opportunity of mature study ought to be regarded by the individual himself, and by all his friends—and will be regarded by both, if they have good sense—as a serious disadvantage; a disadvantage to which nothing short of necessity should induce him to submit; and which can scarcely fail to abridge, and, in all probability, very materially, the usefulness as well as the comfort of all his ministrations.

Besides, let it be considered, that, after doing all we can to raise the standard of ministerial education and character, there will still be some, and, indeed, a considerable number, of those whom we attempt to conform to it, who will fall far short of this standard. Just as in a college—with the best system of instruction, and the best teachers in the world, there will always be some indifferent and even poor scholars. But, surely, it is desirable to have as few of these as possible, and the system of instruction should be so framed and applied, as to lift up as many as possible to the highest grade of excellence. In like manner, too, in a field of corn, with the best plan of culture that ever was or can be adopted, there will be some feeble and small ears of grain. But what then? Because there always will be such, in spite of everything that the best husbandman can do, would it be wise in him to lay his plan in such a manner as should be calculated to make his whole crop to consist of stunted and miserable ears? Common sense says, no. The governors of the college will not utterly reject even the poor scholars; but try to make the best of them. Neither will the wise cultivator of the soil throw away the small and inferior ears; but both will endeavour so to conduct the culture of their respective objects, as to have as few as may be of inferior character. Let the standard be as high as possible, and let the aim be to bring as many up to it as possible, without despising or rejecting those who cannot be raised to the desired elevation.

I have no fear that any of those whom I now address, will suspect me of a design to recommend a cold and heartless erudition in the gospel ministry. On this subject, my own opinion, and that of my colleagues, has been so often and so decisively expressed, as to preclude the possibility of misapprehension. Unfeigned piety—deep, ardent, active piety is, no doubt, the most essential qualification,—the most precious and glorious ornament of the ministerial character. Though a minister had all the learning in the world, yet if he were a stranger to the converting and sanctifying grace of God, there would be no reason to expect him to prove a blessing to the church. The men whom we wish to see trained up for the service of the church, are men of devoted and fervent piety; enlightened and warm friends to revivals of religion; men qualified and disposed to take an active part in forwarding all the laudable Christian institutions of the present day; and, at the same time, so solidly judicious; so intimately acquainted with the Bible, with the system of grace, with the history of the church, and with the human heart, as will prepare them at once, with enlightened discrimination and zeal, to promote all that is good; and to discern and resist everything of a contrary tendency, whether it appear in the form of an angel of light, or of darkness. Such is the ecclesiastical training for which I plead. Such is the model which, next to that of the Chief Shepherd, I would hold up to your view, and commend to your sacred emulation. Let your aims be high. Not high, indeed, on the scale of secular ambition; not high to be merely, or chiefly, great scholars, to be admired as profound divines, to shine as consummate orators, to have the uppermost rooms at feasts, or to be called of men, Rabbi, Rabbi. But let your sanctified emulation be awake and active to be able and faithful workmen; to be skilful as well as courageous soldiers of Christ; to be mighty in the Scriptures; mighty in the knowledge of the faith once delivered to the saints; mighty in the history of the church; mighty in wisdom, prudence, holy love, and active zeal; in a word, mighty in that noble, comprehensive character given by the pen of inspiration to a minister of old—'He was a good man, and full of the Holy Ghost, and of faith, and much people was added to the Lord.'

What do the pages of ecclesiastical history say on this subject? What description of ministers, in all ages, has been found most eminently useful to the church of Christ? Unquestionably those in whom eminent piety, zeal, talents and learning were remarkably united? Let the history of the Apostle Paul;—let the character and services of Augustine, of Ambrose of Milan, of Venerable Bede, of Wycliffe, of Huss, of Luther, of Calvin, of Knox, of Rivet, of Owen, of Baxter, of Doddridge, and to mention no more, of our own Dickinson and Edwards, be pondered well; and they will convince the most sceptical, that, though men of mere piety may, and probably will be, the means of saving good to some souls; and though mere talents and learning may answer another very limited purpose; it is only the union of both, in an eminent degree, that can give a reasonable pledge of that deep, extensive, and permanent usefulness to the church of God, to which every man of the right spirit will not fail to aspire.

I wish it were in my power, my young Friends, to impart to your minds the full impression which my own has received of the importance of this subject. Perhaps I ought rather to say, I feel humbled that it is necessary to plead such a cause before such an audience. And nothing could ever have convinced me that such a necessity exists, but the direful and daily experience which proclaims it;—but the disheartening fact, that so many of your number manifest that you are not yet satisfied of the truth which I have been labouring to establish. How long, my beloved Pupils, shall this humiliating fact continue to stare us in the face? How long shall the concurring voice of youth and of age, of remonstrance and of authority, continue to plead in vain on this subject? How long shall young men of talents worth cultivating, and of piety, which ought to secure a conscientious regard to their cultivation, continue to cheat themselves, and cheat the church of God, by neglecting to prepare for her service; nay by thrusting themselves into that service, while 'novices', and even 'babes in Christ', when they ought to be 'strong men'? Whatever you may think of it now, be assured, you will, one day, find that it is no light matter. You will find that it is a subject which regards, not merely the promotion of sound theological learning, but the advancement of the vital interests of the church of Christ; not merely the honour of our own denomination, which I hope will never be a matter of small moment in your eyes; but the spiritual prosperity of the whole family of the Redeemer on earth.

For my part, so long as I see so many candidates for the holy ministry contenting themselves with superficial and totally inadequate preparation for their exalted and arduous work; and so many actually venturing forth to that work with qualifications which fit them to be only transient meteors, and very humble ones too, rather than bright and steady luminaries in the church of God;—I cannot suppose that the Millennium is very near. I believe that that time will be as much distinguished for mature ministerial preparation, as for ministerial holiness, zeal, fidelity, and activity. If you desire, then, to hasten on that glorious period; if you desire, each one of you, to contribute as much as possible towards preparing the world for its arrival; then give all diligence to imbibe the spirit, and rise to something of the elevation, which that period will assuredly put in requisition. Be not contented with anything short of such furniture, both intellectual and moral, as will qualify you to act a part in harmony with the high commission which you hope to receive, and to be workers together with God in enlightening and blessing the world.

Finally, although I cannot anticipate, beloved Pupils, what effect this earnest appeal may produce on your minds;—especially when it was productive of so little sensible effect on your predecessors, eight years ago;[1]—yet allow me to say, I shall not have gained my purpose, today, unless you let your professors enjoy the pleasure of witnessing, from this time, a new and sacred impulse pervading your ranks. Unless we shall witness, henceforth, a unanimous determination, to think of no term of study short of three years;—to fill up every hour of this term with diligent application;—to attend with punctuality at the opening, and to hold out, with undeviating perseverance, to the closing hour, of every session;—to guard with solicitous care against the loss of a single recitation or lecture;—to cherish a hallowed greediness for every kind of theological knowledge, especially that which is practical and experimental;—to be in no haste to solicit license to preach;—in short, to guard with conscientious care, against the miserable delusion that the Lord hath need of but half-qualified servants. Nay, I shall not consider myself as having addressed you with the desired effect, unless we shall have the satisfaction of finding some of your number disposed

---

[1] The substance of this lecture was delivered at the opening of the winter session in the seminary, November 9, 1821.

to spend not merely three years, but a fourth, and a few even a fifth year, within these walls, for the purpose of more profound biblical and theological study than seems now to be seriously thought of by any. And, let me add, that as soon as a disposition of this kind shall be manifested by any of the sons of the church, I have no doubt provision will be made for its encouragement and support. We have a number of scholarships, founded by the pious liberality of distinguished friends of the seminary, and destined for the aid of those who are pursuing the regular course prescribed in the institution. But we have, as yet, no fellowships, or funds specifically devoted to the support of students who may be desirous of pursuing a course of study considerably more extensive than that which is laid down equally for all, and recommended to all. Only, however, let a few individuals manifest such a thirst for sacred knowledge, and such a devoted and successful diligence in seeking it, as shall evidently render fellowships desirable and necessary, and we shall very soon, I am confident, see one or more of them established. Be it the laudable distinction of some of you, then, my young Friends, to set the first example of this high resolution. It is needed. We must have it. How else shall we hope to see honourably and usefully filled the numerous professorial chairs, in the several theological seminaries which are rising in every part of our land? How else can we reasonably expect that our highly favoured and indebted church will perform her part of the duty which she owes to Christendom, in promoting the culture of profound biblical and theological knowledge? Surely these are considerations which cannot fail of lying with weight on the minds of some whom I address. That they will rouse none of you to corresponding aims and efforts, is a supposition which I cannot possibly admit.

And may he who has the hearts of all flesh in his hands so enlighten and govern your minds; so preside over your studies; and so endow you with gifts and graces adapted to the day of wonders in which you live;—that you may fulfil the high expectations of the Presbyterian Church while you are here;—and that, wherever you go, you may each be found a centre of holy illumination, of wise counsel, and of sanctified impulse in extending the Redeemer's kingdom; so that the blessing of the church, and of distant generations may abundantly come upon you! The grace of our Lord Jesus Christ be with you all! Amen.

HOLDING FAST
THE FAITHFUL WORD[1]

*Holding fast the faithful word, as he hath been taught, that he may be
able, by sound doctrine, both to exhort and to convince the gainsayers.*

Titus 1:9

THE inspired apostle is here giving directions concerning the
proper character and qualifications of ministers of the gospel. Some duties are common to all Christians; while others
belong either exclusively, or in an eminent degree, to pastors and
teachers. The latter is the case with regard to the injunction implied
in our text. On all the disciples of Christ is laid the charge to hold
fast the faithful word; but on the guides and rulers in the house of
God is this obligation especially devolved; among other reasons, for
this, that they may be able, by sound doctrine, both to exhort, and to
convince the gainsayers.

By the 'faithful word', here spoken of, we are evidently to understand the pure, unadulterated doctrines of Christ; the genuine gospel, as revealed by a gracious God for the benefit of sinful men. Not
the doctrines of this or the other particular denomination of Christians, as such, but the doctrines of the Bible. This system of doctrine
is represented as that which we have been taught. The gospel which
we preach, my Friends, is not our gospel. We neither invented it, nor
can we improve it. 'I certify you', says the same apostle who penned
the words of our text—'I certify you, brethren, that the gospel which
was preached by me is not after man. For I neither received it of man,
neither was I taught it but by the revelation of Jesus Christ.'

[1] Samuel Miller, *Holding Fast the Faithful Word: A Sermon, Delivered in the Second
Presbyterian Church, in the City of Albany, August 26, 1829 at the Installation of the Rev.
William B. Sprague, D.D., as Pastor of the Said Church* (Albany: Packard and Van
Benthuysen, 1829).

The original word, here properly translated 'hold fast', is very strong and expressive in its import. It signifies keeping a firm hold of anything, in opposition to those who would wrest it from us. Of course, it implies that gospel truth is and will ever be opposed by enemies and 'gainsayers'; and that maintaining and propagating truth must always be expected, in such a world as this, to require unceasing effort and conflict.

The general position of our text, then, is—*That the ministers of our holy religion, if they desire to convince, to convert, or to edify their fellow men, are solemnly bound to maintain for themselves, and diligently to impart to those around them, sound doctrine, or, in other words, the genuine truths of the gospel.*

To illustrate and confirm this position, let us, first, enquire, *Why we ought to maintain sound doctrine;* and, secondly, *How it ought to be maintained;* or in what manner, and by what means?

I. The first enquiry which demands our attention, is,—*Why ought we to maintain 'sound doctrine'.* Why is it important that all believers, and ministers of religion in particular, should hold fast the faithful word. And here, let me ask,

1. Can anything more be necessary to establish the duty before us, than the consideration that *the faithful word of which we speak is from God;* that it was given to us for our temporal and eternal benefit; and, of course, given not to be disregarded, but to be respected, studied, loved, and diligently applied to the great purposes for which it was revealed? To suppose that we are at liberty lightly to esteem such a gift, coming from such a source; or that we commit no sin in voluntarily permitting a deposit so precious to be corrupted, perverted, or wrested from us, is a supposition equally dishonourable to God, and repugnant to every dictate of reason.

2. But further, holding fast the genuine system of revealed truth, is *frequently and solemnly commanded by the great God of truth.* Both the Old Testament and the New abound with injunctions to this amount. In the former, we are exhorted to cry after knowledge, and lift up our voice for understanding; to seek it as silver, and search for it as for hidden treasures. We are exhorted to buy the truth, and not to sell it. And they are highly commended who are represented as valiant for the truth. In the latter, the language of the Holy Spirit is,

'Hold fast the form of sound words which thou hast received.' And again, 'Contend earnestly for the faith'—that is, the revealed doctrine which is the object of faith—'once delivered to the saints.' And again, 'Be not carried about with every wind of doctrine, and cunning craftiness whereby they lie in wait to deceive.' And again, 'Hold fast the profession of your faith firm without wavering.' And again, 'If there come any unto you, and bring not this doctrine'—that is, the true doctrine of Christ—'receive him not into your house, neither bid him God speed; for he that biddeth him God speed, is a partaker of his evil deeds.' Nay, the inspired apostle pronounces, 'If any man come unto you, and bring any other gospel'—that is, any other system of doctrine concerning the salvation by Christ—'than that which ye have received, let him be accursed' (*Prov.* 2:3, 4; *Prov.* 23:23; *Jer.* 9:3; *2 Tim.* 1:3; *Jude* 3; *Eph.* 4:14; *Heb.* 10:23; *2 John* 10, 11; *Gal.* 1:9).

3. The obligation to hold fast the genuine doctrines of the gospel, appears from considering *the great importance which the Scriptures everywhere attach to evangelical truth.*

I am aware that it is a popular sentiment with many who bear the Christian name, that doctrine is of little moment, and that practice alone is all in all. But such persons surely forget that there can be no settled and habitual good practice, with good principles; and that sound, correct doctrine, is but another name for sound principle. Take away the doctrines of the gospel, and you take away its essential character. You take away everything that is adapted to enlighten, to restrain, to purify, to console, and to elevate. Take away the doctrines of our holy religion, in other words, the great truths of which the glad tidings of great joy are composed, and you take away the essence of the whole message;—the seed of all spiritual life; the aliment on which every believer lives; the vital principles of all experimental piety, and of all holy practice. What is faith, but cordially embracing, with confidence and love, the great truths concerning duty and salvation which the Scriptures reveal? What is repentance, but a holy sorrow for sin, founded on a spiritual perception of those doctrines concerning God, his character, his law, and the plan of mercy which his Word proclaims? What is hope, but looking forward with holy desire and expectation to that exceeding and eternal weight of glory, which the truth as it is in Jesus freely offers to our acceptance? What, in short, is religion, in the largest sense of the term, but the combination of knowledge of the truth, love of the truth, and walking in the truth? What is it but having just apprehensions of those great objects which are revealed in Christian doctrine; just affections and desires toward them; and acting out these desires and affections in the temper and life? No wonder, then, that when the impenitent are converted, they are said to come to the knowledge of the truth; that they are said to be born again by the word of truth; to be made free by the truth, and to obey the truth;—by all which expressions we are plainly taught, that truth, or, which is the same thing, Christian doctrine, is the grand instrument, in the hands of the Holy Spirit, by which spiritual life is begun, carried on, and completed in every subject of redeeming grace.

Hence it is, that the Scriptures everywhere represent bringing the truth, in some way, to men, as absolutely necessary to their conversion and salvation. How shall they believe in him of whom they have not heard? Hence they so plainly teach us, that there can be no real piety where the fundamental doctrines of the gospel are not embraced. Whosoever abideth not in the doctrine of Christ, hath not God. On this principle, too, it is, that the inspired volume, with awful emphasis, declares certain 'heresies' to be 'damnable'—that is, inevitably destructive to the souls of men. And on the same principle it is, that all Scripture, and all experience teach us, that wherever the preaching and the prevalence of true doctrine has declined, there piety, immediately, and in a corresponding ratio, has declined; good morals have declined; and all the most precious interests of the church and of civil society, have never failed to be essentially depressed.

We cannot, indeed, undertake to pronounce how much knowledge of sound doctrine is necessary to salvation; or how much error is sufficient to destroy the soul. But we know, from the nature of the case, and especially from the Word of God, that all error, like poison, is mischievous, and, of course, ought to be avoided. I know not, indeed, how large a quantity of a given deleterious drug might be necessary, in a particular case, to take away life: but of one thing there can be no doubt, that it is madness to sport with it, and that the less we take of it the better. As nothing but nutritious food will support the animal body; so nothing but Zion's provision, which is truth, can either commence, or sustain the life of God in the soul of man.

4. Further, the duty to maintain and hold forth sound doctrine, may be urged from the consideration, that *such doctrine is universally distasteful to the unsanctified heart, and therefore, requires not only to be presented, but also to be importunately pressed on the attention of men, if, by the blessing of God, we may prevail with them to receive it.*

It is, somewhere, justly remarked, by one of the most eloquent of living preachers (Dr Chalmers) that, of all kinds of truth, the pure gospel of Jesus Christ is precisely that, and that alone, for which there is no natural demand among men. All other kinds of truth are called for, even by unsanctified minds. Literary truth; philosophical truth; political truth; commercial truth; mechanical truth;—for all these there is a general, steady, and growing demand, as population becomes more extended and active; because for all of them, there is, among the diversified classes of society, a deep-seated, natural taste. But with regard to the most precious of all truth,—that which relates to God, and the way of salvation, there is no natural demand among the mass of mankind. No, my Brethren, we are perfectly aware that the gospel which we preach—a gospel which proclaims to men their guilt and depravity, and a method of recovery which lays the sinner in the dust, and stains all his pride;—we are perfectly aware that this is a gospel which the natural heart everywhere hates, and is disposed to reject; which, of course, none ever naturally desire or seek; and which, therefore, requires not merely to be held up to the view of men, but to be urged and pressed on their minds, with ceaseless repetition, as long as they continue within the reach of the voice of mercy.

Nor is this all. The same distaste for the holy, humbling, and self-denying doctrines of the gospel, which renders all men, by nature, disposed to reject them;—disposes them also to pervert these doctrines; to contrive, in a thousand ways, to reduce and mutilate them, and thus to endeavour to divest them of their offensive character, and accommodate them to the taste of unsanctified men. This undoubted fact renders it necessary that all who profess to love the religion of Christ, and especially ministers, who are, by divine appointment, the official conservators of evangelical truth, be constantly on the watch to mark these unhallowed attempts at mutilation and perversion; to guard those who are under their care against the insidious arts of error; to distinguish with clearness between truth and falsehood; to recommend the one, and denounce the other; and thus to hold fast and hold forth sound doctrine, for the benefit of themselves and others.

5. Another reason why ministers of religion ought to be vigilant, firm, and unwearied in holding fast sound doctrine, is, that *the enemies of truth are everywhere zealous and indefatigable in opposing it.* This consideration is closely allied with the preceding, but is, nevertheless, worthy of separate notice.

If men were not, everywhere, prone to embrace error; if they did not naturally love error better than truth; and if the advocates of erroneous opinions were not active and unceasing in their efforts to insinuate them into the minds of men; there would be less call for unremitting vigilance and activity on the part of the watchman on the walls of Zion. We know, however, that the advocates of error not only abound in every part of the world, but also that their exertions to propagate their sentiments are equally ceaseless, diversified, ingenious and unwearied. Argument, ridicule, intimidation, flattery, and all the arts which talent, learning, and diligence enable them to apply for extending the dominion of their delusive principles, are constantly employed for effecting this fatal purpose. To say nothing of the avowed rejecter of all revelation, the Unitarian, the Pelagian, the Universalist, and the whole train of errorists, under the Christian name, are incessantly busy, from the pulpit and the press, in public and in private, in disseminating their pestilential doctrines. Indeed it is melancholy to think that the advocate of error, like the other children of this world, are wiser in their generation than the children of light;—that is, more active, more cunning, more watchful, more adroit, more quick-sighted in devising means, and more unwearied in pursuing them; more ingenious in availing themselves of opportunities and prejudices in their favour; and, on all these accounts, more apt to be successful in carrying the multitude with them.

In these circumstances, how important is it that the advocates of truth be awake, active, and faithful in guarding the precious deposit committed to their charge! How wise ought they to be in discriminating and explaining; how courageous in defending; how firm in holding fast, and how diligent in proposing, recommending and enforcing the truth on all around them! The fact is, those whose duty it is to plead the cause of sound doctrine, in the present world, are like mariners rowing against both wind and tide. To make headway, requires incessant exertion. The moment it is intermitted, without a miracle, the current bears them, and all the interests in behalf of which they plead, rapidly down the stream.

6. A further consideration which shows the importance of ministers holding fast, and endeavouring diligently to propagate the genuine doctrines of the Bible, is, that *there is, everywhere, such a deplorable lack of doctrinal information among the mass of the people.*

It might be supposed that in this age of printing and of books, and especially when the press has been, of late, so much enlisted on the side of truth and piety, that there would be found, at any rate among the friends of religion, much more extended reading, and digested knowledge, than in any former times. But I am under a great mistake if this be the fact. Half a century ago, serious professors of religion, and especially those who laid claim to the character of intelligent Christians, were much more, I apprehend, in the habit of retired and careful religious reading, than is now common. Then the Bible, though copies of it were not so multiplied as at present, was daily and abundantly perused. Then the popular writings of Owen, Baxter, Flavel, Charnock, Bunyan, Manton, Halyburton, Watts, Doddridge, Dickinson, Edwards, Bellamy, and a number more of the same class, were found on the shelves of most pious families connected with our church, and other evangelical denominations;—were read with some degree of intelligence and care; and recommended to the rising generation. But has not this laudable habit, within a few years past, fallen into comparative disuse? Do not private Christians, now, commonly spend much less time in storing their minds with scriptural knowledge than formerly? I fear we cannot deny that such is the fact. For this fact perhaps two reasons may be assigned.

The first is, that professing Christians of the present day have so many objects of public enterprise and exertion, to occupy their time, and engage their attention, that they are often tempted to slight the more private, and less attractive duties of retirement and devotion.

There is so much to be done by every man of zeal and energy, in helping forward the multiplied plans of Christian benevolence which characterize the present period, that, unless he be very careful to redeem time, and possess great decision of Christian character, he will often find the duties of the closet crowded into a corner, or, perhaps, occasionally, excluded altogether, by his public engagements. Besides, there is something in the very nature of zealous efforts, and especially of public efforts, to extend the Redeemer's kingdom, so exciting, so warming, so spirit-stirring, that they are adapted to gratify some of the strongest natural feelings as well as the gracious principles of men. Hence they are often more attractive, even to good men, than those duties which include less of public exhibition, and of social excitement. The consequence is, that many, otherwise exemplary professors of religion, who are called to take an active part in the great operations of the day, spend less of their time in retirement and devotion;—meditate less—read less—pray less—examine themselves less than persons equally engaged in religion, were wont to do formerly; and, of course, employ less time in instructing and catechising their children, and in praying with them, and for them. In these circumstances, it is by no means wonderful that both parents and children should manifest much less digested and mature scriptural knowledge, than the multiplied privileges of the day would seem to warrant us in expecting.

A second reason for the undoubted deficiency of doctrinal knowledge, even in the church, may, perhaps, be drawn from the light and ephemeral character of what we may call the religious literature of the day. Have not religious newspapers and other light periodical publications, in a great measure taken the place of the larger and more instructive works before alluded to? Publications which, by their number, have left little time for other reading; and by their superficial character, little taste for reading of a more deep, solid and connected kind. Is it not manifest, that the mass, even of the hopefully pious, have a large portion of their reading time so much occupied, and their taste so much formed, by the details of religious intelligence; by the exciting eloquence of anniversaries; and by the pungent discussion to which new projects and controversies give rise; that they have seldom much relish for the calm study of evangelical truth, or even for the retired and prayerful perusal of the Scriptures? What proportion of private Christians at the present day, with all the multiplication and almost universal circulation of weekly and monthly journals, which profess to diffuse religious knowledge, would be able, think you, to defend their professed creed against a plausible adversary, or to give an intelligent reason of the hope that is in them? I am afraid a very small proportion indeed. Nay, is there not some reason to fear, that even ministers of the gospel, in many cases, have their reading too much confined to the passing periodical works of the day; if not to the exclusion, at least to the lamentable diminution of that profounder and more mature study to which the spiritual teachers and guides of the people ought to be ever habitually addicted?—My Friends, I make no charge; I prefer no accusation against those whom I now address. But I, most respectfully, offer these queries to your serious and impartial consideration. How far they may be considered as applying to the religious population of this city and neighbourhood, I know not. But there are neighbourhoods, to which, my better acquaintance with their state enables me to say, that they are by no means inapplicable.

You will not consider me, I trust, as intending to proscribe, or even to censure, religious periodical publications. When wisely conducted, and not inordinately multiplied, they deserve to be regarded as among the rich blessings of the day in which we live; and those who refuse to patronize them, deprive themselves, and, so far as their example goes, deprive the church of God, of an invaluable auxiliary. But when publications of this kind become so numerous as to impoverish and enfeeble one another, and render it difficult for any to attain the highest excellence: and, especially, when persons altogether inadequate to the task of instructing and guiding the religious public, undertake to be their conductors, merely 'for a piece of bread'; they can only be sources of paltry amusement. Solid intellectual and moral nutrition, it is impossible they should furnish. Wherever this is the case, the consequences cannot fail of being deplorable. There will, almost necessarily, ensue, a diminished attention to Christian doctrine; of course a diminished knowledge of it; and, consequently, a constant liability to be carried about by every wind of doctrine, to which ignorance, vanity, or fanaticism may attempt to give currency in the community. And, accordingly, how often have we seen, to our astonishment, not only individual professors, but, perhaps considerable portions of particular churches, which we once thought as well instructed and exemplary as almost any among us, borne away by the very first onset of some plausible errorist, and making a temporary, if not a final shipwreck of the faith!

Now, such being the deplorable deficiency of sound and discriminating Christian knowledge, among the mass, even of serious, and otherwise exemplary, professors; is it not peculiarly important that some counteracting influence should be found and applied? And to whom are we to look, under God, for this influence, but to the leaders and guides of the church? If, as the prophet informs us, the priest's lips are to keep knowledge, surely there are none to whom we can more rightfully turn for relief, than to the ministers of religion. And I will venture to say, that there cannot be a characteristic prevalence of popular ignorance where they are duly faithful, in the various ways which their office demands, in feeding the people with knowledge and with understanding.

7. The diffusion of sound religious doctrine through all classes of the community is *one of the surest means of establishing and perpetuating our national privileges.*

We often, my Friends, congratulate ourselves on the free constitutions of government under which we are so happy as to live. That our lot is cast in a land where the people, under God, are supreme; where we are not called to bow to the will of a crowned despot, or to the oppressions of privileged orders: where we have no ecclesiastical establishments; but where, under governments of our own choice, and laws of our own formation, all enjoy those equal rights to which the laws of nature, and of nature's God entitle them. And we may well congratulate ourselves, and be thankful for these privileges. The great Governor of the world hath not dealt so with any other nation. The lines are fallen unto us in pleasant places, yea we have a goodly heritage. And our prayer, as patriots, and as Christians ought to be, that these inestimable blessings may be preserved and transmitted, unimpaired, to the latest generations.

But how, think you, my respected hearers, may we rationally hope that these blessings will be preserved inviolate, and transmitted to a distant posterity? I take for granted every individual in this assembly is, in his judgment, convinced that such a hope cannot be realized without the general prevalence of Christian principle. An ignorant people must be an irreligious people. An irreligious people must be an immoral people. And an immoral people must be a miserable people. That such a people should be long free is just as impossible as that light and darkness should agree, or that the relation of cause and effect should cease. Many, indeed, tell us that literature and philosophy, without the fear of God, without the gospel of Christ, will restrain, purify, and regulate men and generate the purest and most efficient patriotism. Nay, it is the favourite theory of some, given up to the insanity of infidel fanaticism—the most blind and senseless of all fanaticism—that the only hope of perfecting and perpetuating the social system, in its best form, is, to reject the religion of Christ; to renounce the laws of marriage and of the Sabbath; and, in short, to throw off most of the restraints which the religious and moral code, under which we are so happy as to live, imposes. But believe them not. As well might they tell us that we must all turn brutes in order to be perfect and happy men. No, the native fruit of their unhallowed system, is, that selfishness, avarice, profligate ambition, fraud, violence, luxury, and unbridled sensuality, which have always been the great destroyers of republics, and which, if ever they become generally characteristic of our population, will as infallibly destroy us, and deliver us up, either to the most horrible anarchy, or to the gloomiest tyranny, as ever they did the most miserable of our predecessors.

These things being so, can anyone possibly doubt that the diligent diffusion of pure religious knowledge is of inestimable importance to the best interests of our beloved country?—That enlightened patriotism, as well as piety, ought to labour unceasingly to impart it to all classes of the community, and especially to the rising generation? No, my Friends, mathematical demonstration never conducted any man to a more unquestionable result. Whether I were called upon, then, to address you as good citizens, or as faithful Christians, I would say to you all, and more particularly to those of your number who bear the office of the holy ministry—Give all diligence to impart pure, Bible knowledge to all within your reach—to old and young, high and low, rich and poor, bond and free. Teach them the character of

God, and the relations which we all equally bear to him. Teach them the condition of our race, by nature, as polluted, guilty sinners in the sight of their heavenly Sovereign. Teach them the way of pardon and sanctification through the atoning sacrifice, and life-giving Spirit of the divine Redeemer, and the endearing ties by which the principles of our 'common salvation' bind together the whole human family. Teach them that all men are by nature equal in the sight of God; and, therefore, that all tyranny and oppression are objects of his righteous abhorrence. Teach them that the kingdom of Christ is not of this world; and, therefore, that every species of alliance between church and state is forbidden, and can never fail to become a curse to both. Teach them to abhor those vices which the laws of man cannot reach, but which do more to undermine and destroy social happiness than a volume could unfold. Teach them to love those graces and virtues, which human authority cannot enforce, but which are vital to the establishment of social prosperity.—Teach them faithfully and diligently these things—and you cannot take a more direct course to lift up their minds above everything that is grovelling and corrupt; to curb their unruly appetites; to restrain their unhallowed passions; to banish fraud, intemperance and voluptuousness, from the land; to promote industry, self-denial, moderation; and universal order, justice, purity and benevolence. You cannot take a more direct and certain course to render the insidious demagogue despised, and to deprive the profligate votary of ambition of all his influence; to inspire a love of liberty, and to promote the prevalence of the purest patriotism. You cannot employ a more infallible means to secure a faithful use of the elective franchise, and, consequently, to exalt the wise and the good to stations of authority. You cannot, in a word, take a more direct course to establish the reign of all those principles, sentiments and habits, which, a thousandfold more than constitutions and laws, tend to perpetuate civil and religious liberty, and social happiness.

Christians! Ministers of the gospel! here lies our country's fairest, best, only hope! To those who love the cause of Christ, is committed, under God, her precious destiny. Spread Christian knowledge in every direction. Never rest satisfied while there is a dark corner of our land unfurnished with faithful Bible instruction; and you will transmit, unimpaired, our precious privileges as a people to that bright and blessed day of millennial glory, when the kingdoms of this world shall become the kingdoms of our Lord, and of his Christ;— and when the knowledge and glory of God shall cover the earth as the waters cover the sea.

8. But further, *the great operations of the day in which we live, call for special attention and diligence in regard to the object for which I plead.*

It is one of the glories, my Friends, of the period in which our lot is cast, that professing Christians of almost every denomination have come together, and are more and more coming together, for the purpose of uniting their efforts to send Bibles, religious tracts, the living missionary, and the system of Sabbath Schools, throughout the world. I repeat it, this is one of the great glories of the day in which we live. Every minister, and every Christian who is so happy as to live at this day, ought to be thankful for it as a great privilege; to enter into the spirit of the hallowed co-operation; and to cheer it on by his example, his exertions, and his substance, as well as by his prayers. If there be a minister or a professing Christian, who looks coldly upon these great plans of Christian benevolence, and refuses to put his hand to the work,—I 'judge him not'; but he really seems to me to stand very near, if not actually in, the ranks of those who will not come up to the help of the Lord against the mighty; and who are placed in no very enviable eminence in the sacred history.

Be it remembered, however, that one fundamental principle of this noble union is, that all the denominations which are parties to it, promise neither to compromit, nor to invade the peculiarities of each other. The publications circulated are of a general character, in which they all agree. The practical language of their union is to the following amount. We will agree to act together, for the sake of acting with more strength, and upon a greater scale. To a certain extent, we are entirely united, both in principle and practice. To that extent, we can cordially co-operate without difficulty. And as to the peculiar doctrines which the pious Presbyterian, the pious Episcopalian, or the pious Methodist may wish to see circulated within the limits of his own denomination; let the pastors and teachers, within the respective bounds of each, take care, in addition to the general measures, which are not sectarian, to provide for conveying that appropriate instruction which each may deem desirable and important.

This is fair, honourable, and Christian-like. But let me request you to take particular notice, that the faithful and happy execution of this admirable plan, not only allows, but really requires, that each particular denomination engaged in carrying it on, be careful not to neglect, or even slight, either of its parts. While, on the one hand, they cordially act upon the principles of their union, and circulate the general publications which they have agreed in forming, through every part of the land; on the other, each party is no less bound, by an implied pledge, to be diligent in instructing its own population, and especially its own children and young people, in its own peculiar views of truth and order. If this be not done, either many discerning and zealous individuals, of each denomination, will withdraw from the union, as not faithfully executed, and as adapted, ultimately, to deceive and ensnare: or, the next generation will grow up in a great measure unindoctrinated; or, to speak in the most guarded terms, very far from being instructed in theological truth in that accurate and discriminating manner which the enlightened guardians of the household of faith know to be important.

Under this impression, if I could speak to every Presbyterian minister and church in the United States, it would be in the following language—If you desire to see different denominations of Christians more and more united in affection and effort; if you wish well to the great institutions of pious benevolence round which, and in behalf of which the followers of Christ, of different names, are rallying with holy zeal; if you wish them to remain, and to become more and more, great public blessings;—if you desire to see them firmly sustained by public sentiment, and adapted to answer public expectation; nay, if you do not wish to find them cheating yourselves and your children into comparative ignorance, or, at least, superficiality, in Christian doctrine;—watch over the Sabbath Schools, and the Bible classes in your respective congregations with intense interest. Carry into them, and unfold, with unremitting diligence, those views of gospel truth which you honestly believe to be agreeable to the Word of God. Add to the Sabbath School lesson, such excellent and scriptural formularies of doctrine, as shall prepare your youthful charge to receive, not merely a meagre outline, but a strong and well delineated portrait of that blessed system of grace and truth, which it is happy for everyone to know, from a child, as distinctly and clearly as possible. Follow the tract, which, as a powerful pioneer, has gone before you, and prepared the way;—follow it, as far as possible, with still deeper instruction in the precious general truths, which it unfolds. Remember that, although the whole Christian world is in motion, the great movements of the day embrace no plan for the dissemination of sound, distinguishing doctrine. There is no institution, no society which has for its object that on behalf of which I plead in this discourse. It is left to be pursued by the pastors and other officers, and, with their aid, by all the members of our respective churches. Thus you will guard against the evils which some have predicted as likely to arise from union in these operations. You will contribute your share to render the institutions of which we speak more extensively useful; more firmly popular; and a richer blessing to yourselves and your children. Nay, strange as it may seem to some, you will do more to harmonize and unite Christians of different denominations in every hallowed affection and enterprise, than by any other course you can possibly pursue.

9. Once more, the great importance of diffusing sound, scriptural knowledge among the people, not only appears from the character of the day in which we live; but also from *the character of those days which we hope and believe are approaching.*

That times of deep interest to the church and the world are hastening on, the watchmen on the walls of Zion seem generally to agree. When we are asked, indeed, what will be the precise aspect and bearing of these coming scenes, we dare not venture to foretell in detail. But that two features will be very prominent and impressive, I think we may venture, without presumption, confidently to anticipate. In the *first* place, we may hope that the approaching time will be distinguished by revivals of religion, more frequent, more extensive, and more glorious than we have ever been accustomed to contemplate: and, *secondly,* by a boldness and bitterness of opposition, on the part of the enemies of the gospel, no less marked, and beyond all former precedent. Now, unless I greatly mistake, it is of the utmost importance, as a preparation for both these events, that care be taken to spread sound doctrine, as deeply and extensively as possible, through every portion of the community, and especially among the rising generation.

With respect to the importance of this preparation for revivals of religion, of extraordinary extent and power, it is so obvious, that I need but hint at the subject. It is known, by painful experience, that powerful effusions of the Holy Spirit are often accompanied by perversions and abuses, which tend, at once, to tarnish their lustre, and to arrest their progress. False zeal, extravagance, ebullitions of animal sympathy, enthusiasm, and various kinds of disorder, have so often followed in the train of undoubted operations of the grace of God, that many have been prejudiced against revivals of religion altogether, and been ready to pronounce them all a miserable delusion, and the very term, a watchword of fanaticism. Now, there is hardly any point respecting which enlightened and pious divines are more agreed, than that the irregularities and extravagancies to which I have just alluded, are most apt to occur among a people comparatively uninstructed on the subject of religion. When such a people have so great a subject powerfully presented to them, not only in the preaching of the Word, but also in the visible triumphs of its divine energy; no wonder they are often excited in a manner, and fall into disorders, which intelligent Christians contemplate with regret. Powerful feeling, without enlightened judgment to control it; ardent zeal, without knowledge to regulate it, have been, in all ages, the bane both of the purity and the order of the church. Whereas all experience testifies, that such excesses and disorders seldom occur, and, certainly, are much less likely to occur, in churches in which the people have been early and carefully trained in the knowledge of divine truth. Such a people will have the best defence against enthusiasm, against fanaticism, against superstition, against all the forms in which 'strange fire' is apt to burst out, and work mischief in seasons of excitement.

If ministers, then, wish the people of their charge to be prepared for revivals of religion; to profit by them most effectually; and to be carried through them in a happy manner;—if they wish revivals to come to them in their most sound and genuine character, and to leave behind them their happiest results;—if it be their desire, in short, that the fruits of these blessed rains of righteousness should be, not stunted, feeble, and short-lived plants, which, having no deepness of earth, will speedily wither away;—but firm, lofty and thriving trees, fixed deep in the soil of Christian instruction and experience;—let them labour without ceasing to imbue every mind within their reach, as early as possible, with sound, Bible doctrine; with clear, discriminating, scriptural knowledge.

Of no less importance is a deep and intimate knowledge of divine truth, as a preparation for days of conflict with the enemies of religion. The great adversary, knowing that his time is short, is stirring up, and will, probably, more and more stir up, infidels, sceptics, heretics, and, perhaps, some formalists who pass for orthodox,—to oppose the claims and the progress of vital piety; and especially the claims and the progress of Christian effort. Effort for honouring the holy Sabbath; for improving, in every form, the intellectual, moral and religious state of society; and for evangelising the world;—For, surely, no ultimate object short of this can bound the ambition of Christians. Now, there seems every prospect that the opposition of which I speak will wax louder and stronger,—wielding the weapons of ridicule, calumny, cruel mockings, and every form of reviling that bigotry, prejudice, or impiety can forge;—until it shall reach that stage of warfare, called in the Apocalypse, the great day of the battle of God Almighty. A 'battle' which is destined, not long hence, to divide, to convulse, and to emancipate the world.

Now, for this conflict, in all its stages, one of the most important preparations is a mature and thorough acquaintance with revealed truth. Hence the inspired apostle, in speaking of the Christian's contest with the powers of darkness, exhorts him to take 'the sword of the Spirit, which is the Word of God', as one of the most indispensable and efficient portions of his armour. Accordingly, it is observable, that our blessed Saviour, in resisting the Devil, when exposed to his severest temptation in the wilderness, resorted to the Scriptures of truth as his principal weapon. To the most insidious attempts to ensnare him, his reply constantly was—'It is written'—'It is written.' Before this weapon even Satan could not stand. He cowered and withdrew, abashed and defeated. And whenever a similar conflict with the powers of darkness and their emissaries, shall come upon any of the dwellers upon earth, to try the spirits of men, and especially to sift as wheat the ranks of professors; happy will those be who shall be found enlightened and confirmed, as well as sincere and warm-hearted Christians! Happy, and only happy, in that day, will those be, who shall be found intelligently holding fast the faithful word, and ready to give a reason of the hope that is in them with meekness and fear! These are the men to triumph in perilous service, and to display the power of Christian courage and magnanimity. These, when the storm rages, will be found stable and safe as the rock on which their feet are placed. A little band of them will do more to strike terror into the ranks of error and sin, and to turn to flight the armies of the aliens, than thousands of your superficial professors, who have little or no root in themselves, and who, when tribulation or persecution ariseth, because of the Word, by and by will be offended; and either openly turn traitors to the best of causes; or, before they are aware, be swept from their apparent standing, by the power of the foe, and fall, with their whole weight, into his unhallowed territory.

Having dwelt so long on the importance of maintaining and diffusing sound doctrine, let us next,

II. *Inquire, in what manner, and by what means this duty ought to be fulfilled?*

Into this wide field we cannot enter at large. A few brief hints can alone be offered. And,

1. *We are to maintain pure evangelical truth firmly and earnestly.* 'Contend', says the inspired apostle,—'Contend earnestly for the faith once delivered to the saints.' Many, indeed, entertain a prejudice against all controversy on the subject of religious doctrine, and imagine that it is never productive of anything but evil. But this is a prejudice merely, and a prejudice as unreasonable as it is unscriptural. If the truth of God's Word be really of sufficient value to be worth defending; if there be multitudes in the world who continually hate and oppose it; and if it cannot be maintained and propagated without frequently pleading in its behalf against gainsayers;—then controversy, even religious controversy, is sometimes unavoidable. The prophets, the apostles, nay Christ himself, often engaged in controversy; and have made it our duty, by precept as well as by example, whenever it is necessary, to do the same. But we need go no further than our context, for an express authority to this effect. The apostle,

in the very next verse, to enforce the duty of holding fast the faithful word, and maintaining sound doctrine, observes—'For there are many unruly and vain talkers and deceivers, whose mouths must be stopped, teaching things which they ought not, for filthy lucre's sake. Wherefore rebuke them sharply, that they may be sound in the faith.' I grant, indeed, that this duty is often a self-denying and painful one. But this is no reason why it should not be considered as sometimes incumbent upon us. It is not pleasant to be called upon to defend our property against robbers, or our lives against assassins. But as long as there are robbers and assassins in the world, we must submit to the necessity of resisting their violence. In like manner, as long as there are opposers and revilers of the truth, it will be a part of that 'good fight of faith', which we are commanded to maintain, to defend it with firmness and zeal against every hostile invader.

2. While we maintain the truth firmly and earnestly, we ought, at the same time, *to do it mildly, and, as far as possible, inoffensively; with the meekness and gentleness of Christ.* Not haughtily, or dogmatically; but in the spirit of Christian benevolence. Not harshly, or with unnecessary severity; but with paternal affection. Not after the manner of the disputers of this world; but, like a messenger from above, intent, not on victory, but on doing good. Not as though we had dominion over the faith of our hearers; but as humble helpers of their spiritual benefit. For this purpose, we ought to make constant appeals to the authority of the Master whose truth we dispense; illustrating Scripture by Scripture; and going continually to the sacred oracles for all our positions, and all our weapons; remembering that one, 'Thus saith the Lord', is worth a thousand of our own philosophical deductions, however plausible or imposing. In short, I am constrained to believe that, even in defending the most precious truth, it is important that we give our defence as little of the polemical character as possible. When we rise before our hearers in the avowed attitude of polemics; with the countenance, the tone, the challenge, and the defiance of polemics; we, almost unavoidably, excite them to take the attitude of counter-polemics, and, with corresponding feelings, to sit in judgment on our arguments, as cold and captious logicians, rather than humble inquirers after truth. Whereas, if we speak the truth in love; if we explain, enforce and defend it with the spirit and weapons

of the Bible alone, they will be apt to throw open their minds to our teaching with the frankest ingenuousness. We shall have, of course, upon every principle both of nature and of grace, the fairest prospect of meeting with a favourable reception, and of 'winning souls' to the love and obedience of the truth.

3. We are to 'hold fast', and hold forth truth *with unremitted constancy and diligence, to the end of life.* It is a work never to be considered as done, and never to be for an hour remitted. As the presence of the elastic fluid in which we live, is necessary to every successive respiration, as long as life continues; and as the aliment by which our bodies are sustained, cannot be received once for all, but must be taken, again and again, day by day;—so it is indispensable that the precious truth of God be brought to bear, unceasingly, upon the understandings, the consciences, and the hearts of all within our reach. As we have seen, it is the food on which the children of God daily and hourly live; and, of course, the more richly, clearly, and faithfully it is applied for their benefit, the more we may hope they will grow in spiritual knowledge and strength. It is also the instrument in the hands of God for slaying the enmity, dispelling the darkness, and winning the hearts of the hardened and impenitent; and, therefore, the more skilfully, and pointedly it is applied for their instruction, warning, and conviction, the greater is the probability of promoting their eternal benefit. There is no class of persons who do not need it urgently and constantly to the end of their course. Hence the duty incumbent on those who are set as trustees and administrators of gospel truth, to hold it forth, and scatter it abroad, daily, in every direction; to dispense it at every opportunity, to saint and sinner; to impart it in public and in private; in the pulpit, and in the lecture-room, in the house, and by the way; to explain it to the ignorant; to urge it on the indifferent; to defend it when attacked; and in every variety of method, consistent with the divine will, to proclaim and apply it for the benefit of the world.

4. Further, it is important that we hold fast, and communicate sound doctrine, *by the use of public formularies, as well as by personal and oral instruction.* As sermons are expositions of scriptural doctrine, by individual ministers; so creeds, confessions of faith, catechisms, and all similar ecclesiastical compends may be said to be expositions

of gospel truth, and public testimonies in its behalf, by the church, in her ecclesiastical capacity. It was thus that the Council of Nice, and the Synods of Dort, and of Westminster, held fast the faithful word, and contended for the faith once delivered to the saints, against hosts of opposers. It was thus that the pious Waldenses, in the Dark Ages, solemnly recorded, at different periods, that testimony to the truth and order of the gospel, which rendered them lights in the world while they flourished; and have served to illuminate and encourage the steps of millions in succeeding times. And it is thus that our beloved church, by her ecclesiastical formularies, bears witness to the truth, amidst the multiplied corruptions in doctrine and order with which she is surrounded. She claims for these formularies no intrinsic authority whatever. The Bible is her only rule of faith and practice. Her Confession of Faith and Catechisms are her public and solemn testimony, as a church, to what she deems the doctrines of the Bible. Of course, to depart from these, is, in her opinion, to depart from the only infallible rule. So far, then, as ecclesiastical formularies are founded on the Word of God;—so long as they speak its language, and breathe its spirit;—and unless they do this, they are unworthy of being received at all;—but so long as they bear this character, it is incumbent on all the members, and especially on all the leaders and guides of the church, to honour them; to hold them fast; and care-fully to employ them for the great purposes which they were intended to answer; that is, for imbuing the youthful mind with the elements of evangelical truth; and for securing soundness in the faith in those who are introduced to the offices of teaching and ruling in the church. When, therefore, these formularies are duly respected, and faithfully employed, in their appropriate character: when ministers, elders, and parents, in their respective charges, are found applying them with diligence to the youth under their care: when the Sabbath School, the catechetical class, and the domestic circle, can all bear testimony to the fidelity with which they are sustained: and, finally, when eccle-siastical judicatories, faithful to the spirit and purpose of these public standards, close the door of admission to office in the church, against all who are known to be unfriendly to them;—then, and then only, can they be said to act, with fidelity, in the spirit of our text.

5. Again, it is important that we maintain and propagate sound doctrine *in its proper connection and order*. Not that it is necessary formally to exhibit to every one a complete system of divinity: or to aim at making all around us systematic divines. Still, in the world of grace, as well as of nature, one thing is connected with another. There is a real plan and order in which gospel truths impart light, strength and glory to each other. And, accordingly, we read in Scripture of the proportion of faith, of the analogy of faith, and of the first principles of the doctrine of Christ; plainly implying, that the genuine gospel of Christ is a connected, proportionate, consistent, orderly system; and that the relation of its parts ought by no means to be neglected, either in studying them for ourselves, or in imparting them to others. The most illiterate and youthful minds, I am persuaded, are often profited by an attention to this point, on the part of their teachers, even before they are capable of perceiving the fact, and far less of understanding its reason.

And here I cannot resist the conviction that a word ought to be said in favour of a method of instruction, highly prized and much practised by our fathers, but which we, their children, have suffered to fall into comparative disuse. I mean that plan of pulpit instruction commonly called expounding, or lecturing. The method of preaching on single, insulated texts, now almost universal, was scarcely known in the church until about the thirteenth century. The effect of this innovation has been, to render the preacher more prominent than the faithful word, which he professes to explain; and, consequently, to diminish a taste for the study of the Scriptures in their connection. What we style lecturing, or expounding large passages of the sacred text, was, undoubtedly, the primitive mode of preaching; and, although certainly the most difficult of execution; yet when well conducted, by far the most profitable, both to the preacher himself, and to his hearers. It constrains the preacher to study the contents of the Bible in their instructive connection; to be familiar with every part of the Scriptures; to treat all classes of subjects; and to be in the habit of explaining the Bible by itself. And, where he expounds a whole book in course, he has his subject, for one part of the day at least, always before him, for weeks if not months together, so that he cannot lose a moment in searching for a text. And what is no less important, he is enabled to discuss in their turn, as they present themselves on the sacred page, the most delicate and unusual topics, either of doctrine or duty, without incurring the charge of either personality, or sinister design. Nor are the advantages less which accrue to the hearers, from this plan of preaching. It leads them to carry their Bibles to the house of God; to meditate much there on the faithful word; to think of it more frequently at home; to trace its connection with more interest, and to feel, from Sabbath to Sabbath, as if they were listening to Jehovah himself, rather than to the humble messenger of his truth. When pulpit discourses shall become less of eloquent orations on announced subjects; and more of simple, affectionate, and faithful expositions and applications of Scripture; they will become, I doubt not, more effectual in convincing and converting sinners, as well as in building up believers in faith and holiness unto salvation.

6. I will only add, it is important that sound doctrine be maintained and propagated in *a distinguishing, practical and pointed manner; in a manner adapted to impress the heart as well as the understanding.* We are not to communicate truth upon a plan calculated to promote mere frigid orthodoxy; but upon a plan suited to address, and to win every part of man's nature; his conscience, his will, and his affections, as well as his intellectual powers:—in short, in a manner which amounts to what the apostle styles, 'rightly dividing the word of truth', and giving to everyone, whether saint or sinner, his portion in due season. The fact is, there is nothing to which depraved man is more prone, even after turning his attention to the subject of religion, than to rely on something formal, external and speculative, instead of the immovable rock which is laid in Zion. Self-righteousness, in a thousand shapes, is the grand delusion of our nature. And it is evident that the spirit of self-righteousness may feed upon doctrines as well as upon works. A man, as one strongly expresses it, may be frozen to the very seat of life, in the ice of orthodoxy. He may have the heart of the veriest Pharisee, while his head is stored with the soundest opinions. It is of the utmost importance, then, that 'sound doctrine' be presented, not as a mere system of speculations; but as a body of vital principles; as ever pointing to experimental piety, and to holy practice, and as of no ultimate value without both. It is in this manner that the great doctrines of the gospel are exhibited in

the Holy Scriptures; and we shall never be so likely to exhibit them profitably, as when we adopt the same plan, and teach as the Holy Ghost teacheth.

The foregoing discussion furnishes matter for a variety of practical inferences; to some of which allow me to request your serious attention.

1. We may learn from this subject what ought to be *the general structure and character of gospel sermons.* Some have supposed, and have explicitly taught, that the only legitimate object of preaching is to convey instruction; to inform the understanding. While others have gone to the opposite extreme, and have insisted that the grand object aimed at in sermons ought to be, not to convey instruction; but to impress the moral and active powers; to excite, to alarm, to awaken, to warm, to impel to action. Now, I apprehend that that discourse is of very little value as a gospel sermon which is formed, exclusively, upon either of these plans. The proclamation of the living teacher is the great ordinance of God for awakening and converting the world. The children of men are asleep in sin; and, therefore, need rousing as well as instruction. On the one hand, then, that sermon which does not feed the people with knowledge and with understanding; which does not distinctly and clearly exhibit truth, gospel truth, as the basis of all genuine feeling; as the groundwork of all scriptural excitement, can be but little better than empty declamation. For no excitement, no feeling, no conviction can be of any value, excepting that which is produced by the operation of truth, or, in other words, of 'sound doctrine', on the conscience and the heart. On the other hand, that sermon which is addressed to the intellect alone, and which, of course, is not fitted to awaken and rouse, labours under a defect quite as essential. It leaves out of view some of the most precious powers and wants of the soul. This is evident from the fact that a man may be doctrinally enlightened in the most thorough manner, and after all, remain a devil still. The celebrated Ganganelli, perhaps the brightest ornament of the Papal throne, since the rise of that enormous ecclesiastical usurpation, in one of his letters, beautifully remarks—'If a preacher only instruct, he does nothing more than prepare the mind. If, on the other hand, he only affect the passions, he does but half his work; he leaves but a slight and temporary

impression. But if he diffuse the light of truth, while he scatters the unction of grace, he well fulfils his duty.' In short, the artillery of the pulpit ought to resemble that of the skies. There ought to be thunder as well as lightning. And then may we hope that, by the divine blessing, a 'rain of righteousness' will plentifully descend.

2. We may infer from what has been said, *how infinitely important it is that ministers carefully study and understand the truth; that they know it deeply, accurately, and systematically!* Perhaps we may say, that the primary and most constant employment of every faithful minister is to present truth—evangelical truth, to the minds of men, for their sanctification. Whether he preaches, or catechises, or converses, or visits from house to house;—whether he opens his mouth in the public sanctuary, or the family, or the Sabbath School, or the social circle, or the street, or the public conveyance, his great object is, or ought to be, to bring truth to bear on the minds of all around him, for their temporal and eternal benefit. Now, it is plain that nothing but truth can be really beneficial to men. And it is, therefore, only so far as we present genuine truth, simple, Bible truth, to those whom we approach, and present it in the spirit of its Author, that we can have any reasonable hope of doing them good. This being the case, how solemn, nay, how fearful is the responsibility of gospel ministers, in reference to the doctrines which they preach! With what diligence and solicitude ought they, above all men, to seek to know the truth! How humbly, impartially, prayerfully, and unceasingly ought they to study it! How ought they to tremble at the thought of giving the people their own notions, instead of the faithful word; giving them that on which they may grow lean, and starve, nay, by which they may be fatally poisoned, instead of dispensing to them the 'bread of life'! That minister, then, I will venture to say, who is ignorant of the truth, or who has but a superficial knowledge of it; who is indifferent to the truth, or disposed to trifle or tamper with it; who is doubtful and wavering respecting the truth, or destitute of that skill which will enable him rightly to divide it—is not qualified to be a guide to immortal souls. Surely that man who is not rooted and grounded in the truth; who is ready to embrace, with little caution, and with less examination, every plausible error which strikes his fancy; and who will not take the trouble diligently and laboriously to compare with

the Word of God every doctrine which he dispenses, both in public and private;—such a man gives too much evidence that he has but little regard for the truth; little reverence for its Author; little sense, either of the difficulty or the importance of finding the truth; and little enlightened concern for the souls of men. I believe it will be found universally true that, in proportion as ministers possess the spirit of their Master, they will be conscientious and careful in studying the doctrines which they preach; slow, cautious and prayerful in embracing new opinions; and deeply solicitous that they preach the truth, the whole truth, and nothing but the truth, in all their ministrations.

3. If the foregoing principles be well founded, then *we ought to regard with the most serious apprehension any material departure from orthodoxy, especially among the teachers and rulers of the church*. If I mistake not, there are those, even among the orthodox themselves, who estimate the mischief and danger of false doctrine as comparatively small; and, as to the mass of society, they are ready to ridicule the ideas of any serious practical evil as likely to flow from doctrinal error. These are matters, as multitudes believe, about which bigoted theologians may be expected to dispute, and to waste their time and strength; but in which the great interests of the community at large, and even of the church, are but little involved. There can scarcely be a greater delusion. Not only does the Bible represent all departures from the faith as evil, and, if they be essential, as destructive of Christian character and hope; but all ecclesiastical history serves at once to illustrate and confirm the melancholy representation. When the leaders of the church, in the second and third centuries, began to swerve from the simple and genuine doctrines of the gospel, vital piety, and holy living began to decline in the same proportion. In the fifth century, when, by means of the labours of Augustine, and his faithful coadjutors, the eyes of thousands were opened to see the error of Pelagian and Semi-Pelagian opinions, and orthodoxy sensibly revived, there was an immediate revival of vital piety, the effects of which were precious and lasting. In several subsequent periods; in the days of Godeschalcus; of Claudius of Turin; of the Waldenses; of Wycliffe; and of Huss and Jerome, it was evident that practical godliness revived or declined, just as sound or erroneous doctrines bore

sway. When gospel truth was brought forth in its genuine lustre by the Reformers, pure and undefiled religion sprung forth, as it were by enchantment, in the same proportion. And, on the contrary, when, toward the close of the sixteenth century, and during the seventeenth, orthodoxy declined in all the Protestant churches, and in some of them to a deplorable degree; there was a corresponding depression, in every one of them, of zeal and of all the great interests of practical religion. Of these churches, the history of few is more melancholy than those of France. For more than three quarters of a century after their first organization, they were among the most pure and flourishing in Reformed Christendom. And as long as their pious pastors continued to be sound in doctrine, faithful in adhering to their excellent Confession of Faith, indefatigable in catechising their children and youth, and in the private as well as the public instruction of all classes of their people;—notwithstanding all the rigours and frowns of a hostile government, they prospered, multiplied, and were comparatively happy. But no sooner did orthodoxy decline in those churches; no sooner did Cameron, Amyraut, and other divines of distinction and influence begin to verge towards Semi-Pelagian opinions, than an immediate and sensible decay ensued in piety, in zeal, and in pure morals. Indeed it seemed as if, from the time that the infection of these errors became in any considerable degree extended, their peace was interrupted; their unity broken; their standing with the government, in the righteous judgment of God, less comfortable; until, on their whole state was written—*Ichabod,* the glory is departed! And, to this day, their glory has never been restored. As they went on to sink lower and lower in error, they became also more and more depressed in everything that constitutes the true excellence and happiness of a church. No less instructive, as to this point, is the history of the established Church of England. The decline and the revival of pure, evangelical doctrine, in that church, have invariably marked a corresponding decline and revival of true, practical religion. Nor can it be doubted that, in all cases whatsoever, the effect of error must be injurious, and the influence of truth healthful and happy, just so far as they respectively prevail. The innocence of error,—nay the entire innocence of any error,—is one of the dreams of infidelity. Little does the ingenious and self-confident advocate of false doctrine think of the mischief he is doing. He may be greatly elated with his philosophical refinements, and plausible novelties. But so far as his speculations affect or approach the fundamental principles of the gospel, and gain prevalence among the people, they will eat as doth a canker; they will eat out piety, peace, brotherly love, revivals of religion, holy living, social order and happiness, and everything which ought to be dear to the friend either of God or man. The Lord preserve his church from such miserable speculations under the name of improvements in theology!

4. From what has been said, we may see, that *all private members of the church, as well as her ministers, ought to consider themselves as having a share, and a very important share, in the duty of holding fast the faithful word.* It is observable that on all classes of persons connected with the church of Crete, where Titus, the person addressed, now was;—on the old and the young; on both sexes; and on persons in office and out of it, the apostle enjoins the duty more particularly inculcated in our text upon ministers. Read the whole epistle, and especially the chapters immediately containing, and immediately following our text; and you will perceive that the inspired writer exempts none from the solemn charge. He exhorts aged men, and aged women likewise; young men, and young women, and even servants—in various forms of expression, indeed, but in the same spirit—to see not only that they were themselves sound in the faith; but also that they all watched over one another; that each and every one might be in doctrine uncorrupt, and adorn the doctrine of God their Saviour in all things.

Do you ask, my Friends, in what manner you, who are not ministers of the gospel, can promote the prevalence of gospel truth? I answer, in the first place,—Never oppose it. Never give countenance, directly or indirectly, to the advocates or the acts of error. Never account your minister your enemy, because he tells you the truth. On the contrary, encourage and support him in all his scriptural fidelity; and never ask him to prophesy smoother things than the Bible prophesies. But, more than this, take care to store your own minds with sound, discriminating, digested, religious knowledge. Let the Word of God dwell in you richly, in all wisdom, and spiritual understanding. Store the minds of your children, also, your servants, and all committed to your care, with the same heavenly treasure. Teach them, as early as possible, to commit to memory portions of the Holy Scriptures, and the excellent Catechisms of our church. Talk to them of the doctrines as well as the duties of religion, when you sit in your houses, and when you walk by the way; when you lie down, and when you rise up. Put them on their guard continually against the insinuations of error, as well as against the pollutions of practical wickedness. In a word, endeavour, from the earliest dawn of reason, until they cease to be under your care, to lodge in their minds as large an amount of rich, assorted gospel truth, as you can induce them to receive. And, finally, make the same efforts, as you may have opportunity, among your neighbours, young and old. Thus may every private Christian, every day and hour that he lives, if he have himself sufficient religious knowledge, and, above all, if he have a heart for the purpose, scatter blessings around him; blessings to his family; to the church of God; to the whole community;—blessings which will not perish in the using, but transmit their hallowed influence far and wide; benefit, it may be, thousands of precious immortals; and stretch into a boundless eternity.

5. This subject *suggests many considerations worthy of being deeply pondered by him who is about to be constituted the pastor of this church.* Beloved, and highly respected Brother in Christ, this is a solemn day for you! You have consented to come hither, to stand as a watchman on this part of the wall of Zion; to guard your Master's honour; to contend for his truth; to plead his cause against gainsayers; to take your station in the front of the battle; to wield the sword of the Spirit daily and hourly; and to cheer and help on, in all its departments and interests, that great cause for which the Saviour laid down his life; which the world is everywhere opposing; and which can be carried on only by fighting for every inch of ground. To aid in bearing forward this cause, in this part of the church, you stand here to pledge yourself today. Solemn pledge! Momentous enterprise! You are not so inexperienced in this warfare, as to dream of victory without hard fighting. The servant is not greater than his Master, nor the disciple above his Lord. The best wish I can form for you, then, my Friend, my Brother, at this interesting moment, is, that you may come girded with the genuine spirit of a good soldier of Jesus Christ. And what is

the spirit of a soldier? In this, as in every other warfare, it is a spirit of undaunted courage; of boundless confidence in your Leader; of implicit obedience to his orders; of prudence, foresight, perseverance, and a readiness to lay down even your life in his service. Cherish this spirit, and act upon it, and all will be well. The result will be blessed to yourself, blessed to this congregation, and blessed to the Redeemer's kingdom in our land. We cordially welcome your entrance into our body; and while we offer you our fraternal salutations, our hopes and our prayers ascend, that the solemn transaction of this hour, may long be matter of joy, not only to yourself, but to all of us who stand here before the Lord!

6. Finally, the subject on which we have been meditating, involves *many considerations, which deserve to be well weighed by the members of this church and society, on the present occasion.* It teaches us, that sound doctrine is in order to godliness; that cold, heartless orthodoxy alone, can avail us nothing, but to aggravate our condemnation; and, of course, that it becomes every gospel hearer to look well to the manner in which he receives the precious truth of God. My respected and beloved Friends of this congregation, you have long enjoyed the privilege of sound instruction in divine things. For the labours of that able, faithful, and beloved man, who was instrumental in forming this church, and who so long ministered to you in holy things,[1] you have a solemn account to give. We are all witnesses with what force, and tenderness, and fidelity he instructed, and warned you, from the pulpit, and by letter, as well as from house to house. And now, before your account with him is finally closed at the bar of God, where you have yet to meet him, you are about to receive another pastor. We congratulate you on your choice and prospects. But while you rejoice in them, rejoice with trembling. Tremble, lest some of you be found to be hearers of the word only, and not doers, deceiving your own souls. Truly, my Friends, it is a solemn thing for a people

[1] It may not be improper to mention, for the sake of readers beyond the bounds of the Presbyterian Church, if the eye of any such should light on this page—that the beloved and lamented man here alluded to is the late Rev. John Chester, D.D., who was for many years the pastor of the congregation here addressed; and the praise of whose talents, piety, pastoral fidelity, public spirit, and peculiarly polished, pleasant and attractive manners, is in all the churches.

to have teacher after teacher, and warning after warning, in sacred things. If they profit not in a saving manner by them, they are only preparing for a more aggravated condemnation. You may love your minister; you may admire his preaching; you may hang upon his lips with delight, from Sabbath to Sabbath; you may become biblical critics, and even sticklers for orthodoxy, under his ministrations; and yet, after all, may 'know nothing', on the subject of religion, 'as you ought to know'. After all, you may have none of that spiritual knowledge of God, of yourselves, and of the Saviour, which is life eternal. While, therefore, I exhort you, my dear hearers, to seek sound doctrinal knowledge, with unceasing diligence, I charge you, in the name of him, whose I am, and whom I serve, not to rest satisfied with mere speculation. You must know the truth in the love and power of it, or it had been better for you that you had never been born. If you have never yet bowed, then, to the power of the gospel, as a practical system, bow to it now. Not tomorrow, for you know not that tomorrow will ever be yours. Now repent and believe the gospel. Now yield yourselves to God, as those that are alive from the dead. Now is the accepted time, behold, now is the day of salvation. Today, while it is called today, harden not your hearts. Grace be with you all! Amen.

A PLEA FOR
AN ENLARGED MINISTRY[1]

Therefore said he unto them, The harvest truly is great, but the labourers
are few: pray ye, therefore, the Lord of the harvest, that he would send
forth labourers into his harvest.
Luke 10:2

THE first ministers of the gospel were called and qualified in
an extraordinary manner. The divine Master himself immediately selected them, gave them their commission, instructed
them in the things pertaining to his kingdom, and endowed them
with the power of working miracles in attestation and aid of their
ministerial labours. With these extraordinary gifts he sent them forth
on the great missionary enterprise of converting the world. After he
had commissioned the twelve apostles in this manner, he sent forth
'other seventy also', on the same great errand, and endowed with
similar powers. It appears to have been when he sent forth this second band of seventy ministers, that he repeated to them what he had
before said to the twelve—'The harvest truly is great, but the labourers are few: pray ye, therefore, the Lord of the harvest, that he would
send forth labourers into his harvest.' As if he had said—'There are
not yet enough of labourers for the great work which is to be done.
Behold the immense field whitening to the harvest which requires to
be gathered in! Pray ye, therefore, the Lord of the harvest, who has
all power in heaven and on earth, that he would raise up, and qualify,
and send forth, many faithful labourers into his harvest.'

[1] Samuel Miller, 'Plea for an Enlarged Ministry', *The Presbyterian Preacher,* Vol.
3, No. 1 (June 1834), pp. 1-15. This sermon was preached in the Central Church,
Philadelphia, May 18, 1834, at the request of, and before, the Board of Education of
the General Assembly of the Presbyterian Church.

Our blessed Saviour was himself 'the Lord of the harvest'. Why, then, it may be asked, did he direct his disciples to pray to *himself*, to do that which he saw was important and indispensable? Why did he not, unsolicited, send forth one company of ministers after another, until a number adequate to the work of gathering in the mighty harvest were actually on the field? I answer, because it was not intended by infinite Wisdom that the method of furnishing ministers by extraordinary means should continue after the first supply. It was necessary that the commencement should be by the immediate agency of the Master himself, because it was impossible to begin the work of instructing the people, and of gathering and organising churches, without a previous supply of living and authorized teachers. But when a beginning had been fairly made, it was judged best that the subsequent supply and increase of preachers should be obtained by the ordinary course of human instrumentality. We are to consider our Saviour, then, in uttering the words of our text, as virtually saying—'I shall extend no further, at present, this extraordinary supply. It is to be carried on, in time to come, by the agency of man. Still the Lord of the harvest alone can prepare ministers for their work, and send them forth; but his church can and must employ the means of attaining this blessing; and to these means let them henceforth address themselves with prayer and diligence.'

And, accordingly, it is well known, that after the day of Pentecost—with a single eminent exception—ministers began to be called, qualified, and set apart to their work in the ordinary way. We find directions given to the teachers and rulers of the church, for selecting and ordaining candidates for the sacred office; and long before the period of miracles and inspiration was ended, we find careful study, and mature knowledge, as well as fervent piety, enjoined as indispensable preparation for the evangelical ministry, and that by an apostle who knew their value by experience, and inculcated them upon principles which apply to all ages.

From the passage before us, I propose to derive, and endeavour to illustrate and enforce the following propositions.

I. *That we now, no less than in the days of our Lord's personal ministry, most urgently need a large additional number of labourers in the gospel field.*

II. *That it is the duty of the church to employ all the means in her power, for the attainment of this blessing.*

I. *We, at present, greatly need a large additional number of gospel labourers.*

It may be confidently asserted, that the declaration of our blessed Lord, that 'the harvest is great, and the labourers few', was never more applicable—more strikingly and affectingly applicable to the state of the world, than at the present hour. With this fact, it is my earnest wish to impress every hearer. And I am so far from being afraid of drawing a more alarming picture than facts will warrant, that my only fear is, that, after all I can say, an adequate impression of the real state of the case will not be left upon your minds.

In the first place, then, there are, at this moment, within the bounds of the Presbyterian Church, more than six hundred vacant congregations: congregations which are not only destitute of pastors, but which cannot possibly be supplied with them, without a corresponding addition to the number of our ministerial labourers. Besides these vacant congregations, many of which are ready and loudly calling for pastors, and languishing and declining for want of them—I say, besides these—there are, at least four or five hundred populous districts, north, south, and west, in which, if we had zealous and able ministers to send to them, large and flourishing congregations might be speedily formed. So that our beloved church, at the present hour, most urgently needs more than a thousand ministers, over and above her present supply. And if they cannot be obtained more rapidly, and in greater numbers, than our means have hitherto furnished, these destitute, complaining, entreating, dying flocks must either fall off to other denominations, and seek a supply of pastors from churches more faithful than ourselves; or be left to sink into all the desolation and death of practical heathenism.

In short, the number of gospel labourers which we are now able annually to send into the field, is scarcely more than a tenth part of what we most pressingly need. And, what is still more appalling, if no means be adopted for obtaining a much larger supply, the deficiency now so serious and distressing, will, every year, become more serious and more distressing, in consequence of the population of our country growing far more rapidly than the supply of ministers;—until, in a few years, myriads of our countrymen, and perhaps some of our own children, or our children's children, must be left without Sabbaths; without sanctuary privileges; without ministers of religion; and thus, virtually, abandoned to heathenism under the name of Christianity.

But besides all these loud calls for many more ministers; beside the large supply demanded for vacant churches, and the extended frontier settlements within our own borders; there is a much larger harvest still, which calls for a far greater number of labourers then any which has been mentioned. I mean the heathen world. Had anyone told the Apostle Paul, in the midst of his arduous and devoted labours, that at the end of eighteen centuries from his time, more than three-fourths of the whole human race would still be covered with pagan darkness, what would have been the feelings of that heroic, noble-minded missionary? Yet so the humbling, appalling fact is! Out of 850, or 900 millions of mankind, more than 600 millions are supposed to be still pagans, or under the dominion of an equally dark and degrading superstition. Over the darkness and misery of these perishing millions, the church of Christ has been criminally slumbering for ages. She is now beginning to awake. I say beginning, for this is all that can be said. She has sent out a few missionaries; but what are they among the uncounted millions who need their labours? It is like sending a single reaper to reap down the whitening fields of an empire! The missionaries who have been sent, are calling in every direction for more labourers. And even the heathen themselves are beginning to join their voices, and to entreat Christians to remember them, and to send to them those who can teach the way of salvation. But when, in consequence of these importunate and heart-affecting calls, we look round for even forty or fifty young men, whose hearts the Lord has touched with love to the souls of men, and especially with love to the heathen—(many hundreds, indeed, might be employed, and are wanted)—but when we look round for even forty or fifty consecrated young heroes, who are willing to carry the glorious gospel to the ends of the earth—we see them not! We cry aloud for them, but we cry in vain! The truth is, for this immense field of service many thousands of labourers are pressingly needed. Nay, for this field several thousands of labourers would be but a fair proportion to be sent by the American churches. But, when I ask myself—where they are to be found—my heart sinks within me. American Christians must be roused to exertions on this subject greatly beyond that which they have ever yet made; or large parts of our country must suffer a grievous 'famine of the word of life', and the heathen world be left to languish for centuries more under all their darkness, and misery, and death.

If these things be so, then we are very naturally conducted to our

II. Second proposition, *viz.: That it is the duty of the church to employ all the means in her power to provide more,—many more—labourers for the great harvest which lies before her.*

The command in our text was originally given to the teachers and guides of the church, and through them, to the church herself in all ages; and especially to those who occupy the place of watchmen on the walls of Zion. Whatever others may feel themselves as at liberty to attempt, or as bound to accomplish—the church—'the household of faith'—the professing body of 'believers'—are solemnly bound to take measures, by their representatives, for carrying into effect this high command of their Master in heaven. And every individual member of the body is bound to co-operate, to the utmost of the power which God has given him, in sustaining and bearing onward all wise efforts for the attainment of an object so momentous to all the interests of Zion.

But while the general obligation to attend with fidelity to this object will be acknowledged by all, some may imagine that it may be safely left to the voluntary enterprise of those individuals who may feel inclined to undertake the task. Now, I maintain, that, while we forbid none who may think proper to engage in the promotion of this great object; while we pray for the prosperity of every wise and scriptural effort to increase the number of evangelical labourers;—*the church of Christ herself, as such*—whatever others may do,—is bound to make this one of her primary and unceasing objects of pursuit. The arguments by which this position may be established are the most direct and simple that can be imagined.

For what purpose, I ask, has a church been founded and sustained in our world by her Almighty Head and Lord? Manifestly, as the Word of God everywhere teaches, for maintaining in their purity the doctrines and ordinances of our holy religion, and for spreading them abroad among those who have them not. In other words, the great end of the church of God is to hold fast, and 'hold forth the word of life', and to send it as far and wide as possible, for enlightening and saving the world. That this is a duty incumbent on the church, is just as evident as that she has any duties to perform. If, besides providing for the ample and faithful support of all gospel ordinances within her own bosom, she does not also remember the destitute and the benighted, who have none to dispense to them the bread and the water of life—she is undoubtedly faithless to a solemn and most important part of her trust.

But if it be incumbent on the church, as that body which is called out of the world, by the authority of Christ, for spreading the knowledge of the gospel;—if it be incumbent on her to send this precious treasure to all within her reach; then it is perfectly obvious that she is also bound to provide the *means* of sending it. Now among the most essential of these means are *living teachers*. The *blessed Bible*, we know, is one of the most important and indispensable means of enlightening and saving men. And, everlasting thanks to him who sits as king upon the holy hill of Zion!—that precious volume, we hope, before the lapse of many years, will be sent to 'every kindred and people, and nation and tongue'. But, suppose the Bible to be actually in the hands of every human being; how are the great mass of mankind to be roused to a sense of its value? How are benighted, hardened, sensual mortals, even in our own land, and much more in pagan lands, to be prevailed upon to read the Bible? How is the Bible to be explained, and brought into contact with the minds of the millions who may have it in their hands? The Bible is, indeed, a plain book, easily comprehended, in all its practical bearings, by all who are willing to know and obey the truth:—and yet, what multitudes in all lands, may reply with that serious reader of the Word of God, from Ethiopia, who, eighteen centuries ago, when asked by a minister of Christ—'Understandest thou what thou readest?' was constrained to answer, 'How can I, except some man guide me?' Nay, suppose every son and daughter of Adam on earth to be furnished with a copy of the Bible;—but to be, at the same time, deprived of all public ordinances; having none to collect them for public worship; none to feed them with the bread of life; none to dispense the sacramental seal; none, in short, to furnish those outward privileges by which the Holy Spirit is wont to convince and convert men, and to build up his people in faith and holiness unto salvation? The fact is, sending forth the living teacher is made just as essential, by the appointment of God, for spreading the gospel, as the distribution of the Bible. 'What, therefore, God has joined together, let not man put asunder.' 'How', asks the inspired apostle—'How shall men believe in him of whom they have not heard? and how shall they hear without a preacher? and how can they preach except they be sent? As it is written, How beautiful are the feet of them that preach the gospel of peace; that bring glad tidings of good things; that say unto Zion, Thy God reigneth!'

The obligation of the church, then, in her ecclesiastical capacity, to train up faithful labourers for the gospel harvest—nay, to provide as many, if it be possible, as the harvest demands—is just as manifest as her obligation to send the Bible, and to send the gospel in any way to every nation under heaven. In fact, if any one department of the church's duty may be represented as radical;—as taking the precedence, in the order of nature and necessity of almost every other;—it is to provide an adequate supply of living teachers, to go everywhere bearing that precious gospel, 'which is the power of God unto salvation to every one that believeth'. What are all missionary plans and enterprises without this? How are the glad tidings of great joy to be imparted to all people, if there be none to carry them? To neglect to raise up living teachers, then, involves, by necessary consequence, the neglect of all the great objects for which the church was founded.

But this general reasoning is not all that demands our attention on this subject. The church is bound to preserve the doctrines and ordinances of the gospel pure and entire as the Master left them. She is expressly appointed to be *a witness of the truth* in the midst of a perverse and corrupt world. It is incumbent on her to 'contend earnestly for the faith once delivered to the saints'; and when the enemy cometh in like a flood, to lift up a standard against him. Hence, as a consequence, she is bound to see that all her ministers be sound in the faith; that they all speak the same thing; and unite in holding forth the same pure and steady light which came down from heaven to enlighten and bless the revolted population of our globe. But can all this be done; nay, *can any part of it be effectually done,* without direct-ing constant and most vigilant attention to the training of those who are to be the teachers and guides of the church? Is it not obviously indispensable that the church herself, with parental care, select and guide the candidates for this high and momentous trust? That she watch over the fountains of knowledge to which they repair, and the course of instruction which they receive? Can she otherwise hope (to employ the language of our fathers more than twenty years ago)

> to form men for the gospel ministry, who shall truly believe, and cor-dially love, and endeavour faithfully to propagate and defend, in its genuineness, simplicity, and fulness, that system of religious belief and practice which is set forth in the Confession of Faith, Catechisms, and Plan of Government and Discipline of the Presbyterian Church.[1]

If we are intelligent and sincere Presbyterians, we, of course, believe that our formularies of doctrine and order are founded on the Word of God. If we really believe this, we shall desire to have them maintained and extended as far as possible. And, if so, can we rationally expect to succeed, if we consent to have our public teachers trained up by other hands, and exposed to the contagion of other sentiments, and other habits than those which characterize our body? It was wisely and forcibly said, by a distinguished minister of our church, several years ago, in an address before the Board now assembled, that a man, with proper vigilance and caution, may be defended against *murder;* but that against *suicide* there is no human defence. As long as the 'watchmen' on the walls of our Zion, and the 'rulers' within the walls, are faithful to their trust;—faithful in warn-ing against error, and faithful in excluding enemies in disguise from our militant ranks—our citadel, under God, is safe. 'The gates of hell will never prevail against it.' But if we deliberately bring in false friends among the number of the 'watchmen', or knowingly allow them to be brought in; if we encourage plans for the preparation of our rising ministry, which shall introduce among the 'teachers' and 'guides' of the church those who have no real love for either her doctrines or her government,—we are, beyond all doubt, preparing

[1] Introduction to the 'Plan of the Theological Seminary at Princeton'—drawn up in 1811. See above, p. 49.

the way for an *ecclesiastical suicide*. Nothing less than a miracle can save us from discord, strife, division, and ruin. The credulity of the ancient Trojans was not more infatuated, when they consented to the introduction within their walls of the fatal wooden horse, which contained in its bowels the instruments of their ignoble subjugation.

We all know what ancient state it was which separated children from their parents at a very early age, and made their whole education a matter of national concern. The declared object of this policy was, that every domestic affection might be swallowed up and lost in general patriotism; that all the children of the state might be trained up with that physical vigour, and that spirit of hardy endurance, which would fit everyone to be a soldier, determined to conquer or to die. This was a plan well adapted to form able-bodied warriors, but not moral beings. It rejected some of the most important elements of human culture, and destroyed some of the strongest bonds of human society. Equally objectionable is the plan of, directly or indirectly, separating the sons of the church from their proper ecclesiastical mother; and resigning their intellectual and spiritual culture, and their professional training to foreign and irresponsible hands. Trained in this manner, they may, perhaps, be as physically and intellectually vigorous as if every part of their education had passed under the immediate eye of that mother. But they will be likely to understand her feelings and her interests less; to love her less; and, of course, to be less desirous, and less qualified to promote the comfort and edification of her immediate household.

In short, if it be our object to train up a set of theological pugilists, who shall keep the church in perpetual agitation by their feats of polemic skill and valour, and expend all their strength in conflicts with one another, then the more diversified the habits and opinions in which our candidates are trained, the better. But if the object be to furnish the Presbyterian Church with spiritual teachers and guides, who shall love her doctrine and order; who will study at once her purity and her peace; and who will labour together, with affectionate harmony, for her edification, and for the conversion of the world;—then no reasonable man can doubt that their selection and training ought to be the object of the church's most anxious and unceasing care; and that none ought to be encouraged to seek the sacred office, in our Zion, but those who give evidence, not only that they love the cause of Christ in general, but also that they sincerely love, as well as outwardly adopt, our ecclesiastical standards, as containing the great system of truth and order taught in the holy Scriptures.

It is no solid objection to the foregoing reasoning, to say, that the interest of the church at large is far more important than the interest of any particular denomination. This is, no doubt, most emphatically correct. But will not an army of good soldiers be most likely to conquer, when every member of it is found fighting bravely in his own appropriate ranks? Besides, if it be our sincere belief that the doctrine and order of our church are most agreeable to the Word of God; then we are not only bound, as the Lord's 'witnesses' to promote their reception and extension as far as possible, but just so far as we accomplish this, we are promoting the extension of the Redeemer's kingdom in the wisest, the best, and the most permanently valuable manner that is possible.

Let the church, then, in all her borders, awake to a deep sense of her great obligation in reference to this matter. Her duty to her Master; her duty to herself; her growth, her strength, her purity, her peace, her power to act with harmony and energy for the conversion of the world,—all—all demand it of her. If she fails here, and in proportion as she fails here, she must ultimately fail in every other department of evangelical exertion. What will become of the largest and the wisest plans of missionary enterprise, if there be not enlightened and sanctified men to carry the 'glad tidings of great joy' to dark and perishing millions? To what purpose shall we organize new churches, as the increasing population and zeal of our body may enable us; if we cannot find living teachers to take charge of them as spiritual guides? In fact, every enterprise for the enlargement of the Redeemer's kingdom must either be abandoned, or deplorably languish, unless a much larger supply of gospel labourers can be sent into the field. And, after all, the mere multiplication of them will not be found to answer the main purpose intended. If they are trained up with other preferences, and other habits than those of our own church, the greater their number, the more will discordant views and divided counsels prevail; and the greater the probability that their discord and strife will destroy our peace, and hold us up to the pity or the scorn of all surrounding denominations.

In applying this subject, I beg to be allowed, in the first place, to address myself to the Board of Education, at whose request, and for whose benefit we are now assembled.

My respected Friends and Brethren! You have committed to your charge one of the most precious and momentous trusts that the church of God can possibly delegate to human hands. Yours is the delicate, the arduous task of selecting and training a large part of those sons of the church, who are hereafter to be her teachers and guides. And if the character of ministers may be said to decide the character and destiny of the church over which they preside, then what arithmetic can calculate the good or the evil which your manner of discharging the trust committed to you, may be preparing for the body of Christ?

It is beyond your power, indeed, to give the most essential of all qualifications for gospel labourers—I mean *vital piety*. In this sense it may be said with special emphasis, the Lord of the harvest can alone send forth labourers into his harvest. For, in regard to this qualification, none but he who made the world can make a minister. But has he ever been wanting when his people were faithful? Is he not now, if I may so speak, running far ahead of our movements, by pouring out his Spirit upon our academies, our colleges, and many of our churches, and bringing into the kingdom of his grace hundreds, perhaps thousands, of young men, who are ready and desirous to devote themselves to the ministry of reconciliation? On you devolves the solemn task of searching them out; putting in the claim of their moral mother, and, still more urgently, the claim of the Master in heaven, to their services; and watching over all their preparation for the great field of labour. To this delicate, weighty, unspeakably important task it is our hope that you will address yourselves, with all that diligence, zeal, faith, and prayer, for *help from on high*, which the solemnity of the trust so evidently demands.

Remember, I pray you, first of all, and above all, that decided piety—ardent piety—is the first, the highest, the most deeply essential qualification that can be named for the sacred office. Let this great principle ever stimulate and guide your operations. Never patronize, as candidates for the ministry, any others than those who give decisive evidence that they are converted men. Though they had the talents of angels, without sincere love to Christ, they would be no blessing to his church. Yet we are not to suppose that every pious youth, or even that every fervently pious youth ought to be introduced into the ministry. Unless he have good native talents; some portion of those gifts which form an impressive public instructor; prudence, and a freedom from striking eccentricity, he will be likely to serve God and his generation, in any other honest calling, far more successfully than as an ambassador of Christ. Many a young man selected and trained for the holy ministry, who gave satisfactory evidence of piety—has been found so feeble-minded, so deficient in the power of public speaking, or so characteristically indiscreet, as to constrain every enlightened friend of religion to wish that he had adorned and sanctified some secular avocation.

Remember, further, my respected Friends, that you have not been appointed to be the board of a party; but to represent and serve the whole Presbyterian Church. And the only plan on which you can successfully attain this object is, not to be swayed by the wishes, or the policy of any individual, or body of individuals; but to keep an eye constantly fixed on the Word of God, and the truly scriptural and apostolic constitution of our church, as that system which we have all equally promised to respect and sustain. The only fair and legitimate index of the church's will is to be found in those public formularies which she has solemnly adopted, and set forth, as containing that system of doctrine and government which, in her judgment, is contained in the holy Scriptures. Let your whole administration be in faithful conformity with the spirit of these; and, with the divine blessing, harmony and edification will follow of course.

Remember, also, as before remarked, that the *mere multiplication* of ministers is not that which the enlightened friends of the Redeemer's kingdom mainly desire, and expect you to seek. In fact, the more ministers are multiplied, unless they be suitably furnished, and of the right spirit,—the greater the burden, and even the curse, which they will inevitably bring on the church of God. We want neither learned drones, nor ignorant fanatics; neither heartless zealots for a mere frigid orthodoxy, nor empty, childish boasters of a zeal without knowledge.

No; the exigencies of the church, and of the world call, more loudly than ever before, for men of enlightened minds, and of hearts warmed with the love of Christ and of souls; men 'full of faith and of the Holy Ghost'; qualified to 'feed the people with knowledge and with understanding'; men who love and desire to promote genuine revivals of religion; men who are wise in winning souls to Christ; men thoroughly devoted, in heart and in life, to the conversion of the world.

Remember, moreover, that such ministers as I have described, can never be furnished (without a miracle) unless candidates for the sacred office can be persuaded to pursue a *regular and adequate course of study*. It will, then, be a most important part of your duty to conjure and constrain such of them as may come under your direction, so far to respect their *Master,* to respect *themselves,* and to respect the *office* which they seek, as not to be found 'novices' when they enter the field of labour. It is the lamentable infatuation of a large majority of our theological students, that, they will, in spite of every dictate of wisdom and of Scripture to the contrary—they will hasten into the pulpit with half, or less than half, an adequate training. In many cases, even after a previous literary course to the last degree stinted and superficial, we cannot persuade them to feel as they ought the importance of extended and mature theological studies. Not more than a fourth part of the candidates for the sacred office whom I have known, have had wisdom and patience enough to complete the course prescribed in the plan of most of our seminaries, as indispensable to form a well-furnished labourer in the gospel harvest. For this deplorable infatuation no remedy has yet been found. Private friends, theological teachers, boards of directors, presbyteries, synods, and general assemblies, have all lifted the voice of remonstrance against the fatal delusion, but they have lifted it in vain. The evil is still going on with undiminished prevalence. The very spirit of *impatience,* and of *superficiality,* seems to have taken possession of the greater part of our candidates for the Lord's harvest. The consequence is, that the proportion of our rising ministry who make attainments in any measure adapted to the day in which we live, is lamentably small. And hence it comes to pass, that so many, when they enter the field, instead of proving 'workmen that need not be ashamed', qualified 'rightly to divide the word of truth'—disappoint the expectations of their friends; are unable to remain, for any length of time, in one place, as acceptable pastors; and finally become rather a burden than a blessing to the church.

I know of no body of men, my respected Friends, in the Presbyterian Church, who have it in their power to do more towards obviating this deplorable evil than the Assembly's Board of Education. To your care, and that of your committees, hundreds of young men will be entrusted from the commencement of their studies. Be entreated ever to inculcate upon them that, with a given amount of piety, he who is the most accurate scholar, and the best furnished divine, will ever be the most useful minister. Assure them also, that these attainments can never be made without unwearied and long-continued labour. There is no royal way to knowledge. I know of no magic by which theological professors can impart adequate furniture to young men who will not study, even while they continue to occupy the place of students, and who are in haste to escape from instruction. And as long as there are presbyteries who will consent to licence, and even ordain, candidates, who have never studied the gospel, and, of course, do not understand it, I can think of no way in which the correction of the evil in question is to be expected from our judicatories. But, if the Board of Education will firmly withhold its patronage from all who will not, in the outset, consent to take a regular and thorough course of study; and, will instantly withdraw its aid from any and every young man who does not in good faith comply with his agreement, unless prevented by unavoidable dispensations of providence;—if this be done, the mass of our candidates may be brought back to listen to the voice of reason, of conscience, and of Scripture, in regard to this matter. There is little hope of relief, unless, under God, it can be afforded by your Board. May the King of Zion enable you to be faithful to this, as well as to every other interest committed to your charge, and crown your labours with an abundant blessing!

But the subject before us demands the solemn attention, not merely of the Board of Education, but of every member and friend of the Presbyterian Church. Are there any of this large class who are ready to ask—What can we do? I answer—There are, probably, at this hour, from four to five thousand young men scattered through our churches, of hopeful piety, and of sound, improvable minds; who might, in seven or eight years, from the present time, be brought into the ministry; if proper measures were forthwith taken to effect the object. Now, let ministers and church sessions search out all such young men;—carefully discriminating between those who have good native talents, and those who have not; and also between those who are modest, humble, prudent, and teachable, and those who, though hopefully pious, have not these qualities. Let them immediately recommend the former to the Board of Education, and encourage them, by all suitable means, to seek the ministry; while they, as carefully, discourage and keep back the latter. Let presbyteries and synods take order on this subject, at every meeting, keeping it constantly before the minds of all the ministers, and elders, and churches, within their bounds, and recommending unceasing attention to it, as one of the most vital parts of their stated business, as judicatories of Christ. Let every congregation ask—Can we not furnish from our number, and support in study, at least one pious young man, to be trained up for the ministry of reconciliation? Let every wealthy Christian, who feels that he cannot preach the gospel himself, ask—Cannot I indirectly become a preacher, by selecting and sustaining one, if not more, beloved youth, 'strong in the grace that is in Christ Jesus' who may go forth, and be made a blessing to perishing thousands? Let pious fathers and mothers ask—Have we no sons, and if we have none, have our neighbours no sons, whose hearts the Lord has enlightened and sanctified, and whom we should be glad to see bearing the gospel far hence to the Gentiles? And let all—all—male and female, who desire the speedy conversion of the world, ask—Can we not, nay, are we not bound, to take a deeper interest and agency in this great subject than we have ever yet done? Can we not pray more, and give more, and make more efforts to rouse and animate others to come to the help of a cause so vital in its character, and so dear to the heart of every intelligent Christian? You see, my Friends, that this is a cause in the prosecution of which everyone, without exception, may contribute some aid. Yes, everyone who has a heart to pray, a tongue to speak, or a cent to give, may be a worker together with God in this great concern, which may be said to lie at the foundation of all enlightened efforts for promoting the best interests of mankind. For it is only when ministers shall be raised up by tens of thousands, that the gospel can possibly be preached to every kindred, and people, and nation, and tongue.

CHRIST THE MODEL OF
GOSPEL MINISTERS[1]

And he saith unto them, Follow me, and I will make you fishers of men.
Matthew 4:19

WE have here at once the *call*, the *commission*, and the *directory* of a gospel minister. Simon Peter and Andrew, his brother, had become the disciples of Christ some time prior to the transaction here recorded. But now they were called habitually to attend upon him; to be 'with him', as the Evangelist Mark expresses it; that is, to be with him statedly. And in a short time afterwards they were regularly set apart, and sent forth among the number of his apostles.

It is observable that these men, when called thus immediately by the Master himself to be his ministers, had enjoyed nothing of what we are accustomed to style a regular learned education. They were illiterate fishermen, taken immediately from their boats and nets, and sent forth to preach the gospel. It is obvious, however, that this is no argument in favour of an unlearned ministry. The apostles were, for three years, under far more able and unerring instruction than any candidates for the sacred office can now enjoy, in the very best colleges and theological seminaries that Christendom affords. Give to ministers now the same advantages which the first bearers of the gospel message enjoyed, and they might well afford to dispense with all the ponderous volumes and unwearied studies which are, at present, and justly, deemed so important. We know, however, that

[1] Samuel Miller, *Christ the Model of Gospel Ministers: A Sermon, Delivered June 1, 1835, in the City of Pittsburgh, before the Association of the Alumni of the Theological Seminary at Princeton* (Princeton: John Bogart, 1835).

this extraordinary state of things did not continue even to the close of the first century. A man of eminent learning was very early introduced among the apostles, and became by far the most laborious and useful of the whole number. That distinguished minister of Jesus, too, knowing by experience the value of mature study, and directed by the Holy Spirit, solemnly exhorts Timothy to 'give himself to reading', as a preparation for his official work; and enjoins upon him, further, not to 'lay hands' upon any who are not 'apt to teach', and, of course, competently instructed in divine things. And, in strong accordance with this injunction, the history of the church, from the apostolic age to this hour, bears uniform testimony to the fact, that those ministers whose labours have been most eminently blessed to the genuine revival of religion, and to the permanent advancement of the Redeemer's kingdom, from time to time, have been men in whom sound learning and fervent piety were remarkably united.

The address of the Saviour to these brethren was simple and plain, and yet most strikingly appropriate; that is, it was, agreeably to his wonted manner, admirably adapted to convey his meaning with force and point, to persons of the occupation and habits of those to whom he spoke. Like most of what he uttered, it was at once level to the capacity of the most illiterate, and adapted to instruct and impress the most elevated and enlightened mind. 'Follow me, and I will make you fishers of men.'

Without further preface, the doctrine which I shall derive from these words is this: *That Christ ought to be the great model of gospel ministers; and that those ministers who are most faithful and diligent in following him, have the best prospect and pledge of success in their work.*

This general doctrine presents *two points* for our consideration, *viz.: What is that 'following Christ' to which the promise is made? And, What is the import of the promise?*

1. To 'follow Christ' is a phrase which, in the language of the Bible, implies much, and expresses much. To 'follow' a *man,* is to adopt his opinions, to come under .his influence, and to be devoted to the advancement of his plans and interest. All this, and more than this, is included in 'following Christ'. Our Saviour himself explains the phrase by the use which he makes of it in other places. 'My sheep',

says he, 'hear my voice, and follow me.' And again, 'If any man will come after me, let him deny himself, and take up his cross, and follow me.' And again, 'If any man will serve me, let him follow me.' And again, 'He that followeth me, shall not walk in darkness, but shall have the light of life.' In all these passages, as well as in our text, the Saviour obviously does not mean merely walking after him, as a mere bodily attendant, during his earthly ministry. Thousands did much of this, who were never his 'followers' in the sense of our text. Neither does he intend the mere reception of a set of speculative opinions; for thousands have done this also, who yet 'held the truth in unrighteousness', and of course never deserved the name of Christ's disciples. But he means something moral; something which implies reverence, affection, discipleship, conformity and devotedness to his holy will. When applied to ministers of the gospel, therefore, we may consider the command to 'follow Christ' as importing, in general, four things;—*implicitly submitting to him as our teacher; diligently imbibing his Holy Spirit; making his example the model of all our public and private ministrations; and being supremely and earnestly devoted to the advancement of his kingdom.*

1. Ministers may be said to 'follow Christ', when they *implicitly yield themselves to his guidance as their teacher;* when they humbly take all the doctrines, which they adopt or preach, from the word of the Master himself. The gospel which we preach, my beloved Brethren, is not our own; it is Christ's gospel. And as man did not invent it, so man is not capable of mending or improving it. 'The gospel which I preach', said the inspired Paul, 'is not of man, nor by man, neither, was I taught it but by the revelation of Jesus Christ'. 'Son of man', said Jehovah to the prophet of the ancient church, 'preach the preaching that I bid thee. Hear the word from my mouth, and give them warning from me.' Ministers, then, while they undertake to teach others, ought ever to place themselves, and to feel, as humble learners at the feet of him 'whose they are, and whom they serve'. Are they servants? and shall they not constantly look for direction to their Master? Are they ambassadors? and shall they not sacredly govern themselves by the instructions of their Sovereign? Are they, stewards, entrusted with the truth and ordinances of the Saviour's household? and shall they dare, for any consideration, to depart from

the declared will of their heavenly Employer? Surely that professed servant of Christ who suffers himself to wander into the regions of speculative philosophy; who subjects Christian doctrine to the torturing ordeal of unsanctified reason; who begins by deciding, upon philosophical principles, what truth ought to be, and must be, and then recurs to the Bible to see what it is; and who is more intent on the honour of being thought an 'inventor' and an 'original' in theology, than on simply ascertaining and proclaiming 'what God the Lord hath spoken'; surely such a servant cannot be said to 'follow Christ'. On the contrary, he may be said to have embraced, whether he be aware of it or not, the radical principle of the worst heresy, and, indeed, of all unbelief. The minister who truly follows Christ; regards his Word as the only infallible rule of faith and practice. He approaches the sacred volume with reverence; studies it with humble and devout diligence; and makes its simple declarations the test of truth. He faithfully employs his reason, indeed, in examining the Bible; but he employs it only to decide two questions—*Has God spoken in that Bible?* and, if he have spoken, *What has he said?* Having ascertained this, he humbly bows every power of his soul to the heavenly message, and is cordially willing, with meekness and docility, to make it 'the man of his counsel', and the sovereign guide of all his instruction. In short, he considers the great subjects of his ministry as made ready to his hand; and feels that his only business is to bear them faithfully, clearly, and without alteration, to a benighted world.

2. Again, to 'follow Christ' is to *imbibe the spirit of Christ;* to have a large portion of 'the same mind that was also in him'. Men may hold the truth with intelligent accuracy, and contend for it with earnestness, without submitting to its power. He who receives with ever so much speculative exactness the genuine doctrines of the gospel, just as the Saviour left them, cannot be said, in the best sense of the word, to 'follow' him, unless 'he give him his heart'; unless he receive his truth in the love of it; unless he unfeignedly yield to him his love and confidence, as his great High Priest and King, as well as his Prophet. That gospel minister, then, who truly follows Christ, is not only 'sound in the faith', but also a *converted man;* a cordial, devoted, experimental Christian; a man 'full of the faith and of the Holy Ghost'; who speaks

that which he knows, and testifies that which he has experienced; who loves his Master and his work above all things; and who accounts it his highest honour to be like Christ, and 'his meat and drink' to do his will. He rejects the aspirings of carnal ambition. He is willing to 'learn of him who was meek and lowly in heart', and to be himself nothing, that Christ may be 'all in all'. In a word, he is one who lives daily under the power of that religion which he preaches to others; who 'walks with God'; who maintains a life of 'fellowship with the Father of his spirit, and with his Son, Jesus Christ'; and who studies daily to 'grow in grace', to 'crucify the flesh with the affections and lusts', and to have his meditations and desires as well as his treasures in heaven. His hatred of sin, his self-denial, his meekness, his forgiveness of injuries, his benevolence, his conscientious regard to truth and justice in everything, his deadness to the world, his condescension to the poorest and weakest of the flock, his disinterestedness, his holy zeal and diligence, all bear witness that the love of Christ constrains him; that the imitation of Christ is his 'ruling passion'; and the glory of Christ the great end for which he lives.

3. Further, the minister who 'follows Christ', *makes the Saviour the great model of all his official labours.* He not only studies to preach the pure gospel; but also in his manner of preaching it to make Christ his guide and pattern. He consults the Word of Christ day and night, not only as a Christian, but also for light and counsel as a preacher. He delights to address his fellow men in 'the words which the Holy Ghost teacheth'. He endeavours to declare the whole counsel of God, and 'rightly to divide the word of truth'; that is, to exhibit every part of gospel truth in that connection, in that proportion, in that order, and under that solemn, practical, heart-affecting aspect, in which it was left by the Saviour and his inspired apostles. He affects no novelties; resorts to no unauthorized modes of doing good; ventures not to teach for ordinances the commandments of men; but makes it his supreme desire, and habitual aim, to imitate, as far as he dare, both in matter and manner, the preaching and the conduct of him who 'spake as never man spake'; who was the most perfect judge of human nature that ever addressed a perishing world; and who promised to be with his ministers as long as they taught men 'to observe all things whatsoever he had commanded them'.

He who 'follows Christ' does not affect either the spirit or the manner of the 'disputers of this world'. He 'contends earnestly, indeed, for the faith once delivered to the saints', and will not, knowingly, give up a single truth of the Bible. But he contends with the 'meekness of heavenly wisdom'; and with as little of the polemical character as possible. 'Speaking the truth in love' is his divinely inspired motto. The great object which fills his mind is not to silence a disputant, or to exult over a vanquished foe; but to recommend his Master's truth, and to win souls to the love and power of his Master's reign. To complete the character of the minister who 'follows Christ',—

4. *He is supremely and earnestly devoted, by all the means in his power, to the advancement of the kingdom of Christ.* He is not content with the strictest doctrinal orthodoxy; with the prevailing hope that he is a converted man; or even with a general consciousness that he desires to imitate Christ, and to walk according to the order of his house. The extension of the Redeemer's kingdom is the great object which fills his mind, which occupies his thoughts, which governs all his plans and calculations, which impels him in going out and coming in, and which prompts him to make every sacrifice for its promotion. Of all this, the Master himself set the most impressive example. 'Though he was rich, yet for our sakes he became poor, that we through his poverty might be rich.' He 'gave himself for us, that he might redeem us' from pollution, misery, and death. He submitted to hunger and thirst, to reproach and shame, to unceasing labour and privation, that we might be delivered from ruin. Nay, he 'humbled himself, and became obedient unto death, even the death of the cross', that we might be rescued from deserved condemnation and wrath, and raised to eternal blessedness. Now the same spirit which actuated the Master in all that he underwent for the salvation of fallen man, must actuate his ministers, and is implied in the language of our text. While we are constrained to say of worldly men, and of worldly-minded ministers of the gospel, 'All seek their own, not the things which are Jesus Christ's'; the occupant of the sacred office who really 'follows Christ', seeks above all 'the things that are Christ's'. He can say, in some good measure, with the devoted and heroic Paul, 'I count all things but loss for the excellency of the knowledge of Christ Jesus my Lord.' Nay, he can say, 'neither count I my life dear

to myself, so that I may finish my course with joy, and the ministry which I have received of the Lord Jesus, to testify the gospel of the grace of God'. The promotion of the Redeemer's kingdom swallows up every other interest in his estimation; and prompts him to say, in spirit, if not in words, 'For Zion's sake I will not hold my peace, and for Jerusalem's sake I will not rest, until the righteousness thereof go forth as brightness, and the salvation thereof as a lamp that burneth.'

Such is a minister of the gospel who 'follows Christ', and to whom the promise before us is given. He is not always the most learned divine, or the most eloquent preacher, that best answers this character: but the most spiritual man; the most humble, heavenly-minded, laborious, self-denied, disinterested, devoted man; who, with unceasing perseverance and zeal, preaches Christ, his divine person, his mediatorial offices, his atoning blood, his justifying righteousness, his sanctifying Spirit, and all the moral duties by which obedience to the Saviour is manifested. He is one who preaches in some degree as his Master preached; who lives, in some humble measure, as his Master lived; who is the active, zealous minister of the gospel out if the pulpit, as well as in it; who 'goes about doing good'; diligently visiting the people of his charge, not to partake of their luxurious hospitality, but to benefit their souls; not to shine in their domestic circles, as an entertaining companion; but to endeavour to promote his Master's reign in their hearts. He is one who carries instruction, as the Saviour always did, into the parlour; into the occasional conversation; and even to the convivial table; who, in short, in every situation and walk of life, abroad and at home, in the house and by the way, in sitting down and rising up, 'watches for souls as one that must give account'; so that none who approach him, can fail of perceiving that he is a holy man of God; a minister of peace and love and salvation to a perishing world; intent, not on his own personal aggrandizement, but on promoting the temporal and eternal welfare of his fellow men.

I will only add, under this head, that he who follows Christ, does all that has been described under the habitual impression that he can effect nothing of himself; and that, unless the Holy Spirit accompany his efforts, they will all be in vain. He is, therefore, as much engaged in *wrestling for* his people at the throne of grace in private, as he is labouring *before them* in public. He remembers that 'he that planteth is nothing, and he that watereth is nothing, but God who giveth the increase'. He, therefore, desires and longs that the power of the Holy Spirit may continually accompany his labours. He often, as it were, agonizes in prayer for this indispensable blessing. He cannot pass a day contented without some visible fruit of his work in winning souls to Christ. His unceasing cry is, 'O Lord, revive thy work! Pour out thine Holy Spirit from on high! O for times of refreshing from the presence of the Lord!'

Such is the minister who may be said to 'follow Christ'. Now to such—

II. *A blessed promise is given.* 'I will make you fishers of men.' This promise, though delivered, originally, to two of the ambassadors of Christ, is certainly not to be considered as confined to them, or as even restricted to the twelve apostles. A promise of the same substantial import is found in various parts of Scripture, as applicable to faithful ministers in every age.

The promise before us, you will perceive, is conveyed in figurative language; language drawn from the original employment of the persons addressed. 'I will make you fishers of men.' Or, as the Saviour said to one of the same brethren, at another time, when astonished, and almost terrified, at the immense draft of fishes, 'Fear not, for henceforth thou shalt catch men.' He intended, perhaps, to intimate that there is an analogy between taking fishes in a net, and drawing men, by the moral influence of truth, applied by the Holy Spirit, into the kingdom of God; and especially an analogy between the qualities requisite for sustaining a fisherman in his laborious occupation, and the fortitude, patience, and indefatigable perseverance necessary for him who would spend his life in 'watching for souls', and endeavouring to 'draw them to Christ'.

But what is it, in the sense of the text, to be fishers of men? Is it merely to ensnare them in the toils of sectarism? Is it to inveigle them, by artifice, into a favourite church? Is it to make them the blind and implicit dupes of some system of ecclesiastical ambition? Such, I fear, have sometimes really been the aims and the efforts of narrow sectarians; and such have been much more frequently the aims charged upon the ambassadors of Christ by an unbelieving world. But nothing can be more opposite to the spirit of the Bible; nothing more foreign from the mind of a faithful minister of Jesus. His supreme object is to win men to the Saviour; to draw them from sin to holiness; from Satan to God; from misery to happiness; from everlasting perdition to an incorruptible crown, an undefiled inheritance, an exceeding and eternal weight of glory. All this, and nothing less than this, is implied in the figurative language of the promise.

The import, then, of the promise under consideration, I understand to be, that, if ministers of the gospel do really follow their Master, in the nature of the gospel which they preach; in the spirit with which they preach it; and in the life and conversation with which they accompany it, their labours shall be crowned with a blessing; they shall succeed in bringing men, some men at least, to the knowledge and love of the Saviour. What precise measure of success they shall have; what number of their fellow men shall be given them as the reward of their labours, is not specified, and cannot be foreknown, from this, or any other promise of Scripture. But the general assurance, that *such* ministerial fidelity and zeal as has been described, shall be crowned with success, shall not be in vain in the Lord, seems to be positive and unquestionable. And I suppose, further, from the language of Scripture, and from the light of experience, that we may, in ordinary cases, anticipate a measure of success in some degree proportioned to the amount of holy fidelity manifested. Not that all truly pious, or even eminently pious ministers, will be precisely alike successful; or that the same man will be alike successful at all times, and in all places. To assert this, would be to contradict all history, divine and human. Still, if I am not greatly deceived, the whole current of God's Word, and the whole experience of his covenanted people, at once illustrate and confirm the spirit of our text; namely, that the most truly spiritual, wise, devoted and faithful ministers will, in general, ever be found the most successful in convincing and converting sinners, and in building up believers in faith and holiness unto salvation.

I know it may be objected here, that even Christ himself, whom his ministers are called to follow, was not, to say the least, a remarkably successful preacher; that notwithstanding all the wisdom, power, and transcendent excellence of his ministrations, the number of converts brought in by his personal ministry was comparatively small. We may grant this to have been the case without at all contravening the doctrine of our text. When the Master himself preached, he did not, for obvious reasons, make a complete disclosure of those precious doctrines concerning his kingdom, which his ministers, after his death and resurrection, freely proclaimed, and which were then found so effectual in turning 'men from darkness to light, and from the kingdom of Satan unto God'. It is also important to recollect that, when the Saviour himself preached, 'the Spirit was not yet given, because Christ was not yet glorified'. The time, in fact, had not yet come for displaying, in their glory, the conquests of the gospel. The New Testament church was not yet set up. But afterwards, when 'the Spirit was poured out from on high', though the disciples were certainly 'not above their Lord' either in skill or fidelity, their preaching was attended with a power before unknown, and was gloriously successful. And although we have reason to believe that the preaching of all the apostles, after the Holy Spirit was given, was attended with success; yet it is worthy of notice that the apostle whose gifts, and graces, and diligence, and devotedness were pre-eminent, even among his brother apostles; who 'laboured more abundantly than they all', seems also to have been by far the most successful of the whole number in bringing men to Christ, and in extending the borders of his kingdom. Not that even the heroic, devoted, and heavenly-minded Paul was equally successful everywhere. He preached as faithfully and powerfully, for aught we know, at refined and polished Athens, and at imperial Rome, as he did in the splendid and luxurious cities of Corinth and Ephesus; yet a far greater blessing seems to have attended his preaching in the latter cities than in the former. But his success was generally signal and extensive; and he appears to have laboured nowhere wholly in vain.

I need not say, indeed, to a Christian assembly, what was before hinted, that every measure of success which ministers of the gospel enjoy, is the result of the Holy Spirit's influence. This, indeed, is plainly implied in the very language of our text. 'Follow me, and *I will make* you fishers of men.' Yes, my Friends, it is a truth, which, while it humbles the faithful minister, at the same time encourages and animates him in his labour, that success is *all of God,* and of a *sovereign God.* Even when the inspired Paul planted, and the eloquent Apollos watered, the increase was not of themselves, but of him alone who sent them forth, and gave them their message. Their most stupendous miracles, and extraordinary gifts, never wrought the conversion of a single heart. The same divine influence which was effectual when the weakest of their contemporaries were the preachers, was just as necessary for their success as for that of any others. And, to this hour, when the most able and faithful minister on earth is made an instrument of saving good to any, we know that 'the excellency of the power is of God', and not of the earthen vessel by whom the treasure is conveyed. Yet, in grace, as well as in nature, there is an *adaptedness,* as well as a *connection,* between means and ends; and a connection which is neither capricious, nor blindly accidental. The ministry of the gospel is the ordinance which God has appointed for bringing men to the knowledge and love of himself,—and which he has promised to bless. And the more simply, earnestly, and perseveringly the ordinance is dispensed, the larger, in general, the amount of blessing which, upon every principle of Scripture and reason, may be anticipated.

The scope of the promise, you will observe, is not that everyone who preaches the gospel shall be crowned with success in his work; not even that every truly pious minister shall be honoured with distinguished success, or even with any visible success. But that those who really 'follow Christ' in their ministry; that is, who follow him with some good degree of *fidelity, consistency,* and *diligence,* shall be crowned with a blessing, in a greater or less degree. It is, no doubt, with ministers of religion as it is with those who fill other stations. Great excellencies, nay, perhaps, even the greatest, may be neutralized, or counteracted by great defects. An instructor of youth, for example, may be an honest man, a profound scholar, and extremely lucid in his mode of imparting knowledge; but he may be, with all, so indolent, so impatient, so undignified, so petulant, or so morose and repulsive, as to conciliate none; arrest the attention of none; and, of course, improve none in knowledge. In like manner, a military commander may have great energy of character, determined bravery, and uncommon quickness of perception and decision; but may be, at the same time, so entirely destitute of judgment, as never to win a battle. So it may be with him who bears the sacred office. A minister may be hopefully pious, and yet, in a great measure, without skill in illustrating and applying truth. He may shine as a 'sermonizer', according to many of the established canons of that art, without being truly a 'gospel preacher'. He may be approved and admired by all in the pulpit; but may manifest so much coldness, levity or worldliness out of it, as wholly to counteract the influence of his preaching; nay, to render him one of the most efficient instruments of the adversary. He may be capable of delighting, by a beautiful discourse, on general truth; while he is so little versed in Christian experience, as to be utterly unqualified wisely and safely to counsel anxious souls. One may have zeal without knowledge or prudence; another may have both knowledge and prudence, but no zeal. One may appear to great advantage in occasional efforts, and fervent appeals; but may have no taste, and scarcely any capacity, for the details of persevering labour. Another may go, year after year, a round of abundant labour; but it may be a dull and lifeless routine, which has not about it a single kindling or spirit-stirring attribute. Now, that *such* ministers should not be found extensively useful; nay, that some of them should never have been apparently instrumental in the awakening and conversion of a single soul, is surely no marvel. It would rather be marvellous if it were otherwise. For it cannot be said of any of them that they really 'follow Christ'. It is not denied, indeed, that a minister who is himself destitute of piety, may be made a channel for conveying piety to others. 'A sovereign God', as an old divine strongly expresses it, 'may, now and then, by way of miracle, raise a man to life, even by the bones of a dead prophet.' He may, and there is reason to believe he sometimes does, honour his own Word so far as to make it effectual to salvation, even though it fall from unhallowed lips. The ministry of Judas Iscariot was, probably, not altogether without benefit to the church of Christ. But such a result is not, in ordinary cases, and certainly not in any considerable degree, to be expected.

But where a minister of Christ really discharges the duties of his office *in the true spirit of his Master;* where his temper, and his life; his preaching and his practice; his labours for his people in public, and his unceasing prayers for them in secret, are all in harmony with his profession; I consider the Word of God, in our text, and in various other passages, as giving a pledge that he shall not labour in vain. Success, in a greater or less degree, will assuredly follow. 'As the rain cometh down from heaven, and returneth not thither, but watereth the earth, and maketh it bring forth and bud, that it may give seed to the sower, and bread to the eater; so shall my word be that goeth out if my mouth, saith Jehovah, it shall not return unto me void, but shall accomplish that which I please, and prosper in the thing whereto I sent it.' A minister, I say again, who thus faithfully, unostentatiously, and perseveringly labours, will not lose his labour. He will see some precious fruit of it, silently, perhaps, but effectually, springing up around him. To some extent, the truth, like leaven, will take effect; the careless will be roused; the ignorant will think and inquire; the obdurate will feel; the secure will become anxious; the impenitent will repent and believe; the dead will live.

Why should it not be so? Was it not thus in apostolic times? Is not the gospel the same now that it ever was? Are not the Holy Spirit and the divine promises the same *now* that they were when Paul preached? Is not that gracious pledge—'Lo, I am with you always even unto the end of the world', as availing and as precious at this hour, as it was eighteen centuries ago? Yes, my Friends, the words of the inspired apostle to the believers of Corinth are as true of the Christian minister, as of any other follower of Christ. 'Be ye, therefore, steadfast, unmovable, always abounding in the work of the Lord, forasmuch as ye know that your labour shall not be in vain in the Lord.'

Let none say, as an objection to this statement, that God is a sovereign, and that some of the best ministers in the church of Christ have been, in a great measure, without success. Jehovah is indeed a sovereign; and every creature ought to rejoice in the glorious truth. But so also is he a sovereign in dispensing temporal blessings. He makes the sun to shine, the rain to descend, and the wind to blow, when and where he pleases. And yet, I suppose it may be laid down, as a general principle, which all experience confirms, that the most wise, vigilant, laborious, and persevering husbandman, will commonly reap the most abundant harvest. Now, the same great principle applies, I believe, quite as extensively, and with even more certainty, in the kingdom of grace. It is true, indeed, in the most favoured portions of the church, and under the most faithful ministerial culture, that the eye of man has ever witnessed, there may be seasons of comparative drought and barrenness. But was there ever a wise, deeply pious, humble, faithful, laborious, devoted minister, who was entirely without success? who had no souls given him for his hire? I will venture to say such a case never existed. Even though a truly faithful servant of Christ were sent to prophesy in a valley of desolation and death, filled with 'dry bones, exceeding dry'; we have never failed to see more or less evidence that his Master was with him, and that his gospel was 'the power of God unto salvation'. We have never failed to see some degree of spiritual verdure and beauty spring up, where all was arid and sterile before. We have heard a shaking, and seen a movement in the valley of vision; 'bone coming to his bone, and flesh to his flesh', until there stood up, if not 'an exceeding great army', at least a 'goodly company of witnesses' to the power of the truth. Was it not so with Whitefield, and Tennent, and Edwards, and Davies, and Schwartz, and Brainerd, and Payson, and Oberlin, and hundreds of others like them? Did *such* men ever labour long together without profit? I firmly believe not. And if the fidelity and zeal of such ministers were habitually kept up to the proper elevation; if even they were not apt, in many cases, to fall into seasons of relaxation and depression in regard both to feeling and action; I will not say that they would be favoured with a perpetual revival of religion; yet I believe they would witness a silent, but constant turning of one and another to the right way. They would seldom, I am persuaded, pass a week without hearing of one or more awakening from the slumber of death, and 'asking the way to Zion, with their faces thitherward'. And, accordingly, when that blessed period shall arrive, of which the evangelical prophet speaks, when the 'watchmen', placed on the walls of Zion, shall be not only really, but uniformly and perseveringly faithful; when they 'shall not cease, day nor night', to instruct and warn, it will be the signal for the arrival of that happy time when the church shall be no longer 'forsaken' or 'desolate'; but when 'the earth shall be full of the knowledge of the Lord, as the waters fill the sea'.

From the foregoing doctrine, we may infer—

1. That the duties of a gospel minister are not only the most *important,* but also the most *delightful* in which a mortal can engage on this

side of heaven. What is the *nature* of these duties, and what is their *object?* The grand purpose for which the faithful minister of Christ studies and lives is to be a 'fisher of men'; to 'win souls' to the best of masters; to persuade his fellow men to be wise, holy and happy; to turn them from rebellion, condemnation and ruin, to obedience, pardon, peace, and eternal blessedness. Can there be an employment more exalted, more delightful, more godlike than this? If the contemplation of happiness, which we have been instrumental in producing, be one of the purest pleasures of which we are capable; what must be the pleasure of that man who spends his life in conveying to those around him the choicest gifts of heaven; in proclaiming, from day to day, the unsearchable riches of grace, and salvation, and glory, to those who must otherwise have perished? What must be his enjoyment *now,* if he have the spirit of his office? And, above all, what must be his enjoyment in *that day,* when the destinies of the soul, and the glories of redemption, shall have the light of eternity poured upon them? Surely, if there be any employment which ought to be 'meat and drink' to him who engages in it, *this* is that employment. Surely, if there be a crown of glory infinitely superior to any earthly diadem, it is that which the faithful minister shall wear. Why, then, O why, is not this office more coveted, more eagerly sought than it is, by enlightened, ingenuous, high-minded young men? And why is it, alas! that those who actually sustain it, are not more completely occupied, delighted, absorbed in its blessed pursuits? 'Verily, this is a lamentation, and shall be for a lamentation!'

2. It is plain, from the foregoing representation, that the gospel ministry is a work, the due performance of which *requires the whole man.* If the duties of the office be such as you have heard, it is self-evident that they demand the whole time, the whole strength, the whole heart of him who undertakes them. The voice of reason, as well as of Scripture, is, *'give thyself wholly to them'.* That minister, then, who thinks to discharge his duty by giving it only a minor part of his time, snatched from secular employment, labours under an awful delusion. And that church, which, by withholding from her pastor a comfortable support, compels him to yield himself to the distraction of worldly cares, is deplorably infatuated. It is truly interesting to observe how some of the ancient servants of Christ were accustomed

to regard this matter. We are told of Ambrose, Bishop of Milan, who lived in the fourth century, that he was, habitually, so incessantly occupied in preaching, catechising, and visiting from house to house; and during the few hours not thus employed, so absorbed in study, that it was difficult to obtain an interview with him, unless on special business. Augustine, when a young man, spent several years in Milan, and though he earnestly desired to enjoy the society of Ambrose, he tells us he found it almost impossible to obtain access to him; not at all on account of any personal reserve; but from the multiplicity, and unceasing urgency of his official engagements.

Let no minister be ready to object, that such an unceasing course of labour will *wear him out*. To be sure it will. And we must wear out in some cause. Every man who does not die prematurely, is worn out in the service of some master. And which is best, to wear out in the service of sensuality, of ambition, of avarice, or of Jesus Christ? Can any man in his senses hesitate? What were life, and health, and talents given for, but to be expended in promoting the kingdom and glory of their adorable Giver? A prudent care of health, indeed, that his life may not be cut short in the midst, is, undoubtedly, the duty of everyone. The minister who, in labouring, goes beyond his strength of body and mind, is a madman. But the spirit of 'self-indulgence' has been strongly, and not improperly, called *the very spirit of Antichrist!* Shall a minister, then, say either to himself, or to anyone else, on this principle, *Spare thyself?* Did our Master 'spare himself', when he came to die for us? Did the apostles 'spare themselves', when they gave up all for Christ? Can we possibly do more than we ought to do, as far as our strength of body and mind permits, for him to whom we owe our being, our talents, our hope, our life, our all, for this world, and the world to come? Surely, then, of all men living, ministers of the gospel ought to feel that they have no time to lounge in the circles of gossip or amusement; or to waste on reading, or any other employment, which has no immediate tendency to prepare them for their momentous work. Surely they ought to be ready to say, with the pious and devoted Nehemiah, to every person or solicitation that would draw them from their appropriate sphere of labour, 'We are doing a great work, so that we cannot come down: why should the work cease, while we leave it, and come down to you?'

3. If our interpretation of the Saviour's words be correct, then, when a minister of the gospel has *no genuine success* in his work, he has reason to be *deeply anxious and alarmed*. Must he not be irresistibly led to the conclusion, that there is something seriously defective in himself, and in the character of his ministry? I am aware, indeed, that when we hear ministers converse on this subject, nothing is more common than to find them referring chiefly to the divine sovereignty, the diversities, and the entire want of success, among the labourers in the gospel vineyard. But I must think, my dear Brethren, that we are apt to 'lay this unction to our souls', much more readily and frequently than either Scripture or reason warrants.

I firmly believe that if we were more like Christ, more devoted, spiritual, diligent, and prayerful, we should all of us be more successful in 'winning souls' to him; and, consequently, that if we are seldom or never thus honoured, it is chiefly because we so little resemble him. If we wish our message, then, to be effectual in rousing others, let us begin with *rousing ourselves*. O, if we were more 'full of faith and of the Holy Ghost'; if we bore about with us more of the spirit and the example of the Lord Jesus, we should find imparted to our sermons, and, our conversation, a life and power; a touching and kindling eloquence, which, without this spirit, can never exist. We, perhaps, all need an improvement in our method of preaching, making it less dogmatical, less philosophical, more simple, more biblical, that is, consisting more in the illustration of Scripture by Scripture; more direct; more pointed; more affectionate; more full of heavenly unction; more, in short, like a message from God, than a human oration. The late excellent and lamented Dr John H. Rice, in the last letter that I ever received from him, made the following remark:

> I am convinced that, in the present state of this country, there is nothing which can control the religious principle, and give it a salutary direction, but *Bible truth, plainly exhibited, and honestly urged on the understanding and conscience*. And I am persuaded that all settled pastors, and all missionaries too, ought to do a great deal more than they now do in *lecturing;* or, as some express it, *expounding*. There is too much reasoning, and too much dogmatizing in the pulpit. I throw out this hint, that, if it is worth anything, you may drop it before the students of your seminary.

The sentiment is worth much, and I repeat and record it for your benefit. 'The word', as the pious and venerable Mr Baxter somewhere observes—'the word is divine; but our preaching is human; and there is scarcely anything we have the handling of, but we leave on it the prints of our fingers'. We need more exclusive devotedness to our great mission; more decision of spiritual character; more ardour and steadfastness of zeal; more urgency in our benevolent suit; more unwearied endeavours to adapt our ministrations to the benefit of the young and the old, the rich and the poor, the bond and the free, the learned and the illiterate. O, if we had more of all this, our labour would, certainly, not be 'in vain in the Lord'. If we desire greater success, then, in our work, the way to it is plain. It is to humble ourselves before God with deeper abasement; to pray with more fervent importunity for the gift of the Holy Spirit; and to gird ourselves with new decision, enterprise and zeal for our work.

4. Finally, we learn from this subject, what *ample encouragement ministers have to plan and labour for Christ*. Surely no labourers ever had higher encouragements set before them than those who are now called of God to the ministry of reconciliation. For such a Master, in such a cause, and for such objects, who would not be willing to live and to die labouring? That brighter days await the church of God, and that those days will be introduced and adorned by a band of ministers more faithful and devoted; more totally absorbed and unwearied in their Master's work, than we have ever seen, cannot, I think, be doubted by any serious believer in God's Word. Such of us as are now in the decline of life, will, probably, not live to see those days ushered in: but cannot the oldest and the feeblest of us contribute something to hasten on their arrival? And can we consent to live another year, or another month, without aspiring, while our time lasts, to the labour and the rewards of such a holy enterprise?

Our lot, beloved Brethren, is cast in a most interesting and momentous period of the world's history. We see a large part of Christendom in a state of excitement and action, such as no generation ever witnessed before since the gospel was preached among men. During the apostolic age, it is true, and for a hundred years afterwards, efforts and sacrifices were made for Christ, at the recital of which the heart of piety warms, and the coldness of modern zeal must hide its head.

But to how small a part of the population of the globe these efforts and sacrifices were confined, and how short their continuance, we all know. During the later portion of the 'Dark Ages' which followed, it may be said, that a large part of the wealth, and power, and activity of the civilized world, was given to the reigning church; but to what objects were that wealth and power devoted?

To the spread of pure and undefiled religion? To the promotion of the virtue and happiness of man? Far from it. But to erect splendid cathedrals; to endow corrupt monasteries; to enrich and pamper a voluptuous and ambitious priesthood. When the Crusades occurred, they caused, it is true, a stupendous and truly memorable movement of the whole Christian church. But to what end? Was it to extend the reign of enlightened piety? By no means. But to prostrate education; to relax morals; to increase ecclesiastical tyranny and profligacy; to destroy two millions of lives; and to clothe almost every household in western Christendom in mourning. That so many blessings were indirectly and ultimately brought out of these enormous evils, is no matter of thanks to the deluded, fanatical actors in the wonderful scene. And, finally, when the Reformation, that 'great moral miracle', electrified Europe, and shook to its foundation, 'the kingdom of the beast', though it was the harbinger of countless blessings to the world, the consequences of which we are enjoying to the present hour; yet how soon was its glory clouded by strife and division; and in how small an amount of immediate exertion for benefiting the human family at large, did it result! But *now* a spirit is poured out, in some measure, if I mistake not, peculiar to the day in which we live. Such a spirit of Christian enterprise; such extensive and active combinations to benefit mankind, and especially to spread the glorious gospel, were, surely, never before known. And, although, it cannot be denied that some features of an unfavourable character mar the face of the day in which our lot is cast; yet, undoubtedly, its prevailing lineaments are those of high moral enterprise, of holy hope, and of animating promise. Such is the period in which the Lord of the harvest has placed us in his vineyard, and commanded us to 'occupy until he come'.

Beloved Alumni of the seminary with which it is the happiness of him who now addresses you to be connected! do you not account it a privilege to live in such a day as this? Do you not regard it as at once an honour and a duty to cheer on, and, by all the means in your power to help forward, the glorious work which is devolved upon the men of this generation—the work of evangelizing the world? I trust there is not one of your number disposed to shrink from the arduous enterprise, or to say, 'I pray thee have me excused.' But remember, I entreat you, that the enjoyment of this privilege is connected with the most solemn responsibility. Yes, your situation is solemn and responsible beyond expression. Have you, or have you not, spirits girded for the plans and efforts of this day? Are you, or are you not, ready and willing to be unreservedly consecrated to Christ, to 'spend and be spent' in his service? O that every one of us may be found ready, with the whole heart, to say, when the call of duty sounds, 'Behold, here am I, Lord! Speak, Lord, for thy servant heareth! Lord, what wilt thou have me to do?'

Perhaps, as I am called to speak this evening, at the request and for the benefit of the Alumni Association of our beloved seminary, it may be expected by some that I shall dwell particularly on the claims, the wants, and the interests of an institution so dear to us all. But I have designedly forborne, and shall forbear to enlarge on this subject, because it appears to me that I have something infinitely more important to speak of than the claims of a single 'school of the prophets', however worthy it may be of our affection and our prayers. My object is to recommend a spirit, and to contribute my humble instrumentality, under the divine blessing, to the formation of a character, which will render every one of you a blessing to the whole church of God, and to the world. Besides, if the beloved Alumni of our seminary possess as much as they ought of that spirit which I have endeavoured to illustrate and enforce, they will, I doubt not, love their theological *Alma Mater* as much as they ought to love her, and will take pleasure in every effort to provide for her wants, and to extend her usefulness. And if it be seen by the religious public that our seminary sends forth many sons largely endowed with this spirit, the Christian community will love her as much as they ought, and will promptly second all your efforts to sustain her interests, and to enlarge her means of doing good. In a word, we can in no way so essentially and permanently benefit the institution for which we are associated to pray and labour, as by 'following Christ', and continually manifesting the power of his Spirit in forming us to be the devoted benefactors of mankind. Cultivate this spirit, and then all will be well. Be filled with this spirit, and then 'your joy will be full'; our churches will smile; our judicatories will be scenes of love, harmony and edification; and that supreme judicatory of our beloved church, which we have come hither to attend, instead of being the theatre of conflicting opinions, and of party strife, will never meet but to bless the city in which it assembles; to rejoice the heart of every friend of Christ who witnesses its proceedings; and to give a new impulse to the progress of truth and righteousness in the world.

Beloved Friends and Pupils! to each one of you is committed a share of this mighty trust. Ponder well the magnitude of your duty, and the weight of your responsibility. Pray without ceasing that the spirit of truth, of peace, of love, and of zeal for the Lord of hosts may ever rest upon you all. Seek the peace of Zion; but remember that her peace may be consulted at the expense of her purity—that she can never be successfully and solidly built up but by a faithful adherence to the truth and order prescribed by her adorable Head; and that he who contributes towards the diffusion of the knowledge and spirit of Christ in our world, does more for the real welfare and happiness of his species, than he could possibly accomplish by the most splendid endowments that wealth, and learning, and patriotism ever devised. Among the trials of the present day is a spirit of restless innovation; a disposition to consider everything that is new as, of course, an improvement. Against this spirit let me warn you. However plausible, it is unwise and delusive. Happy are they, who, taking the Word of God for their guide, and walking 'in the footsteps of the flock', continually seek the purity, the harmony, and the edification of the Master's family! Who, listening with more respect to the unerring oracle, and to the sober lessons of Christian experiences, than to the dreams of morbid excitement, or the delusions of fashionable error; hold on their scriptural way, 'turning neither to the right hand nor the left'; and considering it as their highest honour to be employed in winning souls to Christ, and in building up that 'kingdom which is not meat and drink, but righteousness, and peace, and joy in the Holy Ghost'.

Need I remind you, beloved Friends, that we are all hastening to the judgment seat of Christ? Nearly fourscore of those who once resorted to our seminary, have been already called to give in their final account. Be ye also ready! And remember that the best of all readiness is that which consists in 'following Christ'. In following him, and only in following him, you will be best prepared to meet your Judge. In following him, and only in following him, you will be best qualified to promote the enlargement, the holiness, and the genuine edification of the church of God. May this be your habitual aspiration, this your blessed attainment! And when the Chief Shepherd shall appear, may you all be so happy as to receive a crown of glory that fadeth not away! Amen and Amen.

THE SACRED OFFICE MAGNIFIED[1]

I magnify my office.
Romans 11:13

THE Apostle Paul was eminently a modest and humble man. In all the memorials which he has left of himself we find nothing that savours of arrogance, ambition or selfishness; but everything directly the reverse. He gave up all his worldly prospects for the sake of Christ. He sought neither riches nor honours for himself. He even declined receiving a temporal support from some of those for whose benefit he was wearing out his life. Nay, instead of seeking his own aggrandizement or pleasure, he voluntarily submitted to hunger and thirst, cold and nakedness, bonds and imprisonments, for the sake of serving his fellow men, and extending the reign of truth and righteousness. In the midst of these disinterested and self-denying labours, his mode of speaking of himself is marked with peculiar meekness and humility. He speaks of himself as 'less than the least of all saints'; as 'not worthy to be called an apostle' (*Eph.* 3:8; *1 Cor.* 15:9). But while he abased himself, he 'magnified his office'. 'I speak unto you Gentiles, inasmuch as I am the apostle of the Gentiles, I magnify mine office.'

The 'office' here spoken of is, of course, the apostolical office. This office was, in some respects, confined to the first century. The apostles, in their original, distinctive character; as having 'seen the Lord'; as immediately commissioned by him; and as endowed with

[1] Samuel Miller, *The Sacred Office Magnified: A Sermon, Delivered in the First Presbyterian Church, in the City of Baltimore, September 15, 1836; at the Installation of the Rev. John C. Backus, as Pastor of the Said Church* (Baltimore: Armstrong & Berry, 1836).

inspiration, and the power of working miracles—were to the primitive church what the New Testament is to us—the unerring directory and guide. In this character they had no successors. Their mission was altogether extraordinary; intended to answer special purposes; sustained, by special aids; and endowed with special prerogatives. The necessity of ministrations of this peculiar character was superseded by the inspired writings of those holy men, recorded and embodied as the directory of the church in all succeeding ages. But the apostle probably intended here to speak chiefly of his general ministry, as an ambassador of Christ;—of that authority with which he was invested to preach the gospel; to administer the ordinances of Christ; and to gather the Gentiles as well as the Jews into his fold. For in writing to the Ephesians (3:7, 8), he declares that he was made a minister, and that the requisite grace was given unto him—for what purpose? 'That he might preach among the Gentiles the unsearchable riches of Christ.' Here his inspiration and his miracles are left out of the account, and nothing mentioned but his office as a dispenser of the glorious gospel. This office was intended to be perpetual. In the discharge of its duties, the Saviour promised to be with his ministers 'to the end of the world'. This office,—the apostle declares—*this office*—not himself—he *'magnified'*.

To 'magnify' an object, in popular language, is often intended to express the idea of swelling its importance beyond its real value; in other words, stretching its magnitude inordinately. But no such meaning is intended in our text. The slightest recurrence to the original will show, that the apostle means to say—'I highly esteem, or honour mine office.' Surely there is no pride or ambition in such language. If the humblest and meekest citizen be placed in an elevated and important office in the civil community, if he be a wise man, while he cherishes sentiments of the deepest personal humility, he will not suffer his office to be despised or trampled upon. That he will always endeavour to sustain and to honour, whatever may become of his own individual claims. So in the church of God. An 'ambassador of Christ' ought to be the meekest, and the humblest of men. But while he lies in the dust of abasement himself, he ought to 'magnify his office'; to regard it as one of unspeakable importance, which he is altogether unworthy to bear.

The doctrine of our text, then, is *that the office of the gospel ministry is a great office.* To illustrate this doctrine, and to apply it to the occasion on which we are convened, is the design of the present discourse.

When we say, that the office of a gospel minister is a great office, we have no reference either to those secular honours which ecclesiastical men in past ages have coveted and proudly worn; or to those ghostly prerogatives, which have been so arrogantly claimed and abused by a tyrannical priesthood. There are those among professing Christians who consider the clergy as a great privileged order; as 'lords over God's heritage' (*1 Pet.* 5:3); as having dominion over the faith of men; as the only channel of grace; as empowered to absolve from the guilt of sin; and to dispense the 'covenanted mercies of God'; and, of course, as holding in their hands the eternal destiny of their fellow men. This doctrine we not only reject, but abhor. When such a doctrine is once admitted, there are no bounds to the power which it involves, or to the unhallowed dominion over conscience to which it naturally leads. It is the fundamental principle on which the whole superstructure of Papal tyranny has always rested. It cannot fail to give a despotic triumph to the ecclesiastical over the civil power; and to generate all that array of spiritual penalties and coercions, of which the history of the world presents so many mournful examples.

Neither does our text countenance the doctrine of those who build much of their confidence in the legitimacy and value of the office in question on dreams of ecclesiastical genealogy. There are Protestants who, when speaking of this office, dwell much more on the 'uninterrupted succession' of the 'priesthood', by which gospel ordinances are dispensed, than on that atoning blood, and life-giving Spirit which alone can render ordinances effectual. For this doctrine we are persuaded there is no foundation either in reason or the Word of God. We are very sure that tracing the succession spoken of, from the apostles, as a matter of historical deduction, by any denomination of Christians whatever, is utterly impossible; and if it were possible, would be of little value. To imagine that it is practicable is a delusion; to assert that it has been attained, is a fraud on public credulity; to attach importance to it, is to teach for doctrine a commandment of men. We consider ministers of the gospel as the servants of Christ, and the 'servants of the church for Christ's sake'. We have no doubt that the regular act of the church, for the time being, through her authorized officers, constitutes a sufficient title to office in the visible family of Christ; and we believe that the great work of those who bear the office of which we speak, consists, not in exalting or enforcing their own prerogatives; but in recommending and glorifying their Master, and promoting the salvation of their fellow men. And, therefore, when the Word of God speaks of the highest honours of gospel ministers, it represents them as consisting, not in titles and places; not in establishing a certain course of ancestral descent; not in being 'called of men, Rabbi, Rabbi', or in being loaded with worldly honours; but in humility, in meekness, in benevolence, in purity of heart and life, in zeal for the salvation of men, in resemblance and devotedness to their Master in heaven: and it represents the efficacy of the ordinances, which they administer, as resulting, not from the inherent power of the ordinances themselves, or of those who administer them; but only from the blessing of Christ, and the working of his Spirit in them that by faith receive them. But, to be more particular:

I. The office of the gospel ministry is a great office on account of its *divine origin*. This is an office absolutely peculiar to the religion of Christ. No similar office has ever existed in any of the various forms of false religion. Priests, indeed, those religions had, and still have; but not to perform duties such as those for which the ambassador of Christ is commissioned. The office, as it appears in the Christian church is exclusively and pre-eminently an ordinance of Jesus Christ. To his authority its functions are all to be traced; to his power its usefulness is all to be ascribed. To this consideration the inspired apostle frequently and most pointedly refers. He declares that he was an apostle, 'not of man, nor by man, but by Jesus Christ, and God the Father'. He represents himself as 'an ambassador of Christ'; as 'not taking this honour on himself, but as called of God, as was Aaron'; as having an authority committed to him by the great Head of the church, 'for edification and not for destruction'. And he everywhere represents all true and faithful ministers as 'called of God'; as 'set in the church' by his authority; as 'put in trust with his gospel' (*Gal.* 1:1; *2 Cor.* 5:20; *Heb.* 5:4; *2 Cor.* 10:8; *1 Cor.* 12:18; *1 Thess.* 2:4), and as commanded and commissioned to declare his will. Nor does this representation apply to those only who were clothed with the sacred office in the days, and by the immediate agency of the apostles. The ministry is God's ordinance, and manifestly intended to continue such to the end of the world. The ascending Saviour's last mandate to his disciples implied its perpetuity, as well as its emanation from his authority. 'That which thou hast received of me', said the inspired Paul, 'the same commit thou to faithful men, who shall be able to teach others also' (2 *Tim.* 2:2). And the same apostle has declared, that the office is intended to last until we all come to be 'perfect men in Christ Jesus', that is, until the consummation of all things. And although ministers who are set apart to their office now, by the regular act of the ecclesiastical ministry, are not immediately commissioned by the Saviour himself; yet they are as really his ministers; as really sent by him, as if his own sacred hands had actually been laid on them. They as really bear his office, and are as truly authorized to speak in his name, and to administer his ordinances, as were any of the apostolic men whom our Lord himself immediately commissioned to disciple the nations.

This is a doctrine, my Friends, which, however acknowledged in theory, seems to be but little practically regarded by the mass even of professing Christians:—and as to the unbelieving and impious world, they love to keep out of sight the sacredness and the authority of the gospel ministry, because they do not wish to be pressed by the message which it brings. But if we admit that the gospel is a message from God; that the visible church was constituted by the authority of Christ; and that an order of men to preach the doctrines and to administer the ordinances of his religion, was divinely appointed from the beginning; and intended to last to the end of the world;— all that we desire follows of course. If these premises be admitted, the consequence is inevitable;—that all true ministers of Christ come in his name; clothed with an office which he has appointed; authorized as his servants to announce all that his Word contains; and to administer all the ordinances which he has instituted in his house. We may, therefore, consider the great Head of the church as addressing to every minister the following solemn language of his Word—'Son of man, I have set thee as a watchman on the walls of Zion; therefore preach the preaching that I bid thee: hear the word at my mouth, and give men warning from me. He that receiveth you, receiveth me, and he that despiseth you, despiseth me.' Every time, therefore, that the faithful minister rises in the pulpit, he may, without impropriety, say to every hearer, 'I have a message from God unto thee' (*Ezek.* 3:17; *Matt.* 10:40; *Judg.* 3:20).

How deeply interesting, how unspeakably solemn is this consideration both to those who bear the sacred office, and to those who hear them! Are they 'ambassadors of Christ'? Are they bearers of a message from 'the King of kings, and the Lord of lords'? How can we estimate the solemnity, the awfulness of the trust committed to their charge, or the magnitude of the privilege enjoyed by those to whom they are sent? And if they come, not in their own name, nor bearing their own message; but in the name of Christ, and confining themselves to that preaching which he has enjoined in his Word; how great is the obligation of those who hear them, to receive the Word with meekness from their lips; and to 'esteem them very highly in love for their work's sake' (*1 Thess.* 5:13). And although the fact, that ministers come to us bearing an office which is of divine appointment, ought never to prevent our 'searching the Scriptures daily, to see whether what they say be so', that is, be in conformity with the written Word;—yet as long as they speak to us in conformity with 'the words which the Holy Ghost teacheth', we are bound to honour their office; to hear the word from their mouth with reverence and love; and to consider their message, not as their own, but his who sent them.

Let none object to this statement, that many of those who bear the office of which we speak manifest much weakness and imperfection, and some, the most revolting moral delinquency. Can men, it has been asked, be considered as bearing a divine commission, when they display so much of human error and frailty? I answer, it has pleased God to make the bearers of the gospel to our fallen race, not angels, but men, by nature partakers of the fall, even as others; men 'of like passions' with their fellow creatures, and needing themselves the same pardoning mercy and sanctifying grace with those whom they address. 'He has chosen weak things of the world to confound the mighty, that no flesh might glory in his presence.' We have the treasure of the gospel committed to 'earthen vessels, that the excellency of the power may be of God, and not of us' (*1 Cor.* 1:27; *2 Cor.*

4:7). Besides, in conformity with this sovereign arrangement, let it never be forgotten, that neither the authenticity nor the value of the message which ministers bear, depends on their personal character. The overture which an ambassador to an earthly court brings from his government; is the same whatever his personal conduct may be. He is only the channel by which it is conveyed. And although it is highly desirable that he should not contradict it by his own conduct; yet, whatever that conduct may be, his instructions, and his official functions remain the same. The principle is, in substance, the same with the ambassador of Christ. His office is from God; his message is from God. And although it is unspeakably important to himself and to the church that he set an example corresponding in holiness with his message; yet if he disgrace himself and lose his own soul, still the treasure which he bears remains unsullied; the overtures and the seals of mercy which he dispenses, lose none of their intrinsic value by passing through an unworthy channel. In a word, it is the glory of our system as Protestants, that we regard the *Bible* as the only infallible rule of faith and practice; that we consider the authority of those who bear the sacred office as wholly *ministerial;* that is, that they are, authorized to declare nothing but what the Master has said; to dispense nothing but what he has instituted; and, in judicial decisions, to apply no laws but those which he has promulged for the government of his spiritual family.

II. The office of the gospel ministry will appear to be a *great office,* if we consider its *nature* and *design.*

The importance of any institution or profession is plainly to be measured by the objects which it is intended to promote; by the chief ends which it is appointed and adapted to accomplish. The office of a lawyer is justly deemed important, because he guards our property, and pleads our cause before the dispensers of justice. The office of the physician is still more important to each individual, because he watches over our health, and may be the means of saving our lives, in comparison with which worldly possessions are nothing. For 'all that a man hath will he give for his life' (*Job* 2:4). But, estimated by this standard, how shall we measure the importance of the *gospel ministry?* We cannot measure it. It is literally infinite. What is worldly property; what is even life itself, when compared with the great interests of the soul and eternity? They are 'less than nothing and vanity'. But what is the great design of the gospel ministry? It is nothing less than the eternal salvation of the soul. It is nothing less than to publish, explain, and recommend the religion of Jesus Christ; to proclaim its glad tidings, and to extend its holy reign. But, it may be asked, Is this religion of any real value to mankind? Is it of any real importance that the children of men be instructed in the way of salvation; that they be brought under the genuine power of the gospel; that their sins be pardoned; that their hearts be sanctified; that they be prepared for every holy duty and enjoyment here, and for eternal blessedness hereafter? We need not wait for an answer. Nothing can be plainer than that these are interests in comparison with which all the temporal concerns of men are as the 'small dust of the balance' weighed against 'the everlasting mountains'. Yet these are the great matters about which ministers of the gospel are primarily and constantly conversant. The grand object of their commission is to 'turn men from darkness to light'; from Satan to God; from pollution, condemnation and misery, to purity, pardon and happiness; and, finally, to prepare them for the enjoyment of an 'incorruptible crown', an 'undefiled inheritance', an 'exceeding and eternal weight of glory' in the heavens.

It might be supposed, indeed, that a system so pure, reasonable and glorious as the gospel of Jesus Christ, when once made known, would always be found to work its own way in the world, without the efforts of the living advocate to urge it on the attention and the consciences of men. But the Word of God gives us no reason to expect such a result, and all experience is equally against it. However pressing the need in which human nature stands of such a remedy for its maladies as the gospel presents, it is never itself disposed to seek after it. 'The carnal mind is enmity against God.' 'The natural man receiveth not the things of the Spirit of God; for they are foolishness unto him; neither can he know them because they are spiritually discerned' (*Rom.* 8:7; *1 Cor.* 2:14). So that, left to himself, no one would ever embrace or obey the gospel. To say nothing, therefore, of the unnumbered millions of the world's population, who have never heard of the religion of Jesus Christ, and who can never be expected to hear it 'without a preacher', ministers may be said to be indispensable for maintaining the power of the gospel even where it is already known. To keep alive religion in the world; to prevent Christian knowledge, public worship, the Sabbath, and the various ordinances of the visible church from utterly perishing among men; in short, to preserve those who have enjoyed Christianity from relapsing into real heathenism, it is necessary that ministers of religion be constantly employed to rouse men to a sense of their condition. It is necessary not only that the people be furnished with the written Word, but also with the living teacher, who shall, from Sabbath to Sabbath, and 'from house to house', bring their minds, if I may so express it, into contact with the Word, and constrain them to give it their serious and practical attention. It is necessary that they be called together, instructed, warned, entreated, conjured, again and again, day by day, to attend to the things which belong to their eternal peace. For nearly eighteen centuries the standing means, both of maintaining and extending the knowledge of Christ and his salvation in the world, has been the office of which we speak. And without the use of this divine ordinance still, we have no reason to expect either that sinners will be converted, or saints edified and comforted. It is not, of course, meant to be alleged, either that no conversion is ever effected but by means of the authorized ministry; or that this ministry is ever made effectual to the conversion of a soul by any virtue or power of its own. But the position meant to be maintained is, that God, in his sovereign wisdom, has appointed and promised 'by the foolishness of preaching to save them that believe' (*1 Cor.* 1:21); and that, consequently, on the one hand, where the gospel is not preached, we have no reason to expect that the work of conversion and salvation will, to any extent, go forward; and that, on the other, where it is faithfully and ably dispensed, it will generally be accompanied, in a greater or less degree, with the sanctifying and saving power of the 'Holy Ghost sent down from heaven'.

In short, it is the great design of this office instrumentally to accomplish that for man, which no human laws, no political economy, no physical force can possibly reach. It is to effect the conversion of the world to God; to raise men from the death of sin to the life of holiness; to sanctify the heart; to regulate the practice in secret, as well as before the public eye; to strike at the root of all those vices which disturb society; to render mankind forgiving and benevolent to man; to train up our children in the way they should go; to wipe away the tears of mourners; to comfort the sick and dying; in a word, to furnish the only effectual remedy for all the woes to which flesh is heir; and to prepare for a world of perfect peace and blessedness for ever. Surely, my Friends, an office, the design of which is to promote such objects as these,—objects great, boundless, inestimably precious, and everlasting—may well be styled a *great office*. It is as much, in importance, above any other office known among men, 'as the heavens are higher than the earth'.

III. Once more, the gospel ministry must be pronounced a *great office,* if we consider not only its grand design, but its *actual effects.*

These have not, indeed, been found *in degree,* equal to the great *design* of which we have spoken. Amidst all the labours of gospel ministers, we see not yet all things brought under the power of the benign and holy religion which they announce. But we see a measure of benefit accomplished by the influence of this religion, in proportion to the extent of its reign, which cannot but fill with gratitude and joy every benevolent heart. In every department of life, and with respect to both worlds, its effects are unspeakably beneficial and happy. In respect to all the intellectual and social interests of man; in regard to the life that now is, as well as of that which is to come, it is constantly exerting an influence, which, though silent, is powerful and all-pervading. 'How admirable', said even the sceptical Montesquieu—'How admirable is that religion [and he might have added, that *office*] which, while it seems to have in view only the felicity of the future life, constitutes the happiness of the present!'

A well-qualified and faithful ministry never fails to exert a powerful influence in enlightening, enlarging, and cultivating the public intellect. It is probable that the instructions of the pulpit, and the various labours of the pastoral office, have done more to promote the expansion of the public mind, and the diffusion of useful knowledge, than any other single institution on earth. In confirmation of this remark, an appeal may be confidently made to those ages and countries which have been favoured with an enlightened, pious, and faithful ministry. In those ages, and in those countries, the mass of the population has been, invariably, most enlightened as well as most virtuous. How, indeed, could it possibly be otherwise, when such ministers are everywhere the patrons of learning; when their lives are devoted to the instruction and exhortation of men on the most interesting and important subjects that can come before the human mind; when it is a part of their daily work to put the sacred Scriptures, and other pious books into the hands of the people; when they constantly teach that it is the duty of all to think, to inquire, and to believe for themselves; and to think and inquire, too, on the most sublime and solemn subjects that can engage the intellect of moral agents;—how is it possible, I say, that such an order of men should fail of exerting an influence, in proportion to their fidelity, on the general intelligence of the community? It cannot be. To this statement, I will venture to say, the whole history of the human race furnishes no exception.

No less precious has been the instrumentality of the sacred office in restraining every form of vice, and in promoting social order, domestic happiness, and all the best interests of the commonwealth. True, indeed, it cannot be denied that the office in question, in some ages and countries, has been grievously perverted to the promotion of an opposite influence. When those who styled themselves ministers of the gospel have lent their official character to those miserable superstitions which 'call evil good, and good evil'; when they have 'taught for doctrines the commandments of men'; and have 'made the word of God of none effect by their traditions', and their 'doctrines of devils' (*Isa.* 5:20; *Matt.* 15:9; *Mark* 7:13; *1 Tim.* 4:1); no wonder that their moral influence has been of the worst kind; no wonder that they have ever been panders to the most shocking vices. But where this great office has been true to its Author and its end, its effects, in regard to all the best interests of society, have never failed to be blessed and happy. Its influence has been ever found to strengthen and sanctify all the ties which bind man to man. It makes more regular and amiable members of the society of men on earth, thousands and millions who will never be prepared for 'the inheritance of the saints in light'. How much we are indebted to this office, for the peace and security of our families, no one can estimate. Only suppose, my Friends, the gospel ministry, together with all the ordinances with which it is connected, to be banished from this great city; and you might have left splendid buildings; rich monuments of art; large commerce; and a thousand external ornaments, adapted to gratify 'the lust of the flesh, the lust of the eye, and the pride of life';—but upon every dwelling and monument might be written, *'Ichabod,* the glory is departed'! The real glory of your city would all be gone. The powers of darkness would claim it as their own; and it would, in a little while, more resemble the purlieus of hell, than the abode of civilized and Christian men.

But the effects of this office, in being made instrumental, by the grace of God, to secure the regeneration of the heart, and the eternal welfare of men, are still more precious and glorious. The gospel ministry is that great office, by means of which the religion of Christ is, as it were, brought to the view, and impressed on the minds of men, and made, under God, to accomplish its holiest and most blessed triumphs. It is the great office destined to keep alive in the world, and to propagate that gospel, which, when accompanied by the power of the Holy Spirit, 'opens the blind eyes; raises men from the death of sin to the life of holiness'; and is, in a word, 'the power of God unto salvation to everyone that believeth' (*Isa.* 42:7; *Rom.* 1:16).

How often have we seen the bearers of this sacred office sent to proclaim their message in a region where all was dark and desolate, and miserable; where spiritual death reigned in all its gloomy horror; and where the most degrading profligacy was equally prevalent. And we have seen blessings immediately follow their footsteps. We have seen the whole face of society renovated and transformed. We have beheld light arising in darkness; the careless awakened; the ignorant made to think and inquire; the hardened to relent and feel; the profligate to renounce and forsake their sins; and order, purity, and the song of salvation to take the place of all that was opposite before. We have recorded examples of this in the apostolic age. The inspired Paul, after exhibiting mournful specimens of profligacy and wretchedness, says to the believers of Corinth, 'Such were some of you, but ye are washed, but ye are justified, but ye are sanctified, in the name of the Lord Jesus, and by the Spirit of our God.' Similar effects are also vouched by the early uninspired fathers of the church, as occurring in cases almost numberless, under their own eyes. Nor has the King of Zion left us without ample testimony of the same great fact in modern times. In the frozen regions of Greenland; on the burning plains of Africa; among the degraded Hindus, and over the wilds of the ferocious western savage, we have seen the holy triumphs of the religion of Christ, as far as the office of which we speak has borne it with faithfulness to the nations. And everywhere we have seen it producing the same effects;—enlightening the ignorant; softening the ferocious; humbling the proud; purifying and elevating the slave of corruption; and raising men from brutality to holiness and to God.

Who can tell how many millions have been called by the instrumentality of this sacred office, 'from darkness to light, and from the power of Satan into the glorious liberty of the children of God'? Yes, my Friends, of the ranks of those who are now serving Christ here below; and of the 'multitude which no man can number', now adoring and rejoicing before the throne on high, an immense majority are ready to acknowledge with grateful joy, that it was by 'the ministry of reconciliation', under God, that they were rescued from the power of unbelief and sin, and made the trophies of redeeming grace and love.

Not only so, but it is the invariable plan of our God to lift up the state of the world, by lifting up the character of the gospel ministry. Accordingly, when we are told, in the prophetic Scriptures, of that period of light and glory when 'the knowledge of the Lord shall cover the earth as the waters cover the sea', and when 'there shall be nothing to hurt nor destroy in all God's holy mountain'; we are also informed that the period shall be ushered in by the appearance of watchmen on the walls of Zion more wise, faithful and zealous than ever before; watchmen who shall be filled with wisdom, and inspired with holy zeal; watchmen who shall 'see eye to eye'; watchmen who 'shall not cease day or night', to instruct and warn (*Isa.* 11:9; 62:6); ministers, in a word, who shall be 'clothed with salvation, that the people may shout aloud for joy'.

Such is the greatness of the office of which we speak. Its divine *origin* its grand and infinitely interesting *design;* and its mighty *effects,* all conspire to magnify it, to exalt it, and to clothe it with an importance unspeakable. In short, it is an office so great, that no other on this side of heaven can be compared with it; so great, that no other seems, comparatively, worthy of our attention. Let the men of the world despise or calumniate this office. In their blindness and infatuation they do it. In the estimation of infinite wisdom, it is the greatest, noblest, most blessed office that man or angel can bear on this side of the throne of God.

The foregoing discussion suggests to us a variety of practical reflections, to some of which I beg leave to call your attention before closing the present discourse.

1. It is evident, from what has been said, that the distinction, in popular language, between *'clergy'* and *'laity'*, is a just and scriptural distinction. Mr Gibbon asserts, that this distinction was unknown in the primitive church, and was not introduced into the Christian community until the second century. If by this assertion he meant, that we do not find these 'precise terms, to distinguish between ecclesiastical men and others, in familiar use, in any Christian writings earlier than those of Tertullian, Origen, and Cyprian; and, especially, that the proud and arrogant claims with which one of these terms was afterwards connected, were, before the time of those Fathers in a great measure unknown;—he is probably correct. But if his meaning be that the Christian ministry is not an institution of Jesus Christ; that he did not from the beginning annex to it a specific spiritual authority; that ministers were not, from the very origin of the church, distinguished from the mass of the members of the church; that there were not then appropriate functions assigned to them; and that these functions were not, in the primitive church, confined to ministers, but were common to all Christians;—if this, as would seem, be his meaning, there could hardly be a statement more palpably erroneous;—a statement more unequivocally contradicted by the New Testament itself, and by all the most authentic records of early antiquity.

Nor can I perceive any solid reason for the scruple which even some respectable theological writers have indulged respecting the popular use of the terms, 'clergy' and 'laity' at the present day. Distinguishing ministers of the gospel by the former title has been thought by some good men to savour of arrogance, and by others, of superstition. But wherefore this apprehension? The *term* is of little importance. There is nothing, either in its etymology or bearing, which can be considered as assuming or offensive.[1] It is impossible to read the Acts of

---

[1] The word κληρος properly signifies a lot. And as the land of Canaan was divided among the Israelites by lot, the word, in process of time, came to signify an

the Apostles, and the several Epistles, especially those to Timothy

---

inheritance. In this figurative, or secondary sense, the term is evidently employed in 1 Peter 5:3. Under the Old Testament dispensation, the peculiar people of God were called, (Septuagint translation) his κλερος, or *inheritance*. Of this we have examples in Deuteronomy 4:20, and 9:29. The term in both these passages is, manifestly, applied to the whole body of the nation of Israel, as God's inheritance, or peculiar people. Clemens Romanus, one of the 'Apostolic Fathers', speaking of the Jewish economy, and having occasion to distinguish between the priests and the common people, calls the latter λαικοι. Clemens Alexandrinus, towards the close of the second century, speaks of setting apart such persons for 'clergymen' (κληροι) as were signified by the Holy Ghost. And in the writings of Tertullian, Origen, and Cyprian, the terms 'clergy' and 'laity' occur with a frequency which shows that they were then in familiar use. Jerome observes, that ministers are called *clerici,* either because they are peculiarly the lot and portion of the Lord; or because the Lord is their lot, that is, their inheritance. Hence the learned and pious father takes occasion to infer, 'That he who is God's portion, ought so to exhibit himself, that he may be truly said to possess God, and to be possessed by him' (*Epiet,* 2; *ad Nepotian.* 5). Others have thought, that, in giving this title, some regard was had to the ancient custom of electing persons into sacred offices by lot.

And as we have abundant evidence that ecclesiastical men were familiarly called 'cleric', or 'clergymen', from the second century; so we have the same evidence that this term was employed to designate all ecclesiastical men. That is, all persons who had any public employment in the church, were called by the common name of *clerici,* or 'clergymen'. It was applied, continually to elders and deacons, as well as to bishops or pastors. Nay, in the third century, when not only Prelacy had crept in, and obtained a general prevalence; but when the same spirit of innovation had also brought in a number of inferior orders, such as *sub-deacons, readers, acolyths, etc.,* these inferior orders were all styled *clerici.* Cyprian, speaking of a sub-deacon, and also of a reader, calls them both *clerici.* The ordination of such persons (for it seems they were formally ordained) he calls *ordinationes clericae;* and the letters which he transmitted by them, he styles *literae clericae.* The same fact may be clearly established from the writings of Ambrose, Hilary, and Epiphanius, and from the canons of the Council of Nice. Indeed there seems reason to believe, that, in the fourth and fifth centuries, and subsequently, the title of *clerici* was not only given to all the inferior orders of ecclesiastical men, but was more frequently applied to them than to their superiors; who were generally addressed by their more distinctive titles. Those who recollect that learning, during the Dark Ages, was chiefly confined to the clergy; that few, excepting persons of that profession, were able to read and write; and that the whimsical privilege, commonly called 'benefit of clergy', grew out of the rare accomplishment of being able to read;— will be at no loss to trace the etymology of the word clerk (*clericus*) or secretary, to designate one who officiates as the reader and writer of a public body.

To distinguish the mass of private Christians from the clergy, they were designated and Titus, without perceiving that the distinction between ministers of religion and private Christians was clearly made from the very origin of the Christian church, and uniformly maintained. That the terms 'clergy' and 'laity' were not used at first is of no importance in any view. The thing intended by these terms, as employed by Protestants, was beyond all doubt, familiarly recognized by the whole Christian community in the apostolic age. The titles of 'rulers' in the house of God; 'ambassadors of Christ';—'stewards of the mysteries of God';—'bishops, elders, shepherds, ministers', *etc.*, as distinguished from those to whom they ministered, are so familiar to all readers of the New Testament, that further elucidation, of that point is altogether unnecessary. We contend not, in the use of any ministerial title, for peculiar *honours* or *emoluments;* but for peculiar *duties;* for peculiar *devotedness;* for peculiar *labours;* for peculiar *responsibility* to the Sovereign and Lord of the church.

2. We may learn from this subject *what is the greatest honour of a gospel minister.* Not to receive praise of men. Not to gain titles, emoluments, or rank in society. No, his highest honour is to be distinguished 'by pureness, by knowledge, by long suffering, by the Holy Ghost, by love unfeigned, by the word of truth, by the armour of righteousness, on the right hand and on the left'. His greatest glory is to be like Christ, and to be supremely consecrated to the enlargement of the kingdom of Christ. His laurels are not academical *diplomas,* nor the *hosannas* of admiring crowds; but *conversions.* The highest eulogium ever pronounced on a gospel minister, was that bestowed on Barnabas of old—'He was a good man, and full of the Holy Ghost, and of faith, and much people was added unto the Lord' (*Acts* 11:24). Such seems to have been the estimate of this subject made by the heroic Paul. His talents, his acquirements, and his unparalleled labours entitled him to a great and indisputable pre-eminence among

by several names. They were sometimes called λαικοι, *laici,* 'laymen', from λαος, *populus;* sometimes ἰδιωται, 'private men', from ἰδιος, *privatus* (see *Acts* 4:10.); sometimes βιωτικοι, 'seculars', βιος which signifies a secular life. Soon after the apostolic age, common Christians were frequently called ἀνδρες ἐκκλεσιαστικοι—'men of the church'—that is, persons not belonging either to Jewish synagogues, or heathen temples, or heretical bodies, but members of the church of Christ. Afterwards, however, the title, *ecclesiastics,* became gradually appropriated to persons in office in the church. See *Stephani Thesaurus.* Bingham's *Origines Ecclesiasticae,* B. I.

his brethren in the ministry. But what pre-eminence did he ever seek, unless it were a pre-eminence in privation, in danger, in zeal, and in indefatigable labours for the benefit of his fellow men? O that we might see a similar spirit reigning in the bosom of every minister of Jesus Christ!

3. If the sacred office be so great and weighty as you have heard, then *with what solemn awe ought it to be undertaken, and its duties discharged!* It is an office, the solemnity and responsibility of which might make an angel tremble. Well may we cry out, then, with the apostle, when we think of its being borne by a frail, imperfect man,—'Who is sufficient for these things?' (*2 Cor.* 2:16). The great Reformer, Luther, whom no one ever suspected of lacking moral courage, declared that, even to the close of life, he never ascended the pulpit without trembling. And that minister of Jesus Christ who, whatever his powers or accomplishments may be, when he is about to address an assembly of dying men, and remembers that his sermon will be 'a savour of life unto life, or of death unto death' to those who hear him (*2 Cor.* 2:16), has not 'his spirit stirred within him' at the responsibility of his situation,—has but little of the spirit of Paul, or of Paul's Master.

4. From the view which has been taken of the sacred office, we are led to reflect, *how great is the preparation which ought to be made for it!* The man who undertakes to instruct hundreds, and, perhaps, thousands, of the learned as well as the ignorant, in the most important of all knowledge;—the man who offers himself as an expounder of the Bible, a book the thorough exposition of which requires deep and various learning, theoretical as well as practical;—the man who proposes to act as a spiritual guide to immortal souls;—to enlighten the perplexed; to counsel the tempted; to satisfy the doubting; to silence the bold and literary infidel; to refute the learned and ingenious heretic; and to stop the mouth of the artful caviller:—the man who undertakes to be 'a watchman on the walls of Zion'; to discern when danger is approaching; to estimate its nature and magnitude, and to give warning accordingly:—the man, in a word, who is preparing to go forth into the church and the world, as an adviser, a guide and a helper in all that is good; as a centre of light, and counsel, and instruction, and consolation, and holy activity to thousands; surely such a man ought to have many qualifications which are not

necessary, which do not belong to common Christians. What various and extensive knowledge; especially what rich and familiar knowledge of the Bible;—what deep and ardent piety; what prudence; what knowledge of the world, and of the human heart; what command of his own spirit; what zeal; what patience; what capacity for labour; what diligence; what perseverance, are indispensable here! That no man without unfeigned and ardent piety ought to engage in the duties of this office, is conceded, even by those who have no piety themselves. But there may be truly pious men, who are, nevertheless, totally unqualified for the ministerial work. No ignorant man; no strikingly weak man; no imprudent man; no habitually indolent man; no rash, headstrong, turbulent, contentious man, is fit to be a minister, even if we could suppose him to have the piety of an angel. Then let the candidates for the office of which we speak ever bear in mind, that every consideration which serves to illustrate its greatness, serves at the same time to show how great the intellectual and moral furniture, how mature the preparation, which must be considered as indispensable to a proper fitness for the great undertaking; and how great the infatuation of that young man who ventures to ascend the sacred desk after a hasty and slight preparation for so responsible and weighty an office!

5. It is evident from the view which has been taken of the sacred office that *it demands the whole time, the whole strength, the whole heart of him who undertakes to perform its duties.* It is truly wonderful that any man who has a spark of real love to Christ, or to the souls of his fellow men, can imagine, for a moment, that less than *the whole of all his powers* ought to be devoted to this great office. Who that takes the slightest survey of the duties incumbent on him as an ambassador of Christ; as a leader and guide of immortal souls, as one commissioned, in every variety of way, and to every possible extent, to 'feed the sheep and the lambs' of the great Shepherd;—can suppose that, after a faithful discharge of these numberless, ever recurring, and most weighty duties, he can have time or strength left for any other concerns? The truth is, the occupant of this office, in whatever part of the great vineyard his lot may be cast, if he has a heart for his work, will find every moment of his time, and every power of his soul and body put in constant requisition for the discharge of his duties.

The voice of reason, therefore, as well as of God's Word, is *'give thyself wholly to them'*. How deeply to be pitied is that minister who can find hours to waste in idleness, or on trifles, when a world is dying around him, and when he is surrounded, not only with opportunities, but with importunate calls to labour for the temporal and eternal welfare of his fellow men!

6. Another obvious reflection from what has been said is, *how great the respect and affectionate support which are due from the friends of Christ to his faithful ministers!* We do not ask you, my Friends, to idolize ministers; to load them with praise or adulation; or to follow them with that worldly pampering, which seems to be the only testimonial of esteem which the children of this world ever think of bestowing. Far less do we ask you to surrender your consciences into their hands, or to regard them as the only authorized expounders of the Word of God, and the only medium of intercourse and of grace between God and man. This is not the kind of respect for the gospel ministry for which I plead. On the contrary, against all such idolatrous deference to ecclesiastical authority and power (though not, indeed, a sin of frequent occurrence in our beloved church) I would solemnly warn you. The *Bible,* I again proclaim, is the only infallible rule of faith and practice. To this unerring test you are bound to bring all that ministers say or claim. They cannot be the keepers of your consciences. It is your indefeasible privilege to read, to examine, and to interpret the inspired oracles for yourselves; and for yourselves to believe and obey them. The respect which I call upon you to pay to the sacred office is wholly of another kind. It is, that you regard it as an ordinance of God; that when those who bear this office, faithfully dispense the truth and the ordinances of Christ, you receive them with reverence and affection; that you 'esteem them very highly in love for their work's sake'; that you pray for them; that you be tender of their reputation; and that you endeavour by all the means in your power to strengthen their hands, and encourage their hearts in the arduous work in which they are engaged? These are testimonials of respect which those who possess the spirit of Christ are always ready to give to his ministers. And these are the testimonials of respect which are most dear to the heart of every faithful minister. To be loaded with worldly honours and treasures would not give half so much pleasure

to such a minister, as the obedience of the heart to his message. Such was the sentiment uttered by the excellent and devoted Mr Hervey, and which will be adopted by every pious pastor. When urged to accept the multiplied civilities, and to visit more frequently the luxurious abodes of some of his gay, worldly parishioners, he in substance meekly replied, 'It gives me no pleasure to be found and to receive caresses in those dwellings from which my Master is excluded.'

7. The subject on which we have been meditating suggests many serious reflections to the *beloved young Brother,* who is this evening to take on himself the pastoral charge of this church of Jesus Christ. The great and responsible office, dear Brother, of which we have been speaking, you bear:—and you are now about to pledge yourself for the more immediate and devoted discharge of all its duties in connection with this church. Let me exhort you to *magnify your office;*— not by making great claims; or seeking high honours for yourself; but by making a high estimate of the solemnity and responsibility of the office; by entering deeply into the spirit of its great design, and its hallowed bearing on the glory of Christ, and the salvation of a revolted and lost world; and by being ever supremely devoted to its active duties. Set your heart upon your office. Consider it as your great and single work. Turn not aside from its calls for the sake of the most fascinating objects which this world has to present. When you are solicited by the temptations of secular literature, or worldly wealth, or any temporal object, let your reply be that which was made by a devoted and heroic servant of God, many centuries ago—'I am doing a great work, so that I cannot come down; why should the work cease, while I leave it, and come down to you?' O my Brother, look abroad on the widespread desolation and misery of our sinful world, and think of that gospel which you bear as its only hope; and then say, whether every power you possess to help it, is not put in solemn requisition? Rely on it, the more unreservedly and constantly you are devoted, with your whole heart, to your appropriate work, the happier you will be; the more beloved you will be, by all whose love is worth possessing; the more useful you will be; the more confidently may you hope to be instrumental in extending that kingdom which is 'righteousness, and peace, and joy in the Holy Ghost'.

And, while you 'magnify your office', remember also, beloved Brother, to magnify the support and the aid on which you have a right to rely in the discharge of its duties. 'Thou, therefore, my son, be strong in the grace that is in Christ Jesus' (2 Tim. 2:1). Place no confidence in your own strength; but remember that 'through Christ strengthening you, you can do all things' (Phil. 4:13).

Remember, too, my dear Brother, that in proportion to the magnitude of your office; will be the solemnity of the account you have to render for the manner in which you discharge its duties. Study, and preach, and pray, and visit, with the judgment seat, and the final reckoning of yourself and your hearers, continually before your eyes. And when that solemn scene shall open upon your spirit, may you be enabled to present large numbers of this flock in the arms of pastoral affection, and to say, with grateful joy—'Lord, here am I, and the children thou hast given me' (Isa. 8:18).

8. Finally; the subject on which we have been meditating ought to inspire the most serious reflections in the mind of everyone connected with this church of Christ. We, this evening, my respected Friends, present to you, once more, a beloved young brother, who bears the office of which you have heard. Every word which has been uttered to show its magnitude, furnishes an argument why you ought to receive him who bears it with respect, with confidence, and with thankfulness. If the gospel be the most precious gift of God to fallen man; and if those who bear it sustain an office so essential to the welfare of society, and the conversion of the world to God, as you have heard; then, surely, when you are about to receive another pastor, as we hope, 'after God's own heart', you ought highly to prize the gift.

Never shall I forget the scene in which it was my happiness to participate, sixteen years ago, in which 'a choice young man and a goodly', beloved by me as a son, and highly esteemed by all who knew him, was 'set over you in the Lord'. I had the pleasure to witness the respect and the cordiality with which you received him, and the solemn interest with which he entered on his weighty charge:— and it is but strict justice to both parties to bear this public testimony, on the one hand, to the piety, the zeal, the talent, and the success with which he discharged his duties among you; and on the other, to the kindness and affection with which you ever treated him. We saw him commence his pastoral labours with acceptance, and with high promise. We saw him, by the grace of God, more than redeeming every pledge; rising higher and higher in zeal, fidelity, acceptance and usefulness, to the last year of his active ministry. We saw, with tender sympathy, the mysterious dealings of providence with him, in taking away one after another of his domestic circle; and, finally, in bringing down his own strength in the meridian of life and of usefulness. And we saw him eminently adorning his faith and hope, and setting a seal on his ministry, in the closing scene. Beloved man! his history does indeed form a mysterious, yet instructive and animating page in the volume of God's providence. That you will long cherish his memory with ardent affection, I cannot doubt:—that many of you have savingly benefited by his ministry, and have unspeakable reason to bless God that you ever saw his face, and heard his voice, I am well assured:—and that some of your number, who have not hitherto obeyed the gospel, may yet 'remember how you have received and heard, and hold fast, and repent', is my fervent prayer.

We now present you, my beloved Friends, with a successor to your late-lamented pastor;—a young servant of God, greatly respected and beloved by his teachers, and adapted, as we believe, to be at once an ornament and a blessing to yourselves and your children. Receive him as a minister of Jesus Christ. 'Despise not his youth.' *Magnify his office.* 'Esteem him very highly in love for his work's sake.' Pray for him without ceasing. Study not to add to his burdens, but rather, in every practicable way, to lighten them, and to encourage and aid him in every part of his arduous labours. Hold up his hands, by a punctual attendance on his ministry, and by every kind office, as well as by your daily prayers. Consider the extent, the magnitude, and the exhausting nature of his duties, contrasted with his youth and comparative inexperience; and then say whether he is not entitled to all your sympathy, your indulgence, and your affectionate co-operation? I have no fear, my Friends, of your manifesting toward him any other than a spirit of respect and noble-minded generosity. Your past history furnishes a pledge on this subject, which ought to forbid a doubt. But shall he have to mourn, that, while your external treatment is all that can be desired, some of you turn away from his message, and close your hearts against the grace and love of his heavenly Master? God forbid!

O neglecter of the Saviour! whoever you are, the goodness of God in sending you another pastor, is a new call to repentance and faith. If you wish to give him the sweetest of all the pleasures that can fill the heart of a faithful minister; above all, if you wish to meet your God in peace, neglect not another hour the salvation which he offers you. Remember that for every such offer you must give an account. God grant that, when you meet him who is this evening to be 'set over you in the Lord',—as *meet him you must,* before the bar of your common Judge—it may be a meeting 'of joy and not of grief'! Amen.

ECCLESIASTICAL POLITY[1]

*The elders which are among you I exhort, who am also an elder, and a wit-
ness of the sufferings of Christ, and also a partaker of the glory that shall
be revealed: feed the flock of God which is among you, taking the oversight
thereof, not by constraint, but willingly; not for filthy lucre, but of a ready
mind; neither as being lords over God's heritage, but being ensamples to
the flock.*

1 Peter 5:1-3

THE Bible knows nothing of a solitary religion. The spirit
and duties of Christianity are, characteristically, social. Man,
in his state of primitive rectitude, was made a social creature; and redeemed and restored man, when he shall reach that holy
heaven which is in reserve for him hereafter, will find it to be a state
of perfect and most blessed society. It is true, the Christian, in the
course of the spiritual life, is required, and finds it to be as profitable
as it is delightful, to be often alone with his God. But the object of
this retirement is, like that of Moses in ascending the mount,—not
that he may remain there; but that he may come down with his face
shining; his heart expanding with holy love; and all his graces refined
and invigorated, and thus prepared the better to act his part in those
interesting relations which he sustains to his fellow men. Accordingly,
the visible church, with which we are all bound to be connected, and
which is the means of so many blessings to its members and to the
world, is a social body. It is called in our text a 'flock', under the care
of the great Shepherd and Bishop of souls, and under the immediate
superintendence of the under-shepherds, commissioned and sent for

[1] Samuel Miller, 'Ecclesiastical Polity', *The Spruce Street Lectures: by Several Clergymen.
Delivered during the Years 1831-2. To which Is Added a Sermon on the Atonement by
John De Witt, D.D.* (Philadelphia: James Russell, 1841), pp. 171-212.

this purpose. 'The elders which are among you I exhort, who am also an elder, and a witness of the sufferings of Christ . . . feed the flock of God which is among you.' The word here translated 'feed' literally signifies to perform the work of a *shepherd;*—to *guard* and *govern,* as well as to *dispense food* to the flock. And, accordingly, this rendering is confirmed, not only by many other Scriptures, but also by the charge which immediately follows:—'Taking the oversight thereof;—not as lords over God's heritage, but as examples to the flock.' We have here presented, then, very distinctly, the idea of the church, or the 'flock' of God being under *government.* It is represented as being placed, by its great Head and Lord, under *superintendence* and *regulation.* In all society there must be government, from a family to a nation. There was government in the garden of Eden, where human nature was perfect; and there is now, and ever will be, government in heaven, where the happy inhabitants, redeemed from all the remains of sin, shall be made perfectly blessed in the full enjoyment of God to all eternity.

There have been, indeed, enthusiasts and fanatics, in ancient as well as modern times, who taught that, in the true church there can be no need or place for government; 'because', said they, 'the members of the church being all holy persons, cannot be supposed to require either law or authority to sustain them; nothing but the evangelical law of love, by which they are all spontaneously and, of course, regulated.' But the advocates of this delusive theory forgot that the members of the visible church are not all truly sanctified persons; and that even those of their number who are the sincere friends of Christ, are sanctified only in part, and, therefore, need the salutary application of discipline. They forgot, too, that in almost every page, the New Testament recognizes, either directly or indirectly, the necessity and the actual existence of rule and authority in all the apostolic churches, even in their simplest and purest form. Nor must we forget that the vain theory of these fanatical teachers has been invariably found as worthless, and even mischievous in practice, as it was contrary, at once, to the principles of human nature, and to the instructions of holy Scripture. It has always resulted in disorder, licentiousness, and every evil work.

Quite as erroneous and no less pernicious in its consequences, was the doctrine of Erastus, the learned and ingenious contemporary of the Reformers (see his work, *De Excommunicatione Ecclesiastica*). He taught that the church, as such, can possess no power, and ought not to be allowed to exercise any authority or discipline; upon the alleged principle, that a government within a government is a practical absurdity, and by no means admissible. His theory, of course, was that all lawful authority resides only in the civil government; that the ministers of the church may instruct, persuade and exhort, but nothing more; and that when crimes against religion occur, the offenders can be reached and punished only by the civil magistrate. In short, his doctrine was, that the civil government alone can exercise authority in any community; and, consequently, that no man, as a professor of religion, can incur any penalty, for the most serious delinquency, with regard either to faith or practice, unless he be prosecuted and convicted before the tribunal of the State. A theory more weak and fanciful could scarcely have been proposed. It contradicts the most abundant scriptural testimony in favour of ecclesiastical government, as distinct from the civil, hereafter to be produced: and it is practically refuted by the experience of every day. The authority and discipline exercised in every family, and in every seminary of learning, plainly show that the fundamental principle on which the whole theory rests is altogether delusive; that there may be ten thousand governments within a government, without the least collision or interference.

Accordingly, in whatever direction we turn our eyes among the apostolic churches;—whether to Jerusalem or Antioch, to Ephesus or Crete, to Corinth or Rome, we find the corruption of human nature disclosing itself in various forms; we find the outbreaking of pride, ambition, heresy, and moral irregularity, disturbing the peace of the church, and calling for the application of its wise and wholesome discipline; in other words, for the exercise of its government. Now, if such were the case in the days of inspiration and miracle, under the eyes of the apostles themselves, and when the spirit of love might be said pre-eminently to reign in the church; what is to be expected when these extraordinary aids are taken away, and the covenanted family of Christ left to the ordinary power of the means which he has appointed for its edification?

It is evident, then, that there is, and, from the very nature of the case, must be, ecclesiastical government; that the church of Christ, as such, has essentially vested in her a certain kind and degree of authority, which she is bound, in fidelity to her Lord and Master, to exercise for the great purposes which she was founded to accomplish.

The principal questions in relation to this subject which demand an answer, are the three following: What is the *nature* of this government? What are its *limits?* And what is its legitimate and scriptural *end?* Let me request your serious and candid attention to some remarks intended to furnish a brief answer to each of these questions.

I. Let us begin with inquiring into the *nature* of that ecclesiastical government which the Word of God appears to warrant. And in order to ascertain this with any degree of certainty and clearness, it will be necessary previously to determine what are the *purposes* for which the church was founded: because it is manifest that all that power which is really indispensable to the attainment of these purposes, must, of course, be considered as vested in the church; and she, as not only at liberty, but as bound to exercise.

We are taught, then, in Scripture that the visible church is a body, called out of the world, and established under the authority of her divine Head and Lord, that she may be a faithful depository of gospel truth, worship, and order; that she may carefully maintain, and diligently propagate the genuine doctrines of our holy religion, in opposition to all heresy; that she may preserve in their simplicity and purity the ordinances which the Master has appointed, bearing testimony against all superstition and will-worship; that she may promote holy living among all her members, in the midst of a world lying in wickedness; and that she may thus be a nursery to train immortal souls for the kingdom of heaven. All this is so evident from Scripture that formal proof is unnecessary. And if this representation be correct, then it follows,

1. In the first place, that in all legitimate ecclesiastical government, *the Lord Jesus Christ is the sole fountain of power.* By his authority the church is instituted. He is her divine King and Head. His Word is her statute-book; her only infallible rule of faith and practice. She has no power to institute other rites or ceremonies than those which he has appointed; no right to enjoin anything which is not found in Scripture, or which cannot by good and necessary consequence, be

established by Scripture. All power in heaven, and on earth is given to him. He is the head over all things for the church. 'Call no man master, for one is your Master even Christ.' All the authority, then, of ecclesiastical rulers is derived. They can exercise no power but that which is delegated to them by him in whose name they come, and by whose commission they act.

2. The authorized government of the church is wholly *moral* or *spiritual* in its nature. That is, it has a respect, exclusively, to moral objects, and is to be carried on, exclusively, by moral means. 'My kingdom', said the Saviour, 'is not of this world'; by which he meant to say, that it is wholly separate from, and independent of, all earthly governments. It is not conducted on worldly principles. It is not maintained by 'carnal weapons'. Its laws, its sanctions, and its end are all spiritual. It has nothing to do with corporeal penalties, or secular coercion. No means, in a word, but those which are moral, that is, those which are addressed to the understanding, the conscience, and the heart, can be lawfully employed in that kingdom which 'is not meat and drink, but righteousness, and peace, and joy in the Holy Ghost'.

3. Further, in laying down the nature of ecclesiastical authority, it is plain, from the design of the church, that she must be considered as invested with power *to maintain, within her sacred precincts, the pure doctrines of the gospel.* If these doctrines were delivered to her, that she might be their keeper and guardian, then, surely, she not only has the right, but is bound to adhere to them;—to maintain them against all opposition;—and to publish her testimony in their favour, from time to time, in the form of creeds, confessions, and other formularies, as the state of the church and the world may demand. The church, indeed, has no right to compel anyone to receive her doctrines; no right to impose her creed or confession on the conscience of any human being. But she must, obviously, have power to do that which her Master has commanded her to do, viz., to 'hold fast' for herself the form of sound words once delivered to the saints; and to prevent any, within her bosom, from denying or dishonouring it. Even if the church were a mere voluntary association, she would, of course, have the power, which all voluntary associations have, of declining to receive as members those who are hostile to her essential

design; and also of excluding those who are found, after admission, to entertain and publish opinions subversive of her vital interests as a body. But the church is more than a mere voluntary association. She is a body organized under the authority of her divine Head and Lord; and must, of course, be vested with power to decline all fellowship with those who reject that system of holy doctrine which she is required to maintain. It is perfectly manifest that the exercise of this power is neither inconsistent with the acknowledged supremacy of Christ in his church, nor hostile to the most perfect enjoyment of Christian liberty. It cannot be deemed inconsistent with the supreme authority of Christ; because the church, in forming, publishing, and maintaining her creed, professes to receive no other doctrines than those which Christ has revealed; and to receive them as being, and because they are taught in his Word; and to warn all her members against opposite doctrines, for this very reason, that they are opposed to the will of Christ. Nor is the exercise of the power in question in the least degree hostile to the enjoyment of Christian liberty. Because the church compels no one to enter her communion; she only states what she considers her divine Master as requiring her to believe, and to practise; and practically declares, that those who reject any of the important doctrines, which go to make up the substance of that gospel which he has committed to her to keep and to propagate, cannot be admitted to her fellowship. Is this an invasion of Christian liberty? Nay, is it not rather one of the indispensable means of protecting liberty of conscience? Surely a body of professing Christians have a right to decide, and to profess what doctrines they consider as agreeable to the Word of God, and as represented by that Word as essential to the gospel. And they have, quite as evidently, a further right of agreeing among themselves that none can be admitted to the number of their members, and especially of their public teachers and rulers, who avow opinions adapted, in their view, to destroy their purity and peace. If they have not this right, there is an end of all religious liberty. If an individual, who entertains materially different views of gospel truth and order from those received by such an associated body of Christians, can force himself, contrary to the wishes of the body, into the ranks of their instructors and guides; on whose part, I ask, are the rights of conscience in this case, invaded? Surely the individual who thus intrudes is the invader, and the church which he enters becomes oppressed. If the rights of conscience either mean or are worth anything, they are mutual; and, of course, a body of professing Christians who think alike, have as good a right to enjoy them in undisturbed peace, as any individual who differs from them, and yet wishes to join their body, can possibly have to enjoy without molestation his opinions. If so, every attempt on the part of the latter to intrude himself among the teachers of the former is an invasion of that liberty wherewith Christ came to make his people free.

4. Again, it is manifest, from the purpose for which the church was founded, that she must be, and is vested with the power to exclude from her fellowship those who *violate the laws of practical holiness*. To deny the church this power, would be deny her that which is indispensable to her obeying the Master's command, to have no fellowship with the unfruitful works of darkness, but rather to reprove them. She is said to be the light of the world; to be the salt of the earth; to be a 'witness' of the holiness as well as of the truth of God, in the midst of a rebellious and unbelieving world. She is commanded to withdraw herself from every brother that walketh disorderly, and to keep herself unspotted from the world. But how are these characteristics to be realized; how are these commands to be obeyed, without the possession, and the exercise of a power to exclude from the Christian society those who are found to bear a character inconsistent with the honour of religion and the edification of the sacred family? Without this power to rebuke, to censure, and ultimately, if need be, to banish from the fellowship of the professing people of God, the church can present no visible, effective testimony in favour of gospel holiness; there can be no real separation between the precious and the vile; no sacred fence, enclosing the 'garden of the Lord' from the world. And, without such an enclosure, there may be a congregation, but I will venture to say, there can be no church. Of course, one of the most important purposes which a visible, professing people of God were intended to answer, would be, in this case, virtually abandoned.

5. It is further manifest, that the nature of ecclesiastical government must be such as will enable the church to regulate, agreeably to the laws of Christ, *the choice and investiture of all her officers*. If the church were, in this respect, powerless; if all that pleased, however

ignorant, erroneous in doctrine, or profligate in practice, might thrust themselves into the number of her teachers and rulers, contrary to her wishes and the command of her Master, she would be destitute of the means of self-defence, and self-preservation. Corruption, dishonour, and eventual destruction must inevitably ensue. No society could exist in peace and order for a year together, without the power of regulating the choice and induction of her own officers. Accordingly, the New Testament abounds with directions in reference to this important point of ecclesiastical order. It everywhere represents the church as authorized and required to exercise a sovereign power in this matter; to examine and make trial of those who are candidates for sacred office; and to commit the great work of instruction and rule in the house of God to none but those whose knowledge, soundness in the faith, fidelity and zeal are adapted to promote her edification.

6. It is clear also, from the nature and design of the church, that her government, if it be of any value, must be of such a nature as will enable her *to settle within herself all the ordinary controversies and difficulties which arise within her bosom.* The members of the visible church, even when sincere in their religious profession, are sanctified, as was before remarked, only in part. Of course, they are compassed about with many infirmities; and hence differences of opinion, variance, conflicting claims, and multiplied forms of offence and complaint often arise—between the private members of the same church: between ministers, and the people of their respective charges; between the pastors of different churches; and between different churches of the same denomination. Now, when these complaints and controversies arise, the church ought to be prepared to meet them; and when she is obliged, from the want of appropriate and adequate provision in her form of government, to resort, for settling them, to foreign arbitration, and even to civil courts; she undoubtedly labours under a serious defect in her ecclesiastical organization. It cannot be such an organization as the Master has appointed. The inspired apostle expressly reprobates the practice of Christians going out of the church to reconcile differences, and to adjust matters in controversy. He evidently teaches that the church ought to have tribunals of her own, by which all questions and difficulties, of an ecclesiastical kind,

may be authoritatively decided. And that church which is destitute of such tribunals—however richly and happily furnished in other respects—will undoubtedly find herself unable to carry into effect some very important provisions exhibited in the New Testament for maintaining Christian order and edification.

7. Another characteristic of ecclesiastical polity, indispensable to the attainment of the great purposes for which it was instituted is, that it *be such as will bind all the parts of the church together in one homogeneous body;* and enable all these parts to act together with authority and efficiency, for the benefit of the whole.

There is a visible church catholic, comprising all those of every denomination, who profess the true religion, together with their children. These, though divided from each other by oceans and continents, as well as by names and forms, are all one church, one body in Christ, and everyone members one of another. They do not, nay, they cannot, all worship together. Prejudices and misapprehensions, as well as local separation and numbers, prevent them from all assembling in the same edifice. But still, as they are all united to the same divine Head, so, it is delightful to remember, whether they acknowledge it or not, that, in a very important sense, they are one covenanted people, and are bound to recognize each other as such, as far as circumstances will admit. But if this be so, much more ought those churches which bear the same name, profess the same faith, and are so situated as to admit of their being ecclesiastically connected, to make a point of sustaining this connection with each other in reality, as well as nominally. Now, I say, that such a church cannot be so united as to answer all the purposes which her divine Head, as well as her own peace and edification require, without a form of polity which will enable all the several parts of the body, to meet together, by their representatives, in appropriate judicatories; to plan, consult, and decide for the benefit of the whole body; and that not merely by way of advice, but by authoritative acts, to correct abuses, redress grievances, obviate the approach of error, heal schismatic contention, promote the unity, purity, and co-operation of the whole body; and employ this co-operation in spreading the glorious gospel for the conversion of the world. If the church is commanded to maintain this unity; if she is required, in all her several branches, to walk by the same rule, and to speak the same thing; and if she is commanded, as a church, to be active in sending the gospel to every creature;—then, surely her Master has not withheld from her the means which are indispensable to the attainment of the end. If this principle be admitted, then the system of our Independent brethren, who reject all authoritative synods; all courts of review and control; labour under a defect of the most serious kind. It makes no provision for the churches of the same denomination acting with harmony and authority as one body. And so far as Congregationalism is chargeable with the same deficiency, as it undoubtedly is in some parts of our country, as well as in Great Britain, it is altogether powerless in respect to many of those things in which the church is called to act as a united body.

8. A further and very important feature of that government which the church is warranted in exercising, is, *that it be of such a nature as that it may be carried into execution in all parts of the world, and under any and every form of civil government.* As Christ's kingdom 'is not of this world'; in other words, as the government of the church has no necessary connection, and ought never to be in fact connected, with the government of the State; it can, of course, operate without obstruction, and accomplish all its legitimate objects, without the aid, and even in spite of the enmity of the civil government, whatever may be its form. Of this we need no stronger evidence than the fact, that the Christian church, for nearly three centuries, did exist, and did exercise all the power for which we contend, while it had no connection with the State; nay, while the State frowned and persecuted, and did all in its power to destroy the church. Amidst all this hostility from the world, the rulers of the church went forward, without turning to the right hand or the left, carrying the gospel of the grace of God wherever they were permitted; instructing the people; baptising and receiving to the fellowship of the church those whom they thought worthy; exercising a sacred moral inspection over all their members; admonishing and censuring the disorderly; excluding those who were incorrigibly offensive, with regard either to faith or practice; and, in a word, exercising, for all moral purposes, that authority which the King of Zion had committed to them for the edification of his sacred family. Here was an undoubted example—notwithstanding the dream of Erastus to the contrary—of a government within a

government, and each proceeding without interference; because, as long as each kept in its proper place, they could not possibly come in collision with each other. In like manner, the church of Christ, in all ages, as long as she adheres to the spirit of that government which alone the Saviour has warranted, may carry it into plenary execution in any land, in any state of society, and under any form of civil government; nay, though all the governments of the world should again be, as they once were, firmly leagued against her.

9. The last characteristic which I shall mention of that government which the church is warranted by Scripture to exercise, is, that it be not, in any of its features, *adapted to promote ambition, to excite a lordly and aspiring spirit in the church*. 'Neither', says the apostle, 'as lords over God's heritage, but as examples to the flock.' A love of pre-eminence and of power is natural to man. It is one of the earliest, strongest, and most universal principles of our nature. It reigns without control in wicked men; and has more influence than it ought to have in the minds of the most pious. And when we recollect to what complicated and deplorable mischiefs this spirit has given rise in the church of God,—corrupting her doctrines, alienating her members and ministers, disturbing her peace, and breaking her unity;—it is surely desirable that everything in the form of ecclesiastical polity should be, as far as possible, adapted to obviate and repress the spirit of which we speak. Accordingly, our blessed Saviour, not only while he was on earth, frowned with severity upon everything which looked like aspiring and ambition among his followers, declaring that the question, 'which shall be the greatest?' ought to have no place in his kingdom; for that all his ministers were fellow-servants, and that none of them should seek to be called 'Master' or 'Rabbi'—but he also, as we confidently believe, after his resurrection, appointed a form of ecclesiastical order, which placed all pastors upon an equality, and precluded the possibility of anyone 'lording it' over another in virtue of any official pre-eminence. When, therefore, I find the inspired apostle saying to his son Timothy (*1 Tim.* 3:1), 'If a man desire the office of a bishop, he desireth a good work'—I had almost said that if there were no other text in the Bible declaring against prelacy, this alone would convince me that it was contrary to the mind of Christ. For, if we interpret the

word 'bishop' in this place to mean, what Presbyterians say it means, the pastoral or ministerial office;—an office of great labour and self-denial;—then the whole passage conveys an idea, the seasonableness and importance of which is obvious to everyone, and the consistency of which with the rest of the epistle, and with the spirit of the New Testament, is equally obvious. But if, by this title, we are to understand an office of pre-eminent rank and authority, above that of the ordinary authorized dispensers of the Word and sacraments; no gloss, it appears to me, can prevent our making the Apostle Paul a favourer of ambition and aspiring in the holy ministry. He surely meant to encourage a 'desire' for the office of a 'bishop'; nay, an earnest and eager desire, as the original word undoubtedly signifies; a desire like that of a hungry person to obtain food. But if this be an office of pre-eminent ecclesiastical rank, as our prelatical brethren say it is, then, undoubtedly, Paul, upon this construction, encourages every presbyter eagerly to covet the place of his diocesan. On this supposition the inspired apostle is set at variance with himself, in many other parts of his epistles; at variance with his brother apostle, John, who strongly censures one who loved to have the pre-eminence in the church; at variance with his Master, who, on so many occasions, reprobated all aspiring after mastership, or priority of place among his ministers; and, indeed, at variance with the whole spirit of the gospel.

It is by no means contended that the exercise of individual ambition is either necessarily, or in fact, precluded by the adoption of Presbyterian parity in the holy ministry. This spirit is found, in a greater or less degree, wherever there are men. But, as the constitution of our truly primitive and apostolic church, precludes all official inequality of rank among pastors, their ambition can only take the turn of aspiring to be more learned, more pious, more diligent, and more conspicuously and extensively useful in the same office. An ambition which, in many cases, may be, no doubt, sadly unhallowed; but which is, surely, less dishonourable and corrupting in its influence, than that which exhausts itself in canvassing for titles, chief seats, and emoluments; and which is tempted, of course, to be most intent on the culture of those personal qualities which are most favourable to the attainment of official precedence.

Having endeavoured to show the real nature of that ecclesiastical polity which the Scriptures warrant, by pointing out, in detail, its essential features, and the specific purposes which it ought to be, and must be intended, and adequate to answer; let us now see whether we do not find the apostolic churches actually exercising their ecclesiastical power, in the very cases and for the very purposes which have been specified. If so, the testimony is irresistible, that we have not misapprehended or misapplied the foregoing principles.

We find ministers of the sanctuary, then, in various parts of the New Testament, distinguished by titles which plainly imply that they were invested with authority for the benefit of the church, which they were bound to exercise in the fear of God, and under a deep sense of accountability to the great Shepherd and Bishop of souls. They are called 'rulers' in the house of God; 'shepherds over the flock'; 'stewards of the mysteries of God'; 'overseers'; 'ambassadors of Christ' (*Rom.* 12:8; *1 Tim.* 3:4; *1 Pet.* 5:1-3; *1 Cor.* 4:1; *1 Pet.* 4:10; *Acts* 20:28; *2 Cor.* 5:20)—all implying office in the church;—all implying a delegated power, to be exercised for the edification of that spiritual body of which he who 'sits as King upon the holy hill of Zion' is the sovereign Head. Further, the apostles, again and again, exhort the churches to which they wrote to 'obey them that had the rule over them, and to submit themselves', remembering that those rulers 'watched for their souls as they that must give account' (*Heb.* 13:17; *1 Thess.* 5:12). Our blessed Saviour himself, in giving direction to his disciples respecting offences, evidently authorizes the church, by her proper officers, after due inquiry and evidence, to pass a judicial sentence against incorrigible offenders, cutting them off from the fellowship and privileges of the Christian body (*Matt.* 18:15-19). In conformity with this direction, the actual exercise of ecclesiastical power in the excision of the heretical and the immoral from the apostolic church, is expressly and repeatedly recorded. In several cases the apostles enjoin that those who denied the fundamental doctrines of the gospel, so as to preach 'another gospel', should be refused admission to the church; or, if already admitted, excluded from its privileges. 'The man that is an heretic, after the first and second admonition, reject' (*Titus* 3:10). 'Now I beseech you, brethren, mark them which cause divisions and offences, contrary to the doctrine which ye have learned; and avoid them' (*Rom.* 16:17). 'If any man preach any other gospel unto you than that ye have received, let him be accursed' (*Gal.* 1:9).

> Whosoever transgresseth and abideth not in the doctrine of Christ, hath not God. If there come any unto you, and bring not this doctrine, receive him not into your house, neither bid him God speed:— for he that biddeth him God speed is partaker of his evil deeds (*2 John* 9-11).

Equally undoubted are the examples of judicial censure and exclusion from the church on account of corruption in practice. In the church of Corinth, the rulers are directed to assemble, and authoritatively to cast out of their communion a man who had fallen into gross immorality. 'Wherefore put away from among yourselves', says the inspired apostle, 'that wicked person' (*1 Cor.* 5:1-15). And again, in writing to the Thessalonians, the same apostle directs—'If any man obey not our word by this epistle, note that man, and have no company with him, that he may be ashamed' (*2 Thess.* 3:14). The New Testament, moreover, abounds with directions concerning the proper character, the choice, and the ordination of church officers; prescribing those qualifications without which they ought not to be admitted to office; and committing to the rulers of the church the arduous duty of judging of these qualifications, rejecting the unworthy, and presiding over the choice and investure of those whom they approved. And, to crown all, we have an example in the apostolic church of a synodical assembly, brought together, not by the civil government, but by ecclesiastical men, for deciding matters of great importance, in the name, and for the benefit of the whole church. I refer to the synod of Jerusalem (*Acts* 15) formed by 'the apostles and elders', convened in that place, who decided the question concerning Jewish observances, so interesting at that time, which had been sent up for consideration from Antioch. And, what is no less remarkable, having authoritatively decided, they transmitted their judgement, under the name of 'decrees', to be recorded and observed by all the churches. In a word, ecclesiastical rulers are represented, throughout the New Testament, as entrusted with the 'keys of the kingdom of God', that is, with authority in the visible church; with the power of 'binding and loosing', in the name of the King of Zion; with the power of superintending all the affairs of the church, as such; of judicially directing what appears to be for edification; and seeing that 'all things be done decently and in order'.

Such is the nature of that spiritual government which the church is authorized to maintain. Our next enquiry is,

II. What are the *limits* of that authority which belongs to the church? And in determining these, we shall be aided essentially by keeping in mind that nature and design of this authority which we have already endeavoured to ascertain. For we may rest assured that the church has no superfluous power; no power beyond what is absolutely necessary for the attainment of those great moral purposes for which she was formed by her divine Master. And,—

1. The church can have *no authority over any but her own members*. There have been periods indeed, in which an encroaching, tyrannical church claimed universal dominion; when she arrogated to herself the power to set up and put down whom she would; when she undertook to dispose of crowns and kingdoms at pleasure; and to make kings and emperors bow before her with ignoble homage. I need not say, that this was most presumptuous usurpation; contrary to reason and Scripture; and adapted to destroy the church of God in her appropriate character. It follows, from the very nature and design of the church, that she can have no authority beyond her own pale. And it was, no doubt, because she so frequently transgressed this rule, in former times, that so many adopted, without due examination, the principle before noticed, that a government cannot exist within a government. If the church had not so often transcended her proper limits, this principle would never have occurred to a thinking mind. Be it remembered, then, that she can judge only those who are 'within' her bosom. To those who are 'without' she may send missionaries. She may instruct, invite, and persuade them to come in, and accept of her privileges; but until they comply with her invitation, and become her members, she has no right to extend to them her appropriate authority.

2. Again, the church has no power to control, even her own members, *in any other concerns than those which relate to their moral and spiritual interests*. She has no right to interfere with their political opinions; with their domestic relations; or with any department of

their secular pursuits. As long as they infringe no law of Christ's kingdom, it is no part of her sacred trust to call in question or censure their course. It cannot be too frequently repeated, or too constantly remembered, that Christ's kingdom is not of this world, and can never authorize its rulers to be judges and dividers in the temporal concerns of men. Yet if a member of the Christian church, in the course of his political conflicts, or his professional avocations, be visibly and palpably chargeable with a departure from purity, either in faith or practice, it is incumbent on the church to call him to an account; not for his political partialities, or his secular employments, but solely for his moral delinquency.

3. Further, the church has no power to hold in a state of inspection and discipline, even her own members *any longer than they choose to submit to her authority*. I am not now speaking of the right of these members in the sight of the divine and heart-searching Head of the church. No doubt, all who depart from the body of his professing people, and refuse to submit to the just and scriptural authority of his sacred household, commit sin against him; and, however lightly they may think of it, will be held accountable at his bar for their disobedience. But still the church has no means, and ought not to claim the power, of compelling any to remain under her 'oversight' and authority an hour longer than their judgment and their conscience dispose them to remain. He that will depart, must be allowed to depart. The church can only follow him with her tears, her prayers, and her parental censure.

4. Closely allied to this, or rather involved in this, is another limit to the power of the church; and that is, that *the highest penalty she can inflict upon anyone, however aggravated his offence, is exclusion from her communion*. She can exact no pecuniary fine. She can inflict no corporeal pains or penalties. She cannot confiscate the property, or incarcerate the person, or touch a hair of the head, of the most obstinate offender. When she has shut him out from her fellowship, in other words, disowned him as a Christian brother, she has done the utmost that she has a right to do. Her power is exhausted.

5. Intimately connected with the foregoing, is the last principle of limitation which I shall mention, which is, that *the power of ecclesiastical rulers is strictly ministerial: that is, they have only the power, as*

servants, of communicating what the Master has taught them, and of doing what the Master has commanded them. They derive their power, not from the people whom they serve, and whom they represent, but from Christ, the King and Head of the church. In his name they come. By his authority they speak and act. Their commission is, 'Teach them to observe all things whatsoever I have commanded you. Preach the preaching that I bid thee. Hear the word at my mouth, and give them warning from me.' Their office is 'a ministry', not 'a dominion'. Teachers and rulers have, of course, no right to prescribe terms of communion which the Bible does not warrant; no right to denounce or condemn anything which the Bible does not condemn; no right to enjoin that which the Bible does not enjoin. Like ambassadors at a foreign court, they cannot go one jot or tittle beyond their instructions. I am not ignorant, indeed, that ecclesiastical bodies, calling themselves churches of Christ, have often set up other standards, both of faith and practice. Tradition, the Fathers, general councils, and the judgment of the church, have all been prescribed as authoritative guides both to truth and order. Everything of this kind is an invasion of Christ's supremacy in his church, and a practical denial of the sufficiency of the Scriptures as the great code of laws of his kingdom. It is not maintained, indeed, that there must necessarily be a direct scriptural warrant for every minor detail of ecclesiastical polity. But it *is* maintained, that for every leading, governing feature in the system, there must be the warrant of either scriptural precept, or scriptural example. And, above all, it is maintained, as a radical principle on this subject, that nothing can ever be lawfully made a term of communion for which a warrant from the Word of God cannot be produced. It remains that we consider

III. *The legitimate and scriptural end of church government.* The great end of all good government is the benefit of the community over which it is exercised. For this purpose it was instituted at first by the Governor of the world; and to this end ought its whole administration, in all cases, to be supremely directed. Tyrants in the State, indeed, have taught, and acted upon the principle, that the great end of all civil government is the aggrandisement of a few at the expense of the many. Of course, they supposed that the grand design was most successfully accomplished, when the rulers were most enriched and honoured, and the ruled kept in the most abject and unresisting subjection. And it is deeply to be deplored that the same principle has been too often adopted, if not avowedly, yet really, by bodies calling themselves churches of Christ. Hence the ecclesiastical exactions and edicts to which hood-winked and infatuated millions have so often, in past ages, and so long submitted. Hence the haughty Papal 'bulls' and 'interdicts' by which kings, and even kingdoms have been frequently made to tremble. Nothing can be more opposite than these things to the spirit and law of the Redeemer. The 'authority' which the inspired apostle claims for the rulers of the church, he represents as 'given for edification and not for destruction' (*2 Cor.* 10:8). Not for the purpose of creating and pampering classes of privileged orders, to 'lord it over God's heritage'; not to build up a system of polity which may minister to the pride, the cupidity, or the voluptuousness of an ambitious priesthood; not to form a body under the title of clergy, with separate interests from the laity, and making the latter mere machines and submissive instruments of the former. All this is as wicked as it is unreasonable. No office, no power is authorized by Jesus Christ in his church, but that which is necessary to the instruction, the purity, the edification, and the happiness of the whole body. All legitimate government, here, as well as elsewhere, is to be considered as a means, not an end: not as instituted for the purpose of acquiring dominion over the bodies, the minds, or the property of men; but for promoting their temporal and eternal welfare; and as no further resting on divine authority than as it is adapted to propagate and maintain the truth, to restrain vice, to secure the order and wellbeing of society, and to build up the great family of those who profess the true religion, in knowledge, peace, and holiness, unto salvation.

Accordingly, the divine Founder of our religion himself tells us that he 'came not to be ministered unto, but to minister, and to give his life a ransom for many'; not to gratify himself, but to obey, and suffer, and die, that he might 'seek and save that which was lost' (*Matt.* 20:28; *Luke* 19:10). And, in conformity with this declaration, the inspired apostle, who had drunk deep into the spirit of his Master, declares, 'We preach, not ourselves, but Christ Jesus the Lord, and ourselves your servants for Jesus sake' (*2 Cor.* 4:5). And again: 'Not for that we have dominion over your faith, but are helpers of your joy' (*2 Cor.* 1:24). And again, 'All things', says the same apostle, addressing himself to the body of a Christian church—'all things are yours, whether Paul, or Apollos, or Cephas, all are yours' (*1 Cor.* 3:22). And again, 'Who is Paul and who is Apollos, but ministers by whom you believed, as the Lord gave to every man?' (*1 Cor.* 3:5). Accordingly, the same inspired man reminds his son, Timothy, and commands him to teach, that 'the servants of the Lord must not strive, but be gentle unto all men, apt to teach, patient, in meekness instructing those who oppose themselves, if, peradventure, God will give them repentance to the acknowledging of the truth' (*2 Tim.* 2:24, 25). Accordingly, in pleading before King Agrippa, he declares that the great design of the Saviour in sending gospel ministers to the children of men, is, to 'open their eyes, and to turn them from darkness to light, and from the power of Satan to God, that they might receive forgiveness of sins, and inheritance among them which are sanctified, by faith in Jesus Christ' (*Acts* 26:18). And when he tells the Ephesian church for what purpose apostles, evangelists, pastors and teachers were sent forth, he declares it was not for any purpose of self-aggrandisement, but 'for the perfecting of the saints, for the edifying of the body of Christ; till we all come in the unity of the faith, and of the knowledge of the Son of God, unto a perfect man, unto the measure of the stature of the fulness of Christ' (*Eph.* 4:12).

This subject, my Friends, however dry and speculative it may have appeared to some of my hearers, is all practical. It enters more deeply into the daily walk and duties of the Christian life, than is commonly supposed. Suffer me, then, to trespass a little longer on your patience by stating, and recommending to your attention some of the many *practical inferences* which may be naturally drawn from the subject. And,

1. From what has been said, it is evident that *church government is a very important means of grace*. To many, I know, this whole subject appears unimportant, if not repulsive. They are apt to consider and represent all exercise of ecclesiastical authority, and especially the discipline of the church, which is nothing more than the application of the church's authority, as an officious and offensive intermeddling with Christian liberty. But I need not say to those who take their views of ecclesiastical polity from the Bible, and from the best

experience, that it is not only important, but absolutely essential to the purity and edification of the body of Christ. It ought, undoubtedly, to be regarded as one of the most precious means of grace, by which offenders are humbled, softened, and brought to repentance; by which the church is purged of unworthy members; offences removed; the honour of religion promoted; the office of the Christian ministry regulated and 'magnified'; real Christians stimulated and guided in their spiritual course, faithful testimony borne against error and crime; and the professing family of Christ rescued from disgrace, and made to appear orderly and beautiful in the view of the world. The truth is, the faithful maintenance of church discipline; in other words, the exercise of a faithful watch and care among Christians, over the purity of each other, in doctrine, worship, and life, is so important a part of the purpose for which the church was founded, that we may say with confidence, she cannot flourish, as to her best interests, without it. It may be safely affirmed, that a large part of all that is holy in the church, at the present day, either in faith or practice, may be ascribed, under God, as really to sound ecclesiastical discipline, as to the faithful preaching of the gospel. No matter how many precious plants may be introduced into the garden of the Lord, or how much time and labour may be expended in endeavouring to fertilize the soil, and to apply to it the most skilful and diligent culture: if there be no fence kept up to defend the whole from intruders, all culture will be vain; every beast of the field will devour it; and what ought to be a beautiful and productive enclosure will be a barren and dreary common.

2. If the foregoing representation be correct, then *the plenary and constant exercise of ecclesiastical authority is not usurpation, but simple obedience to Christ.* There is extreme sensitiveness on this subject in the minds of many, who profess to be zealous for the 'rights of conscience'. They believe, and sometimes very clamorously assert, that all ecclesiastical censure on anyone, for any moral delinquency, and especially for any departure from the true faith, is an interference with the prerogative of God, who alone is 'Lord of the conscience'. But if Christ, the divine Head of the church, has solemnly enjoined on his professing people the exercise of this authority, and the faithful infliction of this censure, there is surely an end of all controversy

on the part of those who acknowledge the Scriptures to be the only infallible rule of faith and practice. Suppose the proprietor of a beautiful and valuable garden to have committed it to the entire care of servants, formally chosen and commissioned for that purpose. Suppose the master to have given them a strict and repeated charge, carefully to exclude from it all mischievous intruders, and as soon as possible to banish those who had improperly made their way into the enclosure. And suppose, when these servants faithfully obeyed their orders, anyone were to denounce them as usurping power, and as presumptuously interfering with the liberty of their neighbours. What would be thought of the charge? Would it not be regarded as the most preposterous that could be conceived? Everyone must see, in a moment, that if the servants had not done exactly as they did, they would have been liable to the charge of unfaithfulness and gross disobedience. Precisely so is it in the case before us. The command of Christ, to his commissioned servants, to watch over, rule, and guard the church committed to their care; and to exclude from it all those whose principles or practice are manifestly hostile to its great design; is plain, repeated, and decisive. Can it be for a moment doubted, then, that when they obey this command, they are so far from usurping power, that a failure to obey it, strictly and faithfully, would be an act of direct rebellion against him who is 'Head over all things for the church'.

3. From what has been said, it is plain, that *every departure from the essential principles of gospel order will be likely to exert an unhappy influence on the best interests of the church, and may be productive of the most injurious effects.* It is the habit of many to speak of the established rules of ecclesiastical order, with sneer and contempt, as if they were cold and spiritless forms, the observance of which is rather adapted to repress and hinder, than to promote the real life, the spiritual prosperity of the church. Unless the preacher is greatly deceived, a more erroneous estimate was never made. There is no doubt, indeed, that there may be much pompous and rigid adherence to ecclesiastical form, where there is little or no life. And there is as little doubt that the rigour of church order may be maintained at the expense of more vital interests. But the question is,—Will the garden of the Lord be likely to flourish when its fences are broken down; when not only

old, but important landmarks are disregarded; when rules of order, as wise as they have been long established, are set at nought? Can there be a moment's doubt what answer ought to be given to this question? 'God is not the author of confusion, but of peace and order in all the churches.' Let no one imagine, then, that he will be likely to render God service, or permanently to build up the Redeemer's kingdom, by violating the order of his house; for example, by giving encourage- ment to 'lay-preaching'; by favouring the introduction into the min- istry of men with talents adapted to dazzle as meteors, but destitute of sound principles, and other prescribed qualifications; by violat- ing wholesome scriptural rules, for the purpose of either favouring a friend, or opposing an adversary; by giving countenance to proceed- ings manifestly disorderly, for the purpose of carrying a point, or with the hope of gaining some temporary advantage; or by adopting measures in the public service of the sanctuary, better fitted to inflate or intoxicate, than to enlighten the understanding, convince the con- science, or impress the heart. It is in ecclesiastical affairs, as all wise men acknowledge it to be in civil life, a single departure from some important principle of regularity may lead, directly or indirectly, to mischievous consequences, of which a whole generation may not see the end. Such deviations may appear to do good for a while; but the appearance is delusive. Like the excitement of strong drink, they may stimulate, and even appear to strengthen, for a short time; but they only prepare the way for increased weakness and disease in the issue. It were unwise, indeed, to insist on adhering to form at the expense of substance; but it were equally unwise to cherish the hope, that the substance will long be retained, when form is abandoned. The instructions of history on this subject are most ample and decisive.

4. A further inference from what has been said is obvious and irre- sistible, *viz.: that the Presbyterian form of ecclesiastical polity is mani- festly, and by far, best adapted to strengthen, purify, and build up the church of Christ.* If uniformity of faith, order, and worship, among all the churches which bear the same denomination, and profess to walk by the same rules, be of real importance; if the maintenance of enlightened and faithful discipline, be essential to the purity and genuine health of the body of Christ; and if that ecclesiastical pol- ity which shall be adapted to answer the great purposes for which

the church was founded, must be such as will authoritatively bind all the churches which profess to receive it, in one compact and homogeneous body; then it is manifest that no other form than the Presbyterian is adapted to attain all the purposes, and secure all the advantages which the government of the church was intended by the Master to promote. In saying this, I have no desire to denounce, or even to depreciate, the forms of government preferred by other denominations of our fellow Christians. With the utmost cordiality can I adopt as my own the language of the framers of our excellent ecclesiastical Constitution, when they say, 'We embrace in the spirit of charity those Christians who differ from us, in opinion or in practice, on these subjects.' This, however, is perfectly reconcilable with the conviction, that one form of ecclesiastical government is more scriptural, and better adapted to promote good order, purity, and edification than another. On the one hand, to speak with frankness, we have no doubt that a church formed on the plan of our Episcopal brethren, may be a true church of Christ, and may be, and has been blessed to the everlasting welfare of many souls. Yet we are persuaded, that the peculiar features of that system, besides having no foundation in the Word of God, are by no means adapted to the maintenance of a scriptural discipline in the church, and, indeed, scarcely compatible with it. On the other hand, we are as perfectly confident that the plan of our Independent brethren, and, to a considerable extent, that of our Congregational brethren, is no less materially defective as a means of promoting the unity, and the efficient and authoritative co-operation of all the churches of the same nominal communion. It obviously leaves them entirely powerless in regard to many points, which it would seem no friend of ecclesiastical order can deem of small importance. In both these respects, as well as in many others which might be specified, the Presbyterian system is, at once, liberal and efficient; in the highest degree friendly to the claims of Christian liberty; and yet adapted to maintain the purest discipline, and the most entire harmony and energetic co-operation of the whole body. Much depends, it must be acknowledged, on the spirit with which this system is borne forward. For, although I am not prepared to adopt, in all its extent, in reference to ecclesiastical government, the sentiment which is so often repeated as an admitted maxim, that

'that which is best administered is best', yet I am free to acknowledge, that the Presbyterian form of government and discipline may be administered with so little of the spirit of charity, and of zeal for the glory of God, and the extension of the Redeemer's kingdom, as to make it little more than a course of vexatious and unedifying litigation. But this is only saying, that the infirmity and corruption of man may sometimes mar the beauty, and invalidate the efficacy of the best provisions of a benevolent God. Some adequate and adapted impelling power is necessary to set the most perfect machine in motion. And when the vital spirit of the religion of Christ is present and active, here is the noblest plan of machinery in the world with which it can operate. Where this spirit habitually governs, there is no other plan of ecclesiastical polity so well adapted as the Presbyterian to secure order; to promote peace; to accomplish everything with fraternal counsel and deliberation; to maintain impartial and equitable discipline, at once over ministers and private members; to secure the rights of the people; to protect pastors from injury and oppression; to guard, on the one hand, against the intrusions of laymen into the functions of the clergy, and, on the other, against the encroachments of clerical ambition; to promote uniformity of doctrine and worship; to afford redress in every species of difficulty; to bring the state and proceedings of every part of the church under the distinct and official review of the whole; and to enable the whole to act together as one body, under the authority and guidance of a common head. Are these things desirable? Are they really important to the greatest strength and purity of the body? If so, I will be bold to say, they can be fully attained only by that form of ecclesiastical polity under which we are so happy as to live.

5. From the view which has been given of this subject, it is plain that *diversity in forms of church government ought not to interfere with the communion of saints*. As 'Christ is not divided'; as there is but 'one Christ'; so all who are really united by faith to him who is 'the Head of all principality and power' are 'one body in him, and every one members one of another'. We all grant, that among individual Christians there may be 'diversities of operation', that is great variety in the order, intensity, and aspect of those exercises which mark the entrance as well as the progress of the divine life;—and yet that 'it is

the same spirit which worketh in all'. Why may there not be a similar variety in the modes of organization adopted by ecclesiastical bodies, without destroying their ecclesiastical character? While, therefore, the great importance of the subject of ecclesiastical polity is maintained; and while we may safely assert, that no material departure from the scriptural order of the church can ever occur without subjecting those who are guilty of it to a serious disadvantage; let us guard against the mistake of those who place it among the fundamentals of our holy religion. This, it is apprehended, is an entire and mischievous mistake. The holy Scriptures manifestly do not, like some ecclesiastical men, of narrow views, and of more zeal than knowledge, cut off from the 'covenanted mercies of God' those who reject a certain favourite form of church government;—but only those who reject the gospel of Christ. We undoubtedly sin against the great Head of the church, when we consider and treat as a matter of indifference that which he has appointed; but we may be considered as equally sinning against him, and against the generation of the righteous, when we attempt to place the external order of the church among those things on which its vital character depends; on which the exercise of Jehovah's mercy is suspended.

6. If what has been said be correct, it is evident that *an honest attachment to a particular form of ecclesiastical order, does not, necessarily, deserve the name of high-church and sectarian bigotry.* There is a strong tendency, at the present day, to stigmatize with these epithets everything that indicates a marked preference to any one denomination of Christians. If a book be written, or a plan formed for recommending any particular portion of the Christian community, as, in the estimation of the author, more conformed to Scripture, and more worthy of adoption than others, it is immediately denounced, as a 'high-church' book; as an illiberal, 'sectarian' plan. Nor are any more disposed to utter, and clamorously to urge this denunciation, than those who, under the pretence of a most expanded 'charity', are far more exclusive and intolerant in contending for some opposite peculiarity. None are more severe on bigots and bigotry, than the most intensely bigoted. But can anything be more unreasonable and unjust? If the visible church exist at all, it must be organized in some particular form: and it is manifest that all forms of church

order cannot be equally agreeable to Scripture. Some one is, of course, nearer to the primitive model than the rest. And if anyone honestly believes this to be the case, with the form with which he is particularly connected, and prefers, and endeavours to recommend this form accordingly; provided he do it without uncharitableness, and with due respect to the opinions of others, who has a right to complain? Surely to censure him for this course, is to abridge, instead of maintaining, Christian liberty. The truth is, the sincere and intelligent inquirer must prefer one form of faith and order to others. If he proclaim this preference with bitterness and rancour; if he assail those who cannot agree with him with unsparing denunciation; if he exhibit himself as a fiery, controversial zealot, who can see no evil in his own party, and no good out of it; let the terms 'high churchman', 'bigot', 'sectarian', be heaped upon him without reserve. He richly deserves them all. But, if he meekly and humbly obey those convictions of duty which he considers the Bible as warranting; if he lay no more stress upon modes of faith, and forms of order than the Bible lays upon them; if he, not merely in words, but practically, allow to others the same liberty which he claims for himself; and if he look with unfeigned and equal affection upon all who bear the image of Christ, whether they belong to his own denomination or not;—such an one, whatever opprobrious epithets the latitudinarian, or he who is fierce for moderation may heap upon him, has little reason to fear the abuse of men. Those who would call such an one 'bigot' or 'sectarian' would, undoubtedly, if they had lived in the first century, have applied the same appellation to the Saviour himself and his inspired apostles.

7. From the foregoing discussion it is manifest, *that all alliance between the church and the civil government, is unscriptural, and replete with mischief of the most serious kind.* It is *unscriptural;* contrary alike to the letter and the spirit of the New Testament; and, therefore, solemnly forbidden. It is unhallowed in its origin, the offspring of priestcraft, or statecraft, or both, and, of course, entitled to no countenance from the real friends of the church of Christ. And its tendency and effects are in all cases injurious; necessarily and universally injurious. All civil establishments of religion, then, ought to be opposed to the utmost by those who wish well to the cause of Zion.

Whatever may be their form, or the degree of their rigour; whether they are intended to operate by force, by fear, or by bribery; whether we consider them as a tax on error, or as a bounty on faith; as a legal provision for instructing the people in what the civil magistrate (who may be an infidel or a gross heretic) chooses to say is truth; or as a convenient engine in the hands of government for reaching and controlling the popular mind; in all cases they are corrupt in their principles, and pernicious in their influence; and adapted to generate and encourage hypocrisy; to degrade the Christian ministry; to make the care of souls an affair of secular merchandise; and to prostrate the church of God, with all its officers and ordinances, at the feet of worldly politicians. Such have been the effects of religious establishments from the days of Constantine to the present hour; and such will be their effects as long as human nature remains what it now is. Every friend of Christ, then, ought to recoil with instinctive dread and horror from every attempt to support religion, in any form, by law. Nay, they ought to recoil from every attempt, on the part of the civil government, to interpose in the least degree in the affairs of the church, even to help her. All experience has shown that it is less, far less, injurious to the church to be persecuted by the State, than to be pampered by her caresses, and laden with her treasures.

8. A further practical inference from our subject is, that *the trust committed to church rulers is in the highest degree weighty and solemn.* To conduct the momentous affairs of the Christian society, in which so many interests, divine and human, temporal and eternal, are involved; to sit in judgment in cases in which doctrine and order, Christian character and Christian peace and edification are all deeply concerned; to administer the laws of Christ with fidelity, and yet with prudence; with proper zeal for gospel purity, and at the same time with a sacred regard to the church's peace; surely requires all the wisdom, and all the grace that mortals can exercise. The trust committed to civil rulers is, no doubt, in a high degree important and arduous; and will be felt to be so by every thinking man. But to the ecclesiastical ruler are committed interests unspeakably more momentous; which put in requisition all the sagacity, discretion, meekness, benevolence, and zeal for the honour of Zion's King, which belong to the most intelligent and devoted Christian; and in the view of which, he who

sustains the trust ought, with unceasing solicitude, to implore divine aid and guidance. Into this sacred enclosure, prejudice, passion, partiality, rashness, or unhallowed feelings of any kind ought never to be permitted to enter. The grand, and only leading question to be asked, as a guide to duty, is, not what course will tend most effectually to build up this party, or to defeat that adversary; but what course will be most likely to promote the purity, the harmony, and the edification of the church of God? This is a camp in which every banner that is raised, save that of the Redeemer's glory, ought to be held in the deepest abhorrence. Here, if ever, the tribunal of conscience ought to be consulted with the most sacred vigilance, and the statute book of the Master's kingdom studied with unceasing diligence.

9. Another plain inference from all that has been said, is, *that it is incumbent on professing Christians to make themselves acquainted with the subject of church government.* Is every professing Christian a member of that body called the visible church? Does he bear, of course, intimate and most important relations to that body? And has he, consequently, important duties to that body every day devolving upon him? Can it be necessary, then, to demonstrate, that he ought to know something of the nature and structure of this body; to understand, in some good measure, the constitution and laws under which it is not only authorized, but required to act; and the various obligations resting upon its officers and its members? It were an insult, my Friends, to your understandings, to attempt to reason on a point so perfectly self-evident. As well might I consider it as necessary formally to demonstrate, that a member of civil society ought to understand enough of the government under which he lives, to enable him intelligently to discharge the duties of a good citizen, and to avoid violating the law of the land? I have no doubt, indeed, that a man may be a real Christian, who is in a great measure ignorant of the subject on which I have been addressing you this evening. But a wise and intelligent Christian he cannot be. A Christian ready to perceive, to appreciate, and to discharge the various duties which he owes to his Master in heaven, to his brethren of the church, and to his own best edification, he cannot be. And the only wonder is, that so many professing Christians who would be ashamed of ignorance on a thousand other subjects, of far less importance, are willing, on

this subject, to remain profoundly ignorant. Such persons, however sincere and devout, ought to know that they are in danger every hour, when they undertake to speak or ask in reference to this subject, of giving a touch to the ark of God, the character and effect of which, if they understood the subject, they would deprecate in their inmost souls. Many a real Christian, from ignorance of the very elementary principles of this subject, has spoken and acted in such a way as to inflict wounds on the church of God which no subsequent regret or tears could ever heal.

10. The last inference with which I shall tax your patience, is one which, in closing, I must respectfully and affectionately beg all my hearers to remember and lay to heart. It is, *that a man may be perfectly sound on the subject of church government, and yet be utterly defective as to the essentials of Christian character.* There has been a tendency among those who called themselves Christians, in every age, to attempt a kind of commutation with God for that which his Word requires; to substitute rites and forms for the religion of the heart; to cry out with confidence, 'The temple of the Lord, the temple of the Lord are we', while their hearts were going forth after covetousness or sensuality. Hence that fury of zeal for an ecclesiastical name and connection on which many appear to rely as a passport to heaven. Against this fatal mistake, my beloved Friends, I desire to warn you. It is a mistake not confined to any particular denomination; and a mistake as insidious and dangerous as it is prevalent. It is more than possible that a caution, in connection with the subject which we are now considering, may be neither unseasonable, nor useless.

Be entreated, then, my Friends, to lay no stress whatever, as to the great question of your acceptance with God, on the correctness of your opinions and practice as to church government. In the religion of Jesus Christ, as in other matters, there are outworks, and there are vital parts. Real Christianity may exist without the former, but not without the latter. With respect to the former, you may be perfectly fair and faultless; while, in respect to the latter, you may be as 'whited sepulchres'. It is my earnest desire to see you well informed, intelligent, thorough Presbyterians; because I verily believe, as before stated, that this form of ecclesiastical government is more closely conformed to the apostolic model than any other; and better fitted, by far, than any other, to promote all the great ends of government in the church of Christ. But I beseech you to remember, that you may be zealous Presbyterians, and yet not real Christians. You may contend strenuously and ably for those outward forms which Christ has established in his church, and retain every one of them with scrupulous exactness; and yet be strangers to that 'Spirit without which we are none of his'. Let no one, then, who desires to see the face of God in peace, rest in forms of ecclesiastical order, however scriptural. They are important in their place; but they are not that 'holiness without which no man shall see the Lord'. They are useful as means, but they are not the foundation of that 'hope which maketh not ashamed'. While, therefore, we neglect nothing which Christ has revealed; let our first and highest attention be directed to that regeneration of the heart, by which alone we can be 'made meet for the inheritance of the saints in light'; and to that vital union by faith and love to the blessed Saviour, which alone can give us an interest in his atoning blood, and a title to eternal life. Without the sanctifying and justifying power of that blood, no man is a Christian. To this great foundation of gospel hope, then, be entreated, every one of you, my beloved Brethren, first of all, and above all, to turn your eyes and your hearts. Here rest. Here live. Here rejoice, in holy hope of 'the glory that shall be revealed'. And to Father, Son, and Holy Ghost, our God, and our fathers' God, be glory forever! Amen.

THE DUTY, THE BENEFITS, AND
THE PROPER METHOD OF
RELIGIOUS FASTING[1]

And I set my face unto the Lord God,
to seek by prayer and supplication with fasting.
Daniel 9:3

THIS is the language of the prophet Daniel. He is speaking of that which occurred in Babylon, where he and his brethren were in captivity. It was a dark and distressing day. Religion was at a low ebb among the professing people of God. Even their deep adversity had not led them to repentance and reformation. And idolatry, attended with the most deplorable moral corruption, reigned among the heathen around them. Everything, to the eye of sense, appeared in the highest degree discouraging, not to say desperate. But this holy man trusted in God; and in the exercise of faith, saw, beyond the clouds which encircled him and his people, a ray of light which promised at once deliverance and glory. He perceived nothing, indeed, among the mass of his Jewish brethren which indicated a speedy termination of their captivity; but he 'understood by books', that is, he firmly believed, on the ground of a recorded prophecy, delivered by Jeremiah, that the period of their liberation was drawing nigh. In this situation, what does he do? Instead of desponding, he 'encourages himself in the Lord his God'. And, instead of allowing himself to indulge a spirit of presumption or indolence, on account

---

[1] Samuel Miller, 'The Duty, the Benefits, and the Proper Method of Religious Fasting', *The National Preacher*, Vol. 5 No. 10 (March 1831), pp. 145-60.

of the certainty of the approaching deliverance, he considers himself as called to special humiliation, fasting and prayer; to humble himself before God under a sense of the deep unworthiness of himself and his companions in captivity; and to pray with importunity that their unmerited emancipation might be at once hastened and sanctified. Such is the spirit of genuine piety; it neither despairs in adversity, nor is elated with pride at the approach of help. On the contrary, the firmer its confidence in the divine fidelity, the lower does it lie in humility and penitence, and the more powerfully does it excite to holy action, and to holy desires to be a 'worker together with God'; it was when this man of God distinctly understood that the desolations of seventy years were coming to an end, that he 'set his face unto the Lord God to seek by prayer and supplications with fasting'.

The captive Jews in Babylon, as a body, seem to have been in the habit, before this time, of observing certain stated days of fasting and prayer; but they were evidently observed in a formal and heart-less manner; and, therefore, instead of proving a blessing, had but increased their guilt. The exercise of the servant of God, to which our text refers, was of a very different character. It was with him a season of special, earnest, elevated devotion; prompted by special feelings; consecrated to a special object; and accompanied by those special cir-cumstances of humility which indicated a soul deeply abased before God, and fervently engaged in pleading for his blessing.

I shall take occasion from the example of Daniel to consider the duty of fasting, as a suitable and very important accompaniment of special humiliation and prayer. And in pursuance of this design, I shall request your attention to the *duty,* the *benefits,* and the *proper method of religious fasting.* After which the way will be prepared for some remarks more immediately practical.

I. The *duty of religious fasting* will claim our attention in the first place. It is unnecessary to say that fasting is abstinence from food. It is not, however, every kind of abstinence that constitutes a *religious fast.* Some abstain from their usual aliment because, from indisposi-tion, they loathe it; others, because they cannot obtain it; and a third class, because abstinence is enjoined by medical prescription. But the Christian, as such, refrains from choice, denying his appetite from religious principle, and with a view to spiritual benefit. Now, when it is affirmed that occasional fasting, in this sense, and with this view, is a Christian duty, it is not intended to be maintained that it is one of those stated duties which all are bound to attend upon at certain fixed periods, whatever may be their situation, or the aspect of providence towards them. There is no precept in the Word of God which enjoins the observance of a particular number of fast days in each year. It is to be considered as an occasional, or, perhaps, more properly speaking, a special duty, which, like seasons of special prayer, ought to be regulated, as to its frequency and manner of observance, by the circumstances in which we are placed. But although the times and seasons of religious fasting be left, as they obviously must be, to the judgment and the conscience of each individual, it may be confidently affirmed, that it is a divine institution; that it is a duty on which all Christians are bound, at proper seasons, to attend. This, it is believed, may be firmly established by the following considerations.

1. The *light of nature* seems to recognize this duty. Abstinence from food, either as an aid or an expression of piety, has been common in all ages, and among all nations. Those who have attended to the various forms of paganism, know that in all of them fasting has had a place, and in some of them a very prominent place. In entering on important undertakings, and in preparing for sacrifices of more than common solemnity, their fasts were often protracted and rigid to an almost incredible degree. Now, the question is, how came this practice to be so general, nay universal, among those, whether polished or barbarous, who enjoyed no written revelation? Was it a dictate of nature? Then our position is established. If abstinence from food be a natural expression of deep humiliation and mourning, no further argument is necessary to show that it ought to accompany seasons of special prayer, and peculiar approach to God. Was it the result of tradition, handing down to all generations the practice of the first parents of our race, received from him who made them, and placed them, with the knowledge of his will, under a dispensation of mercy? Then is our position still more firmly established. From one or the other of these sources, the practice must have been derived; and either of them will go far towards furnishing the warrant in question.

2. The *examples* of religious fasting recorded in the Word of God, are multiplied and very decisive in their character. Out of many which might be selected, the following are worthy of special notice:—

Joshua, and the elders of Israel, evidently kept a solemn fast, when their people were defeated by the men of Ai; for they remained all day, from morning till eventide, prostrate on their faces before the ark, with dust on their heads, in exercises of the deepest humiliation and prayer. David, we are expressly told, fasted, as well as prayed, while he humbled himself under a heavy judgment of God, sent on him for his sin in the matter of Uriah. Even the hardened Ahab fasted and cried for mercy, when the judgments of God were denounced against him by the prophet Elijah. The pious and public-spirited Nehemiah, while he was yet in Babylon, set apart a season of special prayer accompanied with fasting, when he heard of the desolations of the city and people of God:—and afterward, when he came to Jerusalem, he proclaimed a public and solemn fast, to deplore the low state of religion, and to pray for pardoning and restoring mercy. Jehoshaphat, king of Judah, appointed a day of fasting and prayer throughout his kingdom, when the confederated forces of Ammon and Moab came up against him. The inhabitants of Nineveh, though pagans, when the prophet of God proclaimed his approaching judgments, immediately set apart a season of special prayer and fasting, in which not only all the adult inhabitants, but also their infants, and the very beasts that served them, were required to abstain from all aliment, 'For it was proclaimed and published by the decree of the king and his nobles, saying,—Let neither man nor beast, herd nor flock, taste any thing; let them not feed nor drink water; but let man and beast be covered with sackcloth, and cry mightily unto God.' When Queen Esther felt herself and her people to be in danger from the conspiracy of Haman, she set apart a season of solemn prayer and fasting; that is, as she explains it, neither eating nor drinking for three days in succession, in which all her maidens in the palace, and all the Jews in Shushan, were united. The devoted and inspired Ezra, when setting out on his important mission to Jerusalem, assembled the returning captives at the river Ahava, and there 'proclaimed a fast, that they might afflict themselves before God, and seek of him a right way for themselves and their little ones, and for all their substance'. And it is remarkable that the blessing of God attended the exercise of fasting in every one of these cases. The armies of Joshua were, thenceforward, victorious. David, though deprived of the child for whose life he prayed, was forgiven his great sin. Nineveh, though exceedingly guilty, was spared. Jehoshaphat was made to triumph over his formidable enemies. Even the impenitent Ahab was favoured with the delay of that dreadful judgment which had been denounced against him. Esther and her people experienced a signal deliverance. And Ezra obtained the blessing which he sought with such humble importunity.

After the coming of Christ, we find the same practice continued, and making a part of almost every extraordinary season of devotion. Jesus Christ himself entered on his public ministry after a long season of preparatory fasting. And although there is no doubt that his was a case of miraculous abstinence, still the general principle held forth and countenanced is the same. We find also the apostles, in almost every instance of setting apart candidates for the gospel ministry, accompanying the ordination solemnities with fasting. The pious Anna, the prophetess, was engaged in 'serving God, day and night, with fastings and prayers'. When the Lord appeared to Cornelius, the 'devout' centurion, and imparted the knowledge of his will to him, we are informed he was engaged in fasting and prayer. And the Apostle Paul speaks repeatedly of his habit of waiting on God by fastings, as well as by prayer, and other means of divine appointment. In short, we scarcely find in all the scriptural record, either in the Old or New Testament, a single example of an extraordinary season of humiliation and prayer which was not accompanied by the abstinence of which we speak.

Now, I ask, can it be supposed that a fact so frequently repeated concerning pious people,—in so great a variety of situations, from early periods of the Bible history to its very close,—could have occurred by mere accident or caprice? It cannot be. That which stands forth sanctioned by the example of the people of God in all ages, and by the author of our holy religion himself, is surely no human device, but an institution of heaven.

3. Again, we may infer that religious fasting is a divine institution from *a variety of precepts and direct intimations found in various parts of Scripture, especially in the New Testament.*

And here I shall say nothing of the fixed periodical fasts solemnly enjoined under the ceremonial economy, as all grant that these are superseded by the new dispensation, and that no specific days have been divinely appointed to succeed them. But it is remarkable that, even under the ceremonial economy, besides the stated fasts, occasional ones were ordered by the express command of God. Thus Jehovah proclaims to the people of Judah, by the prophet Joel, in a day of great political and moral desolation—'Sanctify a fast; call a solemn assembly; gather the elders and all the inhabitants of the land into the house of the Lord your God, and cry unto the Lord.' But there are more than intimations to the same amount in the New Testament. Take, as an example of these, that remarkable passage in our Lord's Sermon on the Mount. 'Moreover, when ye fast, be not as the hypocrites, of a sad countenance; for they disfigure their faces, that they may appear unto men to fast. Verily, I say unto you, they have their reward. But thou, when thou fastest [evidently taking for granted that they must and would fast]—anoint thine head and wash thy face; that thou appear not unto men to fast, but unto thy Father which is in secret; and thy Father which seeth in secret shall reward thee openly.' Again, our blessed Saviour, in speaking of some of the higher attainments in Christian character and power, says—'But this kind goeth not out but by prayer and fasting.' And again, when some persons asked him, 'Why do the disciples of John, and of the Pharisees fast often, but thy disciples fast not?'—he replied—'Can the children of the bride-chamber fast, while the bridegroom is with them! As long as they have the bridegroom with them they cannot fast. But the days will come when the bridegroom shall be taken away from them, and then shall they fast in those days.' And, accordingly, as I have already hinted, we find a number of striking examples of fasting, on occasions of special prayer, after our Lord ascended to heaven, and before the close of the inspired history. And the Apostle Paul, in the seventh chapter of the First Epistle to the Corinthians, in speaking of Christians withdrawing for a time from the ordinary concerns and relations of life, gives it his sanction,—and assigns a reason for it,—'that they may give themselves to prayer and fasting'.

But the duty of religious fasting will be still further illustrated and confirmed, when we consider,—

II. In the second place, the *benefits* which may be expected to result from the proper performance of this duty. And in reference to this point, *it behooves us to be ever upon our guard against the dictates of a vain superstition.* For, as the practice of fasting for religious purposes has probably been in the world ever since the fall of man, and we have every reason to suppose was thus early received from the Author of our being; so this practice began very early, like every other divine appointment, to be perverted and abused. The heathen evidently considered it as highly meritorious, and as purchasing for them the favour of the deities whom they vainly worshipped. And some of the ancient heretics, supposing that there was, as they expressed it, a certain 'malignity in matter', and that the less they had to do, in any shape, with material objects, the better,—taught their followers to consider abstinence, as far as possible, from all aliment, and especially from animal food, as in itself constituting the highest merit in the sight of God, and as one of the most important and essential of all duties. Hence they imagined that the more anyone mortified, enfeebled, and emaciated his body, without destroying life, the nearer he approached to moral perfection. But not only did the early heretics fall into the grossest superstition on this subject, the great body of professing Christians, very soon after the apostles' days, began to pervert the practice of fasting to superstitious purposes. Christians, in fact, began very early to be corrupted by Gnostic dreams, and pagan habits. As early as the close of the second century, they seem to have commenced the practice of observing Wednesday and Friday of every week as days of fasting. Not long after, we find them observing one great annual fast, to commemorate the death of the blessed Saviour. This fast was kept, after its commencement, for different periods of time, by different persons; plainly showing, as indeed many of them confessed, that it had no divine appointment for its origin, but was a mere uncommanded invention of man. Some kept it for one day; but the more common practice was to keep it for precisely forty hours, because they supposed it was just about forty hours from the time of our Lord's death until he rose from the dead. And hence it was called, in the ancient calendars, the *quadragesimal fastut*, or the fast of forty. This time, however, as early as the sixth century after Christ, was extended, by human superstition, to forty days, instead of forty hours; and the reason assigned for this change was, that the Saviour himself fasted forty days and forty nights. Of this annual fast, as well as of all the Fridays in the year, the Romish Church has long been in the habit of making a most superstitious use. The more serious and devout among them make themselves, without any divine warrant, the perfect slaves of this observance, and consider eating meat in Lent, or on Friday, as a mortal sin. Still more servile, if possible, is the rigour of Mohammedan fasting. The votaries of that imposture consider periodical abstinence from food as forming a large part of the duty of an exemplary Mohammedan, and perhaps, next to the pilgrimage to Mecca, as the most important part of the price of heaven. And, in conformity with this delusion, the whole of their month Ramadan, the ninth in their year, is a great fast, during which the law of their religion is that no one shall eat or drink, or suffer the least particle of aliment to pass his lips, from the commencement to the termination of light, on each day.

Now, all this is weakly and criminally superstitious. For 'meat', as the inspired apostle expressly tells us, 'commendeth us not to God; for neither if we eat are we the better; neither if we eat not are we the worse'. And, therefore, in estimating the benefits of religious fasting, we ascribe to it no mystical charm, no sanctifying power. We have no idea that there is any merit in macerating and enfeebling the body; nor can we regard with any other sentiment than that of abhorrence, the doctrine that abstaining from particular kinds of food ever did or can make expiation for sin, or serve, in any form, as the price of our acceptance with God.

But we consider religious fasting, when properly conducted, as attended with the following benefits:—

1. *It is a natural and significant expression of our penitence for sin.* We may say, perhaps, that the primary design, the most obvious and immediate object of fasting is to mortify and afflict the body, as a token of our penitence before God; as an acknowledgment of our entire dependence upon him for all our comforts, and also of our utter unworthiness of them as sinners. For as few things more effectually destroy the inclination for food than great distress of mind, so there seems to be no more suitable emblem of real mourning for sin, than voluntarily refraining from food. Fasting is also a proper

expression of penitence, inasmuch as it carries with it an implied confession that all our comforts, even to a morsel of bread, are forfeited by sin; and that we might justly be deprived of them all, if a holy God should 'deal with us after our sins, or reward us according to our iniquities'. To which may be added, that the inconvenience to which abstinence from food gives rise, is well adapted to make us feel how entirely dependent we are on the bounty of providence, not only for our enjoyment, but also for our very existence, from day to day.

2. Another very important benefit of religious fasting is, *that by denying the animal appetite we 'keep under the body, and bring it into subjection'*. The tendency of the flesh in our fallen nature to gain the mastery over our better part, is that great standing evidence of our depravity which the Word of God everywhere recognizes, and which all history, and daily observation, with melancholy uniformity, establish. This unhallowed dominion is first broken when the 'reign of grace' commences in the heart. But still the carnal principle, 'the flesh', as the Scriptures call it, has too much influence even in the most pious; and to mortify and subdue it is the great object of the spiritual warfare, from its commencement to the last moment of the conflict. When, therefore, the professing Christian indulges the flesh, and pampers appetite over a plentiful table, from day to day, he nourishes this unfriendly principle, gives it strength, and, of course, increases its power over his better part. It is undoubtedly found by universal experience, that when the body is constantly gratified by fulness of aliment, it is more heavy, more sensual, and imparts to the mind a more fleshly and lethargic character, than when the appetite has been wisely denied. Hence it will always be found that habitual luxury, in direct proportion to the degree in which it is indulged, is unfavourable to deep spirituality. Probably they were never found united in any individual, since the world began. On this principle is founded the importance of that self-denial, which our blessed Saviour requires as a distinguishing characteristic of his disciples. Upon this principle rests that great gospel maxim delivered by the apostle; 'They that are Christ's have crucified the flesh with the affections and lusts.' Now, one of the most obvious means of effecting this purpose is to deny the appetite for food. This tends emphatically to 'keep under the body'; to restrain animal desire; to counteract sensuality;

and to promote a holy superiority to all those 'fleshly lusts which war against the soul'. Accordingly, it may be asserted, that in all ages, those Christians who have been most distinguished for 'mortifying the deeds of the body', bringing it 'into subjection', and 'setting their affections upon things above', have been no less remarkable for the frequency and seriousness of their seasons of religious fasting.

3. A third benefit to be derived from fasting, when properly conducted, is, *that it renders the mind more active, clear, and vigorous.* The connection between mind and body, however mysterious, is yet manifest and familiar. And there is, perhaps, no fact in the whole history of this connection which experience more uniformly attests, than that repletion is unfriendly to the highest and most successful mental operations. The seeming exceptions to this law of our nature are so few, and of such a character, as rather to confirm than contradict it. He, therefore, who desires to attain the highest efforts, and the best products of his intellectual faculties, must often abstain, either in whole or in part, from his usual amount of bodily aliment, even though that amount be habitually moderate. Fasting, then, is, beyond all controversy, one of the best preparatives for high intellectual effort. It imparts a degree of acuteness to the understanding, of vigour to the imagination, and of activity and promptness to the memory, which are not experienced in other circumstances. Hence, it is well known, that some of the ancient pagan philosophers, when about to meet their adversaries in public debate, were in the habit of entering on the conflict fasting, that their intellectual powers might be more awake, acute, and active. Did they cheerfully submit to this privation, for the purpose of preparing their minds for meeting with advantage a fellow worm? And shall Christians refuse to submit to the same privation, for preparing them to wait upon God with alacrity, and with holy elevation of sentiment and affection? If any man be desirous of preparing his mind for the highest acts of devotion; for the most complete withdrawment, for a time, from the world; for being lifted above the vanities and sensualities of life; for collecting and fastening his whole soul on God and heavenly things,—among other means of attaining his hallowed object, let him not omit to accompany them with real fasting. He who neglects this precious auxiliary to devotion (for so it assuredly deserves to be called), has

not well considered either the structure of his own frame, or the spirit of the Word of God.

4. A further advantage accruing from well conducted religious fasting is, *that it ministers essentially to the bodily health*. Few things are more severely trying and ultimately undermining to the human body than habitual repletion. A statesman and philosopher of our own country, distinguished at once for his talents, his practical character, his vigorous health, and his long life, was accustomed to observe a fast either total or partial one day in every week, assigning as the reason of it, no religious motive, but that he wished 'to give nature a holiday'. And he had no doubt of its solid benefit to his bodily health. The practice, I am persuaded, was founded in the clearest and soundest principles of physiology. Truly our nature needs such a 'holiday' much oftener than we are willing to yield it. The most enlightened physicians have given it as their opinion, that thousands accounted temperate, and really so in the popular sense of the term, are bringing themselves to premature graves for want of such a frequent respite from the burden of aliment as an occasional day of fasting would furnish. It is plain, then, that any sacred religious habit which secures such a respite; which tends, in the course of each month and week, to preserve us from the effects of habitual indulgence and repletion, cannot fail of contributing to the preservation and vigour of our bodily health, as well as preparing our minds for prompt and active application to the most important of all objects.

5. There is one more advantage of frequent religious fasting by no means to be despised. I mean *making it systematically subservient to the purposes of charity*. Some pious persons, whose pecuniary circumstances were narrow, but whose love to God and their fellowmen was uncommonly fervent, have practised fasting, in part at least, upon this plan. They have constantly omitted one meal in a week, and sometimes more, that they might be able to give to those who were still poorer than themselves, what the meal or meals in question would have cost them. I have no doubt that this will strike some wordly-minded, sensual professors of religion as an extreme, and as almost a ridiculous, if not a contemptible effort of benevolence. But I will say, in the language of a narrator of such a case—'Such charity, instead of being contemptible, shows a strength of principle and a

greatness of soul beyond the ordinary standard; and a self-denial, so applied, adds magnanimity to benevolence.' And I will venture to say, further, that if every professing Christian in the United States, would consent to omit as many meals in each year as upon every principle he ought, and would honestly throw the value of them, annually, into the Lord's treasury, for sending the gospel to the benighted heathen, and to the destitute everywhere; not only would his bodily health be better, his life probably longer and happier, and his soul more richly fed and edified; but were nothing else cast into that treasury, there would the pecuniary means sufficient for sustaining all the Bible and missionary operations that American zeal and instrumentality could carry on, for the benefit of every part of the world.

Let me entreat you, then, my Friends, to lay these considerations seriously to heart. A duty so manifestly founded on the divine will, and attended with so many important benefits, cannot be disregarded without both sin and loss. Remember that it involves interests concerning which you are not at liberty to 'confer with flesh and blood'. And remember, too, that in this whole concern, you have to do with him who 'weigheth the spirits'—who 'cannot be deceived and will not be mocked'.

Having considered the duty and the benefits of religious fasting, we are now to—

III. Consider, in the third place, that *method* of observing a religious fast which will render it truly profitable.

And I begin this head by remarking that the frequency with which every individual Christian ought to fast, and the extent to which he ought to carry his abstinence on each occasion, are questions concerning which no definite rule can be laid down. The Word of God prescribes no precise law, as to either of these points. The whole subject is left, as the subject of almsgiving is left, to every man's conscience in the sight of God. No one can open the Bible without perceiving that we are bound to give alms to those who need them; that 'we have the poor always with us, that whensoever we will we may do them good'. But how often, and how much we are bound to give, is nowhere said. Yet I have no doubt that in the great duty of fasting, as well as of alms giving, where the heart is right with God, and where there is a sincere and humble desire to walk in that course which is adapted to promote our best interest, there will be no material mistake with regard to the path of duty. That degree of abstinence which is salutary and not uncomfortable to one, would be deeply injurious as well as painful to another. The great *end* of the duty is to be regarded. God 'will have mercy and not sacrifice'. Fasting, like the Sabbath, was made for man, and not man for fasting. No one, therefore, ought to carry abstinence to such an extreme as to impair or endanger his bodily health; of which there have been, undoubtedly, some mournful examples, both in ancient and modern times. We have no more right to injure our bodies, than we have to enfeeble or derange our minds. Yet this, it must be acknowledged, is by no means the extreme to which the mass of professing Christians, at the present day, are inclined. On the contrary, it is manifest that the tendency in general is to deficiency rather than excess in this important duty. For one who injures himself by the excessive frequency or protraction of his seasons of abstinence, thousands, it is probable, either wholly neglect this self-denying duty, or perform it in a most superficial and inadequate manner.

The abstinence in religious fasting may be either total or partial. When it is continued for a single day only, it ought in many cases to be total; and, with most persons, may be so, not only without injury, but with profit. Of this everyone must conscientiously judge for himself. But when the fast is continued through several successive days,—as it sometimes ought to be, in a great physical or moral crisis of life;—then, it is obvious, the abstinence should be only partial; that is, aliment ought to be sparingly taken, not to gratify appetite, but merely to sustain nature. The prophet Daniel, in a period of protracted, pious humiliation, tells us that he 'ate no pleasant bread, neither came flesh nor wine into his mouth'. Nor let anyone imagine that it is not his duty to fast, because the abstinence of a single day, and even from a single meal, in some degree incommodes his feelings. This is no valid objection to the duty. In fact, as you have heard, one great design of the privation is to 'afflict the soul', to humble us under a sense of our weakness and dependence, and to remind us, by a feeling of want, of the purpose for which we submit to the privation. If no such feeling were induced, an important purpose of the exercise would be defeated. Thousands were fully persuaded a few years ago that total abstinence from that fell destroyer, ardent spirit, would weaken their bodies and injure their health. But no man ever honestly made the experiment, without finding that his fears had all been delusive. No less delusive, be assured, is the plea that you cannot comply, in an enlightened manner, with the Christian duty of fasting, without injury, either physical or moral. To those who think otherwise, I would say—Have you ever fairly made the trial? If you think you have, make it again, in the fear of God, and with humble prayer for divine direction. And imagine not that a mere feeling of emptiness, and even of importunate hunger, must necessarily mark the approach of mischief. So far from this, they are feelings which you often need, for your physical as well as moral benefit; and no injury will be likely to flow from them, when carried to a proper length, unless unguardedly followed by an excessive indulgence of appetite.

The duty of fasting may be considered as devolving on men in all the circumstances and relations in which they are placed. Seasons of devout fasting ought, undoubtedly, to be observed by individuals, in private, with a special reference to their own personal sins, wants, and trials; by families, who have often much reason as such, for special humiliation and prayer; by particular churches, whose circumstances are frequently such as to call for seasons of peculiar mourning, penitence, and supplication; by whole denominations of Christians, who have very often occasion to humble themselves before God on account of the absence of his Spirit, and the prevalence of some great evils in the midst of them; and, finally, by nations, when suffering under the righteous displeasure of God, or when sensible that, for their sins, they are exposed to his heavy judgments. Of all these we have examples in the Word of God; and if the spirit of the gospel were reigning in the midst of us, we should often see examples of them all at the present day.—But to pursue the inquiry:—

In delineating the *method* in which a religious fast ought to be kept, let it be observed,—

1. First of all, that it will be outwardly kept in vain, *unless the heart be sincerely engaged in the service.* Let pagans, Mohammedans, and nominal Christians, flatter themselves, as you have heard, with the dream that the mere physical observance of abstinence, independent of the state of the soul, will recommend them to God. But let

us remember, that the character and exercises of the inner man are everything here. Yes, my Friends, in fasting, as well as praying, the engagement of the heart is the great and essential matter. There is no piety in merely abstaining from food, aside from the spirit and the purpose with which it is done. It is in this case as in the observance of the Sabbath. A man may shut himself up from all the world on that day; or he may spend the whole of it in the house of God; and yet, if his heart be all the time going after the world, he does not sanctify the Sabbath at all, in the most important sense of the term. So it is in the case before us. We may keep multitudes of fast-days, with all the external exactness of Popish, or even Mohammedan, rigour, and yet be nothing the better for them;—nay, instead of receiving benefit, may contract guilt by them all. A holy God might, and doubtless would, still say unto us, as he did, in substance, to his professing people of old—'Is this such a fast as I have chosen? Have ye fasted to me, even to me, saith the Lord?—This people draweth nigh unto me with their mouth, and honoureth me with their lips; but their heart is far from me;—their appointed fasts are an abomination unto me; I am weary to bear them.'—The primary consideration, then, in keeping a religious fast, is that the whole soul be truly engaged in the work; that while we use the outward symbol of humiliation and penitence, we labour to have our minds deeply occupied and affected with the humbling realities which we express with our lips. A heartless and hypocritical prayer, in any cir-cumstances, is a virtual insult to him to whom it is addressed:—but a heartless and hypocritical fast seems to be a double insult, because offered under the guise of double solemnity and humility. In search-ing, therefore, for the characteristics of an 'acceptable fast', we must begin here. The more deeply, feelingly, and constantly the heart is engaged in the service, the more pleasing to God, and the more profitable to ourselves will it ever be found.

2. While the state of the heart is everything here,—*a real abstinence from aliment is also essential to the proper and acceptable performance of this duty.* Such a remark as this may appear to many unnecessary; and I should certainly so deem it, were there not some serious per-sons who adopt, and endeavour to inculcate, the strange notion, that nothing more is implied in the duty in question, than 'fasting', as they

express it, 'in spirit': meaning, by the phrase, mere moral abstinence, or 'abstinence from sin'.—Hence, those who adopt this opinion suppose that a regular and acceptable gospel fast may be kept, while the animal appetite is fully indulged as usual, provided there be an effort made, for a season, greater than usual to shut out evil, and to maintain a spiritual and devout frame. In this sense they interpret that solemn passage in the fifty-eighth chapter of the prophecy of Isaiah;—'Is not this the fast that I have chosen? to loose the bands of wickedness, *etc.*' In this pointed appeal it is manifest we are to understand Jehovah not as saying that 'loosing the bands of wickedness' includes everything that belongs to a religious fast; but that true penitence, and moral reformation, form, as we have before intimated, its best accompaniment, and its most essential fruits. I am constrained, then, to consider the notion which I am opposing as a mere evasion, and not a very plausible one, of a plain Christian duty. It is nothing less than egregious trifling with the heart-searching God, and cheating ourselves by a miserable subterfuge. We might just as well talk of giving alms 'in spirit', or paying our debts 'in spirit'. No, my Friends, real abstinence from food is, no doubt, intended in all the examples and precepts which are given us on this subject in the Word of God. And we 'rob him', and 'wrong our own souls', when we shrink from the literal self-denial implied in the abstinence in question. In fact those who decline submitting to the literal privation of food of which we speak, not only contravene both the letter and spirit of Scripture, when describing an acceptable fast; but they entirely give up some of the most important benefits to which, as we have seen, this privation is naturally subservient.

3. It is important to the proper observance of a religious fast, that *we retire, during its continuance, as much as possible from the world, shut out its illusions, and endeavour to break its hold of our hearts.* One grand object of observing such days at all is that we may occasionally come to a solemn pause; that we may break the spell which is so apt to bind us down to the grovelling pursuits of time and sense; and take an honest retrospect of our infirmities, failures, and sins. It is of the utmost importance, therefore, that in solemnities which have such an object, we should sacredly withdraw, for the time, from all worldly cares and allurements; that we should put a firm negative upon every appetite and passion which might tend

to drag us down to the dust of earth; and try to get away from the snares and entanglements of this passing scene. With the utmost propriety, then, when a public fast is proclaimed, it is commonly recommended that all servile labour and recreation be laid aside. This is no less important to the spiritual observance of the day, than as a testimony of outward respect. And quite as indispensable is it, when an individual or a family resolve to fast in private, that every occupation be as far as possible suspended, which may even remotely tend to draw off the mind from an entire and unreserved devotion, to the appropriate exercises of the day.

4. Days of religious fasting are to be *devoted to a deep and heartfelt recollection of our sins; and unfeigned repentance for them*. It is true, indeed, that in all seasons of special as well as ordinary prayer, our mercies as well as our sins ought to be recollected and acknowledged. And, therefore, in celebrating a religious fast, thanksgiving is by no means inappropriate or to be forgotten. It is matter of thankfulness to a sinner, in any situation, that he is out of hell; and, surely, the sinner who is truly penitent can never see greater reason for gratitude, than when he is deeply pondering before God the number and aggravation of his sins; and remembers, that to such a rebel, life and glory are offered. Still, it is evident that the primary object of a religious fast is evangelical humiliation. To attempt to keep such a fast, then, without entering deeply into the consideration of our sins, and mourning over them, is really to place out of sight the most prominent object of the observance. This is peculiarly 'a day for a man to afflict his soul' for all the pollutions of his nature, for all the evil he hath done, and for all the abominations which are committed around him. This is a season in which it is incumbent upon us, if ever, to call to mind with cordial penitence our personal sins, our family sins, the sins of the church, and of the nation; to labour, if I may so speak, with concentrated effort, to take strong, profound, and abasing views of their heinousness in the sight of God; to meditate upon them again and again, until the heart is in some measure broken and contrite; to repent, as in dust and ashes; and to apply anew to that atoning blood, by which alone our guilt can be washed away, and to that 'Holy Spirit of promise', who alone can destroy the reign of corruption, and 'heal

all our backslidings'. Such exercises, though humiliating, 'do good as doth a medicine'. Blessed are they who thus mourn,' for 'they shall be comforted'.

5. As days of religious fasting ought ever to be marked by a special recognition, and a deep sense of our sins; *so this recognition, if it be of the right stamp, will ever be followed by genuine reformation.* That confession, which is not succeeded by amendment, is worse than vain. It is manifestly heartless, and, of course, adding sin to sin. Where the heart is really broken and contrite on account of transgression, that transgression will be sincerely loathed and forsaken. If, therefore, a season of humiliation and fasting leave us as much in love with sin, and as hardened in habits of iniquity as it found us, there is abundant evidence, not merely that we have failed of being profited, but that we have contracted guilt by the observance. Hence we find a holy God expressing his righteous displeasure, and denouncing his severest judgments against his professing people of old; because, while they wearied him with their fastings and prayers they remained as obdurate and disobedient as ever. To such he declares, 'When they fast, I will not hear their cry; and when they offer burnt offerings and an oblation, I will not accept them; but I will consume them by the sword, and by the famine, and by the pestilence.'

6. *In keeping a religious fast, everything like ostentation, or self-righteousness, should be put far from us.* The Jewish hypocrites, in the days of our Lord's ministry, displayed much of this unseemly spirit. As they loved to 'pray standing at the corners of the streets, that they might be seen of men'; so even in their private fasts (for to these the Saviour seems to have had a particular reference in reproving them), they put on 'a sad countenance, and disfigured their faces, that they might appear to men to fast'. And when the Pharisee went up to the temple to pray, it was one of the grounds of his boasting, and his confidence toward God, that he 'fasted twice in a week'. In both these cases, our Lord denounces the spirit which they manifested, as diametrically opposed to all true religion, and warns his disciples against it. And, truly, if there be any exercise in the Christian's life, from which a spirit of ostentatious display and of proud self-dependence ought to be shut out with abhorrence, it is when he is prostrate

before the throne of mercy, professing to mourn over his sins, and to acknowledge his ill-desert in the sight of God. Then, surely, if ever, the most unfeigned abasement of soul, the most cordial self-renunciation, the most heart-felt application to and reliance upon the righteousness of the divine Surety, as the only ground of hope, ought not only to be expressed in every word that is uttered by the lips, but to reign in every feeling, affection, and hope of the inmost soul. The only language ever becoming the redeemed sinner, and especially in such a season as this, is, 'God be merciful to me a sinner!' 'God forbid that I should glory, save in the cross of the Lord Jesus Christ, by whom the world is crucified unto me, and I unto the world.'

7. Once more, Christian fasting *ought ever to be accompanied with more or less of sympathy and benevolence to the destitute.* This point has already been alluded to; but a distinct notice of it in this connection is indispensable. The Word of God lays much stress upon it as a concomitant and evidence of acceptable fasting. 'Is not this such a fast as I have chosen', says Jehovah by the prophet, 'that thou deal thy bread to the hungry; that thou bring the poor that are cut out to thy house; when thou seest the naked, that thou cover him; and that you hide not thyself from thine own flesh?' What occasion so appropriate to sympathize with those who are hungry from necessity, as when we submit to the privation from choice, and as an aid to prayer, in approaching him who is the common benefactor of the rich and the poor? With many people, it is almost as much a matter of mortification and self-denial,—that is, it requires almost as much, and, in some cases, even more, of painful effort,—to give a trifle to the poor, as it does to abstain, when hungry, from a favourite meal. It appears peculiarly proper, then, for all professing Christians, and especially for those who feel this backwardness to an important duty, always to make their seasons of special prayer occasions of liberality, in some form, to the indigent. Surely there are few things more reasonable and becoming than that, while we are engaged in mourning over our sins, and confessing our unworthiness of the least of all our comforts, we should practically show mercy to others, as our heavenly Father has done to us. Then is the time to devise plans of mercy and benevolence, to cherish forgiveness of injuries, to make restitution to those whom we may have injured, to feed the hungry,

and clothe the naked, and cause 'the widow's heart to sing for joy'. Above all, such a solemnity is an appropriate season for devising the best of all charity to the benighted, perishing heathen:—for opening the heart in prayer and contributions, that the precious Bible and the living teacher may be sent to the millions who have never heard that 'faithful saying, and worthy of all acceptation, that Jesus Christ came into the world to save sinners'.

The foregoing discussion suggests a number of *practical reflections;* to several of which your serious attention is requested.

1. From what has been said, it is evident that *the great duty of religious fasting is by far too much neglected.* It is a self-denying duty; having nothing in it adapted to gratify either the reign of appetite, or the love of praise. It is an unfashionable duty. Even many serious professors of religion have no taste for fast-days. Indeed, they are agreeable to the natural inclination of no man. They are seldom, there is too much reason to believe, observed in private; and when recommended by public authority, either in church or State, the honest and faithful observance of them is confined, I fear, to a small part even of those who profess to take the Word of God for their guide. This is deeply to be lamented. It argues a low standard of piety in the church generally. If the spirit of the apostolic days were more prevalent, if we had more of the spirit of Baxter, and Flavel, and Brainerd, and Edwards, and Payson, there would be a much more frequent recurrence than there now is, to this important auxiliary of special prayer. It would be much oftener resorted to by individual Christians, and more especially by ministers, in bewailing before God the small measure of their success. We should never hear of an ordination service being disgraced by a sumptuous dinner, instead of solemn fasting. We should be told of churches in every direction availing themselves of this rational and gospel means of adding interest, and feeling, and humiliation to their seasons of special prayer for the descent of the Holy Spirit. In a word, we may say of deep and spiritual piety—'This kind goeth not out but by prayer and fasting.' And until the latter shall be extensively restored, we cannot rationally expect to see the former revived and prevalent. Dear Brethren, we pray in words, we pray abundantly, for the universal revival of religion and the dawn of millennial glory; and, when we hear of those triumphs of the Holy Spirit's power in

various parts of our land, over which, we doubt not, there is 'joy in heaven', as well as on earth,—we feel as if we had ample encouragement to prayer. We have the highest encouragement. But we have no reason to expect that we shall receive these blessings, and certainly shall not be suitably prepared for their arrival, unless we are found waiting for them with that deep contrition and humiliation, as well as longing, importunity of spirit, which belong to the frequent and faithful discharge of the duty now recommended.

2. We are led to reflect, by what has been said, on *the reason why fast-days, even when appointed, and decently observed, are productive of so little beneficial effect.* The plain reason is, that religious fasting, when attempted, is seldom attended upon honestly and sincerely, in the appropriate spirit of the institution. The abstinence from food; the deep and peculiar humiliation of soul, which professedly accompanies it; and the solemn vows and efforts to 'crucify the flesh with the affections and lusts', which it implies,—are all so distasteful to the carnal principle, that they are seldom sincerely, much less thoroughly, carried into effect. The exercise is made, for the most part, a formal and superficial one; and leaves those who undertake to perform it, perhaps, more cold and unfeeling than before. So that, I fear, many of our fast-days, in modern times, as was certainly the case in times of old, become the means of hardening, instead of softening the heart; and of drawing down the hotter displeasure of God upon us, instead of averting his wrath. Unless we enter cordially and in good earnest into the real design of such days, we had better never pretend to observe them. They are but solemn mockery. And, perhaps, on no occasion have we more reason than on the approach of such a season, whether private or public, to pray fervently that the Holy Spirit may enable us to sanctify it in a manner well pleasing to God, and to the furtherance of his cause in our hearts, and around us.

3. Another reflection suggested by what has been said is, that *every part of the service enjoined upon us as Christians is a reasonable service.* None of the commandments of God are grievous. For every duty that he requires of us, there is a just and adequate reason; and a reason which makes as much for our own true welfare and happiness, as for the glory of him who lays the duty upon us. We see, for example, that religious fasting is not enjoined for its own sake; or because it has

any inherent power to recommend us to God; or because he delights to inflict upon us the pain of privation; but because, when properly conducted, it tends to promote the benefit of both our souls and our bodies. It is favourable to our bodily health. It is friendly to the culture and strength of our intellectual faculties. It is an important means of mortifying and subduing our corrupt passions, of weaning us from sin, and of promoting our true happiness here and hereafter. Thus the wisdom as well as the goodness of God appears in all that he requires of us. If our nature were not morally diseased, we should not stand in need of so much discipline, and discipline of the corporeal as well as of the mental kind. But as our nature is deeply diseased, we must not wonder at our constant need of medicine, which, though not commonly pleasant to the taste, is always salutary when properly applied. Instead of repining that we need it, or, needing it, that our heavenly sovereign has placed us under a dispensation which requires us to use it, let us be thankful and submissive. The principles of his government are as benignant as they are holy. 'Godliness is profitable unto all things, having the promise of the life that now is, and of that which is to come.'

4. Finally, from the foregoing view of the subject, the reflection is obvious, *that we have no less reason for fasting and humiliation than our fathers of former ages.* Let us not imagine that there was some special character either in the men or the events of ancient times, which rendered the exercise in question more needful to them than to us. By no means; human nature is the same; religion is the same, and the causes of Christian mourning are the same now, as they were when Joshua, Daniel, Nehemiah, and Paul fasted and laid in the dust before the mercy-seat. What though the number of the hopefully pious be greater in our day than in theirs? What though the God of all grace has gladdened the hearts of his people in many places, by 'pouring out his Spirit', and 'reviving his work'? How many millions of our fellow men around us still remain in hardened rebellion! How many churches in our land, notwithstanding all the precious revivals with which it has pleased God to favour us, are to this hour as cold, as desolate, and almost as lifeless, in a spiritual sense, as the tombs which surround their places of worship! How many personal, domestic, ecclesiastical and national sins press heavily upon us, as a

people, and cry aloud for the judgments of a righteous God! Think of the abounding atheism, and various forms of infidelity, the pride, the degrading intemperance, the profanations of the Sabbath, the fraud, the gross impiety, the neglect and contempt of the gospel, and all the numberless forms of enormous moral corruption, which even in the most favoured parts of our country prevail in a deplorable degree, and in the less favoured hold a melancholy and undisturbed reign;—think of these abounding sins,—and think also in how small a degree multitudes even of the professing people of God seem to be awake to the great responsibilities and duties of their high vocation;—and then say, whether we have not reason for special humiliation and prayer? My beloved hearers, if we see no cause on account of these things for weeping and mourning and fasting before the Lord, it is because we have never had our eyes opened to see the evil of sin, never yet taken our stand among those who bear Jehovah's 'mark upon their foreheads', and who 'sigh and mourn for all the abominations that are done' in the land. Professing Christians! whatever name you bear, unless you be really found in these ranks of the faithful, how can you expect, when the angel of Jehovah's judgment passes by (as pass by he assuredly will), that your habitations will be spared; or that, amid the surrounding darkness, there will be 'light in your dwellings'?

REVIVALS OF RELIGION[1]

CHRISTIAN Brethren, when the real Christian reads or hears of a revival of religion, a chord is touched which vibrates with pleasure to his heart. In no event is a friend of Christ more ready, instinctively, to rejoice, than when he is informed that the Holy Spirit is poured out in large measures, reviving the graces of the people of God; causing multitudes anxiously to enquire what they must do to be saved; and many to rejoice in 'a good hope through grace'. Long may the Presbyterian Church be favoured with genuine revivals of religion, of greater and greater power, in all her borders; and long may she be blessed with ministers and members who love them; who pray for them without ceasing; and who habitually and faithfully use those means for promoting them, which the Scriptures warrant, and which the great Head of the church is wont to own and bless!

This subject appears to me, at the present time, to assume an aspect more than usually interesting, and to indicate a most momentous connection with the future. The frequency, the power, and the precious results of revivals, in almost every part of the American churches, within a few years past, cannot but fill the hearts of intelligent Christians with joy, while they furnish a most animating presage of the rapid manner in which the conversion of the world may be expected to proceed, when 'the set time to favour Zion shall come'; and a no less gratifying pledge of the ease with which the Head of the church can solve that problem so perplexing to human wisdom—How the number of candidates for the ministry may be so rapidly multiplied, as in any good measure to meet the urgent and increasing demand

[1] Samuel Miller, 'Revivals of Religion', *Letters to Presbyterians on the Present Crisis in the Presbyterian Church in the United States* (Philadelphia: Anthony Finley, 1833), pp. 151-91.

for spiritual labourers, both in the domestic and foreign field? Let such revivals as we have been permitted to see, but with augmented power and extent, visit the churches year after year, and fill all lands, and the work will be done. The knowledge and glory of the Lord, without the interposition of what we call miracle, will soon fill the earth; and on every side candidates for carrying the gospel from the rising to the setting sun, will be raised up, saying, with humble readiness to spend and be spent for Christ—'Here are we, send us.' I cannot help recording my conviction that these revivals are the hope of the church and of the world. In other words, the Millennium is at a far greater distance than the most pious and enlightened interpreters of prophecy have supposed; or else the conversion of the heathen, and of all that are afar off, must proceed in a much more rapid manner than it has hitherto done. I am disposed to adopt the latter alternative; and, of course, to believe that the church is warranted in looking and praying for revivals of religion far more extensive, more powerful, and more glorious, than the present generation, or indeed any other, has ever witnessed.

This being my impression, I cannot doubt that it is the duty of all professing Christians, at the present day, to expect great things; to ask for great things; and to employ with increasing diligence all the means which the Spirit of God has warranted, and has promised to follow with his blessing, for the attainment of great things in the way of *revivals*. They are solemnly bound, in that spirit of hallowed enterprise, which becomes a new exigency, and new dawnings in human affairs, to endeavour, by augmented parental care and diligence; by increasing pastoral fidelity; by the more edifying example, and unwearied activity of private Christians in their appropriate sphere; by prayer more humble, importunate, and persevering than heretofore; and by redoubled efforts to sustain and extend all those associations which have for their object the reformation and conversion of the world;—they are bound, I say, by all these means to endeavour to hasten the arrival of that period when 'nations shall be born in a day', and when multitudes shall flock to the ark of safety 'as a cloud, and as doves to their windows', and when 'converts to righteousness shall be numerous as the drops of the morning dew'. In my opinion every professing Christian ought to consider the degree in which he longs, and prays, and exerts himself for the revival of religion, and for the extension of the Redeemer's kingdom, as affording one of the most undoubted and unerring tests of his piety. Show me a professor of religion who manifests but little zeal for these great interests, and I will show you one who has great reason to 'stand in doubt' of himself, and to examine, with new solicitude, whether he has ever taken his stand 'on the Lord's side'.

Assuming, then, the unspeakable importance of this great subject, and the obligation resting upon all Christians, not only to desire revivals, but also to be actively engaged in promoting them;—I beg leave to offer some general remarks on a few points relating to the subject; and it is my wish to do it with all that caution and reverence which becomes everyone in taking a step on consecrated ground.

I. And my first remark is, that it is of the utmost importance *that we be upon our guard against spurious revivals*. If I were called upon to say what I mean by a genuine revival of religion, as distinguished from a spurious one, I should draw the line of distinction by saying, that a genuine revival is one which is produced by the exhibition of gospel truth, faithfully presented to the mind, and applied by the power of the Holy Spirit. And that all high religious excitement or commotion produced by other means than the impression of truth, is the essence of fanaticism. It is a spurious work, adapted to bring genuine revivals into disrepute, and to send a blast instead of a blessing on the church of God; and, of course, the more extended and powerful, the more to be deplored.

It is no uncommon or difficult thing to work upon the animal feelings of assembled multitudes, by mere terror, by sympathy, by vehement addresses, by fine music, by a great variety of means in which gospel truth is not presented, and has no influence. Those who are aware what a 'fearfully and wonderfully made' piece of machinery human nature is, and especially how susceptible of strong and diversified impression are the nerves and sympathies of that nature, will not wonder, though they may not be able fully to explain, why such powerful effects flow from a little adroit management. Who does not know that the far-famed fanatical Unitarians, who call themselves 'Chrystians', have their 'revivals' of a strongly marked character, their 'anxious seats', and all the most imposing and exciting means that have ever been adopted for making a popular impression. Nay, one of the most active and artful leaders of that sect, boasted that he had drawn at least fifty persons to anxious seats, merely by the influence of his own singing, which was, indeed, remarkably touching and powerful. It is surely unnecessary to remark, that such revivals are a disgrace to the name;—that they are the fruit of animal excitement merely; and that every enlightened friend of the Redeemer's kingdom must mourn over their character and tendency.

It is not mere excitement then, in which the animal feelings of many are roused and agitated, and in which the mere principles of nature are addressed, and called into powerful action, that constitute a genuine revival of religion. For, as there can be no real piety in any individual heart, without the reception and love of the fundamental doctrines of the gospel; so we must estimate the real character of every religious excitement which claims to be a revival, by the degree in which pure gospel truth is present, embraced, and obeyed. However widespread and powerful the excitement may be, it ought ever to be brought to this obvious, fair, and decisive test:—Is it produced by a blessing on the truth plainly and faithfully presented? Is it throughout regulated by the truth? And do its professed subjects manifest a general and cordial love of gospel truth? Are their views of the character of God, of his holy law, of sin, of the ground of acceptance, and of Christian hope,—I do not say perfectly—but in the main, accordant with the Bible views of those great subjects? If so, we may hail the work with joy, and bid God speed to those who are instrumental in commencing and giving it direction. If the subjects of it, in 'giving a reason' of their anxiety, or of 'the hope that is in them', appear to be moved by scriptural views of truth, addressed to the conscience and the heart;—if in giving an account of their distress or their peace, they manifest that their views of themselves, of the Saviour, and of Christian confidence towards God, are in substance, those which the Scriptures authorize; and if they evidently bring forth the fruits of holy living,—we must denominate such a revival a work of God,—thank him for it, and rejoice in it as a rich blessing. But if by some strong excitement, addressed to the animal feelings, we could so work upon the nervous system of hundreds, or even thousands in a great assembly, as to constrain them to weep, to cry out with terror, to fall prostrate, and to fill the house with sobbing and groans;—if this were all, we must pronounce it a spurious work, the product of fanaticism and not of the Holy Spirit.

I am persuaded, my Christian Brethren, that this is a point of more practical importance than is commonly imagined. To say that spurious revivals are of no use to the church of God, is to express but a small part of the truth. They are a dreadful curse to any church. They exert a most pestiferous influence. They deceive and destroy the souls of men. They harden the worldly and the infidel in tenfold obduracy. They leave a country over which they have passed arid and desolate, like that over which a ranging fire has swept, and laid it all a gloomy waste. I have more than once witnessed strong and extensive religious excitements, evidently produced by powerful appeals to animal feeling and sympathy, without suitable exhibitions of gospel truth. The effects were, indeed, plausible, and adapted to make a deep popular impression. They did make such an impression; and were trumpeted far and wide as 'glorious revivals of religion'. But, in a few months, the real character of these excitements was painfully disclosed. In a great majority of cases the impressions made, 'like the morning cloud and the early dew', soon entirely passed away; while the small minority who held out long enough to make a public profession of religion, and some who, in the fervour of their first exercises, offered themselves as candidates for the holy ministry—soon made it too evident, by their unhappy mixture of levity, ignorance, censoriousness, and claims of high attainment, that they needed a new conversion before they could be fitted to adorn or to edify the church.

I once knew a minister who took unwearied, and I doubt not, honest pains, to produce a revival of religion in the church under his pastoral care. After employing abundant means, and those of the most exciting and alarming kind, he succeeded in collecting together, at the close of a solemn evening service, in which a powerful impression seemed to have been made, a large number of the professedly 'anxious' and 'enquiring' in his session room. There he met and addressed them—and there, without saying one word to them of their guilt and misery by nature, of Christ, of the gospel plan of acceptance with God, of the nature of evangelical faith and repentance, or of the work of the Holy Spirit as the author of all spiritual life, he spoke to them about 'resolving to be for God';—asked them if they could not 'make up their minds decisively to submit to God';—and assured them that to 'determine in their own minds to engage in the service of God', was regeneration—was to become a Christian. With almost one consent they took the seats assigned to the 'hoping' and came out of the room called, and supposing themselves to be 'converted persons'. Most of them were forthwith hurried into the church; but in the estimation of intelligent Christians few of them appeared to know what they were doing, or turned out to be solid, established Christians. Of such a revival, I should say, with confidence, it has nothing to do with the religion of the gospel.

I repeat it then, experience proves that spurious revivals have been mistaken for genuine, and may be mistaken for them again; and that we ought never to recognize as genuine any revival which is not produced by the instrumentality of truth, which is not regulated by the truth, and which does not bring forth the fruits of truth. All else is fanatical excitement. Like a fever in the human body, it cannot fail of leaving the system relaxed and debilitated, when it declines. Like counterfeit money, it excites deep doubt and distrust wherever it comes, and ultimately interferes with the circulation of genuine coin. 'Beloved', says an inspired apostle, 'believe not every spirit, but try the spirits whether they are of God, for many false prophets have gone out into the world.'

II. Allow me further to suggest, the great importance of *guarding against all those disorders and unwarranted measures which are adapted to arrest or to mar genuine revivals.* I have sometimes heard inconsiderate querists ask, whether it is possible that a work which is really of God, should be arrested in its progress, or marred in its character, by the weakness of man? This question may be answered in the affirmative or negative, according to our understanding of its meaning. Let me answer it by asking another. If an individual were deeply anxious respecting his eternal interests,—and if, in the midst of his anxiety, a large estate were unexpectedly left to him, which, from its extent and situation, was adapted to engross his whole attention;—or, if he were suddenly engaged in all the violence of party politics, or some other angry and absorbing contest, might we not naturally expect, would not all experience teach us to fear—that the new and engrossing subject would soon expel all his former anxiety? Even so, the history of the church has evinced, that even when a genuine and undoubted work of the Holy Spirit has commenced its progress, in the most promising manner, if gross disorders are admitted; if angry contentions arise; or if anything occur powerfully to distract or divide the public mind; the Holy Spirit is wont to depart, and the minds of men to be turned away from the most important concerns, to those subordinate objects which are thus urged on their attention. In these circumstances, where the sanctifying Spirit has taken up his abode in any heart, he will not be totally and finally expelled; but by thousands who had been brought by his strivings to deep conviction, to promising seriousness, and to apparently sincere resolutions, his influences have been quenched, and his presence grieved away from a people who once appeared 'not far from the kingdom of God'. Well meaning, sanguine Christians, may fondly hope, that if the Spirit of God be really present, there is nothing to fear. But his own Word, as well as the history of his dealings with the church, plainly shows that he is a Spirit of order and of love; and that whenever there is a striking departure from either, there he will not remain; but will leave such a people to greater hardness, apathy, and unbelief, than ever.

Let anyone who really desires to know the truth on this subject, look into the apostolical epistles, especially into the fourteenth chapter of the First Epistle to the Corinthians, and he will there see that, even under the ministrations of inspired men, gross disorders creeping into a church were found quite sufficient to mar the work of the Holy Spirit, and to impede the progress of the truth. Let him look into the fourth part of the venerable President Edwards' *Thoughts concerning the Revival of Religion*[1] which appeared in our country more than ninety years ago, and he will perceive that that eminently wise and holy man saw and lamented disorders amidst the glorious revivals which then blessed the church, and had no doubt of the deplorable mischiefs produced by them. Let him read the accounts of the disorders introduced into New England by Davenport and his associates, during the great revivals under the ministry of Whitefield and his excellent coadjutors, many years since; and if he have

[1] Reprinted as Jonathan Edwards, *Thoughts on the New England Revival* (Edinburgh: Banner of Truth, 2005).

a particle of sincere love for the kingdom of Christ, he will mourn over the evils which those disorders occasioned, grieving the hearts of God's people, tearing the churches in pieces, and causing the Holy Spirit to depart, and give them up to strife, and finally to coldness, stupidity, and desolation. Let him notice with care the extravagancies and disorders which have attended revivals of religion within the last thirty years in different parts of the United States; revivals which were in their commencement highly promising; but which soon became marred, disgraced, and terminated, by various forms of fanatical irregularity, which disgusted intelligent and sober-minded Christians, and hardened the enemies of vital religion in deeper hostility. I say, let anyone who sincerely desires to know the truth on this subject, ponder well this recorded experience of the church of God, and then say, whether it is not both reasonable and important to lift, in relation to it, the voice of warning.

If any desire to know what the particular disorders are, to which allusion is intended in these references;—I answer, the very same disorders which the venerable President Edwards, and other eminently wise and pious ministers of the gospel, lamented and opposed nearly a century ago, and which wrought such complicated and widespread mischiefs then, and many years afterwards. Such as the excessive multiplication of public meetings, so as to leave little or no time for the duties of the family and the closet:—continuing the exercises of such meetings to an unseasonably late hour, thereby deranging the order of families, and exhausting both the bodies and the minds of the people: indulging in bodily agitation, groans and outcries in public assemblies: unauthorized and unqualified persons thrusting themselves forward to perform the work of public instruction: a number of persons speaking and praying at the same time: females speaking, and leading in prayer in promiscuous assemblies:—publicly praying for particular individuals by name, as graceless, or opposers of religion: giving vent to the language of harsh censure, and of uncharitable denunciation, as enemies of God, against all who oppose these irregularities: urging the public confession of secret sins, as indispensable to the attainment of a blessing: all these, and many other contrivances of a like kind, the object of which was to produce *strong excitement,* have been tried a hundred times, in various countries and ages;—

have been uniformly found to work ill in the end;—and have been unanimously condemned by judicious Christians as unscriptural and mischievous. They disgust intelligent, reflecting people. They drive many from the house of God, and, perhaps harden them in hopeless infidelity. And they confirm the prejudices of many against revivals altogether. And yet there are those who believe those very means adapted to do good, and who are disposed to try them again! The truth is, there are good people who imagine that unless high popular excitement and agitation be produced, nothing desirable is done. They are ready, therefore, to adopt any new and bold measure which promises to produce the effect. Their delight is in public excitement; in producing effects on large masses of people analogous to the influence of strong drink on the animal body: not remembering that, as in the case of strong drink, such excitement is unnatural; that it is unfriendly to the calm, intelligent and humble exercise of Christian grace; that it cannot long continue; and that it will never fail to be followed by morbid depression, and debility in the end.

But besides these manifest disorders, which have so often drawn a cloud over revivals of religion, and against which judicious Christians, it may be hoped, will be ever on their guard; there are other 'measures' to which the title of 'new' has been given, of which I beg permission to say a word under this head. The principal of these are,—at the end of a warm and pungent discourse—calling upon all who are more or less impressed by it, and who have formed the resolution to attend to the subject of religion, to rise from their seats, and declare their purpose before the public assembly;—or, requesting all who are willing to be prayed for, to rise and come forward to a particular part of the church, and kneel together for that purpose;— or, inviting all who are anxious about their everlasting welfare, to separate themselves publicly from the rest of the congregation, and to occupy certain seats, called 'anxious seats' and vacated for the purpose of being thus filled. In short, this machinery for working on the popular feeling may be, and has been endlessly diversified. Sometimes those who have 'obtained a hope' have been requested to rise in every part of the house, and signify it. At other times, those who have not yet begun to cherish a hope of their good estate, but who resolve that they will attend to this great subject, are urged, on the spot, to signify this resolution in the same way. And sometimes those whose stubborn wills are not yet inclined to bow, and who feel no particular disposition to comply with the gospel call, have been requested to make even this publicly known, by either rising in their seats, or leaving the house.

The great argument urged in favour of this whole system of 'new measures' is, that, as the impenitent are naturally prone to stifle convictions, and to tamper with the spirit of procrastination, it is desirable they should be prevailed upon, as soon as possible, to take some visible step which shall 'commit them' on this great subject. This, however, in my opinion, instead of being an argument in its favour, is precisely the most powerful objection to the whole system. There is no doubt that every impenitent sinner to whom the gospel comes, ought to be called to immediate repentance; and that all delay in embracing the gospel is as unreasonable as it is criminal. But of all the subjects that can come before the human mind, surely religion is that in which every step ought to be taken without rashness, with distinct knowledge, with due consideration, 'counting the cost', and with sacred care not to mistake a transient emotion for a deep impression; or a momentary paroxysm of alarm, or of animal sympathy, for a fixed, practical purpose of the heart. If we call upon those who are 'anxious' about their eternal interest, to take certain seats, or to stand up before the public assembly, as a testimony of their anxiety;—is it wise in them publicly to take such a station, before they know whether their feelings will last an hour, or pass away with the first night's sleep? Or, if we should call upon those who have 'obtained a hope' in Christ, to make it known to a large assembly, by some prescribed signal; would it be right in those into whose minds this hope, whether genuine or spurious, has beamed only a few hours or minutes before the call was made, to stand forth in this high and responsible character, before there was the least opportunity to put their hope to a scriptural test? Of all methods yet devised, this appears to me most directly adapted to fill the church with rash, ignorant, superficial, hypocritical professors, instead of solid, intelligent, truly spiritual and devoted Christians.

Nor is even this, bad as it is, the worst. I feel constrained to add, that when this highly exciting system of calling to 'anxious seats'—

calling out into the aisles to be 'prayed for', *etc.,* is connected, as, to my certain knowledge, it often has been, with erroneous doctrines;—for example, with the declaration, that nothing is easier than conversion;—that the power of the Holy Spirit is not necessary to enable impenitent sinners to repent and believe;—that if they only resolve to be for God—resolve to be Christians—that itself is regeneration—the work is already done:—I say, where the system of 'anxious seats', *etc.,* is connected with such doctrinal statements as these, it appears to me adapted to destroy souls by wholesale! I will not say that such revivals are never connected with sound conversions; but I will be bold to repeat, that the religion which they are fitted to cherish is altogether a different one from that of the gospel. It is, I sincerely believe, a system of soul-destroying deception!

Those of you, my Christian Brethren, who have seen a highly instructive and interesting volume on the subject of revivals by the Rev. Dr Sprague of Albany[1]—a volume which I would earnest recommend to the careful perusal of every Presbyterian in the United States, have no doubt been impressed, not only by the just and luminous views given of the subject before us, by that excellent writer himself; but also by the remarkable unanimity of opinion on the same subject, expressed in the appendix to his work, by a long list of eminent ministers of six different Christian denominations—most of them distinguished for their great wisdom and piety, as well as their ample experience in revivals. From the communications of three of the venerable men—whose competency in every respect to give testimony on the subject before us, will be questioned by none who know them—I beg leave to make a few short extracts.

The following is the testimony of the Rev. President Humphrey of Amherst College, whose character as a tried friend of revivals is well known.

> If you ask me, what means and measures have been most eminently blessed, in the revivals which have fallen under my own personal observation, in college and elsewhere,—I answer, substantially the same as were 'mighty through God to the pulling down of strongholds' in the

[1] Reprinted as W. B. Sprague, *Lectures on Revivals* (Edinburgh: Banner of Truth, 2007).

apostolic age;—the same as were employed by Edwards, and Bellamy, and Brainerd, almost a century ago. Meetings for personal conversation, commonly called 'inquiry meetings' have been held weekly, or oftener, with great spiritual advantage, in all the revivals which have fallen under my notice. The duty of prayer, both secret and social, has been earnestly and daily urged upon Christians; but late meetings have generally been discouraged, as interfering with the religious order of families, and tending in a short time, to exhaust the physical and mental energies of God's people, as well as to mingle 'strange fire' with that which is kindled from the skies. When met for social prayer, neither ministers nor laymen have indulged themselves in loud and boisterous vociferations, in audible groans, or in smiting the hands together in token of their sincerity and earnestness. They have observed, that the most noisy waters are seldom deepest; and have laid more stress upon 'fervency of spirit' than upon strength of lungs, or muscular contortions. With us it has never been customary, either in our larger or smaller religious circles, to pray for sinners who may happen to be present, by name, or to indulge in equivalent personalities. The general tendency of such a practice, it is thought, would be detrimental to the cause of piety, however different the effect might be in solitary instances. Females have kept silence in all our meetings, except such as were composed exclusively of their own sex. Calling anxious sinners into the aisles, to be addressed and prayed for, has not been practised within the circle of my observation; nor have they been requested, before the great congregation, to come forward from any part of the house, and occupy seats vacated for that purpose;—and wherever such measures have been adopted, within my knowledge, I believe the cause of revivals has lost more than it has gained by them. It is unsafe to argue from the present effect of any new system, that it is better than the old. It may accomplish more in a week, but not so much in a year. It may bring a greater number of persons into the visible kingdom of Christ, but not so many into his spiritual kingdom. For myself, every new revival of religion which I am permitted to witness, serves to confirm me in the opinion, that it is safest to walk in the 'old paths' and to employ those means and measures which long experience has sanctioned, and in the use of which the churches in this part of the land, have been so greatly enlarged and edified.

The Rev. President Lord, of Dartmouth College—in reference to the same subject, has the following weighty remarks.

In regard to these revivals of religion, I think it important to remark, that, in every instance, they seemed the product of the Spirit's influence silently affecting different minds with the same truths, and multiplying the trophies of divine mercy. They were an effect, and not a cause of divine interposition; and except as occasionally blemished through human weakness and sinfulness, bore the characteristics of the wisdom that is from above. We have known here nothing except by report, of the 'new measures' for building up the kingdom of Christ. We have no machinery for making converts; and we could allow none to be introduced. We should be afraid to make or suffer an impression upon the young men under our care, many of whom will be ministers of Jesus Christ—that the gospel can be helped, or the work of the Holy Spirit facilitated by human devices. And I think we shall hold, on this subject, to our general principles, too long settled by the experience of ages, and confirmed by the blessing of God, attending the application of them, to be now thrown away in the ardour of questionable excitements, or for the love of innovation, or even to escape the imputation of being the enemies of revivals. When shall the ministers and churches of the Redeemer know effectually their proneness to mar the beautiful simplicity of the gospel, to add something of their own inventions to its sufficient ordinances; to lead instead of following the divine providence, and to mistake their own dreaming for a heavenly impulse; to inflame the sacrifice with unhallowed fire, and to arrogate that power, and that glory which belong to God only? I cannot tell you how much I sometimes fear, when I look abroad upon our country, that Christianity will degenerate in our keeping. Yet let us hold to the old foundations. There are many yet to maintain the right; and the recovering spirit, we are assured, will accomplish the purposes of divine mercy, will correct and convert the world.

President Griffin, of Williams College, than whom few living ministers have had more experience in revivals, employs, on the same subject, the following language:—

Much has been done of late, to lead awakened sinners to commit themselves, in order to get them over that indecision, and fear of man which have kept them back, and to render it impossible for them to return with consistency. For this purpose they are called upon to request public prayers by rising; to come out into the aisles, in token of their determination to be for God; to take particular seats, called in bad English, 'anxious seats'; to come forward and kneel in order to be prayed for; and in very many instances, to promise to give themselves to religion at once. For much the same purpose converts are called upon to take particular seats, and thus virtually to make a profession in a day, and are hurried into the church in a few weeks. These measures, while they are intended to 'commit' the actors, are meant also to awaken the attention of others, and to serve as means of general impression. I would not make a man an offender for a word; but when these measures are reduced to a system, and constantly repeated;— when, instead of the former dignity of a Christian assembly, it is daily thrown into a rambling state by these well meant manoeuvres;—it becomes a solemn question, whether they do not give a disproportionate action to imagination and passion, and lead to a reliance on other means than truth and prayer, and on other power than that of God. I have seen enough to convince me that sinners are very apt to place a self-righteous dependence on this sort of commitment. 'I have taken one step, and now I hope God will do something for me'—is language which I have heard more than once. Against any promises, express or implied, I utterly protest. If they are promises to do anything short of real submission, they will bring up a feeling that more the sinner is not bound to do. If they are promises to submit, they are made in the sinner's own strength, and are presumptuous. The will, which forms resolutions, and utters promises, cannot control the heart. Sinners are bound to love God at once; but they are not bound to promise beforehand to do it, and rely on their own will to change their heart. This is self-dependence. They are bound to go forth to their work at once; but they are not bound to go alone. It is their privilege, and their duty to cast themselves instantly on the Holy Ghost, and not to take a single step in their own strength. In these extorted promises there is another evil,—the substitution of human authority for the divine. It is right for Christians to urge upon sinners the obligation of immediate submission, and they cannot enforce this too much by the authority of God; but to stand over them and say,—'Come, now promise; promise this moment; *do* promise; you *must* promise; promise, and I will pray for you—if you don't, I won't'—is overpowering them with human authority, and putting it in the room of the divine.

The experience and wisdom of the Rev. Mr Nettleton in revivals of religion, for more than twenty years past, are well known throughout the United States. His testimony against the 'new measures' of which I am now speaking is strong and decisive. He informed me, with his own lips, within a few weeks, that a short time before he commenced his career as an evangelist, these very 'measures' (calling upon people in the public assemblies, to proclaim the state of their minds by standing up, going to certain seats—or kneeling in the aisles to be prayed for) had been extensively employed by the Rev. James Davis, a Congregational minister in the eastern part of Connecticut, where he (Mr Nettleton) was subsequently called to labour; that the ultimate fruit of them everywhere, was fanaticism and disorder; that, in more than one place, the spirit which they generated presented such insurmountable obstacles to all rational and sober ministrations, that he was obliged to take leave and go elsewhere; and that in every period of his ministry since, he has found similar 'measures' invariably productive of the same distressing effects. His judgment, therefore, long since formed; tested by much experience both in the Presbyterian Church and in New England; and rendered more and more decisive by every day's additional observation, is, that the whole array of the 'measures' in question, is opposed to the meekness and humility of the gospel; that it tends to nourish a spirit of ostentation, fanaticism, and censoriousness; and that, although it may appear to be productive of a greater number of conversions in the beginning, a less obtrusive system may be expected to produce more genuine and more abundant fruit in the end.

Let it not be said, that calling out enquirers to 'anxious seats' is the only effectual method of ascertaining who are under serious impressions, and who are not. Is it not quite as effectual, and much less exceptionable, to give a public invitation to all who are in any degree seriously impressed, or anxious to remain after the congregation is dismissed; or to meet their pastor the next evening, in some convenient apartment, for the purpose of disclosing their feelings, and of being made the subjects of instruction and prayer? Nay, why is not the latter method very much preferable, in every respect, to the former? It affords quite as good an opportunity to ascertain numbers, and to distinguish persons and cases. It furnishes a far better opportunity to give distinct and appropriate instruction to particular individuals. It prevents the mischief of dragging into public view, and even into the highest degree of publicity, those whose exercises are immature and perhaps transient. And it avoids the danger which to many, and especially to young people, may be very formidable; I mean the danger of being inflated by becoming objects of public attention, and by being forthwith addressed and announced, as is too often the case, as undoubted 'converts'. Surely the incipient exercises of the awakened and convinced ought to be characterized by much calm self-examination, and much serious, retired, closet work. If there be any whose impressions are so slight and transient, that they cannot be safely permitted to wait until the next evening, it will hardly be maintained that such persons are prepared to 'commit themselves', by publicly taking an anxious seat. And if there be any whose vanity would dispose them to prefer pressing forward to such a seat in the presence of a great assembly, to meeting their pastor, and a few friends in a similar state of mind with themselves, in a more private manner, the church, I apprehend, can promise herself little comfort from the multiplication of such members.

After all, what is the ultimate effect of this system of 'new measures', as it is commonly called? Does it continue, like all the ordinances of God's own appointment, to impress and to edify, from year to year, without abatement or weariness? Not at all. In those places in which the practice of calling out the serious, the anxious, and the hoping to the aisles, or to particular seats, as habit or caprice may dictate, has been most extensively and longest in use, all experience testifies, that when the novelty of the expedient has worn off, its exciting character is at an end; and that it soon becomes as powerless and inefficient as any other old story. This is notoriously the case in many parts of the western country; and it will soon be found to be the case in those eastern portions of the church in which similar practices are now in high vogue. The truth is, things of this kind cannot long be tolerated among enlightened, sober-minded Christians. Solid food nourishes the body, and leaves it invigorated and comfortable. But stimulating potations excite to morbid action only, and that for a time; and then leave the system depressed and wretched.

But I must postpone to one more letter some further remarks on the subject of revivals.

SAMUEL MILLER
Princeton,
March 1833

* * * * *

CHRISTIAN Brethren, the subject of revivals of religion is so unspeakably interesting and important, and at the same time, so extensive, that I am persuaded you will not wonder at my making it the subject of another letter. There are several other topics on which I feel desirous of making a few observations.

III. A third remark which I would most respectfully offer, is, that, if we desire to promote genuine and salutary revivals of religion, *we must not undervalue the ordinary means of grace, nor make too common and cheap those which may be called extraordinary.*

When the ancient people of God, in their passage through the wilderness, began to loathe the plain but excellent manna which was provided for them day by day, and to call for some extraordinary supply; we find that, on their request being granted, surfeiting and mischief were the consequence. So it is with respect to Zion's more spiritual provision. When new schemes for making a popular impression begin to occupy the public mind, a love of excitement and of agitation seems to take possession of the people. They begin to suppose that when these are absent, nothing valuable is accomplished. The ordinary exercises of the Sabbath, the weekly lecture, the prayer meeting, and the sacramental table, are esteemed 'light food'. Something stirring; something new; something adapted to produce powerful excitement, analogous to that of strong drink, must be present, or all seems to them vapid and uninteresting. When a spirit of this kind becomes prevalent among a people, it augurs most unhappily for their spiritual interest. The object of these remarks is, not to intimate that extraordinary means of grace ought not sometimes to be employed; but that they ought not so to be employed and regarded as

717

to place the ordinary means which God has appointed 'in the background', and to make the popular impression that where these alone are employed, little good is to be expected.

To exemplify my meaning: I am a warm friend to 'protracted meetings'. They were evidently employed, on special occasions, under the Old Testament economy; but they were not made cheap by too frequent recurrence. They were considered and treated as special services. In the days of our blessed Lord's personal ministry, we know that he kept the people hanging on his lips for three whole days in succession, and, during the greater part of this time, large numbers of them evidently remained on the ground fasting. In the Church of Scotland, protracted meetings, on sacramental occasions, were almost universal, it is believed, for more than a hundred years, and, on many occasions, with richly excellent results. It was on such an occasion that a single sermon by the celebrated Mr John Livingstone, was blessed to the hopeful conversion of five hundred souls.[1] And such protracted meetings, have, beyond all doubt, been made signally instrumental in many parts of our own country, especially within a few years past, to the commencement or the continuance of the most precious revivals of religion. Against protracted meetings, therefore, as such, thus warranted and fortified, it is probable no sincere and intelligent friend of vital piety will venture to speak. But are not such meetings extremely liable to abuse? Nay, is there not reason to believe that they have been abused, and thus made a hindrance, instead of a help, to the cause of pure and undefiled religion? And they may be said to be abused, when professing Christians begin to place their chief dependence upon them; when they look forward to them with eagerness, as the hope of the church; when they are made, as it were, to come in place of an humble tender reliance on the Holy Spirit, and broken-hearted, importunate, persevering prayer for the prosperity of Zion; when they even seem, as they have sometimes been, to be regarded as a kind of machinery which may serve as a substitute for personal religion, and persevering devotion; and, finally, they are greatly abused when they are resorted to so frequently by the same people, as to convert them into stated means of grace, and thus

---

[1] The Life of John Livingstone, recounted in his own words, is found in *Scottish Puritans*, 2 vols. (Edinburgh: Banner of Truth, 2008).

to make the Sabbath, and its ordinary privileges lightly esteemed in comparison with them. This is a sore evil; yet it has happened; and there is a great danger that it will happen again. But if my views of the nature of the economy of grace, as well as distinct information respecting the effects in particular cases, do not deceive me, such an abuse never can happen without mischief; without such frowns and desertion by the great Head of the church, as will leave a people chargeable with it, in a greater or less degree, to the coldness, the stupidity, and the desolation of those who are given up to 'eat the fruit of their own way', and to be 'filled with their own devices'.

The truth is, men have been prone, in all ages, to lay more stress on their own inventions, than on the simple ordinances of Christ. They have honestly, but vainly, thought that the appointments of the Head of the church were not sufficient; or, at any rate, that they might be added to, not only without sin, but with advantage. Every new device for winning the attention, and exciting the mind, they have been ready to adopt; and imagined that in doing so, they 'did God service'. This was, no doubt, the origin of a large number of those human inventions in the worship of God which deform the Romish Church. They began early. They were a long time in reaching that corrupt and revolting maturity which they now exhibit. Good men, in their pious zeal to impress the multitude, and to bring souls into the church, invented device after device for addressing the senses, and working on the feelings of men; until the piety of their inventors, and the force of habit, consecrated these devices in public estimation, as institutions of Christ, and gave them a permanent place in the apparatus of the church; until one after another they built up that mass of superstition which forms the dire machinery by which the 'man of sin', dazzles and deceives the simple. It is, moreover, one of those notorious facts, in the history of human inventions in the worship of God, as humiliating as it is striking, that after a while, more stress is commonly laid upon those inventions than on the ordinances of Christ. Uncommanded festival and fast days in the Romish Church are commonly observed with far more strictness than the Lord's day. And many, if appearances are not deceptive, are beginning to feel as if no good can be hoped for without protracted meetings, and that they are of far more importance than the privileges of the holy Sabbath.

I would say, then, employ protracted meetings. They are fully warranted, by the example, as well as the spirit of the Word of God. But do not make idols of them. Do not imagine that they have an inherent efficacy, independently of the Spirit of God, to produce a revival of religion. Resort to them but seldom; not as stated, but as extraordinary means. Prepare for them with much humble, importunate prayer. Remember that, like all other means, they will only be useful as far as they are attended upon with a believing reference and application to the Spirit of all grace. And be careful not to view or use them in any way which will tend to depreciate in your esteem the ordinary means of grace. Whatever or whoever does this, is a great evil, and will inevitably be followed by the frowns of Zion's King.

IV. It is of great importance in revivals to *guard against a sudden introduction to the church of those who are hopefully made the subjects of converting grace.*

Until recently, the practice here opposed had few or no advocates among intelligent, sober-minded Christians. If it be of any importance, either to themselves or the church, that those who are introduced to her communion be sincere and enlightened believers, then it is, undoubtedly, desirable that, after cherishing the hope that they have become such, they should have some little time to try and know themselves, and to become known to the church. Especially is this caution highly important in seasons of powerful awakening and revival; when many are wrought upon by sympathy, who are strangers even to deep conviction, much more to a genuine conversion;—when many appear serious and promising for a while, but soon draw back, and relapse into deeper carelessness than before. Surely it would be unhappy, in every respect, if such persons were encouraged in their first paroxysms of feeling to enrol themselves publicly as professors of religion! Scarcely anything could be more directly adapted to fill them with delusive hopes, and prevent their genuine conversion. The truth is, the system which I have known to be pursued by some warm-hearted and well-meaning ministers; a system of high animal excitement throughout, unaccompanied with much instruction, and followed up with admission to the communion of the church, within a few days, and sometimes within a few hours, after the commencement of serious feelings; is undoubtedly a system adapted to deceive and destroy immortal souls; to fill the church with ignorant, noisy hypocrites; and, in the end, to destroy, at once, its purity and its peace.

As to the examples found in Scripture, which are supposed to justify the immediate admission of hopeful converts to sealing ordinances—such as the prompt baptising of the Ethiopian eunuch by Philip, and the reception of 3,000 on the day of Pentecost, they are manifestly nothing to the purpose. The cases, when examined, will be found to have been peculiar, and not to have admitted of delay;—not to say, that the peculiar state of the church at that time totally alters the aspect of such facts. Besides, no one doubts that cases may be supposed, and sometimes actually arise, in which immediate reception would be wise and perfectly safe; but the question is, what course is best as a general rule? What course is adapted to fill the church with intelligent, solid, and truly sanctified members? Is it possible to hesitate respecting the proper answer?

I have been struck, and very much gratified with the remarkable unanimity of opinion on this subject, on the part of the distinguished ministers whose communications appear in the appendix to Dr Sprague's excellent *Lectures on Revivals,* before mentioned. The Rev. Dr Hawes of Hartford, in reference to this subject, speaks thus:—

> It is a great error to admit converts to the church before time has been allowed to try the sincerity of their hope. This is an error into which I was betrayed during the first revival among my people, and it has cost me bitter repentance. And yet none were admitted to the church under two months after they had indulged a hope. It is of great importance that young converts, immediately after conversion, should be collected into a class by themselves, and brought under the direct and frequent instruction of the pastor.—And if they are continued from four to six months in a course of judicious instruction, and then admitted to the church, there is very little danger that they will afterwards fall away, or that they will not continue to shine as lights in the world till the end of life.

The Rev. Dr Griffin, in speaking on the same subject, expresses himself thus:—

The means employed in these revivals have been but two—the clear presentation of divine truth, and prayer—nothing to work upon the passions, but sober solemn truth, presented, as far as possible, in its most interesting attitudes, and closely applied to the conscience. We have been anxiously studious to guard against delusive hopes, and to expose the windings of a deceitful heart, forbearing all encouragement except what the converts themselves could derive from Christ and the promises, knowing that any reliance on our opinion was drawing comfort from us and not from the Saviour. We have not accustomed them to the bold and unqualified language, that such a one is converted; but have used a dialect calculated to keep alive a sense of the danger of deception. For a similar reason, we have kept them back from a profession about three months.

The ministry of few pastors in any church has been more honoured by a succession of powerful revivals than that of Dr McDowell of Elizabethtown. In the light of his ample experience on this subject, he speaks of it in the appendix to Dr Sprague's work, before mentioned, in the following terms: 'We have carefully guarded against a speedy admission to the privileges of the church. Seldom in times of revival have we admitted persons to the communion in less than six months after they became serious.'

Closely allied with the too sudden introduction of hopeful converts to the communion of the church is another mistake, as I am constrained to regard it. I mean calling upon such young converts, even before they have been recognized as professors of religion, to lead in public prayer, and even, in some cases, to instruct the anxious and enquiring, and to solve the perplexities of distressed and doubting souls. There are many things which the younger converts may do, as the proper fruit and evidence of conversion; and it is desirable, from the earliest period of their spiritual life, to give them some appropriate employment in the new relation into which they are brought, consistent with the retiring humility which becomes them. But to set 'babes in Christ' to leading in public prayer, is, in most cases, to engage them in a service for the performance of which to edification, their spiritual knowledge and experience are very seldom adequate; and, what is no less worthy of regard, when young converts find themselves called upon to come forward in this public manner, there is danger of their being puffed up, and thus receiving precisely that kind of impression which is most apt to be injurious to the young and inexperienced. I have repeatedly known young persons who, after having undergone what had the appearance of a very decisive conversion, were almost immediately called upon to pray in public; who acknowledged afterwards, that their being thus publicly noticed filled them with spiritual pride; and who subsequently became apostates of the most deplorable and humiliating character. O how much better to have waited awhile, to see what would be the issue of their exercises, and thus to have avoided a train of circumstances which rendered their apostasy more signal, and more injurious to the cause of Christ! Let me say again, then, that encouraging young converts to speak and pray in public, in a few days or hours after their hopeful passage from death to life—is most seriously to endanger the edification of those who hear them; but it is quite as likely, nay more likely, to injure the converts themselves. And allow me to say, that this is especially the case in times of excitement and revival. Then, if ever, wisdom, prudence, and the best experience, are indispensably demanded. Then rashness, and misguided, though well-meant zeal, may do more harm in a single day, than years of laborious diligence can repair.

V. Further, the real friends of revivals of religion *ought to be upon their guard against the confident allegation, that the preaching of certain new opinions is alone favourable to revivals; and that those who adhere to the system of old orthodoxy cannot hope to be, in this respect, extensively if at all useful.*

This allegation has been often and confidently made; yes, and in the face of multiplied and incontrovertible facts, plainly establishing the contrary, has been so often repeated, that many are weak enough, or ignorant enough, to believe it. So that, with not a few, it has come to be a received opinion, that where new opinions are not preached, no revivals are to be expected. But surely, none who have any tolerable acquaintance with the history of revivals, can be imposed upon by a deception so palpable and disingenuous. The preaching of Whitefield was as free from any tincture of the new opinions, as that of the most rigorous old Calvinists among us; and yet all the world knows that the revivals with which his ministry was crowned were more extensive and powerful than have attended the ministry of any other man since his time. The same remark may be made concerning the ministry of the Tennents, President Davies, Dr Finley, and a number of other men of similar spirit and usefulness. That they were guiltless of either holding or preaching those new, or rather revived theological speculations, which many extol, and seem to consider so peculiarly potent in their influence, all know who have read their printed discourses:—yet how few of those who make the arrogant claim, which I am now opposing, have been favoured with equal ministerial success! Nor was this fact, so conclusive against the claim before us, by any means confined to former times. Many individuals, among the living and the dead, within the last thirty years, might easily be mentioned, who preach the same doctrine with Whitefield, Tennent, and Davies, and have been favoured with a success strikingly similar to theirs. Nay, my impression is, that nothing would be easier than to demonstrate, that, in every part of our country, up to the present hour, the more nearly the style of preaching has been conforming to the general spirit of Whitefield, Tennent, Edwards, Davies, and Bellamy, the more deep, sound, scriptural, and consistent, as well as numerous, have been the revivals which have followed its dispensation. Within the last four or five years it has been estimated that at least 1,200 congregations within the bounds of the Presbyterian Church have been graciously visited with revivals of religion:—and of this number it is susceptible of proof, that not only a decided, but a very large majority have occurred under the ministry of men who rejected the new opinions. The testimonies to this amount in every part of the Presbyterian Church, north, south, east, and west, are so indubitable and abundant, that no one, it appears to me, who is not either wonderfully ignorant of facts, or strangely blinded by prejudice, can resist the inevitable inference.

It is not denied, indeed, that some advocates of Old-school orthodoxy, appear to have very little scriptural life and zeal, and very few seals to their ministry. And is not this the case, also, notoriously, with some individuals who are fierce advocates for New-school opinions and measures? What, then, does a fact of this kind prove? It may give reason to fear, that a man, though reputed orthodox, is really leaning upon the crutches of antinomian delusion; or, though truly orthodox, is a stranger to true piety:—or, that, though truly pious, he is lacking in some of those qualities which seem necessary to prepare men for usefulness. I could name New-school men whose ministry is as strikingly without good fruit as that of the veriest drone that ever discredited the Old-school ranks; yet I never heard the most zealous advocates for Old-school principles allege this fact, taken alone, as proof of the unsoundness of their creed.

VI. Finally, I would put the real friends of revivals on their guard, *against the arrogant claims of some to peculiar, nay, to almost exclusive skill and power in this great concern.*

It is well known to attentive observers of passing scenes, that claims of this kind are by no means infrequent. We have heard of both ministers and laymen who applied to one another, with peculiar complacency and emphasis, the title of 'revival-men'. They openly claimed to possess some special skill in the art of producing and conducting revivals. They were announced to the churches in this high and imposing character; and held themselves up to public view as persons to be invited from place to place for the professed purpose of introducing religious excitements. Nay, these men have been known to enter congregations without the request or even consent of the pastor; to commence and pursue a system of measures for the accomplishment of their objects, without consulting him; to proceed altogether independently of him,—not even asking him to make a prayer; in short, to reject entirely the co-operation of all excepting a chosen few; refusing to suffer ministers venerable for age as well as piety, who were present, to take any part with them, for the avowed reason, that they were not 'revival-men' or not 'up to the times'.

And what, in many cases, has been the character of these self-styled 'revival-men'? Were they generally conspicuous for their modesty, their meekness, their humility, their gravity and peculiar spirituality? Did they appear to be deeply acquainted with human nature, and deeply skilled in genuine Christian experience? By no means. It may at least be asserted that this was far from being always the case; but that, in very many instances, rashness, presumption, pride and censoriousness, often intermixed with a heartless levity, were their most prominent characteristics. They appeared, on too many occasions, like men vain of some artful machinery, in the use of which they supposed themselves to be peculiarly expert, to which they looked, and on which they depended for success, far more than on the Spirit of a sovereign God. Nay, we have sometimes seen in the front ranks of these 'revival' preachers, young men scarcely of age; of very small knowledge, and still less experience, denouncing and condemning, as if sure that 'they were the men, and wisdom would die with them'; treating with contempt aged and eminently devoted ministers; ministers who had themselves been brought into the kingdom of Christ in powerful revivals, and had enjoyed for many years more than usual experience in those displays of heavenly grace;—treating such men as these with contempt—as though they knew nothing of the matter, compared with their own deep insight and pre-eminent skill! The truth is, when the thorough-going and highly rectified spirit of which I speak has taken full possession of any individual, young or old, there is no calculating on the lengths to which it may carry him; or the wonderful degree in which it may blind him to the claims of Christian decorum, and even sometimes alas! it would seem, to those of Christian candour and integrity!

It is granted, indeed, that there are men peculiarly adapted to promote revivals of religion. Some ministers, unquestionably, preach the gospel with more spiritual skill, clearness, force, and pungency than others. There is in all their sermons, and in all their prayers, more instruction, more point, and more feeling and solemnity, than in those of most of their brethren. They have a deeper insight into the human heart; know better the avenues which lead to it; and are better versed in the varieties of Christian experience than is common even among pious men. They pray much for the blessing of God on their labours; and their whole conversation and example out of the pulpit, are eminently adapted to make an impression in favour of religion on all whom they approach. These I call 'true revival-men'. If there be men in the world peculiarly adapted to promote genuine revivals of religion, these are the individuals. This, however, is only saying, that men who most resemble the Apostle Paul, or rather Paul's Master, are most likely to be instrumental in promoting real religion. But they would be the last men in the world to call themselves by way of eminence, 'revival-men' or to favour such a claim being made for them by others. Nothing would be more abhorrent from their minds than the thought of attaching that power to their machinery, which every page of the Bible, and all the experience of the church, ascribe to the sovereign agency of him who has declared, 'Not by might, nor by power, but by my spirit saith the Lord.'

A 'revival man' I do know, whose ministry has probably been connected with more numerous and powerful revivals of religion than that of any other man now living:—whose power in such displays of divine glory seems to consist, not in noise, in bustling trickery, or in any kind of artful management; but entirely in simple, pungent exhibitions of gospel truth; in representing to men their true condition as lost sinners; in holding up Christ as an Almighty and willing Saviour; and in constantly referring everything to the power and grace of a sovereign God:—who, instead of loving to be called a 'revival man' shrinks from such an appellation with instinctive aversion:—who, instead of thrusting himself into a congregation, uncalled, for the purpose of making a revival, has ever laboured to avoid everything which might, by possibility, wear such an aspect, or which might lead others to claim for him a revival-making power:—who has always been observed, whenever he entered a congregation, whether in a state of excitement or not, to do honour to the pastor, placing him forward on all occasions, and while he made unceasing efforts to promote the spiritual welfare of the flock, hiding himself, as it were, behind its appropriate shepherd:—whose retiring modesty and humility have ever been as remarkable as his pious zeal:—and whose success is a standing refutation of those who contend that revivals can never be expected to occur excepting under the ministry of those who preach the *new opinions,* and resort to the new measures. May this venerated and beloved brother be long continued an ornament and a blessing to the American church! Though he is not connected with my own particular denomination, I can as cordially rejoice in his labours and success as if he were, and pray that his spirit may fill the land!

But in reference to this momentous subject, my respected Friends, I must now draw to a close. If we wish our beloved church really to prosper, let us never cease to long and pray for revivals of religion. No degree of outward prosperity can compensate for the want of these precious tokens of the divine presence. Let no degree of abuse or disorder with which they have been attended, prejudice you against revivals themselves. Desire them, and pray for them with unwearied importunity. But if we desire to be favoured with revivals in their genuine power, we must never cease to honour the Holy Spirit of God, and importunately to solicit his life-giving influence: and if we would not grieve away the Holy Spirit, when obtained, we must lay aside all human inventions in cherishing his work;—everything tending to nourish pride and self-confidence;—all carnal machinery; all parade, all ostentation, everything, in short, adapted to kindle mere animal excitement, and to bring animal feeling into collision with spiritual exercises, or to give it the predominance over them. Let no persuasion, no plausible example prevail on you to countenance these unscriptural 'measures'. They may promise much for a time; but they have never failed ultimately to corrupt and depress the cause of genuine piety.

It is deeply to be regretted that even this hallowed subject has not escaped the perversion of party violence. Attempts have been made to persuade the religious public that a large portion of our church is unfriendly to revivals of religion. I must cherish the hope that this representation has been rather the result of prejudice than of disingenuousness. I know not of a single synod, or even presbytery in our whole body in which revivals of religion are not constantly and fervently prayed for, and really desired, and would not be cordially welcomed. I know, indeed, a few individual ministers and churches, in the minds of whom the disorders which have really occurred, or been reported to them as occurring, in religious excitements, have created a prejudice against the whole subject; just as, seventy or eighty years ago, in the time of Mr Davenport, and his followers, the same unhappy cause produced a similar effect on the minds of many truly pious and worthy men throughout New England. But let us hope that the prejudice even in such minds will be but temporary. An expression of sentiment on this subject is coming in from the aged, the pious, the wise, and the experienced, in every part of our land, most happily and remarkably concurring; and affording a pledge of united hearts and united prayers in behalf of a general revival, which will do more, I trust, to bind together the affections of American Christians, than all the theories and theoretical persuasives that can be urged by human eloquence. When the Spirit of pure, scriptural revival shall be 'poured out from on high', in its genuine manifestations, and in large measures on our American churches—censoriousness will die. Party violence will cease. The metaphysical refinements and subtleties of a delusive theology will be no more heard. The gospel preached, will be taken from the Bible, and not from the rakings of exploded heresies. And the hearts of Christians, instead of 'doting about questions and strifes of words, whereof come envy, railings, evil surmisings, and corrupt disputings',—'will be knit together in love', and united in counsel and effort for the conversion of the world. May such a revival speedily bless all our churches, and pervade Christendom!

SAMUEL MILLER
Princeton,
March, 1833

CHRISTIAN EDUCATION[1]

THE longer and the more serious the committee have deliberated on the adoption of measures 'for securing to the children and young people of our church more full advantages of Christian education than they have hitherto enjoyed', the deeper has become their impression, at once, of its transcendent importance, and of the exceeding great difficulty, in the present state of our country and of the church, of doing it justice, even in theory, and much more of proposing such plans as will admit of general and convenient execution.

There can be no doubt that one great end for which the church was established by her infinitely wise and gracious Head was, that she might train up a godly seed, enlightened in the truth, and imbued with the sentiments and habits adapted to the maintenance and spread of our holy religion, in all its purity and power.

This great principle is not merely left to be inferred from the general nature and character of the church, but is essentially included in the ordinances appointed by her divine Head, and in the direct and solemn commands with which her statute book abounds. Hence, in the ancient church, her children, while yet infants, were recognized and sealed as members; were carried up at an early age to the great feasts at Jerusalem; and, that they might be taught to take an interest in all that pertained to the people of God, the command of Jehovah was—'These words shall be in thine heart, and thou shalt teach them diligently unto thy children, and shalt talk of them when thou sittest in thine house, and when thou walkest by the way, and when thou liest down, and when thou risest up.' Nay more—it was not

[1] Samuel Miller, 'Report to the General Assembly, on Christian Education', Samuel Miller and J. J. Janeway, *The Christian Education of Children and Youth* (Philadelphia: Wm. S. Martien, 1840), pp. 7-40.

only enjoined on parents under that economy, to teach their children all the commands of God, and continually to inculcate obedience to them, but also to make them familiar with the history of the church—continually reminding them of all Jehovah's dealing with his covenant people; his signal deliverances; his heavy judgments; and the various ways by which he led them on, and accomplished his purposes toward them.

When the New Testament economy was introduced, the same great principles of duty toward the children of the church were not only retained, but with the increasing light and spirituality of the new dispensation, were extended in their application, and urged with new force. Still, while in their infancy, the church, by a solemn rite, was commanded to recognize her children as the members of her body; to regard herself as their moral parent; and to make their early instruction and discipline an object of unceasing care and labour. Some of the examples of this care, and of the happy results of it, recorded in the early history of the church, are at once memorable and instructive.

The pious 'witnesses for the truth' in the Dark Ages, were, perhaps, more remarkable for nothing than for their faithfulness in the instruction and discipline of their children. In particular, the devoted and exemplary Waldenses were probably indebted, under God, to their peculiar diligence in the discharge of this duty, for their remarkable success in keeping their body together; in transmitting their testimony from generation to generation; and in remaining so long as they did, a beacon for the admiration and guidance of the church in after times. Historians tell us that these pious people were in the habit of employing every hour that they could rescue from labour and sleep, in gaining religious knowledge themselves, and in imparting it to the children and young people of their community; that they were careful to prepare excellent catechisms, and other formularies for their youth; and that their pastors made the religious instruction of youth a leading and unceasing object of their labours.

In imitation of their example, the most pure and enlightened of the Reformed churches have ever directed their attention to the education of their children as an object of primary importance in promoting the great interests of religion. Among these churches, that of

Scotland is, on several accounts, most instructive and most interesting to us, as bearing to us, more than any other, the relation of parent. This church, from the earliest period of her establishment, has made careful provision for the early instruction and discipline of her children. By different acts of her General Assembly, from time to time, she has declared their education to be under the supervision and government of her judicatories, and directed the course of their studies accordingly. The General Assembly, soon after its first formation, in 1560, and at different times afterwards, directed the several presbyteries to settle a church school in every parish, and to see that the teacher employed in each was a pious, orthodox, well-qualified man, adapted to instruct youth in the Scriptures, in the Catechism, and in all the most important things, as well as in the elements of literature. By an act of the General Assembly of 1642, a grammar school was erected in every presbytery. The Assembly of 1700 enjoined on all presbyteries to 'take special, particular, and exact notice', of all schoolmasters, governors, and instructors of youth, within their respective bounds, and oblige them to subscribe the Confession of Faith; and, in case of continued negligence (after admonition), error, or immorality, or not being careful to educate those committed to their charge in the Protestant Reformed religion—pointed out the mode in which they were to be punished. By the Assembly of 1706, it was enjoined that presbyteries visit the grammar schools within their respective bounds, twice a year, by some of their number. And, finally, in 1738, the General Assembly revived and ratified the acts of preceding Assemblies, by which visitations of colleges were directed to be kept up by committees of the Assembly; and the principal regents, professors, masters, and doctors within the same were required to be tried concerning their piety, their soundness in the faith, their ability to discharge the duties of their calling, and the honesty of their conversation.

Several other Reformed churches might be cited, as furnishing eminent and instructive examples of fidelity in discharging the great duty which it is the object of this report to recommend. The Church of Holland will alone be noticed at present. By the synodical assemblies of that church it is directed that the consistories in every congregation, shall provide good schoolmasters, who shall be able not only to instruct children in reading, writing, grammar, and the liberal sciences, but also to teach them the Catechism, and the first principles of religion. Every schoolmaster was to be obliged to subscribe the *Confession of Faith of the Belgic Churches,* or the *Heidelberg Catechism.* With regard to instructing children in the Catechism, a threefold attention to it is solemnly enjoined in that church; *viz.:* first, domestic, by parents; second, scholastic, by schoolmasters; and third, ecclesiastic, by pastors, assisted by other members of their consistories; and all whose duty it is to inspect schools, are 'admonished to make this an object of their very first care'. It is further provided, that no person shall be appointed to the charge of any school who is not a member in full communion with the Reformed Belgic Church, and who shall not previously have subscribed the Confession of Faith and Catechism of the church, and solemnly promised to instruct the children committed to his care in the principles contained in the standards of the church. More than this;—it is enjoined that every schoolmaster shall employ two half-days in every week, not only in hearing the children repeat, but in assisting them to understand the Catechism. And to ensure fidelity in these teachers, it is made the duty of the pastors and elders of each church, frequently to visit the schools; to encourage and direct the teachers in the proper method of catechising; to examine the children 'with mild severity'; and to excite them to industry and piety, by holy exhortations, by seasonable commendations, and by little appropriate awards.

Nor is this zealous and persevering labour in the religious training of youth confined to Protestant churches. It is well known, that among some of the Roman Catholic congregations of Europe, the children are imbued with a knowledge of their erroneous system, with an indefatigable diligence and patience which may well put to shame the professors of a more scriptural creed. The consequence is, that so large a number of that denomination of professing Christians have an attachment to their sect, and an expertness in defending their superstitious peculiarities, rarely found among the mass of Protestants.

When your committee contrast these facts with the state of things now existing, and which has for a long time existed, and been manifestly growing in the Presbyterian Church, in regard to the religious training of her children, they experience a degree of mortification which it is not easy to express. For a number of years, indeed, after the planting of our church in this country, that portion of our members which had migrated from Scotland, or the north of Ireland, and their immediate successors, retained much of their European habit in regard to this matter. Their children were, to a considerable extent, trained, as was customary in the land of their fathers, and made perfectly familiar with the Catechisms of the church, and the elementary principles of religion. But even this remnant of European fidelity has, in a great measure, disappeared. The Catechisms of our church have nothing like the currency, even among this class of our young people that they had fifty years ago. From many parts of the church in which they were then habitually taught, they are now, in a great measure, banished. The religious instruction of our youth, instead of becoming more ample and faithful, as the facilities for its accomplishment have multiplied—has undoubtedly declined, both as to extent and fidelity. The children of church members are, in a multitude of cases, totally neglected, and left to ignorance and heathenism. In other instances, they are committed to the tuition of the intemperate, the profane, and the profligate. Not infrequently they are sent to institutions taught by Papists, or other errorists, who are known to make every effort to instil their erroneous opinions into the minds of the youth committed to their care. It may be doubted whether there is a body of people at this time on earth, so orthodox in their creed, and at the same time so deplorably delinquent in the religious education of their children, as the Presbyterian Church in the United States.

In this state of things, no wonder that so many of the children of our beloved church grow up in ignorance, and regardless of the religion of their fathers; some becoming profane and impious; others turning aside to various forms of fatal error; and a large majority feeling little attachment to the good old way, in which they ought to have been faithfully and prayerfully trained. And it is painful to recollect that, amidst this unhappy delinquency, the judicatories of our church have in a great measure slumbered over the evil, and have taken no systematic or efficient order for the removal of it.

The mischiefs flowing from this neglect of early religious instruction are numberless and deplorable.

The first and most serious of these mischiefs is, *its tendency to destroy the souls of our children.*

On the one hand, when the early youth of children is passed without proper instruction in divine things, it is difficult to measure or conceive the thick darkness which generally covers their minds, and appears to defy all ordinary endeavours to impart to them the knowledge of evangelical truth. When men grow old in ignorance, as well as in sin, they are surrounded with a double barrier against the entrance of heavenly light. It becomes almost necessary to teach them a new language before the instructor, in such cases, can be understood. Accordingly the probability of such persons being ever brought to a saving acquaintance with the gospel, is greatly diminished, and, in many cases, rendered in a great measure, hopeless. On the other hand, when the seeds of truth and duty are early and faithfully sown in the minds of youth; though they may long lie buried, there is strong ground of hope that they will eventually spring up, and bring forth a rich harvest. Who can estimate then, the cruelty, the awful guilt of those, whether parents or pastors, who neglect that which is so closely connected, not only with the present happiness, but with the everlasting welfare of every youth committed to their care?

Closely allied with that which was last stated, is another evil resulting from the neglect of a religious education of the children of the church; and that is, *the frequency with which our young people may be expected, in such case, to depart from the church of their fathers, and either stray into communions of the most corrupt character, or become totally regardless of religion in any form.* The fact is, even if the preaching of a pastor be ever so sound and able; yet if he neglect the appropriate training of the young people of his charge, and leave them to the small gleanings of instruction which they will be likely to catch by the ear from the pulpit, they may be expected to grow up little better than heathen in fact, though Christian in name. The consequence must inevitably be, the decay and final ruin of those flocks which have not some other means by which to supply the places of their dying members, than the seed of the church.

Further, the pastor who neglects the religious training of the young people of his charge, *will find them altogether unprepared to profit by his public ministry.* If a pastor desires to render his discourses from the pulpit as profitable as possible to the youth of his flock, he cannot take a more direct course for the attainment of his object, than to attend to them with parental diligence and affection; to become personally acquainted with them; to meet them frequently in private as a body; to catechise them; to render them familiar with his person, his modes of thinking and speaking, and to imbue their minds with those elementary principles of divine knowledge which will prepare them to hear him in the pulpit with intelligence, with respect, and with profit. If a preacher wished for the most favourable opportunity conceivable for preparing the youth of his charge to listen to his sermons to the greatest advantage, it would not be easy to devise one more admirably suited to his purpose, than to meet them, by themselves, once a week, in a paternal and affectionate manner; to teach them the elementary principles of that system which his discourses from the pulpit are intended to explain and inculcate; thus to accustom them to his topics, his phraseology, his manner, his whole course of instruction, and prepare them to receive the richest benefit from his public discourses. There can be no doubt that one great reason why many young people receive so little profit from the pulpit discourses of their minister is, that he has taken so little pains to open their minds by previous instruction; to prepare the soil for the seed; to prepossess them in favour of the substance and mode of his teaching. That minister who desires that his preaching may make the deepest and most favourable impression on the minds of the children and young people of his charge, is an infatuated man, regardless of all the dictates of reason, experience, and the Word of God, if he does not employ himself diligently in labouring to pave the way for their reception of his more formal and public instruction. Young people thus prepared to attend on his preaching, will, of course, understand it better; receive it more readily and respectfully; and be more likely, by the grace of God, to lay it up in their hearts, and practice it in their lives.

Again, the pastor who neglects the religious instruction of the children of his flock *neglects one of the most direct and powerful means of winning the parents themselves to the knowledge and love of the gospel*. It cannot have escaped the notice of any attentive observer of human affairs, that there is no avenue to the hearts of parents more direct and certain than diligent and affectionate attention to their children. On the one hand, it would seem as if they could often bear to be themselves neglected, if their beloved children be followed with manifestations of interest and good will. And, on the other hand, if they see their children overlooked and neglected, scarcely anything in their view can atone for this negligence. Instances of the most striking character have occurred, in which parents appeared to receive the strongest impressions in favour of particular ministers, and in favour of the cause in which they were engaged, chiefly because those ministers had given their children affectionate paternal counsel and instruction, and appeared to manifest a peculiar interest in their temporal and eternal welfare. Nor is this all. It is undoubtedly a fact, that, in some cases, one of the best modes of addressing parents on the great subject of religion, is through the medium of their children. The catechising, instructing, and exhorting of children in the presence of their parents, have frequently proved the means of the conversion of those parents. And it has often happened that the manifest improvement, and especially the hopeful conversion of children in catechetical and Bible classes, have been signally blessed to the spiritual benefit of their parents, and, indeed, of the whole families to which they belonged. What must be thought, then, of the indolence or blindness of that pastor who can willingly forego all these blessings, and incur all the opposite evils, by habitually neglecting the children of the flock committed to his care?

It follows, of course, that the pastor who does not diligently attend to the religious instruction of the young people of his charge, *is blind to the comfort, the acceptance, and the popularity of his own ministry.* Why is it that so many ministers, before reaching an infirm old age, grow out of date with their people, and lose their influence with them? Especially, why is it that the younger part of their flocks feel so little attraction to them, dislike their preaching, and sigh for a change of pastors? There is reason to believe that this has seldom occurred, except in cases in which pastors have been eminently negligent of the religious training of their young people; in which, however respectable they may have been for their talents, their learning, and their worth, in other respects, they have utterly failed to bind the affections of the children to their persons; to make everyone of them revere and love them as affectionate fathers; and, by faithful attentions, to inspire them with the strongest sentiments of veneration and filial attachment. Those whose range of observation has been considerable, have, no doubt, seen examples of ministers, whose preaching was by no means very striking or attractive, yet retaining to the latest period of their lives, the affections of all committed to their care, and especially being the favourites of the young people, who have rallied round them in their old age, and contributed not a little to render their last days both useful and happy. It may be doubted whether such a case ever occurred, excepting where the pastor had bestowed much attention on the young people of his charge.

Such are some of the evils which flow from neglect on the part of the church to train up her children in the knowledge of her doctrines and order. She may expect to see a majority of those children—even children of professors of religion—growing up in ignorance and profligacy; of course forsaking the church of their fathers; leaving her either to sink, or to be filled up by converts from without; turning away from those pastors who neglected them; and causing such pastors to experience in their old age, the merited reward of unfaithful servants.

The truth is, if there be any one part of the pastor's duty, which, more than almost any other, deserves to be considered as vital and fundamental, it is that which bears immediately on the seed of the church—the nursery of Christ's family—that branch of his labour which has for its object the extending and perpetuating the church, by raising up a godly seed to take the place of their parents when they shall be laid in the dust.

In this view of the subject, shall nothing be done by the supreme judicatory of our church, to rouse the attention, and direct the efforts of our churches to this most important, but long neglected concern? That something ought to be done is manifest. It is surely high time to awake out of sleep, and enquire what we can do, and ought to do, as a Christian denomination.

The committee are not unmindful of the difficulties which beset this great subject; and which will render a prompt and thorough return to our duty in regard to it, an arduous, if not an almost impracticable task; difficulties arising from our long continued habits of delinquency—from the scattered state of the population in many parts of our church—from the sentiments in favour of a spurious liberality, which prevail so peculiarly and extensively among many denominations of Christians in the United States, and among none more than Presbyterians—and from the constant and indefatigable labour required for a faithful discharge of the duty recommended. But great as these difficulties are, they may be surmounted by faith, patience, labour, and prayer. And it is evident, that even if the difficulties attending the faithful discharge of the duty in question were far more numerous and formidable than they are, the rewards would, more than an hundredfold, counterbalance all the care and toil bestowed on the object. At any rate, if our delinquency is ever to be repaired, and any real improvement in this great field of Christian effort attained, the sooner we begin the better. The souls of our children are precious—the exigencies of the church are pressing—and every hour we lose in commencing the work of reform, is a loss to all the best interests of the church, and the world—a loss stretching into eternity.

After these preliminary remarks, the committee would beg leave to present a sketch of what they think may and ought to be attempted in reference to this important subject. They are aware that what they are about to propose, has nothing of novelty in it; but, if adopted, would be only returning, in substance, to the forgotten and neglected usages of our venerated fathers, both in Europe and in our own country. And although they are sensible that some of their suggestions may not equally apply, and may not be capable of being carried into execution with equal convenience, in all the churches of our denomination—yet they would fain hope, that a plan may be suggested, which, if carried into effect, may be productive of some benefit to the rising generation. They would, therefore, most respectfully propose to the Assembly the adoption of the following recommendations, to be sent down to all the subordinate judicatories and churches under our care.

I. It is recommended, *that the subject of the Christian education of children be frequently brought before the people, in the instructions and devotional exercises of the pulpit, in a manner so pointed and solemn, as may be adapted to inform the minds, and impress the consciences of*

739

parents and church officers, in regard to a matter so little understood, and so little laid to heart even by many who profess to be truly pious.

II. It is recommended, *that when pastors visit families, whether the visitation be performed formally or otherwise, all the children of every family be attended to with particular care; that their names be taken down; that every important circumstance concerning each, be recorded; that each be affectionately noticed and addressed; that God's claim to them be presented and urged; and that every practicable method be adopted to render such interviews interesting and instructive.* For this purpose, there may be a little tract given to one; an appropriate, striking anecdote related to another; and some expression of interest and regard suited to win the confidence of a third, and so of the whole youthful circle. This would require no expense—nothing, at least, but thought and prayer; as tracts and other little publications suitable to be thus employed, may be had, if not gratuitously, at least on very easy terms, and to almost any extent.

III. It is recommended, *that every congregation shall establish one or more church schools, adapted to the instruction of children between six and ten years of age.* These primary schools had better, usually, be taught by females, decidedly pious, intelligent, and of known attachment to the doctrines and order of our church. These teachers ought to be selected by the church session, and governed by rules formed by that body. Females would be preferable as teachers in such schools; because they may, for the most part, be had on more economical terms than teachers of the other sex; and because, if of a suitable character, they will be apt to train up their pupils with more soft and gentle manners. As children of this tender age cannot travel far to school, there ought to be several of this class of schools in every congregation of any size; as not more than twenty-five, or, at most, thirty scholars of this age ought ever to be placed under one teacher. In these schools, the Bible ought to be used every day, and the Shorter Catechism of the church recited at least once every week; and the pastor and elders ought frequently to visit them, and see that the teachers are faithful; that all the methods of instruction employed are of the best kind; and that the manners and habits of the children are such as become those who are training up for usefulness here, and for the family of Christ hereafter. In these lower schools, it may be proper that the females be sometimes employed, at the discretion of the teachers, in sewing, and in other occupations adapted to their sex. The exercises, every day, should be opened and closed with prayer.

IV. It is recommended, *that in populous towns, infant schools be established as far as circumstances will admit.* These, of course, should be placed under the direction of pious, enlightened females; and it is important that all the religious exercises which take place in them be in conformity with the usages of our own church; and that nothing be admitted which will have a tendency to introduce forms which distinguish other denominations. In these infant schools, the simpler portions of the Holy Scriptures, the Catechism for Young Children, furnished by the Assembly's Board of Publication, and such oral instruction as may be adapted to the weakest capacities, ought to be constantly employed.

V. It is recommended, *that there be established in every presbytery at least one grammar school or academy, and in the larger and more opulent presbyteries more than one, adapted for training youth in the more advanced branches of knowledge, and preparing such of them as may desire it, for an introduction into college.* These academies ought to be under the immediate instruction of ripe and accomplished scholars—men in full communion with the Presbyterian Church; of pious and exemplary deportment; and of known attachment to the faith and order of our church. These institutions ought to be under the supervision of the respective presbyteries in which they are placed, and a committee of ministers and elders appointed by each presbytery to visit them, and to watch over the whole course of instruction and discipline in them. It is by no means, indeed, intended to advise that no pupils be received into such academies but such as are connected with the Presbyterian Church, but it is intended to be earnestly recommended, that all the religious exercises in the same be strictly Presbyterian in their character; and that no youth be allowed to enter them, or to continue a day in them, who is not perfectly correct and unexceptionable in his moral character, and disposed to treat the ordinances of religion with entire respect. In these academies, it is recommended that the Larger Catechism of our church be made a class book; and, if not wholly committed to memory, at least made the subject of recitation and commentary, and accompanied with such other reading and oral instruction as may be adapted to make the pupils familiar with the faith and order of the Presbyterian Church, and with the considerations which explain and vindicate the same.

VI. It is recommended, *that when any of our youth are destined to enjoy the privileges of a college or university, there be the utmost care exercised in selecting for them those institutions in which their moral and religious training will receive the most faithful attention; institutions in which, as far as they can be found, the professors are orthodox and pious, and in which the whole weight of their instruction and influence will be thrown into the scale of pure and undefiled religion, as well as sound learning.* No child of the church ought ever to be sent to any seminary of learning, however high its literary character, in which sound religious instruction is not made a constant and governing object of attention. That parent who selects for his son a college in which his moral and religious interests will run the risk of being sacrificed, or even jeoparded, for the sake of indulging some petty taste or prejudice, is chargeable with an unfaithfulness and cruelty of the most inexcusable kind. In several parts of our church, academies and colleges have been founded by presbyteries and synods, and placed entirely under the direction of the judicatories which founded them. This, where it can be done, is a wise plan; and adapted more effectually to secure to our youth the advantages of thorough and unshackled religious training, than is possible upon any other plan.

VII. It is recommended, *that all parents and heads of families be in the constant habit of assembling the children and youth of their families in the evening of every Lord's day, and spending at least an hour in attending to the recitation of the Catechism, and such other modes of oral instruction in divine things, as the capacity and character of each may require.* Let the head of the family, whether male or female, as the case may be, take this opportunity of speaking seriously to each of the young persons present, and administering an affectionate but solemn rebuke, for any disorderly conduct on that day, or the preceding week, closing with exhortation and a comprehensive prayer. And that this domestic service may not interfere with attendance on public services which, in some churches, are stately held on that evening; in such churches, let the hour devoted to this family interview be the one immediately preceding the evening meal. In all cases in which the Catechism is recited, let one or two proof texts be carefully quoted and committed to memory, for the support of each answer; and let the children be always reminded that the Bible is the only infallible rule of faith and practice, and that the Catechism owes all its authority and value to the fact, that it contains the system of doctrine taught in the Holy Scriptures.

VIII. It is recommended, *that pastors and church sessions be diligently attentive to the catechising and religious instruction of all the children and young people under their care, through the whole course of their childhood and youth.* No recitation of the Catechism in any other school or place ought to supersede this. However constantly and faithfully it may be attended to by the parents, or by Sabbath School teachers; still the pastor and the elders ought to deem it a privilege, as well as a duty, to convene the children of the church, and to endeavour to establish that acquaintance with them, and that influence over them, which will be likely to result in rich advantages to both. Even if a wise and faithful pastor were certain that the religious instruction of the children committed to his care would be adequately discharged without his aid; still he ought, as we have seen, for his own sake, as well as theirs, to desire to bring his personal instruction into contact with their minds; and thus to prepare them to love his person, and profit by his ministry; and to prepare himself to understand, in some measure, the character and want of each, and the best means of doing them good. Nor ought these meetings with the children of the church to be so rare as they too commonly are. Some pastors assemble their children to be catechised and addressed once or twice a year, and others, at most, once in two or three months. It is deliberately believed by the committee that such infrequent meetings are of little or no real value. As a source of instruction to the children, they are of very small advantage, if of any at all; and as a means of making the pastor personally acquainted with the children, and enabling him to judge of the temper, capacity, and disposition of each; to adapt himself to their respective characters; to mark the progress or retrocession of each; and to gain the confidence and affection of all—they might almost as well be omitted. These interviews ought to take place every week—to be attended with as much punctuality as the public exercises of the Sabbath; and to be engaged in with pencil and memorandum book in hand, so that the appearance and outmaking of each may be kept in mind from week to week; and to be conducted throughout with the indefatigable diligence, patience, and affection which are adapted to reach and win the hearts of the children. In large congregations, the members of which are widely scattered, it may not be easy, or even practicable to meet all the children of the same church, in a single body, once in every week. In this case, it may be expedient to have two or three little assemblies of children convened in different parts of the congregation every week; and once in each month, the whole of the children and young people of the congregation may be assembled in the afternoon of the Lord's day, in the church; and there, instead of the usual afternoon service, a service intended especially for their benefit may be conducted, in the presence of their parents and others, in such a manner as to be even more instructive, solemn, and touching to all present than the ordinary service. But this matter may be conducted, where circumstances render it expedient, somewhat differently. Suppose that there are three catechising stations in different parts of the congregation. These may be all punctually attended in the same week, and even on the same day of the week, one by the pastor, and the other two by two of the elders. On the succeeding two weeks, the pastor may change places with his elders; so that he may, in turn, attend every class once a month, and, at the end of the month, meet and address them all in a body, as before suggested. These exercises on the Catechism will be of little value, if the children be merely called upon to repeat by memory the words of the formulary. Every answer ought to be analysed and explained in the most simple and patient manner—condescending to the weakness of the youthful mind, and endeavouring to communicate truth in the most practical and affectionate form. In any and every case, it is important that the elders take a part in this work, that they may become personally acquainted with the children of the church, and also that the work may not be neglected when the pastor is unwell or absent.

IX. It is recommended, *that one or more Bible classes be established in every congregation*. The best methods of conducting these will readily occur to every enlightened pastor, and although they are, and ought to be primarily intended and adapted for the instruction of the young, they may, and ought to include as many, of both sexes and of all ages, as can be prevailed upon to engage in the study of the Bible.

X. It is recommended, *that all the Sabbath Schools in every congregation be under the constant supervision and direction of the pastor and eldership.*

Sabbath schools are too often surrendered to the guidance of irresponsible persons, and sometimes to persons making no profession, and manifesting no practical sense of religion; and whose teaching, of course, must be of a very equivocal character. And sometimes books are introduced from well meaning donors, and regulations formed by no means adapted to promote the spiritual interests of the children. Everything of this kind ought to be avoided. All the teachers employed, all the books used, and all the regulations adopted ought to be such as the pastor and session approve. The pastor, as often as his engagements allow, ought to step in, if it be but for a few minutes, to the various schools, and manifest his interest in them by a word of counsel or of prayer, as the case may be; and thus put himself in the way of knowing personally how everything is conducted, and how everything prospers, and thus qualify himself to preside over the whole with intelligence and fidelity.

XI. It is recommended, *that the baptized children of the church, be assembled three or four times in each year, and be affectionately addressed and prayed with by the pastor.* At these interviews it will be generally advisable to have the parents present, and also the elders, and to accompany the exercises with such tender appeals to parents, as peculiarly charged with the religious training of their offspring; and to the elders, as being the spiritual overseers of the youth of the church, as may tend at once, to remind both of their duty, and to impress on their minds a sense of their solemn obligations. As almost every church may be supposed, of course, to have one or two social services, in the secular evenings of each week, these interviews with baptized children may be made, once in three months, to take the place of one of these meetings, so as to avoid the undue multiplication of public services, which might prove oppressive both to the pastor and the people of his charge.

XII. It is earnestly recommended, *that all our church sessions, presbyteries, and synods direct particular attention to this important subject.* It will be expedient for them once a year, at least, to ascertain how this great concern stands in their bounds. And if they duly appreciate its importance, it will often engage their attention. They will feel that it is impossible too early to enter on the work of forming a large and digested system of religious training, which shall, in some good degree, carry us back to the habits of our venerated fathers, on this subject, with such improvements as the advantages and facilities furnished by modern times may enable us to apply.

XIII. It is recommended, *that the foregoing system, as far as applicable, be enjoined by the General Assembly to be adopted at all our missionary stations among the heathen.* If it be important among the regular and established churches of Christendom, it is in some respects still more vitally important in evangelising the pagan world. It is believed that the advantages of directing special attention to heathen youth, have never yet been either sufficiently appreciated or pursued. When the time shall come, in which, as the Scriptures declare, 'nations shall be born in a day', perhaps nothing will be more likely to prepare the way for such wonders, than having previously scattered amongst youth the seeds of gospel truth.

It may, perhaps, be remarked by some, on a survey of the foregoing recommendations, that they present an amount of attention, and of unceasing labour which cannot fail of pressing heavily on the mind, the heart, and strength of every pastor. This is not denied. To accomplish, from year to year, the aggregate of what has been recommended, must indeed, make large draughts on the time, the thoughts, and the efforts of every spiritual overseer. But surely no faithful minister will complain of this. Can he wear out in any branch of labour more likely to turn to great account? Can he devote himself to any object more worthy of his care; more adapted to reward his work of faith and labour of love; or more fitted to build up the church, and promote his own acceptance and happiness, as an ambassador of Christ, than to train up a generation to serve God, when he shall have gone to his eternal reward?

SOME OTHER PRINCETON TITLES
PUBLISHED BY THE TRUST

WESTMINSTER CONFESSION: A COMMENTARY
A. A. Hodge
ISBN: 978 0 85151 828 2
432pp. clothbound

LIFE OF CHARLES HODGE
A. A. Hodge
ISBN: 978 1 84871 090 0
672pp. clothbound

1&2 CORINTHIANS (GENEVA COMMENTARY SERIES)
Charles Hodge
ISBN: 978 0 85151 185 6
716pp. clothbound

EPHESIANS (GENEVA COMMENTARY SERIES)
Charles Hodge
ISBN: 978 0 85151 591 5
320pp. clothbound

PRINCETON SERMONS
Charles Hodge
ISBN: 978 0 85151 285 3
403pp. clothbound

ROMANS (GENEVA COMMENTARY SERIES)
Charles Hodge
ISBN: 978 0 85151 213 6
732pp. clothbound

BIBLICAL DOCTRINES
B. B. Warfield
ISBN: 978 0 85151 534 2
674pp. clothbound

COUNTERFEIT MIRACLES
B. B. Warfield
ISBN: 978 0 85151 166 5
536pp. paperback

Faith & Life
B. B. Warfield
ISBN: 978 0 85151 585 4
464pp. clothbound

SAVIOUR OF THE WORLD
B. B. Warfield
ISBN: 978 0 85151 593 9
280pp. clothbound

STUDIES IN THEOLOGY
B. B. Warfield
ISBN: 978 0 85151 533 5
690pp. clothbound

PASTOR-TEACHERS OF OLD PRINCETON
Memorial Addresses for the Faculty of
Princeton Theological Seminary
1812-1921
Selected and Introduced by James M. Garretson
ISBN: 978 1 84871 161 7
600pp. clothbound

PRINCETON AND PREACHING
Archibald Alexander and the Christian Ministry
James M. Garretson
ISBN: 978 0 85151 893 0
304pp. clothbound

PRINCETON SEMINARY
Volume 1
Faith & Learning: 1812–1868:
David B. Calhoun
ISBN: 978 0 85151 670 7
528pp. clothbound

PRINCETON SEMINARY
Volume 2
The Majestic Testimony: 1869–1929
David B. Calhoun
ISBN: 978 0 85151 695 0
592pp. clothbound

THE BANNER OF TRUTH TRUST originated in 1957 in London. The founders believed that much of the best literature of historic Christianity had been allowed to fall into oblivion and that, under God, its recovery could well lead not only to a strengthening of the church today but to true revival.

Inter-denominational in vision, this publishing work is now international, and our lists include a number of contemporary authors along with classics from the past. The translation of these books into many languages is encouraged.

A monthly magazine, *The Banner of Truth,* is also published and further information will be gladly supplied by either of the offices below.

THE BANNER OF TRUTH TRUST

3 Murrayfield Road,   PO Box 621, Carlisle,
Edinburgh, EH12 6EL   Pennsylvania 17013,
UK   USA

www.banneroftruth.co.uk

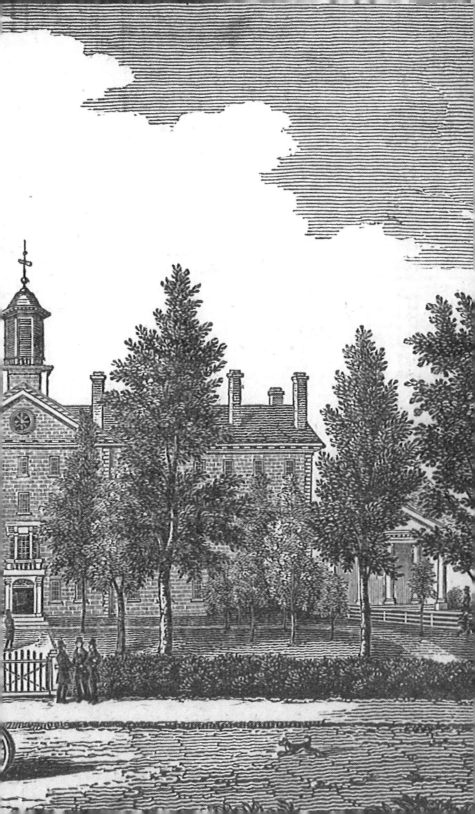

PRINCETON AND THE WORK OF THE CHRISTIAN MINISTRY

VOLUME 2

PRINCETON
AND THE WORK OF THE
CHRISTIAN MINISTRY

---

*A Collection of Addresses, Essays, and Articles
by Faculty and Friends of
Princeton Theological Seminary*

Volume 2

Selected

by

James M. Garretson

THE BANNER OF TRUTH TRUST

THE BANNER OF TRUTH TRUST

Head Office
3 Murrayfield Road
Edinburgh, EH12 6EL
UK

North America Office
PO Box 621
Carlisle, PA 17013
USA

banneroftruth.org

© The Banner of Truth Trust 2012
Reprinted 2020

*

ISBN
This Volume: 978 1 84871 163 1
Two-Volume Ser: 978 1 84871 164 8

*

Typeset in 11/13 Adobe Garamond Pro
at The Banner of Truth Trust, Edinburgh

Printed in the USA by
Versa Press Inc.,
East Peoria, IL.

CONTENTS OF VOLUME 2

Contents

ASHBEL GREEN
1762-1848

LEADING nineteenth-century Presbyterian minister and educator, Ashbel Green was born in Hanover, New Jersey. Green's father worked both as a Presbyterian pastor and a physician; his mother was a descendant of one of the founders of the College of New Jersey. Green was educated and nurtured in a home committed to strict Sabbath observance, routine Bible study, and disciplined catechetical instruction.

Active in the local militia during the American Revolution, Green graduated from the College of New Jersey in 1783. During his collegiate years Green's religious scepticism gave way to new evangelical convictions and membership in the local Presbyterian Church at Princeton. He worked as a tutor at the College for two years after graduation, in turn receiving appointment as Professor of Mathematics and Natural Philosophy. At Princeton he read Theology under Dr John Witherspoon. Licensed to preach in 1786, Green was ordained and installed in 1787 as assistant pastor at the Second Presbyterian Church in Philadelphia. Six years later he became senior pastor, and remained in that position until 1812, when he was appointed President of the College of New Jersey. Green's leadership doubled student enrolment, strengthened the faculty, and introduced the study of the Bible into the curriculum. In this period over thirty students at the college (including John Breckinridge, Charles Hodge and Charles P. McIlvaine) were spiritually influenced by the revival that took place on campus in 1814-15.

Green resigned his presidency in 1822 and returned to Philadelphia, where he spent the remainder of his life. In addition to editing the *Christian Advocate* for twelve years, he maintained active involvement in his denomination and in related benevolent and educational enterprises. A polemicist on behalf of Old-school Presbyterianism, Green was often at the centre of the theological issues that confronted the Presbyterian Church in the early nineteenth century. He was instrumental in the establishment of Princeton Theological Seminary and served as President of its Board of Directors from 1812-48. He was noted for his strength of character, decided convictions, and devout piety. Green's influence, considered by some as intolerant and divisive, was a formidable force in shaping the identity and direction of his denomination. In the years leading up to the 1837 split within the Presbyterian Church, the Princeton faculty were hesitant to support Green's activism in seeking disciplinary action and removal from office of ministers who did not subscribe to the Westminster Standards in the strict sense in which Green did. While the Princeton faculty were not indifferent to Green's concerns, they feared Green's approach more divisive than constructive in dealing with the mounting tensions within the denomination.

A popular preacher and commanding figure, Green's published works include biography, theology, and a variety of sermons and addresses. His theology of ministry is represented in the founding documents of Princeton Theological Seminary approved in 1811 by the General Assembly, *The Plan of the Theological Seminary of the Presbyterian Church in the United States of America*. Ashbel Green's love for the theology of the *Westminster Confession* and *Larger* and *Shorter Catechisms* resulted in publication of the two-volume work, *Lectures on the Shorter Catechism of the Presbyterian Church in the United States of America, addressed to Youth*. Green's autobiography was published in the late 1840s.

Ashbel Green died in 1848 at the age of 86. His death was illustrative of his piety: his friends discovered his lifeless body in the posture of prayer.

Ashbel Green

Green's role in founding and guiding Princeton Theological Seminary in its opening decades is immeasurable. His combination of confessional Calvinism, experimental piety, and Christ-centred preaching gave backbone to the new institution and established its direction for many years to come.

ADDRESS TO THE STUDENTS[1]

MY Young Friends and Brethren—candidates for the gospel ministry; addresses on occasions like the present, have been so frequently made in this place, that the topics peculiarly appropriate to them, have all, perhaps, been preoccupied.—The present is the third service of the kind to which I have myself been called. What therefore, I have now to offer, will be discursive; not confined to a single topic, but touching on a number; and if I deliver nothing that is new, I still hope, if you yield me a careful and candid attention, to say something which, under the divine blessing, may be useful.

Let me first call your attention to a point or two, relative to your course of study in this seminary.

There is scarcely an error to which youth of liberal minds and liberal studies are more prone, if left to themselves, than to take the subjects of study in a wrong order; and, if I mistake not, those whose minds are most active and most comprehensive are, unless well directed, more apt to commit this error than any others. The cause is obvious—their literary curiosity is so intense, and their thirst for knowledge so ardent, that they want to seize on everything at once. They must, at least, have a taste of every subject; they must know something about it. Hence it too often happens, that they acquire a love—a passion even—for miscellaneous reading, which abides with them long, perhaps through the whole of life. The natural, and almost necessary, result is that they know a little of everything, and but a little of anything—I mean, they never become thorough masters of any one branch of knowledge.

[1] Ashbel Green, 'An Address to the Students of the Theological Seminary at Princeton, at the close of the Semi-Annual Examination', *Biblical Repertory and Theological Review,* Vol. 3, No. 3 (July 1831), pp. 350-60.

It is, then, of great importance for liberal youth to pursue improvement in a right method, and to use the self-denial necessary to keep to such a method. There are certain things in every branch of science which are fundamental; they lie, and must lie, at the very foundation of all solid, accurate, and systematic knowledge of that branch of science; and if these elementary parts are not acquired at first, they are seldom acquired afterwards. Their acquisition commonly requires the aid of a teacher, and always requires a good deal of close and continued study; and if a young man does not master them in a school, or a college, or a seminary, he probably will never do it. If even disposed to do it afterwards, he will find it so difficult, that it is a thousand to one that he will get along without it, as well as he can; but always feeling the want of it—feeling it most sensibly, to the very end of life.

Now, what is this elementary fundamental knowledge in Christian theology, considered as a science and a system? I hesitate not to say that the most essential part of it is a knowledge of the Bible, in the languages in which the Bible was given by the inspiration of the Holy Ghost; and a just, accurate, and familiar view of the truths of the Bible, as they are arranged, defended, and illustrated, in our approved systems of theology, and in the Confession of Faith and Catechisms of our church. You may hereafter much more easily make improvement in other things, useful to a theological student, than in the two great departments of study which I have now named. Be assured, my young Brethren; if you do not acquire the ability of studying—I mean studying with pleasure and effect—the Holy Scriptures, in the Hebrew and Greek languages, before you leave this house, there is very little probability that you ever will acquire it; and if you do not acquire it, you will feel the loss—or at any rate you ought to feel it—every time you enter the sacred desk, through the whole of your ministerial course. You ought never to prepare a sermon, especially in the earlier periods of your future ministry, without carefully studying the text, and sometimes its connection too, in the *ipsissima verba*[1] of the Holy Spirit.

In like manner, in regard to systematic theology, if you do not acquire something like a thorough knowledge of it here, the probabil-

[1] the very words.

ity strongly is, that you will die without it. Yet, unless you accustom yourselves to go to the bottom of every point of doctrine and find its basis in the sure Word of God—for every other basis is unstable and worthless—and unless you attain to the ability of looking through the whole system, and of seeing the connection and bearing of every part on every other part—I say, unless you do this before you depart from the seminary, I feel well assured that not one in ten of you will ever do it. Your views, and your exhibitions of divine truth, will forever be disjointed, and frequently discordant. What you say and teach at one time, will be inconsistent with, and even contradictory to, what you say and teach at another. Now, we have quite enough of such teachers in our country already; and I do beseech you, my young Brethren, not to add yourselves to the number: and that you may not, see to it that you do not leave the seminary, till you have fixed every important doctrinal truth, as it lies in your mind and is an object of your faith, on the firm foundation of God's Word; and till you understand the consistency and harmony of all the parts of a theological system.

Are you ready to ask, whether I do not expect and wish, that you should endeavour to make some *improvements* in theology, in your future life? I must answer, as the logicians say—by distinguishing. If, by improvements in theology, the inquiry means an increase of clear perception and deep feeling, in relation to the beauty, glory, excellence, consistency and sweetness of evangelical truth—an increase, too, in a knowledge of the manner in which revealed truth may best be taught, inculcated, and defended—an increase, also, of discernment, as to the errors to which the truth is opposed, and the consequent correction of some minor errors in your own minds—an increase, in a word, of your acquaintance and understanding of the Bible in all its parts, and of the glorious scope and tendency of the whole: if only this, or chiefly this, be intended by an improvement in theology, then, I say, I hope you will make great improvements; for I believe that such improvements will always be made by every minister of the gospel, just in proportion as he grows in grace, and persists in studious habits.

But if, by improvements in theology, I am to understand what some vain talkers seem to intend, the making of some *great and original discoveries* of truths and doctrines, that no searching of the Scriptures has ever yet brought to light; then, I say, I pray God that you may never attempt, or think of making any such improvements; for, if you do, I have not a doubt you will run into false and delusive speculations and conclusions, injurious and perhaps ruinous to your own souls, and the souls of others. The fundamental truths of Holy Scripture have been given for the use and edification of God's people in every age since the canon of Scripture was completed; and I cannot believe that any great practical truth of the Bible has been hidden in such deep darkness as to have escaped the saints of God, and all the pious and learned interpreters of his holy Word, ever since the days of the apostles—escaped their vision, that the clear and satisfactory development of it might be ushered on the world at the present time. For myself, I would not listen for a moment to the man who should tell me that he had found something entirely new, and yet very important, in the doctrinal parts of the sacred Scriptures. If it is very new, I am sure it is not very important; for what is very important now, has certainly been so for many centuries past; and it violates all my maxims in regard to God's revealed will, to admit that it contains fundamental or very important practical truth, of which not a glimpse has been caught by the holiest and wisest men which the church of Christ has hitherto contained.

On this subject, there is sometimes instituted what seems to me a very senseless analogy. It is asked, shall the most brilliant and important discoveries be frequently made in all the natural sciences, and shall no discoveries and improvements be made in theology, the most interesting and sublime of all sciences? But consider, my young Friends, whether there is really any similarity at all between the two cases. On the subject of Christian theology, God has made a revelation of his will, and all the revelation that he will ever make in this world; and he has made this revelation in a book which, as all Protestants believe, he intended for popular use. But have we received a revelation from God of a system of astronomy? No, certainly, unless we profess to be Hutchinsonians; and even then, we must not admit that the system can be improved. Have we gotten a revealed system of natural philosophy? of mathematics? of mechanics? of gravitation? of attraction and repulsion? of hydraulics? of pneumatics? of chemistry? of electricity and galvanism? of heat? of light and colours? of the theory of the tides? of the fluxionary calculus? and of fifty other things, of a like kind, that might be named? Only show me a divine revelation on any one of these subjects—a finished and popular revelation, of all that the great Author of nature ever intends to make known in regard to that subject—and I stand prepared to carry out my principle, and to say, that on that subject you are not to expect to make great discoveries and improvements. No; my young Brethren, there is no resemblance whatever between theology and natural philosophy, that warrants the running of a parallel between them in the matter of improvement and discovery, by mere human intellect and effort—none whatever—and I must think it is a very stupid thing to institute any such analogy, as that which I have shown to be so palpably absurd.

Thus, at much greater length than I at first intended, I have endeavoured to show the prime importance of your leaving this place at least tolerably versed in the Hebrew and Greek of the Bible, that you may be qualified to get at the genuine meaning, and make a sound *exegesis* of any and every text of Holy Scripture; and also of your going to the bottom of every subject of didactic, and, if you please, of polemic theology, but of the former especially; and of learning the bearing of every truth on every other truth, and of understanding the connection and consistency of the whole. You will not understand, however, that I have meant to intimate that any one study of your course here may be neglected. Far from this. It seems to me that there is not a single study in this seminary, which is either superfluous in itself, or carried to a greater extent than will be found useful to you in your future ministerial life. Indeed, the time you spend here is so short, that your professors find, and I believe you must all be sensible, that it is not practicable for you to go as far in any one study as would be desirable and useful, if circumstances did not imperiously forbid it. But, I repeat, my aim has been to make you very sensible, that the languages of the Bible, and systematic theology, are the two things which you must now get, with some accuracy, in their elements at least, or you are never likely to get them; that whatever else you neglect, or are obliged to omit, you must not omit or neglect these; because, among other reasons, you will have a demand for them every time you prepare for, or appear in the pulpit; whereas there are other things for which you will not have such immediate and constant use, and which you can more easily acquire by yourselves, without a teacher, and as opportunity may favour.

In the next place, I would fain guard you against an error which, it would seem, is becoming popular—the error of thinking that close study, and much of it employed in gaining accurate Bible knowledge, and in investigating doctrinal truth, is unfavourable to a highly devout spirit, great sanctity of heart and life, and great zeal in preaching the gospel, and endeavouring to win souls to the Saviour. Now I affirm, and I appeal to facts, and to the experience of the whole Christian church, to support my affirmation, that the apprehension that close study will produce the evil effects specified, is utterly groundless; nay, that it is in direct contrariety to the truth. Yes, I confidently maintain, that the most studious ministers of the gospel, as a general rule—admitting of a few, and but a very few exceptions—have always been, and now are, the most devotedly pious of all their brethren, and the most zealous and the most successful, in their labours for the conversion of sinners, and the edification of saints. If you look into Christian antiquity, whom will you there find, after the apostolic age, to compare with Justin the Martyr, with Irenaeus, and Polycarp, and Cyprian, and Ambrose, and Basil, and Chrysostom, and Augustine, and a number of others like them? And when you come down to the Protestant Reformation, whom will you set in competition with Luther, and Melancthon, and Bucer, and Zwingli, and Calvin, and Beza, and Cranmer, and Jewel, and Ridley, and Knox, and a long list of their coadjutors? And, at a still later period—leaving a glorious evangelical phalanx on the continent or Europe, and keeping to the island of our ancestors, and omitting a long list of worthies in the established Church of England—there were Halyburton and Scougal, and Leighton, and Howe, and Owen, and Charnock, and Baxter, and Bates, and nearly the whole of the Westminster Assembly of divines, who formed our Confession of Faith and Catechisms; and succeeding to these there were Flavel, and Watts, and Doddridge, and Boston, and the Erskines; and coming down to the present time—alas! I cannot say quite to the present time, for the last accounts from Britain have announced the death of Robert Hall and Andrew Thomson—but still there are yet in life, Chalmers, and Jay, and a multitude of their compeers, too numerous to name. In our own country, there have gone to their rest the Mathers, and Shepard, and Edwards, and Dickinson, and Burr, and Davies, and Finley and the Blairs, and Witherspoon, and Rodgers, and Macwhorter, and Dwight, and Mason. Here I stop; for it would be improper to name the eminent gospel ministers who are still living in the United States. You may, however, go over them, if you choose, in your own minds. But what I wish you to note and remember is, that although among the men I have mentioned there were very various degrees of natural talent, and of literary improvement, yet every one of them—yes, every one, without an exception,—was a *studious man,* diligently and perseveringly studious; and many of them ranked among the first scholars of the age and country in which they lived. They were deeply read, especially in the Bible, and in Christian theology; and, at the same time, they were, generally speaking, the most laborious and successful preachers of the gospel, of the day in which they severally appeared. Be certified, my young Brethren, it is idle, and worse than idle—it is absolutely false—to think and say that diligent study—I mean the study of theology and all that is directly auxiliary to it—is unfavourable either to a devout spirit, or to successful preaching. The notion that the last age was the age for speculation, and that this is the age for action, is likely, I fear, to do a great deal of serious mischief. Do not misunderstand me—I am no enemy to action, and to a great deal more of it than I have ever yet seen. But were not the men I have mentioned, the Reformers especially, men of action? Verily they were more active than any men now living, that I have heard of—the blessed missionaries alone excepted. But I do avow myself an enemy to a system of all acting and no thinking. Yes, and an enemy to all neglect of sound doctrinal preaching; for I am satisfied that, without this, we shall soon be overrun with declaiming sciolists, and fanatics, and heretics, who will indeed be active enough, but whose activity will be destructive to the truth as it is in Jesus, and ruinous to precious immortal souls.

I am ready to admit, and do freely admit, that it is very possible a man may be frozen to the core in the ice of biblical criticism, and even of orthodox doctrine. But I deny that the truths and study of the Bible, and the orthodox faith, ever did, by their direct and proper influence, freeze any man. It was something else, or the want of something else, that froze him, if he was frozen; and if he was ever thawed out into spiritual life and vigour, the truths of the Bible and the orthodox faith, in the hand of the Spirit of God, were the instrument of producing this desirable change. Therefore, I counsel and charge you to be habitually diligent students and doctrinal preachers; and if so, then the more action the better.

There is one thing, closely connected with what I have just stated, to which I must, for a moment, draw your attention. It is, that you ought to confirm every important position, or point of doctrine, in a sermon, by a plain and pertinent quotation from the sacred oracles. Believe me, every intelligent and considerate hearer will be more convinced, and more permanently influenced, by one apt text of Holy Scripture, than by all the arguments and eloquence that you can ever use without it. Nothing appears to me more objectionable, in the method of preaching which prevails in our country at the present time, than the sparing use which is made of the Scriptures of truth. Only look into Witherspoon's *Sermons,* or his *Treatise on Regeneration,* which I believe was originally written in the form of sermons, and you will not find a single argument, or important assertion, or exhortation, which is not sustained by a pertinent quotation from the holy oracles; and the weight which this adds to all that he says is felt by every attentive reader. It was, I suppose, in reference to this, among other things, that a very intelligent and discerning man once said to me, while Dr Witherspoon was yet living, that he preached with more *authority,* than any other man he ever heard. It has been with great pleasure that, in the late examination on didactic theology, I have observed that your professor required of, I believe, nearly every student, to confirm his statement of doctrinal truth from the Word of God. This is a habit of inestimable value, in which you ought to persist as long as you live. Give your hearers, if you please, argument and illustration from reason, and sometimes from history, and science, and philosophy; but back and confirm everything you utter by a plain 'Thus saith the Lord': for I say most solemnly, accursed be all that argument, and all that philosophy, and all that eloquence, in the sacred desk, which excludes God's most holy Word, to make room for 'the enticing words of man's wisdom'—the vain words of an arrogant, erring mortal.

Let me now say a few words to you, on the subject of cultivating a missionary spirit. By long and close confinement here on Friday last, I was so much exhausted that I could not attend your missionary meeting, on the evening of that day. But permit me now, not only to exhort you to cherish a missionary spirit, but to say, that I think all of you ought to spend one year, at least, in missionary labours, after you leave the seminary, before you settle as pastors of established churches. Considering the extensive and mournful destitution of all gospel ordinances, which now exists in certain portions of our country, it seems to me that, unless in some very extraordinary case, a young minister of the gospel, not yet encumbered with a family, nor connected with a stated charge, must be considered as lamentably deficient in the spirit of his office, if he is not willing to go and preach, for one year at least, to the hundreds and thousands in our frontier settlements, who are perishing in ignorance and sin, and some of whom are uttering, in a very affecting manner, the Macedonian cry, 'Come over and help us.' The service I would here recommend, besides doing good to others, seems to me admirably calculated to benefit the missionary himself—to fill his heart with that tender compassion for perishing sinners, and to animate him with a holy zeal to instruct and lead them to the Saviour, which will be likely to shed a most benign influence over all his future ministrations.

As to those who are seriously thinking of devoting their whole lives to missionary labours, and of going to the heathen on our own borders, or in foreign lands, we may say of the enterprise to which they are looking forward, what the apostle says of the office of a bishop generally, he that desires it, 'desireth a good work'. And O that there were more—many more than there are—who did *properly* desire this good work! But it is a work to be undertaken from no sudden impulse; from no flash of feeling; from no hasty, however ardent a desire, to do much good. If ever there was a work which demanded much previous thought, much prayer with fasting, much solemn and deep deliberation, and much self-examination, as to the fitness both of the body and the mind—it is the work of a missionary to the heathen, the Jews, or the Mohammedans. You who are making up your minds to this work, as I rejoice to know that some of you are, will scarcely need to be advised to read the lives of Brainerd, of Martyn, of Swartz, of Genecké, and of other devoted men of a similar character. Try to imbibe and cherish their spirit; and if you can and do imbibe it—then, in the name of the Lord, go forth to a work, the most honourable and heavenly, however laborious and painful, in which mortals ever were, or can be, employed.

I did intend to say something to you on the importance of your forming and fixing correct habits, in regard to study, and to deportment, and to care and exactness in all your money transactions, and to everything relative to your visible conduct before the world, But I find myself in danger of running into too much length, and will therefore only remind you, that you are now in that period of life when your habits, in regard to all the points I have mentioned, are fast forming, and will probably be soon unalterably fixed, and that the importance of forming and fixing them in such manner as shall promote, and not hinder your usefulness, is incalculably great. Think on this subject, therefore, very carefully and seriously; for, after all, it is probable you will not estimate it as highly as you ought.

I shall conclude what I have to offer on the present occasion, with a few observations on revivals of religion. We hope and trust there is no student in this seminary, who is not a cordial friend to such a display of divine grace, as is commonly called *a revival of religion;* for he who is a real enemy to this thing, must be hostile to the most glorious work of God in our guilty world, and utterly unfit for that ministerial vocation, that high and holy calling, to which every student of theology professes to aspire; and I think the most of you will do well to spend at least a part of your ensuing vacation, in some place or congregation—easily to be found, blessed be God, at the present time—where a revival of religion exists. But, my dear young Brethren, it is of inconceivable importance that, in regard to revivals of religion, you do not entertain notions, and adopt practices, which are calculated to mar the blessed work which you seek to promote. On this account, it was with more pleasure than I can easily express, that yesterday I heard, in common with yourselves, the scriptural and sound teaching, on this topic, of the learned and eminently pious professor from the Andover Seminary,[1] in a sermon which, in all its parts, was one of the most excellent to which I have ever listened. Fix in your minds, I beseech you, the great principle which he laboured to establish, and inculcate—that no human soul is ever converted, but by the special and almighty energy of the Holy Spirit; and that, in the part which men have to act in this great concern, they are to be careful to do that, and only that, which God has assigned to them as a matter of duty; that they are not to attempt to take the work out of God's hands, nor to use any means which he has not clearly authorized in his holy Word; and that if they do, they commit the sin of preferring their own contrivances before the appointments of his infinite wisdom; on which there is no probability that he will ever confer his blessing. Be exceedingly careful, therefore, to adopt no measures, and to give no advice, but such as are plainly warranted in the Scriptures of truth. But, keeping strictly to your inspired guide, and feeling at every step your dependence on God for success, go forward with a holy zeal and an inflexible perseverance, counting it your highest honour—though the world reproach and infidels sneer, as you must expect that they will—if you may be the humble instruments of saving souls from death; and hiding a multitude of sins. And now, praying that in this holy work, and in all your studies and preparations for the ministry of the gospel of Christ, you may receive a large portion of the grace and blessing of God our Saviour, I affectionately bid you, Farewell.[2]

[1] The Rev. Dr Woods attended a part of the examination of the seminary, and preached in the church in Princeton on the day (the Sabbath) preceding the delivery of this address. The text on which he discoursed was 1 Corinthians 3:7. 'So then, neither is he that planteth any thing, neither he that watereth; but God that giveth the increase.' He had left Princeton before this address was delivered.

[2] This address, in which it was the object of an aged minister of the gospel to give, in a very plain and familiar manner, some useful information, advice, and exhortation to his young brethren, was originally written in great haste, and without a thought that a word of it would ever appear in print. But he has yielded, perhaps indiscreetly, to the request of one of the conductors of the *Biblical Repertory*, to permit it to appear in this work, and with but little variation from the identical terms in which it was delivered.

CHRIST CRUCIFIED, THE CHARACTERISTIC OF APOSTOLIC PREACHING[1]

But we preach Christ crucified
1 Corinthians 1.23

IT appears from internal evidence that the epistle in which we find these words was written to the Corinthians by the Apostle Paul, in answer to one which they had sent to him. In their letter, they had requested him to resolve certain doubts, in regard to Christian duty; and to regulate certain points of order, in their ecclesiastical concerns. On these subjects they seem to have given him distinct information. But there were other things, and things of far greater importance, of which it appears they gave him no information; and which, therefore, it is probable, they were desirous to conceal.

The truth was, that certain false teachers had crept into the church at Corinth, in the absence of the apostle, and had obtained an influence which they had used for the most pernicious purposes. They had endeavoured to persuade the Corinthians that the apostleship of Paul, if not altogether a false assumption, was at least far inferior in dignity and authority to that of those who had been the stated companions of the Saviour in the day of his flesh. They had produced and fomented the most unhappy divisions in the church; and corruption, as usually happens, was the companion of discord. One of the members of that church, probably with the countenance of these false teachers, had been permitted, without censure, to commit and

[1] Ashbel Green, *Christ Crucified, the Characteristic of Apostolic Preaching: A Sermon Delivered in the First Presbyterian Church of Philadelphia, at the Opening of the General Assembly of the Presbyterian Church in the United States, May 19, 1825* (Philadelphia: Clark & Raser, 1825).

continue in a most flagitious immorality. Without opposition from them, if not with their concurrence or connivance, the sacrament of the Lord's Supper had been most awfully profaned. In their public addresses, the false philosophy, and subtle reasonings, and specious eloquence of the sophists, had been substituted for the plain and simple enunciation of evangelic truth. By these, and by whatever other means they could devise, they had courted popularity, and laboured to destroy the influence of the inspired founder of the Corinthian church, who had gathered it from among the heathen.—His doctrines and manner of preaching were, in many respects, in direct opposition to theirs; and unless they could subvert his authority they could not establish their own.

But although the success of these insidious men had been worthy of a better cause, it was not such but that the Corinthian Christians, when serious difficulties and embarrassments arose, resorted to their first and best friend for counsel. He, with his usual address, seized the occasion of answering their letter, not only to reply to their enquiries, but to reprove their vices, to correct their errors, to assert his full apostolic powers, and to recall them to the purity and simplicity of the gospel. Although they had not informed him, yet he tells them frankly, that it had been declared to him by those 'of the house of Chloe', that there were contentions among them. He lets them know that he was apprised of their retaining in their communion an incestuous person, and of the base arts by which the minds of some of them had been alienated from himself. He addresses them, nevertheless, with the utmost tenderness and affection, commends them freely for whatever was praiseworthy among them, and takes occasion, throughout the epistle, to mingle much important doctrinal truth, and much pious sentiment, with all that he says. But he makes no compromise with their erroneous opinions and unlawful practices. He insists peremptorily, in writing, on everything which he had taught and enjoined, when he was personally with them. It is while he is doing this that our text is introduced.—And let it be well observed, that it is introduced among the very first points which the apostle sets himself to maintain. He probably gave it this precedence and prominence, because a right method of preaching, or of publicly teaching and enforcing gospel doctrine, is plainly a matter of the utmost importance in itself, and because this was one of the chief particulars in which he differed from the false teachers, with whom he was at issue.—They preached in one way, and he in another. Their manner of preaching he pointedly condemns. That of his faithful brethren and himself, he not only defends, but declares his determination inflexibly to pursue.—'We preach Christ crucified.'

You are aware, Brethren, that what the apostle here first announces, he afterwards dwells upon, with great emphasis. So soon as he had yielded a little to a tide of holy feeling, by which we often find him borne off to a short distance from his main object, he returns to the subject of our text. In the beginning of the next chapter he says, 'And I, brethren, when I came to you, came not with excellency of speech or of wisdom, declaring unto you the testimony of God. For I determined not to know anything among you, save Jesus Christ and him crucified.'

Here, then, we have the declaration of the great Apostle of the Gentiles, who certainly spake as well as wrote under the divine guidance, in regard to a system of preaching which he had adopted among the Corinthians, to the exclusion of every other; and as we have no reason to believe that he preached to them differently from what he did to others, we may say, without hesitation or reserve, that this was the system, in conformity with which he *always* preached. Must it not, then, be highly important and interesting to all, and especially to the ministers of the gospel, to ascertain distinctly what this system of preaching was and what were the reasons which determined the apostle to adopt it, and to adhere to it with undeviating constancy? These two points I shall endeavour, in a reliance on divine aid, to illustrate, in the sequel of this discourse; and then to make a short application of the subject.

I. What was that system of preaching which the apostle declared that he had adopted, to the exclusion of every other?

In the text, he calls it the preaching of Christ crucified. Here it is manifest, that there is a reference to some one great truth, or doctrine, which formed the substance of the apostle's addresses, both public and private.—I mention private addresses, as well as public, because, from the circumstances in which St Paul was placed among the heathen, much of his preaching was not addressed to large assemblies, but to families or individuals—from house to house. It should also be carefully noted, that it is plain from his declaration, that he used the contemplated doctrine equally in the conversion of the heathen and in the edification of Christian believers.

Now, as the naked and unconnected truth or fact, that Christ was crucified, could be of no use, especially to those who had never before heard of his name, it is too evident to require proof, that the apostle must have connected with this fact, all the information necessary to render it available to the purpose for which he announced it to them. He must have told them from the first, what necessity there was that Christ should be crucified, and what was the great design of God in the life, sufferings and death, of our blessed Redeemer. What this information actually was, we may collect from the writings left us by the apostle; and it is believed that, in a summary statement, it will be nearly this—That all mankind being, by reason of sin, in a lost and helpless state, and exposed to everlasting misery, God our heavenly Father so loved the world, that he gave his only begotten Son, that whosoever believeth in him should not perish, but have everlasting life: That Christ Jesus was this Son of God, who most willingly undertook the work of our redemption, came from heaven to earth on this most benevolent errand, assumed human nature into a personal union with his own divine nature, and thus became God and man, the fit mediator between the parties to be reconciled in the great concern of man's salvation: That the Redeemer, having taken the sinner's place as his substitute and surety, perfectly obeyed and honoured the law which man had disobeyed and dishonoured, satisfied divine justice completely, by enduring the full penalty of the law, in a whole life of humiliation and suffering, and especially by a death of unspeakable agony and infamy—denominated *the cursed death of the cross*—and which, as a principal part of his work, is, for that reason, often put for the whole: That the Redeemer, after being laid in a tomb, rose from the dead on the third day, ascended to heaven, and to the right hand of the Father, there to appear forever as the intercessor and advocate of his people: That thence he sent down the Holy Spirit, to instruct his apostles fully in the nature of his kingdom; to enable them, without study, to speak various languages; to confer on them the power of working miracles; and to complete, without error, the canon of sacred Scripture; and also, in every age, to make a saving application of the Redeemer's work to the human heart, renewing it unto holiness, and implanting and cherishing in it all the Christian graces: That for the sake of what Christ has done, God can now be just and the justifier of him that believeth in Jesus, even though he be the chief of sinners; and that in the preaching of the gospel, he invites and commands every sinner who hears it to come and receive a complete salvation, through this precious and all-sufficient Saviour: That accordingly, whenever a sinner, under the influence of the blessed Spirit, becomes sensible of his guilt and misery, and on the free offer of Christ and his benefits in the gospel, actually commits his soul by faith to the Saviour, as his sole reliance, he is pardoned and justified, and shall never come into condemnation—That by faith he is united to Christ and made one with him; the righteousness of Christ is imputed to him, or reckoned as his; the work of sanctification, by which he is prepared for heaven, is commenced in his soul; and the grace of evangelical repentance, with every other grace, being there begun, shall be cherished and carried on, in a course of sincere but imperfect obedience to all the commands of God; till at death, he shall become perfect in holiness, and rise to the enjoyment of all the bliss of heaven: That thus it shall be with all who accept the gospel offer; while all who hear and do not accept it, shall be consigned to hopeless misery: That there shall be a resurrection of the dead, both of the just and the unjust, when the soul and body of every individual shall be reunited; and when, before the assembled universe, the Redeemer shall award to his friends eternal life, in his kingdom of glory, and to his enemies eternal punishment, with the devil and his angels.

Such, Brethren, it is believed, is a statement, materially correct, of the doctrine of Christ crucified, with its *essential appendages*. It is, indeed, by no means pretended, that this statement is so accurate as to preclude all amendment; or that it may not admit of some modifications, without destroying its essence. But it is maintained, that if this was not the *substance* of what the apostle intended, when he said 'We preach Christ crucified', it will not be practicable to show, in any just or even plausible manner, what he did intend. Much of the subsequent part of this epistle, and much indeed of all his epistles, demonstrates that we have fairly represented the scope and spirit of his meaning in the text.

As to the apostle's determination to know, or preach, *nothing else,* than the doctrine of a crucified Saviour, it may be remarked, that judging of what he delivered orally, by what we find in his writings, he certainly did not confine himself to the dry and incessant reiteration of the truths we have detailed. On the contrary, we find him expressly affirming, that he had not shunned to declare the whole counsel of God; and there is actually apparent in his writings, a whole system of theological truth, and of evangelical ethics, extensively taught and powerfully inculcated. But that all this is perfectly consistent with what we have given as the import of the text, may be shown by an illustration, taken from the words of our Saviour himself. He told the Jews, that on two commandments, relating to the great principle of love—love to God and love to man—hang *all the Law and the Prophets.* In like manner, we affirm, that although the apostle declared many truths, taught many doctrines, and urged many duties, he still knew *nothing but Jesus Christ and him crucified,* because everything was made by him to hang upon the cross. The truths which we have recited, were so much and so often insisted on, that they formed a large and the most prominent part of his system, and thus gave to it its distinctive character and appellation. *All* his teaching, moreover, whatever was the subject or the occasion, *savoured* strongly of the cross; it always had a manifest consistency, and generally a plain connection, with the doctrine of Christ crucified.—From this doctrine it was often immediately derived; frequently it was little else than the ramification, or carrying out, of this doctrine, into its proper consequences; and not seldom, the teaching and illustration of some *related truth,* serving to give it clearness and effect. In a word, the doctrine of Christ crucified, was the *sun* of the apostle's theological system, which imparted lustre to every other truth, directed its course, and kept it to its proper orbit—the sun which threw off its beams of heavenly radiance in all directions, to warm, and cheer, and animate those who were already spiritually alive, and to waken into life those who were yet slumbering in the frost and death of sin; which gave vitality and productive energy to every evangelical principle and precept; and to which every ray of truth might be traced back, as to its proper source; and to whose full-orbed splendour every Christian eye was often directed, to catch some glimpses of a glory too intense for a full and steady vision, till mortality should be swallowed up of life.

Let us now enquire—

II. What were the reasons which determined the apostle to adopt, and inflexibly to adhere to, the system of public teaching, which has been explained—to the preaching of Christ crucified?

There were two reasons for this, which we may collect from the writings of our apostle; and it will appear that they were entirely sufficient to justify the determination he had formed, and to justify the same determination, in every minister of Christ, to the end of the world. In the first place—The apostle knew that it was the purpose of God to *bless* the preaching of Christ crucified, and ordinarily to bless no other kind of preaching than this, both for the conversion of sinners and the edification of saints. This reason is distinctly assigned, and the explanation of it pretty largely stated, in immediate connection with the text. 'Christ', says the apostle,

> sent me not to baptize, but to preach the gospel: not with wisdom of words, lest the cross of Christ should be made of none effect. For the preaching of the cross is to them that perish foolishness; but unto us which are saved, it is the power of God. For it is written—I will destroy the wisdom of the wise, and will bring to nothing the understanding of the prudent. Where is the wise? where is the scribe? where is the disputer of this world? hath not God made foolish the wisdom of this world? For after that, in the wisdom of God, the world by wisdom knew not God, it pleased God, by the foolishness of preaching, to save them that believe. For the Jews require a sign, and the Greeks seek after wisdom. But we preach Christ crucified; unto the Jews a stumblingblock, and unto the Greeks foolishness. But unto them which are called, both Jews and Greeks, Christ the power of God, and the wisdom of God. Because the foolishness of God is wiser than men, and the weakness of God is stronger than men.

No laboured exposition is necessary, to show the direct and decisive bearing of this extended quotation on the point before us. The apostle reminds the Corinthians that the experiment had been fully tried, as to what the wisdom of this world could effect, in teaching the knowledge of God, and in the reformation of mankind. For four thousand years the experiment had been continued, and after all, the world by its boasted wisdom knew not God; but was sunk in the most sottish idolatry, the most degrading vice, and the most horrible wickedness. This had been permitted, in the wisdom and just judgment of God, that contempt might be poured on the proud devices of men; and to prepare the way for the device of God, to instruct and convert the world by the foolishness of preaching—that preaching of a crucified Saviour which the learned and philosophic Greek derided as foolishness, and which the proud and prejudiced Jew found to be a stumbling-block, because it was death to all his hopes of a splendid conquering Messiah, who should raise his nation to supreme worldly dominion. Still, however, the preaching of Christ crucified had been proved, by undeniable facts, to be the power and the wisdom of God, unto the salvation of multitudes. The doctrine of the cross, unaided by philosophical reasonings, and unadorned by a specious eloquence, but in full opposition to both, had done more in a few years, to enlighten and convert the world, than had been done before, by all the wit of man, from the beginning of time till that hour. Thus the foolishness of God—that plan of his which vain mortals had esteemed foolishness—had been proved to be wiser than men, with all their boasted sagacity and refinement. And the weakness of God—the system which they charged with weakness—to be stronger than men:—unspeakably more powerful in turning men to righteousness, than all the fancied force of reason and argument, on which they relied. God, therefore, had set his seal on this system as his own—as such he had blessed it, and would bless it. But as for any different or opposite system, it was of course the *rival* of his, and therefore he had not, and ordinarily would not, use it in his service nor confer on it any blessing.

The sense here given, Brethren, of the passage quoted, is coincident with that which may be found in all the best commentators who have ever expounded it; nor can any other be given, which shall not manifestly appear to be harsh and forced in the extreme.

The reason we are considering consists, you observe, of two parts. The first is, that it is God's purpose to bless the doctrine or preaching of the cross. The second, that he ordinarily blesses nothing else. We shall dispose of the latter part first, and in a very few words.

We say that God *ordinarily* blesses no other preaching than that of Christ crucified, because we ought to admit and remember, that as the author of our text was converted while on his way to persecute the Christians at Damascus, so there have been a few examples in every age, of men who have been met with, and brought to the saving knowledge of the truth, in circumstances, and by means, of the most unpromising character. All such instances are striking exceptions to God's ordinary method of dispensing his grace. They are intended to exhibit the divine sovereignty, and to demonstrate that although he usually employs well-adapted means, he can work without them, and even in opposition to those which he ordinarily uses. The instances of the kind contemplated are exceedingly rare, and by being so, evidently appear to be exceptions to a general rule, and serve, not to invalidate, but to confirm it.

Having shown the nature of this exception, I remark, that the position we maintain—that it is the preaching of Christ crucified, and that only, which God ordinarily blesses—is firmly established by a series of striking and undeniable facts, in every age of the Christian church. Did our limits permit, it would be a pleasing employment to take a general survey of these facts. But we have time only to glance at a few. Others will doubtless occur to many in whose presence I now speak.

First of all, let us turn our attention for a few moments to the apostolic age. Of all the apostles, Paul laboured most, and with the most success. Now we have seen what was exclusively the method of preaching adopted by him, and his immediate associates—'We preach Christ crucified.' All the churches, then, which he gathered from among the heathen, were composed of converts, made and edified by the preaching of the cross. Nor have we the least reason to believe, that the preaching of the other apostles was different from that of Paul. They were all taught and guided by one and the same Spirit, and doubtless pursued the same method of spreading the gospel. Beside, the short notices of their manner of discourse, left us in the Acts, demonstrate that such was indeed the fact. Peter's sermon on the day of Pentecost, his testimony, as the mouth of the whole apostolic college, before the Jewish Sanhedrin, and especially his discourse to Cornelius, and those that were assembled with him, show clearly that it was Jesus Christ and him crucified, that was the burden of his powerful and wonder-working addresses. We may therefore affirm with confidence, that it was the preaching of Christ crucified, by the instrumentality of which the whole primitive church was formed, edified, and established in the world. There was philosophical, and rhetorical, and legal, and logical preaching then, to the utter exclusion or complete disguise of the doctrine of the cross, as there has been in every succeeding age. It was exactly this which was employed by the false teachers in the Corinthian church. And what were its effects? They were noticed, in part, at the entrance of this discourse. They were such as they have commonly been since—formality, self-exaltation, claims to superior knowledge and sagacity, controversy, corruption, immorality, profaning sacred institutions, and alienation from apostolic truth and apostolic men. It probably was never made instrumental to gain a single convert to genuine Christianity, for our apostle solemnly warns Timothy to avoid and oppose it altogether.

Look now to the Protestant Reformation. And here, if we enquire why reformation was necessary—the answer will be, that although there were things innumerable that called for it, yet, in the opinion of the great Reformer himself, no *single* thing demanded it so loudly and imperiously, as this, that the doctrine of justification with God, solely by the merits and righteousness of Christ, had been buried and lost amidst the corruptions and superstition of antichristian Rome. Yet, as fable sometimes indicates that its origin was truth, so, in the very superstition of Popery, we find evidence that the doctrine of which I speak was the doctrine of the apostolic age. Had not the doctrine of the cross been prominent in the faith of the primitive church, and much insisted on by her public teachers, the superstitious notions which afterwards obtained in regard to the cross, had probably never existed. It was in place of the sacred doctrine of Christ crucified, that corrupt superstition and will-worship substituted images of the cross, the worship of the cross, the sign of the cross, and veneration for pretended relics of the cross. To banish the superstition, and to restore the genuine doctrine, was, by his own statement, the most important part of the work of Luther. Justification by the righteousness of Christ, imputed to us and received by faith alone, you know, he declared to be the article of a standing or a falling church. This was the theme on which he dwelt with the greatest earnestness and frequency. He has embodied his sentiments and arguments, in his *Practical Commentary on the Epistle of Paul to the Galatians,* made up of a series of public, popular discourses, which he delivered at Wittenberg. Never have I read an uninspired book in which the very kind of preaching which we now contemplate, is more clearly exhibited—strongly marked, indeed, with the peculiarities—some of them exceptionable peculiarities—of the age and author of the work.

And in the same strain, with little variation, did all the Reformers preach. You know the effect. Apostolic preaching was crowned with apostolic success. While thus they preached and wrote, converts were multiplied like drops of the morning dew. The Reformation, like a mighty torrent, carried all before it. And how was it at last arrested, and brought to a stand? Not so much by the violent opposition of its adversaries, as by the errors and misdirected zeal of its friends. They turned the force of their minds and the vigour of their efforts, from the defence and propagation of essential gospel truth, to wordy and angry controversy, relative to points which probably none of them considered as essential. With these controversies, the minds both of teachers and learners became engrossed, parties were formed and embittered, and vital piety wounded in the house of its friends, languished, till its progress was almost entirely stayed; and the peaceful Melancthon panted for the heavenly rest, that he might escape forever from the disputes of angry theologians.

Leaving the Protestant Reformation, if we examine the origin, and instrumental cause, of every genuine and extensive revival of religion since, I grievously err, if it will not appear, that plain gospel preaching—the preaching of Christ crucified—was manifestly blessed of God, both for commencing and carrying forward his own work of grace. Disputes about unessential points, and forms of religion, visionary extravagance, and corrupt doctrine, taking the place of sober evangelical truth, will be found to have been the usual causes of the declension and termination of these revivals.

Next consider the effects of different kinds of preaching, in particular congregations, and with individual ministers. The distinguished Chalmers has himself told us, that he preached, with all his skill, but without the doctrine of the cross, for more than twelve years; and that he neither made a convert, nor produced a reformation of manners. Since he has preached evangelically, the success that has attended his various labours has been great and extensive. It has been precisely the same with others. Whatever has been the accuracy of their reasoning, the profundity of their speculations, the eloquence of their sermons, or even the purity of moral conduct which they have recommended, if Christ crucified has not been their frequent and animating theme, nothing better has usually been seen in their congregations than decency of deportment, and some regard to the exterior of religion—the form of godliness without its power. Often, indeed, even this has been wanting; and in its place dissipation and profligacy have been notoriously prevalent. On the contrary, the congregation shall rarely if ever be found, in which evangelical truth has been ably, faithfully, and perseveringly preached, without being visibly blessed—often to a marked revival of vital piety; nearly always, to its preservation and increase.

Let us next consult the modern missionaries to the heathen. And here, would your time and my strength permit, I should quote to you largely from the journal of our own Brainerd. If he had written with a view to favour my present design, he could not have written more to the purpose. Take the following short specimens, which would be rendered far more impressive, if I could give you the context of the passages which I shall repeat. 'I can't but take notice', says Brainerd,

> that I have, in the general, ever since my first coming among these Indians in New Jersey, been favoured with that assistance, which to me is uncommon, in preaching *Christ crucified,* and making him the *centre and mark* to which all my discourses among them were directed.—And never did I find so much freedom and assistance, in making all the various lines of my discourses meet together, and *centre in Christ,* as I have frequently done among these Indians.—I don't mention these things as a recommendation of my own performances; for I'm sure I found, from time to time, that I had no skill or wisdom for my great work; and knew not how to choose out acceptable words, proper to address poor benighted Pagans with! But thus God was pleased to help me 'not to know anything among them, save Jesus

Christ and him crucified'. Thus I was enabled to show them their misery and undoneness without him, and to represent his complete fitness to redeem and save them. And *this* was the preaching God made use of, for the awakening of sinners, and the propagation of this work of grace among the Indians.—And 'twas remarkable, from time to time, that when I was favoured with any special freedom in discoursing of *the ability and willingness of Christ to save sinners, and the need they stood in of such a Saviour,* there was *then* the greatest appearance of divine power, in awakening numbers of secure souls, promoting conviction begun, and comforting the distressed.

Such is the testimony, with much of the same import, of the humble, holy, apostolic Brainerd.

And in perfect conformity with this, is the testimony given by the missionaries of the Moravians, or United Brethren, of their success among the Esquimaux Indians. Their account of it is generally known, and is very summarily this. After endeavouring, for a length of time, to indoctrinate their pagan charge, in the knowledge of God, as the Creator, Preserver, and Judge of the world, and by this knowledge to rouse the attention and alarm the fears of the Indians, and prepare them for evangelical truth, they found that they had produced no practical effect whatever; and could scarcely, indeed, gain the attention of their wretched hearers. As a last effort, they directed them at once to 'the Lamb of God, which taketh away the sin of the world'.—They told them of the Son of God, coming from heaven to earth, to suffer, bleed, and die on the cross, to save them from eternal perdition. This was the truth that God blessed. The hearts of the Esquimaux, cold before to the messages of grace as the polar snows with which they were surrounded, melted rapidly under these rays from the Sun of righteousness. They prostrated themselves at the foot of the dying Saviour's cross, and cried 'Lord Jesus, save us, or we perish forever.'

Having mentioned the United Brethren and their missionaries, I cannot forbear to remark, that they have always been distinguished as a Christian sect, for their constant and abundant reference to the Saviour and his cross. And where can we find more self-denial, more gospel simplicity, and greater zeal to promote the cause of the

Redeemer, than have appeared among these excellent people—the pioneers and examples of modern missionaries?

But among the most cultivated, as well as among the most savage, the doctrine of the cross has been pre-eminently blessed. Infidels who had long held out against the most acute and learned reasonings, and even boasted of their triumphs in the field of argument, have sometimes on hearing a plain, practical, gospel sermon, or a private exhibition of gospel truth, been pricked to the heart, humbled in the dust at the feet of that Saviour whom they had before blasphemed, and found redemption and consolation through that precious blood, which once they had impiously trampled under their feet.

As to practical Christians, fully indoctrinated in the truths of the gospel—no matter how dissimilar their circumstances and character—the most erudite as well as the most unlettered, the old and the young, male and female, bond and free—they may all be appealed to with confidence, to decide on the point before us, as a matter of experience with themselves. Ask them, what is the preaching that is most blessed to their souls? What most tends to banish their gloom, to nourish their faith, to encourage their hopes, to dispel their fears? What soonest and most completely dissolves their whole souls into a sweet flow of holy gratitude and love? What fills them with the greatest hatred of all sin, and the strongest desires after an entire deliverance from its thraldom? What animates them most in all duty? What engages them to labour most earnestly and cheerfully for the salvation of others? What disposes them most unreservedly and sincerely to devote all that they have and are to the service and glory of God their Saviour? With one consent they will answer, in the language of the author of our text—'The love of Christ constraineth us'; and they will assign the apostle's reason too:—'Because we thus judge, that if one died for all, then were all dead, and that he died for all, that they which live should not henceforth live unto themselves, but unto him which died for them and rose again.'—With entire unanimity they will testify, that in general those sermons edify, and delight, and animate them the most, in which are set forth in a truly scriptural manner, the all sufficiency and wonderful suitableness of Christ; his dying love; his finished righteousness; his prevalent intercession; his faithfulness to his promises; his perfect example; his sympathy with all his members; the glory of God, as it shines in the union and display of all the divine attributes in the astonishing plan of man's redemption; and the beatific vision of this glory; which his redeemed people shall soon possess, in the immediate presence of their ascended Saviour, and which shall be as lasting as eternity.

But especially, if you observe the believer in the near prospect of death, you shall then find that a crucified Saviour is his all in all. I do not say that all real believers triumph in death. But assuredly many do; and all would, if they could see their state to be what it actually is.—Probably the following language is, in substance, that which a number present have in fact heard—certainly it is such as at least one has heard—from an eminent Christian, when entering the dark valley—

All my hope is in the finished righteousness of my dear, my adored Redeemer. But *there* my hope is strong; it is my anchor within the veil. True it is, I never did see myself to be more polluted and undeserving as a sinner, than I now see myself. But I see such an infinite fulness in Christ, and such a freeness in the offer of all the benefits of his purchase, and I feel such a delight and confidence in trusting my soul with him—simply on his word and warrant, and such an ardent desire to be eternally set free from all sin, and be made perfectly holy in his blissful presence, that I know I am accepted. Yes, most unworthy as I am, 'I know in whom I have believed, and that he is able to keep that which I have committed to him against that day.' Therefore, welcome, thrice welcome, death! 'O death, where is thy sting! O grave, where is thy victory! The sting of death is sin, and the strength of sin is the law, but thanks be to God, who giveth me the victory, through our Lord Jesus Christ.'

Thus, Brethren, I think it clearly appears, from undeniable facts, that God blesses the preaching of Christ crucified, both for the conversion of sinners and the edification of saints; and that he ordinarily blesses nothing else. Now, of this no man that ever lived was more sensible than the Apostle Paul; and hence the inflexible purpose which he formed, that this exclusively should be the matter of his preaching. He surely needed nothing more than this, to bear him out in the determination which he avowed. For if we know that any appointment is of God, although we cannot discern the wisdom of it, yet we certainly know that it must be wise, because it comes from the infinite source both of wisdom and goodness; and therefore it becomes our duty to conform to it promptly and cheerfully. Some of the divine appointments have partaken in a degree of this obscure character. But to those who love the truth, there is no obscurity whatever in this appointment. On the contrary, its wisdom is most apparent; and doubtless it was seen to be so by the apostle for,

Second, it may be shown, that every doctrine and duty of true religion may be best illustrated, and most powerfully enforced, by a reference to a crucified Saviour.[1] To do justice to this position, would require a whole discourse, in place of a small part of one, which is already trespassing on ordinary bounds. We can only advert, in the most cursory manner, to a few leading points of practical Christianity, and show, in a sentence or two, the illustration and enforcement they may receive from the doctrine of Christ crucified.

Human depravity, the evil of sin, God's hatred of it, and his unchangeable determination that it shall never go unpunished, are truths which lie at the foundation of all genuine piety; and all these truths may be most clearly and impressively taught from the cross of Christ. How deeply must that moral being be polluted and depraved, who can never be cleansed, till he is washed in the blood of the Son of God; and never become holy, till he is created anew by the Holy Ghost! And what must be the extent and malignity of that evil, which could not be expiated, so as to render its pardon consistent with the justice of the Deity, but by the inconceivable agonies of Gethsemane, and the accursed death of Calvary—of him who was Emmanuel, God with us? And how must God hate all sin, and never fail to punish it in the most awful manner, when he would make no abatement in the sufferings of a sinless Saviour—his well-beloved Son—when he only stood, and in boundless compassion too, in the sinner's place! 'If these things were done in the green tree, what shall be done in the dry!' Look to the cross of Christ, rather than to the flames of Tophet, if you would have the most impressive view that you can ever take of the evil of sin, of God's abhorrence of it, and of the certainty and severity of its punishment.

[1] When this discourse was delivered, most of the illustration under this particular was omitted.

But 'God is love.'—It is essential that he be so represented, at the same time that he is exhibited as inflexibly just. And 'herein is love: not that we loved God, but that he loved us, and sent his Son to be the propitiation for our sins.—God commendeth his love toward us, in that while we were yet sinners, Christ died for us.—What manner of love the Father hath bestowed upon us, that we should be called the sons of God!' The love, grace, mercy, and compassion of God, can never be shown in any other way, that will, for a moment, bear a comparison with the exhibition made of them in the gift, mission, and sufferings of Christ;—made that guilty rebels might be pardoned, reconciled to himself, become his adopted children, made heirs of God, and joint heirs with his own beloved Son, of 'an inheritance, incorruptible, and undefiled, and that fadeth not away'.

It is also essential to a just system of religion, that the divine attributes be exhibited as harmonious; and the glory of God as secured and illustrated in all that he is represented as having done. Without this, no rightly disposed mind could ever be satisfied, even if complete provision were made for its own safety. Now, in the cross of Christ, all the divine attributes are perfectly harmonised. Here it is, and only here, that 'mercy and truth have met together, righteousness and peace have kissed each other'. By the cross, every attribute of the Deity is shown immaculate, and beaming with a splendour nowhere else to be seen. The highest display of the glory of God ever made to the universe, was made by the cross of Christ. This glory is here seen, not only to be consistent with the salvation of penitent offenders, but to shine the brightest of all, in the *very act* of saving *the chief of sinners*—'where sin abounded, grace did much more abound'.

Guilt is ever suspicious and fearful. Hence the numerous, and often cruel, rites of all false religions, to appease an incensed Deity. But to the gospel penitent, the strongest and most satisfactory evidence is given, of certain pardon and acceptance with God, in the doctrine of a crucified Saviour. Divine justice is perfectly satisfied in the cross of Christ, and unites with mercy, in assuring the believing penitent that he shall never come into condemnation. Here it is, that 'God is faithful and just to forgive us our sins'. United by faith to the Son of God, as the branch is united to the vine—identified with Jesus—the believer can no more come into condemnation, than the Saviour himself. 'Because I live, ye shall live also', is his cheering assurance to all his true disciples.

Again. It is of the utmost importance in religion, that the most powerful motives should be constantly presented to the mind, to avoid all sin, and to discharge all known duty. And where shall we find motives so admirably adapted to this purpose, as we derive from the doctrine of Christ crucified? Can the believer think of the evil of sin, as seen in the cross, and not hate it, loathe it, and flee from it? Can he endure the thought of being in league with the murderers of his adored Lord, and of crucifying him afresh? Must he not fear sin worse than death? And can he refuse any grateful return—for gratitude is the only return he can make—to the Saviour who redeemed him with his own blood? Is there any service, or any sacrifice, that his heart will permit him to withhold from such a Saviour? Is there anything, by which the religion of this Saviour can be either adorned or promoted, that he will not rejoice to do? Here, in fact, are the very motives which, from the time of Paul to the present hour, have rendered real evangelical Christians, the most conscientious, holy, and devoted, of mankind.

Once more. Every sensible sinner, and every real believer, has a clear and affecting perception of his own weakness, frailty, and proneness to sin; and full well he knows that the enemies of his soul, both within him and without him, are numerous, subtle, and powerful. He sees that, left to himself, he must certainly faint and fail, and might therefore despair at once. But he is taught by the doctrine of Christ crucified, that he will never be left to himself. His once crucified Saviour—'his great high priest that is passed into the heavens, Jesus, the Son of God', will help him to 'hold fast his profession'. His glorified Saviour is made head over all things to the church which is his body. He controls, and will ever control, all the enemies of his people. He sympathizes with them, too, in all their trials; and through his strengthening them, 'they can do all things'. While he intercedes for them above, his Spirit intercedes in their hearts, assists their prayers, helps their infirmities, carries on his own work of sanctification, and will carry it on, till they shall be brought off conquerors and more than conquerors, and grace shall be completed in glory.

Finally, heavenly happiness, exquisite and eternal, seems a reward altogether disproportionate to the attainments and services of the best saint that ever lived on earth;—and nothing that is incongruous will ever be awarded by a perfect God. But this incongruity is all removed, by the doctrine of a crucified Saviour. Heavenly happiness is represented by our apostle as 'a purchased possession'. It comes to the believer in the form of an inheritance from his kinsman Redeemer. Between his infinite merits and the happiness of heaven, there is no disproportion, no incongruity. And the reward of the saints, freely bestowed on all, will be apportioned to each according to the measure of his love and his labours. The believer, therefore, rationally and confidently expects to receive his reward, as a gratuitous legacy, from his infinitely meritorious Saviour; and while his heart overflows with gratitude for the unspeakable gift, he anticipates the happy moment, when, in some humble place in heaven, he will begin the eternal song of praise—'Unto him that loved us, and washed us from our sins in his own blood, and hath made us kings and priests unto God and his Father; to him be glory and dominion for ever and ever. Amen.'

From the sketch now given, very imperfect as it is, it may be seen, that, according to the declaration of the apostle in the context, the doctrine of the cross is not only the power of God, but the wisdom of God:—is not only the doctrine to which alone he ordinarily gives efficiency, by the power of his Spirit; but the doctrine also in which the divine wisdom is most wonderfully manifested, in adapting it to all the circumstances of sinful men; to all the principles and powers of their intellectual and moral nature. In using this doctrine to convert the world—to bring sinners to repentance and to edify and comfort saints—the wisdom of God is most apparent in choosing an instrument—an instrument, which, while it is one exactly of which Jews and Greeks, and the children of proud carnal wisdom in every age, never did, and never will see the fitness, is nevertheless fitted, in the most perfect manner, to perform the work to which it is destined,—'The foolishness of God is wiser than men.'

Fathers and Brethren in the Christian Ministry: How unspeakably momentous to us, is the subject that has now been under discussion? Does God bless the preaching of Christ crucified, and ordinarily bless no other kind of preaching? Then, with what solemnity and energy, should the enquiry come home to every one of us—Is this the character of *my* preaching? Ah! it is fearful beyond expression, to speak as a minister and ambassador of Christ, and yet to deliver something which he will never own as his message, or follow with his blessing. O! let us ever keep in mind, that we must, in our humble measure, preach *like* Paul, if we expect to meet with any portion of Paul's success.

In preaching, as in everything else, there may doubtless be different degrees of excellence; a greater or a less degree of conformity to the apostolic example; and God may, and often does, bless his own truth, even when it is mixed with much human error and imperfection. Gold which is mingled with much alloy is still gold, and of real worth. Yet as the value of the metal is greatest when it has no alloy, so evangelical truth is the most precious and useful, when its purity reaches completely the gospel standard. It may therefore be of some use just to mention, both how unqualified counterfeits may be put in its place, and how, when something of it is retained, its worth may be greatly diminished by debasing mixtures.

It is manifest, at once, that those who deny the proper divinity and atonement of our Lord Jesus Christ, never can preach the doctrine of a crucified Saviour, as it was preached by Paul. The cross of the Redeemer, indeed, seems to be a real encumbrance to their whole system; rendering its defence far more difficult than it would be, if he had not expired on a cross, with its attendant sufferings. Their discourses, of consequence, are found to be as different from those of Paul, as if they had been designed to be so. But even those who explicitly admit the divinity of the Saviour, and that, in some sense, he made an atonement for sin, may still have nothing in their preaching of the doctrine of Christ crucified, as it was held and taught by the apostle. In this class—which is indeed a very large one—all those are included, who keep out of their pulpit addresses all the *peculiar doctrines* of the gospel; or only advert to them slightly, or occasionally; as if on purpose to show, that while they do not deny them, they think them of little importance.—All your merely metaphysical, logical, rhetorical, moral, and philosophical preaching in which the name of Jesus Christ is seldom heard, and the doctrine of the cross is never clearly set forth, is of this description. And even when the peculiar doctrines of the gospel are made the subjects of discussion, if they are treated wholly in a dry or abstract way, without close and practical application, and with no animating reference to the cross, there can be very little of the manner of Paul in such pulpit performances. Nor can anything better be said of those representations of something called an *atonement*, to which Paul's language in describing it cannot fairly be applied;—cannot be accommodated, without construing the apostle's expressions in a most unnatural and unwarrantable manner. Neither do they preach Christ crucified as Paul did, who fill a whole discourse with legal terror; with scarcely a word to direct the alarmed sinner to the Saviour. Paul did indeed preach 'the terrors of the Lord', and we ought to preach them, and faithfully too; but always as the apostle did—that we may 'persuade men'—persuade them to flee to the Saviour, while his arms are open to receive them. There may also be, in those who really hold the truth in its purity, such a want of plain language and simplicity of manner in stating it, as to hide much of its excellence from the unlearned, and greatly to abate its power and sweetness with all who love it. There may likewise be a deficiency in the frequency with which the doctrines of the cross are directly and distinctly treated, in a course of preaching; and a deficiency, finally, in making everything, as holy Brainerd well expresses it, 'meet together and centre in Christ'.

Beloved Brethren, let it be understood, that, on the one hand, I solemnly disclaim all personal allusions in anything I have said; and on the other, that I desire not to abate or soften any censure which a declaration of the truth may inflict. Let the truth do its office fairly with the consciences of us all. We may all profit by being warned of the errors that have been specified; and if any of us are conscious of having committed them, let us amend them without delay. Every one of us has continually reason to be on his guard, not to depart, in his preaching, from 'the simplicity that is in Christ'.

As society advances in what is called *refinement*, there is always an increase of danger, that the plain truths of the gospel will be refined away; or in a measure kept back or disguised, by those whose sacred office it is to proclaim them faithfully. Of this danger the whole history of the church hitherto gives us solemn warning. And as learning, and taste, and elegance, and wealth, and luxury, are making progress in our country, who shall say that they will not disadvantageously affect the preaching of the gospel among us, as they have done among others? Who can say and prove, that this effect has not already been experienced, in some portions of our country? Who can affirm that nothing of the kind has yet been indicated in our own church? That with us it has not made great progress, I sincerely believe, and rejoice to say. But it is an evil, against which we should constantly both watch and pray; for Luther's maxim is unquestionably just, that the doctrine we have been considering, is the doctrine of a standing or a falling church. Of the happy part of this alternative we are now the living witnesses. To the blessing of God on the plain and faithful preaching of the doctrines of the cross, the Presbyterian Church in the United States must attribute her remarkable prosperity and increase;—the numerous happy revivals of religion which she has witnessed, the unexampled multiplication of her congregations, and presbyteries, and synods, and the enlargement of her boundaries in all directions. And beyond a peradventure, she will continue to increase and prosper, so long as these doctrines, in their purity and simplicity, shall be loved, and taught, and inculcated. But let these doctrines be corrupted, or become unfashionable; let them even be disguised, or mutilated, or philosophized into obscurity, and the King of Zion will inscribe 'ICHABOD' on our church—her glory will have departed, and her prosperity will terminate. Yes, and in this event it will be desirable that it should terminate; for the salvation of souls is of infinitely more importance than the prevalence of any religious sect, by whatever name it may be called. Wherefore, I repeat, let us use all the means in our power, to guard against the corruption or neglect of the genuine evangelical doctrines, and to cherish the preaching of them plainly, fully, abundantly, closely, and zealously.—That to this end I might contribute my mite, the subject of this address was selected. Being 'such an one', as an aged minister of the gospel, I determined to lay before my brethren on this public occasion, my views of the manner in which the gospel ought to be exhibited and inculcated by those who preach it. This I have endeavoured to do, as in the *near* prospect of my last account; for to me the hour for rendering that account *must* be near. And from none of us, Brethren, can it be far distant—To some, it is probably just at hand. Several of our ministerial brethren, who met in this house at the last General Assembly, are now in eternity. The past year has been marked by the death of more ministers in our communion—some in the prime of life, and others in the meridian of their usefulness—than any other year within my memory. Some of us, it is highly probable, have entered on the last year of our ministry and our life. And O, Brethren! it must be the doctrine of Christ crucified that must afford us support, if we find a stable support, in the hour of death; and ensure our acquittal, if we find an acquittal, at the bar of our final judge.—This precious doctrine, therefore, let us embrace cordially, maintain firmly, and preach, while we may, with fidelity and zeal.

Christian Brethren, who are not in the gospel ministry: be exhorted, in one word, to look well, that it is *on Christ alone,* that you are resting your hopes for eternity; and that you are walking worthily of the high vocation wherewith you are called.

A crucified Saviour has, I know, been faithfully preached to the most of those who now hear me. And it is a most affecting thought, that any who have, to this hour, held out against the Saviour, have done it in opposition to the most effectual means that God has ever devised, to convert sinners, and to reconcile them to himself. Justly may they fear, if their impenitence longer continue, that he may swear in his wrath, that they shall not enter into his rest. Behold, then, O impenitent sinners! one free offer of the Saviour more is now made you; and I entreat you, by all that is dear and sacred, refuse it not, lest it should prove the last. 'Behold, now is the accepted time; behold, now is the day of salvation! Today if ye will hear his voice, harden not your hearts.' Amen.

GARDINER SPRING
1785-1873

RENOWNED preacher and Presbyterian minister, Gardiner Spring was born in Newburyport, Massachusetts in 1785. His early education was received at Berwick Academy in Maine. An 1805 graduate of Yale College, Spring's sense of call to the Christian ministry came a few years after his graduation from the college. Having worked as a teacher for a few years, he attended the recently founded Andover Theological Seminary in 1809.

Following a year of study at Andover, Spring received a call (1810) to the Brick Church in New York City. He began his ministry there when he was just twenty-five years old, and continued in the pastorate there for sixty-three years until he reached the ripe old age of eighty-eight.

Under Spring's leadership, the church grew and eventually relocated to a new building at Fifth Avenue and 37th Street.

A gifted and eloquent preacher, Spring's published sermons were widely read and highly valued. His work on *The Mercy Seat* and his important volume on preaching, *The Power of the Pulpit,* remain in print today, being spiritually rich and full treatments of their subjects.

Gardiner Spring shared the vision for ministerial instruction established by the founders of Princeton Theological Seminary. A long-time friend of the seminary, he also served for a number of years on its Board of Directors. However, by the late 1840s, Spring had growing concerns about the school's curriculum and the quality of students it was graduating. He feared that an academic model of ministerial development had emerged that was not providing the kind of spiritual mentoring and pastorally focused theological learning essential for making effective pastors and preachers. Academic credentials, Spring believed, had taken priority in faculty appointments rather than experience in pastoral ministry; graduates' sermons, he judged, were delivered as if lectures in a classroom and he believed they lacked the vibrant, passionate, personal, Spirit-anointed power that should characterize true gospel preaching. Spring argued that the best corrective to this development was a return to the earlier colonial model of personal mentoring of candidates preparing for ordination to the ministry under the watchful eye of a local pastor. A debate ensued in the pages of the *Biblical Repertory and Princeton Review,* with publication in 1848 of Spring's book, *Power in the Pulpit.* The Princeton faculty acknowledged the challenges but believed the institutional model better suited to meet the needs and demands of their rapidly changing times. The debate continued without resolution.

In the history of American Presbyterianism, Spring is best remembered for a series of resolutions he presented to his denomination at the annual meeting of the General Assembly in 1861. The 'Spring Resolutions', as they came to be known, committed the Presbyterian Church to support the Federal government in suppression of States seeking to secede from the Union. When they were adopted by the General Assembly, Southern commissioners withdrew and formed a new Assembly. The split in national sentiment over secession had now created a division within the church that would not be healed until after the Civil War, and in some respects, not until many years later.

AN ADDRESS TO THE STUDENTS[1]

I have never appreciated the embarrassment of addressing you, My Young Friends, until I am now, in the providence of God, called to this service. I shall not probably suggest a thought that has not frequently been suggested by those who have been called to this service before me. But if I shall be so happy as to present a few topics before your minds in such a light as shall have the least tendency to increase and extend your usefulness as men, as the ministers of Christ, I shall be abundantly gratified in the few moments I am allowed to enjoy with you.

The tendencies of piety are to produce good. 'A good tree bringeth forth good fruit.' The high aim of the true Christian is to be *useful*. This is the tendency of his spirit, his affections, his desires, his hopes, his efforts, his whole renewed character. It is not that he may be a *splendid man,* but a *useful man.*

A minister of the gospel presses after a prize of very questionable lawfulness, when he aims at being a splendid minister; but he has no misgivings of conscience when he honestly aims at being a useful minister. He will be very apt to be disappointed if he aims at being a great and splendid minister; but he will rarely, if ever, miss his mark, if he aims at being a useful minister.

You have a thousand times been told, that to meet the high claims of the work for which you are preparing, you must possess *ardent and uniform piety.* Your usefulness will, in a great measure, depend upon the power which the religion of the gospel exerts upon your own soul. To this, more than any other cause, may be traced the secret power of such men as Baxter, Edwards, Brainerd, and Payson. One reason why so many ministers live to so little purpose is, that

[1] Gardiner Spring, *An Address Delivered at Princeton, New Jersey, at the Annual Examination of the Students of the Theological Seminary, May 1832* (Philadelphia: Russell and Martiens, 1832).

while they may perhaps be good men, they are obviously deficient in that personal piety which has a transforming effect upon the heart and deportment. God and heaven are not the point of attraction towards which their minds and efforts are perpetually tending. I have known ministers of splendid talents not half so useful as many of their humbler brethren; and who probably will not be found in those illumined departments of the heavenly city, where they 'that turn many to righteousness shall shine as the stars for ever and ever'. You never can be faithful ministers, and therefore you never can be useful ministers, without fervent piety. You will not be faithful to the truth of God, nor to the souls of men. You will not take pleasure in your work, nor endure its trials, nor be eminently successful in winning souls to Christ, without fervent piety. Piety, my young Friends, must be your great adornment, and give your character its lustre. The bare hopes of piety, and even its predominating graces, ought not to satisfy you. Her self-denying spirit, her heaven-aspiring affections, her exalted and humbling joys, her unreserved self-devotement, her increasing purity, her sweet sensibility and tenderness, her absorbing confidence in the cross, and her deep and restless solicitude for the best interests of men; these, under a wise direction, will not fail to make you useful ministers.

It is almost too obvious a remark, especially to you, to say, that to be a useful minister, a man must be *well instructed in the oracles of God*. But there are several reasons for making this remark, just at this time. You have the best opportunity for religious instruction of every kind. To say nothing of the excellent instructions you are receiving in the different departments of divine learning, immediately from the Holy Scriptures, which we all know to be the only infallible rule of faith and practice, the standards of faith adopted in this seminary, I am more and more persuaded, must commend themselves to every reflecting and sober man. I know there is a growing prejudice against forming and subscribing creeds or confessions of faith; and it is not surprising that this prejudice should exist in a youthful mind. But if there are essential doctrines of the gospel, and if these doctrines can be ascertained and defined, where is the impropriety of embodying them in some well-digested formula?

By nothing has the baneful influence of error been so generally counteracted, and the cause of truth so generally promoted, as by judicious confessions of faith. New England owes her orthodoxy, under God, to the Assembly's Catechism; and not until that excellent summary of doctrine fell into disuse, did some of her churches decline from the faith of their fathers. Old England, too, owes its remaining orthodoxy to the Thirty-nine Articles. And, where will you find a formula which more clearly ascertains and defines the system of doctrines taught in the Holy Scriptures, than the Catechism and Confessions of Faith of the Presbyterian Church? I am confident you will appreciate these remarks, gentlemen, and you will do so the more, the oftener you reflect upon them, unless you yourselves are carried about with every wind of doctrine, and fall away from the steadfastness of the gospel. Equally confident am I, that you have special cause for appreciating them at the present crisis of the American church. Already are there such departures from the essential truths of the gospel among us; already have so many become wavering and unsettled in their religious sentiments, that there is peculiar obligation on those who are preparing for the sacred office, to investigate and understand the meaning of the Bible. Do not allow yourselves to be satisfied with vague notions of the truth of God. To this we have seen, to our sorrow, not a few of the youthful ministry are exposed. As the guardians of this sacred seminary, the directors have not a little solicitude that no youth should go from these walls before he has formed a well-digested system of religious truth. Let it be a maxim with you to have no views, only so far as they are definite. It were unspeakably better to understand a few truths well, and to know them certainly, than to expatiate vaguely over the extended fields of Christian science. The certainty of knowledge is a very different thing from the extent of knowledge. Because you may have but a partial and imperfect view of divine truth, it does not follow that you must of necessity be in darkness and uncertainty in relation to those truths with which you are familiar. Though no man that ever lived should perfectly know all that God has revealed, this would not prove that he does not know many things with perfect definiteness and certainty. Though our natural eyesight is limited, so that we cannot see beyond a certain circle, nor all things at once in any circle, yet, we can see one thing at a time, and that clearly. The same is true of the understanding. Though we may have no knowledge about some truths, and though we cannot contemplate and compare many truths at once; yet we can contemplate one thing at a time, and compare a few things together, and hence come to a definite and certain knowledge of such things as we can discern and compare, and from one truth clearly discover another, and so make slow, but progressive advancements in knowledge. And thus it is that we shall see clearly, and exhibit impressively the harmony, connection, and consistency of the great truths which the gospel reveals. It is this definiteness of view which we affectionately and urgently recommend to you. One doctrine of the Bible, consistently understood, will almost necessarily lead a devout and inquiring mind to perceive and appreciate the harmony and connection which run through all the peculiar and essential doctrines of the gospel. The student who thoroughly understands one doctrine of the gospel, will be very apt to understand another and another. Once let your views of divine truth be definite, and there is little danger that they will long remain distinct and prominent. Clear and definite views of God's truth, combined with ardent piety, go far to make a useful minister. If the treasures which infinite wisdom has accumulated in the Bible abundantly enrich, and adorn, and give practical utility to the Christian character, how much more to the ministerial? Aim at high attainments in Christian knowledge. If you cannot excel in everything, excel in this. Labour, study, pray, to excel in this. To be burning and shining lights, you must feel the pre-eminent claims of religious truth.

Another characteristic of a useful minister, is *untiring diligence and energy of action*. It was not by his talents merely, nor simply by his fervent piety, nor was it only by his enlarged views of the truth of God, but by his indefatigable diligence and action combined with these, that the Apostle Paul accomplished a greater amount of good than was ever accomplished by any other man. The life of a useful minister is an eventful life. It is fruitful in benevolent results. His energy is not developed so much upon set occasions, or by studied effort: his whole life is full of labours and events that are intimately connected with the best interests of men. I know of no class of men who labour more, or more severely, than *faithful* ministers of the gospel. There are good ministers, pious men, who are called to contend with most inactive and sluggish habits, both of body and mind; and there are those who are never satisfied and happy unless they are in some way actively employed; and the difference in the aggregate of good accomplished by these two classes of men will be found, in the course of years, to be immense, and almost incalculable. Let every young man who is looking toward the sacred office settle it in his mind, that all his indolent habits must be broken up, if he has the most distant hope of becoming a useful minister of Christ! If he is not willing to harness himself for labour, he had better never enter the field. All the springs of his life will run down without effort. His hope and courage will sink and die away, if he has no spirit of enterprise. He will soon become a burden to himself, and a cumberer of the ground. Perhaps I conceded too much, when I said that such ministers might be good men. A slothful minister is a contradiction which it is very difficult to reconcile with the lowest standard of holiness. A man who is born for immortality; ruined by sin; redeemed by the blood and Spirit of Jesus Christ: put into the sacred ministry; set to watch for souls; promised a reward that outweighs all the material universe; and yet, murmur at hardships, and complain that he must spend and be spent in the service of his Redeemer! My young Friends, we hope better things of *you*. God expects better things. The church demands them. The age, the land which gave you birth, and nurtures you for scenes of toil and triumph such as the generations that are gone have never witnessed, expects better things of you, and things that accompany salvation to your own soul, and to this dying world.

To be eminently useful, you must also be *men of prayer*. In this respect every minister would do well to keep before his mind the example of such men as Luther, Knox, Whitefield, and Martyn. Nothing has so powerful a tendency to subdue the unhallowed affections of the mind, and the grosser appetites and passions of the body; nothing will so certainly control and direct your thoughts, and elevate them above all that is base and grovelling, trifling and little, as frequent and intimate fellowship with God. The great secret of mortifying a worldly spirit is to cultivate a heavenly one. 'Walk in the Spirit, and ye shall not fulfil the lusts of the flesh.' 'Be not conformed to this world, but be ye transformed, by the renewing of your minds.' Nowhere does this world appear so much like an empty shadow, and nowhere is its baleful influence so certainly coun-teracted, as in sweet communion with things unseen. You will find also, that prayer furnishes the strongest stimulus, the most powerful incitement to self-denying duty and toil. And who has not observed that intelligent, earnest prayer improves all the powers and properties of the soul, and wakes up the mind from her sluggishness and apathy, to the exercise of the best and most ennobling affections? Nowhere does that wonderful system of truth, that 'mighty range of motive', disclosed in the Bible, obtain its sure and certain dominion over the soul, if not in the frequency, seriousness, and joys of familiarity with God. Were the history of ministers made known, I have no doubt that you might trace the distinguished usefulness of the most distin-guished men to their closets. If you will review your own history, I think you will not fail to see that those periods of it have been most distinguished for usefulness, that have been most distinguished for prayer. The late Dr Payson, in suggesting a few hints to a youthful brother in the ministry, among other most valuable remarks, has the following: 'The disciples, we read, returned to Jesus, and told him all things; what they had done, and what they had taught. I think that if we would every evening come to our Master's feet, and tell him where we have been; what we have done; and what were the motives by which we have been actuated; it would have a salutary effect upon our whole conduct. While reading over each day's page of life, with the consciousness that he was reading it with us, we should detect many errors and defects which would otherwise pass unnoticed.' It is this familiarity with Jesus—they are these unaffected approaches to the throne of grace, through all the sins and duties, the mercies and trials of his course, that make the useful minister. I have seen minis-ters of very reserved habits in their intercourse with men, who were eminently useful because they conversed with God. You will greatly abound in the duty of prayer, if you are ever eminently useful in the sacred office.

It is also indispensable to distinguished and permanent usefulness in a minister of the gospel that he *mortify an aspiring spirit*. Do not contend for pre-eminence. If you are thrown among those who con-tend for it, retire from the conflict. Strive to do good, and if your motives are impeached, let your habitual deportment be your only defence of them. I say again, beware of an aspiring spirit. There is scarcely anything that has a stronger tendency to neutralise and counteract the benevolent designs of good men, than a self-complacent, aspiring spirit. Beware of it. Learn of him who was 'meek and lowly in heart'. 'He that exalteth himself shall be abased, and he that humbleth himself shall be exalted.' 'Pride goes before destruction, and a haughty spirit before a fall.'

A minister of the gospel, to be eminently useful, must also be distinguished for no small share of *earnestness and zeal*. On this point I feel afraid of leaving a wrong impression on your minds. Zeal, without judgment and discrimination, spoils a man for a minister of the gospel. A venerable clergyman once said, 'I would make deficiency in prudence the ground of quite as serious and insurmountable objection against laying hands on a candidate for the ministry, as I would a deficiency in piety or knowledge.' Be ye 'wise as serpents and harmless as doves'. You have seen many a man who possessed commendable qualifications for the sacred office, concerning whom, after all, it might be said, he is not a safe man. You may possess exemplary piety, and distinguished talent, but without practical wisdom, you cannot become a useful minister. And yet discretion may degenerate into timidity; may even lead to a trimming and calculating servility. A minister's character that is formed on the highest models of usefulness, must be distinguished for decision, energy, and zeal, as well as self-diffidence and discretion. There is no danger that your zeal will be too ardent so long as it is the expression of simple benevolence. Seek not your own will, but the will of the Father who hath sent you, and you cannot be too zealous. Only be sure that your heart glows with the benevolence of the gospel, and the flame cannot rise too high. True zeal will find its choicest aliment in cultivating the spirit of Jesus Christ. At a great remove from that false fervour and electric fire which has its origin in a selfish and ambitious mind, which hurries men on to act without consulting the sober dictates of their understanding, and which is distinguished for its subtlety, turbulence, and fickleness, it takes its rise from the meek and gentle spirit of holy love. It is warmed and fanned into flame by every breath of heavenly affection. It is simple, because it has nothing to disguise. It is strong and steady, because it is deliberate and cautious. It is unwearied, because, like the heaven-born charity from which it flows, 'it seeketh not its own'. And where shall we look for such a spirit, if not in the ministers of Christ? Where are there incentives to such a spirit, if not in the cross of Christ? Where did Paul find it, where did the primitive Christians find it, but in the love of Christ? What can support such a spirit, but those awful and touching realities, those weighty and tender truths which are exhibited with such irresistible energy and vividness, in that wonderful redemption of which you hope to become the messengers to your apostate fellow men? A slight and cursory view of your great work, my young Friends, will not answer the purpose of your high calling. Your minds must be roused to the importance of it; you must think intensely, and feel deeply; all your powers of body and mind must be awakened and invigorated in the service of your divine Master; nor should your resolution be impaired, or your efforts relaxed, till you are summoned from the field.

There is another topic on which I will make a few observations, which has an intimate relation to your usefulness, as the ambassadors of the gospel of peace: and that is, the importance of exercising a *kind and fraternal spirit*. Charity suffereth long and is kind. Charity is not easily provoked. Charity thinketh no evil. Charity beareth all things, hopeth all things, endureth all things. O, if this spirit of kindness—this mutual forbearance—this patience of injury—this freedom from suspicion and jealousy—this spirit of fraternal love and confidence were more prominent in the character of the ministers of Christ, how would they adorn the doctrine of God their Saviour, and recommend religion to the world! If I do not misinterpret, nor pervert the signs of the times, the day is near when there will be a peculiar demand for the cultivation of this spirit in the American churches. Deeply does it concern you, to wipe away this dark and foul reproach which stains the ministerial character. 'If a man say, I love God, and hate his brother, he is a liar; for if he love not his brother whom he hath seen, how can he love God, whom he hath not seen?' How often have we seen the usefulness of ministers lamentably circumscribed through the want of a kind and affectionate spirit! There are ministers who need nothing but brotherly kindness to make them patterns of everything that is praiseworthy. I know that the constitutional temperament of good men is various; but there is no apology for the man whose external light is on the wane, because the glow of kindness declines within. You live in such an evil world; a world where there are so many occurrences that are unavoidably painful—so many wrongs to be encountered and forgiven, and where there are such frequent requisitions for the exercise of a kind spirit, that if you do not take special pains to cultivate it, all the better feelings of your hearts will be suppressed, and the manly and generous spirit of a heaven-born religion will lose its glory in the envyings and suspicions of an earthly and selfish mind.

In a word, Gentlemen, strive to possess the uniformity of character which the gospel requires. It is worth much effort, watchfulness, and prayer, to guard against the more common faults and blemishes of ministerial character. It concerns you to cultivate every grace and virtue, and to be adorned with all the beauties of holiness. The usefulness of a minister of the gospel depends much on this uniformity of character. As 'dead flies cause the ointment of the apothecary to send forth a stinking savour, so doth a little folly him that is in reputation for wisdom and honour'. Little things have more to do in the formation of a spotless moral character, than we are at once willing to believe. Especially beware of little deviations from sterling rectitude. 'He that is faithful in that which is least, is faithful also in that which is much; and he that is unjust in the least, is unjust also in much.' Little things exert a prodigious influence on the character of the ministers of the gospel. It is impossible for the man who neglects them to command respect, or to be extensively useful. It is this uniformity of ministerial character which conciliates confidence and veneration, and which everywhere bespeaks a benevolent and elevated mind. Such a minister of the gospel will not live in vain. He may have his superiors in some particular traits of excellence, but in that happy assemblage of excellencies that go to form the useful minister of Jesus Christ, he is one of the lights of the world.

JAMES WADDELL ALEXANDER
1804-1859

PASTOR, educator, theologian, and renowned preacher, James Waddell Alexander was the first-born son of Janetta and Archibald Alexander. Born in Virginia, and later raised in Philadelphia and Princeton, James was a son of the manse and privileged child of one of the nineteenth century's greatest preachers and theological educators. He received his early education in mathematics, algebra, geography, Bible, and classical languages under the tutelage of his father with additional schooling in Philadelphia, graduating from Princeton College in 1820.

Following a public profession of faith in 1821 and sense of call to the pastoral ministry, Alexander enrolled at Princeton Theological Seminary in 1822. After graduation, Alexander served two pastoral charges before receiving appointment in 1833 as Professor of Rhetoric and Belles-Lettres at Princeton College. While a professor at the college, he also served for seven years as pastor of the African American Presbyterian Church whose meeting house was located in Princeton.

Alexander returned to full-time pastoral ministry in 1844 as pastor of the Duane Street Presbyterian Church in New York City. In 1849 he accepted a call to Princeton Theological Seminary as Samuel Miller's successor in the chair of Ecclesiastical History and Church Government. With his background in Rhetoric and Belles-Lettres, Alexander also shared instruction in Homiletics to the students.

Although Alexander's work at the seminary was greatly valued, his love for the pastorate led him to receive a call in 1851 to the pulpit of the Fifth Avenue Presbyterian Church, New York City. During 1857-58 revival broke out in New York City and other locations around the country and Alexander played a prominent role in the events through his preaching and publications.

For reasons that were never diagnosed, Alexander suffered throughout his life from a debilitating nervous condition that led to strong mood swings. He died in 1859 while seeking respite from his condition in his home State of Virginia.

Alexander was a devoted student, polymath in learning, gifted instructor, affectionate pastor, and powerful preacher. He belonged to the 'association of gentlemen' responsible for the material published in the *Biblical Repertory and Princeton Review;* after Charles Hodge, he was the second most active contributor to the journal, supplying articles in a wide range of theological subjects.

Alexander's strong sense of pastoral calling is evident in his many literary publications, most of which were intended for the general reading public. A number of these publications are sermons and popular pieces written to reach the working class and poor members of society. Observations published posthumously in *Forty Years' Familiar Letters of James W. Alexander, D.D., Constituting with Notes, a Memoir of His Life,* evidence a man with a tender pastoral heart for the needs of the downtrodden, poor, and underprivileged; as pastor of a prominent inner-city church, he persistently refused to succumb to the vanity of upper-class New York City society and thereby compromise the integrity of his ministerial calling to minister to people from all walks of life.

Of his many publications, he is probably best remembered for a collection of occasional pieces, letters, and reflections on preaching and pastoral ministry posthumously published as *Thoughts on Preaching.* His writings, like his father's, are practical in nature and marked by remarkable insight into the spiritual condition and needs of the human heart. Devotional in character, they provide testimony to the way Christ-centred, grace-based messages minister to the real needs of people's lives and show the reason why his ministry was so well received.

THE LORD JESUS CHRIST
THE EXAMPLE OF THE MINISTER[1]

FROM the first months of childhood much that we learn is from imitation. What we see others do is thenceforth easier to ourselves, and in accordance with this principle of human action, God addresses us as imitative beings. We are told to be 'imitators of God as dear children'; but lest the splendour and incomprehensibility of the divine model should confound us, 'God manifest in the flesh' is made our example. The words of Christ have a wider application than to the eleven, 'I have given you an example, that ye should do as I have done to you.' And all secondary or intermediate patterns (though Paul himself sit for the picture) are to be compared with the lovely original. It is true of believers in general, that they ought to imitate the example of Christ and all coincident examples. It is true in a higher sense of ministers. To them Paul says, as to the Corinthians, 'be ye imitators of me', or rather of Christ in me. For observe, the holy apostle represents himself as only the reflector of Christ's radiance; and therefore we are justified in leaving the mirror, and directing our views to the sun.

The Lord Jesus Christ is in some way, nay in most respects inimitable. The two natures must be distinguished. In his divine nature Immanuel has no ministerial work; and we can imitate him only in that looser sense in which we imitate Jehovah. In his sacerdotal character Christ cannot be imitated, for 'there is one mediator only between God and man'. But in his human nature, and more particularly as a teacher and preacher, he is imitable; he was imitated by Paul, and he must be imitated by us. Do we deny or forget that Christ is

[1] James W. Alexander, 'The Lord Jesus Christ the Example of the Minister', *Biblical Repertory and Theological Review* Vol. 7, No. 1 (January 1835), pp. 97-109.

very and eternal God, of one substance with the Father? God forbid. To deny this, is to take out the cornerstone of our faith; to forget it, or withhold it, or mask it, or undervalue it, in our ministry, is to betray the truth of God. But, at the same time, we maintain that the exalted person who is very God, is also very man, and that his human nature, united to the divine, was sanctified and anointed with the Holy Spirit above measure; and that we may safely and reverently copy his example, in the whole course of our ministry. The commission has in it something awful: 'As my Father hath sent me, even so send I you.' 'He that receiveth you receiveth me.' Ministers 'are ambassadors for Christ', and it is becoming that they should resemble him whom they represent. They are ministers, or servants, and he has said, 'If any man serve me, let him follow me.' They are pastors, or shepherds, and he is 'the chief Shepherd', 'the good Shepherd'.

We trust that to none of our readers will it seem needless or inappropriate, to exhibit to pastors the ministry of our Lord Jesus Christ, with respect to its subject, manner, and spirit. The subject of Christ's preaching may be dismissed with a few words, for it is the subject of all ministerial labours; and his manner is partly unknown to us, and partly evinced by the spirit of his work; so that we shall pass lightly over the first two points, in order to contemplate the third, But that these may not seem to be slighted, let something be remarked: First, of the *matter* of our Lord's instructions. It was truth; as he was primeval, uncreated truth. It was accordingly divine truth, from God, concerning God, leading to God. It was revealed truth, the same which had streamed in rills or rivers from the prophetic fountains of the Old Testament. And as it was meant for the faith of men, that they might be saved, it was the sole subject of our Lord's communications. It will appear in the sequel, that his wisdom always dispensed it fitly, where and when it was needed. It may be here said, that while Christ was authorized to originate revelations, and while everything he said was vouched by miracle, he still honoured all prior revelation, and that his preaching had reference to the record; it was *scriptural*. The Scriptures were commended to the search of his hearers: 'I have given them thy word'; and when hearers were misled, Jesus thus explained it, 'ye do err, not knowing the Scriptures'. He expounded the law in its severe extent and penetrating spirituality; he held up the divine testimony as the standard, and he died to fulfil its predictions. Our Saviour preached those truths which are *most valuable*. We find in his recorded discourses, no refinements, no ingenious impertinences, no temporal trifles. They contain no disquisitions on natural science, though by him all nature was created; no entertainments for mere taste, though his sermons are unparalleled in exquisite beauty; no metaphysical subtleties, though all the churches know that Jesus is he who 'searcheth the reins and hearts'. When he began to preach, he cried Repent. He taught that the law had now introduced the gospel, and the grand truth was his death. His discourses were searching, faithful, often tremendous in their denunciation. And if we do not find within the four Gospels the same fulness and precision of statement and definition, which occur in the apostolical epistles, we are to remember that Jesus gave the seed rather than the fruit of many doctrines; that he purposely retained some things, enjoining silence on his disciples; and that a great number of his sayings were absolutely unintelligible to his intimate followers, until his death and resurrection made them plain. We may imitate our Saviour, in not giving strong meat to babes, and in not pressing truth prematurely; but we shall greatly err, and sin against the church, if we confine our mature hearers to the milk of elementary principles, or do not, on suitable occasions, bring forward the whole counsel of God, as now revealed in the completed canon of the Scriptures. We are, however, to follow Christ, even as Paul followed him, in the subject of our teaching.

II. A few words will suffice, concerning the *manner* of Christ's preaching and ministry. So far as this is separable from the spirit of our divine Master, we may observe that it was attractive and lovely, but at the same time, simple, clear, unaffected and solemn. Admiration and awe filled the multitude of his hearers. While the rich and great derided or questioned, 'the common people heard him gladly'. Where he meant to be understood on the spot, the manner of his teaching was eminently and inimitably perspicuous. His language, yea his very idiom, was that of the mass of the people; and what he had said obscurely, he explained with patience. Yet the plainness of his words was not that inelegant rudeness which discards ornament. Lovelier ornament than that of the parables, we challenge all human literature to produce. Our Saviour dealt much in illustrations from everyday life, and scenes then under his eye. These were not for embellishment but elucidation; and the result was not so much pleasure, as force. For he was mighty, and there is a pregnancy in his concise observations, which has astonished even the infidel critic. The minister of the gospel will learn more by reading the four Gospels, with the simple purpose of asking *how Christ preached,* than by all the volumes of critics, and all the schools of rhetoric.

III. But we gladly pass to our third and principal topic, which is the *spirit* of Christ's ministry. Thousands have been successful preachers by following Paul; he was the professed model of Chrysostom, Augustine, and Luther. But all that was good in these, is in its source in Jesus.

The spirit of Christ's ministry is to be made the special directory of the preacher's spirit. Could we walk among men as he walked; could our lives breathe, as his life breathed, the gentle hallowed influence of heaven, the church which we serve would be in spirit as it is in doctrine and order, a primitive church. When we contemplate the radiance of this character, we are dazzled; and we must needs sit down and take successive glimpses, inadequate indeed but delightful, of a glory which cannot be comprehended at one view. Cast your eyes towards the Son of God in his ministerial work, passing through the throng of a polluted world, as a purer Being, from a higher sphere. Catch the traits of soul embodied in his walks of painful beneficence, and you shall see among them, love, candour, prudence, courage, tenderness, zeal, lowly meekness, toil, devotion, and self-denial.

1. *Love.* To give the proofs of Christ's love, would be to repeat the whole evangelical history. It shines in his eternal purpose, it irradiates every path of his life, it melts at his cross. In that part of the Redeemer's course which his ministers may imitate, there is a most affecting manifestation of benevolence, compassion, grace, mercy; in a word, all the kindly and charitable outgoings of the soul. The bodies and the souls of men were both his care. With equal sincerity of heart he spake long and often to the multitude, or aided in the handicraft of his disciples, or hung over the bier of the departed. Are any of his wondrous works, miracles of vengeance—is there one of them which was not a miracle of mercy? Is there one sufferer whom he thrusts away? When crowds hemmed him in, some to perplex,

some to deride, and some to murder, did he ever decline to teach the inquiring? Who among us can number up the list of his benefactions? What book could contain the history of his cures? While he healed, he preached; yea, while he gave truth, he gave health, life, salvation. He seemed to repulse a Syrophoenician woman. He seemed to reject her as a heathen—to cast her out among the very dogs; but it was only to enhance the weight of love in that closing word. 'O woman, great is thy faith, be it unto thee even as thou wilt.' It was the spontaneous compassion of Jesus, and not the cry of the multitude, which twice led to the feeding of the thousands. And their need of spiritual food also reached his bursting heart; for 'when he saw the multitudes, he was moved with compassion on them, because they fainted and were scattered abroad, as sheep having no shepherd'. How prompt was his beneficence! My son dieth, said a certain nobleman. Jesus saith unto him, Go thy way, thy son liveth. He was a son of woman, and how much of tender manhood, of social, *human* affection breaks into view in all his intercourse with the family at Bethany—his sadness at the tidings about Lazarus, his condolence, his tears—for *Jesus wept*. As love was his great—his new—his last injunction to the disciples, so it was the reigning grace in his treatment of them: the very inspiration of his farewell discourse, and the crowning characteristic of his conversations after he had risen. Love embraced the infant; actuated his itinerancy, on foot, over the rough hills and torrid plains of Palestine; and flowed out to the poor and the dying in streams of relief; and breathed invitations wide as human woe; and uttered that lamenting cry: 'O Jerusalem, Jerusalem, how often would I have gathered thy children together, even as a hen gathereth her chickens under her wings, and ye would not; behold, your house is left unto you desolate.' It was love that wept over the same city, in view of the very Golgotha where he was to die. It was love that was personified and held up to the view of angels and of God on that 'place of skulls', and that cursed cross. And we may take any discourse, any sentence, any word of Jesus Christ, and find in it the signatures of the same affection. In public and in private, the minister of Christ may walk in these steps, moistened by the toils and the agonies of his loving Saviour. And we might hold your minds for hours upon this single point; but must proceed to name secondly,

57

2. His *candour*. In the Son of man are manifested, openness, ingenuous frankness, transparent sincerity, freeness from guile, craft, finesse, concealment. Is it not superfluous to say so? It might be, if ecclesiastics, in some ages, pretending to follow Christ, had not made church-policy another name for insidious worldly statesmanship. Our blessed Lord has left an example for his ministers, that they should not endeavour to smooth the ruggedness; variegate the sameness, or expand the straitness of that thorny, direct, narrow way which leads to heaven. No converts need to be sought by false pretences. Christ makes no promises of ease, no offers of exemption from the cross; he refrains from no pungency of rebuke in order to gain favour; he wafts no flatteries to the great or the rich. Some would have followed him, whom he dismissed by simply showing that he was more homeless than the birds and foxes, or by explaining that all must be abandoned. 'Think not I am come to send peace on earth—I came not to send peace, but a sword; for I am come to set a man at variance against his father, and the daughter against her mother, and a man's foes shall be they of his own household. I am come to send fire on the earth, and what will I, if it be already kindled!'—There went great multitudes with him, and he turned and said, 'If any man come to me and hate not his family, yea his own life, he cannot be my disciple.' 'It is impossible but that offences will come.' Christ denounced woes against every class of popular leaders, sects, rulers, and cities; and to the wealthy scrupled not an instant to say, 'A rich man shall hardly enter the kingdom.' And in proportion as we try to make the way easier than the Master has made it, we alter it, to the corruption of the church, and the ruin of souls.

3. But in all this, there was no austerity or pride; none of the distant reserve and haughty rigour of the contemporary philosophers; for we discern as a third aspect of Christ's ministerial spirit, his *condescension*. As a man, and as a divine instructor, Jesus has taught us to 'condescend to men of low estate'. It was a token of his mission that he preached to the poor; and a taunt of his foes that he received sinners. Where good was to be done, there Christ was found, whether in the fishing boat of Tiberias, the supper of the publican, or the tumult of the lower people. 'Why eateth your Master with publicans and sinners?' asked the Pharisee. 'Because (answered the Master for himself),

the whole need not a physician, but they that are sick.' So far was he from the affected pomp of monkish virtue, and ascetic moroseness, that men pointed at his company, and falsely cried, 'Behold a man gluttonous and a wine-bibber, a friend of publicans and sinners!' This gentle condescension took the part of children when his followers would have sent them away, for he folded them in his arms, he laid his hands on their little heads, and said, of such is the kingdom of heaven!

4. In this, as in all the deportment of our Lord, there was as much wisdom as grace, as much knowledge of human nature as philanthropy. For we do not derogate from his spirit, when we attribute to it, in the fourth place, heavenly *prudence*. In all our vocabulary, there is scarcely a word more wronged than this. While the wiser heathen enrolled it among the cardinal virtues, the men of our day seem ready to tear it out as synonymous with timid cunning, which is the wisdom of weakness, or politic craft, which is the artifice of the wicked. It is no such thing, for in the words of Chief Justice Hale, prudence is used 'principally in reference to actions to be done, and due manner, means, order, season, and method of doing them'. Prudence is wisdom applied to practice. It is of God: 'I wisdom dwell with prudence.' It is predicated of God, who 'hath abounded toward us in all wisdom and prudence'. The minister of the gospel is as a sheep among wolves, he therefore needs to be wise as a serpent, while he is harmless as a dove. The great Exemplar should be his daily object of contemplation. The whole ministerial activity of Christ was governed by a wise reference to time, place, and circumstances. We do not find him using the same instrument for every work, or meeting all emergencies with an unalterable method. This is the way of the empiric. His discourses were adapted first to the hearers, then to the occasion. As Paul in following Christ, did not quote the rabbins to the Athenians on Mars' Hill, or Aratus and Epimenides to the Hebrews, so the Master himself was wise in observing time and opportunity. He taught, not to cast pearls before swine, nor to put new wine into old skins. Remember the instruction of Nicodemus, the melancholy conference with the young man, the frequent disputations with lawyers, and the memorable dialogue at Jacob's well. Mark the fitness to the occasion of his lessons on humility when 'he took a child and set

it by him' and made it the text of a sermon: or on the bread of life, when the multitude followed him for loaves and fishes.—Jesus came into the world to die, but he did not expose himself to untimely peril. 'No man taketh my life', said he. His unbelieving brethren would have constrained him to go to a Feast of Tabernacles; but he said, 'My time is not yet come; the world hateth me; I go not yet up to this feast.' And at the Passover following, though his soul knew not fear, he departed and did hide himself from them. The Pharisees would fain have entangled him in politics, and made him out a leader of sedition. 'Why tempt ye me, ye hypocrites?', said our Lord, and with a simple coin baffled their malice, so that 'they marvelled, and left him, and went their way'. The Sadducees would gladly have caught him in the meshes of their antinomian sophistry, but the scribe who asked him concerning the law, received in the sum of the Decalogue a conclusive confutation. It would be endless to trace this quality in all its manifestations; if our eyes are open we shall descry it every day in the history of the Evangelists. And if we are wise, we shall use the lesson, to prevent our needlessly raising opposition, laying offences in men's path, bringing gratuitous contempt on the truth, or outraging the useful decorum of life, or precedent of the church. True, in many cases, the proximate effect will be the imputation of pride, lukewarmness, or cowardice; but in the end, and when a man's ways please the Lord, he maketh even his enemies to be at peace with him.

5. But there are extremes in religion, and the extreme of timorous caution is scarcely less to be deprecated than that of reckless fanaticism. When we turn our eyes to our divine example, we behold the golden mean. While our Lord was wise, he was undaunted. *Courage* is the fifth particular in which he is imitable. Not to dwell on the thought, that the whole mediatorial work of our incarnate God was a fearless assault upon the powers of evil, we may observe that holy boldness shone in his ministry. It is no sufficient reason for withholding truth, that it is disagreeable to ungodly men; and our Saviour sometimes so spake that not only were his adversaries filled with rage, but 'many of his disciples went back, and walked no more with him'. Under his piercing discriminations, and his claims to a divine character, the Jews were indignant and even frantic, so that, not content with reviling, they sought to kill him on the spot, and failing of this,

obtained their hellish wish by a more circuitous method. Nevertheless he went right onward; boldly, yet full of love. If we observe the connection, we shall see, that his tears over Jerusalem immediately preceded his fearless expulsion of the traders from the temple: so nearly allied were his courage and his love. Again and again, before large assemblies of the most learned, noble, and arrogant leaders, did he inveigh against them as hypocrites, deceivers, and doomed to unutterable woe. His teaching was the reverse of theirs: the people were astonished at his manner of preaching, 'for he taught them as one having authority, and not as the scribes'. This authority, so far as it pertained to Christ's mediatorial character, the preacher may not assume, but he may, under his commission, 'speak and exhort, and rebuke, with all authority', letting no man despise him; and rebuking them that sin, before all, that others also may fear. There are times, even now, when hearkening to God more than unto men, he may be bold in our God: for if we seek to please men we are not the servants of Christ.

6. Alas! how easily such tempers, in the earthen vessels, become mingled with human passions, so that the gentleness of Christ is scarcely recognized among the turbulence of wrathful, proud, and untender feelings. The spirit of our Master's ministry, was eminently that of *tenderness*. It is the sixth in this constellation of graces. Where shall we begin, where all is the very ideal of gentle, sympathizing affection? It was predicted, 'a bruised reed shall he not break, and smoking flax shall he not quench'. It is impossible to imagine that such sentiments as his were ever uttered with the frown of menace, or the rudeness of objurgation. When his ministry was for the time without effect on some, he gently alludes to a game of Israelitish children, and says, 'we have piped unto you and ye have not danced, we have mourned unto you and ye have not wept'. When a rich young noble turns away, Jesus does not pursue him with a fulmination, but is very sorrowful. The mother of the sons of Zebedee makes a request, so startling, that 'the ten were moved with indignation against the two brethren', but Christ simply, and tenderly, uses the incident to repress ambition. And the spirit of his preaching is well expressed in the kind invitation, 'Come unto me all ye that labour and are heavy laden, and I will give you rest.'

7. In order to show, however, that the tenderness of Christ was not incompatible with fervour, let us further adduce his *zeal*. Zeal is not good in itself, being simply, passionate ardour, which may be for good or evil. Much that passes under the name is strange fire. Such was that of the beloved disciple when he forbade a certain person to cast out devils in Christ's name; or of the same apostle and his brother, when they seemed ready to call fire from heaven to consume the inhospitable Samaritans. But our Redeemer 'turned and rebuked them, and said, Ye know not what spirit ye are of.' The ardour of Jesus was a serener glow, yet it was not inefficient. Under its impulse, he overturned the tables of the money-changers, and scourged them from the temple; but even here it would seem to be only another aspect of love, for it is instantly added, 'and the blind and the lame came to him in the temple and he healed them'. His disciples remembered that it was written: 'The zeal of thine house hath eaten me up.' Even when suffering for food, he declared that it was his meat and drink to do the will of the Father. And in this spirit he lived and died. Could we, Brethren in the ministry, catch the holy ardour which bore forward our Master through cares and anguish—could we, like him, forget our selfish interests in the great work of rescuing souls and glorifying God—could we even, like an humbler model, stand immoveable amidst danger and flattery, so that we might finish our course with joy, and the ministry which we have received of the Lord Jesus, we might justly hope to number a hundred converts where we sadly welcome one, and expect to shine as stars in the firmament of glory.

8. Passing now to other characteristics, let me observe, that *humility* and *meekness* are nearly allied, and that they both adorned the ministry of Christ. It was his oft-repeated maxim, 'whosoever exalteth himself shall be abased'. And he taught that even little ones were not to be despised. How touching was his exemplification of this lowliness. 'The Son of man (such was the language of his conduct) came not to be ministered unto, but to minister.' He humbled himself, and made himself of no reputation: he took upon him the form of a servant; and we are exhorted by Paul to let the same mind be in us. 'Whether is greater',—he once affectingly asked—'he that sitteth at meat, or he that serveth? Is not he that sitteth at meat? But I am

among you as he that serveth?' And when he bowed down to the
menial service of washing his disciples' feet, just when he was about
to die for them, he said: 'Know ye what I have done unto you? Ye call
me Master and Lord, and ye say well; for so I am: if I then, your Lord
and Master, have washed your feet; ye also ought to wash one another's feet; for I have given you an example, that ye should do as I have
done to you. Verily, verily, I say unto you, the servant is not greater
than his Lord; neither he that is sent greater than he that sent him.'
Under injuries, our Lord was exemplary in meekness: 'who when
he was reviled, reviled not again; when he suffered, he threatened
not; but committed himself to him that judgeth righteously.' He
was derided, he was maligned, he was pursued, he was encompassed
with insults. 'Reproach', said he in prophecy, 'hath broken my heart.'
He was accused of sedition, taunted as a madman, a Samaritan, a
demoniac, a blasphemer, yet he resented not. See him in his last sufferings, 'He was oppressed, and he was afflicted, yet he opened not
his mouth: he is brought as a lamb to the slaughter, and as a sheep
before her shearers is dumb, so he opened not his mouth.' Let this
move us to pardon affronts from whomsoever received, forbearing
one another and forgiving one another, if any man have a quarrel
against any: *'even as Christ forgave you, so also do ye'*.

9, A ninth particular, is the *laborious* and *painful assiduity* of the
Lord Jesus Christ. In this he was followed by the Apostle of the Gentiles. In this he must be followed by us, if we would stand clear of the
blood of souls. A minister must not only not be slothful; he must be
above the suspicion of sloth. Paul's language to Timothy conveys the
idea of rapid and pressing activity: 'preach the word—be instant—
in season—out of season'. Be wholly in these things. That is, be in
nothing else. The minister of Christ is not called to be a scientific
inquirer, a politician, an agriculturist, a literary devotee—though the
parsimony of the churches or the desire of avoiding offence, have
sometimes forced holy men into secular pursuits; still less is he called
to be a convivial companion, a fashionable flutterer, or a habitual
idler; but to give himself *continually to prayer and the ministry of the
word*. To such a life he has the sacred incitement of example. *He* went
about doing good. On the mount, on the lake, on the strand, in the
field, in the highway, in the house, by night, by day, in Galilee, in

Samaria, in Judea, in the synagogue, and in the temple, Jesus was labouring. When the plot was maturing, when life was ebbing, when the last Passover was almost begun, he spent his nights on Olivet, and his days teaching in the temple. We read that he began 'early in the morning'. 'I must work the works of him that sent me while it is day: the night cometh, when no man can work.' Wearied with the greatness of his way, he nevertheless taught the Samaritan woman, as he leaned upon the well. And even when apprehended, he turned aside from his own woes, both in Gethsemane and on his way out of the city, to drop gracious words on his followers. In the forty days previous to his ascension, he still taught, and the language of his whole example to each of us is, 'Let the dead bury their dead, but go thou and preach the kingdom of God.'

10. To sustain a gospel minister in such labours, something is necessary beyond habitual diligence, or mere professional zeal. There may be great stir and bustle, and activity, and yet no gospel efficiency. What we need is a spring of holy influence always within us, gushing out like a river-head of living waters. What shall secure this? Answer, the grace of God in the heart, working *holiness* and *devotion*—the tenth trait in our Lord's ministerial character. Oh that every pastor could say to the people whom he serves, or has served, 'Ye are witnesses, and God also, how holily, and justly, and unblamably we behaved ourselves among you that believe.' Paul could say so, for he followed Christ; and Christ was 'holy, harmless, undefiled and separate from sinners'. After a certain tour of preaching and healing, we are told, 'Jesus returned in the power of the Spirit into Galilee, and he taught in the synagogues, being glorified of all.' The indwelling Spirit was in the head, as in the members, a Spirit of grace and supplication, and frequent are the incidental but pathetic notices of our Lord's retreats for private devotion. By these Olivet and Gethsemane were signalized, long before his final agony. Here he 'rejoiced in spirit', here he doubtless groaned and wept, here he cried, 'even so, Father, for so it seemed good in thy sight'. How often did he, after days of weariness, spend the nights in solitary watching and prayer! While the storm was on the lake, Jesus, having dismissed an immense audience, was gone 'up into a mountain apart to pray: and when the evening was come, he was there alone'! When the fame of him

increased, 'he withdrew himself into the wilderness and prayed'. The seventeenth chapter of John is a blessed fragment of his intercessions. In the garden he prayed in agony: he was sorrowful, sore amazed, very heavy, yet he prayed 'with strong crying and tears'. And in that very hour of darkness he exhorts us, 'watch and pray'! On this point we need say no more.

11. Finally. Let us detain the reader only to hint at our Redeemer's *self-denial*. Christ died upon the cross, but his whole foregoing life was a life of cross-bearing, 'For ye know the grace of our Lord Jesus Christ, that though he was rich, yet for your sakes he became poor, that ye through his poverty might be rich.' We are not called to expiatory sufferings, and we are forbidden to attempt neglecting of the body in the sense of meritorious penance. But hear the declaration to all believers, and pre-eminently to ministers: 'If any man will come after me, let him deny himself, and take up his cross daily, and follow me.' When tempted to indolent self-pleasing—the bane of ministerial fidelity—let them remember that 'even Christ pleased not himself'. If the unpleasantness, the shame, the toil, the pain, the danger of any duty, is sufficient to keep them from its performance, they are therein practically renouncing the yoke of him, who has said, 'he that loveth his life shall lose it'. It is, or ought to be understood, that every step of ministerial life is against the course of this world. Is it not enough for preachers to be as their master? 'If they have called the master of the house Beelzebub, how much more shall they call them of his household?' And every minister has reason to suspect himself, when any day occurs in which no tide of opposition, mental or external, is opposed: for he who floats with the current, floats away from God.

May God, of his infinite mercy, make our ministers in the matter, manner, and spirit of their ministry, the followers of all who follow Christ, and especially of himself, whom they call Master and Lord, and who was loving, sincere, wise, undaunted, tender, ardent, lowly, laborious, devout, and self-denying. Whether successful or unsuccessful, they shall then be pleasing to God: for they are unto God a sweet savour of Christ, in them that are saved, and in them that perish; to the one they are the savour of death unto death and to the other the savour of life unto life, And who is sufficient for these things?

CONSIDERATIONS ON FOREIGN MISSIONS ADDRESSED TO CANDIDATES FOR THE HOLY MINISTRY[1]

N O one can so forcibly present the claims of missions as the man who is himself a missionary. Hence there is an urgency in the appeals of Hall, Ward, and Swan, which is almost irresistible. And this might seem to stamp with presumption, if not insincerity, the attempt of a domestic pastor to enlist men for the foreign service. *Physician heal thyself,* might seem a very natural rejoinder. This, however, is simply a prejudice; and the flaw of the objection is betrayed as soon as we hold it up to the light; for the true ground upon which the claims of missions should be rested, is the broad foundation of the Christian ministry itself. And therefore every minister is culpable if he has not, even in his most private toils, the spirit of a missionary. He who becomes a pastor, rather than an evangelist, from fear, selfishness, lukewarmness, or pride, is as unfit to preach in the city as in the wilderness.

Candidates for the sacred office are too much accustomed to think thus: 'I will prepare myself to serve God as a preacher in my native land, and if I should be specially moved, and loudly called, I will become a foreign missionary.' Here there is altogether an error, and an error so great, that we need not be surprised to find him who harbours it, as really unfitted for the ministry at home, as he supposes himself to be for the ministry abroad.

[1] James W. Alexander, 'Considerations on Foreign Missions Addressed to Candidates for the Holy Ministry', *The Annual of the Board of Education of the General Assembly of the Presbyterian Church in the United States,* ed. John Breckinridge (Philadelphia: Russell and Martiens, 1832), pp. 125-37.

Every candidate for this momentous work should consider himself as dedicated to Christ without reserve or exception; not merely devoted to this or that function, or set apart for the more easy employments of the city, or of refined society, but yielded up to the cause of the Lord Jesus, in the spirit of sacrifice, with no limitation or evasion of his bonds. There is something indescribably attractive in the character of such a youth. He is ready, if the Lord will, to go to the pestilent swamps of Burma, or to work at the printing presses of Malta, or to endure the still greater self-denials of teaching the American Indians, no less than to display his moving oratory before a listening crowd in the metropolis, or through the press to rouse or melt the community of readers.

It would seem that there is an idea prevalent among our young men, that a call to the ministry, and a call to the missionary life, are generally different. This is untrue and dangerous. It is undoubtedly right to expect that the concurrence of circumstances and feelings which go to constitute a call to the foreign service, should differ from those which determine one to stay at home. Yet the service is the same, the cause is the same, the qualifications are the same, and the spirit should be the same. The spirit which led Whitefield to the West, and Martyn to the East, is the same which urged on the labours of Fuller and Payson and Rice; nay, is the very same spirit which leads you into the house of your next neighbour, in order to invite him to Christ. It is the love of God joined with the love of souls. Without this, every minister or candidate is a hypocrite, whose place, unless he repent, must be eternally fixed in hell. And with this genuine characteristic spirit of the gospel, the minister or the candidate is as ready, at the call of his Master, to go abroad, as to remain in his native land. Where there is zeal for the glory of God, and the love of mankind, there is a fitness, so far as mere disposition is regarded, for either work; and he who is without this should make all possible haste to clear himself from the horrible stain of blood, the blood of souls, which will adhere to unfaithful ministers.

Let the candidate for the ministry ask himself this question: 'Why do I desire to preach the gospel?' His answer will no doubt be, 'Because I desire to glorify God, by the conversion of souls; to obey the commands of Christ; to turn the talents which I possess to the greatest possible advantage in the service of the Lord.' Now, if the heart be sincere, if this answer spring from conviction and feeling, there will be in him who utters it an entire, unreserved willingness to labour anywhere, without exception, without delay, without one pang of reluctance, where God may be honoured and souls saved. You desire to obey the commandment of Christ, and to be a co-worker with God in saving sinners. You desire it without respect to personal ease, emolument, or honour. You seek the ministry, not as a comfortable profession, or a favourable retreat from the noise of the world, in which you may cultivate literature without interruption, but as a painful, trying service, in which a draught will be made upon all your capabilities in order to convert sinners. Your object is to contribute towards the illumination of the whole world. And why is this your desire? What is your authority for so vast an enterprise, so unusual an expectation? The reply is easy; the Lord has said, in language which no repetition makes uninteresting—'Go ye into all the world and preach the gospel to every creature.' It is the very commission under which you hope to act. This will be your watchword, even if you labour all your days in some little village of America; and because it is so, because the field of motives urging you to the ministry has this extent, and no more; because, if you are a preacher at all, you must be a preacher under this commission; there is every reason why you should cast down the limitations which fence in your views, and regard the field as the world. The same command which makes you a preacher to your own native town, should make you, if duly called, a preacher to the Aborigines or the Islanders.

The terms which are in common use, contribute to perpetuate an error in many minds. We speak of a *missionary* as something unique; and draw a broad demarcation between the respective companies of missionaries and *ministers*. This is not indeed intended, but such is the effect produced. Let it be observed by our youth, that a foreign missionary is a preacher to foreign countries and nothing else. He is one who would be under no necessity of changing his motives, his feelings, or his zeal in labour, if he were suddenly recalled to the domestic service. On the other hand, the country pastor is a preacher to immortal souls at home, and if he is a faithful man, and acts in pursuance of a divine call, will be entirely ready to leave his charge, and exchange his labours for those of the foreign missionary. In a word, the spirit of missions is the ministerial spirit; and where there is not love for souls sufficiently ardent to make one heartily willing to fly to the succour of the Cherokee or the Tartar, there is not enough of the main thing required in pastors to clear a man's conscience or vindicate his profession. Let it not be supposed, as is too common, that the young student or minister must needs have a certain quantum of holy zeal for Christ, in order to make it possible for him to enter the sacred office without sacrilege, and yet that the ardour and love which would make him a missionary, and would send him to the heathen, is something still beyond this, which, though excellent, is not required; a mere supererogation, an angelical quality to which only a favoured few can hope to attain. Let it not be supposed, to put the caution in a single clause, that you are at liberty to mark the line at which your love of souls shall reach its maximum. A graduating process of this kind may be allowed in trade, in literature, in pleasure, but not in serving Christ.

> In this cause we can do nothing aright unless we do all we can. If any one come short of the limits of his ability in aiding this cause, he betrays a criminal indifference which renders all that he does accomplish worthless in the sight of God; and however it may be overruled for good by him who can make the *lukewarmness,* as well as the wrath of man to praise him; yet such a spirit, considered in itself, must be regarded by infinite *purity* and *love* with the loathing occasioned by that which is neither cold nor hot.[1]

The Redeemer must have all; and (blessed be God) not only all that we are and have *now,* but all that with a still expanding capacity we can ever be, or do. And where is the youth, wounded by the ignominy and misery of sinners, bleeding in secret for the hurt of the daughter of Zion, who can sit down deliberately and make terms with Christ; or say 'thus far will I follow thee, but no further'? Where is the beloved youth under the patronage of the church, who can for an instant hesitate as to this entire devotion of himself to her great work—*the evangelizing of the world?*

---

[1] Swan's *Letters.*

To prevent misapprehension, let it be remembered, that it is far from the scope of these remarks to insinuate that every preacher should go to the heathen; or that they who stay at home must of necessity be less zealous and devoted than those who go abroad. Nay, it is the error which lies coiled in these expressions, that is now combated. It is attempted to press upon the minds of all candidates that the spirit of the good pastor is identical with the spirit of the good missionary; and that, so far as the spirit is concerned, he who is faithful and efficient in America, would be equally so in the islands of the Pacific; that every candidate for the work of the ministry should encourage the sentiment, that he is a servant not yet assigned to his field, a soldier awaiting orders; that he has no semblance of a right to determine whither he will go, or whether he will abide at home.

It is high time that the church should take a more cheerful view of Christian missions. It is meet that we should no longer speak and think and pray about the voluntary expatriation of a happy Christian group, bound for distant shores, as if it were a dreary exile; a doubtful enterprise; a jeopardy without promise. It is not so. We wrong our dear missionary brethren if we think it so viewed by them. There may be poignancy in the severance of happy ties, especially, as in Martyn's case, where the temperament of the departing evangelist is delicate. And this is that which makes it a self-denial, a cross-bearing. Were there no pangs, there would be no cross to take up. There are minds indeed so coarse and phlegmatic as to pass even such critical moments as these with apathy; but they are not the more likely, from such a complexion, to rejoice with them that do rejoice, and weep with them that weep. The generous heart will gush forth at such an hour; but I have never doubted, that even then, when the last farewell has been said and betokened, when the last headland of the native coast has sunk and vanished, when the freshening breeze has swelled the canvas, and all has conspired to pronounce the divorce from home—I have never doubted that in this hour of unwonted experience there has been a calm after tumult, a sweet serenity of composed reliance, and a filial repose in that Lord whose power is such, 'that even the winds and the sea obey him',—which together indicate a happiness akin to that of heaven.

Yet it is by no means proper that the candidate for the ministry, especially in the early stages of his course, should definitely choose his field of labour—even though his choice should be the foreign service. Like the cadet who is going through his preparations for military life, without knowing whither he shall be sent upon receiving his commission—the pious student should patiently await the indications of a higher authority. The errors against which he must guard are evidently two. He may precipitately resolve to be a foreign missionary—and this without having any decisive evidence of his fitness for the work. The consequence of such precipitation has, in a number of cases, been, that young men, under the influence of a false impression respecting the mental qualifications required in the missionary life, have neglected their studies, and after all, have retreated from the ground of their original determination. The second error, it must be owned, is far more common. Perhaps a majority of our young ministers have set the question at rest with regard to their own case, by determining that, whatever might be the duty of others, it is theirs to be pastors in their native country. Perhaps a large number have never gravely enquired, as a personal affair, whether the perishing souls of millions of idolaters did not call so loudly upon them, as to make it their duty to become missionaries. Alas! my Brethren, how long shall this spirit of slumber endure? How long will you take it for granted, as a matter admitting of no debate, that your duty is to labour at home,—and that while many who have gone out from us are bearing the heat and burden of the day, you may have a dispensation from all services of the kind? The harvest truly is great, the labourers are few; and when you bow your knees in prayer that God would send forth more labourers into his harvest, does it never flash upon your hearts that you are yourselves the very persons to be sent? Have you no sympathy with the awe and contrition and self-renunciation of the prophet, when he cried, 'Here am I, Lord, send me?'

Consider this plain statement of the case. You expect to be preachers of the gospel. You hold yourselves so entirely devoted to this work, that you are willing to go wherever the Lord may send you. You accordingly look around to ask which those regions are, where the gospel is most needed, or where Christ can be most honoured. The question is, usually, between civilized America and the heathen—and what are the comparative circumstances of the two? In these United States there is enough of divine truth within the reach of every individual (speaking in general terms) to render him inexcusable in the sight of God, if not to save his soul. Is it so in other lands? There are at least five hundred millions who are idolaters, and one hundred millions who are Mohammedans—not to speak of nominal Christians and infidels! And, as has been well remarked,

> we are not to conceive of this vast multitude as collected upon the stage of the world, and *standing still,* waiting till we are able or disposed to make known to them the way of salvation. They are not standing still; they are moving along the stage; and as thousands of them enter every hour on one side of it, as many disappear on the other side; so that the number perpetually fluctuating is still kept up: but twenty millions of them pass away every year—pass away, and are beyond our reach forever!

Now to him who expects to be invested with the ministerial office, these facts cry aloud with a voice of importunate supplication. And who can look over the brink of such an abyss of horror, and contemplate the agony of everlasting exile from God, as realized by so many sinful fellow men, without 'great heaviness', yea even 'continual sorrow' in heart? Other men are called to less direct measures and sacrifices—candidates for the ministry are called to give *themselves.*

Let the proportion be considered, between the six hundred million souls who have never heard of a Saviour from sin, and the comparative handful in Christian America who are in similar ignorance,—and it will be seen at once, that this is not a question which should be in so summary a way set aside; that it is not self-evident that for one who goes to the heathen, a thousand should remain at home: nay, it will be seen by him who devoutly weighs all the grave considerations which encircle the subject, that there is reason to reconsider all his previous determinations. The question is commonly put in the wrong order, namely, thus—*Why should I go on a foreign mission?* Most plainly it ought to be stated thus,—Why am I exempt from the duty of carrying the gospel to perishing millions,—when their number is twenty times greater than that of all the real Christians upon earth? To you, then, dear young Brethren, who feel that there is a claim upon your best services, founded on the death of Jesus—that there is a solace in Christian charity, which you desire to communicate to the desolate Gentile,—that there is a body of Christians whom your very heart pants to see increased by thousands, it may be said,—if there be 'any consolation in Christ, if any comfort of love, if any fellowship of the spirit, if any bowels and mercies', fulfil ye the joy of the church, the joy of Christ, by yielding yourselves to this work. And while we who have gone before you into the ministry, are struggling with a depressing sense of inefficiency, and stung by conscience for our neglects, do you, in fear of like regrets and compunctions,—take that field which no pious missionary has ever yet repented of having sought.

It is high time to awake out of sleep. The church is awakening. Contributions are more like the gifts of those who have 'first given their own selves unto the Lord'; every year witnesses the increase of missionary candidates in our seminaries; every monthly concert in prayer is swelled by the accordant notes of new believers. It is time that every probationer, yea, and every settled minister, should hold himself ready to go abroad as an evangelist; or rather, that the church had at her disposal, for this work, all the youth whom she may deem it desirable to send. Opposition is dying away. We are no longer repelled by objections to this apostolic enterprise; for all are beginning to perceive that no objection can be urged against modern missions which would not have been equally strong against the missions of Paul, Barnabas, and the early preachers. Some there are even now who *please not God,* and are contrary to all men; forbidding us to speak to the Gentiles that they might be saved',—but they are not the friends of Christ, or his cause; and we 'hope better things of you, and things that accompany salvation'.

A few brief counsels will conclude this essay. Though trite, they are momentous, and the profound consideration of them you will never have cause to regret. For the sake of conciseness they are expressed in the form of exhortation, and this must excuse anything magisterial in their style. To candidates for the ministry, then,—whether still abiding under the paternal roof, or pursuing studies in schools, colleges, *etc.,* the friends of missions address themselves with these hints and admonitions:

1. Cultivate that desire for the glory of Christ, which is indispensable in the pastor, no less than in the missionary.

2. Cherish the sentiment that you are not your own, and that, consequently, you have no right to form any habit, or enter into any engagement, employment, or alliance which could give a bias to your determinations, or throw an obstacle in the way of your zeal. Hold yourself disentangled, and in readiness to meet those calls which the church is about to make in behalf of the heathen.

3. As the spirit of missions is the spirit of love for souls, imbibe this now,—cultivate this temper from day to day, from this very moment, by doing all the good you can to the souls of your relatives, friends, neighbours, dependants, classmates. If you are fearful, or ashamed of Christ, at the fireside, or in an academy or college,—what can you expect to be if called to 'speak of his testimonies before kings'?

4. Consider yourselves as agents for foreign missions in every company, and rejoice in the opportunity afforded of contributing to the animation of others, and the simultaneous quickening of your own zeal.

Finally. With earnest prayer for direction, let your language be, 'Lord, what wilt thou have me to do?' This petition you may offer with peculiar interest in the expected reply, for *in the whole compass of human benevolence, there is nothing so grand, so noble, so Christian, so truly god-like, as the work of evangelizing the heathen.*[1]

---

[1] Rev. W. Orme.

THE HISTORY OF CATECHISING[1]

A MONG the works of Augustine, as scholars well know, is one on *Catechising.*[2] It was written at the request of a Carthaginian deacon named Deogratias. Now though it is not pretended that those who were contemplated in this instruction were children, or that the work was done by question and answer, yet when it is considered that the catechumens who came from heathenism were only children of a larger growth, often rudely ignorant, it will be readily believed that this book of the excellent bishop contains useful lessons for ourselves. The Carthaginian friend had lamented to him the hardness and tediousness of the work; and much of Augustine's treatise is intended to prevent this, and to show him how he may shed a most attractive cheerfulness over the whole business of catechising. These advices are just as applicable to the catechist of modern times. 'Remedies', says he, 'are to be sought of God, whereby this narrowness of spirit may be enlarged, that so we may exult in fervour of soul, and take delight in the tranquillity of a good work: for the Lord loveth a cheerful giver.' He urges his correspondent to come cheerfully to the duties of teaching, however annoying, by adducing the example of Christ, and even of human nurses, who reduce the infant's food to the minutest portions, that the child may be able to receive it.

Who that has ever taught a class of children or youth does not perceive that such advices as those which follow proceeded from experience?

> If we grow weary of saying over things which are hackneyed and fit for babes, let us come close to them by fraternal, paternal, maternal love, and when thus joined to them in heart, we shall find even the old things seem new. For such is the power of sympathy, that when

[1] James W. Alexander, 'The History of Catechising', *Biblical Repertory and Princeton Review*, Vol. 21, No. 1 (January 1849), 59-81.
[2] *De Catechisandis Rudibus*

they are affected by our speaking, we also are affected by their learning, and thus the influence is mutual: so, in a manner, they speak the
things which they hear us say, and we learn the things which we are
teaching. Do we not find it thus, in regard to certain spacious and
beautiful places, in city or country, which we have been accustomed
to pass by without any pleasure, but which, when we exhibit to friends
who have never beheld them, we contemplate with all the charm of
novelty? And this the more, the more they are our friends: such being
the bond of friendship, that the more we love them, the more do the
old things become new. But if we have made a little proficiency in the
contemplation of things, we shall not wish those whom we love to be
astonished and delighted by the works of men's hands; but we desire
to lift them to the plan and design of the author, and thence to rise to
admiration and praise of the all-creating God, where we have the end
of a love the most fertile. How much more ought we to delight, when
any approach to learn about God himself, for whose sake all things are
to be learned; and how ought our old instructions to grow fresh, by
sympathy with their feeling of novelty?

These are expressions of our common nature, though uttered fourteen hundred years ago. And what is their principle? That warm love,
and tender sympathy with the young, will make all the repetitions
and labours of catechising delightful.

Augustine lays down rules for arousing the attention of the careless,
which are just as seasonable in a mission assembly or in a parochial
school, as in ancient Carthage or Hippo. And when all means, of
narrative, of sudden question, of gentle remark are exhausted, and
the learner is still hardened and averse, he says, we must 'rather speak
concerning him to God, than concerning God to him'.

So much in earnest is Augustine, that he gives a specimen running through a number of chapters, of the sort of instruction which
a catechist of that day might give to a Gentile, who should come for
instruction. And then he goes over the same, under a shorter form.

The researches of the learned have brought many interesting things
to light respecting the apostolical and primitive catechising. Professor
Walch, of Jena, has treated this subject: we venture to present a few
gleanings from his rich harvest.[1]

---

[1] *Miscellanea Sacra*. See a translation in *Biblical Repertory* for 1827, p. 37ff.

The word *catechise* is almost Greek. The original verb occurs often in the New Testament, but in different senses. In Acts 21:21, it means 'to learn anything by common report'; in Romans 2:18, Galatians 5:6, 1 Corinthians 14:19, 'to be taught about religion'; in Luke 1:4 and Acts 18:25 'to initiate in Christian rudiments'. The word is so used also by early church writers.

This was not new among Hebrew Christians. When in Genesis 18:19, God says that Abraham will *command* his household, the word implies some previous instruction as to the nature of the command. Deuteronomy 1:1-6, is an ordinance of catechising for all ages; so also Exodus 12:26, the rule about instructing children in the meaning of the Passover.[1]

The apostles employed simple teaching, that is catechetical instruction: 'I have fed you with milk', says Paul to the Corinthians; and Clement of Alexandria applies this to catechising. Such summaries as are found in Hebrews 6:1, 2, were by the ancients called *catechetical*, by way of pre-eminence.

The persons submitted to this mode of instruction were called *catechumens*. They were generally, as has been already said, adults, but they were in knowledge no better than children. So they are expressly called, in Scripture; Hebrews 5:13, 14. Paul divides Christians into adults and children or babes, who must be fed with infants' food. So also, 1 Corinthians 3:1, 'And I, brethren, could not speak unto you as unto spiritual, but as unto carnal, even as unto *babes* in Christ.' Apollos, though a learned Alexandrian Jew, and a man of eloquence, was, in a sort, a catechumen. 'This man was instructed (*catechised*, the word is) in the way of the Lord', and a little after, 'Knowing only the baptism of John': he was therefore an unbaptized learner, a catechumen. That excellent woman, Priscilla, and her husband, Aquila, took him 'and expounded unto him the way of the Lord more perfectly'. Some think that the 'form of sound words', which Paul recommends to Timothy (*2 Tim.* 1:13) was some little compend or syllabus of catechetical instruction. It is the better opinion, however, that the apostles left nothing of this kind in writing. We must not ascribe everything to the first age, which we find in use a little later. 'Let it not be supposed', says a learned writer,

[1] See also *Deut.* 12:19; *Josh.* 4:6, 7, 22; *Josh.* 24:15; *1 Sam.* 1:25; *Psa.* 78:4, 5.

that the same kind of catechetical instruction was used in the time of the apostles, which obtained in later ages, especially in the fourth and fifth centuries, when the catechumens were divided into distinct grades and classes. For in that first age of Christianity, when the gospel was preached by the apostles themselves, many extraordinary and miraculous gifts of the Holy Spirit were enjoyed, and especially that peculiar gift, conferred on the apostles, of trying the spirits, whether they were of God.[1]

The method of question and answer is not essential to catechising, as is vulgarly thought, but is nevertheless closely connected with it, and of great importance. Here may be cited the celebrated Hoornbeek, one of the greater lights of Presbyterian Holland, in the seventeenth century.

> The questions, the manner of examining and the explanation, ought to be conformed to the capacity of the catechumens and hearers, so that all things may be done with simplicity and perspicuity, for the edification of all; therefore the first and principal study of the catechist is, to be able to interrogate with dexterity, so to propose and vary his questions, that the mind may be insensibly directed to the answer, and may scarcely avoid seeing it; and nothing is so necessary to this end, as to let down the manner of proposing questions to the capacity of children. *It is more important to interrogate properly than to explain;* for the former enters into the very nature of the catechesis, and the whole answer follows more or less readily, according as the question has been more or less clearly proposed.[2]

It was at a period subsequent to that of the apostles that the regular catechumens came into notice. These were they, whose religious proficiency was not yet enough to warrant their reception into the church. They were also called *auditores* or hearers. They might attend the reading and preaching of the church service, but not the communion. The time of this probation differed with the individual; but the Council of Elvira ordained that it should not be less than two years. Origen speaks of two classes—those who only received

---

[1] Vas Dale, *Historia Baptismeruna,* p. 416.
[2] Hoornbeek: *Misc. Sacra.* I. i. c. 12.

private instruction, and those who frequented assemblies, and were approaching baptism.

Those who gave special instruction to those candidates were called *catechists*. In Carthage and Alexandria, it was thought important to seek out men of knowledge and prudence, if possible also of learning, who might be able to contend with the Gentiles, and resolve their doubts. What is called the Apostles' Creed was probably framed for the use of catechumens. The whole theology of the Grecian world was affected by the famous normal School of Catechists at Alexandria. Of its origin Neander can find no trace. Among its distinguished teachers, who gave fame to the institution, were Pantaenus, Clemens Alexandrinus, Origen, Heraclas, and Dionysius. Origen, when eighteen years of age, was a catechumen at this school. Clement of Alexandria was one of these catechists.[1]

It would be lost labour to endeavour to trace catechetical instruction through the Dark Ages. After all the ingenious efforts of Maitland and others, to show that they were more full of light than our own, it is hard not to perceive that they were more concerned with legends, martyrologies, rosaries, feasts, and relics, than with any solid instruction. Here and there, however, we find attention drawn to the matter. At the Council of Tours, A.D. 1313, and at the second of Mentz, there were decrees enjoining the religious teaching of the young; the same order occurs in the capitulary of Charlemagne. In all these it was ordained that the instruction should be given in the vulgar tongue. From these decrees, and from other documents, we learn what constituted the body of catechetical instruction in that day. It comprised the Ten Commandments, the Apostles' Creed, and the Lord's Prayer; though sometimes one of the three is omitted. Instead of the Commandments, we find an enumeration of capital sins. It was out of regard to the time-honoured usage, in this respect, that the early Reformers followed the same order in their catechism. There is a specimen of middle-age labours, in this line, extant in the Weissenberg Theotisc Catechism of the ninth century.[2] This contains the Lord's Prayer with an exposition, the capital sins, the Athanasian and Apostles' Creed, and the doxology 'Glory to God in the highest.'

[1] Neander, I. p. 900. Eusebius V. 10.
[2] Buddeus, *Isagoge*, p. 333.

Some have attributed this little work to Rabanus Maurus, who is known to have been much concerned about the training of youth. Eccard, the editor of the book, refers it rather to Ottfried, a monk of Weissenberg, and scholar of Rabanus. But the reign of scholastic theology and the plague of superstition brought all labours of this kind to an end. It is only in flourishing periods of Christianity, that Christ's lambs are duly fed. Hence whenever any witnesses for the truth arose, they invariably turned their attention to catechetical instruction. Thus one of the crimes laid to the charge of the Waldenses, was that they gave instruction to one another. From the Catechism which the Waldenses presented to Francis I, king of France, in 1545, it appears that they had not neglected this branch of evangelical labour. The same proved true under John Wycliffe, who set himself to make simple books of instruction for the poor people. John Huss, likewise, wrote a catechetical work, while he was in prison at Constance: it is to be found among his printed works, in the edition of 1715. It is no more than just to add that the great Gerson, Chancellor of the University of Paris, not only wrote a treatise concerning 'the drawing of babes to Christ', but spent much of his latter days in carrying his principles into practice.[1]

The Reformation in the sixteenth century was accompanied by the restitution of catechetical labour. Only a shadow of this instrumentality remained. It was to remedy the brutish ignorance of the German people that Luther prepared his celebrated catechisms. Of these works we propose to speak more particularly in another place. 'The wretched aspect of things', says he, 'lately beheld by me in making a visitation, has impelled me to issue this Catechism, composed with all brevity and plainness. Alas! what calamity did I then see! The common people, especially they who dwell in the country, are so void of knowledge, that it were a shame to tell of it.'

Among many generous traits in the heroic Luther, few are more striking than his zeal for the training of the young. He seemed to be before his age in discerning that on this depended the existence of Protestantism. In 1525 he issued an 'Address to all the Magistrates and Common Councils in all cities of Germany, in behalf of Public

[1] Buddeus, p. 334.

Schools.' The learned historian von Raumer says of this treatise: 'Who can avoid being delighted to become acquainted with this great man as the reformer of German education? His admonitions went to the hearts of innumerable Germans, roused sleeping consciences, and strengthened weak hands: his decisions had, both with princes and people, the cogency of God's own voice.'[1] Some of Luther's rugged, earnest, mighty sentences, will not lose all their force, even in our imperfect translation.

> I entreat you all, therefore, dear masters and friends, on God's behalf, and on behalf of the poor youth, that you would not treat this matter so lightly, as many do, who see not the devices of the prince of this world. For it is a serious and great affair, important to Christ and all the world, that we help and counsel the young. Dear masters, if one must spend so much yearly, on firelocks, roads, bridges, dams, and numberless like things, in order that a city have temporal peace and quietness, why should we not all the rather lay out as much on the poor youth, so as to have a few fit men for schoolmasters?

> Is it not plain, that one can now in three years train a boy, so that in his fifteenth or eighteenth year, he shall know more than hitherto all universities and convents could do? Yea, what hath been learned hitherto in universities and convents, but to be asses, blocks and stocks? Twenty, even forty years have men learned in them, without knowing either Latin or German; to say nothing of the scandalous, vicious lives, whereby noble youth have there been so woefully corrupted.

> God's command by Moses presses and exacts the teaching of children by parents so often, that in the 78th Psalm it is said: 'He commanded our fathers, that they should make them known to their children, and to children's children.' And the fourth [reckoned by us as the fifth] commandment shows this also, where God so earnestly commands obedience to parents, that rebellious sons were to be judicially slain. And why indeed do we elder ones live, but that we may guard and teach and train the younger?

[1] Karl von Raumer, *Gesch. D. Paedagogik,* 1.189.

Woe to the world, forevermore! Here are children daily born and growing up, and alas! there is none to take charge of the poor young generation; so things are suffered to go as they may.

How can even reason, and especially Christian love endure it, that children grow up among us, untutored, and are poison and vermin-eggs to other children, till at last a whole city is corrupted, as befell Sodom, and Gomorrah, and Gaba! In the second place, alas the great mass of parents is unfit for the work, and know not how children should be brought up. For they have learnt nothing themselves, but to care for appetite.

'Our schools', adds Luther, with a noble warmth,

are no longer a hell and a purgatory, in which we were tortured upon *Casualibus* and *Temporalibus;* in which moreover we learned nothing but mere nought, after all our thumping, quaking, anguish and woe. If people take all this time and pains to make their children play cards, sing and dance, why not as much time to teach them reading and other arts, when they are young and at leisure, and fit and cheerful for it? I speak for myself. If I had children, and could do so, I would make them learn not only languages and history, but singing and instrumental music, and all mathematics. For what were all this but child's play, in which the Greeks in old time trained their children, so that they came to be marvellously expert, and afterwards fit for everything? Yea, it grieves me now, that I did not read the poets and histories more, and that no man taught me them. In place of which I had to read the devil's filth, the philosophers and sophists, at great cost, toil, and hurt, so that now I have enough to do to get rid of it.

And then, speaking of the ignorance prevalent in his day, he breaks forth as follows:

. . . therefore we have received what was due, and God has right well repaid our unthankfulness, in not prizing his goodness, and providing while it was yet time, and while it was possible, for the securing of good books and learned persons, and in letting it slip as not concerning us. So, on his part, God, instead of the Bible and good books, suffered Aristotle and innumerable hurtful books to come in, which drew us further and further from the Bible. Besides this, were the devil-masks, friars, college-spectres, maintained at huge expense, with many doctors, preachers, masters, parsons, and monks, that is to say, great gross fat donkeys, decked with red and brown caps, like swine led by a chain of gold and pearls, and we have laden ourselves with these, who have taught us nothing good, but have made us more and more blind and sottish, and, in return, have devoured all our goods, and filled every cloister and every corner, with the ordure of their unsavoury, poisonous books; till to think thereon is horror!

These coarse but powerful passages will do more to show the zeal of Luther for religious education, than pages of dissertation could do.

It has already been said that the Reformation brought with it a revival of catechetical instruction, and mention has been made of the catechisms of Luther. The origin and general character of these compositions belongs to our subject. They were preceded by some smaller works. The Reformation had scarcely dawned before Luther perceived the importance of giving religious training to the young after a regular form. As the result of popular discourses delivered in 1516 and 1517, the Reformer printed in 1518, an exposition of the Decalogue.[1] Two years after he set forth a similar book in German; the Lord's Prayer and Creed being added. And in a preface to his book on the German church service, he wrote, in 1526: 'First of all, we stand in need, for God's service in German, of *a rugged, plain, simple, good Catechism*. Catechism means an instruction, whereby Heathen, who mean to be Christians, may be taught and directed, what they are to believe, do, and know, in Christianity.'

When the visitation of the churches, alluded to above, was made in 1527 and the years following, Luther was so convinced of the wretched ignorance of the parish priests, that in the latter part of 1528, he prepared a catechism. 'Just now', writes he, 'I am busy, making a catechism for the rude pagans'.[2] It was his intention to confine himself to the first and larger work, but afterwards he thought it nec-

---

[1] *Decem Praecepta predicata populo, per Mart. Luther,* Vit. 1518. *Opera,* ed. Welch. tom.x.p. 182.x. 99.
[2] *Letters,* III, p. 417, 426.

essary to afford something more compendious. There has been some question as to the order of their appearance, but it is now well established that the larger one came first; and this is what might be judged from examining it, since it bears every mark of a first draft. Of our two Westminster Catechisms, on the other hand, it is well known, that the Shorter was first written. Both of Luther's were issued in 1529. Both were written by him in his peculiarly nervous[1] German. They began to be extensively used, and good old Mathesius says more than a hundred thousand copies were circulating in the Latin and German schools: so that now they are always included among the symbolical books of the Lutheran Church. The two principal Latin versions were those of Lonicerus and Obsopoeus. The Larger Catechism fills about one hundred and thirty pages of large duodecimo. After a twofold preface, it is divided into six parts, under these heads: the Ten Commandments, the Apostles' Creed, the Lord's Prayer, Baptism, and the Sacrament of the Altar (as he continued to call the Lord's Supper).

Luther's Larger Catechism is not in the form of question and answer, but is a familiar and somewhat diffuse admonition to preachers and teachers, as to the way in which they should explain and inculcate the subjects above mentioned. Some of his sound and pungent sayings will give an idea of his plainness. These instructors, he says, had grown so conceited, and so cloyed with the simplicity of divine truth, that after reading over the Catechism once, they were ready to throw it into a corner, as if they knew all about it; 'a noxious and pestiferous evil'. 'Whereas I', he adds, 'if I may speak of myself, though Doctor and preacher, and not less learned or experienced than those who thus presume, and who have come to so great assurance, am nowise ashamed to do as the boys do. For, as we teach them the Catechism, so do I, in the morning, or at any other spare time, say over to myself, word for word, the Lord's Prayer, the Creed, the Ten Commandments, some Psalms, *etc.*' (Proof, I.§ 6). 'Wherefore', says he,

> I do now once more entreat and conjure all Christians, but especially all pastors and preachers, not to seek to be Doctors before the time, nor falsely to persuade themselves that they know everything. But if

[1] strong, vigorous.

they use diligence, I solemnly promise them, and they shall themselves experience the same, that they shall thence derive great fruit, and that God will make superior men of them, so that they shall one day themselves confess, that the more they repeat and reiterate the doctrine of the Catechism, the less they apprehend and know it, but have need to be ever learning it.

Luther gives some directions as to the way in which the work of catechising shall be conducted. Let the reader judge whether we do not find in them the germ of that household tree, which has borne such goodly fruit in the land of our Presbyterian forefathers.

> The duty of the faithful and watchful father demands, that once a week in the least, he should make trial by examination of his children and family; and discover what they understand or have learnt; solemnly constraining them, in case of ignorance, to learn these things thoroughly.

The treatise (for such it is) abounds in those striking and memorable sayings, which characterize all Luther's writings, but especially those which are in German. The racy idioms often remind us of our own Bunyan: they are as strong, as witty, and as coarse. Writing as Luther did, to draw souls away from the gins and traps of Popery, he loses no opportunity of detecting the Romish snares. 'This (catechetical) way of education,' says he,

> so drives the roots into the heart, that children fear God more than they dread ferule or whip. And the reason I speak so simply is for the youth's sake, that the roots may at length penetrate their inmost mind. For when we teach children, we must prattle in their own tongue.[1]

Speaking of the abuses of the Sabbath, he says:

> Those indeed know full well how to keep holidays and festivals, who are very far from Christ and all piety; since we see all that hive, and idle luxurious throng of our religious orders, who stand daily in churches, chanting and trolling (*singen und klingen*), bawling and vociferating, and yet, with all their stentorian cry and lupine howling, keeping no Sabbath. For they neither teach nor practise any word of God, but

---

[1] (*Cat. Maj.* P.I.§ 64).

express what is quite diverse and opposite, by both their doctrine and their life.

This Larger Catechism of Luther well deserves our study. It was evidently written from a full mind and heart, and with a rapid pen. Being the first deliberate attempt, in this kind, of the Reformation era, it is not to be expected that it should be either so exhaustive or so succinct as later productions. This will be manifest from a comparison of what relates to the Law with the masterly exposition of the Decalogue in our own Catechisms. The division of the Romanists is retained; so that our fourth commandment is Luther's third, and so on, to the tenth, which is numbered ninth and tenth. The view taken of the Sabbath is lower than that of British and American Protestants, being much the same with that of Calvin. The sign of the cross in prayer is commanded. And, in regard to the sacraments, those remnants of popish opinion are of course apparent, in regard to which Luther differed so signally from Calvin, and especially from Zwingli. But the work, as a whole, is a good and great work, and must ever be venerable as the first monument of catechetical Protestantism.

The Shorter Catechism of Luther is in the form of question and answer. It is very simple, and so short as not to take up more than twenty pages, duodecimo. The order is as follows: I. The Decalogue. II. The Apostles' Creed; under three articles, 1. Of Creation, 2. Of Redemption, 3. Of Sanctification. III. The Lord's Prayer. IV. The Sacrament of Baptism. V. The Sacrament of the Altar. There are three appendices: 1. Morning and Evening Prayers; 2. Grace before and after Meat; 3. Economic Maxims.

A specimen of the doctrinal part will scarcely fail to be acceptable; it relates to the second portion of the Creed, *viz.:* 'And in Jesus Christ his only Son, our Lord', *etc.*

Q. What is the meaning of this article?

A. I believe that Jesus Christ, very God, eternally begotten of the Father, and very man, born of the virgin Mary, is my Lord, who redeemed me, a lost and condemned human being [*hominem*], and freed me from all sins, from death, and from the power of Satan, not with silver and gold, but with his own holy and precious blood, and with his innocent passion and death, that I should be wholly his, and should live under him in his kingdom, and should serve him in perpetual righteousness, innocence, and blessedness, as he himself rose from the dead, and liveth and reigneth forever. This is most certainly true.[1]

The Economic Maxims, at the close, are under fourteen heads; of which all are simple texts of Scripture, except the last. They relate to all relative duties. The closing one is a couplet, in three languages, Latin, German, and Greek:

> *Cuique sit imprimis magnae sua lectio curae,*
> *Ut domus officiis stec decorata suis.*
>
> *Ein jeder lern sein Lection,*
> *So wird es wol im Hause ston.*
>
> Let everyone his lesson learn,
> For this to household-good shall turn.

In the preface to this Shorter Catechism, Luther is very urgent upon a point which is essential to catechetical instruction, but which is in danger of being entirely neglected in this day of supposed progress in education; namely, the importance of committing a set form to the memory. He says,

I therefore beseech and conjure all you, who are pastors and preachers, that you solemnly discharge your duty, and take care of the people committed to you by God. And this you will best do, by joining us in inculcating this catechism everywhere, and especially on the young. But if any of you are so unlearned, as to have no knowledge whatever of these things, let not such be ashamed to read to their hearers this prescribed form, word for word, in this manner. First of all, let preachers beware how they set forth the Decalogue, or the Lord's Prayer, or the Creed, or the Sacraments, sometimes in one way, and sometimes in another; but let them constantly use the same form, in the common propounding and explaining these things. And my reason for giving this advice is that I know that the simpler people and youth cannot be successfully taught, *except by one and the same form often proposed and*

[1] Ed. Franke, p. 73.

repeated. For if you present the same things, sometimes in one way and sometimes in another, the more simple minds are apt to be confused, and the result is, that all your pains in teaching go for nothing.

It is another affair, when you teach the gospel in an assembly of learned men; then you may give a specimen of your erudition; and I do not forbid your varying your mode of discussion, offering sometimes one and sometimes another aspect in speaking. But with the more simple, always use the same form, set forth in certain words.

As I have said above, that the simple catechism is to be always taught in the same words, so I would desire, also, that in the explanation of the catechism, the same mode of treatment should be pursued, without altering a single syllable.

The principle contained in these directions is of great moment in all juvenile instruction. It is too commonly thought, that the point is gained with children, when they are known *to understand the matter for the time being;* and this fallacy is encouraged by the slovenly popular methods of abundant questions, to be answered in the pupil's own words. On the contrary, as the basis of every science, as a subject of teaching, is laid in concise and exact definitions; and as the language of these definitions cannot be altered without some loss; so the only safe method of beginning is to charge the memory of the learner with the very words of such definitions. This is equally true of syntax, geometry, physics, metaphysics, and theology. Those more diffuse and tentative methods which are good in the closet are out of place in the school; and the way of discovering truth is not always the way of inculcating it. All first lines of instruction must proceed upon authority; the truth must be given as *dogma.* In a word, though we arrive at principles *analytically,* we teach them *synthetically.* Hence it is not a traditionary but a most philosophic method, to demand the accurate learning by rote of catechetical forms. It is invariably found, that the best theologians are not those who have enjoyed the fullest cursory reading even of the best authors, but those who have enriched their memory with the most complete body of exact definitions.

In the churches of the Reformed, there was no less attention paid to the training of the young. Among their monuments, none is more

venerable than the catechism by John Calvin, commonly called the
Geneva Catechism. This was set forth in French, in 1536, and in
Latin, in 1538.[1] The Geneva edition of 1545 was revised by the author.
It was followed by forms of prayer, both for private use, and for the
church service: these may be seen appended to most old editions of
the French New Testament. This catechism obtained extraordinary
diffusion, being publicly used in Switzerland, Holland, and to some
extent for a time in Scotland and England.[2] Such was its value in
France, that it was expounded in all the Reformed churches of that
country, on Sunday afternoons, until the revocation of the Edict; and
this by decrees of the great National Synods.[3] It was translated into
almost all the modern languages of Europe, besides being put into
Greek by Henry Stephanus, and into Hebrew by Tremellius.

The judgment of Calvin concerning the value of juvenile instruction, may be learnt from his famous letter to Somerset, and from his
preface to the catechism itself. 'Let there besides', he writes to the
Lord Protector of England,

> be published a plain formula or catechism, for the use of children, and
> those who may be more ignorant among the people. Thus the truth
> will be rendered more familiar to them, and at the same time they will
> learn to distinguish it from impostures and corruptions, which are so
> apt to creep in by little and little upon the ignorant and careless. *It
> becomes you to be persuaded, that the church of God cannot be without
> a catechism;* for therein the true seed of doctrine is to be contained,
> from which at length the pure and seasonable harvest will be matured,
> and from this the seed may be multiplied abundantly. Wherefore, if
> you expect to build an edifice of this kind, which shall last long, and
> be safe from destruction, give all care that each child be instructed
> in the faith, by the catechism published for that purpose; that they
> may learn briefly, and as their capacities will admit, in what consists
> true Christianity. The usefulness of the catechism will not be confined
> merely to the instruction of children. The consequence will also be,
> that the people, being taught by it, will be better prepared to profit

[1] Augusti, *Liber. Symb. Ecc. Ref.* p. 647.
[2] L'Enfant, *Discours sur les Catechismes,* p. 101, s. 99.
[3] Buddeus, *Isagoge,* p. 341.

by the ordinary preaching of the word; and also if anyone, puffed up, should introduce any new opinions, he may be detected by an immediate appeal to the rule of the catechism.

In the preface, Calvin uses language which may well seem prophetic to those who in this year of 1848, a little more than three centuries after the date of the Geneva Catechism, observe the National Synod of the French Protestants repudiating the faith of their forefathers, and thus verifying the prediction of the Reformer.

But if this is so needful now, what shall we say of posterity? On this subject I am so anxious, that I scarcely dare to think. *And O that our sons may not some day regard this rather as a vaticination, than a conjecture!* Whence we must give the more pains, to bind up in our writings, such remains of the church, as may survive us, or perhaps emerge into notice. Other sorts of writings may show, indeed, what the religious opinions of us all were; but the doctrinal agreement of our churches cannot be evinced by a more illustrious testimony, than that of catechisms. For there will it appear, not merely what this or that man has taught, but what rudiments have been inculcated among us from boyhood, on all, whether learned or unlearned; all believers having this for a solemn symbol of Christian communion. This indeed was my principal reason for setting forth this catechism.

A little after he adds, in a characteristic passage:

Moreover, I think it is becoming as an example, that it be testified to the world, that we, who endeavour the edification of the church, should everywhere address ourselves faithfully to this, that the use of catechising, which some ages ago was abolished under the papacy, should now as it were be restored to its rights. For we can neither commend this holy institution according to its merits, nor sufficiently rebuke the flagitious popish corruptions, which by turning it into childish fooleries, not only did it away, but basely perverted it to a cloak for their own foul and impious superstition. For they observe no bounds, in adorning that adulterous Confirmation, which they have made to usurp its place, with a great meretricious splendour of ceremonies, and many deckings of pomp: but while they seek to adorn, they really bedeck it with execrable blasphemies, while they vaunt it as a sacrament worthier than Baptism, giving the name of semi-Christians to all who have been anointed with their unsavoury oil: meanwhile their whole action comprises nothing but histrionic gesticulations, or rather the wanton tricks of monkeys.[1]

The Address to the reader is in these words:

It was always an observance of the church, and diligently provided for, that children should be duly trained in Christian doctrine. That this might be done more conveniently, not only were schools opened, of old time, and individuals ordered to instruct their respective families aright, but it was also matter of public injunction and practice, for children to be examined in churches, on each of the articles, which ought to be common and known among all Christians. That this might be orderly done, a formula was drafted, which was called the Catechism, or Instruction. After that time, the devil, miserably lacerating the church of God, and bringing in horrid destruction (the marks of which are even now too visible in most of the earth), overthrew this holy arrangement; nor did he leave anything in its place, but sundry trifles, engendering superstitions only, with no fruit of edification. Such is what they call Confirmation, fraught indeed with postures worse than laughable, quite befitting apes, and resting on no foundation. What therefore we here offer, is nothing else than the practice of those things, which from antiquity were observed by Christians and true worshippers of God, and which were never omitted, but while the church was utterly corrupt.[2]

The starting point of the Geneva Catechism is the same as that of the Westminster, *viz.*: *'What is the chief end of man's life?'* It proceeds then to develop the highest good of man—the knowledge and worship of God—in Jesus Christ—as set forth in the Apostles' Creed, which is then expounded. After this follow the Decalogue, and the Lord's Prayer. Then are treated the Scriptures, and the Sacraments. The plan of the work differs materially from the catechisms with which we are familiar, and we cannot but think that the comparison is in favour of our own. The question is supposed to be asked by the

---

[1] Augusti, p. 462.
[2] *Ibid.*, p. 464.

teacher, and is in some instances longer than the answer; the question is not rehearsed in the answer; and the series of answers do not form a body of connected propositions. For example:

M. How then say you that we are justified by faith?
P. Because, when with certain confidence of heart, we embrace the promises of the gospel, we do, in a manner, obtain possession of this righteousness, of which I speak.

M. This is your meaning then, that the righteousness, as it is offered to us by God through the gospel, so it is received by us by faith?
P. So it is.

The exposition of the fourth commandment will serve more fully as a specimen, and will also show Calvin's doctrine of the Sabbath.

M. Does he command to labour six days, that we may rest the seventh?
P. Not simply: but giving six days to men's labours, he reserves the seventh, on which it is not permitted to labour.

M. Does he forbid all labour on one day of the week?
P. This commandment has a peculiar consideration. For the observance of rest is part of the ceremonies of the old law. And for this cause it was abolished at the coming of Christ.

M. Say you that this commandment pertains properly to the Jews, and was given for the time of the Old Testament?
P. Yes; so far as it is ceremonial.

M. Why? Is there anything in it besides ceremony?
P. It was given for three reasons.

M. What are they?
P. To figure spiritual rest; for ecclesiastical polity; and for the relief of servants.

M. What is spiritual rest?
P. It is to cease from our own works, that the Lord may work in us.

M. How is this accomplished?
P. By mortifying our flesh, that is, renouncing our nature, in order that God may govern us by his Spirit.

M. Should this be done only on one day of the week?
P. It ought to be done continually; for when we have once begun, we must continue all our life.

M. Why then is there a certain day assigned to figure this?
P. It is not required that the figure be in everything like the reality; it is enough that it have some resemblance.

M. Why is the seventh day ordained, rather than any other?
P. The number seven, in Scripture, denotes perfection. It is therefore proper to denote perpetuity. Thus it admonishes us that our spiritual rest is only begun in this present life, and will not be perfected until we depart from this world.

M. But what is the meaning of the reason here alleged by our Lord, that we must rest, as he has done?
P. After having created all his works in six days, he dedicated the seventh to the consideration of these. And to lead us the better to do this, he alleges his own example. For there is nothing so desirable, as to be conformed to him.

M. Must we always meditate on the works of God; or is it enough to do so one day in the week?
P. It should be done every day; but by reason of our infirmity, one day has been specially appointed. And this is the polity of which I spake.

M. What order then should be observed on this day?
P. People should assemble, to be instructed in the truth of God, to offer common prayers, and to render testimony to the faith and religion.

M. How do you understand this precept to be given for the relief of servants?
P. To give some relaxation to those who are under the power of others. And this equally subserves the common polity; for each one accustoms himself to labour the rest of the time, seeing he has a day of rest.

M. Now tell us how this commandment addresses itself to us?
P. Touching the ceremony, it is abolished. For we have the accomplishment in Jesus Christ.

M. How?
P. Because our old man is crucified by the virtue of his death; and because by his resurrection we rise to newness of life.

M. What remains of it then to us?
P. That we observe the order instituted in the church, for hearing the word of the Lord, joining in public prayers and sacraments, and that we do not contravene the spiritual polity which exists among believers.

M. And is the figure of no more use to us?
P. Nay, indeed: for we must return to its reality; which is, that being true members of Christ, we cease from our own works that we may resign ourselves to his government.

In this extract we have followed the French, which differs considerably in point of expression from the conciser Latin. When we consider the time at which this catechism was made, and the generality of its reception, by means of which hundreds of thousands in many countries received from it the lessons of salvation; and its exposition in all the French and Walloon churches, according to its division among the Sundays of the year; we may justly rank this among the most important works of the great Reformer, while we place it by the side of the analogous production of Martin Luther.

The example of Luther and Calvin was followed by many in both divisions of the Protestant body. On the Lutheran side, some proceeded to frame other catechisms, intended to amplify what was in the original, or to supply its defects; others expended labour in commenting more or less largely on the text. Among the former must be numbered Philip Melancthon, John Brentius, John Mathesius (so well known as the affectionate biographer of Luther), Nicholas Selnecker, David Chytraeus, John Wigand, and Nicolas Hemming. Indeed, almost every State in Germany had its respective manual in which the Catechism of Luther was enlarged and explained. The Gotha Catechism, for example, was by Solomon Glassius: the Dantzig Catechism, is noted by Abraham Calovius, and those of Dresden, Frankfort, and Quedlinburg, by Spener, who added to his other labours for Christ a plain exposition of the Smaller Catechism; a work which Buddeus says is marked by his characteristic judgment.

It is called by Mayer 'an incomparable work', on account of its fulness and clearness, the solidity of the Scripture proofs, and the tendency of the whole to promote vital piety in the learner; nothing less was to have been expected from one whom God employed as a chosen vessel for the revival of religion in a cold time. Wittenberg, Tübingen, and Leipsick had their several catechisms.[1]

Other works of catechetical form far transcended the ability of youth, and even rose to the level of theological systems. Such was that of Dietericus, entitled *Catechetical Institutes,* often enlarged upon, in the way of lectures and annotations, by such men as Chemnitius and Bechmann. A similar book by Danhauer, entitled *Catechetical Milk,* has been thought to contain not only milk for babes, but strong meat for men. There were many who published sermons founded on the order of this little book of the Reformer. So that we may bless God that Luther was ever led to such a composition.

On the side of the Reformed, much was also done; as may be read in L'Enfant's work on catechisms. All these were, however, eclipsed by one, which acquired an authority, still existing in our own day; this was the Heidelberg Catechism.

A little explanation will here be necessary. Among those countries in which the Calvinistic doctrines found great favour, one of the most noted was the Palatinate. Under Frederick II, surnamed the Wise, and Otto Henry, the Magnanimous, that is, from 1544 to 1559, the Palatinate was Lutheran. But Frederick III, about the year 1560, introduced the Swiss reform, both in doctrine and worship. He was a pious and distinguished man.[2] He thought it of great importance to fix the opinions which he maintained, by comprehending them in a catechetical formula. For the preparation of this, he employed two eminent theologians, Zachary Ursinus, and Caspar Olevianus; who were aided, some say, by Boquin and Tremellius. Ursinus of Breslau, who is to be carefully distinguished from a Lutheran divine of the same name, was a pupil of Melancthon, and was professor first at Heidelberg and then at Neustadt; he died in 1583. Olevianus became professor at Heidelberg in 1584, and was afterwards at Herborn; he wrote an Exposition of the Apostles' Creed, and died in 1587. The

[1] Buddeus, u. s. p. 335.
[2] Hase, *Kgschte.* § 362.

labour of compiling the new work fell chiefly on Ursinus. When complete, it was subjected to the clergy of the Palatinate in 1562, and in 1563 was published with the sanction of the Elector Palatine. It is a singular fact that his successor, Louis VI, who lived during the days of the celebrated 'Formula of Concord', reverted to Lutheranism, and altered both creed and church service after the Lutheran pattern. After his death, in 1583, Calvinism was restored.[1] Guericke, the representative of old school Lutheranism, commends this work for its warmth and ability, and its general richness of doctrine, but adds, that on the Lord's Supper, it contains the Calvinistic and in part even the Zwinglian doctrine, in most decisive expressions, and that it utters the Calvinistic dogma of Predestination only in an obscure manner.[2] The Heidelberg or Palatine Catechism, for it was known by both names, received respectful attention from many Lutherans, for its method, comprehensiveness, and general truth; but among the Reformed it quickly rose to the authority of a public symbol. Next to the second Helvetic Confession, it is supposed to have been the most valued and widely extended formula. It had currency not only in Germany, but in Hungary, Switzerland, and especially in Holland, from which it came with the Dutch emigration to America. Among the numerous men of learning who have written commentaries upon it, may be mentioned Ursinus himself, Pareus, Mylius, Cocceius, Momma, Alting, Leydecker, Hulsius, Becker, and Reuter. It was vehemently assaulted by Angelo de Monte Bello of Louvain, and was defended against him by Henry Alting of Groeningen, who also defended it against the Arminian objections of the Remonstrants.

The undeniable excellencies of the Heidelberg Catechism ensured it a final triumph, and in the seventeenth session of the Synod of Dort, it was approved by that body and comprehended among the symbolical books of the Reformed Dutch Church. This was further confirmed in the Convention at the Hague, in 1651.[3] Among the rules of church government, established in the Synod of Dort, the sixty-eighth is as follows:

[1] Hase, *Kgschte.* § 362.
[2] Guericke, *Kgschte,* ed. 6. vol. iii. p. 553.
[3] Buddeus, *Isagoge,* p. 339, s. 99.

Every minister shall, in the afternoon service on the Lord's day, briefly explain the system of the Christian doctrine comprehended in the catechism, adopted by the Reformed churches; so that, if practicable, the explanation may be annually completed, according to the sections made for that purpose in said catechism.[1]

It is to be observed, that the catechism is divided into portions for fifty-two Lord's days. While this rule was faithfully observed, it tended to produce that uniformity of orthodox belief which has been the glory of the Dutch churches; and it is much to be deplored, that in our large cities, this venerable usage has fallen somewhat into desuetude. Such importance was ascribed to catechetical instruction by the Reformed churches that it is expressly decreed by the last Synod of Dort, in its seventeenth session, that there should be observed a threefold method of catechising: *viz.*:

1st, Domestic, by Parents.
2nd, Scholastic, by Schoolmasters.
3rd, Ecclesiastic, by Pastors, Elders, Readers, or Visitors of the sick.
And that all whose duty it is to visit and inspect the churches and schools, shall be admonished to make this the first object of their care.

To carry this plan into effect, so far as respects the second method of instruction, there was made another decree, which comprises the following resolutions:

1st. Schools for the education of children and youth shall be established wherever they may be found necessary.

2nd. Provision shall be made for procuring and maintaining suitable teachers.

3rd. The children of the poor must be provided for in these schools, or in others, expressly for them.

4th. No person shall be appointed to the charge of these schools, who is not a member of the Reformed Church, furnished with testimonials of his orthodoxy and good morals, and who shall not previously have subscribed the Confession of Faith, the Belgic Catechism, and

[1] *Const. Ref. Dutch Ch.* ed. NY, 1815, p. 192.

solemnly promised to instruct the children committed to his care, in the principles contained in the church standards.

5th. They shall, according to the age and capacity of the children, employ two half-days in every week, not only in hearing them repeat, but assisting them to understand their catechism; shall examine them frequently, inculcate upon them the necessity of regular attendance upon the ordinances of religion, accompany them to the ordinances, and promote their benefit from them.

6th. To promote fidelity in the teachers, and progress in the children, it shall be the duty of the pastors and elders, frequently to visit these schools, to direct and encourage the teachers in the method of catechising; to examine the children with mild severity, and to excite them to industry, by holy exhortations, by commendations, and with suitable rewards.[1]

It is our purpose, at some more convenient time, to revert to this subject of catechetical history; and we shall probably then find occasion to discuss at greater length the origin and character of the great Heidelberg Catechism.

---

[1] Report to General Synod of R.D.C., 1809.

WILLIAM S. PLUMER
1802-1880

M INISTER, author, and theological professor, William Swan Plumer was one of Princeton Theological Seminary's most well-known students. Born in Griersburg, Pennsylvania, Plumer would graduate from Washington College in Virginia in 1825. Following a year of study at Princeton Theological Seminary in 1826, Plumer began a very active and diverse ministerial career.

During the first several years of Plumer's ministry he helped organize and found churches in Danville, Virginia and Warrenton, North Carolina. After several years of itinerant preaching ministry, he served as a resident pastor in Petersburg, Virginia from 1831 to 1834, and in Richmond, Virginia between the years of 1835 and 1846. During his Richmond pastorate, Plumer founded a religious weekly, the *Watchman of the South*, and an institution to assist the deaf, dumb, and blind.

In 1847, Plumer accepted a pastoral call to Baltimore, Maryland. After eight years of ministry with the congregation there, Plumer became pastor of a church in Allegheny, Pennsylvania, where he also served as a professor at Western Theological Seminary.

Plumer relocated to the Philadelphia area in the mid-1860s. He assisted a congregation in Pottsville, 1865-66, at which time he received appointment to serve as Professor of Didactic and Polemic Theology at Columbia Theological Seminary in Columbia, South Carolina. He served in this position until 1875, when he was transferred to the chair of Historic, Casuistic, and Pastoral Theology. He held this position until shortly before his death.

Plumer was a prolific author and active churchman. His published works include commentaries, biblical studies, articles, essays, sermons, and a volume on pastoral theology. His writings, while profoundly theological in nature, are very practical in focus. A number of his books have remained in print; they represent a high point in the theological-devotional literature produced of nineteenth century American Presbyterianism.

As a churchman, Plumer had the rare distinction of serving as Moderator of the General Assembly of the undivided Presbyterian denomination (1838) and of its southern branch (1871).

In his life and work, William S. Plumer embodied Princeton Theological Seminary's vision for an intelligent and informed piety that rested on the theological foundations of Scripture and the Westminster Standards.

THE SCRIPTURE DOCTRINE OF A CALL TO THE WORK OF THE GOSPEL MINISTRY[1]

Preface

SOME years ago, the writer was entrusted, by the presbytery of which he was then a member, with the special care of that branch of their operations which relates to the education of pious but indigent young men for the ministry. In fulfilling this appointment, frequent demands were made for information on the subject of a call to that work. No satisfactory essay on the subject was known. Things being thus, private application was made to several fathers in the church to write such an essay for publication, but without success. Being thus left, and by office being called to give information, the writer at length reduced his thoughts to something like system; and early in April, 1831, preached the following sermon before the students of the Union Theological Seminary, Virginia. Soon after, an article appeared in the *Biblical Repertory* on the same subject. The author has also within a few days learned that the excellent Thomas Boston published a sermon on this subject, and founded on the portion of Scripture which stands at the head of this discourse. Although he has never seen Mr Boston's discourse, it is believed that he, like the valuable writer in the *Repertory,* treats the subject in a manner applicable to those who are in the ministry, or about to enter it, rather than to those who *think of taking measures that may finally lead to that sacred office.* Respecting the sameness of texts, the language of

[1] William S. Plumer, 'Scripture Doctrine of a Call to the Work of the Gospel Ministry', *The Annual of the Board of Education of the General Assembly of the Presbyterian Church in the United States,* ed. John Breckinridge (Philadelphia: Russell and Martiens, 1832), pp. 20-54.

another on a similar occasion is appropriate. 'The coincidence was entirely accidental; and the text in each instance being employed very much in the manner of a motto, it is hoped the train of thought will be found sufficiently distinct.' So much for the history of this sermon. The serious attention of the reader is invited to a few remarks concerning the spirit with which this subject ought to be studied.

The spirit with which this subject ought to be studied:—that any subject involving moral truth, religious duty, and solemn responsibility, studied in an improper spirit, may be, and most probably will be, determined sinfully, is in full accordance with scriptural principle and careful observation. Besides, a wrong spirit is itself highly criminal, even though it govern not final decisions. If, then, we would innocently enquire into this matter, we must approach it *seriously, solemnly, reverentially.* Thus we ought to approach all subjects of a kindred character—much more, then, this. He who jests, he who trifles, he who feels no solemn awe, when considering this matter, may well doubt not only his fitness for the ministry, but the reality of his piety. When God was about to call Moses, and make him a great prophet, he first appeared to him in the burning bush. And when Moses 'turned aside to see', God said, 'Draw not nigh hither' (remain at a reverential distance): 'put off thy shoes from off thy feet, for the place whereon thou standest is holy ground.' 'And Moses hid his face.' So let all do, who think of becoming 'Ambassadors for Christ', 'Messengers of the LORD of hosts'. Too much solemnity and holy reverence cannot be exercised on this momentous subject.

Another state of the heart, essential to the proper consideration of this matter, is patient waiting on God, producing *caution* and *deliberation.* This subject is often introduced in Scripture in reference to our doubts and difficulties and darkness, and is often of unlimited application. If any think otherwise, an examination of those passages of revealed truth in which the words *wait* and *haste* with their variations occur will satisfy him. Moreover, common observation abundantly proves that purposes respecting duty, if hastily formed, are either foolish, or hastily abandoned. A man who acts without due deliberation is also guilty for so doing, even though his decision be materially right, and carried into effect. *Humility,* producing candour, and a willingness to estimate 'according to truth' one's deficiencies and qualifications, is also indispensable. In this enquiry, 'Pope Self' is one of the important items. He who is entirely ignorant of his faults and deficiencies, his attainments and abilities, cannot judge intelligently or satisfactorily. He who has real piety and much knowledge of himself must have genuine and deep humility, when he contemplates such an undertaking as that of a herald of the cross. Neither will a disposition to deny one's gifts and graces be any less dangerous than an extravagant self-conceit. Humility 'thinks soberly, as it ought to think', and 'judges true judgment'.

Finally. All that is included in the idea of *docility,* is necessary to a right investigation and decision. Of course, the enquirer must possess a deep sense of the folly of mere human wisdom; a spirit of hearty prayer to God for the teaching of the Holy Ghost; a strong desire to know the truth, and an entire willingness to act upon the truth when known. Most, if not all, of the foregoing specifications of spirit are beautifully illustrated in the conduct of Samuel, when God was about to employ him as a publisher of divine truth (*1 Sam.* 3); and in the conduct of Saul of Tarsus, when his bloody purposes were rebuked, and himself about to be sent to preach Christ crucified. So soon as Saul was arrested, he, 'trembling and astonished' (here was reverence), 'said, Lord, what wilt thou have me to do?' (here were prayer for direction, solemn enquiry, and strong desire to know the truth). His prayer was heard—his enquiry was answered—his patience and submission were tried. He was told to 'go into the city', and there learn what he must do. He went, thus manifesting his willingness to obey, and, in obeying, to learn. Soon he did learn, and 'preach Christ in the synagogues, that he is the Son of God' (*Acts* 9:1-20).

Dear youthful Reader! if you have not the spirit just described, read no further, until you look to God through Christ for the influences of the Holy Ghost, to make you solemn, reverential, humble, candid, deliberate, docile, wise, and holy, in your aims and purposes.

* * * * *

Of a Call to the Work of the Gospel Ministry

And Jesus, walking by the sea of Galilee, saw two brethren, Simon called Peter, and Andrew his brother, casting a net into the sea: for they were fishers. And he said unto them, Follow me, and I will make you fishers of men. And straightway they left their nets and followed him. And going on from thence, he saw other two brethren, James the son of Zebedee, and John his brother, in a ship with their father, mending their nets; and he called them. And they immediately left the ship and their father, and followed him (*Matt.* 4:18-22).

In the verses just read, several things are worthy of notice; but the leading idea, *viz.:* the calling of Peter, Andrew, James and John to the discipleship, as a *preparation for the ministry,* will engage our attention at present. Let us view this subject, so that we may take occasion from it to speak of the nature of a call in general, marking the difference between such a call as may be expected now, and such as we know to have been given in the days of the apostles. It may not be amiss to make a few general statements, before we enter into particulars.

The first is, that the subject, although plain in theory, is yet of exceedingly difficult application. Modest, humble, pious men are very apt to be deterred from all thoughts of entering the ministry, by many considerations which naturally present themselves; while others of doubtful piety, having in their compositions a spice of self-conceit and a dash of forwardness, frequently derive encouragement from such things as have in truth no application to their cases. Most men must have witnessed such occurrences. Notwithstanding this difficulty, it is our duty to state scriptural principles with all possible plainness, and endeavour in practice to guard carefully against the abuse of them. Some have taught and practised contrary to the opinion just expressed; but without sufficient reason. All duties ought to be explained and enforced, and all privileges fully and wisely declared. The enquiry, 'Who ought to study the question — Am I *called?'*—admits of several answers. The *first* is, *That no person who is without piety need give the matter his attention.* The first thing for him to do is to 'think on his ways and turn his feet to God's testimonies'; 'to repent and believe the gospel.' Again—*No female is bound to study this subject for personal decision and action.* 'I suffer not a woman to teach' (*1 Tim.* 2:12). Lastly, *It may be a safe rule for every male member of the church to enquire, 'Am I called?'* In a great majority of cases, even an hour's reflection may show clearly that a negative answer should be given. But that men in Christ, who are not far advanced in life, and possess sound minds, may not dismiss the subject without a moment's serious thought, is exceedingly evident.

But let us proceed to consider the nature of a call.

A call, then, is either extraordinary or ordinary. An *extraordinary* call to the ministry is one given under such circumstances as, in a marvellous and clear manner, show the will of God. Thus the call of these four fishermen was extraordinary, not merely because it was given by Christ, the Head of the church (for all genuine calls proceed from him), but because it was given by him in person, and in terms so unequivocal and so plain as to remove all ground of doubt. So also the calling of Barnabas and Saul would seem to have been extraordinary. 'As they ministered to the Lord and fasted, the Holy Ghost said, Separate me Barnabas and Saul, for the work whereunto I have called them' (*Acts* 13:2). An extraordinary call, in its very nature, is confined to the days of miracles.

An *ordinary* call differs from an extraordinary in this, that in ascertaining its reality and genuineness, we pursue the usual course by which duty becomes known, without any supernatural or marvellous indications of the will of God. Such are all calls given since the days of miracles. An ordinary call may be as clear as an extraordinary; yet it must require more patience and longer time to ascertain it. Perhaps Flavel and Baxter and Bunyan and Owen and Edwards and Brainerd had, in the latter part of their lives, no more right to doubt their call, than Paul or Barnabas had. An ordinary call is distinguishable into a general and a special call.

A *general* call is addressed to the pious generally, and arises from the necessities of the world, and from the great principles of the Bible, which command all Christians to 'hold forth the word of life'; to 'say, Come'. This general call is a very loud one. Macedonia, by her necessities, cries for help as loudly as she ever did. Hundreds of millions of this world's mortal, yet immortal inhabitants are sinking to endless night 'for lack of vision'. Gospel precepts are addressed to all the friends of Christ in such manner as requires each one, constrained by amazing love, to stand at his post, and do to the extent of his ability. This general call, however, determines nothing as to the particular method, by the adoption of which, each one shall serve. It barely says to all, 'Be strong.' 'Quit you like men.' 'Let your light shine.' 'Glorify him in your bodies and spirits, which are his', *etc.*

A *special* call to the work of the ministry is such a concurrence of qualities and events on an individual, as, if explained by the principles of the Bible and of common sense, will make it manifest that the will of God is that he, on whom the concurrence is, should enter the ministry. This is the call which every man must have, if he would enter the ministry in an acceptable manner. In determining whether we be thus specially called, we are to give good heed to the word and providences of God as they *separately* shed light on each other, and *unitedly* on this subject; and we are not to give any heed to strange fancies, and unaccountable impulses, and supposed visions.

The first evidence of a call which we shall notice, is a desire for the work. That this desire is necessary, is very evident from Scripture: 'This is a true saying, If a man *desire* the office of a bishop, he desireth a good work' (*1 Tim.* 3:1). Common sense also revolts at the thought of a man engaging in a work, in which his heart is not; especially where, as in the ministry, far more harm than good will be done to all concerned, if the heart be wanting. This desire must not be a transient emotion, but must possess essential permanency. Neither must it be a faint desire, easily overcome by counter-operations. These two ideas of permanency and strength are certainly included in that word 'desire', which first occurs in the passage just quoted. For in the original there are different words corresponding to the English word 'desire'. The first of these, ὀρέγεται, is a word of much more strength than the last, ἐπιθυμεῖ. Doddridge translates the former 'earnestly desire', the latter simply 'desire'. This desire must possess at least such permanence and vehemence as to enable one, with the help of God continually sought, to surmount obstacles as they present themselves; to submit to all the delays and labours necessary to prepare for the work; and to make him willing to take the office and work of a minister, and that only, and for life. This desire, too, must be, not for the learned leisure, the fame, the influence, the ease, or the emoluments of the office, but for the *office itself,* taken in connection with the joys and sorrows, the pains and pleasures, the labours and comforts, the responsibilities and rewards, which God has inseparably connected with a conscientious and faithful discharge of its duties. He that has such a desire, has one quality significant of a call. The more vehement and continuous this desire is, the more weight ought it to have in our determinations.

Another thing of importance in a call, is a deep and abiding sense of personal weakness and unworthiness. In view of the amazing magnitude and tremendous responsibilities, and eternal effects of the work, Paul said: 'Who is sufficient for these things?' (*2 Cor.* 2:16). If an inspired apostle, who had been rapt in visions of the third heavens, had such views, is it any wonder that all who have right conceptions of the matter, should 'exceedingly fear and quake', when they meditate an entrance on this stupendous undertaking! Neither again need we be surprised, if many who are called, should, at least for a time, shrink from any course that would be construed as a pledge or preparation for induction into the ministry. Such feel their weakness, lament their unworthiness, know their insufficiency, and draw back with fearfulness. Here is one of those dangerous places where it is possible for one to be led astray, and sin against God. This is the point on which Jeremiah did well nigh err. When God told him that he had 'ordained him a prophet', he said, 'Ah, Lord God! I cannot speak, for I am a child' (*Jer.* 1:5, 6). Humility is commendable, and, if genuine, cannot be excessive. Let one, therefore, look at the promises, and ask help from on high, and then judge whether he be not warranted in expecting 'out of weakness to be made strong'.

This leads to the remark, that *one part of this call is some comfortable degree of confidence, that, notwithstanding our great unworthiness and insufficiency, God will sustain us.* Thus God assured Jeremiah that he should be supported: 'Say not, I am a child; for thou shalt go to all that I shall send thee, and whatsoever I command thee shalt thou speak. Be not afraid of their faces, for I am with thee to deliver thee, saith the Lord' (*Jer.* 1:7, 8). Here was ground of confidence. On it Jeremiah relied. Can you, in view of all that is discouraging in yourself, and in view of all that is encouraging from God, still say, 'Though I am a worm of the dust, and less than the least of all God's mercies, and the most unworthy of all whom I know, yet God can, and I hope and believe he will bear me up, and bear me through?' To this state of holy confidence the apostle refers in these words: 'And such trust have we through Christ to God-ward: not that we are sufficient of ourselves to think any thing as of ourselves, but our sufficiency is of God, who also hath made us able ministers of the new testament' (*2 Cor.* 3:4-6). Judging from what you can learn of the will of God, honestly, humbly, and earnestly enquired into, can you 'trust' that God will 'make you an able minister of the New Testament'? If you can, 'hold fast your confidence, which hath great recompense of reward'. If you have never sought the will of God in the right manner, an expectation of support can be but presumption; and the absence of it may only prove your guilt.

Another idea which it may be important distinctly to present is, *that we put a high estimate on the office itself, and on its appropriate pleasures, and consolations, and work.* This subject has already been alluded to, but it deserves greater prominence in this discussion than it now possesses. He is not fit to be in the ministry, who cannot find in the discharge of its peculiar duties a satisfaction which he could not find in any other employment. Were you qualified, could it, would it be your meat and drink to do the work assigned you as a minister of the Word of God? Paul says, 'I magnify mine office', as if he had said, 'I commend and extol it. As it occupies a large space in my own eye, so I desire it may in the eyes of others.' Does it present itself to your mind as 'a good work', an excellent employment, in which you would, were it proper, engage rather than in any other service?

To what has been said must be added, *the wishes of judicious, impartial, pious, people (in that part of the church in which our lot is cast) and the consent of the proper authorities.* This rule is to be observed in all ordinary cases, as is evident from the example of the apostles and early Christians, in reference to deacons.

> And in those days, when the number of the disciples was multiplied, there arose a murmuring of the Grecians against the Hebrews, because their widows were neglected in the daily ministration. Then the twelve called the multitude of the disciples unto them and said, It is not reason that we should leave the word of God and serve tables; wherefore, brethren, look ye out among you seven men of honest report,

full of the Holy Ghost and wisdom, whom we may appoint over this business, but we will give ourselves continually to prayer, and to the ministry of the word. And the saying pleased the whole multitude; and they chose Stephen, a man full of faith and of the Holy Ghost and Philip, and Prochorus, and Nicanor, and Timon, and Parmenas, and Nicolas, a proselyte of Antioch, whom they set before the apostles: and when they had prayed, they laid their hands on them (*Acts* 6:1-6).

From this portion of Scripture it is exceedingly evident, that the concurrence of the people's election, and of the ordaining authority's approbation, is necessary to the validity of the commission of even a deacon, whose office extends only to the temporalities of the church. Much more, then, have the people a right to choose the man who is to be their counsellor, and teacher, and guide. Neither can any sufficient reason be given, why the ordaining authority should not also exercise a control over the matter, at least so far as to decline ordaining persons supposed to be unworthy or unfit. Indeed Paul warns Timothy to 'lay hands suddenly on no man', from which warning it is manifest that Timothy was bound to exercise his best judgment, and act accordingly.

The foregoing remarks are made in reference to ordinary times. Cases have occurred, and may again occur, in which one may not wait for a formal expression of the sentiments of either the church or the ministers of Christ; but when a pious and humble man contemplates such a step, he feels the responsibility to be truly tremendous, if not terrific. It is true, that the church and ministers sometimes seem slow in calling and sending one into the sacred office. But in this age and country, there cannot be thought to exist much error of this kind. The great error seems to be of a directly opposite nature. Besides, were the delay ever so great, it may be that God has important ends in view; especially this, that one may have time to become better qualified for the work. Such delay is sometimes seen to have been most benevolently and mercifully ordered by God. For instance, John Newton would have been utterly overwhelmed by the burden and number of his ministerial duties, had it not been for a wholesome, but at the time unwelcome, and, in its instrument, perhaps unkind delay of many months. Whenever judicious, pious, impartial people, with such concord as might fairly be expected, present the subject to one's mind, or when, their judgments being invited, they recommend further serious consideration, their voice ought to be heard, so far at least as to secure mature and religious inquiry into the will of God. Especially does this principle obtain, when those possessing the power of ordination give their consent, or cordial approval. In reference to those who only wish to know whether they ought to pursue a course of study and discipline preparatory to the work of the ministry, let it be said, that even they may arrive at some degree of probability, as to what the views and wishes of the electing and ordaining powers will be, when the proper time shall have come.

Besides these expressions of the wishes and consent of men (over which God, in his providence, exercises sovereign control), *there are various events,* which show more or less distinctly the will of the Head of the church. These leadings of providence are as various and as remarkable, as the striking diversity of occasions requires. In general, however, they relate to the things following, *viz.:*—

The disentangling of one from such engagements or pursuits as would interfere with the duties of a minister, or with due preparation for the holy office:

The furnishing of the means of acquiring the necessary knowledge and discipline, by raising up liberal, and perhaps unexpected friends; by giving success in lawful business; or by disposing someone to instruct us in the rudiments of a suitable education:—

Or, if we already possess the means, perhaps God's will is indicated by defeating our worldly plans; by sending afflictions upon us; or by making us acquainted with the history, written or oral, of someone who has felt and acted very much like ourselves. In many ways, may God indicate his will by his providence. Now, acts of providence, rightly interpreted, are of vast importance in directing the humble in all the affairs of life; and why should not their guidance be especially looked for in this great matter?

A few words of caution and warning belong to this subject. Because you cannot *see* your way clear from your present station to that of a minister, you may not infer that it *is* not clear, or will not *be* clear, as you proceed. It is not given to every man to see clearly far before him, though many think they do. 'The pillar of cloud and of fire', a striking emblem of God's providence, gave not, on one day, any pledge as to the course to be pursued the next day. The question to be decided is this, 'Can I lawfully take a step towards the holy ministry?' If you can, and if it be God's will that you should succeed, the way will, in due time, be opened for you to proceed further and further, until you shall find yourself in that office, at which you had been grasping with pious eagerness for so long a time.

Again, judge nothing before the time. The acts of divine providence, until finished, are holy enigmas; and some of them remain such through our whole lives. If, therefore, God seem for a while to frown on your purposes, be not hasty in inferring that he is about to defeat your plans; but wait, and learn the end of the matter. And if he shall so hedge up your way, as that for a time you cannot proceed, wait and learn whether he will not open it again. When the hosts of Israel had the Red Sea before them and the Egyptians behind them, the unbelieving wished that they had remained in bondage, saying, they had only come out to 'die in the wilderness'. You must learn to 'stand still' if you would 'see the salvation of God'. The obstructions of your way may only be intended as trials of your faith and patience.

To the foregoing evidences of a call must be added the *necessary qualifications, or the capacity, means, and desires of acquiring them*. That no man is called of God to perform a work for which he is not qualified, or cannot be qualified before the time of performance arrives, is so plain a truth as to render proof almost unnecessary. Even fanatics admit the principle, but elude its force, by pleading their extraordinary and supernatural endowments. God would not allow a man even to 'make the tabernacle, the ark of the testimony, the mercy-seat, and the furniture of the tabernacle', until he had 'called him, and filled him with the Spirit of God, in wisdom, and in understanding, and in knowledge, and in all manner of workmanship' (*Exod.* 31:2-7). Certainly then God calls no man to labour in the very delicate, yet grand concerns of salvation, until, in some good degree, 'the Spirit of the Lord shall rest upon him, the spirit of wisdom and understanding, the spirit of counsel and might, the spirit of knowledge and of the fear of the Lord; and shall make him of quick understanding in the fear of the Lord' (*Isa.* 11:2, 3). It is true that these words have their ful-filment in Christ, but the spirit of them is applicable in an important sense to Christ's ministers. In other words, God requires no man to 'divide his word' until he can do it 'rightly'; although he may *call him to prepare to do it.* This was the call of the four fishermen, mentioned in the text: 'Follow me, and I *will make* you fishers of men', said Jesus to two of them. The history of the other two shows their call to have been similar. Accordingly, they did not commence preaching imme-diately, but first learned from him, 'who spake as never man spake'.

As to what the qualifications for the ministry are, let it be remem-bered that among them, *an experimental acquaintance with the truths to be taught* justly holds great prominence. This subject of piety has already been spoken of as a *condecency* to the consideration of this subject. It is here introduced as a requisite to the verity of a call. This piety must be real, not feigned. 'Woe unto you hypocrites', did Jesus often say. It must be practical and consistent. 'Thou, which teachest another, teachest thou not thyself? thou that preachest a man should not steal, dost thou steal? thou that sayest a man should not commit adultery, dost thou commit adultery? thou that abhorrest idols, dost thou commit sacrilege?' (*Rom.* 2:21, 22). The piety required must also be somewhat matured. A minister must be 'not a novice (a young convert) lest, being lifted up with pride, he fall into the condemna-tion of the devil' (*1 Tim.* 3:6). This piety must also be unimpeached by the world. 'Moreover, he must have a good report of them which are without; lest he fall into reproach and the snare of the devil' (*1 Tim.* 3:7). Piety is indispensable to the saving of the soul of the preacher. Ministers must have that 'holiness without which no man shall see the Lord', or terribly perish. It is essential to the honour of Christ and his ordinances. If the 'sons of Eli be sons of Belial', men will 'abhor the offering of the Lord'. It must be at the foundation of any long continued and *cheap* usefulness in the church. The phrase 'cheap use-fulness' is not employed without design. For it is not impossible for a man without piety, and under the influence of ambition, or false zeal, to be useful to some extent; but it will be at a tremendous expense. In compassing some good, he will create a world of mischief. At least his good, which perhaps first appears, will be followed by a train of evils, that may not cease their operation on earth in a century. Indeed, men of some real piety may do this in many ways; and how much more, men without it!

Hence the *inestimable value of prudence as a qualification for the ministry*. Should any say that prudence is included under the last head, inasmuch as it is always, if genuine, the offspring of piety, the answer is, grant it, and still the great importance of the subject requires special notice. Besides, although the kind of prudence required may be the offspring of piety, yet it is no less the offspring of common sense. And, therefore, piety may consist with such constitutional or habitual imprudence, as unfits the subject of it for any important station in the church of God, or in society. It would be impracticable, without destroying the symmetry of this discourse, to do justice to the matter in hand. Reference is therefore made to a valuable discussion of this quality in Smith's work on the sacred office. A few things, however, may not be forgotten or neglected.

In the first place, then, the common consent of serious men is, that, as in a female, so in a minister, imprudence is not merely a foible, a slight obliquity, but it is a positive and glaring vice. Again, the Scriptures insist much upon it, not only under its proper name, but under the names of *wisdom* and *discretion*. 'He that winneth souls is wise' (*Prov.* 11:30). He, who would win many souls, without criminally repelling as many, must be wise. Only 'the words of the wise are as goads, and as nails fastened' (*Eccles.* 12:11). Some, perhaps, may say, 'Will not carnal policy and human cunning be sufficient?' 'Where is the wise? where is the scribe? where is the disputer of this world? hath not God made foolish the wisdom of this world?' (*1 Cor.* 1:20). Jesus also said, 'Behold I send you forth as sheep in the midst of wolves; be ye therefore wise as serpents, and *harmless* as doves' (*Matt.* 10:16). It is proper to add, that if one doubt his call because of a defect in this point, let him by honest and fair trial learn whether his imprudence be incurable. If it can be cured and shall be cured, then his way will be as open before him as if he had not been indiscreet.

The subject next in order, is knowledge. This knowledge must be such as to shield one from the just charge of gross ignorance, or fatal error, or ludicrous mistake, and must respect the message to be communicated. Of course, no man can tell others what he does not know himself. How, or when, or where this knowledge is obtained, is not material. The possession of it is the important point. The knowledge required must be accurate, else it rather merits the name of conjecture. Neither does it consist merely in ideas and notions. These may become knowledge by frequent and deep reflection. This knowledge must also be scriptural. 'The prophet that hath a dream, let him tell a dream; and he that hath my word, let him speak my word faithfully. What is the chaff to the wheat? saith the Lord' (*Jer.* 23:28). It must also be extensive. 'Every scribe which is instructed unto the kingdom of heaven, is like unto a man that is an householder, which bringeth forth out of his treasure things new and old' (*Matt.* 13:52).

To this must be added the *power of communicating knowledge in such a way as is suited to promote the great objects of preaching.* These are the conviction, conversion, and edification of souls. The truth, that it may be effective, must be spoken audibly, boldly, affectionately, earnestly, solemnly, with dignity and animation. So many valuable treatises have been published on this subject, as to make many remarks unnecessary. One remark may be sufficient; it is this: that such a manner of speaking as may become the stage, the bar, the hustings, or even the senate, will not suit the pulpit. Solemnity of a peculiar kind ought ever to rest on the sacred desk.

These four essentials—piety, prudence, knowledge, and the power of communicating knowledge in an appropriate manner—seem to include all that is requisite in the way of qualification. In speaking of them, brevity has been studied, because more than a brief notice would have been ill-timed. Much, however, is comprehended under each specification. These qualifications must be possessed before any man's credentials to the sacred office can be complete. From none of them can a dispensation be had. To ascertain these is the object of the probation pointed out in Scripture. One, however, may not as yet have the necessary knowledge, or the gift of utterance in a sufficient degree, and still may lack nothing else. Let such honestly, humbly, and diligently endeavour the removal of such unfitness; and if he succeed, his call will be clear.

As the last of the evidences of a call, may be noticed a conviction of duty, based on the due consideration of matters already discussed. This conviction may not, need not be so strong as that a man will be able to employ in their entire import the words of Paul, when he says, 'necessity is laid upon me; yea, woe is unto me, if I preach not the gospel' (*1 Cor.* 9:16). Indeed, no man can use this language, as Paul used it, until he is *assured* of his call. Yet his conviction of duty may be as *real,* though not as *firm* as that of Paul. By a *real conviction of duty* in this matter, is meant something like this: that when a man does humbly, seriously, and candidly think of entering the ministry, his mind does incline to the judgment, that in so doing, he would please God; and that in declining to do so, guilt would be contracted. This conviction, from its very nature and basis, grows or diminishes, according to the aspect of things as controlled by providence. Yet it must have permanency, though it may not be exceeding strong. If it be genuine, it will prove itself such by the fact that it is strengthened by the desirableness, and weakened by the undesirableness, of our religious state and sentiments. It was this inward conviction that made the four men named in the text obey the call of Jesus. At the first, the strength of the conviction may be no greater than to justify one in saying: 'So far as I now know my duty, I ought not to lose sight of the ministry as a work upon which I may enter at a future day.' Indeed, this is, perhaps, as far as most can go who are not yet prepared for ordination. A man may be in the ministry for many years before he be *fully convinced, beyond doubt,* that he is pleasing God. Yet no one may enter this holy office whose convictions not only do not oppose, but also incline him to do so. Blessed is he, who, although possessed of a tender and enlightened conscience, doth not condemn himself for becoming a herald of salvation (*Rom.* 14:22).

Let us now seriously consider all that has been said, and say what could be left out without creating a flaw in the call. Might we omit an earnest desire for the work? What would one do in an office for which he had no ardent love? He would presently become a farmer, a merchant, a schoolmaster, a physician, a politician, a lawyer, an owner of mills, a worldling. Could we dispense with a deep sense of personal unworthiness and insufficiency? 'He that teaches humility must himself be humble.' As to 'trust in God', what is a minister without it? He is a reed shaken with the wind; a ship without an anchor; a world without a sun. Dare we leave out a high estimate of the dignity and incalculable importance of the office? 'Woe unto them that call evil good, and good evil; that put darkness for light,

and light for darkness; that put bitter for sweet, and sweet for bitter'
(*Isa.* 5:20). Let all things, especially sacred things, be rightly esteemed.
Shall one commence preaching contrary to the wishes of the church?
How can he edify a people who will not hear him, or, if they do,
wish him to be silent? Or shall one enter on the work, when those
who are at least supposed to be impartial and enlightened judges, tell
him that they dare not 'lay hands' on him, lest they should become
'partakers of other men's sins?' (*1 Tim.* 5:22). Or, shall a man, forgetful
or heedless of the voice of providence, and the duties thereby created
or designated, break through every obstacle, and rush into the ministry, 'as the horse rusheth into the battle'? 'Faith, judgment, mercy,
and piety at home', may on no account be omitted. Can piety be
dispensed with? 'To the wicked God saith, What hast thou to do to
declare my statutes, or that thou shouldest take my covenant in thy
mouth?' (*Psa.* 50:16). We dare not omit prudence. As 'the wicked shall
do wickedly', so the foolish will act foolishly, the imprudent, rashly.
Nothing but a sound mind ever produced sound speech, that could
not be gainsayed, or sober conduct that was irrebukable. Knowledge
is indispensable. 'The priest's lips should keep knowledge' (*Mal.* 2:7).
And knowledge, inappropriately communicated, will be useless to
all, and injurious to many.

He who runs against the convictions of his best judgment, cannot
be strong in the day of trial; and must incur great guilt (*Rom.* 14:23).
Let no man, then, attempt actually to enter the ministry without all
these evidences of a call. If he shall, he will certainly err. If anyone
doubt whether he possess the whole of them, and in such a degree as
is necessary to render it safe for him to proceed, let him wait, humbly
and patiently asking the guidance of Jehovah.

It is due to truth also to state, that the foregoing discussion is
thought to include a summary of all that the Bible teaches respecting
the nature and evidences of a call to the ministry, as a general work.
A call of God to labour in a particular sphere, as on a foreign mission,
or on a domestic mission, or on an agency, or in a system of evangelism, or in the modest, perhaps retired, but delightful and holy work
of pastor, or in the disciplining and instruction of candidates for the
ministry, must be determined by the addition of several distinct principles. But, so far as the subject of a scriptural call to the general

work of the ministry is concerned, what has been said is believed to embrace all the particulars specified in God's Word.

From what has been said, the following seem to be natural and legitimate conclusions:

First: Two men may both be called of God to enter the ministry at the same time; and while one may be well satisfied of his own call, the other may have very painful apprehensions and fears, whether he ought to proceed. So that a man cannot know that he is not called, because he is not as certain about the course of his duty as some of his brethren are respecting the propriety of their course. Again, the clearness or doubtfulness in a man's mind about his own call may arise either from the high or the low character of his piety. Nothing, therefore, positively encouraging or discouraging respecting the amount of personal piety, can be learned from the fact that our minds are doubtful, or that they are decided. How important, then, frequently and impartially to inquire into the state of piety in the soul!

It also follows, from what has been said, that a call may be regarded as clear or doubtful by the subject of it, while other persons may arrive at conclusions very diverse. Through the operation of many undesirable influences a man may think himself clearly called to a work from which impartial, and even charitable men will feel bound to restrain him. On the other hand, one, of whose call others may be satisfied, may, by the undue influence of some principles, in themselves good, but in this case, misapplied, not think himself called to this great work. To this latter class scriptural encouragement should be given. God has set us the example.

Another obvious remark is, that one, who is called to commence preparation for the ministry, ordinarily has a less amount of evidence in favour of his course at that time, than he has afterwards. In other words, he who is but acquiring the rudiments of a suitable education, has less of certainty than the approved candidate for licensure; the licentiate has less than the candidate for ordination; the young minister less than the father in the church. But then the first steps are always, if not less important, less decisive, accompanied with lighter responsibilities, and, if unsuccessful, followed with less disastrous consequences than the subsequent steps. A moderate degree of probability may be the highest result of all the evidence before one's mind, until he shall resolve to make the effort, and, in making it, learn whether he ought to desist or proceed. This remark is intended for such as, having yet before them a large part of the work of preparation, are, nevertheless, demanding a weight of evidence in favour of a call to prepare, equal to that which might be expected, if they were about to be *inducted into office.*

A few observations on two things, necessary to be solemnly considered, shall close this discourse. The first will concern *the resistance of a call.* That such resistance may be offered, few will doubt. If a pious man may enter the ministry uncalled, as certainly some have done confessedly, no reason can be given why even a pious man may not resist when called. This may be done by matrimonial entanglements, which date their existence either before or after the receiving of the call:

Or money-hunting, the spirit of accumulation, the supposed obligation, or the wicked purpose, of maintaining or augmenting hereditaments and patrimonies, may occasion the sinful resistance:

Sinful timidity, creating a wish to lead a quiet and retired life, and indisposing to any public appearance, may produce the same result:

Slothfulness, which loves ease, and dislikes activity, may occasion a refusal to 'bear the heat and burden' of a minister's life:

Ambition for political, scientific, literary, or military fame, may keep one from obeying 'the heavenly calling':

A wicked pride, which is unwilling to be in the ministry without pre-eminence, united with comparative and 'conscious poverty of soul', and weakness of mind, may hinder men from doing their duty:

A 'voluntary humility', which makes its subject deny the graces or the gifts which God has bestowed upon him, has, probably, led many astray:

Or, one who is called, may satisfy himself for not obeying, by pleading the want of good health, when his health is confessedly sufficient for other employments equally *sedentary, or laborious, or active:*

Men, who advise not in the fear of God, especially relatives, perhaps parents, often persuade to sin, in resisting a call:

Sometimes men err through an *unfounded* supposition that their services are necessary for the maintenance of one or more dependants, who might otherwise be provided for, if proper efforts were made:

A foolish and sinful unwillingness to receive aid from the church, while preparing for the ministry, sometimes misleads:

Concealment of personal views and wishes in reference to the ministry from those who might be helpers, may betray into sin:

Or, finally, a man may resist a call through inattention to the providence of God.

If every cause or occasion of resistance has not been named, yet enough has been said to enable each one to supply the deficiency, if personal. The criminality, of course, varies according to the endless diversity of cases; but every resistance is criminal and perilous. If you would know how God regards the matter, read that awful dialogue between God and Moses about leading Israel to Canaan. God told Moses that he should be leader. Moses states, and God sets aside, difficulty after difficulty. Moses still continuing to object, at last it is said, 'And the anger of the Lord was kindled against Moses' (*Exod.* 4:14). If God were thus displeased with Moses, to whom 'he spoke as a man to his friend', can he be otherwise than highly displeased with all who excuse themselves from the work to which they are called? 'Woe unto him that striveth with his Maker!' (*Isa.* 45:9). Remember Jonah. Suppose that Jeremiah, after all the assurances of strength and courage and support which he received, had persisted in crying: 'Ah, Lord God! I cannot speak, for I am a child', God would have been angry with him. Or, suppose the four men mentioned in the text had resisted their call, they had, certainly, never been the instruments of such achievements as sacred story ascribes to them, nor filled the thrones in glory which they now occupy; nor had their names inscribed where John saw them. 'And the wall of the city had twelve foundations, and in them the names of the twelve apostles of the Lamb' (*Rev.* 21:14). If Christ call you even to prepare for the ministry, do you, like the four fishermen, 'straightway, immediately follow'. Blessed is he who, being called, obeys, humbly, heartily, joyfully running at God's command and fulfilling the ministry which he receives. 'For we are unto God a sweet savour of Christ' (*2 Cor.* 2:15). 'And they that be wise shall shine as the brightness of the firmament; and they that turn many to righteousness, as the stars for ever and ever' (*Dan.* 12:3).

The concluding thoughts respect entering the ministry when God does not call. A man may do this in obedience to dreams, supposed voices, and indefinable impulses, thought to be indicative of God's will:

Or the various kinds of false zeal may first destroy modesty and sobriety, and then drive their subject into the ministry:

Some may run uncalled through the influence of an erroneous opinion that every pious man may, if he can, and can, if he will, become 'a preacher of righteousness'. The truth is, pious men are so much needed in every station in life, that the bare necessity of one to fill a place is no evidence of a designation of the person who ought to fill it. Else, every pious man must consider himself called to fill every variety of station:

A man may enter the ministry uncalled, through a desire to lead an easy life, most erroneously thinking a *faithful* minister's such, or, most sadly, forgetting that the only epitaph suitable to an *unfaithful* minister is, 'It had been good for this man, if he had never been born':

Or covetousness, 'that vile idolatry', may induce him to seek the ministry. It is not true that the American churches have nothing to fear from the operation of this principle on the ministry, and on candidates for the ministry:

Again, weak, partial, vain friends, especially parents, may give foolish advice, and cause one to sin, by going unsent:

A man also may be determined for the ministry by a conscious incapacity for any other learned profession, and by a low opinion of the dignity and difficulty of this, and thus 'play the fool':

It sometimes occurs that men under conviction, and in great distress, vow that if God will forgive their sins, and cheer their hearts, they will become preachers. When they hope that they have passed from death unto life, they remember their engagement, and keep it, forgetting that, in many cases, both God and their vow 'would be more honoured by the breach than by the observance':

One may easily be moved by his blind irreverence for the sacredness of the office:

Or an unholy ambition to possess that kind of popularity, and confidence, which faithful ministers generally have, may be the ruling passion in seeking the ministry:

Lastly: A man may enter the ministry, uncalled, by taking imperfect views of the subject of a call, or by denying, or forgetting, the whole matter of a scriptural call, and examining the question, 'Ought I to enter the ministry?' on general grounds, from which no correct decision can be made. Thus do those err who simply enquire, 'Can I be more useful in the ministry, than elsewhere?' a question which no man on earth can answer, unless he can first tell whether he is called of God.

Perhaps the foregoing specifications may be sufficient for ordinary purposes. Illustrations of some of them have perhaps afflicted most of the present race of pious men. There are some very strange and almost unaccountable phenomena in this part of the religious world. Some very weak men have seemed to think that they were raised up in these latter days, to 'turn the world upside down'. Obtuseness of feeling makes them defy ridicule; and want of becoming moral sentiment enables them to live without pain in the midst of moral ruin. By whatever influence one is unscripturally brought into the ministry, guilt rests upon him. In some cases the guilt is less than in others; but, in no instance is the criminality small. One who is in danger of thus transgressing, ought carefully to read, and solemnly to reflect upon the following brief, but alarming narrative: 'And when they came to Nachon's threshing-floor, Uzzah put forth his hand to the ark of God, and took hold of it; for the oxen shook it. And the anger of the LORD was kindled against Uzzah; and God smote him there for his error; and there he died by the ark of God' (2 *Sam.* 6:6, 7). That a man, by entering the ministry, uncalled, may render himself ridiculous, or odious, is not so overwhelming a matter, until we remember that the honour of Christ, the dignity of the gospel institute, and the salvation of souls are involved in his office. Under the ministry of such a man, the lambs and the sheep are not fed. Believers 'grow not up as calves of the stall'. Perhaps the spirit of daring speculation, or wild fanaticism reigns in terror. Or the 'spirit of slumber' works ruin, not the less certain or total, because wrought in the undisturbed stillness of spiritual death. If piety be lacking, such a man will be 'sowing the wind to reap the whirlwind'. As to God, he will be an 'empty vine, and bring forth fruit only unto himself'. If he handle the sword of the Spirit without the skill, which none but the *truly called* have, he will wound whom God has not wounded, and defend whom God has not defended; and thus contract the guilt of a murderer of souls. And 'a man', says Brooks, 'had better have all the blood of all men in all ages of the world to answer for, than the blood of one single soul'. 'No man taketh this honour to himself, but he that is called of God, as was Aaron' (*Heb.* 5:4).

CHARLES HODGE
1797-1878

SCHOLAR, educator, churchman, and distinguished American Presbyterian systematic theologian of the nineteenth century, Charles Hodge was born in Philadelphia in 1797. Following his father's untimely death a few years after he was born, Charles and his brother were raised by their godly widowed mother. In 1812 Hodge's mother moved the family to Princeton in hope of matriculating her sons at Princeton College.

Charles Hodge graduated from Princeton College in 1815. During the 1814-15 school year a revival broke out on the college campus: Charles was one of a number of students converted during this time of spiritual refreshing. At the encouragement of Archibald Alexander, he enrolled at Princeton Theological Seminary, graduating with the class of 1819. Ordained in 1821, his scholarly gifts led to an appointment by his denomination in 1822 to serve as the seminary's third faculty member.

As Professor of Oriental and Biblical Literature, Hodge's primary responsibility was instruction in biblical languages, hermeneutics, biblical criticism, and study of Old Testament texts. During 1826-28, he travelled to Europe to study with the leading European biblical and theological scholars. Hodge focused his studies on theology and biblical interpretation, with additional concentration in Semitic and cognate languages. His studies in Europe made him one of the leading Hebraists teaching in an American theological institution in the early nineteenth century. In the coming decade, Hodge would be assisted by the linguistic talent and philological expertise of Joseph Addison Alexander. With Addison's arrival, Hodge concentrated his labours on New Testament texts and studies, serving as Professor of Exegetical and Didactic Theology from 1840 to 1854. From 1854 until his death in 1878, he served as Professor of Exegetical, Didactic, and Polemic Theology.

During his half-century tenure at Princeton, Charles Hodge held several chairs, but is probably best remembered for the reputation he established as Professor of Systematic Theology. A stout Calvinist with a deep love for the Reformed confessions, his literary labours often involved a polemical thrust, as he sought to defend and expound the Reformed theology of the Protestant Reformation, and the teachings of the Westminster Confession and the Larger and Shorter Catechisms, as received and adopted by the Presbyterian Church in the United States of America.

A prolific author, Hodge served for many years as editor of the seminary journal, *Biblical Repertory and Princeton Review*. Under his editorship, it became the leading theological journal of the nineteenth century: Hodge's personal contributions included articles on biblical studies, spirituality, church history and historical theology, ecclesiological issues, philosophy, politics, slavery, abolition and the Civil War. An active churchman, he was at the forefront of ecclesiastical debates and discussion.

In addition to articles and essays, Hodge published commentaries on Romans, 1 and 2 Corinthians, and Ephesians. A major historical work in defence of Old-school Presbyterian doctrine and practice, *The Constitutional History of the Presbyterian Church in the United States of America,* appeared in 1840. His popular work on piety, *The Way of Life,* was published in 1841. His three-volume *magnum opus, Systematic Theology,* was published in 1872-73, and confirmed him as the outstanding Calvinistic systematic theologian of the nineteenth century. Additional publications on the relationship between Christianity and science, and a collection of essays delivered at the Sabbath Afternoon Conferences, served to further confirm the breadth of his academic competency and the depth of his Christian piety.

THE CHARACTER TRAITS OF
THE GOSPEL MINISTER[1]

THE question which the Apostle Peter proposes, in view of the second advent of the Son of God, is one which Christians, and Christian ministers especially, should often ponder: *What manner of men ought ye to be?* There is, obviously, much which the candidate for the ministry needs, which is equally necessary for every believer. Yet, as every man's duty is more or less modified by the peculiarity of his circumstances, it is evident, that there are some traits of character which are especially important to those who are to be ensamples and leaders of the flock of Jesus Christ. Of these traits, and of those especially which the peculiarity of our circumstances renders important for us, we should form a definite conception; and, having clearly apprehended their nature, steadily labour for their attainment. It is, indeed, much to be feared, that few men adequately feel the necessity of striving to form their characters aright. They neither fix in their minds distinctly what they ought to be, nor endeavour systematically to bring themselves up to the standard. They leave this great concern very much to itself, allowing the circumstances in which they are placed, and the truths which, in the providence of God, are brought to bear upon them, to mould their principles and feelings, without any settled plan or purpose. The result of this course is imperfection and inconstancy. Many faults are left unnoticed, to gain the ascendency, and many tendencies of their situation are unapprehended, and consequently unresisted. It is necessary here, as elsewhere, to act intelligently and rigorously; to feel that we are not passive matter, to be fashioned by all extra influences

---

[1] Charles Hodge, 'Suggestions to Theological Students, on Some of Those Traits of Character, which the Spirit of the Age Renders Peculiarly Important in the Ministers of the Gospel', *Biblical Repertory and Theological Review*, Vol. 5, No. 1 (January 1833), pp. 100-13.

of men and things, but active beings, who must, in dependence on the grace of God, endeavour to make ourselves what God and duty require. We may be allowed, therefore, to call the attention of that class of our readers, for whom these remarks are designed, to a few of those traits of character which, under existing circumstances, it is peculiarly important for them to cultivate.

I. *A sacred regard for the truth of God*. There is an important practical difference between the position occupied by the Christian minister, and the speculative philosopher, whether moralist or theologian. The one is to receive on authority what God has revealed, the other to discover for himself what is truth. The grounds of assault are different. The one believes because God has spoken, the other because he discovers, or fancies that he does, the coincidences between his opinions, and established or intuitive truths. The Christian theologian, indeed, is not required to believe anything which shocks his reason, or does violence to the constitution of his nature; but the ground of his faith is essentially the divine testimony, though he may perceive by the aid of the Spirit, the harmony of the truths which he is called upon to receive, and their coincidence with all other principles which he knows to be correct. The state of mind which this difference of position produces, is very diverse; and, consequently, the theologian, who addresses himself to the study of theology, as the philosopher to the investigation of truth, has placed himself in a false position; his state of mind will necessarily be wrong, and his results, in all probability, erroneous and unstable, destitute of their proper authority for himself or others.

Though the correctness of these remarks may be admitted, yet it is nevertheless the fact, that few things are more common than this initial error among students of theology. They place themselves in a wrong posture. They mistake as to the nature of their work. They commence by settling the principles of moral or mental philosophy, and thence evolve their system of theology; first determine what must be truth, and then, for courtesy sake, turn to the Bible to see what is truth. This course is utterly inconsistent with proper reverence for a divine revelation. It is a practical denial of its necessity; an assertion of an ability to do without it. As this has ever been one of the most prevalent evils of the church, and to no small degree is characteristic of our own age and country, we should sedulously watch against it, remembering, that one important part of the obedience we owe to God is submission to the truth as he has revealed it. As this dependence upon ourselves implies a want of sufficient reverence for the Scripture, as a communication from God, so it tends to produce indifference to the truth. When a large part of a man's theology is made up of the speculations and deductions of his own mind, he is apt to think that the points of difference between himself and others are mere matters of philosophical distinction. Conscious that much of what he holds to be religious truth, he so regards on his own authority, he naturally supposes the same is the case with others, and, of course, regards the difference as of little consequence. The authority of God is, in his view, not concerned, but only human reasoning. It would be strange, therefore, if he felt any very special concern on the subject. He may, indeed, be sufficiently strenuous and positive, but the offence of those who differ from him, is more an offence against reason and common sense than God.

Indifference to truth, and to serious diversity of religious opinion, is, therefore, the natural consequence of this spirit. We accordingly find this result always prevalent, in proportion to the ascendency of this spirit. In some countries, at the present day, theology is professedly regarded as a mere department of philosophy; and the appearance of a new system of religious doctrine is no more regarded than the announcement of a new theory of physics. No one dreams that an opinion can be a crime, or the evidence of it, even though the opinion should involve the denial of the divine Being, or of the existence of sin. Such extreme cases are instructive, as they show the consequence of making theology a branch of philosophy. And this is often practically done, by those who professedly acknowledge and imagine, that they feel the supremacy of the Scriptures. It is not necessary to look beyond the sea, to find abundant illustrations of the truth of this remark. We have examples on every hand, and, doubtless, furnish them not infrequently ourselves. For nothing is more difficult to avoid than this sinful neglect and indifference to the testimony of God, arising from an overweening confidence in the correctness of our own reasonings. The way to avoid the effect is to guard against the cause. To learn practically to regard the Word of God as his Word, worthy of implicit reliance and unhesitating acceptance.

Another cause of this indifference to divine truth, is a false spirit of liberality. This is as insidious, and, perhaps, more so than the other. It comes in the guise of virtue. Liberality, in its genuine exercise, is one of the last attainments of an enlarged and sanctified mind. It presupposes so extended and accurate a knowledge of divine truth, that the distinction between essential and unessential points is easily perceived, and feelings so regulated, that all are affectionately and cordially regarded, who agree as to important points. While, therefore, the truly liberal man is firm and strenuous in maintaining truth, he is no bigot. For bigotry implies the undue regard of trivial matters; a contending for them with a zeal justifiable only when vital truths are concerned. As liberality implies so much excellence, and is so generally attractive and popular, it is not wonderful that we should all desire the reputation of possessing it; and this reputation is very easily gained. Indifference to the truth will commonly answer the purpose; and where obloquy is the portion of those who are not thus indifferent, the temptation is very strong to avoid this evil, by unpardonable concessions. While spurious liberality is thus the offspring, at times, of indifference, at others it is an amiable weakness, or, rather, a weakness of amiable characters: men whose love of peace and kind feelings predominate over other parts of their character, and cause them to sanction opinions which they entirely disapprove of. Whatever may be the source of this spirit, it obviously leads to a disregard of the truth of God. We see men, under its influence, seemingly indifferent to important departures from the faith of the gospel, and unwilling even to avow distinctly their opinions, lest they should be committed, or appear as too strenuous advocates of a particular system. It is plain, that the evils of such a disposition must be extensive, if from no other reason, at least from the fact that the plea and appeal to liberality are always most frequent among those whose departures from the truth are the most serious. The deity of Christ; the doctrines of the atonement, of regeneration, and of the eternal punishment of the finally impenitent, are rejected by men whose claims to liberality are the loudest, and whose appeals to it are the most constant. Those who are surrounded by such men, and still appreciate and maintain the truth and importance of these doctrines, must expect to be regarded as bigots.

The case here, it will be seen, is plain. Everyone acknowledges, that a liberality which can render a man indifferent to such points is inexcusable and destructive. But the difficulty with most minds is to know where to draw the line; what errors may be tolerated, and what strenuously opposed. It commends itself, probably, at first view, to Christian feelings to say, that only such opinions as are inconsistent with piety should be matters of dispute; that so long as enough of the gospel is retained to be a foundation for a good hope and a good life, we must give ourselves no concern. And, indeed, nothing can be plainer, than that duty requires us to recognize men and things as they really are; and hence, if a man be a Christian, we should regard and treat him as such, however much we may differ from him as to points of doctrine. But, to say nothing of the difficulty of deciding what opinions are, and what are not inconsistent with real religion, this rule, though applicable to the terms of communion among Christians generally, is evidently out of place, when applied to the members, or especially the ministers, of the same denomination. The judgment which we form of a man or minister, who is a member of a church professedly Arminian, and who avows the doctrines of his denomination, is very different from what we should entertain toward a member of a Calvinistic society, who should avow the same sentiments. And a mode of treatment highly illiberal towards the one, might be a matter of duty towards the other. Because it is right to regard a Christian as a Christian, it surely does not follow that we must regard an Arminian as a Calvinist.

This distinction between what is due to a man as a follower of Christ, and what is due to him as a member of any particular denomination, professing a particular form of doctrine, though so perfectly obvious, is frequently disregarded. How often is the declaration heard from Presbyterians, 'If a man is only a Christian, and is active in doing good, we care not what doctrines he teaches.' This is meant to be an avowal of a high-minded liberality; but a moment's reflection shows that it is an acknowledgment of the utmost inconsistency, and a disregard of solemn obligations. It is a declaration that every portion of truth, not absolutely essential to salvation, is of little consequence;

and that it matters not whether a man who professes to be a Calvinist is one or not. While we readily grant that it is a duty and privilege to love and cherish all who bear the impress of the Saviour's image, and that we should reject no man from our fellowship whom Christ would receive to his, it is equally plain that no obligation can be more obvious than that which requires men who make a profession of a particular form of doctrine, to be sincere; and those who promise to uphold that form, because they believe it true, to be faithful to their engagement. It is professing, therefore, a freedom from the restraints of morality, to be so liberal as to be indifferent to truth, which we have professed to hold, and engaged to defend.

There are, evidently, therefore, two rules which bind every minister and member of a church; the one which fixes the line of his duty towards Christians, as such, the other towards those who are members of his own society. A man may be a very good Christian, and as such entitled to Christian fellowship, and yet, hold opinions inconsistent with his being an Episcopalian, a Methodist, or a Presbyterian. A neglect of this obvious distinction has led, we doubt not, to much criminal remissness, with regard to the truth as held by our church.

Another and more serious cause of this indifference to truth, is a want of experience of its power and value. No man can lightly esteem that which he knows from his own experience to have a powerful influence in the sanctification or consolation of believers. No man who has not felt the truth of the divine declarations of the evil of sin, nor experienced the power and sovereignty of divine grace, nor rejoiced in the peace which follows the acceptance of Christ, as the propitiation for our sins, can be expected to feel the value or importance of these doctrines. He will regard those who make them essential to the salvation of men, as narrow minded, and will spurn the idea of censuring those who reject them. It will be found, the world over, that truths which men have thus deeply felt, they will cling to and defend, and, therefore, the more thoroughly men are imbued with the spirit of the Word of God, the more they feel the value of its various doctrines, the more consistent and firm will they be in maintaining and promoting them.

While it is evidently our duty to guard against indifference to the truth, from whatever cause it may arise, we should be very careful not to offend on the opposite extreme, by magnifying mole hills into mountains; with undiscriminating zeal, contending with equal warmth for the most trivial technicality and the most essential doctrine. It is plain that the duty of a Christian minister, in reference to this point, is exceedingly difficult. He may, on the one hand, not only offend God but ruin souls by his unconcern as to doctrinal opinions, or, on the other, disgrace and retard religion by unnecessary alarms and clamours. Hence the necessity for every such man carefully and thoroughly to study the Word of God, that he may learn to his own satisfaction what God has taught. Let him form his opinions on mature deliberation; and let him fix the principles which should govern him in their defence and propagation, and then let him calmly, humbly, and firmly pursue his course, through evil and through good report, disregarding the accusation of bigotry from the one side, or latitudinarianism on the other.

If a man properly appreciate his relation to God, the supremacy which he claims over our minds and consciences, as well as our lives, the infinite distance there is between him and us, he will feel the folly and guilt of disregarding what he has revealed. He will feel that he is not to postpone the Bible to his own reasonings; by practically forming his opinions in doctrinal matters in a great measure independently of the Word of God. Let him remember that truth is essential to holiness and salvation; that it has always been repulsive to the majority of men; and, therefore, difficult to maintain and uphold; that the responsibility of thus maintaining and transmitting it, rests mainly with the ministry; and that the fate of many generations may depend on their fidelity. Look at the melancholy desolations of the ancient world. Think you that piety would be so prostrated had the priest's lips kept knowledge? Would the Protestant part of France have exhibited so few signs of life for more than a century? Would her clergy have been ready to close their temples, and join in the worship of reason, at the command of a mad directory? Would Germany, with all her stores of learning and depth of feeling, be now leagued with every antichrist in opposition to the cause of the Redeemer? When we properly appreciate the necessity of truth to piety, the dreadful and long-continued consequences of its neglect, we shall feel that to be indifferent to its interest is one of the greatest sins of which a minister can be guilty; give heed, therefore, to your doctrines; hold fast the form of sound words; contend earnestly for the faith once delivered to the saints. Bear in mind, not only the precepts, but also the example of the Apostle Paul. His life was a protracted conflict with false teachers, his epistles are almost without exception in defence of truth, and opposition to errors of doctrine and practice. Follow his example, however, not only as to zeal, but, like him, let it be evident to your own consciences, and to all men, that your zeal is not for a party, but for the truth; not for victory over men, but for the purity of the gospel, that men may be saved. Like him, too, do not contend about trifles; become all things to all men, within the limits of truth and honesty; but do not let the cry of bigotry, or fear of reproach, drive you from your principles. Depend upon it, you have a difficult part to act. And you cannot act it well without much knowledge, much prayer, and much piety. The spirit of the age, however, admonishes every man who notices its tendency, that fidelity to the truth is one of the most important requisites for the ministry of the present generation.

II. A second requisite of no less importance is *a sacred regard for all moral obligations*. It is a lamentable fact, though one so obvious as to be frequently the subject of remark, that pious men are often less honest, less moral, than many who make no pretensions to religion. That is, they have less regard to truth, are less punctual in their engagements, and less faithful in the discharge of their relative duties. We are not to be understood as guilty of the extravagance of saying that such is generally the case; but that instances often occur of really pious men who are obviously inferior in all these respects to many men of the world. It need hardly be remarked that this is a great disgrace to religion, and the greater when these instances are to be found among ministers of the gospel.

The causes of this lamentable defect of character are numerous. It has its origin at times in the natural constitution. There really seems to be as great a difference among men as to native susceptibility to moral truth, as in their talents, tastes, dispositions, or temperaments. The sentiment which men, thus constitutionally deficient in moral feeling, excite is not that of pity, but of disapprobation. We cannot help regarding them, not as unfortunate but the subject of a moral defect, and therefore, never suffer nor sustain the plea that they are naturally dishonest. Such persons, even when made the subjects of divine grace, often betray this want of moral sensibility, just as the man who is not usually irascible, or improvident, or frivolous, is apt to retain traces of his original temperament. In every such case, there is need of double watchfulness; and the necessity for circumspection is greater in proportion to the seriousness of the besetting infirmity or constitutional defect.

More frequently, however, the evil of which we speak arises from habit, and the want of moral discipline. Early in life the habit is often formed of departing from the path of rectitude as it regards truth, or fidelity, or punctuality. And this habit long cherished, is not always laid aside at conversion. Of course the departures, if the conversion be genuine, cannot be so glaring as before, but they are in many cases both sufficiently frequent and serious to bring great discredit on religion.

Another source of the same evil is to be found in the general want of self-command. When a present gratification can be attained by a violation of strict integrity not sufficiently serious to shock the conscience, or endanger the reputation, the temptation is yielded to without hesitation. How often does a man, for the sake of giving point to an anecdote, or pungency to a remark, or to ward off an attack in argument, knowingly exaggerate or prevaricate. How often too, from indolence, are acknowledged duties, engagements, or promises neglected. How often, for vanity's sake, or self-gratification in some other form, are debts contracted without the reasonable prospect of discharging them. Every man is liable in some such a way, to be led into a violation of the duties which he owes his fellow men, and it therefore cannot be unseasonable to call the attention of those, whose conduct is so narrowly watched, and whose deportment is naturally expected to be exemplary, to this subject.

Many men greatly injure their moral feelings by the nature of their studies, and the character of some of their speculative opinions. There can be no reasonable doubt that pushing our investigations on moral and religious subjects beyond the proper limits of human research, has an unhappy influence on the moral susceptibilities of our nature. As the exclusive study of the exact sciences is found to incapacitate the mind to appreciate moral evidence, and to destroy the susceptibility for the pleasures of taste, so, too, does it often happen, that metaphysical analysis and refinement, when too exclusively indulged, or too far extended, destroy the nice perception of right and wrong. This perception or judgment is guided by the emotion which instinctively rises on the view of the proper objects; but they must be viewed as a whole, the attempt at analysis destroys their power over the feelings, at least for the time. Hence we see professional metaphysicians often maintaining doctrines in morals, which every unsophisticated man knows to be false; and hence, too, such men are frequently withered and dry as a body which has lost its sensibility and vitality; they have no moral pleasures, no moral emotions, the greatest exhibition of excellence does not move them, and the greatest depravity hardly produces disgust.

The same perverting effect is often produced by disputing for disputing's sake, maintaining error for the sake of argument, or starting sentiments which are not really entertained. The moral sense is too delicate to be thus trifled with. The man who often lies in jest, will soon lie in earnest. The remark that speculative opinions are of frequent injurious tendency on the character of those who adopt them, hardly needs illustration. The effects of fatalism, of atheism, of materialism, of pantheism, are so evidently destructive to moral feeling, that none but their advocates can question it. The same is true, in a proportionate degree, with regard to opinions less extravagantly wrong. The Jesuits furnish a standing illustration of the truth in question. Their very name is now the expression, not only for adroit duplicity, but for perverted moral principle. This character was not feigned; supposing them to have acted as though they had no principle, they must really have had none. Their conduct cannot be explained on the principle of passive obedience merely. It would be impossible to take a man of healthful moral feelings, and get him to act the part of a Jesuit, at once, even though he thought his salvation at stake. A long course of demoralisation was necessary to fit men for the work, and this preparatory discipline consisted mainly in the inculcation of false doctrines. It was through their influence the moral sense was withered up. It should, therefore, never be forgotten, that as all truth is in order to holiness, and tends to produce it, so, all error is baneful in its influence on those who espouse it. It is only the grosser forms of error which are sufficiently striking in their effects to be perceptible to our dull vision; but to the eye of God, the hurtful influence of all false principles and doctrines is apparent. And hence he warns men from error, as he warns them from sin.

The only other source of a perverted moral sense, and want of moral rectitude among pious men, which need be mentioned, is a spirit of party. It is wonderful that the mere congregating of men in large numbers should have the effect which we often observe. A man, though peaceable and harmless when by himself, if introduced into an excited crowd, is no longer the same person. He seems to lose his individuality, and to become but a constituent member of a great monster. He is no longer governed by his own individual principles, or feelings, but catching the spirit of the throng, he acts under its guidance, without reflection or remorse.

There is more or less of this observable, whenever men are brought to act in large numbers, even in deliberative bodies. The individual is more or less lost, and the spirit of the whole, or of the party, becomes the spirit of each member. Hence men are frequently guilty of acts of moral turpitude, as members of such bodies, from which, as individuals, they would have revolted. It is, indeed, a common saying, 'that corporations have no consciences'. The reason of this is not to be sought in divided responsibility merely; for in fact, the moral responsibility is not divided. He that votes that injustice should be done, is not the less guilty, because ten or a hundred others do the same. The cause is frequently to be found in the deadening influence on the moral sense of the spirit by which such bodies are often pervaded. The spirit of party, when it once has gained possession of a man, is not confined in its influence to these casual exacerbations; it governs in a great measure the whole course of the individual in reference to all subjects which his party has in view. He becomes habituated to view things, not as right or wrong, but in their party bearings. He often feels that he must either do wrong, and sin against his private judgment, or abandon the cause. As he is but one of a multitude, and if they will go wrong, he cannot hinder them; he commonly, therefore, unscrupulously advances, gathering strength as he goes, until he arrives at a state of complete demoralisation, acting, all but avowedly, on the principle that the end sanctions the means. Respectable and honourable men, who have run the course of politics, have often been heard to hoot at the idea of there being any morality or conscience in politicians as such; and instances are not infrequent where editors of newspapers, professedly pious men, and sufficiently exemplary in other respects to avoid reproach, knowingly publish the most malicious falsehoods to injure a political opponent.

Now, Brethren, is this fell spirit confined to the world? Does it fear to mingle with the sons of God in their holy convocations? Does it dread to pass the threshold of the church? Would that this were the case; but it is not. It has ever existed in every large community where there was diversity of views and interests, and its baneful influence has not been less apparent in the church than elsewhere. Here, alas, we see men, and even good men, carried along by its power; asking with regard to every measure, not whether it is right, but how it will operate, for or against their own party. We see them too, resorting to all the expedients of political men for the accomplishment of their objects; plotting, manoeuvring, perverting truth and facts; and doing all this as though they were doing God service. Such is the perverting influence of the spirit of party; blinding the moral perceptions, and deadening the moral sensibilities of the heart. Against this spirit you should be ever on your guard. It is infectious and insidious in the highest degree. It enters at every pore by some mysterious sympathy; and when the demon is in, we are as men possessed. There is but one way of preventing this: let the soul always be so full of the Holy Ghost, that it shall always be pre-occupied; and let the determination be graven on both tablets of the heart, always to do what is right in the sight of God, not what is politic, nor what a party wishes.

It is enough to make one weep to think that from one or the other of the causes mentioned, or from others of similar tendency, there is so general a perversion of moral feeling, such a weakening of the principles of moral rectitude, that it is now high, if not the highest praise, to say that a Christian man or minister is *honest;* that is, that he acts from moral principle, not from policy and party feeling; that he always means what he says; that there is no prevarication, double dealing, or chicanery about him; that, in debate or controversy, he never misstates facts, or misrepresents arguments, but uniformly in speech and conduct is frank, ingenuous, above board, and sincere.

There are obviously few subjects in the present state of the church and the world of greater practical importance than that to which we have ventured in these remarks to call your attention. Do endeavour to be honest men, men of unquestionable integrity, on whose word everyone can implicitly rely, of whose purity of motive and purpose no one can doubt. Impress deeply upon your mind that morality is a great part of religion, a great and essential part of the service which we owe to God. Habituate yourselves always to look at the moral character of everything you are called upon to do. Determine always to do what is right, regardless of consequences. Never trifle with your moral feelings; it is trifling with God. Never suffer yourselves to do wrong in little matters; to neglect little duties; but be punctual and faithful in all engagements, and obligations. You are now forming your characters and fixing your principles, and if you accustom yourselves now to the disregard of duties, and violation of engagements in matters which may appear of little importance, you are educating yourselves for more serious departures from rectitude in future life. Such matters cannot be considered little, for, if not in themselves, yet in their influence on character, they are greatly and permanently important.

The influence of Chatham, in the British senate, is said to have resulted not more from his commanding intellect and eloquence, than from his honesty. His audience could not resist the impression that he was sincere and pure in his principles and aims; and there is enough of power yet in stern integrity, and enough of moral feeling in every human heart, to give the honest man a real, though a reluctantly yielded ascendency, over the hearts of those around him. In nothing are the honour of religion, and the usefulness of ministers more involved.

III. Another characteristic which should distinguish ministers of the present age, is *activity in doing good*. This it is the tendency of the spirit of the times to produce, and, therefore, though feeling and acknowledging its importance, we shall not dwell on the subject, having considered it more useful to call the attention of our younger brethren to subjects to which the spirit of the age is rather hostile than friendly.

The demand for activity is now such, that a minister cannot get along without it; and this, so far, is a great blessing. The Bible speaks of nothing with greater disapprobation than sloth, even where the things of this world are in view, and for a man who professes to have it as his object to win souls, to be a sluggard, must be peculiarly offensive in the sight of God. Only be careful that your activity does not arise from the mere desire of being busy, or of avoiding the irksomeness of retired study, or from the love of excitement, or for the reputation which attends it, but from deep impressions of the guilt and misery of unconverted men, and a proper sense of your obligations to Jesus Christ.

IV. The age in which we live calls for *unusual mental discipline and furniture*. The necessity of an enlightened and well-educated ministry arises, indeed, from the essential nature of the work which ministers have to perform, and therefore always exists. But at the present time it is peculiarly important because the tendency of circumstances is to break down this hedge around the sacred office, and to let in a flood of uneducated, undisciplined men. The demand is so much greater than the supply, that the temptation is strong to hasten the entrance on active duty, of all who are looking forward to the work, and this temptation, addressing itself to excited feelings, has more than wonted force. It is precisely, however, in such a state of things that an ignorant ministry is to be most dreaded. There are men who will be prepared to substitute fanaticism for spiritual piety; to overturn all the landmarks of truth and order, and to turn the church over with a fierce fanatical spirit, and thus reduce it to lasting barrenness. When the religious opinions and character of large and growing communities are to be formed; when new forms of doctrine are broached on every hand, and when a spirit of excitement and action is abroad in the land, then, if ever, should ministers be thoroughly instructed, wise, well disciplined, and faithful. Let it then be impressed on your minds, Brethren, that the circumstances of the church and country render it peculiarly important for you to be thoroughly furnished for your work; that you can hardly do a greater injury to the cause of religion, than by plunging into the agitated and conflicting elements around you, unprepared by well-digested knowledge, and well-considered principles. This state of things, while it renders ignorance dangerous, furnishes to the properly qualified minister, the prospect of doing good for ages to come, of laying the foundations for many generations.

V. Our limits will hardly permit us to mention what ought to have been the chief topic of discourse, were it not the one which is most frequently inculcated, and that is, *a spirit of elevated piety, as a requisite for the ministry, which the circumstances of the times render peculiarly important.*

When things are all in regular training, when the battle in a country is well-nigh fought, and the land possessed and secured, we may feel less sensibly the value of eminent spirituality in the preachers of the gospel. But, when almost everything is to be done; when those who enter in the ministry, if not animated by a right spirit, are sure to be filled and excited by an evil one; when temptations, dangers, and difficulties are multiplied on every hand; when men need so much teaching and so much guidance, which can only come from the indwelling of the Holy Ghost, then it is we look around for those who are deeply and sincerely pious; who live near to God and the cross, as the hope and stay, under Jesus Christ, of the church.

ON THE NECESSITY OF A KNOWLEDGE OF THE ORIGINAL LANGUAGES OF THE SCRIPTURES[1]

T HE clergy have ever been one of the most influential classes in society. They address themselves to the most powerful and universally operative feelings of the human heart. As the great dispensers of moral and religious truth, their power over the opinions and principles of their fellow men is such as to involve the most solemn responsibility. In the Dark Ages and portions of the church, this influence was, and still is, mainly official. The fact that a man is a minister of religion, with the ignorant and superstitious, secures for him respect, and often reverence and submission. This is not the case where the people are enlightened, and especially, where they have been taught to revolt at all kinds of authoritative dictation. Under such circumstances, the influence of the clergy depends much more upon their personal qualifications than mere respect for their office. An ignorant or immoral man can pretend to no right, and has no prospect of being able, to guide the opinions and form the character of men superior to himself, merely because he may be invested with the sacred office. It is only by being superior in intellectual and moral culture that he can secure any salutary influence over his fellow men. The usefulness of the clergy, the progress of religion, and the best interests of the Redeemer's kingdom, depend, therefore, under God, in a great measure on the intellectual and moral character of the ministers of the gospel. That this is really the case, experience abundantly proves. Wherever ministers of the gospel have been ignorant, religion

---

[1] Charles Hodge, 'On the Necessity of a Knowledge of the Original Languages of the Scriptures', *The Annual of the Board of Education of the General Assembly of the Presbyterian Church in the United States,* ed. John Breckinridge (Philadelphia: Russell and Martiens, 1832), pp. 195-214.

has degenerated into superstition or fanaticism. The uneducated have been the victims of one or other of these forms of error, and the cultivated portions of society have fallen a prey to infidelity. On the other hand, wherever the teachers of religion have taken the lead in intellectual and moral excellence, there piety has flourished. How solemn, then, is the responsibility which rests on every candidate for the sacred office, to attend to the cultivation of his mind. It is not for his personal advancement, for his own happiness or honour, that he is bound to labour in this vocation, but it is because by becoming a minister, he identifies himself with the cause of religion, and he has no right to degrade that cause by allying it, in his own person, with imbecility and ignorance.

There are many who endeavour to free themselves from this responsibility, as to mental improvement, by saying they expect to spend their days among the poor, where much learning will not be requisite. But who has revealed to these men where they are to spend their days? The providence of God may cast their lot among the most educated and refined classes of society. A friend of the writer, who made this the excuse for neglecting a regular and faithful course of theological study, has had a succession of charges in which intellectual culture was peculiarly desirable. His usefulness and respectability have suffered materially, and for life, from the false step of his youth. Besides, in our country, the rich and poor, the educated and ignorant, are so intermingled, that a congregation or community formed exclusively of either class is not to be met with. Wherever you may go, you will find your usefulness depending, next to piety and zeal, mainly on your knowledge.

The candidate for the ministry, therefore, cannot but be regarded as criminally negligent of his duty to his Master, who neglects any opportunity of intellectual improvement.

As to the kinds of knowledge which a minister should cultivate, they ought undoubtedly to be principally professional; and in this class are included subjects of sufficient compass and importance to occupy the most devoted attention and comprehensive talents. But among professional subjects, there is ground of preference. Some are intrinsically more important than others; and some become especially important on account of the peculiar character of the age, or state of the church. On the ground of intrinsic value, and peculiar adaptation to the circumstances of the candidates for the ministry of the present day, there is no department of knowledge which more imperiously demands their attention, than *the original languages of the sacred Scriptures.*

To evince the justice of this assertion, let the following considerations be duly weighed.

I. *No translation can make a full and fair exhibition of its original.* This inadequacy results from the necessary difference which exists between different languages, which renders it impossible that words can be put for words, so that the meaning, force, and beauty should be unchanged. This difference includes a variety of particulars. In the first place, there is a general disparity, which it may be difficult to define, yet is sensibly felt. Any person acquainted with more than one language, needs no other proof of this than his own experience. He is constantly sensible that there is something in the original which his translation does not reach. And it is evident this must be the case, because much of the excellence of every writer depends on his style—all this is lost in the version. You have, necessarily, the style of the translator, not that of his author. If the former be on a par in the talent for writing with the latter, and if the two languages be in all respects equal, the translation may, as a composition, be equal to the original. But even if the advantage in each respect was on the side of the translator, it does not affect our position. The version is not, and cannot be, an exact representation of the original. It may be better, or worse, but it is not the same. It is with the mind of the translator we have to do, in every translation. Who knows anything of Homer from Pope, or Cowper, or Voss, or Sotheby? It is not the Grecian poet we learn by reading these versions. They are indeed all excellent, all to a sufficient extent faithful; yet each and all fail of bringing us acquainted with the father of profane poetry. We learn what Pope, and Cowper, and Sotheby were as poets, but we are ignorant of Homer. The facts, indeed, of his story are retained, but he is not the narrator. We have, as it were, the body without the soul.

This is a point at once so obvious, and so important, that it has ever been acknowledged and regarded in respect to classic authors. No one pretends to an acquaintance with these writers, who is indebted for his knowledge to translators. It seems to be on all hands conceded, that a knowledge of what the author has himself written is necessary to qualify any man, in that department, to speak of the merits of an author, and much more to authorize anyone to expound his meaning. But why should this be conceded in reference to the writers of Greece, and not to those of Palestine? Why should the lecturer on the classics, who could not read a word of them, be an object of ridicule, and the equally ignorant lecturer on the Bible, an object of respect?

There is therefore such an acknowledged difference between languages, that all translations must differ materially from their originals. The vital characteristic spirit of the one, cannot be infused into the other. The mind of the translator is interposed between the reader and the original author. The thoughts and sentiments are transmuted by the process of translation; divested of their characteristic impress, they fall chilled and enfeebled on the heart of the reader. If this were the only evil of a translation, and if the only advantage of a knowledge of the original was, that it secured us immediate access to the minds of the sacred writers, it would be enough to compensate for all the time and labour which the acquisition requires. To have their language a direct medium of thought, and to be admitted to immediate communion with minds 'moved by the Holy Ghost', is a pleasure and a benefit sufficient to recompense the severest toil.

But this, which may be considered as merely a matter of enjoyment, is not all. There are more solid benefits to be derived from reading the Scriptures in their original languages, than the vividness of impression, and the freshness of the truth as it comes from the lips of the servants of God. The difference between languages extends beyond the attributes of style. It pertains to their general character and structure, to the precision and compass of the meaning of terms; and is so serious as to render every translation defective as to its meaning as well as its manner. Some languages are rude, others polished; some are highly figurative, and others the reverse; some remarkably precise in the use of words, in the force of particles, in the use of the tenses and other grammatical forms; others the reverse in all these particulars. It is obvious, therefore, that the translator must often express, literally, what is conveyed by figure; must render definite, what is ambiguous; must use a form which may express various modifications of the meaning of a word, for one which admits of no such latitude. He may be right or wrong as to the sense which he expresses, but whether right or wrong, he is different from his author; for he renders definite what was left undeterminate, or makes ambiguous what admits of but one interpretation.

Again, all the characteristic peculiarities of a language must be passed over, or very inadequately expressed. The particles, which add so much, not only to the grace, but also to the precision and force of the Greek writers, must, in Latin and English, be almost entirely neglected. Phrases properly idiomatic, must be new modified, or remain uncouth deformities in the version, and often lead the reader into error. Again, very few words belonging to different languages are precisely synonymous. Some classes of terms, of course, more nearly correspond than others. In a few, the correspondence may be considered as complete; as in those which express simple ideas, or natural objects, or the necessary relations of life. But beyond these, and a few other classes, it will be almost impossible to find any two words belonging to different languages which exactly agree. The one either expresses more or less than the other, or admits of applications which the other does not allow. Hence we see foreigners constantly making the mistake of using our terms in all the extent of meaning, and variety of application, which the nearest corresponding word of their own language admits. This too is a source of endless error to the readers of mere translations of the Scriptures. Because the word 'hell', for example, in a certain connection, may mean the abode of lost spirits, how natural the inference that the Hebrew or Greek word which it represents, may, in the same connection, have the same meaning; and yet this, to any reader of the original, may be seen to be impossible. And how often are arguments and doctrines built upon the assumption, that the original will bear every interpretation which the version admits. This therefore is a point of vital importance. Translations must, to a greater or less extent, make a false representation. We might submit to a loss of beauty or force, but it appears we cannot have in all cases the precise sense. There can be no doubt that languages do so differ in their general structure, in their peculiar expressions and idioms, in the extent of meaning and variety of application of their nearest corresponding terms, that no version can be a faithful exhibition of its original. It will either say more or less, it will make what is figurative literal, or literal figurative; what is definite ambiguous, or ambiguous definite. If this be so, need the question be asked, Whether preachers and expounders of the Word of God are not bound to go to what he has himself said, and not trust in the inadequate and faulty reports of others?

II. A second consideration, which should impress on the mind of every candidate for the ministry a sense of the importance of studying the original languages of Scripture, is but an inference from the preceding. *He cannot otherwise be qualified to explain the Word of God.* The grand official duty of the minister of the gospel is 'rightly to divide the word of God', and by the presentation of the truth to instruct, rebuke, and exhort with all longsuffering and meekness. How is this to be done, unless he himself knows the truth; and how is this knowledge to be obtained? He finds it revealed through the medium of a written language, which he is to understand, not by inspiration or miracle, but by applying to its interpretation those simple rules of exegesis which govern the exposition of all language. He must examine accurately the meaning of the words and phrases used by the sacred writers, by ascertaining how these writers themselves employ them in other passages, and in what way they were used by the persons to whom they were addressed; and by investigating the etymology as well as usage of every important term. The application of these, and other equally obvious rules of interpretation, of course, suppose a knowledge of the language used by the sacred penman. It may indeed be said, that this process has all been gone through by the translator, who furnishes us with the result. But we are bound to verify his report for ourselves. It has already been remarked, that the best translation cannot be an exact exhibition of the original. Even when most correct, it may be the source of error to the ignorant. The words of the version may answer to the original in one of the various senses which those words will bear, but not in others.

The translator may be right, and yet we, by concluding that the original admits of every interpretation which his version allows, may be seriously wrong. We cannot be sure, with any enlightened confidence, when expounding a translation, that we are not wandering far from the text which it proposes to represent. But versions are very often positively incorrect. Among the thousand translations by churches and individuals, no two precisely agree. Some are so loose and inaccurate, that important doctrines are obscured, and important errors inculcated. Which version shall we choose? Who shall insure us from error in this choice?

It is however self-evident, that no man can be qualified to explain an ancient document of which he knows nothing but a translation. He is unavoidably exposed to ludicrous or fatal mistakes by the faultiness or insufficiency of his guide. This, as we before remarked, is a matter universally admitted with regard to every other document than the Word of God. That is, it is universally admitted in every case, except precisely the one in which it is most evident and most important.

We do not of course deny that the most faulty of the translations of the sacred Scriptures contain much of their genuine sense, and consequently may convey this saving knowledge to those who peruse them. But the question now is, whether the man who must expound the Scriptures to the people, is not bound to do all that he can to understand them fully and accurately; and whether the knowledge of something better than a faulty and inadequate translation, is not, of all qualifications, one of the most obvious and important for the discharge of this duty. If this be admitted (and who will deny it?)—then is it admitted that few obligations are more solemn and imperious, than that which binds the ministers of the gospel to study the Scriptures in their original languages.

III. Another of the most important duties of the minister of the gospel is to *defend the faith, to resist and put to silence gainsayers—for the proper discharge of this duty, a knowledge of the original Scriptures is essential.* This is evident, not only from the consideration that this knowledge is necessary to any accurate and well-grounded acquaintance with the contents of the sacred volume, but it alone can enable us to meet and answer that large class of objections founded on the misapprehensions or mistakes of translators. Many arguments in which the opponents of the truth most confidently rely, have no better foundation than such mistakes. How then are these to be detected or answered, if we know nothing of the original? Besides, no version is acknowledged by all parties as the standard of divine truth. If we are brought into collision with Roman Catholics, we shall find that they not only deny the authority of our version of the Word of God, but charge its authors with wilfully perverting and misrepresenting the sacred text. Are our lips to be closed by such an assertion? Are those whose duty it is to defend and uphold the truth, to be thus easily vanquished? And yet what can we say? The accomplished Catholic appeals to the original; he affirms that it teaches all the peculiarities of his own faith, and overturns the doctrines of Protestants; and must we sit silent, with the seal of ignorance upon our lips? Is this the way we are to clear our conscience of the solemn duty of defending the truth on which the salvation of men depends? The common Catholic will show us in his Douay Bible, the frequently reiterated command 'to do penance'. The Saviour is made to say to men, 'Unless ye do penance ye shall all perish.' How are we to answer his argument in favour of penances founded on such passages? Not by appealing to our translation, for to him it is of no authority. The only possible method is to turn to the original, and satisfy everyone capable of understanding it, that no such doctrine is contained in the Word of God. But this, if ignorant of the sacred languages, we, of course, shall not be able to do. If it is our lot to encounter Socinians, all our arguments are met and answered by the easy assertion, that they rest on false translations. However unfounded the assertion, it is sufficient to silence the ignorant advocate of orthodoxy. Let any candidate for the sacred ministry put it to his conscience, whether this is the kind of defence which the truth merits at his hands; whether he can justify himself either in the sight of God or man, in assuming the responsibility of a defender of the faith delivered to the saints, and yet be no better prepared for his work.

It is not, however, only in controversy with those who differ thus seriously from us in matters of belief, that the knowledge in question is essential. The English version is not the standard to which appeal is made in any doctrinal discussion. On every subject, the original alone is regarded as authoritative. Any disputant, therefore, can at once carry the controversy beyond our depth, and inflict on us and our cause the disgrace and injury of defeat, at pleasure. Will it not then be admitted that a knowledge of the original languages is essential to qualify us for the discharge of one of the most obvious and important duties of the ministry; that without this knowledge, no man can defend the truth, satisfy the doubting, stop the mouths of gainsayers, or even, in an enlightened manner, satisfy his own mind. How poor an excuse, then, is disinclination or sloth, for the neglect of a duty so obvious and so important.

IV. *Ignorance of the sacred languages will prevent our access to the best sources of theological knowledge.*

It is so much taken for granted that ministers are acquainted with what are considered the rudiments of their science, that all works of consequence which refer to the Bible at all, refer to the Scriptures in the original. It is the original which they criticize and explain; it is this on which they rest their arguments and found their remarks. If therefore we are ignorant of the sacred languages, such works must be to us uninteresting and unintelligible. The magnitude of this difficulty will be felt by all those who mean to extend the range of their studies beyond the most contracted limits. The standard works in all departments, the best commentaries, the best systems of divinity, the best polemical, and even the best practical writers, must, to all such, remain hermetically sealed. The department of Biblical Literature must be in a great measure neglected. Everything which belongs to the first step in theology, ascertaining the true text of the Scriptures, must be passed over, and we be left at the mercy of everyone who chooses to assert that this or that passage is a false reading or interpolation. All that pertains to the science of interpretation presupposes a knowledge of the sacred languages; the literary history of the sacred volume, the discussion of the canonical authority and authenticity of every book, requires the same acquisition. In short, without this knowledge, two-thirds of theological literature must remain to us an unknown land. How anyone who does not determine to be an ignorant minister, can neglect this subject, it is hard to conceive. And how any man can determine to be an ignorant minister, who admits that the interests of religion depend in a great measure on the character and standing of the clergy, it becomes those who make the determination to explain.

V. In this connection it may be remarked, that *the acquisition of which we are speaking is becoming so common, that we cannot be expected to maintain without it a respectable standing among our fellow clergymen.*

It has already been remarked, that in different ages of the church, certain subjects have received an importance independent of their intrinsic worth. There was a time when a man's standing depended on his metaphysical acumen; and useless as were the subjects on which that acumen was exercised, yet to obtain the influence necessary to usefulness, even a good man would be justified in its cultivation. But when the subject which demands our attention, because it is a matter of general interest, is in itself of great value, the motive to exertion is proportionably increased. A knowledge, then, of the sacred languages should be obtained, because public sentiment requires it in the rising ministry. The inconvenience of ignorance will become every day more seriously felt, as the acquisition becomes more common. Let it be remembered, too, that the enemies of the truth are often the most accomplished in knowledge of this kind, and that it therefore becomes its friends and advocates to maintain a standing which shall place them on equal terms. The appeal we make on this subject is to feelings of piety, to zeal for the truth and honour of religion. It is not for the pleasure or the pride of knowledge, it is for higher objects, and from purer motives, we would urge the study of the sacred languages in all candidates for the ministry.

VI. *A knowledge of these languages has been made a requisite for admission into the office of the ministry by almost every denomination of Christians.*

If this should, in any case, become a dead letter, it will be a matter of reproach, and proof of degeneracy, in whatever section of the church it occurs. These requisitions were enjoined in the purest and most enlightened period of our ecclesiastical existence, and they form an abiding testimony of the estimate which our fathers made of the importance of this subject. This testimony is sustained by the opinion of the great body of the eminently pious and useful men, who have adorned the church of Christ. The Reformers were all learned men, men familiar with the Scriptures in the languages in which they were revealed. This was the case with Luther and Calvin, with Melancthon and Beza. It was the case with Knox, though born in a land comparatively ignorant, and although he had to make the acquisition in a great measure, when he was of full age and an exile. It was the case with the English Reformers, and the English Puritans, with Owen and Baxter and Howe, and in short with almost every man whose memory has come down embalmed in the blessings of his generation. It was an attainment, which these men not only made, but which they highly prized, which they, in many cases, made great sacrifices to secure, and which, as Luther says, they would not exchange for all the treasures of the world. An impression of the importance of this subject, so general, so strong, and so lasting, is not likely to prove unfounded. Shall we, then, be dead to all the considerations which have thus impressed the purest churches and the most favoured of God's servants? Shall we regard an attainment which they so highly prized, as unworthy a serious effort?

VII. *This acquisition requires no great labour, and will prove a source of constant pleasure.*

It might doubtless be easily made by every minister in half the number of hours which he has already wasted.

In most cases, the difficulty is in a great measure overcome, with regard to the Greek, before professional studies are commenced. As it respects Hebrew, the difficulty is greatly overrated. It is far more simple in its structure and syntax than either of the classic languages; and the repulsive features of the vowel system become familiar after a few months' attention. There is therefore no excuse to be found in the irksomeness of the task, for its neglect. The language of the Old Testament has its own peculiar claims. It was, peradventure, the primitive language of our race. It is confessedly the repository of the oldest literature, of the most sublime productions, of the purest ideas of God and religion of the ancient world. The language in which Moses wrote, in which Isaiah breathed the eloquence of heaven, and through which the soul of David poured forth itself to God. No one can be insensible to the interest which belongs to the language of the patriarchs and prophets, and which has formed the medium of so large a portion of God's communications to men. It is, however, not merely for its own sake, or for the sake of a proper understanding and appreciation of the Old Testament Scriptures, that the Hebrew is important. The New Testament is Hebraic. It is so completely impressed with this character, that no rule in its interpretation is of more frequent application than that which requires us to explain its terms in accordance with the meaning of the corresponding Hebrew word. It is no extravagant assertion, that an individual ignorant of the language of the Old Testament, is incapable of properly explaining the New.

Let candidates for the ministry lay this subject to heart. Let them feel the responsibility which rests upon them to prepare, not in the easiest, but the best, manner their circumstances permit, to understand, explain, and defend the truth of God. Let them resolve to be Bible men—men mighty in the Scriptures; let them determine to read a portion of the Word of God in the original every day; what they commence as a task, they will soon continue as a delight. If the remarks which we have made are well founded, it must be admitted, that a knowledge of the sacred languages is one of the most essential qualifications for the ministry; and if this be admitted, then may we confidently hope, that no conscientious candidate for the sacred office will neglect to make this important attainment.

> *Haec eo dicta sunt, ut intelligamus nos evangelium nunquam retenturos esse, nisi fiat linguarum notitia.*[1]

---

[1] He said these things that we might understand that we will never hold on to the gospel unless we develop a knowledge of languages.

REVIEW OF SPRAGUE'S
LECTURES TO YOUNG PEOPLE[1]

IT is the highest wisdom of man to endeavour to discover, and to follow, the plan of God. This plan is manifested in the nature of his creatures, in the dispensations of his providence, and in his word. It is our business to fall in with this; never, from vain ideas of doing more good, venturing to counteract it. Thus, the different natures which God has given the sexes, renders it necessary, in order that the greatest perfection should be attained, and the greatest good effected, that the difference should be carefully preserved; that the man should not assume the position, or discharge the duties of the woman; and that the woman should not step out of her appropriate sphere into the province of the man. This is, however, a common evil. Unenlightened zeal in religion often leads to a greater or less infringement of the plan of God in this respect. Women take a stand and undertake to discharge duties which force them out of their place in the great scheme of infinite wisdom, and the result is invariably injurious to themselves and to society. To be where and what God wills us to be is our perfection and highest usefulness. It is of more practical importance than men are wont to imagine thus to eye and follow the divine arrangements.

As God has given a diversity of constitution to the sexes suited to the different purposes they are to accomplish, so he has given to different periods of life different susceptibilities and powers, which are intimations of his will, and consequently of our duty with regard to them. The dependence of the young on their parents; the feelings of parents towards their children; the susceptibility of the youthful

---

[1] Charles Hodge, 'Review of Sprague's *Lectures to Young People*', *Biblical Repertory and Theological Review* Vol. 3, No. 3 (July 1831), pp. 295-306.

mind; the quickness of perception; the tenacity of the memory and pliability of the feelings, all declare that this is the forming period of life; that God designs it to be employed and improved as such. This is, indeed, a universally admitted truth; and education has ever been one of the most absorbing subjects of interest.

Though this be admitted, it is still true that the formation of character in the young has been and is still lamentably neglected. The development of the intellect and communication of knowledge have ever been the grand if not exclusive objects of education. How is it, at present, in our schools, academies and colleges? Is not the whole course of instruction directed almost exclusively to these objects? Is not the cultivation of the social virtues and the religious feelings, in a great measure, left to take care of itself? We cannot but think that there is here a lamentable deficiency in all our systems; that the intellectual, in opposition to the moral powers of the soul, are too exclusively the objects of assiduous care. No one will pretend that the latter are second in importance to the former. We all admit, that it is the moral nature of man which raises him into the sphere of immortal beings, connects him with the infinite, and stamps an incomprehensible value on the soul. The subordinate part, therefore, assigned to the cultivation of these feelings in youth, cannot be accounted for on the assumption of their inferior importance. It may be, there is an impression on many minds that these powers are less susceptible, or stand less in need of cultivation. That this impression is erroneous, it needs only a moment's reflection to perceive. Were this the case, it would be an anomaly in our whole constitution. All the other faculties, whether of mind or body, which God has given us, are susceptible of cultivation, and are dependent on it, for their right development and exercise. What would the mind be without truth on which to exert its powers?—and what would the body be, if never exercised in the manner adapted to its improvement? All experience shows, moreover, that the moral faculties are just as susceptible of culture as any other of our powers. If it were possible to bring up a child entirely removed from the influence of moral truths, his moral powers would be as dormant as his mind would be, were he confined from birth in a dark and solitary cell. This, however, is impossible. Everyone born into the world is brought under ten thousand influences, favourable and unfavourable, by which his character is formed; and it depends, not entirely, but predominantly, on the nature of these influences, what form the character assumes. We say not *entirely*, because man is a free agent, and may resist the tendencies, good or bad, of the influences under which he is placed. Still, the history of the world proves that evil communications corrupt good manners; which is but the statement of one aspect of the more general truth, that the character is formed by the *ab extra* influences brought to bear upon it. If this were not the case, where would be the use of religious education? For what purpose would we labour for the establishment of Sunday Schools, or take any other means to form the character of the young? Can men differ more in any respect, than do the children of a well-ordered Christian family, and those of superstitious and licentious pagans? A proportionate difference is found in the character of children of different Christian countries, of the various sections of the same land, and of different families.

It will, doubtless, be suggested, that we often see the best adapted means ineffectual, and the children of the pious becoming profligate; and, on the other hand, the children of the profligate moral and exemplary. True; and so, too, we see the means of intellectual culture often thrown away on those unwilling, or unable, to profit by them; and, on the contrary, minds rising from the greatest obscurity in brightness, developing themselves with the greatest strength, under very unfavourable circumstances. Do these instances shake the confidence of any man, in the general efficacy of proper means of intellectual culture? Does it not still remain true, that education forms the man?

The individual cases of the inefficacy of moral culture in securing its appropriate result, may be traced often to various causes. In a multitude of instances, it is erroneously assumed that because a child has had pious parents, or at least professing parents, he has therefore had good moral and religious culture. The truth is, there is no point in which such parents are more frequently lamentably deficient in duty. The immoral or irreligious character of their children, is nothing more than might naturally be expected from the mode of their education. They are often brought up, as completely surrounded by the influence of the world—of its manners, opinions and spirit—as though their parents did not belong to the church of God. Such cases are not to be appealed to, therefore, in proof of the uselessness of moral and religious instruction. In many instances, there are counteracting causes, which cannot be traced; and there is much to be referred to the wilful opposition of the heart to all good, and the determined resistance to salutary impressions.

There is, moreover, the same diversity in the moral susceptibilities of men, as in their intellectual and bodily powers or appearance. There is a native integrity and strength of character in some, which enables them to withstand the temptations which lead others astray. There is a liveliness of feeling, which admits of impressions which the more callous never experience. Admitting these and other causes, which prevent a uniform result from the same system of means, it still remains a truth sanctioned by Infinite Wisdom and general experience, that if a child be trained up in the way he should go, when he is old, he will not depart from it.

We are not leaving out of view either the doctrine of human depravity, or the necessity of divine influence, doctrines as clearly taught in Scripture, as they are intimately related to each other, and inwoven in all Christian experience; and we consider every system of education, and every mode of operation in which their practical influence is not pervadingly felt, as radically defective. Neither the difficulty to be encountered, nor the means of surmounting it, are at all in view, where these great truths are kept out of sight. But what is the remedy which God in his wisdom has revealed for the 'diseases of the mind'—what is the appropriate corrective of the hidden evils of the human heart? Not ignorance—not error—but divine truth. And it is clearly taught that the Spirit operates with and by the truth, on our hearts. Where that truth is never presented, we never see the effects of the Spirit's influences. God has determined that men should honour his Word—for his Word is truth—and that they should honour his Spirit, not taking to themselves the glory, by ascribing to the skill or felicity of their exhibition, the effect which the Holy Ghost only can produce. It is the union, therefore, of the faithful presentation of the truth, with a consciousness of entire dependence on the power of the Holy Spirit, which constitutes the whole duty of men in bringing sinners, whether young or old, to Christ and salvation.

When, therefore, we contend for the efficacy of religious education, we are only maintaining that the gospel is the wisdom of God, and the power of God unto salvation; that God blesses obedience, and frowns on disobedience; blesses the faithful and humble use of the means of his own appointment, and punishes their neglect by a loss of their appropriate results. The world is full of instruction on this subject, both for encouragement and warning. The success of the preached gospel is more uniformly in proportion to the degree of attention paid to the religious instruction of the young, than to any other circumstance.

There are, indeed, doubtless many other things which influence this success: the frequency, purity, pointedness and humility of the manner of exhibition. Still, our remarks, we think, will bear the test of experience. We see revivals of religion most frequent and most pure in those portions of the country, where religious instruction of the young is the most general and faithful; and how often is the fact recorded that the members of Bible classes have been the subject of renewing grace, during such special visitations of mercy. If this is true—if, as a general fact, the religious instruction of the young is of all means the most efficacious in bringing them to the saving knowledge of the truth, then is it clear that, of all duties, none can be more obvious, none more imperious, than that of faithfully using this means. This duty presses with peculiar force on parents, pastors and instructors. Did parents but duly feel how much, under God, the salvation of their children depended upon them, the solemnity of their responsibility would weigh constantly and heavily on their hearts.

In reference to this subject, we would remark that the end to be effected, *viz.,* the right formation of the moral and religious character, can only be accomplished through the instrumentality of the truth. This, as the sun, is the source of those quickening and forming influences which call forth and mould the moral and religious principles of our nature. The question, therefore, is, how can parents most efficaciously bring the truth of God to bear on the expanding hearts of their children? To do this requires much skill, and much spirituality. It is obvious that the mode of exhibition must be adapted to the comprehension of the child. Nothing is gained, where nothing is understood. The mere storing the memory with abstract propositions, although embodying the most important truth, can have no effect on the present character of the child. It is true, that these propositions may be retained in the mind, until it is sufficiently advanced to be able to comprehend them, and they may then become effective. But until this period arrives, they must be inoperative.

The evil, however, of pursuing this course, is not merely negative; there is more than the loss of a good, which might be attained. It is not to be expected that the mind can receive cordially what it does not understand. There is always more or less of opposition excited to the repulsive statements which the child is obliged to commit, without comprehending their import. We think, therefore, it is one of the most important principles with regard to early education that the child should not be made to get anything entirely beyond its comprehension, and there is happily no necessity for this course. All the leading doctrines of the gospel may be so exhibited as to be as adequately comprehended by a child, for all moral or spiritual effect, as by those of maturer years. That there is a God, who is a Spirit, *i.e.,* a Being of the same nature with the thinking principle of which the child is conscious in his own breast; that this Spirit knows, loves, disapproves—not imperfectly, but perfectly—a child may understand as adequately as persons of maturer years. That this God is good and merciful, the child may be made to feel. And a consciousness of its relation to this Being, must be at once attended by a sense of its obligations. So the doctrines of the sinfulness of the heart, of regeneration and redemption, may be brought within its grasp. It is a matter of great importance that the facts of the Bible should be early impressed upon the minds of children, and the character of the blessed Saviour be clearly exhibited. We think there is no more effectual method of conveying religious instruction than from the Bible itself. It is adapted to every age. The child can treasure up its facts, and when properly aided, be made to understand its leading truths. Were parents sufficiently attentive to this duty, they would be surprised to find how rapid would be the progress of their children in divine knowledge.

But truth must not only be communicated in a form suited to the power of comprehension, it must be urged on the heart and conscience. A constant application to the case of the child should therefore be made, and made with love. The power of love is almost without limit. We can hardly conceive of the effect of a constant exhibition of divine truth urged with tenderness and skill on the youthful mind. Parents never should forget too that their children are always learning; that it is not merely in the hours allotted to instruction, their minds are receiving ideas and impressions. Their eyes and ears are ever open. All their parents say, all the manifestations of character which they make, affect deeply their minds. Hence the indispensable importance of a constant exhibition of the true spirit of the gospel. How can an exhortation to meekness, kindness and love, counteract the effect of an exhibition of anger or malice on the part of the parent? How can the command of Christ to 'seek first the kingdom of God', be effectually urged by a father, whom the child sees evidently more anxious to secure this world than heaven? Parents cannot be too much under the influence of the truth, that their habitual spirit and conversation exert a more powerful influence over the minds of their children, than all their occasional instructions. Here as everywhere else, to do good we must be good. We must try to bring up our children under the influence of the true, full, consistent spirit of the religion of Jesus Christ.

Parents perhaps too seldom expect present fruit from their labours. They seem to act under the impression that youth is the seed time when truth is to be deposited in the mind, while its fruit is only to be expected in riper years. That youth is the seed time, no one will question; and that the full benefit of religious instruction is not exhibited immediately is also true. But it is no less true that the infant heart is susceptible of piety. That God can, and often does, produce a saving change in the very morning of life. This result therefore should be desired, aimed at, prayed for, and expected.

Though we have said thus much on the duty and hopefulness of early religious instruction, we would by no means have it supposed that we imagine that any degree of fidelity in the exhibition of the divine truth, can of itself effect the sanctification of the infant mind. We firmly believe, as others have strongly expressed the idea, that the unrenewed soul of man would expand unsanctified in the midst of the light and purity of heaven. Nothing is more clearly taught in the

Word of God than that the influence of the Holy Spirit is essential to give his truth effect. Parents therefore dishonour God, and labour for nought, who do not bear this truth constantly in mind, and act under its influence; commending their children to that God to whom they are dedicated, for the renewing and sanctifying influence of his grace. This feeling of dependence is not only consistent with fidelity in the use of means, but is urged in Scripture as the strongest motive to diligence. Though we would be far from presuming to affirm, that all parents who thus depend on divine aid, and thus appropriately, constantly, and tenderly bring up their children in the nurture and admonition of the Lord, will have the unspeakable joy of seeing them walking in the ways of God, yet we think it clear from the Scriptures and experience, that this will be the general result, and that a fearful responsibility, therefore, in this matter, rests on all those to whom God has committed young immortals to train up for eternity. We recently heard an anecdote on this subject, which strongly impressed our mind, and may be useful to others. A mother of a large family, whose children all seemed to evince the spirit of genuine religion from their infancy, being asked how it was that her children were so early pious, answered, she did not know; but that she never remembered taking any of them to her arms, without silently lifting up her heart to God for his saving blessing to rest upon them.

The care of the young is not, however, confined to their parents; teachers and pastors have a most important duty to discharge, in respect of their religious instruction. It is a question of the deepest interest, how religious instruction can be most advantageously secured for the rising generation throughout our land. That there are hundreds and thousands of families where the parents, from want of disposition or capacity, neglect this business, no one will question. It is therefore clear that some other provision must be made for this object, or we shall have a large portion of our population growing up ignorant of the first principles of moral and religious truth. The evils which must result from such a state of things, to the temporal and eternal interests of our fellow men, are beyond calculation. This is admitted; but the question is, how shall they be prevented? How shall the truth of God be brought to bear clearly and uniformly on the minds of our youth during the forming period of their being? That much may be, that much has been accomplished by our infant and Sabbath Schools, and that much more may be accomplished by these means than has yet been effected, we have no disposition to question. We believe there are few institutions of the present age more extensively useful than the American Sabbath School Union. Still, this system does not and cannot embrace all our rising population; and being confined to one day in the week, cannot be so thoroughly operative as is desirable. We think, therefore, that it should be a constant object with the friends of religion, to try to secure a religious character to the instructions of the common school. Here everything depends upon the teacher and the system. If a proper sentiment pervaded the community, it would be universally felt that the Bible is the best book to be used in forming the minds and hearts of children, and should, therefore, be made the basis of instruction in all our common schools; not to be used as a reading book, merely, but to be studied, much on the plan which is pursued in the Sabbath Schools. If there were one lesson of this kind a day, the children would obtain a familiarity with the sacred volume, and a degree of moral and religious knowledge which would serve to enlarge and purify their minds, to enlighten their consciences and impress on them a holy character. It would be well, too, if this plan could be introduced into our higher schools, so that at every stage of advancement the mind might be brought under the influence of divine truth. This, in more advanced seminaries for English education, might easily be effected, and in our grammar schools the Greek Scriptures might form most profitably the subject of one of the daily exercises of the students. Even our colleges would be greatly benefited by the adoption of the same plan.

It is not to be expected, however, that in a country like ours any one system will ever be universally introduced. Hence the necessity of suggesting various means of accomplishing the same grand object, some of which may be suited to one region, and some to another. The importance of having teachers of every grade, properly qualified, both as to their mind and heart, for this work, cannot be questioned. And until some means be devised for securing a supply of competent instructors, the business of education can never be satisfactorily conducted. Would it not be well for every church, or congregation,

to have its own school? Wherever there are Presbyterians, or Episco-
palians, or Methodists enough to form a congregation, there must be
children to form a school. And this school might then be conducted
in a manner fitted to train up Christians. Or if the different denominations were, in any place, willing to have a school in common, they
might unite on the same principle which secures their cordial cooperation in the Sabbath School system.

We have recently heard from a friend of the cause of religious education, the idea suggested, that much good might be accomplished
in many parts of our country, by having properly qualified and pious
men employed to teach a school for a couple of hours every day on
the plan of a Sabbath School. The children being previously prepared,
would attend, say, early in the morning, and spend two hours with
the teacher and then return to their other duties. These two hours
would, no doubt, be as profitable as the six spent in the usual manner. On this plan, the same teacher might conduct several schools at
the same time, assembling at different hours of the day, and in different neighbourhoods. In destitute regions where the population is
scattered and poor, this plan, we think, might be very advantageously
adopted.

Our limits forbid our enlarging on this interesting subject. We had
intended to offer a few remarks on the importance of pastors paying
more special attention to the religious instruction of the young, but
we must wait for some other opportunity. We were led into this train
of reflection from the mere title of Dr Sprague's work, *Lectures to the
Young*. We regret that we have not had an opportunity of expressing at an earlier date our sense of the service which the author has,
in the publication of these *Lectures,* rendered to the cause of religion. As they have already reached a second edition, it is certainly
unnecessary for us to descant on their merits, or to enter on any
detailed account of their contents. With these, the public are already
acquainted. The 'Introductory Address', by Dr Miller, on the peculiar
importance of religion to the young, and especially to the young in
this favoured country, has served to deepen our impression of the
importance of this subject. His remarks on the necessity of bringing
educated youth, the children of the rich, under the influence of religious instruction, ought to be very deeply pondered. We venture to

extract the following paragraph on the bearing of this subject on the prospects of our country.

> There is another thought of deep interest which occurs in this connection. The highly favoured, but most responsible population of this land, is now conducting an experiment of incalculable importance to ourselves and to mankind:—the experiment whether men are capable of self-government? In other words, whether they can live permanently in peace under rulers of their own choice, and laws of their own formation; or whether they are destined, until the millennium shall open on our world, continually to vibrate between anarchy and despotism;—between the manacles of privileged orders, and the exactions of an established church—and the infuriated licentiousness of popular profligacy, which refuses to obey any law, either of God or man? This experiment, as I said, is now going on; and it will probably be decided by the men of the next generation; by those whose principles and characters are now forming. Of course, every youth who is decisively won to the side of Christian knowledge and practice, is so much gained to the cause of our national hopes. If, then, we wish to transmit all our privileges, civil and religious, unimpaired, to the latest posterity, let our young men be deeply imbued with the spirit of the Bible.—If we wish to avert from our country the curse of an ecclesiastical establishment, that bane of both church and State, let the Bible, and *nothing but the Bible,* be impressed upon the minds of our youth, as the *only infallible rule of faith and practice.* Here, and here only, do we find those principles which are equally opposed to slavery and licentiousness. Every young man who has been trained in the spirit of the Bible, will be, as far as his influence goes, an impregnable barrier against every species of oppression, civil or religious; and equally against every species of disorder. Only let the great mass of our population, for the next forty years, drink deep into the spirit of the *Bible,* and we may probably consider our stability and happiness as a nation finally secured.

Dr Miller expresses the following opinion of the work before us:—

> So far as my opportunity of examination has extended, it is rich and judicious in matter; neat, perspicuous, and attractive in style; and

peculiarly adapted to engage and reward the attention of enlightened, reflecting, and literary youth. Indeed, if I were asked to point out a manual, better suited than any other within my knowledge, to be put into the hands of students in the higher literary institutions, I know not that it would be in my power to name one more likely to answer the purpose than this volume.

A judgment which the voice of the public has sustained.

Dr Sprague's first lecture is on 'The Importance of the Period of Youth'. Those which immediately follow are on the various peculiar dangers to which the young are exposed, and are introductory to those discourses which are intended to arouse the attention of the careless, to guide the enquiries of the anxious, to exhibit the nature and evidence of real religion, and to direct the course of the young convert. Our limits forbid our indulging ourselves in making extracts. We close with an earnest recommendation of the book to our youthful readers, and the expression of our sincere desire that it may be made extensively useful.

THE NATURE OF THE ATONEMENT[1]

> *When we were enemies we were reconciled unto God*
> *by the death of his Son.*
> Romans 5:10

THE truth that man is a moral, and consequently an accountable being, is the foundation of all religion. It is necessarily involved in this truth that our happiness depends on the favour of God, and that his favour is forfeited by sin. Just so far, and so clearly, therefore, as men are conscious of sin, are they convinced that they are the objects of the divine displeasure. As the consciousness of sin is universal, so also is the apprehension of God's anger. The question, therefore, forces itself on the attention of every considerate human being, with an energy and importunity which cannot be resisted: How is the favour of God to be regained? The answer to this question decides the religious character and the destiny of him who gives it. For, if he is mistaken here, if he adopts a wrong method of securing this object, he is, on his own principles, undone. Here, then, more immediately than anywhere else, are we in contact with the vital principle of religion. For as there can be no real happiness, so there can be no holiness except in the enjoyment of God's favour (*Rom.* 6:14), and consequently there can be no true religion where the method of securing his favour, whatever that may be, is denied or neglected. Such being confessedly the importance of this question, it need hardly be remarked, that this of all others is the subject on which mere speculation and theorising should be forborne. When a man is seeking for himself a footing on which he can stand alone

---

[1] Charles Hodge, 'Nature of the Atonement', *The Spruce Street Lectures: by Several Clergymen. Delivered During the Years 1831-2. To which is Added a Sermon on the Atonement by John De Witt, D.D.* (Philadelphia: James Russell, 1841), pp. 143-69.

in the presence of his God, or on which he is willing to assume the responsibility of exhorting others to stand, he needs, if ever, the rock of the divine testimony beneath his feet.

Happily we are not left in uncertainty on this subject. There is no one doctrine of the Bible more frequently asserted, more variously implied, more intimately interwoven with all the rest, than that which teaches the method of regaining the forfeited favour of God. The declaration is so explicit, and so frequently repeated, that we are reconciled unto God by the death of his Son, that no class of men, professing to recognize the authority of the Scriptures, venture to deny that it is in some way through the death of Christ this result is secured. But the question here arises, what is the nature of this connection—how is it that the sufferings of the Son of God secure the remission of sins? It must be admitted that there is no little diversity of opinion as to the answer which should be given to this question. But why need the question be agitated? Why not be contented with the general statement, we are saved by the death of Christ, without perplexing ourselves or others by enquiring how these events are related? We should be at a loss for an answer to these interrogations, and feel ready to admit that all such enquiries are worse than useless, if the Bible was silent on the subject. Did the Scriptures teach us the fact only, that the death of Christ is connected with the pardon of sin, without explaining the nature or mode of that connection, then indeed would enquiry on the subject be vain, if not impious. But this is not the case. The manner in which the sufferings of the Redeemer are connected with our salvation, is as much revealed as the object of our faith and ground of our hope, as the fact itself. Besides, this question is most intimately connected with all true piety. If the death of Christ has no other connection with the remission of sins, than as it confirms his doctrines, then must our views of the divine character, of the ground of a sinner's confidence towards God, of the nature of faith, and mode of salvation, all be changed; then have we another gospel; and all those exercises of piety, which suppose a different view of this subject, are fanatical delusions. We are not, therefore, travelling beyond the limits of revealed truth, nor instituting an enquiry unconnected with practical religion, when we ask, How it is that the death of Christ secures the remission of sins? Various as are the opinions entertained on this subject, they may all, it is believed, be reduced to these three general views.

The first is that which represents the death of Christ, not as the immediate or proximate ground of pardon, but as securing this result only so far as it is instrumental in producing a change of character in the sinner himself. Its tendency to effect this change is ascribed either to the confirmation which it gives to the gospel in the general, or to some one truth in particular; to the exhibition which it makes of the divine mercy, or the excellence of the Redeemer; or to some more mysterious and indefinable influence. The effect, however, in whatever way it may be produced, is on the sinner himself, and it is in virtue of this effect that pardon is secured. According to this view, every constituent idea of the doctrine of atonement is rejected, and Christianity is either a modified system of natural religion, or of mystical philosophy.

The second general view proceeds on the assumption, that as the end of punishment is the prevention of crime, if this end can be otherwise attained, the obstacle to the exercise of mercy would be removed. The death of Christ is designed to accomplish this object, by making an impression on the intelligent universe at least as efficacious in deterring from sin, as the punishment of the actual offender would have produced. Such being the object of the atonement, it consists in sufferings not of a penal character, nor inflicted in the execution of the law, but endured under circumstances adapted to produce the desired impression. Its effect is to remove a governmental difficulty to the dispensation of pardons.

The third view proceeds on the principle, that the necessity of punishment does not arise merely out of the necessity of making an impression on the universe, and on the sinner himself, adapted to deter from sin, but also and primarily out of the inherent ill-desert of sin itself, and the infinite rectitude of the divine character, in which the idea of distributive justice is included. Consequently, while the atonement is designed and adapted to produce the deepest impression of the holiness and justice of God on all intelligent beings, its primary object is to answer the demands of divine justice. It is, therefore, of the nature of a satisfaction, consisting in vicarious punishment, or in the infliction of the penalty of the law on Jesus Christ as the substitute of the sinner. And its effect is to secure reconciliation on the condition of faith and repentance.

It is the object of this discourse to endeavour to show that the third of these views is the form in which the doctrine is presented in the Word of God. Before entering on the subject, it may be necessary to state the sense in which the terms here employed are used. When it is said, the sufferings of Christ were of the nature of punishment, the word punishment is used in its ordinary acceptation, for suffering judicially inflicted, or sufferings imposed in execution of a legal sentence. The idea, of course, is not included, that the sufferer himself must be chargeable with sin in a moral sense. This would be no less abhorrent to the feelings of those who use this expression, than inconsistent with the plainest declarations of Scripture. Again, when it is said that the penalty of the law was executed on the Redeemer, it is not intended that his sufferings were, either in nature or degree, any more than in duration, the same as would have come on the sinner himself. Such an idea is not necessarily, nor properly, conveyed by the expression. The penalty of the law is not any specific degree or character of pain which the law imposes, but it is any and all pain, which sustains to the law the relation of a sanction. Thus, the word death, according to its scriptural use, does not import any one definite form or amount of suffering, but all evil, however varied in nature or intensity, by which sin is punished. Even with regard to human laws, the penalty never involves precisely the same kind and degree of pain in its execution. The terms may remain the same, but the character and amount of suffering are modified by ten thousand circumstances in the moral character, natural temperament, and physical constitution of the individual. A youth of tender feelings, susceptible conscience, alive to the good opinion of society, with fair prospects and many friends, suffers unspeakably more and differently under the same sentence, than a hardened offender differently circumstanced in all these respects. It is, therefore, of all objections, the least worthy of notice, that Christ's sufferings were not penal, because they were not the same in character as those which the actual sinner would have experienced. There may be even an entire commutation of the punishment, without the penal character of the infliction being lost.

We cling to these expressions, not from any fondness for terms, but because those which we are urged to substitute for them do not express the idea we mean to convey. It is, therefore, in the sense just stated, we maintain, in accordance with the language of the Scriptures, that Christ suffered the penalty of the law. The law threatened death—and Christ suffered death—in the proper scriptural meaning of the term; that is, misery or pain judicially inflicted in support of the claims of the law.

The definition of the phrase vicarious punishment, we give in the words of a modern Lutheran divine, 'It is suffering judicially inflicted on condition of the exemption of the actual offender.'[1] It derives its character from its being judicially substituted for the punishment of the real transgressor, with a view to his pardon. The correctness of this definition is evident from the nature of the transaction, and from all the examples and illustrations of vicarious sufferings recorded in the Scriptures. It is true, the exemption of the offender need not be, and in the case before us, is not, absolute and immediate, but may be suspended on any condition the judge and substitute have pleased to determine.

Christ, then, saves us from the penalty of the law by vicariously suffering that penalty in his own person. That this is the doctrine of the Word of God, on this subject, we think can easily be shown, if the two following principles of interpretation be admitted, and faithfully applied. The first is, that as the sacred writers unquestionably meant to be understood by the persons to whom they wrote, they must have employed the terms which they use in the sense which they knew would be attached to them by their readers or hearers, and, consequently, that the business of an interpreter is to ascertain the sense in which the contemporaries of the sacred writers employed the terms these writers used, and the mode in which they would naturally conceive the doctrines which they presented. In doing this, he ascertains the mode in which the inspired penmen meant to be understood; and the mode in which we are bound to receive their meaning. This simple rule lies at the foundation of all certainty in the interpretation of written documents, ancient or modern.

[1] Storr, *Object of the Death of Christ.*

The other principle is, that although it is not only proper in itself, but absolutely necessary in a teacher to accommodate himself to the capacity, the modes of thinking and speaking of his hearers, it is not consistent with fidelity or honesty to employ such a mode of instruction as would naturally lead them into error; or, by adopting their false opinions, to confirm and sanction them. Much less would such a course be consistent with the character of inspired teachers, and least of all when teaching the plan of salvation. We are, therefore, never at liberty to assume that the sacred writers really meant something different from the obvious import of their language, on the ground of their having accommodated themselves to the opinions of those to whom they wrote. To attempt to draw a distinction between what is exegetically true, and what is doctrinally correct, is at once and entirely to destroy the authority of the Scriptures as a rule of faith. The Scriptures become a mere set of cabbalistic signs for every man to interpret as he pleases. Nothing more is necessary than this principle to enable anyone, not only to explain away every doctrine of the Bible, but to make the Scriptures teach any conceivable system of opinions. And in point of fact, they have thus been made to contain every form of doctrine, from icy deism to ideal pantheism; and the apostles alternately presented as heathen moralists, and mystic philosophers. It is clearly impossible to prove anything from Scripture, to the satisfaction of those who either avowedly, or practically, adopt such a principle of interpretation. If we are not to take the simple exegetical meaning of the Bible for its true meaning, then we can never know what its meaning is. Let us, under the guidance of the simple rule of construction, that the sacred writers say what they mean, and mean what they knew their readers would understand them to say, enquire in what way they teach the doctrine of atonement. That they represent the death of Christ as a vicarious punishment of our sins, we think clear from the following considerations:

I. *This doctrine is taught in all those passages in which Christ is said 'to bear our sins'.* Thus, repeatedly, in the fifty-third chapter of Isaiah. 'The Lord hath laid on him the iniquity of us all.' 'He was numbered with the transgressors: and he bare the sins of many.' 'By his knowledge shall my righteous servant justify many, for he shall bear their iniquities.' It is our duty simply to enquire, what was the import of this phrase among the ancient Hebrews; what idea did they attach to the expression, 'to bear sin', for this must be the idea which the sacred writer meant to convey. This point is easily decided, as the phrase is one of frequent occurrence in the Scriptures. Thus, in Leviticus 5:1, it is said of the man who gives false testimony, 'he shall bear his iniquity'. As an equivalent expression in the next verse, it is said of him who touches anything unclean, 'he also shall be guilty'. In verse 17, he who violates the law, though he does it ignorantly, 'yet is he guilty, and shall bear his iniquity'. In chapter 7:18, he that eateth of a peace-offering on the third day, 'shall bear his iniquity'. So, 17:16, he that does not wash his clothes, and bathe his flesh after eating anything torn by a wild beast, 'shall bear his iniquity'. Numbers 9:13, he that does not partake of the Passover 'shall be cut off from among his people—he shall bear his sins'. This expression is sometimes interchanged (and thereby explained) with the phrase 'he shall die', 'he shall be cut off from among the people' (*Num.* 19:20) or, 'he shall be guilty'. In all the numerous passages, therefore, in which these words occur in reference to men, the meaning is obvious and uniform: for a man to bear his sins, is to bear the blame of them, to be punished for them. And, accordingly, to bear the sins of another, is to bear the blame of them—to be punished for them. So, in Numbers 14:33, Jeremiah's Lamentations 5:7, and Ezekiel 18:19, 20, 'The son shall not bear the iniquity of the father, neither shall the father bear the iniquity of the son, but the soul that sinneth it shall die.' Where the sense is too obvious to be at all questionable. That this is the meaning of the phrase as applied to Christ, by the prophet, is not only evident from the constant usage of the Bible, but from the prophet's own explanation: 'to bear our sins', is to bear our sorrows, stripes, sickness, chastisement; that is, our punishment. It is to be afflicted, wounded, smitten, and that of God, for our sins. It is plain, too, from its use in the sacrificial services. After the imposition of hands, and confession, *i.e.,* after the act of substitution, and the symbolical transfer of sin, the dying victim was said to bear the sins of the offerer. And, finally, the same thing is evident from the admitted opinions of ancient nations in reference to this subject. The case, indeed, is so plain, that the interpretation just given has secured the assent of all impartial commentators, orthodox or infidel. One of the most distinguished of the latter class, remarks on this phrase, 'If we wish to understand such expressions, we must revert to the opinion of all early nations, and especially of the Hebrews, that all calamities, particularly those of more than ordinary severity, were punishments inflicted immediately by God, and that they could only be removed by an innocent victim undergoing the punishment as a substitute, and thus stilling the anger of the offended Deity.'[1] Another of the same class says, in reference to representations contained in this chapter (*Isa.* 53), 'The majority of Hebrew readers, having their minds filled with the ideas of sacrifice and substitution, must, of necessity, have so understood these passages; and it is not to be doubted, that the mode in which the apostles presented the atoning death of Christ, rests mainly on this ground.'[2] It is, therefore, with the fullest authority of scriptural usage, Grotius asserts, that 'To bear sins by suffering, that others may be pardoned, can mean nothing else than to bear the punishment of those sins.'[3] And Archbishop Magee, though he is willing, for the sake of peace, to give up the word punishment, says, 'But it is evident, that it (the suffering of Christ) is, notwithstanding, a judicial infliction';[4] the very idea which the word is intended to express.

Although, therefore, the expression, 'to bear sin', may to our ears mean either, first, to remove it; second, to suffer on the occasion of it; or, third, to suffer its punishment; to the Jews, it could in such connections, convey only the last idea, and consequently, to substitute for this either of the two former, is to make it express a sense, which, as we have shown, is contrary to Scripture usage, the opinions of the people to whom the prophet wrote, and therefore contrary to the obvious intention of the sacred writer, and mind of the Spirit.

It is in this sense, too, the New Testament writers, in addressing those 'whose minds were filled with the ideas of sacrifice and substitution', who were imbued with the ideas and language of the Old Testament, assert that Christ 'was offered to bear the sins of many' (*Heb.* 9:28), that he 'bare our sins in his own body on the tree' (*1 Pet.*

---

[1] Martini on Isaiah 53.
[2] Gesenius on Isaiah 53.
[3] Grotius *Opera Theologia,* Vol. iv, p. 300.
[4] *On the Atonement,* Vol. I, p. 347. See also p. 346.

2:24). So in John 1:29, 'Behold the Lamb of God which beareth the sin of the world' (according to the reading of the margin), and 1 John 3:5, 'He was manifested to take away our sins.'

II. *Precisely the same idea is clearly expressed by the apostle in Galatians 3:13.* In this chapter the apostle is engaged in proving that faith in Christ is the only means by which we can attain the favour of God. One of his arguments is the following: 'As many as are of the works of the law, are under the curse; for it is written, cursed is every one who continueth not in all things written in the book of the law to do them.' But 'Christ has redeemed us from the curse of the law, being made a curse for us: for it is written, cursed is every one who hangeth on a tree.' It will of course be admitted that 'the curse of the law' is its penalty, and that to be under this curse, and to be 'a curse' mean the same thing, the apostle himself teaches, as he substitutes for both expressions, the word 'cursed'. We are 'under the curse', because it is written, 'cursed', *etc.,* and Christ was 'made a curse', for it is written, 'cursed', *etc.* There can be no doubt, therefore, that the literal meaning of this passage is, 'no one can be saved by obedience to the law, because, as the law demands perfect obedience, he who violates the least commandment is exposed to its penalty; but Christ has redeemed us from this penalty by bearing it in our stead.' It hardly seems possible to interpret the apostle's language in any other way. That Christ was properly considered as suffering a penalty, the apostle confirms by appealing to a declaration of the law, that everyone judicially condemned was accounted accursed of God (as the expression is in the passage quoted, *Deut.* 21:23), *i.e.,* exposed as an object of divine displeasure; one on whom, by the divine law, a penalty has fallen. So far, therefore, is this reference to the Old Testament from explaining away the previous assertion, that it is intended to confirm it. According to the doctrine of the apostle, then, we are saved from the penalty of the law, by Christ bearing it in our stead. And this seems to be the ground of his arguing so often that Christ's death is tantamount to our death, and that it is not by the relaxation of the law, as to its penalty, but by its execution that we are saved, 'For I, through the law, am dead to the law' (*Gal.* 2:19), *i.e.,* free from its demands, so that there is now no condemnation to me, nor to any who are in Christ Jesus.

III. *Romans 8:3.* The same course of reasoning occurs in Romans 8:3. 'The salvation which men in vain look for through the law, God has secured in another way. For as the law was insufficient, God having sent his Son in a nature the same with our own, and as a sin offering, punished sin in him, that thus the demands of the law might be satisfied by us.' This seems to be the view of the passage best suited to the context, and the peculiar expressions which the apostle here employs. In this passage God is said to have sent his Son 'in the likeness of sinful flesh', and it was in this flesh (or nature) 'that he punished or condemned sin', not in our flesh, for this the context will not allow, but in the flesh in which his Son appeared, *i.e.,* in his person, and the object of this vicarious condemnation is our exemption.

IV. *The same representation is found in 2 Corinthians 5:21.* The apostle had stated 'that God was reconciling the world unto himself, not imputing their trespasses unto them'; and then states how it is that pardon was thus secured; 'God made him to be sin for us, who knew no sin, that we might be made the righteousness of God in him.' He treated the Redeemer as though he were the sinner—that we might be treated as though we were righteous. As, 'to be made the righteousness of God', means to be justified, so, 'to be made sin', is to be condemned or made subject to the penalty of the law. As we are not constituted morally righteous by the death of Christ, so is it infinitely far from the apostle's intention to say that Christ was made, morally, a sinner. Both expressions are obviously used in their usual forensic sense.

V. *We may now refer to those numerous passages in which Christ is said, 'to die for us', 'to suffer the just for the unjust', etc.* These texts all prove the doctrine of substitution, *i.e.,* that Christ died in our stead. It is true that taken by itself this expression might mean nothing more than that Christ suffered for our benefit, but the following reasons seem sufficient to prove that this is not all the sacred writers mean by it.

1. One of the prepositions (ἀντι) thus translated, seldom has any other meaning than, 'in the place of'.

2. In some connections this sense is required, as when it is said, 'he gave his life a ransom for many', where the force of the word ransom requires the last words to be rendered, 'in the place of many'.

3. In Romans 5:7, it is said 'scarcely for a righteous man will one die', which seems clearly to mean, in the place of a righteous man; and, therefore, when it is said, 'but when we were yet sinners Christ died for us', it must mean, in our place.

4. The very expression, to die for a man, who is exposed to death, that he may live, seems with sufficient clearness to express the idea of dying in his stead.

5. The manner in which the death of Christ is said to benefit us, requires this interpretation—it is by bearing our sins—being made a curse for us, *i.e.,* enduring the punishment we had incurred.

6. Finally, if the sacred writers clearly elsewhere teach, as we have seen they do, the doctrine of legal substitution, then, as their meaning is ascertained as to this point by passages which are obvious as to their import, it can be no longer doubtful what they intended when they declare that Christ 'died for us'.

VI. *Another important class of text is that in which Christ is called a ransom, and his work a redemption.* It is freely admitted that the words 'to redeem' and 'redemption' are often used when merely the general idea of deliverance is meant to be conveyed. As when God is said to have redeemed his people out of Egypt. Their primary and proper meaning, however, as is on all hands admitted, is to deliver by the payment of a ransom. That it is in this, and not in the more general sense of mere deliverance, they are used in reference to the work of Christ, is evident from the simple consideration that the ransom, or price paid for our deliverance, is expressly stated. Thus in Ephesians 1:7, 'In whom we have redemption through his blood.' 1 Corinthians 6:20, 'Ye are bought with a price.' 1 Peter 1:18, 19, 'Ye are not redeemed with corruptible things, as silver and gold, but with the precious blood of Christ, as of a lamb without spot or blemish.' Galatians 3:13, 'Christ has redeemed us from the curse of the law, having been made a curse for us.' In all these cases, it is not mere deliverance that is asserted, but deliverance by a specific method; by a ransom, by the payment of a price. It is true these and all similar representations are figurative, but figurative language is so often as intelligible as literal, and sometimes more so. The simple question is, what idea would this language naturally excite in the minds of men accustomed to regard their sacrifices as ransoms, and familiar with the mode of deliverance which these expressions properly describe? It is impossible that this mode of representation should fail of exciting the idea of deliverance on the ground of a satisfaction. This Christ and his apostles knew; and this idea, therefore, they must have intended to convey.

VII. *We may appeal to the frequently recurring passages in which Christ is said to propitiate God, or to make reconciliation for the sins of the people; or to be himself a propitiation, which all imply that the object of the atonement is to satisfy divine justice.* God is represented as angry with the wicked, and the death of Christ as the means by which he is propitiated. As anger among men is commonly a modification and expression of malice, we know that from association these expressions are apt to excite ideas derogatory to the divine perfection, and furnish an easy topic of declamatory misrepresentation. But it should be remembered, that these are scriptural expressions, expressions intended to convey important truth, and to represent ideas, which, so far from being inconsistent with divine excellence, necessarily enter into the conception of infinite perfection. The anger of God is the expression of his disapprobation of sin; the exhibition of his holiness in view of moral evil; or, in other words, the manifestation of his justice. It is to turn off from us this anger, by rendering our pardon consistent with the justice of the divine Being, that Christ died. And this is expressed in the terms just mentioned. For when God is said to reconcile the world unto himself, or we to be reconciled to him; (in such connections) the idea is not that we are led to lay aside our enmity towards him, but that this favour is propitiated for us, as the word means 'to restore to the favour of anyone'. It is thus used, in the command of our Saviour, 'If thou bring thy gift to the altar, and there rememberest that thy brother hath ought against thee, first go and be reconciled to thy brother', *i.e.,* first go and satisfy him and regain his favour. And in Romans 5:11, 'In whom we have obtained reconciliation', *i.e.,* restoration to the divine favour. In the phrase 'making reconciliation for sin', Hebrews 2:17, it, of course, can have no other meaning. That this is the sense of these expressions is further evident from the means by which this reconciliation is effected, it is 'by the death of his Son', by his cross, by Christ being made sin for us.

VIII. The only other class of texts to which our limits will permit us to refer is perhaps the largest and most important of all. *The work of Christ is at least more fully illustrated, if not more frequently expressed, by a reference to the sacrifices of the Old Testament than in any other way.* He is called the Lamb of God, John 1:29, a propitiation, or propitiatory sacrifice, Romans 3:25, a sin offering Romans 8:3, an acceptable sacrifice, Ephesians 5:2. He is declared and proved to be a Priest, Hebrews 5, and all the duties of the office are ascribed to him: the sacrifice, which he offered, was himself. 'He offered himself without spot unto God', Hebrews 9:14. 'He was once offered to bear the sins of many', Hebrews 9:28. He offered a sacrifice for sin, 'once when he offered up himself', Hebrews 7:27. The effects of his sufferings are in like manner described in terms borrowed from the sacrificial services. 'Having by himself purged our sins', Hebrews 1:3. If the blood of bulls and of goats was of any avail, 'how much more shall the blood of Christ purge your consciences from dead works', Hebrews 9:14. 'He appeared to put away sin by the sacrifice of himself', Hebrews 9:26. 'We are sanctified through the offering of the body of Christ', Hebrews 10:10. 'The blood of Jesus Christ cleanses from all sin', 1 John 1:7. All these expressions refer, not to moral purification, but to the removal of the guilt of sin, by atonement. So also the mode of application of the benefits of his death is expressed, by sprinkling his blood on the conscience, to indicate its pardoning efficacy; or on the throne of God, as expressive of its influence in propitiating the divine favour.

Is it conceivable that such representations, made not casually, or by allusion, but dwelt upon, urged, defended and argued, could fail to produce in the minds of those, who from their youth had been familiar with sacrificial rites, the conviction that the sacred writers meant to teach, that Christ was really a sacrifice in their sense of the term, that his death saves us from the penalty of the law in the same way as the sacrifices of the old dispensation saved the Jews from the consequences of the transgression of the law of Moses? If this be admitted, then must we admit, that the sacred writers intended to produce this conviction. For who will maintain they designedly led their readers into error; that inspired men were intentional deceivers while propounding the method of salvation?

In what light, then, are the sacrifices of the Old Testament presented in the Scriptures? We are clearly taught that they sustained a twofold relation; the one to the theocratical polity of the Jewish State, and the other to the great truths which were afterwards to be revealed.

In the former respect, we learn, in the first place, that they were concerned about God, designed to propitiate his favour, and thus secure the pardon of sin; and in the second that this was effected through the medium of vicarious punishment. Both of these points seem evident from the language, rites, and opinions of the ancient Hebrews, and the ancient world in general. The design of these services, is, indeed, clearly indicated by the expressions 'to propitiate', 'make reconciliation for', and others of similar import, as already remarked; and the nature of the observance shows how this was to be accomplished. When a man had violated any of the laws of Moses, the penalty was excision from among the people. The method prescribed by the judge and head of the Jewish State for averting this evil, was to present a victim to suffer in his place. But suffering, judicially imposed on one with the view to the exemption of another, is the definition of vicarious punishment. This idea of substitution and transfer of sin was clearly expressed by the imposition of hands and confession of sin over the head of the sacrifice. And hence, after this ceremony, the victim was said to bear the sins of the offender, *i.e.,* to bear the blame or guilt of them, and being thus laden, was considered unclean, and, at times, burnt without the camp, and all who touched it were regarded as defiled. All this to be sure is figurative, but these figures are designed to teach something, to teach that pardon was to be obtained only through the medium of vicarious punishment. This is the essential, formal idea of a sin-offering. In the language of Grotius, 'They secured pardon, by inducing God to forgive, on the ground of a satisfaction' (p. 330). Such being the obvious nature and import of those rites in relation to the Mosaic ceremony, their connection with the Christian dispensation is not less clear, and far more important. As typical institutions, they were designed to teach by significant actions, by prefiguring, to predict and explain the method of salvation through Jesus Christ, the Lamb of God, who was to bear the sins of the world. Their own efficacy, in securing pardon, did not extend beyond the mere ceremonial and civil penalties of the old dispensation. As it was impossible that the blood of bulls or of goats could take away sin, they had no bearing on the relation of the offender to God as judge and moral governor of the universe. But if, as the apostle reasons, they availed to the purifying of the flesh, to the removal of mere external disabilities, how much more shall the blood of Christ, who, possessed of an eternal spirit, *i.e.,* a divine nature, offered himself unto God, avail to the pardon of sin? In the comparisons so frequently instituted between Christ and the ancient sacrifices, it is to be remarked that it is not the result or effect merely that is taken into view. He is called a sacrifice, not merely because he secures pardon, but the mode in which this is done is the very point of the comparison; he is a sacrifice, because he takes our place, bears our sins, is made a curse for us, and thus propitiates God in our behalf. All the ideas, therefore, of substitution, legal transfer of sin, vicarious punishment, and propitiation, which enter into the Jewish idea of a sacrifice are, over and over, asserted to meet in the great atonement of Jesus Christ. It is, therefore, in the Jewish sense of the term, that he is called a sacrifice for sin.

It is easy, indeed, to get over all this, by simply substituting for the ancient view of sacrifices, our own idea of what they were, or ought to have been. To assert that they were merely symbols, or signs of God's disapprobation of sin, designed to exhibit and impress that truth on the minds of all concerned; and thence infer that in this sense, and to this extent, Christ was a sacrifice. Or, as others have done, maintain that they were only intended to make the sinner feel his guilt, and assure him of pardon, and then limit the death of Christ to the same objects. This, however, is interpreting Scripture not according to the views of its writers, but according to our own views of the nature and fitness of things. It is not taking the sense of the Bible as we find it, but interposing a sense of our own. It is obvious if we once abandon the rule of interpretation so often referred to, if we do not understand the Bible in the way in which the inspired writers knew they would be understood by their readers; then are we far and hopelessly at sea, without a star to guide us. One man has as good a right to interpose his sense of the terms of Scripture as another; one may as well say, a sacrifice was designed to impress the offerer, as another it was intended to impress spectators. Which is right, or whether either, is a matter to be debated at the bar of reason; and the plan of salvation is made to await the decision. Our only hope of any solid foundation for faith, or of any security for truth, is to receive the Scriptures in the sense which they were designed and adapted to convey to the minds of their original readers.[1]

When, Christian Brethren, we remember that the representations just given are not casual or incidental, but that they pervade the sacred volume, are insisted upon, illustrated, established and defended, made the grounds of doctrinal and practical inferences; when we remember that Christ is said to have borne the punishment of our sins, in the plainest terms the language of the Old Testament admits of; that he was made sin, or treated as a sinner in our place; that he bore the curse of the law; that he died in our stead; that he gave his life as our ransom; bought us with his blood; that he propitiated God on our behalf, and saved us as a sacrifice; can we hesitate to admit that the very constituent idea of atonement is vicarious punishment?

This doctrine, thus clearly taught in the Word of God, has an advocate even in natural conscience; for this is the light in which sacrificial rites have been viewed in all ages, and among all people, Gentiles as well as Jews. No matter how various the offerings, nor how diversified the ceremonies, the object of such rites was the satisfaction of divine justice, and the means, vicarious punishment. And it may be assumed that this is the form in which the doctrine presents itself to every pious unsophisticated reader of the Bible. When oppressed with a sense of sin, he feels that some atonement must be made to God. The attribute which leads him to punish, the convinced sinner sees to be perfectly lovely and excellent, and it is not until he discovers some method by which the exercise of mercy can be reconciled with justice, that pardon appears possible. Such a method he finds revealed in the cross of Christ. There he sees that the penalty of the broken law has been endured in his stead. It is this that reconciles him so cordially to the gospel, and enables him to embrace, without any misgivings, the offers of mercy there presented. It is not until he has been taught by others what is called, the philosophy of the subject, that he is

---

[1] The limitations to which this principle is subject, do not affect the view here given.

led to imagine all this is a delusion, that the atonement, instead of being designed as a satisfaction or propitiation to God, is intended either to impress his own heart, or to symbolise a general truth for the instruction of the universe. And even when thus instructed, he reverts in his ordinary exercises of faith and devotion to the scriptural representations of the subject. This too, let me add, is the form in which the doctrine has been held in the Christian church from first to last. For although during the ages in which the Scriptures were buried, many absurd ideas were entertained on this subject; yet when the Reformation brought them again to light, this was the doctrine which burst with redeeming brightness from the sacred pages. Much and bitterly as the men of that day disputed about other points, in this they were agreed. Lutherans and Calvinists, the Huguenots of France and the Reformed of Holland, the Scotch Presbyterians and English Reformers, all conspired to represent this as the cardinal doctrine of the gospel, the article of a rising or a falling church.

The atonement, then, Christian Brethren, as exhibiting the mode of the sinner's salvation, is the characteristic doctrine of the gospel. Its direct object is the reconciliation of men to God; to secure pardon of sin, the sanctification of their nature, and eternal life. In this light, who can comprehend the importance of the work of Christ! Let anyone endeavour to estimate the value of these results in the case of any one individual. Let him ask, what it is for one soul to be delivered from hell and raised to heaven; to be freed from eternal degradation and misery, and raised to eternal purity and happiness; let him strain his powers to the utmost to take in the full blessedness of such a redemption. And when he finds how vain is the effort, let him ask himself what he ought to think and feel in view of the ten thousand times ten thousand, and thousands of thousands redeemed out of every nation, and kindred, and tongue under the whole heaven, a multitude which no man can number, whose robes have been made white in the blood of the Lamb.

Inconceivably great as is the amount of blessedness thus effected, its accomplishment is not the sole object of the death of Christ. The rays from the cross are cast far onward to the utmost verge of the universe of God. Wherever there are immortal minds to see or learn the exhibition here made of the divine character, there do the effects of the atonement reach. So far from supposing that the view of the subject, which we have endeavoured to present, excludes the idea of a moral impression on the world of intelligent spirits, we consider that the atonement derives its adaptedness to produce this impression, from the fact of its being a satisfaction to divine justice. When that most wonderful of all commands was heard in heaven, 'Awake O sword, against the man that is mine equal, saith the Lord', then was it seen and felt, that though heaven and earth should perish, the law of God must stand; that sin was indeed an evil so enormous that to pass it with impunity was impossible. Only so far as the atonement involves an exercise of justice, is it a manifestation of justice. Viewed in the light, not of setting aside the penalty of the law, but as involving its execution, it is better adapted to seal the conviction on all minds of the immutability of the law, and of the certainty of sin being punished, than the eternal condemnation of ten thousand worlds. It is, as the apostle informs us, the fact that Christ was possessed of an eternal spirit, or divine nature, Hebrews 9:14, and thus was equal with God, Philippians 2:6, which gives the atonement its efficacy. It is this that fills the wondering universe with awe, and constitutes the most effective of all exhibitions of the divine holiness and justice. Whatever moral impression, therefore, the exhibition of divine justice can produce, is thus most effectually made, and whatever benefit, in deterring from sin, this impression can effect, is thus secured. The law is sustained and vindicated, by being executed; or its transgression, with impunity, by man or seraph, is felt through all worlds to be impossible.

This truth is made to bear with all its force upon the sinner. 'If these things be done in the green tree, what shall be done in the dry',—if it was not possible that the cup of wrath should pass from the Saviour's lips, from whose lips shall it pass? Where is the man who believes the doctrine of atonement, who does not feel that his destruction is just and inevitable, if he neglect the salvation of the gospel? Who does not feel that it is the utmost limits of infatuation to believe that the sinner can escape, if God spared not his own Son?

The ill-desert of sin, and the certainty of its punishment, are, however, not the only truths exhibited in the death of Christ. God commendeth his love towards us, in that while we were yet enemies

Christ died for us. God so loved the world that he sent his Son. It is this attribute which is most conspicuously displayed in the cross of Christ. It is this, therefore, which is the constant theme of praise with the sacred writers; a love whose height, and depth, and length, and breadth, are beyond our knowledge. As it is by the exhibition of truth, and especially of the character of God, that holiness is sustained and exercised in all created minds; so does the atonement become of all means perhaps the most effective in promoting holiness throughout the whole universe. It is the exhibition here made, which commonly leads men to repentance. It is here they see the evil of sin; the holiness and love of God; the wonderful grace of their Redeemer. It is here they learn the vileness and ingratitude of their conduct; it is when they look on him whom they have pierced, that they mourn and turn unto God with contrition and penitence. It is from the cross, too, that the Christian derives his most active impulses to duty and self-denial. Constrained by the love of Christ, Paul laboured and suffered with constancy and alacrity. And it is the same influence which now restrains from sin, and urges on to duty, all faithful followers of the Redeemer. Nor is the effect confined to our world. If, when God spread these garnished heavens, and called these countless worlds, with their endless variety of happy inhabitants, into being, a shout of rapture was heard in heaven, at this display of his wisdom, power, and goodness; we need not wonder that the sons of God regard with interest the work of redemption. It is into the deeper wonders and brighter glories of this new creation, they desire to look; and thence they derive their chief materials of praise. As a means of promoting holiness and happiness, therefore, among all orders of intelligent beings, and throughout all eternity, the cross of Christ is perhaps of all others the most effective.

The effect which the consideration of this doctrine ought to have on Christians, time does not permit us to indicate. Paul tells us, that having such a High Priest, we should hold fast our profession, never be tempted to give up either the faith or hope of the gospel; that we should come with boldness to the throne of grace; that we should live for him who died for us; that, having experienced the unsearchable riches of Christ, we should esteem it the chief business and honour of our lives to endeavour to bring others to the enjoyment of its blessing; that we should fix no limits to our desire for the extension of the knowledge of the Saviour, until it covers the earth as the waters do the great deep. We should esteem all sacrifices and all efforts slight for the attainment of this object. Do what we will, suffer what we may, for the salvation of others, it will all be little, compared with what Christ has done and suffered for us. And it will all appear little in our own eyes when we enter in the eternal world.

Though this doctrine has always proved a stumbling-block in the way of some, and foolishness in the eyes of others; it is nevertheless the wisdom of God unto salvation. Presenting the plan which infinite wisdom has devised for the redemption of men, it teaches most clearly to those who refuse to accede to its terms, that they make their own destruction sure. The refuges of lies to which they betake themselves will not stand a moment before the coming storm of divine wrath. Their prayers or penances, their deeds of charity or honesty, will avail nothing in averting the sword of divine justice. Rejecting the offering of Christ, there remains no other sacrifice for sin; refusing this Saviour, there is no other name given under heaven whereby they can be saved. The obvious imperative duty of all such, is an immediate return to God through Jesus Christ, a sincere and penitent acquiescence in the plan of salvation proposed in the gospel. Hear, then, and obey the voice of the dying Saviour from the cross, 'Look unto me all ye ends of the earth, and be ye saved.'

And now, unto him who loved us and gave himself for us, be blessing, and honour, and glory, and power, even unto him that sitteth on the throne, and unto the Lamb for ever and ever. Amen.

THE TEACHING OFFICE
OF THE CHURCH[1]

Go ye, therefore, and teach all nations, baptizing them in the name of the
Father, and of the Son, and of the Holy Ghost; teaching them to observe all
things whatsoever I have commanded you; and, lo, I am with you alway,
even unto the end of the world.
Matthew 28:19, 20.

WE learn from the first chapter of Acts that Christ showed himself alive after his passion, by many infallible proofs, being seen of the apostles forty days, and speaking to them of the things pertaining to the kingdom of God. We have four, more or less independent, histories of these forty days. Circumstances mentioned by one historian are omitted by another, so that all must be collated in order to obtain a full account of the parting instructions of Christ to his disciples. The passage just recited, however, contains the substance of his last injunctions. According to the Evangelist Matthew, our Lord, on the morning of his resurrection, appeared to the women who visited his sepulchre, and said to them, 'All hail! Be not afraid: go tell my brethren that they go into Galilee, and there shall they see me.'

Then the eleven disciples went away into Galilee, into a mountain where Jesus had appointed them, and when they saw him they worshipped him. It was on that mountain, and to those worshipping disciples, that Jesus addressed the words of the text.

[1] Charles Hodge, *The Teaching Office of the Church: A Sermon by the Rev. Charles Hodge, D.D., Preached in the church on University Place, New York, on Sabbath evening, May 7, 1848, at the request of the Executive Committee of the Board of Foreign Missions of the Presbyterian Church* (reprinted from the *Missionary Chronicle*, June 1848).

If special interest and authority are due to any one communication of Christ more than to others, they must attach to words uttered under these peculiar circumstances. He had finished his work on earth; he had risen from the dead; he was on the eve of his final departure; he was now constituting his church; he was in the act of delivering its charter. He then and there gave his disciples their commission, prescribed their duties, and gave them the promise of his perpetual presence.

To whom is the commission given? What duty does it prescribe? How is that duty to be performed? What are the powers here conveyed? And what is the import of the promise here given? These are questions on which volumes have been written, and on whose solution the most momentous interests depend.

I propose to call your attention to only one of these questions, *viz.:* How is the duty prescribed in this commission to be performed? or how is the end here set before the church to be accomplished? We answer, by teaching.

I. *This appears in the first place from the nature of the end to be accomplished, and from the express words of the commission.* The command is to make disciples of all nations. A disciple, however, is both a follower and a learner. If the nations are to be made the disciples of Christ, they must know his doctrines and obey his commands. This is to be done by baptism and by teaching. The command is to make disciples of all nations by baptizing and teaching. These are, therefore, the two divinely appointe means for attaining the end contemplated.

Baptism, as a Christian ordinance, is a washing with water in the name of the Father, of the Son, and of the Holy Ghost. Its main idea is that of consecration. The person baptized takes God the Father to be his father, Jesus Christ his Son to be his Lord and Redeemer, and the Holy Ghost to be his sanctifier. That is, he accepts the covenant of grace and professes allegiance to his covenant God. Everyone therefore who is baptized becomes a disciple. He is enrolled among the professed children of God and worshippers of Christ.

Baptism, however, in the case of adults implies faith. It is in fact the public avowal of faith. And faith supposes knowledge. No man can take God to be his father unless he knows who God is. Nor can he take Christ to be his Redeemer unless he knows who Christ is and what he has done. Nor can he take the Holy Ghost to be his sanctifier unless acquainted with his person and office. Knowledge lies at the foundation of all religion, and therefore Christ has made it the great comprehensive duty of his church to teach. She does nothing unless she does this, and she accomplishes all other parts of her mission just in proportion as she fulfils this, her first and greatest duty.

II. *In the second place, the paramount importance of this duty appears from the kind of knowledge which is necessary to make men the true and worthy disciples of Christ.* It will not be denied that the church is bound to teach what God has revealed in his Word. If, then, we would understand the nature of the duty Christ has enjoined upon his church, we must consider that system of truth which he has commanded her to communicate to all nations. It comprehends a knowledge of the Being and attributes of God and of his relation to the world. These, however, are the profoundest themes of human thought; the most difficult subjects to be rightly comprehended, and yet absolutely essential to all true religion. The God, moreover, whom we are to make known, is revealed as the Father, Son, and Holy Spirit. He must be received and worshipped as such by every man who becomes a Christian. This cannot be done without knowledge, and this knowledge can only be communicated by teaching. Even in a Christian country it requires early and long-continued instruction to imbue the mind with any correct apprehension of the nature of God as he is revealed in the Bible. Among heathen nations the task must be an hundred fold more difficult. The pagan mind is prepossessed with false conceptions of the divine Being: the terms by which he is designated are all associated with degraded ideas of his nature. The very medium of instruction has to be created. A proposition which to our minds, and in our sense of the words employed, expresses truth, must of necessity convey error to the minds of those who attach a different meaning to the words we use. What is God to the mind of a heathen? What is law? What is sin? What is virtue? Not what we mean by these terms, but something altogether different. Without a miracle, correct knowledge can be communicated to such minds only by a long process of explanations or corrections. The heathen have a great deal to unlearn before they can learn anything aright.

Their minds must be emptied of the foul and deformed images with which they are filled, before it is possible that the forms of purity and truth can enter and dwell there.

The same remarks are applicable to what the Bible teaches concerning man; his origin, his apostasy, his present state, his future destiny. No man can be a Christian without a competent knowledge of these subjects. They are, however, subjects in themselves of great difficulty: the prepossessions of the heathen are opposed to the scriptural representations on these topics: all their previous opinions and convictions must be renounced, before the truth concerning the nature and condition of man can be communicated to their minds.

Again, to be Christians, men must understand the plan of salvation; they must know Jesus Christ, the constitution of his person, and the nature of his work; they must know how we are made partakers of the redemption purchased by Christ, and the nature and office of the Holy Spirit.

Again, to be Christians, men must know the law of God, that perfect rule of duty which unfolds the obligations which we owe to him as creatures, as sinners, and as the subjects of redemption. But the heathen, alas, have been taught to call evil good, and good evil, to put sweet for bitter, and bitter for sweet. Their moral perceptions are darkened and their moral sensibilities hardened; so that the acquisition of correct knowledge on their part of the pure law of God must be a tedious and gradual operation.

Such is a meagre outline of the knowledge which the church is bound to communicate, and without which the nations cannot be saved. We have no adequate conception of the magnitude or difficulty of the task. We forget that we have been slowly acquiring this knowledge all our lives; that our mothers gave us our first lessons in this divine science before we could speak; that from our infancy it has been constantly inculcated in the family, in the sanctuary, and in the school-room; that this heavenly light has always beamed around us and upon us from the Bible, from the institutions of the country, and from innumerable other sources. Can the heathen then learn it in a day? Because the English language is familiar to us, can it be taught to foreigners in an hour? If we undertake the work of making disciples of all nations, we ought to understand what it is we have to do. It is no work of miracle or magic. As far as we are concerned it is a sober, rational enterprise. We undertake to change the opinions and convictions of all the inhabitants of the world on the whole department of religious and moral truth, the widest domain of human knowledge. This is the work which Christ has assigned to his church. And it is to be accomplished by the ordinary process of teaching; not by inspiration, nor by miraculous interference of any kind. It is, indeed, a stupendous work, and no man can address himself to it in a proper spirit who does not so regard it. It would be comparatively a small matter to bring all nations to speak our language and to adopt the civil and social institutions of our country. Stupendous as is the work assigned us, we cannot flinch from it. It must be done, and we must do it.

There is another aspect of this subject which must not be overlooked. The system of truth of which we have spoken cannot be taught in abstract propositions, as though it were a mere philosophy. It must be taught by the church, just as God has taught it in his Word; in history, in types, in allegories, in prophecies, in psalms, in didactic assertions, in exhortations, warnings and precepts. No man can understand the truths of the Bible without understanding the Bible itself. He must know the history of the creation, of the fall and of God's dealings with his ancient people. He must be acquainted with the Mosaic institutions, and with the experience of the saints as recorded in the Psalms. He must know the history of Christ as predicted by the prophets and as recorded by the Evangelists. He must hear Christ's own words and read for himself what the apostles have delivered. If we teach Christianity, we must teach the Bible and the whole Bible. We must convey the truth to others in the very facts and forms in which God has communicated it to us. The two are absolutely inseparable; and woe to those who would attempt to divide them—who would undertake to tell men, in their own way and in their own forms, what they think the Bible means, by popular discourse or otherwise, instead of teaching the Bible itself. Let us then, Christian Brethren, calmly look our work distinctly in the face. The precise, definite task which Christ has enjoined upon his church is to teach the Bible, and the whole Bible, to every creature under heaven.

It never could have entered into the mind of any man that this work could be accomplished in any other way than by a regular process of education, were it not for some vague impression that the work of the Holy Spirit in some way supersedes the necessity of the ordinary methods of instruction. This is a fatal delusion. The Bible teaches us that the Spirit operates with and by the truth upon the hearts of men. As far as we know, either from Scripture or observation, he never operates on the minds of adults in any other way. The knowledge of the truth is therefore a preliminary condition to the experience of this divine influence. This knowledge the Spirit does not communicate. He has revealed it in the Word. It is the business of the church to make it known. The office of the church and that of the Spirit are therefore perfectly distinct. Both are necessary. Neither supersedes the other. The church teaches the truth; the Spirit gives that truth effect. He opens the mind to perceive the excellence of the things of God, he applies them to the conscience, he writes them upon the heart; but the truth must be known before it is thus effectually applied to the sanctification and salvation of the soul. It is therefore in perfect consistency with the doctrine of the Spirit's influence that we assert the absolute necessity of knowledge, and therefore of instruction.

III. *A third argument in support of the doctrine that the great duty of the church is to teach is drawn from the fact that the church from the beginning of the world has, by divine appointment, been an educational institute.* This is and ever has been her distinctive character. She is indeed an association for the worship of God and for the cure of souls, but she is peculiarly and distinctively an organization for maintaining and promoting the truth.

To the ancient church were committed the oracles of God, not only to be preserved and transmitted, but to be taught to the people. The whole ritual service was a mode of teaching. The morning and evening sacrifice was a daily lesson on sin and atonement. Every rite was the visible form of some religious truth. Every festival was a commemoration and a prophecy. The Sabbath was a perpetual annunciation of the creation of the world and of the Being of a personal God. There were thus daily, monthly, and yearly services all designed for the instruction of the people. The sabbatical year and the year of jubilee were prolonged periods for setting forth the great truths of morals and redemption. Besides all this there was a distinct order of men, one-twelfth of the whole population, set apart for this purpose. The priests were devoted to the service of the temple, the august school of God, and the Levites scattered over the whole land. Into this system the synagogues were incorporated, where the Scriptures were read and expounded to the people. It must also be borne in mind that the whole literature of the Hebrews was religious. Their only histories were the record of God's dealings with his church; their poetry was devotional or didactic; their fictions were divine parables; their orators, inspired prophets. We cannot conceive of a set of institutions better adapted to imbue a whole nation with religious knowledge than those ordained of God under the old dispensation.

Another very instructive fact, is this: when God designed to extend the offer of salvation beyond the limits of Judea he subjected the surrounding nations for three centuries to a course of preliminary education. Two hundred and eighty years before Christ the Scriptures, or at least the Pentateuch, were translated into Greek, the language of the civilized world. Jews were congregated in every city of the Roman empire. Synagogues were everywhere established, in which the true God was worshipped and his Word expounded. Hundreds and thousands of devout proselytes were gathered from among the heathen and instructed out of the law and the prophets, and taught to look for the salvation that was to come out of Zion. A broad foundation was thus silently and laboriously laid for the Christian church in every part of the civilized world. It was the special mission of the apostles to go over the Roman empire and, selecting those points where the ground had been thus previously prepared, to establish churches as centres of light to the surrounding regions. They always when they entered a city went first to the synagogue, and there endeavoured to convince the Jews and proselytes that Jesus was the Christ, and that there was no other name given under heaven whereby men must be saved. Sometimes the whole assembly, with their elders, believed and became a Christian church. At others only a portion embraced the gospel. Those the apostles separated and organized into a new church or Christian synagogue.

We are apt to forget all this, and to think the work of the apostles was analogous to that of our modern missionaries. It was, however, essentially different. The apostles preached in a great measure to the worshippers of Jehovah; to men whose hearts and consciences had been educated under his Word and institutions; to men who had comparatively little to unlearn, whose general views of the nature of religion were correct, and who were in earnest expectation of the salvation which the apostles preached, and with whom they could communicate in a competent language. We need not remark on the different character and condition of the people among whom the modern messengers of the gospel are called to labour; men whose minds are dark, degraded and inaccessible, having no ideas in common with us and no terms of correct religious import. Our missionaries have to do the long preparatory work, which the apostles found done to their hands. We should therefore commit a fatal error if we should infer from the itinerant character of the apostles' labours that our missionaries should pass in like manner from city to city, abiding only a few months at any one place. It would be most unreasonable to expect that this mode of operating would now be attended with a success analogous to that which followed similar labours of the apostles, under circumstances essentially different. The great fact however is undeniable and most instructive, that God did prepare the way for the apostles, by subjecting the population of the chief cities of the Roman empire, for nearly three centuries, to a preliminary process of religious culture.

As then God made the church under the old dispensation an educational institute, as he prepared the way for the dissemination of the gospel by previously causing Judaism to be extensively diffused, so also in the organization of the Christian church, he gave it a distinctive educational character. Christ appointed a set of men as teachers; he made provision for their being continued; he promised to be with them in all ages, and to give them by his Spirit the qualifications for their work. When the apostles went forth, it was in the character of teachers. They everywhere established churches, which were schools presided over by διδασκαλοι [*didaskaloi,* teachers]. Aptness to teach was made an essential requisite for the office of a presbyter. Ministers were commanded to give attendance to reading, to exhortation, to doctrine or instruction, that their profiting might appear unto all. In support of the doctrine that the great business of the church is to teach, that this is the divinely appointed means by which she is to make disciples, we appeal, therefore, not to this or that particular passage of Scripture, but to the whole design or organization of the church as laid down in the Word of God.

IV. What God has thus clearly taught in his Word, he has not less impressively taught by his providence. If the history of the church teaches any one lesson more distinctly than any other, it is that *just in proportion as she has been faithful as a teacher, she has been successful in promoting the Redeemer's kingdom; and just in proportion as she has failed in teaching, she has failed in everything pure and good.*

In proof of this point we appeal in the first instance to the contrast between the Romish and Protestant portions of Christendom. The characteristic difference between the popish and Protestant churches is that the former is a ritual and the latter a teaching church. In the former the minister is a priest, in the latter he is an instructor. The functions of the Romish priesthood are the offering of sacrifices, the administration of rites, and the absolution of penitents. Public worship in the Romish Church is conducted in a language which the people do not understand, and consists largely in ceremonies which they do not comprehend. The Scriptures are a sealed book among them, and the necessity of knowledge to faith or holiness is expressly denied. The consequence is that under a dread uniformity of outward show there is in the Romish Church a mass of ignorance, heresy, irreligion, superstition, immorality, such as probably never existed within the pale of any Christian communion on earth.

On the other hand, among Protestants the minister is a teacher. He leads indeed in the worship of the sanctuary and he administers the sacraments, but his great official business is to minister in word and doctrine. The sacraments in his hands are not magic rites, but methods of instruction, as well as seals of the covenant. It is in Protestant countries, accordingly, we find knowledge and religion in a far higher state than in any other portions of the world.

Again, if we compare different Protestant countries we shall find that religion flourishes uniformly and everywhere exactly in proportion as the church performs her duty as a teacher. In England, notwithstanding the abundant provision made for the support of the clergy, yet from the enormous extent of many of the parishes and from the predominance of the liturgical element in the constitution of the Established Church, a large part of the population has been left uninstructed, and, were it not for the exertions of other denominations, would be in a state little better than heathenism. In Scotland, on the other hand, religion is more generally diffused and has a stronger hold on the mass of the people than in any other country in the world. The reason is that the Church of Scotland has from the beginning been pre-eminently a teaching church. Notwithstanding the trammels of an establishment and patronage under which she has acted, she understood her vocation; she recognized her duty to teach the people, and the whole people, Christianity as a system of doctrines and duties, and she has therefore succeeded in making Scotland the most religious country in the world.

It matters not, however, where we look, wherever we find a teaching church there we find religion prosperous; and wherever we find a ritual, an indolent, or a ranting or merely declaiming church, there we find religion degenerated either into superstition or fanaticism.

As a final appeal on this subject we refer to the history of missions. There are only three methods by which Christianity has ever been established among heathen nations. The first is that adopted by the apostles, who established churches in various important places where the ground had been long under a process of preparatory culture, which churches became centres of radiation for the surrounding people. From such centres the gospel was extended in ever-widening circles, until their circumferences met and compassed the whole Roman world.

The second method is that in which, by force or fraud, a people has been brought to submit to Christian rites, and to an external compliance with the forms of Christian worship. Thus the Franks were converted under Clovis, and the Saxons under Charlemagne; and thus was Christianity introduced into Mexico and Peru, and by the Jesuits into Paraguay, China, and the Indies. The characteristic of this method is that it is conversion without instruction. It implies no change of opinions, no change of heart, no change of life. It is simply a change of name and external ceremonies. In some cases this nominal conversion is followed sooner or later by instruction, and a real reception of the gospel is the ultimate result. The Saxons, who long remained baptized heathen, are now the stamina of the Lutheran and Reformed churches. In other cases instruction does not follow, and then the consequence is that the people remain Christians only in name, or, when the external pressure is removed, they relapse into heathenism. The Indians of Mexico and Peru are no more Christians now than they were in the days of Cortes and Pizarro, and the once flourishing missions of the Jesuits, with their thousands and even millions of converts, have perished without leaving a trace behind them.

The third method of propagating the gospel is a process of education; that is, actually teaching the people, so that they come to know God and Jesus Christ his Son, and the way of salvation through him. Unless God works miracles, unless he subverts all the revealed or known methods of his operation, this is the only means by which the nations can be converted. This is the method which all Protestant churches have been forced to adopt, and it is the only one that has ever been successful. No instance can be produced of the establishment of the gospel in a heathen land by any other means. This was the course pursued by the faithful Moravians in Greenland, in the West Indies and in this country. They uniformly established permanent missions and laboriously taught the people. This was the method adopted by Eliot and Brainerd. To this mode of procedure, after many experiments and failures, the missionaries were obliged to resort in Tahiti, the Sandwich Islands, in India, and South Africa.

It is a very humble and self-denying work thus to teach the first principles of the oracles of God; it is a very slow process; there is no éclat about it; it is very trying to the faith of the missionaries and to the patience of the churches. But it is God's appointment. It is as much a law of his gracious dispensation that the minds of men must be imbued with the divine knowledge before the Spirit quickens them into life, as it is a law of his providence that the seed must first be properly deposited in the earth before, by his rain and sun, he calls forth the beautiful and bountiful harvest. No man expects to raise a crop of wheat by casting seed broadcast in swamps, forests and jungles; and just as little reason have we to expect a harvest of souls or the secure and permanent establishment of the gospel in heathen lands by any such short and easy method of disseminating truth. God will not depart from his wise ordinations to gratify either our ease or love of excitement. If we would bring our sheaves to his garner, we must go forth with tears and patient labour, bearing the precious seed of truth.

This is the true apostolic method. The apostles converted the world by teaching. They established churches at Jerusalem, at Antioch, at Ephesus, and at Rome, just as we are now labouring to establish churches at Lodiana, Furrukhabad, Agra, and Allahabad. The only difference is that the apostles found the ground cleared, broken up, and prepared for the reception of the seed, while our poor missionaries, with but a small portion of their strength or grace, have to go into the jungles and forests, and clear the ground as well as sow the seed. The same God, however, who wrought effectually in the apostles, is mighty in the weaker messengers whom he has sent to do this harder work. In both cases the excellency of the power is of God, and not of man. But do not let us add to all the other trials and discouragements of our missionaries the heavy burden of our impatience. Let us not forget that the work to be done is, of necessity, in its first stages a very slow work—that the harvest does not follow immediately after seed-time,

That teaching, then, is the great vocation of the church, that by no other means can she make disciples of all nations, is evident—1. From the express command of Christ, in the commission given to his disciples. 2. From the nature of that system of doctrines, the knowledge and cordial belief of which are essential to salvation. 3. From the nature, design, and constitution of the church, as revealed in the Scriptures; and, 4. From the whole history of the church, and especially from the whole history of missions.

It may, however, be asked, What is meant by teaching? What is this educational process which is so necessary to the propagation of the gospel? We answer, it is that process by which men are brought really to know what the Bible reveals. The end to be attained is the actual communication of this divine knowledge. There are, of course, different methods of instruction, some better adapted to one class of learners, and some to another; no one of which should be neglected.

The principal agencies which God has put into our hands for this purpose are the pulpit, the school-room, and the press. All these are employed in Christian countries, and all must be used among the heathen. The danger is, that a disproportionate importance be given to one of these methods of instruction to the neglect of the others. The great temptation is to overvalue the first. This arises from several sources.

1. In the first place, we are apt to attach to the word *preaching*, as used in the Bible, the sense which it now has in common life. We mean by preaching, the public and authoritative enunciation of the gospel; whereas, in the Bible, the word comprehends all methods of communicating divine truth. When Paul says, 'It pleased God, by the foolishness of preaching to save them that believe', he does not mean that the public oral proclamation of the gospel is the only method of saving sinners; but that God had determined to save men by the gospel, and not by the wisdom of this world. Human wisdom is entirely inadequate to that end, as the world by wisdom knew not God, and therefore God determined to save them by the gospel, which Paul calls the true or hidden wisdom. Any method by which that wisdom is communicated comes within the compass of that foolishness of preaching of which Paul speaks. The parent, the teacher, the author, are all preachers in the scriptural sense of the word, so far as they are engaged in holding forth the word of life. The power is in the truth, not in the channel or method of communication. It is this transferring to the Bible the modern restricted meaning of the word *preaching* which has led many good men to undervalue other methods of instruction. They suppose that all the Scriptures say about preaching is to be understood of the oral enunciation of the gospel, whereas it relates to the inculcation of divine truth, in any and all ways by which it can be conveyed to the human mind.

2. But secondly, we do not make due allowance for the difference between the state of the heathen and that of our own people. Because the majority of persons in a Christian land are prepared, in a good degree, to understand a public discourse, we are apt to take it for granted that this method of instruction is equally adapted to the heathen. A moment's reflection, however, is sufficient to correct this mistake. A certain degree of previous knowledge is requisite to enable

us to profit by public discourses; and we accordingly find, the world over, that the effect of public preaching is just in proportion to the previous religious training of the hearers.

3. In the third place, as we know from Scripture and experience that many single sentences of the Word of God contain truth enough to save the soul, and as the Spirit of God does sometimes make one such sentence fasten on the conscience, and from that single germ, by his inward teaching, evolves enough of the system of truth to enable the sinner to receive Christ, to the saving of the soul, it is very natural for us to be anxious to scatter the truth as rapidly and as widely as possible. And this is a good and sufficient reason why, even in heathen countries, the public proclamation of the gospel should never be neglected, but on the contrary, should be as assiduously employed as possible that some one grain, here and there, may take root and bring forth fruit. But no harvest is ever raised in that way. Neither has any heathen nation ever been converted by the itinerant proclamation of the gospel. To raise grain enough to feed our families or to sustain a nation, we must plough and harrow, as well as sow; and to save souls enough to found a church or convert a nation, we must slowly and labouriously indoctrinate the people in the knowledge of the Bible.

The mistake to which we have referred is one into which the missionaries themselves almost uniformly fall, at the beginning; and those new to the work are apt to think that their more experienced brethren rely too little on preaching, and too much on the slower method of instruction. A missionary from Ceylon told me that soon after his arrival in that field, he ventured to suggest his doubts on this subject to the oldest and certainly one of the ablest and most devoted of his brethren. That elder brother was then ill, lying on his bed, opposite an open window. He said to his doubting brother, 'From that window you can cast your eye over a number of villages, embowered in trees: as I lie here, I can in my mind go from house to house through all those villages, and tell you the names and character of every family. In a course of years I visited them so often, I so often conversed with them and preached to them, that I know them all, and know them intimately; yet I never saw my fruit from all that labour. Their minds were so darkened, their moral feelings so degraded, that the truth could gain no access, and made no impression. We were literally forced to adopt the method of regular teaching; and you see the result. A Christian nation is rising up around us.' Another missionary from the same field, who had been twenty-five years on the ground, expressed his firm conviction that if God would continue to bless their labours for the next five and twenty years as he had hitherto done, the whole Tamil people would be as thoroughly Christianized as any nation in Europe.

Let it, however, be distinctly understood that we advocate no exclusive method of instruction. The business of the church is to teach, and to teach in all the ways by which the truth of God can be conveyed to the understanding; but that work must be accomplished.

We have endeavoured to show that teaching is the great duty of the church, and how she ought to teach; the only other question is, What is she to teach? Is she to teach secular knowledge? The proper answer to this question undoubtedly is that the church is bound to teach the Bible; and other things, only so far as they are necessary or important to the right understanding of the Bible. This exception, however, covers the whole field of human knowledge. The Bible is a wonderful book. It brings everything within its sweep. Its truths radiate in every direction, and become implicated with all other truth, so that no form of knowledge—nothing which serves to illustrate the nature of God, the constitution of the universe, or the powers of the human soul—fails to do homage and render service to the book of God. We cannot teach the doctrines of creation and providence without teaching the true theory of the universe, and the proper office of the laws of nature; we cannot teach the laws of God without teaching moral philosophy; we cannot teach the doctrines of sin and regeneration without teaching the nature and faculties of the soul. Christianity, as the highest form of knowledge, comprehends all forms of truth.

Besides this, every false religion has underlying and sustaining it a false theory concerning God, concerning the world, and concerning the human soul. If you destroy these false theories, you destroy the religion. The Hindu religion cannot stand without the Hindu astronomy and cosmogony. Science undermines the pillars of heathenism, and frightens its votaries from its tottering walls. The native population of Calcutta is beginning to quake under the silent operation of

199

Dr Duff's school in that great city. They feel the ground trembling beneath their feet, and they are well aware if the truth in any form is taught, the whole system of error must soon crumble into dust. On the other hand, the true religion necessarily supposes a true theory concerning God, the universe, and the soul; so that you cannot teach the Bible without teaching what is commonly called human science. All knowledge comes from God, and leads to God. We must remember that ignorance is error, and not merely the absence of knowledge. The mind is never empty. If it has not right views, it has wrong views. If it has not right apprehensions concerning God, the universe, and itself, it has wrong ones. And all error is hostile to the truth. It is right, therefore, to pull up these noxious weeds, that the seeds of divine truth may the better take root and grow.

While, therefore, the church is mindful that her vocation is to teach the Bible, she cannot forget that the Bible is the friend of all truth, and the enemy of all error. The church is the light of the world. She has the right to subsidize all departments of knowledge, those principalities and powers, and force them to do homage to him to whom everything that has power must he made subservient. She has always acted under the consciousness that knowledge is her natural ally. She is the mother of all the universities of Europe. Harvard, Yale, Nassau Hall, and a numerous progeny besides, are all her children. She knows she is most effectually fulfilling her vocation, and honouring her divine Master, when she is most effectually bringing men to know him, to whom all knowledge bows and to whom all truth leads.

It is, Christian Brethren, an infelicity incident to the prominent exhibition of any one truth, that other not less important truths are, for the moment, cast into the shade. Because we have insisted on the importance of communicating a knowledge of the truth, it may seem as though we forget that the truth is powerless without the demonstration of the Spirit. Must we ever undulate between these two cardinal points? Because the Spirit alone can give the truth effect, must we do nothing? Or because the Spirit operates only with and by the truth, are we simply to teach, and forget our dependence upon God? Cannot we unite these two great doctrines in our faith and practice? Cannot we believe that it is the office of the church to teach, and the prerogative of the Spirit to give that teaching effect? Cannot we be at once diligent and dependent, doing all things commanded, and yet relying exclusively on the power of God for success? In his commission to his church, Christ says, 'Go teach, and, lo, I am with you always, to give your teaching effect.' Here, then, is at once our duty and our hope.

ARE THERE TOO MANY MINISTERS?[1]

U NTIL recently this question would have sounded strangely in the ears of Presbyterians. We have been accustomed to regard increase in the number of ministers as the evidence and index of the favour of God. To ask whether we had too many ministers was regarded as equivalent to asking whether we had too many converts, too many revivals, too much of a missionary spirit, too much benevolence, too much zeal for Christ's glory, or too much devotion to his service. Were we and our fathers wrong in this view of the matter? Since when have the harvest ceased to be great, and the labourers few? When and how has our Lord recalled his command, 'Pray ye the Lord of the harvest, that he would send forth labourers into his harvest'? We hardly know how to enter on the discussion of this subject; and yet we are told that there is an urgent necessity for it. We are assured, that not only among men of the world, not only among those who are habitually disposed to take low views of everything, or who stand aloof from all benevolent efforts, but among many of the best men of the church and the best friends of our boards, the impression is gaining ground, and often finds utterance, that we have too many ministers—that the supply is greater than the demand. It is very obvious that if this is true—if the supply of ministers is greater than we need—then it is the duty of the church to lessen the supply—to cease all efforts to increase the number of the preachers of the gospel. And it is no less obvious, that just in proportion as this conviction, whether well or ill-founded, spreads among the churches, will all effort to increase the number of ministers cease. It is very clear, therefore, that this is a vital subject, affecting the life of the church and her cherished institutions.

[1] Charles Hodge, 'Are there too many Ministers?' *Biblical Repertory and Princeton Review,* Vol. 34, No. 1 (1862), pp. 133-46.

We have said that the assertion that we have too many ministers, once sounded as strangely as the declaration that we had too many Christians, or too much piety. Whether the state of mind which led to regarding these things as equivalent, was right or scriptural, or whether the present impression which is said to be gaining prevalence in the church, that the number of our ministers is in fact too great, is reasonable and right, depends on the view taken of the nature and office of the church. If the church is a voluntary society in the sense in which the State is, or in which the army or navy within the State are, then the question whether its members or its officers are too many or too few, is a question of fact to be determined by prudential considerations. The citizens of a country may easily increase beyond the limits of comfortable support or profitable employment. The State would then be called upon to take measures to prevent such increase, and by emigration or otherwise, to remedy the evil. Still more frequently does it happen, that applicants for service in the army or navy are more numerous than the exigencies of the country demand. Then it becomes the duty of the authorities to stop all recruiting, and to refuse to make any new appointments. Now if men are disposed to regard the church in the light of a civil institution, it is to be dealt with on the same principles. If its converts become inconveniently numerous, we must stop preaching; or, if too many candidates for the ministry present themselves, we must refuse to receive them. This, however, is not the view which Presbyterians have been in the habit of taking of the church. And it is because the complaint that we have too many ministers betrays the influence (secret it may be) of this low theory over the minds and feelings of our brethren, that it has given rise to so much painful surprise.

In the Scriptures, in our own standards, and in the inmost convictions of God's people, the church is the body of Christ, filled and animated by his Spirit. Every man by his regeneration becomes united to that body as a living member. Every member has its place and its office, determined not by its own will, not by human appointment, but by the Spirit of God. To one he gives one gift, to another another, dividing to each one severally as he wills. 'We, being many', says the apostle, 'are one body in Christ, and every one members one of another. Having then gifts differing according to the grace that is

given to us, whether prophecy, let us prophesy according to the proportion of faith; or ministry, let us wait on our ministering; or he that
teacheth, on teaching; or he that exhorteth, on exhortation' (*Rom.*
12:5-8). If this be the true view of the matter, then the complaint that
we have too many ministers, terminates, not on the church, but on
the Holy Spirit. The church has nothing to do with it. It is not her
office to call men into the ministry. She can only sit in judgment on
the question, whether the candidate is really called of God. She puts
him upon trial; she examines into his experience, into his qualifications or gifts. If satisfied, she pronounces her judgment to that effect,
and thenceforth, until the contrary is made manifest, those whom
the church approves as called by the Spirit, are to be so regarded and
treated. Those who complain that we have too many ministers, know
not what they do. They can escape the guilt of charging the Spirit
with distributing his gifts unwisely or too profusely, only by denying that there is any divine call to the ministry. But this they cannot
do without denying the plain doctrine of God's Word, and the faith
of our own, and of every other Christian church. The candidate is
expressly asked in the ordination service of the Episcopal Church,
and impliedly in the inducting ceremonies and services of our own
and of all other churches, 'Do you believe that you are called of God
to take upon you this office?' If the candidate believes that he is thus
called, if the church is satisfied that he is neither a hypocrite nor a
self-deceiver; if he gives every scriptural evidence of being the subject
of this divine call, what shall we do? Shall we refuse to recognize
it? Shall we say that we have ministers enough? Shall we decline to
aid those thus called in preparing for the work to which God has
called them, or in sustaining them in their labours? No one would
dare consciously to take this ground. And yet this is the very ground
taken by those who complain that we have too many ministers. To
divest this complaint of its irreligious character, it must be directed
not against the number, but against the character of our ministers.
The only rational ground of complaint is, that the church introduces
into the ministry men who are not called of God. This may well be;
nay, it is impossible but that in some cases it must be; just as it is
impossible but that offences must come. The church is not infallible
in her judgment, and is not always faithful in the exercise of her

prerogative of judging. It is here, as in the admission of men to the full communion of the church. When a man is called of God into the kingdom of Christ, he has the right to come to the Lord's table, and it is the duty of the church to receive him. But it is not her duty to receive all who profess to be thus called, or who sincerely believe in their own vocation. It is the duty of the church to see that they have the qualifications for church fellowship laid down in the Word of God. In like manner, if any man is called by the Spirit to the work of the ministry, it is his right and duty to preach the gospel, and it is the duty of the church to aid him in preparing for his work, and to sustain him when he enters upon it. But it is not every one who professes or believes that he is called to be a minister, who is really called of God. And therefore it is the duty of the church carefully and faithfully to examine into the matter; to put him through a protracted trial, and be fully satisfied that he gives all the evidence of a divine vocation which she is authorized to demand. When she has done this, her responsibility ceases. Whether they be few or many whom God thus calls, she must joyfully receive, sustain, and encourage them, assured that if God calls men into his service he will find work for them to do.

The complaint, however, as we understand, is not that our presbyteries have become of late more remiss than formerly, in the discharge of their important and responsible duty in this matter, nor that the character of our ministers and candidates has deteriorated, giving evidence that the church is, so to speak, in advance of God's Spirit, receiving more candidates for the ministry than the Spirit calls to that work. Of any such charge we bear no intimation, and we believe that there is no ground for it. It must of course be admitted, that as unworthy members are received to the fellowship of the church, so unworthy men are sometimes admitted to the ministry. This is an evil against which no human foresight or fidelity can effectually guard. But we presume that no intelligent person will venture to assert, that the character of our church membership, or of our ministers and candidates, is lower now than it was twenty or thirty years ago. So far from this being the case, we believe that on an average the character of both our membership and ministry is higher now than it ever was. So far at least as we have the opportunity or ability to judge, we can confidently say, that the candidates for the ministry are now, and for some years past have been, of higher promise as to their spirit, piety, and general qualifications, than at any former period. We cannot see, therefore, that the complaint that we have too many ministers can be seriously entertained by any who believe that the Spirit of God, and not presbyteries, is the author of the call to the sacred office. It is our duty to hail the increase in the number of those whom the Spirit thus calls, with the same grateful joy with which we would hail any other manifestation of the Spirit's presence.

It may be said, however, that this is all theory, that there is no reasoning against facts, and the fact is that we have more good ministers and good candidates than we need, or than can find profitable employment. If this be so, it is something which never happened before since the world began. The clearest possible evidence should be demanded, to satisfy any Christian man that the Holy Spirit calls more men to the ministry than there is any necessity for. What is the evidence relied upon to sustain this extraordinary assertion? So far as we have heard, the evidence consists of two particulars; first, that many of our candidates after licensure are unable to find suitable fields of labour; and second, that when a vacancy occurs in any self-sustaining church, there is always a crowd of applicants for the situation. The former of these allegations is easily disposed of. The fact assumed is not true to any extent justifying the allegation. The graduates of our theological seminaries are generally settled in the ministry, or profitably employed in the service of the church, within a few months after leaving their respective institutions. It was publicly asserted months ago that every student who left the Western Seminary at Allegheny last spring, was already a settled pastor; and of the sixty recent graduates of Princeton, we are informed, that there are not ten who remain unemployed, excepting such as are still pursuing their studies or preparing for the foreign field. If, however, the graduates of our seminaries did remain unsettled to a much greater extent than is actually the case, this would not prove that the Spirit calls too many men into the ministry. This is the very last hypothesis to which we ought to resort to explain the fact. It may arise from the peculiar and transient state of the country; from the want of proper guidance, or the deficiency of energy, or tact, or of popular talents on the part of the candidates. It is far from being true that the best and most useful men are the soonest called. Showy, superficial gifts, often secure attention when those of higher value remain for a while unnoticed. But suppose it should be admitted that five or ten per cent of our candidates for the ministry are failures; that that proportion of their number are either unworthy, or deceived as to their call; may not the same be said of our church members? Must we then close our churches? Must we refuse to send into the harvest ninety men, really called of God, because ten men join them who are not called? No enlightened Christian conscience could justify such a course. We must do the best we can to sift the tares from the wheat, but let us not throw away the wheat; let us not refuse to receive those whom God really calls, for fear we shall receive some whom he has not called. We are bound to receive the former, and to do what we can to avoid receiving the latter. The rest belongs to God.

The great argument, however, relied upon to prove that we have too many ministers, is that there are on our list some three hundred without charge, and that whenever any vacancy occurs in a self-supporting congregation there is a crowd of applicants for the post. Of these three hundred ministers without charge, we are not told how many are disqualified by age or infirmity for active duty; how many are voluntarily engaged in other pursuits; how many have mistaken their calling and have not the gift of preaching, If proper deductions were made from this class, the number would probably be greatly reduced. We do not believe there are one hundred Presbyterian ministers, qualified and willing to preach the gospel, who are unemployed. That there are numerous applicants for every desirable vacant church is indeed true. But this only proves that there are comparatively few congregations in this region able or willing to give a minister an adequate support. There might be only a dozen such congregations in the State of Pennsylvania, and yet a million of her population be destitute of the means of grace. Would this prove that thirteen ministers were too many for Pennsylvania? Does the fact that there is not one self-supporting church in all Africa prove that its teeming thousands need no missionaries? According to the moral statistics from great cities, not one half of the people are supplied with the stated ministrations of the gospel. Every unemployed minister in our church could find abundant employment in any one of these great centres of our population. If from one fourth to one half of the people of every State in this Union are not living without the stated ministration of the gospel, then our statistics are greatly at fault, and then is our country far better off in this respect than most other Christian nations. According to the most reliable information furnished to the public, there are some six millions of people in the United States who are under no pastoral care. We are commanded to preach the gospel to every one of those millions. Their blood will be required at our hands if we fail to do it. Yet we are told that we have too many ministers! Common sense and common honesty, it is said, forbid the increase of the number of preachers. The churches are exhorted to refuse to sustain any more candidates, to stop the supplies of our Board of Education, and to turn our theological seminaries into manufactories and arsenals. We have nothing to say to this. Giving is a matter of free will. The church has no right to constrain its members to contribute to any particular object. Each man must exercise his own judgment and his own choice. To his own Master he stands or falls. God does not beg any man to give. He only permits it. The Bible leaves everyone perfectly sovereign in the disposition of his money. He may spend it wisely and liberally for the glory of God, or he may keep it all and carry it with him to the judgment, and say, Here, Lord, is thy talent. His fellow men have no right to prescribe or to control in this matter. The churches, therefore, need have no fear of being pestered, much less disciplined, into giving to any cause which their reason and conscience do not approve. It is, however, a duty to disabuse the minds of the brethren, and not permit them to be deceived, or to deceive themselves as to what the true interests of the Saviour's kingdom demands.

Even if we confine our attention to our own denomination, the want of ministers is deplorably great. According to the Minutes of the Assembly of 1861, the number of our churches exceeds that of our ministers by nine hundred and seventeen. Deducting, on the one hand, from the number of congregations, those who are united under one minister, and on the other, from the whole number of ministers reported, those who are disabled, or engaged in other departments of labour at home or abroad, we have still such a deficiency, 'that if every available minister in our church were settled in a pastoral charge, there would remain from eight hundred to one thousand churches for which there would not be a single minister'. We make this statement, in full confidence of its correctness, from data furnished from the office of one of our boards in Philadelphia. This, however, is not all: we learn from the same source, that although the last decade has been the most active and successful in the operations of the Board of Education, yet, so far from keeping up the supply of ministers, we have fewer preachers now, in proportion to our membership, than we had ten years ago! One half of our ministers now in the service of the church have been aided by the Board of Education, whose operations it is proposed to suspend. What would have been our position as a church had the views now advanced been acted upon in 1851? Would we now exhibit the condition of one of the most efficient and honoured ecclesiastical bodies on the face of the earth, or one of the most inefficient and dishonoured? This question admits of but one answer; and it requires no spirit of prophecy to predict what will be our condition ten years hence, if these new views are to control our action. Should God withdraw from our young men his Spirit, so that few or none should be called to the ministry, or from the churches the gift of Christian liberality in their support, we have little reason to hope for other manifestations of his presence. Where the Spirit dwells, he dwells in the plenitude and harmony of his gifts. If he gives a man faith, he gives him repentance; if he gives a church zeal and spirituality, he will give to her children the grace to preach the unsearchable riches of Christ.

There is another consideration which cannot be overlooked. The average number of deaths among our ministers can be hardly less than fifty annually. In 1855 it was forty-eight; in the year 1856 and '57 it was forty-six. To this must be added the number annually rendered unfit for active service by old age or sickness. Those causes cannot deduct annually less than sixty ministers from the number of our working clergy. For the last ten years, the average number of graduates from our two largest and oldest seminaries, Princeton and Allegheny, has hardly amounted to that number; those seminaries, therefore, can barely supply the yearly loss of ministerial strength, leaving it to the other institutions to make provision for the demands of a population which nearly doubles itself every twenty years.

Hitherto we have not raised our eyes from the ground. We have been looking at our feet, and at what lies immediately around them. The commission of Christ to our church is not, Preach the gospel to the thirty millions of Americans, but to every creature under heaven. Preach the gospel to the thousand millions of your dying fellow men, and, lo, I am with you always; with you, to endue your sons with the gifts of preaching, and you with the grace to aid and sustain them. To this we answer, Stay thy hand, O Lord, we have already more preachers than we know what to do with. What! more than enough for the thirty millions of your countrymen, and for the thousand millions of your fellow sinners! Then, stand aside; I will give my gifts to those who are not so easily satisfied. May God in mercy preserve our church from such reprobation!

The brethren who complain that we have too many ministers, have their eye on a real and portentous evil of our system; but they fatally mistake as to its cause. It is not that we have too many ministers, but that inadequate means are provided for their support. This they acknowledge by contradicting themselves. They tell us, and tell us truly, that there are heathen enough in our cities to give full employment to every minister without charge in our church—and yet they say we have more than we need! That is, the cities would absorb our whole supply, and leave all the other abounding desolations of the land unsupplied. By their own showing, therefore, we have not a tenth part of the number of ministers we need; what we lack is adequate means of supporting them. The reason why so many applicants are found for the vacant pulpits of self-supporting churches, is not that we have too many ministers, but that it is so hard for them to find means of supporting themselves and their families. This support they are entitled to by the laws of justice and by the express ordinance of Christ. Read the apostle's argument and revelations on this subject in 1 Corinthians 9. 'Who goeth to war on his own charge?' he asks; 'who planteth a vineyard, and eateth not of the fruit thereof? or who feedeth a flock, and eateth not of the milk of the flock?' Is this merely a human usage? Does not the law recognize the same principle even in its application to brutes, when it says, 'Thou shalt not muzzle the ox that treadeth out the corn'? What human and divine law thus recognize as right, has its foundation in simple justice; 'for if we have sown unto you spiritual things, is it a great thing if we shall reap your carnal things?' Under the old dispensation, by divine command, they who ministered about holy things, lived of the things of the temple; 'even so', he adds, 'hath the Lord ordained that they who preach the gospel should live of the gospel.' On this point there can be no dispute. If, therefore, there are well qualified ministers unemployed, it must be either because they are unwilling to labour, which is neither asserted nor believed, or because they have not the means of support. If the latter, whose fault is it? Can the church complain that we have too many ministers, when there are thousands and millions of our fellow men perishing for lack of knowledge, if she fails in providing the means of sustaining them in the field? Here is the difficulty; and it is inherent in our system. We almost tremble while we write the sentence; but does not truth demand that it should be written? The Presbyterian Church is not a church for preaching the gospel to the poor. She has precluded herself from that high vocation by adopting the principle that the support of the minister must be derived from the people to whom he preaches. If, therefore, the people are too few, too sparse, too poor, to sustain a minister, or too ignorant or wicked to appreciate the gospel, they must go without it. We have attempted to obviate this evil by aiding feeble congregations through the Board of Domestic Missions, and great good has been thus accomplished. But, 1st, this leaves the principle untouched. It is the object of the board to aid, in the main, those churches which promise to become self-supporting. People living where congregations cannot be formed, or who fail to reach the self-sustaining standard, are either not reached, or are sooner or later dropped. 2nd. The scale on which the limited resources of our board force its officers to dispense their contributions, is far below the reasonable and righteous demands of the ministry. The families of our home missionaries are kept but little above the starvation point; therefore it is, that while the field is white for the harvest, ministers with families dependent upon them hesitate to enter into the harvest. If the church will not support them, how can they go? Do we refuse to send missionaries to the heathen until the heathen are willing and able to support them? If not, why should we refuse to sustain those whom we send to our own people?

Our system, which requires the minister to rely for his support on the people to whom he preaches, has had the following inevitable results:—

1. In our cities we have no churches to which the poor can freely go, and feel themselves at home. No doubt, in many of our city congregations there are places in the galleries, in which the poor may find seats free of charge, but, as a general thing, the churches are private property. They belong to those who build them, or who purchase or rent the pews after they are built. They are intended and adapted for the cultivated and thriving classes of the community. There may be exceptions to this remark, but we are speaking of a general fact. The mass of the poor in our cities are excluded from our churches. The Presbyterian Church is practically, in such places, the church for the upper classes (we do not mean the worldly and the fashionable) of society.

2. In large districts of the country—as in the pines of New Jersey, for example—where the people are poor and widely dispersed, we can have no churches. So far as we are concerned, such districts are left entirely deserted.

3. Hundreds of our best and most laborious ministers, settled over new or feeble congregations, are subjected to the greatest privations and trials; often unable to provide for the support of their families, or the education of their children.

4. Many such ministers, unable to sustain themselves, are constrained to engage in secular pursuits, and to devote more or less of their time to making money; others give up in despair, resign their charges, and wait and look for some vacant church able to support them—hence the number of applications for every such vacancy.

5. Our present system interferes with the progress and efficiency of the church. It can go only where there are people who are rich and good enough to support the gospel for themselves. On this plan, it is almost impossible that we should adequately fulfil our duty to preach the gospel to every creature.

On the other hand, the system which secures an adequate support of the minister, independent of the people whom he immediately serves, has the precisely opposite effects.

1. The churches are common property. They do not belong to individuals who build or rent them. They belong to the people. The

high and low, the rich and poor, have a common and equal right to them, as they have to the common highway. They resort to the one with the same freedom with which they walk on the other. The consequence is, that there are few or no class churches, none from which, by force of circumstances, the poor are excluded. Anyone who has visited Europe must have been struck with this fact. Not only in Catholic, but also in Protestant countries, the places of worship are seen crowded with a promiscuous throng—the peasant, the student, the professor, the merchant, the noble, unite in one worshipping assembly. This is a right of which the poor avail themselves freely, and the gospel, or at least the benefits of public worship, are as open to them as to any class in the community.

2. Ministers can be sent and sustained among people unwilling or unable to support a religious teacher for themselves.

3. It is rare where this system prevails to see ministers engaged in any secular pursuits.

In countries where the church and State are united, the support of the clergy is provided for, in some cases, as in England and Scotland, by a system of tithes, in others, by endowments, in others by stipends from the government, and in others, as formerly in New England, by a tax on property for the support of public worship, just as the free schools are now supported. Where the church is independent of the State, and acts on the voluntary principle, one plan is adopted by the Free Church of Scotland, another by the Methodists, both here and in Europe. The question now under consideration, is not how this should be done in our case, but rather the importance of, in some way, accomplishing the object. As long since as July 1847, this subject was discussed in the pages of this journal. The two principles insisted upon are, first, that every minister devoted exclusively to his work is entitled to a competent support; and, secondly, that the obligation to provide that support does not rest exclusively on the people to whom he ministers, but upon the church at large. As to the way in which duty can be best discharged, opinions may differ. The main point, however, is to secure the general and cordial recognition of the duty itself. In some of our cities it may be expedient to erect churches and provide an endowment for the pastor, or secure his support by outside contributions. In others, it may be wise to have district missionaries sustained as are ministers in our seamen's chapels. But, as it seems to us, the most feasible plan is simply to enlarge the resources of the Board of Domestic Missions, so as to enable them to give an adequate support to those aided by its funds. To accomplish this the plan adopted by the Free Church of Scotland might be found as available here as it has proved there.

The proposition to provide an adequate support for the clergy, independent of their congregations, righteous and scriptural as it appears to us, met with strenuous opposition, not only on the ground of the expense which it would involve, but on the assumption, that if ministers are secure of a support independent of their people, they will neglect their work. To this we answer,

1. That it supposes that ministers have no higher motive of action than the desire to get money out of their people. If the love of money governs the ministry of our church, they are a very silly set of men. There is not one in ten of them who could not secure that object in some other way more effectually than by preaching the gospel.

2. It is not found that the teachers of our free academies and schools, whose salaries are not dependent on the favour of the parents of their pupils, neglect their work. These teachers are not constrained by higher motives than ministers, nor are they held to a stricter responsibility.

3. Our foreign missionaries have a support independent of the people among whom they labour. And yet, as a body, they are as faithful, diligent, and successful, to say the least, as any other equal number of our clergy.

4. This is no new plan, it has been acted on for centuries. Whatever may be said of the orthodoxy or spirituality of the stipendiary clergy of Prussia, for example, they are as hard-working a class of men as any to be found in this country. They not only conduct public worship on Sundays and festivals, but they must attend to the sick, and to the burial of the dead, and devote certain hours every week to the religious instruction of the young in the public schools. Every child in Prussia, male or female, passes through a course of religious training by the clergy, and you cannot find a barefooted boy in the streets of Berlin, who cannot read and write, and give an intelligible account of the historical facts of the Bible, and, if approaching the

age of fourteen, who cannot repeat the Creed, the Lord's Prayer, and Luther's Catechism. These results imply an amount of faithful and systematic labour, which the plan of making the clergy dependent on their own people has never yet secured.

We are not concerned about the way, if only the end be secured. Let the church remember that her field is the world, that she is bound gratefully to receive, and, if need be, to educate, every young man whom the Holy Spirit mercifully calls to preach the gospel, and then to sustain him in that great work. Let those who feel for unemployed ministers not raise the standard of rebellion against God, nor reject the proffered gifts of the Spirit, nor strive to impede the progress of the church, but devote their energy to enable her to carry into effect the ordinance of Christ, that they who preach the gospel shall live by the gospel. Then, should we have too many ministers, the proper remedy will be the deposition of those who refuse to work, and not arresting the increase of faithful labourers.

WHAT IS PRESBYTERIANISM?[1]

B RETHREN:—We are assembled this evening as a Presbyterian Historical Society. It has occurred to me that it would not
be inappropriate to discuss the question, What is Presbyterianism? You will not expect from me an oration. My object is neither
conviction nor persuasion; but exposition. I propose to occupy the
hour devoted to this address in an attempt to unfold the principles
of that system of church polity which we, as Presbyterians, hold to be
laid down in the Word of God.

Setting aside Erastianism, which teaches that the church is only
one form of the State; and Quakerism, which does not provide for
the external organization of the church, there are only four radically
different theories on the subject of church polity.

1. The Popish theory, which assumes that Christ, the apostles and
believers, constituted the church while our Saviour was on earth, and
this organization was designed to be perpetual. After the ascension
of our Lord, Peter became his vicar, and took his place as the visible
head of the church. This primacy of Peter, as the universal bishop, is
continued in his successors, the bishops of Rome; and the apostleship
is perpetuated in the order of prelates. As in the Primitive Church,
no one could be an apostle who was not subject to Christ, so now
no one can be a prelate who is not subject to the Pope. And as then
no one could be a Christian who was not subject to Christ and the
apostles, so now no one can be a Christian who is not subject to the
Pope and the prelates. This is the Romish theory of the church. A
vicar of Christ, a perpetual college of apostles, and the people subject
to their infallible control.

[1] Charles Hodge, *What is Presbyterianism? An Address Delivered Before the Presbyterian Historical Society at their Anniversary Meeting in Philadelphia, on Tuesday evening, May 1, 1855* (Philadelphia: Presbyterian Board of Publication, 1855).

2. The Prelatical theory assumes the perpetuity of the apostle-ship as the governing power in the church, which therefore consists of those who profess the true religion, and are subject to apostle-bishops. This is the Anglican or High-Church form of this theory. In its Low-Church form, the Prelatical theory simply teaches that there was originally a three-fold order in the ministry, and that there should be now. But it does not affirm that mode of organization to be essential.

3. The Independent or Congregational theory includes two principles; first, that the governing and executive power in the church is in the brotherhood; and secondly, that the church organization is complete in each worshipping assembly, which is independent of every other.

4. The fourth theory is the Presbyterian, which it is our present business to attempt to unfold. The three great negations of Presbyterianism—that is, the three great errors which it denies are— 1. That all church power vests in the clergy. 2. That the apostolic office is perpetual. 3. That each individual Christian congregation is independent. The affirmative statement of these principles is—1. That the people have a right to a substantive part in the government of the church. 2. That presbyters, who minister in word and doctrine, are the highest permanent officers of the church, and all belong to the same order. 3. That the outward and visible church is, or should be, one, in the sense that a smaller part is subject to a larger, and a larger to the whole. It is not holding one of these principles that makes a man a Presbyterian, but his holding them all.

I. *The first of these principles relates to the power and rights of the people.* As to the nature of church power, it is to be remembered that the church is a theocracy. Jesus Christ is its head. All power is derived from him. His Word is our written constitution. All church power is, therefore, properly ministerial and administrative. Everything is to be done in the name of Christ, and in accordance with his directions. The church, however, is a self-governing society, distinct from the State, having its officers and laws, and, therefore, an administrative government of its own. The power of the church relates, 1. To matters of doctrine. She has the right to set forth a public declaration of the truths which she believes, and which are to be acknowledged by all who enter her communion. That is, she has the right to frame creeds or confessions of faith, as her testimony for the truth, and her protest against error. And as she has been commissioned to teach all nations, she has the right of selecting teachers, of judging of their fitness, of ordaining and sending them forth into the field, and of recalling and deposing them when unfaithful. 2. The church has power to set down rules for the ordering of public worship. 3. She has power to make rules for her own government; such as every church has in its Book of Discipline, Constitution, or Canons, *etc.* 4. She has power to receive into fellowship, and to exclude the unworthy from her own communion.

Now, the question is, Where does this power vest? Does it, as Romanists and Prelatists affirm, belong exclusively to the clergy? Have they the right to determine for the church what she is to believe, what she is to profess, what she is to do, and whom she is to receive as members, and whom she is to reject? Or does this power vest in the church itself—that is, in the whole body of the faithful? This, it will be perceived, is a radical question—one which touches the essence of things, and determines the destiny of men. If all church power vests in the clergy, then the people are practically bound to passive obedience in all matters of faith and practice; for all right of private judgment is then denied. If it vests in the whole church, then the people have a right to a substantive part in the decision of all questions relating to doctrine, worship, order, and discipline. The public assertion of this right of the people, at the time of the Reformation, roused all Europe. It was an apocalyptic trumpet, *i.e.,* a trumpet of revelation, *tuba per sepulchra sonans,* calling dead souls to life; awakening them to the consciousness of power and of right; of power conveying right, and imposing the obligation to assert and exercise it. This was the end of church tyranny in all truly Protestant countries. It was the end of the theory that the people were bound to passive submission in matters of faith and practice. It was deliverance to the captive, the opening of the prison to those who were bound; the introduction of the people of God into the liberty wherewith Christ has made them free. This is the reason why civil liberty follows religious liberty. The theory that all church power vests in a divinely constituted hierarchy, begets the theory that all civil power vests, of divine right, in kings and nobles. And the theory that church power vests in the church itself, and all church officers are servants of the church, of necessity begets the theory that civil power vests in the people, and that civil magistrates are servants of the people. These theories God has joined together, and no man can put them asunder. It was, therefore, by an infallible instinct, the unfortunate Charles of England said, 'No bishop, no king'; by which he meant, that if there is no despotic power in the church, there can be no despotic power in the State; or, if there be liberty in the church, there will be liberty in the State.

But this great Protestant and Presbyterian principle is not only a principle of liberty, it is also a principle of order. 1st. Because this power of the people is subject to the infallible authority of the Word; and 2nd. Because the exercise of it is in the bands of duly constituted officers. Presbyterianism does not dissolve the bands of authority, and resolve the church into a mob. Though delivered from the autocratic authority of the hierarchy, it remains under the law to Christ. It is restricted in the exercise of its power by the Word of God, which bends the reason, heart, and conscience. We only cease to be the servants of men, that we may be the servants of God. We are raised into a higher sphere, where perfect liberty is merged in absolute subjection. As the church is the aggregate of believers, there is an intimate analogy between the experience of the individual believer, and of the church as a whole. The believer ceases to be the servant of sin, that he may be the servant of righteousness; he is redeemed from the law, that he may be the servant of Christ. So the church is delivered from an illegitimate authority, not that she may be lawless, but subject to an authority legitimate and divine. The Reformers, therefore, as instruments in the hands of God, in delivering the church from bondage to prelates, did not make it a tumultuous multitude, in which every man was a law to himself, free to believe, and free to do what he pleased. The church, in all the exercise of her power, in reference either to doctrine or discipline, acts under the written law of God, as recorded in his Word.

But besides this, the power of the church is not only thus limited and guided by the Scriptures, but the exercise of it is in the hands of legitimate officers. The church is not a vast democracy, where everything is decided by the popular voice. 'God is not the author of confusion, but of peace, (*i.e.,* of order) as in all churches of the saints.' The Westminster Confession, therefore, expressing the common sentiment of Presbyterians, says:—'The Lord Jesus Christ, as King and Head of his Church, hath therein appointed a government in the hands of Church officers, distinct from the civil magistrate.' The doctrine that all civil power vests ultimately in the people, is not inconsistent with the doctrine that that power is in the hands of legitimate officers, legislative, judicial, and executive, to be exercised by them according to law. Nor is it inconsistent with the doctrine that the authority of the civil magistrate is *jure divino.* So the doctrine that church power vests in the church itself, is not inconsistent with the doctrine that there is a divinely appointed class of officers, through whom that power is to be exercised. It thus appears that the principle of liberty and the principle of order are perfectly harmonious. In denying that all church power vests exclusively in the clergy, whom the people have nothing to do but to believe and to obey, and in affirming that it vests in the church itself, while we assert the great principle of Christian liberty, we assert the no less important principle of evangelical order.

It is not necessary to occupy your time in quoting either from the Reformed Confessions or from standard Presbyterian writers, that the principle just stated is one of the radical principles of our system. It is enough to advert to the recognition of it involved in the office of ruling elder.

Ruling elders are declared to be the representatives of the people. They are chosen by them to act in their name in the government of the church. The functions of these elders, therefore, determine the power of the people; for a representative is one chosen by others to do in their name what they are entitled to do in their own persons; or rather to exercise the powers which radically inhere in those for whom they act. The members of a State legislature, or of Congress, for example, can exercise only those powers which are inherent in the people.

The powers, therefore, exercised by our ruling elders, are powers which belong to the lay members of the church. What then are the powers of our ruling elders? 1. As to matters of doctrine and the great office of teaching, they have an equal voice with the clergy in the formation and adoption of all symbols of faith. According to Presbyterianism, it is not competent for the clergy to frame and authoritatively set forth a creed to be embraced by the church, and to be made a condition of either ministerial or Christian communion, without the consent of the people. Such creeds profess to express the mind of the church. But the ministry are not the church, and, therefore, cannot declare the faith of the church, without the cooperation of the church itself. Such confessions, at the time of the Reformation, proceeded from the whole church. And all the confessions now in authority in the different branches of the great Presbyterian family, were adopted by the people through their representatives, as the expression of their faith. So, too, in the selection of preachers of the Word, in judging of their fitness for the sacred office, in deciding whether they shall be ordained, in judging them when arraigned for heresy, the people have, in fact, an equal vote with the clergy.[1]

2. The same thing is true as to the *jus liturgicum,* as it is called, of the church. The ministry cannot frame a ritual, or liturgy, or directory for public worship, and enjoin its use on the people to whom they preach. All such regulations are of force only so far as the people themselves, in conjunction with their ministers, see fit to sanction and adopt them.

3. So too, in forming a constitution, or in enacting rules of procedure, or making canons, the people do not merely passively assent, but actively co-operate. They have, in all these matters, the same authority as the clergy.

4. And finally, in the exercise of the power of the keys, in opening and shutting the door of the communion with the church, the people have a decisive voice. In all cases of discipline, they are called upon to judge and to decide.

There can, therefore, be no doubt that Presbyterians do carry out the principle that church power vests in the church itself, and that the people have a right to a substantive part in its discipline and government. In other words, we do not hold that all power vests in the clergy, and that the people have only to listen and obey.

But is this a scriptural principle? Is it a matter of concession and courtesy, or is it a matter of divine right? Is our office of ruling elder

---

[1] This point is argued at length by Turrettin, in his chapter, *De Jure Vocaiionis.* He proves that the right to call and appoint ministers belongs to the whole church.

only one of expediency, or is it an essential element of our system, arising out of the very nature of the church as constituted by God, and, therefore, of divine authority?

This, in the last resort, is, after all, only the question, Whether the clergy are the church, or whether the people are the church. If, as Louis XIV said of France, 'I am the State', the clergy can say, 'We are the church', then all church power vests in them, as all civil power vested in the French monarch. But if the people are the State, civil power vests in them; and if the people are the church, power vests in the people. If the clergy are priests and mediators, the channel of all divine communications, and the only medium of access to God, then all power is in their hands; but if all believers are priests and kings, then they have something more to do than merely passively to submit. So abhorrent is this idea of the clergy being the church to the consciousness of Christians, that no definition of the church for the first fifteen centuries after Christ, was ever framed that even mentioned the clergy. This is said to have been first done by Canisius and Bellarmine.[1] Romanists define the church to be 'those who profess the true religion, and are subject to the Pope'. Anglicans define it as 'those who profess the true religion, and are subject to prelates'. The Westminster Confession defines the visible church, 'Those who profess the true religion, together with their children.' In every Protestant symbol, Lutheran or Reformed, the church is said to be the company of faithful men. Now, as a definition is the statement of the essential attributes or characteristics of a subject; and as, by the common consent of Protestants, the definition of the church is complete without even mentioning the clergy, it is evidently the renunciation of the radical principles of Protestantism, and, of course, of Presbyterianism, to maintain that all church power vests in the clergy. The first argument, therefore, in support of the doctrine that the people have a right to a substantive part in the government of the church is derived from the fact that they, according to the Scriptures and all Protestant confessions, constitute the church.

2. A second argument is this. All church power arises from the indwelling of the Spirit; therefore those in whom the Spirit dwells are

[1] Sherlock on the Nature of the Church, p. 36.

the seat of church power. But the Spirit dwells in the whole church, and therefore the whole church is the seat of church power.

The first member of this syllogism is not disputed. The ground on which Romanists hold that church power vests in the bishops, to the exclusion of the people, is that they hold that the Spirit was promised and given to the bishops as a class. When Christ breathed on his disciples, and said, 'Receive ye the Holy Ghost; whose soever sins ye remit, they are remitted unto them; and whose soever sins ye retain, they are retained'; and when he said, 'Whatsoever ye shall bind on earth shall be bound in heaven; and whatsoever ye shall loose on earth shall be loosed in heaven'; and when he further said, 'He that heareth you heareth me; and lo, I am with you alway, even to the end of the world'; they hold that he gave the Holy Ghost to the apostles and to their successors in the apostleship, to continue unto the end of the world, to guide them into the knowledge of the truth, and to constitute them the authoritative teachers and rulers of the church. If this is true, then, of course, all church power vests in these apostle-bishops. But on the other hand, if it is true that the Spirit dwells in the whole church; if he guides the people as well as the clergy into the knowledge of the truth; if he animates the whole body, and makes it the representative of Christ on earth, so that they who hear the church hear Christ, and so that what the church binds on earth is bound in heaven, then, of course, church power vests in the church itself, and not exclusively in the clergy.[1]

If there be anything plain from the whole tenor of the New Testament, and from innumerable explicit declarations of the Word of God, it is that the Spirit dwells in the whole body of Christ; that he guides all his people into the knowledge of the truth; that every believer is taught of God, and has the witness in himself, and has no need that any should teach him, but the anointing which abideth in him teacheth him all things. It is, therefore, the teaching of the church, and not of the clergy exclusively, which is ministerially the teaching of the Spirit, and the judgment of the church, which is the

---

[1] 'For assuredly, this tyranny did spring from the pride of the pastors, that those things which appertain unto the common state of the whole church are subject (the people being excluded) to the will, I will not say lust, of a few.'—Calvin on Acts 15:22.

judgment of the Spirit. It is a thoroughly antichristian doctrine that the Spirit of God, and therefore the life and governing power of the church, resides in the ministry, to the exclusion of the people.

When the great promise of the Spirit was fulfilled on the day of Pentecost, it was fulfilled not in reference to the apostles only. It was of the whole assembly it was said, 'They were all filled with the Holy Ghost, and began to speak with other tongues, as the Spirit gave them utterance.' Paul, in writing to the Romans, says, 'We being many, are one body in Christ, and every one members one of another. Having, therefore, gifts differing according to the grace given unto us, whether prophecy, let us prophesy according to the proportion of faith; or ministry, let us wait on our ministering; or he that teacheth, on teaching.' To the Corinthians he says: 'To every one is given a manifestation of the Spirit to profit withal. To one is given by the Spirit the word of wisdom, to another the word of knowledge by the same Spirit.' To the Ephesians he says: 'There is one body and one Spirit; but unto every one is given grace according to the measure of the gift of Christ.' This is the uniform representation of Scripture. The Spirit dwells in the whole church, animates, guides, and instructs the whole. If, therefore, it be true, as all admit, that church power goes with the Spirit, and arises out of his presence, it cannot belong exclusively to the clergy.

3. The third argument on this subject is derived from the commission given by Christ to his church, 'Go ye into all the world and preach the gospel to every creature; and lo, I am with you alway, even to the end of the world.' This commission imposes a certain duty; it conveys certain powers; and it includes a great promise. The duty is to spread and to maintain the gospel in its purity over the whole earth. The powers are those required for the accomplishment of that object, *i.e.,* the power to teach, to rule, and to exercise discipline. And the promise is the assurance of Christ's perpetual presence and assistance. As neither the duty to extend and sustain the gospel in its purity, nor the promise of Christ's presence is peculiar to the apostles as a class, or to the clergy as a body, but as both the duty and the promise belong to the whole church, so also of necessity do the powers on the possession of which the obligation rests. The command, 'Go teach all nations', 'go preach the gospel to every creature', falls on the ear of

the whole church. It wakens a thrill in every heart. Every Christian feels that the command is addressed to a body of which he is a member, and that he has a personal obligation to discharge. It was not the ministry alone to whom this commission was given, and therefore it is not to them alone that the powers which it conveys belong.

4. The right of the people to a substantive part in the government of the church is recognized and sanctioned by the apostles in almost every conceivable way. When they thought it necessary to complete the college of apostles, after the apostasy of Judas, Peter, addressing the disciples, the number being an hundred and twenty, said, 'Men and brethren, of these men which have companied with us, all the time the Lord Jesus went in and out among us, beginning from the baptism of John unto that same day he was taken up from us, must one be ordained to be a witness with us of his resurrection.' And they appointed two, Joseph called Barsabas, who was surnamed Justus, and Matthias. And they prayed and cast lots, and the lot fell on Matthias, and he was numbered with the apostles.' Thus, in this most important initiatory step, the people had a decisive voice. So, when deacons were to be appointed, the whole multitude chose the seven men who were to be invested with the office. When the question arose as to the continued obligation of the Mosaic law, the authoritative decision proceeded from the whole church. 'It pleased', says the sacred historian, 'the apostles and elders, with the whole church, to send chosen men of their own company to Antioch.' And they wrote letters by them after this manner: 'The apostles, elders, and brethren, (οἱ ἀποστολλοι και οἱ πρεσβυτεροι και οἱ ἀδελφοι) send greeting unto the brethren which are of the Gentiles in Antioch, and Syria, and Cilicia.' The brethren, therefore, were associated with the ministry in the decision of this great doctrinal and practical question. Most of the apostolic epistles are addressed to churches, *i.e.,* the saints or believers, of Corinth, Ephesus, Galatia, and Philippi. In these epistles, the people are assumed to be responsible for the orthodoxy of their teachers, and for the purity of church members. They are required not to believe every spirit, but to try the spirits; to sit in judgment on the question whether those who came to them as religious teachers were really sent of God. The Galatians are severely censured for giving heed to false doctrines, and are called to pronounce even an

apostle anathema, if he preached another gospel. The Corinthians are censured for allowing an incestuous person to remain in their communion; they are commanded to excommunicate him, and afterwards, on his repentance, to restore him to their fellowship. These and other cases of the kind determine nothing as to the way in which the power of the people was exercised; but they prove conclusively that such power existed. The command to watch over the orthodoxy of ministers and the purity of members, 'was not addressed exclusively to the clergy, but to the whole church. We believe that, as in the synagogue, and in every well ordered society, the powers inherent in the society are exercised through appropriate organs. But the fact that these commands are addressed to the people, or to the whole church, proves that they were responsible, and that they had a substantive part in the government of the church. It would be absurd in other nations to address any complaints or exhortations to the people of Russia in reference to national affairs, because they have no part in the government. It would be no less absurd to address Roman Catholics as a self-governing body. But such addresses may well be made by the people of one of our states to the people of another, because the people have the power, though it is exercised through legitimate organs. While, therefore, the epistles of the apostles do not prove that the churches whom they addressed had not regular officers through whom the power of the church was to be exercised, they abundantly prove that such power vested in the people; that they had a right and were bound to take part in the government of the church, and in the preservation of its purity.

It was only gradually, through a course of ages, that the power thus pertaining to the people was absorbed by the clergy. The progress of this absorption kept pace with the corruption of the church, until the entire domination of the hierarchy was finally established.

The first great principle, then, of Presbyterianism is the re-assertion of the primitive doctrine that church power belongs to the whole church; that that power is exercised through legitimate officers, and therefore that the office of ruling elders as the representatives of the people, is not a matter of expediency, but an essential element of our system, arising out of the nature of the church, and resting on the authority of Christ.

II. *The second great principle of Presbyterianism is, that presbyters who minister in word and doctrine are the highest permanent officers of the church.*

1. Our first remark on this subject is that the ministry is an office, and not merely a work. An office is a station to which the incumbent must be appointed, which implies certain prerogatives, which it is the duty of those concerned to recognize and submit to. A work, on the other hand, is something which any man who has the ability may undertake. This is an obvious distinction. It is not every man who has the qualifications for a governor of a State, who has the right to act as such. He must be regularly appointed to the post. So it is not everyone who has the qualifications for the work of the ministry, who can assume the office of the ministry. He must be regularly appointed. This is plain; (a) From the titles given to ministers in the Scriptures, which imply official station. (b) From their qualifications being specified in the Word of God, and the mode of judging of those qualifications being prescribed. (c) From the express command to appoint to the office only such as, on due examination, are found competent. (d) From the record of such appointment in the Word of God. (e) From the official authority ascribed to them in the Scriptures, and the command that such authority should be duly recognized. We need not further argue this point, as it is not denied, except by the Quakers, and a few such writers as Neander, who ignore all distinction between the clergy and laity, except what arises from diversity of gifts.

2. Our second remark is, that the office is of divine appointment, not merely in the sense in which the civil powers are ordained of God, but in the sense that ministers derive their authority, from Christ, and not from the people. Christ has not only ordained that there shall be such officers in his church—he has not only specified their duties and prerogatives—but he gives the requisite qualifications, and calls those thus qualified, and by that call gives them their official authority. The function of the church in the premises, is not to confer the office, but to sit in judgment on the question, whether the candidate is called of God; and if satisfied on that point, to express its judgment in the public and solemn manner prescribed in Scripture.

That ministers do thus derive their authority from Christ, follows not merely from the theocratical character of the church, and the relation which Christ, its King, sustains to it, as the source of all authority and power, but,

(*a*) From the fact that it is expressly asserted, that Christ gave some apostles, some prophets, some evangelists, some pastors and teachers, for the edifying of the saints, and for the work of the ministry. He, and not the people, constituted or appointed the apostles, prophets, pastors, and teachers.

(*b*) Ministers are, therefore, called the servants, the messengers, the ambassadors of Christ. They speak in Christ's name, and by his authority. They are sent by Christ to the church, to reprove, rebuke, and exhort with all long-suffering and doctrine. They are indeed the servants of the church, as labouring in her service, and as subject to her authority—servants as opposed to lords—but not in the sense of deriving their commission and powers from the church.

(*c*) Paul exhorts the presbyters of Ephesus, 'to take heed to all the flock over which the *Holy Ghost* had made them overseers'. To Archippus he says, 'Take heed to the ministry which thou hast received in the Lord.' It was then the Holy Ghost that appointed these presbyters, and made them overseers.

(*d*) This is involved in the whole doctrine of the church as the body of Christ, in which he dwells by his Spirit, giving to each member his gifts, qualifications, and functions, dividing to every one severally as he wills; and by these gifts making one an apostle, another a prophet, and another a teacher, another a worker of miracles. It is thus that the apostle reconciles the doctrine that ministers derive their authority and power from Christ, and not from the people, with the doctrine that church powers vest ultimately in the church as a whole. He refers to the analogy between the human body and the church as the body of Christ. As in the human body, the soul resides not in any one part to the exclusion of the rest; and as life and power belong to it as a whole, though one part is an eye, another an ear, and another a hand; so Christ, by his Spirit, dwells in the church, and all power belongs to the church, though the indwelling Spirit gives to each member his function and office. So that ministers are no more appointed by the church, than the eye by the hands and feet. This is the representation which pervades the New Testament, and necessarily supposes that the ministers of the church are the servants of Christ, selected and appointed by him through the Holy Ghost.

3. The third remark relates to the functions of the presbyters. (*a*) They are charged with the preaching of the Word and the administration of the sacraments. They are the organs of the church in executing the great commission to make disciples of all nations, teaching them, and baptizing them in the name of the Father, Son, and Holy Ghost. (*b*) They are rulers in the house of God. (*c*) They are invested with the power of the keys, opening and shutting the door of the church. They are clothed with all these powers in virtue of their office. If sent where the church does not already exist, they exercise them in gathering and founding churches. If they labour in the midst of churches already established, they exercise these powers in concert with other presbyters, and with the representatives of the people. It is important to notice this distinction. The functions above mentioned belong to the ministerial office, and, therefore, to every minister. When alone he of necessity exercises his functions alone, in gathering and organizing churches; but when they are gathered, he is associated with other ministers, and with the representatives of the people, and, therefore, can no longer act alone in matters of government and discipline. We see this illustrated in the apostolic age. The apostles, and those ordained by them, acted in virtue of their ministerial office, singly in founding churches, but afterwards always in connection with other ministers and elders. This is, in point of fact, the theory of the ministerial office included in the whole system of Presbyterianism.

That this is the scriptural view of the presbyterial office, or that presbyters are invested with the powers above referred to, is plain,

(*a*) From the significant titles given to them in the Word of God; they are called teachers, rulers, shepherds or pastors, stewards, overseers or bishops, builders, watchmen, ambassadors, witnesses.

(*b*) From the qualifications required for the office. They must be apt to teach, well instructed, able rightly to divide the Word of God, sound in the faith, able to resist gainsayers, able to rule their own families; for if a man cannot rule his own house, how can he take care of the church of God? He must have the personal qualities which give him authority. He must not be a novice, but grave, sober, temperate, vigilant, of good behaviour, and of good report.

(*c*) From the representations given of their duties. They are to preach the Word, to feed the flock of God, to guide it as a shepherd; they are to labour for the edification of the saints; to watch for souls as those who must give an account; they must take heed to the church to guard it against false teachers, or, as the apostle calls them, 'grievous wolves'; they are to exercise episcopal supervision, because the Holy Ghost, as Paul said to the presbyters of Ephesus, had made them bishops, Acts 20:28, and the Apostle Peter exhorts presbyters to feed the flock of God, taking episcopal oversight thereof, (ἐπισκοπουντες) not of constraint, but willingly. They are, therefore, bishops. Every time that word, or any of its cognates, is used in the New Testament, in relation to the Christian ministry, it refers to presbyters, except in Acts 1:20, where the word *bishopric* is used in a quotation from the Septuagint, applied to the office of Judas.

4. The office of presbyters is a permanent one.

This is plain: (*a*) Because the gift is permanent. Every office implies a gift of which it is the appointed organ. If, therefore, a gift be permanent, the organ for its exercise must be permanent. The prophets of the New Testament were the recipients of occasional inspiration. As the gift of inspiration has ceased, the office of prophet has ceased. But as the gift of teaching and ruling is permanent, so also is the office of teacher and ruler. (*b*) As the church is commissioned to make disciples of all nations, to preach the gospel to every creature; as saints always need to be fed, and built up in their most holy faith, she must always have the officers which are her divinely appointed organs for the accomplishment of this work.

(*c*) We accordingly find that the apostles not only ordained presbyters in every city, but that they gave directions for their ordination in all subsequent time, prescribing their qualifications, and the mode of their appointment.

(*d*) In point of fact, they have continued to the present time. This, therefore, is not a matter open to dispute; and it is not, in fact, disputed by any with whom we are now concerned.

5. Finally, in relation to this part of our subject, presbyters are the highest permanent officers of the church.

(*a*) This may be inferred, in the first place, from the fact that there are no higher permanent functions attributed in the New Testament to the Christian ministry, than those which are therein attributed to presbyters. If they are charged with the preaching of the gospel, with the extension, continuance, and purity of the church—if they are teachers and rulers, charged with episcopal powers and oversight, what more, of a permanent character, is demanded?

2. But, secondly, it is admitted that there were, during the apostolic age, officers of a higher grade than presbyters, *viz.,* apostles and prophets. The latter, it is conceded, were temporary. The only question, therefore, relates to the apostles. Prelatists admit that there is no permanent class or grade of church officers intermediate between apostles and presbyters. But they teach that the apostleship was designed to be perpetual, and that prelates are the official successors of the original apostles. If this is so, if they have the office, they must have the gifts of an apostle. If they have the prerogatives, they must have the attributes of the original messengers of Christ. Even in civil government every office presumes inward qualifications. An order of nobility, without real superiority, is a mere sham. Much more is this necessary, in the living organism of the church, in which the indwelling Spirit manifests himself as he wills. An apostle without the 'word of wisdom', was a false apostle; a teacher without 'the word of knowledge', was no teacher; a worker of miracles without the gift of miracles, was a magician; anyone pretending to speak with tongues without the gift of tongues, was a deceiver. In like manner an apostle without the gifts of an apostle, is a mere pretender. There might as well be a man without a soul.

Romanists tell us that the Pope is the vicar of Christ; that he is his successor as the universal head and ruler of the church on earth. If this is so, he must be a Christ. If he has Christ's prerogatives, he must have Christ's attributes. He cannot have the one without the other. If the Pope, by divine appointment, is invested with universal dominion over the Christian world; if all his decisions as to faith and duty are infallible and authoritative; if dissent from his decisions or disobedience to his commands forfeits salvation, then is he heir to the gifts as well as to the office of Christ. If he claims the office, without having the gifts, then is he Antichrist, 'the man of sin, the son of perdition, who opposeth and exalteth himself above all that is called God, or that is worshipped, so that he, as God, sitteth in the temple of God, showing himself that he is God'. Romanists concede this principle. In ascribing to the Pope the prerogatives of Christ, they are forced to ascribe to him his attributes. Do they not enthrone him? Do they not kiss his feet? Do they not offer him incense? Do they not address him with blasphemous titles? Do they not pronounce anathemas against, and debar from heaven, all who do not acknowledge his authority?

This is the reason why opposition to Popery in the breasts of Protestants is a religious feeling. Caesar Augustus might rule the world; the Czar of Russia may attain to universal dominion, but such dominion would not involve the assumption of divine attributes; and therefore submission to it would not involve apostasy from God, and opposition to it would not of necessity be a religious duty. But to be the vicar of Christ, to claim to exercise his prerogatives on earth, does involve a claim to his attributes, and therefore our opposition to Popery is opposition to a man claiming to be God.

But if this principle applies to the case of the Pope, as all Protestants admit, it must also apply to the apostleship. If any set of men claim to be apostles—if they assert the right to exercise apostolic authority, they cannot avoid claiming the possession of apostolic endowments; and if they have not the latter, their claim to the former is an usurpation and pretence.

What, then, were the apostles? It is plain from the divine record that they were men immediately commissioned by Christ to make a full and authoritative revelation of his religion; to organize the church; to furnish it with officers and laws, and to start it on its career of conquest through the world.

To qualify them for this work, they received, first, the word of wisdom, or a complete revelation of the doctrines of the gospel; secondly, the gift of the Holy Ghost, in such manner as to render them infallible in the communication of the truth, and in the exercise of their authority as rulers; thirdly, the gift of working miracles in confirmation of their mission, and of communicating the Holy Ghost by the imposition of their hands.

The prerogatives arising out of these gifts, were, first—absolute authority in all matters of faith and practice; secondly, authority equally absolute in legislating for the church as to its constitution and laws; thirdly, universal jurisdiction over the officers and members of the church.

Paul, when he claimed to be an apostle, claimed this immediate commission, this revelation of the gospel, this plenary inspiration, and this absolute authority and general jurisdiction. And in support of his claims, he appeals not only to the manifest cooperation of God through the Spirit, but to the signs of an apostle, which he wrought in all patience, in signs, and wonders, and mighty deeds (*2 Cor.* 12:12).

It followed necessarily from the actual possession by the apostles of these gifts of revelation and inspiration, which rendered them infallible, that agreement with them in faith, and subjection to them were necessary to salvation. The Apostle John, therefore, said, 'He that knoweth God heareth us; and he that is not of God, heareth not us. Hereby we know the spirit of truth and the spirit of error' (*1 John* 4:6). And the Apostle Paul pronounced accursed even an angel should he deny the gospel which he preached, and as he preached it. The writings of the apostles, therefore, have in all ages and in every part of the church, been regarded as infallible and authoritative in all matters of faith and practice.

Now, the argument is, that if prelates are apostles, they must have apostolic gifts. They have not those gifts, therefore they are not apostles.

The first member of this syllogism can hardly need further proof. It is evident from the nature of the case, and from the Scriptures, that the prerogatives of the apostles arose out of their peculiar endowments. It was because they were inspired, and consequently infallible, that they were invested with the authority which they exercised. An uninspired apostle is as much a solecism as an uninspired prophet.

As to the second point, *viz.*, that prelates have not apostolic gifts, it needs no argument. They have no special revelation; they are not inspired, they have not either the power of working miracles, or of conferring miraculous gifts, and, therefore, they are not apostles.

So inseparable is the connection between an office and its gifts, that prelates, in claiming to be apostles, are forced to make a show of possessing apostolic gifts. Though not inspired individually, they claim to be inspired as a body; though not infallible singly, they claim to be infallible collectively; though they have not the power of conferring miraculous gifts, they claim the power of giving the grace of orders. These claims, however, are not less preposterous than the assumption of personal inspiration. The historical fact, that the prelates collectively, as well as individually, are uninspired and fallible, is not less palpable than that they are mortal. Those of one age differed from those of another. Those of one church pronounced accursed those of another—Greeks against Latins, Latins against Greeks, and Anglicans against both. Besides, if prelates are apostles, then there can be no religion and no salvation among those not subject to their authority. He is not of God, said the Apostle John, who heareth not us. This is a conclusion which Romanists and Anglicans admit, and boldly assert. It is, however, a complete *reductio ad absurdum*. It might as well be asserted that the sun never shines out of Greenland, as that there is no religion beyond the pale of prelatical churches. To maintain this position, necessitates the perversion of the very nature of religion. As faith in our Lord Jesus Christ, repentance towards God, love, and holy living, are found outside of prelatical churches, prelatists maintain that religion does not consist in these fruits of the Spirit, but in something external and formal. The assumption, therefore, that prelates are apostles, of necessity leads to the conclusion that prelates have the gifts of the apostles, and that to the conclusion that submission to their teaching and jurisdiction, is essential to salvation; and that again, to the conclusion that religion is not an inward state, but an external relation. These are not merely the logical, but the historical sequences of the theory that the apostolic office is perpetual. Wherever that theory has prevailed, it has led to making religion ceremonial, and divorcing it from piety and morality. 'We would beg those who love Christ more than their order, and those who believe in evangelical religion, to lay this consideration to heart. The doctrine of a perpetual apostleship in the church, is not a mere speculative error, but one, to the last degree, destructive.

We cannot pursue this subject further. That the apostolic office is temporary, is a plain historical fact. The apostles, the twelve, stand out just as conspicuous as an isolated body in the history of the church, without predecessors, and without successors, as Christ himself does.

They disappear from history. The title, the thing itself, the gifts, the functions, all ceased when John, the last of the twelve, ascended to heaven.

If it is a fearful thing to put the Pope in the place of Christ, and to make a man our God; it is also a fearful thing to put erring men in the place of infallible apostles, and make faith in their teaching, and submission to their authority, the condition of grace and salvation.

From this awful bondage, Brethren, we are free. We bow to the authority of Christ. We submit to the infallible teachings of his inspired apostles; but we deny that the infallible is continued in the fallible, or the divine in the human.

But if the apostolic office was temporary, then presbyters are the highest permanent officers of the church, because, as is conceded by nine-tenths, perhaps by ninety-nine hundredths of prelates, the Scriptures make no mention of any permanent officers intermediate between the apostles and the presbyter-bishops of the New Testament. There is no command to appoint such officers, no record of their appointment, no specification of their qualifications, no title for them, either in the Scriptures or in ecclesiastical history. If prelates are not apostles, they are presbyters, holding their pre-eminence by human, and not by divine authority.

III. As then presbyters are all of the same rank, and as they exercise their power in the government of the church, in connection with the people, or their representatives, this of necessity gives rise to sessions in our individual congregations, and to presbyteries, synods, and assemblies, for the exercise of more extended jurisdiction. *This brings into view the third great principle of Presbyterianism, the government of the church by judicatories composed of presbyters and elders, etc.* This takes for granted the unity of the church in opposition to the theory of the Independents.

The Presbyterian doctrine on this subject is, that the church is one in such a sense that a smaller part is subject to a larger, and the larger to the whole. It has one Lord, one faith, one baptism. The principles of government laid down in the Scriptures bind the whole church. The terms of admission, and the legitimate grounds of exclusion, are everywhere the same. The same qualifications are everywhere to be demanded for admission to the sacred office, and the same grounds for deposition. Every man who is properly received as a member of a particular church, becomes a member of the church universal; every one rightfully excluded from a particular church, is excluded from the whole church; every one rightfully ordained to the ministry in one church, is a minister of the universal church, and when rightfully deposed in one, he ceases to be a minister in any. Hence, while every particular church has a right to manage its own affairs and administer its own discipline, it cannot be independent and irresponsible in the exercise of that right. As its members are members of the church universal, and those whom it excommunicates are, according to the scriptural theory, delivered unto Satan, and cut off from the communion of the saints, the acts of a particular church become the acts of the whole church, and therefore the whole has the right to see that they are performed according to the law of Christ. Hence, on the one hand, the right of appeal; and, on the other, the right of review and control.

This is the Presbyterian theory on this subject; that it is the scriptural doctrine appears,

1. From the nature of the church. The church is everywhere represented as one. It is one body, one family, one fold, one kingdom. It is one because pervaded by one Spirit. We are all baptized into one Spirit so as to become, says the apostle, one body. This indwelling of the Spirit which thus unites all the members of Christ's body, produces not only that subjective or inward union which manifests itself in sympathy and affection, in unity of faith and love, but also outward union and communion. It leads Christians to unite for the purposes of worship, and of mutual watch and care. It requires them to be subject one to another in the fear of the Lord. It brings them all into subjection to the Word of God as the standard of faith and practice. It gives them not only an interest in each other's welfare, purity, and edification, but it imposes the obligation to promote these objects. If one member suffers, all suffer with it; and if one member is honoured, all rejoice with it. All this is true, not merely of those frequenting the same place of worship, but of the universal body of believers. So that an independent church is as much a solecism as an independent Christian, or as an independent finger of the human body, or an independent branch of a tree. If the church is a

living body united to the same head, governed by the same laws, and pervaded by the same Spirit, it is impossible that one part should be independent of all the rest.

2. All the reasons which require the subjection of a believer to the brethren of a particular church, require his subjection to all his brethren in the Lord. The ground of this obligation is not the church covenant. It is not the compact into which a number of believers enter, and which binds only those who are parties to it. Church power has a much higher source than the consent of the governed. The church is a divinely constituted society, deriving its power from its charter. Those who join it, join it as an existing society, and a society existing with certain prerogatives and privileges, which they come to share, and not to bestow. This divinely constituted society, which every believer is bound to join, is not the local and limited association of his own neighbourhood, but the universal brotherhood of believers; and therefore all his obligations of communion and obedience terminate on the whole church. He is bound to obey his brethren, not because he has agreed to do so, but because they are his brethren—because they are temples of the Holy Ghost, enlightened, sanctified, and guided by him. It is impossible, therefore, to limit the obedience of a Christian to the particular congregation of which he is a member, or to make one such congregation independent of all others, without utterly destroying the very nature of the church, and tearing asunder the living members of Christ's body. If this attempt should be fully accomplished, these separate churches would as certainly bleed to death, as a limb when severed from the body.

3. The church, during the apostolic age, did not consist of isolated, independent congregations, but was one body, of which the separate churches were constituent members, each subject to all the rest, or to an authority which extended over all. This appears, in the first place, from the history of the origin of those churches. The apostles were commanded to remain in Jerusalem until they received power from on high. On the day of Pentecost the promised Spirit was poured out, and they began to speak as the Spirit gave them utterance. Many thousands in that city were added to the Lord, and they continued in the apostles' doctrine and fellowship, and in breaking of bread and prayer. They constituted the church in Jerusalem. It was one not only

spiritually, but externally, united in the same worship, and subject to the same rulers. When scattered abroad, they preached the word everywhere, and great multitudes were added to the church. The believers in every place were associated in separate, but not independent churches, for they all remained subject to a common tribunal.

For, secondly, the apostles constituted a bond of union to the whole body of believers. There is not the slightest evidence that the apostles had different dioceses. Paul wrote with full authority to the church in Rome before he had ever visited the imperial city. Peter addressed his epistles to the churches of Pontus, Cappadocia, Asia, and Bithynia, the very centre of Paul's field of labour. That the apostles exercised this general jurisdiction, and were thus the bond of external union to the church, arose, as we have seen, from the very nature of their office. Having been commissioned to found and organize the church, and being so filled with the Spirit as to render them infallible, their word was law. Their inspiration necessarily secured this universal authority. We accordingly find that they everywhere exercised the powers not only of teachers, but also of rulers. Paul speaks of the power given to him for edification; of the things which he ordained in all the churches. His epistles are filled with such orders, which were of binding authority then as now. He threatens the Corinthians to come to them with a rod; he cut off a member of their church, whom they had neglected to discipline; and he delivered Hymenaeus and Alexander unto Satan, that they might learn not to blaspheme. As a historical fact, therefore, the apostolic churches were not independent congregations, but were all subject to one common authority.

In the third place, this is further evident from the Council at Jerusalem. Nothing need be assumed that is not expressly mentioned in the record. The simple facts of the case are, that a controversy having arisen in the church at Antioch, concerning the Mosaic law, instead of settling it among themselves as an independent body, they referred the case to the apostles and elders at Jerusalem, and there it was authoritatively decided, not for that church only, but for all others. Paul, therefore, in his next missionary journey, as he 'passed through the cities, delivered to them', it is said, 'the decrees for to keep, which were ordained of the apostles and elders which were at Jerusalem' (*Acts* 16:4). It matters not whether the authority of that council was due to the inspiration of its chief members or not. It is enough that it had authority over the whole church. The several congregations were not independent, but were united under one common tribunal.

In the fourth place, we may appeal to the common conscious-ness of Christians, as manifested in the whole history of the church. Everything organic has what may be called a *nisus formativus;* an inward force, by which it is impelled to assume the form suited to its nature. This inward impulse may, by circumstances, be impeded or misdirected, so that the normal state of a plant or animal may never be attained. Still, this force never fails to manifest its existence, nor the state to which it tends. What is thus true in nature, is no less true in the church. There is nothing more conspicuous in her history than the law by which believers are impelled to express their inward unity by outward union. It has been manifested in all ages, and under all circumstances. It gave rise to all the early councils. It determined the idea of heresy and schism. It led to the exclusion from all churches of those who, for the denial of the common faith, were excluded from any one, and who refused to acknowledge their subjection to the church as a whole. This feeling was clearly exhibited at the time of the Reformation. The churches then formed, ran together as naturally as drops of quicksilver; and when this union was prevented by internal or external circumstances, it was deplored as a great evil. It may do for men of the world to attribute this remarkable characteristic in the history of the church, to the love of power, or to some other unwor-thy source. But it is not thus to be accounted for. It is a law of the Spirit. If what all men do, is to be referred to some abiding principle of human nature; what all Christians do, must be referred to some-thing which belongs to them as Christians.

So deeply seated is this conviction that outward union and mutual subjection is the normal state of the church, that it manifests itself in those whose theory leads them to deny and resist it. Their Consocia-tions, Associations, and Advisory Councils, are so many devices to satisfy an inward craving, and to prevent the dissolution to which it is felt that absolute Independency must inevitably lead.

That then, the church is one, in the sense that a smaller part should be subject to a larger, and a larger to the whole, is evident. 1. From its nature as being one kingdom, one family, one body, having one head, one faith, one written constitution, and actuated by one Spirit; 2. From the command of Christ that we should obey our brethren, not because they live near to us; not because we have covenanted to obey them; but because they are our brethren, the temples and organs of the Holy Ghost; 3. From the fact that during the apostolic age the churches were not independent bodies, but subject in all matters of doctrine, order, and discipline, to a common tribunal; and 4. Because the whole history of the church proves that this union and mutual subjection is the normal state of the church towards which it strives by an inward law of its being. If it is necessary that one Christian should be subject to other Christians; it is no less necessary that one church should be subject in the same spirit, to the same extent, and on the same grounds, to other churches.

We have now completed our exposition of Presbyterianism. It must strike everyone that it is no device of man. It is not an external framework, having no connection with the inward life of the church. It is a real growth. It is the outward expression of the inward law of the church's being. If we teach that the people should have a substantive part in the government of the church, it is not merely because we deem it healthful and expedient, but because the Holy Ghost dwells in the people of God, and gives the ability and confers the right to govern. If we teach that presbyters are the highest permanent officers of the church, it is because those gifts by which the apostles and prophets were raised above presbyters, have, in fact, ceased. If we teach that the separate congregations of believers are not independent, it is because the church is, in fact, one body, all the parts of which are mutually dependent.

If this is so—if there is an outward form of the church which corresponds with its inward life, a form which is the natural expression and product of that life, then that form must be most conducive to its progress and development. Men may, by art, force a tree to grow in any fantastic shape a perverted taste may choose. But it is at the sacrifice of its vigour and productiveness. To reach its perfection, it must be left to unfold itself according to the law of its nature. It is so with the church. If the people possess the gifts and graces which qualify and entitle them to take part in the government, then the exercise of that right tends to the development of those gifts and graces; and the denial of the right tends to their depression. In all the forms of despotism, whether civil or ecclesiastical, the people are degraded; and in all forms of scriptural liberty, they are proportionably elevated. Every system which demands intelligence tends to produce it. Every man feels that it is not only one of the greatest advantages of our republican institutions that they tend to the education and elevation of the people, but that their successful operation, demanding popular intelligence and virtue, renders it necessary that constant exertion should be directed to the attainment of that end. As republican institutions cannot exist among the ignorant and vicious, so Presbyterianism must find the people enlightened and virtuous, or make them so.

It is the combination of the principles of liberty and order in the Presbyterian system, the union of the rights of the people with subjection to legitimate authority, that has made it the parent and guardian of civil liberty in every part of the world. This, however, is merely an incidental advantage. The church organization has higher aims. It is designed for the extension and establishment of the gospel, and for the edification of the body of Christ, till we all come to the unity of the faith and knowledge of the Son of God; and that polity must be best adapted to this end, which is most congenial with the inward nature of the church. It is on this ground we rest our preference for Presbyterianism. We do not regard it as a skilful product of human wisdom; but as a divine institution, founded on the Word of God, and as the genuine product of the inward life of the church.

PREACHING THE GOSPEL
TO THE POOR[1]

ONE of the evidences of our Lord's Messiahship was that the gospel was preached to the poor. 'God hath chosen the poor.' 'Look at your calling, brethren, not many wise men after the flesh, not many mighty, not many noble are called, but God hath chosen the foolish, the weak, the base, the despised, those who are nothing. that no flesh should glory in his presence.' In the Old Testament, 'the poor', and 'the people of God' are almost equivalent expressions. They constitute much the larger part of mankind. They have the same right to the gospel as other classes of men. It was intended for them as well as for others. The command to preach the gospel to every creature of course includes them. They have special need of its consolations and supports: no Christian, therefore, has ever doubted that it is the duty of the church to preach the gospel to the poor. To preach the gospel, and to teach the gospel, are inter-changeable expressions. The thing to be done is to bring the poor to the knowledge of the gospel, and therefore every means of communicating that knowledge is included in preaching the gospel, in the scriptural sense of the words.

It being admitted that it is the duty of the church to preach the gospel to the poor, it must also be admitted that any church which fails to bring the gospel to bear upon the poor, fails in its duty to Christ. It refuses or neglects to do what he has specially commanded; and sooner or later its candlestick will be removed out of its place. In spiritual things at least, those who fail to communicate fail to possess. A candle under a bushel soon goes out.

[1] Charles Hodge, 'Preaching the Gospel to the Poor', *Biblical Repertory and Princeton Review,* Vol. 43, No. 1 (1871), pp. 83-95.

The most superficial survey of the Christian world is sufficient to satisfy anyone that some churches are much more faithful, or at least much more successful, in bringing religion within reach of the poor, than others. Such survey also proves that, in some cases, those churches which are in other respects most what they ought to be, are most deficient in this one duty. It will further prove that the degree in which a church succeeds in reaching the poor depends quite as much, if not more, on the principles which underlie its organization and modes of action, than upon the character of its ministers or members.

The Roman Catholic Church, for example, does reach the poor. In Roman Catholic countries, as in France, in Spain, in Italy, the poor are in the church. They are all baptized in the name of Christ. They are all confirmed. They all participate in the ministrations of the priesthood. They crowd the sanctuaries, even when the houses of worship are forsaken by the educated and rich. This one thing the Romish Church does do. This, however, does not counteract the evils flowing from the false doctrines and superstitious observances of that church. But as to the point in hand, it is an example to the whole Christian world.

The same may be said of the Church of Scotland during a long period of its history. It is a clear proof that John Knox was one of the greatest men of his own, and perhaps of any age, that, in that period of the world's history, he formed and carried out the plan of having an university in each of the great divisions of Scotland, an academy in every county, and a school in every parish. These schools were under the care of the pastor or the elders of the church. The children were all instructed in the principles of religion. The population being to a great degree homogeneous, the mass of the people were brought under the power of the gospel. After its adoption by the Church of Scotland, the Westminster Catechism was taught in all the parish schools. A people imbued with the truths and spirit of that matchless compend of Christian doctrine, could not fail, under the ordinary blessing of God, to be intellectual, moral, religious, energetic, and independent. And such were the Scotch as a nation. The late Archbishop Hughes, of New York, had good reason for what he is reported to have said in one of his public addresses, *viz.,* That if

Ireland had been peopled by Presbyterians, they would have driven the English into the sea two hundred years ago.

Immigration and political causes have in a measure changed this state of things in Scotland; but still, both in the established and free churches of Scotland, the poor are reached to a greater extent than in most other Christian countries.

The Church of England has in a great measure failed in preaching the gospel to the poor. Nearly one half of the people of England are outside of the established church; and in the larger cities the great mass of the population live and die in ignorance of the first principles of Christianity. In the rural districts and among the peasantry that church has been more successful in the accomplishment of its mission. It is foreign to our present purpose to inquire into the reasons why that richly endowed establishment has not more successfully accomplished its work.

In Prussia the poor are effectually reached by all the ministrations of the church. There are two ways in which the religious character of a nation may be determined. The one is, the character of the people; the other is, the character of its institutions. If we adopt the former standard, the United States may be pronounced to be one of the most Christian nations on the face of the earth; if the latter, we must admit that it is one of the most irreligious. Prussia, if judged by her institutions and laws, must be regarded as the most thoroughly Christian nation in the world. The law requires that everyone born in the land (unless of Jewish parents), shall not only profess, but be taught the Christian religion. A certificate of baptism and confirmation is required before any citizen of Prussia can he received as an apprentice, before he can marry, or enter upon any profession. In confirmation he makes a profession of faith in Christianity. And he cannot be confirmed unless he is familiar with the Old and New Testament history, and can repeat the Apostles' Creed (which he must adopt as his own), the Ten Commandments and Luther's Catechism. These laws are not obsolete or inoperative. As the Prussian system secures that every man shall be a soldier, so it secures that every man shall be a Christian, so far as knowledge and profession are concerned. No child, although barefooted, of twelve years of age, can be found in Berlin or Halle who cannot read and write, and who is not familiar with Scripture history. The experiment has been often made. The children are all required to go to school. The pastors are required to devote so many hours a week to their religious instruction. The churches are all free, and whatever may be the character of the sermons, the Scriptures are read, an evangelical liturgy is used, and devout hymns are sung. The hymnology of Germany is probably richer than that of any other Christian people, if not than that of all other nations combined. The Germans are a musical people, and these hymns are sung not only in the churches but in the homes of the poor all over the land. Hence, while the French soldiers are roused by the 'Marseillaise', the Germans nerve themselves by singing the grand old hymn of Luther, 'A sure defence is our God, a trusty shield and weapon'. The churches throughout Prussia, as a general thing, are crowded with worshippers. The rich and titled mayor may not be there in curtained stalls, but the body of the church is thronged by the common people. While, therefore, in Prussia, as elsewhere, many of the educated, and especially of the scientific class, have given themselves up to scepticism, the nation, as a nation, is eminently Christian.

In this country the work of evangelization is not in the hands of any one denomination, and things seem tending to the result that one denomination will address itself principally to one class, and another to a different. But this is antichristian. No church can afford systematically and of set purpose to neglect the poor, or, in point of fact, fail to reach them.

Of the Protestant denominations in the United States, it must be admitted that the Methodists have been the most successful in accomplishing this great object of the Christian church. Wesley began his career by preaching to the poor, and he employed his great constructive genius in organizing a system that should secure that object. His followers, especially in this country, have followed his example; and the good which has thus been accomplished is beyond all estimate.

It is with great reluctance that we are constrained to acknowledge that the Presbyterian Church in this country is not the church for the poor. It is not meant that they are excluded, nor that we fail entirely to reach them. But it is true that our system does not make adequate provision for their instruction. In purely agricultural districts, where the poor hardly exist as a class, this evil is not felt; but in all our larger towns and cities it is great and apparent. Great efforts are, indeed, made to accomplish the object by means of city missions and chapels. But these means are inadequate. A very small part of the poor, much smaller than is our proper portion, belong to the Presbyterian Church. We, as a church, are not doing, and never have done, what we were bound to do, in order to secure the preaching of the gospel to the poor. We are not disposed to refer this neglect to any special want of intelligence or zeal in the ministry or members of our church. They may compare favourably in these respects with the ministers and members of any other church in our land. The evil is to be referred to our system. The Presbyterians early adopted in this country, and have always adhered to the principle, that, as a general rule, a minister should look for his support to the particular congregation to which he preaches. We have, indeed, never been unmindful of the wants of those who were not able to sustain the gospel by their own resources. Our church from the beginning has laboured in the field of domestic missions, and made systematic efforts to aid feeble congregations in the support of their pastors. This, however, was regarded as a temporary expedient, and at one time the rule was adopted by our Board of Missions that if, in the course of a few years a church did not become self-sustaining, it should be dropped from the list. The error, however, complained of, is not in the Board of Missions, either in its principles or its operations. It is in the church itself. The error is that no general provision has been made for the support of the preachers of the gospel. Every minister has been left to depend on those to whom he preached. The inevitable consequence of this system is, that those who are unwilling or unable to support the gospel are left in ignorance. Had those who went before us acted on this principle, we should be without the gospel to this day.

There are two principles which have been generally recognized in the church, but which we, as a denomination, have not adequately carried out into practice. The one is, that every minister, devoted to his work, is entitled to an adequate support. The other is, that the obligation to furnish that support does not rest exclusively on the particular congregation which he serves, but upon the church as a whole.

The first of these principles does not admit of dispute. Our Lord says in reference to his ministers, 'the labourer is worthy of his hire'. He has a right to it. To withhold it from him is an act of injustice. It is dishonest. It is not very euphonious to speak of ministers as hirelings, and of their salaries as their hire. But it is the idea, not the word, with which we are concerned. The principle is of universal application, in all departments of life, and among all classes of men; emperors, statesmen, generals, have their 'hire' as well as poor ministers. 'Who', asks the apostle, when speaking of this subject, 'goeth a warfare at any time at his own charges? Who planteth a vineyard, and eateth not of the fruit thereof? or who feedeth the flock, and eateth not of the milk of the flock?' This principle, he tells us, is recognized in Scripture even in its application to brutes, for it is written: 'Thou shalt not muzzle the mouth of the ox that treadeth out the corn.' 'If we have sown unto you spiritual things, is it a great thing if we shall reap your carnal things?' 'Do ye not know, that they which minister about holy things live of the things of the temple? and they which wait at the altar are partakers with the altar? Even so hath the Lord ordained, that they which preach the gospel should live of the gospel.' There is no need of arguing this question. This the apostle has done for us. He has not only argued it on the general principles of justice and of established usage, but announced it as an express command of Christ; that they who preach the gospel shall live of the gospel.

As to the amount of a minister's salary, there is no other principle laid down in Scripture than that it should be adequate, *i.e.,* adequate to enable him to 'live of the gospel' without resorting to other means of support. This scriptural rule is rarely carried out. Even in the most richly endowed churches, while there are princely incomes for the few, the mass of the working clergy have an utterly inadequate support. In England it is said that the average income of the lower clergy is only a hundred and fifty pounds. In our own church there are whole synods in which not one minister in twenty is supported by his salary. A distinguished gentleman from New England told us he had two brothers: one, an able and highly educated man, had preached for years to a church in Massachusetts, on a salary of six hundred dollars; the other, of whom he spoke as a 'chub of a boy', who had only received a common-school education, was in a Boston store, where he received $1,500 a year for rolling out carpets. When this circumstance was mentioned to a merchant of Boston, his reply was: 'A thing always brings what it is worth!'

We do not intend to dwell on this subject. The inadequacy of ministerial support has always been an evil in the church, and we presume it will continue to be so. All we have to say is, that it involves a violation of the express command of Christ, and that it is a great injury to the church itself. Ministers must be supported. If they are not supported by their salaries, they must earn money for themselves. This demands a large part of their time and attention, which is so much detracted from their official work; and its tendeney, and in many cases its effect, is to secularize the ministry itself. God no doubt will carry on his work, whether his ministers are supported or not. He may furnish men, as he did Paul, with such a plenitude, not only of grace, but of knowledge, and of gifts, that they may, as he did, labour night and day with their own hands, and yet preach the gospel in season and out of season. But this is not God's ordinance. He requires the church to do its duty, and ministers to do theirs, in sending and preaching the gospel to every creature.

The second principle above mentioned is more open to debate, or, at least, is less generally recognized and adopted, and that is, that it is the duty of the church, as a whole, to sustain those of its members whom God calls to preach the gospel. The grounds on which this obligation rests are:—

1st. That the command of Christ to preach the gospel is given to the whole church. The obligation which it imposes does not rest exclusively on the clergy. Nor is it satisfied when a man does what he can to secure the knowledge of the gospel for his own family, or for his immediate neighbours, or for those who may choose to unite with him in the support of a minister. In times of pestilence and famine, no man feels justified in confining his efforts for relief to those immediately around him. Why then should he not be bound to send the gospel to those perishing for the bread of life? Not only, therefore, the command of Christ, but the moral obligation which rests upon every man to do what he can to secure the salvation of his fellow men, prove that our obligation to sustain the gospel is not limited to the narrow sphere of the congregation to which we happen to belong.

2nd. The church is one. It constitutes a body more intimately and permanently united than any other association on earth, not excepting even the family. Believers have not only one Lord, one faith, one baptism, and one God and Father of all, but they are members of the mystical body of Christ by the indwelling of the Holy Ghost, so that, as the apostle says, if one member suffer, all the members suffer with it, and if one member be honoured, all the members rejoice with it. The consciousness of this unity, sympathy with our fellow believers, a readiness to help them, is laid down in Scripture as a principal evidence of our own union with Christ. 'Hereby we know that we have passed from death unto life, because we love the brethren.' 'He that seeth his brother have need, and shutteth up his bowels of compassion from him, how dwelleth the love of God in him?'

3rd. Ministers are ordained to the service of the whole church, not to that of a particular congregation. When a man receives a commission in the army of the United States, he is a servant of the general government. He may be sent first to one place and then to another. He receives his support, not from the particular community whom he may be sent to protect, but from the general government, whose servant he is, and whom he is bound to obey. In like manner the minister is the servant of the church as a whole. He is bound to obey the church. His obligation is not limited to the particular congregation to which he is sent to preach. And, therefore, the obligation to provide for his support is not limited to that congregation. It rests upon the body to whom his service belongs, and to whom it is rendered.

4th. This principle has been generally recognized in the church, although it has not always been carried into effect. During the apostolic age the effective operative labourers, those at least of whom we have any special mention in the New Testament, were not pastors of particular churches, but men without charge, who went wherever the providence of God presented an open door, and who were supported by the general contributions of the churches. The idea, borrowed from congregational independency, that local pastors are the only real ministers of the church, and are alone authorized to exercise the prerogatives of ministers, is utterly foreign to the New Testament economy. So far as we know there is not a single local pastor named in the New Testament, unless James of Jerusalem be an exception.

Such pastors may be mentioned in the salutations appended to some of the epistles, but they were not the men that did the great work of the church during the apostolic age. This fact is not referred to to depreciate the pastoral office. In the present state of the church it is indispensable, and its value above all estimate. The fact referred to is here adduced simply as evidence that the apostles gave no sanction to the principle that the preachers of the gospel were to rely for their support on the congregations to whom they preached. The great work of extending the gospel was carried on by men who had no such congregations, and, therefore, were supported by their own labour or by general contributions. Even Paul acknowledges the contributions which he received time and again from churches with which he had no pastoral relations.

As under the old dispensation the priests and Levites were supported by a sustentation fund derived from the general contributions of the people, so throughout the greater part of the history of the Christian church the clergy have not been left to depend upon their several separate congregations. Their support was derived either from the resources of the church or of the State. The entire separation of church and State is a modern idea. A Christian community organized in one form and for one purpose was a State, and the same community organized in another form and for a different purpose was a church. The functions of these organizations were not sharply defined or distinct, as the community as such felt bound to uphold both tables of the Decalogue, and, therefore, to provide for the maintenance of the true religion. We, in keeping the two organizations distinct, have, in a manner, lost sight of the idea that we are a community, a united whole; having common obligations, and especially the obligation of securing the preaching of the gospel to all classes of the people.

5th. Apart, however, from all other considerations, it is decisive in support of the principle in question, that no church can fulfil the great duty of preaching the gospel to the poor, which adopts the plan of making the preacher depend for his support on those to whom he preaches. This is almost self-evident. It is, at any rate, an historical fact, that no church does, or ever has, effectually reached the poor which acts on that plan. The opposite plan is adopted by the Romanists, in the Church of Scotland, in Prussia, and by the Methodists. The illustrious Chalmers knew that it would never do to allow the Free Church to depend exclusively upon their separate congregations, and, therefore, before the separation, he had, with a constructive genius equal to that of Wesley, organized an effective plan for a sustentation fund, so that those who left their pleasant manses and fixed stipends, were assured of at least an adequate support. We cannot shut our eyes to this fact. We have our Board of Domestic Missions to aid feeble congregations; we send missionaries to the heathen, and assume the responsibility of supporting them. We know and admit that we cannot do our duty to the poor without departing from the principle of making our ministers dependent on the people to whom they preach. The complaint is, that we cling to that principle to a degree which prevents our doing our whole duty. We fail in adequately reaching the poor. We fail to a far greater degree than those churches which boldly recognize the opposite principle. We cannot deny the fact that in our cities and larger towns the poor are not in our churches. We cannot get them in. They will not occupy 'free seats' set apart for their accommodation. They instinctively go with their class.

How is this evil to be remedied? How is the Presbyterian Church to be made a church which characteristically and pre-eminently preaches the gospel to the poor? Without pretending to give an exhaustive answer to this question, this much may be safely assumed:—

1st. We must adopt and faithfully carry out the principle that every man who is called of God to the work of the ministry, and devotes himself to his work, shall receive an adequate support. This does not mean that every man ordained to the ministry shall be supported by the church. Many men thus ordained are found disqualified for the office, and should be allowed to demit it. Others are disabled by sickness and infirmity. These should, perhaps, be placed on the retired list (as is done in the army), and suitably provided for. Others, again, are in whole or in part engaged in secular pursuits, and get a support in that way. Others are professors in our literary institutions, although often effective and diligent preachers of the gospel. These limitations greatly reduce the number of ordained ministers who are entitled to look to the church for their support. But the principle remains, that all whom God calls to preach the gospel, and who are devoted to that work, the church, as a whole, or in its collective capacity, is bound to support, provided that support be not otherwise secured.

2nd. A support being thus provided, the presbyteries should exercise the prerogative, which belongs to them, of assigning a field of labour to all their unoccupied ministers and licentiates.

3rd. There should in all our large cities, and wherever necessity calls for them, be established absolutely free churches. To these the people may come without restraint; and when made the subjects of grace, they will gladly of their poverty aid in sending the gospel to others. Not long since a minister who had declined the most flattering calls elsewhere, determined to try and establish a church among the most degraded class of the population of Glasgow. Such a church was gathered, and in a few years became the parent of several others in the same neighbourhood.

4th. Besides such free churches, there should be a class of itinerant missionaries going from place to place within a given district, and even preaching the gospel from house to house. Forty or fifty years ago this was the principal mode in which our Board of Missions conducted its operations. As a general rule, every young man on his licensure took a commission from the Board, and travelled about preaching in destitute places for six months, or a year, or for a longer period.

5th. This plan requires no new organization to carry it into effect. All that is necessary is that the Board of Domestic Missions should be authorized and enabled to promise every man, approved by the church, and devoted to the work of preaching the gospel, an adequate support; and that the several presbyteries should see to it, that all their ministers and licentiates, capable of service, should be diligently employed.

6th. The location and control of ministers and licentiates being thus distributed among the presbyteries, there would be no concentration of power in one central board, which is not only inconsistent with the principles of Presbyterianism, but, as experience teaches, is liable to great abuse.

We do not see that any formidable objections can be urged against this plan. It does not propose any equalization in the salaries of ministers. Every church would remain at liberty to give its pastor what salary it pleased. This might be done while enough was given to others to enable them to live. There are rich and poor in every other department of life and always have been. The same is true with regard to the ministry. Such is the will of God as revealed in his providence, 'The poor ye have always with you.' It would be chimerical to attempt to change this ordinance. It is a consolation to know that the poor are often as happy and as useful as the rich. It has been urged as an objection to this plan, that if a minister is independent of his people as to his support, he will not work. It is a sufficient answer to that objection that our foreign missionaries are independent of the people to whom they are sent, and yet they work. There are other principles of action in all men than the desire of support; and ministers are no exception to that rule. Besides, ministers are responsible to their presbyteries, whose duty it is to see that all their members are faithful. The dependence therefore would only be shifted from the people to the presbytery.

A DISCOURSE DELIVERED AT THE RE-OPENING OF THE CHAPEL[1]

It pleased God by the foolishness of preaching to save them that believe.
1 Corinthians 1:21

THE Bible assumes all primary truths—whether principles of reason or facts of consciousness—and by assuming,
authenticates them. It assumes:—

1. That man has a soul capable of conscious existence and activity
without the body; and that the soul is the man—that in which his
personality and identity reside. Abraham, Isaac and Jacob are alive,
and are now the same persons as when they dwelt on earth.

2. It assumes that man is a free moral agent: dependent, responsible
and immortal.

3. It assumes that the well-being of all creatures depends on their
preserving their normal relation to God.

4. It assumes that man has by sin lost his normal relation to God,
and that by no effort of his own, and by no aid from any creature, can
he be restored to the divine fellowship and favour.

These are among the assumptions of the Bible; and they are all
self-evident truths. They enter into the convictions of all men in all
ages of the world.

The Bible teaches concerning fallen men:

1. That it pleased God, out of his mere good mercy, to determine
not to leave them in their estate of sin and misery but to bring them
into an estate of salvation by a Redeemer.

2. That the only Redeemer of men is the Lord Jesus Christ, who,
being the eternal Son of God became man, and so was, and continues

---

[1] Charles Hodge, *A Discourse Delivered at the Re-opening of the Chapel, September 27, 1874* (Princeton: Charles H. Robinson, 1874).

to be, both God and man, in two distinct natures, and one person forever.

3. That Christ effects our redemption by exercising in our behalf the offices of Prophet, Priest, and King. He is Prophet or teacher, not only as he is the logos, the Word, the Revealer, the ἀπαυγασμα or effulgent image of God, but specially as he reveals to us the will of God for our salvation. He is our Priest in that he offered himself unto God as a sacrifice to satisfy divine justice, and in that he ever lives to make intercession for us. He is our King because he subdues us unto himself, rules in, and reigns over us, and conquers all his and our enemies.

4. The Bible further teaches that the divinely appointed means for applying to men the benefits of Christ's redemption is 'the foolishness of preaching'. It is so called because, so far as the method of salvation is concerned, the wisdom of men is foolishness with God; and the wisdom of God is foolishness with man. In the beginning the gospel was a stumbling-block to the Jews and foolishness to the Greek. We ought not, therefore, to be either surprised or concerned when, in our day, we hear the hierarchs of science proclaiming from their high places, that the supernatural is impossible, and that all faith is superstition. It has always been so and always will be so. Nevertheless, in spite of the opposition of the Jews and of the contempt of the Greek, the gospel was, is, and will continue to be the wisdom of God and the power of God unto salvation.

Two things are included in preaching. First, *the communication to be made is of the nature of a message.* Paul says, 'It pleased God to save men μωρίας τοῦ κηρύγματος.' The preacher, therefore, is a κηρυξ, a herald. It is the office of a herald to proclaim what he is commanded to announce. He is not responsible for the truth or wisdom of what he communicates. If sent to a besieged city, should he presume to modify the message he was commissioned to deliver, he would be false to the very idea of his office. And so the preacher, who is the messenger of God, if he delivers his own speculations, what he thinks is true and right instead of what God has taught, he too is false to the nature of his office.

In the context Paul contrasts philosophy and the gospel. The former is the product of human reason; the speculations of men as to God, the universe, man, the future state, and the means of delivery from moral and physical evil. Philosophy in this sense the apostle pronounces to be foolishness. He says that it is 'vain'; that is, empty, worthless, powerless. In contrast with this, he says that he as a preacher proclaimed the wisdom of God; that is, truths which had never entered in the mind of man, but which God had revealed by his Spirit. A preacher, therefore, in the scriptural sense of the word, is a herald, a messenger, one sent to tell men what God has revealed in the Scriptures—nothing more and nothing less. This every minister of the gospel vows to do. Vows are not to be taken except on proper occasions and after due deliberation. They are voluntary; but when taken they bind the conscience with the stringency of an oath. The baptismal service involves a vow, so does attendance on the Lord's Supper, so does ordination, and so does the act of seeking the ministry. The man who seeks the office of a herald does thereby promise to deliver simply and faithfully the message entrusted to him. So also the man who seeks the office of the ministry does by that very act vow, that is, promise to God, that, if permitted to enter on that work, he will not deliver his own speculations, or doctrines which rest on mere human authority, but simply and solely what God has revealed in his Word. This is a truth which should be engraved not only on the heart and conscience of every minister and of every candidate for the ministry, but also on the palms of his hands, that it may be ever before his eyes. To no one thing in the whole history of the church is so much evil to be attributed as to ministers forgetting that they are mere messengers, and presuming to substitute their wisdom for the wisdom of God, preaching for doctrines the commandments of men.

The second idea included in preaching is, *that it is a method of oral instruction*. It hath pleased God to make the proclamation of the gospel by the living teacher the great means of salvation. Other methods of instruction are important, this is indispensable. The ordinances of God are not arbitrary: they are founded on the nature or the present circumstances of man. God has so made us that the human voice is the most effective instrument for conviction and persuasion. Therefore it is that God has adopted it as his great instrument in saving men. Whitefield's sermons as delivered stirred the hearts of thousands: as read they are almost powerless.

5. The Bible teaches that as preaching is the appointed means of salvation, God has ordained that there shall be in his church a class of men specially set apart to that service. No religion has ever been sustained or propagated without a priesthood or a ministry. Under the old dispensation the whole tribe of Levi was set apart for the instruction of the people. Our Lord chose twelve apostles and commanded them to preach the gospel to every creature. They, in the execution of their commission, ordained pastors and teachers in every city. They prescribed the qualifications for the work of the ministry, and gave directions as to the mode in which men should be set apart to the office. Accordingly, from the apostolic age to the present time, in all parts of the church, there has been a class of men set apart as preachers.

But if the ministry be an office, it cannot be assumed at pleasure, by any man. He must be duly called to the work. That call is from God. Paul charged the presbyters of Ephesus to take heed to the flock over which the Holy Ghost had made them overseers. The province of the church in the premises is to authenticate and certify this divine vocation.

The call to the ministry is not made by any audible voice from heaven, nor by any blind impulses. It consists first, in the gift of the requisite qualifications for the office; second, in an earnest desire for it, springing from right motives; third, the purpose to consecrate the whole life to the work.

The qualifications for the office are of three kinds; first natural, the ability to learn and the ability to teach orally; second, acquired, *viz.,* knowledge and the art of effective public speaking; third, supernatural or gracious; a firm faith in the Bible as the Word of God; a faith founded on the demonstration of the Spirit, which works by love, purifies the heart, and overcomes the world; supreme love for the Lord Jesus Christ; zeal for his glory, for the advancement of his kingdom, and for the salvation of men.

The possession of these qualifications is essential, as without them there can be neither any fitness for the office, nor any divine warrant for its assumption. The natural qualifications are taken for granted. As God does not call the blind to see or the dumb to speak, so neither does he call any man to the office of teacher who has not the ability to acquire and to impart knowledge. The cultivation of the gracious gifts above mentioned, must, from the nature of the case, be left in great measure to the candidate himself. It is a matter between his own soul and God. He should, however, lay to heart that his happiness and usefulness in the ministry will depend on the measure of his faith, love, and zeal. It should, therefore, be his fixed purpose constantly to grow in grace.

It is the acquired qualifications, *viz.,* knowledge, and the art of effective public speaking, which in an institution like this specially demand attention.

As the preacher is a teacher, he must of course have the knowledge which he is required to communicate; and as he is a teacher of the Bible, the Bible must be the great and constant subject of his studies. First, he must know the languages in which the Bible is written. How can a man be qualified to proclaim a message unless he understands the language in which that message is delivered? He should not be obliged to depend on bystanders to tell him what that message means. Secondly, he must know the principles on which the Scriptures are to be interpreted. Thirdly, he should know the origin, contents, and design of the several books which constitute the sacred canon, and their relation to each other. Fourthly, he should know the doctrines which the Bible reveals and which men are bound to believe. And as these doctrines are not dogmatically stated in a few sentences, but one element here and another element there throughout the Scriptures, to learn what the Bible teaches on any subject, requires great labour, patience, and fidelity. It took the church six hundred years before it could frame a satisfactory statement of the doctrines of the Trinity and of the person of Christ. How long will it take geologists to learn the contents of the strata of the earth? Fifthly, as the Bible is not only a rule of faith but also of the duties of men as individuals and as members of society, the whole field of moral and social science lies before the candidate for the ministry.

Besides all this, it is to be remembered that the minister must not only teach the faith but defend it. He must be able to resist gainsayers; and as the assaults against the Bible come from the three departments of philosophy, historical criticism, and science, the whole realm of human knowledge demands the attention of those who are set for the defence of the gospel. The more of this illimitable field that is mastered by any man, the better will he be fitted, other things being equal, to be an able minister of the New Testament, rightly dividing the Word of God. There are some men who seek the ministerial office who regard it as a small matter, requiring no laborious preparation. Such men have reason to doubt whether they are really called to the work. If God calls any man to an office, it is reasonable to assume that he will give him some due sense of its importance, and the purpose to make the best possible preparation for its duties.

The second of the acquired qualifications for the ministry, is the art of effective public speaking. This includes correct pronunciation, distinct articulation, and the proper modulation of the voice. This a matter of great importance, as the difference between a good and bad public speaker is not merely the difference between the agreeable and the disagreeable, but between power and weakness. It is not given to every man to be a great orator, but any man can, by due culture, make himself an agreeable and effective speaker.

The question here arises, How can the knowledge and culture requisite for the sacred office be best attained? in other words, What is the best method of theological education? There are only two methods, private and public—under an approved pastor or in a public institution. Each doubtless has its advantages. The church has decided for the latter. It is reasonable to assume that the candidate will learn more from four or six instructors devoted to the work of teaching, than from one man whose attention must be principally given to other duties. In all parts of the world young men have been gathered into colleges and universities with their several faculties of law, medicine, and theology, so that we have the testimony of almost universal experience in favour of public education. With us this is not an open question. If Presbyterians should refuse to establish theological seminaries, their young men would resort to such institutions under the control of other denominations.

Influenced by these and other considerations, the General Assembly of our church, in the year 1812, founded this seminary; and God has smiled upon the enterprise.

The first signal manifestations of the divine favour to this institution was the selection of Dr Archibald Alexander and Dr Samuel

Miller as its first professors, and their being spared for nearly forty years to devote themselves to its service. It is admitted that the most important part of a man's life is the formative period of youth. The same is true of communities and institutions. If a college be dependent on the State, its character may vary with the change of parties in the State; but if it be independent, it bids fair to retain its original character from generation to generation. If a father commit his child to incompetent and wicked tutors and governors, the fate of the child is sealed; but if it be confided to faithful guardians, as a rule, it will grow up to be an ornament and a blessing. The favour of God to this infant seminary was manifested in its being entrusted to the hands of men pre-eminently qualified for the sacred trust.

They were in the first place eminently *holy* men. They exerted that indescribable but powerful influence which always emanates from those who live near to God. Their piety was uniform and serene; without any taint of enthusiasm or fanaticism. It was also biblical. Christ was as prominent in their religious experience, in their preaching, and in their writings, as he is in the Bible. Christ's person, his glory, his righteousness, his love, his presence, his power, filled the whole sphere of their religious life. When men enter a Roman Catholic church, they see before them a wooden image of Christ extended upon a cross. To this lifeless image they bow. When students entered this seminary, when its first professors were alive, they had held up before them the image of Christ, not graven by art or man's device, but as portrayed by the Spirit on the pages of God's Word; and it is by beholding that image that men are transformed into its likeness from glory to glory. It is, in large measure, to this constant holding up of Christ, in the glory of his person and the all-sufficiency of his work, that the hallowed influence of the fathers of this seminary is to be attributed.

It often happens, however, that men are very pious without being very good. Their religion expends itself in devotional feelings and services, while the evil passions of their nature remain unsubdued. It was not so with our fathers. They were as *good* as they were pious. I was intimately associated with them, as pupil and colleague, between thirty and forty years. In all that time I never saw in either of them any indication of vanity, of pride, of malice, of envy, of jealousy, of insincerity, of uncharitableness, or of disingenuousness. I know that what I say is incredible. Nevertheless it is true. And it is my right and my duty to scatter these withered flowers upon their graves. Most men have reason to rejoice that their bosoms are opaque, but these holy men, as it always seemed to me, might let the sun shine through them.

Another characteristic of the men of whom I speak was their *firm and simple faith in the Scriptures and in the system of doctrine contained in the standards of our church.* Their faith was founded on the demonstration of the Spirit, and therefore could not be shaken. No Sunday School scholar, no mother in Israel, could be more entirely submissive to the teachings of the Scriptures than were these venerable men. There was something sublime and beautiful in the humility of old Doctor Alexander when he found himself at the feet of Jesus. There was no questioning of the reason, no opposition of the heart. The words of Scripture were received as the revelation of what is true and right from the highest source of truth and goodness. No one can estimate the influence of this trait of the character of our first professors operating through forty years on successive generations of their pupils.

There are theologians, however, who, although firm believers in the authority of the Bible, have such a high idea of the dignity of man and of the prerogatives of the understanding, that they constantly exhort men to think for themselves and to receive nothing on authority. This is all very well so far as the authority of man is concerned. It is to be remembered, however, that the portal to the temple of divine truth is very low, and that the high-headed find it very difficult to enter. Our Lord says a man must be converted and become as a little child in order to enter the kingdom of heaven. And the apostle says a man must become a fool in order to attain the wisdom which comes from God. As God does not often convert those who think they can convert themselves, so he rarely teaches those who think they can teach themselves.

Again, there are men who tire of what is old: they crave novelty, and aspire after originality. They advocate progress and development. What suited the sixteenth century, they say, cannot suit the nineteenth. They tell us that we might as well insist on retaining the dress of the Reformers as their theology. We must have clothes as well as they, but the fashion must be altered; so we may retain the substance of their doctrines, but the whole spirit, aspect, and mode of presentation must be changed. There is some truth in this. We must, however, remember that God cannot change; and that the form of a thing is the thing itself. If you change the form of a statue, what becomes of the statue? If you reject the form of a doctrine, you thereby reject the doctrine. The Bible sets forth Christ under the form of a priest; to deny his priesthood is to reject his salvation.

Other theologians, again, have a philosophical disposition. All doctrines must be put into an alembic and distilled; and then they are received not as matters of revelation but of demonstration—not as matters of faith, but of knowledge.

It pleased God that the first professors in this seminary should belong to neither of these classes. They exhorted their students to be *humble* rather than high minded. They had *no fondness for new doctrines,* or for new ways of presenting old ones; and they dreaded the thought of transferring the ground of faith from the rock of God's Word to metaphysical quicksands. For this reason Princeton Theological Seminary was regarded by the *illuminati* in every part of the land as very umbrageous, impenetrable to any ray of new light. This did not move the men of whom we speak. They had heard Christ say of certain men that the light that is in them is darkness. And knowing that man is blind as to the things of God, they thought it safer to submit to be guided by a divine hand, rather than, with darkness within and darkness without, to stumble on they knew not whither.

As to the method of instruction adopted by our first professors, little need be said. They both used text-books where they could be had. Dr Alexander's text-book in theology was Turretin's *Theologia Elenchtica,* one of the most perspicuous books ever written. In the discussion of every subject it begins with the *Status Quaestionis,* stating that the question is not this or that; neither this nor that, until every foreign element is eliminated, and then the precise point in hand is laid down with unmistakable precision. Then follow in distinct paragraphs, numbered one, two, three, and so on, the arguments in its support. Then come the *Fontes Solutionum,* or answers to objections. The first objection is stated with the answer; then the second, and so on to the end. Dr Alexander was accustomed to give us from twenty to forty quarto pages, in Latin, to read for a recitation. And we did read them. When we came to recite, the professor would place the book before him and ask, What is the state of the question? What is the first argument? What is the second, *etc.*? Then what is the first objection and its answer? What the second, *etc.*? There were some of my classmates, Dr Johns the present bishop of the Episcopal Church in Virginia, for example, who would day after day be able to give the state of the question, all the arguments in its support in their order, all the objections and the answers to them, through the whole thirty or forty pages, without the professor saying a word to him. This is what in the College of New Jersey used to be called rowling. Whatever may be thought of this method of instruction, it was certainly effective. A man who had passed through that drill never got over it. Some years ago I heard the late Bishop McIlvaine preach a very orthodox sermon in the Episcopal Church in this place. When we got home, it being a very warm day, he threw himself on the bed to rest. In the course of conversation he happened to remark that a certain professor failed to make any marks on the minds of his students. I said to him, 'Old Turretin, it seems, has left his mark on your mind.' He sprang from the bed, exclaiming, 'That indeed he has, and I would give anything to see his theology translated and made the text-book in all our seminaries.' The Jesuits are wise in their generation, and they have adopted this method of instruction in their institutions.

Dr Alexander, however, did not confine himself to his text-book. He lectured from time to time on those doctrines which were exciting general attention. These lectures from year to year became more numerous, until they constituted an important part of his course. He was accustomed also to give out lists of theological questions, which the students were expected to answer in writing. On the departments of mental and moral philosophy, polemic and pastoral theology, his instructions were by lectures, so that his mind was constantly brought into contact with those of his students. His lectures on pastoral theology were devotional exercises, which we attended as we would attend church.

Dr Miller also had a text-book on ecclesiastical history which he supplemented and corrected by a running commentary at each recitation. He too gave out lists of questions covering the whole course of biblical and church history. His instructions on church government and discipline, and on the composition and delivery of sermons, were by lectures. These venerable men were remarkably punctual and faithful in attending on all their official duties.

Their influence on the students was after all mainly religious, arising from the doctrines which they taught, the character which they exhibited, and the principles which they inculcated. To this must be added the power of calling the religious feelings into exercise which Dr Alexander possessed beyond any man whom I have ever known. He had the gift of searching the heart; of probing the conscience; of revealing a man to himself; of telling him his thoughts, feeling, doubts and conflicts. As with a lighted torch he would lead a man through the labyrinth of his heart, into places which his intelligent consciousness had never entered. He would thus humble him, instruct him, comfort or strengthen him. He could melt his hearers to penitence, make their hearts burn within them, inspire them with zeal, and give them a foretaste of the joy that is unspeakable. This power he exerted not only in the pulpit, but in our Sabbath afternoon conferences, and in his addresses to the students at evening prayers. There are three of his sermons which I specially remember; one on Abraham's offering up Isaac; one on the transfiguration of Christ; and one on our Lord's passion. The only way in which I can give an idea of the impression produced by these discourses, is by saying that his hearers felt, in a measure, as they would have done had they been present at the scenes described. We left this chapel after his sermon on the transfiguration, feeling that we had seen the Lord in his glory, at least as through a glass darkly. His sermon on the passion of Christ was delivered in the church on a communion Sunday. The impression which it made was profound. The students became clamorous: they would take no denial of their request for its possession. I do not think that it was printed; but the manuscript came into our hands; and when I read it, there was nothing there, but what is in the Gospels. So that the mystery of its power remained unsolved.

There was another peculiarity in Dr Alexander's preaching. He would sometimes pause and give utterance to a thought which had no connection with his subject, and then resume the thread of his discourse. He seemed to think that these thoughts were given to him for a purpose, and he sent them forth as arrows shot at a venture. When a boy I attended a service which he conducted in the old school house, which stood on the ground now occupied by the First Presbyterian Church. I sat in the back part of the room, on a shelf with my feet dangling half-way to the floor. The Doctor suddenly paused in his address, and stretching out his arm to attract attention, deliberately uttered this sentence, 'I don't believe a praying soul ever enters hell.' That bolt, I suspect, pierced more hearts than one. It may well be believed that more than one poor sinner in that little assembly, said to himself, 'If that be so, I will keep on praying, while I keep on breathing.'

We all know that the man who is instrumental in bringing us near to God, who enables us to see the glory of Christ, who stirs up our hearts to penitence and love, becomes sacred in our eyes, and that the place in which we have enjoyed these experiences can never be forgotten. Hence the feeling which our old Alumni cherish for this seminary, is not pride, but a tender, sacred, love, as for the place in which they passed some of the holiest, happiest, and most profitable hours of their lives.

Owing to the peculiar power of Dr Alexander over the feelings, the students were more demonstrative of their regard for him than for Dr Miller. But in their heart of hearts, in the place where reverence dwells, in the inner temple of the soul, neither of these holy men stood higher than the other.

Dr Addison Alexander was appointed teacher of Hebrew in this seminary in 1833. In 1836 he was elected Professor of Biblical and Oriental Literature. He did not consent, however, to be inaugurated until two years later, although he discharged the duties of the chair to which he had been appointed. He continued connected with the seminary as one of its professors until his death, February 1860.

I believe that I was rash enough to say on the floor of the General Assembly of 1860, that I thought Dr Addison Alexander the greatest man whom I had ever seen. This was unwise; both because there are so many different kinds of greatness, and because I was no competent judge. I feel free to say now, however, that I never saw a man who so constantly impressed me with a sense of his mental superiority—with his power to acquire knowledge and his power to communicate it. He seemed able to learn anything and to teach anything he pleased. And whatever he did, was done with such apparent ease as to make the impression that there was in him a reserve of strength, which was never called into exercise. The rapidity with which he accomplished his work was marvellous. The second volume of his *Commentary on Isaiah,* a closely printed octavo volume of five hundred pages, with all its erudition, was written, as I understand, during one summer vacation, which he passed in the City of New York. Few literary achievements can be compared to that.

He had two marked peculiarities. One was that although he had apparently the power to master any subject, he could not do what he did not like. Being in his youth very precocious and very much devoted to intellectual pursuits, he needed neither excitement nor guidance. He was, therefore, allowed to pass from one subject to another at pleasure. A habit of mind was thus induced which rendered it almost impossible for him to fix his attention on subjects which were disagreeable to him. There were consequently some departments of knowledge of which he was purposely ignorant. This was true of psychology, or mental philosophy. I never knew him to read a book on that subject. He never would converse about it. If, when reading a book, he came across any philosophical discussion, he would turn over the leaves until he found more congenial matter. When Dr Schaff's work on *The Apostolic Age* came out, he was greatly delighted with it. The theory of historical development which it broached, he took no notice of. He did not even know it was there. When, therefore, he reviewed the book, he never adverted to one of its most marked characteristics. The same thing was true, in good measure, of natural science, to which he devoted very little attention. It was specially true of physiology and hygiene. It would be hard to find an educated man more profoundly ignorant of the structure of the human body or of the functions of its organs. Hence he was constantly violating the laws of health. He was a whole year seriously ill without knowing it; and only two or three days before his death, he said to me, 'Don't look so sad, I'm as well as you are.'

The other peculiarity referred to was his impatience of routine. He could not bear to go over and over the same ground, or to attend

long to any one subject. Hence he was constantly changing his subjects of study and methods of instruction. He would begin to write
a book, get it half done, and then throw it aside. Or, he would begin
to write on one plan, and then change it for another. He occupied
three different chairs in this seminary. He first had the Old Testament
department; then Ecclesiastical History; then the Language and Literature of the New Testament. The friends of the seminary cared little
what he did, for whatever he undertook, he was sure to do so grandly
that everyone would be more than satisfied. As he advanced in life,
these peculiarities became less apparent. He was constantly getting
his powers more under his own control. At the time of his death we
flattered ourselves that he had before him twenty or thirty years for
steady work. Then suddenly our great treasure ship went down—disappearing under the waves—a dead loss—leaving us, as we then felt,
utterly bankrupt.

The departments in which he took the most interest were languages,
literature, history, and above all, the Bible. His earliest reputation
was as a linguist. It was known that he had without any instruction
made himself so familiar with the Arabic that he had read the Qur'an
through before he was fourteen. In the same way he learned Persian,
and while but a lad delighted in reading the Persian poets. He then
learned Hebrew, Chaldee, and Syriac. He kept up his familiarity with
the Greek and Latin classics through life. He read all the modern
languages of Europe, unless the Slavonic dialects be excepted. His
object in these studies was not simply the vocabulary and grammar of
these languages, but their mutual relations, and specially the literary
treasures which they contained. He was specially master of his own
tongue. He had read all the leading English authors of every age.
His style was a model of precision, perspicuity, felicity of expression,
purity and force. His command of language did not seem to have
any limit. He could speak in correct and polished English as easily as
he could breathe. Extemporary speaking is an every day matter. But
I have known Dr Addison to come into this chapel, without having
committed or written his sermon, and read it off from blank paper
from beginning to end without hesitation or correction. He was constantly doing such things, which made those around him think he
could do whatever he pleased.

As to his qualifications as a theological professor, the first in importance was his sincere and humble piety. Religion, however, even when
genuine, assumes different forms in different persons. Some men it
impels to live before the public as well as for the public. In others it
leads rather to self-culture and intercourse with God. Dr Addison's
life was in a great measure hidden. He never appeared in church
courts or in religious conventions. But although he lived very much
by himself, he did not live for himself. All his powers were devoted
to the service of Christ, as writer, teacher, and minister of the gospel.
His temper was naturally irritable; but if it ever got the better of him
in the classroom, the next prayer he offered in the oratory was sure
to manifest how sincerely he repented. The students, on leaving the
prayer room, would sometimes ask each other, What has Dr Addison
been doing for which he is so sorry?

The second great qualification for his office was his firm faith in
the Bible and his reverence for it as the Word of God. He believed in
it just as he believed in the solar system. He could not help believing. He saw so clearly its grandeur as a whole, and the harmonious
relation of its several parts, that he could no more believe the Bible
to be a human production than he could believe that man made the
planets. He never seemed to have any doubts or difficulty on the
subject. Although perfectly familiar with the writings of the German rationalists and sceptics from Ernesti to Baur and Strauss, they
affected him no more than the eagle is affected by the dew on his
plumage as he soars near the sun. The man who studies the Bible as
he studied it, in the organic relation of its several parts, comes to see
that it can no more be a collection of the independent writings of
uninspired men, than the human body is a haphazard combination
of limbs and organs. It was in this light that he presented it to his
students, who were accustomed to say that he glorified the Bible to
them, that is—he enabled them to see its glory, and thus confirmed
their faith and increased their reverence.

Another of his distinguishing gifts as a professor was his ability as
a teacher. The clearness, rapidity, and force with which he communicated his ideas aroused and sustained attention; and the precision
and variety of his questions, in the subsequent catechetical exercise
on the subject of the lecture, drew out from the student everything

he knew, and made him understand himself and the matter in hand. Students from all the classes often crowded his lecture room, which they left drawing a long breath as a relief from overstrained attention, but with their minds expanded and invigorated.

As a preacher his sermons were always instructive and often magnificent. He would draw from a passage of Scripture more than you ever imagined it contained; show how many rays concentrated at that point; and how the truth there presented was related to the other great truths of the Bible. This was not so much an exhibition of the philosophical or logical relation of the doctrine in hand with other doctrines, as showing the place which the truth or fact in hand held in the great scheme of Scripture revelation. Thus in his sermon on the words of Paul to the Jews at Rome, 'Be it known unto you, that the gospel of God is sent unto the Gentiles, and they will hear it', he showed that everything Moses and the Prophets had taught, culminated in the proclamation of the religion of the Bible as the religion of the world. At times he gave his imagination full play; and then he would rise in spiral curves, higher and higher, till lost to sight; leaving his hearers gazing up into heaven, of which they felt they then saw more than they had ever seen before. These three men, Dr Archibald Alexander, Dr Samuel Miller, and Dr Addison Alexander, are our galaxy. They are like the three stars in the belt of Orion, still shining upon us from on high. Their lustre can now never be dimmed by the exhalations of the earth.

I have not forgotten two others of our professors, now we doubt not in heaven, Dr John Breckinridge and Dr James W. Alexander. These men, however, were never given to the seminary; they were only lent to it for a short time. Dr Breckinridge was elected in 1836 and resigned in 1838: Dr James Alexander was elected in 1849 and resigned in 1851. God had fitted and designed them for other fields of action. They were both eminent, each in his own way; but we cannot claim them specially as our own. Dr Breckinridge was one of the leaders of the church in its conflicts. Dr Alexander was a man of varied scholarship and accomplishments. The former was proud of calling himself a Kentuckian. His State, however, had as much reason to be proud of him, as he had of his State. He was tall, handsome, spirited, and courteous. He made a friend of almost every man he met. Being a natural orator, his appropriate place was the pulpit and the platform. Dr James Alexander, as you all know, was one of the most eminent and useful preachers of his day.

The second signal manifestation of God's favour to this institution is to be seen in the munificent patrons which he has raised up for its support. Mr James Lenox, to whom we are indebted for our library building and the extensive grounds on which it is erected; for one of our professor's houses, and for liberal contributions to our general funds. Messrs Robert L. and Alexander Stuart, who have contributed $60,000 to our scholarship, library, and miscellaneous funds, a professor's house, and who have recently purchased land for the erection of a handsome building for our recitation rooms. Mrs George Brown of Baltimore, to whom we are indebted for Brown Hall; Mr Levi P. Stone, who founded the Stone Lectureship: Mr John C. Green, who endowed the Helena Professorship of Ecclesiastical History, purchased a house for a professor, contributed generously to our permanent funds, and at whose expense this chapel has been transformed from what it was to what it is; so that we can never enter this room without being reminded of his kindness.

There is another class of benefactors, who, not having gold or silver to bestow, gave their prayers, their counsels and their disinterested labours. Dr Ashbel Green, Dr John McDowel, Dr William Philips, head a long list of friends who should always be held in grateful remembrance.

A mother's pride, however, is in her children. Much as she may love and reverence her parents, she turns her fondest gaze on those whom she has nurtured at her bosom and fondled on her knees. So our *Alma Mater,* while she cherishes with reverence the memory of her fathers, turns her streaming eyes with gratitude to heaven, and says, 'Here, Lord, am I and the children whom thou hast given me.' More than three thousand ministers of the gospel have been trained within these walls. With rare exceptions they have been faithful men. They have laboured in every part of our own land and in almost every missionary field. This goodly company of ministers, confessors, and even martyrs, is God's best gift and our crown.

To the present members of the seminary I would say, you have assumed grave responsibilities in coming to this place. This is sacred ground. A sanctuary is a place to which men come to enquire of the Lord. For that purpose you have come here. You have come to learn what he would have you teach your fellow men. You should, therefore, preserve a spirit and deportment becoming those who are preparing to be the ambassadors of God, and who must be instrumental in saving or destroying the souls of men. If you are really called of God to the ministry of his Son, you are highly favoured. God gives to men no higher gift than the grace to preach the unsearchable riches of Christ. But if you are not called of God, you are greatly to be pitied. Your whole life, whatever it may be in semblance, in reality, must be a failure.

Your first duty, therefore, is to make your calling and election sure. If an honest scrutiny of your hearts satisfies you that you seek the ministry from love to Christ, zeal for his glory, and a desire to save your fellow men; if you have the fixed purpose to be diligent in your studies in order to be prepared to become preachers and defenders of the faith; and if you are determined to consecrate your lives to this work; then you will be humble, for those gifts of God which are graces, or fruits of his Spirit, never produce self-complacency or self-exaltation. Nevertheless, you may rejoice in the assurance that you are among those who are destined to shine as stars in the firmament of heaven. It matters not what is before you; whether you are cheered with visible success, or whether you are forced to join the lamentation of the prophet, 'Lord, who hath believed our report?' It will be a cause for joy and not for grief, if on the review of life you can say with the apostle, that for the sake of Christ, you had suffered afflictions, necessities, distresses, stripes, imprisonments, tumults, labours, watchings, fastings, cold, nakedness, perils by sea and perils by land. Paul would not willingly erase one item from this long catalogue. Each of them is now a brilliant in his diadem of glory.

Your second duty is to throw your whole heart into the work, and, while here, into the work of preparation, and into the life of the seminary. When a man joins a particular church, he is bound to identify himself with it, and to strive to sustain and promote its church life. He must attend its services and co-operate in its measures. He must not go first to one church and then to another, to gratify his curiosity or his taste. He must be governed by a sense of duty and not by inclination: thus only can he promote his own edification and the welfare of the church. Every institution like this has its distinctive life, and its members are under a solemn obligation to sustain and promote it, by a faithful attendance on its services, whether in the classroom, the chapel, the conference, or prayer meeting. As the character of the church depends on its members, so the character of this seminary depends, at least for the time being, on you.

Finally, in the name of my colleagues, I have one request to make of you. It is a small matter to you, but a great matter to us. We beg that each of you, as long as he lives, would daily pray that the officers and students of this seminary may be full of faith and of the Holy Ghost. Let others believe and say what they please, we believe and know that God is the hearer of prayer. If each of the two thousand surviving *Alumni* of this institution would daily offer that prayer, what a place Princeton would be!

FAITH IN CHRIST
THE SOURCE OF LIFE[1]

The life which I now live in the flesh I live by the faith of the
Son of God, who loved me and gave himself for me.
Galatians 2:20

THE churches in Galatia were founded by the Apostle Paul.
He had appeared among them in much weakness. There
was something either in his personal appearance, or in his
external circumstances, which tended to excite contempt. But the
Galatian converts did not on that account reject him, but received
him as an angel of God, and even as Christ Jesus. This devotion to
him, and to the gospel which he preached, was very short-lived. He
begins his epistle to them by expressing his astonishment that they
had so soon turned unto another gospel. It is plain from the course of
his argument, that this apostasy was Judaism. The Galatians had been
induced to live after the manner of the Jews, to consider circumcision and keeping the law necessary to salvation. Paul's object is to
convince them that this apostasy, if persisted in, must be fatal. There
are but two methods of salvation—the one by the law, the other by
grace—the one by works, the other by faith. These methods are perfectly incompatible. They cannot be combined. The adoption of the
one is the rejection of the other. Salvation must be wholly by works,
or entirely by grace. Paul, therefore, says:—'I testify to every man
that is circumcised, that he is a debtor to do the whole law. Christ
is become of no effect to you; whosoever of you are justified by the
law, ye are fallen from grace.' By adopting the legal, you have rejected
the gracious method of justification. It was his deep conviction, both

---

[1] Charles Hodge, 'Faith in Christ the Source of Spiritual Life', *The Princeton Pulpit*,
ed. John T. Duffield (New York: Charles Scribner, 1852), pp. 74-94.

from the revelation of God, and his own experience, that the law, in none of its forms, could give life. Neither the Mosaic institutions nor the Decalogue, neither ritualism nor morality, could avail to restore sinners from death to the life of God, and life with God. The law, he argues, cannot free us from condemnation, because we are sinners, and it is the very province of the law to condemn sin. How can we be justified by that which condemns? Neither can the law give spiritual life. It can only present the form of knowledge and truth. It cannot change the heart. On the contrary, it exasperates its opposition by the extent of its inexorable demands, so that it slays, instead of giving life. Paul says, he found the law which was ordained unto life, to be unto death. What the law could not do, in that it was weak through the flesh, God has accomplished by the gospel. He has set forth his Son as the author of life, as the redeemer from judicial death, and the giver of inward spiritual life. There are two indispensable conditions on which our interest in his salvation is suspended. The one is, the renunciation of the law, or of the legal method of salvation; and the other is, union with Christ, so that we become partakers of the merit of his death, and the virtue of his life. I am dead to the law, says the apostle. 'I am crucified with Christ; nevertheless, I live; yet not I, but Christ liveth in me; and the life which I now live in the flesh, I live by the faith of the Son of God, who loved me and gave himself for me.'

The doctrine of this passage is, *that faith of Christ is the necessary condition and source of spiritual life.*

By 'faith of Christ' is not meant the faith which Christ had. The faith which is the life of the soul, is not mere belief of the existence of God, and of those great moral and religious truths which are the foundation of all religion. Those who would bring revelation down to the level of philosophy, and resolve all its doctrines into truths of the reason, tell us that all the Bible means when it says we are saved by faith and not by works is, that confidence in God, and in moral and religious truth, is not only the source of virtue, but the test of character. What a man is, is determined more by this habitual state of mind, than by individual and outward acts. When it is said, Abraham was justified by faith, they would have us understand that it was his inward posture of mind toward God that was approved and recognized as the source of all true piety. Here, as in most other cases, error is negative. The evil lies not in what is affirmed, but in what is denied. It is true that faith in God is the principle of all religion; but it is far from being true that this is the whole import of the Scripture doctrine of salvation by faith. It is characteristic of the doctrines of the Bible, that they comprehend all that is true in other forms of religion, while they contain a divine element to which their power is due, which is to be found nowhere else. The faith, therefore, by which the Christian lives, is something more than mere faith in God.

Neither does the faith of Christ, of which our text speaks, mean faith in that unseen world which Christ has revealed. It is, indeed, true that the life of the Christian is regulated by the objects of faith, as distinguished from the objects of sight. It is true that he walks by faith, and not by sight; that he looks not at the things which are seen, but at the things which are not seen. It is true the Christian has a faith which is the evidence of things not seen, and the substance of the things hoped for. It is true that faith, as the organ of perceiving what neither sense nor reason knows, as the cognition of the things of the Spirit, does regulate the Christian's life, determine his conduct, sustain him in trial, comfort him in affliction, and open for him the perennial fountain of life. Still, this is not all the Scriptures teach on this subject; nor is this the doctrine which they mean to inculcate, when they teach that we are saved by faith; and when they represent faith as the source of spiritual life to the soul.

Neither is the truth in question either exhausted or accurately stated by saying, the faith which has this life-giving power has the whole Word of God for its object. It is, indeed, admitted that faith has respect to the whole revelation of God. It receives all his doctrines, bows to all his commands, trembles at his threatenings, and rejoices at his promises. This, however, is not the faith by which the apostle lived; or, rather, it is not those acts of faith which have the truth of God in general for their object, which give life to the soul. The doctrine of the text and of the whole New Testament is, that the soul is saved, that spiritual life is obtained, and supported, by those acts of faith which have Christ for their object. Other things in the Word of God we may not know, and, therefore, may not consciously believe, but Christ we must know. About other things true Christians may differ; but they must all agree as to what they believe concerning Christ. He is in such a sense the object of faith, that saving faith consists in receiving and resting on him alone for salvation as he is offered to us in the gospel. It consists in receiving Christ—*i.e.*, in recognizing, acknowledging, accepting, and appropriating him, as he is held forth to us in the Scripture. It includes therefore a resting on him alone for salvation—*i.e.*, for justification, sanctification, and eternal life.

That this is the true doctrine on the subject is plain from the common form of expression employed in Scripture when the Bible speaks of faith in connection with justification and life. It is not of faith as general confidence in God, nor faith as assent to divine revelation, but specifically 'faith of Christ', that is, faith of which Christ is the object. Thus the apostle, in the earnest and important passage whence the text is taken, and in which he condenses the whole substance of the gospel, says three times over, that the only method of obtaining justification and life, is by those acts of faith which terminate on Christ. In the third chapter of the Epistle to the Romans, from verse 21 to the end, where we have another of those condensed exhibitions of the gospel, the same form of expression occurs. We are said to be saved by 'the faith of Christ'. So, too, in that remarkable passage, Philippians 3:1-14, in which he contrasts the two systems—the legal and evangelical—Judaism and the gospel, he ascribes the power of the latter to secure justification and life to 'the faith of Christ'. The same doctrine is taught in all those passages in which we are required to *believe in Christ* in order to salvation. The specific act which is everywhere declared to be essential, is to believe on the Son of God. 'He that believeth on the Son', it is said, 'hath life; he that believeth not the Son, shall not see life, but the wrath of God abideth on him.' The Apostle John insists much on this point. 'Whosoever believeth that Jesus is the Christ, is born of God.' 'Whosoever shall confess that Jesus is the Son of God, God dwelleth in him, and he in God.' 'Believe in the Lord Jesus Christ and thou shalt be saved', is the message which the gospel brings to every creature. This doctrine is taught, also, by all those passages which declare Christ to be our life. It is by union with him we live. 'Our life is hid with Christ in God.' It is not we that live, but Christ that liveth in us. The life which we now live in the flesh is by faith of the Son of God. The whole scheme of redemption is founded on this truth. Men are dead in trespasses and sins. They cannot be delivered from this state by any works or efforts of their own. Neither can they come to God without a mediator. Christ is the only medium of access; therefore faith in him is the indispensable condition of salvation. Whatever else we may believe, it will avail us nothing unless we exercise faith in him; and therefore, the specific act which sinners are called upon to perform, is to come to Christ; to look to him; to flee to him as a refuge; to lay hold on him as a helper; to confide in him as the propitiation for their sins; to commit themselves to him as their High Priest. In all these, and in many other ways, are we clearly taught that Christ is the immediate object of that faith which is connected with life and salvation. This is so plain and so important that our Catechism defines the faith which saves the soul to be that grace, whereby we receive and rest on Christ alone for salvation, as he is offered to us for salvation. It is not, therefore, by faith in God as God, nor by faith in divine revelation; but by faith in Christ, that is, by those acts of faith which have him for their immediate object, that the soul is freed from condemnation, and made partaker of divine life.

But what is meant by faith in Christ? What are those truths concerning Christ which we are required to believe? Thanks be to God for the distinctness with which this all-important question is answered in his Word. We have that answer summed up in the passage before us. There are three things which we must believe, or our faith is dead. First, That Christ is the Son of God. Second, That he loves us. Third, That he gave himself for us.—All these are essential elements in that faith which gives life to the soul.

First, We must believe that *Christ is the Son of God.* Both the divinity and incarnation of the object of our faith are included in this expression. The designation, Son of God, is applied in Scripture to the divine nature of Christ, and implies his essential equality with God. God is in such a sense his Father that he is equal with God, of the same nature or substance, possessing the same attributes, bearing the same titles, performing the same works, and entitled to the same confidence, obedience, and worship. In this light he is set forth as the object of hope in the Old Testament. In this light he exhibited himself when he appeared on earth, teaching in his own name, working miracles by his own power, claiming for himself the love, confidence, and obedience due to God alone, asserting his power to save all who come to him, promising to raise the dead, and foretelling his coming to judge the world at the last day. These claims were authenticated by the manifestation of the glory of God in his character and life, so that those who were with him beheld his glory as of the only begotten Son of God, and knew he was indeed the true God and eternal life. God confirmed these claims by a voice from heaven, saying: 'This is my beloved Son in whom I am well pleased'; by the works which he gave him to do, and by raising him from the dead, thereby proclaiming with power that he was the Son of God. The apostles received, worshipped, and preached him as the true God. They proclaimed themselves and all their fellow Christians to be the worshippers of Christ, and the great object of their mission (as it is to this day the great end of the ministry) was to bring men to know, worship, and obey Christ as God. It is, therefore, one of the essential elements of faith in Christ to believe in his divinity. This, however, necessarily includes faith in his incarnation, because all the designations applied to Christ belong to him as an historical person. Jesus Christ is the name of a person who was born of the Virgin Mary, who suffered under Pontius Pilate, was crucified, dead, and buried, who rose again on the third day, ascended into heaven, and is now seated at the right hand of God. Everything taught concerning Christ, is taught concerning that person. He, that is, the person who was thus born, who thus suffered, died, and rose again, is the Son of God, that is, a divine person. This, of course, supposes that he became flesh and dwelt among us. Faith of the Son of God is, therefore, necessarily faith in the incarnation. It is faith in Christ as God manifest in the flesh. This is so prominent and so important an element in saving faith, that it may be said to include all others. Hence the apostle says: 'Whosoever believeth that Jesus is the Son of God, God dwelleth in him, and he in God'; and, 'Every spirit that confesseth that Jesus Christ is come in the flesh, is of God.' That faith, therefore, which has power to give life, has the incarnate God for its object. It contemplates and receives that historical person, Jesus Christ, who was born in Bethlehem, who lived in Judea, who died on Calvary, as God manifest in the flesh.

Any other faith than this is unbelief. To believe in Christ, is to receive him in his true character. But to regard him, who is truly God, as a mere creature, is to deny, reject, and despise him. It is to refuse to recognize him in the very character in which he is presented for our acceptance. If this truth be hid, 'it is hid', says the apostle, 'to them that are lost; in whom the God of this world hath blinded the eyes of them that believe not, lest the light of the glorious gospel of Christ, who is the image of God, should shine unto them. For God, who commanded the light to shine out of darkness, hath shined into our hearts, to give the light of the knowledge of the glory of God in the face of Jesus Christ.' Saving faith, then, is the knowledge of the glory of God in the face of Jesus Christ. It is perceiving and recognizing him to be the brightness of the Father's glory, and the express image of his substance. This is that knowledge for which Paul said he was willing to suffer the loss of all things; and which our blessed Lord himself declared to be eternal life.

The necessity of faith in the divinity and incarnation of our Lord, to the saving power of faith, is further plain, because a Saviour less than divine, is no Saviour. The blood of no mere man is an adequate atonement for the sins of the whole world. The righteousness of no creature is an adequate foundation for the justification of sinners. The assurance of the gift of eternal life is mockery from any other lips than those of God. It is only because Jesus is the Lord of glory, the Son of God, God manifest in the flesh, that his blood cleanses from all sin, that his righteousness is infinite in value, sufficient to cover the greatest guilt, to hide the greatest deformity, and to secure even for the chief of sinners admission into heaven. The ranks of angels give way to allow anyone to enter and ascend, who appears clothed in the righteousness of God. Yes, the righteousness of God; and any righteousness short of his, would be of no avail. Faith draws her power to give life to the soul; to free from the sentence of death; to speak peace to the troubled conscience only from the divine character of its object. It is only an almighty, an ever present, an infinite Saviour, who is suited to the exigencies of a ruined immortal.

It must also be remembered, that it is to the spiritually dead to whom Christ is declared to be the author of life. But no creature is life-giving. It is only he who has life in himself that is able to give life unto others. It is because Christ is God, because all the fulness of the Godhead dwells in him, that he is the source of spiritual life to us. God only hath life in himself, and all creatures live in him. If, therefore, Christ is our life, he must be our God.

Spiritual life, moreover, supposes divine perfection in the object on which its exercises terminate. It is called the life of God in the soul, not only because God is its source, but also because he is its object. The exercises in which that life consists, or by which it is manifested, must terminate on infinite excellence. The fear, the admiration, the gratitude, the love, the submission, the devotion, which belong to spiritual life, are raised to the height of religious affections only by the infinitude of their object. It is impossible, therefore, that the soul can live by the faith of the Son of God, unless it believes him to be divine. It is the exhibition of divine perfection in the person of Jesus Christ, through the power of the Holy Ghost, that calls forth, in the benumbed and lifeless soul, the aspirations and outgoings of the spiritual life. It is the glory of God as thus made known, thus softened, and brought down to our apprehension, and revealed in its manifold relations to us, that brings us into that communion with the divine nature in which our life consists. Nothing is more clearly taught in Scripture than that Christ is the object of the life of God in the souls of his people. He is the object of their supreme love, of their adoration, of their confidence, of their devotion and obedience. The whole New Testament is a hymn of praise to Christ. The whole church is prostrate at his feet; and whenever heaven has been opened to the eyes of mortals, its inhabitants were seen bowing before the throne of the Lamb. To live by faith of the Son of God, therefore, is to live by believing him to be divine. The faith which gives life to the soul, is the cognition, or spiritual apprehension of the glory of God in the person of Jesus Christ. Without this, faith is dead, and the soul turns its leaden eye on an eclipsed sun.

The second great truth we must believe concerning Christ is *his love*. It is not enough that we believe he loves others, we must believe that he loves us. Paul said, 'I live by the faith of the Son of God, who loved *me,* and gave himself for *me.'* This means, first negatively, that we do not exclude ourselves from the number of those who are the objects of Christ's love. This is really to reject him as our Saviour, while we admit he may be the Saviour of others. This is a very common form of unbelief. The soul under a sense of sin is disposed to think there is something peculiar in its case; something either in the number or the aggravation of its sins, which makes it an exception. It, therefore, does not believe that Christ loves it. It thinks this would be presumptuous, supposing that to be the object of Christ's love we must be lovely. It forgets the great, salient, life-giving truth of the gospel, that God loves his enemies, the ungodly, the polluted, and by loving makes them lovely. Alas! Did he not love us until we loved him, we should perish in our sins. The love of God is the love of a father—it has a hidden source, and is not founded on the character of its objects. It is unbelief, therefore, however it may assume the specious garb of humility, to exclude ourselves from the number of those whom Christ loves. So long as we do this we exclude ourselves from his salvation.

The second or positive aspect of the truth contained in this part of our text is, that we must appropriate to ourselves, personally and individually, the general assurance and promise of the love of Christ. Faith is not mere assent to the proposition that God is merciful; but trust in his mercy to us. It is not a mere assent to the truth that Christ loved sinners; but it is the appropriation of his love to ourselves; a believing that he loves us. It is not necessary in order to justify this appropriation, that there should be any special revelation that we, as distinguished from others, are the objects of divine love. The general declaration is made that God is merciful. The general promise is made that he will receive all who come to him through Christ. To appropriate these general declarations, is to believe that they are true, not in relation to others merely, but to us. We credit the assurance of God's love; we look up to him as propitious; we say to him, 'Our Father'; we regard him not as an enemy, but as a friend, for Christ's sake. This is faith. It is precisely because it is so hard to believe that, notwithstanding our unworthiness, God loves us, that the Scriptures are so full of assurances of his mercy, and that so many illustrations are employed to set forth the greatness and freeness of his love. God, it is said, hath commended his love towards us, in that while we were yet sinners, Christ died for us. 'Herein is love, not that we loved God, but that he loved us, and sent his Son to be the propitiation for our sins.' This also is the reason why the way in which God can be just and yet justify the ungodly is so distinctly set forth in his Word; and why we are exhorted to come with boldness to the throne of grace; to draw nigh with confidence; to come with even the full assurance of faith. This, too, is the reason why we are reproved for doubting the mercy of God, for distrusting his promises, or questioning his love. And this is the reason why such blessings are pronounced on those who trust in the Lord. This again is faith. Trusting in the Lord is believing. It is taking him at his word when he offers us his mercy, and assures us of his love. These are all degrees of this faith. It may be exercised with an assurance which excludes all doubt, or with a diffidence which scarcely admits of hope. It may alternate with doubt, and be attended with many misgivings. Still, the thing believed is, that Christ loves us. When, says Calvin, the least drop of faith is instilled into our minds, we begin to see the serene and placid face of our reconciled Father, dimly and afar it may be, but still it is seen. A man in a dungeon may have no light but through a crevice. Oh! how different is this from the bright light of day. It is, however, light. Thus the feeblest faith and the strongest assurance differ in degree and not in their nature or their object. The love of God in Christ is the object of both. The one sees that love glancing through the clouds, or stealing through a crevice; the other sees it as the sun at noon. Still, the thing seen, and the act of seeing are in both cases the same.

Faith in Christ, therefore, includes faith in his love towards us. The life of the soul consists in communion with God. There can be no communion with God, without faith in his love. We must believe that he loves us, in order that we should love him. We love God, says the apostle, because he first loved us. His love is the light and heat which calls our love into being and exercise; and the faith which gives life to the soul, must include the belief that Christ loves us. This is the fountain of life. That a Being so exalted and glorious should love us, who are so unworthy and worthless, fills the soul with wonder and gratitude. It calls forth all its activity, and fills it with joy unspeakable and full of glory.

The third element included in the life-giving faith of which the apostle speaks, is *believing that Christ gave himself for us, i.e., that he died for us*. This again includes two things—first, faith in his vicarious death as an atonement for sin; and second, faith in his death as a propitiation for our own individual or personal sins. Both of these are necessary. We must believe not only that Christ has made an atonement for sin; but that he died for us, that our sins are washed away in his blood. This is plain, because faith in Christ is the act of receiving and resting on him, as he is offered in the gospel, for our own personal salvation.

It cannot be necessary to prove before a Christian audience, that Christ is set forth in the gospel as a propitiation for sin, and that faith in him involves the receiving and resting upon him in that character. The Bible clearly teaches on this subject—first, in general terms, that Christ died for us; secondly, that the design of his death was to reconcile us to God; thirdly, that his death accomplishes this design, because it was a sacrifice, or propitiation for sin, or because he bore our sins in his own body on the tree; fourthly, that we are, therefore, justified meritoriously, not by works, but by the blood or righteousness of Christ, and, instrumentally, by faith. These are plain scriptural doctrines. Faith in Christ, therefore, must include the belief of these doctrines. To regard him merely as a teacher, or merely as a sovereign, or merely as the means by which a new and divine element has been introduced into our nature, is to reject him as a sacrifice for sin. It is to refuse to be saved by his blood. It is not, however, sufficient that we should believe the doctrine of atonement. This angels believe; this devils believe; this millions of our race believe, who yet die in their sins. It is not enough that we should stand as wondering spectators round the cross of the Lord of glory. It is not enough that we should see others wash their robes and make them white in the blood of the Lamb; we must appropriate the merit of his death; we must lay our hand on the head of the victim; we must have his blood sprinkled on our own conscience; we must accept him as the propitiation of our sins, and believe that God, for his sake, is reconciled to us. This is faith indeed! To believe that God, for Christ's sake, is propitious; that he loves us; that he regards us as his children, and has adopted us as his sons and daughters. Until we thus take Christ for our own, we have nothing wherewith to satisfy the demands of the law, or claims of justice; nothing wherewith we can appease a guilty conscience. But being justified by faith, we have peace with God and rejoice in hope of his glory.

He, then, that has the faith by which Paul lived, is able to say with Paul, I believe Jesus is the Son of God, or God manifest in the flesh. I believe he loves me, and gave himself for me. However weak and faltering our faith may be, if we have any saving faith at all, this is what we believe.

If such be the doctrine of the text and of the Scriptures, it answers two most important questions.—

First, *it tells the anxious inquirer definitely what he must do to be saved.* There are times of exigency in every man's experience—times in which the question, what we must do to be saved, must be answered without delay, and with clearness and authority. It is well to have the answer which God has given to this question graven on the palms of our hands. We shall need to read it sometimes when our sight is very dim. In such seasons of emergency, the soul is apt to get confused, and its vision wandering and indistinct. The mind becomes distracted in the multitude of its thoughts; it looks inward to determine the character of its own experience; it looks outward, and with unsteady eye gazes all around for some source of help. The voice of the Son of God on the cross is: Look unto me. The voice of his messengers is: Believe in the Lord Jesus Christ and thou shalt be saved. This is much. But still the anxious question arises—What must I believe? Here comes the definite answer from the lips of Paul: Believe that Jesus is the Son of God—that he loves you—that he gave himself for you. If you believe this, you will also believe that God for Christ's sake is reconciled to you; that your sins are forgiven; that Christ is made of God unto you wisdom, righteousness, sanctification, and redemption. Do not then, in these hours of trial, allow yourself to be careful and troubled about many things. This is the one thing needful. If you thus believe, your salvation is secure. But must I not be born again in order to enter into the kingdom of heaven? Certainly you must. Regeneration, however, is something to be experienced. Believing is something to be done. The former is God's work—the latter is yours. Do your part, and you will find that his is already done. When Christ said to the man with the withered arm: 'Stretch forth thy hand'; he did not wait to ascertain whether his arm was restored before he obeyed, although stretching forth his hand pre-supposed the restoration of his limb. Let not the man, therefore, who is seeking his salvation, be deluded by a false philosophy, and because faith implies regeneration, refuse to believe until he knows he is regenerated. His simple duty is to believe that Jesus is the Son of God; that he loved us, and died for us; and that God for his sake is reconciled to us. Let him do this and he will find peace, love, joy, wonder, gratitude and devotion filling his heart and controlling his life.

The second question answered by the doctrine of the text is: *How the divine life in the soul of the believer is to be sustained and invigorated.* Paul said the life which he lived, he lived by faith in the Son of God, who loved him, and gave himself for him. The clearer the views we can attain of the divine glory of the Redeemer, the deeper our sense of his love, and the stronger our assurance that he gave himself for us, the more of spiritual life shall we have; the more of love, reverence, and zeal; the more humility, peace, and joy; and the more strength to do and suffer in the cause of Christ. We should then regard all things but loss for the excellency of the knowledge of Christ Jesus our Lord. We should glory even in infirmities and afflictions, that his strength might be the more manifested in our weakness. Death would bear a smiling aspect, for we should have a constant desire to depart and be with Christ.

The great duty, then, inculcated in the text is to look away from ourselves, and to look only unto Christ; to contemplate him as God manifested in the flesh, loving us, and giving himself for us. The text calls upon us to suppress all doubts of his love as the suggestions of an evil heart of unbelief; to cherish the assurance that nothing can separate us from him; that having loved us while enemies, and died for us while sinners, he will love us unto the end. Believing this, we shall not only have perfect peace, but we shall feel that the entire devotion of our heart and life is the only return we can make for the love of Christ which passes knowledge.

'Now, unto him that loved us, and washed us from our sins in his blood, and hath made us kings and priests unto God and his Father, to him be glory and dominion for ever and ever. Amen.'

CHRISTIANITY WITHOUT CHRIST[1]

I
N one sense of the word, Christianity is the system of truth taught by Christ and his apostles. In this sense the question, What is Christianity? is simply an historical one. It may be answered intelligently and correctly by a man who does not profess to be a Christian, just as he may answer the question, what is Brahmanism? or, what is Buddhism?

In another sense, Christianity is that state of one's mind produced by faith in the truths revealed concerning Christ. In this sense, Christianity without Christ is an impossibility. It would be an effect without its proximate cause. Nevertheless. there is a form of religion, widespread and influential, which is called Christianity, in which Christ fails to occupy the position assigned to him in the Bible.

The Bible teaches us, that the same divine person by whom and for whom the universe was created, is the Jehovah of the Old Testament and the Jesus of the New. And as natural religion (in the subjective sense of the word) is that state of mind which is, or should be, produced by the revelation of God in the works of nature, and by our relation to him as his rational creatures; and as the religion of the devout Hebrew consisted in the state of mind produced by the revelation of the same God, made in the Law and the Prophets, and by their relation to him as their covenant God and Father; so Christianity is that state of mind produced by the knowledge of the same God, as manifest in the flesh, who loved us and gave himself for us, and by our relation to him as the subjects of his redemption.

Three things follow from this: First, as the same divine person is the Creator of heaven and earth, the Jehovah of the Old Testament and the Jesus of the New, there can be no inconsistency between the religion of nature, the religion of the Hebrews, and the religion of

[1] Charles Hodge, 'Christianity without Christ', *The Presbyterian Quarterly and Princeton Review*, Vol. 5 No. 18 (1876), pp. 352-62.

Christians. The one does not assume that to be true which either of the others assumes to be false. The only difference is that which arises from increased knowledge of the object of worship, and the new relations which we sustain to him. The Hebrews, in worshipping Jehovah, did not cease to worship the God of nature; and the Christian, in worshipping Christ, does not cease to worship the God of the Hebrews.

Second, it is impossible that the higher form of religion should be merged into a lower. It is impossible that the religion of a Hebrew should sink into natural religion. That would imply that he ceased to be a Hebrew, that he rejected the revelations of Moses and the prophets, and that he renounced his allegiance to Jehovah as the God of his fathers. In like manner, it is impossible that the religion of a Christian can sink into that of the Old Testament, or into that of nature. That would imply that he ceased to be a Christian; that he rejected or ignored all that the New Testament reveals concerning God and Christ. There could be no true religion in the mind of a Hebrew that was not determined by his relation to Jehovah as his covenant God; and there can be no true religion in the mind of a Christian that is not determined by his relation to Christ as God manifested in the flesh.

Third, the Christian, in worshipping Christ, does not cease to worship the Father and the Spirit. He does not fail to recognize and appreciate his relation to the Father, who loved the world and gave his Son for its redemption; nor does he fail to recognize his relation to the Holy Spirit, on whom he is absolutely dependent, and whose gracious office it is to apply to men the redemption purchased by Christ. In worshipping Christ, we worship the Father and the Spirit; for these three are one—one only living and true God, the same in substance and equal in power and glory. Christ says, I am in the Father and the Father in me. I and the Father are one. He that hath seen me, hath seen the Father; and therefore, he that worships the Son, worships the Father. Hence, it is written, 'Whosoever denieth the Son, the same hath not the Father'; but, 'Whosoever shall confess that Jesus is the Son of God, God dwelleth in him, and he in God.' 'He that hath the Son hath life; he that hath not the Son of God, hath not life.' It is to be remembered, however, that in the mysterious constitution of the Godhead, the second person of the Trinity is the *Logos,* the Word, the Revealer. It is through him that God is known. He is the brightness of his glory, revealing what God is. We should not know that there is a sun in the firmament, if it were not for his ἀπαυγασμα. So we should not know that God is, or what he is, were it not for his Son. 'No man knoweth the Father but the Son, and he to whom the Son shall reveal him.' In having Christ, therefore, we have God; for in him dwelleth the fulness of the Godhead.

It does not need to be proved that Jehovah was the God of the Hebrews; the object of their worship, of their love, gratitude, and trust. They recognized him as their absolute and rightful sovereign, whose authority extended over their inward as well as their outward life. On him they were dependent, and to him they were responsible. His favour was their life, and they could say, 'Whom have we in heaven but thee, and there is none on earth we desire beside thee.'

As little does it require proof that Christ is the God of Christians. In the New Testament all divine titles are given to him. He is called God, the true God, the great God, God over all, Jehovah. He is declared to be almighty, omnipresent, immutable, and eternal. He created heaven and earth; all things visible and invisible were made by him and for him, and by him all things consist. He upholds all things by the word of his power. This divine person became flesh; he was found in fashion as a man, and in the form of a servant. Having been born of a woman, he was made under the law, and fulfilled all righteousness. He redeemed us from the curse of the law by being made a curse for us. He bore our sins in his own body on the tree. He died the just for the unjust, to bring us unto God, and having died for our offences, and risen again for our justification, has ascended to heaven, where he is seated on the right hand of God, all power in heaven and earth being committed to his hands, and where he ever lives to make intercession for his people. This Christ, God and man, in two distinct natures and one person forever, was to the writers of the New Testament all and in all. He was their wisdom; from him they derived all their knowledge of divine things, and to his teaching they implicitly submitted. He was their righteousness; renouncing all dependence on their own righteousness, they trusted exclusively on the merit of his obedience and death for their acceptance with God.

He was their sanctification. Their spiritual life was derived from him and sustained by him. They were in him as the branch is in the vine, or the members in the body, so that it was not they who lived, but Christ who lived in them. Without him they could do nothing; they could no more bring forth the fruits of holy living separated from him than a branch can bear fruit when separated from the vine, nor than the body can live when separated from the head. They felt themselves to be in him in such a sense, that what he did, they did. They died with him. They rose with him. What he is, they become. What he has, they receive, all in their measure—that is, as much as they can hold. They are filled with the fulness of God in him.

This being so, it follows, of course, that Christ was to them the object of divine worship and of all the religious affections, of adoration, of supreme love, of trust, of submission, of devotion. He was their absolute sovereign and proprietor by the double right of creation and redemption. Love to him was the motive, his will the rule, his glory the end of their obedience. It was Christ for them to live. Living or dying, they were the Lord's. They enforced all moral duties out of regard to him; wives were to obey their husbands, children their parents, servants their masters, for Christ's sake. Christians were commanded not to utter a contaminating word in a brother's ear because he belonged to Christ; they endeavoured to preserve their personal purity, because their bodies were the members of Christ. The blessedness of heaven in their view consisted in being with Christ, in beholding his glory, enjoying his love, in being like him, and in being devoted to his services. It is a simple fact, that such was the Christianity of the writers of the New Testament. Their religious life terminated on Christ, and was determined by their relation to him. He was their God, their Saviour, their Prophet, Priest, and King; they depended on his righteousness for their justification; they looked to him for sanctification. He was their life, their way, their end. If they lived, it was for him; if they died, it was that they might be with him. They did not attempt to reform or to save men on the principles of natural religion, or by a process of moral culture. These had their place, but they are inadequate and absorbed in a higher moral power. Paul, in writing to Titus, speaking of Christians before their conversion, says: 'They were sometimes foolish, disobedient, deceived, serving diverse lusts and pleasures, living in malice and envy, hateful, and hating one another. But after the kindness and love of God our Saviour toward man appeared, not by works of righteousness which we have done, but according to his mercy, he saved us, by the washing of regeneration and the renewing of the Holy Ghost, which he shed on us abundantly, through Jesus Christ our Saviour, that, being justified by grace, we should be heirs according to the hope of eternal life.' They, therefore, laboured for the reformation and salvation of men by going everywhere preaching Christ as the only Saviour from sin.

What Christianity was in the hearts of the apostles, it has been in the hearts of Christians of all ages, and in all parts of the world. Of this, every Christian has the evidence in his own experience. Christ is to him both God and man—God manifest in the flesh; God surrounded by the rainbow of humanity, which softens, diversifies, and beautifies his rays. Christ he worships, trusts, loves, and obeys. Christ is his wisdom, his righteousness, his sanctification, his redemption. Christ is ever near him, so that he can be spoken to, appealed to, and communed with; a present help in every time of need. Christ is the Christian's portion for time and for eternity. With Christ he has everything, and without him he has nothing.

The experience of one Christian is the experience of all. This is the conscious bond of their union. The hymns which live through all ages, are hymns of praise to Christ. All Protestants can join with St Bernard, when he says:

> Jesus, the very thought of Thee
> With sweetness fills my breast;
> But sweeter far Thy face to see,
> And in Thy presence rest.
>
> When once Thou visitest the heart,
> Then light begins to shine,
> Then earthly vanities depart,
> Then kindles love divine.
>
> Jesus, our only joy be Thou,
> As Thou our prize shalt be;
> Jesus, be Thou our glory now
> And through eternity.

'Jesus our being's hope and end.' They can also join with that other
Bernard, who says of heaven:

> The Lamb is all thy splendour,
> The Crucified thy praise,
> His laud and benediction,
> His ransomed people raise.

What is true of the Christianity of the medieval saints, is true of
believers now. Toplady's hymn, 'Rock of Ages, cleft for me', finds a
response in every Christian heart. So does his hymn,

> Compared with Christ, in all besides,
> No comeliness I see;
> The one thing needful, dearest Lord,
> Is to be one with Thee.
>
> Thyself bestow; for Thee alone,
> I absolutely[1] pray.
> Less than Thyself will not suffice,
> My comfort to restore.
>
> More than Thyself I cannot have;
> And Thou canst give no more.

Cowper expresses the hopes and feelings of every believer in his
hymn,

> There is a fountain filled with blood
> Drawn from Immanuel's veins;
> And sinners, plunged beneath that flood,
> Lose all their guilty stains.

Every Christian can join with Newton in saying,

> How sweet the name of Jesus sounds
> In a believer's ears;
> It soothes his sorrows, heals his wounds,
> And drives away his tears.

---

[1] *Absolutely* means here *unconditionally,* and is the proper word.

> It makes the wounded spirit whole,
> And calms the troubled breast;
> 'Tis manna to the hungry soul,
> And to the weary rest.

He is a rock, a shield, a hiding-place, a never-failing treasury.

> Jesus, my Shepherd, Husband, Friend,
> My Prophet, Priest, and King,
> My Lord, my Life, my Way, my End,
> Accept the praise I bring.
>
> When I see Thee as Thou art,
> I'll praise Thee as I ought.

In like manner, Keble makes Christ everything to the believer.

> Sun of my soul, Thou Saviour dear,
> It is not night, if Thou be near.
>
> Abide with me from morn to eve,
> For without Thee, I cannot live;
> Abide with me when night is nigh;
> For without Thee, I dare not die.
>
> Come near to bless us when we wake,
> Ere through the world our way we take;
> Till, in the ocean of Thy love,
> We lose ourselves in heaven above.

Wesley's hymn, 'Jesus, lover of my soul', is on the lips of every English-speaking Christian. All look up to him as a guide, as their refuge, their trust, their only source of strength, as their all, more than all—as the source of spiritual and eternal life. In another hymn he says:

> I thirst, I pine, I die to prove,
> The wonders of redeeming love,
> The love of Christ to me.
>
> Thy only love do I require:
> Nothing on earth beneath desire,

> Nothing in heaven above.
> Let earth, and heaven, and all things go,
> Give me Thy only love to know,
> Give me Thy only love.

Again,

> Oh, for a thousand tongues to sing
> My dear Redeemer's praise,
> The glories of my God and King,
> The triumphs of his grace. *etc., etc.*

So Dr Watts,

> Dearest of all the names above,
> My Jesus and my God.

> Till God in human flesh I see,
> My thoughts no comfort find.

> But, if Immanuel's face appear,
> My hope, my joy begins.

> Jesus, my God, Thy blood alone,
> Has power sufficient to atone;
> Thy blood can make me white as snow;
> No Jewish type could cleanse me so.

> To the dear fountain of Thy blood,
> Incarnate God, I fly,
> There let me wash my guilty soul
> From sins of deepest dye.

> A guilty, weak, and helpless worm,
> On Thy kind arms I fall,
> Be Thou my strength and righteousness,
> My Jesus and my all.

Volumes might be filled with such proofs of what Christianity is in the hearts of Christians. It will be observed, it is not mainly Christ as a teacher, as an example, nor even as the expiator of our sins—it is not mainly what he has done that is rendered thus prominent;

but what he *is*. He is God clothed in our nature, ever with us, ever in us—our life, our present joy, our everlasting portion; the one to whom we owe everything, from whom we derive everything, who loves us with a love that is peculiar, exclusive (that is, such as he entertains for no other class of beings), and unspeakable.

In painful contrast with the Christianity of the Bible and of the church, there is a kind of religion, very prevalent and very influential, calling itself Christianity, which may be properly designated Christianity without Christ. It might be all that it is, though Christ had never appeared, or, at least, although our relation to him were entirely different from what it really is.

The lowest form of this kind of religion is that which assumes Christ to be a mere man, or, at most, merely a creature. Then, of course, he cannot be an object of adoration, of supreme love, of trust, and of devotion. The difference is absolute between the inward religious state of those who regard Christ as a creature, and that of those who regard him as God. If the one be true religion, the other is impiety.

The second form of this religion admits of higher views of the person of Christ, but it reduces Christianity to benevolence. And by benevolence is often meant nothing more than philanthropy. The gospel is made to consist in the inculcation of the command, 'Love your neighbour as yourself.' All who approximately do this are called Christians. Hence it is said, that if all records concerning Christ should be blotted out of existence, his religion could be evolved out of our own nature. And hence, too, an avowed atheist is told, that if he sits up all night with a sick child, he is a Christian, whatever he may think. A popular poem—popular because of the sentiment which it teaches—represents the recording angel as placing at the head of those who love God, the name of the man who could only say; 'Write me as one who loves my fellow men.' The love of our fellow men is thus made the highest form of religion. This is below even natural religion. It ignores God as well as Christ. Yet this is the doctrine which we find, variously sugared over and combined, in poetry, in novels, in magazines, and even in religious journals.

The doctrine which makes benevolence, the desire or purpose to promote the happiness not of our fellow men merely, but of being in general, or all beings, logically, and often actually, results essentially in the same thing. All religion, all moral excellence, consists in benevolence. Our only obligation is so to act as to promote the greatest good. This is the motive and the end of obedience, According to the New Testament, the motive to obedience is the love of Christ, the rule of obedience is the will of Christ, and its end the glory of Christ. Every Christian is benevolent; but his benevolence does not make him a Christian; his Christianity makes him benevolent. Throughout all ages the men who have laboured most and suffered most for the good of others, have been Christians—men animated and controlled by Christ's love to them, and by their love to Christ. It is evident that the spiritual life—the inward religious state—of the man to whom it is Christ to live, is very different from that of the man who lives for the happiness of the universe. A man might thus live if there were no Christ.

Another form of religion in which Christ fails to occupy his proper position, is that which assumes God to be merely a moral governor, of infinite power and benevolence. Being infinitely benevolent, he desires the well-being of his kingdom. To forgive sin without some suitable manifestation of his disapprobation of sin, would be inconsistent with a wise benevolence. Christ makes that manifestation in his sufferings and death. Then he retires; henceforth we have nothing to do with him; we have to deal with God on the principles of natural religion; we must submit to his authority, obey his commandments, and expect to be rewarded, not merely according to, but for, our works. Christ merits nothing for us, we are not to look to him for sanctification, or any other blessing. All he has done, or does, is to make it consistent with the benevolence of God to forgive sin. Forgiveness of sin, therefore, is the only benefit which God bestows on us on account of Christ.

This theory changes everything. Men are rebellious subjects. It is now consistent in God to forgive them. He calls on them to submit, to lay down their arms, then he is free to deal with them as though they had never sinned. They must merit, not forgiveness—for that is granted on account of what Christ has done—but the reward promised to obedience; justification is simply pardon. Conversion is that change which takes place in a man when he ceases to be selfish, and becomes benevolent; ceases making his own happiness the end of his life, and determines to seek the happiness of the universe. The essence of faith is love, *i.e.,* benevolence. It is hard to see, according to this theory, in what sense Christ is our Prophet, Priest, and King; how he is our wisdom, righteousness. sanctification, and redemption; what is meant by our being in him as the branch is in the vine; or, what our Lord meant when he said, 'without me, ye can do nothing'; what was in Paul's mind when he said, 'it is Christ for me to live', 'it is not I that live, but Christ liveth in me', and so on to the end. This is a different kind of religion from that which we find in the Bible and in the experience of the church. As the religion (in the subjective sense of the word) is different, so is the preaching different, and so are the modes of dealing with sinners, and of promoting reformation among men. Some go so far as to hold, that there can be morality without religion; men are exhorted to be moral because it is right, because it will promote their own welfare, and make them respected and useful. They are to become morally good by a process of moral culture, by suppressing evil feelings and cherishing such as are good ones, by abstaining from what is wrong and doing what is right.

Others take the higher ground of theism, or of natural religion, and bring in considerations drawn from our relation to God as an infinitely perfect being, our creator and preserver and father, who has rightful authority over us, who has prescribed the rule of duty, and who rewards the righteous and punishes the wicked.

All this is true and good in its place. But it is like persuading the blind to see and the deaf to hear. This is not the gospel. Christ is the only Saviour from sin, the only source of holiness, or of spiritual life. The first step in salvation from sin is our reconciliation to God. The reconciliation is effected by the expiation made by the death of Christ (*Rom.* 5:10). It is his blood, and his blood alone, that cleanses from sin. As long as men are under the law, they bring forth fruit unto death; it is only when freed from the law, freed from its inexorable demand of perfect obedience and from its awful penalty, that they bring forth fruit unto God (*Rom.* 7:4-6). Christ delivered us from the law as demanding perfect obedience, by being made under the law, and fulfilling all righteousness for us; and he redeems us from the curse of the law, by being made a curse for us—dying the just for the unjust, and bearing our sins in his own body on the tree. Being thus reconciled unto God by his death, we are saved by his life. He sends the Holy Spirit to impart to us spiritual life, and transforms us more and more into his own image. The Spirit reveals to us the glory of Christ and his infinite love. He makes us feel not only that we owe everything to him, but that he himself is everything to us—our present joy and our everlasting portion—our all in all. Thus every other motive to obedience is absorbed and sublimated into love to Christ and zeal for his glory. His people become like him, and as he went about doing good, so do they. All this of course, is folly to the Greek. God, however, has determined by the foolishness of preaching to save them who believe.

Pulmonary consumption is more destructive of human life than the plague. So Christianity without Christ, in all its forms, the phthisis of the church, is more to be dreaded than scepticism, whether scientific or philosophical. The only remedy is preaching Christ, as did the apostles.

Two important facts are to be borne in mind. First, the inward religious life of men, as well as their character, and conduct, are determined by their doctrinal opinions. Even the *Edinburgh Review,* years ago, said, 'The character of an age is determined by the theology of that age.' Therefore, any system of doctrine which assigns to Christ a lower position than that which he occupies in the New Testament, must, in a like degree, lower the standard of Christianity—that is, the religious life of those calling themselves Christians. Second, nevertheless, it is equally true that men are more governed by their practical than by their speculative convictions. The idealist does not feel and act on his belief that the external world has no real existence. In like manner, the religious life of men is often determined more by the plain teaching of the Scriptures and by the common faith of the church than by their theological theories. Hence, men have often more of Christ in their religion than in their theology. It is, however, of the last importance to remember, that sound doctrine is, under God, our only security for true religion and pure morals. If we forsake the truth, God forsakes us.

NICHOLAS MURRAY
1802-1861

ESTEEMED pastor, eloquent preacher, and active churchman with a passion for missions and ministerial instruction, Nicholas Murray was born into a Roman Catholic home on December 25, 1802, in the county of Westmeath, Ireland. Murray's father died while Nicholas was still a young boy. Following a few years of schooling, he was apprenticed as a merchant's clerk. Harsh treatment in this position led him to run away and return home. Determined to make a new life for himself, he sailed for New York in 1818.

Murray soon found employment as a proof-reader for the Harper publishing company. In a strange providence, Murray's reading of the New Testament led him to abandon Roman Catholicism, whereupon he renounced Christianity and became a professed infidel. But his life was soon to change. A sermon preached by Dr John Mason convinced Murray of his sin and pointed him to God's mercy in Christ. Seeking spiritual counsel, he had opportunity to meet Dr Gardiner Spring. Spring's interest in Murray facilitated his spiritual growth and eventual membership in Spring's church. It was during this period of his life that Murray began to pursue a call to the ministry.

After completing a course of study at Amherst Academy and graduating from Williams College in 1826, Murray worked as an agent of the American Tract Society before entering Princeton Theological Seminary. Murray worked intermittently with the American Tract Society during his time at the seminary.

Licensed to preach by the Presbytery of Philadelphia in 1828, Murray served as a domestic missionary before accepting a pastoral call to Wilkesbarre, Pennsylvania. In 1833 he accepted a call to serve in Elizabethtown, New Jersey, where he remained until his death in 1861.

A gifted preacher and devoted pastor, Murray twice turned down the offer of seminary professorships as well as numerous invitations to more prominent churches in major cities. Contemporaries considered him one of the outstanding Presbyterian preachers of his day.

Murray's keen intellect and Irish wit were suffused with an eminent piety that drew people to his ministry. An active churchman, he also served as one of the directors of Princeton Theological Seminary. As a student, he was profoundly influenced by Archibald Alexander and Samuel Miller. Their vision for ministerial training captured his heart and became a mainstay in his approach to pastoral ministry and support for the seminary in later years.

Murray's labours as a pastor were offset by his accomplishments as an author. A number of his sermons and addresses were published in volumes such as *Parish and other Pencillings* and *The Happy Home;* but his most popular volume—printed in a number of editions in both Great Britain and America, and also translated into several foreign languages—was his *Letters to Bishop Hughes.*

Murray's stirring address at the 1854 inauguration of Alexander T. M'Gill as Professor of Pastoral Theology, Church Government and the Composition and Delivery of Sermons, at Princeton Theological Seminary, bears testimony to his passionate eloquence and burden for the preparation of future generations of faithful ministers and powerful preachers of the gospel.

THE MINISTRY WE NEED[1]

REVEREND Directors of the Theological Seminary, and Respected Friends of this venerable institution:

We are here assembled for the performance of a most solemn and important duty. To the chair which Dr Alexander filled with such distinguished ability for about forty years, and which was left vacant by his universally lamented death, the last General Assembly elected the Reverend Alexander T. M'Gill, D.D., and he having signified his acceptance of the appointment, we are here assembled for his inauguration. And by my brethren, who are the agents of the Assembly in the direction of this institution, it is made my duty to deliver the charge to the newly-elected professor on the present occasion.

It is expected that the hour devoted to this service should be occupied with those reflections suited to the occasion; to the character we sustain; and to the relations of our theological seminary to the world, which is to be restored to its allegiance to God, mainly, through the labours of the ministry. And the topics to which we now invite your attention are *the characteristics of an able minister of the New Testament,* and *the world's great need of such ministers.*

The word 'minister' means a servant; and 'ministry' means service. The word usually translated minister, διακονος, is the name given in the ancient church to those who collected alms for the poor, and distributed them; but, when connected with the words Κριστου, Θεου, Εὐγγελιου [Christ, God, gospel], and the like, it means religious instructors, or preachers of the gospel. Yet the leading character of a

[1] Nicholas Murray, 'The Ministry We Need', *Discourses at the Inauguration of the Rev. Alexander T. M'Gill, D.D., as Professor of Pastoral Theology, Church Government, and the Composition and Delivery of Sermons in the Theological Seminary at Princeton, NJ* (Philadelphia: C. Sherman, 1854), pp. 3-34.

minister is that of a servant, and the ministry is a service of a special kind. Every Christian is a servant of Christ, but every Christian is not a minister of the gospel. Every deacon is a servant, as the word implies; but his service respects temporal things, and the office was instituted that the ministry of the Word might fully devote itself to the high duty of spiritual instruction.

As to the ministry, there are obviously two extremes in the church; one among ministers, the other among the people. That among ministers, is an abuse of their office, so as to make it a stepping-stone to power, and to the exercise of undue dominion over their brethren. That among the people, arises from the idea that, because ministers are servants, therefore they are their masters. The one extreme has given rise to hierarchies, which, in their most modified forms, have been a calamity to the church and the world;—and the other has given rise to insubordination, springing from the assumption that ministers, as such, were accountable to the people, and not to Jesus Christ. These extremes exist and are producing one another; as in the State, anarchy produces despotism, and despotism anarchy. Whilst the people owe obedience to scriptural officers, exercising due authority in the Lord, ministers should ever regard the precept of their Master, 'He that will be great, let him be the servant of all', and the example of their Master, who said, 'I have been among you as one that serveth.' They should aim to be, in every respect, 'able ministers of the New Testament, not of the letter, but of the Spirit; for the letter killeth, but the Spirit giveth life'. But what are the characteristics of an able minister of the New Testament? We would place among these:

1. *Decided piety.*—Piety is a firm and right apprehension of the Being, perfections, and providence of God, with suitable affections to him, resemblance to his moral perfections, and a constant obedience to his will. To be an able minister and faithful, this must be decidedly possessed. Otherwise, the great spring of ministerial life is wanting, or defective. No gifts, however splendid or attractive, can compensate for the lack of piety. It requires but a small degree of this for a young man to go through our required course of training for the ministry, and to sustain a respectable character. Its trial commences with the active duties of the ministry. There is difficulty in finding

a field of labour, and division attending his settlement, his salary is inadequate, his labours are exhausting, his people are lukewarm, he is opposed in his labours, the world murmurs, his preaching is not successful, his talents are depreciated, and he is apparently neglected by his brethren. Now comes the trial of faith, piety, and principles, which soon makes apparent the real state of a minister's heart. And unless his heart is deeply imbued with the Spirit of Christ, he fails to accomplish many of the great ends for which the ministry was instituted.

The lack of that Spirit also manifests itself in efforts to become what the world calls a popular preacher. One is truly popular by the force of his talents and the fervour of his piety; another, because he makes it his main object. Between these there is a great difference. One is simple and solemn; the other, magniloquent and self-complacent. The one impresses by his thoughts; the other by his language. The one collects his flowers from Calvary; the other from Parnassus. The one wins converts to Christ: the other, makes admirers of himself. The one moistens the eye with a tear; the other, curls the lip with a smile of admiration. The one preaches strongly and boldly the doctrines of the cross; the other withholds them, lest they should offend, and blunts his arrows lest they should penetrate;—emulous of the reputation of a popular preacher. These nice and pretty preachers are too rapidly multiplying; and they will continue to increase or diminish in the proportion of the degree of serious piety in the ministry. Such are not ambassadors for Christ; they are but Sabbath-day performers before fashionable audiences, that seek amusement alternately at the church, the opera, and the theatre!

How sadly the Jewish church suffered from false prophets and priests! How soon the early church was rent and torn by ungodly ministers! For how many ages, not excepting our own, the boasted successors of the apostles were the vilest of men! How even, at the present day, in some countries nominally Protestant, the lowest infidelity is decked in the robes of the ministry; and how, in communions regarded as evangelical, an unsanctified clergy are prostituting the order and ordinances of God's house, to the supplanting of a spiritual by a formal and ritual religion! And, when we examine the history of the church, we find that true piety was the great element of the success of those who have most blest it by their ministry. It was the piety of Paul that sustained him amid his manifold trials and persecutions and untiring labours. We owe the glorious Reformation far more to the piety than to the policy or talents of the Reformers. What but the piety of our Presbyterian fathers sustained and animated them amid the glens, and the rocks, and the mountains of Scotland, when the bloody trooper was sent out for their murder by those who worshipped in cathedrals. And if we look into the character of such men as Baxter, Doddridge, Edwards, Dickinson, Davies, Tennent, or to come down to some of our own *Alumni,* whose names are as fragrant ointment among us, we find that decided, warm-hearted piety was the great element of their success.

2. *To be an able minister requires due qualification for the work.* In the magnitude of its objects, the preaching of the gospel far surpasses every other employment in which man can engage. There is scarcely any intellectual culture, civil liberty, or social order, but through its influence. And it is alike God's appointed instrument for the salvation of men, and for the moral illumination of our world. To the scheme of redemption all objects and events in our world are subordinate and subservient. This is the point where all the attributes of God converge into a blaze of glory. And the means appointed to make known the redemption which is in Christ Jesus to our world, is the preaching of the gospel. If angels, without being satisfied, are prying into its wonders; if Paul, the eloquent and aged, could say, 'Who is sufficient for these things?', then a pious, uninspired man should seek the highest possible qualifications for the ministry.

The distinguishing mark of a faithful minister is this, 'he shall feed his people with knowledge and understanding'. Unless he possesses these, how can he mete them out to his people? What, but sound, can an empty vessel send forth? Regarding an uneducated ministry as unfit to instruct the people, as unfitted to obtain for the gospel the attention and the respect of the thoughtful, and as very liable to become the dupes of error, and the promoters of fanaticism and folly, our church, from its origin, has insisted on an educated ministry. Hence, it has ever been the patron of the school, the academy, the college, and of schools for the instruction of her rising prophets. Hence, the erection of this seminary, and of its sister institutions, that the future pastors of the churches may have the benefit of a thorough training for their high duties. Mere piety will exert an influence; but it requires an alliance with talent and education to arrest the attention of the vicious, and to reform public morals. It required all the talent and education of Paul, to cross the Rubicon of Jewish prejudice; to confute the Pharisee and Sadducee in the synagogue the sophist in the school of Tyrannus, and the subtle heathen in all the courts of the Gentiles. It required all the talent and education of Luther and Melancthon to breast the storm of Papal wrath that fell upon them; and, like the towering cliff, to bear unmoved and uninjured, the tempest, the thunder, and the lightning, that played around them. And wherever the gospel has made signal and permanent conquests, in changing the face of society, in moulding civil and moral institutions, in correcting the opinions and reforming the lives of the intelligent and influential, it has been always preached by men of high mental endowment, and of great and varied acquisition.

The living historian of the Reformation tells us, that 'the Reformers always connected deep study with the laborious ministry; the ministry was the end, study was but the means'. And this we might learn from their works. And here we have revealed one of the great elements of their success. The great defect of the ministry of our day is a neglect of study; and this is induced by causes which we cannot now stop to state. They are known of all men. A young man of fine promise concludes his course of study and becomes a pastor, exciting high hopes of eminence and usefulness. Amid the calls and rewards of active life, books and studies are neglected. Applauded by those who praise without stint, because without sense, he soon learns to lean upon his unassisted genius and natural sagacity. He soon discovers a way to reputation other and shorter than the dull and beaten one of industry. He soon cuts the knot that he cannot untie, and jumps the difficulty that he cannot remove, and depends less upon patience of investigation than upon his intuition to comprehend causes, and subjects, and methods of argumentation. And soon his mind, naturally fertile and productive, becomes barren. Now his sermons are alike, whatever may be the text. All have something old, but nothing new. His people complain; but habits are now formed which cannot be mended. His people cry for meat, and he gives them milk. Unprofited by his labours, they seek a dismission; and he must retire from a field where diligent habits of study would make him an honoured and useful man until the almond blossoms flourished upon his head. He began a man; he ends a boy. As a rule, the minister should make everything give way to a due and full preparation for the pulpit. The pulpit is the place from which to instruct the people. There, pre-eminently, he is to prove himself an able minister of the New Testament. He should ever feel that the image of God is not to be re-instamped upon our world by those who are talkers, and exhorters, and storytellers, instead of preachers and teachers; and whose best prepared nutriment is but milk for babes.

3. *To be an able minister of the New Testament requires the full presentation of its great doctrines.* It is by the preaching of the gospel, that God has ordained to save men. Everything else, so far as saving men is concerned, is but giving scorpions for eggs, and serpents for fish. The grand object of the Saviour during his incarnation, was to prove that he was the promised Messiah by the miracles which he wrought and by showing that in himself all the lines of history and prophecy met and blended. His life he closed upon the cross agreeably to the Scriptures; being made a sin offering for his people that they might be made the righteousness of God in him. And with the cup of sorrow in his hand, and with the agonies of Gethsemane and Calvary in full view, he uttered this memorable sentiment, 'And I, if I be lifted up from the earth, will draw all men unto me.' This refers, primarily, to his crucifixion, but in a secondary and important sense to the preaching of the doctrines of the cross. And, hence, after the resurrection had completed the circle of testimony to his Messiahship, and the Spirit had been granted, the work of the apostles was to preach a crucified Christ as God's great remedy for the moral diseases of man. This was the theme of Peter amid the gatherings at the feast of Pentecost—and of Paul amid all the cities of the Gentiles. Their grand theme was 'repentance towards God, and faith in the Lord Jesus Christ'. And, hence, their ministry was mighty, through God, to the pulling down of strongholds. And such is the course which must be pursued by all their successors in office who desire to approve themselves as able ministers of the New Testament.

When we look into the ages of conflict between truth and error, we find that those have been always the victors who presented the doctrines of the cross most simply and purely. And in every branch of the church that ministry has been most successful which has been thus characterized. The preaching of Christ and him crucified, produced the Reformation, and has sustained it. If any doubt this, let them read D'Aubigné, and Luther on the Galatians, and the Life of John Knox, and Howe's Living Temple, and his nine sermons on Friendship with God, and Flavel's forty-two sermons on the Character of Christ, and his thirty-four on the Method of Grace, and Owen on the Spirit, and on the Person and Glory of Christ. A Christ crucified for the sins of sinners, as their substitute, and in their law place, is the great central truth of our religion. And to the directing of the eyes of all men to the Lamb of God that taketh away the sins of the world, an able minister of the New Testament will make everything subservient. The *Alumni* of this seminary will all testify that thus we have been emphatically taught by the venerated professor in whose vacated chair we place today a successor. And our heartfelt supplication will ascend to the God of all grace, that in this, as in all other respects, the mantle of Elijah may fall upon Elisha.

And is there not need for warning upon this subject, when so many are turning away from the simplicity of Christ, spoiling the gospel, 'through philosophy, and vain deceit, after the tradition of men, after the rudiments of this world'? Instead of preaching Christ, and simply expounding his Word, how many are seeking, above all things, to make adherents to their own peculiarities! One has his theory of moral suasion,—another, of inspiration,—another, as to original sin,—another, as to regeneration,—another, as to the atonement; another, as to interpretation,—another, as to the efficacy of sacraments and ceremonies,—another, of moral and social reform. In many portions of the church there is a raging controversy as to the mint, anise, and cumin, amid which the lifting up of the Son of Man is sadly neglected. It is the preaching of the cross that gives power to the ministry; and when that is neglected for anything else, we cut off the lock of our strength. The truth as it is in Jesus is the only successful weapon of the ministry; and the history of the church is pregnant with the most important lessons upon this subject. As the truth died out from the ancient church, fancy and credulity and corruption had a freer play; the tokens of departing glory and of a coming night fearfully multiplied. Shade thickened after shade. Each succeeding age came wrapped in a deeper gloom, until the sun which rose over Judea set at Rome,—until the flood of light which it poured upon the world had to retreat before that long, long night, called the 'Dark Ages', which seemed to roll on as if it were never to end!

And what, in some quarters, has been made the reproach of our beloved institution, is its true glory; and is the great cause of the rejoicing of all its friends, and of its influence in all sections of our country, and in all branches of the church, that amid the currents and counter-currents of erroneous doctrine; amid the conflicts of philosophy falsely so called; amid the storms which have blown over the church, and which have made some of its men of might to bow; amid the reproaches of lukewarmness and time-serving by its friends, and of bigoted attachment to antiquated formularies, and of blind submission to authority by its enemies; it has continued steadfast and immovable in the faith once delivered to the saints. So may it ever continue. And the prayer of all of us will ascend to the God of all grace that the beloved brother placed among its professors by the election of the church, may strengthen every cord that tends to bind it, in immovable anchorage under the shelter of the Rock of Ages.

4. *An able minister must be impressive.* If true, as the notable reviewer of Milton affirms, that 'as civilization advances poetry necessarily declines', it is equally true, and for the same reasons, that in the proportion people are enlightened, is it difficult to impress them! In the age of Moses the Jews were more easily impressed than in that of Isaiah; and as the unsanctified mind becomes accustomed to the light of science and religion, does it lose its susceptibility of impression from the public exhibitions of divine truth! And hence the inelegant but descriptive phrase, 'a gospel-hardened sinner', to describe a person who, under the influence of light, has lost, measurably, that susceptibility. We state the principle, not as an argument for the blessedness of ignorance, but for an impressive ministry. It is by the preaching of the gospel that men are to be saved instrumentally; and no effort should be left untried to raise up a ministry prepared to preach, so as to impress men with a sense of its eternal importance. And especially

should this be the case in our country, where, more than in any other, the public mind is swayed by popular addresses; where the current to worldliness is so proverbially strong, and where, perhaps, more than in any other, the difficulty may be greater of arresting attention and turning away the heart from the pursuit of vanity. Ours, beyond all others, is the country for a Whitefield, a Summerfield, a Larned, a John Breckinridge; men peculiarly adapted to sway the masses, and whose dispensation was public impression. Such men may leave no monuments to their learning; but they give out impulses which may be absorbed by other minds, and plans of action, and thus pass away from view, but never die.

May it not be that to this point too little attention is directed in our seminaries; and by our young brethren who resort to them for instruction? Their chairs of Theology, and of History, and of Criticism, are filled with the best, and best furnished minds in the church; but in many of them there is no adequate provision made for instruction in the art of preaching. In the field which is the world, the power of impression is the main thing; is it not regarded as too secondary in our theological schools? Is it not even sometimes the subject of the sneer of the dull scholastic? Notwithstanding the positive and accumulated evidence upon the subject, there is a way of talking about popular talent as if it were necessarily disconnected with profound thought; and also a way of talking about mere scholarship, and the power of accumulation, as if they could accomplish everything. And the whole machinery of our preparation for the ministry, is calculated thus to impress our candidates for the pulpit. Hence, many of our young ministers can read their Hebrew Bibles fluently, who cannot in public read a chapter of the English version, without stumbling and mispronouncing from the beginning to the end. Many can read Homer and Horace, with accuracy and fluency, who cannot read a hymn of Watts or Newton, with the emphasis or elegance of a young lady from some of our best boarding schools. Many can write a sermon according to rule, and of power both as to truth and argument; but when they come to preach it, so dull and slovenly is their manner, and so drawling and holy is their tone, that to their hearers it has neither sense, point, truth, or force. As spiritual fishermen they cast the net so clumsily as to drive off, instead of drawing up the fishes. And so little skill in adapting themselves to circumstances have many of our best educated licentiates, that they wander through our vacancies for years, without meeting with a congregation willing to extend a call to their educated dullness. We are far from believing that too much is done to secure the full education of our ministry; we would rather increase than diminish the time for preparation, and the course of study; but the conviction is deep and heartfelt, that far too little is done to give it power and impressiveness in public. We may differ as to the cause, but the fact is obvious, that our ministry, to a lamentable degree, fails to impress the masses.

The necessary ingredients to impressiveness in the preacher are, good writing, good speaking, and a manner at once solemn and earnest. When these are accompanied with a character for consistent piety, they cannot fail to attract and to impress. And hence they should be sedulously cultivated in order to usefulness. To be sure, education cannot supply everything where nature has been parsimonious of her gifts. But it can do much; and what we plead for, is, that far more attention should be given to that side of the education of our ministry which fits it for impressively preaching the gospel, so as to reach the great masses that are out in ways of wandering from God.

When we add to these characteristics of an able minister of the New Testament, that of *entire consecration to the work of the ministry,* our picture is complete. The injunction of our Lord is, 'pray ye the Lord of the harvest, that he will send forth labourers unto his harvest'. The Lord's harvest requires labourers, not idlers. Those who enter the field in answer to this prayer, enter it, not to seek the lordship of it, nor yet to fatten on the labours of others, but to work in it during the whole day of their lives, whether it be long or short.

It is not sufficient for a true minister to feel a general desire to be useful; he must be possessed by a desire for the salvation of men, which will give him no rest but as he seeks to gratify it. Souls are his hire; and many waters cannot quench the love which inflames his heart to obtain them. It is this one great, absorbing feeling, which takes him to his study, to his closet, to the chamber of sickness, to the pulpit. It inspires every sermon he writes, gives energy to every address he makes, and fervency to every prayer he utters, and marks all his intercourse with all men. He is seeking a place among those who, by turning many to righteousness, will shine as the stars forever, and forever. A church with such a ministry is a growing and glorious church.

But will any say, this is a fancy sketch, unattainable by ordinary men? But is not Christ the pattern for our imitation? And his meat and drink was, to do the will of his Father. But will any say he was divine? Then look at Paul; from the hour the scales fell from his eyes, until the hour he went up to receive his crown from his exalted Saviour, he lived but for one object: to save men by the preaching of the truth. But will any say, he was inspired? Then look at Whitefield and Wesley. 'When you see them dividing their lives between the pulpit and the closet; sacrificing every comfort, crossing the ocean many times, moving populous cities, often rising from the bed of sickness to preach to multitudes, and under circumstances which rendered it not improbable that they might exchange the pulpit for the tomb'; when you look at the lives and labour of these, and such men as Heywood, and Baxter, and Chalmers, and others among the dead and the living, you will see that we have drawn no fancy sketch. When it was announced to the dying Backus, whose ministry was greatly protracted and useful, that he could not survive an hour, 'Then', said he, 'place me on my knees, that I may offer up another prayer for the church of God before I die.' He was placed upon his knees; and upon his knees, praying for the church of God, he died.

Such being what we consider the characteristics of an able minister of the New Testament, we proceed briefly to state:—*The world's great need of such ministers.*

Our country is incomparably the most inviting field for Christian exertion which the world contains. Its territory is vast, its soil productive, its wealth beyond computation,—its mind, intelligent and active; its institutions free. We possess the broadest liberty, and the most perfect security. And as free as is the air to the electric fluid, so free is our country to the exchange of thought, and open to manly discussion on all kinds of subjects.

It is also the point towards which almost all the streams of emigration rising in the old world are flowing. The strangers weekly landed on our shores, under the genial influence of our institutions, are soon moulded into fellow citizens. And a minister must possess the gift of tongues who can in their own language preach to the few hundred inhabitants of any of our rising villages on the banks of the Ohio, or on the shores of our Lakes. As a nation, our physical power is vigorous, and it is all driven as by steam. The most enterprising people of Europe, in comparison with our own, are but as the sluggish Rhine as it flows through Holland, to our Niagara. Indeed, we possess all the great elements of power, with room to grow, and nurture to sustain. But these elements are not yet fully combined; and a few generations are to determine whether we will be governed by infidelity and Popery, or by morality and religion. Unless the gospel gains the ascendency in this nation, the astonishment excited by our unexampled progress to greatness, will give way to the greater astonishment of our sudden fall. And whether or not the gospel shall obtain the ascendency depends, under God, upon the fact whether or not it is supplied with an able ministry. And what but a ministry earnest as was that of Paul and Whitefield, truthful as was that of Davies and Brainerd, self-sacrificing as was that of our Scottish and Irish ancestry, can scatter the salt from the Lakes to the Gulf of Mexico, and from the east across the Great River, through Texas, Nebraska, New Mexico, Oregon, and California, in such quantities as to preserve their rapidly growing communities from moral putrefaction? Let but a tithe of the enterprise which reigns in the world around us, glow in the bosom of the ministry of our land, and soon the Rocky Mountains will cry to the Alleghenies, and the Sacramento to the Hudson, and the Columbia to the Ohio: 'O, magnify the Lord with me, let us exalt his name together.'

Nor, when we look at the state of the world, is the kingdom of heaven as near as many would imagine? This age does not answer the description of that which is to precede the setting up of the kingdom of our Lord. Before Jesus Christ becomes the King of nations, there will be a conflict which will make the earth to tremble. The signs of the times are already portentous in the old world. Popery is yet what it was in the days of its Gregories, Clements, and Johns. The lion is caged, but his natural ferocity and tusks remain. And Mohammedanism is yet what it was in the days of its Alis and Omars. It is civilly weak; it has lost its bold spirit of enterprise and imposture; but its heart is the same. Nor has heathenism lost any of its stupid and sullen resistance to the truth. 'The prince of the powers of the air' yet rules the heathen world with a strong hand. Nor will these powers always look quietly on, and without resistance see their territories won over to the Prince of Peace. There is yet a battle to be fought, when, as seen in vision by the prophet, the blood may come up to the horse's bridles. True, the result is not doubtful. Victory will eventually perch upon the banner under which are ranged the people and saints of the Most High. But an able ministry is needed to prepare the church for the conflict; to lead on the hosts of the elect, and to guide them in the coming struggle.

And the present state of the visible church loudly calls for such a ministry. A wasting and multiform fanaticism, claiming almost prophetic revelations, is deluding multitudes. A religion of forms, and sacraments, and priestly interferences, is deluding multitudes more. Prelacy, for reasons baseless as the fabric of a vision, is urging its exclusive claims to be the true church; and in some quarters, with a narrowness and bigotry better suited to the dotage of the 'Latin sister'. Popery, too, is lifting up its wounded head, and is stretching its aged limbs, and is urging its grey hairs and furrowed brow, its decrepitude, its wounds, and its weakness, to make unto itself friends. And amid our evangelical churches, old heresies are rising under new names, and old errors are returning in a new dress, distracting the councils of the wise and the good, and arraying brethren against one another, who should stand shoulder to shoulder in the conflict with the common enemy. In any of our villages of one thousand inhabitants we meet with the rationalism of Germany, the infidelity of France, the apostasy of Oxford, and the stupid Popery of Ireland. And everywhere is human nature in ruins, and the carnal heart with its errors and prejudices. To silence these adversaries; to repel their assaults upon the truth, and to save men from their snares, we need minds trained, sanctified, and active, that can pour forth light like the sun. A feeble opposition to these is worse than none, as they measure their strength, not by the volume of their own muscle, but by the dexterity with which they cause a weak opponent, like a silkworm, to wind himself up in the web of his own weaving.

In our age and country, mind is unshackled,—and with the chains of superstition it has thrown aside reverence for orders, office, station.

We make the statement only to record an historical fact. Nothing is now received without investigation, but error and nonsense. The attachments of clans, parties, sects descending from one generation to another, are here unknown. The fact that a man is a minister obtains no notes for his opinions; and in many portions of the land, secures many against them. The most catholic principles are here discussed, as if but just stated; and creeds and confessions, sealed by the blood of martyrs, and which have received the sanction of ages, are searched and sifted as if but just published. Amid such an array of opposition, the advocacy of truth requires the ablest minds that God has created. Efficacy as to the success of the truth is from God, but the instrumentality is with man; and the more able our ministry, the surer the hopes of its speedy triumphs. As we cannot expect every lawyer to be a Blackstone, nor every judge to be a Marshall, nor every physician to be a Rush, nor every soldier to be a Washington, nor every philosopher to be a Newton, so neither can we expect every minister to be a Paul, a Chalmers, a Miller, or an Alexander. There are various departments and fields of labour in the church to occupy every variety of talent in the ministry; and every man sustaining that relation to the world should occupy their every talent to the full; and, like the stars in heaven, should fill up the orbit in which they move with their light. A minister in our age and country, where so much is to be done, and yet finding nothing to do! Out upon such ministers! Had they lived in the days of Noah, they would have found themselves in lack of water when the waves of the deluge were rising around them.

Such, my Brother, is the ministry needed in our day by the church and the world. It was for the education of such a ministry that our fathers founded the theological seminary located in this town; and that through the years of its history, it has been fostered and cherished by the General Assembly. And it is to aid to the utmost of your ability, in the education of such a ministry, that you have been called by the church from a sister seminary to be a professor in this institution. No higher mark of their confidence could the directors of this seminary give you than their unanimous nomination of you to the Assembly which has transferred you here; and we feel assured that that confidence will be justified, by a life consecrated to the high interests which we cheerfully commit to your trust.

The department, my Brother, over which you are especially to preside, embraces subjects and topics, the most important in their bearings upon all the interests of the church. To you is committed instruction in the sacraments of the church, as to their authority, history, administration and meaning. I need not say to you, who have spent so many of your years in laborious study, and successful instruction, that it is through the door of the sacraments the most fearful and desolating errors have entered the church of God. There is scarcely a shade of error from their denial as positive institutions, up to the giving to them the power which the Holy Ghost alone exercises, which has not existed in reference to them, and which do not now exist. It will be for you to clear these rites from the clouds and mists with which the fanaticism of a Fox, and the superstition of Papists and Puseyites have cast around them, and to hold them up before our rising ministry in their true scriptural simplicity and meaning.

To you is also committed the work of instruction in church government; and at a time when Popery, Prelacy, and Independency are urging their claims with quenchless zeal, and great power. Whilst as a people we have ever insisted less upon the external organization of the church, than upon its system of doctrines, and its inner life, yet our entire history proves that we have not been indifferent to it. Where has purity of doctrine long survived the introduction of grades into the ministry? And where now is the truth, the life, the holy zeal of the church to be found, save where the purity of the ministry, and the radical principles of Presbyterianism, are maintained? Our fathers were not contending for airy speculations, or for unmeaning peculiarities, when they refused to bow to a bishop's sceptre—when they surrendered life rather than the principles of presbytery—when they preferred to be hunted like wild beasts through the glens and over the mountains of Scotland, by troopers set on by those who worshiped in cathedrals, rather than surrender their simple faith as to the polity of the church. They have transmitted to us a church organized upon the foundation of the apostles and prophets, with its three orders of ministers, elders, and deacons; and so organized as to secure promptness and efficiency without tyranny,—the free action of the people, without confusion or anarchy;—and the oversight and government of each member without interfering with the freedom of any. And the maintenance of these principles, endeared to us because taught us in the New Testament, and purchased by the blood and treasures of our fathers, we regard as essential to the maintenance of the civil rights of man and the sacred liberties of the church. Your own early training, your vows and your services as a minister, and your antecedents as a professor, lead us with entire confidence to commit this department of instruction to your care. We want not our young brethren to be bigots; but we charge you to make them thorough Presbyterians.

To you also is committed the work of preparing our young brethren here, for the duties of the pastor, and of the preacher of the gospel. The brethren associated with you teach them theology, and the history of the church, and the literature of the Bible; and then pass them over to you, to be prepared by you for actual service in the field. If others furnish the weapons of warfare, it will be for you to teach their use. Here is the point of greatest deficiency in the present mode of educating our ministry. In everything pertaining to scholastic education, we have made a great advance beyond the systems of our fathers, nor do we admit that our existing ministry, as some would assert, is inferior in pastoral or pulpit ability to any generation of their predecessors; but we have not made advance in the practical, proportional to that made in the scholastic, departments of education. And unless we mistake, it is the strong desire of the directors of this seminary, and of the church, that the department of instruction committed to you should assume, at once, its due importance. The churches need sympathising pastors, and skilful, who are fully instructed as to the duties of good shepherds, and who will faithfully discharge them. The good pastor should be as the good physician who watches the rise and progress of diseases—who seeks to know the diseases of his patients—who wisely prescribes for them—and who visits them to see the effect of his remedies. They need also preachers; not merely men who can write good sermons—who can analyse a text—who can deliver a discourse with a correct coldness which chills the hearer; but men who feel that the object of preaching the gospel is to stir the hearts of others by the great truths which fill their own,—that the preaching of the gospel is an ordinance upon whose improvement or neglect the life or the death of men hangs suspended. The church needs preachers of sermons, not readers of essays,—men who prefer the walks about the Sea of Galilee, and in the garden of Gethsemane, and over Calvary, to the dreamy regions of transcendentalism,—who would as soon quote Paul as Coleridge, or Carlyle,—who prefer the obscurity to which the resolve 'to know nothing but Christ and him crucified' may consign them, to the notoriety obtained by converting the pulpit into a stage from which all kinds of lectures are delivered, upon all kinds of subjects, and before all kinds of people. It cannot be denied that 'Young America', in many parts of the country, is seeking its way into the pulpit. It prophesies smooth things. It prefers the word in fashion, for the 'word in season'; pleasing generalities, to the doctrines 'piercing even to the dividing asunder of soul and spirit'; unoffending truisms, or shallow sophisms, to unpalatable truths. It courts popularity by every art. It exchanges old creeds for new ones; and is evermore seeking new ways of reforming men, to the neglect of holding forth the doctrines of the cross, the only adequate means of re-instamping on our world the image of its Creator. The church, the world, needs a ministry penetrated with the belief that the salvation of the world is suspended on the cross of Christ;—not the cross as wrought on the banners of armies—nor as borne by crusaders—nor as glittering from the steeples of churches—nor as worked on the slipper of a Pope—nor as braided on the back of a priest—nor as dangling on the bosom of a young Miss, or a vain bishop; but the cross, preached in the fulness of its doctrines, as the power of God to the salvation of all who believe them. It was for the purpose of raising up such a ministry that this beloved institution was founded, and it is to aid in the training of such a ministry that you, my Brother, are this day inaugurated as professor. And, in the name of my brethren, I charge you, to the utmost of your ability, to see to it that these ends are attained.

It is with no cold or faltering words we welcome you to this oldest seat of theological instruction in our church. We hesitate not to pledge to you the kind and fraternal cooperation of the existing faculty, who adorn the chairs they occupy not less by their amiable virtues, than by their profound learning. And whilst we pledge to you the support and affectionate sympathy of our directors, we would implore that the mantle of the sainted Alexander and Miller may rest upon you;—that, like them, you may live, blessing the church, to a good old age—that like them you may die, wearing the robes of your office—and that your sun, like theirs, may set without a cloud, leaving behind it an undying radiance.

ALEXANDER TAGGART M'GILL
1807-1889

Pastor, winsome preacher, and Professor of Practical Theology and Church History, Alexander Taggart M'Gill was born in Canonsburg, Pennsylvania, in 1807. Of Scots-Irish lineage, he was raised in the Scottish Seceder tradition.

A graduate of Jefferson College, M'Gill initially served as a tutor at the same college before relocating to Georgia, where he served as principal of an academic academy. A student of law, he worked for a time in varying capacities for the State of Georgia before pursuing a call to the ministry. He enrolled as a student at the Associate Reformed Presbyterian Church Seminary in Canonsburg, Pennsylvania (1831-34), after which he served as a pastor in several of the denomination's churches, before receiving a call to the Second Presbyterian Church in Carlisle, Pennsylvania. M'Gill transferred his ministerial credentials to the Presbyterian Church and served as pastor of this congregation from 1838 to 1842.

M'Gill's pastoral leadership, preaching, and scholarship earned him a reputation as an effective minister, and a call soon followed to serve as Professor of Ecclesiastical History and Church Government at Western Theological Seminary. He accepted the call and served at the school from 1842 to 1852. Following his years at Western, he served for one year at Columbia Theological Seminary, South Carolina, before moving to Princeton Theological Seminary in 1854 to serve as Professor of Pastoral Theology, Church Government and Homiletics.

M'Gill's immediate responsibilities were to teach the classes in practical theology following the death of Archibald Alexander in 1851. Although not a graduate of Princeton, M'Gill shared the educational vision and ministerial convictions of his predecessors, Samuel Miller and Archibald Alexander, and was faithful in maintaining the perspective on practical theology that they had established.

During the years of his professorship at Princeton, M'Gill's responsibilities were somewhat varied: from 1854 to 1859 he was Professor of Pastoral Theology, Church Government and Homiletics; from 1859-60 he was Professor of Church History and Practical Theology; from 1860 to 1861 he served as Professor of Ecclesiastical History and Church Government; and from 1861 to 1883 he carried out his duties as Professor of Ecclesiastical History, Homiletics and Pastoral Theology. M'Gill's primary publication, *Church Government: A Treatise Compiled from His Lectures in Theological Seminaries,* was published one year before his death in 1889.

Throughout his years of service, M'Gill's pastoral heart and congeniality won him the affection of his congregations and students alike. He brought a wealth of understanding and insight to his lectures on pastoral theology during his three decades of teaching at the seminary.

PRACTICAL THEOLOGY[1]

FATHERS and Brethren: it is a result, worthy of the wisdom which has ever directed this great school of theology, that, on the demise of the fathers, who reared it from the beginning, there should be assigned to their successors, a distribution of labour, so distinct and complete, in every department. Fragmentary as may appear to some the tradition of its several parts, the chair, to which I am now inducted, is as perfectly unique and definite as any other. It is *practical* theology, as distinguished from *theoretical*. It is the complement of that perfect cycle, in which exegetic, systematic, and historic theology, are primary and main departments in theological training. It is necessary to these, as art is to science, as speech is to thought, as action is to life and vigour: sharing with them, also, difficult investigations, which demand the highest culture and discipline of mind. A more perfect separation to itself of what logically pertains to this department, was never made, in any age or country, than is indicated in the title you have given it, with the sanction of our General Assembly. That mastermind in Scottish education, Dr Campbell of Aberdeen, sketches the four departments of a complete divinity course precisely as they are now arranged in this institution; making systematic and polemic theology to be appropriately one, and the whole province of 'instructing and governing' to be another department, distinct from any other, and properly denominated practical.

A sixfold division of subjects, may be fairly detailed, under the threefold denomination bestowed.

I. Pastoral theology, strictly considered; embracing the theory of the pastor's office, its origin, its end, its importance, its qualifications,

---

[1] Alexander T. M'Gill, 'Practical Theology: An Inaugural Address', *Discourses at the Inauguration of the Rev. Alexander T. M'Gill D.D., as Professor of Pastoral Theology, Church Government, and the Composition and Delivery of Sermons in the Theological Seminary at Princeton, NJ* (Philadelphia: C. Sherman, 1854), pp. 35-60.

its care of souls, and discernment of their diversities, its rights and relations, trials, encouragements, and rewards. The warrant for a standing ministry, the nature and degree of its separation from the body of the faithful; what constitutes a call to the ministry, what maintains the evidence of such vocation, and cultivates the pre-eminent holiness which must characterize the office,—these are some of the topics that belong to this division, and involve many questions of great importance and difficulty, which are distinct from didactic theology; and yet need the teacher, as much as any other study, in the work of preparation.

II. Homiletics; the whole range of sacred rhetoric; comprehending as much instruction as renowned academies in ancient times were instituted to impart, with those great peculiarities engrafted, which a Sabbath, a sanctuary, a divine Word, and a witnessing omnipotence impress on the eloquence of man. It proposes to fit the orator for the noblest achievements of human speech; for all that ancient eloquence ever accomplished, and immeasurably more; a miracle, which man's eloquence never dreamed of achieving,—the creation, instrumentally, of a new nature, instinct with regenerate emotions, to which its appeals may be ever effectively directed.

Combined with the composition and delivery of sermons, will be the cultivation of criticism and review; in circumstances the most favourable for imbuing the critic with candour, kindness, and fraternal magnanimity.

The faithfulness and delicacy, the unwearied attention, patient labour, and careful discrimination of individual varieties of taste and talent, which this department demands, have led the founders of separate theological seminaries in some European States, to limit the number of students admitted, to one-fourth of the attendance customary in these halls. There, however, it may be seen, that too great a reduction to one standard of public preaching has resulted already, from the minuteness and artificial exactness of homiletic discipline. Better than limitation of number for such an object, will be wakeful concern to promote a fair development of each candidate's own native talent and sectional taste; which the minuteness of artificial criticism would tend to repress while it chastens. We would have the bold and ready exhorter, the quick and cogent debater, the smooth and elegant writer, all trained together; with free and right propulsion on the part of the teacher, and by the interaction of their own diversified genius; under the conditions of a vigilant oversight, and firm retrenchment of whatever the sensibilities of true Christian refinement would anywhere condemn in the pulpit.

III. A third division may be denominated Catechetics; embracing the whole variety of means, for the instruction of youth and ignorance, other than public preaching. These were never so many and important, as at the present day. We live in the great era of means. And it requires even painful discrimination, to guard the rights of the pulpit, amid the bustle of platforms, which would jostle and disparage it, in the hurry to do good. We would train our ministers to superlative regard for 'the foolishness of preaching', as an instrumentality in the salvation of men; and to confide in the wisdom of other instrumentalities only so far as they conduce to the honour and success of preaching, by the living minister.

Hence there is need for careful indoctrination on the subject of subsidiary means; their relative importance; and how far they should be controlled by the church, in her appropriate organization, or left to the management of voluntary combinations.

The relation of the church and her ministers to the great work of general education—the pedagogies, which a preacher may properly connect with his holy office,—and that entire capacity of Christian ministers, which seems to have been set off distinctly, in primitive times, and times of Scottish reformation, under the denomination of teachers, should be studied here.

So, also, the missionary field, as far as the work of imparting elementary instruction, dealing with the superstitions of the heathen, and managing the education of their children, constitute the errand of missionaries.

Here belong lessons for the guidance of young ministers in times of revival; when the visitations of power from on high call them to multiplied exertions and peculiar toils: casuistry, also, for all times and seasons of pastoral life, with its difficult problems, and balancing principles.

Many a prelection of great value may be given, under this humble head, on Sabbath Schools, Bible classes, parochial visits, and diets of examination; provinces of ministerial work and skill, which cannot be valued too highly; and which are all underlaid with principles, that must be studied, and must anticipate experience, if the ardour of youth would enter on its career safely, and turn its own experience to wisdom and efficiency, without the loss of time and labour.

A normal school for teachers, whose main calling must ever give them paramount influence in educating the world—may we call this particular branch of practical theology; in which we would make them know how they ought to behave themselves, in the school, the convention, the author's study, the editor's chair, the secretary's desk, the agent's itinerancy, and the colporteur's broadcast of dissemination—all of which may appertain to 'the house of God, which is the church of the living God, the pillar and ground of the truth'.

IV. Liturgics may be called a fourth division; though we reluctantly abide by the title. It will embrace the Sabbath, and those ordinances of religion, which are distinctively worship, and formal solemnity. Puritanical protest will, itself, require a careful study of rites and ceremonies—to know what they are, by the sanction of God's Word, what the authority of the church, in relation to them, and what the proprieties of their actual administration.

With the ordinance of prayer, must be studied the question of liturgical forms; and many important counsels and directions. With that of singing praises, questions which separate branches of the Presbyterian family; as well as many a minor topic of interest, within our own denomination. With reading the Word, that emphasis, which interprets without comment, and that emotion, which becomes the words, that are, themselves, 'spirit and life'.

Baptism and the Lord's Supper afford a rich domain, after ceding much to theoretic theology, on every side. Fasting and thanksgiving will connect asceticism for investigation; and lead us to distinguish the mortification, which our Saviour, and his apostles, and all men exercised unto godliness, in every age, have practised, from that mere bodily exercise, and voluntary humility, and austere virginity, with which the Catholic Church revolted from the liberty of the gospel, and sunk to bondage, terror, and death.

The ordinance of 'making collections for the poor, and other pious purposes', which, it might be thought, any deacon would understand, without elaborate teaching, is one that a Chalmers deemed worthy of his head and heart and pen, without finding its problems easily solved, with all his gigantic power: one which my predecessor in pastoral theology loved to investigate and teach, with the dint of his massive intellect, and the deep earnest of his capacious heart: one, too, which our own General Assembly has just devolved on theological professions, with strong recommendation; under the title of 'Systematic Benevolence'.

V. A fifth division is the Church, and her proper visibility; the true theory of her constitution, membership, and government. This itself is a great theme; complicated with the most important discussions of the age; and presenting, perhaps, the only subject that has not yet been fairly settled in the suffrages and literature of evangelical Christendom.

Opposite extremes of error, in the true church of God, have probably but one battle more, in which to perish; and the golden moderation of the gospel may triumph in millennial joy. That battle is to be here. The last thing for the church, in her militancy, to know conclusively, is her own self. And, it would be strange anomaly, indeed, if the result of this ultimate struggle be the attainment of a mere abnegation; and the triumph of true moderation consist, in restoring the moderatism of a feeble and supine indifference to any particular form.

We cannot believe it; and, therefore, determine to stand on the watchtower, of a proper *jus divinum* for the parity of ministers, the existence of ruling elders, and church courts, original and appellate.

We seek to place on higher ground than man's expedience, a polity like this; which gives the germ of civil and political freedom to the nations, and conserves, with the force of a great psychological bond, which history has ever illustrated, the soundness of redeeming truth, in the belief and practice of men. Though not honoured with instruction from the lips of Dr Miller, his type of Presbyterianism was impressed upon my youth by his writings; and the researches of years in the study of church government have only confirmed that early tuition.

In refuting the figment of apostolic succession on the one hand, and no succession at all upon the other—the continuance of priesthood, in a particular class, on the one hand, and priesthood in the people, which repudiates the authority of office, on the other—a depository of power in the hands of individuals, apart from assemblies, on the one hand, and engrossment of power in the masses, without representation, on the other,—we have some of the appropriate exercises of this department; in which we shall seek to find and hold 'the present truth'.

VI. The sixth division may be designated, Ecclesiastical law and discipline; the diacritical power and practice of the church. It is not canon law, the offspring of church and State united, which rivalled civil and common law, for centuries, as a pathway to fame and influence; but that declarative legislation and execution of law in the church herself, which is far more a profound and profitable study.

The statute book of our own particular denomination, containing so many wise enactments, and valuable interpretations of the constitution, and important regulations of that vast machinery for doing good, which employs the alms and prayers and abilities of more than 2,000 ministers, and 200,000 members, ought now to be taught with diligence to the rising ministry. And still more, the principles and Book of Discipline, which embody so much of Christian ethics, as well as forms of justice, that symbolize the doctrines of human right.

To construe offences fairly, to conduct the process righteously, to graduate the conviction justly, to inflict the censure faithfully, and restore the penitent offender seasonably, require a cultivation which must be one of liberal study, as well as sound judgment and careful experience. Judges of both law and fact, whose decisions involve the honour and safety of the Saviour's kingdom, and depend so much upon their manifest propriety, for any force and credit among men, must be learned in the law; and qualified to uphold the judiciary of our spiritual courts, in comparison with that of secular courts; or, in a great nation like ours, of jurists and jurymen, the law of Christ will be disparaged, if not entirely despised.

Such is an outline of the department proper, to my apprehension. The singularly excellent usage, in this institution, of making the Bible a text-book, to be studied exegetically, in every department, with reference to the subjects belonging to each, respectively, will be followed, with delight; and interesting portions, historical and epistolary, may fall to this practical chair, for critical and thorough examination.

Other studies, which are ancillary, will not be neglected; such as lead to the knowledge of human nature—spiritual anthropology—man as debased or developed in every age, by the religious sentiment, as it has been called, under its various manifestations.

Practical theology must ever attempt to explain the contact and confluence of religion with civilization. And, though many questions, greatly agitated elsewhere, respecting the relation of civil magistracy to sacred things, are of little interest to this country, they are of much importance to our missionaries; and many yet remain, along this line, ever important to ourselves, which cannot be understood by superficial thought or observation.

It was only by the most learned of our ministers, and not without help from this hall of theological education, that the true doctrine of 'the higher law', came to be fairly understood, on a late memorable occasion of national disturbance. And it will require yet a laborious culture, in the seats of sacred science, to qualify the ministers of reconciliation for a judicious exercise of their ability and influence, on the heaving masses, which may be tempted, in the day of passion, to tear in pieces the most beautiful result of modern civilization,—the constitution of this great republic. Questions of vital concernment to the welfare of our nation, continually press upon such a department as this; and it is not, perhaps, extravagant to say, that a single question of discipline, in our own church, if it had been settled as other churches have settled it, or left it unsettled, would have already severed the cords of this American Union.

Great conflicts are coming; if not in relation to social and domestic institutions, certainly, in relation to a vast political system, which is ecclesiastical in its history and claims; and must be countervailed on the arena of ecclesiastical discussion; and there is not one division of this study which may not be made an armoury for the preparation of champions in the contest with Popery. When we teach that the pastor is not a priest, but a minister of Jesus—that preaching truth from the oracles of God, in the language of the people, is to be his principal function—that the Bible, in some vernacular tongue, should be,

first and last, at home and at school, the handbook of all catechumens—that forms of worship, which have no warrant in the Word of
God for their use, are to be discarded, as the mere commandments of
men—that all gradation of rank in the ministry of Christ is unscriptural and unjust—that the true administration of discipline must
aim to make the church visible and invisible entirely coincident—we
touch the whole circle of practical theology, and subvert the whole
fabric of Papal idolatry.

But, far within this margin of our holy religion, the department
of which we speak deals with central interest, and claims a memorial
of peculiar renown. The 'applied science' of theological study, it governs all the resources which any other department can furnish, with
adaptation to the end of the whole, the glory of God, in the salvation
of men; and must have, therefore, all the value, which this proximity
to such an end confers upon means. Think of marshalling the educated energies of scores in the ardour of youth, and vigour of high
discipline on the verge of such a field, as this wonder-working age is
opening daily to 'the glorious gospel of the blessed God'! Think of
but one lesson, the first and most obvious, which this function must
impress on such instrumentalities—that of true consecration, the call
of God, the crucifixion of self, the value of souls, the glory of Christ,
and that holiness of heart and life, without which this ministry were
usurpation, and the whole acquirements of theoretic theology a perversion, of deadly bane to the church and the world!

From the earliest germ of revealed religion, we may scan a seminal
importance in this branch of sanctified learning. Primeval divinity
was almost entirely comprehended here. Catechetics and liturgics
were the cyclopaedia of sacred science, from Adam to Christ. And
where is the Christian minister, who does not repair to the orators,
and bards, and historians, of regular and irregular attendance on the
schools of the prophets during that long period of time, for the richest illustrations of doctrine and duty, with which to adorn the pulpit
now?

The great Teacher himself, within his college of disciples, dwelt
most on themes of pastoral theology and church government; on a
call to the ministry, and its qualifications, its cross, and its crown; on
the nature of his kingdom, its separation from the State, its parity of

ministers, its bench of elders, and even its method of process for the exercise of discipline; not omitting, by any means, important hints in his own example and precept, for the composition and delivery of sermons. His valedictory charge on a mountain of Galilee, where all the disciples were present, and five hundred besides, was arranged with so much care, and delivered in so significant a manner, that the great commission fell upon the bosom of the church, as well as the shoulders of particular men; to bar the roots of religious pedigree, and provide for emergencies of reformation, while the world endures.

The apostles followed the example of their Master; all of them abounding in lessons of practical theology. Whole epistles were written for text-books in this department; and their author, the great polemic of that primitive and sainted school, has mingled on every page of his other epistles, ecclesiastical and pastoral lessons, with his profound elucidation of doctrines.

Passing the Apostolic Fathers, whose scanty literature is nearly all in this department only; the first theological seminary of the Christian church began at Alexandria as a catechetical school; and was probably conducted altogether within the range of practical theology, in its exercise and studies.

In the balmy age of Patristic theology, when systematic divinity had not yet shapen a creed, and church history was only beginning its annals, and polemics were little more than Catholic anathema on heresy, the noblest ministers, whether Greek or Latin, vied in the advanced cultivation of this study. Augustine, Chrysostom, and Cyril, furnished manuals, which may yet be studied with profit: not to mention the labours of Jerome and others, in the department of church government and discipline.

The darkness and torpor of succeeding ages could pall the life of Christianity everywhere but here. Pulsations of power might always be felt in the hands of this religion. Asceticism, with its ceaseless activity of change, images, investitures, offices, patronage, pilgrimage, councils, and crusades,—everything that tumultuated in the life of medieval Christendom, belonged, in some way, to this practical domain; and shows how vastly important it must be, to guide such irrepressible vitality with careful and true enlightenment.

When that great revival of Christianity, the Reformation, awakened men to the light of the Bible, exegesis, didactics, polemics, and history were suddenly restored to their usefulness and rights; but the imperfections of men could not escape the weakness of extreme reaction. The greatest fault of Luther and Calvin's age was the disparagement of practical theology; arising from the fact, that such theology, in its perversion, had been everything of religion, under the darkness and tyranny from which they had just revolted. But for such a tacit disparagement, Luther would not have left his church burdened with ceremonies, benighted on the doctrine of a sacrament, and deformed with the most diversified accidents of polity and discipline. And, but for the same disparagement, though less, incomparably, Calvin would not have left his, a mixture of form and opinion, so mottled, that presbytery and prelacy, charity, bigotry, and latitudinarianism, could have claimed, with any colour of right, the same denomination.

The reaction of Popery punished the former; the troubles of Puritans punished the latter. And it was in the next century, an age of giants, the seventeenth and greatest, in the chronicles of modern time, that practical theology regained its just consideration, and took its high place in the literature and schools of our holy reformed religion. Baxter and Owen, and Henderson and Baillie, and Rutherford and Gillespie, and Selden and Lightfoot, and Claude and Grotius, and a host of others, bestowed their energies on this department with peculiar fondness; and full three-fourths of the time employed by the Westminster divines to prepare the greatest monument of uninspired talent which the world has seen, our Confession of Faith and its Catechism, was engrossed with the subjects of this study; for which, indeed, that venerable body was primarily convened. Worthy of the most favoured church that ever adopted the Westminster Confession, and worthy of the most favoured land that ever obtained from its divinely sanctioned scheme of polity, the model of well-regulated liberty, is the discretion with which, for the first time in Presbyterian history, you have made it completely one, and given it a separate chair.

Many an illustration, from the decline of presbytery in England, its trials in Scotland, its extinction in France, its transplantation to

America, and vigorous growth on our shores, might be adduced to show the importance of our study, and enhance the greatness of its memorial. History, to which my labours have been much devoted heretofore, and in which, as a great framework, every important part of human knowledge may be set and included, will come to my aid, as peculiarly and indispensably subservient.

That such a province of sacred learning should be left to the mere observation and experience of pupils, or to a discipleship with men of practical efficiency and success, without other qualifications for teaching, must be regarded as a grave mistake, if we have not wholly mistaken the nature and scope of this office. Rather say, that imitation is better than science, in teaching the elements of any liberal art; that empiricism is better than study, in teaching the work of any other profession, than that the line of any one pastor's experience is better than great principles, embodied by careful induction from many experiences, in teaching the lessons of practical theology. Could a city pastor, merely from his own particular life, however long and favoured in the pastoral care, teach the student how to behave himself in a country charge, or at a missionary station? 'The care of souls', says Vinet, a great name in pastoral theology, 'will not be the same in city and country, in a farming and a manufacturing district, in the bosom of a population of simple manners, and with refined and effeminate people.'

Besides, the man of right conduct for himself, is not always the man to explain even his own conduct, for the benefit of others. In daily intercourse we often find an incapacity of practical men to give intelligible reasons for the success with which they direct their own business and meet the changes and emergencies of life; and in the most elevated spheres of magisterial vocation the same ineptitude has been frequent and striking. It was said of a renowned executive in our own country, that no man ever ruled with more unerring direction in the right way, and no man ever blundered with more entire confusion, in giving reasons for his conduct as a ruler. So, we apprehend, the discreet and successful pastor may be found, who seldom fails to turn the exigencies of his great vocation to the very best account, in the tact of his own administration, and yet is disqualified, by the cast of his mind, and the habitudes of office, as he fills it, dealing so much in the concrete, for that quick analysis and broad rationale, which must furnish the learner with principles that govern the office, and fit him to meet with versatile application, stations of life and duties, with which his teacher has never been conversant. All education were stagnant, if the tuition of great principles be not a pioneer to particular experience.

While, therefore, we bow to the practical pastor, as the noblest of human characters, and eagerly seek, at all times, to learn from his lips, the art of caring for souls, there may be an extravagant estimate of practice alone, as a qualification for teaching the rising ministry, to the disadvantage of any department; and especially those great theoretic departments, which demand the studies of a lifetime, intensely given, to furnish a proper defence of the gospel, against the erudite and subtle enemies which now 'come in like a flood'. Yet, in this particular chair, though its themes might well demand illimitable stores of erudition, and cannot be handled by merely empirical tact, experience is indispensable; experience of the world, the pastor's office, and the teacher's art. Without having had a fair and full experiment of pastoral life, and surpassing fondness for its duties, along with previous training of many a kind in common life, including the brief pursuit of another profession, which brings a man most fully into contact with human nature, as well as fits him somewhat for the last two branches here detailed, my own consent to adventure on this high office could not have been obtained.

And yet, the first idea, in premeditating an address for this occasion, was to make apology for being here, and venturing to touch a responsibility which was shared by Dr Alexander and Dr Miller, both, in part. Assuredly, it is not done, without a diffidence, which trembles to despondency at times. But, we owe it to those illustrious men themselves, not to speak of the church they loved better than themselves, that the generation they instructed and left behind them, should not allow the greatness of their names to injure the work of their hands, or cause an institution for which they laboured and prayed through forty years, to be declined and forsaken, because there is no one to sustain the position as they did. There must be a sacrifice, just here. And is it not worth the martyrdom of half a score of men, so far as reputation is concerned, to fill a breach like this; and carry on God's work in this venerable seat, through all disparagement; perpetuating, in some way, a monument so precious, of their toil and consecration?

Exchanging, at what seemed to be a wish of the church at large, as well as peculiar indications of my Master's will, the pride of remaining in a place built up for myself in one sense, where the demands of the position and my own qualifications were supposed to be commensurate, for the peril of this new responsibility, of standing in a place already built by others—and more than built—adorned with living talent, which enlightened Christendom confesses, and with festooned memories, which might well oppress the spirit of any successor who is not led by a simple sense of duty, I come to relinquish self on the altar of this service; knowing, that, even my preference of this chair to any other imposes a more aggravated obligation.

Indulge me then, Fathers and Brethren, with kind extenuation. We are not always most successful in the duties which we fancy most; and in the very scheming, which I make at this inauguration, a field of overpowering magnitude spreads itself before me. God only, with his own rich grace and abounding mercy, can make me equal to the work.

And whatever be the results of this accession, or any other, from this time, one thing is obvious, that we may not expect the same superiority of numbers, as in times that are past. It is, manifestly, the will of our church, that her sons be distributed among many theological nurseries; and that the usefulness of this original seminary be maintained, in the high standard and faithful care of its instruction, rather than a throng of students in attendance. Nor has this ordination been made against your own will, either as guardians or benefactors of this institution. 'The rivalship of numbers', it has been well said, by one of yourselves, 'is unworthy of these seats of sacred science. Numbers may ruin us.' Your own best patrons have aided, with munificent help, as I can attest with gratitude, even the nearest competition for students, until it is at length completely established, and claims a common interest in almost every part of our field. The reduction of numbers, then, we consent to, as no evil or decline, when it redounds to the prosperity of sister institutions, and does not indicate a loss at large to the work of 'the harvest'.

And for the goodwill, with which the friends of this seminary have aided others in their efforts to become similar centres of attraction;

for the unrivalled benefactions, that she has shed over all this land and other lands; for the honour of that peerless unity, which binds our beloved church together in conspicuous harmony; and, above all, for the glory of that Blessed One, whose we are, and whom we serve, compactly in the common salvation, may we not hope, that the loan of love will be repaid; and that these halls will ever be prospered with the best wishes and constant prayers of all the churches that have been gladdened with streams from this fountain, and all the seminaries that have been profited by its issues of living ministers and lasting literature? Cheered by this hope, so reasonable, yet confiding only in God, the God of our fathers, we give ourselves wholly to do what our hands find to do; prepared, alike, to suffer and rejoice, as he may mete the evil and the good, which are mingled in any allotment of life.

'But, this I say, brethren, the time is short.' Death, which made a desolation here, by removing the patriarchs to their seats in 'the general assembly and church of the firstborn' in heaven, reverses with amazing persistency, the roll of ministers; and the young, or the mature at the meridian of usefulness are called away, with a frequency which is without parallel in the memory of this generation. How soon may we, also, that labour to recruit those wasting hands, on the high places of the field, fall at the quiet fountain; where, indeed, from the venerable Matthews to the lamented Sampson, almost every year is laying some professor in the dust. Honoured directors yet live, whose hands have managed this ancient institution from its origin, and whose vigour in this high trust is not yet abated. Long may they linger to counsel and befriend us. But the burden of their years and the frailty of their juniors admonish us, that the sequel of our history here will be one of quicker challenge, in the progress of mortality. God grant us all, 'mercy to be faithful',—'faithful unto death', that we may obtain 'a crown of life'.

WILLIAM MILLER PAXTON
1824-1904

D EVOTED pastor, gifted preacher, and beloved seminary professor, William Miller Paxton was born June 7, 1824 in Adams
County, Pennsylvania. He was raised in a godly home at Gettysburg, Pennsylvania. His godly ancestry included a grandfather who
served for a number of years as pastor of Lower Marsh Creek Presbyterian Church, not far from where Paxton was born.

After graduation from Pennsylvania College (later renamed
Gettysburg College) in 1843, Paxton pursued the study of law. By 1845
he sensed a call to the ministry and enrolled at Princeton Theological
Seminary. Having completed his studies at Princeton in 1848, he served
as a pastor for two years in Greencastle, Pennsylvania.

As Paxton's preaching and pastoral gifts became more widely known,
he was called to the First Presbyterian Church of Pittsburgh, where he
served from 1851 to 1865. A gifted orator, he also found service as Professor of Sacred Rhetoric at Western Theological Seminary from 1860 to
1867. In 1866 he accepted a call from First Church in New York City,
where he remained as pastor until 1883; from 1872 to 1875 he also served
as a lecturer at Union Theological Seminary.

In 1883 Paxton was appointed to serve as a Professor of Ecclesiastical, Homiletical and Pastoral Theology at Princeton Theological Seminary, and here he laboured in this office until his retirement in 1902. After a long and full life of pastoral and professorial service in the ministry of the Presbyterian Church, Paxton died in 1904.

William M. Paxton was an effective and admired professor at Princeton. A careful student of the Scriptures and conscientious composer of skilfully crafted sermons which were rooted in the Bible and relevant in application, he set a high standard for instruction in preaching among his students. He believed in the preached Word as a means of grace and impressed upon his classes the importance of careful sermon preparation for powerful and persuasive pulpit proclamation. His small publication, *Homiletics: Classification of Divisions,* provides helpful observations on his homiletical method.

Paxton's homiletical instruction was also accompanied with rich insight from his experience in pastoral ministry. His strong emphasis on the practical nature of theology was a strong deterrent to scholasticizing influences in the theological instruction students received at Princeton. Paxton warned against the deadening influences in pulpit and pastoral ministry of a merely intellectual theology that was not accompanied by a lively, Spirit-wrought piety; throughout his career at Princeton, he sought to maintain the priorities of the founders and early faculty with an academic programme focused on training men to be godly and effective pastors, whose preaching would be marked by the 'power and demonstration of the Spirit'.

THE MINISTRY FOR THIS AGE[1]

M Y Dear Brother: if a corporal were commanded to teach a general how to marshal an army, he would, no doubt, attempt to perform the duty—not because the general needed to be taught, nor because the corporal felt competent to instruct, but simply because in the army every soldier is expected to obey orders. Upon the same principle, I undertake to charge you as to the duties of your high office, not because you need instruction, nor because I am competent to impart it, but simply because this Board has so ordered, and I have no alternative but to obey.

It is a sublime thought, my Brother, that God has spoken; that he has spoken to man; that he has spoken to man by men, and in the forms of human speech. If this be so, then to expound God's words, to explain his meaning, to arrange and systematize the diversified expressions of his thought, to embody it in the forms of human logic, and to exhibit it so as to enlighten, impress, and win the souls of others, is at once a sublime work, and an august responsibility.

To this momentous work you are called at a period when the circumstances of the times, and the tendencies of thought and feeling which give character to the age, render its performance peculiarly difficult.

In theology, as in every other department of instruction, the teaching must be adapted to the times. The matter of your teaching, the Word of God, never changes. Like its Author, it is 'the same yesterday, today, and forever'. What God said in the days of Paul, Augustine, and Calvin, is just what God says now. This book with its chapters

---

[1] William M. Paxton, 'The Charge', *Addresses at the Inauguration of Rev. Archibald Alexander Hodge, D.D., LL.D., as Associate Professor of Didactic and Polemic Theology, in the Theological Seminary at Princeton, NJ, November 8, 1877* (Philadelphia: Sherman & Co., Printers, 1877), pp. 5-16.

and verses is the sum total of all that God has ever uttered; and, as if to stay the hand of him who would evolve from this book more than God means, all the woes that are written in it are denounced against him who 'adds thereto'; and, as if to strike with awe the man who would diminish its truths, deny its doctrines, or explain away or belittle its teachings, the warning is given that 'if any man shall take away from the words of this book, God shall take away his part out of the Book of Life'.

But whilst the truth itself never changes, the method of teaching, the mould in which it is to be cast, and the manner in which it is to be exhibited, must change with the progress of the age, and to suit the ever-changing conditions of the human mind. The long, prolix, syllogistic statements of the Schoolmen are surely not adapted to an age of telegrams. The mental conditions of a people who travel in a stagecoach at the rate of five miles an hour, must differ greatly from those of a people who travel in a railroad car at a speed of forty miles. In an age when mind is intensely active, and all other ideas come to men on the wing, it will not do for the truth of God to crawl like a snail, or slumber like a crow. It must fly with the celerity of a carrier pigeon to bring its messages to men in the thick of life's battle, or it must mount like an eagle to command attention and to carry its glad tidings upon swift wing to every corner of the earth.

Your lot as a teacher is cast in an age which differs materially from that of either of your predecessors. Dr Alexander lived in one age—a formative age—in which the foundations had to be laid deep and strong. Your father's teaching was in another age—an age of change and controversy—requiring distinct lines of demarcation and clear-cut statements of truth. But you, my Brother, stand as a teacher in the midst of an age in which (as I shall afterwards show) the conditions of your work are greatly changed.

Your venerated predecessors were both men who were wise to discern the time and to adapt themselves to it. They were not weak men to bend to the times, but strong men to resist the times, or to reform the times, if need be, or to guide and direct the spirit of the times into better and other channels. In the same manner, it devolves upon you to look out and study the age in which you live, and then, placing yourself in intense sympathy with its spirit, to look in upon your work and to ask yourself, How can I teach theology so as to qualify these young men so to handle the truth, as to leave the image and superscription of God upon the age in which they live? This question, my dear Brother, I cannot answer for you. The response must be found in the depths of your own soul, under the teaching of God's Spirit. The best that I can do is to utter a few suggestions in the direction of that line of thought.

It is plain to me that an inefficient church is a curse to the world, an inefficient ministry is a curse to the church, and the seeds of this efficiency or inefficiency lie in the theological seminary.

There stands that venerable institution. What does it mean? What is the idea which it expresses, to the farmer who passes in his wagon, to the student who enters its halls, and to the professors who occupy its chairs? Is it a place where young men get a profession by which they are to make their living? Is it a school in which a company of educated young men are gathered to grind out theology, to dig Hebrew roots, to read Patristic literature, to become proficients in ecclesiastical dialectics, to master the misty technics of the school men, and to debate about fate, free will, and the divine decrees? If this be its purpose or its chief purpose, then bring the torch and burn it; take the young men and place each one upon a horse, with the Bible in one side of the saddle bags and *Cruden's Concordance* in the other, and send them out to tell, without a professor, without a lecture, out of the simple Bible, that Jesus Christ has died to save the souls of men. We do not in any way depreciate a learned ministry. We must have learning. The age demands it; but whenever, in a theological seminary, learning takes the precedence, it covers as with an icicle the very truths which God designed to warm and melt the hearts of men.

No, no, this is not the meaning of a theological seminary. Nor is this the idea which the history and influence of this seminary is calculated to give. It is a school of learning, but it is also a cradle of piety. I remember well that when I was a student, no young man could pass through his first year without being constrained to re-examine his personal hope and motives for seeking the sacred office. The founders of this institution were men of faith. Its professors and friends now are godly men. To their eye of faith the cross of Christ gleams above it, and from that cross they hear the mandate 'Go ye into all the world, and preach the gospel to every creature.' This then is the idea which this seminary is designed to express. It is a place where educated young men are imbued with the doctrine of the cross, and with this truth as a burning power in their hearts, they go out into the world to kindle and fire the hearts of others.

The question then with you, my Brother, and with every professor in this institution is, How to teach and how to influence these young men so as to realize this idea? They are put into your hands to do this thing, and anything short of it is failure.

The world trains its young men for its specific purposes, and why should not the church? Let me illustrate. There, in the sight of the windows of the seminary, runs the railroad train. You step aboard and you find that the world has trained men, with that acute sagacity which the love of gain imparts, to hitch its thousand interests to that rapid locomotive. The merchant has hitched his goods, the editor his papers, the publisher his books, the jobber his wares, and the farmer his produce. Now, why may we not train men with equal sagacity to hitch the gospel to every locomotive, nay, to attach it to all the world's machinery, that it may mingle with every industry and sanctify every enterprise?

In yonder harbour lies a ship. It is an enemy's man-of-war. We have men in our navy so trained that they know precisely how to go and attach a torpedo to the bottom of that vessel and blow it to atoms. And why may we not train men of equal daring to know how to blow the enemies' guns out of the water, or how to attach the gospel to every sail that is unfurled, that it may mingle its blessed influence with every cargo that is loaded, and carry its glad message to every port into which commerce carries its banner? This is the end to be accomplished. The gospel must be brought into close contact with every department of the world's work. As long as religion is confined to *Sundays,* the world will lie in wickedness. It must be made to interpenetrate *every day* and *every thing*. As long as the gospel is confined to Gothic churches, it is in bonds; it must be loosed and let go out everywhere.

Now, the purpose of a theological seminary is to train men to accomplish this end. But to this you reply, 'That is not my department, my work is simply to teach doctrinal theology.' Ah, *there, there,* my Brother, we have just hit the secret of weakness. One says, 'This does not belong to my department.' Another says, 'It does not belong to mine', and thus the sense of responsibility is shifted, and the professor settles down to his work with the idea that when he has communicated a certain quantum of information upon a given subject, his responsibility is discharged. No, no, let me tell you that whenever the teaching in a theological seminary sinks to this perfunctory level, the guilt and curse of an inefficient ministry lies at its door. It is not simply instruction, it is the whole work of training and inspiring men to save souls that belongs to your department. I stand here today to say this to you and to every member of this faculty, *'This is your department.'* Can it be that your work is done when you have demonstrated a truth or deposited an intellectual dogma in the memory of a student? No, no, your responsibility continues until you have sent that truth as a lighted torch into his soul to kindle there its light and to warm his whole being as with fire.

To bring this matter closer, let me ask, When a professor sits down to prepare his lecture, what is his aim? This point was put to me once by an aged minister with such power that it meets me every time I enter my study. He said, 'When you prepare a sermon, *what are you in favour of?'* I asked him what he meant. He replied, 'Some ministers are in favour of *preparing a discourse,* some of *discussing a subject before the public,* and some of *saving souls.* What are you in favour of?' We all know too well the difference between a minister who aims at preaching a discourse, and one who aims at saving souls. Precisely the same is true of a professor. Should he be content simply to give a clear exposition and truth of a doctrine? or, over and beyond this, should he not aim, by the help of the divine Spirit, to lodge that truth as a living power in the soul of the student?

It is just at this point that the question of the future efficiency or inefficiency of the minister is determined. If, in his first study of a truth, he is made to feel its quickening influence in his own experience, it will abide with him as one of the forces of his life. He will never think of it again without being warmed by it, and it will be his pleasure to talk of it to others. The measure of every minister's power is just the number of these truths which he has received as living forces into his own soul. Upon the other hand, if a divine truth is simply studied and mastered by the intellect, it is laid away upon the shelf as a dead, inoperative thing, of little more value to him than a theorem in conic sections. He cannot seize and wield it with effect, for he is ignorant of its value. It has never been a light in his own soul, and he cannot make it shine. He has never felt its kindling power himself, and therefore he cannot shoot it as a flaming arrow into the hearts of others. It follows therefore that the aim of each professor should be to produce a vitalizing impression upon the student. Give them theology, give them orthodoxy, give them exposition, proof, demonstration, give them learning, but give it to them *warm*.

This quickening power must come from the presence of the divine Spirit. I know well that a sermon that is not conceived in the Spirit, and delivered in the Spirit, is of little value. So a lecture upon theology must be conceived by the help of the Holy Ghost, delivered under his melting influence, and received by the student under his blessed illumination. Hence the professor's study must be a Bethel in direct communication with heaven; and a theological seminary must be a Bochim, from which strong cries for help are constantly going up. A ministry trained to realize this idea will be a power in the world mightier than armies. The gospel has come to them 'not in word only but in power', and they can utter it in the confidence that it is 'the power of God unto salvation'. They well know that there is but one thing to do, and that is to save souls, and that anything short of this is failure. They will feel that they have in their possession the remedy for the woes of the world, and they will burn to apply it. They will go out from the seminary with the glad feeling of a man who is carrying provisions to a family that is starving, or with the feeling of the commander of a lifeboat who is hurrying to the wreck where souls are perishing. They will come before their audiences like a breathless messenger of good news with their hearts bursting to tell it.

Now, my Brother, there is no use in evading it. Theological seminaries cannot afford to shut their eyes to the fact that it is only such a ministry as this that can meet the wants of the world, and satisfy the demands of the age in which you live.

Look at the facts for a moment.

First. This is an age in which there is a *dissatisfaction with the pulpit.* It is a dissatisfaction that has been growing for years. The proof of this is patent in the expedients which the pulpit has adopted to evade this dissatisfaction. Some, imagining that the gospel had become trite, have gone off into the fields of literature and philosophy for subjects of discourse, elaborating intellectual essays, and complimenting the Bible by prefixing a verse as a motto to indicate the point of their departure. Others have sought to mingle religion with everyday life by taking their topics from the newspapers, by discussing whatever is uppermost in the public mind, and by making the pulpit a platform for Sunday entertainment. As a reaction from both these, some have endeavoured to satisfy the public demand by a more interesting kind of biblical preaching, treating of Oriental manners and customs, giving pictorial views of history, with lessons upon the geography and agriculture of the Bible, embracing, after the manner of Solomon, everything from the 'cedar of Lebanon to the hyssop that springs from the wall'.

Now, the remedy for all this is such a ministry as we have indicated. Men whose hearts are filled and thrilled with the 'truth as it is in Jesus' will not need to discourse of geography or agriculture, nor to go for themes of interest to literature or philosophy. No, Jesus to them is the centre of all interest, and out of the freshness of their own experience they will set forth his preciousness with such cogent persuasion that men will look up with surprise and say, 'We never saw it before. We will have none but Jesus, none but Jesus.'

Secondly. This is an age in which *doctrine is at a discount.* Disguise it as you may, it is nevertheless true that the popular mind has a dread of doctrine. Erratic preachers and theological adventurers, who know no theology, and have not logic enough to comprehend a formulated statement, have thrown gibes at dogmas; but, strange to say, the public mind has caught these gibes, and the impression has passed from mind to mind until people everywhere are saying, 'Oh, don't preach doctrine. Give us something interesting, something that will attract the young.' Now, as reasonable as all this is, we dare not conceal from ourselves the *fact.* There is doubtless a reason for it. Doctrine has been abused. It has been preached in such a dull, heavy, lifeless way that people have gone to sleep over it. Students have gone out from the seminary under the impression that the professor's lecture is just the thing they are to present in the pulpit, and some have given out half a lecture in a single sermon, whilst others have been generous enough to give the whole. They suppose a theological lecture to be fixed ammunition, and that they are to load and fire the very cartridge which has been given to them.

Now, the remedy for all this is a ministry that can preach doctrine *all ablaze*. If a man can put the light of his own living experience inside of the deadest dogma, he will make it a spiritual transparency that will interest and attract. A heart that is full of Christ will gild every doctrine with the halo of his glory.

Thirdly. Closely allied with this is another characteristic of the times. This is an age of *action,* of action so intense, that all life loses much of its inwardness by the intensity of its outwardness. Hence men have readily caught at the idea that religion is a *life,* and that its expression is *action.* It is of little consequence what a man believes, if he is busy in good works. Hence the inwardness of religion is forgotten, and all piety is made to consist in *doing.* Here is a great error, but it is an error that springs out of the tendencies of the times. True indeed, religion is a life, but it is a life that springs from truth believed. All the fruits of well-doing spring from the 'incorruptible seed' of truth planted within. All this busy doing of good works which does not spring from this root must either be a flower without a root, or the galvanism of a false zeal which will end when the spasm subsides. Now this alarming error must be met by a ministry that knows, from a heart experience, whence life comes. Some, in ignorance of this, are attempting to galvanize churches by *organization.* We have heard of generals who organized victories, but we have no confidence in *organized piety,* or in good works that do not proceed from the germ of living doctrines embedded in the soul.

Fourthly. Bear with me again whilst I advert to another feature of the times which a theological teacher must regard with alarm. It is *the growing tendency to preach only half the gospel.* There are some who sum up the whole message of God to man in the words 'Come to Jesus.' To them God has but one attribute, and that is love, and into this all others are merged. These are precious parts of the gospel, but only parts, and to magnify a part into the whole, or to hold up these isolated truths so constantly to the light as to ignore or eclipse others, is perilous. It divides Christ, it bisects the gospel, it separates 'what God has joined together'. The effect of this is not only to produce an ill-shaped and distorted religion, not only to open an easy way to universalism, but these neglected truths rise up and come back upon us in the retributive form of errors and heresies, which seem to meet the want in man, which this neglect of the whole truth has failed to supply.

Now to counterbalance this tendency you must, with the help of the divine Spirit, train up men who know how to preach a *full-orbed* gospel, how to present a *whole Christ,* not only for justification but also for sanctification, who will teach that there is not only a 'coming to Christ' but *an abiding in him'* for all that the soul needs. You must send out preachers who not only know about God, but who *know God,* that he is a God of justice as well as of love, a Sovereign as well as a Father. To preach only half the gospel is to commit a worse sin than Ananias, who kept back half the price.

But we cannot pursue these thoughts further. In one word, a ministry with a living experience of the truth is the remedy for the evils of the age, and the answer to the demands of the world.

One word more in conclusion. You, my Brother, stand in a historic position. The name of this seminary is known in all the world. Its chief distinction is its biblical teaching. The ground of its faith is the *Bible*. Its only question is, 'What has God said?' Its only proof is God's Word. Its professors have never reached the point of thinking that they knew more than the Bible. This seminary has always taught that there are but two questions to be considered. *First.* Is this the Word of God? *Secondly.* What does it mean? and this ascertained, there is nothing left but to believe and adore. The preaching which has always been taught in this seminary and illustrated in the pulpits of its graduates has been simple biblical preaching; not that kind of biblical preaching which strings texts together, and repeats them like a Romish saint his beads in an endless rote and in a sacred monotone which charms to sleep, but that intelligent biblical preaching which makes the text emit thought as the sun emits light, which couples God's Word and man's doctrine like voice and echo, and which puts such life and interest into discussion as to make the Word a living oracle. The Princeton student has always been known by the honour which he puts upon the divine Word.

My dear Brother, I need only to say to you, *'continue in these things'*. You have the footsteps of godly and illustrious men before you. Shall I say to you 'follow them'? Nay, there is a more sacred footprint before you. Better take your position here, as Mr Standfast did in the River Jordan, and say,

> My foot is fixed upon that which the feet of the priests that bare the ark of the covenant stood, while Israel went over this Jordan . . . I am going now to see that head that was crowned with thorns, and that face that was spit upon for me . . . Wherever I have seen the print of his shoe in the earth, there I have coveted to set my foot too . . . His voice to me has been most sweet; and his countenance I have more desired than they that have most desired the light of the sun.

May God bless you, my Brother, and prepare you for your solemn work.

THE CHURCH, THE PREACHER, THE PASTOR—THE INSTRUMENTS OF GOD'S SALVATION[1]

WHEN Horace was writing his 'Art of Poetry', he felt embarrassed with the apprehension that he who professed to teach the art would be regarded as assuming for himself a position of pre-eminence among poets. To repel this inference, he reminds the reader that 'a whetstone, though in itself incapable of cutting, is of excellent use in the sharpening of steel'. Upon this same principle, one who accepts the position of an instructor may, without assuming any proficiency for himself, aim at the humble office of a whetstone—sharpening others while he wastes himself—content to be nothing if by his own hardness and dullness he may sharpen other intellects to the keenness of a Damascus blade, or point a spear to pierce the hearts of the King's enemies. It is not, however, the humble instrument you have chosen, but the great department in which he is called to labour, that now claims your attention.

Paul Richter said, 'Christ has lifted empires off their hinges, turned the stream of centuries out of its channel, and he still governs the ages.' But by what agencies has he achieved these wonderful results? By his church, in which he dwells with his all-conquering power; by his truth, which his Spirit makes 'mighty to the pulling down of strongholds'; by his ministry, which goes into all the world and wins the hearts of men by his messages of love; by his pastors, who care for the flock, who lead the young by the tenderest sympathies, and

[1] *Discourses at the Inauguration of the Rev. William M. Paxton, D.D., LL.D., as Professor of Ecclesiastical, Homiletical and Pastoral Theology in the Theological Seminary at Princeton, NJ, May 13, 1884* (Philadelphia: Sherman & Co. Printers, 1884), pp. 15-30.

'who go their way forth by the footsteps of the flock and feed the kids beside the shepherd's tents'. In other words, the three great agencies included in this department of instruction, the church, the preacher, and the pastor, are the very instrumentalities by which Christ has conquered in the past, and by which he still rules the ages.

These agencies are also the points to which the awakened interest and keenest thought of the present time are directed. The great life questions of the future gather around them.

By some it is said that the church is growing feeble, it no longer goes forth with the might of conquest; that the ministry is shorn of its strength, and utters no more the word of power; that the pastors are not now in sympathetic contact with the people; that the masses are falling off from the church, and the common people no longer 'hear the word of God gladly'. The anxieties awakened by such statements have so stimulated public thought, that there is perhaps now no subject which engages more general attention than the question how to bring the gospel to bear upon the masses, and how to maintain the church in its position of power and blessing in the world.

But a little thought will convince anyone that the statements upon which these anxious questions are based are exaggerated. They originate usually with enemies, whose chief desire is that the church may prove a failure, and who are watching with a lynx-eyed jealousy to interpret every mistake as a disaster, and a single faltering step as senile weakness. Sometimes also these complaints come from revolutionists who wish to run the church upon worldly principles. They are eager for change, and would retire the old scriptural methods and instrumentalities in favour of the novel expedients of the world's prosperity. Such statements, once uttered, are eagerly caught up and intensified by the alarms of timid Christians, who mistake every distant sound for a tornado; or by specious worldlings, who are willing to compromise to suit all tastes and preferences, and adjust both the principles and methods of the church to the dominant tendencies of the times.

No, no; such alarms are needless. The church gives no evidence of decay. It has been frequently shown by statistics that her progress for the last ten years compares most favourably with the former decades in her history. Her preparation and equipment for her work in the world is more complete than in any former period. At this very moment 'the name of Jesus is above every name', and his church is the grandest, mightiest power this world has ever seen. It is true indeed that the church in all its history has had its times of diminished as well as accelerated progress. It has had struggles as well as victories, its days of cloud and sunshine, its times of action and reaction. But this cloud and struggle and reaction may not arise from inherent feebleness or ineffective instrumentalities, but from a combination of adverse influences without. Just here, we think, lies the solution of this problem. Allowing for such a measure of truth as may exist in these adverse statements, we may fully account for every diminution of growth in the present period by a single glance at the state of the world, in the midst of which the mission of the church is now cast.

We live in an age in which a sudden accumulation of adverse influences has come in on the church like a flood. The progress of science has opened up the whole world to the sphere of trade, and brought its most distant points into intimate connection. The limit of a man's business is no more the circuit of the village or the city, but the circumference of the earth. This has induced an intense spirit of competition, and stimulated an unnatural excitement. Speculation has grown to gigantic proportions. Christian principle, and even the sentiment of common honour, is disappearing as the struggle becomes desperate. The news, coming every hour from the ends of the earth, absorbs public thought, and cultivates a morbid craving for novelty. The increased facilities for rapid communication create a taste for travel, throw the populations of the earth together, disseminate vice, communicate the moral contagions of one people to another, transport the habits and customs of luxurious civilization to Christian countries, and bring the vices and abominations of heathenism to the doors of our own homes.

In our own country, a multitude of causes combine to increase and intensify these adverse influences. The recent war created a tide of vice and immorality which has swept through every city and village, and penetrated to the remotest borders of the land. The crowding together of vast masses of human beings almost in one common herd has made our great cities prolific centres of corruption, into parts of which it is scarcely possible for a gospel influence to penetrate.

The adoption of such various foreign elements into our civilization, has in many places displaced the old-fashioned, Christian home,
with the happy family circle gathered around its warm hearth-stone,
and the pastor a beloved guest; and has substituted in its stead the
tenement house and the flat, or at best the brownstone palace, with
no warm hearth-stone, no Bible or catechism, but with parlours filled
with gaiety and fashion, with the card table and the dance—a home
in which the pastor has no welcome, and religion no altar.

To all this we must add the influence of the evil virus of religious
doubt and sceptical opinion coming to us from foreign sources under
the specious names of advanced thought, liberal opinion, and higher
culture. The effect is to unsettle opinion, to break down the barriers
of moral and religious constraint, to produce a contempt for law and
government, to puff up the young with the idea that they are wiser
than their parents, to encourage the expectation of change: that all
that is old will pass away, that the age of reconstruction has come,
and that all things in religion as well as in science will become new.

Now, grouping together all these adverse influences, we are able
to see in a single view that the church is opposed and hedged in by
an environment of difficulties and obstacles, greater perhaps in their
combination than ever before in her past history. She is doubtless
able to meet and surmount them all. She is divinely organized for
this purpose. Christ, her living head, dwells in the midst of her. Her
past history is the guarantee of her future success. But the agencies
by which she works are human. It is, therefore, very unreasonable to
expect that her success shall be instantaneous, or that her existence
and work in the world should have prevented the rise and development of these evils. As well might we hold the officers of the Signal
Service responsible for the occurrence of a tornado. Nor can we expect
that when these hostile influences have arisen, she can strike down
every enemy at a blow, or remove all obstacles with a single struggle.
As her instrumentalities are human, she must have time and opportunity. It will require patience and conflict. But in the meantime it is
most unreasonable to raise the cry of complaint, or to make charges
of inefficiency. Surely it cannot be expected that the church will
make a uniform advance under all circumstances. An ocean steamer,
no matter how effective the machinery, or skilful the management,

does not make the same speed every day. Suppose a timid passenger, observing a diminution of speed, should say, 'The ship is a failure, the machinery is giving out, we must have new adjustments and a different management or we shall never cross the stormy ocean.' It would be easy to spread the alarm among the ship's company, and to raise vociferous murmurings. But to all this the captain readily answers: 'Why this alarm? The ship is sound and strong, the machinery is in perfect condition, she has carried us safely through many perils. True, our speed is not so great today as yesterday, but do you not see that we are breasting a storm? Our diminished speed is not the result of internal weakness, but of great waves piled up by adverse winds; and even now do you not see how she rides every billow?' It is just so with the church. The old ship is sound and strong, built by a divine architect: its machinery is planned by unerring wisdom and needs no change. Its administration is watched over by its ever-living head, and requires no new adjustments. For eighteen hundred years she has ridden stormy seas, and risen above mountain billows. Just now she is breasting a storm. The sea of human thought and life is driven by contrary winds. But alarms are needless. She has surmounted every wave. The Master is at the helm, and it only requires the ear of faith to hear his voice, saying, 'It is I; be not afraid.' 'Lo, I am with you alway.'

Such then being the inevitable conclusion to which a wide observation of the state of the church and the world must bring us, the problem of the future is cleared of much of its difficulty, and the scope of our enquiry reduced to a narrower range. The factors for all our work for the good of the world must be the church, the preacher and the pastor, and the question is how to organize and direct these agencies, so potent in the past, so as to realize their utmost efficiency in breasting this storm of opposition from without.

To this question there are some who reply: Adjust the church in all its aspects and agencies to the circumstances of the times. This is an age, say they, of philosophic thought, scientific activity, and aesthetic culture. These are the great formative influences which are now working everywhere in our national, political and social life, shaping our literature and moulding our civilization. Let the church, say they, place itself under these same formative influences. Let its architectural structures, its music and methods of worship be determined by the most approved principles of aesthetic taste. Educate pastors to develop the social spirit of the church in harmony with the manners and customs of the most refined worldly society. Imbue the ministry with the highest spirit of philosophic criticism, and with a literary culture in sympathy with the most advanced progress. Train the preacher to cast the expression of moral and religious truth in the most scientific moulds, and to adapt the utterances of the gospel to the choicest ideals of beauty, and to the most recent developments of refined taste. This, they say, will show that the church is not a mediæval relic, floundering in the wake of an advancing age, but a living institution, abreast of the age, and in harmony with its ideal of progress.

The simple answer to all this is that which was given by the apostles to the Sanhedrin of the Jews. 'Whether it be right in the sight of God to hearken unto men more than unto God, judge ye.' Who that has heard the command, 'Preach the preaching which I bid thee', can take his text from philosophy, and his spirit from the dominant excitement of the times? Is not this reversing God's method? He placed his church on the earth to be the great formative influence that is to mould and transform the world; but this is a proposal that the world shall mould and transform the church. Is it science or is it the gospel that is appointed to be the power of God unto salvation? Is this world to be drawn to God by aesthetic taste, or by the attractions of the cross? Is the church a social institution in which fashion is baptized with the name of religion, or is it the temple of the living God, to be adorned with the beauties of holiness? Is the boasted progress of an age which leaves the church of God in its wake, progress toward heaven, or is it progress in the broad road that leadeth to destruction?

Setting aside, then, this and kindred proposals, the question returns: How are we most effectively to meet and resist the combination of adverse influences by which we are now surrounded? We answer, By accepting and employing God's own institutions, ordinances and agencies, just as he has appointed them, and so far as these instrumentalities are human to put them in a condition of complete equipment, and give them all the power and efficiency which training, qualification and skill can impart to human instruments.

In order to do this we are,—

First, *To emphasize the church as God's own ordained and organized institution, for the regeneration, education, culture and sanctification of the world.* He laid its foundation stone in Zion; its walls composed of living stones are growing to an holy temple in the Lord; he hath chosen it as his abode, saying, 'Here will I dwell forever.' He has ordained its officers, commissioned its ministers, appointed its government, designated its functions. 'He has set his king on the hill of Zion', and promised the 'uttermost parts of the earth as his possession'. He has 'built his church upon a rock', and his word of truth is pledged that the 'gates of hell shall never prevail against it'. Hence the efficacy of the church as God's instrument for the salvation of the world is certain, no matter what influences may combine against it. To doubt is simply to disbelieve either God's power or his promise. To trust to any other means is simply dishonesty to God. Shall God's appointed agency fail of its destined results?

Hence we are to maintain the divine efficacy of the church as against those who are prone to conceive of it as a human device—a society for religious purposes—rather than a divine institution; its organization as an arrangement of human expediency rather than a divine appointment; its government and administration as a matter of prudent policy; and its forms and methods of worship as details which are to be conformed to the prevalent taste and fashion of the times.

To all such human perversions of the church, we conceive that God's language is just that which he addressed to the Jews when they perverted the institutions of worship, 'When ye come to appear before me, who hath required this at your hands to tread my courts?'

In the same manner also we must maintain the divine institution of the church against those who are disposed to look upon it as an ancient family home for comfort and enjoyment, but who imagine that to work for the world's good they must go outside and form voluntary organizations to convert souls, to care for the young men of our cities and towns, and win the masses to give attention to the gospel.

This is saying very broadly to the world, but perhaps thoughtlessly, that they prefer their own wisdom to God's wisdom, and choose to work by a human voluntary agency rather than through the church which God has appointed to save the world. Perhaps it would be well to remember in these days that to men in old times who presumed to do divine work upon their own motion, God said, 'I have not sent these prophets, yet they ran; I have not spoken to them, yet they prophesied.'

But whilst we bear our testimony to the church in its divine authority and sanction as the one ordained instrumentality for the salvation of the world, we are also to see to it that all its agencies, appliances and methods of work are kept in a state of effective operation. Hence we are,—

Secondly, *To emphasize the ministry as God's chosen instrument for the utterance of his truth, for the enlightenment of the world, for the education of the family, and the salvation of souls.*

There is a disposition in the present age to depreciate the preacher. Philosophy and science both claim to be the world's instructors, and they turn away from the preacher as an ancient, enfeebled champion whom they have bound with withes, and shorn of his strength. But they have forgotten that the power of God is in him, and that no Philistine withes can bind his hands, and no gates of Gaza can withstand his strength when he rises in his might. No, no; it is the old story. Men may account the preaching foolishness, but 'it is by the foolishness of preaching that God saves them that believe'. It is 'to them that perish' that 'the preaching of the cross is foolishness', but to them that are saved it is the 'power of God'.

The press also assumes to be the great teacher, but it has utterly failed to cast out the evil spirits from the world. They recognize the press as their companion and fellow labourer, but not as master. Hence when the press attempts to exorcise the evil spirits, they turn as in times of old and say, 'Jesus I know, and Paul I know, but who are you?'

We need not stay to argue. The proof is summed up in one divine witness, 'The preaching of the cross is the power of God.'

The facts of history endorse this testimony. All the great victories in behalf of truth, civilization and salvation have been achieved by the preacher's power. It was he who carried the light of life into the deep darkness of the heathen world. It was the preacher who, by God's authority and with God's Word on his lips, stood and cried, 'Let there be light', and there was light. It was he who smote the pagan altars, and they fell. It was when he spoke the heathen oracles grew dumb. It was at his advance that the popular shout, 'Great is Diana of the Ephesians', died away from the ears of men. It was the preacher who carried the tidings of the resurrection to the Areopagus at Athens. It was the preacher who planted the banner of the cross upon the palace of the Caesars. It was he who converted the dark ages into the Reformation. He spoke, and the light of life came out of darkness, as the light of day came out of chaos. It was his Word that rocked thrones, and broke the fetters of tyrants. It was he who laid the foundations of civil liberty, disenthralled and elevated woman, sanctified the family, reared our institutions of learning, and disseminated the principles of Christian civilization to the ends of the earth. A power that has accomplished such results is immortal. It has the perpetual youth of the living Word, and the quenchless energy of truth. Its power is as elastic today as when Paul preached on Mars Hill, or Luther thundered the resurrection note to a sleeping church, or when the hills of Scotland echoed to the voice of John Knox, proclaiming 'the crown rights of Jesus Christ'.

But if the preacher is God's ordained instrument of power, we must not forget that the instrument is human, and may become feeble and ineffectual from a want of vital piety, or from deficient learning and culture, or from a worldly spirit, or from a lack of adaptation to the wants of the age; but upon the other hand it may be preserved in power by such training and education as will invest it with the attributes of efficiency requisite for the exigencies of the present conflict. Just here lies the responsibility of our theological seminaries. They are to train men to meet every exigency.

For this age we must have a learned ministry. The enemy meets us upon the field of philosophy and science, and we must prepare men fully armed to accept the issue. We assume this as a matter of course.

But there are elements of practical qualification to which I wish specially to point.

First, we must train *a believing ministry,* a ministry that believes the Bible upon the authority of God, a ministry that goes forth in the confidence that this Word of truth is the Word of life, that it is the appointed instrument by which God works in the world, that through this Word of truth as a medium the Holy Ghost communicates his saving power to the heart, that it is the one single implement which God has put into our hands for the conversion of the world, that it is the one agency to which the power of God is bound by promise and therefore cannot fail. In this confidence the preacher will speak with power, and his message will carry with it a resistless energy.

We must have a ministry also that believes in the Son of God, that he became incarnate, that he suffered and died as the only expiation of human guilt. This is to be received not as a theological statement, but realized in a living experience in the preacher's own soul. He must have in his own heart a thrilling conviction that he himself was a sinner, that he was perishing, that he deserved to perish, and would have perished if Christ had not rescued him, and washed him in his atoning blood. This alone will enable him to go to thoughtless and sinful men and testify of Jesus with such urgency as will fasten upon their souls the conviction that there is nothing between them and eternal death but the blood of Jesus Christ.

If the truth is simply received into the intellect as a matter of dogmatic belief, it is laid away upon the shelf as a dead, inoperative thing. The preacher cannot seize and weigh it with effect, for he is ignorant of its value. He has never felt its kindling power himself, and therefore he cannot shoot it as a flaming arrow into the hearts of others. But if in his first study of the truth he is made to feel its quickening efficacy, it will abide with him as one of the forces of his life. The measure of every minister's power is just the number of these truths which he has received as living forces into his own soul.

Again, we must train *men for the times.* Here we must distinguish. There are men who are made *by* the times, products of the times. Their character and opinions are the mere efflorescence of the times in which they live. Their voice is simply the world's echo, their principles are caught from the current sentiment of the hour. They compromise with the times, court the smiles of the age, and barter the truth of God for popular favour.

But as distinguished from these, there are men who are made *for* the times, to resist the times, to reform the times, to mould the age in which they live, courageous men who are not afraid to maintain the truth of God in the face of the world's opposition, men of settled convictions who cannot compromise with popular errors. These are the men the necessities of the church demand. These are the men the world respects. The recreant who surrenders the truth of God at the challenge of a boasting scepticism should be beaten with a scourge of small cords from the sanctuary. The dilettante who truckles for the world's favour receives the world's scorn. He alone has power to resist and control the age who can stand and say like John Knox, 'The truth I speak, impugn it whoso list.'

Again, we must train men *to save souls*. Whatever other ends the ministry may accomplish, if it fails in this it fails in the very purpose for which it was instituted. A military company which is trained simply for the purposes of holiday exhibition is of little account in the actual battle. So a ministry trained for learned display or pulpit exhibition is of little value in the real work of the world's conversion. The single purpose for which the ministry is commissioned is to save souls. The soul, the undying soul, was the keynote of our Lord's ministry. 'What shall it profit a man if he gain the whole world and lose his own soul?' This is the point to which all must concentrate. All else in the education of the ministry is of little avail if they are not taught that the one great aim of all their preparation and work is to save souls.

We must also emphasize *the pastorate*. The pastor is Christ's mediatorial gift. The shepherd is not more necessary to the flock than the pastor is to the church. The pastorate is a divinely appointed function of the ministry for special purposes: to win souls by the attraction of personal sympathy, to sanctify the family by bringing the sacred influences of religion into every household, to educate the young by stimulating and guiding their instruction, and to gather men to the cross one by one, through the attractive power of man on man, and by the mystic charm of individual influence. One of the complaints of this age is the disposition of the masses to stand aloof from the church. If this be so, the pastor has lost his cunning. Just here the fault should be searched and the remedy applied. If in the churches the sacredness of the pastoral relation is ignored, and the minister regarded as a hireling instead of a mediatorial gift, if in our theological seminaries pastoral instruction and training is overshadowed and depreciated by the aggressions of the more learned departments, if ministers are sent forth without any thrilling realizations of the important issues and solemn responsibilities of the pastoral office, then it is no marvel that this potent arm of the church's work is paralysed, and that the masses stand aloof from a ministry that has no sympathy to attract and no charm to bind them to the church of God. To meet this peril we must enthuse the ministry with the pastoral spirit. We must raise up and send forth men who are in intense sympathy with the poor, and who can carry the affection of warm Christian hearts into every struggling family and into every home darkened by sorrow. Then again will the blessing of the poor come upon the church, and she 'shall arise and shine and put on her beautiful garments, the glory of the Lord having arisen upon her'.

But time would fail to pursue the subject further. These few thoughts we present towards the solution of the problem of the hour. The *church,* the *preacher,* and the *pastor* are the factors with which we must work. They have been the power of God in the past, and we believe they are still the instruments of might by which Christ rules the ages.

THE CALL TO THE MINISTRY[1]

THERE are some special reasons which urge this subject upon our attention.

First. There is an attempt in some directions to lower the choice of the ministry to the same level with that of any other profession or avocation in life. It is claimed that men are called to the ministry in the same way in which they are called to be farmers, merchants, lawyers, or physicians. The question would then be one simply of expediency and aptitude. The conditions of the choice would be the tastes and preferences of each individual, together with his talents and qualifications and such outward indications of providence as seemed more favourable to the ministry than to any other occupation.

This theory overlooks the *divine character* of the ministerial office. The minister is no longer a *mediatorial gift* to the church.

It ignores also the *immediate headship* of Jesus Christ over his church. He no longer can say to ministers, 'Ye have not chosen me, but I have chosen you.'

It sets aside also the *divine call of the Spirit*. It is no longer 'the Holy Ghost who' makes them overseers of the flock.

A *second* reason which urges this subject upon our attention is the fact that while some go to the extreme which I have just mentioned and deny the necessity of the Spirit's call, there are others who fly to the opposite extreme, and so emphasize the internal call of the Spirit as to render appointment to office or ordination or any authentication by the church entirely unnecessary. Upon this theory any man who can persuade himself that he is called by the Spirit to preach the gospel may take up the office of the minister and discharge its function when and where he please.

[1] William M. Paxton, 'The Call to the Ministry', *The Presbyterian Review*, Vol. 10, No. 37 (1889), pp. 1-16.

This theory ignores the church as the divinely appointed organization for the salvation of the world, and ordination or official relation
to the church as the divinely appointed means for the authentication
of a true ministry. It makes each individual minister the sole judge of
his own calling and qualifications; it sends him out in violation of the
law and order of God's house to act as an adventurer upon his own
authority and guidance, and to fall at last under the condemnation,
'Woe unto the foolish prophets, that follow their own spirit, that
prophesy out of their own heart. I am against the prophets that steal
my words. I sent them not, neither commanded them, therefore they
shall not profit this people at all.'

With this view of the urgency of the subject, and of the dangerous
extremes which lie upon each side of our pathway, let us advance to
inquire, *What is the true view, according to the Scriptures, of a call to
the ministry?*

We freely concede that it is both the privilege and the duty of
every believer to preach the gospel both with his lips and his life. If a
man has found salvation for his own soul, he immediately turns with
a natural, gracious, and imperative instinct to seek to save the souls
of others. If he has found the good Word of God to be precious to
his own soul, his lips are immediately opened to say, 'Oh, come and
taste and see that the Lord is good.' It is not only the privilege, but
the imperative duty of every Christian to utter the gospel invitation,
'The Spirit and the Bride say, Come. And let him that heareth say,
Come. And let him that is athirst come. And whosoever will, let him
take the water of life freely.'

Nor should this privilege be restricted or hedged about by unnecessary limitations.

The idea of a Christian is that of a consecrated worker for
Christ, and the idea of the church in the New Testament is that of
a self-expanding missionary organization. There is a place for every
individual and the largest sphere for personal exertion.

The church will never rise to greatness and power until we realize
that nothing can absolve the individual Christian from the responsibility of doing all that he can by personal work to save the souls of men.

But this is a very different thing from assuming an official relation to the church. It is one thing to testify for Christ and to work

for the salvation of men, but it is an entirely different thing to be a minister, to assume upon one's own motion an official relation to the church, which implies his appointment from the Head of the church, which invests him with spiritual authority, which calls him not only to preach, but to bear rule in the church, which requires him to separate himself from all secular pursuits and to devote his whole life to this one work.

If, then, this distinction is so clear, if the position and function of the minister are so different from those of the private Christian, if they are so much higher, so much more sacred, and so much nearer in their spiritual relations to Christ and his people, then the question comes back, Can any man be justified in assuming this higher office without a divine call?

The Scriptures certainly teach the necessity of a call from the great head of the church to the office and work of the ministry. This necessity may be shown,—

First. From the fact that the ministry is from its very nature an *office*. What is the ministry? It is not simply a work, but an office. Thought upon this subject is often confused from failure to make this distinction. Some think only of the work, and conclude that this is something they can take up for themselves; but they fail to see the office to which the work belongs. What, then, is an office? An office under the government is such a relation to that government as involves authority, duties, privileges, and responsibilities. The work may be that of a clerk, a postmaster, a soldier, or premier, but the official relation in each case is the same—it involves authority, duties, privileges. Office under a government can only be constituted by a call, appointment, or investiture; without this the office cannot exist.

In the same manner as an official relation to the government can only be created by a call or appointment from the government, so the ministry, as an official relation to the church, can only be created by a call from the head of the church, and authentication by the officers of the church. A simple illustration will make this plain.

A good citizen feels bound to do what he can to uphold and enforce the civil law; but because he feels this to be his duty, shall he assume upon his own motion to execute the office of a magistrate? No man can be a magistrate until he is called and inducted into the office.

In the same manner shall a Christian, because he feels it to be his duty to speak and work for Christ, assume on his own motion to perform the functions of a minister? As no man can be a magistrate until he is appointed and sworn into office, so no man can be a minister until he is called and ordained.

That the ministry is such an official relation, and can only be constituted by a divine call, is proved, *first, by all the names and designations by which it is described in the New Testament.*

For example, a minister is an *'ambassador of Jesus Christ',* but an ambassador is one who is selected, called, and commissioned under special instructions from one government to another. How absurd would it be for any man to assume to go as an ambassador to a foreign court without a call or commission! Can, then, a man be an ambassador of Jesus Christ except by his immediate call and commission?

Again, a minister is *'a steward of the mysteries of God'.* But can a steward act without the authority of the master? A self-constituted steward is a fraud and impostor.

A minister is also called *'a herald'.* But a herald never goes unsent, and the very message he is to proclaim is given to him. The same idea is conveyed by every appellation given to the ministry. Is he *'a pastor'?* he is called to the care of the flock by the chief Shepherd. Is he *'a watchman'?* he is sent or placed upon the walls of Zion. Is he *'a ruler'?* it is by the authority which Christ has given him. Is he *'a soldier'?* it is because he bears commission from the great Captain of salvation.

Thus it is that the very nature of the ministry as an official relation to the church, and every name by which it is designated, implies the necessity of vocation from Christ as the source of all church power and authority.

Secondly. The necessity of a call to the ministry is proven from the fact that both under the Old and New Testaments every official relation to the church required *divine call and investiture, and the most terrible punishments were threatened against and visited upon those who intruded uncalled into any sacred office.*

I need not stay to show how true this was of Moses and all the prophets, of Aaron and all the priests, of Paul and all the apostles. So minute and extensive was the application of this principle, that God would not permit the mechanical work of the tabernacle to be done until he had called Bezaleel and 'filled him with the Spirit of God in wisdom and in understanding and in all manner of workmanship'. But does anyone say these were all miraculous calls, and are therefore no precedent now as to the call of an ordinary minister? True, they were all miraculous and extraordinary, and as to the *manner* of the call are no precedent; but as to the *principle,* it is the same now as then. All these cases embody most expressly the principle that all official relation to the church must be authenticated by a divine call.

The Apostle Paul teaches this clearly in Hebrews 5:4, when he says, speaking of the priesthood, 'No man taketh this honour unto himself, but he that was called of God, as was Aaron.' In other words, he assumes it as a general principle that official relation to the church implies an appointment or call as opposed to an unauthorized assumption of the office. If this is not admitted, then it must be proved upon the other side that something has supervened to stay the operation of a principle that has hitherto been universal and imperative. If this cannot be done, then the divine woe is as operative against an uncalled ministry now as it ever was. 'Woe unto these prophets . . . I have not sent them, neither commanded them.'

So unvarying and imperative is this connection between a divine call and a sacred office that the Lord Jesus Christ himself was no exception; he came not upon self-constituted, but upon delegated authority. 'He glorified not himself to be made a high priest, but was called of God, as was Aaron.' If a divine call was necessary for Aaron and all the priests, and the Lord Jesus as the great High Priest, then it is much more necessary in all inferior cases.

Thirdly. The necessity of a divine call to the ministry is proven still more distinctly by the fact that *the Scriptures teach most expressly that the call and mission of the ordinary ministry comes from God.*

The pervading implication of the Scriptures is that Christ dwells now in the midst of his church, influencing by his Spirit and controlling by his providence all its operations; that he is the immediate author of all church power and church blessings, bestowing and authenticating ministerial gifts and ministerial authority according to his own will. It is his prerogative to call whom he will into his church, to give them gifts generally as he wills, and to call them from sources and to positions according to his own pleasure.

Accordingly, we find the apostles laying such significant stress upon their own vocation; they were not self-appointed ministers, but called to be apostles by the will of God.

Paul constantly announces himself as 'an apostle of Jesus Christ', 'an apostle not of men, neither by man, but by Jesus Christ and God the Father, who raised him from the dead'.

But if you make a distinction between the vocation of the apostles and that of ordinary ministers, then it is still more striking to notice that when these apostles come to speak of the calling and mission of ordinary ministers, they use precisely the same language which they had employed as descriptive of their own. Paul, sending a message to Archippus, says, 'Take heed unto the ministry which thou hast received of the Lord Jesus, that thou fulfil it.' Here was an ordinary minister, but he had received his ministry of the Lord Jesus, just as Paul had received his.

When the elders or presbyters of Ephesus met Paul at Miletus, he charged them to 'feed the flock over which the Holy Ghost had made them overseers'. No language can be constructed to convey more clearly the idea of a divine call than this. They were elders, presbyters, overseers, pastors of the flocks, but they had been made so by the Holy Ghost.

The New Testament idea of a minister is one who has received the 'ministry of reconciliation', and who 'in Christ's stead entreats men to be reconciled to God'. Surely he who stands in Christ's stead must have a call and mission from him whom he represents. The office of Timothy, whom Paul speaks of as an evangelist, is expressly stated to have been 'the gift of God'. The work of Barnabas when he was sent forth as an evangelist is styled a work to which 'the Holy Ghost had called him'. Paul's teaching upon this point in Ephesians 4:11 is so clear that there can be no mistake. When our Lord 'ascended up on high he gave gifts unto men'. What were these gifts? Church officers—men set apart and qualified for various works. 'He gave some apostles, some prophets, some evangelists, and some pastors and teachers.' Here, then, are Christ's 'ascension gifts'. They are not simply offices, but officers for the church. Some of these are ordinary and some extraordinary, but they all alike have a call and mission from the ascended Redeemer.

But as if to leave no question about the divine vocation of the ministry, Paul gives us a whole chapter on this subject. In the twelfth chapter of First Corinthians, the apostle shows that God has set officers in his church, just as he has set the members in the body. In other words, the constitution and officers of the church are just as much a divine work as the organism of the human body. After developing the figure of the human body, with all its different members, and showing how God has given to each member its peculiar office, he says, 'Now, ye are the body of Christ and members in particular. And God hath set some in the church, first, apostles; secondarily, prophets; thirdly, teachers; after that miracles, then gifts of healing, helps, governments, diversities of tongues.' Here, then, is the enumeration of the officers of the church; each is a gift of God, and each qualified and placed in position by the Lord's hand, just as he has placed the members in the body. 'The design of the whole chapter', says Dr Charles Hodge, 'is to show that Christ through his Spirit gives these gifts and offices, ordinary and extraordinary, to each one as he wills, and that to him alone they are to be referred.'

But the teaching of our Lord himself upon this subject is so plain as to foreclose the argument.

In that beautiful parable in the tenth chapter of John, in which he represents the church as a sheepfold, and himself as the good Shepherd, and ministers or pastors as the under-shepherds, he says, 'I am the door—namely, the door of ministerial entrance to the care of the flock. 'He who enters in by the door—*viz.,* he who enters in by his divine commission—'is the shepherd of the sheep', while those who 'climb up some other way'—*viz.,* those who enter without his call and authority—'are thieves and robbers'.

Again, on another occasion he points our attention to the harvest perishing for want of labourers, and says, 'Pray ye the Lord of the harvest that he send forth more labourers into the harvest.' The harvest is the millions of perishing souls in the world; he himself is the Lord of the harvest; ministers are the labourers who are to enter and reap. But how are these ministers to be secured? He does not say to the church, 'Go ye into the market-place and hire as many as ye find, and send them into the field.' Nor does he say to men to look at the perishing harvest and then go in of their own accord and labour. But he does say, 'Pray ye the Lord of the harvest to send labourers into the harvest.' The men who are to reap the harvest are to be men whom Christ himself sends.

In the Book of Revelation the expression of this idea is very striking. The churches are represented as 'golden candlesticks'; in the midst of these churches Christ, as the risen and living head, lives and walks with eyes 'as of a flame of fire', making a most minute inspection of their condition and exercising a more direct supervision over them. The ministers of the churches are represented as stars which Christ holds in his right hand. By this representation he expresses more forcibly than he could do by words his own sovereignty in the vocation and control of his ministers. He holds them in his right hand, he fills them with light, he elevates them to their position, and revolves them in the orbit of ministerial duty.

This obviously closes the argument. How can it be possible for anyone, without blinding his eyes to the teaching of the Word of God, to assume the duties of the ministry without a divine call from Christ himself as the head of the church?

This point being settled, the question arises, *How is this divine call to be so authenticated to the individual himself as to induce him to obey it?*

Upon this point the thought of young men seeking the ministry is sometimes confused and anxious. They are disposed to say, 'I do not understand this idea of a call to the ministry; there seems to be something mysterious, supernatural, miraculous about it.' To this we answer that it is not miraculous; the days of immediate revelation have ended. We are not, therefore, to expect to be called by a special messenger, or to be summoned by an audible voice to preach the gospel, or be constrained by the spirit of inspiration to testify of Jesus.

God's method of dispensation to the church has changed. This is the dispensation of the Spirit, and a call to the ministry is now a call from the Lord Jesus Christ as the head of the church by his Spirit. But this, you say, is mysterious and supernatural and difficult to understand.

To this we answer, Yes, everything in religion is supernatural, and to that extent it carries with it the element of the mysterious.

If you are a Christian you have experienced a supernatural change, the divine Spirit has wrought a new birth in your soul, and abides in you in the power of a supernatural life. And yet all this is a *reality* to you, and something that you comprehend as an experience. There is nothing more mysterious or supernatural in a call to the ministry than this. Your conversion is a calling; the old writers styled it 'effectual calling'. The general call of the gospel goes out to all men; some close their ears and disregard it, others hear and obey it; in them it is effectual, in the others it is not. Now, why is it effectual in some? Because the divine Spirit carries it home to their hearts, and disposes and enables them to hear and obey. Hence our 'effectual calling is the work of God's Spirit whereby, convincing us of our sin and misery, enlightening our minds in the knowledge of Christ and renewing our wills, he doth persuade and enable us to embrace Jesus Christ, freely offered to us in the gospel'. This call you have heard and obeyed; it has been effectual in you; you have been so convinced that you are called of God that you have confessed Christ before men, and taken your place at the sacramental table. This is your *calling* as a Christian. Now, is there anything more mysterious, more difficult to understand in a call to the ministry than in this call to be a Christian?

They are both divine, both immediate and personal. The effectual call is authenticated to the individual by the operation of the Spirit in his heart, and is recognized first in the sphere of his own consciousness, and then in the life by the fruits of faith, hope, and charity.

And may not a call to the ministry be authenticated to the individual in the same way, by the working of God's Spirit in his heart, giving him such views of truth, such an experience of the preciousness of Christ, and such love for the souls of men, as will enkindle a burning desire in his heart to go out and preach the unsearchable riches of Christ? Hence, following the suggestion of the Catechism definition of effectual calling, we may formulate in general a description of what a call to the ministry is.

A call to the ministry is the inward operation of the Spirit, enlightening the mind to apprehend truth and duty, imparting right views and motives, and influencing us to desire and seek to be employed by Christ in the discharge of ministerial functions. A definition comprehending the whole subject is given by Dr Charles Hodge: 'A call to the ministry is such an expression of God's will to an individual through his grace, through his providence, and through his constituted authorities as empower him to exercise the functions of the ministry, without which he is no minister, and with which he is a minister.' The late Bishop Simpson, of the Methodist Church, said, 'The first evidence of a divine call is in the consciousness of the individual, and is a persuasion which, slight as it may be at first, deepens into an intense conviction that he is called of God to preach the gospel. In its slightest form this call is a persuasion that he who receives it ought to preach the gospel. In its strongest form, that God requires him to do this work upon the peril of his soul. It is God's voice to the human conscience saying, "You ought to preach."'

From this general view we are able to point out some indications which should accompany and authenticate this divine call.

Generally, we may say that these evidences are connected with an inward operation of the divine Spirit upon the heart, leading a man to seek the office of the ministry from right motives; and as all right affections come from God, we may infer that an intelligent desire to preach the gospel from scriptural motives comes from the Holy Spirit. But to make this more tangible and practical, we may particularize and mention some of the more obvious indications of a divine call.

First, we mention *a strong conviction that it is our duty to preach the gospel.* This seems to be indicated by the analogy which I have before alluded to between a call to the ministry and our effectual calling. In our call to be Christians the first thing is conviction—a conviction of sin as something to be repented of and abandoned—and this is followed with a conviction of duty to embrace Christ and serve him. From this analogy may we not infer that in a call to the ministry the divine Spirit sends in upon our hearts a conviction of duty, a sense of obligation from which it would be sinful to withdraw? If Christ has done so much for me, what shall I do for him? This is that sense of *oughtness* to which Bishop Simpson refers in his account of a call to the ministry. This sense of duty is prominent in all the divine calls recorded in the Scriptures. In each case, obedience to the call was rendered under the pressure of a divine command. Moses seemed to be lacking at first in this sense of duty, and he displayed when first called upon to stand before Pharaoh an unworthy hesitancy, because he was slow of speech; and his brother Aaron was advanced to the position of chief speaker.

When Jeremiah was called, he showed reluctance and said, 'Ah, Lord God, behold I cannot speak, for I am a child'; but God said, 'Say not, I am a child, for thou shalt go to all that I shall send thee, and whatsoever I command thee, thou shalt speak.' Isaiah had a vision of the glory of the Lord, 'high and lifted up in the temple', and when the call came, 'Whom shall I send?', he answered, 'Here am I, send me.' The very first utterance of Paul's new life sprang from this conviction of duty—'Lord, what wilt thou have me to do?' As he grew in experience, this sense of oughtness deepened, and he said, 'A necessity is laid upon me. Woe is me if I preach not the gospel.' Vinet, writing upon this point, says, 'When conscience commands and obliges us to perform a certain task, we have that which next to a miracle best merits the name of a call. And it must be *nothing less*. To exercise legitimately the ministry, we must have a call to it.'

The *second* indication of a call to the ministry is *a strong and abiding desire for the work springing from love to Christ.*

This intense desire to accomplish his work was one of the striking characteristics of our Lord's ministry. Dr Bridges, in his book on the *Christian Ministry*,[1] noticing this point, says, 'While he was in the bosom of the Father and in anticipation of his work, his delights were with the sons of men.' When he came into the world for the accomplishment of his mission, the same earnest desire distinguished him. His delight in his Father's work was greater than in his necessary food. He said to his disciples, 'I have food to eat that ye know not of. My meat is to do the will of him that sent me.' Some such earnest desire must certainly characterize our experience as ministers. Paul's desire amounted to a painful agony. He 'laboured and travailed in birth for souls.' It was said of Dr Alleine that 'he was infinitely and insatiably greedy for the conversion of souls'.

Vinet, in his *Pastoral Theology*, says, 'When fitness for the ministry exists, will not this supply the place of desire and be sufficient evidence of a call?' 'Fitness', we reply, 'does not exist where the desire

---

[1] Charles Bridges, *The Christian Ministry* (1830: Edinburgh: Banner of Truth, repr. 2009), 400 pp. ISBN: 978 0 85151 087 3.

does not. Where the desire is wanting, there is not that harmony of the man with his duties which is so essential to the success of the work. We do not say that the Christian will do no good who engages in the work without a taste or desire for it—we only say that he has no call and ought to leave this office to others.'

But Vinet presses this point further. He says, 'While desire is the first sign of vocation, it is an equivocal sign. It is necessary to ascertain what is the object of this desire, whether it be the ministry itself, or something in the ministry that suits our tastes. The taste, the inclination we feel for the ministry may be superficial, carnal, or erroneous as to its object. It may be that what we like in the ministry is a respectable, honoured profession, or the sphere and occasions which it offers for the exercise of talents with which we may think ourselves endowed; or a vague religious sentimentalism; or an unreflecting enthusiasm; an ideal image; the poetry of the thing. The imagination in these cases is apt to take the place of the conscience and the heart.'

In order to be fully assured that we have a true call, our desire for the ministry must in some degree at least spring from love for the glory of God. Nothing is more foreign to the natural heart than this desire for the glory of God, nothing marks more decisively our birth to a new life.

'When one perceives unfolding in himself this strange desire, so chimerical to the natural man, this desire that God be honoured and glorified in the world, then he may think himself called to the ministry.'

A *third* indication of a call to the ministry is *the possession or the opportunity to acquire the proper gifts and qualifications.*

Dr Bridges says, 'A desire for the ministry does not of itself attest a divine vocation. We cannot suppose that the Lord would send unqualified labourers, however willing, into the vineyard, and none but he can qualify them.'

It is a dictate both of reason and Scripture that God does not call a man to the discharge of any duty without furnishing him with the requisite qualifications. God, in his providence, does not call the blind to be artists nor the deaf to be musicians. So neither in his church does he call the ignorant to be the guides and instructors of his people, nor the feeble-minded to be the expositors of his will. These qualifications are,

First, *physical*. If God forbade a sickly or puny animal to be offered to him in sacrifice, how will he regard those who present a feeble or diseased body as a living sacrifice in the work of the ministry? If men are chosen for military service who have strength and vigour of body, shall there be less care in the selection of those who are to 'endure hardness as good soldiers of Jesus Christ'?

The ministry has doubtless often been injured by the strange mistake of parents who give their strong and healthy sons to the plough and the business of the world, while they educate the feeble or invalid boy for the service of God.

Dr Crosby, in his Yale lecture, says, 'For a weak-bodied man to undertake the onerous duties of a preacher seems to me to be a tempting of providence. When there is organic difficulty of lungs, heart, or nerves, the work of God is to be done in some other way than in the ministry.'

Upon these physical conditions we need not particularize except to say that voice is one of the first conditions of our work. It is essential to a minister as sight is to an alpine guide. A man who has a feeble vocal utterance has certainly reason to inquire whether he is called to the ministry. This weakness may sometimes be remedied by careful culture, and the student who neglects it is doing great injustice to himself and to his Master's work. A preacher cannot command attention or produce an impression on his audience without clearness of voice and distinctness of articulation.

These qualifications are, second, *mental*. If the physical qualifications are important, the mental are still more so. Mind is the one factor with the minister. In everything that he does he brings his mind to bear upon other minds. Hence Vinet pronounces the ministry as 'the art *par excellence*', because it is that of governing minds.

The one instrument with which he works is mind, Whether he preaches or prays or visits or talks, he looks for results by the action of his mind upon other minds; and not only so, his mind is the medium through which the divine mind operates upon the souls of men. He is mentally a co-worker with God. The aim of his whole work is 'to awaken and strengthen in men thought, which must determine and control their lives.' It is his work 'to govern by purely moral means a multitude of very different minds and dispositions'. He must subjugate the acts and thoughts of others, and this by persuasion. 'The minister has to conduct men where they do not wish to go. He has to induce them to receive unlooked-for ideas which they are not disposed to receive, and which they regard as foolishness.' Hence it is plain that a minister must not be a feeble-minded man; he ought to have mental faculties stronger, keener, and better cultivated than the men whom he is expected to influence.

As mind is the one implement with which he works, it should be of the best quality, and much of his success will depend upon his natural force and ability. Paul laid stress upon this qualification when directing Timothy to whom the gospel should be committed; he says to faithful men, 'who shall be able to teach others also' (2 *Tim.* 2:2). Still more expressly describing a minister, he says, he must be 'apt to teach', *viz.,* not only capable of learning, but also of impressing others by the force of his teaching.

To this end he should have acuteness of perception to see the truth, a well-balanced mind to judge of truth in its connections and relations, a good memory to retain what is acquired; but, above all, a sound judgment to protect him against prejudices and one-sided views of truth.

The qualifications which indicate a call to the ministry are, third, *spiritual.* The physical and intellectual qualifications are important, but spiritual qualifications are absolutely essential.

John Newton said,

> None but he who made the world can make a minister of the gospel. If a young man has capacity, culture, and application he may make a scholar, or a philosopher, or an orator; but the true minister must have certain motives, principles, feelings, and aims which no industry or endeavours of men can either acquire or communicate. They must be given from above or they cannot be received.

Erasmus said with fine point, 'He who wishes to be apt to teach must first be taught of God.' Where there is no divine teaching, there certainly is no divine calling. He who has not the unction from the Holy One cannot understand the truths of the gospel. He may receive them into his intellect and preach them, but he is like a blind man talking about colours, or like a deaf man discoursing about music. All the great truths of theology may be learned by the mind, but if we have not an experience of religion they will remain in the intellect as dead dogmas, as cold and inoperative as a theorem of geometry. It is when these doctrines are studied in a devotional spirit and fused into our own experience by prayer and meditation that they become living forces in our own hearts, and it is only when we are warmed and quickened and fired by these truths ourselves that we can send them out in our preaching as blazing arrows or burning forces to kindle and fire the hearts of others. Here, then, is the one qualification without which all other qualifications are useless—an experience of the power of religion in our own hearts.

A fourth qualification involved in a call to the ministry is *soundness in the faith*. We cannot suppose that God calls errorists to be the teachers of his truth. This is expressly enjoined as one of the qualifications of a minister. 'He is to speak the things that become sound doctrine', 'he is to hold fast the faithful word as he hath been taught, that he may be able by sound doctrine both to exhort and to convince the gainsayers'. Having laid down this qualification, God would not surely call a man to the ministry who does not possess it.

If there is any doubt upon this subject, a man should stand in awe before obtruding himself into the ministry, for the apostle, as if to utter a warning that cannot be mistaken, declares that no matter what evidence a man or an angel may give of a divine call, if he has not this he is to be regarded as accursed. 'Though we or an angel from heaven preach any other gospel unto you than that which we have preached unto you, let him be accursed.'

This may suffice upon the point of qualifications.

A *fourth* indication of a call to the ministry is *the manifest blessing of God upon your efforts to do his work*. If the Spirit of God attends the words which we speak to others, this may be taken as a token of his approval.

It sometimes happens that young men after their conversion are filled with a most earnest desire to bring other souls to Christ; they talk with them in private, or address them in prayer meetings, or teach them in a Bible class, and a manifest blessing attends these efforts to convert others. In such cases the inquiry very properly starts up in the young man's mind, 'May it not be that God by these tokens of success is calling me to the ministry?' Such experiences are so encouraging that I feel reluctant to break their force by a single precaution. If this experience of success leads the young man to a deeper humility and self-distrust, and to a more profound dependence upon God, it is surely a call to take this great question into serious consideration.

But occasionally it happens that apparent success fills a man with pride and inflates him with a conceit of his superior piety; he is flattered by injudicious friends, who predict that the 'young man is the making of a wonderful preacher'.

When this occurs, it is far more probable that the young man has fallen into what the apostle calls the 'snare of the devil' than that he has found the leading of the Spirit. The most dangerous men that I know anything of are men who are filled with the conceit of their own piety. It leads them to a spirit of crimination, they reflect upon others, their piety puts on the aspect of arrogance, and they seem to think themselves inspired; hence whatever they think is right, and they can brook no opposition. It is certainly a most unfortunate thing when such a man gets it into his head that he is called to the ministry.

But while all this is true, it should not be permitted to detract from the force of the indication which I have just mentioned.

Where God grants a man success, and at the same time maintains his humility and self-distrust, he should certainly be encouraged to feel that God is calling him to higher spheres of usefulness. Paul, you remember, appeals to the divine blessing that attended his labour as the proof of his divine mission. Thus to the Corinthians he says, 'The seals of mine apostleship are ye in the Lord.' And again he says, 'Need we epistles or commendation to you, or letters of commendation from you? Ye are our epistle written in our hearts, known and read of all men.' When God uses a man to turn others to righteousness, it is certainly a strong proof that he is called to the work.

The *fifth* and last indication of a call to the ministry consists of *such providential leadings as remove obstacles and open up the way for a man to enter the ministry.* Some writers upon this subject speak of a call to the ministry as having two aspects—*external* and *internal*. The internal call consists of such indications as I have already mentioned, and the external of such providential directions as open up the way to a preparation for and an entrance upon the work. This distinction does not seem to me to be necessary. The call is *one,* and a division of the subject seems to be artificial and tends to confuse thought. Divine providence and divine grace work in a beautiful harmony. Whenever God puts a strong desire into the heart of a man to preach, he opens the way to the work.

If the secret history of ministers could be written, there would be some marvellous chapters upon this subject. I have known instances in which difficulties have been removed and the way opened up as clearly as if an angel had come and said, 'This is the way, walk ye in it.'

Sometimes this opening is at the beginning. A young man is filled with a desire to preach, but he has no means to pursue his education, and possibly others are dependent on him for support; his way seems hedged up by difficulties, which he can only interpret as a prohibition. But unexpectedly these difficulties are removed, the hedge is opened, and the crooked path becomes straight.

Sometimes the orderings of providence are such as to try a young man's patience and trust in God and his spirit of submission to what seems to be adverse providence. He is filled with a great desire to preach, and a burning zeal to do something for the salvation of men; but the way is not open. Under such circumstances it is difficult to restrain a feeling of impatience or discouragement, but perseverance and trust often have their reward, and the young student is led forward in a plain path.

ARCHIBALD ALEXANDER HODGE
1823-1886

PASTOR, preacher, missionary, theologian, educator, and
churchman, Archibald Alexander Hodge was the first-born son
of Charles and Sarah Hodge. Born and raised in the pleasant
and intellectually stimulating environment of Princeton, New Jersey,
the young Hodge enjoyed the inestimable privilege of being nurtured
in the home of Presbyterianism's greatest biblical scholar and theologian
in mid-nineteenth century America.

Charles Hodge was a devoted husband and loving father to his children. The loving atmosphere that characterized the Hodge family home
bore a rich spiritual harvest in the life of A. A. Hodge. Named after his
father's spiritual mentor and surrogate father, Archibald Alexander, A.
A.'s life was embedded in the rich spiritual soil of the Calvinistic orthodoxy and redolent piety for which Princeton Theological Seminary was
so well known.

A. A. Hodge graduated from Princeton College in 1841 and Princeton Theological Seminary in 1846. Having developed a love for missions, he and his young bride set sail to serve as Presbyterian missionaries in Allahabad, India. The couple ministered in India for only a few short years; health-related complications necessitated their return to the United States, whereupon A. A. served as a pastor in rural congregations in Maryland and Pennsylvania.

During these years A. A. began writing his major work, *Outlines on Theology,* which was first published in 1860 and later in a revised and enlarged edition in 1879. He was an emotional and captivating preacher whose popularity grew during the years of his pastoral charges. His gifts as a preacher, teacher, pastor, and author led to his receiving a call, in 1864, to serve as Professor of Systematic Theology at Western Theological Seminary in Allegheny, Pennsylvania.

In 1878 he returned to Princeton Theological Seminary as Professor of Didactic and Exegetical Theology. A beloved professor, he continued the theological legacy begun by Archibald Alexander and perpetuated by his father. His publications on *The Atonement,* a popular series of talks published as *Lectures on Theology,* and *A Commentary on the Westminster Confession of Faith,* all demonstrate his self-conscious commitment to the Reformed confessional heritage, as well as the purposeful integration of piety and learning that Princeton Theological Seminary was founded upon. He also co-authored with B. B. Warfield an important article on the inspiration of the Scriptures that remains a classic statement on the subject.

An active spokesman against the dangers of nationalized government-sponsored public education based upon a foundation of scientific naturalism, A. A. Hodge supported an amendment to the United States Constitution that would affirm recognition of the lordship of Jesus Christ over the United States government. His outlook predates modern evangelicalism's interest in the integration of faith with learning and the development of a Christian worldview which seeks to integrate all aspects of the created order under Christ's lordship.

Additional publications by A. A. Hodge include an important intellectual and spiritual biography of his father, *The Life of Charles Hodge.*[1] This *Life* provides rich insights into the spiritual culture and theological issues that characterized American Presbyterianism in his father's

---

[1] A. A. Hodge, *The Life of Charles Hodge* (Edinburgh: Banner of Truth, 2011), 672 pp. ISBN: 978 1 84871 090 0

lifetime and the way in which Princeton Theological Seminary carried out the founders' vision for preparing future generations of ministers.

A compassionate man with a burden for the lost, Archibald Alexander Hodge's life-long passion for missions and earnest preaching of the gospel—often with tears streaming down his cheeks—endeared him to his students, congregations, and community. He lived as a man who walked with God and whose life was spent bringing others into the same true and living way.

DOGMATIC CHRISTIANITY, THE ESSENTIAL GROUND OF PRACTICAL CHRISTIANITY[1]

FATHERS and Brethren of the Board of Directors: in obedience to your call, I am here to assume the solemn trust involved in teaching Christian theology in this seminary. Doubtless the design of associating an inaugural address with the induction of a new professor into such a charge is to afford him an opportunity of satisfying you, as the responsible guardians of the institution, with respect to his theological convictions and method.

I therefore affirm my belief that the Scriptures of the Old and New Testaments in their integrity *are* the Word of God, as a whole and in every part infallible and binding the conscience, and the only divinely authentic informant and rule of faith in matters of religion. Christian theology is wholly in the Scriptures, and is to be drawn from them only by legitimate interpretation. This is true of systematic as absolutely as of exegetical or of biblical theology. The system lies in the relations of the facts, and their relations are determined by their nature, as that is disclosed by the words of the Holy Ghost. The systematic theologian as well as the exegete is only an interpreter; the one interprets the words and develops the revealed truths; the other interprets these separate lessons in their mutual light and reciprocal relations, and develops the revealed system.

More definitely I affirm, not as a professional propriety, but as a personal conviction, that the Confession and Catechisms of the

---

[1] A. A. Hodge, 'Inaugural Address: Dogmatic Christianity, the Essential Ground of Practical Christianity', *Addresses at the Inauguration of Rev. Archibald Alex. Hodge, D.D., LL.D., as Associate Professor of Didactic and Polemic Theology, in the Theological Seminary at Princeton, NJ, November 8, 1877* (Philadelphia: Sherman & Co., Printers, 1877), pp. 17-39.

Westminster Assembly contain the system taught in the Holy Scriptures. Or rather, in the more absolute terms of subscription imposed upon intrants by the Scottish Presbyterian churches, 'I do sincerely own and believe the *whole doctrine* contained in the Confession of Faith, approved by former General Assemblies of this church, to be founded upon the Word of God, and do acknowledge the same as the confession of my personal faith, and will firmly and constantly adhere thereunto, and to the utmost of my power will assert, maintain, and defend the same.' This is affirmed, not only because I believe this 'whole doctrine' to be true, but because I also believe this 'system of doctrine' to be the most complete and adequate presentation as yet attained by the church of that truth revealed in the Holy Scriptures, which the Holy Ghost has declared to be 'the power of God unto salvation'. For therein Christ and his work is exhibited in their relation to human needs, experiences, duties, and destinies, and it is, therefore, the efficient instrument of forming character, of ruling action, and of effecting salvation.

It is precisely this last position which in the present day is so earnestly and in such various quarters denied. Besides the numerous classes of professed unbelievers, who positively reject Christianity, or the integrity and authority of its records, or at least some of its essential doctrines, there are many more, because of their position of professed friendliness, doing incalculably more harm, who, expressing no opinion as to the objective truthfulness of the church system of doctrines, maintain that it is at any rate unessential because impractical and unprofitable. Hence, they insist that the careful elaboration and the prominent and ceaseless emphasis which the church gives to doctrine imperils the interests of religion, by dividing those otherwise agreed, by rendering the candid examination of new truth impossible through the bias of foregone conclusions, and by diverting the attention of Christian people from the great practical and moral interests of life to matters of barren speculation. They charge the church with exalting creed above morals, and faith above character. They insist upon it, that the norm of Christianity is to be found in the Sermon on the Mount, and as such it is proved to be a religion of character, not of creed; and hence, that it is the duty of the church to regard immoral action as the only heresy.

This tendency to depreciate the importance of clearly discrimin-ated views of religious truth rests in the case of different objectors upon very different grounds, and is carried to very different degrees. But against this entire tendency, which opposes creed and morals, faith and character, in all its forms and intensities, we protest, and proclaim the opposite principle as fundamental—that truth is in order to holiness, and that knowledge of the truth is an essential prerequisite to right character and action.

The force of the objections against the importance of clearly dis-criminated truth in the sphere of religion is mainly the result of the vagueness with which the objections are stated. When it is charged against the church, as its record stands in history, that it has subordi-nated moral and practical interests to those of scholastic speculation and party contests, there is a colouring of truth in the charge which commands attention, and disguises the real animus and ultimate aim of the objectors.

In order to clear the question of accidental complications, which constantly confuse the current discussions of it, we make the follow-ing admissions and distinctions:

First, we concede that one of the sins most easily besetting theo-logians has been a tendency to over-refinement in speculation, over-formality of definition, and an excess of rigidity of system. Logical notions, creatures of the understanding, have too often been substituted for the concrete form of spiritual truth presented by the Holy Ghost to faith. Theologians have often practised a rationalism as real as that of their modern opponents, when their ambition to be wise beyond what is written has urged them to explore and explain divine mysteries, to philosophize on the basis of scriptural facts, and to form rational theories, as, for instance, of the relation of the divine and human natures in the person of Christ, and of the concursus of the first with second causes in providence.

Second, we admit also that zeal for doctrine has in too many instances been narrow and prejudiced, mingled with the infirmities of personal pride and party spirit, and has hence led to the unneces-sary divisions and alienations of those who were in reality one in faith, and to the conditioning of communion, and even of salva-tion, upon unessential points. Human nature has operated among earnest theological advocates with the uniformity and blindness of a physical law, leading each to choose a position as far as possible from his opponent—to unduly emphasize some Scriptures and depreciate others—to confine his attention to the fragment of truth he champions, exaggerating its proportions, and denying or minimizing the qualifying truths represented by his antagonist. This law has led to the multiplying of special theological tendencies, and to their development in all possible directions and to every possible extent, and has thus been providentially overruled to the extension of our knowledge, and to the ultimate establishment of the truth in wider relations. But the habit is in itself obviously evil, since for the individuals immediately concerned it sacrifices the truth as a whole to special elements, which by exaggeration or dissociation from their natural relations become virtually untruths. This is illustrated in the whole history of controversies, *e.g.,* between Nestorians and Monophysites, Lutherans and Reformed as to the person of Christ, between Supralapsarian Calvinists and Arminians, Churchmen and Puritans, Mystics and Formalists. It is plainly the duty of the individual to understand as fully as possible the position of his respondent, and to incorporate the other's fragment of truth with his own into the catholic whole.

Third, we must admit also that some advocates of theological dogma have lacked the courage of their convictions, and have betrayed their want of perfect confidence in the foundations on which they have builded by a disposition to discourage the fearless investigations of new truth in all directions, and to put an ungenerous interpretation upon all opinions to which their own minds were unaccustomed.

We claim to be sincere advocates of free investigation, in the true sense of that word, in every direction open to man. The believer in the supernatural revelation contained in God's Word is placed on a higher and more central point of vision than that of the mere naturalist, and he is thus rendered free of the whole sphere of truth. The true relation of the successive realms of the universe of being and knowledge can be read by one looking upon them from within outward and not from without inward, from above downward and in the direction in which the supreme light of revelation radiates, and not from below upward upon the side on which the shadows fall.

But it is absurd to suppose that true intellectual progress consists in a mere change of opinions, or that it is consistent with the destruction of the foundations which have been laid in the verified knowledge of the past. Truth once adequately established must be held fast forever, while we stand prepared to add to it all new truth substantiated by equal evidence. And it is a law which all educated men should be ready to acknowledge as axiomatic, that truth in any department, once established, must ever after hold the place of valid presumptions, influencing the course of new investigations in every department. Ruskin well testifies, 'It is the law of progressive human life that we shall not build in the air, but in the already high-storied temple of the thoughts of our ancestors', and that any addition successfully made can 'never be without modest submission to the Eternal Wisdom, nor ever in any great degree except by persons trained reverently in some large portion of the wisdom of the past'.

It cannot be doubted that what is held by men as truth in any one department of knowledge must, in the long run, be brought into conscious adjustment with all that they hold as truth in every other department. That which is false in philosophy cannot long be believed to be true in religion, and conversely, that which is false in religion can never be rightly regarded true in philosophy. Consequently, in the rapid development of the physical sciences which characterizes the present age, it is inevitable that there should be serious difficulty in so adjusting all the elements as to allow us to become clearly conscious of the congruity in all respects of the new knowledge with the old. It is not to be wondered at even that at several points there is an apparently irreconcilable antagonism. But when we recall the obvious distinction between facts and theories, between established knowledge and provisional hypothesis, we are readily reassured by the recollection it suggests that the historic track of human thought is strewn with the wrecks of systems, of cosmogonies, and anthropologies, as certainly believed and as influential in their day as any of the anti-theological systems of the present day.

We should unquestionably open our doors wide, with a joy equal to her own, for all the facts which science gathers in her harvest-time. But is it not absurd to ask the believers in the great church creeds of Christendom to abandon, to modify, or to mask that ancient and coherent mass of knowledge which roots itself in the profoundest depths of human nature, and in all human history, which has verified itself to reason and every phase of experience for two thousand years, which has moulded the noblest characters, inspired the most exalted lives, and inaugurated the very conditions which made modern science and civilization possible—to modify or abandon all this in deference to one or the other of the variant and transient speculations which each in his little day claims to speak in the venerable name of science?

We admit also that all Christian doctrine, like all other truth, rests on evidence appropriate in kind and adequate in degree. Nor is it denied that human reason legitimately exercised is the organ by which alone this divine truth is to be apprehended and its credentials examined and verified. These evidences ought to be subjected to the most thorough legitimate examination. He is a false or a mistaken advocate of the truth who would impede such investigation or who fears the result. Most of those who depreciate Christian dogma as incapable of certain verification, or as impractical and unprofitable, simply beg the question as to these evidences. All such we refer to the Christian apologist, who is fully prepared to meet all reasonable demands. At present we assume the truth of our dogma, and claim, that being true, every fragment of it is of transcendent importance as to the God-appointed means of effecting the moral and spiritual regeneration of human character and life.

Fourth. We moreover admit without hesitation that theologians must themselves be held to their own principle that truth is in order to holiness; that the great end of dogma is not the gratification of the taste for speculation, but the formation of character and the determination of the activities of our inward and outward life in relation to God and our fellow men. There is a patent distinction between the logical and the moral aspects of truth, between that manner of conceiving and stating it which satisfies the understanding and that which affects the moral nature and determines experience. Neither can be neglected without injury to the other. For if the laws of the understanding are essentially outraged, the moral nature cannot be either healthfully or permanently affected; that which is apprehended as logically incongruous by the understanding, cannot be rested in as certainly true and trustworthy by the heart and conscience and will. But all the great doctrines of the Scriptures may be apprehended on the side and in the relations which immediately determine the moral attitude of the soul in relation to God. It is possible, for instance, to treat the biblical teaching as to the sinful estate into which man has fallen and from which he has been redeemed by Christ, as a metaphysical or a psychological problem, in which its reality and bearings, as a matter of experience, may be to a great degree disguised. On the other hand, it may be set forth, as it always is in Scripture, as it is realized in consciousness, and as it enters into all religious experience. If, as is asserted, religious experience is only the personal experience of the truth of the great doctrines of Christianity, as we are personally concerned with them, it follows that they must be conceived and stated in a form in which they admit of being realized in the experience. Any theological method which sacrifices the moral and experiential aspects of the truth to a metaphysical and speculative interest will soon lose its hold upon the consciences of men, and itself experience that law of change which determines the fluctuations of all mere speculative systems.

With these admissions and distinctions, we return to our theme, that the truth revealed in the Scriptures, and embraced in what evangelical Christians style Christian dogma, is the great God-appointed means of producing in men a holy character and life. At present neither the general truth of Christianity, nor that of any particular system of theology claiming to represent it, is the question. But the truth of Christianity being assumed, we affirm that the truths set forth in the Word of God in their mutual relations are necessary means of promoting holiness of heart and life. That is, that dogmatic Christianity is the essential ground of practical Christianity.

First. This will be made evident when we consider what Christianity really is and what is the essence of Christian doctrine. Unlike all philosophies, it is not a speculative system built up on certain principles or seminal ideas. It is, on the contrary, a divinely authenticated statement of certain facts concerning God, his nature, his attitude towards man as fallen, his purpose with regard to man's redemption from sin, and several stages of his actual intervention to effect that end. This redemptive work Christ has been, and is now, engaged in accomplishing by several actions in chronological succession. The revelation of these purposes and redemptive actions has been evolved through an historic process, the separate facts of which are as definitely ascertainable as those which constitute any other history. Christian doctrine, therefore, is just God's testimony with regard to certain matters of fact, with which the religious life of the race is bound up. A distinction has been pressed, beyond all reason, between the matter of fact taught in Scripture and doctrines which, it is asserted, men have inferred from or have superadded to the facts, as hypothetical explanations of them. By matters of fact the liberal school means the external events of Christ's history as these were observed by the bodily senses of human witnesses, and assured to us by their testimony; and these external facts of sense, perception, and nothing more, they admit to be valid objects of faith, forgetful that a more advanced and consistent school of their fellow rationalists overset these external facts just as confidently as they themselves flippantly relegate dogma to the region of the unknowable. These men admit, for instance, that we know, as a matter of 'fact' that Christ died on the cross, and rose from the dead the third day; but they hold that the design with which he died or that the relation which his death sustains to man's restoration to the divine favour are matters of speculative opinion, but no matter of 'fact'.

The word 'fact' in universal usage signifies not merely an action, a thing done, but as well any objective reality, and by way of eminence, a reality of which we have adequate certainty, in distinction from a matter of opinion or probable reality. Now that Christ died and rose again as our representative, that his death was a vicariously endured penalty, is plainly as purely *a matter of fact, i.e.,* objective reality, as definitely and certainly verifiable on the direct testimony of God, as the dying and rising again themselves. All that a witness in the Hall of Independence on July 4, 1776, would have seen with his bodily eyes would have been the physical acts of certain men subscribing their names to a written paper; that was the optical perception, and nothing more. But no man would be absurd enough to deny that it is just as much a 'fact', and just as certain a 'fact', that they subscribed their names as the representatives of certain political communities, with the design and effect of changing their political constitutions and relations. The sensible transaction and its legal intent and effect were equally matters of 'fact', and ascertainable with equal precision and certainty upon adequate evidence. Now the matter of fact of which Christian dogmas are the revealed expression and attestation are those which more than any other conceivable facts are of transcendent importance and of immediate practical interest to mankind. The tri-personal constitution of the Godhead, and his essential attributes and eternal purposes—his relation to the world as Creator, Providential Ruler, and Moral Governor—his judgment of man's present guilt, corruption, and impotence as a sinner—his purposes of grace, and the provision made for their execution, in the incarnation of the second person of the Trinity and in the life, death, resurrection, and ascension to universal dominion of the God-man—the work of the Holy Ghost—the institution of the church—the resurrection of the body, the judgment and eternal condemnation of the finally impenitent and glorification of believers—these are the *facts*.

In every department of life all practical experience and activity is constantly determined by the external facts into relation to which we are brought, and upon our knowledge of and voluntary conformity to these facts. All modern life, personal, social, and political, is notoriously being changed through the influence of the facts brought to our knowledge in the advances of the physical sciences. All moral duties spring out of relations, as those of husband and wife, parent and child, citizen and community. All religion is morality lifted up to the sphere of our relations to God, as Father, Son, and Holy Ghost, as Creator, Moral Governor, Redeemer, Sanctifier, and Father. Our question, at present, is not whether our theological dogmas are true, but whether, being true, they are of practical importance. Much of the cavil against their use is only a disingenuous begging the question as to their truth. We prove them to be true in the department of apologetics, which draws upon all the resources of philosophy and historical criticism. And having proved them to be true, we now assert, in advance, that morality and religion are possible only so far as these facts are recognized, and our inward and outward life adjusted to them. It would be incomparably more reasonable to attempt to accomplish all the offices pertaining to the departments of agriculture, navigation, and manufactures, while ignoring all the ascertained facts of the natural world, than it would be to attempt to accomplish the offices of morality and religion while ignoring the facts of the spiritual world signified and attested to us in Christian dogma.

Second. Again, our proposition that knowledge and belief of scriptural truth is the essential means of the production of holiness in heart and life may be demonstrated upon universally admitted psychological principles. Knowledge is the act of the subject knowing, apprehending the truth. Truth is the object apprehended and recognized in the act of knowledge. In every act of apprehension there is required the object to be apprehended, and the apprehensive power upon the part of the agent apprehending. 'The eye sees what it brings the power to see.' All truth of every kind stands related to the human mind, and the mind is endowed with the constitutional faculties adjusted to it, and effecting its apprehension. As an actual fact, however, in the present state of the race, many individuals are found incapable of apprehending and recognizing some kinds of truth. For the apprehension of some truth a special endowment and cultivation of the understanding is necessary; for the recognition of other truth a special temperament and cultivation of taste is requisite, and for the apprehension of other truth again a special condition and habit of the moral and spiritual nature. In the actual condition of human nature, the truths revealed in the Scriptures cannot be discerned in their spiritual quality as the things of God. But when the soul is quickened to a new form of spiritual life by the baptism of the Holy Ghost, this very truth, now discerned, becomes the instrument whereby the new spiritual life is sustained and developed. This accords with the analogy of the constitutional action of the soul in every sphere of its activity. The perception of beauty depends upon the possession of the aesthetic faculty. But that being possessed, the aesthetic culture of the soul depends upon the contemplation of beautiful objects, and the knowledge of the law of beauty in the endless variety of its forms. It is a law having no exception that the exercise of the perceptive faculty necessarily precedes and conditions the exercise of the affections and the will. Beauty must be apprehended before it can be appreciated and loved. Moral truth must be apprehended before it can be loved or chosen, and only thus can the moral affections be trained and strengthened. Mere feeling and mere willing without knowledge are absolutely impossible experiences, and if possible, they would be irrational and immoral. It is the grand distinction of Christianity that it is ethical and not magical in all its processes and spirit. It rests on facts. It moves in the sphere of personal relations. It is a spiritual power acting through the instrumentality of truth addressed to the reason, and made effectual upon the soul by the power of the divine Spirit. And the truth, through the medium of knowledge spiritualized, acts on the emotions and will, and transforms character and governs life.

It is unquestionable that every one of the dogmas of Christianity, when spiritually apprehended, bears directly upon the moral and spiritual attitude and experience of the soul. A man can experience due sense of sin and repentance thereof only as he apprehends the truth of the scriptural teaching as to the guilt, pollution, and impotence inherent in the condition of our race as sinful. A man can realize a true evangelical attitude and experience of soul in relation to the several persons of the Godhead only as he receives the scriptural doctrine as to redemption in all its elements and in all its fulness. Christian doctrine thus acts upon and sets into spiritual exercise every one of the faculties of the human soul after its special kind, and thus instrumentally forms and disciplines to a perfect growth each of these spiritual habits or special modes of the action of those faculties which we call the Christian graces. And the spiritualized soul, in the exercise of faith, 'acteth differently upon that which every' doctrine 'containeth, yielding obedience to the commands, trembling at the threatenings, and embracing the promises of God for this life and that which is to come'. And thus Christians grow in the unity of the faith and 'of the knowledge of the Son of God unto a perfect man, unto the measure of the stature of the fulness of Christ'.

Third. Having thus seen the relation which the knowledge of the truth sustains to spiritual character and experience, as determined by the constitutional laws of human nature, I now assert, in addition, that the Scriptures clearly affirm that God has recognized this constitutional principle and availed himself of it by ordaining the doctrines of his Word to be his instruments in effecting his purposes of regenerating human nature. Christ prays, 'Sanctify them through thy truth, thy word is truth.' In his great commission he commanded his apostles to disciple all nations by teaching them whatsoever he had commanded them. He that believeth, *i.e.,* knows and accepts and obeys the truth, shall be saved, he that believeth not shall be damned. The doctrine as a whole is declared to be the power of God unto salvation, and to be quick, and powerful, and sharper than any two-edged sword, piercing even to the dividing asunder of soul and spirit, and of the joints and marrow, and is a discerner of the thoughts and intents of the heart. The psalmist, whom the Holy Ghost honoured to be his organ in instructing the church by presenting to it the expression of a typical religious experience, celebrates the uses of theological dogma under a variety of descriptive titles, 'The *testimony* of the Lord is sure, making wise the simple; the *statutes* of the Lord are right, rejoicing the heart; the *commandment* of the Lord is pure, enlightening the eyes; the *fear* of the Lord is clear, enduring forever; the *judgments* of the Lord are true and righteous altogether.' To which the great Christian apostle adds, that 'all Scripture is profitable for doctrine, for reproof, for correction, and for instruction in righteousness'.

Fourth. In confirmation of this truth, we appeal in the last place to the history of the church in all ages. While we acknowledge that an unspiritual scholasticism has often done its best to transform the great concrete truths of revelation into mere general notions and verbal propositions, yet we confidently affirm that marked activity in the cultivation of theology on a biblical basis and in an evangelical spirit has always been one of the essential conditions of every revival or advance of general church life, whether *intensive* in the elevation of the ideal of Christian character, or *extensive* in the development of missions.

It is notorious that secular critics affirm that the prevalent moral catastrophes occurring in the ranks of professed Christians, and the comparative failures of the church to raise the moral standard of the community, are due to an unacknowledged want of confidence in the objective reality of Christian dogmas which prevails in secret. This is a virtual confession of our affirmation that in the existing state of human nature the prevalence of morality and religion among the masses of men is possible only in proportion as the facts expressed by Christian dogma are known and realized as true.

But it may be rejoined by the depreciator of scientific theology, 'Admitting all you have claimed as to the use and necessity of the truth in the form and order in which it is stated in the very language of Scripture, what is the authority for your system-making; and what the use of your theological dogma in its systematic form?'

To this challenge we answer:

First. The Scriptures themselves suggest the systematic construction of the truths they communicate, and afford inspired examples of all the various processes by which theological dogma is generated.

(1) As before pointed out, Christian doctrine is God's own account and interpretation of the historical facts of his interventions for human redemption. The facts themselves have occurred in historical order. The inspired account has also been gradually developed through the successive Scriptures in an historical order. There has been a progressive evolution of divine teaching by the concurrent action of a supernaturally ordered history and a supernaturally inspired order of prophets from the beginning. Each prophet received the entire antecedently accumulated volume of revelations from his predecessors, and has transmitted it to his successors enlarged and illuminated with his own specific contribution. The revelation does not consist in set categorical statements, but in this historical evolution through sixteen centuries, through successive dispensations, through sixty-six separate books, composed by about forty different writers in every form of composition, the germs and shadowy outlines of truths gradually unfolded into the complete disclosures of the finished canon. This method of revelation of course necessitates the interpretation of the Bible as an organic whole—the tracing of the divine teaching in every element of it from its dawn to its culmination—the determination of the mutual relations of each part to each other part and to the whole, and thus by directly disclosing a system of revelation running through dispensations and centuries, it incidentally discloses the systematic relations of the facts and principles revealed.

(2) The apostolical writing and preaching afford constant examples of all the processes by which theological dogma is generated, as, for instance, analysis, logical inference, generalization, dogmatic definition.

(a) Peter and Stephen, in their great addresses recorded in Acts, and Paul, in all his epistles, draw inferences from selected passages of the Old Testament.

(b) They all subject the data of Old Testament history to a logical treatment, and generalize Christian doctrine from a wide historical induction—Acts. 2:14-36, 7:2-53, Rom. 4 and Heb. 2.

(c) They continually appeal to the rational and moral intuitions of men.—Acts 17:27-29, Rom. 1:19, 20, 2:12-15. They assume and incorporate into their teaching a definite psychology, and their doctrines as to sin and grace correspond to the human faculties of knowing, thinking, feeling, and willing. They assert (i) That man possesses a spiritual nature, which is the true seat of his personality; (ii) The validity and finality of intuitive truth as shown above; (iii) That man is a free agent, and therefore responsible; (iv) The relation of the affections and desires to volition; James 1:15, and see usage of θελημα and θεληματα, 1 Cor. 7:37 and Phil. 2:13; (v) The supremacy of conscience, Rom. 14:14, 1 Cor. 10:27-29, Rom. 2:14, 15; (vi) That responsibility is not measured by ability, Rom. 7:14-25 and 8:7; (vii) The law of habit ἕξις, Heb. 5:14, Rom. 1:21-31.

(d) In their epistles, the apostles characteristically settle practical questions not by mere positive directions, but by appeals to principles grounded in the widest relation of revealed facts and doctrines, as, for example, the debate as to circumcision among the Galatians, and as to the position of women in the church among the Corinthians. They, moreover, were determined in the subject and form of their doctrinal developments by the collisions into which they were providentially brought with errorists either within or without the church, *e.g.,* the tendency to latitudinarianism among the Corinthians, and the tendency to relapse into Judaistic legality and ritualism among the Galatians. This polemic principle has determined the development of doctrine in all subsequent time.—See *Delivery and Development of Christian Doctrine,* by Principal Rainy, pp. 87, 208.

(e) The Epistle to the Romans is a dogmatic treatise of the most systematic kind, as any competent analysis of the epistle will show down to the minutest ramification of the argument.

(f) Paul also, with characteristic boldness, exhibits the broad analogies and systematic articulations of the divine scheme of redemption, as, for instance, when he traces the parallelisms between Adam and Christ, or the relations of the Mosaic law, moral and symbolical, to the gospel, or when he sketches a complete *ordo salutis* from the eternal purpose through effectual calling, justification, sanctification to glorification.

Second. Our second argument is derived from the fact that however much men and schools may differ as to the degree of dogmatic construction which they regard as admissible, yet it is unquestionable that some good degree of it is universal because absolutely unavoidable. Indeed, there is no class of men who dogmatize more dogmatically than the agnostics themselves, or who show a more malignant spirit in controversy, as in the conspicuous instance of Mr Matthew Arnold. 'To disbelieve is to believe', as Dr Whately truly affirms. The difference is that the dogmatism of each agnostic is founded on his own personal unsupported reason and self-will. While the dogmatism of the Christian church is an act of obedience to the teaching authority of Christ, and is the consenting and mutually supporting experience and confession of an innumerable company of elect saints of all ages.

(1) The formation of dogma is absolutely necessary for the simplest exegetical unfolding of the text of Scripture. If the whole Bible is admitted to be one as the Word of Jehovah, it must be interpreted in all its parts as every other book must be, in the light of the analogy of the whole. The mind of God expressed in one passage must throw light upon his mind expressed in another passage. If one Scripture declares that Christ is less than the Father, it can be interpreted only in connection with the limiting statements that he is equal to and one with the Father. All said of his birth must be interpreted in the light of what is said of his pre-existence; all taught of his humanity must be interpreted in the light of that which is affirmed as to his divinity. The teachings of the Scriptures as to redemption, justification, regeneration, *etc.,* necessarily presuppose all that they teach as to human sinfulness.

(2) Doctrinal construction is also rendered absolutely inevitable by the laws of human intelligence. All the objects of our knowledge are necessarily believed to be mutually consistent. They cannot be believed to be true if they are seen to be mutually contradictory. And there is in every mind, even the most sluggish, a gradual process of unintentional, if not of unconscious, co-ordination, by which the whole mass of our knowledge tends to be digested into systematic

unity. Glaring incongruities of faith may coexist for a time, but in the long run one or other element of belief gains the mastery, and adjusts the whole to itself. Every reader of the Scriptures, however ignorant or sceptical, has, as a matter of fact, a dogmatic system of his own, however crude. The only question is whether we will have a true or a false one; one formed by ourselves alone, or one which we freely and intelligently reach by aid of all of the associated Christian thought and experience of all the ages.

(3) This necessity is made, if possible, more evident when we recognize the fact that the Scriptures are given to the church as a community of individuals. As such the church must come to a common understanding as to what the Scriptures teach, and as such she must teach that truth to others, and defend it from all errorists. This necessity for a common understanding at once leads to the necessity for common statements of doctrine, for conventions as to technical terms, definitions, and extended creeds. The duty of defending the truth from errorists must lead to controversies, and through them, as all history shows, to more precise definitions and to more articulate systematizing.

(4) It is only through such a process that the church has been able to advance towards a complete knowledge of all the contents of Scripture. Since, as before shown, objective truth forms character and governs conduct upon condition of its being subjectively apprehended in knowledge, it follows that the more comprehensive our knowledge of the truth the more complete will be our experience of its beneficial influence upon character and conduct. Now it is evident that this comprehensive knowledge of the contents of Scripture can be attained only through this process of systematic construction of dogma, in constant union with an ever fresh and spiritual exegesis of the text. The nature of the *truth* determines the relations of the *truths,* and is discerned by the same mental acts by which the relations are discriminated. The most abstruse and transcendental doctrines, such as the Trinity, the person of Christ, the eternal decrees, providential and gracious concursus, have, as all religious history proves, the most intimate and vital relations with all other truth taught in Scripture, and with every condition of religious experience. A man's conceptions of these gives form, whether he will or not, to all his thinking,

feeling, or teaching upon religious subjects. They are articulated in every possible involution of thought and experience as expressed in all Christian liturgies and sacred hymns. At the same time they tend to build up theology into system, and to mould religious life into conformity to God.

Besides this, it is an accepted axiom that all error is partial truth, that is, truth dissevered from its relations in the entire system. Yet error is no less misleading and morally corrupting because its elements are dislocated half-truths. It is only a counter process that can cure the evil by giving us the whole truth in its integrity—that is, the truth as a whole, which is synonym for system. To see the truth as a whole is to know the only pure truth. As the essence of error consists in an apprehension of a part out of its relations, so the essence of the truth is its integrity, a perfect sphere, comprehending all of its parts in their true relations.

Third. Finally, another necessity for systematic construction of explicitly defined dogma, eminently important in this age of general disintegration, is found in the unparalleled power of a coherent system of truth to resist pressure from without. This is a property which distinguishes systems of truths and systems of error. A system of error, when once undermined in its radical principles, must collapse at once by very force of the general coherence of the parts. But an articulate system of truth, on the other hand, rooted in fact, touching history, experience, consciousness at every point, and braced together by the reciprocal support of every part, has proved to be invincible. An apparently overwhelming pressure at any one point leads to a reaction, induced by the elasticity of the coherent parts of the whole.

In the face of the deluge of aggressive unbelief, we are invited by not a few sentimental friends to disembarrass ourselves of the incumbrance of system in order that each man of us may escape with some dislocated fragment in his grasp. From their slowly dissolving islands of half-truths—slowly dissolving according to their own vociferous affirmation—they call us to leave the old continent which has survived the convulsions of ages, because bound together and buttressed by the primary granite rocks of God's truth entire. They fear the continent will break down of its own weight, while they hope that their soft, undulating islands will escape destruction by yielding, if not overlooked because of their insignificance. Whether this policy of preserving the truth by means of its disintegration be urged upon us by subtle enemies or by silly friends, we intend to refuse it utterly. We will maintain the whole truth to be the only pure truth, and the whole truth to be the truth as a whole—a complete system divinely revealed in all its parts, and invincible through the comprehension of all the parts in the whole.

Fathers and Brethren of the Board of Directors, your representative in his charge has reminded me that the chair to which I am called is historical, having for sixty-five years from the beginning been occupied only by Archibald Alexander and Charles Hodge. Alas, sirs, when I think of myself, I often cry, 'Woe is me, that such a one as I should be called to inherit the responsibilities descending in such a line.' And when I think of the church, I cry with a far sorer wonder, 'What times are these when such a man as I should be made to stand in such a place?' But God has done it. He has chosen a vessel earthen indeed, that the excellency of the power may be the more conspicuously shown forth to be his own alone. Directors, since your responsibilities in the matter are at least equal to my own, I can surely claim your prayers that in this service today inaugurated *God's* strength may be made perfect in *weakness*.

BENJAMIN BRECKINRIDGE WARFIELD
1851-1921

PASTOR, biblical scholar, and eminent theologian, Benjamin Breckinridge Warfield was born near Lexington, Kentucky in 1851. He studied at the College of New Jersey and afterwards enrolled as a student at Princeton Theological Seminary. He completed his seminary degree in 1876 and afterwards spent two additional years of study abroad under leading European theological tutors.

After returning to America, Warfield served as pastor at First Presbyterian Church, Baltimore, Maryland (1877-78). In 1878 he accepted a call to serve as a Professor of New Testament at Western Theological Seminary in Allegheny, Pennsylvania, where he remained for the next nine years. Following the sudden and premature death of A. A. Hodge in 1887, Princeton Theological Seminary again looked to Western Theological Seminary to fill a faculty vacancy, as it had done nine years earlier when it procured A. A. Hodge's assistance for his father in the department of Systematic Theology. Warfield accepted the call to Princeton and began a distinguished teaching and publishing career that would conclude with his death in 1921, just a few hours after completing what would be his final lecture at the seminary.

Warfield was a competent linguist and gifted exegete; his studies in textual transmission and the related field of biblical criticism provided a strong scriptural foundation for his work as Professor of Polemic and Didactic Theology at Princeton. Warfield's individual mastery of theological encyclopedia represents the highpoint in the history of the gifted faculty who helped establish Princeton's reputation for profound scholarship and eminent piety.

Warfield devoted his life to meticulous research, learned and pious publications, and the care for his invalid wife, who had suffered a nervous breakdown not long after they were married. Warfield's domestic responsibilities limited his involvement in denominational activities and travels beyond Princeton. His time spent in study, however, paid rich dividends of lasting value for the Christian church through the steady stream of articles, reviews, lectures, collections of sermons, and monographs that flowed from his pen. Warfield's publications are often in-depth analyses of specific biblical topics or doctrinal issues in the field of historical theology; a number of his publications were critical reviews of contemporary theological trends. A selection of his most important articles, reviews, lectures, and monographs can be found in *The Works of Benjamin Breckinridge Warfield,* a ten-volume collection published posthumously (1927-32).

Warfield sought to perform his work at Princeton as a continuation of the spirit and theological contours of Charles Hodge's legacy. As editor of *The Princeton Review* for over twenty years, he helped reestablish the journal as a major presence in the world of theological academia. He cherished his Calvinistic theological heritage and spoke in glowing terms of the beauty, depth, and practical benefits of documents such as the Westminster Confession of Faith and the Larger and Shorter Catechisms for nurturing vital piety in the believer's life.

As a theologian, Warfield's efforts were often drawn to an apologetic defence of the reliability of the Scriptures and the intellectual truth claims of biblical doctrine. Scientific naturalism, theological liberalism, and the effects of autonomous human reason were all brought under the searchlight of Scripture and exposed for the different species of unbelief that they each were. Warfield's evidentialist approach to biblical apologetics places emphasis on the facts of divine revelation and the ability of the human mind to interpret the data in a way that should lead to responsive faith, but never at the expense of omitting the need for the work of the Holy Spirit in illumination and regeneration for the data to be properly interpreted and Christ embraced with genuine saving faith.

Like his colleagues, Warfield was a man possessed of a deep, heart-felt love for Christ and his church. He understood well the dynamics of the life of piety and its proper relationship to theological scholarship. He sought to instil the importance of both in the hearts and minds of his students, just as his predecessors had done so well before him, to become godly pastors, Spirit-anointed preachers, and able divines.

OUR SEMINARY CURRICULUM[1]

MUCH of the confusion into which opinion as to the proper curriculum of a theological seminary is apparently drifting, seems to arise from altering, or perhaps we would better say varying, conceptions of the functions of the ministry for which the theological seminary is intended to provide a training. A low view of the functions of the ministry will naturally carry with it a low conception of the training necessary for it. A rationalistic view of the functions of the ministry entails a corresponding conception of the training which fits for it. An evangelical view of the functions of the ministry demands a consonant training for that ministry. And a high view of the functions of the ministry on evangelical lines inevitably produces a high conception of the training which is needed to prepare men for the exercise of these high functions.

Our Episcopalian brethren are complaining bitterly of the difficulties they are experiencing in obtaining candidates for orders with anything like adequate equipment. They may enact canons galore requiring real and precise tests to be applied. What they find impossible is to convince either examiners or examined that these tests should be seriously applied. They do not see the use of it, when all that is required of the clergy is *Ut pueris placeant et declamationes fiant.*[2] Pretty nearly anybody seems to them 'to know enough to get along in a parish'. Similar difficulties are not unknown to Presbyterians. All the requirements which can be stuffed into a Form of Government will not secure that a high standard of training will be maintained, if a suspicion forms itself in the minds of the administrators of this Form of Government that a minister does not need such learning. And this suspicion will inevitably form itself—and

[1] B. B. Warfield, 'Our Seminary Curriculum', *The Presbyterian,* Sept. 15, 1909, pp. 7, 8.
[2] To please the boys and make rhetorical speeches.

harden into a conviction—if the functions of the minister come to be conceived lowly: if the minister comes to be thought of, for example, fundamentally as merely the head of a social organization from whom may be demanded pleasant manners and executive ability; or as little more than a zealous 'promoter' who knows how to seek out and attach to his enterprise a multitude of men; or as merely an entertaining lecturer who can be counted upon to charm away an hour or two of dull Sabbaths; or even—for here we have, of course, an infinitely higher conception—as merely an enthusiastic Christian eager to do work for Christ. If a minister's whole function is summed up in these or such things—we might as well close our theological seminaries, withdraw our candidates from the colleges and schools, and seek recruits for the ministry among the capable young fellows about town. The 'three R's' will constitute all the literary equipment they require; their English Bible their whole theological outfit; and zeal their highest spiritual attainment.

It has not been characteristic of the rationalistic bodies to think meanly of the functions of the minister or of the equipment requisite to fit him to perform them. Their tendency has been to treat the minister rather as an intellectual than as a religious guide; and they have rather secularized than vulgarized his training. For a hundred years, now, our Unitarian friends have been urging upon us this secularized conception of the ministerial functions and of the minister's training. Ex-president Charles W. Eliot, of Harvard, for example, winningly commended it to us a quarter of a century ago in a much-talked of article in *The Princeton Review,* but was happily set right by Dr. F. L. Patton in the next number. What now attracts attention is that this secularized conception has begun to wander away from home in these last days, and to invade evangelical circles. It is a highly honoured Presbyterian elder, whose voice carries far over the land, who has lately told us that the proper function of the ministry is to mediate modern advances in knowledge to the people, through the churches. Were that true, the ministry would no longer be a spiritual office, but only an educational agency; and training for it should be sought not in theological seminaries, but in the universities.

He would be the best-equipped minister who had obtained the most thorough knowledge, not of the ways of God with men and the purposes of God's grace for men, but of the most recent currents of thought and fancy which flow up and down in the restless hearts of men. Extremes meet. Pietist and Rationalist have ever hunted in couples and dragged down their quarry together. They may differ as to why they deem theology mere lumber, and would not have the prospective minister waste his time in acquiring it. The one loves God so much, the other loves him so little, that he does not care to know him. But they agree that it is not worth while to learn to know him. The simple English Bible seems to the one sufficient equipment for the minister, because, in the fervour of his religious enthusiasm, it seems to him enough for the renovating of the world just to lisp its precious words to man. It seems to the other all the theological equipment a minister needs, because in his view the less theology a minister has the better. He considers him ill employed in poring over Hebrew and Greek pages, endeavouring to extract their real meaning—for what does it matter what their real meaning is? The prospective minister would, in his opinion, be better occupied in expanding his mind by contemplation of the great attainments of the human spirit, and in learning to know that social animal Man, by tracing out the workings of his social aptitudes and probing the secrets of his social movements. If the minister is simply an advance agent of modern culture, a kind of university-extension lecturer, whose whole function it is to 'elevate the masses' and 'improve the social organism'—why, of course, art and literature should take the place of Greek and Hebrew, and 'sociology' the place of theology in our seminary curriculum. If the whole function of the minister is 'inspirational' rather than 'instructional', and his work is finished when the religious nature of man is roused to action, and the religious emotions are set surging, with only a very vague notion of the objects to which the awakened religious affections should turn, or the ends to which the religious activities, once set in motion, should be directed—why, then, no doubt we may dispense with all serious study of Scripture, and content ourselves with the employment of its grand music merely to excite religious susceptibilities.

But, if the minister is the mouthpiece of the Most High, charged with a message to deliver, to expound and enforce; standing in the name of God before men, to make known to them who and what this God is, and what his purposes of grace are, and what his will for his people—then, the whole aspect of things is changed. Then, it is the prime duty of the minister to know his message; to know the instructions which have been committed to him for the people, and to know them thoroughly; to be prepared to declare them with confidence and with exactness, to commend them with wisdom, and to urge them with force and defend them with skill, and to build men up by means of them into a true knowledge of God and of his will, which will be unassailable in the face of the fiercest assault. No second-hand knowledge of the revelation of God for the salvation of a ruined world can suffice the needs of a ministry whose function it is to convey this revelation to men, commend it to their acceptance and apply it in detail to their needs—to all their needs, from the moment that they are called into participation in the grace of God, until the moment when they stand perfect in God's sight, built up by his Spirit into new men. For such a ministry as this the most complete knowledge of the wisdom of the world supplies no equipment; the most fervid enthusiasm of service leaves without furnishing. Nothing will suffice for it but to know; to know the Book; to know it at first hand; and to know it through and through. And what is required first of all for training men for such a ministry is that the Book should be given them in its very words as it has come from God's hand and in the fulness of its meaning, as that meaning has been ascertained by the labours of generations of men of God who have brought to bear upon it all the resources of sanctified scholarship and consecrated thought.

How worthily our fathers thought of the ministry! And what wise provision they made for training men for it, when they set out the curriculum of their first theological seminary! This curriculum was framed with the express design that those who pursued it should come forth from it these five things: 'a sound biblical critic'; 'a defender of the Christian faith'; 'an able and sound divine'; 'a useful preacher and faithful pastor'; and a man 'qualified to exercise discipline and to take part in the government of the church in all its judicatories'. A well-rounded minister this, one equal to the functions which belong to a minister of the New Testament order. But that we may have such ministers, we must provide such a training for the ministry as will produce such ministers. And that means nothing less than that our theological curriculum should provide for the serious mastery of the several branches of theological science. A comprehensive and thorough theological training is the condition of a really qualified ministry. When we satisfy ourselves with a less comprehensive and thorough theological training, we are only condemning ourselves to a less qualified ministry.

THE PURPOSE OF THE SEMINARY[1]

IT is customary to say that the theological seminaries are training schools for the ministry. Properly understood, that is the right thing to say. But it is not very difficult, and it is very common, seriously to exaggerate the function of the seminary under this definition. It is not the function of the seminary to give young men their entire training for the ministry. That is the concern of the presbytery; and no other organization can supersede the presbytery in this business. The seminary is only an instrument which the presbytery uses in training young men for the ministry. An instrument, not the instrument. The presbytery uses other instruments also in this work.

There is the academy, for example; and the university. It being once understood that the ministry is to be an educated ministry, the academy and the university become instruments which the church uses in training young men for its ministry. And there is the local church. It is to the local church that the presbytery commits its candidates for the ministry, for moral and spiritual oversight and training. The seminary cannot properly undertake the work of these other instrumentalities. It is essential, if the ministry is to be an educated body, that the minister shall know his ABC's. It does not follow that the seminary ought to teach young men their ABC's. It is absolutely necessary, if the ministry is to be a religious body, that every minister should be a converted man. It is not therefore the function of the seminary to convert its students.

No one will suspect me of suggesting that the seminary need not be a 'nursery of piety'—any more than that it need not be a 'nursery of learning'. But no one ought to contend that the seminary ought to be either expected or permitted to begin with either piety or learning

[1] B. B. Warfield, 'The Purpose of the Seminary', *The Presbyterian*, Nov. 22, 1917, pp. 8-9.

at the beginning. The illiterate and the ungodly have simply no place in the seminary. And if they actually are found there, the remedy is not that the seminary should enlarge its borders and take on the functions either of a primary school or of a confirmation class. The seminary has its own specific work to do, and that work presupposes in its pupils attainments both in literature and in piety. Young men go to it only after they have acquired the education which is common to all educated men, and have made such progress in piety as ranks them with the especially pious men of the community. Basing on this foundation, the seminary undertakes to give to candidates for the ministry the specific training which is peculiar to them as ministers; which fits them, in a word, for the worthy prosecution of the particular work of a minister. It is, in this sense, the finishing school of the ministry; and it must give itself strictly to those things which the deeply pious man of liberal culture still requires, in order that he may fulfil the office of a minister with credit to himself and to the advantage of the church.

What precisely must be taught in a theological seminary will be determined by our conception of the ministry for the exercise of the functions of which it offers preparation. And that will be determined ultimately by our conception of the church. On the sacerdotal theory of the church, the business of the minister is to perform certain rites, by the correct performance of which the effect sought is obtained. The seminary, in this view, becomes a training school in the exact sense of that term. It is the place where the prospective minister is trained to perform these rites properly. On the rationalistic theory, the church is simply a club for intellectual entertainment, or, at the best, a society for ethical culture, or a benevolent organization. The function of the preacher is to be the leader of the group which he serves in such activities; and his training ought to be such as will fit him for this. Great stress will naturally be laid on literary culture, and the masters of thought will take a large place in the theological curriculum. Or, perhaps, the best course in the seminary will be one in sociology—possibly an investigation as to the housing problem in manufacturing towns, possibly a census of the inhabitants within a given radius of a country church.

None of these things are bad. Even the evangelical minister would do well to know how to conduct the services of the church acceptably. And it will not hurt him a bit to be on speaking terms with Plato and Emerson—and Galsworthy and H. G. Wells and Marie Corelli! Certainly it will be of advantage to him to be at least aware of the social unrest growling around him, and of the terrible distress which it may lie within his power to do something to mitigate or relieve. But all this will not make him a good minister of the gospel of Christ. Do not even the heathen the same? Christ has sent him not to baptize, but to preach the gospel; not to ameliorate the lot of men, but to carry to them salvation. On the evangelical view, the church is the communion of saints, gathered out of a lost world; and the business of the minister is to apply the saving gospel to lost men for their salvation from sin—from its guilt and from its corruption and power. Palpably, what he needs for this is just the gospel; and if he is to perform his functions at all, he must know this gospel, know it thoroughly, know it in all its details, and in all its power. It is the business of the seminary to give him this knowledge of the gospel. That is the real purpose of the seminary.

It is important that we think worthily of the minister, and understand exactly what the great task which is laid upon him involves. The ministry is not a handicraft, a certain skill in the performance of which may be acquired simply by practice. It is a 'learned profession': one of the three, or at the most four, learned professions which divide between them the expert care of man in his several relations. Man is a composite being, with body and soul, set in a social organism, dependent on a physical environment. He needs expert guidance in every sphere of his existence. Science mediates between him and nature. It is the lawyer who advises him in his social relations. The physician cares for his body. The minister is his guide in spiritual things.

It is possible to argue that we can do very well without any of these guides. It is easier to argue it than to practise it. The Lord has not intended his people to hobble along in their religious living. He has appointed ministers in the churches, and given them the task of shepherding the flock. And no minister is fitted for the position he occupies, unless he is prepared to act as spiritual adviser of the community which he serves. We may talk of 'the simple gospel' being enough; and we may thank God that the gospel is simple, and that it is enough. But it is no simple matter rightly to apply this simple gospel in all the varied relations of life, in the multiform emergencies which arise in the tangled business of living. Read but the Epistle to the Romans. Was the right exposition of the gospel in the conditions then obtaining at Rome, given us in the first eleven chapters of this epistle, so simple a matter that Paul might just as well have left it to the Romans themselves to work it out? Was the application of this gospel to life at Rome in the first Christian century, added in the remaining chapters, so simple a matter that it did not need a Paul to make it rightly? Perhaps we nowhere see the minister more plainly at work than in the First Epistle to the Corinthians. These questions which the Corinthians put to Paul, and he answered with so much care—did they really not need to be asked of him or answered by him? The minister in his place, as Paul in his, is the spiritual guide and adviser of his people.

For this, we say, he needs to know the gospel: to know it at first hand, and to know it through and through. All the work of the seminary must be directed just to this end. For one thing, the minister must learn the code in which the gospel message is written. He must be able to decode it; to decode it for himself. No trusting the decoding to another! This is the message of salvation, and he is the channel by which it is conveyed to men. He cannot take it at second-hand. He must get it for himself, and convey it first-handed to those entrusted to his care. He must, in other words, know the languages in which the gospel is written; and he must be skilled in drawing out from the documents the exact meaning. And, then, he must know the message, thus drawn out, thoroughly, and all its compass, and in all its details, in its right perspective, and in its just proportions. Otherwise he cannot use it aright. Of course, he must also be skilled in winningly presenting this message, thus thoroughly known, and in helpfully applying it, point by point, to emerging needs. These things constitute the core of the seminary's teaching. There are others that stand very close to them; so close that they cannot be dispensed with as props and stays. The minister must know how to defend the gospel he preaches. And he should know something of the history this gospel has wrought for itself in the world. These things not for themselves, but for the aid they bring him for understanding the gospel better for himself, and for commending it more powerfully to others.

Without this much equipment, the evangelical minister is robbed of his dignity and shorn of his strength. He cannot be the spiritual guide and adviser of the community, as the lawyer is the legal guide and the physician the medical adviser. He sinks into a mere handicraftsman plying a manual trade, learned by rote; or into a mere lecturer to a club or leader in benevolent activities. Of course, 'the simple preaching' of the 'simple gospel' will not fail of its effect. The loving lisping of the name of Jesus by the lips of a child may carry far. But that is no reason why we should man our pulpits with children lisping the name of Jesus. The foolishness of preaching is one thing: foolish preaching is another. Let us not deceive ourselves: in religion as in everything else knowledge is power. That is a platitude. But platitudes have this to be said for them—they are true. Nothing—not fervour, not devotion, not zeal—can supersede the necessity of knowledge. If knowledge without zeal is useless; zeal without knowledge is worse than useless—it is positively destructive. This is Reformation year: let us ask ourselves why was William Farel, consumed with zeal, burning with evangelical fervour, proclaiming the pure gospel, helpless at Geneva—until 'with dreadful imprecations' he brought to his aid John Calvin: John Calvin, scholar become saint, scholar-saint become preacher of God's grace? What we need in our pulpits is scholar-saints become preachers. And it is the one business of the theological seminaries to make them.

THE RELIGIOUS LIFE OF
THEOLOGICAL STUDENTS[1]

A minister must be both learned and religious. It is not a matter of choosing between the two. He must study, but he must study as in the presence of God and not in a secular spirit. He must recognize the privilege of pursuing his studies in the environment where God and salvation from sin are the air he breathes. He must also take advantage of every opportunity for corporate worship, particularly while he trains in the theological seminary. Christ himself leads in setting the example of the importance of participating in corporate expressions of the religious life of the community. Ministerial work without taking time to pray is a tragic mistake. The two must combine if the servant of God is to give a pure, clear, and strong message.[2]

* * * * *

I am asked to speak to you on the religious life of the student of theology. I approach the subject with some trepidation. I think it the most important subject which can engage our thought. You will not uspect me, in saying this, to be depreciating the importance of the intellectual preparation of the student for the ministry. The importance of the intellectual preparation of the student for the ministry is the reason of the existence of our theological seminaries. Say what you will, do what you will, the ministry is a 'learned profession'; and the man without learning, no matter with what other gifts he may be endowed, is unfit for its duties. But learning, though indispensable, is not the most indispensable thing for a minister. 'Apt to teach'—yes, the ministry must be 'apt to teach'; and observe that what I say—or

---

[1] B. B. Warfield, 'The Religious Life of Theological Students', (n.p., 1911).
[2] The prefatory abstract is an editorial addition to the original article.

rather what Paul says—is 'apt to teach'. Not apt merely to exhort, to beseech, to appeal, to entreat; nor even merely, to testify, to bear witness; but to teach. And teaching implies knowledge: he who teaches must know. Paul, in other words, requires of you, as we are perhaps learning not very felicitously to phrase it, 'instructional', not merely 'inspirational', service. But aptness to teach alone does not make a minister; nor is it his primary qualification. It is only one of a long list of requirements which Paul lays down as necessary to meet in him who aspires to this high office. And all the rest concern, not his intellectual, but his spiritual fitness. A minister must be learned, on pain of being utterly incompetent for his work. But before and above being learned, a minister must be godly. Nothing could be more fatal, however, than to set these two things over against one another. Recruiting officers do not dispute whether it is better for soldiers to have a right leg or a left leg: soldiers should have both legs. Sometimes we hear it said that ten minutes on your knees will give you a truer, deeper, more operative knowledge of God than ten hours over your books. 'What!', is the appropriate response, 'than ten hours over your books, on your knees?' Why should you turn from God when you turn to your books, or feel that you must turn from your books in order to turn to God? If learning and devotion are as antagonistic as that, then the intellectual life is in itself accursed, and there can be no question of a religious life for a student, even of theology. The mere fact that he is a student inhibits religion for him. That I am asked to speak to you on the religious life of the student of theology proceeds on the recognition of the absurdity of such antitheses. You are students of theology; and, just because you are students of theology, it is understood that you are religious men— especially religious men, to whom the cultivation of your religious life is a matter of the profoundest concern—of such concern that you will wish above all things to be warned of the dangers that may assail your religious life, and be pointed to the means by which you may strengthen and enlarge it. In your case there can be no 'either/or' here—either a student or a man of God. You must be both.

Perhaps the intimacy of the relation between the work of a theological student and his religious life will nevertheless bear some emphasizing. Of course you do not think religion and study incompatible. But it is barely possible that there may be some among you who think of them too much apart—who are inclined to set their studies off to one side, and their religious life off to the other side, and to fancy that what is given to the one is taken from the other. No mistake could be more gross. Religion does not take a man away from his work; it sends him to his work with an added quality of devotion. We sing—do we not?—

> Teach me, my God and King,
>   In all things Thee to see—
> And what I do in anything,
>   To do it as for Thee.
>
> If done t'obey Thy laws,
>   E'en servile labours shine,
> Hallowed is toil, if this the cause,
>   The meanest work divine.

It is not just the way George Herbert wrote it. He put, perhaps, a sharper point on it. He reminds us that a man may look at his work as he looks at a pane of glass—either seeing nothing but the glass, or looking straight through the glass to the wide heavens beyond. And he tells us plainly that there is nothing so mean but that the great words, 'for thy sake', can glorify it:

> A servant, with this clause,
>   Makes drudgery divine,
> Who sweeps a room as for Thy laws,
>   Makes that, and the action, fine.

But the doctrine is the same, and it is the doctrine, the fundamental doctrine, of Protestant morality, from which the whole system of Christian ethics unfolds. It is the great doctrine of 'vocation', the doctrine, to wit, that the best service we can offer to God is just to do our duty—our plain, homely duty, whatever that may chance to be.

The Middle Ages did not think so; they cut a cleft between the religious and the secular life, and counselled him who wished to be religious to turn his back on what they called 'the world', that is to say, not the wickedness that is in the world—'the world, the flesh and the devil', as we say—but the work-a-day world, that congeries of occupations which forms the daily task of men and women, who perform their duty to themselves and their fellow men. Protestantism put an end to all that. As Professor Doumergue eloquently puts it,

> Then Luther came, and, with still more consistency, Calvin, proclaim- ing the great idea of 'vocation', an idea and a word which are found in the languages of all the Protestant peoples—*Beruf, Calling, Vocation*— and which are lacking in the languages of the peoples of antiquity and of medieval culture. 'Vocation'—it is the call of God, addressed to every man, whoever he may be, to lay upon him a particular work, no matter what. And the calls, and therefore also the called, stand on a complete equality with one another. The burgomaster is God's burgomaster; the physician is God's physician; the merchant is God's merchant; the labourer is God's labourer. Every vocation, liberal, as we call it, or manual, the humblest and the vilest in appearance as truly as the noblest and the most glorious, is of divine right.

Talk of the divine right of kings! Here is the divine right of every workman, no one of whom needs to be ashamed, if only he is an hon- est and good workman. 'Only laziness', adds Professor Doumergue, 'is ignoble, and while Romanism multiplies its mendicant orders, the Reformation banishes the idle from its towns.'

Now, as students of theology your vocation is to study theology; and to study it diligently, in accordance with the apostolic injunc- tion: 'Whatsoever ye do, do it heartily, as to the Lord.' It is precisely for this that you are students of theology; this is your 'next duty', and the neglect of duty is not a fruitful religious exercise. Dr Charles Hodge, in his delightful autobiographical notes, tells of Philip Lindsay, the most popular professor in the Princeton College of his day—a man sought by nearly every college in the central States for its presidency—that 'he told our class that we would find that one of the best preparations for death was a thorough knowledge of the Greek grammar'. 'This', comments Dr Hodge, in his quaint fashion, 'was his way of telling us that we ought to do our duty.' Certainly, every man who aspires to be a religious man must begin by doing his duty, his obvious duty, his daily task, the particular work which lies before him to do at this particular time and place. If this work happens to be studying, then his religious life depends on nothing more fundamentally than on just studying. You might as well talk of a father who neglects his parental duties, of a son who fails in all the obligations of filial piety, of an artisan who systematically skimps his work and turns in a bad job, of a workman who is nothing better than an eye-servant, being religious men as of a student who does not study being a religious man. It cannot be: you cannot build up a religious life except you begin by performing faithfully your simple, daily duties. It is not the question whether you like these duties. You may think of your studies what you please. You may consider that you are singing precisely of them when you sing of 'e'en servile labours', and of 'the meanest work'. But you must faithfully give yourselves to your studies, if you wish to be religious men. No religious character can be built up on the foundation of neglected duty.

There is certainly something wrong with the religious life of a theological student who does not study. But it does not quite follow that therefore everything is right with his religious life if he does study. It is possible to study—even to study theology—in an entirely secular spirit. I said a little while ago that what religion does is to send a man to his work with an added quality of devotion. In saying that, I meant the word 'devotion' to be taken in both its senses—in the sense of 'zealous application', and in the sense of 'a religious exercise', as the Standard Dictionary phrases the two definitions. A truly religious man will study anything which it becomes his duty to study with 'devotion' in both of these senses. That is what his religion does for him: it makes him do his duty, do it thoroughly, do it 'in the Lord'.

But in the case of many branches of study, there is nothing in the topics studied which tends directly to feed the religious life, or to set in movement the religious emotions, or to call out specifically religious reaction. If we study them 'in the Lord', that is only because we do it 'for his sake', on the principle which makes 'sweeping a room' an act of worship. With theology it is not so. In all its branches alike, theology has as its unique end to make God known: the student of theology is brought by his daily task into the presence of God, and is kept there. Can a religious man stand in the presence of God, and not worship? It is possible, I have said, to study even theology in a purely secular spirit. But surely that is possible only for an irreligious man, or at least for an unreligious man. And here I place in your hands at once a touchstone by which you may discern your religious state, and an instrument for the quickening of your religious life. Do you prosecute your daily tasks as students of theology as 'religious exercises'? If you do not, look to yourselves: it is surely not all right with the spiritual condition of that man who can busy himself daily with divine things, with a cold and impassive heart. If you do, rejoice. But in any case, see that you do! And that you do it ever more and more abundantly.

Whatever you may have done in the past, for the future make all your theological studies 'religious exercises'. This is the great rule for a rich and wholesome religious life in a theological student. Put your heart into your studies; do not merely occupy your mind with them, but put your heart into them. They bring you daily and hourly into the very presence of God; his ways, his dealing with men, the infinite majesty of his being form their very subject-matter. Put the shoes from off your feet in this holy presence!

We are frequently told, indeed, that the great danger of the theological student lies precisely in his constant contact with divine things. They may come to seem common to him, because they are customary. As the average man breathes the air and basks in the sunshine without ever a thought that it is God in his goodness who makes his sun to rise on him, though he is evil, and sends rain to him, though he is unjust; so you may come to handle even the furniture of the sanctuary with never a thought above the gross earthly materials of which it is made. The words which tell you of God's terrible majesty or of his glorious goodness may come to be mere words to you—Hebrew and Greek words, with etymologies, and inflections, and connections in sentences. The reasonings which establish to you the mysteries of his saving activities may come to be to you mere logical paradigms, with premises and conclusions, fitly framed, no doubt, and triumphantly cogent, but with no further significance to you than their formal logical conclusiveness. God's stately stepping in his redemptive processes may become to you a mere series of facts of history, curiously interplaying to the production of social and religious conditions, and pointing mayhap to an issue which we may shrewdly conjecture; but much like other facts occurring in time and space, which may come to your notice. It is your great danger.

But it is your great danger, only because it is your great privilege. Think of what your privilege is when your greatest danger is that the great things of religion may become common to you! Other men, oppressed by the hard conditions of life, sunk in the daily struggle for bread perhaps, distracted at any rate by the dreadful drag of the world upon them and the awful rush of the world's work, find it hard to get time and opportunity so much as to pause and consider whether there be such things as God, and religion, and salvation from the sin that compasses them about and holds them captive. The very atmosphere of your life is these things; you breathe them in at every pore; they surround you, encompass you, press in upon you from every side. It is all in danger of becoming common to you! God forgive you, you are in danger of becoming weary of God!

Do you know what this danger is? Or, rather, let us turn the question—are you alive to what your privileges are? Are you making full use of them? Are you, by this constant contact with divine things, growing in holiness, becoming every day more and more men of God?

If not, you are hardening! And I am here today to warn you to take seriously your theological study, not merely as a duty, done for God's sake and therefore made divine, but as a religious exercise, itself charged with religious blessing to you; as fitted by its very nature to fill all your mind and heart and soul and life with divine thoughts and feelings and aspirations and achievements. You will never prosper in your religious life in the theological seminary until your work in the theological seminary becomes itself to you a religious exercise out of which you draw every day enlargement of heart, elevation of spirit, and adoring delight in your Maker and your Saviour.

I am not counselling you, you will observe, to make your theological studies your sole religious exercises. They are religious exercises of the most rewarding kind; and your religious life will very much depend upon your treating them as such. But there are other religious exercises demanding your punctual attention which cannot be neglected without the gravest damage to your religious life. I refer particularly now to the stated formal religious meetings of the seminary. I wish to be perfectly explicit here, and very emphatic. No man can withdraw himself from the stated religious services of the community of which he is a member, without serious injury to his personal religious life. It is not without significance that the apostolic writer couples together the exhortations, 'to hold fast the confession of our hope, that it waver not', and 'to forsake not the assembling of ourselves together'. When he commands us not to forsake 'the assembling of ourselves together', he has in mind, as the term he employs shows, the stated, formal assemblages of the community, and means to lay upon the hearts and consciences of his readers their duty to the church of which they are the supports, as well as their duty to themselves. And when he adds, 'as the custom of some is', he means to put a lash into his command. We can see his lip curl as he says it.

Who are these people, who are so vastly strong, so supremely holy, that they do not need the assistance of the common worship for themselves; and who, being so strong and holy, will not give their assistance to the common worship?

Needful as common worship is, however, for men at large, the need of it for men at large is as nothing compared with its needfulness for a body of young men situated as you are. You are gathered together here for a religious purpose, in preparation for the highest religious service which can be performed by men—the guidance of others in the religious life; and shall you have everything else in common except worship? You are gathered together here, separated from your homes and all that home means; from the churches in which you have been brought up, and all that church fellowship means; from all the powerful natural influences of social religion—and shall you not yourselves form a religious community, with its own organic religious life and religious expression? I say it deliberately, that a body of young men, living apart in a community life, as you are and must be living, cannot maintain a healthy, full, rich religious life individually, unless they are giving organic expression to their religious life as a community in frequent stated diets of common worship. Nothing can take the place of this common organic worship of the community as a community, at its stated seasons, and as a regular function of the corporate life of the community. Without it you cease to be a religious community and lack that support and stay, that incitement and spur, that comes to the individual from the organic life of the community of which he forms a part.

In my own mind, I am quite clear that in an institution like this the whole body of students should come together, both morning and evening, every day, for common prayer; and should join twice on every Sabbath in formal worship. Without at least this much common worship I do not think the institution can preserve its character as a distinctively religious institution—an institution whose institutional life is primarily a religious one. And I do not think that the individual students gathered here can, with less full expression of the organic religious life of the institution, preserve the high level of religious life on which, as students of theology, they ought to live. You will observe that I am not merely exhorting you 'to go to church'. 'Going to church' is in any case good. But what I am exhorting you to do is go to your own church—to give your presence and active religious participation to every stated meeting for worship of the institution as an institution. Thus you will do your part to give to the institution an organic religious life, and you will draw out from the organic religious life of the institution a support and inspiration for your own personal religious life which you can get nowhere else, and which you can cannot afford to miss—if, that is, you have a care to your religious quickening and growth. To be an active member of a living religious body is the condition of healthy religious functioning. I trust you will not tell me that the stated religious exercises of the seminary are too numerous, or are wearying. That would only be to betray the low ebb of your own religious vitality. The feet of him whose heart is warm with religious feeling turn of themselves to the sanctuary, and carry him with joyful steps to the house of prayer. I am told that there are some students who do not find themselves in a prayerful mood in the early hours of a winter morning; and are much too tired at the close of a hard day's work to pray, and therefore do not find it profitable to attend prayers in the late afternoon: who think the preaching at the regular service on Sabbath morning dull and uninteresting, and who do not find Christ at the Sabbath afternoon conference. Such things I seem to have heard before; and yours will be an exceptional pastorate, if you do not hear something very like them, before you have been in a pastorate six months. Such things meet you every day on the street; they are the ordinary expression of the heart which is dulled or is dulling to the religious appeal.

They are not hopeful symptoms among those whose life should be lived on the religious heights. No doubt, those who minister to you in spiritual things should take them to heart. And you who are ministered to must take them to heart, too. And let me tell you straight out that the preaching you find dull will no more seem dull to you if you faithfully obey the Master's precept: 'Take heed how ye hear'; that if you do not find Christ in the conference room it is because you do not take him there with you; that, if after an ordinary day's work you are too weary to unite with your fellows in closing the day with common prayer, it is because the impulse to prayer is weak in your heart. If there is no fire in the pulpit it falls to you to kindle it in the pews. No man can fail to meet with God in the sanctuary if he takes God there with him.

How easy it is to roll the blame of our cold hearts over upon the shoulders of our religious leaders! It is refreshing to observe how Luther, with his breezy good sense, dealt with complaints of lack of attractiveness in his evangelical preachers. He had not sent them out to please people, he said, and their function was not to interest or to entertain; their function was to teach the saving truth of God, and, if they did that, it was frivolous for people in danger of perishing for want of the truth to object to the vessel in which it was offered to them.

When the people of Torgau, for instance, wished to dismiss their pastors, because, they said, their voices were too weak to fill the churches, Luther simply responded, 'That's an old song: better have some difficulty in hearing the gospel than no difficulty at all in hearing what is very far from the gospel.' 'People cannot have their ministers exactly as they wish', he declares again, 'they should thank God for the pure word', and not demand St Augustines and St Ambroses to preach it to them. If a pastor pleases the Lord Jesus and is faithful to him,—there is none so great and mighty but he ought to be pleased with him, too. The point, you see, is that men who are hungry for the truth and get it ought not to be exigent as to the platter in which it is served to them. And they will not be.

But why should we appeal to Luther? Have we not the example of our Lord Jesus Christ? Are we better than he? Surely, if ever there was one who might justly plead that the common worship of the community had nothing to offer him it was the Lord Jesus Christ. But every Sabbath found him seated in his place among the worshipping people, and there was no act of stated worship which he felt himself entitled to discard. Even in his most exalted moods, and after his most elevating experiences, he quietly took his place with the rest of God's people, sharing with them in the common worship of the community. Returning from that great baptismal scene, when the heavens themselves were rent to bear him witness that he was well pleasing to God; from the searching trials of the wilderness, and from that first great tour in Galilee, prosecuted, as we are expressly told, 'in the power of the Spirit'; he came back, as the record tells, 'to Nazareth, where he had been brought up, and'—so proceeds the amazing narrative—'he entered, as his custom was, into the synagogue, on the Sabbath day'. 'As his custom was'! Jesus Christ made it his habitual practice to be found in his place on the Sabbath day at the stated place of worship to which he belonged. 'It is a reminder', as Sir William Robertson Nicoll well insists, 'of the truth which, in our fancied spirituality, we are apt to forget—that the holiest personal life can scarcely afford to dispense with stated forms of devotion, and that the regular public worship of the church, for all its local imperfections and dullness, is a divine provision for sustaining the individual soul.' 'We cannot afford to be wiser than our Lord in this matter. If anyone could have pled that his spiritual experience was so lofty that it did not require public worship, if anyone might have felt that the consecration and communion of his personal life exempted him from what ordinary mortals needed, it was Jesus. But he made no such plea. Sabbath by Sabbath even he was found in the place of worship, side by side with God's people, not for the mere sake of setting a good example, but for deeper reasons. Is it reasonable, then, that any of us should think we can safely afford to dispense with the pious custom of regular participation with the common worship of our locality?' Is it necessary for me to exhort those who would fain be like Christ, to see to it that they are imitators of him in this?

But not even with the most assiduous use of the corporate expressions of the religious life of the community have you reached the foundation stone of your piety. That is to be found, of course, in your closets, or rather in your hearts, in your private religious exercises, and in your intimate religious aspirations. You are here as theological students; and if you would be religious men, you must do your duty as theological students; you must find daily nourishment for your religious life in your theological studies, you must enter fully into the organic religious life of the community of which you form a part. But to do all this you must keep the fires of religious life burning brightly in your heart; in the inmost core of your being, you must be men of God.

Time would fail me, if I undertook to outline with any fulness the method of the devout life. Every soul seeking God honestly and earnestly finds him, and, in finding him, finds the way to him. One hint I may give you, particularly adapted to you as students for the ministry: Keep always before your mind the greatness of your calling, that is to say, these two things: the immensity of the task before you, the infinitude of the resources at your disposal.

I think it has not been idly said, that if we face the tremendous difficulty of the work before us, it will certainly throw us back upon our knees; and if we worthily gauge the power of the gospel committed to us, that will certainly keep us on our knees. I am led to single out this particular consideration, because it seems to me that we have fallen upon an age in which we very greatly need to recall ourselves to the seriousness of life and its issues, and to the seriousness of our calling as ministers to life. Sir Oliver Lodge informs us that 'men of culture are not bothering', nowadays, 'about their sin, much less about their punishment', and Dr Johnston Ross preaches us a much needed homily from that text on the 'light-heartedness of the modern religious quest'. In a time like this, it is perhaps not strange that careful observers of the life of our theological seminaries tell us that the most noticeable thing about it is a certain falling off from the intense seriousness of outlook by which students of theology were formerly characterized. Let us hope it is not true. If it were true, it would be a great evil; so far as it is true, it is a great evil. I would call you back to this seriousness of outlook, and bid you cultivate it, if you would be men of God now, and ministers who need not be ashamed hereafter. Think of the greatness of the minister's calling; the greatness of the issues which hang on your worthiness or your unworthiness for its high functions; and determine once for all that with God's help you will be worthy. 'God had but one Son', says

Thomas Goodwin, 'and he made him a minister.' 'None but he who made the world', says John Newton, 'can make a minister'—that is, a minister who is worthy. You can, of course, be a minister of a sort, and not be Godmade.

You can go through the motions of the work, and I shall not say that your work will be in vain—for God is good and who knows by what instruments he may work his will of good for men? Helen Jackson pictures far too common an experience when she paints the despair of one whose sowing, though not unfruitful for others, bears no harvest in his own soul.

> O teacher, then I said, thy years,
> Are they not joy? each word that issueth
> From out thy lips, doth it return to bless
> Thine own heart manyfold?

Listen to the response:

> I starve with hunger treading out their corn,
> I die of travail while their souls are born.

She does not mean it in quite the evil part in which I am reading it. But what does Paul mean when he utters that terrible warning: 'Lest when I have preached to others, I myself should be a castaway?' And there is an even more dreadful contingency. It is our Saviour himself who tells us that it is possible to compass sea and land to make one proselyte, and when we have made him to make him twofold more a child of hell than we are ourselves. And will we not be in awful peril of making our proselytes children of hell if we are not ourselves children of heaven? Even physical waters will not rise above their source: the spiritual floods are even less tractable to our commands.

There is no mistake more terrible than to suppose that activity in Christian work can take the place of depth of Christian affections. This is the reason why many good men are shaking their heads a little today over a tendency which they fancy they see increasing among our younger Christian workers to restless activity at the apparent expense of depth of spiritual culture. Activity, of course, is good: surely in the cause of the Lord we should run and not be weary. But not when it is substituted for inner religious strength. We cannot get along without our Marthas. But what shall we do when, through all the length and breadth of the land, we shall search in vain for a Mary? Of course the Marys will be as little admired by the Marthas today as of yore. 'Lord', cried Martha, 'dost thou not care that my sister hath left me to serve alone?' And from that time to this the cry has continually gone up against the Marys that they waste the precious ointment which might have been given to the poor, when they pour it out to God, and are idle when they sit at the Master's feet.

A minister, high in the esteem of the churches, is even quoted as declaring—not confessing, mind you, but publishing abroad as something in which he gloried—that he has long since ceased to pray: he works. 'Work and pray' is no longer, it seems, to be the motto of at least ministerial life. It is to be all work and no praying; the only prayer that is prevailing, we are told, with the same cynicism with which we are told that God is on the side of the largest battalions—is just work. You will say this is an extreme case. Thank God, it is. But in the tendencies of our modern life, which all make for ceaseless—I had almost said thoughtless, meaningless—activity, have a care that it does not become your case; or that your case—even now—may not have at least some resemblance to it. Do you pray? How much do you pray? How much do you love to pray? What place in your life does the 'still hour', alone with God, take?

I am sure that if you once get a true glimpse of what the ministry of the cross is, for which you are preparing, and of what you, as men preparing for this ministry, should be, you will pray, 'Lord, who is sufficient for these things', your heart will cry; and your whole soul will be wrung with the petition: 'Lord, make me sufficient for these things.' Old Cotton Mather wrote a great little book once, to serve as a guide to students for the ministry. The not very happy title which he gave it is *Manductio ad Ministerium*. But by a stroke of genius he added a sub-title which is more significant. And this is the sub-title he added: *The angels preparing to sound the trumpets*. That is what Cotton Mather calls you, students for the ministry: *the angels, preparing to sound the trumpets!* Take the name to yourselves, and live up to it. Give your days and nights to living up to it! And then, perhaps, when you come to sound the trumpets the note will be pure and clear and strong, and perchance may pierce even to the grave and wake the dead.

SPIRITUAL CULTURE IN THE THEOLOGICAL SEMINARY[1]

I T is natural that at the opening of a new session the minds of
both professors and students, especially of those students who
are with us for the first time, should be bent somewhat anxiously
upon the matter which has brought us together. How are we who
teach best to fulfil the trust committed to us, of guiding others in
their preparation for the high office of minister of grace? How are
you who are here to make this preparation, so to employ your time
and opportunities as to become in the highest sense true stewards
of the mysteries of Christ? Standing as you do at the close of your
university work and at the beginning of three years more of mental
labour—looking back at the conquests you have already made and
forward at unconquered realms still lying before you—it would not
be strange if your thoughts as they busy themselves with the preparation you require for your ministerial work should be predominately
occupied with intellectual training. It is the more important that we
should pause to remind ourselves that intellectual training alone will
never make a true minister; that the heart has rights which the head
must respect; and that it behoves us above everything to remember
that the ministry is a spiritual office.

I should be sorry to leave the impression that it is questionable
whether the church may not have laid too strong an emphasis on
the intellectual outfit that is needed for her ministry. I must profess,
indeed, that I am incapable of understanding the standpoint of those
(for such there seem to be) who talk of the over-intellectualization of
the ministry. The late Dr Joseph T. Duryea spoke rather strongly, but

[1] An address delivered to the incoming students, Sabbath afternoon, September 20,
1903, in the Oratory of Stuart Hall, Princeton Theological Seminary. B. B. Warfield,
'Spiritual Culture in the Theological Seminary', *Princeton Theological Review*, 2
(1904), pp. 65-87.

with substantial justice, when he declared it to be 'high time that the question whether culture and learning do not unfit preachers for the preaching of the gospel to ordinary men and women, were referred back without response to the stupidity that inspires it'. It is not to be denied, of course, that there are learned men who are perfectly useless in the ministry; and even, what is more surprising, that there are men of broad and varied and, one would have thought, humanizing culture, who seem to be unable to turn their culture to any practical use. But it is yet to be shown that these same men, without knowledge and destitute of the culture which might have been expected to humanize them, would have been any more useful. Are there no ignorant men, no men innocent of all culture, who are unpractical and of no possible use in the ministry? The fact is that when our Lord decreed that the religion he founded should be propagated by preaching, or, to put it more broadly, when he placed it in the world with the commission to reason its way to the hearts of men, he put a premium on intellectual endowments, and laid at the basis of ministerial equipment a demand for intellectual training, which no sophistry can cloud. The minister must have good tools with which to work, and must keep these tools in good condition.

You will find nothing in the curriculum which will be offered to you in this seminary, the mastery of which is not essential to your highest efficiency in your ministry. The intellectual training at present provided for candidates for the ministry is not above either their prospective needs or the easy possibilities of their present powers. You will be wise to give yourselves diligently to making full account of it. It would not be easy to exaggerate the intimacy of the relation between sound knowledge and sound religious feeling; and the connection between sound knowledge and success in ministerial work is equally close. 'Without study', says an experienced bishop of the Church of England, with his eye on the daily life of the minister it is true, but no less applicably to his preparation—'without study we shall not only fail to bring to our people all the blessings which God intends for them, but we shall gradually become feeble and perfunctory in our ministrations: our life may apparently be a busy one, and our time incessantly occupied, but our work will be comparatively fruitless: we shall be fighting as one that beateth the air.'

So intimate is the connection between the head and the heart and hand, indeed, that it is not unfair to say broadly that if undue intellectualism exhibits itself in those preparing for the ministry, the fault is relative, not absolute: that, in a word, there is not a too muchness in the case at all, but a too littleness somewhere else. The trouble with those whom a certain part of the world persists in speaking of as over-educated for an effective ministry is not that they are too highly trained intellectually, but that they are sadly undertrained spiritually; not that their head has received too much attention, but that their heart has received too little. Of course, I shall not deny that it is possible to find men who are naturally lacking in sufficient mental power to pursue a seminary course profitably; and I am far from saying that there are none of these 'unlearned and ignorant men' who have been so baptized with the Holy Spirit that the church may profitably induct them into the ministry to which God has obviously called them. But these are rare exceptions; and I do not think it characteristic of this humble but honourable class that they refuse to make the best use possible of the mental powers that have been vouchsafed to them. Certainly it would be perilous for us to make the existence of such a class the excuse for neglecting to stir up the gift that is in us. Rather I think it may be fairly inferred that when students for the ministry fail to take full advantage of the opportunities for intellectual culture offered them, the fault is usually to be found in the heart itself. When too much blood seems to have gone to the head, we may ordinarily justly presume that this is only because too little has gone to the heart; and similarly when little or none is thrown to the head, we may quite generally suspect it is because the heart has too little within it to supply the needs of any organ.

I. I have missed my mark in what I have been saying if, while insisting on the need of a strenuous intellectual preparation for the ministry, I have not also suggested that *the deepest need is a profound spiritual preparation*. An adequate preparation for the gospel ministry certainly embraces much more than merely the study of certain branches of learning. When Bishop Wilberforce opened Cuddesden College in 1854, he wrote: 'Threefold object of residence here: 1. Devotion; 2. Parochial Work; 3. Theological Reading.' The special circumstances of 'candidates for holy orders' in the Church of England suggested, as we shall subsequently see, the order in which these three elements in their preparation are mentioned. In our special circumstances a different order might be suggested. But does it not, even on first sight, commend itself to you with clear convincingness, that any proper preparation for the ministry must include these three chief parts—a training of the heart, a training of the hand, a training of the head—a devotional, a practical, and an intellectual training? Such a training, in a word, as that we may learn first to know Jesus, then to grasp the message he would have us deliver to men, and then how he would have us work for him in his vineyard. We are told by the Evangelist Mark (3:14) that when Jesus appointed his twelve apostles, it was first that they might be with him, and then that he might send them forth to preach. And surely we may believe that we who are the successors of the apostles as the evangelizers of the world have been called like them first of all to be with Jesus and only then to go forth to preach. It may not be without significance that out of the fourteen or fifteen qualifications which, according to the Apostle Paul, must unite in order to fit a man to be a bishop, only one requires an intellectual preparation. The bishop must be 'apt to teach'. But aptness to teach is only the beginning of his fitting. All the other requirements are rooted in his moral or spiritual fitness.

I am not going to lose myself in a vain—perhaps worse than vain—inquiry as to which of the three lines of preparation I have hinted at is the most essential. Why raise a question between three lines of training, each of which is essential both in itself and to the proper prosecution of the others? If intellectual acuteness will not of itself make a man an acceptable minister of Christ, neither will facility and energy in practical affairs by themselves, nor yet piety and devotion alone. The three must be twisted together into a single three-ply cord. We are not to ask whether we will cultivate the one or the other; or whether we will give our chief attention to the one or the other. We must simultaneously push our forces over all three lines of approach, if we are to capture the stronghold of a successful ministry at all. Doing so, they will interact, as we have suggested, each to secure the others. Do we wish to grow in grace? It is the knowledge of God's truth that sanctifies the heart. Do we desire a key to the depths of God's truth? It is the Spirit-led man who discerns all things. Are our souls in travail for the dying thousands about us? How eager, then, will be our search in the fountain of life for the waters of healing? Is the way weary? Do we not know whence alone can be derived our strength for the journey of life? There is no way so surely to stimulate the appetite for knowledge as to quicken the sense of the need of it in the wants of our own spiritual life or in the calls of practical work for others. There is no way so potent for awakening a craving for personal holiness or for arousing a love of souls in our hearts, as to fill the mind with a knowledge of God's love to man as revealed in his Holy Book.

The reciprocal relation in which the several lines of preparation for the ministry stand to one another supplies me with my first remark as I address myself to the task immediately before me—of attempting to outline in a practical way some account of how your spiritual training may be advanced during your stay in the seminary. This remark takes a negative form and amounts to saying with some emphasis that your spiritual growth will not be advanced by the neglect of the very work for which you resort to the seminary. Such a remark may seem to some of you out of place: it is perhaps not so entirely unnecessary as it may appear. There is a valuable bit from his own personal experience given us by the late Phillips Brooks in his *Yale Lectures*,[1] which I shall repeat here for our admonition also. He is impressing on his readers the important truth that the first and most evident element in a true preparation for the ministry consists in a mastery of the professional studies leading up to it. He writes as follows:

> Most men begin really to study when they enter on the preparation for their professions. Men whose college life, with its general culture, has been very idle, begin to work when at the door of the professional school the work of their life comes into sight before them. It is the way in which a bird who has been wheeling vaguely hither and thither sees at last its home in the distance and flies toward it like an arrow. But shall I say to you how often I have thought that the very transcendent motives of the young minister's study have a certain tendency to bewilder him and make his study less faithful than that of men seeking other professions from lower motives? The highest motive often

[1] p. 43.

dazzles before it illuminates. It is one of the ways in which the light within us becomes darkness. I never shall forget my first experience of a divinity school. I had come from a college where men studied hard but said nothing about faith. I had never been at a prayer meeting in my life. The first place I was taken to at the seminary was the prayer meeting; and never shall I lose the impression of the devoutness with which those men prayed and exhorted one another. Their whole souls seemed exalted and their natures were on fire. I sat bewildered and ashamed and went away depressed. On the next day I met some of these men at a Greek recitation. It would be little to say of some of the devoutest of them that they had not learnt their lesson. Their whole way showed that they had never learnt their lessons; that they had not got hold of the first principles of hard, faithful, conscientious study. The boiler had no connection with the engine. The devotion did not touch the work which then and there was the work, and the only work, for them to do. By and by I found something of where the steam did escape to. A sort of amateur, premature preaching was much in vogue among us. We were in haste to be at what we called 'our work'. A feeble twilight of the coming ministry we lived in. The people in the neighbourhood dubbed us 'parsonettes'. Oh, my fellow-students, the special study of theology and all that appertains to it, that is what the preacher must be doing always; but he can never do it afterward as he can in the blessed days of quiet in Arabia, after Christ has called him, and before the apostles lay their hands upon him. In many respects an ignorant clergy, however pious it may be, is worse than none at all. The more the empty head glows and burns the more hollow and thin and dry it grows. 'The knowledge of the priest', said St Francis de Sales, 'is the eighth sacrament of the church.'

Well, it was not at Princeton Seminary that Dr Brooks saw these evils. Perhaps they do not exist here; let us hope that they do not, at least in the measure in which he portrays them. Nevertheless his experience may fitly be laid to heart by us for our warning. The religious training which a minister needs to get in his days of preparation assuredly cannot be had by neglecting the very work he is set to do, in favour of any show of devoutness which does not affect the roots of his conduct, or of any show of zeal in another work which it is not yet his to do.

Of course, there is, another side to it. This religious training is not already obtained by the mere refusal to be led away from our primary work at the seminary by practical calls upon our energies. Our primary business at the seminary is, no doubt, to obtain the intellectual fitting for our ministerial work, and nothing must be allowed to supersede that in our efforts. But neither must the collateral prosecution of the requisite training of the heart and hand be neglected, as opportunity offers. Nor will a properly guarded attention to these injure the discharge of our scholastic duties; it will, on the contrary, powerfully advance their successful performance. The student cannot too sedulously cultivate devoutness of spirit. The maxim has been often verified in the experience of us all: *bene orasse est bene studuisse.*[1] When the heart is thoroughly aroused, the slowest mind starts into motion and an impulse is given it which carries it triumphantly over intellectual difficulties before which it quailed afraid. And equally a proper taste of the practical work of the ministry is a great quickener of the mind for the intellectual preparation. We cannot do without these things. And the student must be very careful, therefore—even on this somewhat low ground—while not permitting any distractions to divert him from his primary task as a student, yet to take full advantage of all proper opportunities that may arise to train his heart and hand also. Preparation for ministerial service is very much like building a machine—say a locomotive. The intellectual work may have been accomplished and the machine may stand perfect before us. But it will not go unless the vital force of devotion is throbbing through it. Knowledge is a powerful thing; and practical tact is a powerful thing. And so is a locomotive a powerful thing—provided it has steam in it! Though I know all mysteries and all knowledge, and though I bestow all my goods to feed the poor, if I have not the love of God and man welling up in invincible power beneath it all and lifting it all and transmuting it all into effective working force—it profits me nothing.

II. But the question comes back to us, How are we to obtain this spiritual culture in the seminary? Well, theological students, in becoming theological students, have not ceased to be men; and there

---

[1] To have prayed well is to have studied well.

is no other way for them to become devout men than that which is common to man. There is but one way, Brethren, to become strong in the Lord. That way is to *feed on the Bread of Life!* This is the way other men who would fain be devout take, and it is the way we, if we would fain be devout, must take. We are simply asking ourselves then, as theological students, what opportunities are offered us by our residence in the seminary for the cultivation of faith in Jesus Christ and obedience to him. What we are eager to know is how we cannot merely keep alive, but fan into a brighter flame the fires of our love for our Lord and Saviour. I desire to be perfectly plain and simple in attempting to suggest an answer to this question. I shall, therefore, only enumerate in the barest manner some of the ways in which the devout life may be assisted in the conditions in which we live in the seminary.

First of all, I must point you to the importance of a *diligent use of the public means of grace.* Public means of grace abound in the seminary. There is the stated Sabbath-morning service in the chapel; and no student who is not prevented from attending it by some imperative duty should fail to be in his seat at that service, adding whatever his presence and his prayers can bring to the spiritual forces at work there. Then there is our weekly Conference on Sabbath afternoon, in which we talk over together the blessed promises of our God and seek to learn better his will for the ordering of our lives. There have been those in times past whose hearts have been stirred within them at these conferences; and they may be made by the seeking spirit very precious seasons of social meditation and prayer. Then, faculty and students meet daily, at the close of the day's work, to listen to a fragment of God's Word, mingle their voices in praise to God, and ask his blessing on the labour of the day. Indeed, we proceed to no one of our classroom exercises without pausing a moment to lift up our hearts to God in prayer. And every effort is made by all of us who teach, I know, in all our teaching—however it may appear from moment to moment to be concerned with mere parts of speech, or the signification of words, or the details of history, or the syllogisms of formal logic—to preserve a devout spirit and a reverent heart, as becomes those who are dealing even with the outer coverings that protect the mysteries of God. I need not stay to speak with particularity of the more rarely occurring stated services, such as the monthly concert of prayer for missions and the like. Enough has been said to suggest the richness of provision made in the seminary for public worship; and assuredly amid such abounding opportunities for the quickening of the religious life it ought to be a comparatively easy thing to cultivate devoutness of spirit.

You will doubtless observe that I have said nothing, so far, of additional opportunities for social worship afforded by public services open to the attendance of the students outside the boundaries of the seminary, or by voluntary associations for religious culture among the students themselves. These also are abundant, and have their parts to play in your edification. They may be justly accounted supplementary means of grace, useful to you, each in its own place and order. But what I am insisting on now is something which no such services, whether without or within the seminary walls, can supply: something which by the grace of God can go much deeper into the bases of your religious nature and lay much broader foundations for the building up of a firm and consistent and abiding Christian character. I am exhorting you to give great diligence to the cultivation of the stated means of grace provided by the seminary, to live in them and make them the full and rich expression of the organic religious life of the institution. I am touching on something here that seems to me to be of the utmost importance and which does not seem to me to have received the attention from the students which it deserves. Every body of men bound together in as close and intimate association as we are, must have an organic life; and if the bonds that bind them together are fundamentally of a religious character, this organic life must be fundamentally a religious one. We do not live on the top of our privileges in such circumstances unless we succeed in giving this organic religious life full power in our own lives and full expression in the stated means provided for its expression. No richness of private religious life, no abundance of voluntary religious services on the part of members of the organism, can take the place of or supersede the necessity for the fullest, richest and most fervent expression of this organic religious life through its appropriate channels. I exhort you, therefore, Brethren, with the utmost seriousness, to utilize the public means of grace afforded by the seminary, and to make them instruments for the cultivation and expression of the organic religious life of the institution. We shall not have done our duty by our own souls until we find in these public services the joy of our hearts and the inspiration of our conduct.

Let me go a step further and put into plain words a thought that is floating in my mind. The entire work of the seminary deserves to be classed in the category of means of grace; and the whole routine of work done here may be made a very powerful means of grace if we will only prosecute it in a right spirit and with due regard to its religious value. For what are we engaging ourselves with in our daily studies but just the Word of God, the history of God's dealings with his people, the great truths that he has revealed to us for the salvation of our souls? And what are we doing when we engage ourselves day after day with these topics of study and meditation, but just what every Christian man strives to do when he is seeking nutriment for his soul? The only difference is that what he does sporadically, at intervals, and somewhat primarily, it is your privilege to give yourselves to unbrokenly for a space of three whole years! Precious years these ought to be to you, Brethren, in the culture of the spiritual life. If such contact as we in the seminary have the privilege of enjoying with divine truth does not sanctify our souls, should we not infer either that it is a mistake to pray in Christ's own words, 'Sanctify us in the truth; thy word is truth', or else that our hearts are so indurated as no longer to be capable of reaction even to so powerful a reagent as the very truth of God?

I beseech you, Brethren, take every item of your seminary work as a *religious* duty. I am emphasizing the adjective in this. I mean do all your work religiously—that is, with a religious end in view, in a religious spirit, and with the religious side of it dominant in your mind. Do not lose such an opportunity as this to enlighten, deepen and strengthen your devotion. Let nothing pass by you without sucking the honey from it. If you learn a Hebrew word, let not the merely philological interest absorb your attention: remember that it is a word which occurs in God's holy Book, recall the passages in which it stands, remind yourselves what great religious truths it has been given to it to have a part in recording for the saving health of men. Every biblical text whose meaning you investigate treat as a biblical text, a part of God's holy Word, before which you should stand in awe. It is wonderful how even the strictest grammatical study can be informed with reverence. You cannot read six lines of Bishop Ellicott's *Commentaries, Critical and Grammatical,* on Paul's epistles without feeling through and through that here is a man of God studying the Word of God. *O si sic omnes!*[1] Let us make such commentators our models in our study of the Word, and learn like them to keep in mind whose Word it is we are dealing with, even when we are merely analysing its grammatical expression. And when, done with grammar, we begin to weigh the meaning, O let us remember what meaning it has to us! Apply every word to your own souls as you go on, and never rest satisfied until you feel as well as understand. Every item of God's dealing with his church to which your attention is directed, contemplate reverently as an act of God and search out the revelation it carries of God and his ways with man. And the doctrines—need I beg you to consider these doctrines not as so many propositions to be analysed by your logical understanding, but as rather so many precious truths revealing to you God and God's modes of dealing with sinful man? John Owen, in his great work on Justification, insists and insists again that no man can ever penetrate the significance of this great doctrine unless he persistently studies it, not in the abstract light of the question, How can man be just with God? but in the searching light of the great personal question, How can *I,* sinner as I am, be accepted of God? It is wonderful how inadequacies in conceiving what is involved in justification fall away under the illumination of this personal attitude toward it. And is it conceivable that it can be so studied and the heart remain cold and unmoved? Treat, I beg you, the whole work of the seminary as a unique opportunity offered you to learn about God, or rather, to put it at the height of its significance, to learn God—to come to know him whom to know is life everlasting. If the work of the seminary shall be so prosecuted, it will prove itself to be the chief means of grace in all your lives. I have heard it said that some men love theology more than they love God. Do not let it be possible to say that of you. Love theology, of course; but love theology for no other reason

---

[1] O if we were all thus!

than that it is *Theology*—the knowledge of *God,* and because it is your meat and drink to know God, to know him truly, and as far as it is given to mortals, to know him whole.

There is yet another aspect of the seminary life the value of which as a means of spiritual development cannot easily be overestimated. I do not know how better to express what I mean than by calling the seminary a three years' *retreat.* The word 'retreat' may strike somewhat strangely upon our Protestant ears: though even our Presbyterian ministry has been learning of late what a 'retreat' is. Well, that is what a seminary life very largely is—a period of three years' duration during which the prospective minister withdraws from the world and gives his time exclusively to study and meditation on God's Word, in company with a select body of godly companions.

> Here man more purely lives, less oft doth fall,
> More promptly rises, walks with stricter heed.

Possibly with our natural Protestant objection to all that in the remotest way savours of the monastery, we may be prone to take little account of this feature of seminary life—much to our hurt. Much to our hurt, I say; for a 'retreat' is what a seminary life is, and it will have its effect on us as such—one way or another, according as we do or do not prepare for it, and are or are not receptive of it.

Our brethren of the Church of England, who have only comparatively lately taken to multiplying distinctively theological colleges, because they look to the universities as the places where their candidates are to be educated for the holy office, consider this element in the life at a theological college one of its most characteristic and helpful features, It was because he viewed it thus that Bishop Wilberforce declared the three objects of residence at Cuddesden to be: 1. Devotion; 2. Parochial Work; and 3. Theological Reading. It is as a matter of fact inevitable that the practical withdrawal from the world and the congregation together of a hundred or two young men, all consecrated to the work of the Lord, and living in that closeness of intimacy which only community life can induce, should have a very powerful effect on their religious development. What, Brethren, can you draw coals together without creating a blaze? I beseech you, esteem very highly and cultivate with jealous eagerness this unique privilege of long and intimate association with so many of God's children. No such opportunities of interaction of devout lives upon one another can ever come to you again in all your life. If no fire of Christian love breaks out among you, look well to yourselves: you may justly suspect there is something wrong with your souls. In the daily intercourse of scores of Christian men there must arise innumerable opportunities of giving and receiving spiritual impressions. See to it that all you give shall conduce to the quickening of the religious life, and that all you receive shall be food on which your own hearts feed and grow strong in the Lord. When you leave the seminary you will miss this intercourse sorely; but by God's help you may so use it while here that in the strength derived from it you may go many days.

III. But we must penetrate beneath even such means of grace as those I have enumerated before we reach the centre of our subject. It is not to the public ordinances, not to your professors, and not even to your companions, that you can look for the sources of your growth in religious power. As no one can give you intellectual training except at the cost of your own strenuous effort, so no one can communicate to you spiritual advancement apart from the *activities of your own eager souls.* True devoutness is a plant that grows best in seclusion and the darkness of the closet; and we cannot reach the springs of our devout life until we penetrate into the sanctuary where the soul meets habitually with its God. If association with God's children powerfully quickens our spiritual life, how much more intimate communion with God himself. Let us then make it our chief concern in our preparation for the ministry to institute between our hearts and God our Maker, Redeemer, and Sanctifier such an intimacy of communion that we may realize in our lives the command of Paul to pray without ceasing and in everything to give thanks, and that we may see fulfilled in our own experience our Lord's promise not only to enter into our hearts, but unbrokenly to abide in them and to unite them to himself in an intimacy comparable to the union of the Father and the Son.

Lectio, meditatio, oratio, the old Doctors used to say, *jaciunt theologum.*[1] They were right. Take the terms in the highest senses they

---

[1] Reading, meditation and prayer, these are the making of the theologian.

will bear, and we shall have an admirable prescription of what we must do would we cultivate to its height the Christian life that is in us.

Above all else that you strive after, cultivate *the grace of private prayer*. It is a grace that is capable of cultivation and that responds kindly to cultivation; as it can be, on the other hand, atrophied by neglect. Be not of those that neglect it, but in constant prayer be a follower of Paul, or rather of our Lord himself; for, God as he was, our blessed Lord was a man of prayer, and found prayer his ceaseless joy and his constant need. Of course, the spirit of prayer is the main thing here, and the habit of 'praying without ceasing', of living in a prayerful frame, is above all what is to be striven for. But let us not fall into the grave error of supposing this prayerful habit of mind enough, or that we can safely intermit the custom of setting apart seasons for formal prayer. Let me read you a few appropriate words here from one of Dr. H. C. G. Moule's delightful devotional treatises: 'To speak in terms of the simplest practicality', he says,[1]

> the living Christian will do anything rather than make his 'life' an excuse for indolence, and for want of method and self-discipline, in secret devotion; or for want of adoring reverence in the manner of it; or for neglect of the Written Word as a vital element in it, and as the one sure guide and guard of it all along. He will most specially take care that Christ is thus 'in his life', in respect of morning intercourse with him. His 'morning watch' will be a time of sacred necessity and blessed benefit. He will not merely confess the duty of 'meeting God before he meets man'. He will understand that he cannot do without it, if indeed he would deal with the unfolding day as it should be dealt with by one whose 'life is hid with Christ in God'; one who possesses the priceless treasure of the blessed Union, 'joined to the Lord, one Spirit', and who has his treasure at hand, in hand for use. And he will be not less watchful over his evening interview with him who is at once his Master and his Life; coming with punctual reverence *to* him who meanwhile liveth *in* him, to report the day's bond-service, to confess the day's sin in contrite simplicity, to look again deliberately upon his Master's face mirrored in his Word, to feel again the bond

---

[1] *Life in Christ and for Christ,* p. 37.

of the Union, tested and handled through the promises and then to lie down in the peace of God. And will he not see whether some *midday* interval, if but for a few brief minutes, cannot be found and kept sacred, for a special prayer and watch half-way? Such stated times are not substitutes for the spiritual attitude in which the 'eyes are ever toward the Lord', but they are, I believe, quite necessary in order to the proper preparedness of the soul for that attitude, and for the right use, too, of all public and social ordinances. Nothing can annul the vital need of secret and deliberate communion with him in whom we live, by whom we move.

Next to the prayerful spirit, the habit of *reverent meditation on God's truth* is useful in cultivating devoutness of life. It is commonly said around us that the old gift of meditation has perished out of the earth. And certainly there is much in our nervous, fussy times which does not take kindly to it. Those who read nowadays like to do it running. It is assuredly worth our while, however, to bring back the gracious habit of devout meditation. Says Jeremy Taylor in the opening page of his *Holy Living,* in his quaint, old-world words:

> The counsels of religion are not to be applied to the distempers of the soul as men used to take hellebore; but they must dwell together with the spirit of a man, and be twisted about his understanding for ever: they must be used like nourishment, that, is, by a daily care and meditation; not like a single medicine, and upon the actual pressure of a present necessity.

It is the same lesson that Mr Spurgeon expounds in his illuminating way in a passage like the following:

> We ought to muse upon the things of God, because we thus get the real nutriment out of them. Truth is something like the cluster of the vine: if we would have wine from it, we must bruise it; we must press and squeeze it many times. The bruiser's feet must come down joyfully upon the bunches, or else the juice will not flow; and they must well tread the grapes, or else much of the precious liquid will be wasted. So we must, by meditation, tread the clusters of truth, if we would get the wine of consolation therefrom. Our bodies are not supported by merely taking food into the mouth, but the process which really

supplies the muscle, and the nerve, and the sinew, and the bone, is the process of digestion. It is by digestion that the outward food becomes assimilated with the inner life. Our souls are not nourished merely by listening awhile to this, and then to that, and then to the other part of divine truth. Hearing, reading, marking, and learning, all require inwardly digesting to complete their usefulness, and the inward digesting of the truth lies for the most part in meditating upon it. Why is it that some Christians, although they hear many sermons, make but slow advances in the divine life? Because they neglect their closets, and do not thoughtfully meditate on God's Word. They love the wheat, but they do not grind it; they would have the corn, but they will not go forth into the fields to gather it; the fruit hangs upon the tree, but they will not pluck it; the water flows at their feet, but they will not stoop to drink it. From such folly deliver us, O Lord, and be this our resolve this morning, 'I will meditate in thy precepts.'[1]

Meditation is an exercise which stands somewhere between thought and prayer. It must not be confounded with mere reasoning; it is reasoning transfigured by devout feeling; and it proceeds by broodingly dissolving rather than by logically analysing the thought. But it must be guarded from degenerating into mere day-dreaming on sacred themes; and it will be wise in order to secure ourselves from this fault to meditate chiefly with the Bible in our hands and always on its truths. As meditation, then, on the one side takes hold upon prayer, so, on the other, it shades off into devotional Bible-reading, the highest exercise of which, indeed, it is. Life close to God's Word, is life close to God. When I urge you to make very much while you are in the seminary of this kind of devotional Bible study, running up into meditation, pure and simple, I am but repeating what the General Assembly specifically requires of you. 'It is expected', says the Plan of the Seminary, framed by the Assembly as our organic law, 'that every student will spend a portion of time, every morning and evening, in devout meditation and self-recollection and examination; in reading the Holy Scriptures solely with a view to a personal and practical application of the passage read to his own heart, character, and circumstances; and in humble, fervent prayer and praise to God in secret.'

[1] *Morning by Morning*, October 12.

And do we not find in the practice here recommended the remedy for that lamentable lack of familiarity with 'the English Bible'—as it is fashionable now to speak of it—which is distressing us all in candidates for the ministry? Brethren, you deceive yourselves if you fancy anyone can *teach* you 'the English Bible' in the sense in which knowledge of it is desiderated. As well expect someone to digest your food for you. You must taste its preciousness for yourselves, before you can apply its preciousness to others' needs. You must assimilate the Bible and make it your own, in that intimate sense which will fix its words fast in your hearts, if you would have those words rise spontaneously to your lips in your times of need, or in the times of the need of others. Read, study, meditate on your Bible: take time to it—much time; spend effort, strength, yourselves on it; until the Bible is in you. Then the Bible will well up in you and come out from you in every season of need.

It is idle to seek aids for such reading and meditation. The devout and prayerful spirit is the only key to it. Nevertheless there are helps which may be temporarily used as crutches if the legs halt too much to go. Dean Alford has a couple of little books on *How to Study the Scriptures,* and Dean Goulburn has a little volume on *The Practical Study of the Bible* which may be profitably consulted for general direction. Our fathers used to read their Bibles with Thomas Scott's *Family Bible with Notes,* or Matthew Henry's *Exposition of the Old and New Testaments,* or William Burkitt's *Expository Notes on the New Testament* (which turns every passage into a prayer), on their knee; and a worse practice can be conceived. The pungent quaintness of Henry especially remains until today without a rival; and no one can read his comments with his heart set on learning of God without deriving from them perennial profit. Direction for your thoughts in meditating on divine truth may be sought also in the numerous books now in such general use for morning and evening religious reading. Bogatzky's *Golden Treasury* is the book of this sort our grandfathers used. William Jay's *Morning and Evening Exercises* is still one of the most useful of them. By its side may be fairly placed at least Mr Spurgeon's *Chequebook of the Bank of Faith.* And the little books of Frances Ridley Havergal have won for themselves a good report. In the use of such aids it is wise to be constantly on guard lest, on the one side, we permit the aid to supplant the direct use of the Word of God as the basis of our meditation, and, on the other, we grow so accustomed to the crutch that we never learn to walk alone. Let neither Matthew Henry nor Charles Spurgeon supplant either the Word of God or the Spirit of God as the teacher of your soul.

IV. In speaking of such aids to the devotional study of Scripture and prayerful meditation, we are already making the transition to a further class of helps to which I must advert before closing. 'Every student', says the Plan of the Seminary, 'at the close of his course . . . must' [I beg you to observe that *'must'*] 'have read a considerable number of *the best practical writers on the subject of religion.'* Even without such admonition we certainly could not have failed to recognize this source of quickening for the religious life. The question that is pressing is, Which are 'the best practical writers on the subject of religion'? In the multitude clamouring for our attention, some good, many bad, and not a few indifferent, the need of guidance in the choice of our practical reading becomes very acute.

Four great movements have been especially prolific in books of edification, each, of course, after its own fashion and with peculiarities of its own. These are the great mystical movement which runs through all ages of the church; the Puritan movement of the seventeenth century; the Evangelical movement in the latter part of the eighteenth and early nineteenth centuries; and more lately and to a less extent the Anglican revival of the nineteenth century. The characteristic mark of the works which have emanated from the mystical writers is a certain aloofness combined with a clear and piercing note of adoration. The Puritan literature is marked by intense devotion to duty and strong insistence on personal holiness. Its message is apt to be couched in a somewhat unadorned literary style. But when the graces of style happen to be added to its clear good sense and profound piety, nothing could be more charming. I can never forget my 'discovery' of John Arrowsmith, for example, when, reading a mass of Puritan literature for another purpose, I suddenly passed from the plain goodness of Anthony Burgess to his delightful pages. The evangelical fervour of the writers of the Great Awakening, and the churchly fervour of the Anglican writers are naturally their most marked characteristics. Our task is to select from this varied literature just the books which will most feed our souls.[1]

Thinking that in the multitude of counsellors there was likely to be strength, I made bold a few years ago to write to a number of religious teachers, each of them justly famous as a writer of books of devotional character, and asked their aid in making out a short list of 'the best practical writers on the subject of religion' for the use of the students of the seminary. I will give you one or two of the answers I received, and these may serve as preliminary guides to your practical reading. Dr James Stalker, now a professor in the United Free Church College, Aberdeen, thought the following, on the whole, the five most helpful books of practical religion: Thomas à Kempis' *Imitation of Christ,* Richard Baxter's *Reformed Pastor,* Jeremy Taylor's *Life of Christ,* John Owen's *Holy Spirit,* Adolph Monod's *Saint Paul.* The late Rev. Dr William M. Taylor, of New York, gave the preference to the following five: Dean Goulburn's *Thoughts on Personal Religion,* Phelps' *Still Hour,* Tholuck's *Hours of Christian Devotion,* Alexander's *Thoughts on Religious Experience,* Faber's *Hymns.* Our own Dr William M. Paxton recommends especially: Hodge's *Way of Life,* Bishop Ryle's *Holiness,* Doddridge's *Rise and Progress of Religion in the Soul,* Owen's *Spiritual Mindedness,* and Faber's *Thoughts on Great Mysteries.* These are all good books and would richly repay your loving study. A hundred others could be added just as good.

It would be useless, however, to draw out a long list of books to be especially recommended. I shall venture to set down the titles of just a round dozen, which I look upon as indispensable. Each must

---

[1] We have no good history of edifying literature in English. The amazing diligence of Hermann Beck has given the Germans two admirable books in this department of knowledge: *Die Erbauungsliteratur der evang. Kirche Deutschlands* (Erlangen: Deichert, 1883, Part I) and *Die relig. Volksliteratur d. ev. Kirche Deutschlands in eine Abriss ihrer Geschichte* (Gotha: Perthes, 1892). A volume on *Books of Devotion,* by the Rev. Charles Bodington, has lately appeared in the series of practical treatises called *The Oxford Library of Practical Theology,* edited by the Rev. W. C. E. Newbold, M.A., and the Rev. Darwell Stone, M.A. (London and New York: Longmans, Green & Co., 1903). It is written from an extreme Anglican point of view; and I am afraid l shall have to add that it is high and dry to a degree and, beyond giving some account of the contents of a number of books of devotional tenor in English, largely of Romish origin, is of little value.

be read for what it can give us; and in none of them shall we seek inspiration and instruction in vain. They come from every part of the church and from every age, and they include representatives of every type of Christian thought, from the mariolatrous Romanism of Thomas à Kempis or the bald Pelagianism of Sir Thomas Browne to the penetrating mysticism of the *Theologia Germanica* and the plain evangelicalism of John Newton. But they all are veritable devotional classics, and each of them has power in it to move and instruct the heart of whoever would live in the Spirit. Get at least these dozen booklets, keep them at your elbow, and sink yourselves in them with constant assiduity. They are: Augustine's *Confessions;*[1] *The Imitation of Christ;*[2] the *Theologia Germanica;*[3] Bishop Andrewes' *Private Devotions;*[4] Jeremy Taylor's *Life of Christ;*[5] Richard Baxter's *The Saints' Everlasting Rest;*[6] Samuel Rutherford's *Letters;*[7] John Bunyan's *Pil-*

---

[1] The editions are numerous. The best Latin text is that of Pius Knöll, which is accessible in the Teubner series of Latin texts (Leipzig, 1898). Of the English translations of the whole work, Dr Pusey's is best both for the translation and its admirable notes. Dr Shedd's edition or Watt's version contains an interesting Introduction. An excellent new translation of the first nine books, with introduction and notes, by Dr. C. Bigg, was published by Methuen in 1898.

[2] The editions are numerous and easily accessible in both Latin and English. Much the best English translation is that by Dr Charles Bigg, published in Methuen's series of Devotional Books. A new departure was made by the publication at Berlin in 1814, by Dr C. Hirsche, of an edition the text of which is presented 'metrice'. The English version of this metrically arranged text, published by A. D. F. Randolph, New York, 1889, is somewhat diffuse but interesting.

[3] Get the edition in Macmillan's *Golden Treasury Series,* edited by Dr Pfeiffer, and translated by Susanna Winkworth.

[4] There are many editions. The best is The *Preces Privatæ of Bishop Andrewes,* edited by F. E. Brightman, M.A. (London: Methuen, 1903). I recommend for the English reader also Dr Alexander Whyte's edition (Edinburgh: Oliphant, Anderson & Ferrier, 1896), to which is prefixed an admirable 'Biography' and still more admirable 'Interpretation'.

[5] Printed in Vol. 2 of Heber's edition of his *Works.*

[6] An edition is published by the Presbyterian Board of Publication, and another in Methuen's series of Devotional Books.

[7] Dr Bonar's edition is the best (New York: Carter): cf. Dr A. Whyte's *Samuel Rutherford and Some of His Correspondents.* The Messrs. Longmans publish an excellent selection from the letters, edited by Miss Lucy M. Soulsby, under the title of *Christ and His Cross.*

grim's Ptogress;[1] Sir Thomas Brownes *Religio Medici;*[2] William Law's *Serious Call;*[3] John Newton's *Cardiphonia;*[4] Bishop Thomas Wilson's *Sacra Privata.*[5] To these twelve I should add two or three others which have peculiar interest to us as Princetonians, and which I am sure are worthy of association with them—Jonathan Edwards' *Treatise Concerning Religious Affections,* Archibald Alexander's *Thoughts on Religious Experience,* and Charles Hodge's *Way of Life.*

I have purposely omitted from this list collections of hymns and (in general) of prayers, in order that I might recommend the use of both to you in a separate category. I strongly advise you to make yourselves familiar with the best religious verse, and occasionally to support your devotions with the best prayers to which saintly men have given permanent form. Faber's *Hymns* have a quality of intense adoration in them which recommends them to many as the best for such a purpose: Miss Rosetti's devotional poems are unsurpassed for elevation of feeling: many prefer the quieter note of Keble's *Christian Year:* others still love best the evangelical sobriety of *The Olney Hymns,* or the exotic flavour of Miss Winkworth's *Lyra Sacra Germanica:* others find more attractive the variety afforded by such a book as Dr Schaff's *Christ in Song.* On the whole, I fancy most of you will find that Palgrave's *Treasury of Sacred Song* will meet your needs as well as any other single volume: it is a veritable treasure-house of the best of English religious poetry. As to collections of prayers, nothing is more inspiring than Lancelot Andrewes' *Private Devotions,* which I have already named in the general list of recommended devotional books, unless it be Anselm's *Meditations and Prayers,*[6] which, despite the deforming hagiolatry which sometimes invades them, remain

[1] A good edition is issued by the Presbyterian Board of Publication.
[2] *The Golden Treasury* edition (Macmillan) is particularly to be recommended.
[3] Get the edition in Dent's *Temple Classics.*
[4] An edition is printed by the Presbyterian Board of Publication.
[5] Keble's edition (Oxford, 1860) is the standard. A good edition is Bishop Wilson's *Sacra Privata,* edited by A. E. Burn, B.D. (London: Methuen, 1903).
[6] An English translation, with prefatory matter by Dr Pusey, was published at Oxford in 1856. A good edition is that of London, 1872. The latest edition, *The Devotions of St Anselm,* edited by C. C. J. Webb, M.A. (London: Methuen, 1903), contains only (along witb the *Proslogion* and some letters) four each of the *Meditations* and *Prayers.*

an example for all ages of how a great heart lifts itself up greatly to
God.

There is yet another branch of religious reading which I think you
will scarcely be able to neglect, if you would build yourself up into
the full stature of manhood in Christ by the example of his saints. I
refer to religious biography. Only let us remember that in selecting
religious biographies to read with a view to our spiritual improvement, we must bear in mind that the adjective must be understood as
qualifying the *Life* as well as the life: it must be the biographies themselves that are religious. It must be confessed that many of the greatest
saints have been unfortunate in their biographers. Not only are their
lives often written without a particle of literary skill, but equally often
much of the religious impression of their holy walk has evaporated in
the telling. Nevertheless, from at least the time when the great Athanasius himself edified the church with a life of Anthony—written, we
fear, not without some imitation in form and content alike of the
popular romances of the time[1]—the church has never lacked a series
of religious biographies which have in them the promise and potency
of religious life for their readers. Dr Stalker thinks the best of these
for your use are Augustine's *Confessions,* Baxter's *Reliques,* Hanna's *Life
of Chalmers,* Blaikie's *Life of Livingstone,* Witte's *Life of Tholuck,* and
Brown's *Life of Rabbi Duncan.* The late Dr William M. Taylor recommended Bonar's *Memoirs of M'Cheyne,* Hanna's *Life of Chalmers,*
Arnot's *Memoir of James Hamilton,* Guthrie's *Memoirs,* Blaikie's *Life of
Livingstone,* J. G. Paton's *Autobiography,* and Dr Prentiss' *Life and Letters of Mrs Prentiss.* You will not fail to observe how Scotch Dr Taylor's
list is. Tastes will differ: the late Dean Goulburn wrote me simply
that there were no religious biographies equal to Isaac Walton's. I shall
not undertake to add a list of my own, which doubtless would have
its peculiarities also. I shall content myself with a bare hint that you
must not miss reading the great books. Such, for example, is Bunyan's
Grace Abounding—the seventeenth century replica of Augustine's
Confessions. Such also is John Newton's *Authentic Narrative.* Such also
is Boston's *Memoirs,* which can now be had in a worthy form.[2] Such,

[1] See a very interesting essay on 'Greek and Early Christian Novels', pp. 357 *sqq.* of
Mr T. R. Glover's *Life and Letters in the Fourth Century* (Cambridge, 1901).
[2] Edited by Rev. G. H. Morrison (Edinburgh: Oliphant, Anderson & Ferrier, 1899).

also, is probably Doddridge's account of James Gardiner's remarkable life. And such certainly is Edwards' *Life of David Brainerd*. And if I am to judge by my own experience of its religious impression, such also is the *Life of Adolph Monod* by one of his daughters.

Along with religious biography may I venture to mention also religious fiction—the portrayal of the religious life under the cover of imagined actors? Take the *Chronicles of the Schoenberg-Cotta Family*. Take the *Heir of Redcliffe*. Who in the face of the experience of a generation can doubt the quickening influence of such books? A book that has played a part such as that played by the *Heir of Redcliffe* in the lives of men like Dr A. Kuyper and Mr William Morris is surely worthy of our serious attention as a religious force in the world. And speaking of these books brings to my lips the exclamation, 'What women the church of Victorian England gave the world! Elizabeth Rundell Charles, Charlotte Mary Yonge, Frances Ridley Havergal, Dora Greenwell, Dora Pattison—the *Lives* of all of these are accessible to you as well as their writings, though some of them, I am sorry to say, are rather dully written. Put them by the side of the *Life of Mrs Prentiss* recommended to us by Dr Taylor, and learn from them what women Christianity is still making all around us.

Of *Sermons* I shall say nothing: they form a department of religious literature by themselves. But I have reserved for the last mention a class of religious literature which, for my own part, I esteem the very highest of all for spiritual impression. I refer to the great creeds of the church. He who wishes to grow strong in his religious life, let him, I say, next to the Bible, feed himself on the great creeds of the church. There is a, force of religious inspiration in them which you will seek in vain elsewhere. And this for good reasons. First, because it is ever true that it is *by the truth that sanctification is wrought*. And next, because the truth is set forth in these creeds with *a clearness and richness* with which it is set forth nowhere else. For these creeds are not the products of metaphysical speculation, as many who know infinitesimally little about them are prone to assert, but are the compressed and weighted utterances of the Christian heart. I am not alone, of course, in so esteeming them. You will remember with what insistence Cardinal Newman warns us against 'an untheological devotion', and with what force he expounds in his *Grammar of Assent* the spiritual import of the creeds and catechisms of the church. For himself, he tells us, the Athanasian Creed has always seemed the most devotional formulary that Christianity has ever given birth to; and certainly readers of Dr Gore's beautiful exposition of it as 'the Battle-hymn of Christians' will not be slow to feel the truth of Dr Newman's estimate. Dr Alexander Whyte, in commenting on Andrewes' *Private Devotions,* takes up the theme afresh and remarks on the exemplification it receives in Andrewes' treatment of the Apostles' and Nicene Creeds. 'When Andrewes takes up any of these things', he observes, 'into his intellect, imagination and heart, he has already provided himself and his readers with another great prayer and another great psalm. So true is it that all true theology is directly and richly and evangelically devotional.'

I do not think I go astray, therefore, when I say to you in all seriousness that the second and third volumes of Dr Schaff's *Creeds of Christendom* have in them more food for your spiritual life—are 'more directly, richly and evangelically devotional'—than any other book, apart from the Bible, in existence. Nor can I think myself wrong in directing you specifically to the Reformed creeds as, above all others, charged with blessing to those who will read and meditate on their rich deposit of religions truth. Our Scotch forefathers turned for spiritual nourishment especially to the *Sum of Saving Knowledge and the Practical Use Thereof,* which had come to be a stated portion of the current editions of the Confession of Faith, just because that volume circulated at first chiefly as a devotional book and a directory for practical religion. This treatise has never been a part of our 'Church Book'. But in the Westminster Confession we have something even better. Read what Dr Thornwell tells us of what the study of the Confession did for his soul,[1] and then ask yourselves whether it may not do the same for you too. By the side of the Westminster Confession put the Heidelberg Catechism: where will you find more faithful, more probing Christian teaching than this? I beg you, Brethren, feed your souls on the Christian truth set forth with so much combined clearness of apprehension and depth of feeling in these great formularies.

And so we come around at the end to the point from which we took our start. Religious knowledge and religious living go hand in

[1] See Palmer's *Life of Thornwell,* pp. 162, 165.

hand. 'It might be instructive to inquire', writes good Dr Andrew A. Bonar,[1]

> why it is that whenever godliness is healthy and progressive we almost invariably find learning in the church attendant on it: while, on the other hand, an illiterate state is attended sooner or later by decay of vital godliness.

We deceive ourselves if we think we can give a portion of our being only to God. If we withhold the effort requisite to learn to know the truth, we cannot hope to succeed in any effort to do his will. Unknown truth cannot sanctify the soul; and it is by the truth that we are to be sanctified. Mind, heart, and hand—true religious cultivation must embrace them all and carry on their training all together. We must indeed rebuke the lordly understanding if it essays to supersede the necessity of holy living. Our heart thrills responsively when the monk of Deventer, at the opening of his pungent book, asks us pointedly, How will it advantage you to know all things if you have no love?

> 'What is the profit', he demands, 'of high argument on the Trinity if you lack humility and are offensive to the Trinity? Great words assuredly make no man holy and righteous, but by virtuous living he becomes dear to God. Far better feel compulsion than have skill in defining it. Though you know the whole Bible and all the sayings of the philosophers, what would it all advantage you without God's love and grace? It is natural to man to desire knowledge; but knowledge without the fear of God—of what avail is it?'

Yes, yes, our hearts reply: it is all true, greatly true! But beneath our assent does there not lurk an underlying sense, as we read on deeper into the exhortation, that there is something of the narrowness of mysticism in the sharp 'either/or' that is thrust upon us? If we must choose between knowledge and life, why of course give us life! But why put the alternative so sharply? Must it be knowledge *or* life? Must it not rather be knowledge *and* life? *Non comprehenditur Deus per investigationem sed per imitationem,*[2] says Hugh of St Cher. Ah,

[1] Introduction to his ed. of *Rutherford's Letters,* NY, 1851, p. xvi.
[2] God is not apprehended by investigation but by imitation.

but 'investigation' is the first step in 'imitation'; for how shall I strive
to be like God, except by first discovering what God is like? And
'imitation' itself—is it after all the key word of Christianity? It is, no
doubt, a great word. But it is not the greatest. 'Trust' is greater. And
by the side of 'trust' there stand but two others. 'But now abideth',
says Paul, 'faith, hope, love, these three; and the greatest of these is
love.'

Happily we have not been left to ourselves to make the correction.
The church has had greater teachers than even Thomas à Kempis.
And a greater than he begins a greater book than his with greater
words than he could give us:

> Great art Thou, O Lord, and highly to be praised; great is Thy power
> and Thy understanding is infinite. Yet Thee would man praise—
> though but a little particle of Thy creation: even man, who bears
> about with him his mortality, bears about with him the proof of his
> sin, even the proof that Thou resisteth the proud: yea, Thee still would
> man praise, this little particle of Thy creation. 'Tis Thou that dost
> excite us to delight in Thy praise; for Thou didst make us for Thyself
> and our heart is restless till it find its rest in Thee. Grant me, Lord, to
> know whether I should first call upon Thee or praise Thee; whether I
> should first know Thee, or call upon Thee . . . Alas! Alas! tell me for
> Thy mercies' sake, O Lord, my God, what Thou art unto me. Say unto
> my soul, 'I am thy salvation.' So speak that I may hear. Behold, the
> ears of my heart are before Thee, O Lord: open Thou them and say to
> my soul, 'I am thy salvation.' Make me to run after Thy voice and lay
> hold on Thee. Hide not Thy face from me. Let me die that I die not:
> only let me see Thy face. Narrow is my soul's house; enlarge Thou it,
> that Thou mayest enter in. It is fallen into ruins: repair Thou it. There
> is that within it which must offend Thine eyes: I confess, I know it.
> But who shall cleanse it? Or to whom but to Thee shall I cry?'

Here, I venture to say, is the essence of all true religion. *Humility of
spirit is here rather than depreciation of intellect:* trust in the mercy of
God to sinners rather than dependence on deeds of man. There is no
such note struck here as this: 'Even though I knew everything in all
the world and were not in charity, what would it advantage me in the
sight of God, who will judge me *ex facto*.' *Ex facto* indeed! Who that

is judged by his works shall stand? It is not an antithesis of knowledge and works that Augustine draws. It is an antithesis of man and God; and its note is, 'In thee only do I put my trust, O Lord, for in thee only is there salvation.' *Dic 'Habeo'*, says he tersely, *sed, 'Ab Eo.'*[1] It is an execrable word play, but excellent theology, and the very quintessence of religion. And when we have learned this well,—learned it so that it sounds in all the chambers of our hearts and echoes down through all the aisles of our lives,—we shall have learned the great lesson of practical religion.

[1] Say 'I have', but, 'from Him'.

THE SIGNIFICANCE OF
THE WESTMINSTER STANDARDS
AS A CREED[1]

FATHERS and Brethren:—it would be difficult for me adequately to express the pleasure which it gives me to respond to your invitation to join with you today in celebrating the fifth jubilee of the gift of the Westminster Standards to the world. The task you have laid upon me, of seeking to set forth the significance of that gift, though it has its difficulties arising from its magnitude, cannot fail to appeal powerfully to one who has, in all sincerity and heartiness, set his hand to these Standards as 'containing the system of doctrine taught in the Holy Scriptures'. It is not merely a duty but a pleasure to bear witness to the truth of God as we apprehend it, and to give a reason from time to time for the faith that is in us. I cannot, indeed, hope to tell over today all that the Westminster Standards are to us—to unfold in detail all that has for two centuries and a half made them precious to a body of Christians who have been second to none in intelligence of conviction, evangelistic zeal and faithfulness of confession. But if I were to essay to express in one word what it is in them which has proved so perennial a source of strength to generation after generation of Christian men, and which causes us still to cling to them with a devotion no less intelligent than passionate, I think I should but voice your own conviction were I to say that it is because these precious documents appeal to us as but the embodiment in fitly chosen language of the pure gospel of the grace of God. The high

---

[1] B. B. Warfield, *The Significance of the Westminster Standards as a Creed. An Address Delivered before the Presbytery of New York, November 8, 1897, on the occasion of the celebration of the Two Hundred and Fiftieth Anniversary of the Completion of the Westminster Standards* (New York: Charles Scribner's Sons, 1898).

value that we attach to them and that leads us to gather here today to remember with gratitude before God the men who gave them to us, and to thank God for this supreme product of their labours, is but the reflection of our conviction that in these forms of words we possess the most complete, the most fully elaborated and carefully guarded, the most perfect, and the most vital expression that has ever been framed by the hand of man, of all that enters into what we call evangelical religion, and of all that must be safeguarded if evangelical religion is to persist in the world.

How they came to be this, it is to be my task this afternoon to attempt to recall to our remembrance.

I. It is a humbling exercise to reflect on *the difficulty which has been experienced by the gospel of God's grace—or evangelical religion, as we currently call it nowadays—in establishing and preserving itself in the world.* The proclamation of this gospel constitutes the main burden of the scriptural revelation. And, after the varied and insistent statement which it received at the hands of the great company of inspired men whose writings make up the complex of the Scriptures—and especially after its rich prophetic announcement by Isaiah; its marvellous exposition in the language of living fact in the fourfold narrative of the life of Jesus; its full dialectical development and explanation by Paul, as over against almost every possible misconception; its poignant assertion by John, cut with the sharpness and polished to the brilliancy of a gem—one might well suppose that it had been made the permanent possession of men, etched into the very substance of human thought with such boldness that even he that ran could not fail to read it, with such depth that it could never again be erased or obscured. But it was not so. There is no other such gulf in the history of human thought as that which is cleft between the apostolic and the immediately succeeding ages. To pass from the latest apostolic writings to the earliest compositions of uninspired Christian pens, is to fall through such a giddy height that it is no wonder if we rise dazed and almost unable to determine our whereabouts. Here is the great fault—as the geologists would say—in the history of Christian doctrine. There is every evidence of continuity—but, oh, at how much lower a level! The rich vein of evangelical religion has run well-nigh out; and, though there are masses of apostolic origin lying everywhere, they are but fragments, and are evidently only the talus which has fallen from the cliffs above and scattered itself over the lowered surface. Thus it came about that the deposit of divine truth in the apostolic revelation did not supply the starting-point of the development of doctrine in the church, but has rather from the beginning stood before it as the goal to which it was painfully to climb.

Through how many ages men needed to struggle slowly upward before they even measurably recovered the lost elevation! No doubt the essence of evangelical religion remained the implicit possession of every truly Christian heart, and this implicit presence of so great a light lent a glow to every Christian age. No doubt the constituent elements of evangelical doctrine found disjointedly more or less explicit recognition at the hands of every really great Christian thinker, and we may piece these fragments together into a mosaic picture of the real Christian heart of each period. No doubt there persisted everywhere and always an instinctive protest, fed by the Word and quickened by the demands of the Christian life, against the deteriorated conceptions of the day; and this protest flared up from time to time into a flame of vehement resistance to some more than usually widespread, or some more than usually aggressive, or some more than usually deadly assault upon some essential element of that truth by which alone men could live, and would not be allayed until the whole truth in question had been brought to clear consciousness and guarded expression. Early monuments of such struggles for fundamental elements of evangelical religion we possess in those forms of sound words which we know as the Nicene Creed and the Chalcedonian Formulary, in which the evangelical doctrines of the Trinity in unity and of the person of Christ receive such lucid, comprehensive, and circumspect statement as has safeguarded them through all subsequent time, and against every hitherto conceivable encroachment of misbelief. But it was not until four centuries had dragged by that, in reaction upon an incredibly audacious onslaught upon the very core of evangelical religion, the church was enabled to rise upon the broad and strong wings of a great religious genius, to something like a full-orbed apprehension of the treasures she possessed in the gospel of God's grace.

Augustine compassed for her the privilege of this splendid vision, and for a season she basked in its glory. But what that generation thus achieved, it lacked the power fully to secure for its successors. It fixed its own attainments in no firmly outlined and detailed formulary of ecumenical authority; and it had not itself passed away before the lines drawn so sharply and boldly by the master hand of Augustine began to fade again out of the consciousness of men. We can trace the increasing obscuration from age to age. Not more than a century had elapsed before the tenacity and distinctness with which the gospel in its entirety was grasped had so far relaxed, that it was possible even for the best Christians of the time, men like the great and good Cæsarius, to betray it into one of those futile and fatal compromises with its persistent enemy which have proved in all ages the snare of good men and the ruin of the truth. No wonder that three centuries later it lay languishing and dying in chains in the person of one who nobly bore the fit name of the 'Servant of God',[1] and to whose honour, as to a light shining in a dark place, we should do well to pause to pay some grateful tribute today. Then the pall of ecclesiasticism was dragged over the corpse, and the dense primeval night seemed to have settled again upon the face of the earth.

But it is a long night that knows no dawn; and just when the darkness seemed most hopeless, a streak of light appears again on the horizon and the sun springs suddenly up and climbs the heavens. The Reformation we call it: Zwingli, Luther, Calvin, these are its heralds; and what it really is is the gospel of God's grace brought back to earth. Ah! how men greet it! Crushed under the weight of their sin, with nothing but their poor, human strength to lift it, and nought reached to their help but the hand of a church much too obviously human, how joyously they welcome again the outstretched hand of God! And how the glad news spreads until all Europe is filled with its echo, and men everywhere rise from the ashes of their despondency, stretch themselves awake, put on new courage, and go forward in the hope of God. Surely now, we will say, flung into the midst of this mass of awakened men, with the memory of their despair fresh on them and the experience of their deliverance keen in their hearts, the gospel has come to stay. But no: the clouds at once gather again. Melancthon himself, trusted helper and worthy companion

---

[1] *Fulgentius Gotteschalcus:* 'illustrious servant of God'.

of Luther, first systematic expounder of the newly recovered gospel, Melancthon himself readmits the old 'evil leaven of synergism', and, amid the turmoils that ensue, the Lutheran churches succeed in only partially recovering the lost ground. They are able, accordingly, to establish themselves, not on the pure gospel of the grace of God, but as their *Formula Concordiae* witnesses, only on a somewhat neutral territory over which the old humanitarianism could urge some sort of claim. Thus these churches lost the hope of giving its final and complete formulation to the principles of evangelical religion.

Meanwhile, in the grace of God, better things were being wrought by the Reformed. They it was who were most cruelly ground under the heel of the oppressor; they it was, consequently, who most passionately cast their hearts' hope upon the God of salvation. And so, all over the Reformed world, voices were raised giving expression to the doctrines of grace with a fulness, a richness, an absoluteness never before known. Reformed confessions sprang up everywhere in a luxuriant growth, written often by the hands of martyrs, wet always with their blood, and each and all declaring through martyr lips, which spoke not only in the fear of God but out of ardent love to him, and face to face as dying men with their Judge and their Redeemer, all the words of this life.

It is a century of struggle and suffering which is distilled into these confessions—a century of patient endurance and faithful testimony which, in their glowing and uncompromising language, speaks out, with a firmness and clearness and fulness never before attained, the principles of that gospel by which alone the soul can live, and the full sweetness and strength of which men taste only in times like those. At last the gospel had come to its rights; at last men seemed to have laid hold upon it with a clearness of apprehension and an ardour of embrace which could never more be loosed.

But the treasure was not even yet to be retained without a final and supreme struggle. One evil had hitherto been spared the Reformed churches. Every conceivable assault had been made upon them from without, but no serious internal treason had as yet endangered the purity of their confession. With the second century of their existence even this trial was to fall upon them. It came in what we know as the Remonstrant Controversy, in which the old humanitarian conceptions, the violent assertion of which had been the occasion of Augustine's republication of the gospel of grace, and by the more measured and subtle working of which evangelical religion had been gradually throttled in the Latin church, reappeared in the very bosom of the Reformed churches themselves and jeopardized the purity of their assertion of the gospel. We all know how the new danger was transcended. Met in ecumenical synod at Dort, the Reformed churches gave renewed and serious consideration, in the light of Scripture alone, to those elements of evangelical religion to which exception had been taken, and with one tongue, voicing the testimony of the whole Reformed world, bore their solemn witness to them as essential elements in the gospel of God's grace. But the end was not even yet. Transferred to English ground, the assault was continued for a third of a century longer under circumstances which gave it the highest conceivable force and speciousness. Here sacerdotalism, in the form of Anglican prelacy, presented itself in the disguise of the Reformed religion itself. Here humanitarianism put on the garments of light, allied itself with religious fervour, and ran up by insensible stages into a mysticism which confounded human claims with the very voice of God. This is the meaning of what we call the Puritan conflict which, from the theological side, was nothing else than the last deadly struggle of evangelical religion—the gospel of God's grace—to preserve itself pure and sweet and clean in the midst of the most insidious attacks which could be brought against it—attacks, the strength of which resided just in the fact that now its old-time foes approached it with the sword in hand, indeed, and with no loss of their undying hatred, but under its own banner and clothed in its own uniform.

It was a battle to the death; and the arts of war could not but be learned in its progress. To meet so protean a foe, attacking at every point with weapons of unexampled fineness and tactics of unimagined subtlety, a skill of fence and a wariness of defence unknown before were necessarily developed; and, with them, those high qualities which underlie them—keenness of perception, clearness of vision, firmness of purpose, accuracy of aim, precision of movement straight to the essential goal. Men trained in this school could not be content with merely general statements of the truth by which they lived, and which would long since have been wrested from them had they held to it with only a broad and, therefore, loose grasp. In the strenuousness of the conflict they had not only learned how to state the gospel sharply, distinctly, precisely; they had, so to speak, lost the power of stating it otherwise than with clearness and exactitude and force. As well expect the veteran fresh from the wars to bungle in his fence; nay, his blade takes instinctively the correct attitude of guard, and eye and wrist move in such organic harmony that it would be only with an effort that either could prove false to its fellow. As well expect the mountaineer who has trodden the peaks from infancy to stumble heavily over his arrêtes and passes; he knows not how to do otherwise than to step cleanly and surely and firmly, and he instinctively plants his feet where they cannot be moved. So, when this company of Puritan pastors was gathered from the parishes of England which they had saved for the gospel, and was bidden, 'Write down this gospel', they could not do otherwise than write it down with that rich completeness which had nourished their own souls and the souls of their flocks in those times of conflict and often almost of despair, and with that precision in which alone it could preserve its integrity and power in the face of the violent and insidious foes to the attacks of which it had been, in their own experience, exposed.

It is because the Westminster Standards are the product of such men, working under such circumstances, that they embody the gospel of the grace of God with a carefulness, a purity, and an exactness never elsewhere achieved, and come to us as, historically, the final fixing in confessional language of the principles and teachings of evangelical religion. Sixteen centuries of struggle toward the pure apprehension of the gospel lay behind them, culminating in that ultimate proclamation of evangelical truth which we call the Reformation. More specifically, a hundred and fifty years of the development of Reformed theology lay behind them, culminating in the vindication of the purity of the gospel by the Reformed world as over against the Remonstrant adulterations.

Most specifically of all, there lay behind them the half-century of the Puritan conflict—a half century of working and polishing the jewel of the gospel beneath every hammer that the cruelty of men, and every chisel and file that the ingenuity of men could devise, until it was beaten and cut into the most compact and sharply outlined possible expression of the pure gospel of the grace of God. It is to these historical conditions of their origin that the Westminster Standards owe their high significance and value. Historically speaking, this is the significance of the Westminster Standards as a creed.

II. But when we thus say that the historical origin of the Westminster Standards operated directly to give them peculiar completeness and precision as a statement of the gospel, that is as much as to say that *they appeal to us not more because they are historically the ultimate crystallization of the principles of evangelical religion, than because of the high scientific perfection which they attain, considered as a product of human thought, in their statement of these principles.* The scientific quality of the Chalcedonian Formulary, for example, was not due to any speculative interest dominating the minds of its framers, nor to any singular speculative ability characterizing them, but to the thoroughness with which the whole problem with which the document deals was threshed out in the course of the keen and prolonged controversies which preceded its formulation and prepared the material for its use. This effect is not best expressed by representing the vital processes which go on in a long discussion, affecting the basis of the religious life, as simulating in their results a scientific product; it would be more nearly correct to conceive the processes of scientific statement as imitating, and that at a considerable interval, the work of organic controversy.

The scientific investigator makes all due effort carefully to consider every possible solution of the problem brought before him, candidly to weigh every conceivable element which may affect the result, and thoroughly to canvass every combination of the elements possible to imagine; and he hopes, by strenuous diligence, watchful impartiality and thorough manipulation of his material, to reach a result which will do full justice to all considerations, and which will therefore stand permanently in the face of all criticism. But it would seem to be obvious that such a sifting and weighing cannot go on in a single coolly working mind with anything like the same searching completeness, or ultimate in anything like the same perfection of result, as when they take place in the cauldron of an aroused and deeply moved mass of men striving earnestly to comprehend and express the elements of their faith. Scientific construction, therefore, bears to vital processes in this sphere, too, very much the same relation as in chemical synthesis: not until the manipulation of the laboratory can outdo the subtle alchemy of life can we expect scientific care to surpass living controversy in producing a truly scientific statement of vital truth. Whenever the elements cast into the crucible of life include all those that enter into the case, and the ferment is violent enough and sufficiently long continued, we may expect the ultimate eliminations and combinations to be in the highest sense natural—that is to run on the lines of essential rightness—and the final crystallization to be a scientific product of the first quality. It is to the fact that just this was the process by which the Westminster Standards came into being that they owe their high scientific character.

For, consider how richly represented in the religious life of Europe during the formative period of the Reformed theology, and especially in the religious life of Britain during the era when the Westminster theology was in preparation, were all those constructions which can with any show of attractiveness be given to the Christian religion. I think it may be said that there are only three main forms in which this religion may be plausibly presented to the acceptance of men; which can acquire—certainly which have ever acquired—a completeness, a self-consistency, a power of presentation, such as tend to give them any extended empire over men's minds. We may, for our convenience, label these the Sacerdotal, the Humanitarian, and the Evangelical gospel; and it is among them that the battle of the faith must needs be fought out. Possibly there never will be a time when all three will not, in one form or another, be represented in the world; certainly up to today, and apparently as far into the future as our conjecture can penetrate, the supreme task of each has been and will continue to be to make good its position as over against the other two, and to protect its territory from absorption by them. Every attack that has ever been made, or apparently can ever be made, upon evangelical religion—be it as violent or as insidious as it may—will, on analysis, be found to be a more or less gross, or a more or less subtle, manifestation of one or the other of these opposing tendencies. No statement of evangelical religion can stand, therefore, which does not differentiate it, and in differentiating protect it, from these its two perennial and ever-encroaching foes. And the statement that does perfectly differentiate it from them both will be the highest and most perfect scientific statement of which evangelical religion is capable.

It was thus incident to the historical circumstances of their origin that the Westminster Standards should attain the high water mark of a differentiated statement of the elements of evangelical religion. For the most complete and the most powerful embodiment of the sacerdotal tendency is found, of course, in the Church of Rome; and never was this tendency so active in its propaganda, so impassioned, so filled with the courage of intense conviction and utter devotion as in those days of the Counter Reformation, when the Jesuit hosts flung themselves into the work of recovering every inch of the ground lost in the Protestant revolt with a fiery zeal and a fertility of resource which remain until today the wonder and example of the world. And while the most complete embodiment of the humanitarian tendency is to be sought in more extreme developments, such as for example Socinianism or rationalizing naturalism, to the workings of which the Reformed churches were no strangers; its most effective elaboration within the limits of a church claiming to believe in God and his Christ has ever exhibited itself in that great middle system which under the name of Semi-Pelagianism early allied itself with Roman ecclesiasticism and in later Romanism became the characterizing feature of the Jesuit theology, and which broke out afresh in the churches of the Reformation in the forms of Lutheran synergism and Remonstrant humanism and sought to poison the fountains of evangelical religion in their sources. The simple enumeration of these facts will serve to indicate the fires in which the Reformed theology was forged. It would have been a marvel had it emerged from its century of conflict with these forces without having been beaten into something like shape. There was indeed but a single alternative open: that it should be crushed out of existence and pounded into the dust that is spurned by the foot of man, or else that it should come forth from the forging compacted into adamant and polished into perfection.

And yet the process of the forging of that exquisite product of scientific theology which we call the Westminster Standards is but half revealed when we recite these broad facts. It was under those hammers that the Reformed theology was beaten into that perfected shape in which it lay in the minds of its adherents throughout Europe in the seventeenth century. Thus it was fashioned into the noble shape in which it was spoken out by the assembled Reformed world at the Synod of Dort or by the Swiss theologians in their Formula Consensus; and thus it would have been spoken out in every centre of Reformed life in all Europe, from Scotland to Hungary. It was already in a high and true sense a finished product. But in a higher and finer sense there was a finish yet to be given it: a finish which could be acquired only by passage through the yet more severe ordeal that awaited it on English ground. There can be no need to recite again the details of the story of how narrow the lines were there drawn within which he must walk who would preserve his good confession: of how sacerdotalism seized the reins of the Reformed Church of England itself and drove rough-shod over the hearts and consciences of her only faithful children; of how, in the dreadful confusion of the times, humanitarian self-assertiveness obtained control of some of the finest spiritual sinew in the land and set it to demolishing the foundations of the gospel. No wonder that many of the very elect were deceived and lost the purity of their testimony. But no wonder, on the other hand, that those who endured, because—how else?—they saw the Invisible One and in the light of that vision were enabled to keep the word of God's patience, emerged from the ordeal as from a furnace seven times heated, purified and refined and shaking the very smell of the smoke from their undefiled garments. These were they, who, sitting in solemn conclave in the Jerusalem Chamber, gave forth that serious expression of the faith by which they lived which we call the Westminster Standards; and this is the reason why this, their enunciation of the elements of the gospel of God's grace, has a perfection of finish upon it elsewhere unattained,—which could not have been equalled by the work of any other body of men then on the face of the earth, which we can never hope to surpass, and which we can lightly lose or rashly cast from us only when our grasp upon evangelical religion becomes weak or our love for it grows cold.

It belongs to the very essence of the situation that an enunciation of the elements of the gospel, springing out of such conditions, should be supremely well guarded from the sides of both its most obdurate foes,—between which it was at the time, only by the great-est circumspection, preserving itself from being crushed, as between the upper and nether millstones. No wonder, then, that even the most cursory reader of the Westminster Standards is impressed with the exquisite precision and balance of their statements, with the clearness and purity with which they bring out just the essence of the gospel, and the drastic thoroughness with which they separate from it every remainder of sacerdotal and humanitarian leaven. To read over a chapter or two of the Westminster Confession gives one fresh from the obscurities and confusions of much modern theo-logical discussion a mental feeling very nearly akin to the physical sensation of washing one's hands and face after a hot hour's work. Here the truth is shelled out clean. No doubt there are those whose perverted appetites seem to like more or less chaff in their bread, and who may therefore manage to take offence at this very perfection of statement. And it may be easy to find fault with what we may be pleased to call the polemic flavour of documents so formulated, and to ask whether it is not time to smooth out the frowns of war from our countenance and to speak out our testimony to the gospel of love with the unbroken serenity of a universal peace. As if truth could ever be stated without offence to falsehood: as if the very essence of defini-tion lay not in exclusion: as if it were not self-evident that perfect and clean inclusion must always work equally perfect and clean exclusion, and the more complete and perfect the exclusion the more complete and perfect the definition. The wall that protects the citadel must needs be too narrow in its compass to enclose the foeman's camp as well: the flask that preserves the precious essence must needs be tight enough to shut out corrupting germs. The Westminster fathers placed nothing in their Standards which they did not think worth fighting for,—nay, which they had not already been called upon to fight for; and it marks the height of their service that they have given it a form securely guarded on every side, on the well-polished surface of which, in particular, the chiefest and most persistent foes of the gospel will seek in vain for a foothold.

So long, then, as the leavens of Sacerdotalism and Humanitarian-ism—of externality in religion and of dependence on flesh—remain, in one form or another, the most dangerous perils to which the gospel is exposed (and it would seem as if this must be as long as human nature endures), so long the statement given the gospel of grace in the Westminster Standards must remain the ultimate scientific enunciation of the principles of evangelical religion. In the same sense in which the Nicene and Athanasian creeds attained the final expression of the doctrine of the Trinity, and the Chalcedonian definition the final expression of the doctrine of the person of Christ, the Westminster Standards attained the final expression of the elements of evangelical religion.

Of course, nothing like divine inspiration is attributed to any of these documents; nor is it necessary to invoke any special or peculiar divine superintendence over their production, though he who believes in a God will not fail to perceive his providential working, nor will he who believes in the God of the Bible fail to perceive the fulfilment of his promises, in such supreme products of human thought on divine things as these. What we discover on the surface of these documents, however, is the product of historical processes and of historical conditions which not only enabled but compelled their framers firmly to grasp in all their relations and clearly, cleanly, and guardedly to express the truths with which they deal. They mark, in a word, epochs in the history of human reflection on the truths of the gospel—epochs in the attainment and registry of special truths; and they, therefore, in the nature of the case, give these special truths their complete and final scientific expression. All subsequent attempts to restate them can but repeat these older statements—which were struck out when the fires were hot and the iron was soft—or else fall helplessly away from the purity of their conceptions or the justness of their language. In this fact resides, scientifically speaking, the significance of the Westminster Standards as a creed.

III. *It is sufficiently clear that a scientific statement of truth, originating in the manner described and owing its scientific character not merely to closet reflection but to the interaction of the varied interests and requirements of men's souls, need not—nay, cannot—lack in vital quality.*

It will necessarily bear in its very fibre a colouring from the heart. A product of the intensest intellectual activity, and exhibiting in its forms of statement the niceties of scientific construction, it is nevertheless the product of intellect working only under impulse from and dictation of the heart, and in its very forms of statement will be the vehicle of the expression of the needs and attainments of the spiritual life. And thus it comes about that the Westminster Standards appeal to us not merely as, historically, the deposited faith of the best age of evangelical development, and not merely as, scientifically, the most thoroughly thought out and most carefully guarded statement ever penned of the elements of evangelical religion, but also as, vitally, filled with the expressed essence and breathing the finest fragrance of spiritual religion.

They gravely err who picture to themselves the fathers to whom we owe the formulation of any of the great doctrines of our religion as dominated by merely speculative interests, or nerved for their task mainly by metaphysical considerations. It has never been so. Restless speculation and philosophical pretension have ever been rather the boasts and, let us frankly admit it, the characteristic possessions of the purveyors of heresies and the fomenters of those fatal conciliations with the thought of the world which have, from the beginning, been the bane of the church and one of the most serious perils of the gospel. It is not only in the infancy of Christianity that it has been a true testimony that 'not many wise are called'. A certain speculative inertness, we might almost say, has marked the church, and even those to whom God, in his providence, has committed the formulation of its treasures of truth, until, goaded into action by intolerable assaults on the very penetralium of their spiritual life, their minds have taken fire from their hearts and risen to compass and proclaim the elements of the higher wisdom of God. The accents which smite our ears, out of our creeds, with such tremendous emphasis do not indicate the crisp, cold, sharp movements of mere intellection; they are the pulsations of great hearts heaving in emotion and rising to the assertion of the precious truth by which they live. If we read them as merely speculative discriminations, the fault lies in us, not in them. It is because our hearts cannot, like theirs, stand up and answer, 'We have felt!'[1]

---

[1] 'A warmth within the breast would melt
   The freezing reason's colder part,
And like a man in wrath the heart
   Stood up and answer'd, 'I have felt!'
         —*In Memoriam*, cxxiv.

The scoffer who mocks, for example, at the Nicene Fathers wrangling over a mere iota in framing their definition of the Trinitarian relation,[1] but uncovers the poverty of his own spiritual life and betrays the shallowness of his own religious experience. He that knows his Lord, that has in his periods of despair fled to his sheltering arms and in his periods of comfort rested upon his bosom, I do not say will not, I say cannot, abate one jot or one tittle of his passionate assertion of his divine majesty. We treat these cleanly cut and nicely balanced phrases as if they were intellectualistic scales weighing minute differences of merely speculative import, only because, and only so long as, we have not vitally experienced the spiritual truths which underlie them, to which they give just expression and for which they form the bulwarks. 'Nothing could be more mistaken', says Professor Sabatier in one of his lapses into sound reason,[2]

> than to represent the Fathers of the councils or the members of the synods as theorists, or even as professional theologians, brought together in conference by speculative zeal alone in order to resolve metaphysical enigmas. They were men of action, not of speculation; courageous priests and pastors who thought of their work as like that of soldiers in open battle, and who were ready to die as one dies for his country.

The creeds have been given to the church, not by philosophers but by the shepherds of the flocks, who loved the sheep; not in a speculative but in a practical interest; not to advance or safeguard what we may speak of as merely intellectual, but distinctively spiritual needs; and to every seeing eye—that is, to every eye open to spiritual vision—they bear their corresponding appearance.

Of no creed is all this more true than of the Westminster Standards. Perhaps I may even venture to say, of no creed is it true in an equal measure as of the Westminster Standards. Men of learning they were, no doubt, who framed these standards; men of speculative power and philosophical grasp; men who were the heirs of all the Christian ages, and who had consciously entered into their

---

[1] This is the difference between the orthodox formula (ὁμοούσιος) and the Semi-Arian (ὁμοιούσιος); the decided Arian affirmed ἑτεροούσιος. Of course, the whole doctrine of the Trinity in unity and of the proper deity of Christ resides in the iota.

[2] *Discours sur l'évolution des dogmes*, pp. 23-4.

inheritance; in whose minds were stored the well-ordered fruits of serious study of the whole product of Christian thought and living up to their time.[1] But their chief claim to greatness does not lie in this. 'Some of the Assembly', is the testimony of one who, though not in sympathy with them, strives hard to do them justice—'some of the Assembly were great men; most of them were sincerely good.'[2] They were above and before all else—and that too consciously to themselves—men of God, men of strenuous and devout lives, who had known what it was to suffer for Christ's sake, and who spared not themselves in the work of his vineyard. They were, in one word, just a picked body of Puritan pastors—'the flower of the Puritan clergy', as the secular historian calls them[3]—the best men of the best age of British Protestantism. And they were met together not to air their conceits, but to save the good ship of the Church of England alike from the rocks of sacerdotalism and the shoals of humanitarianism, on one or the other of which it seemed likely to founder; and above all, to speak out heartily and without circumlocution, all the words of the divine life. It results, therefore, from the very nature of the case that it is above everything else a religious document which they have given us—a document phrased in theological language, no doubt, as all religious instruments must be, for such is the language of religion when seeking to express itself in terms of thought—but a document which, in the highest and most distinctive sense of those words, is a religious document; a document transfused with the very spirit of the age of religious revival which gave it birth, and bearing to every age which will receive it the spirit of devotion enshrined in its bosom. Speaking of the Puritans of London, one of the soberest of historians is forced to give utterance to the admiring cry that 'aiming to be a

[1] 'It was an age of great religious knowledge, and now for thirty years of free and violent discussion.'—Marsden, *History of the Later Puritans,* p. 53. 'The Presbyterian party [in the Assembly, *i.e.,* the great majority] were not ordinary men, nor men of fickle minds . . . Most of them left to the world some records of ministerial ability, of solid learning, and of zeal and piety, which time has not destroyed.'—*Ibid.,* p. 64. On the knowledge and power displayed by the Westminster divines in the work of preaching, see p. 88.

[2] Marsden, *History of the Later Puritans,* p. 106.

[3] S. R. Gardiner, *History of the Great Civil War,* I, p. 272. 'It [the Assembly of Divines] comprised the flower of the Puritan clergy.'

saint, each man unconsciously became a hero'.[1] The description may be applied in an eminent sense to the divines of the Westminster Assembly. If they have become intellectual heroes to us, as we wonder over the solidity and circumspection of their theological structure, it is not because their prime aim was scholastic. They wrote these definitions aiming before all things to be saints: is it strange that we see the saint through the theologian and have our hearts warmed by the contact? Certain it is that the Westminster Standards have a spiritual significance to us which falls in no wise short of their historical and scientific significance.

Open these standards where you will and you will not fail to feel the throb of an elevated and noble spiritual life pulsing through them. They are not merely a notably exact scientific statement of the elements of the gospel: they are, in the strictest sense of the words, the very embodiment of the gospel. They not only know what God is; they know God; and they make their readers know him—know him in his infinite majesty, in his exalted dominion, in his unlimited sovereignty, in the immutability of his purpose and his almighty power and universal providence, but know him also in that strangest, most incomprehensible of all his perfections, the unfathomableness of his love. Their description of him transcends the just limits of mere definition and swells into a paean of praise—praise to him who is 'most loving, gracious, merciful, longsuffering, abundant in goodness and truth, forgiving iniquity, transgression and sin, the rewarder of them that diligently seek him'. And how profound their knowledge is of the heart of man—its proneness to evil, its natural aversion to spiritual good, its slowness of response to spiritual influence, the deviousness of its path even under the leading of the Holy Ghost. But, above all, they know, with a fulness of apprehension which startles and instructs and blesses the reader, the ways of God with the errant souls of men—how he has condescended to open the way to them of having fruition of him as their blessedness and reward, how he has redeemed them unto himself in the blood of his Son, and how he deals with them, as only a loving Father may, in disciplining and fitting them for the heavenly glory. Where elsewhere may

---

[1] Marsden, *History of the Later Puritans*, p. 111.

we find more vitally set forth the whole circle of experience in the Christian life—what conversion is and how God operates in bringing the soul to knowledge of him and faith in its Saviour, what are the joys of justifying grace and of adoption into the family of God, and what the horrors of those temporary lapses that lie in wait for unwary steps, and what the inconceivable tenderness of God's gracious dealings with the stumbling and trembling spirit until he brings it safely home? Who can read those searching chapters on perseverance and assurance without feeling his soul burn within him, or without experience of a new influx of courage and patience for the conflicts of life? It is not a singular experience which Dr Thornwell records, when he sets down in his journal his thanksgiving to God for this blessed Confession. 'I bless God', he writes, 'for that glorious summary of Christian doctrine contained in our noble Standards. It has cheered my soul in many a dark hour, and sustained me in many a desponding moment.' We do not so much require as delight, with consentient mind, in his testimony, when he declares that he knows of 'no uninspired production in any language, or of any denomination, that for richness of matter, soundness of doctrine, scriptural expression and edifying tendency can for a moment enter into competition with the Westminster Confession and Catechisms'.[1] The Westminster Standards, in a word, are notable monuments of the religious life as well as of theological definition, and, speaking from the point of view of vital religion, this is their significance as a creed.

I have sought, Fathers and Brothers, nothing more than to indicate, with a brevity suitable to the nature of the occasion, what may be thought to be the chief sources of the significance of the Westminster Standards as a creed—to suggest in broad outline why, after two centuries and a half, they are still enshrined in the affections of the churches which have been blessed by their possession, and why we feel impelled to gather here today to express before the world our sense of benefits received from them and of satisfaction in them. It would be easy to enlarge upon the theme. It would be easy to show, for example, how freely the best thought of the best age of Protestantism was poured into them; how fully and genially they represent

[1] B. M. Palmer, *The Life and Letters of James Henley Thornwell, D.D., LL.D.*, pp. 162, 165.

the consensus of Reformed doctrine in its most developed and most catholic form; how strictly they are held in every definition to the purity of the biblical conceptions and enunciations of truth. These and similar grounds of appeal to our admiration and acceptance may be considered, however, to be implicitly included in what has been broadly adduced, and we may agree that the hold of the Westminster Standards upon our hearts and suffrages is due proximately to the fact that we see in them, historically speaking, the final crystallization of the very essence of evangelical religion—scientifically speaking, the richest and most precise and best guarded statement possessed by man, of all that enters into evangelical religion and of all that must be safeguarded if evangelical religion is to persist in the world—religiously speaking, the very expressed essence of vital religion. Surely blessed are the churches which feed upon this meat! Surely the very possession of Standards like these differentiates the fortunate churches which have inherited them as those best furnished for the word and work of the Christian proclamation and the Christian life. May God Almighty infuse their strength into our bones and their beauty into our flesh, and enable us to justify our inheritance by unfolding into life, in all its completeness and richness and divinity, the precious gospel which they have enfolded for us in their protecting envelope of sound words!

THE IDEA OF SYSTEMATIC THEOLOGY CONSIDERED AS A SCIENCE[1]

FATHERS and Brethren of the Board of Directors:—The signature which I have just affixed to the pledge which with great propriety, as I believe, you require of those whom you call to the responsible position of teachers in this seminary, will have assured you already of the matter of the doctrinal teaching which is still to be expected in this institution. Mourning as you do here today, with the renewed grief which is brought back upon us all by the business of the hour, with its teeming memories of those great men of the past who have shed lustre on the whole church from the chair into which you are now inducting a new incumbent, may you not take some comfort in being assured that, with however diminished power, the same theology is still to be taught here that for three-quarters of a century gave to Princeton Seminary a noble name in the world? It was not my lot to know him who was called of God to plant the first seeds in this garden of the Lord. But it was my inestimable privilege to sit at the feet of him who tended it and watered it until its fragrance went out over the whole earth. And I rejoice to testify to you today that though the power of Charles Hodge may not be upon me, the theology of Charles Hodge is within me, and that this is the theology which, according to my ability, I have it in my heart to teach to the students of the coming years. Oh, that the mantle of my Elijah might fall upon my shoulders; at least the message that was given to him is set within my lips.

[1] B. B. Warfield, 'The Idea of Systematic Theology Considered as a Science', *Inauguration of the Rev. Benjamin B. Warfield, D.D., as Professor of Didactic and Polemic Theology* (New York: Anson D.F. Randolph & Company, 1888).

In casting about for a subject germane to the occasion on which I might address you, I have lighted upon a line of thought which leads me to cast what I have to say into the form of some somewhat desultory remarks directed toward outlining the implications that arise from our regarding systematic theology as a science. I venture to state my subject, then, as *the idea of systematic theology considereed as a science.*

I am not sure that we always realize how much we have already determined about theology, when we have made the simple assertion concerning it, that it is a science. In this single predicate is implicitly included a whole series of affirmations which, taken together, will give us a rather clear conception not only of what theology is, but also of what it deals with, whence it obtains its material, and for what purpose it exists. It will be my object in this address to make this plain to you.

I. *The Subject-Matter of Systematic Theology*—First of all, then, let us observe that to say that theology is a science is to deny that it is a historical discipline, and to affirm that it seeks to discover not what has been or is held to be true, but what is ideally true; in other words, it is to declare that it deals with absolute truth and aims at organizing it into a concatenated system all the truth in its sphere. Geology is a science, and on that very account there cannot be two geologies; its matter is all the well-authenticated facts in its sphere, and its aim is to digest all these facts into one all-comprehending-system. There may be rival psychologies, which fill the world with vain jangling; but they do not strive together in order that they may obtain the right to exist side by side in equal validity, but in strenuous effort to supplant and supersede one another: there can be but one true science of mind. In like manner, just because theology is a science there can be but one theology. This all-embracing system will brook no rival in its sphere, and there can be two theologies only at the cost of one or both of them being imperfect, incomplete, false. It is because theology is often looked upon, in accordance with a somewhat prevalent point of view, as a historical rather than a scientific discipline, that it is so frequently spoken of and defined as if it were but one of many similar schemes of thought. There is no doubt such a thing as Christian theology, as distinguished from Buddhist theology or

Muhammadan theology; and men may study it as the theological implication of Christianity considered as one of the world's religions. But when studied from this point of view, it forms a section of a historical discipline and furnishes its share of facts for a history of religions; on the data supplied by which a science or philosophy of religion may in turn be based. We may also, no doubt, speak of the Pelagian and Augustinian theologies, or of the Calvinistic and Arminian theologies; but, again, we are speaking as historians and from a historical point of view. The Pelagian and Augustinian theologies are not two co-ordinate sciences of theology; they are rival theologies. If one is true, just so far the other is false, and there is but one theology. This we may identify, as an empirical fact, with either or neither; but it is at all events one, inclusive of all theological truth and exclusive of all else as false or not germane to the subject.

In asserting that theology is a science, then, we assert that in its subject-matter, it includes all the facts belonging to that sphere of truth that we call theological; and we deny that it needs or will admit of limitation by a discriminating adjectival definition. We may speak of it as Christian theology just as we may speak of it as true theology, if we mean thereby more fully to describe what, as a matter of fact, theology is found to be; but not, if we mean thereby to discriminate it from some other assumed theology thus erected to a co-ordinate position with it. We may describe our method of procedure in attempting to ascertain and organize the truths that come before us for building into the system, and so speak of logical or inductive, of speculative or organic theology; or we may separate the one body of theology into its members, and, just as we speak of surface and organic geology or of physiological and direct psychology, so speak of the theology of grace and of sin, or of natural and revealed theology. But all these are but designations of methods of procedure in dealing with the one whole, or of the various sections that together constitute the one whole, which in its completeness is the science of theology, and which, as a science, is inclusive of all the truth in its sphere, however ascertained, however presented, however defended.

II. *The Presuppositions of Systematic Theology*—There is much more than this included, however, in calling theology a science. For the very existence of any science, three things are presupposed:

(1) the reality of its subject-matter;

(2) the capacity of the human mind to apprehend, receive into itself, and rationalize this subject-matter; and

(3) some medium of communication by which the subject-matter is brought before the mind and presented to it for apprehension. There could be no astronomy, for example, if there were no heavenly bodies. And though the heavenly bodies existed, there could still be no science of them were there no mind to apprehend them. Facts do not make a science; even facts as apprehended do not make a science; they must be not only apprehended, but also so far comprehended as to be rationalized and thus combined into a correlated system. The mind brings somewhat to every science which is not included in the facts considered in themselves alone, as isolated data, or even as data perceived in relation to one another. Though they be thus known, science is not yet; and is not born save through the efforts of the mind in subsuming the facts under its own intuitions and forms of thought. No mind is satisfied with a bare cognition of facts: its very constitution forces it on to a restless energy until it succeeds in working these facts not only into a network of correlated relations among themselves, but also into a rational body of thought correlated to itself and its modes of thinking. The condition of science, then, is that the facts which fall within its scope shall be such as stand in relation not only to our faculties, so that they may be apprehended; but also to our mental constitution so that they may be so far understood as to be rationalized and wrought into a system relative to our thinking. Thus a science of aesthetics presupposes an aesthetic faculty, and a science of morals a moral nature, as truly as a science of logic presupposes a logical apprehension, and a science of mathematics a capacity to comprehend the relations of numbers. But still again, though the facts had real existence, and the mind were furnished with a capacity for their reception and for a sympathetic estimate and embracing of them in their relations, no science could exist were there no media by which the facts should be brought before and communicated to the mind. The transmitter and intermediating wire are as essential for telegraphing as the message and the receiving instrument. Subjectively speaking, sense perception is the essential basis of all science of external things; self-consciousness, of internal things. But objective media

are also necessary. For example, there could be no astronomy, were there no trembling ether through whose delicate telegraphy the facts of light and heat are transmitted to us from the suns and systems of the heavens. Subjective and objective conditions of communication must unite, before the facts that constitute the material of a science can be placed before the mind that gives it its form. The sense of sight is essential to astronomy: yet the sense of sight would be useless for forming an astronomy were there no objective ethereal messengers to bring us news from the stars. With these an astronomy becomes possible; but how meagre an astronomy compared with the new possibilities which have opened out with the discovery of a new medium of communication in the telescope, followed by still newer media in the subtle instruments by which our modern investigators not only weigh the spheres in their courses, but analyse them into their chemical elements, map out the heavens in a chart, and separate the suns into their primary constituents.

Like all other sciences, therefore, theology, for its very existence as a science, presupposes the objective reality of the subject-matter with which it deals; the subjective capacity of the human mind so far to understand this subject-matter as to be able to subsume it under the forms of its thinking and to rationalize it into not only a comprehensive but also a comprehensible whole; and the existence of trustworthy media of communication by which the subject-matter is brought to the mind and presented before it for perception and understanding. That is to say:

(1) The affirmation that theology is a science presupposes the affirmation that God is, and that he has relation to his creatures. Were there no God, there could be no theology; nor could there be a theology if, though he existed, he existed out of relation with his creatures. The whole body of philosophical apologetics is, therefore, presupposed in and underlies the structure of scientific theology.

(2) The affirmation that theology is a science presupposes the affirmation that man has a religious nature, *i.e.,* a nature capable of understanding not only that God is, but also, to some extent, what he is; not only that he stands in relation with his creatures, but also what those relations are. Had man no religious nature he might, indeed, apprehend, certain facts concerning God, but he could not

so understand him in his relations to man as to be able to respond to those facts in a true and sympathetic embrace. The total product of the great science of religion, which investigates the nature and workings of this element in man's mental constitution, is therefore presupposed in and underlies the structure of scientific theology.

(3) The affirmation that theology is a science presupposes the affirmation that there are media of communication by which God and divine things are brought before the minds of men, that they may perceive them, and in perceiving, understand them. In other words, when we affirm that theology is a science, we affirm not only the reality of God's existence and our capacity so far to understand him, but we affirm that he has made himself known to us,—we affirm the objective reality of a revelation. Were there no revelation of God to men, our capacity to understand him would lie dormant and unawakened; and though he really existed it would be to us as if he were not. There would be a God to be known and a mind to know him; but theology would be as impossible as if there were neither the one nor the other. Not only, then, philosophical, but also, if there be a written revelation, the whole mass of historical apologetics by which the reality of a written revelation is vindicated, is presupposed in and underlies the structure of scientific theology.

III. *The Definition of Systematic Theology*—In thus developing the implications of calling theology a science, we have already gone far toward determining our exact conception of what theology is. We have in effect, for example, settled our definition of theology. A science is defined from its subject-matter; and the subject-matter of theology is God in his nature and in his relations with his creatures. Theology is therefore that science which treats of God and of the relations between God and the universe. To this definition most theologians have actually come. And those who define theology as 'the science of God', mean the term God in a broad sense as inclusive also of his relations; while others exhibit their sense of the need of this inclusiveness by calling it 'the science of God and of divine things'; while still others speak of it more loosely, as 'the science of the supernatural'. These definitions fail rather in precision of language than in correctness of conception. Others, however, go astray in the conception itself. Thus theologians of the school of Schleiermacher usually derive their definition from the sources rather than the sub-ject-matter of the science,—and so speak of theology as 'the science of faith' or the like; a thoroughly unscientific procedure, even though our view of the sources be complete and unexceptionable, which is certainly not the case with this school. Quite as confusing is it to define theology, as is very currently done and often as an out-growth of this same subjective tendency, as 'the science of religion', or even—pressing the historical conception which as often underlies this type of definition, to its greatest extreme,—as 'the science of the Christian religion'. Theology and religion are parallel products of the same body of facts in diverse spheres; the one in the sphere of thought and the other in the sphere of life. And the definition of theology as 'the science of religion' thus confounds the product of the facts concerning God and his relations with his creatures working through the hearts and lives of men, with those facts themselves; and consequently, whenever strictly understood, bases theology not on the facts of the divine revelation, but on the facts of the religious life. This leads ultimately to a confusion of the two distinct disciplines of theology, the subject-matter of which is objective, and the science of religion, the subject-matter of which is subjective; with the effect of lowering the data of theology to the level of the aspirations and imag-inings of man's own heart. Wherever this definition is found, either a subjective conception of theology which reduces it to a branch of psychology, may be suspected, or else a historical conception of it, a conception of 'Christian theology' as one of the many theologies of the world parallel with, even if unspeakably truer than, the others with which it is classed and in conjunction with which it furnishes us with a full account of religion. When so conceived, it is natural to take a step further and permit the methodology of the science, as well as its idea, to be determined by its distinguishing element: thus theology, in contradiction to its very name, becomes Christocentric. No doubt, 'Christian theology', as a historical discipline, is Christo-centric; it is by its doctrine of redemption that it is differentiated from all the other theologies that the world has known. But theology as a science is and must be theocentric. So soon as we firmly grasp it from the scientific point of view, we see that there can be but one science of God and of his relations to his universe, and we no longer seek a point of discrimination, but rather a centre of development; and we quickly see that there can be but one centre about which so comprehensive a subject-matter can be organized,—the conception of God. He that hath seen Christ, has beyond doubt seen the Father; but it is one thing to make him the centre of theology so far as he is one with God, and another thing to organize all theology around him as the *theanthropos* and in his specifically theanthropic work.

IV. *The Sources of Systematic Theology*—Not only, however, is our definition of theology thus set for us: we have also determined in advance our conception of its sources. We have already made use of the term 'revelation', to designate the medium by which the facts concerning God and his relations to his creatures are brought before men's minds, and so made the subject-matter of a possible science. The word accurately describes the condition of all knowledge of God. If there be a God, it follows by stringent necessity, that he can be known only so far as he reveals himself. And it is but the converse of this, that if there be no revelation, there can be no knowledge, and, of course, no systematized knowledge or science of God. Our reaching up to him in thought and inference is possible only because he condescends to make himself intelligible to us, to speak to us through word or work, to reveal himself. We hazard nothing, therefore, in saying that, as the condition of all theology is a revealed God, so, without limitation, the sole source of theology is revelation.

In so speaking, however, we have no thought of doubting that God's revelation of himself is 'in divers manners'. We have no desire to deny that he has never left man without witness of his eternal power and Godhead, or that he has multiplied the manifestations of himself in nature and providence and grace, so that every generation has had abiding and unmistakable evidence that he is, that he is the good God, and that he is a God who marketh iniquity. Under the broad skirts of the term 'revelation', every method of manifesting himself which God uses in communicating knowledge of his Being and attributes, may find shelter for itself—whether it be through those visible things of nature whereby his invisible things are clearly seen, or through the constitution of the human mind with its causal judgment indelibly stamped upon it, or through that voice of God that we call conscience, which proclaims his moral law within us, or through his providence in which he makes bare his arm for the government of the nations, or through the exercises of his grace, our experience under the tutelage of the Holy Ghost—or whether it be through the open visions of his prophets, the divinely-breathed pages of his written Word, the divine life of the Word himself. How God reveals himself—in what divers manners he makes himself known to his creatures, is thus the subsequent question by raising which we distribute the one source of theology, revelation, into the various methods of revelation, each of which brings us true knowledge of God, and all of which must be taken account of in building our knowledge into one all-comprehending system. It is the accepted method of theology to infer that the God that made the eye must himself see; that the God who sovereignly distributes his favours in the secular world may be sovereign too in grace; that the heart that condemns itself but repeats the condemnation of the greater God; that the songs of joy in which the Christian's happy soul voices its sense of God's gratuitous mercy, are valid evidence that God has really dealt graciously with it. It is with no reserve that we accept all these sources of knowledge of God—nature, providence, Christian experience—as true and valid sources, the well-authenticated data yielded by which are to be received by us as revelations of God, and as such to be placed alongside of the revelations in the written Word and wrought with them into one system. As a matter of fact, theologians have always so dealt with them; and doubtless they always will so deal with them.

But to perceive, as all must perceive, that every method by which God manifests himself is, so far as this manifestation can be clearly interpreted, a source of knowledge of him, and must, therefore, be taken account of in framing all our knowledge of him into one organic whole, is far from allowing that there are no differences among these various manifestations, in the amount of revelation they give, the clearness of their message; the case and certainty with which they may be interpreted, or the importance of the special truths which they are fitted to convey. Far rather is it *a priori* likely that if there are 'divers manners' in which God has revealed himself, he has not revealed precisely the same message through each; that these 'divers manners' correspond also to divers messages of divers degrees of importance, delivered with divers degrees of clearness. And the mere fact that he has included in these 'divers manners' a copious revelation in a written Word, delivered with an authenticating accompaniment of signs and miracles, proved by recorded prophecies with their recorded fulfilments, and pressed, with the greatest solemnity, upon the attention and consciences of men as the very Word of the Living God, who has by it made foolishness all the wisdom of men; nay, proclaimed as containing within itself the formulation of his truth, the proclamation of his law, the discovery of his plan of salvation:—this mere fact, I say, would itself and prior to all comparison, raise an overwhelming presumption that all the others of 'the divers manners' of God's revelation were insufficient for the purposes for which revelation is given, whether on account of defect in the amount of their communication or insufficiency of attestation or uncertainty of interpretation or fatal onesidedness in the character of the revelation they are adapted to give. We need not be surprised, therefore, that on actual examination, all these imperfections are found undeniably to attach to all forms of what we may, for the sake of discrimination, speak of as mere manifestations of God; and that thus the revelation of God in his written Word—in which are included the only authentic records of the revelation of him through the incarnate Word—is easily shown not only to be incomparably superior to all other manifestations of him in the fulness, richness, and clearness of its communications, but also to contain the sole discovery of all that it is most important for the soul to know as to its state and destiny, and of all that is most precious in our whole body of theological knowledge. The superior lucidity of this revelation makes it the norm of interpretation for what is revealed so much more darkly through the other methods of manifestation. The glorious character of the discoveries made in it, drives all other manifestations back into comparative insignificance. The amazing fulness of its disclosures renders the little that they can tell us of small comparative value. And its absolute completeness for the needs of man, taking up and reiteratingly repeating in the clearest of language all that can be, only after much difficulty and with much uncertainty, wrung from their enigmatic indications, and then adding to this a vast body of still more important truth undiscoverable through them, all but supersedes their necessity. With the fullest recognition of the validity of all the knowledge of God and his ways with men, which can be obtained through the manifestations of his power and divinity in nature and history and grace; and the frankest allowance that the written Word is given, not to destroy the manifestations of God, but to fulfill them; the theologian must yet refuse to give these sources of knowledge a place alongside of the written Word, in any other sense than that he gladly admits that they, alike with it, but in unspeakably lower measure, do tell us somewhat of God. And nothing can be a clearer indication of a decadent theology or of a decaying faith, than a tendency to neglect the Word in favour of some one or of all of the lesser sources of theological truth, as fountains from which to draw our knowledofe of divine things. This were to prefer the flickering rays of a taper to the blazing light of the sun; to elect to draw our water from a muddy run rather than to dip it from the broad bosom of the pure fountain itself.

Nevertheless, men have often sought to still the cravings of their souls with a purely natural theology; and there are men today who prefer to derive their knowledge of what God is and what he will do for man from an analysis of the implications of their own religious feelings: not staying to consider that nature, 'red in tooth and claw with ravin', can but direct our eyes to the God of law, whose deadly letter killeth; or that our feelings must needs point us to the God of our imperfect apprehensions or of our unsanctified desires,—not to the God that is, so much as to the God that we would fain should be. The natural result of resting on the revelations of nature is despair; while the inevitable end of making our appeal to even the Christian heart is to make for ourselves refuges of lies in which there is neither truth nor safety. We may, indeed, admit that it is valid reasoning to infer from the nature of the Christian life what are the modes of God's activities toward his children: to see, for instance, in conviction of sin and the sudden peace of the new-born soul, God's hand in slaying that he may make alive. His almighty power in raising the spiritually dead. But how easy to overstep the limits of valid inference; and, forgetting that it is the body of Christian truth known and consciously assimilated that determines the type of Christian experience, confuse in our inferences what is from man with what is from God, and condition and limit our theology by the undeveloped Christian thought of the man or his times. The interpretation of the data included in what we have learned to call 'the Christian consciousness', whether of the individual or of the church at large, is a process so delicate, so liable to error, so inevitably swayed to this side or that by the currents that flow up and down in the soul, that probably few satisfactory inferences could be drawn from it, had we not the norm of Christian experience and its dogmatic implications recorded for us in the perspicuous pages of the written Word. But even were we to suppose that the interpretation was easy and secure, and that we had before us in an infalhble formulation, all the implications of the religious experience of all the men who have ever known Christ, we have no reason to believe that the whole body of facts thus obtained, would suffice to give us a complete theology. After all, we know in part and we feel in part; it is only when that which is perfect shall appear that we shall know or experience all that Christ has in store for us. With the fullest acceptance, therefore, of the data of the theology of this feelings, no less than of natural theology, when their results are validly obtained and sufficiently authenticated as trustworthy, as divinely revealed facts which must be wrought into our system, it remains nevertheless true that we should be confined to a meagre and doubtful theology were these data not confirmed, reinforced, and supplemented by the surer and fuller revelations of Scripture; and that the Holy Scriptures are the source of theology in not only a degree, but also a sense in which nothing else is.

There might be a theology without the Scriptures,—a theology of nature, gathered by painful, and slow, and doubtful processes from what man saw around him in external nature and the course of history, and what he saw within him of nature and of grace. In like manner there may be and has been an astronomy of nature, gathered by man in his natural state without help from aught but his naked eyes, as he watched in the fields by night. But what is this astronomy of nature to the astronomy that has become possible through the wonderful appliances of our observatories? The Word of God is to theology as, but vastly more than, these instruments are to astronomy. It is the instrument which so far increases the possibilities of the science as to revolutionize it and to place it upon a height from which it can never more descend. What would be thought of the deluded man, who, discarding the new methods of research, should insist on acquiring all the astronomy which he would admit, from the unaided observation of his own myopic and astigmatic eyes? Much more deluded is he who, neglecting the instrument of God's Word written, would confine his admissions of theological truth to what he could discover from the broken lights that play upon external nature, and the faint gleams of a dying or even a slowly reviving light, which arise in his own sinful soul. Ah, no! the telescope first made a real science of astronomy possible: and the Scriptures form the only sufficing and thoroughly infallible source of theology.

V. *The Place of Sysyematics in the Theological Encylopaedia*—Under such a conception of its nature and sources, we are driven to consider the place of systematic theology among the other theological disciplines as well as among the other sciences in general. Without encroaching upon the details of theological encyclopaedia, we may adopt here the usual fourfold distribution of the theological disciplines into the Exegetical, the Historical, the Systematic, and the Practical, with only the correction of prefixing to them a fifth department of Apologetical Theology. The place of systematic theology in this distribution is determined by its relation to the preceding disciplines, of which it is the crown and head. Apologetical theology prepares the way for all theology by establishing its necessary presuppositions without which no theology is possible—the existence and essential nature of God, the religious nature of man which enables him to receive a revelation from God, the possibility of a revelation and its actual realization in the Scriptures. It thus places the Scriptures in our hands for investigation and study. Exegetical theology receives these inspired writings from the hands of apologetics, and investigates their meaning; presenting us with a body of detailed and substantiated results, culminating in a series of organized systems of biblical history, biblical ethics, biblical theology, and the like, which provide material for further use in the more advanced disciplines. Historical theology investigates the progressive realization of Christianity in the lives, hearts, worship, and thought of men, issuing not only in a full account of the history of Christianity, but also in a body of facts which come into use in the more advanced disciplines, especially in the way of the sifted results of the reasoned thinking and deep experience of Christian truth during the whole past, as well as of the manifold experiments that have been made during the ages in Christian organization, worship, living, and creed-building. systematic theology does not fail to strike its roots deeply into this matter furnished by historical theology; it knows how to profit by the experience of all past generations in their efforts to understand and define, to systematize and defend revealed truth; and it thinks of nothing so little as lightly to discard the conquests of so many hard-fought fields. It therefore gladly utilizes all the material that historical theology brings it, accounting it, indeed, the very precipitate of the Christian consciousness of the past; but it does not use it crudely, or at first hand for itself, but accepts it as investigated, explained, and made available by the sister discipline of historical theology which alone can understand it or draw from it its true lessons. It certainly does not find in it its chief or primary source, and its relation to historical theology is, in consequence, far less close than that in which it stands to exegetical theology which is its true and especial handmaid. The independence of exegetical theology is seen in the fact that it does its work wholly without thought or anxiety as to the use that is to be made of its results; and that it furnishes a vastly larger body of data than can be utilized by any one discipline. It provides a body of historical, ethical, liturgic, ecclesiastical facts, as well as a body of theological facts. But so far as its theological facts are concerned, it provides them chiefly that they may be used by systematic theology as material out of which to build its system. This is not to forget the claims of biblical theology. It is rather to emphasize its value, and to afford occasion for explaining its true place in the encyclopaedia, and its true relations on the one side to exegetical theology, and on the other to systematics,—a matter which appears to be even yet imperfectly understood in some quarters. Biblical theology is not a section of historical theology, although it must be studied in a historical spirit, and has a historical face; it is rather the ripest fruit of exegetics, and exegetics has not performed its full task until its scattered results in the way of theological data are gathered up into a full and articulated system of biblical theology. It is to be hoped that the time will come when no commentary will be considered complete until the capstone is placed upon its fabric by closing chapters gathering up into systematized exhibits, the unsystematized results of the continuous exegesis of the text, in the spheres of history, ethics, theology, and the like. The task of biblical theology, in a word, is the task of co-ordinating the scattered results of continuous exegesis into a concatenated whole, whether with reference to a single book of Scripture or to a body of related books or to the whole scriptural fabric. Its chief object is not to find differences of conception between the various writers, though some recent students of the subject seem to think this is so much their duty, that when they cannot find differences, they make them. It is to reproduce the theological thought of each writer or group of writers in the form in which it lay in their own minds, so that we may be enabled to look at all their theological statements at their angle, and to understand all their deliverances as modified and conditioned by their own point of view. Its exegetical value lies just in this circumstance, that it is only when we have thus concatenated an author's theological statements into a whole, that we can be sure that we understand them as he understood them in detail. A light is inevitably thrown back from biblical theology upon the separate theological deliverances as they occur in the text, such as subtly colours them, and often, for the first time, gives them to us in their true setting, and thus enables us to guard against perverting them when we adapt them to our use. This is a noble function, and could students of biblical theology only firmly grasp it, once for all, as their task, it would prevent the bringing this important science into contempt through a tendency to exaggerate differences in form of statement into divergences of view, and so to force the deliverances of each book into a strange and unnatural combination, in their effort to vindicate a function for their discipline.

The relation of biblical theology to systematic theology is based on a true view of its function. Systematic theology is not founded on the direct and primary results of the exegetical process; it is founded on the final and complete results of exegesis as exhibited in biblical theology. Not exegesis itself, then, but biblical theology, provides the material for systematics. It is not, then, a rival of systematics; it is not even a parallel product of the same body of facts, provided by exegesis; it is the basis and source of systematics. Systematic theology is not a concatenation of the scattered theological data furnished by

the exegetic process; it is the combination of the already concatenated data given to it by biblical theology. It uses the individual data
furnished by exegesis, in a word, not crudely, not independently for
itself, but only after these data have been worked up into biblical
theology and have received from it their final colouring and subtlest
shades of meaning—in other words, only in their true sense, and
only after exegetics has said its last word upon them. Just as we shall
attain our finest and truest conception of the person and work of
Christ, not by crudely trying to combine the scattered details of his
life and teaching as given in our four Gospels into one patchwork
life and account of his teaching; but far more rationally and far more
successfully by first catching Matthew's full conception of Jesus, and
then Mark's, and then Luke's, and then John's, and combining these
four conceptions into one rounded whole:—so we gain our truest
systematics not by at once working together the separate dogmatic
statements in the Scriptures, but by combining them in their due
order and proportion as they stand in the various theologies of the
Scriptures. Thus we are enabled to view the future whole not only in
its parts, but in the several combinations of the parts, and, looking
at it from every side, to obtain a true conception of its solidity and
strength, and to avoid all exaggeration or falsification of the details
in giving them place in the completed structure. And thus we do not
make our theology, according to our own pattern, as a mosaic, out of
the fragments of the biblical teaching; but rather look out from ourselves upon it as a great prospect, framed out of the mountains and
plains of the theologies of the Scriptures, and strive to attain a point
of view from which we can bring the whole landscape into our field
of sight. From this point of view, we find no difficulty in understanding the relation in which the several disciplines stand to one another,
with respect to their contents. The material that systematics draws
from other than biblical sources may be here left out of account, seeing that we are now investigating its relations, considered as a biblical
discipline, to its fellow biblical departments. The actual contents of
the theological results of the exegetic process, of biblical theology,
and of systematics, with this limitation, may be said to be the same.
The immediate work of exegesis may be compared to the work of a
recruiting officer: it draws out from the mass of mankind the men

who are to constitute the army. Biblical theology organizes these men into companies and regiments and corps, arranged in marching order and accoutred for service. Systematic theology combines these companies and regiments and corps into an army drawn up in battle array against the enemy of the day. It, too, is composed of men—the same men which were recruited by exegetics; but it is composed of these men, not as individuals merely, but in their due relations to the other men of their companies and regiments and corps. The simile not only illustrates the mutual relations of the disciplines, but also suggests the historical element that attaches to biblical theology, and the polemic or practical element which is inseparable from systematic theology as distinguished from a merely biblical dogmatic. It is just this polemico-practical element, determining the spirit and therefore the methods of systematic theology, which, along with its greater inclusiveness, discriminates it from all forms of biblical theology the spirit of which is purely historical.

VI. *The Place of Systematic Theology among the Sciences*—The place that theology claims for itself, as the scientific presentation of all the facts that are known concerning God and his relations, within the circle of the sciences, is an equally high one. Whether we consider the topics which it treats, in their dignity, their excellence, their grandeur; or the certainty with which its data can be determined; or the completeness with which its principles have been ascertained and its details classified; or the usefulness and importance of its discoveries: it is as far out of all comparison above all other sciences as the eternal health and destiny of the soul are of more value than this fleeting life in this world. It is not so above them, however, as not to be also within them. There is no one of them all which is not in some measure touched and affected by it, or, we may even say, which is not in some measure included in it. As all nature, whether mental or material, may be conceived of as only the mode in which God manifests himself, every science which investigates nature and ascertains its laws, is occupied with the discovery of the modes of the divine action, and as such might be considered a branch of theology. Its closest relations are, no doubt, with the highest of the other sciences, ethics. Any discussion of our duty to God must rest on a knowledge of our relation to him; and much of our duty to man is undiscoverable, save through knowledge of our common relation to the one God and Father of all, and one Lord the Redeemer of all, and one Spirit the Sanctifier of all,—all of which it is the function of theology to supply. This is not inconsistent with the existence of a natural ethics; but an ethics independent of theological conceptions would be a meagre thing indeed, while the theology of the scriptural revelation for the first time affords a basis for ethical investigation at once broad enough and sure enough to raise that science to its true dignity. Neither must we on the ground of this intimacy of relation confound the two sciences of theology and ethics. Something like it in kind and approaching it in degree exists between theology and every other science, no one of which is so independent of it as not to touch and be touched by it. Much of theology is presupposed in all metaphysics and physics alike. It alone can determine the origin of either matter or mind, or of the mystic powers that have been granted to them. It alone can explain the nature of second causes and set the boundaries to their efficiency. It alone is competent to declare the meaning of the ineradicable persuasion of the human mind that its reason is right reason, its processes trustworthy, its intuitions true. All science without God is mutilated science, and no account of a single branch of knowledge can ever be complete until it is pushed back to find its completion and ground in him. It is as true of sciences as it is of creatures, that in him they all live and move and have their being. The science of him and his relations is thus the necessary ground of all science. All speculation takes us back to him; all inquiry presupposes him; and every phase of science consciously or unconsciously rests at every step on the science that makes him known. Theology, thus, both lies at the root of all sciences, and brings to each its capstone and crown. Each could, indeed, exist without it, in a sense and in some degree; but through it alone can any one of them reach its true dignity. Herein we see not only the proof of its greatness, but also the assurance of its permanence. 'What so permeates all sections and subjects of human thought, has a deep root in human nature and an immense hold on it. What so possesses man's mind that he cannot think at all without thinking of it, is so bound up with the very being of intelligence that ere it can perish, intellect must cease to be.'[1]

[1] Principal Fairbairn.

VII. *Systematic Theology a Progressive Science*—The interpretation of a written document, intended to convey a plain message, is infinitely easier than the interpretation of the teaching embodied in facts themselves. It is therefore that systematic treatises on the several sciences are written. Theology has, therefore, an immense advantage over all other sciences, inasmuch as it is more an inductive study of facts conveyed in a written revelation, than an inductive study of facts as conveyed in life. It was, consequently, the first-born of the sciences. It was the first to reach relative completeness. And it is today in a state far nearer perfection than any other science. This is not, however, to deny that it is a progressive science. In exactly the same sense (though not in equal degree) in which any other science is progressive, this is progressive. It is not meant that new revelations are to be expected, or new discoveries made, of truth which has not been before within the reach of man. There is a vast difference between the progress of a science and increase in its material. All the facts of psychology, for instance, have been in existence so long as mind itself has existed; and the progress of this science has been dependent on the progressive discovery, understanding, and systematization of these facts. All the facts of theology have, in like manner, been within the reach of man for nearly two millennia; and the progress of theology is dependent on men's progress in gathering, defining, mentally assimilating, and organizing these facts into a correlated system. So long as revelation was not completed, the progressive character of theology was secured by the progress in revelation itself. And since the close of the canon of Scripture, the intellectual realization and definition of the doctrines revealed in it, in relation to one another, have been, as a mere matter of fact, a slow but ever advancing process. The affirmation that theology has been a progressive science is no more, then, than to assert that it is a science that has had a history,—and a history which can be and should be genetically traced and presented. First, the objective side of Christian truth was developed: pressed on the one side by the crass monotheism of the Jews and on the other by the coarse polytheism of the heathen, and urged on by its own internal need of understanding the sources of its life, Christian theology first searched the Scriptures that it might understand the nature and modes of existence of its God and the person of its divine Redeemer. Then, more and more conscious of itself, it more and more fully wrought out from those same Scriptures a guarded expression of the subjective side of its faith; until through throes and conflicts it has built up the system which we all inherit. Thus the body of Christian truth has come down to us in the form of an organic growth; and we can conceive of the completed structure as the ripened fruit of the ages, as truly as we can think of it as the perfected result of the exegetical discipline. As it has come into our possession by this historic process, there is no reason that we can assign why it should not continue to make for itself a history. We do not expect the history of theology to close in our own day. However nearly completed our realization of the body of truth may seem to us to be; however certain it is that the great outlines are already securely laid and most of the details soundly discovered and arranged; no one will assert that every detail is as yet perfected, and we are all living in the confidence so admirably expressed by old John Robinson, 'that God hath more truth yet to break forth from his holy Word'. Just because God gives us the truth in single threads which we must weave into the reticulated texture, all the threads are always within our reach, but the finished texture is ever and will ever continue to be before us until we dare affirm that there is no truth in the Word which we have not perfectly apprehended, and no relation of these truths as revealed which we have not perfectly understood, and no possibility in clearness of presentation which we have not attained.

The conditions of progress in theology are clearly discernible from its nature as a science. The progressive men in any science are the men who stand firmly on the basis of the already ascertained truth. The condition of progress in building the structures of those great cathedrals whose splendid piles glorify the history of art in the middle ages, was that each succeeding generation should build upon the foundations laid by its predecessor. If each architect had begun by destroying what had been accomplished by his forerunners, no cathedral would ever have been raised. The railroad is pushed across the continent by the simple process of laying each rail at the end of the line already laid. The prerequisite of all progress is a clear discrimination which as frankly accepts the limitations set by the truth already discovered, as it rejects the false and bad. Construction is not destruction; neither is it the outcome of destruction. There are abuses no doubt to be reformed; errors to correct; falsehoods to cut away. But the history of progress in every science and no less in theology, is a story of impulses given, corrected and assimilated. And when they have been once corrected and assimilated, these truths are to remain accepted. It is then time for another impulse, and the condition of all further progress is to place ourselves in this well-marked line of growth. Astronomy, for example, has had such a history; and there are now some indisputable truths in astronomy, as, for instance, the rotundity of the earth and the central place of the sun in our system. I do not say that these truths are undisputed; probably nothing is any more undisputed in astronomy, or any other science, than in theology. At all events he who wishes, may read the elaborate arguments of the 'Zetetic' philosophers, as they love to call themselves, who in this year of grace are striving to prove that the earth is flat and occupies the centre of our system. Quite in the same spirit, there are 'Zetetic' theologians who strive with similar zeal and acuteness to overturn the established basal truths of theology,—which, however, can never more be shaken; and we should give about as much ear to them in the one science as in the other. It is utter folly to suppose that progress can be made otherwise than by placing ourselves in the line of progress; and if the temple of God's truth is ever to be completely built, we must not spend our efforts in digging at the foundations which have been securely laid in the distant past, but must rather give our best efforts to rounding the arches, carving the capitals, and fitting in the fretted roof. What if it is not ours to lay foundations? Let us rejoice that that work has been done! Happy are we if our God will permit us to bring a single capstone into place. This fabric is not a house of cards to be built and blown down again an hundred times a day, as the amusement of our idle hours: it is a miracle of art to which all ages and lands bring their various tribute. The subtle Greek laid the foundations; the law-loving Roman raised high the walls; and all the perspicuity of France and ideality of Germany and systematization of Holland and deep sobriety of Britain have been expended in perfecting the structure; and so it grows. We have heard much in these last days of the phrase, 'progressive orthodoxy', and in somewhat strange connections. Nevertheless, the phrase itself is not an inapt description of the building of this theological house. Let us assert that the history of theology has been and ever must be a progressive orthodoxy. But let us equally loudly assert that progressive orthodoxy and retrogressive heterodoxy can scarcely be convertible terms. Progressive orthodoxy implies that first of all we are orthodox, and secondly that we are progressively orthodox, *i.e.,* that we are ever growing more and more orthodox as more and more truth is being established. This has been and must be the history of the advance of every science, and not less, among them, of the science of theology. Justin Martyr, champion of the orthodoxy of his day, held a theory of the inter-trinitarian relationship which became heterodoxy after the Council of Nice; the ever-struggling Christologies of the earlier ages were forever set aside by the Chalcedon Fathers; Augustine determined for all time the doctrine of grace, Anselm the doctrine of the atonement, Luther the doctrine of forensic justification. In any progressive science, the amount of departure from accepted truth which is possible to the sound thinker becomes thus ever less and less, in proportion as investigation and study result in the progressive establishment of an ever increasing number of facts. The physician who would bring back today the medicine of Galen would be no more mad than the theologian who would revive the theology of Clement of Alexandria. Both were men of light and leading in their time; but their time is past, and it is the privilege of the child of today to know a sounder physic and a sounder theology than the giants of that far past yesterday could attain. It is of the very essence of our position at the end of the ages that we are ever more and more hedged around with ascertained facts, the discovery and establishment of which constitute the very essence of progress. Progress brings progressive limitation, just because it brings progressive knowledge. And as the orthodox man is he that teaches no other doctrine than that which has been established as true; the progressively orthodox man is he who is quick to perceive, admit, and condition all his reasoning by all the truth down to the latest, which has been established as true.

VIII. *Systematic Theology a Practical Science*—When we speak of progress our eyes are set upon a goal. And in calling theology a progressive science we unavoidably raise the inquiry, what the end and purpose is toward an ever-increasing fitness to secure which it is continually growing. When we consider the surpassing glory of the subject-matter with which it deals, it would appear that if ever science existed for its own sake, this might surely be true of this science. The truths concerning God and his relations are, above all comparison, in themselves the most worthy of all truths of study and examination. Yet we must vindicate for theology rather that it is an eminently practical science. The contemplation and exhibition of Christianity as truth, is far from the end of the matter. This truth is specially communicated by God for a purpose, for which it is admirably adapted. That purpose is to save and sanctify the soul. And the discovery, study, and systematization of the truth is in order that, firmly grasping it and thoroughly comprehending it in all its reciprocal relations, we may be able to make the most efficient use of it for its holy purpose. Well worth our most laborious study, then, as it is, for its own sake as mere truth; it becomes not only absorbingly interesting, but inexpressibly precious to us when we bear in mind that the truth with which we thus deal constitutes, as a whole, the engrafted Word that is able to save our souls. The task of thoroughly exploring the pages of revelation, soundly gathering from them their treasures of theological teaching and carefully fitting these into their due places in a system whereby they may be preserved from misunderstanding, perversion, and misuse, and given a new power to convince the understanding, move the heart, and quicken the will, becomes thus a holy duty to our own and our brothers' souls as well as our eager pleasure of our intellectual nature. That the knowledge of the truth is an essential prerequisite to the production of those graces and the building up of those elements of a sanctified character for the production of which each truth is especially adapted, probably no one denies: but surely it is equally true that the clearer, fuller, and more discriminating this knowledge is, the more certainly and richly will it produce its appropriate effect; and in this is found a most complete vindication of the duty of systematizing the separate elements of truth into a single soundly concatenated whole, by which the essential nature of each is made as clear as it can be made to human apprehension. It is not a matter of indifference, then, how we apprehend and systematize this truth. On the contrary, if we misconceive it in its parts or in its relations, not only do our views of truth become confused and erroneous, but also our religious life becomes dwarfed or contorted. The character of our religion is, in a word, determined by the character of our theology: and thus the task of the systematic theologian is to see that the relations in which the separate truths actually stand are rightly conceived, in order that they may exert their rightful influence on the development of the religious life. As no truth is so insignificant as to have no place in the development of our religious life, so no truth is so unimportant that we dare neglect it or deal deceitfully with it in adjusting it into our system. We are smitten with a deadly fear on the one side, lest by fitting them into a system of our own devising, we cut from them just the angles by which they were intended to lay hold of the hearts of men: but on the other side, we are filled with a holy confidence that, by allowing them to frame themselves into their own system as indicated by their own natures,—as the stones in Solomon's temple were cut each for its place,—we shall make each available for all men, for just the place in the saving process for which it was divinely framed and divinely given.

From this point of view the systematic theologian is pre-eminently a preacher of the gospel; and the end of his work is not merely the logical arrangement of the truths which come under his hand, but the moving of men through their power to love God with all their hearts, and their neighbours as themselves; to choose their portion with the Saviour of their souls; to find and hold him precious; and to recognize and yield to the sweet influences of the Holy Spirit whom he has sent. With such truth as this he will not dare to deal in a cold and merely scientific spirit, but will justly and necessarily permit its preciousness and its practical destination to determine the spirit in which he handles it, and to awaken the reverential love with which alone he should investigate its reciprocal relations. For this he needs to be suffused at all times with a sense of the unspeakable worth of the revelation which lies before him as the source of his material, and with the personal bearings of its separate truths on his own heart and life; he needs to have had and to be having a full, rich, and deep religious experience of the great doctrines with which he deals; he needs to be living close to his God, to be resting always on the bosom of his Redeemer, to be filled at all times with the manifest influences of the Holy Spirit. The teacher of systematic theology needs a very sensitive religious nature, a most thoroughly consecrated heart, and an outpouring of the Holy Ghost upon him, such as will fill him with that spiritual discernment, without which all native intellect is in vain. He needs to be not merely a student, not merely a thinker, not merely a systematizer, not merely a teacher,—he needs to be like the beloved disciple himself in the highest, truest and holiest sense, a divine.

Fathers and Brethren, as I speak these words, my heart fails me in a deadly anxiety. 'Who is sufficient for these things?' it cries to me in a true dismay. We all remember how but a short decade ago one stood in this place where I now stand, who, in the estimation of us all, was richly provided by nature and grace for the great task which now lies before me, but which then lay before him. 'Alas ! sirs', said he, with a humility which was characteristic of his chastened and noble soul,—'Alas ! sirs, when I think of myself, I often cry, "Woe is me, that such an one as I, should be called to inherit the responsibilities descending in such a line." And when I think of the church, I cry with a far sorer wonder, "What times are these, when such a man as I should be made to stand in such a place?"' With far more reason may I be allowed to echo these words today. With far more need may I demand now, as he demanded then, your prayers for me, that in 'the service today inaugurated, God's strength may be made perfect in my weakness'.

THE INDISPENSABLENESS OF SYSTEMATIC THEOLOGY TO THE PREACHER[1]

PROFESSOR Flint, of Edinburgh, in closing his opening lecture to his class a few years ago, took occasion to warn his students of what he spoke of as an imminent danger. This was a growing tendency to 'deem it of prime importance that they should enter upon their ministry accomplished preachers, and of only secondary importance that they should be scholars, thinkers, theologians'. 'It is not so', he is reported as saying, 'that great or even good preachers are formed. They form themselves before they form their style of preaching. Substance with them precedes appearance, instead of appearance being a substitute for substance. They learn to know truth before they think of presenting it . . . They acquire a solid basis for the manifestation of their love of souls through a loving, comprehensive, absorbing study of the truth which saves souls.'[2] In these winged words is outlined the case for the indispensableness of systematic theology for the preacher. It is summed up in the propositions that it is through the truth that souls are saved, that it is accordingly the prime business of the preacher to present this truth to men, and that it is consequently his fundamental duty to become himself possessed of this truth that he may present it to men and so save their souls. It would not be easy to overstate, of course, the importance to a preacher of those gifts and graces which qualify him to present this truth to men in a winning way—of all, in a word, that goes to make him an 'accomplished preacher'. But it is obviously even more important to him that he

[1] B. B. Warfield, 'The Indispensableness of Systematic Theology to the Preacher', *Homiletic Review* (February 1897), pp. 99-105.
[2] As reported in the *Scotsman* for Nov. 13, 1888.

should have a clear apprehension and firm grasp of that truth which he is to commend to men by means of these gifts and graces. For this clear apprehension and firm grasp of the truth its systematic study would seem certainly to be indispensable. And systematic theology is nothing other than the saving truth of God presented in systematic form.

The necessity of systematic study of any body of truth which we need really to master will scarcely be doubted. Nor will it be doubted that he who would indoctrinate men with a given body of truth must needs begin by acquiring a mastery of it himself. What has been made matter of controversy is whether Christian truth does lie so at the basis of the Christian hope and the Christian life that it is the prime duty of the preacher to possess himself of it and to teach it. It has been argued that the business of the preacher is to make Christians, not theologians; and that for this he needs not a thorough systematic knowledge of the whole circle of what is called Christian doctrine, but chiefly a firm faith in Jesus Christ as Saviour and a warm love toward him as Lord. His function is a practical, not a theoretical one; and it matters little how ignorant he may be or may leave his hearers, so only he communicates to them the faith and love that burn in his own heart. Not learning but fervour is what is required; nay, too much learning is (so it is often said) distinctly unfavourable to his best efficiency. Engagement of the mind with the subtleties of theological construction excludes that absorption in heart-devotion and in the practical work of the ministry, which on its two sides forms the glory of the minister's inner life and the crown of his outer activity. Give us not scholars, it is said, but plain practical men in our pulpits—men whose simple hearts are on fire with love to Christ and whose whole energy is exhausted in the rescue of souls.

Surely, if the antithesis were as is here implied, no voice would be raised in opposition to these demands. If we are to choose between a chilly intellectualistic and a warmly evangelical ministry, give us the latter by all means. A comparatively ignorant ministry burning with zeal for souls is infinitely to be preferred to a ministry entirely absorbed in a purely intellectual interest in the relations of truths which are permitted to exercise no influence on their own lives and which quicken in them no fervour of missionary love. But the matter cannot be settled by fixing the eye on this extreme only. What should we do with a ministry which was absolutely and blankly ignorant of the whole compass of Christian truth? Obviously it would not be a Christian ministry at all. Let it be admitted, then, that it is possible for men to become so occupied with the purely intellectual aspects of Christian truth as to be entirely unfitted for the prosecution of the Christian ministry. It must be equally allowed that they must have a sound knowledge of Christian truth in order to be qualified to undertake the functions of the Christian ministry at all. The possibility of the abuse of systematic theology has no tendency to arraign its usefulness or even its indispensableness to the preacher. A high capacity and love for mathematics may live in a sadly unpractical brain, and, for aught I know, the world may be full of pure mathematicians who are absolutely useless to it; but it does not follow that the practical worker in applied mathematics can get on just as well without any mathematics at all. In like manner, though there may be such a thing as a barren knowledge of even such vital truth as the Christian verities, there is not and cannot be such a thing as a fruitful Christian ministry without a sound and living knowledge of these verities. And it is very much to be deprecated that men should sometimes permit themselves to be driven, through their keen sense of the valuelessness of an inoperative knowledge, to speak as if no importance attached to that vitalizing knowledge of divine truth without which any true ministry is impossible. The warning given us by the lamented Aubrey Moore is sorely needed in our times. He says: 'There are many earnest-minded Christians who are so morbidly afraid of a barren belief that they sometimes allow themselves to talk as if to hold fast to any form of sound words must be formalism; as if, in fact, the belief in a creed were rather dangerous than helpful. It is true, of course, as we all know well, that a right creed cannot save a man and that when the bridegroom comes many may be found with lamps that have no oil; but surely if we discard our lamps, much of the precious oil we have may be lost.'[1]

The fundamental principle on which the indispensableness to the preacher of a sound knowledge of Christian truth rests is not more surely rooted in a true psychology than it is illustrated by universal

---

[1] *Some Aspects of Sin,* p. 20.

experience. That 'conduct in the long run corresponds with belief', as Bishop Westcott puts it, 'all experience goes to show'. And certainly he is entitled to add that 'this unquestionable principle carries with it momentous consequences'. 'Patient investigation', he continues, 'will show that no doctrine can be without a bearing on action . . . The influence of a dogma will be good or bad—that is an important criterion of dogma, with which we are not now concerned—but if the dogma be truly maintained, it will have a moral value of some kind. Every religion, and every sect of every religion, has its characteristic form of life; and if the peculiarities of these forms of life are smoothed away by time, it is only because the type of belief to which they correspond has ceased to retain its integrity and sharpness.'[1] It is therefore that Principal Wace rebukes the 'tendency of some modern historians to undervalue the influence upon human nature of variations in religious and moral principles', as 'strangely at variance with the evidence before them'.[2] 'The history of the world', he adds, 'would appear to be in great measure a history of the manner in which religious ideas, often of an apparently abstract and subtle character, can determine the future of whole races and of vast regions of the earth . . . The facts of history thus afford conclusive evidence that the instinct of the Christian world, or rather the instinct of mankind, has not been mistaken in attributing extreme importance to those variations in faith, even on points apparently secondary, by which Christendom has been and is still so grievously divided.' The whole case is most concisely put in a comprehensive passage in the *Systematic Theology* of the late Prof. John Miley:

> A religious movement with power to lift up souls into a true spiritual life must have its inception and progress in a clear and earnest presentation of the vital doctrines of religion. The order of facts in every such movement in the history of Christianity has been, first, a reformation of doctrine, and then, through the truer doctrine, a higher and better moral and spiritual life . . . Such has ever been and must forever be the chronological order of these facts, because it is the logical order. When souls move up from a sinful life or a dead formalism into a true spiritual life they must have the necessary reasons and

[1] *The Gospel of Life,* pp. 48, 57.
[2] *The Foundations of Faith,* pp. 194-8.

motives for such action . . . If we should be consecrated to God in a life of holy obedience and love, it must be for reasons of duty and motives of spiritual well-being which are complete only in the distinctive doctrines of Christianity. These doctrines are not mere intellectual principles or dry abstractions, but living truths which embody all the practical forces of Christianity. The spiritual life takes a higher form under evangelical Christianity than is possible under any other form, whether ritualistic or rationalistic, because therein the great doctrines of Christianity are apprehended in a living faith and act with their transcendent practical force upon all that enters into this life.[1]

If there be any validity at all in these remarks, the indispensableness of systematic theology to the preacher is obvious. For they make it clear not only that some knowledge of Christian truth is essential to him who essays to teach that truth, but that the type of life which is produced by his preaching, so far as his preaching is effective, will vary in direct relation to the apprehension he has of Christian truth and the type and proportion of truth he presents in his preaching. As Bishop Westcott puts it: 'Error and imperfection in such a case must result in lives which are faulty and maimed where they might have been nobler and more complete'; and, on the other hand, 'right doctrine is an inexhaustible spring of strength, if it be translated into deed'.[2] In directly the same line of remark, that saint of God, Dr Horatius Bonar, urges that:

> All wrong thoughts of God, whether of Father, Son, or Spirit, must cast a shadow over the soul that entertains them. In some cases the shadow may not be so deep and cold as in others; but never can it be a trifle. And it is this that furnishes the proper answer to the flippant question so often asked: Does it really matter what a man believes? All defective views of God's character tell upon the life of the soul and the peace of the conscience. We must think right thoughts of God if we would worship him as he desires to be worshipped, if we would live the life he wishes us to live, and enjoy the peace which he has provided for us.[3]

[1] Vol. I, pp. 48-49. Cf. also p. 40.
[2] *The Gospel of Life*, p. 58.
[3] *The Gospel of the Spirit's Love*, p. 22.

And what is true of the doctrine of God is true of every other doctrine about his ways and works; as Dr Westcott phrases it, 'The same law which holds good of the effect of the ideas of God and of a future life and of the incarnation in their most general form, holds good also of the details of the view upon which they are realized.'[1]

Accordingly Dr Alexander Whyte testifies to the relation of right belief and all the highest devotion, in a striking passage which we cannot forbear quoting somewhat in full. He writes:

One of the acknowledged masters of the spiritual life warns us against 'an untheological devotion'. 'True spirituality', he insists, 'has always been orthodox.' And the readers of the *Grammar of Assent* will remember with what masterly power and with what equal eloquence it is there set forth that the theology of the Creeds and Catechisms, when it is rightly understood and properly employed, appeals to the heart quite as much as to the head, to the imagination quite as much as to the understanding. And we cannot study Andrewes' book [his *Private Devotions*], his closet confession of faith especially, without discovering what a majesty, what a massiveness, what a depth, and what a strength, as well as what an evangelical fervour and heartsomeness, his theology has given to his devotional life . . . In the *Grammar* its author says that for himself he has ever felt the Athanasian Creed to be the most devotional formulary to which Christianity has given birth. We certainly feel something not unlike that when Andrewes takes up the Apostles' Creed, or the Nicene Creed, or the Life of our Lord, or his Names, or his Titles, or his Offices. When Andrewes takes up any of these things into his intellect, imagination, and heart, he has already provided himself and his readers with another great prayer and another great psalm. So true is it that all true theology is directly and richly and evangelically devotional.[2]

Readers of Dr Palmer's *Life of Thornwell* will recall a parallel testimony to what the reading of the Westminster Confession did for Thornwell's soul; and we can ourselves testify from experience to the power of the Westminster Confession to quicken religious emotion, and to form and guide a deeply devotional life. 'So true is it', to

[1] *Op. cit.,* p. 58.
[2] *Lancelot Andrewes and His Private Devotions,* pp. 49-51.

repeat Dr Whyte's words, that 'all true theology is directly and richly and evangelically devotional.'

It cannot be a matter of indifference, therefore, what doctrines we preach or whether we preach any doctrines at all. We cannot preach at all without preaching doctrine; and the type of religious life which grows up under our preaching will be determined by the nature of the doctrines which we preach. We deceive ourselves if we fancy that because we scout the doctrines of the creeds and assume an attitude of studied indifference to the chief tenets of Christianity we escape teaching a system of belief. Even the extremest doctrinal indifferentism, when it ascends the pulpit, becomes necessarily a scheme of faith. As a bright writer in *The Atlantic Monthly* puts it, men are always found believers in either the head or the tail of the coin. Even 'Renan's followers have their pockets crammed with beliefs of their own, bawling to the public to try them; they trundle their push-carts down the boulevard, hawking new creeds: *Par ici, mes amis, par ici! Voici des croyance neuves, voici la Verité!*'[1] Beliefs old or beliefs new, we all have them; and when we take our place in the rostrum in their behalf we perforce become their teachers. There may be Christian truths of which we speak as if they were of infinitesimally little importance, because, as Aubrey Moore caustically puts it, 'from first to last we know infinitesimally little about them';[2] but we need not fancy that we are teaching nothing in so speaking of them, or are failing to preach a dogmatic faith or by it to mould lives in essaying to occupy a position of indifference. To withhold these truths from our hearers is not merely a negative act, nor can their loss act merely negatively upon their spiritual development. A mutilated gospel produces mutilated lives, and mutilated lives are positive evils. Whatever the preacher may do, the hearers will not do without a system of belief; and in their attempt to frame one for the government of their lives out of the fragments of truth which such a preacher will grant to them, is it any wonder if they should go fatally astray? At the best, men will be 'driven to a kind of empirical theologizing, attempting with necessarily imperfect knowledge to co-ordinate for themselves

[1] Henry T. Sedgwick, Jr, in *The Atlantic Monthly*, August 1896, p. 188. 'This way, my friends, this way! Here are some (brand) new beliefs; here is the Truth!'
[2] *Op. cit.*, p. 26.

the truths of religion and those which follow as consequences from them';[1] and so will build up an erroneous system of belief which will mar their lives. At the worst, they will be led to discard the neglected or discredited truths, and with them the whole system of Christianity—which they see, even though the preacher does not see, to be necessarily correlated with them; and so will lapse into unbelief. In either case, they may rightly lay their marred or ruined lives at the preacher's door. It is not given to one who stands in the pulpit to decide whether or no he shall teach, whether or no he shall communicate to others a system of belief which will form lives and determine destinies. It is in his power only to determine what he shall teach, what system of doctrine he shall press upon the acceptance of men, by what body of tenets he will seek to mould their lives and to inform their devotions.

By as much, however, as the communication of a system of belief is the inevitable consequence of preaching, by so much is the careful formation of his system of belief the indispensable duty of the preacher. And this is but another way of saying that the systematic study of divine truth, or the study of systematic theology, is the most indispensable preparation for the pulpit. Only as the several truths to be presented are known in their relations can they be proclaimed in their right proportions and so taught as to produce their right effects on the soul's life and growth. Systematic theology is, in other words, the preacher's true text-book. Its study may be undertaken, no doubt, in a cold and unloving spirit, with the mind intent on merely scholastic or controversial ends. In that case it may be for the preacher an unfruitful occupation. But so undertaken it has also lost its true character. It exists not for these ends, but to 'make wise unto salvation'. And when undertaken as the means of acquiring a thorough and precise knowledge of those truths which are fitted to 'make wise unto salvation', it will assuredly bear its fruit in the preacher's own heart in a fine skill in rightly dividing the word of truth, and in the lives of the hearers as a power within them working a right attitude before God and building them up into the fulness of the stature of symmetrical manhood in Christ.

---

[1] Aubrey Moore, *Some Aspects of Sin,* p. 25.

THE CHRIST THAT PAUL PREACHED[1]

'THE monumental introduction of the Epistle to the Romans'—it is thus that W. Bousset speaks of the seven opening verses of the epistle—is, from the formal point of view, merely the address of the epistle. In primary purpose and fundamental structure it does not differ from the addresses of Paul's other epistles. But even in the addresses of his epistles Paul does not confine himself to the simple repetition of a formula. Here too he writes at his ease and shows himself very much the master of his form.

It is Paul's custom to expand one or another of the essential elements of the address of his epistles as circumstances suggested, and thus to impart to it in each several instance a specific character. The address of the Epistle to the Romans is the extreme example of this expansion. Paul is approaching in it a church which he had not visited, and to which he apparently felt himself somewhat of a stranger. He naturally begins with some words adapted to justify his writing to it, especially as an authoritative teacher of Christian truth. In doing this he is led to describe briefly the gospel which had been committed to him, and that particularly with regard to its contents.

There is very strikingly illustrated here a peculiarity of Paul's style, which has been called 'going off at a word'. His particular purpose is to represent himself as one authoritatively appointed to teach the gospel of God. But he is more interested in the gospel than he is in himself; and he no sooner mentions the gospel than off he goes on a tangent to describe it. In describing it, he naturally tells us particularly what its contents are. Its contents, however, were for him summed up in Christ. No sooner does he mention Christ than off

[1] B. B. Warfield, 'The Christ That Paul Preached', *The Expositor,* 8th ser., xv, 1918, pp. 90-110 (repr. *Biblical Doctrines,* [Edinburgh: Banner of Truth, 2002], pp. 235-52).

he goes again on a tangent to describe Christ. Thus it comes about that this passage, formally only the address of the epistle, becomes actually a great Christological deliverance, one of the chief sources of our knowledge of Paul's conception of Christ. It presents itself to our view like one of those nests of Chinese boxes; the outer encasement is the address of the epistle; within that fits neatly Paul's justification of his addressing the Romans as an authoritative teacher of the gospel; within that a description of the gospel committed to him; and within that a great declaration of who and what Jesus Christ is, as the contents of this gospel.

The manner in which Paul approaches this great declaration concerning Christ lends it a very special interest. What we are given is not merely how Paul thought of Christ, but how Paul preached Christ. It is the content of 'the gospel of God', the gospel to which he as 'a called apostle' had been 'separated', which he outlines in these pregnant words. This is how Paul preached Christ to the faith of men as he went up and down the world 'serving God in his spirit in the gospel of his Son'. We have no abstract *theologoumena* here, categories of speculative thought appropriate only to the closet. We have the great facts about Jesus which made the gospel that Paul preached the power of God unto salvation to every one that believed. Nowhere else do we get a more direct description of specifically the Christ that Paul preached.

The direct description of the Christ that Paul preached is given us, of course, in the third and fourth verses. But the wider setting in which these verses are embedded cannot be neglected in seeking to get at their significance. In this wider setting the particular aspect in which Christ is presented is that of 'Lord'. It is as 'Lord' that Paul is thinking of Jesus when he describes himself in the opening words of the address—in the very first item of his commendation of himself to the Romans— as 'the slave of Christ Jesus'. 'Slave' is the correlate of 'Lord', and the relation must be taken at its height. When Paul calls himself the slave of Christ Jesus, he is calling Christ Jesus his Lord in the most complete sense which can be ascribed to that word (*cf. Rom.* 1:1; *Gal.* 1:10). He is declaring that he recognizes in Christ Jesus one over against whom he has no rights, whose property he is, body and soul, to be disposed of as he will. This is not because he abases himself. It is because he exalts Christ. It is because Christ is thought of by him as one whose right it is to rule, and to rule with no limit to his right.

How Paul thought of Christ as Lord comes out, however, with most startling clearness in the closing words of the address. There he couples 'the Lord Jesus Christ' with 'God our Father' as the common source from which he seeks in prayer the divine gifts of grace and peace for the Romans. We must renounce enervating glossing here too. Paul is not thinking of the Lord Jesus Christ as only the channel through which grace and peace come from God our Father to men; nor is he thinking of the Lord Jesus Christ as only the channel through which his prayer finds its way to God our Father. His prayer for these blessings for the Romans is offered up to God our Father and the Lord Jesus Christ together, as the conjoint object addressed in his petition. So far as this Bousset's remark is just: 'Prayer to God in Christ is for Pauline Christianity, too, a false formula; adoration of the *Kyrios* stands in the Pauline communities side by side with adoration of God in unreconciled reality.'

Only, we must go further. Paul couples God our Father and the Lord Jesus Christ in his prayer on a complete equality. They are, for the purposes of the prayer, for the purposes of the bestowment of grace and peace, one to him. Christ is so highly exalted in his sight that, looking up to him through the immense stretches which separate him from the plane of human life, 'the forms of God and Christ', as Bousset puts it, 'are brought to the eye of faith into close conjunction'. He should have said that they completely coalesce. It is only half the truth—though it is half the truth—to say that, with Paul, 'the object of religious faith, as of religious worship, presents itself in a singular, thoroughgoing dualism'. The other half of the truth is that this dualism resolves itself into a complete unity. The two, God our Father and the Lord Jesus Christ, are steadily recognized as two, and are statedly spoken of by the distinguishing designations of 'God' and 'Lord'. But they are equally steadily envisaged as one, and are statedly combined as the common object of every religious aspiration and the common source of every spiritual blessing. It is no accident that they are united in our present passage under the government of the single preposition, 'from',—'Grace to you and peace from God our Father and the Lord Jesus Christ.' This is normal with Paul. God our Father and the Lord Jesus Christ are not to him two objects of worship, two sources of blessing, but one object of worship, one source of blessing. Does he not tell us plainly that we who have one God the Father and one Lord Jesus Christ yet know perfectly well that there is no God but one (*1 Cor.* 8:4, 6)?

Paul is writing the address of his Epistle to the Romans, then, with his mind fixed on the divine dignity of Christ. It is this divine Christ who, he must be understood to be telling his readers, constitutes the substance of his gospel proclamation. He does not leave us, however, merely to infer this. He openly declares it. The gospel he preaches, he says, concerns precisely 'the Son of God . . . Jesus Christ our Lord'. He expressly says, then, that he presents Christ in his preaching as 'our Lord'. It was the divine Christ that he preached, the Christ that the eye of faith could not distinguish from God, who was addressed in common with God in prayer, and was looked to in common with God as the source of all spiritual blessings. Paul does not speak of Christ here, however, merely as 'our Lord'. He gives him the two designations: 'the Son of God . . . Jesus Christ our Lord'. The second designation obviously is explanatory of the first. Not as if it were the more current or the more intelligible designation. It may, or it may not, have been both the one and the other; but that is not the point here. The point here is that it is the more intimate, the more appealing designation. It is the designation which tells what Christ is to us. He is our Lord, he to whom we go in prayer, he to whom we look for blessings, he to whom all our religious emotions turn, on whom all our hopes are set—for this life and for that to come. Paul tells the Romans that this is the Christ that he preaches, their and his Lord whom both they and he reverence and worship and love and trust in. This is, of course, what he mainly wishes to say to them; and it is up to this that all else that he says of the Christ that he preaches leads.

The other designation—'the Son of God'—which Paul prefixes to this in his fundamental declaration concerning the Christ that he preached, supplies the basis for this. It does not tell us what Christ is to us, but what Christ is in himself. In himself he is the Son of God; and it is only because he is the Son of God in himself, that he can be and is our Lord. The Lordship of Christ is rooted by Paul, in other words, not in any adventitious circumstances connected with his historical manifestation; not in any powers or dignities conferred on him or acquired by him; but fundamentally in his metaphysical nature. The designation 'Son of God' is a metaphysical designation and tells us what he is in his Being of being. And what it tells us that Christ is in his Being of being is that he is just what God is. It is undeniable—and Bousset, for example, does not deny it,—that, from the earliest days of Christianity on, (in Bousset's words) 'Son of God was equivalent simply to equal with God' (*Mark* 14:61-63; *John* 10:31-39).

That Paul meant scarcely so much as this, Bousset to be sure would fain have us believe. He does not dream, of course, of supposing Paul to mean nothing more than that Jesus had been elevated into the relation of Sonship to God because of his moral uniqueness, or of his community of will with God. He is compelled to allow that 'the Son of God appears in Paul as a supramundane Being standing in close metaphysical relation with God'. But he would have us understand that, however close he stands to God, he is not, in Paul's view, quite equal with God. Paul, he suggests, has seized on this term to help him through the frightful problem of conceiving of this second divine Being consistently with his monotheism. Christ is not quite God to him, but only the Son of God. Of such refinements, however, Paul knows nothing. With him too the maxim rules that whatever the father is, that the son is also: every father begets his son in his own likeness. The Son of God is necessarily to him just God, and he does not scruple to declare this Son of God all that God is (*Phil.* 2:6; *Col.* 2:9) and even to give him the supreme name of 'God over all' (*Rom.* 9:5).

This is fundamentally, then, how Paul preached Christ—as the Son of God in this super-eminent sense, and therefore our divine Lord on whom we absolutely depend and to whom we owe absolute obedience. But this was not all that he was accustomed to preach concerning Christ. Paul preached the historical Jesus as well as the eternal Son of God. And between these two designations—Son of God, our Lord Jesus Christ—he inserts two clauses which tell us how he preached the historical Jesus. All that he taught about Christ was thrown up against the background of his deity: he is the Son of God, our Lord. But who is this that is thus so fervently declared to be the Son of God and our Lord? It is in the two clauses which are now to occupy our attention that Paul tells us.

If we reduce what he tells us to its lowest terms it amounts just to this: Paul preached the historical Christ as the promised Messiah and as the very Son of God. But he declares Christ to be the promised Messiah and the very Son of God in language so pregnant, so packed with implications, as to carry us into the heart of the great problem of the two-natured person of Christ. The exact terms in which he describes Christ as the promised Messiah and the very Son of God are these: 'Who became of the seed of David according to the flesh, who was marked out as the Son of God in power according to the Spirit of holiness by the resurrection of the dead.' This in brief is the account which Paul gives of the historical Christ whom he preached.

Of course there is a temporal succession suggested in the declarations of the two clauses. They so far give us not only a description of the historical Christ, but the life-history of the Christ that Paul preached. Jesus Christ became of the seed of David at his birth and by his birth. He was marked out as the Son of God in power only at his resurrection and by his resurrection. But it was not to indicate this temporal succession that Paul sets the two declarations side by side. It emerges merely as the incidental, or we may say even the accidental, result of their collocation. The relation in which Paul sets the two declarations to one another is a logical rather than a temporal one: it is the relation of climax. His purpose is to exalt Jesus Christ. He wishes to say the great things about him. And the two greatest things he has to say about him in his historical manifestation are these—that he became of the seed of David according to the flesh, that he was marked out as the Son of God in power according to the Spirit of holiness by the resurrection of the dead.

Both of these declarations, we say, are made for the purpose of extolling Christ: the former just as truly as the latter. That Christ came as the Messiah belongs to his glory; and the particular terms in which his Messiahship is intimated are chosen in order to enhance his glory. The word 'came', 'became' is correlated with the 'promised afore' of the preceding verse. This is he, Paul says, whom all the prophets did before signify, and who at length came—even as they signified—of the seed of David. There is doubtless an intimation of the pre-existence of Christ here also, as J. B. Lightfoot properly instructs us: he who was always the Son of God now 'became' of the seed of David. But this lies somewhat apart from the main current of thought. The heart of the declaration resides in the great words, 'of the seed of David'. For these are great words. In declaring the Messiahship of Jesus Paul adduces his royal dignity. And he adduces it because he is thinking of the majesty of the Messiahship. We must beware, then, of reading this clause depreciatingly, as if Paul were making a concession in it: 'He came, no doubt, . . . he came, indeed, . . . of the seed of David, but . . .' Paul never for an instant thought of the Messiahship of Jesus, as a thing to be apologised for. The relation of the second clause to the first is not that of opposition, but of climax; and it contains only so much of contrast as is intrinsic in a climax. The connection would be better expressed by an 'and' than by a 'but'; or, if by a 'but', not by an 'indeed . . . but', but by a 'not only . . . but'. Even the Messiahship, inexpressibly glorious as it is, does not exhaust the glory of Christ. He had a glory greater than even this. This was but the beginning of his glory. But it was the beginning of his glory. He came into the world as the promised Messiah, and he went out of the world as the demonstrated Son of God. In these two things is summed up the majesty of his historical manifestation.

It is not intended to say that when he went out of the world, he left his Messiahship behind him. The relation of the second clause to the first is not that of supersession but that of superposition. Paul passes from one glory to another, but he is as far as possible from suggesting that the one glory extinguished the other. The resurrection of Christ had no tendency to abolish his Messiahship, and the exalted Christ remains 'of the seed of David'. There is no reason to doubt that Paul would have exhorted his readers when he wrote these words with all the fervour with which he did later to 'remember Jesus Christ, risen from the dead, of the seed of David' (*2 Tim.* 2:8). 'According to my gospel', he adds there, as an intimation that it was as 'of the seed of David' that he was accustomed to preach Jesus Christ, whether as on earth as here, or as in heaven as there. It is the exalted Jesus that proclaims himself in the Apocalypse 'the root and the offspring of David' (*Rev.* 22:16; 5:5), and in whose hands 'the key of David' is found (3:7).

And as it is not intimated that Christ ceased to be 'of the seed of David' when he rose from the dead, neither is it intimated that he then first became the Son of God. He was already the Son of God when and before he became of the seed of David; and he did not cease to be the Son of God on and by becoming of the seed of David. It was rather just because he was the Son of God that he became of the seed of David, to become which, in the great sense of the prophetic announcements and of his own accomplishment, he was qualified only by being the Son of God. Therefore Paul does not say he was made the Son of God by the resurrection of the dead. He says he was defined, marked out, as the Son of God by the resurrection of the dead. His resurrection from the dead was well adapted to mark him out as the Son of God: scarcely to make him the Son of God. Consider but what the Son of God in Paul's usage means; and precisely what the resurrection was and did. It was a thing which was quite appropriate to happen to the Son of God; and, happening, could bear strong witness to him as such; but how could it make one the Son of God?

We might possibly say, no doubt, with a tolerable meaning, that Christ was installed, even constituted, 'Son of God in power' by the resurrection of the dead—if we could see our way to construe the words 'in power' thus directly with 'the Son of God'. That too would imply that he was already the Son of God before he rose from the dead,—only then in weakness; what he had been all along in weakness he now was constituted in power. This construction, however, though not impossible, is hardly natural. And it imposes a sense on the preceding clause of which it itself gives no suggestion, and which it is reluctant to receive. To say, 'of the seed of David' is not to say weakness; it is to say majesty. It is quite certain, indeed, that the assertion 'who was made of the seed of David' cannot be read concessively, preparing the way for the celebration of Christ's glory in the succeeding clause. It stands rather in parallelism with the clause that follows it, asserting with it the supreme glory of Christ.

In any case, the two clauses do not express two essentially different modes of Being through which Christ successively passed. We could think at most only of two successive stages of manifestation of the Son of God. At most we could see in it a declaration that he who always was and continues always to be the Son of God was manifested to men first as the Son of David, and then, after his resurrection, as also the exalted Lord. He always was in the essence of his being the Son of God; this Son of God became of the seed of David and was installed as—what he always was—the Son of God, though now in his proper power, by the resurrection of the dead. It is assuredly wrong, however, to press even so far the idea of temporal succession. Temporal succession was not what it was in Paul's mind to emphasize, and is not the ruling idea of his assertion. The ruling idea of his assertion is the celebration of the glory of Christ. We think of temporal succession only because of the mention of the resurrection, which, in point of fact, cuts our Lord's life-manifestation into two sections. But Paul is not adducing the resurrection because it cuts our Lord's life-manifestation into two sections; but because of the demonstration it brought of the dignity of his person. It is quite indifferent to his declaration when the resurrection took place. He is not adducing it as the producing cause of a change in our Lord's mode of Being. In point of fact it did not produce a change in our Lord's mode of Being, although it stood at the opening of a new stage of his life-history. What it did, and what Paul adduces it here as doing, was that it brought out into plain view who and what Christ really was. This, says Paul, is the Christ I preach—he who came of the seed of David, he who was marked out in power as the Son of God, by the resurrection of the dead. His thought of Christ runs in the two moulds—his Messiahship, his resurrection. But he is not particularly concerned here with the temporal relations of these two facts.

Paul does not, however, say of Christ merely that he became of the seed of David and was marked out as the Son of God in power by the resurrection of the dead. He introduces a qualifying phrase into each clause. He says that he became of the seed of David 'according to the flesh', and that he was marked out as the Son of God in power 'according to the Spirit of holiness' by the resurrection of the dead. What is the nature of the qualifications made by these phrases?

It is obvious at once that they are not temporal qualifications. Paul does not mean to say, in effect, that our Lord was Messiah only during his earthly manifestation, and became the Son of God only on and by means of his resurrection. It has already appeared that Paul did not think of the Messiahship of our Lord only in connection with his earthly manifestation, or of his Sonship to God only in connection with his post-resurrection existence. And the qualifying phrases themselves are ill-adapted to express this temporal distinction. Even if we could twist the phrase 'according to the flesh' into meaning 'according to his human manifestation' and violently make that do duty as a temporal definition, the parallel phrase 'according to the Spirit of holiness' utterly refuses to yield to any treatment which could make it mean, 'according to his heavenly manifestation'. And nothing could be more monstrous than to represent precisely the resurrection as in the case of Christ the producing cause of—the source out of which proceeds—a condition of existence which could be properly characterized as distinctively 'spiritual'. Exactly what the resurrection did was to bring it about that his subsequent mode of existence should continue to be, like the precedent, 'fleshly'; to assimilate his post-resurrection to his pre-resurrection mode of existence in the matter of the constitution of his person. And if we fall back on the ethical contrast of the terms, that could only mean that Christ should be supposed to be represented as imperfectly holy in his earthly stage of existence, and as only on his resurrection attaining to complete holiness (*cf. 1 Cor.* 15:44, 46). It is very certain that Paul did not mean that (*2 Cor.* 5:21).

It is clear enough, then, that Paul cannot by any possibility have intended to represent Christ as in his pre-resurrection and his post-resurrection modes of Being differing in any way which can be naturally expressed by the contrasting terms 'flesh' and 'spirit'. Least of all can he be supposed to have intended this distinction in the sense of the ethical contrast between these terms. But a further word may be pardoned as to this. That it is precisely this ethical contrast that Paul intends has been insisted on under cover of the adjunct 'of holiness' attached here to 'spirit'. The contrast, it is said, is not between 'flesh' and 'spirit', but between 'flesh' and 'spirit of holiness'; and what is intended is to represent Christ, who on earth was merely 'Christ according to the flesh'—the 'flesh of sin' of course, it is added, that is 'the flesh which was in the grasp of sin'—to have been, 'after and in consequence of the resurrection', 'set free from "the likeness of (weak and sinful) flesh"'. Through the resurrection, in other words, Christ has for the first time become the holy Son of God, free from entanglement with sin-cursed flesh; and, having thus saved himself, is qualified, we suppose, now to save others, by bringing them through the same experience of resurrection to the same holiness. We have obviously wandered here sufficiently far from the declarations of the apostle; and we have landed in a *reductio ad absurdum* of this whole system of interpretation. Paul is not here distinguishing times and contrasting two successive modes of our Lord's Being. He is distinguishing elements in the constitution of our Lord's person, by virtue of which he is at one and the same time both the Messiah and the Son of God. He became of the seed of David with respect to the flesh, and by the resurrection of the dead was mightily proven to be also the Son of God with respect to the Spirit of holiness.

It ought to go without saying that by these two elements in the constitution of our Lord's person, the flesh and the spirit of holiness, by virtue of which he is at once of the seed of David and the Son of God, are not intended the two constituent elements, flesh and spirit, which go to make up common humanity. It is impossible that Paul should have represented our Lord as the Messiah only by virtue of his bodily nature; and it is absurd to suppose him to suggest that his Sonship to God was proved by his resurrection to reside in his mental nature or even in his ethical purity—to say nothing now of supposing him to assert that he was made by the resurrection into the Son of God, or into 'the Son of God in power' with respect to his mental nature here described as holy. How the resurrection—which was in itself just the resumption of the body—of all things, could be thought of as constituting our Lord's mental nature the Son of God passes imagination; and if it be conceivable that it might at least prove that he was the Son of God, it remains hidden how it could be so emphatically asserted that it was only with reference to his mental nature, in sharp contrast with his bodily, thus recovered to him, that this was proved concerning him precisely by his resurrection. Is Paul's real purpose here to guard men from supposing that our Lord's bodily nature, though recovered to him in this great act, the resurrection, entered into his Sonship to God? There is no reason discoverable in the context why this distinction between our Lord's bodily and mental natures should be so strongly stressed here. It is clearly an artificial distinction imposed on the passage.

When Paul tells us of the Christ which he preached that he was made of the seed of David 'according to the flesh', he quite certainly has the whole of his humanity in mind. And in introducing this limitation, 'according to the flesh', into his declaration that Christ was 'made of the seed of David', he intimates not obscurely that there was another side—not aspect but element—of his Being besides his humanity, in which he was not made of the seed of David, but was something other and higher. If he had said nothing more than just these words: 'He was made of the seed of David according to the flesh', this intimation would still have been express; though we might have been left to speculation to determine what other element could have entered into his Being, and what he must have been according to that element. He has not left us, however, to this speculation, but has plainly told us that the Christ he preached was not merely made of the seed of David according to the flesh, but was also marked out as the Son of God, in power, according to the Spirit of holiness by the resurrection of the dead. Since the 'according to the flesh' includes all his humanity, the 'according to the Spirit of holiness' which is set in contrast with it, and according to which he is declared to be the Son of God, must be sought outside of his humanity. What the nature of this element of his Being in which he is superior to humanity is, is already clear from the fact that according to it he is the Son of God. 'Son of God' is, as we have already seen, a metaphysical designation asserting equality with God. It is a divine name. To say that Christ is, according to the Spirit of holiness, the Son of God, is to say that the Spirit of holiness is a designation of his divine nature. Paul's whole assertion therefore amounts to saying that, in one element of his Being, the Christ that he preached was man, in another God. Looked at from the point of view of his human nature, he was the Messiah—'of the seed of David'. Looked at from the point of view of his divine nature, he was the Son of God. Looked at in his composite personality, he was both the Messiah and the Son of God, because in him were united both he that came of the seed of David according to the flesh and he who was marked out as the Son of God in power according to the Spirit of holiness by the resurrection of the dead. We may be somewhat puzzled by the designation of the divine nature of Christ as 'the Spirit of holiness'. But not only is it plain from its relation to its contrast, 'the flesh', and to its correlate, 'the Son of God', that it is his divine nature which is so designated, but this is made superabundantly clear from the closely parallel passage, Romans 9:5. There, in enumerating the glories of Israel, the apostle comes to his climax in this great declaration,—that from Israel Christ came. But there, no more than here, will he allow that it was the whole Christ who came—as said there from the stock of Israel, as said here from the seed of David. He adds there too at once the limitation, 'as concerns the flesh',—just as he adds it here. Thus he intimates with emphasis that something more is to be said, if we are to give a complete account of Christ's Being; there was something about him in which he did not come from Israel, and in which he is more than 'flesh'. What this something is, Paul adds in the great words, 'God over all'. He who was from Israel according to the flesh is, on the other side of his Being, in which he is not from Israel and not 'flesh', nothing other than 'God over all'. In our present passage, the phrase, 'Spirit of holiness', takes the place of 'God over all' in the other. Clearly Paul means the same thing by them both.

This being very clear, what interests us most is the emphasis which Paul throws on holiness in his designation of the divine nature of Christ. The simple word 'Spirit' might have been ambiguous: when 'the Spirit of holiness' is spoken of, the divine nature is expressly named. No doubt, Paul might have used the adjective, 'holy', instead of the genitive of the substantive, 'of holiness'; and have said 'the Holy Spirit'. Had he done so, he would have as expressly intimated deity as in his actual phrase. But he would have left open the possibility of being misunderstood as speaking of that distinct Holy Spirit to which this designation is commonly applied. The relation in which the divine nature which he attributes to Christ stands to the Holy Spirit was in Paul's mind no doubt very close; as close as the relation between 'God' and 'Lord' whom he constantly treats as, though two, yet also one. Not only does he identify the activities of the two (*e.g.,* *Rom.* 8:9ff.); but also, in some high sense, he identifies them themselves. He can make use, for example, of such a startling expression as 'the Lord is the Spirit' (*2 Cor.* 3:17). Nevertheless, it is perfectly clear that 'the Lord' and 'the Spirit' are not one person to Paul, and the distinguishing employment of the designations 'the Spirit', 'the Holy Spirit' is spread broadcast over his pages. Even in immediate connection with his declaration that 'the Lord is the Spirit', he can speak with the utmost naturalness not only of 'the Spirit of the Lord', but also of 'the Lord of the Spirit' (*2 Cor.* 3:17f.). What is of especial importance to note in our present connection is that he is not speaking of an endowment of Christ either from or with the Holy Spirit; although he would be the last to doubt that he who was made of the seed of David according to the flesh was plenarily endowed both from and with the Spirit. He is speaking of that divine Spirit which is the complement in the constitution of Christ's person of the human nature according to which he was the Messiah, and by virtue of which he was not merely the Messiah, but also the very Son of God. This Spirit he calls distinguishingly the Spirit of holiness, the Spirit the very characteristic of which is holiness. He is speaking not of an acquired holiness but of an intrinsic holiness; not, then, of a holiness which had been conferred at the time of or attained by means of the resurrection from the dead; but of a holiness which had always been the very quality of Christ's Being. He is not representing Christ as having first been after a fleshly fashion the son of David and afterwards becoming by or at the resurrection from the dead, after a spiritual fashion, the holy Son of God. He is representing him as being in his very nature essentially and therefore always and in every mode of his manifestation holy. Bousset is quite right when he declares that there is no reference in the phrase 'Spirit of holiness' to the preservation of his holiness by Christ in his earthly manifestation, but that it is a metaphysical designation describing according to its intrinsic quality an element in the constitution of Christ's person from the beginning. This is the characteristic of the Christ Paul preached; as truly his characteristic as that he was the Messiah. Evidently in Paul's thought of deity holiness held a prominent place. When he wishes to distinguish Spirit from spirit, it is enough for him that he may designate Spirit as divine, to define it as that Spirit the fundamental characteristic of which is that it is holy.

It belongs to the very essence of the conception of Christ as Paul preached him, therefore, that he was of two natures, human and divine. He could not preach him at once as of the seed of David and as the Son of God without so preaching him. It never entered Paul's mind that the Son of God could become a mere man, or that a mere man could become the Son of God. We may say that the conception of the two natures is unthinkable to us. That is our own concern. That a single nature could be at once or successively God and man, man and God, was what was unthinkable to Paul. In his view, when we say God and man we say two natures; when we put a hyphen between them and say God-man, we do not merge them one in the other but join the two together. That this was Paul's mode of thinking of Jesus, Bousset, for example, does not dream of denying. What Bousset is unwilling to admit is that the divine element in his two-natured Christ was conceived by Paul as completely divine. Two metaphysical entities, he says, combined themselves for Paul in the person of Christ: one of these was a human, the other a divine nature; and Paul, along with the whole Christian community of his day, worshipped this two-natured Christ, though he (not they) ranked him in his thought of his higher nature below the God over all.

The trouble with this construction is that Paul himself gives a different account of the matter. The point of Paul's designation of Christ as the Son of God is not to subordinate him to God, as Bousset affirms, but to equalize him with God. He knows no difference in dignity between his God and his Lord; to both alike, or rather to both in common, he offers his prayers; from both alike and both together he expects all spiritual blessings (*Rom.* 1:7). He roundly calls Christ, by virtue of his higher nature, by the supreme name of 'God over all' (*Rom.* 9:5). These things cannot be obscured by pointing to expressions in which he ascribes to the divine-human Christ a relation of subordination to God in his saving work. Paul does not fail to distinguish between what Christ is in the higher element of his Being, and what he became when, becoming poor that we might be made rich, he assumed for his work's sake the position of a servant in the world. Nor does he permit the one set of facts to crowd the other out of his mind. It is no accident that all that he says about the historical two-natured Christ in our present passage is inserted between his two divine designations of the Son of God and Lord; that the Christ that he preached he describes precisely as 'the Son of God—who was made of the seed of David according to the flesh, who was marked out as the Son of God in power according to the Spirit of holiness by the resurrection of the dead—Jesus Christ our Lord.' He who is defined as on the human side of David, on the divine side the Son of God, this two-natured person, is declared to be from the point of view of God, his own Son, and—as all sons are—like him in essential nature; from the point of view of man, our supreme Lord, whose we are and whom we obey. Ascription of proper deity could not be made more complete; whether we look at him from the point of view of God or from the point of view of man, he is God. But what Paul preached concerning this divine Being belonged to his earthly manifestation; he was made of the seed of David, he was marked out as God's Son. The conception of the two natures is not with Paul a negligible speculation attached to his gospel. He preached Jesus. And he preached of Jesus that he was the Messiah. But the Messiah that he preached was no merely human Messiah. He was the Son of God who was made of the seed of David. And he was demonstrated to be what he really was by his resurrection from the dead.

This was the Jesus that Paul preached: this and none other.

AUTHORITY, INTELLECT, HEART[1]

THE exact nature of the intimate relation between religion and theology is not always perceived. Sometimes religion is made the direct product of theology; more frequently theology is conceived as directly based on religion. The truth is that while they react continually upon each other, neither is the creation of the other. They are parallel products of the same body of truths in different spheres. Religion is the name we give to religious life; theology is the name we give to the systematized body of religious thought. Neither is the product of the other, but both are products of religious truth, operative in the two spheres of life and thought. Neither can exist without the other. No one but a religious man can be a true theologian. No one can live religiously who is innocent of all theological conceptions. Man is a unit; and the religious truth which impinges upon him must affect him in all his activities, or in none. But it is in their common cause—religious truth—that religion and theology find their deepest connection. The truth concerning God, his nature, his will, his purposes is the fundamental fact upon which both religion and theology rest. The truth of God is, therefore, the greatest thing on earth. On it rest our faith, our hope, and our love. Through it we are converted and sanctified. On it depends all our religion, as well as all our theology.

There are three media or channels through which the truth of God is brought to man and made his possession, that it may affect his life and so make him religious, or that it may be systematized in his thinking and so issue in a theology. These three media or channels of communication may be enumerated briefly as authority, the intellect, and the heart. They are not so related to one another that any one of

[1] B. B. Warfield, 'Authority, Intellect, and Heart', *The Presbyterian Messenger*, January 30, 1896, pp. 7-8.

521

them may be depended upon to the exclusion of the others. In any sound religion and in any true religious thinking, that is theology, all three must be engaged, and must work harmoniously together as the proximate sources of our religion and of our knowledge. The exaltation of any one of the three to the relative exclusion of the others will, therefore, mar our religious life and our religious thought alike, and make both one-sided and deformed. We cannot have a symmetrical religious life or a true theology except through the perfect interaction of all three sources of communication of the truth.

It may, indeed, be plausibly pleaded that the three reduce ultimately to one; and this one channel of truth may, with almost equal plausibility, be found in each of the three in turn. Thus it may be urged that our confidence in the processes of our intellects and in the deliverances of our feelings, rests ultimately on the trustworthiness of God; so that, after all, authority is the sole source of our information concerning God. We know only what and as God tells us. Similarly it may be argued that all the *dicta* of authority are addressed to the intellect, which, also, is the sole instrument for ascertaining the implications of the feelings; so that all our sources of knowledge reduce at last to this one source—the intellect. We know only what our intellect grasps and formulates for us. Still again, it may be contended that not the logical reason but the facts of life, our upward strivings, our feelings of dependence and responsibility, supply the points of contact between us and God, without which all the thunders of authority and all the excursions of thought into the realm of divine things would be as unintelligible to us and as inoperative upon us as a babbling of colours would be to a blind man. There is truth in each of these representations; but they do not avail to show that we have but one means of access to divine things, but rather emphasize the fact that the three sources so interlace and interact that one may not be exaggerated to the exclusion of the others as our sole channel of knowledge concerning God and divine things.

The exaggeration of the principle of authority to the discrediting of the others would cast us into *traditionalism,* and would ultimately deliver us bound hand and foot to the irresponsible dogmatism of a privileged caste. This is the pathway which has been trodden by the Church of Rome, and we have as the result a nerveless submission to the *dicta,* first of an infallible church, then of an infallible class, and lastly of an infallible person. Here neither the heart nor the intellect is permitted to speak in the presence of lordly authority; but men are commanded docilely to receive, on authority alone, even what contradicts their most primary intuitions (as in the doctrine of transubstantiation) or what outrages their most intimate feelings (as in the use of indulgences).

The exaggeration of the principle of intellect to the discrediting of the others would bring us to *rationalism,* and leave us helplessly in the grasp of the merely logical understanding. This pathway has been followed by the rationalists, and we have as the result any number of *a priori* systems built up on the sole credit of the reasoning faculty. Here neither revelation nor the conscience is permitted to raise a protest against the chill processes of intellectual formulae, but all things are reconstructed at the bidding of *a priori* fancies, and men are required to reject as false all for which they have not a demonstration ready even though God has spoken to assert its truth (as in the doctrine of the Trinity) or the heart rises up and answers, I have felt (as in original sin).

The exaggeration of the principle of the heart to the discrediting of the others would throw us into *mysticism,* and deliver us over to the deceitfulness of the currents of feeling which flow up and down in our souls. This pathway has been travelled by the mystics, and we have as the result the clash of rival revelations, and the deification of the most morbid of human imaginations. Here neither the objective truth of a revealed word nor adherence to rational thinking is allowed to check the wild dreaming of a soul that fancies itself divine, or the confusion of our weakest sentiments with the strong voice of God; and men are forbidden to clarify their crude fancies by right reason (as in the doctrine of absorption in God), or to believe God's own testimony to his real nature (as with reference to his personality).

Thus authority, when pressed beyond its mark and becoming traditionalism, intellect when puffed up into rationalism, and the heart when swamped in mysticism, alike illustrate the danger of one-sided construction. Authority, intellect, and the heart are the three sides of the triangle of truth. How they interact is observable in any concrete instance of their operation. Authority, in the Scriptures, furnishes the matter which is received in the intellect and operates on the heart. The revelations of the Scriptures do not terminate upon the intellect. They were not given merely to enlighten the mind. They were given through the intellect to beautify the life. They terminate on the heart. Again, they do not, in affecting the heart, leave the intellect untouched. They cannot be fully understood by the intellect, acting alone. The natural man cannot receive the things of the Spirit of God. They must first convert the soul before they are fully comprehended by the intellect. Only as they are lived are they understood. Hence the phrase, 'Believe that you may understand', has its fullest validity. No man can intellectually grasp the full meaning of the revelations of authority, save as the result of an experience of their power in life. Hence, that the truths concerning divine things may be so comprehended that they may unite with a true system of divine truth, they must be: first, revealed in an authoritative word; second, experienced in a holy heart; and third, formulated by a sanctified intellect. Only as these three unite, then, can we have a true theology. And equally, that these same truths may be so received that they beget in us a living religion, they must be: first, revealed in an authoritative word; second, apprehended by a sound intellect; and third, experienced in an instructed heart. Only as the three unite, then, can we have a vital religion.

WHAT IS CALVINISM?[1]

I T is very odd how difficult it seems for some persons to understand just what Calvinism is. And yet the matter itself presents no difficulty whatever. It is capable of being put into a single sentence; and that, one level to every religious man's comprehension. For Calvinism is just religion in its purity. We have only, therefore, to conceive of religion in its purity, and that is Calvinism.

In what attitude of mind and heart does religion come most fully to its rights? Is it not in the attitude of prayer? When we kneel before God, not with the body merely, but with the mind and heart, we have assumed the attitude which above all others deserves the name of religious. And this religious attitude by way of eminence is obviously just the attitude of utter dependence and humble trust. He who comes to God in prayer, comes not in a spirit of self-assertion, but in a spirit of trustful dependence. No one ever addressed God in prayer thus: 'O God, thou knowest that I am the architect of my own fortunes and the determiner of my own destiny. Thou mayest indeed do something to help me in the securing of my purposes after I have determined upon them. But my heart is my own, and thou canst not intrude into it; my will is my own, and thou canst not bend it. When I wish thy aid, I will call on thee for it. Meanwhile, thou must await my pleasure.' Men may reason somewhat like this; but that is not the way they pray. There did, indeed, once two men go up into the temple to pray. And one stood and prayed thus to himself (can it be that this 'to himself' has a deeper significance than appears on the surface?), 'God, I thank thee that I am not as the rest of men.' While the other smote his breast, and said, 'God be merciful to me a sinner.' Even the former acknowledged a certain dependence on God; for he thanked God for his virtues. But we are not left in doubt in which

[1] B. B. Warfield, 'What is Calvinism?', *The Presbyterian*, March 2, 1904, pp. 6-7.

one the religious mood was most purely exhibited. There is one who has told us that with clearness and emphasis.

All men assume the religious attitude, then, when they pray. But many men box up, as it were, this attitude in their prayer, and shutting it off from their lives with the Amen, rise from their knees to assume a totally different attitude, if not of heart, then at least of mind. They pray as if they were dependent on God's mercy alone; they reason—perhaps they even live—as if God, in some of his activities at least, were dependent on them. The Calvinist is the man who is determined to preserve the attitude he takes in prayer in all his thinking, in all his feeling, in all his doing. That is to say, he is the man who is determined that religion in its purity shall come to its full rights in his thinking, and feeling, and living. This is the ground of his special mode of thought, by reason of which he is called a Calvinist; and as well of his special mode of acting in the world, by reason of which he has become the greatest regenerating force in the world. Other men are Calvinists on their knees; the Calvinist is the man who is determined that his intellect and heart and will shall remain on their knees continually, and only from this attitude think and feel and act. Calvinism is, therefore, that type of thought in which there comes to its rights the truly religious attitude of utter dependence on God and humble trust in his mercy alone for salvation.

There are at bottom but two types of religious thought in the world—if we may improperly use the term 'religious' for both of them. There is the religion of faith; there is the 'religion' of works. Calvinism is the pure embodiment of the former of these; what is known in church history as Pelagianism is the pure embodiment of the latter of them. All other forms of 'religious' teaching which have been known in Christendom are but unstable attempts at compromise between the two. At the opening of the fifth century, the two fundamental types came into direct conflict in remarkably pure form as embodied in the two persons of Augustine and Pelagius. Both were expending themselves in seeking to better the lives of men. But Pelagius in his exhortations threw men back on themselves; they were able, he declared, to do all that God demanded of them—otherwise God would not have demanded it. Augustine on the contrary pointed them in their weakness to God; 'He himself', he said, in his pregnant speech, 'He himself is our power.' The one is the 'religion' of proud self-dependence; the other is the religion of dependence on God. The one is the 'religion' of works; the other is the religion of faith. The one is not 'religion' at all—it is mere moralism; the other is all that is in the world that deserves to be called religion. Just in proportion as this attitude of faith is present in our thought, feeling, life, are we religious. When it becomes regnant in our thought, feeling, life, then are we truly religious. Calvinism is that type of thinking in which it has become regnant.

'There is a state of mind', says Professor William James in his lectures on 'The Varieties of Religious Experience', 'known to religious men, but to no others, in which the will to assert ourselves and hold our own has been displaced by a willingness to close our mouths and be as nothing in the floods and waterspouts of God.' He is describing what he looks upon as the truly religious mood as over against what he calls 'mere moralism'. 'The moralist', he tells us, 'must hold his breath and keep his muscles tense'; and things go well with him only when he can do so. The religious man, on the contrary, finds his consolation in his very powerlessness; his trust is not in himself, but in his God; and 'the hour of his moral death turns into his spiritual birthday'. The psychological analyst has caught the exact distinction between moralism and religion. It is the distinction between trust in ourselves and trust in God. And when trust in ourselves is driven entirely out, and trust in God comes in, in its purity, we have Calvinism. Under the name of religion at its height, what Professor James has really described is therefore just Calvinism.

We may take Professor James' testimony, therefore, as testimony that religion at its height is just Calvinism. There are many forms of religious teaching in the world which are not Calvinism. Because, teaching even in religion often (ordinarily even) offers us only 'broken lights'. There is no true religion in the world, however, which is not Calvinistic—Calvinistic in its essence, Calvinistic in its implications. When these implications are soundly drawn out and stated, and the essence thus comes to its rights, we obtain just Calvinism. In proportion as we are religious, in that proportion, then, are we Calvinistic; and when religion comes fully to its rights in our thinking, and feeling, and doing, then shall we be truly Calvinistic. This is why those who have caught a glimpse of these things love with passion what men call 'Calvinism', sometimes with an air of contempt; and why they cling to it with enthusiasm. It is not merely the hope of true religion in the world: it *is* true religion in the world—as far as true religion is in the world at all.

J. GRESHAM MACHEN
1881-1937

NEW Testament scholar, author, and minister, J. Gresham Machen was born at Baltimore, Maryland on July 28, 1881. Raised in a well-educated family with genteel tastes and a Southern heritage, Machen's Presbyterian upbringing was firmly rooted in the theological convictions of 'Old-school' Presbyterianism.

Machen's early academic aptitude for classical literature and languages resulted in his completion of an undergraduate degree in Classics at Baltimore's Johns Hopkins University, where he graduated in 1901. Following a post-graduate year of study in Classics at Hopkins, he enrolled at Princeton Theological Seminary while simultaneously completing studies at Princeton University for a Master's degree in Philosophy. Machen graduated from the university in 1904 and the seminary in 1905. After graduation from the latter, he travelled to Germany to study at the Universities of Marburg and Gottingen. He returned to

Princeton Theological Seminary in 1906, where he served as an instructor in the New Testament department. From 1914 until his resignation in 1929 he served as Assistant Professor of New Testament Literature and Exegesis.

During World War I, Machen volunteered and served with the YMCA on the European front (1917-18). He returned to Princeton with a renewed sense of the brevity of life and the devastating effect of sin on the human race.

A meticulous scholar and maturing churchman, Machen made significant contributions to New Testament studies and played an active role in identifying and addressing the changing theological currents within mainstream American Protestantism and the Northern Presbyterian Church. His important books, *The Origin of Paul's Religion* (1921) and *The Virgin Birth of Christ* (1930), were impressive works of scholarship, demonstrating the theological continuity between the teaching of Paul and that of Jesus while vindicating the biblical and historical validity of Christ's virgin birth. Machen's Greek grammar, *New Testament Greek for Beginners* (1923), remains in print as a standard treatment of its topic.

In response to the changing theological trajectories affecting his denomination and seminary, Machen published what may be his most enduring work, *Christianity and Liberalism* (1923). In a compelling yet clear manner, he addressed the profound ideological differences which exist between Protestant liberalism and historic Christianity, concluding they were, at root, two fundamentally different religions.

Machen's efforts to reverse and mitigate the impact of Protestant liberalism within his denomination and school would culminate in the founding of Westminster Theological Seminary in 1929, and, following his defrocking from the ordained ministry, a new Presbyterian denomination in 1936 (The Presbyterian Church of America, later renamed The Orthodox Presbyterian Church)—both of which new institutions were intended to carry on the theological heritage of 'Old-school' Presbyterianism which he believed had been forfeited within his former denomination, the Presbyterian Church in the U.S.A.

Machen's published writings include works in biblical studies, apologetics, sermons, and a variety of occasional addresses and articles, many of which remain of ongoing theological and pastoral value for maintaining both the orthodoxy of the church's beliefs and orthopraxy of the church's witness.

CHRISTIANITY AND CULTURE[1]

ONE of the greatest of the problems that have agitated the church is the problem of the relation between knowledge and piety, between culture and Christianity. This problem has appeared first of all in the presence of two tendencies in the church—the scientific or academic tendency, and what may be called the practical tendency. Some men have devoted themselves chiefly to the task of forming right conceptions as to Christianity and its foundations. To them no fact, however trivial, has appeared worthy of neglect; by them truth has been cherished for its own sake, without immediate reference to practical consequences. Some, on the other hand, have emphasized the essential simplicity of the gospel. The world is lying in misery, we ourselves are sinners, men are perishing in sin every day. The gospel is the sole means of escape; let us preach it to the world while yet we may. So desperate is the need that we have no time to engage in vain babblings or old wives' fables. While we are discussing the exact location of the churches of Galatia, men are perishing under the curse of the law; while we are settling the date of Jesus' birth, the world is doing without its Christmas message.

The representatives of both of these tendencies regard themselves as Christians, but too often there is little brotherly feeling between them. The Christian of academic tastes accuses his brother of undue emotionalism, of shallow argumentation, of cheap methods of work. On the other hand, your practical man is ever loud in his denunciation of academic indifference to the dire needs of humanity. The scholar is represented either as a dangerous disseminator of doubt, or else as a man whose faith is a faith without works. A man who

[1] J. Gresham Machen, 'Christianity and Culture', *The Princeton Theological Review* Vol. 11, No. 1 (1913), pp. 1-15.

investigates human sin and the grace of God by the aid solely of dusty volumes, carefully secluded in a warm and comfortable study, without a thought of the men who are perishing in misery every day!

But if the problem appears thus in the presence of different tendencies in the church, it becomes yet far more insistent within the consciousness of the individual. If we are thoughtful, we must see that the desire to know and the desire to be saved are widely different. The scholar must apparently assume the attitude of an impartial observer—an attitude which seems absolutely impossible to the pious Christian laying hold upon Jesus as the only Saviour from the load of sin. If these two activities—on the one hand the acquisition of knowledge, and on the other the exercise and inculcation of simple faith—are both to be given a place in our lives, the question of their proper relationship cannot be ignored.

The problem is made for us the more difficult of solution because we are unprepared for it. Our whole system of school and college education is so constituted as to keep religion and culture as far apart as possible and ignore the question of the relationship between them. On five or six days in the week, we were engaged in the acquisition of knowledge. From this activity the study of religion was banished. We studied natural science without considering its bearing or lack of bearing upon natural theology or upon revelation. We studied Greek without opening the New Testament. We studied history with careful avoidance of that greatest of historical movements which was ushered in by the preaching of Jesus. In philosophy, the vital importance of the study for religion could not entirely be concealed, but it was kept as far as possible in the background. On Sundays, on the other hand, we had religious instruction that called for little exercise of the intellect.

Careful preparation for Sunday School lessons as for lessons in mathematics or Latin was unknown. Religion seemed to be something that had to do only with the emotions and the will, leaving the intellect to secular studies. What wonder that after such training we came to regard religion and culture as belonging to two entirely separate compartments of the soul, and their union as involving the destruction of both?

Upon entering the seminary, we are suddenly introduced to an entirely different procedure. Religion is suddenly removed from its seclusion; the same methods of study are applied to it as were formerly reserved for natural science and for history. We study the Bible no longer solely with the desire of moral and spiritual improvement, but also in order to know. Perhaps the first impression is one of infinite loss. The scientific spirit seems to be replacing simple faith, the mere apprehension of dead facts to be replacing the practice of principles. The difficulty is perhaps not so much that we are brought face to face with new doubts as to the truth of Christianity. Rather is it the conflict of method, of spirit that troubles us. The scientific spirit seems to be incompatible with the old spirit of simple faith. In short, almost entirely unprepared, we are brought face to face with the problem of the relationship between knowledge and piety, or, otherwise expressed, between culture and Christianity.

This problem may be settled in one of three ways. In the first place, Christianity may be subordinated to culture. That solution really, though to some extent unconsciously, is being favoured by a very large and influential portion of the church today. For the elimination of the supernatural in Christianity—so tremendously common today—really makes Christianity merely natural. Christianity becomes a human product, a mere part of human culture. But as such it is something entirely different from the old Christianity that was based upon a direct revelation from God. Deprived thus of its note of authority, the gospel is no gospel any longer; it is a cheque for untold millions—but without the signature at the bottom. So in subordinating Christianity to culture we have really destroyed Christianity, and what continues to bear the old name is a counterfeit.

The second solution goes to the opposite extreme. In its effort to give religion a clear field, it seeks to destroy culture. This solution is better than the first. Instead of indulging in a shallow optimism or deification of humanity, it recognizes the profound evil of the world, and does not shrink from the most heroic remedy. The world is so evil that it cannot possibly produce the means for its own salvation. Salvation must be the gift of an entirely new life, coming directly from God. Therefore, it is argued, the culture of this world must be a matter at least of indifference to the Christian. Now in its extreme form this solution hardly requires refutation. If Christianity is really found to contradict that reason which is our only means of apprehending truth, then of course we must either modify or abandon Christianity. We cannot therefore be entirely independent of the achievements of the intellect. Furthermore, we cannot without inconsistency employ the printing-press, the railroad, the telegraph in the propagation of our gospel, and at the same time denounce as evil those activities of the human mind that produced these things. And in the production of these things not merely practical inventive genius had a part, but also, back of that, the investigations of pure science animated simply by the desire to know. In its extreme form, therefore, involving the abandonment of all intellectual activity, this second solution would be adopted by none of us. But very many pious men in the church today are adopting this solution in essence and in spirit. They admit that the Christian must have a part in human culture. But they regard such activity as a necessary evil—a dangerous and unworthy task, necessary to be gone through with under a stern sense of duty in order that thereby the higher ends of the gospel may be attained. Such men can never engage in the arts and sciences with anything like enthusiasm—such enthusiasm they would regard as disloyalty to the gospel. Such a position is really both illogical and unbiblical. God has given us certain powers of mind, and has implanted within us the ineradicable conviction that these powers were intended to be exercised. The Bible, too, contains poetry that exhibits no lack of enthusiasm, no lack of a keen appreciation of beauty. With this second solution of the problem we cannot rest content. Despite all we can do, the desire to know and the love of beauty cannot be entirely stifled, and we cannot permanently regard these desires as evil.

Are then Christianity and culture in a conflict that is to be settled only by the destruction of one or the other of the contending forces? A third solution, fortunately, is possible—namely consecration. Instead of destroying the arts and sciences or being indifferent to them, let us cultivate them with all the enthusiasm of the veriest humanist, but at the same time consecrate them to the service of our God. Instead of stifling the pleasures afforded by the acquisition of knowledge or by the appreciation of what is beautiful, let us accept these pleasures as the gifts of a heavenly Father. Instead of obliterating the distinction between the kingdom and the world, or on the other hand withdrawing from the world into a sort of modernized intellectual monasticism, let us go forth joyfully, enthusiastically to make the world subject to God.

Certain obvious advantages are connected with such a solution of the problem. In the first place, a logical advantage. A man can believe only what he holds to be true. We are Christians because we hold Christianity to be true. But other men hold Christianity to be false. Who is right? That question can be settled only by an examination and comparison of the reasons adduced on both sides. It is true, one of the grounds for our belief is an inward experience that we cannot share—the great experience begun by conviction of sin and conversion and continued by communion with God—an experience which other men do not possess, and upon which, therefore, we cannot directly base an argument. But if our position is correct, we ought at least to be able to show the other man that his reasons may be inconclusive. And that involves careful study of both sides of the question. Furthermore, the field of Christianity is the world. The Christian cannot be satisfied so long as any human activity is either opposed to Christianity or out of all connection with Christianity. Christianity must pervade not merely all nations, but also all of human thought. The Christian, therefore, cannot be indifferent to any branch of earnest human endeavour. It must all be brought into some relation to the gospel. It must be studied either in order to be demonstrated as false, or else in order to be made useful in advancing the kingdom of God. The kingdom must be advanced not merely extensively, but also intensively. The church must seek to conquer not merely every man for Christ, but also the whole of man. We are accustomed to encourage ourselves in our discouragements by the thought of the time when every knee shall bow and every tongue confess that Jesus is Lord. No less inspiring is the other aspect of that same great consummation. That will also be a time when doubts have disappeared, when every contradiction has been removed, when all of science converges to one great conviction, when all of art is devoted to one great end, when all of human thinking is permeated by the refining, ennobling influence of Jesus, when every thought has been brought into subjection to the obedience of Christ.

If, to some of our practical men, these advantages of our solution of the problem seem to be intangible, we can point to the merely numerical advantage of intellectual and artistic activity within the church. We are all agreed that at least one great function of the church is the conversion of individual men. The missionary movement is the great religious movement of our day. Now it is perfectly true that men must be brought to Christ one by one. There are no labour-saving devices in evangelism. It is all hard work.

And yet it would be a great mistake to suppose that all men are equally well prepared to receive the gospel. It is true that the decisive thing is the regenerative power of God. That can overcome all lack of preparation, and the absence of that makes even the best preparation useless. But as a matter of fact God usually exerts that power in connection with certain prior conditions of the human mind, and it should be ours to create, so far as we can, with the help of God, those favourable conditions for the reception of the gospel. False ideas are the greatest obstacles to the reception of the gospel. We may preach with all the fervour of a Reformer and yet succeed only in winning a straggler here and there, if we permit the whole collective thought of the nation or of the world to be controlled by ideas which, by the resistless force of logic, prevent Christianity from being regarded as anything more than a harmless delusion. Under such circumstances, what God desires us to do is to destroy the obstacle at its root. Many would have the seminaries combat error by attacking it as it is taught by its popular exponents. Instead of that they confuse their students with a lot of German names unknown outside the walls of the universities. That method of procedure is based simply upon a profound belief in the pervasiveness of ideas. What is today matter of academic speculation begins tomorrow to move armies and pull down empires. In that second stage, it has gone too far to be combated; the time to stop it was when it was still a matter of impassionate debate. So as Christians we should try to mould the thought of the world in such a way as to make the acceptance of Christianity something more than a logical absurdity. Thoughtful men are wondering why the students of our great eastern universities no longer enter the ministry or display any very vital interest in Christianity. Various totally inadequate explanations are proposed, such as the increasing attractiveness of other professions—an absurd explanation, by the way, since other professions are becoming so over-crowded that a man can barely make a living in them. The real difficulty amounts to this—that the thought of the day, as it makes itself most strongly felt in the universities, but from them spreads inevitably to the masses of the people, is profoundly opposed to Christianity, or at least—what is nearly as bad—it is out of all connection with Christianity. The church is unable either to combat it or to assimilate it, because the church simply does not understand it. Under such circumstances, what more pressing duty than for those who have received the mighty experience of regeneration, who, therefore, do not, like the world, neglect that whole series of vitally relevant facts which is embraced in Christian experience—what more pressing duty than for these men to make themselves masters of the thought of the world in order to make it an instrument of truth instead of error? The church has no right to be so absorbed in helping the individual that she forgets the world.

There are two objections to our solution of the problem. If you bring culture and Christianity thus into close union—in the first place, will not Christianity destroy culture? Must not art and science be independent in order to flourish? We answer that it all depends upon the nature of their dependence. Subjection to any external authority or even to any human authority would be fatal to art and science. But subjection to God is entirely different. Dedication of human powers to God is found, as a matter of fact, not to destroy but to heighten them. God gave those powers. He understands them well enough not bunglingly to destroy his own gifts. In the second place, will not culture destroy Christianity? Is it not far easier to be an earnest Christian if you confine your attention to the Bible and do not risk being led astray by the thought of the world? We answer, of course it is easier. Shut yourself up in an intellectual monastery, do not disturb yourself with the thoughts of unregenerate men, and of course you will find it easier to be a Christian, just as it is easier to be a good soldier in comfortable winter quarters than it is on the field of battle. You save your own soul—but the Lord's enemies remain in possession of the field.

But by whom is this task of transforming the unwieldy, resisting mass of human thought until it becomes subservient to the gospel—

by whom is this task to be accomplished? To some extent, no doubt, by professors in theological seminaries and universities. But the ordinary minister of the gospel cannot shirk his responsibility. It is a great mistake to suppose that investigation can successfully be carried on by a few specialists whose work is of interest to nobody but themselves. Many men of many minds are needed. What we need first of all, especially in our American churches, is a more general interest in the problems of theological science. Without that, the specialist is without the stimulating atmosphere which nerves him to do his work.

But no matter what his station in life, the scholar must be a regenerated man—he must yield to no one in the intensity and depth of his religious experience. We are well supplied in the world with excellent scholars who are without that qualification. They are doing useful work in detail, in biblical philology, in exegesis, in biblical theology, and in other branches of study. But they are not accomplishing the great task, they are not assimilating modern thought to Christianity, because they are without that experience of God's power in the soul which is of the essence of Christianity. They have only one side for the comparison. Modern thought they know, but Christianity is really foreign to them. It is just that great inward experience which it is the function of the true Christian scholar to bring into some sort of connection with the thought of the world.

During the last thirty years there has been a tremendous defection from the Christian church. It is evidenced even by things that lie on the surface. For example, by the decline in church attendance and in Sabbath observance and in the number of candidates for the ministry. Special explanations, it is true, are sometimes given for these discouraging tendencies. But why should we deceive ourselves, why comfort ourselves by palliative explanations? Let us face the facts. The falling off in church attendance, the neglect of Sabbath observance—these things are simply surface indications of a decline in the power of Christianity. Christianity is exerting a far less powerful direct influence in the civilized world today than it was exerting thirty years ago.

What is the cause of this tremendous defection? For my part, I have little hesitation in saying that it lies chiefly in the intellectual sphere. Men do not accept Christianity because they can no longer be convinced that Christianity is true. It may be useful, but is it true? Other explanations, of course, are given. The modern defection from the church is explained by the practical materialism of the age. Men are so much engrossed in making money that they have no time for spiritual things. That explanation has a certain range of validity. But its range is limited. It applies perhaps to the boom towns of the West, where men are intoxicated by sudden possibilities of boundless wealth. But the defection from Christianity is far broader than that. It is felt in the settled countries of Europe even more strongly than in America. It is felt among the poor just as strongly as among the rich. Finally, it is felt most strongly of all in the universities, and that is only one indication more that the true cause of the defection is intellectual. To a very large extent, the students of our great eastern universities—and still more the universities of Europe—are not Christians. And they are not Christians often just because they are students. The thought of the day, as it makes itself most strongly felt in the universities, is profoundly opposed to Christianity, or at least it is out of connection with Christianity. The chief obstacle to the Christian religion today lies in the sphere of the intellect.

That assertion must be guarded against two misconceptions. In the first place, I do not mean that most men reject Christianity consciously on account of intellectual difficulties. On the contrary, rejection of Christianity is due in the vast majority of cases simply to indifference. Only a few men have given the subject real attention. The vast majority of those who reject the gospel do so simply because they know nothing about it. But whence comes this indifference? It is due to the intellectual atmosphere in which men are living. The modern world is dominated by ideas which ignore the gospel. Modern culture is not altogether opposed to the gospel. But it is out of all connection with it. It not only prevents the acceptance of Christianity. It prevents Christianity even from getting a hearing.

In the second place, I do not mean that the removal of intellectual objections will make a man a Christian. No conversion was ever wrought simply by argument. A change of heart is also necessary. And that can be wrought only by the immediate exercise of the power of God. But because intellectual labour is insufficient it does not follow, as is so often assumed, that it is unnecessary. God may, it is true, overcome all intellectual obstacles by an immediate exercise of his regenerative power. Sometimes he does. But he does so very seldom. Usually he exerts his power in connection with certain conditions of the human mind. Usually he does not bring into the kingdom, entirely without preparation, those whose mind and fancy are completely dominated by ideas which make the acceptance of the gospel logically impossible.

Modern culture is a tremendous force. It affects all classes of society. It affects the ignorant as well as the learned. What is to be done about it? In the first place, the church may simply withdraw from the conflict. She may simply allow the mighty stream of modern thought to flow by unheeded and do her work merely in the back-eddies of the current. There are still some men in the world who have been unaffected by modern culture. They may still be won for Christ without intellectual labour. And they must be won. It is useful, it is necessary work. If the church is satisfied with that alone, let her give up the scientific education of her ministry. Let her assume the truth of her message and learn simply how it may be applied in detail to modern industrial and social conditions. Let her give up the laborious study of Greek and Hebrew. Let her abandon the scientific study of history to the men of the world. In a day of increased scientific interest, let the church go on becoming less scientific. In a day of increased specialization, of renewed interest in philology and in history, of more rigorous scientific method, let the church go on abandoning her Bible to her enemies. They will study it scientifically, rest assured, if the church does not. Let her substitute sociology altogether for Hebrew, practical expertness for the proof of her gospel. Let her shorten the preparation of her ministry, let her permit it to be interrupted yet more and more by premature practical activity. By doing so she will win a straggler here and there. But her winnings will be but temporary. The great current of modern culture will sooner or later engulf her puny eddy. God will save her somehow—out of the depths. But the labour of centuries will have been swept away. God grant that the church may not resign herself to that. God grant she may face her problem squarely and bravely. That problem is not easy. It involves the very basis of her faith. Christianity is the proclamation of an historical fact—that Jesus Christ rose from the dead. Modern thought has no place for that proclamation. It prevents men even from listening to the message. Yet the culture of today cannot simply be rejected as a whole. It is not like the pagan culture of the first century. It is not wholly non-Christian. Much of it has been derived directly from the Bible. There are significant movements in it, going to waste, which might well be used for the defence of the gospel. The situation is complex. Easy wholesale measures are not in place. Discrimination, investigation is necessary. Some of modern thought must be refuted. The rest must be made subservient. But nothing in it can be ignored. He that is not with us is against us. Modern culture is a mighty force. It is either subservient to the gospel or else it is the deadliest enemy of the gospel. For making it subservient, religious emotion is not enough, intellectual labour is also necessary. And that labour is being neglected. The church has turned to easier tasks. And now she is reaping the fruits of her indolence. Now she must battle for her life.

The situation is desperate. It might discourage us. But not if we are truly Christians. Not if we are living in vital communion with the risen Lord. If we are really convinced of the truth of our message, then we can proclaim it before a world of enemies, then the very difficulty of our task, the very scarcity of our allies becomes an inspiration, then we can even rejoice that God did not place us in an easy age, but in a time of doubt and perplexity and battle. Then, too, we shall not be afraid to call forth other soldiers into the conflict. Instead of making our theological seminaries merely centres of religious emotion, we shall make them battlegrounds of the faith, where, helped a little by the experience of Christian teachers, men are taught to fight their own battle, where they come to appreciate the real strength of the adversary and in the hard school of intellectual struggle learn to substitute for the unthinking faith of childhood the profound convictions of full-grown men. Let us not fear in this a loss of spiritual power. The church is perishing today through the lack of thinking, not through an excess of it. She is winning victories in the sphere of material betterment. Such victories are glorious. God save us from the heartless crime of disparaging them. They are relieving the misery of men. But if they stand alone, I fear they are but temporary. The things which are seen are temporal; the things which are not seen are eternal. What will become of philanthropy if God be lost? Beneath the surface of life lies a world of spirit. Philosophers have attempted to explore it. Christianity has revealed its wonders to the simple soul. There lie the springs of the church's power. But that spiritual realm cannot be entered without controversy. And now the church is shrinking from the conflict. Driven from the spiritual realm by the current of modern thought, she is consoling herself with things about which there is no dispute. If she favours better housing for the poor, she need fear no contradiction. She will need all her courage. She will have enemies enough, God knows. But they will not fight her with argument. The twentieth century, in theory, is agreed on social betterment. But sin, and death, and salvation, and life, and God—about these things there is debate. You can avoid the debate if you choose. You need only drift with the current. Preach every Sunday during your seminary course, devote the fag-ends of your time to study and to thought, study about as you studied in college—and these questions will probably never trouble you. The great questions may easily be avoided. Many preachers are avoiding them. And many preachers are preaching to the air. The church is waiting for men of another type. Men to fight her battles and solve her problems. The hope of finding them is the one great inspiration of a seminary's life. They need not all be men of conspicuous attainments. But they must all be men of thought. They must fight hard against spiritual and intellectual indolence. Their thinking may be confined to narrow limits. But it must be their own. To them theology must be something more than a task. It must be a matter of inquiry. It must lead not to successful memorizing, but to genuine convictions.

The church is puzzled by the world's indifference. She is trying to overcome it by adapting her message to the fashions of the day. But if, instead, before the conflict, she would descend into the secret place of meditation, if by the clear light of the gospel she would seek an answer not merely to the questions of the hour but, first of all, to the eternal problems of the spiritual world, then perhaps, by God's grace, through his good Spirit, in his good time, she might issue forth once more with power, and an age of doubt might be followed by the dawn of an era of faith.

LIBERALISM OR CHRISTIANITY[1]

THE attack upon the fundamentals of the Christian faith is not a matter merely of theological seminaries and universities. It is being carried on vigorously by Sunday School 'lesson-helps', by the pulpit, and by the religious press. The remedy, therefore, is not to be found in the abolition of theological seminaries, or the abandonment of scientific theology, but rather in a more earnest search after truth and a more loyal devotion to it when once it is found.

At the seminaries and universities, the roots of the great issue are more clearly seen than in the world at large; among students the reassuring employment of traditional phrases is often abandoned, and the advocates of a new religion are not at pains, as they are in the church at large, to maintain a pretence of conformity with the past. In discussing the attack against the fundamentals of Christianity 'from the point of view of colleges and seminaries', therefore, we are simply discussing the root of the matter instead of its mere superficial manifestations. What, at bottom, when the traditional phrases have all been stripped away, is the real meaning of the present revolt against historic Christianity?

That revolt, manifold as are its manifestations, is a fairly unitary phenomenon. It may all be subsumed under the general head of 'naturalism'—that is, the denial of any entrance of the creative power of God (in distinction from the ordinary course of nature) in connection with the origin of Christianity. The word 'naturalism' is here used in a sense somewhat different from its philosophical meaning. In this non-philosophical sense it describes with fair accuracy the real root of what is called, by a common degradation of an originally

[1] J. Gresham Machen, 'Liberalism or Christianity', *The Princeton Theological Review,*, Vol. 20, No. 1 (1922), pp. 93-117.

noble word, 'liberal' religion. What then, in brief, are the teachings of modern liberalism, as over against the teachings of Christianity?

At the outset, we are met with an objection. 'Teachings', it is said, are unimportant; the exposition of the teachings of liberalism and the teachings of Christianity, therefore, can arouse no interest at the present day; creeds are merely the changing expression of a unitary Christian experience, and provided only they express that experience they are all equally good.

Whether this objection be well-founded or not, the real meaning of it should at least be faced. And that meaning is perfectly plain. The objection involves an out-and-out scepticism. If all creeds are equally true, then since they are contradictory to one another, they are all equally false, or at least equally uncertain. We are indulging therefore in a mere juggling with words. To say that all creeds are equally true, and that they are based upon experience, is merely to fall back upon that agnosticism which fifty years ago was regarded as the deadliest enemy of the church. The enemy has not really been changed into a friend merely because he has been received within the camp. Very different is the Christian conception of a creed. According to the Christian conception, a creed is not based upon Christian experience, but on the contrary it is a setting forth of those facts upon which experience is based.

But, it will be said, Christianity is a life, not a doctrine. The assertion is often made, and it has an appearance of godliness. But it is radically false, and to detect its falsity one does not need to be a Christian. For to say that 'Christianity is a life' is to make an assertion in the sphere of history. The assertion does not lie in the sphere of ideals; it is far different from saying that Christianity ought to be a life, or that the ideal religion is a life. The assertion that Christianity is a life is subject to historical investigation exactly as is the assertion that the Roman Empire under Nero was a free democracy. Possibly the Roman Empire under Nero would have been better if it had been a free democracy, but the historical question is simply whether as a matter of fact it was a free democracy or no. Christianity is an historical phenomenon, like the Roman Empire, or the Kingdom of Prussia, or the United States of America. And as an historical phenomenon it must be investigated on the basis of historical evidence.

Is it true, then, that Christianity is not a doctrine but a life? The question can be settled only by an examination of the beginnings of Christianity. Recognition of that fact does not involve any acceptance of Christian belief; it is merely a matter of common sense and common honesty. At the foundation of the life of every corporation is the incorporation paper, in which the objects of the corporation are set forth. Other objects may be vastly more desirable than those objects, but if the directors use the name and the resources of the corporation to pursue the other objects they are acting '*ultra vires*' of the corporation. So it is with Christianity. It is perfectly conceivable that the originators of the Christian movement had no right to legislate for subsequent generations; but at any rate they did have an inalienable right to legislate for all generations that should choose to bear the name of 'Christian'. It is conceivable that Christianity may now have to be abandoned, and another religion substituted for it; but at any rate the question what Christianity is can be determined only by an examination of the beginnings of Christianity.

The beginnings of Christianity constitute a fairly definite historical phenomenon. The Christian movement originated a few days after the death of Jesus of Nazareth. It is doubtful whether anything that preceded the death of Jesus can be called Christianity. At any rate, if Christianity existed before that event, it was Christianity only in a preliminary stage. The name originated after the death of Jesus, and the thing itself was also something new. Evidently there was an important new beginning among the disciples of Jesus in Jerusalem after the crucifixion. At that time is to be placed the beginning of the remarkable movement which spread out from Jerusalem into the Gentile world—the movement which is called Christianity.

About the early stages of this movement definite historical information has been preserved in the epistles of Paul, which are regarded by all serious historians as genuine products of the first Christian generation. The writer of the epistles had been in direct communication with those intimate friends of Jesus who had begun the Christian movement in Jerusalem, and in the epistles he makes it abundantly plain what the fundamental character of the movement was.

But if any one fact is clear, on the basis of this evidence, it is that the Christian movement at its inception was not just a way of life in the modern sense, but a way of life founded upon a message. It is perfectly clear that the first Christian missionaries did not simply come forward with exhortation; they did not say: 'Jesus of Nazareth lived a wonderful life of filial piety, and we call upon you our hearers to yield yourselves as we have done to the spell of that life.' Certainly that is what modern historians would have expected the first Christian missionaries to say; but it must be recognized at least that as a matter of fact they said nothing of the kind. They came forward, not merely with an exhortation or with a programme, but with a message,—with an account of something that had happened a short time before. 'Christ died for our sins', they said, 'according to the Scriptures; he was buried; he has been raised on the third day according to the Scriptures.'

This message, even the small excerpt from it quoted by Paul in 1 Cor. 15:3ff., contains two elements—it contains (1) the facts and (2) the meaning of the facts ('for our sins'). The narration of the facts is history; the setting forth of the meaning of the facts is doctrine. These two elements are always contained in the Christian message. 'Suffered under Pontius Pilate, was crucified, dead and buried'—that is history. 'He loved me and gave himself for me'—that is doctrine. Without these two elements, inextricably intertwined, there is no Christianity.

The character of primitive Christianity, as founded upon a message, is summed up in the words of the eighth verse of the first chapter of Acts—'Ye shall be my witnesses both in Jerusalem, and in all Judea and Samaria, and unto the uttermost part of the earth.' It is entirely unnecessary, for the present purpose, to argue about the historical value of the book of Acts or to discuss the question whether Jesus really spoke the words just quoted. In any case the verse must be recognized as an adequate summary of what is known about primitive Christianity. From the beginning Christianity was a campaign of witnessing. And the witnessing did not concern merely what Jesus was doing within the recesses of the individual life. To take the words of Acts in that way is to do violence to the context and to all the evidence. On the contrary, the epistles of Paul and all the sources make it abundantly plain that the testimony was primarily not to inner spiritual facts but to what Jesus had done once for all in his death and resurrection.

Christianity is based, then, upon an account of something that happened, and the Christian worker is primarily a witness. But if so, it is rather important that the Christian worker should tell the truth. When a man takes his seat upon the witness stand, it makes little difference what the cut of his coat is, or whether his sentences are nicely turned. The important thing is that he tell the truth, the whole truth, and nothing but the truth. If we are to be truly Christians, then, it does make a vast difference what our teachings are, and it is by no means aside from the point to set forth the teachings of Christianity in contrast with the teachings of the chief modern rival of Christianity.

The chief modern rival of Christianity is 'liberalism'. An examination of the teachings of liberalism will show that at every point the liberal movement is in opposition to the Christian message. That examination will now be undertaken, though necessarily in a summary and cursory way.[1]

Christianity, it has already been observed, is based upon an account of something that happened in the first century of our era. But before that account can be received, certain presuppositions must be accepted. These presuppositions consist in what is believed first about God, and second about man. With regard to the presuppositions, as with regard to the message itself, modern liberalism is diametrically opposed to Christianity.

It is opposed to Christianity, in the first place, in its conception of God. But at this point we are met with a particularly insistent form of that objection to doctrinal matters which has already been considered. It is unnecessary, we are told, to have a 'conception' of God; theology, or the knowledge of God, is the death of religion; we should not seek to know God, but should merely feel his presence.

With regard to this objection, it ought to be observed that if religion consists merely in feeling the presence of God, it is devoid of any moral quality whatever. Pure feeling, if there be such a thing, is non-moral. What makes affection for a human friend, for example,

---

[1] The principal divisions of what follows were suggested by the Rev. Paul Martin, of Princeton.

such an ennobling thing is the knowledge which we possess of the character of our friend. Human affection, apparently so simple, is really just bristling with dogma. It depends upon a host of observations treasured up in the mind with regard to the character of our friend. But if human affection is thus really dependent upon knowledge, why should it be otherwise with that supreme personal relationship which is at the basis of religion? Why should we be indignant against slanders directed against a human friend, while at the same time we are patient about the basest slanders directed against our God? Certainly it does make the greatest possible difference what we think about God.

In the Christian view of God as set forth in the Bible, there are many elements. But one attribute of God is absolutely fundamental in the Bible; one attribute is absolutely necessary in order to render intelligible all the rest. That attribute is the awful transcendence of God. From beginning to end the Bible is concerned to set forth the awful gulf that separates the creature from the Creator. It is true, indeed, that according to the Bible God is immanent in the world. Not a sparrow falls to the ground without him. But he is immanent in the world not because he is identified with the world, but because he is the free Creator and Upholder of it. Between the creature and the Creator a great gulf is fixed.

In modern liberalism, on the other hand, this sharp distinction between God and the world is broken down, and the name 'God' is applied to the mighty world process itself. We find ourselves in the midst of a mighty process, which manifests itself in the indefinitely small and in the indefinitely great—in the infinitesimal life which is revealed through the microscope and in the vast movements of the heavenly spheres. To this world-process, of which we ourselves form a part, we apply the dread name of 'God'. God, therefore, it is said in effect, is not a person distinct from ourselves; on the contrary our life is a part of his. Thus the gospel story of the Incarnation, according to modern liberalism, is sometimes thought of as a symbol of the general truth that man at his best is one with God.

It is strange how such a representation can be regarded as anything new, for as a matter of fact, pantheism is a very ancient phenomenon. And modern liberalism, even when it is not consistently pantheistic, is at any rate pantheizing. It tends everywhere to break down the separateness between God and the world, and the sharp personal distinction between God and man. Even the sin of man on this view ought logically to be regarded as part of the life of God. Very different is the living and holy God of the Bible and of Christian faith.

Christianity differs from liberalism, then, in the first place, in its conception of God. But it also differs in its conception of man. Modern liberalism has lost all sense of the gulf that separates the creature from the Creator; its doctrine of man follows naturally from its doctrine of God. But it is not only the creature limitations of mankind which are denied. Far more important is another difference. According to the Bible, man is a sinner under the just condemnation of God; according to modern liberalism, there is really no such thing as sin. At the very root of the modern liberal movement is the loss of the consciousness of sin.[1]

The consciousness of sin was formerly the starting-point of all preaching; but today it is gone. Characteristic of the modern age, above all else, is a supreme confidence in human goodness; the religious literature of the day is redolent of that confidence. Get beneath the rough exterior of men, we are told, and we shall discover enough self-sacrifice to found upon it the hope of society; the world's evil, it is said, can be overcome with the world's good; no help is needed from outside the world.

What has produced this satisfaction with human goodness? What has become of the consciousness of sin? The consciousness of sin has certainly been lost. But what has removed it from the hearts of men?

In the first place, the War has perhaps had something to do with the change. In time of war, our attention is called so exclusively to the sins of other people that we are sometimes inclined to forget our own sins. Attention to the sins of other people is, indeed, sometimes necessary. It is quite right to be indignant against any oppression of the weak which is being carried on by the strong. But such a habit of mind, if made permanent, if carried over into the days of peace, has its dangers. It joins forces with the collectivism of the modern

[1] For what follows, compare 'The Church in the War', in *The Presbyterian*, for May 29, 1919, pp. 10f.

State to obscure the individual, personal character of guilt. If John Smith beats his wife nowadays, no one is so old-fashioned as to blame John Smith for it. On the contrary, it is said, John Smith is evidently the victim of some more of that Bolshevistic propaganda; Congress ought to be called in extra session in order to take up the case of John Smith in an alien and sedition law.

But the loss of the consciousness of sin is far deeper than the War; it has its roots in a mighty spiritual process which has been active during the past seventy-five years. Like other great movements, that process has come silently, so silently that its results have been achieved before the plain man was even aware of what was taking place. Nevertheless, despite all superficial continuity, a remarkable change has come about within the last seventy-five years. The change is nothing less than the substitution of paganism for Christianity as the dominant view of life. Seventy-five years ago, Western civilization, despite inconsistencies, was still predominantly Christian; today it is predominantly pagan.

In speaking of 'paganism', we are not using a term of reproach. Ancient Greece was pagan, but it was glorious, and the modern world has not even begun to equal its achievements. What, then, is paganism? The answer is not really difficult. Paganism is that view of life which finds the highest goal of human existence in the healthy and harmonious and joyous development of existing human faculties. Very different is the Christian ideal. Paganism is optimistic with regard to unaided human nature, whereas Christianity is the religion of the broken heart.

In saying that Christianity is the religion of the broken heart, we do not mean that Christianity ends with the broken heart; we do not mean that the characteristic Christian attitude is a continual beating on the breast or a continual crying of 'Woe is me.' Nothing could be further from the fact. On the contrary, Christianity means that sin is faced once for all, and then is cast, by the grace of God, forever into the depths of the sea. The trouble with the paganism of ancient Greece, as with the paganism of modern times, was not in the superstructure, which was glorious, but in the foundation, which was rotten. There was always something to be covered up; the enthusiasm of the architect was maintained only by ignoring the disturbing fact of sin. In Christianity, on the other hand, nothing needs to be covered up. The fact of sin is faced resolutely once for all, and is removed by the grace of God. But then, after sin has been removed by the grace of God, the Christian can proceed to develop joyously every faculty that God has given him. Such is the higher Christian humanism—a humanism founded not upon human pride but upon divine grace.

But although Christianity does not end with the broken heart, it does begin with the broken heart; it begins with the consciousness of sin. Without the consciousness of sin, the whole of the gospel will seem to be an idle tale. But how can the consciousness of sin be revived? Something no doubt can be accomplished by the proclamation of the law of God, for the law reveals transgressions. The whole of the law, moreover, should be proclaimed. It will hardly be wise to adopt the suggestion (recently offered among many suggestions as to the ways in which we shall have to modify our message in order to retain the allegiance of the returning soldiers) that we must stop treating the little sins as though they were big sins. That suggestion means apparently that we must not worry too much about the little sins, but must let them remain unmolested. With regard to such an expedient, it may perhaps be suggested that in the moral battle we are fighting against a very resourceful enemy, who does not reveal the position of his guns by desultory artillery action when he plans a great attack. In the moral battle, as in the Great European War, the quiet sectors are usually the most dangerous. It is through the 'little sins' that Satan gains an entrance into our lives. Probably, therefore, it will be prudent to watch all sectors of the front and lose no time about introducing the unity of command.

But if the consciousness of sin is to be produced, the law of God must be proclaimed in the lives of Christian people as well as in word. It is quite useless for the preacher to breathe out fire and brimstone from the pulpit, if at the same time the occupants of the pews go on taking sin very lightly and being content with the moral standards of the world. The rank and file of the church must do their part in so proclaiming the law of God by their lives that the secrets of men's hearts shall be revealed.

All these things, however, are in themselves quite insufficient to produce the consciousness of sin. The more one observes the condition of the church, the more one feels obliged to confess that the conviction of sin is a great mystery, which can be produced only by the Spirit of God. Proclamation of the law, in word and in deed, can prepare for the experience, but the experience itself comes from God. When a man has that experience, when a man comes under the conviction of sin, his whole attitude toward life is transformed; he wonders at his former blindness, and the message of the gospel, which formerly seemed to be an idle tale, becomes now instinct with light. But it is God alone who can produce the change.

Only, let us not try to do without the Spirit of God. The fundamental fault of the modern church is that she is busily engaged in an impossible task—she is busily engaged in calling the righteous to repentance. Modern preachers are trying to bring men into the church without requiring them to relinquish their pride; they are trying to help men avoid the conviction of sin. The preacher gets up into the pulpit, opens the Bible, and addresses the congregation somewhat as follows: 'You people are very good', he says; 'you respond to every appeal that looks toward the welfare of the community. Now we have in the Bible—especially in the life of Jesus—something so good that we believe it is good enough even for you good people.' Such is modern preaching. It is heard every Sunday in thousands of pulpits. But it is entirely futile. Even our Lord did not call the righteous to repentance, and probably we shall be no more successful than he.

Modern liberalism, then, has lost sight of the two great presuppositions of the Christian message—the living God, and the fact of sin. The liberal doctrine of God and the liberal doctrine of man are both diametrically opposite to the Christian view. But the divergence concerns not only the presuppositions of the message, but also the message itself.

According to the Christian view, the Bible contains an account of a revelation from God to man, which is found nowhere else. It is true, the Bible also contains a confirmation and a wonderful enrichment of the revelations which are given also by the things that God has made and by the conscience of man. 'The heavens declare the glory of God; and the firmament showeth his handywork'—these words are a confirmation of the revelation of God in nature; 'all have sinned and fall short of the glory of God'—these words are a confirmation of what is attested by the conscience. But in addition to such reaffirmations of what might conceivably be learned elsewhere—as a matter of fact, because of men's blindness, even so much is learned elsewhere only in comparatively obscure fashion—the Bible also contains an account of a revelation which is absolutely new. That new revelation concerns the way by which sinful man can come into communion with the living God.

The way was opened, according to the Bible, by an act of God, when, almost nineteen hundred years ago, outside the walls of Jerusalem, the eternal Son was offered as a sacrifice for the sins of men. To that one great event the whole Old Testament looks forward, and in that one event the whole of the New Testament finds its centre and core. Salvation then, according to the Bible, is not something that was discovered, but something that happened. Hence appears the uniqueness of the Bible. All the ideas of Christianity might be discovered in some other religion, yet there would be in that other religion no Christianity.

For Christianity depends, not upon a complex of ideas, but upon the narration of an event. Without that event, the world, in the Christian view, is altogether dark, and humanity is lost under the guilt of sin. There can be no salvation by the discovery of eternal truth, for eternal truth brings naught but despair, because of sin. But a new face has been put upon life by the blessed thing that God did when he offered up his only begotten Son.

Thus the revelation of which an account is contained in the Bible embraces not only a reaffirmation of eternal truths—itself necessary because the truths have been obscured by the blinding effect of sin— but also a revelation which sets forth the meaning of an act of God.

The contents of the Bible, then, are unique. But another fact about the Bible is also important. The Bible might contain an account of a true revelation from God, and yet the account be full of error. Before the full authority of the Bible can be established, therefore, it is necessary to add to the Christian doctrine of revelation the Christian doctrine of inspiration. The latter doctrine means that the Bible not only is an account of important things, but that the account itself is true, the writers having been so preserved from error, despite a full maintenance of their habits of thought and expression, that the resulting Book is the 'infallible rule of faith and practice'. The Christian, then, if he make full use of his Christian privileges, finds the seat of authority in the whole Bible, which he regards as the very Word of God.

Very different is the view of modern liberalism. The modern liberal rejects the unique authority of the Bible. But what is substituted for the Christian doctrine? What is the liberal view as to the seat of authority in religion?

The impression is sometimes produced that the modern liberal substitutes for the authority of the Bible the authority of Christ. He cannot accept, he says, what he regards as the perverse moral teaching of the Old Testament or the sophistical arguments of Paul. But he regards himself as being the true Christian because, rejecting the rest of the Bible, he depends upon Jesus alone.

This impression, however, is utterly false. The modern liberal does not really hold to the authority of Jesus. Even if he did so, he would be impoverishing very greatly his knowledge of God and of the way of salvation. The words of Jesus, spoken during his earthly ministry, could hardly contain all that we need to know about God and about the way of salvation; for the meaning of Jesus' redeeming work could hardly be fully set forth before that work was done. It could be set forth indeed by way of prophecy, and as a matter of fact it was so set forth by Jesus even in the days of his flesh. But the full explanation could naturally be given only after the work was done. And such was actually the divine method. It is doing despite, not only to the Spirit of God, but also to Jesus himself, to regard the teaching of the Holy Spirit, given through the apostles, as at all inferior in authority to the teaching of Jesus.

As a matter of fact, however, the modern liberal does not hold fast even to the authority of Jesus. Certainly he does not accept the words of Jesus as they are recorded in the Gospels. For among the recorded words of Jesus are to be found just those things which are most abhorrent to the modern liberal church, and in his recorded words Jesus also points forward to the fuller revelation which afterwards to be given through his apostles. Evidently, therefore, those words of Jesus which are to be regarded as authoritative by modern liberalism must first be selected from the mass of the recorded words by a critical process. The critical process is certainly very difficult, and the suspicion often arises that the critic is retaining as genuine words of the historical Jesus only those words which conform to his own preconceived ideas. But even after the sifting process has been completed, the liberal scholar is still unable to accept as authoritative all the sayings of Jesus; he must finally admit that even the historical Jesus said some things that are untrue.

So much is usually admitted. But, it is maintained, although not everything that Jesus said is true, his central 'life-purpose' is still to be regarded as regulative for the church.[1] But what then was the life-purpose of Jesus? According to the shortest, and if modern criticism be accepted, the earliest of the Gospels, the Son of Man 'came not to be ministered unto, but to minister, and to give his life a ransom for many' (*Mark* 10:45). Here the vicarious death is put as the 'life-purpose' of Jesus. Such an utterance must of course be pushed aside by the modern liberal church. The truth is that the life-purpose of Jesus discovered by modern liberalism is not the life-purpose of the real Jesus, but merely represents those elements in the teaching of Jesus—isolated and misinterpreted—which happen to agree with the modern programme. It is not Jesus, then, who is the real authority, but the modern principle by which the selection within Jesus' recorded teaching has been made. Certain isolated ethical principles of the Sermon on the Mount are accepted, not at all because they are teachings of Jesus, but because they agree with modern ideas.

It is not true at all, then, that modern liberalism is based upon the authority of Jesus. It is obliged to reject a vast deal that is absolutely essential in Jesus' example and teaching—notably his consciousness of being the heavenly Messiah. The real authority, for liberalism, can only be 'the Christian consciousness' or 'Christian experience'. But how shall the findings of the Christian consciousness be established? Surely not by a majority vote of the organized church. Such a method would obviously do away with all liberty of conscience. The only authority, then, can be individual experience; truth can only be that

---

[1] Compare 'For Christ or Against Him', in *The Presbyterian,* for January 20, 1921, p. 9.

which 'helps' the individual man. Such an authority is obviously no authority at all; for individual experience is endlessly diverse, and when once truth is regarded only as that which works at any particular time, it ceases to be truth. The result is an abysmal scepticism.

The Christian man, on the other hand, finds in the Bible the very Word of God. Let it not be said that dependence upon a book is a dead or an artificial thing. The Reformation of the sixteenth century was founded upon the authority of the Bible, yet it set the world aflame. Dependence upon a word of man would be slavish, but dependence upon God's Word is life. Dark and gloomy would be the world, if we were left to our own devices, and had no blessed Word of God.

It is no wonder, then, that liberalism is totally different from Christianity, for the foundation is different. Christianity is founded upon the Bible. It bases upon the Bible both its thinking and its life. Liberalism, on the other hand, is founded upon the shifting emotions of sinful men.

Three points of difference between liberalism and Christianity have now been noticed. The two are different (1) in their view of God, (2) in their view of man, and (3) in their choice of the seat of authority in religion. A fourth difference concerns the view of Christ. What does modern liberalism believe about the person of our Lord?

At this point a puzzling fact appears—the liberal preacher is often perfectly ready to say that 'Jesus is God.' The plain man is much impressed. The preacher, he says, believes in the deity of our Lord; obviously then his unorthodoxy must concern only details; and those who object to his presence in the church are narrow and uncharitable heresy-hunters. But unfortunately language is valuable only as the expression of thought. The English word 'god' has no particular virtue in itself; it is not more beautiful than other words. Its importance depends altogether upon the meaning which is attached to it. When, therefore, the liberal preacher says that 'Jesus is God', the significance of the utterance depends altogether upon what is meant by 'God'.

But it has already been observed that when the liberal preacher uses the word 'God', he means something entirely different from that which the Christian means by the same word. 'God', at least according to the logical trend of modern liberalism, is not a person separate from the world, but merely the unity that pervades the world. To say, therefore, that Jesus is God means merely that the life of God, which appears in all men, appears with special clearness or richness in Jesus. Such an assertion is diametrically opposed to the Christian belief in the deity of Christ.

Equally opposed to Christian belief is another meaning that is sometimes attached to the assertion that Jesus is God. The word 'God' is sometimes used to denote simply the supreme object of men's desires, the highest thing that men know. We have given up the notion, it is said, that there is a Maker and Ruler of the universe. Such notions belong to 'metaphysics', and are rejected by the modern man. But the word 'God', though it can no longer denote the Maker of the universe, is convenient as denoting the object of men's emotions and desires. Of some men, it can be said that their God is mammon—mammon is that for which they labour, and to which their hearts are attached. In a somewhat similar way, the liberal preacher says that Jesus is God. He does not mean at all to say that Jesus is identical in nature with a Maker and Ruler of the universe, of whom an idea could be obtained apart from Jesus. In such a Being he no longer believes. All that he means is that the man Jesus—a man here in the midst of us, and of the same nature as ours—is the highest thing we know. It is obvious that such a way of thinking is far more widely removed from Christian belief than is Unitarianism, at least the earlier forms of Unitarianism. For the early Unitarianism no doubt at least believed in God. The modern liberals, on the other hand, say that Jesus is God not because they think high of Jesus, but because they think desperately low of God.

In another way also, liberalism within the 'evangelical' churches is inferior to Unitarianism. It is inferior to Unitarianism in the matter of honesty. In order to maintain themselves in the evangelical churches and quiet the fears of their conservative associates, the liberals resort constantly to a double use of language. A young man, for example, has received disquieting reports of the unorthodoxy of a prominent preacher. Interrogating the preacher as to his belief, he receives a reassuring reply. 'You may tell everyone', says the liberal preacher in effect, 'that I believe that Jesus is God.' The inquirer goes away much impressed.

It may well be doubted, however, whether the assertion, 'I believe that Jesus is God', or the like, on the lips of liberal preachers, is strictly truthful. The liberal preacher attaches indeed a real meaning to the words, and that meaning is very dear to his heart. He really does believe that 'Jesus is God.' But the trouble is that he attaches to the words a different meaning from that which is attached to them by the simple-minded person to whom he is speaking. He offends, therefore, against the fundamental principle of truthfulness in language. According to that fundamental principle, language is truthful, not when the meaning attached to the words by the speaker, but when the meaning intended to be produced in the mind of the particular person addressed, is in accordance with the facts. Thus the truthfulness of the assertion, 'I believe that Jesus is God', depends upon the audience that is addressed. If the audience is composed of theologically trained persons, who will attach the same meaning to the word 'God' as that which the speaker attaches to it, then the language is truthful. But if the audience is composed of old-fashioned Christians, who have never attached anything but the old meaning to the word 'God' (the meaning which appears in the first verse of Genesis), then the language is untruthful. And in the latter case, not all the pious motives in the world will make the utterance right. Christian ethics do not abrogate common honesty; no possible desire of edifying the church and of avoiding offence can excuse a lie.

At any rate, the deity of our Lord, in any real sense of the word 'deity', is of course denied by modern liberalism. To the modern preacher, Jesus is an example for faith, and Christianity consists in having the same faith in God that Jesus had. To the Christian, on the other hand, Jesus is the object of faith, and upon him alone depends the eternal welfare of the individual soul and of humanity.[1]

Finally, liberalism differs from Christianity in the account which is given of the way of salvation. The two give exactly opposite answers to the question, 'What must I do to be saved?' Liberalism finds salvation in man; Christianity finds it only in an act of God.

The difference with regard to the way of salvation concerns, in the first place, the basis of salvation in the redeeming work of Christ.

[1] For the distinction between Jesus as an example for faith and Jesus as the object of faith, see Denney, *Jesus and the Gospel,* 1909.

According to Christian belief, Jesus is our Saviour, not by virtue of what he said, not even by virtue of what he was, but by what he did. He is our Saviour not because he has inspired us to live the same kind of life that he lived, but because he took upon himself the dreadful guilt of our sins and bore it instead of us on the cross. Such is the Christian conception of the cross of Christ. It is ridiculed as being a subtle 'theory of the atonement'. In reality, though it involves mysteries, it is itself so simple that a child can understand it. 'We deserved eternal death, but the Lord Jesus because he loved us died instead of us on the cross'—surely there is nothing so very intricate about that. It is not the Bible doctrine of the atonement which is difficult to understand—what are really incomprehensible are the elaborate modern efforts to get rid of the Bible doctrine in the interests of human pride.

To modern liberalism the cross of Christ is an inspiring example of self-sacrifice. But since there have been many acts of self-sacrifice in the history of the world, why should we pay such exclusive attention to this one Palestinian example? We are perfectly ready, men say in effect, to admit Jesus into the noble fellowship of those who have sacrificed themselves in a noble cause. But further we will not go. Men used to say with reference to Jesus, 'There was no other good enough to pay the price of sin.' They say so no longer. On the contrary, every man is now regarded as plenty good enough to pay the price of sin if he will only go bravely over the top in a noble cause.

It is no wonder that men adopt this patronizing attitude toward the cross; for the liberal conception of the cross follows naturally from the liberal conception of man and the liberal conception of Christ. If there be no such thing as sin, no such thing as the just condemnation of God's law, then of course we can get along perfectly well without a sacrifice for sin. And if Jesus be a man like the rest of men, then of course his death cannot possibly be a sacrifice for the sins of others. One mere man cannot possibly pay the penalty of another man's sin. But it does not follow that the Son of God cannot pay the penalty of the sins of men. When we come to see that it was no mere man, but the Lord of glory, who suffered on Calvary, then we shall be willing to say, as men used to say, that the precious blood of Jesus alone—and not all the rivers of blood that have flowed on the battlefields of history—is of value as a ground for our own salvation and for the hope of the world.

With the liberal view of the basis of salvation goes the liberal view of the application of salvation to the individual man, and that also is entirely different from the teaching of the Bible. According to the Bible, salvation is applied to the individual man by the Spirit of God. The work of the Spirit is mysterious. But the human accompaniment of the Spirit's action is a very simple thing—it is faith. Faith means simply receiving a gift. To have faith in Christ means to cease trying to win God's favour by one's own character; the man who believes in Christ simply accepts the sacrifice which Christ offered on Calvary. The result of such faith is a new life and all good works; but the salvation itself is an absolutely free gift of God.

Liberalism, on the other hand, seeks the welfare of men by urging them to 'make Christ Master in their lives'. In other words, salvation is to be obtained by our own obedience to the commands of Christ. Such teaching is just a sublimated form of legalism. Not the sacrifice of Christ, on this view, but our own obedience to God's law is the ground of hope.

In this way the whole achievement of the Reformation has been given up, and there has been a return to the religion of the Middle Ages. At the beginning of the sixteenth century, God raised up a man who began to read the Epistle to the Galatians with his own eyes. The result was the rediscovery of the doctrine of justification by faith. Upon that rediscovery has been based the whole of our evangelical freedom. As expounded by Luther and Calvin, the Epistle to the Galatians became the 'Magna Carta of Christian liberty'. But modern liberalism has returned to the old interpretation of Galatians which was urged against the Reformers. Thus Professor Burton's elaborate commentary on the epistle, with all its valuable modern scholarship, is at bottom a thorough mediaeval book; it has returned to an anti-Reformation exegesis, by which Paul is thought to be attacking in the epistle only the piecemeal morality of the Pharisees. In reality, of course, the object of Paul's attack is the thought that in any way man can earn his acceptance with God. What Paul is primarily interested in is not spiritual religion over against ceremonialism, but the free grace of God over against human merit.

The grace of God is rejected by modern liberalism. And the result is slavery—the slavery of the law, the wretched bondage by which man undertakes the impossible task of establishing his own righteousness as a ground of acceptance with God. It may seem strange at first sight that 'liberalism', of which the very name means freedom, should in reality be wretched slavery. But the phenomenon is not really so strange. Emancipation from the blessed will of God always involves bondage to some worse task-master.

Thus it may be said of the modern liberal church, as of the Jerusalem of Paul's day, that 'she is in bondage with her children'. God grant that she may turn again to the liberty of the gospel of Christ!

Such is the present situation. It is a great mistake to suppose that liberalism is merely a heresy—merely a divergence at isolated points from true Christian teaching. On the contrary, it proceeds from a totally different root. It differs from Christianity in its view of God, of man, of the seat of authority, of Christ, and of the way of salvation. Christianity is being attacked from within by a movement which is antichristian to the core.

What is the duty of laymen at such a time? What is the duty of the ruling elders in the Presbyterian Church?

In the first place, they should encourage those who are engaging in the intellectual and spiritual struggle. They should not say, in the sense in which some laymen say it, that more time should be devoted to the propagation of Christianity, and less to the defence of Christianity. Certainly there should be propagation of Christianity. Believers should certainly not content themselves with warding off attacks, but should also unfold in an orderly and positive way the full riches of the gospel. But far more is usually meant by those who call for less defence and more propagation. What they really intend is the discouragement of the whole intellectual defence of the faith. And their words come as a blow in the face of those who are fighting the great battle. As a matter of fact, not less time, but more time, should be devoted to the defence of the gospel. Indeed, truth cannot be stated clearly at all, without being set over against error. Thus a large part of the New Testament is polemic; the enunciation of evangelical truth was occasioned by the errors which had arisen in the churches. So it will always be, on account of the fundamental laws of the human mind. Moreover, the present crisis must be taken into account. There may have been a day when there could be propagation of Christianity without defence. But such a day at any rate is past. At the present time, when the opponents of the gospel are almost in control of our church, the slightest avoidance of the defence of the gospel is just sheer unfaithfulness to the Lord. There have been previous great crises in the history of the church, crises almost comparable to this. One appeared in the second century, when the very life of Christendom was threatened by the Gnostics. Another came in the Middle Ages when the gospel of God's grace seemed forgotten. In such times of crisis, God has always saved the church. But he has always saved it not by pacifists, but by sturdy contenders for the truth.

In the second place, ruling elders should perform their duty as members of presbyteries. The question, 'For Christ or against him?', constantly arises in the examination of candidates for licensure or ordination. Attempts are often made to obscure the issue. It is often said: 'The candidate will no doubt move in the direction of the truth; let him now be sent out to learn as well as to preach.' And so another opponent of the gospel enters the councils of the church, and another false prophet goes forth to encourage sinners to come before the judgment seat of God clad in the miserable rags of their own righteousness. Such action is not really 'kind' to the candidate himself. It is never kind to encourage a man to enter into a life of dishonesty. The fact often seems to be forgotten that the Presbyterian Church is a purely voluntary organization; no one is required to enter into its service. If a man cannot accept the belief of the church, there are other ecclesiastical bodies in which he can find a place. The belief of the Presbyterian Church is plainly set forth in the Confession of Faith, and the church will never afford any warmth of communion or engage with any real vigour in her work until her ministers are in whole-hearted agreement with that belief. It is strange how in the interests of an utterly false kindness to men, Christians are sometimes willing to relinquish their loyalty to the crucified Lord.

In the third place, the ruling elders of the Presbyterian Church should show their loyalty to Christ in their capacity as members of the individual congregations. The issue often arises in connection with the choice of a pastor. Such and such a man, it is said, is a brilliant preacher. But what is the content of his preaching? Is his preaching full of the gospel of Christ? The answer is often evasive. The preacher in question, it is said, is of good standing in the church, and he has never denied the doctrines of grace. Therefore, it is urged, he should be called to the pastorate. But shall we be satisfied with such negative assurances? Shall we be satisfied with preachers who merely 'do not deny' the cross of Christ? God grant that such satisfaction may be broken down! The people are perishing under the ministrations of those who 'do not deny' the cross of Christ. Surely something more than that is needed. God send us ministers who, instead of merely avoiding denial of the cross shall be on fire with the cross, whose whole life shall be one burning sacrifice of gratitude to the blessed Saviour who loved them and gave himself for them!

A terrible crisis has arisen in the church. In the ministry of evangelical churches are to be found hosts of those who reject the gospel of Christ. By the equivocal use of traditional phrases, by the representation of differences of opinion as though they were only differences about the interpretation of the Bible, entrance into the church was secured for those who are hostile to the very foundations of the faith. And now there are some indications that the fiction of conformity to the past is to be thrown off, and the real meaning of what has been taking place is to be allowed to appear. The church, it is now apparently supposed, has almost been educated up to the point where the shackles of the Bible can openly be cast away and the doctrine of the cross of Christ can be relegated to the limbo of discarded subtleties.

Yet there is in the Christian life no room for despair. Only, our hopefulness should not be founded on the sand. It should be founded, not upon a blind ignorance of the danger, but solely upon the precious promises of God. Laymen, as well as ministers, should return, in these trying days, with new earnestness, to the study of the Word of God.

If the Word of God be heeded, the Christian battle will be fought both with love and with faithfulness. Party passions and personal animosities will be put away, but on the other hand, even angels from heaven will be rejected if they preach a gospel different from the blessed gospel of the cross. Every man must decide upon which side he will stand. God grant that we may decide aright! God grant that instead of directing men, as modern liberalism does, to the village of Morality, where dwells a gentleman whose name is Legality, said to have skill in easing men of their burdens, we may direct them on the old, old way, through the little wicket gate, to a place somewhat ascending, where they shall really see the cross, that when at that sight the burden of their sin has fallen away, they may press on past the Hill Difficulty, past the Valley of Humiliation and the Valley of the Shadow of Death, past the allurements of Vanity Fair, up over the Delectable Mountains, and so, at length, across the last river, into the City of God.

GEERHARDUS VOS
1862-1949

THEOLOGIAN, author, and long-time Professor of Biblical Theology at Princeton Theological Seminary, Dutch immigrant Geerhardus Vos was born on March 14, 1862 at Heerenveen, Netherlands. Raised in a pious home, Vos graduated from Amsterdam Gymnasium in 1881.

Immigrating to the United States with his family, Vos studied at the Theologische School (later renamed Calvin Theological Seminary) in Grand Rapids, Michigan, from 1881 to 1883 and afterwards at Princeton Theological Seminary (1883-85). Upon graduation from Princeton, he studied abroad at the University of Berlin (1885-86) and the University of Strasburg where he was awarded a Ph.D in Arabic.

Returning to the United States, Vos served as Professor of Didactic and Exegetical Theology at the Theologische School from 1888 to 1893 before receiving a call from Princeton Theological Seminary in 1893 to serve as the school's first Professor of Biblical Theology. Vos retired from Princeton in 1932 and spent his remaining days in Pennsylvania, California, and Grand Rapids, Michigan, where he died on August 13, 1949. His remains were buried beside his wife, Catherine, in Roaring Branch, Pennsylvania, a rural community in the central part of the State, where Vos and his wife spent many quiet and enjoyable summer months together throughout the years of their marriage.

Vos's publications established him as a premier exegete and influential voice in the emerging discipline of biblical theology. Sensitive to the historical development of Scripture and the progressive character of God's self-disclosure in redemptive revelation, Vos's research provides valuable new light on the Christological centre of the Bible's unfolding message, the relationship of eschatology to soteriology, and the complementary but distinct roles of systematic and biblical theology in how they each organize and interpret the canon of Scripture.

A prolific author, Vos's published writings include articles, essays, reviews, poems, a collection of sermons, and biblical-theological studies on both Old and New Testament topics. *The Teaching of Jesus Concerning the Kingdom of God* (1903) and Vos's study of Pauline theology, *The Pauline Eschatology* (1930), remain two of his most important works. Vos's approach to the theology of the Old and New Testaments was published in 1948 as *Biblical Theology.* A stirring collection of Christ-centred sermons delivered to the student body in the chapel at Princeton Theological Seminary and published in 1922, *Grace and Glory,* presents the application of his biblical-theological perspective to pulpit proclamation.

While Vos's primary vocation was as a theological professor, his writings are characterized by an evident orthodoxy and devout faith which breathe a spirit of reverence and adoration into all his publications and explain why they are still highly prized among readers interested in a Reformed approach to biblical theology.

THE MORE EXCELLENT MINISTRY[1]

But we all, with unveiled face, beholding as in a mirror the glory of the
Lord, are transformed into the same image from glory to glory,
even as from the Lord, the Spirit.

2 Corinthians 3:18

THE Second Letter of Paul to the Church at Corinth is marked by a pronounced polemic strain. In this respect it somewhat resembles the Epistle to the Galatians. In each instance a serious crisis in the life of the church had evoked it. It is further common to both writings that in certain passages the polemic assumes a sharply personal character. In neither case is this due to any temperamental difficulty on Paul's part to control his outraged feelings, although even if this had been so, much could have been said in excuse of the apostle. His opponents had certainly not been sparing in personalities. He had been represented as a deceiver, as one who preached himself and praised himself. It had been charged that in his quasi-apostolic authority he lorded it over the church, employed his usurped power for casting down instead of for building up, and that, in spite of all this bluff and bluster of prestige, he lacked the ability to make good his pretensions, being indeed weighty and strong in his letters, but weak in his bodily presence, and in his speech, of no account. The insinuation had been made that Paul himself was aware of the hollowness of his claims, because he would not take from the church the support to which, if a true apostle, he ought to have felt himself entitled. He had been held up as a man who by his fickleness betrayed the duplicity of his position.

---

[1] Geerhardus Vos, 'The More Excellent Ministry', *Grace and Glory* (Edinburgh: Banner of Truth, 1994), pp. 82-102.

The apostle had not even been spared that meanest of all aspersions—that he was spending money collected for the poor saints in Judea on his own person. His sincerity as a minister of the truth had been called into question. It was charged that, while aware of his subordination to the original apostles, he was disloyal to them, and substituted for their gospel an entirely different one spun out of his own mind. Thus the truth of the very substance of his preaching was challenged. In this respect again a certain resemblance to the tactics of his Galatian opponents may be observed. The charge in both instances was that he preached 'a different gospel'. Nevertheless the point of attack had been somewhat shifted. In Galatia the main question had been that of salvation with or without the law. Here in Corinth, on the other hand, the controversy raged around Paul's teaching concerning the Christ. It was with another Jesus that his opponents had approached the Corinthians. No effort had been spared to prove this the true Jesus, by the side of whom the Christ of Paul's preaching was a pure figment of the imagination. Suspicion had been cast on the source of his knowledge of the Saviour on the ground that the visions through which it was obtained belonged to the class of wild, fantastic experiences, and that these marked Paul as one beside himself, not merely in this one point, but in the entire tone and temper of his religious life. The exalted, spiritual, heavenly nature, in which his gospel clothed the glorified Christ, was construed as convincing proof of the darkness and incomprehensibleness of the apostle's message. He preached a gospel that was veiled. And over against these elusive and intangible things had been placed the palpable institutions of the Mosaic covenant, carrying with them the demand for a Messiah correspondingly substantial and realistic in his make-up. This is an early illustration of the principle which from that time onward has shaped all forms of teaching in the church. For in each instance the view about the method of salvation is reflected in the conception of the Saviour. A certain gospel requires a certain kind of Christ, and a certain type of Christ a certain gospel.

It might have seemed as if the attack upon the apostle had therewith reached its logical conclusion and could not possibly go farther. Still this was not the case. With a curious retroversive movement the issue had been carried back from this point to the question of the personality of Paul, with this difference only, it was now his dignity in office that had been assailed. Paul's office as such was made out to be mean and contemptible. Such a Christ and such a cause could engage one who laboured for them only in the weakest and most ignoble kind of service. Paul was not permitted to escape the immemorial stigma reflected upon the minister from the apparent foolishness and weakness of the cross. And the apostle was sensitive, if anywhere, on this point of the nobility and glory of his office. Moral aspersions against his character he might, had it not been for fear of danger to the churches, have passed by as unworthy of notice. But the pride of office was stronger in him than the sense of personal honour. And thus it happens that we are indebted to these disturbers of the Corinthian church, whose names have long been forgotten, for an encomium upon the gospel service, which for power and splendour has no equal in the records of Christian apology. It deserves to be placed beside the song of triumph in the eighth chapter of the Epistle to the Romans. As there the apostle is carried on the crestwave of assurance of salvation, so here he moves with the full tide of enthusiasm over the excellence of his calling. The very words are, as it were, baptized in the glory of which they speak.

Let us briefly examine the several elements that enter into this high consciousness. The form of argument which Paul adopts is evidently determined by the method of his detractors. At the climax of their calumny they had concentrated their attack on the meanness and weakness of his message. Consequently he chooses to defend himself on the same basis by arguing from the glory of the message to the distinction of the bearer. While thus adjusted to the manner of attack, this method was also in keeping with Paul's innate modesty, still further refined by grace.

But there was another tactical motive besides. Paul recognized that by thus approaching the subject a more substantial title to official prestige could be made out than in any other way, such, perhaps, as calling attention to outward results. After all, it is not so much by what the minister contributes of himself to the cause of Christ, but rather by what he is enabled to draw out and utilize from the divine resources, that his office and work will be tested. It is not chiefly the question whether we are strong in the cause, but whether the cause is strong in and through us. And herein lies the practical value of the argument in its application to the servants of Christ under all conditions. If Paul had staked the issue on the personal factor, then there could be in his testimony but little comfort and encouragement for others, for there are not many Pauls. Now that the subject is dealt with in the other way the apostle's words contain something heartening for you and me and the simplest, obscurest bearer of the gospel.

We are too often told at the present day that the official, professional distinction of the minister is a matter of the past, that it has become purely a question of what is called personal magnetism whether he shall earn success or failure. Paul certainly was far from this opinion. To be sure, to such things as ecclesiastical position or rank he would hardly have attributed much importance. Even the difference between the apostolate and other forms of service in the church seems scarcely to enter into the reckoning here. But within the realm of the invisible and spiritual there remains such a thing as an intrinsic prestige. Paul is conscious of belonging to a veritable elite of the Spirit. I beg you to notice on how large a scale this thought is projected. It gives rise to the conception of a ministry of God's covenant, that is, a ministry identified with an all-comprehensive dispensation of divine grace. Thus Moses was a minister of the Old and Paul is a minister of the New Covenant.

To have such a covenant-ministry means to be identified with God in the most intimate manner, for the covenant expresses the very heart of God's purpose. It means to be initiated into the holiest mysteries of redemption, for in the covenant these are transacted. It means to be enrolled on the list of the great historic servants of God, for in the organism of the covenant these are united and salute each other across the ages. It means to become a channel through which supernatural currents flow. In the covenant the servant is, as it were, made part of the wonder-world of salvation itself. The apostle has embodied this grandiose thought in a most striking figure. 'Thanks be to God', he exclaims, 'who always leadeth us in triumph in Christ.' The onward march of the gospel is a triumphal procession, God the victorious conqueror, Paul a follower in God's train, burning the incense to his glory, making manifest the savour of his knowledge in every place!

What has been said so far applies to the ministry of the covenant of grace under both dispensations. It describes a glory common to Moses and Paul. The apostle ungrudgingly recognizes that the Old Testament had its peculiar distinction. To be a prophet or priest of the God of Israel conferred greater honour than any secular prominence in the pagan history of the race. Even the ministration written and engraven on stones came with glory. This excellence of the Old Covenant found a symbolic expression in the light upon the face of Moses after his tarrying with God upon the mount, a light so intense that the children of Israel could not steadfastly look upon its radiance. Paul's purpose, however, is not to emphasize what the two dispensations have in common, but that in which the New surpasses the Old.

Since the opponents had clothed their attack upon him in the invidious form of a comparison with the Mosaic administration, it was natural for him to take up the challenge and fight out the battle along the same line. None the less the comparison, as followed up by Paul, is startling in its exceeding boldness. A more impressive disclosure of his exalted sense of office is scarcely conceivable. In order to feel the full force of this we ought to make clear to ourselves that not two single persons but two pairs of persons are set over against each other. On the one side stand God and Moses, the reflector of his glory, on the other Christ and Paul, the reflector of his glory.

It would be interesting, but beside our present purpose, to consider what it implies as to the nature and rank of Christ, that the apostle feels free simply to put him on a line with God as a fount and dispenser of glory in the New Covenant after no different fashion than God was under the Old Covenant. Without pursuing this further, we now wish to make the point, that the comparison lies not between Moses and Christ, but between Moses and Paul. Than Moses no greater name was known in the annals of Old Testament redemption. Prophet, priest, lawgiver in one, he towers high above all the others. And to Paul, the son of Israel, all this wealth of sacred story gathered round the head of Moses must have been a thousand times more impressive than it can be to us. What an overwhelming sense, then, of the greatness of his own ministry must Paul have possessed, when he dared conceive the thought of being greater than

Moses! 'Verily that which has been made glorious has been made not-glorious in this respect, by reason of the glory that surpasseth.'

The apostle, however, does not give expression to this lofty consciousness in an outburst of unreasoning enthusiasm. He carefully specifies wherein the surpassing excellence of his ministry above that of Moses consists. *The first point relates to the contrast between transitoriness and eternity.* Putting it in terms of the figure, Paul affirms that the glory of the Old Covenant had to pass away, whereas that of the New Covenant must remain. When Moses descended from the mount his face shone with a refulgence of the divine glory near which he had been permitted to dwell for a season.

But his face could not retain this brightness for any length of time. It soon disappeared. Thus what Moses stood for was glorious but lacked permanence. The day was bound to come when its splendour would vanish. On the other hand, the New Covenant is final and abiding. The times cannot outgrow, the developments of history cannot age it, it carries within itself the pledge of eternity. But not only did such a difference actually exist—both Moses and Paul were aware of the state of things in each case. Moses was aware of it, for we are told that he put the veil on his face for the purpose of hiding the disappearance of the glory. And Paul was, since in pointed contrast to this procedure, he professes to minister with open face: 'Not as Moses, who put a veil over his face.' It was further inevitable that in Paul's estimation the speedy abrogation of Moses' work detracted from his glory as a servant of the covenant, and that, on the other hand, the enduring character of his own work added greatly to the honour wherewith Paul felt it clothed him and the satisfaction he derived from it. Time, especially time with the wasting power it acquires through sin, is the arch-enemy of all human achievement. It kills the root of joy which otherwise belongs to working and building. All things which the succeeding generations of mankind have wrought in the course of the ages succumb to its attacks. The tragic sense of this accompanies the race at every step in its march through history. It is like a pall cast over the face of the peoples. In revealed religion, through the grace of redemption, it is in principle removed, yet not so that under the Old Covenant the dark shadow entirely disappears. The complaint of it is in Moses' own psalm: 'Thou turnest man to destruction—thou carriest them away as with a flood.' And something of this bitter taste of transitoriness enters even into the Old Testament consciousness of salvation.

Now put over against this the triumphant song of life and assurance of immortality that fills the glorious, spacious days of the New Covenant, especially where first it issues from the womb of the morning bathed in the dew of imperishable youth. The note of futility and depression has disappeared, and in place of this the rapture of victory over death and decay, the exultant feeling of immersion in the atmosphere of eternity prevail. And this particularly communicated itself to the spirit in which the covenant-ministration was performed. The joy of working in the dawn of the world to come quickens the pulse of all New Testament servants of Christ. Paul felt that the product of his labours, the output of his life, would shine with unfading splendour in the palace of God. Thus also the honour of being a fellow labourer of God first obtains its full rich meaning. It is the prerogative of God, the Eternal One, to work for eternity. As the King of the Ages he discounts and surmounts all the intervening forces and barriers of time. He who is made to share in this receives the highest form which the divine image can assume in its reproduction in man. Neither things present nor things to come can conquer him, he reigns in life with God through Jesus Christ, his Lord.

In the second place, there is a difference operating to the advantage of Paul between the two ministries in regard to the measure of openness and clearness with which they are conducted. Moses ministered with covered, Paul ministers with open, that is uncovered, face. As regards Moses this was that the children of Israel should not perceive the passing away of the glory underneath the veil. Not that Moses acted as a deceiver of his people. Paul means to say, that in receiving the glory, and losing it, and hiding its loss, he served the symbolic function of illustrating, in the first place, the glory of the Old Covenant, in the second place its transitoriness, and in the third place the ignorance of Israel in regard to what was taking place. The chief point of ignorance of the people related to the eclipse and abrogation of their institutions would suffer. But the symbolism permits generalization, so as to include all the limitations of self-knowledge and self-understanding under which the Old Covenant laboured. As a matter of fact, Paul immediately afterwards extends it to Israel's entire reading of the law, that is, to Israel's self-interpretation and Scripture-interpretation on a large scale. Ignorance as to the end would easily produce ignorance or imperfect understanding with reference to the whole order of things under which the people were living.

Everything temporal and provisional, especially if it does not know itself as such, is apt to wear a veil. It often lacks the faculty of discriminating between what is higher and lower in its composition. Things that are ends and things that are mere means to an end are not always clearly separated. Every preparatory stage in the history of redemption can fully understand itself only in the light of that which fulfils it. The veil of the Old Covenant is lifted only in Christ. The Christian standpoint alone furnishes the necessary perspective for apprehending its place and function in the organism of the whole. So it came about that the Mosaic covenant moved through the ages a mystery to itself and to its servants. According to Paul this tragical process reached its climax when Israel came face to face with him who alone could interpret Israel to itself. It is not for us to unravel the web of self-misinterpretation and unbelief wrought by the Jews on the ancient loom previously to the appearance of Christ. Paul implies that both causes contributed to the sad result. There was an element of original guilt as well as of subsequent hardening involved. Their minds were blinded. The veil was on the reading of Moses, but the veil was also on their hearts. And the apostle's word still holds true: the veil remains until the present day. It can be taken away only when Israel shall turn to the Lord. Then, and not until then, that ghost of the Old Covenant which now accompanies Israel on its wandering through the ages will vanish from its side. As a double gift of grace it will then receive the treasures of Moses and those of Paul from the hand of Christ.

It is in sharp contrast to all this that Paul describes his own mode of ministering under the New Covenant. He serves with unveiled face, and in this one figure all the openness, the self-intelligence, the transparency of his ministry find expression. The proclamation of the word of the gospel has left behind all the old reserve and restrictions and limitations under which Moses and his successors laboured. Its ministers can now speak fully and freely and plainly the whole counsel of God. Paul glories in being able to do this. He uses great boldness of speech. There is nothing to withhold, nothing to conceal: the entire plan of redemption has been unfolded, the mystery hidden through the ages has been revealed, and there is committed to every ambassador of Christ an absolute message, no longer subject to change. Not the delicate procedure of the diplomat, who hides his aim, but the stately stepping forward of the herald who renders an authoritative pronouncement characterizes his task to Paul's own mind. He discards all human artifice and invention, all insincere and undignified devices evidently employed by some at that time, as they are still not infrequently at the present time, to render the gospel palatable to his hearers. He scorns, where principles are concerned, all compromise and concession: 'Therefore, seeing we have this ministry, even as we obtained mercy, we faint not, but we have renounced the hidden things of shame, not walking in craftiness, nor handling the word of God deceitfully, but by the manifestation of the truth commending ourselves to every man's conscience in the sight of God.'

There is a straightforwardness, a simplicity in preaching, which is proportionate to the preacher's own faith in the absoluteness, and inherent truthfulness of his message. No shallow optimism about the adjustableness of Christianity to ever-changing conditions, about its self-rejuvenating power after apparent decline, can possibly make up for a lack of this fundamental conviction. Unless we are convinced with Paul that Christianity has a definable and well-defined message to bring, and are able to tell wherein it consists, all our talk about its vitality or adaptability will neither comfort ourselves nor deceive others. A thing is not immortal because it is long-lived and dies hard. Only when through all changes of time it preserves unaltered its essence and source of power, can it be considered worthwhile as a medicine for the sickness of the world. Something that needs the constant use of cosmetics to keep up the appearance of youth is a caricature of the Christianity of the New Testament. Its case is worse than it imagines: it has not merely passed its youth, but is in danger of losing its very life.

In the next place, the greater distinction of the ministry of the New Covenant springs from this, that it is in the closest conceivable manner bound up with the person and work of the Saviour. It is a Christ-

dispensation in the fullest sense of the word. What is possessed by the New Covenant is not the glory of God as such, but the glory of God in the face of Jesus Christ. Moses had a great vision on the mountain, but Paul had a greater one, even as Moses himself had a greater when he stood with Elias on the New Testament mount of transfiguration. Paul beholds the glory of Christ as in a mirror, or, according to another rendering, reflects it as a mirror. His entire task, both on its communicative and on its receptive side, can be summed up in his reflecting back the Christ-glory, caught by himself, unto others. To behold Christ and to make others behold him is the substance of his ministry.

All the distinctive elements of Paul's preaching relate to Christ, and bear upon their face his image and superscription. God is the Father of our Lord Jesus Christ. The Spirit is the Spirit of Christ. In the procuring of righteousness Christ is the one efficient cause. In Christ believers were chosen, called, justified, and will be glorified. To be converted is to die with Christ and to rise with him. The entire Christian life, root and stem and branch and blossom, is one continuous fellowship with Christ. But to say that the gospel is full of Christ is still too general a statement. What the apostle affirms is that it is particularly the gospel of the glory of Christ, and that, therefore, its ministry also has specifically to do with this.

Now this is not a mere metaphorical way of speaking, as if it meant no more than that in every possible manner the gospel-preaching brings out and promotes the honour of the Saviour. Paul intends it in a far more literal sense. The glory of Christ transmitted by his gospel is an objective reality. It is that which effects the Saviour's exalted state since the resurrection. While including the radiance of his external appearance, it is by no means confined to this. Paul reckons among this glory the whole equipment of grace and power and beauty, all the supernatural potencies and forces stored up in the risen Lord. It consists of energy no less than of splendour. Taken in this comprehensive, realistic sense, it is equivalent to the content of the gospel, and determines the nature of its ministry. The rendering, 'beholding as in a mirror', admirably fits into this representation. As a mirror is not an end in itself but exists for the sake of what is seen through it, so the gospel serves no other purpose than to bring men face to face with the glory of Christ. It is nothing else but a tale of Christ, a Christ in words, the exact counterpart of Christ's person and work in their glorious state.

Because of the consciousness of this Paul felt himself greater than Moses, for the partial light that shone on the latter's face has now become omnipresent and fills the New Covenant. Under the old dispensation, the servants of God saw only from afar the brightness of the Messiah's rising. Now he is visible from nearby, the One filling all in all, occupying the entire field of vision. The humblest of preachers surpasses in this respect the greatest of Old Testament evangelists. He carries a gospel all-fragrant and all-radiant with Christ.

In the fourth place, the excellence of the ministry of the New Covenant is seen in this, that it is a ministry of abundant forgiveness and righteousness. This aspect of it also is intimately connected with the glory of the Lord, although it requires a somewhat closer inspection to perceive this. It should be remembered that the glory possessed by Christ in heaven is, to Paul, the emphatic, never-silent declaration of his absolute righteousness acquired during the state of humiliation. It sprang from his obedience and suffering and self-sacrifice in our stead. It is righteousness translated into the language of effect, the crown set upon his work of satisfaction. Consequently, the servant of the New Covenant can attach his ministry of pardon and peace to the glory of Christ. Hence Paul in working out the comparison between Moses and himself with special reference to the question of righteousness reduces the difference to terms of glory: 'For if the ministry of condemnation is glory, much rather does the ministry of righteousness exceed in glory.'

In a broad sense the Old Testament was the economy of conviction of sin. The law revealed the moral helplessness of man, placed him under a curse, worked death. There was, of course, gospel under and in the Old Covenant, but it was for its expression largely dependent on the silent symbolic language of altar and sacrifice and lustration. Under it the glory which speaks of righteousness was in hiding. In the New Covenant all this has been changed. The veil has been rent, and through it an unobstructed view is obtained of the glory of God on the face of Jesus Christ. And with this vision comes the assurance of atonement, satisfaction, access to God, peace of conscience, liberty, eternal life. For Paul, the commission to proclaim these things constitutes no small part of the excellence of his task. As Jesus delighted in announcing release to the captives, in setting at liberty those who were bruised, in proclaiming the acceptable year of Jehovah, so Paul, even more because of the accomplishment of the redemptive work, rejoiced in the ministry of reconciliation. Beautiful to him upon the mountains were the feet of those who bring good tidings, that publish peace.

The fifth and principal reason why the service of the New Covenant excels in honour, Paul adds, is this: that the Christ-glory is a living and self-communicating power, transforming both those who mediate it and those who receive it from glory to glory into the likeness of the Lord. Paul here again has in mind the difference between Moses and himself. Moses' own condition and appearance were only externally and temporarily affected by the vision on the mount. After a while his face became as before. And what he was unable to retain for himself he was unable to communicate unto others.

Over against this the apostle places the two facts, first that the servants of the New Covenant are internally and permanently transformed by beholding the image of the Lord, and second that they effect a similar transformation in others to whom through their ministry the knowledge of the glorified Saviour comes. In its first part this representation was doubtless connected with the apostle's personal experience. There had been a point in his life at which the perception of the glorified Lord had been for him attended with the most marvellous change it is possible to undergo. The glory that shone around him on the road to Damascus had in one moment, in the twinkling of an eye, swept away all his old beliefs and ideals, his sinful passion and pride, and made of him a new creature, to whom the past things were like the faint memory of some distant phase of existence. And what had happened there Paul had afterwards seen repeating itself thousands of times, less conspicuously, to be sure, but not on that account less truly, less miraculously. To express this aspect of his ministry he employs the formula that it is a ministry of the Spirit, that is of the Holy Spirit, whereas that of Moses was one of the letter. The Spirit stands for the living, energizing, creative grace of God, the letter for the inability of the law as such to translate itself into action.

Now, in saying that the ministry of the New Covenant is a ministry of the glory of Christ and that it is a ministry of the Spirit, Paul is not really affirming two different things but one and the same fact. The glory and the Spirit to him are identical. As we have seen, the glory means the equipment, with supernatural power and splendour, of the exalted Christ. And this equipment, described from the point of view of its energizing source, consists of the Holy Spirit. It was at the resurrection that the Spirit in this high, unique sense was received by him. There the Spirit transformed the Lord's human nature and made it glorious beyond conception. Besides this, the Spirit is with Christ in continuance as the indwelling principle, the element, as it were, in which the glorified life of the Saviour is lived. We need not wonder, then, that a little later the apostle gives almost paradoxical expression to this truth by declaring, 'The Lord is the Spirit', and that we are transformed from 'the Lord, the Spirit'.

This language is not, of course, intended to efface the distinction between the second and the third persons of the Trinity, but simply serves to bring out the practical inseparableness of the exalted Christ and the Holy Spirit in the work of salvation. So we begin to understand at least a little of the mystery, how the glory of Christ can communicate itself to and reproduce itself in the believer and transform him. As Spirit-glory it cannot fail to do this, for it is of the nature of the Spirit so to act. Hence also we read elsewhere that Christ 'became a quickening Spirit'. The main point to be observed, however, is how all this adds to the high conception held by Paul about the honour of his ministry as compared with that of Moses. The minister of the law, the letter, can never taste that sweetest joy of seeing the message he brings incarnate and reincarnate itself in the lives of others. The minister of the New Covenant does taste of this joy: he writes with the Spirit of the living God in tables that are hearts of flesh. This means more than what we sometimes speak of and feel as pleasure in the consciousness of power set free or good accomplished.

Paul undoubtedly knew this also, but to confine what he here describes to that would rob it of its most distinctive quality. Paul had the sensation of coming through his ministry into the closest touch with the forthputting of the saving energy of God himself. He was aware that to his preaching of the gospel there belonged an invisible background, that at every step his presentation of the truth was accompanied by a ministry from heaven conducted by the Christ of glory. His work was for him imbued with divine power, the lifeblood of the supernatural pulsed through it. His service, at each point where it touched men, marked the line and opened channels for the introduction of divine creative forces into human souls. So vivid was this consciousness of involvement in the supernatural, that nothing short of a comparison of God's word through him with the divine word at the first creation could adequately express it to Paul's mind: 'God who said, Let light shine out of darkness, has shined into our hearts for the purpose of our imparting the light of the knowledge of his glory in the face of Jesus Christ.'

Nor was this close participation with God in a transforming spiritual process something glorious merely in itself. Paul also took into account its comprehensive effect. When the apostle says, 'We all are transformed', it is evident that the statement is not limited to the apostles or preachers of the gospel, but includes, so far at least as the passive experience is concerned, all believers. To the joyous consciousness of exerting extraordinary power there was added the delight of witnessing extraordinary results. There is a note of genuine Christian universalism in this. It was a reason for profound satisfaction to Paul that he need not stand in the midst of the congregation of God as another Moses, partaking of a light from God in which the others could not share, solitary in his splendour, but that the larger share of what he affirmed of himself had through him become the possession of the simplest believer, a transfiguration of spirit like his own by the beholding of the Lord. Refracted from numberless mirrors, the light multiplied and intensified itself for each on whom it fell. Nevertheless, even so a measure of incommunicable distinction remained. Since the reproduction into the likeness of Christ is dependent on and proportionate to the vision of the Saviour, and since this vision from the nature of the case is more constantly present to the minister of the gospel than to the common believer, it follows that in the former an altogether unique result may be expected.

So it was undoubtedly with Paul. He had no need of testing the principle in others; a more direct and convincing evidence lay in its effect upon himself. He was aware of a renewal of the inner man, progressing from day to day, and in which there was observable this law of increase, that the more he did to make Christ known, the deeper the lineaments of the character of Christ were impressed upon his soul. Even the hardships befalling his flesh in the service of the Lord were contributory to this: 'We are always bearing about in the body the dying of Jesus, that the life also of Jesus may be manifested in our mortal flesh.' And: 'Our light affliction, which is for the moment, works for us more exceedingly an eternal weight of glory.' 'Therefore we faint not; though our outward man decay, yet the inner man is renewed day by day.' Thus the apostle's ministry, while exercised upon others, became unto him a continual ministry to his own soul, ever increasingly assimilating him to the glory of Christ.

Such was Paul's conception of the ministry of the New Covenant. It bears upon its face the marks of the historical situation in which he was called upon to present it. None the less it has abiding validity, for it is drawn from the nature of the gospel itself, and the gospel is the gospel of him who remains the same yesterday and today and forever. Even of the errors over against which Paul placed these glorious views it is in a certain sense true that they are not of one age but of all ages; they lead a life of pseudo-immortality among men. In the Judaistic controversy which shook the early church, forces and tendencies were at work deeply rooted in the sinful human heart. In modernized apparel they confront us still to the present day. There are still abroad forms of a Christless gospel. There prevails still a subtle form of legalism which would rob the Saviour of his crown of glory, earned by the cross, and would make of him a second Moses, offering us the stones of the law instead of the life-bread of the gospel. And, oh the pity and shame of it, the Jesus that is being preached but too often is a Christ after the flesh, a religious genius, the product of evolution, powerless to save!

Let us pray that it may be given to the church to repudiate and cast out this error with the resoluteness of Paul. There is need for her ministers of placing themselves ever afresh in the light of the great apostolic consciousness revealed in our text. They should learn once more to bear their message out of the fulness of conviction that it is an unchangeable message, reliable as the veracity of God himself.

God grant that it may become on the lips of his servants more truly from age to age a gospel from which the name of Christ crowds out every other human name, good tidings of atonement and righteousness and supernatural renewal; to preacher and people alike, what it was to Paul and his converts, a mirror of vision and transfiguration after the image of the Lord.

MAITLAND ALEXANDER
1867-1940

P RESBYTERIAN pastor, graduate of Princeton College (1889) and Princeton Theological Seminary (1892), and grandson of Archibald Alexander, Maitland Alexander played a pivotal role in his service on the Board of Directors of Princeton Theological Seminary.

Pastor of the First Presbyterian Church in Pittsburgh, Pennsylvania, Maitland succeeded Ethelbert Warfield in 1904 as President of Princeton's Board of Directors. Faithful to the goals and purposes for which the seminary had been founded and for which his grandfather had selflessly devoted many years of his life, Maitland provided steady leadership in the ensuing years during a period of significant change in his denomination's direction and theological convictions.

By the 1920s the American Presbyterian Church faced a period of unprecedented theological turbulence. Divisions within the faculty at Princeton Theological Seminary were representative of divisions within the church. Sympathetic to the issues identified and addressed by faculty member J. Gresham Machen, a majority of the directors of the board affirmed their support for Machen's scholarship and competency as an instructor at a time when Modernist sympathizers opposed his appointment to the chair of Apologetics at Princeton Theological Seminary. Alexander's efforts in addressing issues which had divided the president, board, and faculty came at a critical point in the life of the seminary—issues which would ultimately be resolved at an institutional level in a reorganization of the seminary's boards and executive authority of the seminary's president.

Maitland Alexander's piety, churchmanship, and theological competency are evident in the stirring charge delivered on October 11, 1921 at the seminary inauguration of Caspar Wistar Hodge, Jr. as Charles Hodge Professor of Didactic and Polemic Theology. Recognizing the important role Hodge would play in the preservation and promotion of biblical orthodoxy at a time of significant doctrinal deviation in American Presbyterianism, Alexander charged Hodge to be vigilant in his responsibilities as a guardian and example of the Reformed confessional orthodoxy which he had inherited from his predecessors and upon which the institutional integrity of the seminary's future depended. Alexander's brief charge is an eloquent retrospect of the seminary's glorious spiritual history and a cautionary warning on what the future would hold if the doctrinal and pietistic foundations of the institution were exchanged for the tenets of Protestant Modernism.

THE CHARGE[1]

THERE are few things that I have been called upon to do which give me greater pleasure than to charge you, my dear Friend, in the name of the Board of Directors of this seminary as you are inducted into this chair so filled with associations to you, which must be weighing you down with those responsibilities which great men pass on to their successors. I am glad to have been chosen, because the names of Alexander and Hodge have been associated through all the years of this seminary's history. The friendships, between your grandfather and mine, between my father and yours, and again between us in the third generation, make the links in a chain of ancestral and life-long friendship which I am sure will never be broken.

In charging you, as is required by this seminary, I shall not presume to charge you what you shall teach, or how you shall teach it. I know that your teaching will accept the principle of external authority in religion and find that authority in the Word of God and not in the Christian consciousness; and that you will teach the Reformed faith, undiluted and unweakened,—the great system which believes in the deity of our Lord, atonement through his blood and the absolute dependence of the sinner on divine grace. And knowing this I feel confident that the department of which you are now the head will maintain the proud position which it has always enjoyed in the field of dogmatic theology and the training and grounding of ministers to preach these great truths.

---

[1] Maitland Alexander, 'The Charge', *Addresses Delivered at the Inauguration of Reverend Caspar Wistar Hodge, Ph.D., as Charles Hodge Professor of Didactic and Polemic Theology in Princeton Theological Seminary, October 11, 1921*, pp. 3-7.

If I were a learned man instead of a plain preacher and pastor, I might charge you more scientifically as to your duty in the hour in which you find yourself today. All I can do, however, is to say a word to you which I hope you will remember again and again while you teach, and that it may be to you a kind of call from one who fights with the weapons you forge, and receives his reinforcements from your training camp.

The conception of this seminary and its purpose is twofold. One purpose existed when it was founded and the other has grown more and more evident in the last fifty years.

Princeton Seminary was founded as a training school for the sons of the prophets. Since her foundation she has filled another and equally great duty to the church. She has had a polemic duty to perform, a position to maintain, error to combat. And I charge you to remember that on you comes the responsibility of continuing this great work. By your pen, by your classroom work, by your public utterances, in the impress you put on students, maintain this great duty. We hear today of the Princeton position. It is a misnomer. True, we occupy a position, we defend it, we are uncompromising in our warfare against those who would attack it; but it is not the Princeton position. It is the apostolic position; it is the position of the Lord Jesus Christ, who revealed God not as the creature of our imagination, or man as needing no second birth, or himself as a good man martyr to his zeal, or the Scriptures as a moral manual; but himself as God, one with the Father, man as lost save by the efficacy of divine grace, and the Bible as the inspired Word of God.

I do not need to tell you of the need of maintaining this position which we hold—you know it better than I do. One of our colleagues has said that 'the wardrobe of Christianity is ample enough to clothe with moral and religious respectability types of thought which fall far short of the religion embodied in the New Testament'. He describes a religion which he says shall soon come, but which I think is already here, 'which reveres the name of Jesus, sees in him the ideal man, gets lessons in philanthropy from his life, looks for a sociological millennium, but leaves us to go down in the dark valley with no lamp to our feet or light to our path'.

The attacks which menace the church today are the same as those spoken of by our Lord when he said 'Beware of false prophets which come to you in sheep's clothing but inwardly they are ravening wolves.' There is a catholicity which is good, a liberality which is the liberality of Jesus. There is an attitude of tolerance which believes there is room for every shade of opinion within the church. But I charge you to remember that there are hundreds of ministers who in the battle will fire the ammunition that you prepare, and follow the plan of campaign that you devise; and to whom you can be a great and inspiring leader, as they strive to exalt Christ the Son of God, uplift his precious cross and stand with the doctrine of grace in the path of the hopeless sinner. Never let the isolation sometimes felt in the cloistered seclusion of your study or classroom make you forget us your fellow ministers who look to you for leadership and who again and again, when the fight is hot, seek to see your face and hear your voice in the thickest of the battle.

I charge you therefore to remember that you have a position to maintain, not in these secluded walks or amid these friendly walls, but in the world where enemies have said, 'Let us take for ourselves the whole pastures of God.' I make you with your colleagues responsible for this, in your life and teaching.

But I remind you of another thing for which you are even more responsible and concerning which I hope you will think and pray.

You must *compel*, and I use this word as Christ used it, the students in your classes to believe what you teach. It is not enough to deliver what you believe to be the truth. It is not enough to demand an examination in what you have said. It is not duty well done if you say 'Here it is. Take it or leave it.' You must teach with so much conviction, impart with so much skill and tact, deal so powerfully with your students, that they will carry away an impression that they will never forget.

The most abiding part of my seminary training, the most stimulating knowledge I received for my pulpit work, was in the department of which you are now the head and which was imparted to me by your distinguished predecessor, and in the classroom where your honoured father opened the New Testament to his students. The defect in the modern pulpit today is the substitution of social preaching for doctrinal preaching. I do not mean doctrinal preaching in the sense of the theological discussion. But the way of salvation cannot be preached without a theological knowledge of the meaning of the cross and the atonement. Without that knowledge the path to Calvary cannot be made plain to the sinner or the Eternal Son be seen by those who walk in darkness.

Theology is the heart of preaching. You must see to it that the students sent out from here shall have for free, familiar use a body of doctrine that has become so much a part of their thought that they cannot escape it.

We hear that the Department of Homiletics teaches men to preach, that it is here that they are developed; and too often the other departments of our curriculum disavow responsibility for what men are in the pulpit. You cannot make bricks out of straw or iron without ore, but I charge you so to conduct your department that the fascination of it shall be contagious and that the men whom you teach shall be constrained to preach those magnificent truths, the understanding of which and power of which they owe to you.

I therefore pray that the Holy Spirit may in turn teach you, that as you review the past history of the theological department of this seminary and its achievements, as you look forward to its administration in the most difficult days of its history, you may hear the voice of him 'whose mercy is from everlasting to everlasting upon them that fear him and whose righteousness is unto children's children', even the Lord God of the covenant, saying 'Be thou strong and very courageous, that thou mayest observe to do according to all the law which my servant Moses commanded thee: turn not from it to the right hand or to the left . . . for then thou shalt make thy way prosperous and then thou shalt have good success.' If such be the case, the 'great cloud of witnesses', yes even the angels of God, shall say to each other, 'The spirit of Elijah doth rest on Elisha.'

CASPAR WISTAR HODGE
1870-1937

G IFTED educator and successor to B. B. Warfield, Caspar Wistar Hodge Jr. was born at Princeton, New Jersey on September
22, 1870. Grandson of Charles Hodge, Caspar was named after
his father, who also served for many years on the Princeton Theological
Seminary faculty as Professor of New Testament Literature and Exegesis.

Educated at Princeton College, Princeton Theological Seminary,
Heidelberg University, and the University of Berlin, he initially served
as an instructor of Philosophy at Princeton College during 1895-97, and
later as Associate Professor of Ethics at Lafayette College (1897-98).

In 1901 Caspar became an instructor in the New Testament department at Princeton Theological Seminary, serving alongside William
Park Armstrong. He also served as an assistant in Dogmatic Theology

from 1901 to 1907; from 1907 to 1915 he held was Assistant Professor of Didactic and Polemic Theology. Between the years 1915 and 1921 he served as Professor of Dogmatic Theology. Following B. B. Warfield's death on February 16, 1921, Caspar was appointed as Charles Hodge Professor of Didactic and Polemic Theology—a position which he held with distinction from 1921 to 1937.

Noted for his deep piety and careful scholarship, Caspar upheld the noble theological heritage made famous by his grandfather, Charles Hodge, and famous uncle, A. A. Hodge. Profoundly influenced by the example and friendship of B. B. Warfield, Caspar embodied the Warfieldian approach to the study of Scripture and theological formulation in his publications and instruction to his students.

Well-versed in the history of theology, Caspar provided penetrating analyses of the various schools of theological thought popular in his time. Like his colleagues B. B. Warfield and J. Gresham Machen, Caspar was especially gifted at identifying, examining, and refuting naturalistic and apostate theological methodologies whose theological trajectories would lead to the abandonment of a biblical, Reformed, and confessional orthodoxy in the life of his denomination with an accompanying disintegration of piety and spiritual vitality in the life of the local church.

Caspar Wistar Hodge was one of the last living representatives of the 'Old Princeton' theology who continued teaching in the seminary after its reorganization in 1929. A sympathetic supporter of J. Gresham Machen, he elected to finish his remaining years as a theological professor at Princeton rather than accompany his friend and other colleagues in the founding of Westminster Theological Seminary in Philadelphia. With his death in 1937, the near 'endless succession' of Hodges and Alexanders serving professorships at Princeton Theological Seminary concluded.

THE SIGNIFICANCE OF THE
REFORMED THEOLOGY TODAY[1]

MR President, Gentlemen of the Board of Directors, Fathers and Brethren:—I have a very profound sense of unworthiness in taking up the duties of the chair to which you have called me—a chair made famous by the illustrious men who have preceded me, and whose labours have helped to give Princeton Seminary a fame throughout the world for sound learning and true piety. We think today of Archibald Alexander, that man of God, the first professor in this seminary; of Charles Hodge, whose *Systematic Theology* today remains as probably the greatest exposition of the Reformed Theology in the English language; of Archibald Alexander Hodge, a man of rare popular gifts and of unusual metaphysical ability; and last, but not least, excelling them all in erudition, of Dr Warfield, whose recent death has left us bereft of our leader and of one of the greatest men who have ever taught in this institution.

I would pause a moment to pay a tribute to his memory. He was my honoured teacher and friend. For twenty years I had the privilege of helping him in this department, and drew inspiration from his broad-minded scholarship. At the time of his death he was, I think, without an equal as a theologian in the English-speaking world. With Doctors Kuyper and Bavinck of Holland, he made up a great trio of outstanding exponents of the Reformed faith. His loss is simply irreparable. But he has gone to his reward, to meet the Lord he loved and served, and we must seek to carry on the work he did so faithfully and well.

[1] Caspar Wistar Hodge, Jr., 'The Inaugural Address: The Significance of the Reformed Theology Today', *Addresses Delivered at the Inauguration of Reverend Caspar Wistar Hodge, Ph.D., as Charles Hodge Professor of Didactic and Polemic Theology in Princeton Theological Seminary,* October 11, 1921, pp. 9-22.

I am oppressed, I say, by a sense of unworthiness in following such men as these. But their example is an inspiration. Hallowed memories crowd upon us in this place. We are surrounded by the spirits of just men made perfect, who consecrated great powers and learning to the Master whom they loved. Relying on the help of God, I shall teach the same theology they taught, and give myself whole-heartedly to its exposition and defence. And so I wish to say a few words to you today about: *the significance of the Reformed Theology today.*

We hear much nowadays about the difference between the old and new theology.

The old theology, as one of its leading opponents in this country admits, is characterized by definiteness, and gives us a great reinforcement of power from dependence on God. It has a profound view of the infinitude and transcendence of God as the Creator and Ruler of the universe. It therefore makes a clear distinction between the world and God, and between the spheres of nature and of grace. It views man as created in God's image, as fallen and ruined by sin, which is no mere incident in human evolution, but a transgression of and want of conformity to God's law. God himself, therefore, must intervene in the world-process for man's salvation. This he does by giving man a supernatural revelation recorded in a supernaturally inspired Bible, which consequently gives us truth concerning God and his plan of redemption. The old theology views Christ the Redeemer as very God in essence, become man for our salvation; not merely God *in* man, but God *and* man. With its profound sense of the justice of God and the guilt of sin, the old theology makes the cross of Christ central, and proclaims expiation through his blood. With no less deep a sense of the power of sin, this theology cannot look for salvation to the natural perfectibility of man, or any change in his social environment, but asserts the regeneration of the sinner by the almighty power of God. And with this thorough-going supernaturalism, this theology cannot see in Christianity a religion chiefly for the betterment of this world, but is profoundly eschatological in its outlook, and sees the final realization of God's eternal purpose and kingdom in a future consummation brought in by mighty acts of God. The distinctive mark of the old theology, then, is supernaturalism and the realization of the infinitude and transcendence of God, in opposition to paganism which finds God only in the world.

The new theology likewise is not a matter of date but of principles. It is not the result of the needs of the heart but of an intellectual revolution going back to English Deism, the French Revolution, and the German Illumination. It is claimed by its advocates that it is a theology determined by the modern scientific movement, but in reality it is the product of a philosophical dogma rooted in Kant and Darwin. It takes on a multitude of forms in Schleiermacher, Coleridge, Sabatier, and Roman Catholic Modernism. Thus, in contrast with the old theology, it is lacking in definiteness. It has no formal creed; no official representative. Indeed, if, one looks at the attacks of the Ritschlians on the Hegelians, of the Radicals on the Liberals, of Loisy on Harnack, one is tempted to believe that here are fundamental differences.

Yet this is not the fact. There are common principles underlying the various forms of the new theology. What are these common principles?

First, there is its idea of God. This theology has no adequate sense of the majesty and transcendence of God. He is not distinct and separate from the world, but only a name for the immanent law of the world; of an ever present Spirit in the world; or the divine in man. In this, the new theology is akin to paganism which, whether polytheistic or pantheistic, finds God only in the world. The advocates of the new theology like to call this a conception of the world as a unity, and assert that it does away with what they term the dualism of the old theology. But in seeking to escape from a false dualism, they have done away with any real distinction between God and the world, and the contrast between the natural and the supernatural, fundamental for the old theology, has vanished. 'Nature', says a new theologian, 'expresses the law of development in process, the supernatural is only the end to which it tends.'

In harmony with this low conception of God and his relation to the world is also the exalted idea of this theology concerning the natural perfectibility of man, and its low view of sin. Man is naturally divine, or destined to become so. He is not in a natural state of sin, and redeemed by the supernatural grace and power of God. He is by nature both natural and supernatural, they tell us, *i.e.,* at once the product of mere natural causes, yet destined for an ethical end. In consequence of this view of man and sin, there is the view of man's religious knowledge. Man has not a natural knowledge of God from reason, and a supernatural revelation from God. The terms natural and supernatural express only two aspects of knowledge. All of man's religious knowledge is natural and psychologically mediated in origin, and supernatural only in the religious purpose which it serves. Hence there is no real distinction between natural and supernatural revelation, and the Bible is not regarded as different from other religious books, but is subjected to a naturalistic reconstruction. It gives us no revealed truths; it simply nourishes the religious life from which doctrine is supposed to spring. Its uniqueness is found only in its spiritual content as the nourishment of religious life.

Furthermore, with its naturalistic idea of redemption, this theology needs no divine and supernatural Redeemer. Its low conception of God makes it easy to call Christ divine, for all men are divine in the same way. Christ is not God and man, but only God in man. He has, as this theology acknowledges, many brethren. And there being no conception of the guilt of sin, all idea of expiation vanishes, and the cross and Calvary become only an illustration of the principle of all religious life. Instead of regeneration by the power of God, we have the false hope of the natural evolution of man, and his perfecting through adjustment to his environment and the improvement of the latter. Christianity is no longer a religion for the future with tremendous issues of life and destiny, but is chiefly a religion for this present world, looking toward its social betterment and the rule of ethical principles on earth.

Such then, in general, is the new theology. To understand it and its underlying causes, we must go back and see how the logic of its principles has worked itself out relentlessly. Speaking broadly, this theology has come to us from Germany. To understand the situation today, no less than formerly, it is necessary to go back to Schleiermacher. The rapid development of the historical and exegetical theological disciplines, with their claim to exact scientific knowledge and their attitude of indifference or hostility to dogmatics, led to a denial of the scientific character of the latter, and to a sharp separation between history and dogmatics. The historical group of theological disciplines was supposed to be scientific and to have no practical motive; whereas dogmatics was supposed to be purely practical and non-scientific, and to serve the practical interests of the church. Consequently dogmatic theology turned from the statement of objectively valid doctrines to set forth the ideas implicated in Christian experience. It was this situation, as Troeltsch points out,[1] which led to an attempt to justify theoretically this separation between the theological disciplines which had already taken place. The supposedly practical and non-scientific character of dogmatics had to be justified. This was done by means of an agnostic theory of religious knowledge and a sharp distinction between religious and theoretic or scientific knowledge. This unfortunate point of view is quite generally recognized as a distinguishing mark of modern theology, as contrasted with the old evangelical theology and the old rationalism. This religious agnosticism denotes the impossibility of adequate scientific knowledge in the sphere of religious truth, and the practical, experiential character of religious knowledge. And more than this; it means the inadequate and symbolical form of all doctrinal statements which embody this religious knowledge. Thus dogmatic theology separated itself from the historical theological disciplines and assumed a purely practical character.

In order, however, to avoid falling into bare natural religion, Schleiermacher emphasized the fact that it was *Christian* experience, *i.e.,* an experience connected with the influence of Christ, which was the source and norm of Christian truth. But his emphasis on the experience of the individual was so strong that he failed to do justice to the Christian revelation.

In order to avoid the danger of making Christian doctrine purely subjective and of reducing Christianity to the natural religious sentiment of man, it was necessary to give more emphasis to the objective revelation in the historical Christ; and in order to avoid the speculative construction of Christian truth of the mediating theology, it was thought to be necessary to reassert the practical character of religious

---

[1] E. Troeltsch, 'Rückblick auf ein halbes Jahrhundert der theologischen Wissenschaft', in *Zeitschrift für wissetlschaftliche Theologie Jahrgang* 51, N. F. Heft 2, p. 105. I have also previously outlined this situation in an article 'Modern Positive Theology', *Princeton Theol. Review,* No. II, pp. 179ff.

knowledge and its distinction from scientific knowledge as well as from metaphysics. It was the significance of the Ritschlian school that it sought in these respects to carry out Schleiermacher's ideas more thoroughly than he had done. In doing this, Ritschl reacted from Schleiermacher so much that, though he rejected the old doctrine of the authority of Scripture, he nevertheless laid so much stress on the teaching of Jesus and the apostolic conception of Christianity, that he was inconsistent with his fundamental principles. Some of his followers were more consistent. Herrmann, for example, regards Christian faith simply as trust in God's providence brought about by the impression which Jesus makes on the soul. All ideas about God and Christ, *i.e.,* all Christian doctrines, are merely the way in which we think about Christ and God in view of our experience of God's presence in Christ. Dogmatic theology which formulates these doctrines is purely an individual and subjective matter. It can lay no claim to universal validity. All that is permanent is the experience and life; doctrine is subjective and changing.

While, therefore, this theology sought to be conservative, its conservatism is only apparent. It sought to escape naturalism, but let it in by the back door in giving up as unessential to Christianity all that naturalism demanded. It would keep Christianity free from metaphysics, yet it depends on a philosophical theory of knowledge. It asserted independence of historical criticism, yet used it to separate a human Jesus from unhistorical surroundings. It was determined by a naturalistic philosophy, and yet would isolate Christianity as the final religion.

In opposition to the Ritschlians, the school of comparative religions arose, Troeltsch being its theologian. The isolation of Christianity from other religions, and of Christ from history, is abandoned as a remnant of dogmatism. A thorough application of historical method is demanded, which changes Christian doctrine into a chapter in the evolution of religious ideas. All is an unbroken evolution, naturalistically conceived. Troeltsch speaks of defending an 'inclusive supernaturalism' in contrast with the old 'exclusive supernaturalism'; but by this he means only that some contact with God is back of all religions. The religion of Israel is connected with old oriental religious traditions; late Judaism, from which Christianity is supposed to have sprung, is thought to be influenced by oriental and Greek thought, and New Testament Christianity is regarded as the product of a syncretistic religious evolution. Naturalism determines the whole procedure, and Troeltsch acknowledges that the application of these principles renders the uncertainty of the portrait of Christ in the Gospels 'a heavy burden'. How is the Christ of apostolic tradition related to the actual Jesus? To what extent, in the Gospels, do we get the dogma of Christ's followers instead of history? How did this dogma arise? From such a point of view the gospel narrative is treated more and more sceptically, until it is doubted if Jesus claimed to be Messiah; the tradition in the so-called *Logia* is shattered; the difference between the Johannine and the Synoptic tradition is laid aside; and any certain historical knowledge of Jesus is questioned. The so-called historical Jesus has become a continually changing, even a vanishing quantity, so that any faith at all in Jesus is rendered difficult. We are left to choose between a divine Christ in a wholly mythical gospel and a purely human Jesus in a gospel which is supposed to be true only in so far as it is desupernaturalized.

And what has been said of Christ and Christianity is true of the entire sum of Christian truth. All Christian doctrine is merged in the stream of evolution, the result being that all that is distinctive of supernatural Christianity, *i.e.,* the Christianity of the New Testament, is explained away. For Christian truth is not the product of man's nature, and every attempt to explain Christianity as the culmination of the naturalistic evolution of religious thought must end in the reduction of the doctrinal content of Christianity to that of bare natural religion.

In this situation more positive theologians judged rightly that the Christian faith had been destroyed. But the attempt to mediate between the old theology and the modern consciousness has proved a failure and the so-called 'modern positive theology'—a new mediating theology—seems to have had little vitality and influence.

Since the War the dogmatics which have appeared show either a return to the old mediating theology, though with differences, as for example Lemme's *Glaubenslehre*, or to a line of thought which goes back to Schleiermacher, Ritschl, and Herrmann, as in the recent *Dogmatics* of Martin Schulze and Stephan.

When, now, we enquire what are the causes underlying this whole movement of modern theology, we should note that the chief cause alleged by modern theologians is not the real cause. It is usually claimed that, while the old theology is at variance with modern science, the new theology is the product of modern scientific thought. But such is not the case. There is nothing in the ascertained results of the modern natural sciences which need cause such a theological revolution. It is only when natural science fails to observe the limitations of its knowledge, and attempts to construct a naturalistic view of the world—in a word, when it becomes unscientific, speculative, and dogmatic—that it can be claimed as the cause of the new theology.

The real causes of this new theology are: first, agnosticism in religious knowledge, which reduces religion to mere feeling, making doctrine of no objective validity and purely symbolic. This is the result of the false anti-intellectualism which sprang from Kant's philosophy, and which is a widespread and potent error of modern thought. Under the false plea that religion is a matter of life and feeling only, the new theology brands the old theologians as 'rationalists' because they believe in the rational basis of religion.

This religious agnosticism can be met by showing that its alleged grounds lead to agnosticism in regard to all metaphysical questions, and that this kind of agnosticism leads in its turn to a complete scepticism which is self-contradictory. But this is not enough. It can be met in a constructive way only by a vindication of our natural knowledge of God from the point of view of Augustine and Calvin and the Reformed Theology which recognizes the innate religious sense in all men, or the *semen religionis* as it was called. This alone will give an adequate basis by which to meet the religious agnosticism which underlies the new theology.

A second cause and fundamental characteristic of the new theology is that it rejects all external authority in religious knowledge, and rests upon the Christian consciousness instead of on the Bible as the Word of God, as did the old theology. Again, under the specious plea that, because faith is trust which springs from the heart, and not a mere intellectual assent to truth, therefore it cannot have its doctrinal content given to it by revelation or accept it on authority, the new theology changes our whole conception of revelation and of the Bible. Revelation cannot give us truth objectively revealed, and the Bible does not contain such truth. Revelation consists in quickening our religious life, and the Bible is not intended to teach truth, but to nourish life.

It would not be difficult to point out the speciousness of the plea upon which this view of revelation and of faith rests. But we must hasten on to the real cause of this position. The real cause of this fundamental difference between the old and new theology runs back to the difference between naturalism and supernaturalism. Here we strike the third, the fundamental, and the underlying difference between the old and new theology. It is not, then, the evangelical conception of faith which is at the basis of the rejection of the authority of the Bible by the new theology, as it claims, but a naturalistic philosophy which denies all supernatural revelation, which demands a revolutionary and absolutely naturalistic reconstruction of the Bible, which sees revelation only in man's thoughts about God or in the Christian feelings, and which asserts man's ability and power of moral reformation over against a supernatural new birth from God. It is this naturalism which underlies the reconstruction of the Old Testament history and the Gospel criticism from Reimarus to Wrede, as well as all the doctrines of theology. By naturalism in this sense we do not mean simply the denial of teleology, and the assertion that the mechanical view of the world is final. We mean the denial of the power of God to make bare his arm and intrude in the world for man's salvation. *This,* chiefly, nay we may say, *this* almost alone, is the false root from which the whole movement of the new theology has sprung.

This all-engulfing speculative philosophy—for such it is—cannot be met by half-way measures. We cannot withdraw into the citadel of our heart, and suppose that thereby we have saved the Christian religion. We cannot set up an apologetic minimum and hope to defend it and escape with the essence of Christianity from the flood of this naturalistic stream. Only by a bold assertion and adequate defence of the opposite principle,—that of *Christian supernaturalism*—can we maintain our common Christian faith; by the defence of a supernatural Bible as the Word of God, and a supernatural salvation which comes from the power of Almighty God.

This pure supernaturalism can be upheld only from the standpoint of a pure theism which interprets all events as the unfolding of the purpose of God, and which sets no limits to his power; of a pure religion which acknowledges our absolute dependence on God, and rejects the naturalistic or Pelagian principle of dependence on self; and of pure grace or our absolute dependence on God for salvation.

This pure theism and pure religion and pure grace are just the essence of the Reformed faith, which is really just Christian supernaturalism come to its full rights, and in which alone it comes to its full rights.

For what is the Reformed Theology? Goebel, Schneckenburger, Schweizer, and many others, have defined it chiefly from its points of distinction from Lutheranism. But Dr Warfield,[1] calling it Calvinism, has taught us to distinguish between its distinctive differences and its formative principle. Its formative principle is, as Dr Warfield said, the vision of God in his majesty, and, we may add, the realization of our absolute dependence on God, and the immediacy of the relation of the soul to God. The Reformed Theology, therefore, is essentially just three things, as Dr Warfield put it—pure theism, pure religion at the height of its conception, and pure grace or evangelicalism in 'its pure and only stable expression'.

It is, I repeat, pure theism. For theism is just the interpretation of the universe from the standpoint of God's purpose. And pure theism is just the construction of all that happens in the physical and mental spheres as the unfolding of the eternal purpose of God, and the refusal to limit God either by the world of nature or the human will. And this is precisely the view of the Reformed Theology. Withdraw the acts of free agents from the purpose of God, under the false notion that an event cannot be certain as to the fact of its futurition and free as to the mode of its occurrence, and you must also withdraw such acts from the foresight and providence of God which render them equally certain. The next step is to deny creation by this blind and helpless God, and to end in an ultimate dualism or else in the modern notion of a finite God. Your theism is gone, and the flood of naturalism sweeps away your Christianity. Go the

---

[1] B. B. Warfield, *Calvin as a Theologian and Calvinism Today.* Three Addresses in Commemoration of the Four Hundredth Anniversary of the Birth of John Calvin.

opposite way and merge God in the world-process, and you end in pantheism, and then the flood of naturalism not only overwhelms yourself but God as well. To maintain theism you must keep it pure and regard God as the Almighty Creator, Preserver, and Governor of the universe, whose purpose and power are not limited. This is the Reformed faith.

The Reformed Theology is secondly, I repeat, pure religion as absolute dependence on God, and not on the human will, using God only as a helper in our struggle against the world. Take this attitude of pure religion; let it have its way in all your thought, in all your feeling, and in all your life, and you have taken just the position of the Reformed faith, and are in a position to defend yourself against naturalism in religion.

The Reformed Theology is thirdly, I repeat, the conception of pure grace or the absolute dependence of the sinner upon God for salvation. All the power in our salvation it ascribes to God; all the glory to him alone; all to his wondrous grace. Only in this consistent form can evangelicalism be adequately defended against naturalism in soteriology. Subtract from this pure evangelicalism in any degree, and you fall into the idea and attitude of dependence in some degree on human merit and human power for salvation. You are in unstable equilibrium between the Reformed Theology and a bald naturalism and Pelagianism in which this relentless philosophy has now entered the centre of your life and attacked the very ground of your hope for yourself and the world.

Only as the Christian church defends her faith against this naturalism in all spheres can she hope adequately to propagate it.

We must conclude, therefore, that, since the essence of the new theology is naturalism, it can be opposed adequately only from that viewpoint which gives us the opposite principle of supernaturalism in its purity and thoroughly grounded on an adequate basis, *i.e.*, from the point of view of the Reformed Theology.

It is true that this theology emphasizes Christian supernaturalism especially in the sphere of soteriology. But you cannot deny it there, and hope to maintain it in regard to the origin of Christianity and the Christian revelation. Hence there follows the tremendous signifi-cance of the Reformed Theology for us today in giving us the only adequate support for supernaturalism against a naturalism which, when it has run its logical course and borne its bitter fruit, not only robs us of a supernatural salvation, but of supernatural Christianity and a supernatural Bible, and which indeed does not stay in its course till it has robbed us of Christ and even of God.

We are being told that the Reformed faith or Calvinism is dead today, or at least about to pass away. Doubtless it has not many representatives among the leaders of religious thought, nor does it court a place alongside of the wisdom of this world. But wherever humble souls catch the vision of God in his glory, and bow in adoration and humility before him, trusting for salvation only in his grace and power, there you have the essence of the Reformed faith. Once let this life-blood of pure religion flow from the heart to nourish the anaemic brain and work itself out in thought, and it will wash away many a cobweb spun by a dogmatic naturalism claiming to be modern, but in reality as old as Christianity itself.

And if amongst professed theologians we find not many who accept this faith, let us thank God that here in America and in our church, the influence of Charles Hodge, Robert Breckinridge, James Thornwell, Robert Dabney, W. G. T. Shedd, and Benjamin Warfield, still lives on.

What other hope have we than that which this Reformed faith gives us? The forces of evil are powerful in the world today in the sphere of human life. In the realm of religious thought sinister shapes arise before us, threatening our most sacred possessions. And if we look within our own hearts, often we find there treachery from the lust of the flesh and the pride of life, when we would fain keep our eye single for the glory of God. With foes on every hand around us and within; with dark clouds of yet unknown potency for harm forming on the horizon; we dare not put our trust in human help or in the human will, but only in the grace and power of God. We must take the standpoint of the Reformed faith, and say with the psalmist:

> My soul, wait thou only upon God; for my expectation is from him. He only is my rock and my salvation; he is my defence; I shall not be moved. In God is my salvation and glory: the rock of my strength and my refuge is in God (*Psa.* 62:5-7).

OTHER PRINCETON TITLES
PUBLISHED BY THE TRUST

THOUGHTS ON RELIGIOUS EXPERIENCE
Archibald Alexander
ISBN:978 0 85151 757 5
368pp. paperback

GOD IS LOVE
J. W. Alexander
ISBN: 978 0 85151 459 8
368pp. paperback

REMEMBER HIM
J. W. Alexander
ISBN: 978 0 85151 790 2
64pp. paperback

ACTS (GENEVA COMMENTARY SERIES)
J. A. Alexander
ISBN: 978 0 85151 309 6
984pp. clothbound

EVANGELICAL THEOLOGY
A. A. Hodge
ISBN: 978 0 85151 582 3
456pp. clothbound

OUTLINES OF THEOLOGY
A. A. Hodge
ISBN: 978 0 85151 160 3
680pp. clothbound

WESTMINSTER CONFESSION: A COMMENTARY
A. A. Hodge
ISBN: 978 0 85151 828 2
432pp. clothbound

LIFE OF CHARLES HODGE
A. A. Hodge
ISBN: 978 1 84871 090 0
672pp. clothbound

1&2 CORINTHIANS (GENEVA COMMENTARY SERIES)
Charles Hodge
ISBN: 978 0 85151 185 6
716pp. clothbound

EPHESIANS (GENEVA COMMENTARY SERIES)
Charles Hodge
ISBN: 978 0 85151 591 5
320pp. clothbound

PRINCETON SERMONS
Charles Hodge
ISBN: 978 0 85151 285 3
403pp. clothbound

ROMANS (GENEVA COMMENTARY SERIES)
Charles Hodge
ISBN: 978 0 85151 213 6
732pp. clothbound

BIBLICAL DOCTRINES
B. B. Warfield
ISBN: 978 0 85151 534 2
674pp. clothbound

COUNTERFEIT MIRACLES
B. B. Warfield
ISBN: 978 0 85151 166 5
536pp. paperback

Faith & Life
B. B. Warfield
ISBN: 978 0 85151 585 4
464pp. clothbound

SAVIOUR OF THE WORLD
B. B. Warfield
ISBN: 978 0 85151 593 9
280pp. clothbound

STUDIES IN THEOLOGY
B. B. Warfield
ISBN: 978 0 85151 533 5
690pp. clothbound

PASTOR-TEACHERS OF OLD PRINCETON
Memorial Addresses for the Faculty of
Princeton Theological Seminary
1812-1921
Selected and Introduced by James M. Garretson
ISBN: 978 1 84871 161 7
600pp. clothbound

PRINCETON AND PREACHING
Archibald Alexander and the Christian Ministry
James M. Garretson
ISBN: 978 0 85151 893 0
304pp. clothbound

PRINCETON SEMINARY
Volume 1
Faith & Learning: 1812–1868:
David B. Calhoun
ISBN: 978 0 85151 670 7
528pp. clothbound

PRINCETON SEMINARY
Volume 2
The Majestic Testimony: 1869–1929
David B. Calhoun
ISBN: 978 0 85151 695 0
592pp. clothbound

THE BANNER OF TRUTH TRUST originated in 1957 in London. The founders believed that much of the best literature of historic Christianity had been allowed to fall into oblivion and that, under God, its recovery could well lead not only to a strengthening of the church today but to true revival.

Inter-denominational in vision, this publishing work is now international, and our lists include a number of contemporary authors along with classics from the past. The translation of these books into many languages is encouraged.

A monthly magazine, *The Banner of Truth,* is also published and further information will be gladly supplied by either of the offices below.

THE BANNER OF TRUTH TRUST

3 Murrayfield Road, Edinburgh, EH12 6EL UK

PO Box 621, Carlisle, Pennsylvania 17013, USA

www.banneroftruth.co.uk